ROTHMANS
RUGBY UNION
YEARBOOK 1996-97

**Editors: Mick Cleary
and John Griffiths**

ROTHMANS

HEADLINE

First published in 1996
by HEADLINE BOOK PUBLISHING

Cover photographs.
Front: Will Carling, who retired as England's captain after 59 internationals at the helm,
pictured in the Murrayfield match which squashed Scotland's hopes of a
Grand Slam in the 1996 Five Nations Championship.
Back: Gregor Townsend eludes Olivier Roumat in Scotland's memorable triumph
against France.

All photographs by Colorsport unless otherwise credited.

10 9 8 7 6 5 4 3 2 1

ISBN 0 7472 7771 0

Typeset by Letterpart Limited, Reigate, Surrey

Printed and bound in Great Britain by
The Bath Press, Bath

HEADLINE BOOK PUBLISHING
A division of Hodder Headline PLC
338 Euston Road
London NW1 3BH

CONTENTS

EDITORIAL PREFACE

To celebrate our silver jubilee we invited Fran Cotton, former Lions and England prop and manager of next summer's Lions tour to South Africa, to choose his world side from the players of the past 25 years. Welshmen predominate in a team which might surprise English readers. Yet with six of the famous 1971 Lions in his selection and four distinguished All Blacks in the pack, few, we suggest, would fancy facing the Anniversary XV.

The past season saw Rugby Union accelerate towards its professional destiny with important competitions launched worldwide. Our coverage reflects the shifting emphasis in the sport by providing details of the inaugural Super-12 series, the new Heineken European Cup and the first Latin Cup. Moreover, our correspondents are preparing to file reports from the recent Tri-Nations and Pacific Rim tournaments for inclusion in the next edition of the Yearbook.

Another feature of this edition is the Rothmans Awards review. After lengthy deliberations our panel presents Lawrence Dallaglio as the Player of the Year, Toulouse are the Team of the Year, and the former Irish internationals Hugo MacNeill and Trevor Ringland jointly become the first recipient of the Personality of the Year award. Elsewhere the Yearbook offers it customary mix of reviews and statistics which, for international records, are complete **up to 30 April 1996**.

Readers will no doubt appreciate the difficulties of producing an accurate fixtures list for the coming season. Even at the time of going to press uncertainties regarding arrangements for Five Nations, Anglo-Welsh and League matches remained. Consult the press, therefore, for confirmation of venues and fixtures at the relevant time.

Warm thanks, once again, go to the team of correspondents who provide copy from all corners of rugby's expanding globe. Over the past 25 years the Yearbook has enjoyed growing support overseas and we are grateful to the reliable net of enthusiasts in New Zealand, South Africa, Australia, Fiji, Canada, France, Italy and Argentina as well as those in the Home Unions who answer queries and contribute amendments to our databases.

Finally, special thanks to Caroline North, our house editor. In her 14th consecutive season on our team she has again worked with characteristic good humour and efficiency to oversee production of the Yearbook.

Mick Cleary
John Griffiths

ROTHMANS 25TH ANNIVERSARY WORLD XV

To mark the 25th edition of *Rothmans Rugby Union Yearbook* we invited Fran Cotton, manager of the Lions tour to South Africa in May 1997 and distinguished British Lion himself, to select his World XV from the players of the past 25 years. There were no restrictions on nationalities. Fran had only one problem: 'Who the hell do you leave out?'

It was only after he had picked his side that Fran realised that there was not one Englishman in the ranks. 'And me, of all people, not to pick an Englishman,' he said. If nothing else, the exercise gave Fran an insight into the tortuous and challenging business of picking a Lions squad for next year's tour to South Africa. But, even for this little exercise in fantasy rugby, there was no swaying the Lions manager once he had made up his mind. Solid on the pitch; solid off the pitch. What he sought above all else for this squad was balance and integration. There were so many players of real quality pressing their claims that the deciding factor was how they would work with those alongside them. In only one case, that of fly-half, did Fran more or less toss a coin. 'Barry John or Phil Bennett – there's nothing between them,' said Fran. 'I played a lot with Phil and not with Barry. That's all it came down to.' This is the team he finally chose.

FRAN COTTON'S WORLD XV 1971–96

Full-back: **J P R Williams** (Wales)
Right wing: **Gerald Davies** (Wales)
Centre: **Danie Gerber** (South Africa)
Centre: **Mike Gibson** (Ireland)
Left wing: **Jonah Lomu** (New Zealand)
Fly-half: **Phil Bennett** (Wales)
Scrum-half: **Gareth Edwards** (Wales)
Loose-head: **Ray McLoughlin** (Ireland)
Hooker: **Sean Fitzpatrick** (New Zealand) *(capt)*
Tight-head: **Graham Price** (Wales)
Lock: **Gary Whetton** (New Zealand)
Lock: **John Eales** (Australia)
Blindside: **Ian Kirkpatrick** (New Zealand)
No 8: **Mervyn Davies** (Wales)
Openside: **Michael Jones** (New Zealand)

Here are Fran's observations on the other contenders.

Full-back

Serge Blanco is a magnificent attacking player but had occasional lapses. Andy Irvine had maybe more edge than J P R Williams in attack, but he was not in the same class in defence, while someone like Gavin Hastings was not consistent enough at this level. J P R offered so much in both attack and defence. I never saw him have a poor game.

J P R Williams.

Gerald Davies.

Danie Gerber.

Mike Gibson.

Jonah Lomu.

Phil Bennett.

Wings

There was some competition here. How could you leave out John Kirwan and David Campese? Well, you can if you've got Gerald Davies and Jonah Lomu. Gerald was the best I've ever come across, and not just in attack. He was a tremendous defender too. As for Lomu, he is the most influential player I've ever seen on a rugby field. He transforms matches on his own.

Centres

I've gone for balance here. There was some quality in the field, but I've opted for Danie Gerber's penetration allied to the vision, timing and silky skills of Mike Gibson. Sella, Guscott, Carling, Horan and Little all had plenty to offer, but for me this is the best combination.

Fly-half

How do we pass over Michael Lynagh, Jonathan Davies, Mark Ella and John Rutherford? It's not easy, but if you've got Barry John and Phil Bennett to call upon as well, then you can only go in one direction. I played with Phil, which is the only reason I've picked him ahead of Barry. Benny could play any game, in attack or defence.

Scrum-half

No contest here, even though there are some great candidates, including Steve Smith, who is sitting alongside me as I write this, Nick Farr-Jones and the South African Joost van der Westhuizen. But there is only one Gareth Edwards. Lomu might have a great impact on a match but Gareth is the best player of them all. He had everything: he is a notch above all the others, even in this great team, in that regard. On the 1974 Lions tour we just worked on getting the ball to him, and he did the rest.

Loose-head

'Mighty Mouse' McLauchlan is a strong candidate, and Jason Leonard is a solid international, but Ray McLoughlin stands head and shoulders above them. He played on either side and was so good technically that on the 1971 Lions tour coach Carwyn James handed the coaching of the front row over to him after just a few days.

Hooker

Of course, Peter Wheeler would slot into any team; so would John Pullin. But a player who has managed to hold off all comers in New Zealand for ten years has to be something special. So Sean Fitzpatrick it is. I don't think I've seen him have a bad game. He's become a great leader as well, so we'll ask him to captain the team.

Tight-head

There's only one name which really jumps out at you here, that of Graham Price. I've played with him and against him, and he's a great, great player.

Locks

Gordon Brown on his day could take on anyone. Paul Ackford is probably the best front jumper of recent times. Big Wade Dooley had immense physical presence. However, I think the principal criteria for the modern era are mobility and athleticism. Gary Whetton was a terrific player round the field, while John Eales is an all-round outstanding athlete. All the same, there were some very good people left out.

Blindside

Jean-Claude Skrela was very close here, and Roger Uttley also had a claim on the position. But in the early 1970s, Ian Kirkpatrick was unstoppable.

Gareth Edwards.

Ray McLoughlin.

Sean Fitzpatrick.

Graham Price.

Gary Whetton.

John Eales.

No 8
Buck Shelford was some player, as was Jean-Pierre Bastiat. Dean Richards, in his own style, could affect a game. Mervyn Davies, though, had everything. Merv was top drawer: a great ball-player, good at the line-out and a far better tackler than many gave him credit for. And what a partnership he had with Gareth Edwards.

Openside
There was tremendous competition here. Peter Winterbottom, Jean-Pierre Rives, Tony Neary, Fergus Slattery, John Taylor . . . who do you leave out? Any of them would do the job for you, but the one man they all talk about is Michael Jones. Even in a great All Black side he was something else.

That's my team. Now, where's the opposition?

Ian Kirkpatrick.

Mervyn Davies.

Michael Jones.

9

ROTHMANS AWARDS 1995-96

We have decided to change the format of awards this season. In order to salute as wide a range of personnel as possible, there will be three awards: Player of the Year, Team of the Year and Personality of the Year.

Player of the Year

The first category speaks for itself. Every season there is at least one player who thrusts himself into the spotlight for one reason or another. It might simply be the quality of his play, or the unselfish and unstinting contribution made to a team effort, his leadership qualities at club or international level, or perhaps the commitment he shows to a particular cause. There were several candidates to consider. Jonah Lomu might have been marginally less significant over the past year than he was in those devastating earlier months of 1995. He had a particularly quiet tour of France with New Zealand last autumn. Closer to home there were the mercurial talents of Gregor Townsend to admire, particularly his tormenting of the French defence in Scotland's victory against them in the Five Nations Championship. Ultimately, though, not even Townsend, for all his prompting, was able to take Scotland to a first-ever victory over New Zealand. Wales offered us Robert Howley, who had a vivid debut international season at scrum-half, as did Leigh Davies in the centre. Their day will surely come. In a short space of time it was Lawrence Dallaglio of Wasps and England who made the biggest impression on us and is a worthy recipient of the title Rothmans Player of the Year.

LAWRENCE DALLAGLIO

Dallaglio had a fine season as a player, winning his first cap as a replacement against South Africa in November and then, a month later, marking his full debut with a try. By the end of England's international season he had made the troublesome No 7 position his own. But these achievements will tell you only part of the story. Dallaglio made perhaps an even greater contribution to the cause of his club, Wasps.

Wasps have always prided themselves on their tight-knit spirit, their homely, unpretentious air, their sense of camaraderie, which more than made up for any shortfall in facilities and resources. Harlequins could have the glamour and the stars: Wasps had a sense of community which money couldn't buy. And then, suddenly, it all blew up in their faces. Rob Andrew's departure in September was bad enough, but when he then recruited from within, enticing Wasps captain Dean

Lawrence Dallaglio winning his first full cap against Western Samoa.

Ryan, former England scrum-half Steve Bates and Ireland prop Nick Popplewell to join him at Newcastle, it seemed as if the family was turning in on itself. Dallaglio, 23, was asked to take over. He did a superb job in helping the club through a difficult year. At one point it seemed as if they might miss out on that critical fourth placing in the League, the cut-off point for entry into Europe. But Wasps, under Dallaglio's level-headed and spirited captaincy, rallied to finish three points clear of Sale. Dallaglio resisted overtures from several clubs – Bath, Leicester and Harlequins among them – to stay with Wasps. His loyalty was undoubtedly a factor in helping them to secure the £3 million backing of music and media magnate Chris Wright. 'I did have offers,' said Dallaglio, 'but I have said all along that my loyalty was to Wasps. I intend to help them build something worthwhile here.'

Dallaglio made a real mark three years ago when his blistering speed off the mark made him a powerful influence in the victorious England squad at the World Sevens in Edinburgh. He showed there that he had good hands, immense power in the tackle and in breaching the gain-line as well as an alert rugby mind. In some ways he was too versatile. He played in all three positions in the back row for Wasps and went on England's tour to South Africa in 1994, but missed out on World Cup selection in favour of Neil Back. However, this past year has belonged to Dallaglio. He has now dedicated himself to the open side, and his lines of running have become much sharper, his ability to read the game from No 7 more assured.

Dallaglio learned his rugby at Ampleforth College. His life was thrown into turmoil at the age of 16 when his sister, Francesca, became one of the 51 victims of the *Marchioness* boat disaster. 'It took me a long time to get over that,' says Dallaglio. 'The only good thing, I suppose, is that you don't get too wound up by the little things any more. Rugby was a big help: it got me going again and gave me a focus.'

Dallaglio has played for England at every level – 18 Group, Colts, Under-21, Emerging England, Students and A team. He has just finished an estate management degree at Kingston University. Such is his impact that he is a strong contender to succeed Will Carling as England captain. The good times might just be beginning.

Personality of the Year

This category is designed to acknowledge the contributions of those who make the sport happen, who make it come alive and who give it shape and meaning. It may be a player who, by his long service or selfless efforts, has portrayed the game in its best light. He might be an unsung hero, slogging away in the foothills of the sport, uncom-

Hugo MacNeill and Trevor Ringland observe a minute's silence before the Peace International. *(Billy Stickland/INPHO)*

plaining and unnoticed. There might be those who strive for years and are finally rewarded with representative honours. We could honour a coach who has taken an ordinary bunch of players, made them believe in themselves and turned them into a class act. In recent years we would have considered Paul Turner of Sale or Barry Corless at Northampton. There are administrators to salute, those who are too easily vilified and too infrequently applauded. Both Vernon Pugh of Wales and Tony Hallett of England had their admirers, as well as their critics, over the last year. We decided, though, that there was one event last season which seemed to encapsulate so much of what rugby is supposed to be about – and which it rarely is these days. This was the Peace International between Ireland and the Barbarians in Dublin on 18 May 1996, organised by Hugo MacNeill and Trevor Ringland.

HUGO MacNEILL/TREVOR RINGLAND

Sport and politics do and should mix. You can't divorce yourself from the society in which you live, no matter how convenient it might be to do so on occasions.

Those who have played their rugby for Ireland are all too aware of the unique position their sport occupies in that it blends players from both sides of the border. Whatever their background, the players are all affected by the problems in the north. So when the IRA ceasefire broke down in the early months of the year, former team-mates, full-back Hugo MacNeill, a native of Dublin, and wing Trevor Ringland of Belfast were not alone in feeling a profound sense of depression. They were alone, however, in deciding to do something about it. They set about organising a match whose sole aim was to promote peace, to show to the world that ordinary rugby folk do care and do want their voices to be heard.

'Of course there will be sceptics,' said MacNeill at the time. 'But this gesture is for real. Irish people are sick and tired of terrorists setting the agenda. You cannot say that often enough or loud enough. All the people who come are making their own statement of intent. We all want peace. It's as simple as that.'

In the end some 30,000 came to Lansdowne Road to see the Barbarians win 70-38. The Barbarians attracted their strongest side for years. François Pienaar and David Campese turned up even though they were injured and could not play. They thought the day was that important, and so do we.

Team of the Year

The final award goes to the team which we feel has achieved some-

Toulouse in festive mood after their European Cup final win.

15

thing special during the season. It may be that they have dominated their own domestic championship; it may be that they have swept all before them on the international stage. Of course, it might just be that they have battled against the odds and simply come through a very difficult period in their own history. It's tempting, and indeed almost inevitable, to look solely at the top tiers for our winner. There are many, though, who are on their way up – teams like Rotherham, who have risen through the English divisions with assurance and self-confidence. Nine years ago they were in North-East 1; this year they are in National League 2. It's a fabulous success story. Bath are, as ever, strong candidates. They won their sixth League title and their tenth knock-out Cup to complete their fourth double. It was close, though. We might have chosen Auckland for their winning of the Super-12, but their season is yet to finish. And so we have decided to honour Stade Toulousain, the French and European champions.

Stade Toulousain

This French club are renowned throughout the world for their stylish endeavours. It was only this year, though, that British audiences had a chance to see for themselves the full power and majesty of France's premier club side. They may only have shaded the final of the Heineken European Cup in extra time, beating Cardiff 21-18, but it was the manner of their play which so took the breath away. If the sheer beauty and ebullience of their approach can be encapsulated in one player, then look no further than Emile Ntamack, their charismatic winger and captain. He is both graceful and deadly. Alongside there is the youthful swagger of Thomas Castaignède, the underrated threat of Stephane Ougier, the thrust of Jerome Cazalbou, all complemented by a rugged pack spearheaded by the dynamic front row of Christian Califano, Patrick Soula and Claude Portolan. We were new to the Toulouse experience, but the French have long rejoiced in it. Stade Toulousain won the coveted French championship last season for the third time in succession, becoming the first French club ever to do so twice. They achieved the hat-trick first in 1922-24 and completed the run this time by beating Brive 20-13. This was their 13th French title in all. Only Béziers, with 11 titles, come close to their record. Now, with the English and Scottish in the fray for the first time, can Stade Toulousain hang on to their European crown? It would take a brave man to bet against them.

TOO MUCH TALK; NOT ENOUGH PLAY

REVIEW OF THE 1995-96 SEASON
Mick Cleary

The 1996 Five Nations Championship was neither particularly rivet-ing nor scintillating. Sure there was drama and tension in the air at Murrayfield as England throttled Scottish Grand Slam aspirations. Or rather, one big, lumbering, gap-toothed old warhorse called Dean Richards throttled them. Deano proved once again that sport is about character and presence as much as it is about pace and fitness. There ought to be no place for Dean Richards in the slick, fast modern game, say the theorists. There ought to be no place for Dean Richards in the England side, said Jack Rowell and many others at the start of the season. We were all proved wrong. The Grand Slam match may not have been spectacular, but it was nonetheless theatre of the highest order.

There were many lulls in between. When the tempo did drop, there was an easy remedy for those who get their kicks from witnessing bloody confrontation. One quick turn of the head away from the pitch and there, high up at the back of the stand in the committee rooms, was a punch-up of the highest order. Even the most blood-thirsty of us had our fill last year. Perhaps we shouldn't try to lighten with a dash of mocking humour the sombre air which hung over much of the season. For these are serious times for the game. There is a grievous split among the Home Unions; a deep fissure in the RFU, temporarily mended with the equivalent of a 5p plaster, and enough bad blood and suspicion between the leading clubs and their respec-tive unions for us all to fear that the season ahead may be just as tangled and fraught as the past one has been. Out there circling too are the likes of Kerry Packer, Ross Turnbull and other entrepre-neurial sharks looking for an easy kill. The 1995 close season involved the chasing of whispers. Rumours that many of the southern hemi-sphere players were being signed up for massive sums of money to play in a rebel circus buzzed along the wires almost daily. Finally the main men – notably François Pienaar and Sean Fitzpatrick – were wooed back into the fold. Yet even as one putative rebel tournament collapsed, so another was being proposed in these parts. As late as January 1996 there was talk of 100 English and Welsh players having agreed to play in a £50 million venture. It was all talk. Of course players expressed an interest. Who in their right mind would abso-lutely veto a salary of £150,000 when a mere nod of the head was all the commitment needed in the early stages?

Such projects may have bitten the dust, and their viability in any circumstances may be shaky, but these fast-buck men could rise just as quickly again in the coming 12 months if there were a serious enough rift between players, clubs and unions. At the moment the threat of a bust-up is as alarmingly likely as it was at any stage over the last year. How uplifting it would be to write solely in these pages of the audacious talent of Scotland's Gregor Townsend; the thrilling emergence of a new All Black star in Christian Cullen; the brash new adventure called the Super-12; Thomas Castaignède's winning dropped goal against England; the arrival in England of Michael Lynagh, Philippe Sella and Bob Dwyer; the dismantling of the barriers between the two codes encapsulated in the appearance at Twickenham, not once but twice, of Wigan. All these great events came to pass in a truly astonishing season, but, regrettably if inevitably, it was politics, not players, which hogged the headlines.

As we write there is a very real prospect that the 1997 Five Nations Championship will be the last in the form we know and so dearly love – indeed, even that tournament was under threat as we went to press. The decision of the RFU to go it alone in negotiating TV rights for all matches at Twickenham prompted a furious backlash from the other Home Unions. In April 1996 the RFU withdrew from the joint committee of the Home Unions which has traditionally negotiated the television deal. Immediately, the Celtic countries warned of the consequences of such unilateral activity. 'I believe that this will mean that England are out of the Five Nations,' said Vernon Pugh, chairman of the Welsh Rugby Union and of the Home Unions' TV committee. 'This is selfishness gone mad. What infuriates the other unions is that the deal has been done in a deceitful way. The RFU, in taking this decision, have done it in the knowledge that the other countries will no longer play them.'

It was only a short time before the RFU showed their hand. Their dalliance with satellite television had been well flagged through the season, and eventually they announced an £87.5 million deal over five years with BSkyB for all matches at Twickenham. Again, the other Home Unions, who see the Five Nations as an entity, not a series of individual matches, were incensed that the RFU should sell off piecemeal a tournament which was not theirs to sell in the first place.

'It is inevitable that England will be expelled if they carry on like this,' declared Irish president Syd Millar. But the RFU carried on like this. 'We have not taken this decision lightly,' said RFU secretary Tony Hallett. 'We don't want to go it alone, but feel we have been forced into it by a lack of return from the current negotiations. We have many interests to serve and feel it only reasonable that we should seek the best possible way to fund those concerns.'

Those interests include a bank loan of £35 million to service and the clamour from the leading clubs for help to fund professionalism. It's worth bearing in mind that the RFU was threatened with a breakaway by its leading clubs for the best part of the season, and the BSkyB deal went a long way to satisfying the clubs' demands. Of course, this does not necessarily justify the RFU's action: it merely lays down some markers by way of explanation. All along the RFU claimed in private that they had been frustrated in their attempts to get the other unions to listen to their pleas for a greater share of the cake and an early start to the negotiations themselves. The old three-year £27 million deal with the BBC still had 18 months to run when the RFU first started putting out feelers. The RFU wanted to get things on the move for two reasons. First, they needed some idea of the value of the contract so that they could appease their clubs by offering them a substantial share of the monies. Secondly, there was also a fear that a parliamentary lobby group might succeed in getting the championship recognised as a listed event and therefore not available to satellite television.

The RFU insist that they made all the proper overtures to their Home Union partners. (Along the way, the Celts have claimed that the French, who do actually negotiate their own TV rights on the grounds that they operate in a different language and on a different legal territory, would side with them and ostracise England. We'll believe it when we see it.) If this was the case, it's difficult to know why the others did not at least make some acknowledgement of the RFU's cause. They didn't have to agree with it, just recognise that it existed as a possible line of argument. There's no doubt that personalities as well as principles have played a large part in this explosive rift – too large a part, in fact. The leading Welsh and English officials do not see eye to eye on many matters. The Celts are furious that the established procedure was not adhered to, angry that the usual timetable was ignored and apoplectic that the English should consider themselves bigger and more deserving than their neighbours. The term 'typical arrogant English' was heard more than once from the Celtic fringes.

It wasn't long before these countries received their own offers from BSkyB. Wales were offered £40.5 million, Scotland £20 million and Ireland £18 million. Wales rejected the approach out of hand. 'We were offered twice as much as the others in an attempt to break us up,' said Vernon Pugh. 'But there is no way we'll abandon them, because to do so would be to abandon ourselves. We were being asked to surrender control of the game in Wales. There was also the consideration that England were offered more than the other three nations combined. That wasn't acceptable.' BSkyB immediately dismissed Pugh's assertion that the satellite company was trying to dictate terms to the union. All they had asked for, they said, was that a certain percentage of the monies should find its way to the clubs and that an Anglo-Welsh League should be put in place, a competition which the clubs themselves had been asking for.

In July, only 24 hours after the RFU's AGM failed to produce any new initiative to resolve the impasse, Scotland, Wales and Ireland, with the agreement of France, called England's bluff by throwing them out of the Five Nations Championship with immediate effect and announcing the formation of a new Four Nations tournament for 1997. The row rumbled along and will continue to do so.

There are many points to consider here, not least of which is that the whole affair is potentially ruinous. It's simply not good enough that both sides should state blithely that they will go off and play in different competitions. The impasse must never get that far. To allow this would be a heinous dereliction of duty on the part of the administrators – a massive blow to all supporters and players for whom the Five Nations is the centre of the season. Even if games against the southern hemisphere nations, the suggested alternative for England, might carry greater technical worth, they do not come anywhere near rivalling the social and emotional impact of a Five Nations match.

The Celts may feel that they have generations of perceived injustice to call upon when asking for the support and loyalty of their followers. That solidarity will not last long. As soon as it sinks in that England are not on the agenda for that year, enthusiasm will wane. The reason for this is simple, and in many ways explains why the Home Unions are themselves at loggerheads with the RFU. Everyone – player, fan, administrator – wants to put one over on the arrogant, aloof, insufferable English. This attitude lasts only 80 minutes for some, a good deal longer for others. Both sides have got to abandon their sense of injured pride and moral self-righteousness. There is right on both sides.

The RFU should have courted their Home Union partners for longer; the Celts, for their part, ought to have sent out more positive signals. England should not have cited their bigger constituency as a prime justification for more money. New Zealand has a smaller rugby population than England, yet no one would dream of reducing their right to equal shares in, say, the World Cup. That line of argument is simplistic as well as elitist and offensive. Yet the old ways are no longer good enough, either. The whole face of the game has changed radically: there are new imperatives and different, pressing commercial realities. TV negotiations are a relatively new practice, and as recently as ten years ago were conducted on the basis of minimal discussion, a good lunch and a handshake. The time is right for a new approach, be it separate deals or whatever, and personal antipathies and old prejudices have to be buried. No one will thank any of the administrators if they are not.

The emotive issue of selling rights to satellite television is not as black and white as it is painted. There are those who would argue that to put a sport into the hands of such blatant commercial operators is a reckless, uncaring act. No sooner are the precious jewels handed over than they might be melted down, changed or simply flogged off elsewhere. Those fears would seem to have no basis in reality. BSkyB have had exclusive rights to Premiership football for several years now, and the appeal of the sport has not been as high for many, many years. And those cricket followers who yearned for so long for a glimpse of winter cricket but never got it from terrestrial TV now have it right across the schedules.

Yet it has to be said that there would indeed be cause for concern if one TV company had absolute rights in both northern and southern hemispheres. If that were to happen then the scope for tinkering with laws, competitions even, the transfer of players and much more would be so great as to require constant policing. There has to be some sort of terrestrial involvement to safeguard control of the sport as well as to spread the word to a wider audience in the short term. The RFU's deal, which allows for full transmission on terrestrial television two hours after the finish of the game, seems a reasonable compromise. I would also be happier if the proposed contract were for three rather than five years.

It's a fair bet that the internal wrangling of each union will continue. There was dissent in Scotland between the clubs and the SRU as to whether clubs or districts should be entered for Europe; in Wales and England there has been ongoing strife between the clubs and the union over money, power and structures. The heat was really turned up in England with the election of Cliff Brittle as chairman of the executive ahead of John Jeavons-Fellows, the nomination of the RFU executive itself. For the rest of the season Brittle and the leading clubs fought an acrimonious battle as to who should get what from the spoils of the new professional game. In April the leading clubs, operating under the banner of EPRUC (English Professional Rugby Union Clubs) declared that they would quit the RFU competitions for the 1996-97 season over disagreement about the structure of the game. It was only in late May, on the eve of the Bath-Wigan return match at Twickenham, that both sides pulled back from the brink. In the end there seemed to be no real point of fundamental disagreement. The clubs got their way on a 12-club First Division, a dangerous trade-off by the RFU, as well as a say in new sponsorship negotiations, an eminently sensible development. The RFU retained overall control, which is exactly how it should be. There was little need for it to have been such a drawn-out affair.

The club scene was volatile. New money brought many new names into the frame. First up in September was Sir John Hall, who expanded his soccer fiefdom into rugby when he bought up Newcastle Gosforth. Rob Andrew followed a few weeks later as his designated supremo for a reputed £150,000 a year. Andrew was not timid in opening the chequebook. Former Wasps team-mates Dean Ryan, Nick Popplewell and Steve Bates were enticed north, and

21

joining them for the coming season will be Tony Underwood, Gary Armstrong, Doddie Weir, Peter Walton and Garath Archer.

Other clubs reacted swiftly. Saracens signed up in November with City businessman Nigel Wray, a Saracens member, for £2.5 million. By the end of the season Michael Lynagh, Philippe Sella, Eddie Halvey, Tony Copsey and Kyran Bracken had pledged themselves to Saracens' cause. The club will play at Enfield FC this season and have hopes for a £5 million multi-purpose, 10,000-capacity sports complex within the next couple of years. In February Ashley Levett, a millionaire commodities trader, ploughed £2.5 million into Richmond, a lot of which went straight back out as Ben Clarke, Adrian Davies, Andy Moore and brothers Scott and Craig Quinnell headed to the Athletic Ground. Brian Moore will come out of retirement to play for them, too.

Harlequins went down the sponsorship route, signing a deal worth £1.5 million over three years with NEC. This was followed by a £3 million partnership with the Riverside Leisure group. The French liked the sound of that, and two of their internationals, prop Laurent Bénézech and Laurent Cabannes, will be among the new faces at the Stoop this season. Wasps waited until after the end of the season to get in on the act. Chris Wright, head of entertainment group Chrysalis, invested £3 million in the club. Wasps also have the prospect of playing their major matches at Loftus Road, the home of Queens Park Rangers, in which Wright also has an interest. Frank Warren, meanwhile, is looking to reawaken a slumbering giant. His Sports Network group are backing Bedford. First new arrivals were former England manager Geoff Cooke, and Paul Turner, once of Wales, latterly of Sale, who was unceremoniously booted out of the northern club at the season's end.

On the playing field itself we had an earnest rather than an uplifting year. The three best individual international matches all involved France. Their victory over the All Blacks in Toulouse was a stupendous effort; the All Black riposte the following week in Paris even more so. In the Five Nations Championship France were on the receiving end of a great Scottish performance at Murrayfield. The French also figured in one of the great innovations of the season. Toulouse carried the French colours right to the end of the inaugural Heineken European Cup, winning the final after extra time by 21-18 against Cardiff. Neither the English nor Scottish teams were allowed to enter in this first year, but they'll all be there for the coming season, which kicks off in October and promises to be a magnificent addition to the calendar.

In the southern hemisphere the new Super-12 produced some dazzling rugby, an average of over six tries a match, and worthy winners in Auckland, who saw off Natal in the final, 45-21. The new laws compelling all eight forwards to stay bound to the scrummage and the bonus-points scheme both helped to generate more positive attacking rugby.

The Welsh bonus-points system had its critics but, if nothing else, it helped sustain interest right down to the last moments of the League season. Just minutes from the final whistle, Neath No 8 Steve Williams plunged over for the decisive try which earned Neath the maximum three bonus points in their 45-25 victory over Pontypridd. At the same time Cardiff were beating Llanelli 65-13, scoring 11 tries in all and securing maximum bonus points, but to no avail. Neath and Cardiff finished on 72 points apiece but Neath took the title by virtue of scoring 121 tries to Cardiff's 119. It was a cruel irony for Cardiff that they beat Neath twice and would have retained the title but for the new system. Neath were denied a double by Pontypridd, who defeated them 29-22 in what many regarded as the best of all SWALEC Cup finals. It was a personal triumph for their legendary 40-year-old captain, Nigel Bezani.

Wales also saw many comings and goings. Jonathan Davies returned from Warrington and Rugby League in November only to have his rehabilitation thwarted by injury. The new raiders with chequebooks now come from across the Severn Bridge. The Llewellyn brothers have both ended up in London, Adrian Davies and Andy Moore at Richmond, Colin Stephens and Phil Davies at Leeds. Robert Howley almost went to Saracens but eventually wound up at Cardiff, along with the other finds of the season, centre Leigh Davies and openside flanker Gwyn Jones. New coach Kevin Bowring restored some much-needed steel to the national side, although the hefty summer defeats by Australia show that there is still much to do.

Scotland too suffered Down Under in the close season. They were competitive but nonetheless convincingly beaten in both Tests by the All Blacks. Yet their season once again exceeded expectations. The 15-15 draw with Western Samoa and defeat by Italy A forecast a season of mediocrity. Instead, superbly led by Rob Wainwright, they were denied a Grand Slam only by that damned man Richards. Melrose won the League title for the fifth time in seven seasons, coming from behind to eclipse Stirling County only on points difference. The inaugural SRU Tennents Cup, won by Hawick, who beat Watsonians 17-15 in the final, was a great success.

Ireland had a new coach in New Zealander Murray Kidd. Their season had no clear logic to it. They were hammered by a record margin in Paris only to reply with a record score themselves against Wales a fortnight later. They were committed and rugged, even in defeat in their final match, against England. Simon Mason showed promise at full-back, as did David Humphreys at fly-half. The real black note was prop Peter Clohessy stamping on Olivier Roumat in the match against France. Clohessy was spotted by TV cameras and subsequently banned for six months. Limerick once again cornered

Will Carling marks his last season as England captain with the Five Nations Trophy. Could it prove to be the end of an era for the championship itself in the form we know and love?

the domestic market, with Shannon becoming the first club to take the League title back to back.

England struggled through a difficult, at times dark season to emerge as champions on points difference. They blooded many new caps, most impressively Bath winger Jon Sleightholme, who also enjoyed success on the club front as Bath won both League and Cup. As in Wales the League went to the closing minutes, John Liley's penalty miss for Leicester enabling Bath, who drew 38-38 on the last day with Sale, to edge home. In the Pilkington Cup final Bath needed the assistance of referee Steve Lander, who awarded a penalty try against Leicester enabling Bath to squeak a 16-15 win. Leicester's Neil Back completely lost his cool at the final whistle and pushed Lander to the ground. Back was banned for six months. The Bath players had no respite even then. They still had the money-spinning cross-code challenge against Wigan to face. Predictably, both games were something of a farce, Wigan winning at League, played at Maine Road, by 82-6. Martin Offiah scored six tries. Bath had their revenge at Twickenham a couple of weeks later by 44-19. In between, in this weird season, Wigan won the Middlesex Sevens.

Rugby made an appearance in the law courts during the year. In April the High Court ruled that a referee was responsible for the paralysis of a player during a match in which he had been officiating. In the first ruling of its kind the player, Ben Smoulden, who has been a tetraplegic since the incident in 1991, won his case against match referee Michael Nolan. Smoulden was injured at the age of 17 when a scrum collapsed during a game between his team, Sutton Coldfield Colts, and Burton-on-Trent Colts. Mr Justice Curtis ruled that Nolan had not exerted proper control.

On a much lighter note, one familiar pair of brackets will be missing in 1996-97. No longer will the name of Will Carling be accompanied by the title of captain. Carling, after 59 games in charge, during which he oversaw 44 victories, announced his retirement from the role. It won't seem the same without him.

TOURS 1995

WESTERN SAMOA TO SOUTH AFRICA

Western Samoa had been happy to accept invitations to play against the best in their build-up to the World Cup. They had been to New Zealand in 1993 and Australia a year later, and just a month before the tournament they made their first international visit to South Africa. It was an arduous trail.

In the Test South Africa broke their international record, scoring 60 points (their previous best was 52 against Argentina). Gavin Johnson broke the individual record for a Springbok in Test rugby with his 28-point contribution, which consisted of three tries, five conversions and a penalty goal. An appreciative crowd of 30,000 applauded the home side's willingness to run the ball at every opportunity.

Chester Williams scored two tries and had a direct influence on two of Johnson's. However, the charismatic winger was forced to leave the field with a hamstring injury which was eventually to rule him out of the start of the World Cup. Johnson followed him, again with a hamstring problem.

Brian Lima scored a consolation try for Western Samoa from a charge-down late in the game.

THE TOURING PARTY

Manager T Simi   **Coach** P Schuster   **Captain** P Fatialofa
Technical Director B G Williams

FULL-BACKS

T Fa'amasino (Vaimoso)
M T Umaga (Wellington, NZ)

THREEQUARTERS

B P Lima (Marist)
G Harder (Auckland, NZ)
T M Vaega (Counties, NZ)
G E Leaupepe (Counties, NZ)
F Tuilagi (Marist)
L Langkilde (King Country, NZ)

HALF-BACKS

E Puleitu (Auckland, NZ)
F Sini (Marist)
T Nu'uali'itia (Auckland, NZ)
J Young (North Harbour, NZ)

FORWARDS

B P Reidy (Marist, Wellington, NZ)
T Leiasamaivao (Wellington, NZ)
M A N Mika (Otago U, NZ)
G Latu (Vaimoso)
P Fatialofa (Auckland, NZ)
P L Leavasa (Apia)
F L Falaniko (Marist)
D R Williams (Colomiers, France)
D Mika (Marist, Auckland, NZ)
P J Paramore (Manurewa, NZ)
S L Vaifale (Marist)
M Iupeli (Marist)
P R Lam (Auckland, NZ)

TOUR RECORD

All matches   Played 3   Lost 3   Points for 38   Against 104
International matches   Played 1   Lost 1   Points for 8   Against 60

SCORING DETAILS

All matches					**International matches**				
For:	4T	3C	4PG	–	38 Pts	For:	1T	–	1PG	8 Pts
Against:	12T	7C	8PG	2DG	104 Pts	Against:	9T	6C	1PG	60 Pts

MATCH DETAILS

1995	OPPONENTS	VENUE	RESULT
4 Apr	Northern Transvaal	Pretoria	L13-23
8 Apr	Natal	Durban	L17-21
13 Apr	SOUTH AFRICA	Johannesburg	L8-60

MATCH 1   4 April, Loftus Versfeld, Pretoria

Northern Transvaal 23 (1G 1PG 1DG 2T)   **Western Samoa XV 13** (1G 2PG)
Northern Transvaal *Tries:* F P Naude, Otto, D du Toit   *Conversion:* Van
As   *Penalty Goal:* Van As   *Dropped Goal:* Van As
Western Samoa XV *Try:* Vaega   *Conversion:* Umaga   *Penalty Goals:* Umaga (2)

MATCH 2   8 April, King's Park, Durban

Natal 21 (6PG 1DG)   **Western Samoa XV 17** (2G 1PG)
Natal *Penalty Goals:* Reece-Edwards (6)   *Dropped Goal:* Reece-Edwards
Western Samoa XV *Tries:* Puleitu, Umaga   *Conversions:* Sini (2)
Penalty Goal: Sini

MATCH 3   13 April, Ellis Park, Johannesburg   Test Match

SOUTH AFRICA 60 (6G 1PG 3T)   **WESTERN SAMOA 8** (1PG 1T)
SOUTH AFRICA: G K Johnson (Transvaal); J T Small (Natal), J C Mulder
(Transvaal), H P le Roux (Transvaal), C M Williams (Western Province); J T
Stransky (Western Province), J H van der Westhuizen (Northern Transvaal); J P du
Randt (Free State), C L C Rossouw (Transvaal), I S Swart (Transvaal), J J Wiese
(Transvaal), M G Andrews (Natal), J F Pienaar (Transvaal) *(capt)*, R A W Straeuli
(Transvaal), R J Kruger (Northern Transvaal)   *Replacements* C Badenhorst (Free
State) for Williams (55 mins); H W Honiball (Natal) for Johnson (66 mins); M Visser
(Western Province) for Rossouw (72 mins); I Macdonald (Transvaal) for Wiese (79
mins)
Scorers *Tries:* Johnson (3), Williams (2), Andrews, Small, Rossouw,
Stransky   *Conversions:* Johnson (5), Stransky   *Penalty Goal:* Johnson
WESTERN SAMOA: Umaga; Lima, Vaega, Leaupepe, Harder; Puleitu,
Nu'uali'itia; M Mika, Leiasamaivao, Fatialofa (capt), Falaniko, Williams, Vaifale,
Lam, Iupeli   *Replacements* Latu for M Mika; Paramore for Vaifale; Sini for Vaega
Scorers *Try:* Lima   *Penalty Goal:* Umaga
Referee J Meuwesen (Namibia)

CANADA TO FIJI AND NEW ZEALAND

This short tour might have seemed like a good idea at the time, to
build morale and knock the squad into shape before the World Cup,
but in the event it had the opposite effect. The results were poor,
confidence was shattered by the huge loss to the All-Blacks and key
players were injured. Dan Jackart, the tight-head prop and long-time

cornerstone of the Canadian scrum, was hurt in the Fijian Test, struggled for the rest of the tour and missed the World Cup.

Canada laboured in the heat of Nadi before finally overcoming Fiji. Worse was to come in New Zealand. Two defeats from three matches left the team in questionable form for the Test match against New Zealand. Their worst fears were exceeded as the All Blacks ran in ten tries, showing the sort of breathtaking form which was to become a feature of the World Cup and take them to the final shortly afterwards. Andrew Mehrtens, the New Zealand fly-half, scored 28 points, more than any other debutant in history, from a try, seven conversions and three penalty goals.

Canada had desperate luck with injuries. New cap on the wing Barry Ebl broke his shoulder; centre Steve Gray fractured his cheekbone while Paul le Blanc (ribs) and lock Mike Jamer (back) were also replaced. The experiment of playing Gareth Rees in the centre was deemed unsuccessful.

THE TOURING PARTY

Manager R Skett   **Coach** I Birtwell   **Assistant Coach** R Holloway
Captain G L Rees

FULL-BACK

D S Stewart (UBCOB)

THREEQUARTERS

R Toews (Meraloma)
D C Lougheed (Toronto Welsh)
C Smith (Meraloma)
S D Gray (Vancouver Kats)
C Stewart (Western Province, SA)
S J MacKinnon (Ex-Britannia Lions)
S T T Brown (Ex-Britannia Lions)
S Lytton (Meraloma)
B G Ebl (Vancouver Kats)

HALF-BACKS

B Ross (James Bay)
G L Rees (Oak Bay Castaways & Newport)
J D Graf (UBCOB)
A P C Tynan (Meraloma)

FORWARDS

E A Evans (UBCOB & IBM Tokyo)
D C Jackart (UBCOB)
P G le Blanc (Vancouver Kats)
R Snow (Dogs, Newfoundland)
M E Cardinal (James Bay)
K F Svoboda (Ajax Wanderers)
M B James (Burnaby Lake)
C M Whittaker (James Bay)
G I MacKinnon (Ex-Britannia Lions)
J Hutchinson (UBCOB)
A J Charron (Ottawa Irish)
G D Ennis (Kats & Suntory Japan)
C J McKenzie (UBCOB)
C D Michaluk (Vancouver Rowing)
G D Rowlands (Velox Valhallians)
J D Knauer (Meraloma)

TOUR RECORD

All matches   Played 5   Won 2   Lost 3   Points for 104   Against 175
International matches   Played 2   Won 1   Lost 1   Points for 29   Against 83

SCORING DETAILS

All matches

For:	10T	9C	12PG	-	104 Pts
Against:	21T	17C	11PG	1DG	175 Pts

International matches

For:	4T	3C	1PG	29 Pts
Against:	11T	8C	4PG	83 Pts

MATCH DETAILS

1995	OPPONENTS	VENUE	RESULT
8 Apr	FIJI	Nadi	W22-10
12 Apr	South Island	Timaru	L18-19
15 Apr	New Zealand XV	Palmerston North	L17-38
18 Apr	North Island	Rotorua	W40-35
22 Apr	NEW ZEALAND	Auckland	L7-73

MATCH 1   8 April, Nadi   Test Match

FIJI 10 (1G 1DG)   CANADA 22 (2G 1PG 1T)

FIJI: F Rayasi; J Vidiri, S Sorovaki, L Little, P Bale; O Turuva, J McLennan;
R Williams (*capt*), E Batimala, J Veitayaki, A Nadolo, I Savai, I Tawake, D Rouse,
M Korovou   *Replacements* R Bogisa for Rayasi (30 mins); J Rauluni for McLennan
(60 mins); A Mocelutu for Savai (45 mins); E Katalau for Rouse (50 mins)
Scorers *Try:* Sorovaki   *Conversion:* Turuva   *Dropped Goal:* Turuva
CANADA: S Stewart; Toews, C Stewart, Gray, Lougheed; Rees (*capt*), Graf; Evans,
Svoboda, Jackart, James, Ennis, G MacKinnon, McKenzie, Charron   *Replacements*
P le Blanc for Jackart (40 mins); J Hutchinson for James (40 mins); S MacKinnon for
Ennis (60 mins); M Cardinal for Charron (61 mins)
Scorers *Tries:* C Stewart, Evans, Rees   *Conversions:* Rees (2)   *Penalty Goal:* Rees
Referee P Marshall (Australia)

MATCH 2   12 April, Alpine Energy Stadium, Timaru

South Island XV 19 (1G 4PG)   **Canada XV 18** (6PG)
South Island XV *Try:* Matthews   *Conversion:* Culhane   *Penalty Goals:* Culhane (4)
Canada XV *Penalty Goals:* Ross (6)

MATCH 3   15 April, Showgrounds Oval, Palmerston North

New Zealand XV 38 (3G 4PG 1T)   **Canada XV 17** (2G 1PG)
New Zealand XV *Tries:* Berryman (2), Howarth, M N Jones
Conversions: Culhane (3)   *Penalty Goals:* Culhane (4)
Canada XV *Tries:* Graf, C Stewart   *Conversions:* Rees (2)   *Penalty Goal:* Rees

MATCH 4   18 April, Rotorua International Stadium

North Island XV 35 (5G)   **Canada XV 40** (4G 4PG)
North Island XV *Tries:* Davis (2), S Stone (2), Falcon
Conversions: Cunningham (5)
Canada XV *Tries:* A Tynan (2), Ebl, Knauer   *Conversions:* Ross (4)
Penalty Goals: Ross (4)

MATCH 5   22 April, Eden Park, Auckland   Test Match

NEW ZEALAND 73 (7G 3PG 3T)   CANADA 7 (1G)

NEW ZEALAND : G M Osborne (North Harbour); M C G Ellis (Otago),
F E Bunce (North Harbour), W K Little (North Harbour), J W Wilson (Otago);
A P Mehrtens (Canterbury), G T M Bachop (Canterbury); C W Dowd (Auckland),
S B T Fitzpatrick (Auckland) (*capt*), O M Brown (Auckland), I D Jones (North
Harbour), R M Brooke (Auckland), J W Joseph (Otago), M R Brewer (Canterbury),
J A Kronfeld (Otago)
Scorers *Tries:* Bunce (2), Ellis (2), Osborne (2), Bachop, Mehrtens, Brown,
Wilson   *Conversions:* Mehrtens (7)   *Penalty Goals:* Mehrtens (3)

CANADA: S Stewart; Ebl, Gray, Rees (*capt*), Lougheed; Ross, Graf; Evans, Cardinal, Le Blanc, James, Ennis, Charron, McKenzie, G MacKinnon
Replacements A Tynan for Ebl (27 mins); C Stewart for Gray (25 mins); Snow for Le Blanc (42 mins); Rowlands for James (46 mins)
Scorers *Try:* C Stewart   *Conversion:* Ross
Referee W J Erickson (Australia)

ARGENTINA TO AUSTRALIA

The Argentinians had a new coaching team for this five-match build-up tour to the World Cup. They can only have been disappointed with the outcome. The squad was a mixture of youth and experience, and the Pumas found any sort of real form only in the first part of the Second Test. Just one match was won, against Queensland B. That game was more notable for the return to competitive rugby after a year's absence of Australian centre Tim Horan, whose career had been almost brought to an end by a knee injury. Horan was making a late bid for the World Cup. After this showing his team-mate, David Campese, reckoned he was not yet ready.

The Argentinians' opening match, against ACT, degenerated into a brawl involving all 30 players. Diego Cuesta-Silva was somehow singled out from the mass of potential culprits and sent off.

The Pumas were well beaten in the First Test as Australia's Michael Lynagh weighed in with an individual record of 28 points from two tries, three conversions and four penalty goals. The second international was Lynagh's last home game for Australia. David Campese scored two tries in the match (his 62nd and 63rd respectively), perhaps his last in international rugby. The Pumas at least finished the tour on a decent note, playing well enough in the Second Test to lead 13-3 at half-time.

THE TOURING PARTY

Manager L Chaluleu   **Coaches** A Petra, R Paganini   **Captain** S Salvat

FULL-BACKS

S E Meson (San Isidro Club)
E Jurado (Jockey Club, Rosario)

THREEQUARTERS

D L Albanese (San Isidro Club)
F Garcia (Alumni)
S Salvat (Alumni)
D Cuesta-Silva (San Isidro Club)
F del Castillo (Jockey Club, Rosario)
G J del Castillo (Jockey Club, Rosario)
M J Teran (Tucumán RC)
L Arbizu (Belgrano AC)

HALF-BACKS

J L Cilley (San Isidro Club)
G F Camardon (Alumni)
R H Crexell (Jockey Club, Rosario)
A Pichot (CA San Isidro)

FORWARDS

R A le Fort (Tucumán RC)
M Urbano (Buenos Aires C & RC)
F E Mendez (Mendoza RC)
M E Corral (San Isidro Club)
R D Grau (Liceo, Mendoza)
E P Noriega (Hindu)
G A Llanes (La Plata)

P L Sporleder (Curupayti)
N Bossicovich (Esgrima, Rosario)
P M Buabse (Los Tarcos, Tucumán)
R A Martin (San Isidro Club)
M Sugasti (Jockey Club, Rosario)

A M Macome (Tucumán RC)
S L Irazoqui (Bajo Palermo, Cordoba)
C E Viel (Cardinal Newman)
J M Santamarina (Tucumán RC)

TOUR RECORD
All matches   Played 5   Won 1   Lost 4   Points for 86   Against 182
International matches   Played 2   Lost 2   Points for 20   Against 83

SCORING DETAILS

All matches						International matches				
For:	8T	8C	9PG	1DG	86 Pts	For:	2T	2C	2PG	20 Pts
Against:	23T	11C	15PG	-	182 Pts	Against:	10T	3C	9PG	83 Pts

MATCH DETAILS

1995	OPPONENTS	VENUE	RESULT
22 Apr	Australian Capital Territory	Canberra	L16-33
25 Apr	Queensland B	Brisbane	W34-24
30 Apr	AUSTRALIA	Brisbane	L7-53
3 May	New South Wales B	Orange	L16-42
6 May	AUSTRALIA	Sydney	L13-30

MATCH 1   22 April, Manuka Oval, Canberra

Australian Capital Territory 33 (2G 3PG 2T)   **Argentina XV 16** (1G 3PG)
Australian Capital Territory: *Tries:* Roff (2), Fenukitau, Grimmond   *Conversions:* O'Connor (2)   *Penalty Goals:* O'Connor (2), Friend
Argentina XV *Try:* Camardon   *Conversion:* Meson   *Penalty Goals:* Meson (3)

MATCH 2   25 April, Ballymore Oval, Brisbane

Queensland B 24 (3G 1PG)   **Argentina XV 34** (4G 1PG 1DG)
Queensland B *Tries:* Horan, Mandrusiak, Flanagan   *Conversions:* Mandrusiak (3)   *Penalty Goal:* Mandrusiak
Argentina XV *Tries:* Camardon (2), Crexell, Santamarina   *Conversions:* Crexell (4)   *Penalty Goal:* Crexell   *Dropped Goal:* Arbizu

MATCH 3   30 April, Ballymore Oval, Brisbane   1st Test

AUSTRALIA 53 (3G 4PG 4T)   ARGENTINA 7 (1G)

AUSTRALIA: M J Pini (Queensland); D I Campese (NSW), D J Herbert (Queensland), J S Little (Queensland), D P Smith (Queensland); M P Lynagh (Queensland) (*capt*), G M Gregan (ACT); D J Crowley (Queensland), P N Kearns (NSW), E J A McKenzie (NSW), R J McCall (Queensland), J A Eales (Queensland), V Ofahengaue (NSW), B T Gavin (NSW), D Wilson (Queensland)   *Replacement* M N Hartill (NSW) for McKenzie (65 mins)
Scorers *Tries:* Lynagh (2), Eales, Pini, Ofahengaue, Smith, Campese   *Conversions:* Lynagh (3)   *Penalty Goals:* Lynagh (4)
ARGENTINA: Meson; Camardon, Salvat (*capt*), Garcia, Teran; Arbizu, Pichot; Corral, Mendez, Noriega, Sporleder, Llanes, Viel, Santamarina, Martin   *Replacements* Jurado for Camardon (47 mins); Buabse for Llanes (51 mins)
Scorers *Try:* Pichot   *Conversion:* Arbizu
Referee C J Hawke (New Zealand)

31

MATCH 4   3 May, Wade Park, Orange

New South Wales B 42 (3G 2PG 3T)   **Argentina XV 16** (1G 3PG)
New South Wales B *Tries:* Harry (2), Hardy, Harrison, Magro, Madz   *Conversions:* Momsen (3)   *Penalty Goals:* Momsen (2)
Argentina XV *Try:* Pen try   *Conversion:* Cilley   *Penalty Goals:* Cilley (3)

MATCH 5   6 May, Sydney Football Stadium, Sydney   2nd Test

AUSTRALIA 30 (5PG 3T)   ARGENTINA 13 (1G 2PG)

AUSTRALIA: M J Pini (Queensland); D I Campese (NSW), D J Herbert (Queensland), J S Little (Queensland), D P Smith (Queensland); M P Lynagh (Queensland) (*capt*), G M Gregan (ACT); D J Crowley (Queensland), P N Kearns (NSW), E J McKenzie (NSW), R J McCall (Queensland), J A Eales (Queensland), T Coker (Queensland), B T Gavin (NSW), D Wilson (Queensland)
Replacements M N Hartill (NSW) for McKenzie (63 mins); V Ofahengaue (NSW) for Coker (40 mins)
Scorers *Tries:* Campese (2), Wilson   *Penalty Goals:* Lynagh (5)
ARGENTINA: Meson; Salvat (*capt*), Garcia, Teran, Jurado ; G del Castillo, Crexell; Corral, Mendez, Noriega, Sporleder, Llanes, Viel, Santamarina, Martin
Replacement Arbizu for Meson (11 mins)
Scorers *Try:* Arbizu   *Conversion:* Crexell   *Penalty Goals:* Meson, Crexell
Referee D J Bishop (New Zealand)

SCOTLAND TO SPAIN

Preparing for the Rugby World Cup in South Africa, Scotland visited Spain for two games and a training camp at Navacerrada, 50 miles from Madrid in the shadow of the Sierra de Guadarrama. Victories were achieved in both games, though not without bother in the first match, against a Madrid selection. The Scots were struggling even before a thunderstorm swept across the brand-new Madrid City Stadium, and they had to come from behind three times to win by 27-16. Three tries by Craig Joiner brightened an otherwise dull performance, and the Melrose wing, just 21, registered another hat-trick as the Scots beat the Spanish national XV, much more comfortably, at the Madrid University Stadium. The visitors ran in ten tries in a 62-7 victory.

THE TOURING PARTY

Manager D S Paterson   **Captain** A G Hastings   **Coach** D W Morgan
Assistant Coach J R Dixon

FULL-BACKS	
A G Hastings (Watsonians)	
S Hastings (Watsonians)	

D A Stark (Boroughmuir)

HALF-BACKS

C M Chalmers (Melrose)
A G Shiel (Melrose)
D W Patterson (West Hartlepool)
B W Redpath (Melrose)

THREEQUARTERS

I C Glasgow (Heriot's FP)
I C Jardine (Stirling County)
C A Joiner (Melrose)
K M Logan (Stirling County)
A G Stanger (Hawick)

FORWARDS

A P Burnell (London Scottish)
D I W Hilton (Bath)

J J Manson (Dundee HSFP)
P H Wright (Boroughmuir)
K D McKenzie (Stirling County)
M W Scott (Orrell)
S J Campbell (Dundee HSFP)
D F Cronin (Bourges)
A E D Macdonald (Heriot's FP)

J F Richardson (Edinburgh Acads)
G W Weir (Melrose)
I R Morrison (London Scottish)
E W Peters (Bath)
I R Smith (Gloucester)
R I Wainwright (West Hartlepool)
P Walton (Northampton)

TOUR RECORD
Played 2   Won 2   Points for 89   Against 23

SCORING DETAILS

For:	15T	7C	–	–	89 Pts
Against:	2T	2C	2PG	1DG	23 Pts

MATCH DETAILS

1995	OPPONENTS	VENUE	RESULT
2 May	Madrid XV	Madrid City Stadium	W 27-16
6 May	Spain	Madrid University	W 62-7

Appearances: 2 – Campbell*, S Hastings*, Jardine*, Joiner, McKenzie, Peters, Shiel, Stanger; 1 – Burnell, Chalmers, Cronin, Glasgow, A G Hastings, Hilton, Logan, Manson, Morrison, Patterson, Redpath, Richardson, Scott*, Smith, Wainwright, Walton, Weir, Wright   *includes appearances as replacement
Scorers: 30 – Joiner (6T); 22 – A G Hastings (2T 6C); 10 – Wainwright (2T); 5 – Chalmers, Logan, Morrison, Richardson, pen try (1T each); 2 – Shiel (1C)

MATCH 1   2 May, Madrid City Stadium

Madrid XV 16 (1G 2PG 1DG)   **Scotland XV 27** (1G 4T)
Madrid XV: F Puertas; D Saenz, N Dubroscq, P Polidori, R Robles; A Kovalenko, J Hernandez; L Lelievre, J Aguiar (*capt*), A Sanz, A Ravier, T Nicaudie, P Monzon, J Gutierrez, S Samalo *Replacements* F Diez for Kovalenko; R Bartolome for Lelievre; M Andueza for Bartolome
Scorers *Try:* Dubroscq   *Conversion:* Dubroscq   *Penalty Goals:* Kovalenko, Dubroscq   *Dropped Goal:* Kovalenko
Scotland XV: S Hastings; Joiner, Stanger, Jardine, Glasgow; Shiel, Patterson; Manson, McKenzie (*capt*), Burnell, Richardson, Campbell, Walton, Peters, Smith
Scorers *Tries:* Joiner (3), Richardson, pen try   *Conversion:* Shiel
Referee J Mostaza (Madrid)

MATCH 2   6 May, Madrid University

Spain XV: 7 (1G)   **Scotland XV 62** (6G 4T)
Spain XV: F Puertas; D Saenz, F Fernandez, A Mino, P Gutierrez; X Geregiada, J Hernandez; J Alvarez, F de la Calle, J Diez, J Villau, J Escobar, A Malo, J Gutierrez (*capt*), J Exetbarria *Replacements* I Laskurain for Escobar; P Calderon for Mino; J Torres Morote for Hernandez; I de Lazaro for Diez
Scorers *Try:* P Gutierrez   *Conversion:* Geregiada
Scotland XV: A G Hastings (*capt*); Joiner, Stanger, Shiel, Logan; Chalmers, Redpath; Hilton, McKenzie, Wright, Cronin, Weir, Wainwright, Peters, Morrison *Replacements* Campbell for Cronin; Jardine for Shiel; S Hastings for Stanger; Scott for Morrison
Scorers *Tries:* Joiner (3), A G Hastings (2), Wainwright (2), Chalmers, Logan, Morrison   *Conversions:* A G Hastings (6)
Referee J Dumé (France)

ENGLAND A TO AUSTRALIA AND FIJI

THE TOURING PARTY

Manager Peter Rossborough **Coaches** Keith Richardson, Mike Slemen
Captain P Hull

FULL-BACKS

P **Hull** (Bristol)
T **Stimpson** (West Hartlepool)

THREEQUARTERS

J **Naylor** (Orrell)
S **Hackney** (Leicester)
J **Sleightholme** (Bath)
P **Holford** (Gloucester)
S **Potter** (Leicester)
P **Mensah** (Harlequins)
J **Keyter** (Bristol)
W **Greenwood** (Harlequins)

HALF-BACKS

P **Grayson** (Northampton)
D **Pears** (Harlequins)
A **Gomarsall** (Wasps)
M **Dawson** (Northampton)

R **Kitchin** (Harlequins)

FORWARDS

R **Hardwick** (Coventry)
K **Yates** (Bath)
G **Adams** (Bath)
M **Regan** (Bristol)
D **Crompton** (Bath)
D **Garforth** (Leicester)
D **Sims** (Gloucester)
G **Archer** (Newcastle Gosforth)
J **Fowler** (Sale)
R **Metcalfe** (Newcastle Gosforth)
M **Corry** (Newcastle Gosforth)
R **Jenkins** (Harlequins)
C **Sheasby** (Harlequins)
D **Eves** (Bristol)
R **Hill** (Saracens)
T **Diprose** (Saracens)

TOUR RECORD

Played 6   Won 3   Lost 3   Points for 239   Points Against 157

MATCH DETAILS

1995	OPPONENTS	VENUE	RESULT
20 May	South Australia	Adelaide	W 66-9
24 May	Victoria	Melbourne	W 76-19
28 May	Queensland	Brisbane	L 15-20
31 May	Australian Universities	Sydney	L 30-32
7 June	Australia A	Brisbane	W 27-19
10 June	Fiji	Suva	L 25-28

SCOTLAND TO ZIMBABWE

While the 1995 Rugby World Cup was being contested in South Africa, Scotland's reserves were lying in wait across the border in Zimbabwe. They were not idle: to maintain match sharpness for the call (which never came) they took on a tour, winning all four games, including two non-cap international matches.

In fact it was the Scots in Zimbabwe who needed a replacement. Derek Turnbull, Hawick's international wing forward, had to be sent out after captain Fergus Wallace broke an ankle in the first international. Stuart Reid, the Boroughmuir No 8 who was to win his first cap against Western Samoa six months later, took over as tour captain, while Jim Hay, Hawick's hooker, led the Scots in the midweek match against Zimbabwe A.

The tour did not have an auspicious start. The Scots were down 3-13 at half-time against Mashonaland Country Districts in Banket, and it was midway into the second half before they went ahead for the first time, John Kerr kicking ahead for a Michael Dods try. The Scots went on to win 42-13, and over the tour they maintained an average of more than 40 points per game.

Stuart Laing, Instonians' Glasgow-born fly-half, kicked four conversions and three penalty goals in the opening match and went on to score 59 of the Scots' 165 points with a strike rate of nearly 75 per cent – 23 goals from 31 kicks. Derek Stark, Boroughmuir's international wing, was the top try-scorer on the tour with four.

THE TOURING PARTY

Manager A B Hastie   **Captain** F D Wallace   **Coach** D I Johnston
Assistant Coach H Campbell

FULL-BACKS

M Dods (Gala)
R J S Shepherd (Edinburgh Acads)

THREEQUARTERS

M P Craig (Waterloo)
B R S Eriksson (London Scottish)
H R Gilmour (Heriot's FP)
A J Kerr (Watsonians)
S A Nichol (Selkirk)
D A Stark (Boroughmuir)

HALF-BACKS

D W Hodge (Watsonians)
S R Laing (Instonians)
G G Burns (Stewart's-Melville FP)
K Troup (Edinburgh Acads)

FORWARDS

M G Browne (Melrose)
A J Kittle (Stewart's-Melville FP)
S W Paul (Heriot's FP)
A G J Watt (GHK)
J A Hay (Hawick)
M W Scott (Orrell)
I Elliot (Hawick)
M B Rudkin (Watsonians)
R Scott (London Scottish)
G F Dall (Heriot's FP)
G N Flockhart (Stirling County)
S J Reid (Boroughmuir)
B L Renwick (Hawick)
*D J Turnbull (Hawick)
F D Wallace (GHK)

*Replacement during tour

TOUR RECORD

All matches   Played 4   Won 4   Points for 165   Against 71
International matches   Played 2   Won 2   Points for 82   Against 45

SCORING DETAILS

All matches						International matches					
For:	17T	13C	16PG	2DG	165 Pts	For:	8T	6C	9PG	1DG	82 Pts
Against:	5T	5C	11PG	1DG	71 Pts	Against:	3T	3C	8PG	–	45 Pts

MATCH DETAILS

1995	OPPONENTS	VENUE	RESULT
31 May	Mashonaland CD	Banket	W 42-13
3 June	ZIMBABWE	Bulawayo	W 39-23
7 June	Zimbabwe A	Mutare	W 41-13
10 June	ZIMBABWE	Harare	W 43-22

Appearances: 4 – Elliot*, Shepherd**; 3 – Dall, Eriksson, Gilmour, Laing, R Scott, Stark, Troup*; 2 – Browne, Burns, Craig, Dods, Flockhart*, Hay, Hodge, Kerr, Kittle, Nichol, Paul, Reid, Renwick, Rudkin, M W Scott, Turnbull, Wallace, Watt   *includes appearances as replacement
Scorers: 59 – Laing (10C 12PG 1DG); 20 – Stark (4T); 18 – Dods (2T 1C 2PG); 15 – Eriksson (3T), Shepherd (1T 2C 2PG); 10 – Gilmour (2T); 8 – Troup (1T 1DG); 5 – Craig, Dall, Renwick, Turnbull (1T each)

MATCH 1   31 May, Banket

Mashonaland Country Districts 13 (1G 2PG)   **Scotland XV 42** (4G 3PG 1T)
Mashonaland Country Districts: M Steenkamp; B Saunders, N Crabb, M Saunders, H Thomas; S Rugg, R Hoarde; A Voon, G Frangoulis, S Arnold, A Hopper, M Hopper, G Waterfall, G O'Neil, A Bruk-Jackson *Replacement* D Wyrley-Birch for Frangoulis
Scorers *Try:* O'Neil   *Conversion:* Rugg   *Penalty Goals:* Rugg (2)
Scotland XV: Dods; Gilmour, Craig, Hodge, Kerr; Laing, Troup; Browne, Hay, Kittle, R Scott, Rudkin, Wallace (*capt*), Renwick, Flockhart *Replacements* Elliot for Rudkin (temp) and Scott (temp); Shepherd for Kerr
Scorers *Tries:* Craig, Dods, Gilmour, Renwick, Troup   *Conversions:* Laing (4) *Penalty Goals:* Laing (3)
Referee M Leresche (Harare)

MATCH 2   3 June, Hartsfield, Bulawayo

Zimbabwe XV 23 (2G 3PG)   **Scotland XV 39** (4G 1PG 1DG 1T)
Scotland set themselves up for victory with a try in the first minute, Stuart Reid's scrummage pick-up and Graeme Burns' link putting Derek Stark over in the blindside corner. They stretched their lead to 15-0 after 19 minutes, and were out of sight at 32-6 by half-time. Zimbabwe cut the margin to 16 points when Craig Brown's reverse pass in his own 22 sent Ian Noble clear for a try.

Rowen Shepherd, intruding from full-back, made the Scots safe at 39-16, and after Fergus Wallace, their captain, broke an ankle, the game's only other score was an Aron Jani try for Zimbabwe.

Zimbabwe XV: E Chimbima; A Jani, I Noble, D Walters (*capt*), J Muchepa; C Brown, S Day; R Moore, B Beattie, N Mujaji, S Landsman, P Stephenson, B Dawson, T Tabvuma, D Kirkman *Replacement* B Norman for Muchepa
Scorers *Tries:* Jani, Noble   *Conversions:* Noble (2)   *Penalty Goals:* Noble (3)
Scotland XV: Shepherd; Gilmour, Nichol, Eriksson, Stark; Laing, Burns; Watt, M W Scott, Paul, Elliot, R Scott, Wallace (*capt*), Reid, Dall
Replacements Flockhart for Wallace; Troup for Burns (temp)
Scorers *Tries:* Dall, Gilmour, Shepherd, Stark (2)   *Conversions:* Laing (4) *Penalty Goal:* Laing   *Dropped Goal:* Laing
Referee M Wild (Bulawayo)

MATCH 3   7 June, Mutare Sports Club

Zimbabwe A 13 (1G 1PG 1DG)   **Scotland XV 41** (2G 3PG 1DG 3T)
Zimbabwe A: M Steenkamp; B Buckley, W Lunga, P Watson, M Nyahoda; M Grobler, E McMillan; R Pierce, W Barratt (*capt*), S Arnold, B Chivandire, M Hopper, B Lynch, J Putterill, K Cooke
Scorers *Try:* Nyahoda   *Conversion:* Grobler   *Penalty Goal:* Grobler *Dropped Goal:* Grobler
Scotland XV: Dods; Stark, Craig, Eriksson, Kerr; Hodge, Troup; Browne, Hay (*capt*), Kittle, Elliot, Rudkin, Turnbull Renwick, Dall *Replacement* Shepherd for Dods
Scorers *Tries:* Dods, Eriksson, Hodge, Stark (2)   *Conversions:* Dods, Shepherd   *Penalty Goals:* Dods (2), Hodge   *Dropped Goal:* Troup
Referee B O'Dwyer (Harare)

MATCH 4   10 June, Police Ground, Harare

Zimbabwe XV 22 (1G 5PG)   **Scotland XV 43** (2G 8PG 1T)
Zimbabwe put up a far stiffer performance in the second international than they had in the first, even though Derek Turnbull's scrum-based try put the Scots 11-6 up after 16 minutes. Ian Noble's fourth penalty goal gave the home team a 12-11 lead midway through the first half, and an Aron Jani try left them 22-17 in front at the interval. The Scots, however, had a strong third quarter. Two Ronnie Eriksson tries were converted by Stuart Laing, who in that time also kicked two of his eight penalty goals. Eriksson's first try, which put the Scots ahead for the fourth time, was created by Ian Elliot's line-out take, and the second was from simple exploitation of a tapped penalty.

Zimbabwe XV: E Chimbima; A Jani, I Noble, D Walters (*capt*), B Norman; C Brown, S Day; R Moore, B Beattie, N Mujaji, S Landsman, P Stephenson, B Dawson, T Tabvuma, D Kirkman
Replacements W Barratt for Beattie; B Chivandire for Kirkman
Scorer *Try:* Noble   *Conversion:* Noble   *Penalty Goals:* Noble (5)
Scotland XV: Shepherd; Gilmour, Nichol, Eriksson, Stark; Laing, Burns; Watt, M W Scott, Paul, Elliot, R Scott, Turnbull, Reid (*capt*), Dall
Scorers *Tries:* Eriksson (2), Turnbull   *Conversions:* Laing (2)
Penalty Goals: Laing (8)
Referee M Wild (Bulawayo)

WALES TO SOUTH AFRICA

Wales got their season off to an early start with this two-match tour, which was seen as a return favour for South Africa's vote clinching the 1999 World Cup for the Principality. Wales had cleared out many of the players who had been in South Africa for the World Cup only a couple of months earlier, notably scrum-half Robert Jones and lock Gareth Llewellyn. New captain Jonathan Humphreys was chosen with a view to helping build for the next tournament in four years' time. The squad was very young and inexperienced and the omens for the Test match looked bleak when the warm-up game against South-East Transvaal, effectively a third-division province, resulted in a heavy defeat by 47-6. Yet by the final whistle of the international in Johannesburg, much of the faith placed in youth by the management seemed to have been vindicated.

THE TOURING PARTY
Manager T G Evans   **Coach** R A C Evans   **Assistant Coach** D John
Captain J M Humphreys

FULL-BACKS

W J L Thomas (Cardiff IHE & Llanelli)

THREEQUARTERS

A R Harris (Swansea)
G H Jones (Bridgend)
M Taylor (Pontypool)

S D Hill (Cardiff)
I C Evans (Llanelli)
G Thomas (Bridgend)

HALF-BACKS

N R Jenkins (Pontypridd)
D A Williams (Swansea)
A P Moore (Cardiff)
P John (Pontypridd)

FORWARDS

A L P Lewis (Cardiff)
L Mustoe (Cardiff)
C D Loader (Swansea)
J D Davies (Neath)
J M Humphreys (Cardiff)
G R Jenkins (Swansea)
D Jones (Cardiff)

P Arnold (Swansea)
A Gibbs (Newbridge)
A M Bennett (Cardiff)
C Wyatt (Neath)
H T Taylor (Cardiff)
G Prosser (Pontypridd)
A P Moore (Swansea)

TOUR RECORD

All matches   Played 2   Lost 2   Points for 17   Against 87
International match   Played 1   Lost 1   Points for 11   Against 40

SCORING DETAILS

All matches					International match			
For:	1T	-	4PG	-	17 Pts	For:	1T	-	2PG	11 Pts
Against:	10T	8C	6PG	1DG	87 Pts	Against:	5T	3C	3PG	40 Pts

MATCH DETAILS

1995	OPPONENTS	VENUE	RESULT
27 Aug	South-East Transvaal	Witbank	L6-47
2 Sept	SOUTH AFRICA	Johannesburg	L11-40

MATCH 1   27 August, Johann van Riebeek Stadium, Witbank

South-East Transvaal 47 (5G 3PG 1DG)   **Wales XV 6** (2PG)
South-East Transvaal: J Bodenstein: M Benade, C Greef, G Gendall, S Naude;
J Benade, G Erasmus; H Swart, F Engelbrecht, J Espag, M Bosman, P de Lange,
F Rossouw, T Oosthuizen (*capt*), R Fourie   *Replacement* J Visagie for Naude
(29 mins)
Scorers *Tries:* Erasmus, Visagie, Bosman, Fourie, Bodenstein
Conversions: J Benade (5)   *Penalty Goals:* J Benade (3)   *Dropped Goal:* J Benade
Wales XV: J Thomas; Harris, G Jones, M Taylor, Hill; Williams, John (*capt*); Lewis,
G Jenkins, Mustoe, D Jones, Arnold, Gibbs, Wyatt, Bennett   *Replacements* N Jenkins
for Thomas (29 mins); Prosser for Arnold (40 mins); H Taylor for Wyatt (40 mins);
A Moore (Cardiff) for John (61 mins); Humphreys for G Jenkins (61 mins); Loader
for Prosser (78 mins)
Scorer *Penalty Goals:* Williams (2)
Referee I Rogers (South Africa)

MATCH 2   2 September, Ellis Park, Johannesburg   **Test**

SOUTH AFRICA 40 (3G 3PG 2T)   **WALES 11** (2PG 1T)

This was billed as the first professional Test match. In this context, Wales
were very much the poor relations: the Springbok players were on at least
£100,000 apiece a season while the Welsh were still haggling for anything
at all.

The financial differential did not make itself evident on the field until
the closing stages of this keenly contested match – too keenly contested at
times. Swansea hooker Garin Jenkins was sent off shortly before the end
for striking Van der Westhuizen. South African Kobus Wiese was cited
after the match for flooring his opposite number, Derwyn Jones, after just

five minutes, a punch which necessitated Jones' departure from the field. Wiese was later suspended for 30 days. Two other Welsh players, Gibbs and Gareth Thomas, were also forced to retire with concussion.

Wales, despite their defeat, had cause to feel pleased: indeed, for 60 minutes there was little to choose between the teams. The tourists fielded three new caps: Justin Thomas, Gareth Jones and Chris Loader. Ieuan Evans, playing in his 55th international, equalled the record set by J P R Williams. The pack worked well, with Arnold and Moore causing the Springboks problems, Justin Thomas and Gareth Thomas impressed in defence.

For South Africa, Gary Teichmann was the only new Springbok on view. Wing James Small could consider himself lucky to have been on view at all since he had allegedly stamped on his international team-mate Chester Williams in a Currie Cup match just prior to the Test. Two tries in two minutes in the second half finally ended Wales' challenge after first-half tries from Wiese and Pienaar. A well-worked move sent Small over for the Springboks' third, and a fluffed Welsh restart then saw Joubert carve up the field for Teichmann to touch down.

SOUTH AFRICA: A J Joubert (Natal); J T Small (Natal), J C Mulder (Transvaal), H P le Roux (Transvaal), J Olivier (Northern Transvaal); J T Stransky (Western Province), J H van der Westhuizen (Northern Transvaal); I S Swart (Transvaal), J Dalton (Transvaal), M H Hurter (Northern Transvaal), J J Wiese (Transvaal), M G Andrews (Natal), J F Pienaar (Transvaal) (*capt*), G H Teichmann (Natal), R J Kruger (Northern Transvaal)
Scorers *Tries:* Wiese, Pienaar, Small, Teichmann, Mulder
Conversions: Stransky (3)   *Penalty Goals:* Stransky (3)
WALES: J Thomas; Evans, G Jones, G Thomas, Hill; N Jenkins, A Moore (Cardiff); Loader, Humphreys (*capt*), Davies, Arnold, D Jones, Gibbs, H Taylor, Bennett
Replacements A Moore (Swansea) for D Jones (4 mins); G Jenkins for Gibbs (40 mins); M Taylor for G Thomas (69 mins)
Scorers *Try:* Bennett   *Penalty Goals:* N Jenkins (2)
Referee J Dumé (France)

FIJI TO WALES AND IRELAND

The Fijians might have been forced to leave behind some elements of their romantic past (no *cava* drinking-bowl, no pre-match *ciba* war dance and no sevens magician Waisale Serevi), but there were still enough glimpses of their unique style to satisfy purists, particularly in the early matches, against Wales A, Neath and Treorchy.

Former All Blacks Brad Johnstone and Bernie Fraser were brought in as coaches to temper Fijian flair with Kiwi steel for the nine-match tour. A change in selection policy for the trip enabled overseas players to be chosen, and half the squad had played provincial rugby in New Zealand and Australia. The Fijians had a testing schedule, playing against the top five Welsh sides from the previous season before heading across the Irish Sea to meet Connacht and Ireland. In the

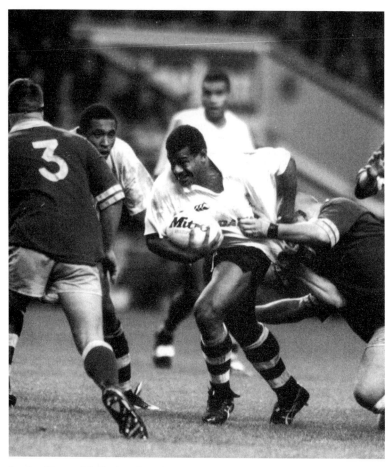

Lyndon Mustoe (No 3) closes in on Rasolosolo Bogisa of Fiji during Wales' narrow win in Cardiff.

end their failings were familiar ones: not enough muscle and technique up front and too many mistakes under pressure. Even so, Fiji were unlucky to lose to Wales, whom they led 15-13 shortly after half-time, although the Test match in Ireland, which was lost 44-8, exposed their limitations.

THE TOURING PARTY

Manager S Vuetaki   **Coach** M Kurisaru   **Captain** J Veitayaki
Technical Adviser B Johnstone

FULL-BACKS	THREEQUARTERS
F Rayasi (King Country, NZ)	**J Vidiri** (Counties, NZ)
R Bogisa (Nadi)	**P Bale** (Canterbury, NZ)

M **Bari** (Tavua)
W **Rokotuiviwa** (Rewa)
L **Little** (King Country, NZ)
S C **Sorovaki** (Wellington, NZ)
E **Bolobolo** (Tavua)

HALF-BACKS

O **Turuva** (Nadi)
J **Waqa** (Nadroga)
J **Rauluni** (Easts, Brisbane)
J **McLennan** (Auckland, NZ)

FORWARDS

J **Veitayaki** (King Country, NZ)
V **Cavubati** (Wellington, NZ)

S **Sadria** (Suva)
E **Natuivau** (Suva)
G **Smith** (Waikato, NZ)
E **Batimala** (Nadroga)
E **Katalau** (Poverty Bay, NZ)
A **Nadolo** (Suva)
W **Masirewa** (Counties, NZ)
T **Tamanivalu** (Brothers, Brisbane)
L **Vatureva** (Wellington, NZ)
M T **Korovou** (Nadi)
I **Tawake** (Nadroga)
D **Rouse** (Nadi)
S **Vonalagi** (Suva)

TOUR RECORD

All matches   Played 9   Won 3   Lost 6   Points for 217   Against 209
International matches   Played 2   Lost 2   Points for 23   Against 63

SCORING DETAILS

All Matches						**International matches**				
For:	31T	13C	11PG	1DG	217 Pts	For:	3T	1C	2PG	23 Pts
Against:	22T	15C	21PG	2DG	209 Pts	Against:	8T	4C	5PG	63 Pts

MATCH DETAILS

1995	OPPONENTS	VENUE	RESULT
21 Oct	Wales A	Bridgend	W 25-10
25 Oct	Neath	Neath	L 22-30
28 Oct	Cardiff	Cardiff	L 21-22
1 Nov	Treorchy	Treorchy	W 70-14
4 Nov	Pontypridd	Pontypridd	L 13-31
7 Nov	Llanelli	Llanelli	W 38-12
11 Nov	WALES	Cardiff	L 15-19
14 Nov	Connacht	Galway	L 5-27
18 Nov	IRELAND	Dublin	L 8-44

Appearances: 8 – Bari*, Katalau*; 7 – Sorovaki, Bale, Bogisa**, Masirewa*; 6 – Little, Veitayaki, Tawake, Rouse, Waqa, Nadolo; 5 – Natuivau, Tamanivalu, Rauluni, Smith; 4 – Rayasi, McLennan, Batimala, Bolobolo, Rokotuiviwa, Turuva, Cavubati, Vonolagi*; 3 – Sadria, Vatureva, Korovou   *includes appearances as replacement
Scorers: 49 – Waqa (2T 9C 6PG 1DG); 30 – Bari (6T); 25 – Bogisa (4T 1C 1PG); 18 – Turuva (3C 4PG); 15 – Bale, Bolobolo, Rokotuiviwa (all 3T); 10 – Masirewa (2T); 5 – Rayasi, Little, McLennan, Nataivau, Rouse, Tawake, Vatureva, Korovou (all 1T)

MATCH 1   21 October, Brewery Field, Bridgend

Wales A 10 (1G 1PG)   **Fiji XV 25** (1G 1PG 3T)
Wales A: W J L Thomas (Llanelli); A R Harris (Swansea), M Taylor (Swansea), G Thomas (Bridgend), W T Proctor (Llanelli); A Davies (Cardiff), P John (Pontypridd), (*capt*); A L P Lewis (Cardiff), R C McBryde (Llanelli), S C John (Llanelli), G Prosser (Pontypridd), A P Moore (Swansea), A Gibbs (Newbridge), S M Williams (Neath), O Lloyd (Llanelli) *Replacements* M Voyle (Newport) for Prosser (51 mins); L Mustoe (Cardiff) for Lewis (78 mins)
Scorers *Try:* pen try   *Conversion:* Davies   *Penalty Goal:* Davies
Fiji XV: Rayasi; Bari, Sorovaki, Little, Bale; Bogisa, McLennan; Veitayaki (*capt*), Batimala, Natuivau, Katalau, Tawake, Tamanivalu, Rouse, Masirewa
Scorers *Tries:* Bale (2), Bari, Masirewa   *Conversion:* Bogisa   *Penalty Goal:* Bogisa
Referee P Thomas (France)

41

MATCH 2   25 October, The Gnoll, Neath

Neath 30 (2G 2PG 2T)   **Fiji XV 22** (2G 1PG 1T)
Neath: G Davies; C Higgs, L Davies, J Funnell, R Jones; P Williams, P Horgan;
D Morris, K Allen, J Davies, Glyn Llewellyn, Gareth Llewellyn (*capt*), J Burnell,
S Williams, C Scott
Scorers *Tries:* Funnell, L Davies, Scott, Higgs   *Conversions:* P Williams (2)   *Penalty Goals:* P Williams (2)
Fiji XV: Waqa; Bolobolo, Little, Rokotuiviwa, Bari; Turuva, Rauluni; Sadria, Smith,
Cavubati, Nadolo, Vatureva, Katalau, Vonalagi (*capt*), Masirewa
Scorers *Tries:* Waqa, Bari, Vatureva   *Conversions:* Turuva (2)   *Penalty Goal:* Turuva
Referee E F Morrison (England)

MATCH 3   28 October, Cardiff Arms Park, Cardiff

Cardiff 22 (1G 5PG)   **Fiji XV 21** (1G 3PG 1T)
Cardiff: M Rayer; S Ford, M Ring, C John, S Hill; A Davies (*capt*), A Moore;
A Lewis, J Humphreys, L Mustoe, J Wakeford, D Jones, V Davies, E Lewis,
O Williams *Replacements* A Booth for Moore (temp); H Stone for Williams (temp)
Scorers *Try:* Moore   *Conversion:* A Davies   *Penalty Goals:* A Davies (5)
Fiji XV: Rayasi; Bale, Sorovaki, Little, Bari; Turuva, Rauluni; Veitayaki (*capt*), Smith,
Cavubati, Katalau, Tawake, Tamanivalu, Rouse, Korovou
Replacement Bogisa for Rayasi (28 mins)
Scorers *Tries:* Korovou, Bogisa   *Conversion:* Turuva   *Penalty Goals:* Turuva (3)
Referee E Murray (Greenock)

MATCH 4   1 November, The Oval, Treorchy

Treorchy 14 (2G)   **Fiji XV 70** (6G 1PG 5T)
Treorchy: D Lloyd; A Harries, C Hacker, R Morgan, A Lewis; D Evans,
C Hammans; M Smith, A Thomas, M Powell, A Gregory, A Freeman, N Jones,
G Owen (*capt*), I Davies *Replacement* W Booth for Evans (6 mins); S Eggar for
Harries (25 mins); D Owen for Jones (51 mins); C Rees for Booth (72 mins)
Scorers *Tries:* Thomas, Hammans   *Conversions:* Lloyd (2)
Fiji XV: Waqa; Bolobolo, Sorovaki, Rokotuiviwa, Bale; Bogisa, McLennan;
J Veitayaki (*capt*), Batimala, Natuivau, Nadolo, Katalau, Tawake, Rouse, Masirewa
Replacement Vonalagi for Tawake (50 mins)
Scorers *Tries:* Bolobolo (3), Rokotuiviwa (2), Natuivau, Waqa, McLennan, Rouse,
Bale, Bogisa   *Conversions:* Waqa (6)   *Penalty Goal:* Waqa
Referee R Duhau (France)

MATCH 5   4 November, Sardis Road, Pontypridd

Pontypridd 31 (2G 4PG 1T)   **Fiji XV 13** (1PG 2T)
Pontypridd: C Cormack; D Manley, J Lewis, S Lewis, G Jones; N Jenkins, Paul
John; N Bezani (*capt*), Phil John, N Eynon, G Prosser, M Rowley, M Spiller,
M Lloyd, P Thomas *Replacements* N Lloyd for Paul John (64 mins); R Collins for
M Lloyd (68 mins)
Scorers *Tries:* Phil John, Manley, S Lewis   *Conversions:* Jenkins (2)
Penalty Goals: Jenkins (4)
Fiji XV: Waqa; Bolobolo, Rokotuiviwa, Bogisa, Bari; Turuva, McLennan; Sadria,
Batimala, Cavubati, Nadolo, Vatureva, Tamanivalu, Vonolagi (*capt*), Korovou
Replacement Masirewa for Tamanivalu (47 mins)
Scorers *Tries:* Bari, Rokotuiviwa   *Penalty Goal:* Waqa
Referee R McDowell (Ireland)

MATCH 6   7 November, Llanelli

Llanelli 12 (2PG 2DG)   **Fiji XV 38** (2G 2PG 1DG 3T)
Llanelli: S Pearce; D Evans, N Boobyer, M Wintle, G Evans; M McCarthy, H Harries; H Williams-Jones, R McBryde (*capt*), S John, L Williams, P Jones, O Lloyd, P Morris, G Jones *Replacements* R Moon for Harries (50 mins); J Hyatt for McBryde (67 mins)
Scorers *Penalty Goals:* Pearce (2)   *Dropped Goals:* McCarthy (2)
Fiji XV: Bogisa; Bale, Sorovaki, Little, Bari; Waqa, Rauluni; Veitayaki (*capt*), Smith, Natuivau, Katalau, Nadolo, Tawake, Rouse, Masirewa
Scorers *Tries:* Tawake, Bogisa, Little, Bari (2)   *Conversions:* Waqa (2)
Penalty Goals: Waqa (2)   *Dropped Goal:* Waqa
Referee S Lander (England)

MATCH 7   11 November, Cardiff Arms Park   Test Match

WALES 19 (3PG 2T)   **FIJI 15** (1G 1PG 1T)

Wales came into this match having lost three games in succession at the Arms Park. How easily they might have made it four. Only desperate defence in the last quarter kept the Fijians at bay and earned Wales only their second victory in nine matches. The rain sluicing down made it an inauspicious day for running and handling but Fiji, particularly Rayasi and Bale, showed glorious touches of all their fabled skills. Not so prominent was Ieuan Evans, who might have wished for more opportunities to celebrate his record-breaking 56th cap, which eclipsed the old mark set by J P R Williams. At the other end of the scale Craig Quinnell, 20, added another chapter to a famous family history by making his debut.

Wales came out of the blocks well, scoring two tries within 16 minutes through Moore and Jenkins. By half-time Fiji were on equal terms at 10-10, Bari's try and Waqa's conversion and penalty goal bringing the scores level. Within ten minutes of the restart Rayasi's wonderful try put Fiji two points in front, Jenkins having put over a penalty. Two more followed from the Welsh fly-half's boot and Fijian dreams perished.

WALES: W J L Thomas (Llanelli); I C Evans (Llanelli), G Thomas (Bridgend), N G Davies (Llanelli), W T Proctor (Llanelli); N R Jenkins (Pontypridd), A P Moore (Cardiff); C D Loader (Swansea), J M Humphreys (Cardiff) (*capt*), L Mustoe (Cardiff), A P Moore (Swansea), D Jones (Cardiff), J C Quinnell (Llanelli), H T Taylor (Cardiff), A M Bennett (Cardiff) *Replacements* D A Williams (Swansea) for Davies (23 mins); G R Jenkins (Swansea) for Humphreys (temp)
Scorers *Tries:* A P Moore (Cardiff), N Jenkins   *Penalty Goals:* N Jenkins (3)
FIJI: Rayasi; Bale, Sorovaki, Little, Bari; Waqa, Rauluni; Veitayaki (*capt*), Smith, Natuivau, Katalau, Tawake, Tamanivalu, Rouse, Masirewa *Replacement* Bogisa for Waqa (40 mins)
Scorers *Tries:* Bari, Rayasi   *Conversion:* Waqa   *Penalty Goal:* Waqa
Referee P D O'Brien (New Zealand)

MATCH 8   14 November, Sportsground, Galway

Connacht 27 (3G 2PG)   **Fiji XV 5** (1T)
Connacht: A White (Corinthians); M Devine (Buccaneers), M Murphy (Galwegians), R Corrigan (Lansdowne), M O'Reilly (Old Belvedere); E Elwood

43

(Lansdowne), D Reddan (Old Crescent); D Kavanagh (Blackrock Coll), B Mulcahy (Skerries), C Shanley (DLSP), G Heaslip (Galwegians), R McCarthy (Sunday's Well), R Rogers (Blackrock Coll), N Mannion (Buccaneers), K Devlin (St Mary's Coll) *(capt)* *Replacements* K Lawless (Clontarf) for Reddan; N Culliton (Wanderers) for McCarthy
Scorers *Tries:* Devine, Devlin, Rogers   *Conversions:* Elwood (3)
Penalty Goals: Elwood (2)
Fiji XV: Bogisa; Bolobolo, Sorovaki, Rokotuiviwa, Bale; Turuva, McLennan; Sadria, Batimala, Cavubati, Vatureba, Nadolo, Vonalagi *(capt)*, Rouse, Korovou
Replacements Bari for Bale; Katalau for Korovou
Scorer *Try:* Bogisa
Referee J Pearson (England)

MATCH 9   18 November, Lansdowne Road, Dublin   Test Match
IRELAND 44 (4G 2PG 2T)   FIJI 8 (1PG 1T)

If there was a breath of fresh air about Lansdowne Road it had much to do with the fact that Ireland were parading a new manager, Pat Whelan, a new coach, Murray Kidd, and a new captain, Jim Staples. There were two new caps on view in the Irish side, too: converted lock Jeremy Davidson at wing forward and, a surprise choice, Sale scrum-half Chris Saverimutto. With Paul Burke at fly-half the Irish had pledged themselves to a more expansive game. Fiji made two changes, one in personnel, and one positional, from the side which lost to Wales.

If that game had raised Fijian hopes they were suitably smashed here. Showing unfamiliar traits of method and discipline, Ireland ran in six tries and dominated the match from first whistle to last. Fiji had barely had a touch of the ball before Ireland scored their opening try through Paddy Johns in the ninth minute. Ireland's tall back five produced a stream of possession from the line-out. Neil Francis went over for a soft try before Burke struck two penalties. Staples' try in the 50th minute, after great build-up work from the pack, was the best of the afternoon. Then the Wallace brothers emulated the Hewitt brothers' feat of 1924 in scoring tries either side of one by Geoghegan. Masirewa's try in injury time was scant consolation for Fiji.

IRELAND: J E Staples (Harlequins) *(capt)*; R M Wallace (Garryowen), M J Field (Malone), J C Bell (Northampton), S P Geoghegan (Bath); P A Burke (Cork Const), C Saverimutto (Sale); N J Popplewell (Newcastle), T J Kingston (Dolphin), P S Wallace (Blackrock Coll), G M Fulcher (Cork Const), N P J Francis (Old Belvedere), J W Davidson (Dungannon), P S Johns (Dungannon), D S Corkery (Cork Const) *Replacements* A T H Clarke (Northampton) for Kingston (45 mins); H D Hurley (Old Wesley) for Popplewell (temp); W D McBride (Malone) for Davidson (75 mins); S A McCahill (Sunday's Well) for Field (temp)
Scorers *Tries:* R Wallace, P Wallace, Geoghegan, Johns, Francis, Staples   *Conversions:* Burke (4)   *Penalty Goals:* Burke (2)
FIJI: Rayasi; Bale, Sorovaki, Little, Bari; Waqa, Rauluni; Veitayaki *(capt)*, Smith, Natuivau, Katalau, Nadolo, Tamanivalu, Tawake, Masirewa
Scorers *Try:* Masirewa   *Penalty Goal:* Waqa
Referee P D O'Brien (New Zealand)

NEW ZEALAND TO ITALY AND FRANCE

At the end of an arduous season the All Blacks knew that they could not afford to seek mental refuge in excuses about fatigue and staleness. Their eight-match itinerary encompassed six games in France, an excursion into one of the most hostile terrains on the touring map. There was also the little matter of revenge to stir any flagging spirits – France had beaten New Zealand in a series on their home patch just a year before. New Zealand, whatever their weariness, were ready and up for it.

What they didn't need was to lose one of their key men, fly-half Andrew Mehrtens, in the opening game in Sicily against Italy A.

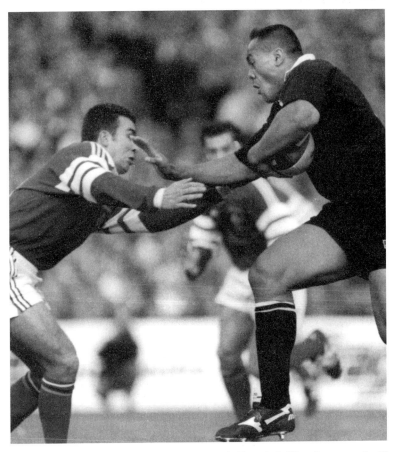

Jean-Luc Sadourny tackles the mighty Jonah Lomu in France's thrilling victory over the All Blacks in the First Test in Toulouse.

Mehrtens' knee injury forced him to return home and he was replaced by 20-year-old Aucklander Carlos Spencer. At that juncture the loss did not seem to affect the All Blacks greatly as they ran in 70 points against Italy in Bologna. However, they were to stutter throughout the tour, during which the boy wonder Jonah Lomu was a shadow, albeit still an intimidating one, of his World Cup self.

The First Test against France in Toulouse was lost, but, fired by pride and the thought of potential shame, the All Blacks hit stunning form to win one of the great modern Tests in Paris the following week and squared the series.

Coach Laurie Mains retired after four years in charge.

THE TOURING PARTY

Manager C E Meads   **Coach** L W Mains   **Captain** S B T Fitzpatrick

FULL-BACKS

J W Wilson (Otago)
G M Osborne (North Harbour)

THREEQUARTERS

J T Lomu (Counties)
E J Rush (North Harbour)
F E Bunce (North Harbour)
W K Little (North Harbour)
A I Ieremia (Wellington)
*J T F Matson (Canterbury)

HALF-BACKS

A P Mehrtens (Canterbury)
S D Culhane (Southland)
*C J Spencer (Auckland)
S T Forster (Otago)
J W Marshall (Southland)

FORWARDS

C W Dowd (Auckland)

O M Brown (Auckland)
M R Allen (Taranaki)
R W Loe (Canterbury)
S B T Fitzpatrick (Auckland)
N J Hewitt (Southland)
I D Jones (North Harbour)
R M Brooke (Auckland)
R T Fromont (Auckland)
*M S B Cooksley (Waikato)
B P Larsen (North Harbour)
J A Kronfeld (Otago)
M N Jones (Auckland)
L J Barry (North Harbour)
T J Blackadder (Canterbury)
T C Randell (Otago)
Z V Brooke (Auckland)

Replacement during tour

TOUR RECORD

All matches   Played 8   Won 7   Lost 1   Points for 339   Against 126
International matches   Played 3   Won 2   Lost 1   Points for 122   Against 40

SCORING DETAILS

	All matches					International matches				
For:	40T	26C	28PG	1DG	339 Pts	For:	14T	8C	12PG	122 Pts
Against:	14T	10C	11PG	1DG	126 Pts	Against:	5T	3C	3PG	40 Pts

MATCH DETAILS

1995	OPPONENTS	VENUE	RESULT
25 Oct	Italy A	Catania	W51-21
28 Oct	ITALY	Bologna	W70-6
1 Nov	French Barbarians	Toulon	W34-19
4 Nov	Languedoc-Roussillon	Béziers	W30-9

7 Nov	Côte Basque-Landes	Bayonne	W47-20
11 Nov	FRANCE	Toulouse	L15-22
14 Nov	French Selection	Nancy	W55-17
18 Nov	FRANCE	Paris	W37-12

Appearances: 7 – Rush, Osborne*, Lomu*; 6 – Little*, Larsen*, Marshall*; 5 – Culhane, Bunce, I Jones, Barry, Loe*; 4 – Wilson, Fitzpatrick, Blackadder, Ieremia, Hewitt, Allen, M Jones, Z Brooke, Randell, R Brooke, Brown, Dowd, Fromont; 3 – Matson, Forster, Spencer*; 1 – Mehrtens, Cooksley *includes appearances as a replacement
Scorers: 76 – Culhane (11C 17PG 1DG); 32 – Spencer (10C 4PG); 30 – Rush, Osborne (both 6T); 25 – Lomu (5T); 24 – Wilson (2T 4C 2PG); 17 – Mehrtens (1C 5PG); 15 – Bunce (3T); 10 – Little, Marshall, Fitzpatrick, Blackadder, I Jones, Ieremia (all 2T); 5 – Barry, Hewitt, Allen, M Jones, Z Brooke, Matson (all 1T)

MATCH 1   25 October, Santa Maria Goretti Stadium, Catania

Italy A 21 (1G 2PG 1DG 1T)   **New Zealand XV 51** (3G 5PG 3T)
Italy A: P Dotto (Treviso); F Roselli (Roma), M Visentin (Treviso), M Piovene (Padova), N Mazzuccato (Padova); G Filizzola (Calvisano), G Guidi (Livorno); A Castellani (L'Aquila), G de Carli (Roma) (*capt*), F Properzi-Curti (Milan), R Favaro (Treviso), D Scaglia (Treviso), C Caione (L'Aquila), R Piovan (Padova), R Saetti (Padova) *Replacements* F Scipioni (L'Aquila) for Visentin (60 mins); P Donati (Treviso) for Dotto (63 mins); R Cassina (Piacenza) for Piovan (65 mins); P Menapace (Padova) for Castellani (66 mins)
Scorers *Tries:* Castellani, Favaro   *Conversion:* Filizzola
Penalty Goals: Filizzola (2)   *Dropped Goal:* Filizzola
New Zealand XV: Osborne; Wilson, Bunce (*capt*), Ieremia, Rush; Mehrtens, Marshall; Allen, Hewitt, Loe, Larsen, Fromont, Randell, Blackadder, Barry
Replacement Little for Mehrtens (57 mins)
Scorers *Tries:* Blackadder (2), Ieremia, Bunce, Wilson, Osborne
Conversions: Wilson (2), Mehrtens   *Penalty Goals:* Mehrtens (5)
Referee C Giacomel (Italy)

MATCH 2   28 October, Stadio dall'Arra, Bologna   Test

ITALY 6 (2PG)   NEW ZEALAND 70 (7G 2PG 3T)

Many in the record crowd of 30,000 had come to witness and salute that great phenomenon, Jonah Lomu. For most of the first half, however, they spent their time cheering their own side's valiant display and fostering hopes of an unlikely victory. Reality set in in the second half, when the All Blacks found form. They ran in ten tries, several of them prompted by devastating counter-attacking from the back three of Lomu, Wilson and Rush, the latter standing in for Osborne. Bonomi had a poor afternoon with the boot for Italy. The crowd finally got their treat when Lomu, brushing off tacklers as if they were bothersome confetti, ran 90 metres for a score. 'These All Blacks are of a different world,' said Italian coach Georges Coste afterwards.

ITALY: M Ravazzolo (Calvisano); P Vaccari (Calvisano), S Bordon (Rovigo), I Francescato (Treviso), F Mazzariol (Treviso); M Bonomi (Milan), A Troncon (Treviso); Massimo Cuttitta (Milan) (*capt*), C Orlandi (Piacenza), F Properzi-Curti (Milan), P Pedroni (Milan), M Giacheri (Treviso), M Giovanelli (Milan), C Checchinato (Rovigo), A Sgorlon (Milan) *Replacements* O Arancio (Catania) for Giovanelli (61 mins); M Piovene (Padova) for Bordon (69 mins), G Filizzola (Calvisano) for Piovene (75 mins)
Scorer *Penalty Goals:* Bonomi (2)
NEW ZEALAND: Wilson; Rush, Bunce, Little, Lomu; Culhane, Forster; Dowd, Fitzpatrick (*capt*), Brown, I D Jones, R M Brooke, B P Larsen, Z V Brooke, M N Jones

Scorers *Tries:* Little (2), Lomu (2), M Jones, Z Brooke, I Jones, Fitzpatrick, Rush, Wilson   *Conversions:* Culhane (7)   *Penalty Goals:* Culhane (2)
Referee G Gadjovich (Canada)

MATCH 3   1 November, Stade Mayol, Toulon

French Barbarians 19 (2G 1T)   **New Zealand XV 34** (2G 4PG 1DG 1T)
French Barbarians: O Toulouze (Grenoble); P Bernat-Salles (Bègles), S Glas (Bourgoin), D Charvet (Racing Club de France) (*capt*), D Venditti (Bourgoin); D Camberabero (Grenoble), A Hueber (Toulon); J-L Jordana (Pau), M de Rougemont (Toulon), J-L Crenca (Agen), J A Eales (Queensland), O Roumat (Dax), M Lièvremont (Perpignan), X Blond (Racing Club de France), A Carminati (Brive)
Replacements P Bondouy (Narbonne) for Charvet (69 mins); J-P Alarcon (Toulon) for Carminati (69 mins)
Scorers *Tries:* Toulouze (3)   *Conversions:* Charvet, Camberabero
New Zealand XV: Osborne; Rush, Little, Ieremia, Lomu; Culhane, Marshall; Allen, Hewitt, Loe, I D Jones, Fromont, Barry, Z V Brooke (*capt*), Blackadder
Scorers *Tries:* Rush (2), Hewitt   *Conversions:* Culhane (2)
Penalty Goals: Culhane (4)   *Dropped Goal:* Culhane
Referee R G Davies (Wales)

MATCH 4   4 November, Stade de la Mediterranée, Béziers

Languedoc-Roussillon 9 (3PG)   **New Zealand XV 30** (3G 3PG)
Languedoc-Roussillon: O Laffitte (Béziers); P Fabre (Perpignan), P Arlettaz (Perpignan), P Bondouy (Narbonne), L Arbo (Perpignan); B Bellot (Perpignan), A Macabiau (Perpignan); P Gallart (Béziers), A Racine (Narbonne), F Tournaire (Narbonne), G Bourguignon (Narbonne), F Dejean (Narbonne) (*capt*), T Lievremont (Argeles), C Labit (Narbonne), G Majoral (Perpignan)
Replacements S Chinaro (Perpignan) for Bourguignon (24 mins); A Vercruysse (Béziers) for Macabiau (68 mins)
Scorer *Penalty Goals:* Bellot (3)
New Zealand XV: Wilson; Osborne, Bunce, Little, Matson; Culhane, Forster; Dowd, Fitzpatrick (*capt*), Brown, I D Jones, R M Brooke, Larsen, Randell, M N Jones *Replacements* Lomu for Osborne (41 mins); Spencer for Culhane (41 mins); Marshall for Wilson (78 mins)
Scorers *Tries:* Bunce (2), Fitzpatrick   *Conversions:* Wilson (2), Culhane
Penalty Goals: Wilson (2), Culhane
Referee J M Fleming (Scotland)

MATCH 5   7 November, Parc Municipal des Sports, Bayonne

Côte Basque-Landes 20 (2G 2PG)   **New Zealand XV 47** (4G 3PG 2T)
Côte Basque-Landes: C Lamaison (Bayonne); P Hontas (Biarritz), E Vergniol (Dax), C Pomme (Dax), P Labeyrie (Dax); D Arrieta (Biarritz), P Maillot (Bayonne); G Lascubé (Bayonne), R Ibanez (Dax), D Laperne (Dax), P Beraud (Dax) (*capt*), J Condom (Bayonne), C Milheres (Dax), R Berek (Dax), C Dongieu (Bayonne) *Replacement* H Durquety (Bayonne) for Milheres (66 mins)
Scorers *Tries:* Berek, Arrieta   *Conversions:* Lamaison (2)
Penalty Goals: Lamaison (2)
New Zealand XV: Osborne; Rush, Matson, Ieremia, Lomu; Spencer, Marshall; Allen, Hewitt, Loe (*capt*), Larsen, Fromont, Barry, Blackadder, Randell
Scorers *Tries:* Osborne (2), Allen, Rush, Ieremia, Marshall   *Conversions:* Spencer (4)   *Penalty Goals:* Spencer (3)
Referee B Campsall (England)

MATCH 6 11 November, Stade Municipal, Toulouse 1st Test

FRANCE 22 (2G 1PG 1T) NEW ZEALAND 15 (5PG)

This was a momentous afternoon. As the wind howled and the crowd roared, the French team contrived a storm of their own making, and one which completely unhinged the All Blacks. The omission of the 'South African Three' – Cabannes, Roumat and Lacroix – had created a bond of solidarity among the squad. They boycotted a civic function two days before the match, causing a split which provoked the resignation of team manager André Herrero. 'This will bring them together,' warned All Black captain Sean Fitzpatrick.

He was right. France scored three tries, and the young centres Dourthe and Castaignède tackled as if their lives depended on it. Sadourny, with a mesmerising, swerving run, scored France's first in the 16th minute. Dourthe's charge-down of Culhane's attempted clearance and subsequent follow-up gave France their second try ten minutes before half-time.

France missed five penalties and four dropped goals in the match, and their 17-3 interval lead was cut to just two points by Culhane's four penalties with 20 minutes still remaining. French captain Saint-André had the fitting last word of a memorable week by squeezing under Lomu for a try four minutes from time.

FRANCE: J-L Sadourny (Colomiers); E Ntamack (Toulouse), R Dourthe (Dax), T Castaignède (Toulouse), P Saint-André (Montferrand) *(capt)*; A Penaud (Brive), P Carbonneau (Toulouse); L Bénézech (Racing Club de France), M de Rougemont (Toulon), C Califano (Toulouse), O Merle (Montferrand), F Pelous (Dax), P Benetton (Agen), A Benazzi (Agen), A Carminati (Brive) *Replacement* D Berty (Toulouse) for Sadourny (46 mins)
Scorers *Tries:* Sadourny, Dourthe, Saint-André *Conversions:* Castaignède (2) *Penalty Goal:* Castaignède
NEW ZEALAND: Wilson; Rush, Bunce, Little, Lomu; Culhane, Forster; Dowd, Fitzpatrick *(capt)*, Brown, I D Jones, R M Brooke, Larsen, Z V Brooke, M N Jones *Replacement* Osborne for Wilson (54 mins)
Scorer *Penalty Goals:* Culhane (5)
Referee P Marshall (Australia)

MATCH 7 14 November, Stade Marcel Picot, Nancy

French Selection 17 (2G 1PG) New Zealand XV 55 (6G 1PG 2T)
French Selection: G Danglade (Tarbes); F Corrihons (Grenoble), L Burg (Grenoble), Y Delaigue (Toulon), F Tauzin (Bègles); P Favre (Bourgoin), S Bonnet (Brive); C Soulette (Béziers), H Guiraud (Nîmes), P Collazo (Toulon), O Brouzet (Grenoble), J-P Versailles (Montferrand), A Costes (Montferrand), C Juillet (Montferrand) *(capt)*, M Malafosse (Bourgoin) *Replacements* L Dehez (Bègles) for Collazo (48 mins); F Aymard (Grenoble) for Guiraud (72 mins)
Scorers *Tries:* Costes, Juillet *Conversions:* Favre (2) *Penalty Goal:* Favre
New Zealand XV: Osborne; Rush, Matson, Ieremia, Lomu; Spencer, Marshall; Allen, Hewitt, Loe *(capt)*, Cooksley, Fromont, Blackadder, Randell, Barry *Replacement* Larsen for Fromont (temp)
Scorers *Tries:* Osborne (2), Lomu (2), Rush, Barry, Matson, Marshall *Conversions:* Spencer (6) *Penalty Goal:* Spencer
Referee G Black (Ireland)

MATCH 8   18 November, Parc des Princes, Paris   2nd Test

FRANCE 12 (1G 1T)   **NEW ZEALAND 37** (1G 5PG 3T)

The All Blacks responded to that most powerful of motivating forces, the fear of humiliation, to produce one of their most stunning performances of recent years. The match was full of sustained running and shuddering clashes, played out before the Parc des Princes first-ever capacity crowd for a touring team. New Zealand made significant changes to their line-up after the previous week's reverse. Canterbury's Justin Marshall made his debut at scrum-half in place of Stu Forster, while Liam Barry, a third-generation All Black, came in at open side for his first cap. Jeff Wilson failed a fitness test and was replaced by Glen Osborne. Culhane put over the first of his five penalties after three minutes, only for Saint-André to reply by rounding off a thrilling movement for France. Eric Rush left tacklers in his slipstream to put New Zealand 15 points clear at the interval.

Osborne's audacious try five minutes after half-time set the tone for the second period. Lomu obliged with a typical blockbusting effort.

This was Laurie Mains' last match in charge. 'I retire a very happy man,' he said.

FRANCE: J-L Sadourny (Colomiers); E Ntamack (Toulouse), R Dourthe (Dax), T Castaignède (Toulouse), P Saint-André (Montferrand) (*capt*); A Penaud (Brive), P Carbonneau (Toulouse); L Bénézech (Racing Club de France), M de Rougemont (Toulon), C Califano (Toulouse), O Merle (Montferrand), F Pelous (Dax), P Benetton (Agen), A Benazzi (Agen), A Carminati (Brive) *Replacements* S Graou (Colomiers) for Bénézech (40 mins), M Lièvremont (Perpignan) for Carminati (65 mins)
Scorers *Tries:* Saint-André (2)   *Conversion:* Castaignède
NEW ZEALAND: Osborne; Rush, Bunce, Little, Lomu; Culhane, Marshall; Dowd, Fitzpatrick (*capt*), Brown, I D Jones, R M Brooke, M N Jones, Z V Brooke, Barry *Replacement* Loe for Dowd (80 mins)
Scorers *Tries:* Rush, Osborne, I Jones, Lomu   *Conversion:* Culhane
Penalty Goals: Culhane (5)
Referee P Marshall (Australia)

WESTERN SAMOA TO SCOTLAND AND ENGLAND 1995

The Samoans are a welcoming people, even if they know that on a rugby tour several of those dropping by at the team hotel may well be Rugby League scouts aiming to lure away yet another of their party. In 1995, for the second tournament running, Western Samoa had reached the quarter-final of the World Cup, yet by the time they began this demanding 12-match tour five months later they had lost six of their squad to League, another to Japan and one more, Saini Lemamea, to the outback, where he wandered off and never returned. In terms of their tiny playing base, they are perhaps the most talented rugby nation of all. The poaching depredations, and the arduousness of the weather, took their toll here. The side lost heavily to Scotland's North & Midlands, Cambridge University and England A. Superbly led by their captain, No 8 Pat Lam, the team showed their true colours in drawing with Scotland and challenging England strongly. The scouts will have noted the impressive displays of Leaupepe, Vaifale and Vaega.

THE TOURING PARTY

Manager Rev Dr F Talapusi **Coach** B G Williams
Assistant Coach T M Salesa **Captain** P R Lam

FULL-BACKS

V Patu (Vaiala)
A Autagavaia (Suburbs, NZ)

THREEQUARTERS

A T Telea (Petone, NZ)
T Fa'aiuaso (Police)
G E Leaupepe (Te Atatu)
F Fereti (Apia)
T M Vaega (Te Atatu)
S Leaega (Suburbs, NZ)
K Tuigamala (SCOPA)
B Lima (Marist, NZ)

HALF-BACKS

C Burnes (Auckland U, NZ)
D J Kellett (Ponsonby, NZ)
J Filemu (Wellington, NZ)
M Vaea (Marist, NZ)

FORWARDS

M A N Mika (Otago U)
P Fatialofa (Manukau/Marist, NZ)
G Latu (Vaimoso)
T Leota (Te Atatu)
T Leiasamaivao (Wellington, NZ)
B P Reidy (Marist St Pats, NZ)
M L Birtwistle (Suburbs, NZ)
P L Leavasa (Apia)
F L Falaniko (Marist, NZ)
S Lemamea (SCOPA)
S L Vaifale (Marist, NZ)
S Smith (Helensville, NZ)
L Ta'ala (Police)
M Iupeli (Marist, NZ)
S P Kaleta (Ponsonby, NZ)
P R Lam (Auckland/Marist, NZ)
*O Matauiau (Moataa)

*Replacement during tour

TOUR RECORD

All matches Played 12 Won 5 Drawn 1 Lost 6 Points for 253 Against 330
International matches Played 2 Drawn 1 Lost 1 Points for 24 Against 42

SCORING DETAILS

All matches						International matches				
For:	29T	15C	25PG	1DG	253 Pts	For:	2T	1C	4PG	24 Pts
Against:	35T	22C	35PG	2DG	330 Pts	Against:	2T	1C	10PG	42 Pts

MATCH DETAILS

1995	Opponents	Venue	Result
8 Nov	Edinburgh	Inverleith	W35-22
12 Nov	Scotland A	Hawick	W26-9
14 Nov	North & Midlands	Perth	L9-43
18 Nov	SCOTLAND	Murrayfield	D15-15
21 Nov	Oxford University	Oxford	W47-15
25 Nov	Cambridge University	Cambridge	L14-22
29 Nov	London & South East	Twickenham	W40-32
2 Dec	Midlands	Leicester	L19-40
5 Dec	North	Huddersfield	L8-34

9 Dec	South & South-West	Gloucester	W31-16
12 Dec	England A	Gateshead	L0-55
16 Dec	ENGLAND	Twickenham	L9-27

Appearances: 9 – Vaega*; 8 – Birtwistle, Kaleta, Lam, Vaifale*, Smith***; 7 – Patu, Lima, Telea, Filemu, Mika, Falaniko, Leiasamaivao*, Latu*; 6 – Burnes, Leaega, Kellett, Fatialofa, Tuigamala, Matauiau*, Vaea*, Reidy*, Autagavaia*; 5 – Leaupepe, Leavasa, Fa'aiuaso; 4 – Fereti, Lemamea, Ta'ala, Iupeli, 1 – Leota   *includes appearances as a replacement Scorers: 60 – Kellett (9C 13PG 1DG); 47 – Burnes (1T 6C 10PG); 31 – Patu (5T 2PG); 20 – Lima, Fa'aiuaso (both 4T); 10 – Vaifale, Lam, Birtwistle, Telea (all 2T); 5 – Leiasamaivao, Leaupepe, Kaleta, Matauiau, Vaega, Tuigamala, Autagavaia (all 1T)

MATCH 1   8 November, Inverleith

Edinburgh 22 (1G 5PG)   **Western Samoa XV 35** (2G 2PG 3T)
Edinburgh: N Mardon (Boroughmuir); D Macrae (Boroughmuir), D Laird (Boroughmuir), G Lawrie (Heriot's FP), C Glasgow (Heriot's FP); A Donaldson (Currie) *(capt)*, G Beveridge (Boroughmuir); R McNulty (Stewart's-Melville FP), P Haslett (Edinburgh Acads), S Paul (Heriot's FP), D Burns (Boroughmuir), S Murray (Edinburgh Acads), B Ward (Currie), T McVie (Heriot's FP), G Dall (Heriot's FP) *Replacements* F Henderson (Watsonians) for Macrae (71 mins); B Stewart (Edinburgh Acads) for McNulty (temp)
Scorers *Try:* Burns   *Conversion:* Donaldson   *Penalty Goals:* Donaldson (5)
Western Samoa XV: Patu; Lima, Leaupepe, Vaega, Telea; Burnes, Vaea; Reidy, Leiasamaivao, Latu, Leavasa, Birtwistle, Kaleta, Lam *(capt)*, Vaifale
Scorers *Tries:* Patu (3), Leiasamaivao, Lima   *Conversions:* Burnes (2)
Penalty Goals: Patu, Burnes
Referee G Simmonds (Wales)

MATCH 2   12 November, Mansfield Park, Hawick

Scotland A 9 (3PG)   **Western Samoa XV 26** (2G 3PG 1DG)
Scotland A: S Lang (Heriot's FP); H Gilmour (Heriot's FP), S Nichol (Selkirk), I Jardine (Stirling County), D Stark (Boroughmuir); S Welsh (Hawick), G Armstrong (Jedforest) *(capt)*; G Wilson (Boroughmuir), G Ellis (Currie), S Paul (Heriot's FP), I Elliot (Hawick), S Campbell (Dundee HSFP), B Renwick (Hawick), E Peters (Bath), J Amos (Gala) *Replacement* S Scott (Melrose) for Ellis (temp)
Scorer *Penalty Goals:* Welsh (3)
Western Samoa XV: Leaega; Patu, Vaega, Leaupepe, Telea; Kellett, Filemu; Mika, Leiasamaivao, Fatialofa, Falaniko, Leavasa, Kaleta, Lam *(capt)*, Vaifale *Replacement* Latu for Fatialofa (77 mins)
Scorers *Tries:* Vaifale, Lam   *Conversions:* Kellett (2)   *Penalty Goals:* Kellett (3)
Dropped Goal: Kellett
Referee A Spreadbury (England)

MATCH 3   14 November, McDiarmid Park, Perth

North & Midlands 43 (3G 4PG 2T)   **Western Samoa XV 9** (3PG)
North & Midlands: S Burns (Edinburgh Acads); N Renton (Kirkcaldy), P Rouse (Dundee HSFP), A Carruthers (Kirkcaldy), J Kerr (Watsonians); M McKenzie (Stirling County), K Harper (Stirling County); W Anderson (Kirkcaldy), R Cairney (Stirling County), D Herrington (Kirkcaldy), S Hamilton (Stirling County), S Grimes (Watsonians), D McIvor (Edinburgh Acads) *(capt)*, M Waite (Edinburgh Acads), G Flockhart (Stirling County) *Replacements* B Easson (Boroughmuir) for Rouse (64 mins); Easson for Carruthers (temp)
Scorers *Tries:* Kerr (3), Renton, Rouse   *Conversions:* McKenzie (3)
Penalty Goals: McKenzie (4)

Western Samoa XV: Autagavaia; Fa'aiuaso, Tuigamala, Leaega, Fereti; Burnes, Vaea; Reidy, Leota, Latu, Birtwistle, Lemamea, Ta'ala, Smith, Iupeli (*capt*)
Replacement Leiasamaivao for Leota (49 mins)
Scorer *Penalty Goals:* Burnes (3)
Referee A Lewis (Ireland)

MATCH 4   18 November, Murrayfield   Test Match
SCOTLAND 15 (5PG)   WESTERN SAMOA 15 (1G 1PG 1T)

The moral victory belonged to Western Samoa, who scored the only tries of the match, both of them in the second half as the tourists ate into Scotland's lead. There were three new caps in the Scottish side: hooker Jim Hay, Stuart Reid at No 8 and Rowen Shepherd at full-back trying to fill the biggest shoes of all – those of the retired Gavin Hastings. Shepherd had a reasonable debut, although his one slip, a failure to take a high ball, led to the Samoans' first try in the 48th minute through George Leaupepe. By that stage, Michael Dods, younger brother of 1984 Grand Slam-winning full-back Peter, had put over four penalties in reply to one from Darren Kellett. Samoa were much quicker and sharper all round the field, and both locks, Lio Falaniko and Potu Leavasa, were involved in the build-up to their second try four minutes from time. The move eventually led to a penalty from which flanker Sam Kaleta scored. Dods finished with five penalty goals to his credit while Kellett will rue the miss of an easy conversion of the opening try.

SCOTLAND: R J S Shepherd (Melrose); M Dods (Northampton), G P J Townsend (Northampton), A G Shiel (Melrose), K M Logan (Stirling County); C M Chalmers (Melrose), B W Redpath (Melrose); D I W Hilton (Bath), J A Hay (Hawick), A P Burnell (London Scottish), G W Weir (Melrose), D F Cronin (Bourges), R I Wainwright (West Hartlepool) (*capt*), S J Reid (Boroughmuir), I R Smith (Gloucester) *Replacements* S J Campbell (Dundee HSFP) for Smith (temp); Campbell for Reid (temp)
Scorer *Penalty Goals:* Dods (5)
WESTERN SAMOA: Patu; Lima, Vaega, Leaupepe, Telea; Kellett, Filemu; Mika, Leiasamaivao, Fatialofa, Falaniko, Leavasa, Kaleta, Lam (*capt*), Vaifale *Replacements* Vaea for Filemu (83 mins); Smith for Leavasa (83 mins)
Scorers *Tries:* Leaupepe, Kaleta   *Conversion:* Kellett   *Penalty Goal:* Kellett
Referee T Henning (South Africa)

MATCH 5   21 November, Iffley Road, Oxford

Oxford University 15 (1G 1PG 1T)   **Western Samoa XV 47** (4G 3PG 2T)
Oxford University: J J Sackree; S J Rush, Q A de Bruyn, J M D Riondet, T G Howe (*capt*); D G Humphreys, M P Butler; C G B Norton, K F Svoboda, D N Penney, N J Basson, P F Coveney, C A P McCarthy, R S Yeabsley, M G P S Orsler
Scorers *Tries:* Howe, Riondet   *Conversion:* Humphreys   *Penalty Goal:* Humphreys
Western Samoa XV: Autagavaia; Fa'aiuaso, Vaega (*capt*), Leaega, Fereti; Burnes, Filemu; Mika, Leiasamaivao, Latu, Birtwistle, Falaniko, Smith, Iupeli, Kaleta
Replacement Matauiau for Leiasamaivao (5 mins)
Scorers *Tries:* Fa'aiuaso (4), Burnes, Matauiau   *Conversions:* Burnes (4)
Penalty Goals: Burnes (3)
Referee R Davies (Wales)

MATCH 6   25 November, Grange Road, Cambridge

Cambridge University 22 (4PG 2T)   **Western Samoa XV 14** (3PG 1T)
Cambridge University: A P Spencer; S Sexton, T A Q Whitford, S R Cottrell
(*capt*), N J Walne; R W Ashforth, B C I Ryan; L T Mooney, J Evans, N J Holgate,
R A Bramley, C R A Simpson, M J Hyde, S D Surridge, R D Earnshaw
Replacement J Rutter for Walne (71 mins)
Scorers *Tries:* Cottrell, Walne   *Penalty Goals:* Ashforth (4)
Western Samoa XV: Patu; Lima, Vaega, Tuigamala, Telea; Burnes, Vaea; Reidy,
Matauiau, Fatialofa, Lemamea, Falaniko, Ta'ala, Lam (*capt*), Vaifale
Scorers *Try:* Patu   *Penalty Goals:* Burnes (2), Patu
Referee G Crothers (Ireland)

MATCH 7   29 November, Twickenham

London & South-East 32 (3G 2PG 1T)   **Western Samoa XV 40** (3G 3PG 2T)
London & South-East: J Ufton (Wasps); D O'Leary (Harlequins), N Greenstock
(Wasps), P Mensah (Harlequins), A Adebayo (Bath); D Pears (Harlequins), S Bates
(Wasps) (*capt*); J Leonard (Harlequins), B Moore (Harlequins), I Dunston (Wasps),
A Snow (Harlequins), M Watson (Harlequins), L Dallaglio (Wasps), A Diprose
(Saracens), R Jenkins (Harlequins) *Replacement* G Gregory (Wasps) for Pears (40
mins)
Scorers *Tries:* Watson (2), Dallaglio, Mensah   *Conversions:* Gregory (3)
Penalty Goals: Pears (2)
Western Samoa XV: Autagavaia; Lima, Leaega, Leaupepe, Fa'aiuaso; Kellett,
Filemu; Mika, Leiasamaivao, Latu, Birtwistle, Leavasa, Smith, Lam (*capt*), Kaleta
Replacements Vaifale for Leavasa (28 mins); Vaega for Leaupepe (54 mins)
Scorers *Tries:* Lima (3), Lam, Vaifale   *Conversions:* Kellett (3)
Penalty Goals: Kellett (3)
Referee N Lasaga (France)

MATCH 8   2 December, Welford Road, Leicester

Midlands 40 (3G 3PG 2T)   **Western Samoa XV 19** (2G 1T)
Midlands: J Quantrill (Rugby); R Subbiani (Bedford), M Allen (Northampton),
B Whetstone (Bedford), H Thorneycroft (Northampton); P Grayson
(Northampton), M Dawson (Northampton); G Rowntree (Leicester), R Cockerill
(Leicester), D Garforth (Leicester), J Phillips (Northampton), M Bayfield
(Northampton), T Rodber (Northampton) (*capt*), C Tarbuck (Leicester), N Back
(Leicester) *Replacement* A Smallwood (Nottingham) for Subbiani (26 mins)
Scorers *Tries:* Rodber, Allen, Dawson, pen tries (2)   *Conversions:* Grayson (3)
Penalty Goals: Grayson (3)
Western Samoa XV: Patu; Lima, Vaega, Tuigamala, Telea; Kellett, Filemu; Mika,
Matauiau, Fatialofa, Birtwistle, Falaniko, Kaleta, Lam (*capt*), Vaifale
Scorers *Tries:* Birtwistle, Telea, Vaega   *Conversions:* Kellett (2)
Referee C Thomas (Wales)

MATCH 9   5 December, McAlpine Stadium, Huddersfield

North 34 (4G 2PG)   **Western Samoa XV 8** (1PG 1T)
North: T Stimpson (West Hartlepool); J Naylor (Orrell), P Johnson (Orrell) (*capt*),
W Greenwood (Harlequins), J Mallinder (Sale); R Liley (Sale), A Healey (Orrell);
G Baldwin (Wakefield), S Diamond (Sale), M Shelley (West Hartlepool),
M Greenwood (Wasps), J Fowler (Sale), R Arnold (Newcastle), C Vyvyan (Sale),
N Ashurst (Sale) *Replacement* T Herbert (West Hartlepool) for Diamond (20 mins)
Scorers *Tries:* Naylor, Mallinder, Liley, Arnold   *Conversions:* Liley (4)
Penalty Goals: Liley (2)

Western Samoa XV: Autagavaia; Fa'aiuaso, Leaega, Tuigamala, Fereti; Burnes, Vaea; Reidy, Matauiau, Latu, Lemamea, Birtwistle (*capt*), Ta'ala, Smith, Iupeli
Scorers *Try:* Tuigamala   *Penalty Goal:* Burnes
Referee I Ramage (Scotland)

MATCH 10   9 December, Kingsholm, Gloucester

South & South-West 16 (2DG 2T)   **Western Samoa XV 31** (1G 3PG 3T)
South & South-West: P Hull (Bristol) (*capt*); N Beal (Northampton), A Turner (Exeter), S Enoch (Pontypridd), P Holford (Gloucester); R Dix (Harlequins), B Fenley (Gloucester); T Windo (Gloucester), K Dunn (Wasps), D Hinkins (Bristol), D Sims (Gloucester), C Yandell (Saracens), P Glanville (Gloucester), E Rollitt (Bristol), J Pearson (Bristol) *Replacement* B Stafford (Brunel U) for Dix (64 mins)
Scorers *Tries:* Yandell, Enoch   *Dropped Goals:* Dix (2)
Western Samoa XV: Patu; Lima, Vaega, Tuigamala, Telea; Kellett, Filemu; Mika, Matauiau, Fatialofa, Falaniko, Birtwistle, Kaleta, Lam (*capt*), Vaifale *Replacements* Smith for Lam (15 mins); Reidy for Kaleta (40 mins); Autagavaia for Kellett (70 mins)
Scorers *Tries:* Patu, Birtwistle, Autagavaia, Telea   *Conversion:* Kellett
Penalty Goals: Kellett (3)
Referee D Méné (France)

MATCH 11   12 December, Gateshead

England A 55 (6G 1PG 2T)   **Western Samoa XV 0**
England A: T Stimpson (West Hartlepool); J Sleightholme (Bath), A Blyth (West Hartlepool), W Greenwood (Harlequins), J Naylor (Orrell); A King (Bristol U), A Gomarsall (Wasps); K Yates (Bath), P Greening (Gloucester), D Garforth (Leicester), G Archer (Bristol), R West (Gloucester), M Corry (Bristol), A Diprose (Saracens) (*capt*), R Hill (Saracens)
Scorers *Tries:* Gomarsall (2), Greenwood (3), Greening, Hill, Garforth   *Conversions:* Stimpson (6)   *Penalty Goal:* Stimpson
Western Samoa XV: Autagavaia; Fa'aiuaso, Leaega, Tuigamala, Fereti; Burnes, Vaea; Reidy, Matauiau, Latu, Lemamea, Birtwistle (*capt*), Ta'ala, Iupeli, Smith
Referee K McCartney (Scotland)

MATCH 12   16 December, Twickenham   Test Match

ENGLAND 27 (1G 5PG 1T)   WESTERN SAMOA 9 (3PG)

England's margin of victory may have looked comfortable on the scoreboard, but it was anything but comfortable on the pitch. Two tries within two minutes of each other midway through the second half, both of which had a mundane point of origin in the scrummage, put a decent distance between the teams, but they could not fool the capacity crowd of 72,000, who took to jeering an England side which had pledged themselves to playing expansive rugby.

England had made changes of personnel, and another two of position, to the team beaten by South Africa. Northampton half-backs Matt Dawson and Paul Grayson came in for their first caps, while Lawrence Dallaglio also had his first full outing after impressing as a replacement against the Springboks. Mike Catt was moved from fly-half in a bid to find a strike full-back, and Jason Leonard was switched to tight head. The new boys were entitled to feel reasonably pleased with their performance – Grayson directed his kicks well and Dawson looked lively round the base – but overall, England lacked shape, desire and momentum. The alignment and passing of the backs were lamentable.

It took them an hour to settle the result. Grayson had put them 15-6 ahead with five penalty goals to two from Kellett. Clarke's pick-up and feed put Dallaglio over from a close-range scrum. The pair featured again in England's second try two minutes later, making good ground before the ball moved to the blind side, where Catt's pass put Rory Underwood in. It was Western Samoa, though, who finished the stronger.

ENGLAND: M J Catt (Bath); D P Hopley (Wasps), W D C Carling (Harlequins) (*capt*), J C Guscott (Bath), R Underwood (Leicester & RAF); P J Grayson (Northampton), M J S Dawson (Northampton); G C Rowntree (Leicester), M P Regan (Bristol), J Leonard (Harlequins), M O Johnson (Leicester), M C Bayfield (Northampton), T A K Rodber (Northampton & Army), B B Clarke (Bath), L B N Dallaglio (Wasps)
Scorers *Tries:* Dallaglio, Underwood   *Conversion:* Grayson
Penalty Goals: Grayson (5)
WESTERN SAMOA: Patu; Lima, Vaega, Leaupepe, Telea; Kellett, Filemu; Mika, Leiasamaivao, Fatialofa, Leavasa, Falaniko, Kaleta, Lam (*capt*), Vaifale *Replacement* Smith for Falaniko (73 mins); Smith for Kaleta (temp)
Scorer *Penalty Goals:* Kellett (3)
Referee I Rogers (South Africa)

SOUTH AFRICA TO ITALY AND ENGLAND

This was the briefest of tours, but perhaps it was an indication of the shape of things to come. Defeat in a one-off international match can hurt the pocket as much as the morale these days, so a warm-up game to the main match is put on the agenda. Thus South Africa stopped off in Italy en route to England. It was a shrewd move, judging by later events. Against Italy the world champions were below par. Only a late flurry of scoring saw them home against a well-organised, battling Italian side; indeed, when Orlandi crossed for Italy's second try in the 56th minute, defeat looked on the cards for the 'Boks. Their line-out struggled and Dalton's throwing was poor, while wingers Small and Williams were out of touch. Italy's half-backs, Dominguez and Troncon, both had a fine game.

Joubert's stylish counter-attack set up the opening try for Mulder and scrummage pressure led to a penalty try for the 'Boks. Stransky's kicking kept South Africa in the hunt. Loose-head prop Van der Linde was the only new cap on show.

12 November, Olympic Stadium, Rome   **Test**

ITALY 21 (1G 3PG 1T)   **SOUTH AFRICA 40** (4G 4PG)

ITALY: F Williams (Milan); P Vaccari (Milan), S Bordon (Rovigo), I Francescato (Treviso), N Mazzuccato (Padova); D Dominguez (Milan), A Troncon (Treviso);

Chester Williams, South Africa's charismatic wing, breaks Jon Callard's tackle to score in the Twickenham international.

M Cuttitta (Milan) (*capt*), C Orlandi (Milan), F Properzi-Curti (Milan), P Pedroni (Milan), M Giacheri (Treviso), M Giovanelli (Milan), O Arancio (Catania) A Sgorlon (San Dona) *Replacement* R Crotti (Rovigo) for Mazzuccato (74 mins)
Scorers *Tries:* Arancio, Orlandi *Conversion:* Dominguez
Penalty Goals: Dominguez (3)
SOUTH AFRICA: A J Joubert (Natal); J T Small (Natal), J C Mulder (Transvaal), H P le Roux (Transvaal), C M Williams (Western Province); J T Stransky (Western Province), J H van der Westhuizen (Northern Transvaal); A van der Linde (Western Province), J Dalton (Transvaal), T G Laubscher (Western Province), J J Wiese (Transvaal), M G Andrews (Natal) R J Kruger (Northern Transvaal), J F Pienaar (Transvaal) (*capt*), F J van Heerden (Western Province) *Replacement* J Olivier (Northern Transvaal) for Joubert (78 mins)
Scorers *Tries:* Mulder, pen try, Pienaar, Le Roux *Conversions:* Stransky (4)
Penalty Goals: Stransky (4)
Referee S Lander (England)

18 November, Twickenham   **Test**

ENGLAND 14 (3PG 1T)   SOUTH AFRICA 24 (3PG 3T)

As a celebration of the new 78,000-capacity Twickenham the game backfired, since England failed to lift their supporters at any stage of a mediocre match. Openside Andy Robinson was recalled after an absence of six years in a bid by England to play a more dynamic game. The game plan spluttered. They struggled to find any sort of rhythm as South Africa ran out comfortable winners. Brian Moore, Rob Andrew and Dean Richards were missing from the England teamsheet. Instead Bristol hooker Mark Regan won his first cap and Wasps centre Damian Hopley his second, this time as a winger. Hopley's club colleague Lawrence Dallaglio made his first international appearance as a replacement for Tim Rodber, and captain Will Carling was also replaced, by Phil de Glanville, after damaging his neck. De Glanville scored England's only try two minutes from time. By then Chester Williams, with two tries, in the 39th and 66th minutes, and another disallowed, had shown England the way home. Van der Westhuizen added a third for South Africa, a marvellous solo try, in the 41st minute.

ENGLAND: J E B Callard (Bath); D P Hopley (Wasps), W D C Carling (Harlequins) *(capt)*, J C Guscott (Bath), R Underwood (Leicester & RAF); M J Catt (Bath), K P P Bracken (Bristol); J Leonard (Harlequins), M P Regan (Bristol), V E Ubogu (Bath), M O Johnson (Leicester), M C Bayfield (Northampton), T A K Rodber (Northampton & Army), B B Clarke (Bath), R A Robinson (Bath) *Replacements* L B N Dallaglio (Wasps) for Rodber (69 mins); P R de Glanville (Bath) for Carling (79 mins)
Scorers *Try:* De Glanville *Penalty Goals:* Callard (3)
SOUTH AFRICA: A J Joubert (Natal); J Olivier (Northern Transvaal), J C Mulder (Transvaal), H P le Roux (Transvaal), C M Williams (Western Province); J T Stransky (Western Province), J H van der Westhuizen (Northern Transvaal); A van der Linde (Western Province), J Dalton (Transvaal), T G Laubscher (Western Province), J J Wiese (Transvaal), M G Andrews (Natal), R J Kruger (Northern Transvaal), J F Pienaar (Transvaal) *(capt)*, F J van Heerden (Western Province) *Replacements* J T Small (Natal) for Olivier (46 mins); R A W Straeuli (Transvaal) for Kruger (62 mins)
Scorers *Tries:* Williams (2), Van der Westhuizen *Penalty Goals:* Stransky (3)
Referee J M Fleming (Scotland)

STOP PRESS TOURS AND INTERNATIONALS

WALES TO AUSTRALIA

MATCH DETAILS

1996	OPPONENTS	VENUE	RESULT
29 May	Western Australia	Perth	W62-20
2 Jun	ACT	Canberra	L30-69
5 Jun	NSW	Sydney	L20-27
8 Jun	**AUSTRALIA**	**Brisbane**	**L25-26**
12 Jun	Australia B	Brisbane	L41-51
15 Jun	NSW Country	Moree	W49-3
18 Jun	Victoria	Melbourne	W42-9
22 Jun	**AUSTRALIA**	**Sydney**	**L3-42**

SCOTLAND TO NEW ZEALAND

MATCH DETAILS

1996	OPPONENTS	VENUE	RESULT
28 May	Wanganui	Wanganui	W49-13
31 May	Northland	Whangarei	L10-15
5 Jun	Waikato	Hamilton	L35-39
8 Jun	Southland	Invercargill	W31-21
11 Jun	S Island Divisional XV	Blenheim	W63-21
15 Jun	**NEW ZEALAND**	**Dunedin**	**L31-62**
18 Jun	Bay of Plenty	Rotorua	W35-31
22 Jun	**NEW ZEALAND**	**Auckland**	**L12-36**

WESTERN SAMOA TO NEW ZEALAND

MATCH DETAILS

1996	OPPONENTS	VENUE	RESULT
26 May	Wellington	Wellington	L30-52
29 May	Counties	Pukekohe	W31-19
1 Jun	Taranaki	New Plymouth	W26-18
3 Jun	Wairarapa-Bush	Masterton	W23-18
7 Jun	**NEW ZEALAND**	**Napier**	**L10-51**
11 Jun	King Country	Taupo	W27-20
14 Jun	NZ Maoris	Auckland	L15-28

CANADA TO AUSTRALIA

MATCH DETAILS

1996	OPPONENTS	VENUE	RESULT
15 Jun	Queensland B	Rockhampton	L6-23
19 Jun	NSW	Sydney	L19-44
22 Jun	South Australia	Adelaide	W19-13
25 Jun	Australian Us	Sydney	W19-6
29 Jun	**AUSTRALIA**	**Brisbane**	**L9-74**

FRANCE TO ARGENTINA

MATCH DETAILS

1996	OPPONENTS	VENUE	RESULT
10 Jun	Cordoba Selection	Cordoba	W22-19
15 Jun	Buenos Aires Selection	Buenos Aires	L26-29
18 Jun	Tucumán Selection	Tucumán	W20-10
22 Jun	**ARGENTINA**	**Buenos Aires**	**W34-27**
25 Jun	San Juan Selection	San Juan	W51-0
29 Jun	**ARGENTINA**	**Buenos Aires**	**W34-15**

FIJI TO NEW ZEALAND AND SOUTH AFRICA

MATCH DETAILS

1996	OPPONENTS	VENUE	RESULT
15 Jun	Northland	Whangarei	W49-18
19 Jun	Poverty Bay	Gisborne	W49-6
23 Jun	Waikato	Hamilton	W33-25
2 Jul	**SOUTH AFRICA**	**Pretoria**	**L18-43**

PACIFIC RIM SERIES

11 May: United States 19, Canada 12 (San Francisco); Japan 34, Hong Kong 27 (Tokyo)

18 May: Canada 24, United States 20 (Vancouver); Hong Kong 33, Japan 9 (Hong Kong)

1 Jun: Hong Kong 12, Canada 18 (Hong Kong)

8 Jun: Hong Kong 19, United States 22 (Hong Kong)

9 Jun: Japan 18, Canada 45 (Tokyo)

16 Jun: Japan 24, United States 18 (Tokyo)

29 Jun: United States 42, Hong Kong 23 (San Francisco)

6 Jul: Canada 57, Hong Kong 9 (Vancouver); United States 74, Japan 5 (San Francisco)

13 Jul: Canada 51, Japan 30 (Vancouver)

Series winners: Canada

TRI-NATIONS SERIES

6 Jul: New Zealand 43, Australia 6 (Wellington)

13 Jul: Australia 21, South Africa 16 (Sydney)

20 Jul: New Zealand 15, South Africa 11 (Christchurch)

New Zealand led the series at the halfway mark

MIDDLING TEAM WIN A MIDDLING CHAMPIONSHIP

THE INTERNATIONAL CHAMPIONSHIP 1996

So much was expected of the Five Nations Championship; so little was delivered. Does it matter? In a purely sporting sense, of course it does. The All Blacks had showed us in the World Cup just how riveting and exciting rugby can be if played with imagination, skill and nerve. Yes, they lost the final, and perhaps that was the biggest blow of all, for in so doing they failed to convince every player and team in these isles of the way forward. So we had a middling championship won by a middling team, England.

If sporting aspirations were not fulfilled, the social desires of every weekend tripper were once again more than adequately catered for. It's important to reaffirm this aspect at a time when administrators are proposing to heave the tournament into May – not to mention threatening to exclude England, as was happening as we went to press. To do either would be folly: the ties to tradition and to the calendar are strong. Tamper with them at your peril.

Logic dictated that France would breeze to the title, Ireland would be reasonable contenders, England would be in transition and Scotland would be blown away. Those who begrudge England their championship win – their 22nd in all, bringing them level at the top of the all-time table with Wales – should think again. It's true that England were lumpy and dishevelled for much of the year; it's true also that they took the trophy only on points difference from Scotland, and with the lowest ever return of tries (three). But sport is about character as much as it is about fine skills; guts as much as glory. In adversity England pulled together superbly, and nowhere more emphatically and dramatically than in Edinburgh, where they confronted the hype and passion to deny Scotland a Grand Slam.

England's young players will have learned a huge amount about themselves in the course of a difficult season. Rowntree, Dallaglio, Regan, Archer, Dawson, Grayson and Sleightholme were all new as first choices for the championship. One Englishman wasn't – Dean Richards. Left out of the squad initially, he returned to throttle Scottish aspirations. 'He looks so strange,' remarked Scotland's Jim Telfer, 'but what a player.'

Scotland were the success story of the championship. They rallied from the trauma of defeat in Italy a fortnight before the tournament to play fast, positive rugby. Led by Rob Wainwright, their team spirit was quite superb, their collective desire unquenchable, as France discovered at Murrayfield in what was the match of the tournament. Scotland had the most impressive middle five of the Five Nations;

Redpath and Townsend at half-back were always prompting, always asking questions. In the end, England's greater bulk and Dean Richards were to deny them their moment of glory.

Ireland were true to their traditions: completely unpredictable. They were expected to do well, but got off to a poor start against Scotland, plummeted still further in Paris – conceding a record score – staged a magnificent revival against Wales – accumulating a record score – and finished in competitive mood at Twickenham. No crystal ball could tell you where they go from here, except that Peter Clohessy won't be going anywhere for some time yet. He was banned for 26 weeks for stamping on Roumat.

The whole of Wales was on the look-out for a new dawn, but was forced to sit through long, anxious hours before the first confirmed sighting of it. New coach Kevin Bowring's side played with great verve and spirit, but without success. They went into the last match against France staring an unprecedented back-to-back whitewash in the face and pulled off a stirring victory. Now, buoyed by newcomers Leigh Davies and Gwyn Jones, and the leadership of Jonathan Humphreys, they can step out with confidence into the new day.

As for France, they once again beat themselves. After defeating the All Blacks in Toulouse they had the makings of a great side. By the end of the championship only three of the team remained in their original positions. Exit Philippe Sella; enter Thomas Castaignède. But at least they gave us some glimpses of magic.

FINAL TABLE

	P	W	D	L	F	A	Pts
England	4	3	0	1	79	54	6
Scotland	4	3	0	1	60	56	6
France	4	2	0	2	89	57	4
Wales	4	1	0	3	62	82	2
Ireland	4	1	0	3	65	106	2

The championship yielded 355 points, comprising 30 tries, 17 conversions, 50 penalty goals and 7 dropped goals.

Leading scorers: 64 – Paul Grayson (E); 47 – Michael Dods (S); 26 – Thomas Castaignède (F); 21 – Arwel Thomas (W).

Most tries: 3 – Michael Dods (S), Emile Ntamack (F)

20 January, Lansdowne Road
IRELAND 10 (1G 1PG)   SCOTLAND 16 (1PG 1DG 2T)

The winds howled, blowing away the hopes of Irish supporters that, at last, this would be a season to remember. Instead this defeat extended their miserable record against Scotland, whom they have not beaten since 1988. It was also Ireland's 60th loss at home in the Five Nations, the worst return of all the countries.

Expectations had been fuelled by a decent build-up against Fiji and the USA. Ireland recalled Peter Clohessy at prop and Jeremy Davidson at flanker. Scotland, on the other hand, appeared in a much worse state following their 29-17 loss to Italy a fortnight earlier. Chalmers and Logan were notable absentees from this match, passed over in favour of Townsend and Dods, the latter chosen for his goal-kicking, and Weir was restored to the second row. Wainwright, confirmed as captain for the championship, moved across to the blind side.

The match had a degree of energy and excitement about it, induced largely by the number of errors and the siege of the Scottish line in the closing stages. A more generous referee would have awarded a penalty try against Scotland; as it was, with the elements against them, they held firm to complete only the second scoreless second half in the Five Nations since 1985. Redpath and Wainwright were outstanding for Scotland. Ireland were too loose and casual.

Scotland had opened the scoring in the 11th minute when hooker McKenzie took advantage of poor Irish protection to pounce on a loose line-out ball. Elwood brought Ireland back to 5-3 six minutes later with a penalty goal, but Irish hearts sank in the 21st minute when Dods slipped in at the corner for a try. A Dods penalty and Townsend dropped goal gave Scotland a comfortable 16-3 cushion as half-time approached. But then, in one of the moves of the match, Clohessy rounded off the scoring with a fine try. Elwood's conversion made it 10-16. It was as close as Ireland were to get.

IRELAND: J E Staples (Harlequins) (*capt*); R M Wallace (Garryowen), J C Bell (Northampton), K P McQuilkin (Bective Rangers), S P Geoghegan (Bath); E P Elwood (Lansdowne), C Saverimutto (Sale); N J Popplewell (Newcastle), T J Kingston (Dolphin), P M Clohessy (Young Munster), G M Fulcher (Cork Const), N P J Francis (Old Belvedere), J W Davidson (Dungannon), P S Johns (Dungannon), D S Corkery (Cork Const)
Scorers *Try:* Clohessy *Conversion:* Elwood *Penalty Goal:* Elwood
SCOTLAND: R J S Shepherd (Melrose); C A Joiner (Melrose), S Hastings (Watsonians), I C Jardine (Stirling County), M Dods (Northampton); G P J Townsend (Northampton), B W Redpath (Melrose); D I W Hilton (Bath), K D McKenzie (Stirling County), P H Wright (Boroughmuir), S J Campbell (Dundee HSFP), G W Weir (Melrose), R I Wainwright (West Hartlepool) (*capt*), E W Peters (Bath), I R Smith (Gloucester)
Scorers *Tries:* McKenzie, Dods *Penalty Goal:* Dods *Dropped Goal:* Townsend
Referee B Campsall (England)

20 January, Parc des Princes
FRANCE 15 (3PG 2DG)   ENGLAND 12 (2PG 2DG)

The bogeyman almost got France again. They were strong favourites, yet it took a snap dropped goal from 20-year-old centre Thomas Castaignède in the last minute to finally wrest the game their way.

England had won eight times in succession before France finally broke the sequence with victory in the third-place play-off in the World Cup, and France had gone on to beat New Zealand in the first of two Tests in the autumn. The French made six changes, one positional, from that series. Most significantly, Roumat, Lacroix and Cabannes were brought back after their exile. Loose-head prop Michel Périé was the only new cap. England, meanwhile, had struggled in their early-season Tests. Bath winger Jon Sleightholme, replacing Damian Hopley, became England's fifth new cap of the season. The 23-year-old was to typify England's defiance and resolve.

The Northampton half-backs, Dawson and Grayson, turned the French time and again with well-placed box kicks, but it was a strategy of containment rather than adventure. England offered little in the way of creativity, although Underwood got a hand, but not downward pressure, to a Catt kick-through in the opening minute. The Leicester winger was also involved in a move shortly afterwards initiated by Sleightholme, carried on by Clarke and Carling, which floundered when Underwood's pass was flung at Catt's knees.

France had by far the best of the match. Benazzi and Pelous cleaned up in the line-out; Lacroix, though, chose to be cautious. It almost cost France dear. With England ahead 6-3 at the interval, Lacroix kicked a dropped goal in the 54th minute, followed by penalties in the 63rd and 75th. Grayson dropped a beautiful 40-metre goal to level the scores just three minutes from time. It looked to be enough, but Castaignède had other ideas.

The day afterwards, BBC TV cameras detected a kick by Richard Dourthe on Ben Clarke, and the French centre was suspended.

FRANCE: J-L Sadourny (Colomiers); E Ntamack (Toulouse), R Dourthe (Dax), T Castaignède (Toulouse), P Saint-André (Montferrand) (*capt*); T Lacroix (Dax), P Carbonneau (Toulouse); M Périé (Toulon), J-M Gonzalez (Bayonne), C Califano (Toulouse), O Merle (Montferrand), O Roumat (Dax), A Benazzi (Agen), F Pelous (Dax), L Cabannes (Racing) *Replacement* P Bernat-Salles (Bègles-Bordeaux) for Sadourny (55 mins)
Scorers *Penalty Goals:* Lacroix (3) *Dropped Goals:* Lacroix, Castaignède
ENGLAND: M J Catt (Bath); J M Sleightholme (Bath), W D C Carling (Harlequins) (*capt*); J C Guscott (Bath), R Underwood (Leicester & RAF); P J Grayson (Northampton), M J S Dawson (Northampton); G C Rowntree (Leicester), M P Regan (Bristol), J Leonard (Harlequins), M O Johnson (Leicester), M C Bayfield (Northampton), S O Ojomoh (Bath), B B Clarke (Bath), L B N Dallaglio (Wasps) *Replacement* D Richards for Clarke (temp)
Scorer *Penalty Goals:* Grayson (2) *Dropped Goals:* Grayson (2)
Referee D T M McHugh (Ireland)

Emile Ntamack of France lies in wait for England's Ben Clarke in the match at Parc des Princes, won narrowly by France in the last minute.

3 February, Murrayfield
SCOTLAND 19 (3PG 2T)   FRANCE 14 (3PG 1T)

No one plays rugby like the French, with their flair, invention, running from deep, reverse inside flick-passes, unshackled ambition. No one, that is, except Scotland. From the very first ball they received they were off and away, triggered by the intelligent, sniping prompts of Redpath at scrum-half and the audacious, sublime talent of Townsend at fly-half. It was too much for the French.

Scotland exacted ample revenge for the shattering World Cup defeat and enjoyed the best opening quarter of the entire championship. They ran everything, and stretched France across the field. When Dods scored the first of his two tries, in the ninth minute, French flanker Laurent Cabannes, who had chased everywhere, could only jog back in despair as he raced past. Dods finished with 19 points in all, a new individual record for this fixture, eclipsing the mark set (twice) by Gavin Hastings. Hastings' successor at full-back, Rowen Shepherd, was instrumental in initiating Scottish attacks from deep. Once again the Scottish back row of Peters, Smith and Wainwright were to the fore.

For all the thrust and vigour of Scotland's opening, they were pegged back to 11-8 by the 22nd minute. Dods put over two penalties after his opening try while Benazzi went over from short range following good build-up work from Sadourny and Saint-André. Prior to that, Castaignède had kicked a goal. In the 52nd minute, though, Dods was able to put a more appropriate Scottish gain on the scoreboard. Scotland ran a penalty in the French 22, from where the ball finally arrived in the hands of Redpath. The Scottish scrum-half spotted Dods free on the left and flung a long pass in his direction. Dods juggled the ball but held on and was in at the corner. Lacroix's second penalty goal saw him pass Camberabero's French points record (354) and narrowed the gap here to a couple of points. Dods, though, was to have the last word, sealing a memorable Scottish victory with his third penalty goal four minutes from time. Murrayfield rose as one to salute the moment.

SCOTLAND: R J S Shepherd (Melrose); C A Joiner (Melrose), S Hastings (Watsonians), I C Jardine (Stirling County), M Dods (Northampton);
G P J Townsend (Northampton), B W Redpath (Melrose); D I W Hilton (Bath), K D McKenzie (Stirling County), P H Wright (Boroughmuir), S J Campbell (Dundee HSFP), G W Weir (Melrose), R I Wainwright (W Hartlepool) (*capt*), E W Peters (Bath), I R Smith (Gloucester)
Scorers *Tries:* Dods (2) *Penalty Goals:* Dods (3)
FRANCE: J-L Sadourny (Colomiers); E Ntamack (Toulouse), A Penaud (Brive), T Castaignède (Toulouse), P Saint-André (Montferrand) (*capt*); T Lacroix (Dax), P Carbonneau (Toulouse); M Périé (Toulon), J-M Gonzalez (Bayonne), C Califano (Toulouse), O Merle (Montferrand), O Roumat (Dax), A Benazzi (Agen), F Pelous (Dax), L Cabannes (Racing) *Replacement* S Glas (Bourgoin) for Lacroix (temp)
Scorers *Try:* Benazzi *Penalty Goals:* Lacroix (2), Castaignède
Referee C Thomas (Wales)

3 February, Twickenham
ENGLAND 21 (1G 3PG 1T)   WALES 15 (1G 1PG 1T)

For Wales it was a new beginning; for England yet another attempt to kick-start their new approach. Wales will have emerged the happier, playing what little rugby there was on offer and finishing the stronger. England again failed to impress. The crowd was flat and muted at the final whistle.

Wales had picked a fledgling half-back combination, Robert Howley, making his debut at scrum-half, teaming up with the fresh-faced Arwel Thomas. This was Wales' sixth different partnership in seven matches. The tone of the whole side was callow: four of the backs had only five caps between them, while three of the forwards boasted only seven in total.

This immaturity was to show in dramatic fashion. Wales were in hearty contention at 7-5 shortly after the interval when Grayson, who had a wretched afternoon all round, skewed a drop-goal attempt way to the left. Full-back Justin Thomas dithered fatally. Guscott charged the kick, the ball landed kindly and the England centre touched down. Wales rallied, scoring a late try through Howley, who had a superb debut, but their recklessness had cost them dear.

Welsh heart and ambition brought them a wonderfully speculative try in the 11th minute. Wales were awarded a penalty on the right, just inside the 22. England trotted back for the expected shot at goal. Instead, the impudent Arwel Thomas tapped and set off. Gwyn Jones, Proctor and Leigh Davies took it on before Hemi Taylor blasted through a double tackle and over the line.

Underwood put England on the board with his 50th Test try two minutes before the interval. Again, a tap penalty saw the ball move wide, Catt finally sending his winger clear. Grayson, who missed five kicks in all, slotted three second-half penalties in reply to one from Thomas. England, for whom Rodber was recalled, were badly beaten in the line-out. More damningly, they were all toil and little sparkle.

ENGLAND: M J Catt (Bath); J M Sleightholme (Bath), W D C Carling (Harlequins) (*capt*), J C Guscott (Bath), R Underwood (Leicester & RAF); P J Grayson (Northampton), M J S Dawson (Northampton); G C Rowntree (Leicester), M P Regan (Bristol), J Leonard (Harlequins), M O Johnson (Leicester), M C Bayfield (Northampton), T A K Rodber (Northampton & Army), B B Clarke (Bath), L B N Dallaglio (Wasps) *Replacement* P R de Glanville (Bath) for Carling (52 mins)
Scorers *Tries:* Underwood, Guscott *Conversion:* Grayson *Penalty Goals:* Grayson (3)
WALES: W J L Thomas (Llanelli); I C Evans (Llanelli), L B Davies (Neath), N G Davies (Llanelli), W T Proctor (Llanelli); A C Thomas (Bristol), R Howley (Bridgend); A L P Lewis (Cardiff), J M Humphreys (Cardiff) (*capt*), J D Davies (Neath), G O Llewellyn (Neath), D Jones (Cardiff), E W Lewis (Cardiff), H T Taylor (Cardiff), R G Jones (Llanelli) *Replacements* S Williams (Neath) for E Lewis (temp) and G Jones (temp); G R Jenkins (Swansea) for Humphreys (56 mins)
Scorers *Tries:* Taylor, Howley *Conversion:* A Thomas *Penalty Goal:* A Thomas
Referee K W McCartney (Scotland)

17 February, Parc des Princes
FRANCE 45 (5G 2T) IRELAND 10 (1G 1PG)

Paris is one of the most popular destinations for millions of people. How is it, then, that 15 blokes with green shirts and a shamrock always break out in a terrible sweat at the very mention of the place? You need look no further than this match for the answer.

This was Ireland's worst-ever defeat in the championship and the 12th time in succession they have lost to France. Even the rare landmark of a try – an injury-time penalty try – their first in the French capital since 1980, gave little cheer. Prop Peter Clohessy was cited and subsequently banned for 26 weeks for stamping on Roumat. Ireland also lost their captain, Jim Staples, to concussion.

Ireland were disrupted beforehand when Geoghegan cried off with a hamstring problem. There was hope that new fly-half David Humphreys would trigger things around him; instead he was left grasping at the inadequate pass of his partner, Niall Hogan.

France, after the trauma of Edinburgh, had reverted to type and sacked almost half their side. Castaignède swapped places with Lacroix at fly-half, to be partnered inside by Accoceberry. Why France put Benazzi in the second row is a mystery. There was no mystery about the French play: it was fast, imaginative and lethal.

Saint-André was over the try-line after 11 minutes, followed by his fellow winger Ntamack eight minutes later. Castel took a short inside pass for his try in the 29th minute before Accoceberry scored France's fourth from a blindside break just before half-time. Humphreys managed a lone penalty in reply.

Three more tries – from Ntamack, Castel and Campan – followed during the second half to help France accumulate their highest score and biggest winning points margin for a Five Nations match.

FRANCE: J-L Sadourny (Colomiers); E Ntamack (Toulouse), O Campan (Agen), T Lacroix (Dax), P Saint-André (Montferrand) (*capt*); T Castaignède (Toulouse), G Accoceberry (Bègles-Bordeaux); C Califano (Toulouse), J-M Gonzalez (Bayonne), F Tournaire (Narbonne), A Benazzi (Agen), O Roumat (Dax), R Castel (Toulouse), F Pelous (Dax), L Cabannes (Racing) *Replacements* S Glas (Bourgoin) for Lacroix (21 mins); M Périé (Toulon) for Califano (51 mins); M de Rougemont (Toulon) for Gonzalez (67 mins); S Dispagne (Toulouse) for Roumat (49 mins)
Scorers *Tries:* Ntamack (2), Castel (2), Saint-André, Campan, Accoceberry *Conversions:* Castaignède (5)

IRELAND: J E Staples (Harlequins) (*capt*); R M Wallace (Garryowen), J C Bell (Northampton), K P McQuilkin (Bective Rangers), N K P J Woods (Blackrock Coll); D G Humphreys (London Irish), N A Hogan (Terenure Coll); N J Popplewell (Newcastle), T J Kingston (Dolphin), P M Clohessy (Young Munster), P S Johns (Dungannon), G M Fulcher (Cork Const), J W Davidson (Dungannon), V C P Costello (St Mary's Coll), D S Corkery (Cork Const) *Replacement* M J Field (Malone) for Staples (41 mins)
Scorer *Try:* penalty try *Conversion:* Humphreys *Penalty Goal:* Humphreys
Referee E Morrison (England)

17 February, Cardiff Arms Park
WALES 14 (3PG 1T) SCOTLAND 16 (1G 3PG)

Judging by the result alone, the whole of Wales should have been beating their breast with woe afterwards. This was their seventh consecutive defeat in a Five Nations match, their worst-ever run, and the promise of the new dawn already seemed to be clouding over with doubt. Statistics, though, tell you only part of the story. Even in defeat there was promise and hope in the Welsh performance. Indeed, they created the better chances in what was an exuberant, passionate and dramatic game, culminating in the point when Arwel Thomas's attempted conversion drifted fractionally wide in the last seconds.

Three times in the second half Wales had opportunities for scores which would have broken the 9-9 stalemate. They all went begging. Scotland, by contrast, had the killer instinct. They were resourceful and resilient, withstanding pressure, and struck with chilling precision when their chance came six minutes from time. Logan, who had come on as a replacement for Joiner, was sent clear with an inside pass from Townsend. The movement was overhauled by the Welsh defence, but from the resultant scrum a crisply executed move saw Townsend stretch over. Just when it seemed the game had slipped away, Wales came back and fashioned a try for Proctor following great build-up work by both centres, then Gwyn Jones and Justin Thomas. The two kickers, Dods and Arwel Thomas, had matched each other throughout the game with three penalty goals each.

Wales had been unchanged for the first time in three years, and the selectors' loyalty was rewarded with particularly fine performances from Howley, Gwyn Jones, Justin Thomas and both locks, Jones and Llewellyn. Scotland, too, fielded the same team. Now, after three successes, the holy grail of the Grand Slam beckoned.

WALES: W J L Thomas (Llanelli); I C Evans (Llanelli), L B Davies (Neath), N G Davies (Llanelli), W T Proctor (Llanelli); A C Thomas (Bristol), R Howley (Bridgend); A L P Lewis (Cardiff), J M Humphreys (Cardiff) (*capt*), J D Davies (Neath), G O Llewellyn (Neath), D Jones (Cardiff), E W Lewis (Cardiff), H T Taylor (Cardiff), R G Jones (Llanelli)
Scorers *Try:* Proctor *Penalty Goals:* A Thomas (3)
SCOTLAND: R J S Shepherd (Melrose); C A Joiner (Melrose), S Hastings (Watsonians), I C Jardine (Stirling County), M Dods (Northampton); G P J Townsend (Northampton), B W Redpath (Melrose); D I W Hilton (Bath), K D McKenzie (Stirling County), P H Wright (Boroughmuir), S J Campbell (Dundee HSFP), G W Weir (Melrose), R I Wainwright (West Hartlepool) (*capt*), E W Peters (Bath), I R Smith (Gloucester) *Replacement* K M Logan (Stirling County) for Joiner (39 mins)
Scorers *Try:* Townsend *Conversion:* Dods *Penalty Goals:* Dods (3)
Referee J Dumé (France)

2 March, Lansdowne Road
IRELAND 30 (2G 2PG 2T)　　WALES 17 (2G 1PG)

From the depths to the heights: who can make sense of Irish rugby? A record defeat in Paris was turned around within a fortnight as Ireland amassed their highest score in a Five Nations match in this the 100th meeting between the countries. They also equalled their record of four tries in a game against Wales. Their third win in a row over the visitors matched their best sequences against them (1923-25 and 1966-68).

For Wales, who had brought some 20,000 supporters to Dublin, there was a resounding crash as their previously buoyant morale fell to earth. No one's chin hit the deck with more force than that of Arwel Thomas. The young fly-half had the sort of nightmare game that will bring him out in a cold sweat whenever he thinks back to it. If he can remember much of it, that is – he was flattened early on in the match and was certainly dazed, if not officially concussed. Thereafter he fluffed routine clearance kicks, two of which were run back by Ireland to produce tries.

Wales fielded an unchanged side for the third time in a row, only the fifth occasion in their history that this has happened. Ireland, by contrast, made six changes, and three more of position. Simon Mason, the 22-year-old Orrell full-back, made his debut, and the captaincy passed to Hogan.

Geoghegan successfully chased Humphreys' chip for Ireland's first try in the sixth minute before Ieuan Evans hit back for Wales with a converted try six minutes later. A Thomas miss-kick was returned with interest by Woods in the 24th minute, the Irish winger chipping and acrobatically readjusting. The best try of the match belonged to Wales, and it came in the 64th minute, a counter-attack from deep featuring Leigh Davies most prominently, finished off by Evans. Fulcher and Corkery added two more for Ireland in the closing 12 minutes.

IRELAND: S J P Mason (Orrell); S P Geoghegan (Bath), J C Bell (Northampton), M J Field (Malone), N K P J Woods (Blackrock Coll); D G Humphreys (London Irish), N A Hogan (Terenure Coll) (*capt*); N J Popplewell (Newcastle), A T H Clarke (Northampton), P S Wallace (Blackrock Coll), G M Fulcher (Cork Const), J W Davidson (Dungannon), D S Corkery (Cork Const), V C P Costello (St Mary's Coll), W D McBride (Malone)
Scorers *Tries:* Geoghegan, Woods, Fulcher, Corkery *Conversions:* Mason (2) *Penalty Goals:* Mason (2)
WALES: W J L Thomas (Llanelli); I C Evans (Llanelli), L B Davies (Neath), N G Davies (Llanelli), W T Proctor (Llanelli); A C Thomas (Bristol), R Howley (Bridgend); A L P Lewis (Cardiff), J M Humphreys (Cardiff) (*capt*), J D Davies (Neath), G O Llewellyn (Neath), D Jones (Cardiff), E W Lewis (Cardiff), H T Taylor (Cardiff), R G Jones (Llanelli)
Scorers *Tries:* Evans (2) *Conversions:* A Thomas (2) *Penalty Goal:* A Thomas
Referee D Mené (France)

Niall Woods races over the line to make his contribution to Ireland's record Five Nations score of 30 points in the defeat of Wales.

2 March, Murrayfield
SCOTLAND 9 (3PG)   ENGLAND 18 (6PG)

Amid the rubble of a nation's dreams, the man who had toppled tartan hopes merely punched the air and smiled a toothy grin. The image of Dean Richards, in a rare show of emotion, will fill Scottish nightmares for years to come.

Richards was awesome, controlling the ball and with it the tempo of the match. The pace was pedestrian, the life squeezed from it by the Leicester No 8. Scotland failed utterly to move him and so to establish their faster, looser game. By the time Richards limped from the field three minutes from time, the die was well and truly cast.

Richards had been a surprise call-up for his 47th cap, as had 21-year-old Bristol lock Garath Archer, for his first. Rodber and Bayfield were the selectorial casualties. Scotland began the match with an unchanged team, Scott Hastings winning his 61st cap to equal the Scottish record held by his brother Gavin. It was only the second time in the history of the championship that Scotland started with the same 15 in all four matches. The previous occasion was in 1990, when they won the Grand Slam.

But here they never looked likely to break the Richards stranglehold. A try never looked very likely either, a lone 60-metre break-out by Townsend early in the second half apart. England went into the interval 12-3 ahead, with four penalty goals from Grayson and Dods replying with one successful shot for Scotland. Dods had a variable afternoon, landing only three from six attempts. Grayson was going well until near the end, when four shots (two of them drops) were missed. Scotland closed to 12-9 in the 57th minute, but if they had any thoughts that Richards and England were to be denied they quickly evaporated. Grayson's fifth penalty went over in the 71st minute, and his sixth, in injury time, completed England's seventh win in a row against Scotland, matching the series record.

SCOTLAND: R J S Shepherd (Melrose); C A Joiner (Melrose), S Hastings (Watsonians), I C Jardine (Stirling County), M Dods (Northampton); G P J Townsend (Northampton), B W Redpath (Melrose); D I W Hilton (Bath), K D McKenzie (Stirling County), P H Wright (Boroughmuir), S J Campbell (Dundee HSFP), G W Weir (Newcastle), R I Wainwright (Watsonians & Army) *(capt)*, E W Peters (Bath), I R Smith (Gloucester)
Scorer *Penalty Goals:* Dods (3)
ENGLAND: M J Catt (Bath); J M Sleightholme (Bath), W D C Carling (Harlequins) *(capt)*; J C Guscott (Bath), R Underwood (Leicester & RAF); P J Grayson (Northampton), M J S Dawson (Northampton); G C Rowntree (Leicester), M P Regan (Bristol), J Leonard (Harlequins), M O Johnson (Leicester), G S Archer (Bristol & Army), B B Clarke (Bath), D Richards (Leicester), L B N Dallaglio (Wasps) *Replacement* T A K Rodber (Northampton) for Richards (77 mins)
Scorer *Penalty Goals:* Grayson (6)
Referee W D Bevan (Wales)

16 March, Cardiff Arms Park
WALES 16 (1G 3PG)   FRANCE 15 (1G 1PG 1T)

If anyone doubted that in this professional era emotional fulfilment is infinitely more valuable, as well as more elusive, than a mere fat cheque, then they had to do no more than look at the scenes after this match. The Welsh celebrated as if the Grand Slam itself had been brought home. Wales, who had played with relish and style throughout the tournament, yet thus far without reward, had won their first championship match in two years and had staved off the ignominy of an unprecedented second successive whitewash. The fact that their victory had handed the title to England was overlooked.

Neil Jenkins, restored after Arwel Thomas's torrid afternoon in Dublin, became Wales' most-capped fly-half in his 30th game in the position. He rounded off a solid performance with the winning penalty six minutes from time, and the second of his three penalties took him past the 100 mark in Test rugby.

The Welsh forwards set the platform. Llewellyn and Derwyn Jones dominated the line-out, Gwyn Jones was an ever-present around the loose ball and hooker Jonathan Humphreys again proved an inspirational leader. France were classically chaotic in selection and build-up. Lacroix was axed, and the great Cabannes was making what would perhaps be his last appearance for France.

Robert Howley cemented his claim as the outstanding scrum-half of the championship. His try in the tenth minute was a cameo of all he has to offer. France hit back within eight minutes, a counter-attack from deep ending with Castaignède going over. Jenkins' penalty in the 30th minute gave Wales a 10-5 lead at the interval.

Castaignède and Jenkins exchanged penalties in the 49th and 61st minutes before Ntamack sent a shiver through Welsh supporters 13 minutes from time with a try which edged France in front at 15-13. But with his final penalty, Jenkins sent a nation home in rapture.

WALES: W J L Thomas (Llanelli); I C Evans (Llanelli), L B Davies (Neath), N G Davies (Llanelli), G Thomas (Bridgend); N R Jenkins (Pontypridd), R Howley (Bridgend); C D Loader (Swansea), J M Humphreys (Cardiff) *(capt)*, J D Davies (Neath), G O Llewellyn (Neath), D Jones (Cardiff), E W Lewis (Cardiff), H T Taylor (Cardiff), R G Jones (Llanelli)
Scorers *Try:* Howley *Conversion:* Jenkins *Penalty Goals:* Jenkins (3)
FRANCE: J-L Sadourny (Colomiers); E Ntamack (Toulouse), S Glas (Bourgoin), O Campan (Agen), P Saint-André (Montferrand) *(capt)*; T Castaignède (Toulouse), G Accoceberry (Bègles); C Califano (Toulouse), J-M Gonzalez (Bayonne), F Tournaire (Narbonne), A Benazzi (Agen), O Roumat (Dax), R Castel (Toulouse), S Dispagne (Toulouse), L Cabannes (Racing) *Replacements* F Galthié (Colomiers) for Accoceberry (20 mins); O Brouzet (Grenoble) for Dispagne (63 mins); R Ibanez (Dax) for Castel (75 mins)
Scorers *Tries:* Castaignède, Ntamack *Conversion:* Castaignède *Penalty Goal:* Castaignède
Referee B W Stirling (Ireland)

16 March, Twickenham
ENGLAND 28 (1G 6PG 1DG)   IRELAND 15 (4PG 1DG)

This match, the England captain's last in charge, was billed as the Carling farewell extravaganza. It was always unlikely to happen: the Irish are renowned for gatecrashing premature celebrations. In the end it was an anti-climax. Fate decreed that he should catch his studs in the turf in the 33rd minute, yards away from the action, and crumple to the ground with torn ankle ligaments. He was stretchered from the field. He was fit enough to hobble up the steps at the end to collect the Millennium Trophy, awarded to the winners of the match, but the Five Nations Trophy itself had to be whipped back from Wales to be presented at the banquet that night.

England played with more ambition and fluency than in previous matches, almost as if they were intent on making up the 21-point difference between themselves and France. It proved an unnecessary chase. They were pushed all the way by a battling Irish side which led by 15-12 at the interval. Humphreys, again impressing at fly-half, had opened the scoring for Ireland in the first minute with a 30-metre dropped goal. Mason, looking comfortable at full-back, struck four penalties thereafter. Grayson was to do likewise for England.

It was only when England tightened the game in the second half that they began to dominate. Richards, as ever, was at the core of their strategy. Grayson kicked his goals from the pressure exerted by the pack, in the 45th and 67th minutes, with a dropped goal in between. Finally, that rarest of things, a try, arrived – just three minutes from time. Dallaglio and Johnson featured in the build-up. The ball was fed back to Grayson, and Guscott set off on a dummy run, leaving Sleightholme to cut through a narrow channel to the line. Grayson's conversion, just infield from the touchline, wrapped things up. The England fly-half finished with 23 points, a record for the fixture.

ENGLAND: M J Catt (Bath); J M Sleightholme (Bath), W D C Carling (Harlequins) (*capt*), J C Guscott (Bath), R Underwood (Leicester & RAF); P J Grayson (Northampton), M J S Dawson (Northampton); G C Rowntree (Leicester), M P Regan (Bristol), J Leonard (Harlequins), M O Johnson (Leicester), G S Archer (Bristol & Army), B B Clarke (Bath), D Richards (Leicester), L B N Dallaglio (Wasps) *Replacements* P de Glanville (Bath) for Carling (33 mins); T A K Rodber (Northampton) for Dallaglio (temp)
Scorers *Try:* Sleightholme *Conversion:* Grayson *Penalty Goals:* Grayson (6) *Dropped Goal:* Grayson

IRELAND: S J P Mason (Orrell); S P Geoghegan (Bath), J C Bell (Northampton), M J Field (Malone), N K P J Woods (Blackrock Coll); D G Humphreys (London Irish), N A Hogan (Terenure Coll) (*capt*); N J Popplewell (Newcastle), A T H Clarke (Northampton), P S Wallace (Blackrock Coll), G M Fulcher (Cork Const), J W Davidson (Dungannon), D S Corkery (Cork Const), V C P Costello (St Mary's Coll), W D McBride (Malone) *Replacement* C M McCall (Bangor) for Field (19 mins)
Scorers *Penalty Goals:* Mason (4) *Dropped Goal:* Humphreys

Referee E Murray (Scotland)

FRANCE FIND THE RIGHT MIX

LATIN CUP 1995

The inaugural Latin Cup, a biennial tournament for Argentina, France, Italy and Romania, took place in mid-October 1995. A six-match round robin effectively culminated in the final desired by the organisers: Argentina, the host nation, against France, winners of the World Cup play-off against England only four months earlier.

For new French coach Jean-Claude Skrela, who had succeeded Pierre Berbizier in September, the Cup was an opportunity to prepare for the home Tests against New Zealand and the Five Nations tournament. In addition, with Thierry Lacroix, Laurent Cabannes and Olivier Roumat remaining in South Africa on Currie Cup duty, there was room to experiment with those younger players who are likely to carry France's challenge into the next World Cup.

Newcomers to the French squad were the Toulouse backs Thomas Castaignède and Philippe Carbonneau, who had been the centres in their club's championship success in May. Skrela had originally recruited Carbonneau as a scrum-half to the Toulouse club back in 1990. After France struggled to beat Italy in their opening match of the tournament, the coach turned to his former protégé, installing him as scrum-half for the midweek game against Romania. He was paired with Castaignède, who collected 22 points on his Test debut, including a full house of scoring actions in an easy win.

Unbeaten France thus went forward to meet unbeaten Argentina in the final match of the week. On the opening Saturday, the Pumas had disposed of Romania, whose injured captain, Sandu Ciorascu, was unable to take part in any of the matches. A 51-16 win against an inexperienced side who defended soundly to keep the score to 15-9 at the break included 31 points – an Argentinian Test record – by José-Maria Luna.

Undoubtedly, the highlight of the tournament for the hosts was their midweek success against Italy. Earlier in the year, the Pumas had lost to Italy in the World Cup, but at Tucumán they exacted revenge with a convincing three-tries-to-nil win. Luna, who finished as the tournament's leading scorer with 54 points, chipped in with 11. Italy were clearly missing their chief play-maker, Diego Dominguez, who had withdrawn from the original party for professional reasons. Their subsequent rout of Romania was no more than a consolation win for a team which had upcoming Tests against the All Blacks and Springboks.

There were 10,000 spectators at the Ferrocarril Oeste Stadium to witness the showdown between France and Argentina. The Pumas had humiliated the French in Nantes only three years earlier, but

Thomas Castaignède of Toulouse, who made his international debut in the Latin Cup, went on to become a feature of the French national side in 1995-96. Here he celebrates his match-winning dropped goal against England in the Five Nations Championship.

there were no French jitters on this occasion. Captain Philippe Saint-André's try in the 19th minute put his side 11-6 ahead before another score from the skipper, also converted by Christophe Deylaud, took France to a comfortable 20-6 lead at the break. Although Luna landed two more penalties early in the second half, France ran in five tries to post their biggest winning points margin against the Pumas and take the Cup in style.

The next tournament will be held in France in 1997.

ARGENTINA Captain S Salvat **Manager** L Chaluleu **Coach** A Petra

---

Full-backs: E Jurado (Jockey Club, Rosario), J-M Luna (Jockey Club, Cordoba) *Threequarters:* D L Albanese (San Isidro Club), P Cremaschi (Los Tordos), D Cuesta-Silva (San Isidro Club), S Salvat (Alumni), M J Teran (Tucumán RC) *Half-backs:* L Arbizu (Belgrano AC), J L Cilley (San Isidro Club), R H Crexell (Jockey Club, Rosario), A Pichot (CA San Isidro) *Forwards:* R D Grau (Liceo, Mendoza), O J Hassan Jalil (Natación y Gimnasia), F E Mendez (Mendoza RC), M Urbano (Buenos Aires Cricket & Rugby Club), J J Angelillo (San Isidro Club), R A le Fort (Tucumán), J-M Lerga (Pucara), G A Llanes (La Plata), R N Pérez (Duendes), S L Irazoqui (Bajo Palermo, Cordoba), R A Martin (San Isidro Club), C E Viel (Cardinal Newman), J M Santamarina (Tucumán RC)

FRANCE Captain P Saint-André **Manager** A Herrero **Coach** J-C Skrela

---

Full-back: J-L Sadourny (Colomiers) *Threequarters:* E Ntamack (Toulouse), R Dourthe (Dax), P Carbonneau (Toulouse), T Castaignède (Toulouse), A Hyardet (Castres), P Arlettaz (Perpignan), P Saint-André (Montferrand) *Half-backs:* C Deylaud (Toulouse), Y Delaigue (Toulon), G Accoceberry (Bègles-Bordeaux) *Forwards:* C Califano (Toulouse), L Bénézech (RCF), F Tournaire (Narbonne), S Graou (Colomiers), J-M Gonzalez (Bayonne), O Azam (Montferrand), O Merle (Montferrand), F Pelous (Dax), O Brouzet (Grenoble), P Benetton (Agen), M Lièvremont (Perpignan), A Carminati (Brive), C Juillet (Montferrand)

ITALY Captain Massimo Cuttitta **Manager** G Dondi **Coach** G Coste

---

Full-backs: P Vaccari (Calvisano), M Ravazzolo (Calvisano), J Pertile (Roma) *Threequarters:* S Bordon (Rovigo), I Francescato (Treviso), F Mazzariol (Treviso), M Platania (Milan), F Roselli (Roma) *Half-backs:* M Bonomi (Milan), G Filizzola (Calvisano), A Troncon (Treviso) *Forwards:* Massimo Cuttitta (Milan), M dal Sie (San Dona), A Moscardi (Rovigo), C Orlandi (Milan), A Castellani (L'Aquila), C Caione (L'Aquila), D Scaglia (Treviso), M Giacheri (Treviso), O Arancio (Catania), M Giovanelli (Milan), A Sgorlon (San Dona), P P Pedroni (Milan), C Checchinato (Treviso)

ROMANIA Captain S Ciorascu **Manager** M Paraschivescu **Coach** C Fugigi

---

Full-back: V Maftei (Cluj U) *Threequarters:* I Rotaru (Dinamo Bucharest), M Nedelcu (Steaua Bucharest), T Luca (Grivita Bucharest), G Solomie (Timisoara U), M Olarasu (Grivita Bucharest), R Fugigi (CSM Foresta Sibiu) *Half-backs:* V Besarau (Farul Constanta), V Popisteanu (Steaua Bucharest), V Flutur (Cluj U), C Dragnea (Stiinta Petrarea) *Forwards:* L Costea (Steaua Bucharest), G Vlad

(Dinamo Bucharest), A Salageanu (Dinamo Bucharest), N Dragos (Steaua Bucharest), I Negreci (CFR Constanta), M Radoi (Dinamo Bucharest), C Cojocariu (Bayonne), N Marin (Farul Constanta), A Girbu (Farul Constanta), C Draguceanu (Steaua Bucharest), A Gealapu (Steaua Bucharest), A Guranescu (Dinamo Bucharest), S Ciorascu (Auch, France)

MATCH 1   14 October, Ferrocarril Oeste Stadium, Buenos Aires

FRANCE 34 (4G 2PG)   **ITALY 22** (1G 4PG 1DG)

FRANCE: Sadourny; Ntamack, Hyardet, Delaigue, Saint-André (*capt*); Deylaud, Accoceberry; Califano, Gonzalez, Tournaire, Merle, Brouzet, Lièvremont, Carminati, Benetton
Scorers *Tries:* Sadourny (2), Ntamack, Carminati   *Conversions:* Deylaud (4)
Penalty Goals: Deylaud (2)
ITALY: Vaccari; Roselli, Bordon, Francescato, Mazzariol; Bonomi, Troncon; Cuttitta (*capt*), Orlandi, Dal Sie, Pedroni, Giacheri, Arancio, Checchinato, Sgorlon
Replacements Platania for Bordon (38 mins); Giovanelli for Arancio (65 mins); Ravazzolo for Mazzariol (temp)
Scorers *Try:* Troncon   *Conversion:* Bonomi   *Penalty Goals:* Bonomi (4)
Dropped Goal: Bonomi
Referee N Chiciu (Romania)

MATCH 2   14 October, Ferrocarril Oeste Stadium, Buenos Aires

ARGENTINA 51 (4G 6PG 1T)   **ROMANIA 16** (1G 2PG 1DG)

ARGENTINA: Jurado; Luna, Cuesta-Silva, Salvat (*capt*), Teran; Arbizu, Pichot; Mendez, Angelillo, Urbano, Perez, Llanes, Martin, Santamarina, Viel
Scorers *Tries:* Cuesta-Silva (2), Luna, Mendez, Jurado   *Conversions:* Luna (4)
Penalty Goals: Luna (6)
ROMANIA : Maftei; Rotaru, Nedelcu, Luca, Solomie; Bezarau, Flutur; Costea, Negreci, Vlad, Cojocariu (*capt*), Girbu, Gelapu, Marin, Draguceanu *Replacements* Salageanu for Costea (temp); Dragos for Costea (61 mins); Guranescu for Draguceanu (67 mins)
Scorers *Try:* Girbu   *Conversion:* Bezarau   *Penalty Goals:* Bezarau (2)
Dropped Goal: Bezarau
Referee N Lasaga (France)

MATCH 3   17 October, Stadio Atlético, Tucumán

FRANCE 52 (4G 2PG 1DG 3T)   **ROMANIA 8** (1DG 1T)

FRANCE: Sadourny; Ntamack, Arlettaz, Dourthe, Saint-André (*capt*); Castaignède, Carbonneau; Bénézech, Azam, Graou, Merle, Pelous, Lièvremont, Juillet, Carminati
Replacements Delaigue for Sadourny (51 mins); Benetton for Lièvremont (61 mins)
Scorers *Tries:* Carminati, Castaignède, Pelous, Arlettaz (2), Lièvremont, Delaigue   *Conversions:* Castaignède (4)   *Penalty Goals:* Castaignède (2)
Dropped Goal: Castaignède
ROMANIA: Maftei; Olarasu, Nedelcu, Luca, Solomie; Popisteanu, Dragnea; Costea, Radoi, Salageanu, Marin, Cojocariu (*capt*), Guranescu, Draguceanu, Gealapu *Replacements* Negreci for Radoi (30 mins); Girbu for Marin (50 mins); Flutur for Dragnea (52 mins)
Scorers *Try:* Negreci   *Dropped Goal:* Maftei
Referee E Sklar (Argentina)

MATCH 4   17 October, Stadio Atlético, Tucumán

ARGENTINA 26 (1G 3PG 2T)   **ITALY 6** (2PG)
ARGENTINA: Jurado; Luna, Cuesta-Silva, Salvat (*capt*), Teran; Arbizu, Pichot;
Mendez, Le Fort, Urbano, Perez, Llanes, Martin, Santamarina, Viel *Replacement*
Cremaschi for Cuesta-Silva (40 mins)
Scorers *Tries:* Martin, Teran, Salvat   *Conversion:* Luna   *Penalty Goals:* Luna (3)
ITALY: Pertile; Vaccari, Bordon, Francescato, Ravazzolo; Bonomi, Troncon;
Cuttitta (*capt*), Orlandi, Dal Sie, Pedroni, Giacheri, Giovanelli, Checchinato, Sgorlon
Replacements Mazzariol for Pertile (58 mins); Castellani for Dal Sie (68 mins)
Scorer *Penalty Goals:* Bonomi (2)
Referee N Lasaga (France)

MATCH 5   21 October, Ferrocarril Oeste Stadium, Buenos Aires

ITALY 40 (3G 3PG 2T)   **ROMANIA 3** (1PG)
ITALY: Vaccari; Roselli, Platania, Francescato, Mazzariol; Bonomi, Troncon;
Cuttitta (*capt*), Orlandi, Castellani, Pedroni, Giacheri, Giovanelli, Checchinato,
Sgorlon *Replacements* Moscardi for Orlandi (65 mins); Caione for Sgorlon (78 mins);
Filizzola for Bonomi (80 mins)
Scorers *Tries:* Checchinato (2), Moscardi, Mazzariol, Roselli
Conversions: Bonomi (3)   *Penalty Goals:* Bonomi (3)
ROMANIA: Maftei; Solomie, Nedelcu, Luca, Fugigi; Bezarau (*capt*), Flutur; Vlad,
Negreci, Salageanu, Marin, Cojocariu, Guranescu, Girbu, Gealapu *Replacements*
Rotaru for Maftei (49 mins); Draguceanu for Marin (57 mins); Dragos for Salageanu
(69 mins)
Scorer *Penalty Goal:* Bezarau
Referee E Sklar (Argentina)

MATCH 6   21 October, Ferrocarril Oeste Stadium, Buenos Aires

ARGENTINA 12 (4PG)   **FRANCE 47** (3G 2PG 4T)
ARGENTINA: Jurado; Luna, Cuesta-Silva, Salvat (*capt*), Teran; Arbizu, Pichot;
Mendez, Angelillo, Urbano, Perez, Llanes, Martin, Irazoqui, Viel *Replacements*
Albanese for Teran (38 mins); Lerga for Llanes (temp)
Scorer *Penalty Goals:* Luna (4)
FRANCE: Sadourny; Ntamack, Dourthe, Castaignède, Saint-André (*capt*);
Deylaud, Carbonneau; Bénézech, Gonzalez, Califano, Merle, Pelous, Benetton,
Juillet, Carminati *Replacements* Azam for Gonzalez (49 mins); Lièvremont for
Carminati (64 mins); Hyardet for Dourthe (70 mins); Brouzet for Pelous (73 mins);
Graou for Califano (temp)
Scorers *Tries:* Saint-André (2), Carbonneau (2), Ntamack (2),
Castaignède   *Conversions:* Deylaud (3)   *Penalty Goals:* Deylaud (2)
Referee J Morandin (Italy)

RESULTS OF INTERNATIONAL MATCHES *(up to 30 April 1996)*

Cap matches only.
Years for Five Nations matches are for the second half of the season: eg 1972 means season 1971-72. Years for matches against touring teams from the Southern Hemisphere refer to the actual year of the match.

Points-scoring was first introduced in 1886, when an International Board was formed by Scotland, Ireland and Wales. Points values varied between countries until 1890, when England agreed to join the Board, and uniform values were adopted.

Northern Hemisphere seasons	Try	Conversion	Penalty goal	Dropped goal	Goal from mark
1890-91	1	2	2	3	3
1891-92 to 1892-93	2	3	3	4	4
1893-94 to 1904-05	3	2	3	4	4
1905-06 to 1947-48	3	2	3	4	3
1948-49 to 1970-71	3	2	3	3	3
1971-72 to 1991-92	4	2	3	3	3*
1992-93 onwards	5	2	3	3	–

*The goal from mark ceased to exist when the free-kick clause was introduced, 1977-78.
WC indicates a fixture played during the Rugby World Cup finals. LC indicates a fixture played in the Latin Cup.

ENGLAND v SCOTLAND
Played 113   England won 57, Scotland won 39, Drawn 17

1871 Raeburn Place (Edinburgh) **Scotland** 1G 1T to 1T
1872 The Oval (London) **England** 1G 1DG 2T to 1DG
1873 Glasgow **Drawn** no score
1874 The Oval **England** 1DG to 1T
1875 Raeburn Place **Drawn** no score
1876 The Oval **England** 1G 1T to 0
1877 Raeburn Place **Scotland** 1 DG to 0
1878 The Oval **Drawn** no score
1879 Raeburn Place **Drawn** Scotland 1DG England 1G
1880 Manchester **England** 2G 3T to 1G
1881 Raeburn Place **Drawn** Scotland 1G 1T England 1DG 1T
1882 Manchester **Scotland** 2T to 0
1883 Raeburn Place **England** 2T to 1T
1884 Blackheath (London) **England** 1G to 1T
1885 No Match
1886 Raeburn Place **Drawn** no score
1887 Manchester **Drawn** 1T each
1888 No Match
1889 No Match
1890 Raeburn Place **England** 1G 1T to 0
1891 Richmond (London) **Scotland** 9-3
1892 Raeburn Place **England** 5-0
1893 Leeds **Scotland** 8-0
1894 Raeburn Place **Scotland** 6-0
1895 Richmond **Scotland** 6-3
1896 Glasgow **Scotland** 11-0
1897 Manchester **England** 12-3
1898 Powderhall (Edinburgh) **Drawn** 3-3
1899 Blackheath **Scotland** 5-0
1900 Inverleith (Edinburgh) **Drawn** 0-0

1901 Blackheath **Scotland** 18-3
1902 Inverleith **England** 6-3
1903 Richmond **Scotland** 10-6
1904 Inverleith **Scotland** 6-3
1905 Richmond **Scotland** 8-0
1906 Inverleith **England** 9-3
1907 Blackheath **Scotland** 8-3
1908 Inverleith **Scotland** 16-10
1909 Richmond **Scotland** 18-8
1910 Inverleith **England** 14-5
1911 Twickenham **England** 13-8
1912 Inverleith **Scotland** 8-3
1913 Twickenham **England** 3-0
1914 Inverleith **England** 16-15
1920 Twickenham **England** 13-4
1921 Inverleith **England** 18-0
1922 Twickenham **England** 11-5
1923 Inverleith **England** 8-6
1924 Twickenham **England** 19-0
1925 Murrayfield **Scotland** 14-11
1926 Twickenham **Scotland** 17-9
1927 Murrayfield **Scotland** 21-13
1928 Twickenham **England** 6-0
1929 Murrayfield **Scotland** 12-6
1930 Twickenham **Drawn** 0-0
1931 Murrayfield **Scotland** 28-19
1932 Twickenham **England** 16-3
1933 Murrayfield **Scotland** 3-0
1934 Twickenham **England** 6-3
1935 Murrayfield **Scotland** 10-7
1936 Twickenham **England** 9-8
1937 Murrayfield **England** 6-3
1938 Twickenham **Scotland** 21-16
1939 Murrayfield **England** 9-6

1947 Twickenham **England** 24-5
1948 Murrayfield **Scotland** 6-3
1949 Twickenham **England** 19-3
1950 Murrayfield **Scotland** 13-11
1951 Twickenham **England** 5-3
1952 Murrayfield **England** 19-3
1953 Twickenham **England** 26-8
1954 Murrayfield **England** 13-3
1955 Twickenham **England** 9-6
1956 Murrayfield **England** 11-6
1957 Twickenham **England** 16-3
1958 Murrayfield **Drawn** 3-3
1959 Twickenham **Drawn** 3-3
1960 Murrayfield **England** 21-12
1961 Twickenham **England** 6-0
1962 Murrayfield **Drawn** 3-3
1963 Twickenham **England** 10-8
1964 Murrayfield **Scotland** 15-6
1965 Twickenham **Drawn** 3-3
1966 Murrayfield **Scotland** 6-3
1967 Twickenham **England** 27-14
1968 Murrayfield **England** 8-6
1969 Twickenham **England** 8-3
1970 Murrayfield **Scotland** 14-5
1971 Twickenham **Scotland** 16-15
1971 Murrayfield **Scotland** 26-6
Special centenary match – non-championship

1972 Murrayfield **Scotland** 23-9
1973 Twickenham **England** 20-13
1974 Murrayfield **Scotland** 16-14
1975 Twickenham **England** 7-6
1976 Murrayfield **Scotland** 22-12
1977 Twickenham **England** 26-6
1978 Murrayfield **England** 15-0
1979 Twickenham **Drawn** 7-7
1980 Murrayfield **England** 30-18
1981 Twickenham **England** 23-17
1982 Murrayfield **Drawn** 9-9
1983 Twickenham **Scotland** 22-12
1984 Murrayfield **Scotland** 18-6
1985 Twickenham **England** 10-7
1986 Murrayfield **Scotland** 33-6
1987 Twickenham **England** 21-12
1988 Murrayfield **England** 9-6
1989 Twickenham **Drawn** 12-12
1990 Murrayfield **Scotland** 13-7
1991 Twickenham **England** 21-12
1991 Murrayfield *WC* **England** 9-6
1992 Murrayfield **England** 25-7
1993 Twickenham **England** 26-12
1994 Murrayfield **England** 15-14
1995 Twickenham **England** 24-12
1996 Murrayfield **England** 18-9

ENGLAND v IRELAND
Played 109   England won 63, Ireland won 38, Drawn 8

1875 The Oval (London) **England** 1G 1DG
    1T to 0
1876 Dublin **England** 1G 1T to 0
1877 The Oval **England** 2G 2T to 0
1878 Dublin **England** 2G 1T to 0
1879 The Oval **England** 2G 1DG 2T to 0
1880 Dublin **England** 1G 1T to 1T
1881 Manchester **England** 2G 2T to 0
1882 Dublin **Drawn** 2T each
1883 Manchester **England** 1G 3T to 1T
1884 Dublin **England** 1G to 0
1885 Manchester **England** 2T to 1T
1886 Dublin **England** 1T to 0
1887 Dublin **Ireland** 2G to 0
1888 No Match
1889 No Match
1890 Blackheath (London) **England** 3T to 0
1891 Dublin **England** 9-0
1892 Manchester **England** 7-0
1893 Dublin **England** 4-0
1894 Blackheath **Ireland** 7-5
1895 Dublin **England** 6-3
1896 Leeds **Ireland** 10-4
1897 Dublin **Ireland** 13-9
1898 Richmond (London) **Ireland** 9-6
1899 Dublin **Ireland** 6-0
1900 Richmond **England** 15-4
1901 Dublin **Ireland** 10-6
1902 Leicester **England** 6-3
1903 Dublin **Ireland** 6-0
1904 Blackheath **England** 19-0
1905 Cork **Ireland** 17-3

1906 Leicester **Ireland** 16-6
1907 Dublin **Ireland** 17-9
1908 Richmond **England** 13-3
1909 Dublin **England** 11-5
1910 Twickenham **Drawn** 0-0
1911 Dublin **Ireland** 3-0
1912 Twickenham **England** 15-0
1913 Dublin **England** 15-4
1914 Twickenham **England** 17-12
1920 Dublin **England** 14-11
1921 Twickenham **England** 15-0
1922 Dublin **England** 12-3
1923 Leicester **England** 23-5
1924 Belfast **England** 14-3
1925 Twickenham **Drawn** 6-6
1926 Dublin **Ireland** 19-15
1927 Twickenham **England** 8-6
1928 Dublin **England** 7-6
1929 Twickenham **Ireland** 6-5
1930 Dublin **Ireland** 4-3
1931 Twickenham **Ireland** 6-5
1932 Dublin **England** 11-8
1933 Twickenham **England** 17-6
1934 Dublin **England** 13-3
1935 Twickenham **England** 14-3
1936 Dublin **Ireland** 6-3
1937 Twickenham **England** 9-8
1938 Dublin **England** 36-14
1939 Twickenham **Ireland** 5-0
1947 Dublin **Ireland** 22-0
1948 Twickenham **Ireland** 11-10
1949 Dublin **Ireland** 14-5

1950 Twickenham **England** 3-0
1951 Dublin **Ireland** 3-0
1952 Twickenham **England** 3-0
1953 Dublin **Drawn** 9-9
1954 Twickenham **England** 14-3
1955 Dublin **Drawn** 6-6
1956 Twickenham **England** 20-0
1957 Dublin **England** 6-0
1958 Twickenham **England** 6-0
1959 Dublin **England** 3-0
1960 Twickenham **England** 8-5
1961 Dublin **Ireland** 11-8
1962 Twickenham **England** 16-0
1963 Dublin **Drawn** 0-0
1964 Twickenham **Ireland** 18-5
1965 Dublin **Ireland** 5-0
1966 Twickenham **Drawn** 6-6
1967 Dublin **England** 8-3
1968 Twickenham **Drawn** 9-9
1969 Dublin **Ireland** 17-15
1970 Twickenham **England** 9-3
1971 Dublin **England** 9-6
1972 Twickenham **Ireland** 16-12
1973 Dublin **Ireland** 18-9
1974 Twickenham **Ireland** 26-21

1975 Dublin **Ireland** 12-9
1976 Twickenham **Ireland** 13-12
1977 Dublin **England** 4-0
1978 Twickenham **England** 15-9
1979 Dublin **Ireland** 12-7
1980 Twickenham **England** 24-9
1981 Dublin **England** 10-6
1982 Twickenham **Ireland** 16-15
1983 Dublin **Ireland** 25-15
1984 Twickenham **England** 12-9
1985 Dublin **Ireland** 13-10
1986 Twickenham **England** 25-20
1987 Dublin **Ireland** 17-0
1988 Twickenham **England** 35-3
1988 Dublin **England** 21-10
Non-championship match
1989 Dublin **England** 16-3
1990 Twickenham **England** 23-0
1991 Dublin **England** 16-7
1992 Twickenham **England** 38-9
1993 Dublin **Ireland** 17-3
1994 Twickenham **Ireland** 13-12
1995 Dublin **England** 20-8
1996 Twickenham **England** 28-15

ENGLAND v WALES
Played 102   England won 42, Wales won 48, Drawn 12

1881 Blackheath (London) **England** 7G 1DG 6T to 0
1882 No Match
1883 Swansea **England** 2G 4T to 0
1884 Leeds **England** 1G 2T to 1G
1885 Swansea **England** 1G 4T to 1G 1T
1886 Blackheath **England** 1GM 2T to 1G
1887 Llanelli **Drawn** no score
1888 No Match
1889 No Match
1890 Dewsbury **Wales** 1T to 0
1891 Newport **England** 7-3
1892 Blackheath **England** 17-0
1893 Cardiff **Wales** 12-11
1894 Birkenhead **England** 24-3
1895 Swansea **England** 14-6
1896 Blackheath **England** 25-0
1897 Newport **Wales** 11-0
1898 Blackheath **England** 14-7
1899 Swansea **Wales** 26-3
1900 Gloucester **Wales** 13-3
1901 Cardiff **Wales** 13-0
1902 Blackheath **Wales** 9-8
1903 Swansea **Wales** 21-5
1904 Leicester **Drawn** 14-14
1905 Cardiff **Wales** 25-0
1906 Richmond (London) **Wales** 16-3
1907 Swansea **Wales** 22-0
1908 Bristol **Wales** 28-18
1909 Cardiff **Wales** 8-0
1910 Twickenham **England** 11-6
1911 Swansea **Wales** 15-11

1912 Twickenham **England** 8-0
1913 Cardiff **England** 12-0
1914 Twickenham **England** 10-9
1920 Swansea **Wales** 19-5
1921 Twickenham **England** 18-3
1922 Cardiff **Wales** 28-6
1923 Twickenham **England** 7-3
1924 Swansea **England** 17-9
1925 Twickenham **England** 12-6
1926 Cardiff **Drawn** 3-3
1927 Twickenham **England** 11-9
1928 Swansea **England** 10-8
1929 Twickenham **England** 8-3
1930 Cardiff **England** 11-3
1931 Twickenham **Drawn** 11-11
1932 Swansea **Wales** 12-5
1933 Twickenham **Wales** 7-3
1934 Cardiff **England** 9-0
1935 Twickenham **Drawn** 3-3
1936 Swansea **Drawn** 0-0
1937 Twickenham **England** 4-3
1938 Cardiff **Wales** 14-8
1939 Twickenham **England** 3-0
1947 Cardiff **England** 9-6
1948 Twickenham **Drawn** 3-3
1949 Cardiff **Wales** 9-3
1950 Twickenham **Wales** 11-5
1951 Swansea **Wales** 23-5
1952 Twickenham **Wales** 8-6
1953 Cardiff **England** 8-3
1954 Twickenham **England** 9-6
1955 Cardiff **Wales** 3-0

1956 Twickenham **Wales** 8-3
1957 Cardiff **England** 3-0
1958 Twickenham **Drawn** 3-3
1959 Cardiff **Wales** 5-0
1960 Twickenham **England** 14-6
1961 Cardiff **Wales** 6-3
1962 Twickenham **Drawn** 0-0
1963 Cardiff **England** 13-6
1964 Twickenham **Drawn** 6-6
1965 Cardiff **Wales** 14-3
1966 Twickenham **Wales** 11-6
1967 Cardiff **Wales** 34-21
1968 Twickenham **Drawn** 11-11
1969 Cardiff **Wales** 30-9
1970 Twickenham **Wales** 17-13
1971 Cardiff **Wales** 22-6
1972 Twickenham **Wales** 12-3
1973 Cardiff **Wales** 25-9
1974 Twickenham **England** 16-12
1975 Cardiff **Wales** 20-4
1976 Twickenham **Wales** 21-9

1977 Cardiff **Wales** 14-9
1978 Twickenham **Wales** 9-6
1979 Cardiff **Wales** 27-3
1980 Twickenham **England** 9-8
1981 Cardiff **Wales** 21-19
1982 Twickenham **England** 17-7
1983 Cardiff **Drawn** 13-13
1984 Twickenham **Wales** 24-15
1985 Cardiff **Wales** 24-15
1986 Twickenham **England** 21-18
1987 Cardiff **Wales** 19-12
1987 Brisbane *WC* **Wales** 16-3
1988 Twickenham **Wales** 11-3
1989 Cardiff **Wales** 12-9
1990 Twickenham **England** 34-6
1991 Cardiff **England** 25-6
1992 Twickenham **England** 24-0
1993 Cardiff **Wales** 10-9
1994 Twickenham **England** 15-8
1995 Cardiff **England** 23-9
1996 Twickenham **England** 21-15

ENGLAND v FRANCE
Played 73   England won 40, France won 26, Drawn 7

1906 Paris **England** 35-8
1907 Richmond (London) **England** 41-13
1908 Paris **England** 19-0
1909 Leicester **England** 22-0
1910 Paris **England** 11-3
1911 Twickenham **England** 37-0
1912 Paris **England** 18-8
1913 Twickenham **England** 20-0
1914 Paris **England** 39-13
1920 Twickenham **England** 8-3
1921 Paris **England** 10-6
1922 Twickenham **Drawn** 11-11
1923 Paris **England** 12-3
1924 Twickenham **England** 19-7
1925 Paris **England** 13-11
1926 Twickenham **England** 11-0
1927 Paris **France** 3-0
1928 Twickenham **England** 18-8
1929 Paris **England** 16-6
1930 Twickenham **England** 11-5
1931 Paris **France** 14-13
1947 Twickenham **England** 6-3
1948 Paris **France** 15-0
1949 Twickenham **England** 8-3
1950 Paris **France** 6-3
1951 Twickenham **France** 11-3
1952 Paris **England** 6-3
1953 Twickenham **England** 11-0
1954 Paris **France** 11-3
1955 Twickenham **France** 16-9
1956 Paris **France** 14-9
1957 Twickenham **England** 9-5
1958 Paris **England** 14-0
1959 Twickenham **Drawn** 3-3
1960 Paris **Drawn** 3-3
1961 Twickenham **Drawn** 5-5
1962 Paris **France** 13-0

1963 Twickenham **England** 6-5
1964 Paris **England** 6-3
1965 Twickenham **England** 9-6
1966 Paris **France** 13-0
1967 Twickenham **France** 16-12
1968 Paris **France** 14-9
1969 Twickenham **England** 22-8
1970 Paris **France** 35-13
1971 Twickenham **Drawn** 14-14
1972 Paris **France** 37-12
1973 Twickenham **England** 14-6
1974 Paris **Drawn** 12-12
1975 Twickenham **France** 27-20
1976 Paris **France** 30-9
1977 Twickenham **France** 4-3
1978 Paris **France** 15-6
1979 Twickenham **England** 7-6
1980 Paris **England** 17-13
1981 Twickenham **France** 16-12
1982 Paris **England** 27-15
1983 Twickenham **France** 19-15
1984 Paris **France** 32-18
1985 Twickenham **Drawn** 9-9
1986 Paris **France** 29-10
1987 Twickenham **France** 19-15
1988 Paris **France** 10-9
1989 Twickenham **England** 11-0
1990 Paris **England** 26-7
1991 Twickenham **England** 21-19
1991 Paris *WC* **England** 19-10
1992 Paris **England** 31-13
1993 Twickenham **England** 16-15
1994 Paris **England** 18-14
1995 Twickenham **England** 31-10
1995 Pretoria *WC* **France** 19-9
1996 Paris **France** 15-12

ENGLAND v NEW ZEALAND
Played 18   England won 4, New Zealand won 14, Drawn 0

1905 Crystal Palace (London) **New Zealand**
   15-0
1925 Twickenham **New Zealand** 17-11
1936 Twickenham **England** 13-0
1954 Twickenham **New Zealand** 5-0
1963 *1* Auckland **New Zealand** 21-11
   2 Christchurch **New Zealand** 9-6
   New Zealand won series 2-0
1964 Twickenham **New Zealand** 14-0
1967 Twickenham **New Zealand** 23-11
1973 Twickenham **New Zealand** 9-0

1973 Auckland **England** 16-10
1978 Twickenham **New Zealand** 16-6
1979 Twickenham **New Zealand** 10-9
1983 Twickenham **England** 15-9
1985 *1* Christchurch **New Zealand** 18-13
   2 Wellington **New Zealand** 42-15
   New Zealand won series 2-0
1991 Twickenham *WC* **New Zealand** 18-12
1993 Twickenham **England** 15-9
1995 Cape Town *WC* **New Zealand** 45-29

ENGLAND v SOUTH AFRICA
Played 13   England won 4, South Africa won 8, Drawn 1

1906 Crystal Palace (London) **Drawn** 3-3
1913 Twickenham **South Africa** 9-3
1932 Twickenham **South Africa** 7-0
1952 Twickenham **South Africa** 8-3
1961 Twickenham **South Africa** 5-0
1969 Twickenham **England** 11-8
1972 Johannesburg **England** 18-9
1984 *1* Port Elizabeth **South Africa** 33-15

   2 Johannesburg **South Africa** 35-9
   South Africa won series 2-0
1992 Twickenham **England** 33-16
1994 *1* Pretoria **England** 32-15
   2 Cape Town **South Africa** 27-9
   Series drawn 1-1
1995 Twickenham **South Africa** 24-14

ENGLAND v AUSTRALIA
Played 19   England won 7, Australia won 12, Drawn 0

1909 Blackheath (London) **Australia** 9-3
1928 Twickenham **England** 18-11
1948 Twickenham **Australia** 11-0
1958 Twickenham **England** 9-6
1963 Sydney **Australia** 18-9
1967 Twickenham **Australia** 23-11
1973 Twickenham **England** 20-3
1975 *1* Sydney **Australia** 16-9
   2 Brisbane **Australia** 30-21
   Australia won series 2-0
1976 Twickenham **England** 23-6

1982 Twickenham **England** 15-11
1984 Twickenham **Australia** 19-3
1987 Sydney *WC* **Australia** 19-6
1988 *1* Brisbane **Australia** 22-16
   2 Sydney **Australia** 28-8
   Australia won series 2-0
1988 Twickenham **England** 28-19
1991 Sydney **Australia** 40-15
1991 Twickenham *WC* **Australia** 12-6
1995 Cape Town *WC* **England** 25-22

ENGLAND v NEW ZEALAND NATIVES
Played 1   England won 1

1889 Blackheath **England** 1G 4T to 0

ENGLAND v RFU PRESIDENT'S XV
Played 1   President's XV won 1

1971 Twickenham **President's XV** 28-11

ENGLAND v ARGENTINA
Played 6   England won 4, Argentina won 1, Drawn 1

1981 *1* Buenos Aires **Drawn** 19-19
   2 Buenos Aires **England** 12-6
   England won series 1-0 with 1 draw
1990 *1* Buenos Aires **England** 25-12

   2 Buenos Aires **Argentina** 15-13
   Series drawn 1-1
1990 Twickenham **England** 51-0
1995 Durban *WC* **England** 24-18

ENGLAND v ROMANIA
Played 3   England won 3

1985 Twickenham **England** 22-15
1989 Bucharest **England** 58-3

1994 Twickenham **England** 54-3

ENGLAND v JAPAN
Played 1   England won 1

1987 Sydney *WC* **England** 60-7

ENGLAND v UNITED STATES
Played 2   England won 2

1987 Sydney *WC* **England** 34-6

1991 Twickenham *WC* **England** 37-9

ENGLAND v FIJI
Played 3   England won 3

1988 Suva **England** 25-12
1989 Twickenham **England** 58-23

1991 Suva **England** 28-12

ENGLAND v ITALY
Played 2   England won 2

1991 Twickenham *WC* **England** 36-6

1995 Durban *WC* **England** 27-20

ENGLAND v CANADA
Played 2   England won 2

1992 Wembley **England** 26-13

1994 Twickenham **England** 60-19

ENGLAND v WESTERN SAMOA
Played 2   England won 2

1995 Durban *WC* **England** 44-22

1995 Twickenham **England** 27-9

SCOTLAND v IRELAND
Played 108   Scotland won 57, Ireland won 45, Drawn 5, Abandoned 1

1877 Belfast **Scotland** 4G 2DG 2T to 0
1878 No Match
1879 Belfast **Scotland** 1G 1DG 1T to 0
1880 Glasgow **Scotland** 1G 2DG 2T to 0
1881 Belfast **Ireland** 1DG to 1T
1882 Glasgow **Scotland** 2T to 0
1883 Belfast **Scotland** 1G 1T to 0
1884 Raeburn Place (Edinburgh) **Scotland** 2G 2T to 1T
1885 Belfast **Abandoned** Ireland 0 Scotland 1T
1885 Raeburn Place **Scotland** 1G 2T to 0
1886 Raeburn Place **Scotland** 3G 1DG 2T to 0
1887 Belfast **Scotland** 1G 1GM 2T to 0
1888 Raeburn Place **Scotland** 1G to 0
1889 Belfast **Scotland** 1DG to 0
1890 Raeburn Place **Scotland** 1DG 1T to 0
1891 Belfast **Scotland** 14-0
1892 Raeburn Place **Scotland** 2-0
1893 Belfast **Drawn** 0-0

1894 Dublin **Ireland** 5-0
1895 Raeburn Place **Scotland** 6-0
1896 Dublin **Drawn** 0-0
1897 Powderhall (Edinburgh) **Scotland** 8-3
1898 Belfast **Scotland** 8-0
1899 Inverleith (Edinburgh) **Ireland** 9-3
1900 Dublin **Drawn** 0-0
1901 Inverleith **Scotland** 9-5
1902 Belfast **Ireland** 5-0
1903 Inverleith **Scotland** 3-0
1904 Dublin **Scotland** 19-3
1905 Inverleith **Ireland** 11-5
1906 Dublin **Scotland** 13-6
1907 Inverleith **Scotland** 15-3
1908 Dublin **Ireland** 16-11
1909 Inverleith **Scotland** 9-3
1910 Belfast **Scotland** 14-0
1911 Inverleith **Ireland** 16-10
1912 Dublin **Ireland** 10-8
1913 Inverleith **Scotland** 29-14
1914 Dublin **Ireland** 6-0

1920 Inverleith **Scotland** 19-0
1921 Dublin **Ireland** 9-8
1922 Inverleith **Scotland** 6-3
1923 Dublin **Scotland** 13-3
1924 Inverleith **Scotland** 13-8
1925 Dublin **Scotland** 14-8
1926 Murrayfield **Ireland** 3-0
1927 Dublin **Ireland** 6-0
1928 Murrayfield **Ireland** 13-5
1929 Dublin **Scotland** 16-7
1930 Murrayfield **Ireland** 14-11
1931 Dublin **Ireland** 8-5
1932 Murrayfield **Ireland** 20-8
1933 Dublin **Scotland** 8-6
1934 Murrayfield **Scotland** 16-9
1935 Dublin **Ireland** 12-5
1936 Murrayfield **Ireland** 10-4
1937 Dublin **Ireland** 11-4
1938 Murrayfield **Scotland** 23-14
1939 Dublin **Ireland** 12-3
1947 Murrayfield **Ireland** 3-0
1948 Dublin **Ireland** 6-0
1949 Murrayfield **Ireland** 13-3
1950 Dublin **Ireland** 21-0
1951 Murrayfield **Ireland** 6-5
1952 Dublin **Ireland** 12-8
1953 Murrayfield **Ireland** 26-8
1954 Belfast **Ireland** 6-0
1955 Murrayfield **Scotland** 12-3
1956 Dublin **Ireland** 14-10
1957 Murrayfield **Ireland** 5-3
1958 Dublin **Ireland** 12-6
1959 Murrayfield **Ireland** 8-3
1960 Dublin **Scotland** 6-5
1961 Murrayfield **Scotland** 16-8
1962 Dublin **Scotland** 20-6

1963 Murrayfield **Scotland** 3-0
1964 Dublin **Scotland** 6-3
1965 Murrayfield **Ireland** 16-6
1966 Dublin **Scotland** 11-3
1967 Murrayfield **Ireland** 5-3
1968 Dublin **Ireland** 14-6
1969 Murrayfield **Ireland** 16-0
1970 Dublin **Ireland** 16-11
1971 Murrayfield **Ireland** 17-5
1972 No Match
1973 Murrayfield **Scotland** 19-14
1974 Dublin **Ireland** 9-6
1975 Murrayfield **Scotland** 20-13
1976 Dublin **Scotland** 15-6
1977 Murrayfield **Scotland** 21-18
1978 Dublin **Ireland** 12-9
1979 Murrayfield **Drawn** 11-11
1980 Dublin **Ireland** 22-15
1981 Murrayfield **Scotland** 10-9
1982 Dublin **Ireland** 21-12
1983 Murrayfield **Ireland** 15-13
1984 Dublin **Scotland** 32-9
1985 Murrayfield **Ireland** 18-15
1986 Dublin **Scotland** 10-9
1987 Murrayfield **Scotland** 16-12
1988 Dublin **Ireland** 22-18
1989 Murrayfield **Scotland** 37-21
1990 Dublin **Scotland** 13-10
1991 Murrayfield **Scotland** 28-25
1991 Murrayfield *WC* **Scotland** 24-15
1992 Dublin **Scotland** 18-10
1993 Murrayfield **Scotland** 15-3
1994 Dublin **Drawn** 6-6
1995 Murrayfield **Scotland** 26-13
1996 Dublin **Scotland** 16-10

SCOTLAND v WALES
Played 100   Scotland won 44, Wales won 54, Drawn 2

1883 Raeburn Place (Edinburgh) **Scotland** 3G to 1G
1884 Newport **Scotland** 1DG 1T to 0
1885 Glasgow **Drawn** no score
1886 Cardiff **Scotland** 2G 8T to 0
1887 Raeburn Place **Scotland** 4G 8T to 0
1888 Newport **Wales** 1T to 0
1889 Raeburn Place **Scotland** 2T to 0
1890 Cardiff **Scotland** 1G 2T to 1T
1891 Raeburn Place **Scotland** 15-0
1892 Swansea **Scotland** 7-2
1893 Raeburn Place **Wales** 9-0
1894 Newport **Wales** 7-0
1895 Raeburn Place **Scotland** 5-4
1896 Cardiff **Wales** 6-0
1897 No Match
1898 No Match
1899 Inverleith (Edinburgh) **Scotland** 21-10
1900 Swansea **Wales** 12-3
1901 Inverleith **Scotland** 18-8
1902 Cardiff **Wales** 14-5
1903 Inverleith **Scotland** 6-0
1904 Swansea **Wales** 21-3

1905 Inverleith **Wales** 6-3
1906 Cardiff **Wales** 9-3
1907 Inverleith **Scotland** 6-3
1908 Swansea **Wales** 6-5
1909 Inverleith **Wales** 5-3
1910 Cardiff **Wales** 14-0
1911 Inverleith **Wales** 32-10
1912 Swansea **Wales** 21-6
1913 Inverleith **Wales** 8-0
1914 Cardiff **Wales** 24-5
1920 Inverleith **Scotland** 9-5
1921 Swansea **Scotland** 14-8
1922 Inverleith **Drawn** 9-9
1923 Cardiff **Scotland** 11-8
1924 Inverleith **Scotland** 35-10
1925 Swansea **Scotland** 24-14
1926 Murrayfield **Scotland** 8-5
1927 Cardiff **Scotland** 5-0
1928 Murrayfield **Wales** 13-0
1929 Swansea **Wales** 14-7
1930 Murrayfield **Scotland** 12-9
1931 Cardiff **Wales** 13-8
1932 Murrayfield **Wales** 6-0

1933 Swansea **Scotland** 11-3
1934 Murrayfield **Wales** 13-6
1935 Cardiff **Wales** 10-6
1936 Murrayfield **Wales** 13-3
1937 Swansea **Scotland** 13-6
1938 Murrayfield **Scotland** 8-6
1939 Cardiff **Wales** 11-3
1947 Murrayfield **Wales** 22-8
1948 Cardiff **Wales** 14-0
1949 Murrayfield **Scotland** 6-5
1950 Swansea **Wales** 12-0
1951 Murrayfield **Scotland** 19-0
1952 Cardiff **Wales** 11-0
1953 Murrayfield **Wales** 12-0
1954 Swansea **Wales** 15-3
1955 Murrayfield **Scotland** 14-8
1956 Cardiff **Wales** 9-3
1957 Murrayfield **Scotland** 9-6
1958 Cardiff **Wales** 8-3
1959 Murrayfield **Scotland** 6-5
1960 Cardiff **Wales** 8-0
1961 Murrayfield **Scotland** 3-0
1962 Cardiff **Scotland** 8-3
1963 Murrayfield **Wales** 6-0
1964 Cardiff **Wales** 11-3
1965 Murrayfield **Wales** 14-12
1966 Cardiff **Wales** 8-3
1967 Murrayfield **Scotland** 11-5
1968 Cardiff **Wales** 5-0

1969 Murrayfield **Wales** 17-3
1970 Cardiff **Wales** 18-9
1971 Murrayfield **Wales** 19-18
1972 Cardiff **Wales** 35-12
1973 Murrayfield **Scotland** 10-9
1974 Cardiff **Wales** 6-0
1975 Murrayfield **Scotland** 12-10
1976 Cardiff **Wales** 28-6
1977 Murrayfield **Wales** 18-9
1978 Cardiff **Wales** 22-14
1979 Murrayfield **Wales** 19-13
1980 Cardiff **Wales** 17-6
1981 Murrayfield **Scotland** 15-6
1982 Cardiff **Scotland** 34-18
1983 Murrayfield **Wales** 19-15
1984 Cardiff **Scotland** 15-9
1985 Murrayfield **Wales** 25-21
1986 Cardiff **Wales** 22-15
1987 Murrayfield **Scotland** 21-15
1988 Cardiff **Wales** 25-20
1989 Murrayfield **Scotland** 23-7
1990 Cardiff **Scotland** 13-9
1991 Murrayfield **Scotland** 32-12
1992 Cardiff **Wales** 15-12
1993 Murrayfield **Scotland** 20-0
1994 Cardiff **Wales** 29-6
1995 Murrayfield **Scotland** 26-13
1996 Cardiff **Scotland** 16-14

SCOTLAND v FRANCE
Played 68   Scotland won 32, France won 33, Drawn 3

1910 Inverleith (Edinburgh) **Scotland** 27-0
1911 Paris **France** 16-15
1912 Inverleith **Scotland** 31-3
1913 Paris **Scotland** 21-3
1914 No Match
1920 Paris **Scotland** 5-0
1921 Inverleith **France** 3-0
1922 Paris **Drawn** 3-3
1923 Inverleith **Scotland** 16-3
1924 Paris **France** 12-10
1925 Inverleith **Scotland** 25-4
1926 Paris **Scotland** 20-6
1927 Murrayfield **Scotland** 23-6
1928 Paris **Scotland** 15-6
1929 Murrayfield **Scotland** 6-3
1930 Paris **France** 7-3
1931 Murrayfield **Scotland** 6-4
1947 Paris **France** 8-3
1948 Murrayfield **Scotland** 9-8
1949 Paris **Scotland** 8-0
1950 Murrayfield **Scotland** 8-5
1951 Paris **France** 14-12
1952 Murrayfield **France** 13-11
1953 Paris **France** 11-5
1954 Murrayfield **France** 3-0
1955 Paris **France** 15-0
1956 Murrayfield **Scotland** 12-0
1957 Paris **Scotland** 6-0
1958 Murrayfield **Scotland** 11-9
1959 Paris **France** 9-0

1960 Murrayfield **France** 13-11
1961 Paris **France** 11-0
1962 Murrayfield **France** 11-3
1963 Paris **Scotland** 11-6
1964 Murrayfield **Scotland** 10-0
1965 Paris **France** 16-8
1966 Murrayfield **Drawn** 3-3
1967 Paris **Scotland** 9-8
1968 Murrayfield **France** 8-6
1969 Paris **Scotland** 6-3
1970 Murrayfield **France** 11-9
1971 Paris **France** 13-8
1972 Murrayfield **Scotland** 20-9
1973 Paris **France** 16-13
1974 Murrayfield **Scotland** 19-6
1975 Paris **France** 10-9
1976 Murrayfield **France** 13-6
1977 Paris **France** 23-3
1978 Murrayfield **France** 19-16
1979 Paris **France** 21-17
1980 Murrayfield **Scotland** 22-14
1981 Paris **France** 16-9
1982 Murrayfield **Scotland** 16-7
1983 Paris **France** 19-15
1984 Murrayfield **Scotland** 21-12
1985 Paris **France** 11-3
1986 Murrayfield **Scotland** 18-17
1987 Paris **France** 28-22
1987 Christchurch *WC* **Drawn** 20-20
1988 Murrayfield **Scotland** 23-12

87

Scotland's Doddie Weir, with Peter Wright in support, confronts Abdel Benazzi of France in the 68th international between the two countries, played at Murrayfield.

1989 Paris **France** 19-3
1990 Murrayfield **Scotland** 21-0
1991 Paris **France** 15-9
1992 Murrayfield **Scotland** 10-6
1993 Paris **France** 11-3

1994 Murrayfield **France** 20-12
1995 Paris **Scotland** 23-21
1995 Pretoria *WC* **France** 22-19
1996 Murrayfield **Scotland** 19-14

SCOTLAND v NEW ZEALAND
Played 18   Scotland won 0, New Zealand won 16, Drawn 2

1905 Inverleith (Edinburgh) **New Zealand**
    12-7
1935 Murrayfield **New Zealand** 18-8
1954 Murrayfield **New Zealand** 3-0
1964 Murrayfield **Drawn** 0-0
1967 Murrayfield **New Zealand** 14-3
1972 Murrayfield **New Zealand** 14-9
1975 Auckland **New Zealand** 24-0
1978 Murrayfield **New Zealand** 18-9
1979 Murrayfield **New Zealand** 20-6
1981 *1* Dunedin **New Zealand** 11-4

   2 Auckland **New Zealand** 40-15
   New Zealand won series 2-0
1983 Murrayfield **Drawn** 25-25
1987 Christchurch *WC* **New Zealand** 30-3
1990 *1* Dunedin **New Zealand** 31-16
   2 Auckland **New Zealand** 21-18
   New Zealand won series 2-0
1991 Cardiff *WC* **New Zealand** 13-6
1993 Murrayfield **New Zealand** 51-15
1995 Pretoria *WC* **New Zealand** 48-30

SCOTLAND v SOUTH AFRICA
Played 9   Scotland won 3, South Africa won 6, Drawn 0

1906 Glasgow **Scotland** 6-0
1912 Inverleith **South Africa** 16-0
1932 Murrayfield **South Africa** 6-3
1951 Murrayfield **South Africa** 44-0
1960 Port Elizabeth **South Africa** 18-10

1961 Murrayfield **South Africa** 12-5
1965 Murrayfield **Scotland** 8-5
1969 Murrayfield **Scotland** 6-3
1994 Murrayfield **South Africa** 34-10

SCOTLAND v AUSTRALIA
Played 14   Scotland won 7, Australia won 7, Drawn 0

1927 Murrayfield **Scotland** 10-8
1947 Murrayfield **Australia** 16-7
1958 Murrayfield **Scotland** 12-8
1966 Murrayfield **Scotland** 11-5
1968 Murrayfield **Scotland** 9-3
1970 Sydney **Australia** 23-3
1975 Murrayfield **Scotland** 10-3
1981 Murrayfield **Scotland** 24-15

1982 *1* Brisbane **Scotland** 12-7
  2 Sydney **Australia** 33-9
  Series drawn 1-1
1984 Murrayfield **Australia** 37-12
1988 Murrayfield **Australia** 32-13
1992 *1* Sydney **Australia** 27-12
  2 Brisbane **Australia** 37-13
  Australia won series 2-0

SCOTLAND v SRU PRESIDENT'S XV
Played 1   Scotland won 1

1973 Murrayfield **Scotland** 27-16

SCOTLAND v ROMANIA
Played 7   Scotland won 5, Romania won 2

1981 Murrayfield **Scotland** 12-6
1984 Bucharest **Romania** 28-22
1986 Bucharest **Scotland** 33-18
1987 Dunedin *WC* **Scotland** 55-28

1989 Murrayfield **Scotland** 32-0
1991 Bucharest **Romania** 18-12
1995 Murrayfield **Scotland** 49-16

SCOTLAND v ZIMBABWE
Played 2   Scotland won 2

1987 Wellington *WC* **Scotland** 60-21   1991 Murrayfield *WC* **Scotland** 51-12

SCOTLAND v FIJI
Played 1   Scotland won 1

1989 Murrayfield **Scotland** 38-17

SCOTLAND v ARGENTINA
Played 3   Scotland won 1, Argentina won 2

1990 Murrayfield **Scotland** 49-3
1994 *1* Buenos Aires **Argentina** 16-15

2 Buenos Aires **Argentina** 19-17
Argentina won series 2-0

SCOTLAND v JAPAN
Played 1   Scotland won 1

1991 Murrayfield *WC* **Scotland** 47-9

SCOTLAND v WESTERN SAMOA
Played 2   Scotland won 1, Drawn 1

1991 Murrayfield *WC* **Scotland** 28-6   1995 Murrayfield **Drawn** 15-15

SCOTLAND v CANADA
Played 1   Scotland won 1

1995 Murrayfield **Scotland** 22-6

SCOTLAND v IVORY COAST
Played 1   Scotland won 1

1995 Rustenburg *WC* **Scotland** 89-0

SCOTLAND v TONGA
Played 1   Scotland won 1

1995 Pretoria *WC* **Scotland** 41-5

IRELAND v WALES
Played 100   Ireland won 36, Wales won 58, Drawn 6

1882 Dublin **Wales** 2G 2T to 0
1883 No Match
1884 Cardiff **Wales** 1DG 2T to 0
1885 No Match
1886 No Match
1887 Birkenhead **Wales** 1DG 1T to 3T
1888 Dublin **Ireland** 1G 1DG 1T to 0
1889 Swansea **Ireland** 2T to 0
1890 Dublin **Drawn** 1G each
1891 Llanelli **Wales** 6-4
1892 Dublin **Ireland** 9-0
1893 Llanelli **Wales** 2-0
1894 Belfast **Ireland** 3-0
1895 Cardiff **Wales** 5-3
1896 Dublin **Ireland** 8-4
1897 No Match
1898 Limerick **Wales** 11-3
1899 Cardiff **Ireland** 3-0
1900 Belfast **Wales** 3-0
1901 Swansea **Wales** 10-9
1902 Dublin **Wales** 15-0
1903 Cardiff **Wales** 18-0
1904 Belfast **Ireland** 14-12
1905 Swansea **Wales** 10-3
1906 Belfast **Ireland** 11-6
1907 Cardiff **Wales** 29-0
1908 Belfast **Wales** 11-5
1909 Swansea **Wales** 18-5
1910 Dublin **Wales** 19-3
1911 Cardiff **Wales** 16-0
1912 Belfast **Ireland** 12-5
1913 Swansea **Wales** 16-13
1914 Belfast **Wales** 11-3
1920 Cardiff **Wales** 28-4
1921 Belfast **Wales** 6-0
1922 Swansea **Wales** 11-5
1923 Dublin **Ireland** 5-4
1924 Cardiff **Ireland** 13-10
1925 Belfast **Ireland** 19-3
1926 Swansea **Wales** 11-8
1927 Dublin **Ireland** 19-9
1928 Cardiff **Ireland** 13-10
1929 Belfast **Drawn** 5-5
1930 Swansea **Wales** 12-7
1931 Belfast **Wales** 15-3
1932 Cardiff **Ireland** 12-10
1933 Belfast **Ireland** 10-5
1934 Swansea **Wales** 13-0
1935 Belfast **Ireland** 9-3
1936 Cardiff **Wales** 3-0
1937 Belfast **Ireland** 5-3
1938 Swansea **Wales** 11-5
1939 Belfast **Wales** 7-0

1947 Swansea **Wales** 6-0
1948 Belfast **Ireland** 6-3
1949 Swansea **Ireland** 5-0
1950 Belfast **Wales** 6-3
1951 Cardiff **Drawn** 3-3
1952 Dublin **Wales** 14-3
1953 Swansea **Wales** 5-3
1954 Dublin **Wales** 12-9
1955 Cardiff **Wales** 21-3
1956 Dublin **Ireland** 11-3
1957 Cardiff **Wales** 6-5
1958 Dublin **Wales** 9-6
1959 Cardiff **Wales** 8-6
1960 Dublin **Wales** 10-9
1961 Cardiff **Wales** 9-0
1962 Dublin **Drawn** 3-3
1963 Cardiff **Ireland** 14-6
1964 Dublin **Wales** 15-6
1965 Cardiff **Wales** 14-8
1966 Dublin **Ireland** 9-6
1967 Cardiff **Ireland** 3-0
1968 Dublin **Ireland** 9-6
1969 Cardiff **Wales** 24-11
1970 Dublin **Ireland** 14-0
1971 Cardiff **Wales** 23-9
1972 No Match
1973 Cardiff **Wales** 16-12
1974 Dublin **Drawn** 9-9
1975 Cardiff **Wales** 32-4
1976 Dublin **Wales** 34-9
1977 Cardiff **Wales** 25-9
1978 Dublin **Wales** 20-16
1979 Cardiff **Wales** 24-21
1980 Dublin **Ireland** 21-7
1981 Cardiff **Wales** 9-8
1982 Dublin **Ireland** 20-12
1983 Cardiff **Wales** 23-9
1984 Dublin **Wales** 18-9
1985 Cardiff **Ireland** 21-9
1986 Dublin **Wales** 19-12
1987 Cardiff **Ireland** 15-11
1987 Wellington *WC* **Wales** 13-6
1988 Dublin **Wales** 12-9
1989 Cardiff **Ireland** 19-13
1990 Dublin **Ireland** 14-8
1991 Cardiff **Drawn** 21-21
1992 Dublin **Wales** 16-15
1993 Cardiff **Ireland** 19-14
1994 Dublin **Wales** 17-15
1995 Cardiff **Ireland** 16-12
1995 Johannesburg *WC* **Ireland** 24-23
1996 Dublin **Ireland** 30-17

IRELAND v FRANCE
Played 70   Ireland won 25, France won 40, Drawn 5

1909 Dublin **Ireland** 19-8
1910 Paris **Ireland** 8-3
1911 Cork **Ireland** 25-5
1912 Paris **Ireland** 11-6
1913 Cork **Ireland** 24-0
1914 Paris **Ireland** 8-6
1920 Dublin **France** 15-7
1921 Paris **France** 20-10
1922 Dublin **Ireland** 8-3
1923 Paris **France** 14-8
1924 Dublin **Ireland** 6-0
1925 Paris **Ireland** 9-3
1926 Belfast **Ireland** 11-0
1927 Paris **Ireland** 8-3
1928 Belfast **Ireland** 12-8
1929 Paris **Ireland** 6-0
1930 Belfast **France** 5-0
1931 Paris **France** 3-0
1947 Dublin **France** 12-8
1948 Paris **Ireland** 13-6
1949 Dublin **France** 16-9
1950 Paris **Drawn** 3-3
1951 Dublin **Ireland** 9-8
1952 Paris **Ireland** 11-8
1953 Belfast **Ireland** 16-3
1954 Paris **France** 8-0
1955 Dublin **France** 5-3
1956 Paris **France** 14-8
1957 Dublin **Ireland** 11-6
1958 Paris **France** 11-6
1959 Dublin **Ireland** 9-5
1960 Paris **France** 23-6
1961 Dublin **France** 15-3
1962 Paris **France** 11-0
1963 Dublin **France** 24-5
1964 Paris **France** 27-6

1965 Dublin **Drawn** 3-3
1966 Paris **France** 11-6
1967 Dublin **France** 11-6
1968 Paris **France** 16-6
1969 Dublin **Ireland** 17-9
1970 Paris **France** 8-0
1971 Dublin **Drawn** 9-9
1972 Paris **Ireland** 14-9
1972 Dublin **Ireland** 24-14
Non-championship match
1973 Dublin **Ireland** 6-4
1974 Paris **France** 9-6
1975 Dublin **Ireland** 25-6
1976 Paris **France** 26-3
1977 Dublin **France** 15-6
1978 Paris **France** 10-9
1979 Dublin **Drawn** 9-9
1980 Paris **France** 19-18
1981 Dublin **France** 19-13
1982 Paris **France** 22-9
1983 Dublin **Ireland** 22-16
1984 Paris **France** 25-12
1985 Dublin **Drawn** 15-15
1986 Paris **France** 29-9
1987 Dublin **France** 19-13
1988 Paris **France** 25-6
1989 Dublin **France** 26-21
1990 Paris **France** 31-12
1991 Dublin **France** 21-13
1992 Paris **France** 44-12
1993 Dublin **France** 21-6
1994 Paris **France** 35-15
1995 Dublin **France** 25-7
1995 Durban *WC* **France** 36-12
1996 Paris **France** 45-10

IRELAND v NEW ZEALAND
Played 13   Ireland won 0, New Zealand won 12, Drawn 1

1905 Dublin **New Zealand** 15-0
1924 Dublin **New Zealand** 6-0
1935 Dublin **New Zealand** 17-9
1954 Dublin **New Zealand** 14-3
1963 Dublin **New Zealand** 6-5
1973 Dublin **Drawn** 10-10
1974 Dublin **New Zealand** 15-6

1976 Wellington **New Zealand** 11-3
1978 Dublin **New Zealand** 10-6
1989 Dublin **New Zealand** 23-6
1992 *1* Dunedin **New Zealand** 24-21
    2 Wellington **New Zealand** 59-6
    New Zealand won series 2-0
1995 Johannesburg *WC* **New Zealand** 43-19

IRELAND v SOUTH AFRICA
Played 10   Ireland won 1, South Africa won 8, Drawn 1

1906 Belfast **South Africa** 15-12
1912 Dublin **South Africa** 38-0
1931 Dublin **South Africa** 8-3
1951 Dublin **South Africa** 17-5
1960 Dublin **South Africa** 8-3
1961 Cape Town **South Africa** 24-8

1965 Dublin **Ireland** 9-6
1970 Dublin **Drawn** 8-8
1981 *1* Cape Town **South Africa** 23-15
    2 Durban **South Africa** 12-10
    South Africa won series 2-0

IRELAND v AUSTRALIA
Played 16   Ireland won 6, Australia won 10, Drawn 0

1927 Dublin **Australia** 5-3
1947 Dublin **Australia** 16-3
1958 Dublin **Ireland** 9-6
1967 Dublin **Ireland** 15-8
1967 Sydney **Ireland** 11-5
1968 Dublin **Ireland** 10-3
1976 Dublin **Australia** 20-10
1979 *1* Brisbane **Ireland** 27-12
     2 Sydney **Ireland** 9-3
     Ireland won series 2-0

1981 Dublin **Australia** 16-12
1984 Dublin **Australia** 16-9
1987 Sydney *WC* **Australia** 33-15
1991 Dublin *WC* **Australia** 19-18
1992 Dublin **Australia** 42-17
1994 *1* Brisbane **Australia** 33-13
     2 Sydney **Australia** 32-18
     Australia won series 2-0

IRELAND v NEW ZEALAND NATIVES
Played 1   New Zealand Natives won 1

1888 Dublin **New Zealand Natives** 4G 1T to 1G 1T

IRELAND v IRU PRESIDENT'S XV
Played 1   Drawn 1

1974 Dublin **Drawn** 18-18

IRELAND v ROMANIA
Played 2   Ireland won 2

1986 Dublin **Ireland** 60-0

1993 Dublin **Ireland** 25-3

IRELAND v CANADA
Played 1   Ireland won 1

1987 Dunedin *WC* **Ireland** 46-19

IRELAND v TONGA
Played 1   Ireland won 1

1987 Brisbane *WC* **Ireland** 32-9

IRELAND v WESTERN SAMOA
Played 1   Ireland won 1

1988 Dublin **Ireland** 49-22

IRELAND v ITALY
Played 2   Ireland won 1, Italy won 1

1988 Dublin **Ireland** 31-15

1995 Treviso **Italy** 22-12

IRELAND v ARGENTINA
Played 1   Ireland won 1

1990 Dublin **Ireland** 20-18

IRELAND v NAMIBIA
Played 2   Namibia won 2

1991 *1* Windhoek **Namibia** 15-6

2 Windhoek **Namibia** 26-15
Namibia won series 2-0

IRELAND v ZIMBABWE
Played 1   Ireland won 1

1991 Dublin *WC* **Ireland** 55-11

IRELAND v JAPAN
Played 2   Ireland won 2

1991 Dublin *WC* **Ireland** 32-16   1995 Bloemfontein *WC* **Ireland** 50-28

IRELAND v UNITED STATES
Played 2   Ireland won 2

1994 Dublin **Ireland** 26-15   1996 Atlanta **Ireland** 25-18

IRELAND v FIJI
Played 1   Ireland won 1

1995 Dublin **Ireland** 44-8

WALES v FRANCE
Played 70   Wales won 38, France won 29, Drawn 3

1908 Cardiff **Wales** 36-4	1964 Cardiff **Drawn** 11-11
1909 Paris **Wales** 47-5	1965 Paris **France** 22-13
1910 Swansea **Wales** 49-14	1966 Cardiff **Wales** 9-8
1911 Paris **Wales** 15-0	1967 Paris **France** 20-14
1912 Newport **Wales** 14-8	1968 Cardiff **France** 14-9
1913 Paris **Wales** 11-8	1969 Paris **Drawn** 8-8
1914 Swansea **Wales** 31-0	1970 Cardiff **Wales** 11-6
1920 Paris **Wales** 6-5	1971 Paris **Wales** 9-5
1921 Cardiff **Wales** 12-4	1972 Cardiff **Wales** 20-6
1922 Paris **Wales** 11-3	1973 Paris **France** 12-3
1923 Swansea **Wales** 16-8	1974 Cardiff **Drawn** 16-16
1924 Paris **Wales** 10-6	1975 Paris **Wales** 25-10
1925 Cardiff **Wales** 11-5	1976 Cardiff **Wales** 19-13
1926 Paris **Wales** 7-5	1977 Paris **France** 16-9
1927 Swansea **Wales** 25-7	1978 Cardiff **Wales** 16-7
1928 Paris **France** 8-3	1979 Paris **France** 14-13
1929 Cardiff **Wales** 8-3	1980 Cardiff **Wales** 18-9
1930 Paris **Wales** 11-0	1981 Paris **France** 19-15
1931 Swansea **Wales** 35-3	1982 Cardiff **Wales** 22-12
1947 Paris **Wales** 3-0	1983 Paris **France** 16-9
1948 Swansea **France** 11-3	1984 Cardiff **France** 21-16
1949 Paris **France** 5-3	1985 Paris **France** 14-3
1950 Cardiff **Wales** 21-0	1986 Cardiff **France** 23-15
1951 Paris **France** 8-3	1987 Paris **France** 16-9
1952 Swansea **Wales** 9-5	1988 Cardiff **France** 10-9
1953 Paris **Wales** 6-3	1989 Paris **France** 31-12
1954 Cardiff **Wales** 19-13	1990 Paris **France** 29-19
1955 Paris **Wales** 16-11	1991 Paris **France** 36-3
1956 Cardiff **Wales** 5-3	1991 Cardiff **France** 22-9
1957 Paris **Wales** 19-13	*Non-championship match*
1958 Cardiff **France** 16-6	1992 Cardiff **France** 12-9
1959 Paris **France** 11-3	1993 Paris **France** 26-10
1960 Cardiff **France** 16-8	1994 Cardiff **Wales** 24-15
1961 Paris **France** 8-6	1995 Paris **France** 21-9
1962 Cardiff **Wales** 3-0	1996 Cardiff **Wales** 16-15
1963 Paris **France** 5-3	

WALES v NEW ZEALAND
Played 16   Wales won 3, New Zealand won 13, Drawn 0

1905 Cardiff **Wales** 3-0
1924 Swansea **New Zealand** 19-0
1935 Cardiff **Wales** 13-12
1953 Cardiff **Wales** 13-8
1963 Cardiff **New Zealand** 6-0
1967 Cardiff **New Zealand** 13-6
1969 *1* Christchurch **New Zealand** 19-0
    2 Auckland **New Zealand** 33-12
    New Zealand won series 2-0

1972 Cardiff **New Zealand** 19-16
1978 Cardiff **New Zealand** 13-12
1980 Cardiff **New Zealand** 23-3
1987 Brisbane *WC* **New Zealand** 49-6
1988 *1* Christchurch **New Zealand** 52-3
    2 Auckland **New Zealand** 54-9
    New Zealand won series 2-0
1989 Cardiff **New Zealand** 34-9
1995 Johannesburg *WC* **New Zealand** 34-9

WALES v SOUTH AFRICA
Played 9   Wales won 0, South Africa won 8, Drawn 1

1906 Swansea **South Africa** 11-0
1912 Cardiff **South Africa** 3-0
1931 Swansea **South Africa** 8-3
1951 Cardiff **South Africa** 6-3
1960 Cardiff **South Africa** 3-0

1964 Durban **South Africa** 24-3
1970 Cardiff **Drawn** 6-6
1994 Cardiff **South Africa** 20-12
1995 Johannesburg **South Africa** 40-11

WALES v AUSTRALIA
Played 16   Wales won 8, Australia won 8, Drawn 0

1908 Cardiff **Wales** 9-6
1927 Cardiff **Australia** 18-8
1947 Cardiff **Wales** 6-0
1958 Cardiff **Wales** 9-3
1966 Cardiff **Australia** 14-11
1969 Sydney **Wales** 19-16
1973 Cardiff **Wales** 24-0
1975 Cardiff **Wales** 28-3
1978 *1* Brisbane **Australia** 18-8

    2 Sydney **Australia** 19-17
    Australia won series 2-0
1981 Cardiff **Wales** 18-13
1984 Cardiff **Australia** 28-9
1987 Rotorua *WC* **Wales** 22-21
1991 Brisbane **Australia** 63-6
1991 Cardiff *WC* **Australia** 38-3
1992 Cardiff **Australia** 23-6

WALES v NEW ZEALAND NATIVES
Played 1   Wales won 1

1888 Swansea **Wales** 1G 2T to 0

WALES v NEW ZEALAND ARMY
Played 1   New Zealand Army won 1

1919 Swansea **New Zealand Army** 6-3

WALES v ROMANIA
Played 3   Romania won 2, Wales won 1

1983 Bucharest **Romania** 24-6
1988 Cardiff **Romania** 15-9

1994 Bucharest **Wales** 16-9

WALES v FIJI
Played 4   Wales won 4

1985 Cardiff **Wales** 40-3
1986 Suva **Wales** 22-15

1994 Suva **Wales** 23-8
1995 Cardiff **Wales** 19-15

WALES v TONGA
Played 3   Wales won 3

1986 Nuku'Alofa **Wales** 15-7
1987 Palmerston North *WC* **Wales** 29-16

1994 Nuku'Alofa **Wales** 18-9

WALES v WESTERN SAMOA
Played 4   Wales won 2, Western Samoa won 2

1986 Apia **Wales** 32-14
1988 Cardiff **Wales** 28-6

1991 Cardiff *WC* **Western Samoa** 16-13
1994 Moamoa **Western Samoa** 34-9

WALES v CANADA
Played 3   Wales won 2, Canada won 1

1987 Invercargill *WC* **Wales** 40-9
1993 Cardiff **Canada** 26-24

1994 Toronto **Wales** 33-15

WALES v UNITED STATES
Played 1   Wales won 1

1987 Cardiff **Wales** 46-0

WALES v NAMIBIA
Played 3   Wales won 3

1990 *1* Windhoek **Wales** 18-9
    2 Windhoek **Wales** 34-30
    Wales won series 2-0

1993 Windhoek **Wales** 38-23

WALES v BARBARIANS
Played 1   Barbarians won 1

1990 Cardiff **Barbarians** 31-24

WALES v ARGENTINA
Played 1   Wales won 1

1991 Cardiff *WC* **Wales** 16-7

WALES v ZIMBABWE
Played 2   Wales won 2

1993 *1* Bulawayo **Wales** 35-14

2 Harare **Wales** 42-13
Wales won series 2-0

WALES v JAPAN
Played 2   Wales won 2

1993 Cardiff **Wales** 55-5

1995 Bloemfontein *WC* **Wales** 57-10

WALES v PORTUGAL
Played 1   Wales won 1

1994 Lisbon **Wales** 102-11

WALES v SPAIN
Played 1   Wales won 1

1994 Madrid **Wales** 54-0

WALES v ITALY
Played 2   Wales won 2

1994 Cardiff **Wales** 29-19

1996 Cardiff **Wales** 31-26

FRANCE v NEW ZEALAND
Played 32   France won 8, New Zealand won 24, Drawn 0

1906 Paris **New Zealand** 38-8
1925 Toulouse **New Zealand** 30-6
1954 Paris **France** 3-0
1961 *1* Auckland **New Zealand** 13-6
     2 Wellington **New Zealand** 5-3
     3 Christchurch **New Zealand** 32-3
     New Zealand won series 3-0
1964 Paris **New Zealand** 12-3
1967 Paris **New Zealand** 21-15
1968 *1* Christchurch **New Zealand** 12-9
     2 Wellington **New Zealand** 9-3
     3 Auckland **New Zealand** 19-12
     New Zealand won series 3-0
1973 Paris **France** 13-6
1977 *1* Toulouse **France** 18-13
     2 Paris **New Zealand** 15-3
     Series drawn 1-1
1979 *1* Christchurch **New Zealand** 23-9
     2 Auckland **France** 24-19
     Series drawn 1-1
1981 *1* Toulouse **New Zealand** 13-9

     2 Paris **New Zealand** 18-6
     New Zealand won series 2-0
1984 *1* Christchurch **New Zealand** 10-9
     2 Auckland **New Zealand** 31-18
     New Zealand won series 2-0
1986 Christchurch **New Zealand** 18-9
1986 *1* Toulouse **New Zealand** 19-7
     2 Nantes **France** 16-3
     Series drawn 1-1
1987 Auckland *WC* **New Zealand** 29-9
1989 *1* Christchurch **New Zealand** 25-17
     2 Auckland **New Zealand** 34-20
     New Zealand won series 2-0
1990 *1* Nantes **New Zealand** 24-3
     2 Paris **New Zealand** 30-12
     New Zealand won series 2-0
1994 *1* Christchurch **France** 22-8
     2 Auckland **France** 23-20
     France won series 2-0
1995 *1* Toulouse **France** 22-15
     2 Paris **New Zealand** 37-12
     Series drawn 1-1

FRANCE v SOUTH AFRICA
Played 24   France won 5, South Africa won 14, Drawn 5

1913 Bordeaux **South Africa** 38-5
1952 Paris **South Africa** 25-3
1958 *1* Cape Town **Drawn** 3-3
     2 Johannesburg **France** 9-5
     France won series 1-0, with 1 draw
1961 Paris **Drawn** 0-0
1964 Springs (SA) **France** 8-6
1967 *1* Durban **South Africa** 26-3
     2 Bloemfontein **South Africa** 16-3
     3 Johannesburg **France** 19-14
     4 Cape Town **Drawn** 6-6
     South Africa won series 2-1, with 1 draw
1968 *1* Bordeaux **South Africa** 12-9
     2 Paris **South Africa** 16-11
     South Africa won series 2-0
1971 *1* Bloemfontein **South Africa** 22-9

     2 Durban **Drawn** 8-8
     South Africa won series 1-0, with 1 draw
1974 *1* Toulouse **South Africa** 13-4
     2 Paris **South Africa** 10-8
     South Africa won series 2-0
1975 *1* Bloemfontein **South Africa** 38-25
     2 Pretoria **South Africa** 33-18
     South Africa won series 2-0
1980 Pretoria **South Africa** 37-15
1992 *1* Lyons **South Africa** 20-15
     2 Paris **France** 29-16
     Series drawn 1-1
1993 *1* Durban **Drawn** 20-20
     2 Johannesburg **France** 18-17
     France won series 1-0, with 1 draw
1995 Durban *WC* **South Africa** 19-15

FRANCE v AUSTRALIA
Played 25   France won 13, Australia won 10, Drawn 2

1928 Paris **Australia** 11-8
1948 Paris **France** 13-6
1958 Paris **France** 19-0
1961 Sydney **France** 15-8
1967 Paris **France** 20-14
1968 Sydney **Australia** 11-10
1971 *1* Toulouse **Australia** 13-11
     2 Paris **France** 18-9
     Series drawn 1-1
1972 *1* Sydney **Drawn** 14-14
     2 Brisbane **France** 16-15
     France won series 1-0, with 1 draw
1976 *1* Bordeaux **France** 18-15

     2 Paris **France** 34-6
     France won series 2-0
1981 *1* Brisbane **Australia** 17-15
     2 Sydney **Australia** 24-14
     Australia won series 2-0
1983 *1* Clermont-Ferrand **Drawn** 15-15
     2 Paris **France** 15-6
     France won series 1-0, with 1 draw
1986 Sydney **Australia** 27-14
1987 Sydney *WC* **France** 30-24
1989 *1* Strasbourg **Australia** 32-15
     2 Lille **France** 25-19
     Series drawn 1-1

1990 *1* Sydney **Australia** 21-9
    2 Brisbane **Australia** 48-31
    3 Sydney **France** 28-19
    Australia won series 2-1

1993 *1* Bordeaux **France** 16-13
    2 Paris **Australia** 24-3
    Series drawn 1-1

FRANCE v UNITED STATES
Played 5   France won 4, United States won 1

1920 Paris **France** 14-5
1924 Paris **United States** 17-3
1976 Chicago **France** 33-14
1991 *1* Denver **France** 41-9

2 Colorado Springs **France** 10-3★
★Abandoned after 43 mins
France won series 2-0

FRANCE v ROMANIA
Played 43   France won 33, Romania won 8, Drawn 2

1924 Paris **France** 59-3
1938 Bucharest **France** 11-8
1957 Bucharest **France** 18-15
1957 Bordeaux **France** 39-0
1960 Bucharest **Romania** 11-5
1961 Bayonne **Drawn** 5-5
1962 Bucharest **Romania** 3-0
1963 Toulouse **Drawn** 6-6
1964 Bucharest **France** 9-6
1965 Lyons **France** 8-3
1966 Bucharest **France** 9-3
1967 Nantes **France** 11-3
1968 Bucharest **Romania** 15-14
1969 Tarbes **France** 14-9
1970 Bucharest **France** 14-3
1971 Béziers **France** 31-12
1972 Constanza **France** 15-6
1973 Valence **France** 7-6
1974 Bucharest **Romania** 15-10
1975 Bordeaux **France** 36-12
1976 Bucharest **Romania** 15-12
1977 Clermont-Ferrand **France** 9-6

1978 Bucharest **France** 9-6
1979 Montauban **France** 30-12
1980 Bucharest **Romania** 15-0
1981 Narbonne **France** 17-9
1982 Bucharest **Romania** 13-9
1983 Toulouse **France** 26-15
1984 Bucharest **France** 18-3
1986 Lille **France** 25-13
1986 Bucharest **France** 20-3
1987 Wellington *WC* **France** 55-12
1987 Agen **France** 49-3
1988 Bucharest **France** 16-12
1990 Auch **Romania** 12-6
1991 Bucharest **France** 33-21
1991 Béziers *WC* **France** 30-3
1992 Le Havre **France** 25-6
1993 Bucharest **France** 37-20
1993 Brive **France** 51-0
1995 Bucharest **France** 24-15
1995 Tucumán *LC* **France** 52-8
1996 Aurillac **France** 64-12

FRANCE v NEW ZEALAND MAORIS
Played 1   New Zealand Maoris won 1

1926 Paris **New Zealand Maoris** 12-3

FRANCE v GERMANY
Played 15   France won 13, Germany won 2

1927 Paris **France** 30-5
1927 Frankfurt **Germany** 17-16
1928 Hanover **France** 14-3
1929 Paris **France** 24-0
1930 Berlin **France** 31-0
1931 Paris **France** 34-0
1932 Frankfurt **France** 20-4
1933 Paris **France** 38-17

1934 Hanover **France** 13-9
1935 Paris **France** 18-3
1936 *1* Berlin **France** 19-14
    2 Hanover **France** 6-3
    France won series 2-0
1937 Paris **France** 27-6
1938 Frankfurt **Germany** 3-0
1938 Bucharest **France** 8-5

FRANCE v ITALY
Played 18   France won 18

1937 Paris **France** 43-5
1952 Milan **France** 17-8
1953 Lyons **France** 22-8

1954 Rome **France** 39-12
1955 Grenoble **France** 24-0
1956 Padua **France** 16-3

1957 Agen **France** 38-6
1958 Naples **France** 11-3
1959 Nantes **France** 22-0
1960 Treviso **France** 26-0
1961 Chambéry **France** 17-0
1962 Brescia **France** 6-3

1963 Grenoble **France** 14-12
1964 Parma **France** 12-3
1965 Pau **France** 21-0
1966 Naples **France** 21-0
1967 Toulon **France** 60-13
1995 Buenos Aires *LC* **France** 34-22

FRANCE v BRITISH XVs
Played 5   France won 2, British XVs won 3

1940 Paris **British XV** 36-3
1945 Paris **France** 21-9
1945 Richmond **British XV** 27-6

1946 Paris **France** 10-0
1989 Paris **British XV** 29-27

FRANCE v NEW ZEALAND ARMY
Played 1   New Zealand Army won 1

1946 Paris **New Zealand Army** 14-9

FRANCE v ARGENTINA
Played 27   France won 22, Argentina won 4, Drawn 1

1949 *1* Buenos Aires **France** 5-0
    2 Buenos Aires **France** 12-3
    France won series 2-0
1954 *1* Buenos Aires **France** 22-8
    2 Buenos Aires **France** 30-3
    France won series 2-0
1960 *1* Buenos Aires **France** 37-3
    2 Buenos Aires **France** 12-3
    3 Buenos Aires **France** 29-6
    France won series 3-0
1974 *1* Buenos Aires **France** 20-15
    2 Buenos Aires **France** 31-27
    France won series 2-0
1975 *1* Lyons **France** 29-6
    2 Paris **France** 36-21
    France won series 2-0
1977 *1* Buenos Aires **France** 26-3
    2 Buenos Aires **Drawn** 18-18
    France won series 1-0, with 1 draw
1982 *1* Toulouse **France** 25-12

    2 Paris **France** 13-6
    France won series 2-0
1985 *1* Buenos Aires **Argentina** 24-16
    2 Buenos Aires **France** 23-15
    Series drawn 1-1
1986 *1* Buenos Aires **Argentina** 15-13
    2 Buenos Aires **France** 22-9
    Series drawn 1-1
1988 *1* Buenos Aires **France** 18-15
    2 Buenos Aires **Argentina** 18-6
    Series drawn 1-1
1988 *1* Nantes **France** 29-9
    2 Lille **France** 28-18
    France won series 2-0
1992 *1* Buenos Aires **France** 27-12
    2 Buenos Aires **France** 33-9
    France won series 2-0
1992 Nantes **Argentina** 24-20
1995 Buenos Aires *LC* **France** 47-12

FRANCE v CZECHOSLOVAKIA
Played 2   France won 2

1956 Toulouse **France** 28-3

1968 Prague **France** 19-6

FRANCE v FIJI
Played 3   France won 3

1964 Paris **France** 21-3
1987 Auckland *WC* **France** 31-16

1991 Grenoble *WC* **France** 33-9

FRANCE v JAPAN
Played 1   France won 1

1973 Bordeaux **France** 30-18

FRANCE v ZIMBABWE
Played 1   France won 1

1987 Auckland *WC* **France** 70-12

FRANCE v CANADA
Played 3   France won 2, Canada won 1

1991 Agen *WC* **France** 19-13   1994 Besançon **France** 28-9
1994 Nepean **Canada** 18-16

FRANCE v TONGA
Played 1   France won 1

1995 Pretoria *WC* **France** 38-10

FRANCE v IVORY COAST
Played 1   France won 1

1995 Rustenburg *WC* **France** 54-18

NEW ZEALAND v SOUTH AFRICA
Played 42   New Zealand won 18, South Africa won 21, Drawn 3

1921 *1* Dunedin **New Zealand** 13-5
   2 Auckland **South Africa** 9-5
   3 Wellington **Drawn** 0-0
   Series drawn 1-1, with 1 draw
1928 *1* Durban **South Africa** 17-0
   2 Johannesburg **New Zealand** 7-6
   3 Port Elizabeth **South Africa** 11-6
   4 Cape Town **New Zealand** 13-5
   Series drawn 2-2
1937 *1* Wellington **New Zealand** 13-7
   2 Christchurch **South Africa** 13-6
   3 Auckland **South Africa** 17-6
   South Africa won series 2-1
1949 *1* Cape Town **South Africa** 15-11
   2 Johannesburg **South Africa** 12-6
   3 Durban **South Africa** 9-3
   4 Port Elizabeth **South Africa** 11-8
   South Africa won series 4-0
1956 *1* Dunedin **New Zealand** 10-6
   2 Wellington **South Africa** 8-3
   3 Christchurch **New Zealand** 17-10
   4 Auckland **New Zealand** 11-5
   New Zealand won series 3-1
1960 *1* Johannesburg **South Africa** 13-0
   2 Cape Town **New Zealand** 11-3
   3 Bloemfontein **Drawn** 11-11
   4 Port Elizabeth **South Africa** 8-3
   South Africa won series 2-1, with 1 draw

1965 *1* Wellington **New Zealand** 6-3
   2 Dunedin **New Zealand** 13-0
   3 Christchurch **South Africa** 19-16
   4 Auckland **New Zealand** 20-3
   New Zealand won series 3-1
1970 *1* Pretoria **South Africa** 17-6
   2 Cape Town **New Zealand** 9-8
   3 Port Elizabeth **South Africa** 14-3
   4 Johannesburg **South Africa** 20-17
   South Africa won series 3-1
1976 *1* Durban **South Africa** 16-7
   2 Bloemfontein **New Zealand** 15-9
   3 Cape Town **South Africa** 15-10
   4 Johannesburg **South Africa** 15-14
   South Africa won series 3-1
1981 *1* Christchurch **New Zealand** 14-9
   2 Wellington **South Africa** 24-12
   3 Auckland **New Zealand** 25-22
   New Zealand won series 2-1
1992 Johannesburg **New Zealand** 27-24
1994 *1* Dunedin **New Zealand** 22-14
   2 Wellington **New Zealand** 13-9
   3 Auckland **Drawn** 18-18
   New Zealand won series 2-0, with 1 draw
1995 Johannesburg *WC* **South Africa** 15-12
   (*aet*)

NEW ZEALAND v AUSTRALIA
Played 100   New Zealand won 68, Australia won 27, Drawn 5

1903 Sydney **New Zealand** 22-3
1905 Dunedin **New Zealand** 14-3
1907 *1* Sydney **New Zealand** 26-6
   2 Brisbane **New Zealand** 14-5
   3 Sydney **Drawn** 5-5
   New Zealand won series 2-0, with 1 draw
1910 *1* Sydney **New Zealand** 6-0

   2 Sydney **Australia** 11-0
   3 Sydney **New Zealand** 28-13
   New Zealand won series 2-1
1913 *1* Wellington **New Zealand** 30-5
   2 Dunedin **New Zealand** 25-13
   3 Christchurch **Australia** 16-5
   New Zealand won series 2-1

99

1914 *1* Sydney **New Zealand** 5-0
  2 Brisbane **New Zealand** 17-0
  3 Sydney **New Zealand** 22-7
  New Zealand won series 3-0
1929 *1* Sydney **Australia** 9-8
  2 Brisbane **Australia** 17-9
  3 Sydney **Australia** 15-13
  Australia won series 3-0
1931 Auckland **New Zealand** 20-13
1932 *1* Sydney **Australia** 22-17
  2 Brisbane **New Zealand** 21-3
  3 Sydney **New Zealand** 21-13
  New Zealand won series 2-1
1934 *1* Sydney **Australia** 25-11
  2 Sydney **Drawn** 3-3
  Australia won series 1-0, with 1 draw
1936 *1* Wellington **New Zealand** 11-6
  2 Dunedin **New Zealand** 38-13
  New Zealand won series 2-0
1938 *1* Sydney **New Zealand** 24-9
  2 Brisbane **New Zealand** 20-14
  3 Sydney **New Zealand** 14-6
  New Zealand won series 3-0
1946 *1* Dunedin **New Zealand** 31-8
  2 Sydney **New Zealand** 14-10
  New Zealand won series 2-0
1947 *1* Brisbane **New Zealand** 13-5
  2 Sydney **New Zealand** 27-14
  New Zealand won series 2-0
1949 *1* Wellington **Australia** 11-6
  2 Auckland **Australia** 16-9
  Australia won series 2-0
1951 *1* Sydney **New Zealand** 8-0
  2 Sydney **New Zealand** 17-11
  3 Brisbane **New Zealand** 16-6
  New Zealand won series 3-0
1952 *1* Christchurch **Australia** 14-9
  2 Wellington **New Zealand** 15-8
  Series drawn 1-1
1955 *1* Wellington **New Zealand** 16-8
  2 Dunedin **New Zealand** 8-0
  3 Auckland **Australia** 8-3
  New Zealand won series 2-1
1957 *1* Sydney **New Zealand** 25-11
  2 Brisbane **New Zealand** 22-9
  New Zealand won series 2-0
1958 *1* Wellington **New Zealand** 25-3
  2 Christchurch **Australia** 6-3
  3 Auckland **New Zealand** 17-8
  New Zealand won series 2-1
1962 *1* Brisbane **New Zealand** 20-6
  2 Sydney **New Zealand** 14-5
  New Zealand won series 2-0
1962 *1* Wellington **Drawn** 9-9
  2 Dunedin **New Zealand** 3-0
  3 Auckland **New Zealand** 16-8
  New Zealand won series 2-0, with1 draw
1964 *1* Dunedin **New Zealand** 14-9
  2 Christchurch **New Zealand** 18-3

  3 Wellington **Australia** 20-5
  New Zealand won series 2-1
1967 Wellington **New Zealand** 29-9
1968 *1* Sydney **New Zealand** 27-11
  2 Brisbane **New Zealand** 19-18
  New Zealand won series 2-0
1972 *1* Wellington **New Zealand** 29-6
  2 Christchurch **New Zealand** 30-17
  3 Auckland **New Zealand** 38-3
  New Zealand won series 3-0
1974 *1* Sydney **New Zealand** 11-6
  2 Brisbane **Drawn** 16-16
  3 Sydney **New Zealand** 16-6
  New Zealand won series 2-0, with 1 draw
1978 *1* Wellington **New Zealand** 13-12
  2 Christchurch **New Zealand** 22-6
  3 Auckland **Australia** 30-16
  New Zealand won series 2-1
1979 Sydney **Australia** 12-6
1980 *1* Sydney **Australia** 13-9
  2 Brisbane **New Zealand** 12-9
  3 Sydney **Australia** 26-10
  Australia won series 2-1
1982 *1* Christchurch **New Zealand** 23-16
  2 Wellington **Australia** 19-16
  3 Auckland **New Zealand** 33-18
  New Zealand won series 2-1
1983 Sydney **New Zealand** 18-8
1984 *1* Sydney **Australia** 16-9
  2 Brisbane **New Zealand** 19-15
  3 Sydney **New Zealand** 25-24
  New Zealand won series 2-1
1985 Auckland **New Zealand** 10-9
1986 *1* Wellington **Australia** 13-12
  2 Dunedin **New Zealand** 13-12
  3 Auckland **Australia** 22-9
  Australia won series 2-1
1987 Sydney **New Zealand** 30-16
1988 *1* Sydney **New Zealand** 32-7
  2 Brisbane **Drawn** 19-19
  3 Sydney **New Zealand** 30-9
  New Zealand won series 2-0, with 1 draw
1989 Auckland **New Zealand** 24-12
1990 *1* Christchurch **New Zealand** 21-6
  2 Auckland **New Zealand** 27-17
  3 Wellington **Australia** 21-9
  New Zealand won series 2-1
1991 *1* Sydney **Australia** 21-12
  2 Auckland **New Zealand** 6-3
1991 Dublin *WC* **Australia** 16-6
1992 *1* Sydney **Australia** 16-15
  2 Brisbane **Australia** 19-17
  3 Sydney **New Zealand** 26-23
  Australia won series 2-1
1993 Dunedin **New Zealand** 25-10
1994 Sydney **Australia** 20-16
1995 Auckland **New Zealand** 28-16
1995 Sydney **New Zealand** 34-23

NEW ZEALAND v UNITED STATES
Played 2   New Zealand won 2

1913 Berkeley **New Zealand** 51-3   1991 Gloucester *WC* **New Zealand** 46-6

NEW ZEALAND v ROMANIA
Played 1   New Zealand won 1

1981 Bucharest **New Zealand** 14-6

NEW ZEALAND v ARGENTINA
Played 7   New Zealand won 6, Drawn 1

1985 *1* Buenos Aires **New Zealand** 33-20
    2 Buenos Aires **Drawn** 21-21
    New Zealand won series 1-0, with 1 draw
1987 Wellington *WC* **New Zealand** 46-15
1989 *1* Dunedin **New Zealand** 60-9

    2 Wellington **New Zealand** 49-12
    New Zealand won series 2-0
1991 *1* Buenos Aires **New Zealand** 28-14
    2 Buenos Aires **New Zealand** 36-6
    New Zealand won series 2-0

NEW ZEALAND v ITALY
Played 3   New Zealand won 3

1987 Auckland *WC* **New Zealand** 70-6   1995 Bologna **New Zealand** 70-6
1991 Leicester *WC* **New Zealand** 31-21

NEW ZEALAND v FIJI
Played 1   New Zealand won 1

1987 Christchurch *WC* **New Zealand** 74-13

NEW ZEALAND v CANADA
Played 2   New Zealand won 2

1991 Lille *WC* **New Zealand** 29-13   1995 Auckland **New Zealand** 73-7

NEW ZEALAND v WORLD XVs
Played 3   New Zealand won 2, World XV won 1

1992 *1* Christchurch **World XV** 28-14   *3* Auckland **New Zealand** 26-15
    2 Wellington **New Zealand** 54-26   *New Zealand won series 2-1*

NEW ZEALAND v WESTERN SAMOA
Played 1   New Zealand won 1

1993 Auckland **New Zealand** 35-13

NEW ZEALAND v JAPAN
Played 1   New Zealand won 1

1995 Bloemfontein *WC* **New Zealand** 145-17

SOUTH AFRICA v AUSTRALIA
Played 33   South Africa won 23, Australia won 10, Drawn 0

1993 *1* Cape Town **South Africa** 17-3
    2 Durban **Australia** 21-6
    3 Johannesburg **South Africa** 12-3
    4 Port Elizabeth **South Africa** 11-0
    5 Bloemfontein **Australia** 15-4
    South Africa won series 3-2

1937 *1* Sydney **South Africa** 9-5
    2 Sydney **South Africa** 26-17
    South Africa won series 2-0

1953 *1* Johannesburg **South Africa** 25-3
    2 Cape Town **Australia** 18-14
    3 Durban **South Africa** 18-8
    4 Port Elizabeth **South Africa** 22-9
    South Africa won series 3-1

1956 *1* Sydney **South Africa** 9-0
    2 Brisbane **South Africa** 9-0
    South Africa won series 2-0

1961 *1* Johannesburg **South Africa** 28-3
    2 Port Elizabeth **South Africa** 23-11
    South Africa won series 2-0

1963 *1* Pretoria **South Africa** 14-3
    2 Cape Town **Australia** 9-5

    3 Johannesburg **Australia** 11-9
    4 Port Elizabeth **South Africa** 22-6
    Series drawn 2-2

1965 *1* Sydney **Australia** 18-11
    2 Brisbane **Australia** 12-8
    Australia won series 2-0

1969 *1* Johannesburg **South Africa** 30-11
    2 Durban **South Africa** 16-9
    3 Cape Town **South Africa** 11-3
    4 Bloemfontein **South Africa** 19-8
    South Africa won series 4-0

1971 *1* Sydney **South Africa** 19-11
    2 Brisbane **South Africa** 14-6
    3 Sydney **South Africa** 18-6
    South Africa won series 3-0

1992 Cape Town **Australia** 26-3

1993 *1* Sydney **South Africa** 19-12
    2 Brisbane **Australia** 28-20
    3 Sydney **Australia** 19-12
    Australia won series 2-1

1995 Cape Town *WC* **South Africa** 27-18

SOUTH AFRICA v WORLD XVs
Played 3   South Africa won 3

1977 Pretoria **South Africa** 45-24
1989 *1* Cape Town **South Africa** 20-19

    2 Johannesburg **South Africa** 22-16
    South Africa won series 2-0

SOUTH AFRICA v SOUTH AMERICA
Played 8   South Africa won 7, South America won 1

1980 *1* Johannesburg **South Africa** 24-9
    2 Durban **South Africa** 18-9
    South Africa won series 2-0

1980 *1* Montevideo **South Africa** 22-13
    2 Santiago **South Africa** 30-16
    South Africa won series 2-0

1982 *1* Pretoria **South Africa** 50-18
    2 Bloemfontein **South America** 21-12
    Series drawn 1-1

1984 *1* Pretoria **South Africa** 32-15
    2 Cape Town **South Africa** 22-13
    South Africa won series 2-0

SOUTH AFRICA v UNITED STATES
Played 1   South Africa won 1

1981 Glenville **South Africa** 38-7

SOUTH AFRICA v NEW ZEALAND CAVALIERS
Played 4   South Africa won 3, New Zealand Cavaliers won 1

1986 *1* Cape Town **South Africa** 21-15
    2 Durban **New Zealand Cavaliers**
    19-18

    3 Pretoria **South Africa** 33-18
    4 Johannesburg **South Africa** 24-10
    South Africa won series 3-1

SOUTH AFRICA v ARGENTINA
Played 4   South Africa won 4

1993 *1* Buenos Aires **South Africa** 29-26
    2 Buenos Aires **South Africa** 52-23
    South Africa won series 2-0

1994 *1* Port Elizabeth **South Africa** 42-22
    2 Johannesburg **South Africa** 46-26
    South Africa won series 2-0

SOUTH AFRICA v WESTERN SAMOA
Played 2   South Africa won 2

1995 Johannesburg **South Africa** 60-8   1995 Johannesburg *WC* **South Africa** 42-14

SOUTH AFRICA v ROMANIA
Played 1   South Africa won 1

1995 Cape Town **South Africa** 21-8

SOUTH AFRICA v CANADA
Played 1   South Africa won 1

1995 Port Elizabeth *WC* **South Africa** 20-0

SOUTH AFRICA v ITALY
Played 1   South Africa won 1

1995 Rome **South Africa** 40-21

AUSTRALIA v UNITED STATES
Played 5   Australia won 5

1912 Berkeley **Australia** 12-8   1987 Brisbane *WC* **Australia** 47-12
1976 Los Angeles **Australia** 24-12   1990 Brisbane **Australia** 67-9
1983 Sydney **Australia** 49-3

AUSTRALIA v NEW ZEALAND MAORIS
Played 10   Australia won 4, New Zealand Maoris won 4, Drawn 2

1928 Wellington **New Zealand Maoris** 9-8   *3* Sydney **Australia** 18-3
1931 Palmerston North **Australia** 14-3   *Series drawn 1-1, with 1 draw*
1936 Palmerston North **Australia** 31-6   1958 *1* Brisbane **Australia** 15-14
1946 Hamilton **New Zealand Maoris** 20-0   *2* Sydney **Drawn** 3-3
1949 *1* Sydney **New Zealand Maoris** 12-3   *3* Melbourne **New Zealand Maoris**
    2 Brisbane **Drawn** 8-8   13-6
      Series drawn 1-1, with 1 draw

AUSTRALIA v FIJI
Played 15   Australia won 12, Fiji won 2, Drawn 1

1952 *1* Sydney **Australia** 15-9   1972 Suva **Australia** 21-19
    2 Sydney **Fiji** 17-15   1976 *1* Sydney **Australia** 22-6
    Series drawn 1-1   *2* Brisbane **Australia** 21-9
1954 *1* Brisbane **Australia** 22-19   *3* Sydney **Australia** 27-17
    2 Sydney **Fiji** 18-16   *Australia won series 3-0*
    Series drawn 1-1   1980 Suva **Australia** 22-9
1961 *1* Brisbane **Australia** 24-6   1984 Suva **Australia** 16-3
    2 Sydney **Australia** 20-14   1985 *1* Brisbane **Australia** 52-28
    3 Melbourne **Drawn** 3-3   *2* Sydney **Australia** 31-9
    Australia won series 2-0, with 1 draw   *Australia won series 2-0*

AUSTRALIA v TONGA
Played 3   Australia won 2, Tonga won 1

1973 *1* Sydney **Australia** 30-12   1993 Brisbane **Australia** 52-14
    2 Brisbane **Tonga** 16-11
    Series drawn 1-1

AUSTRALIA v JAPAN
Played 3   Australia won 3

1975 *1* Sydney **Australia** 37-7
    2 Brisbane **Australia** 50-25
    Australia won series 2-0

1987 Sydney *WC* **Australia** 42-23

AUSTRALIA v ARGENTINA
Played 11   Australia won 7, Argentina won 3, Drawn 1

1979 *1* Buenos Aires **Argentina** 24-13
    2 Buenos Aires **Australia** 17-12
    Series drawn 1-1
1983 *1* Brisbane **Argentina** 18-3
    2 Sydney **Australia** 29-13
    Series drawn 1-1
1986 *1* Brisbane **Australia** 39-19
    2 Sydney **Australia** 26-0
    Australia won series 2-0

1987 *1* Buenos Aires **Drawn** 19-19
    2 Buenos Aires **Argentina** 27-19
    Argentina won series 1-0, with 1 draw
1991 Llanelli *WC* **Australia** 32-19
1995 *1* Brisbane **Australia** 53-7
    2 Sydney **Australia** 30-13
    Australia won series 2-0

AUSTRALIA v WESTERN SAMOA
Played 2   Australia won 2

1991 Pontypool *WC* **Australia** 9-3

1994 Sydney **Australia** 73-3

AUSTRALIA v ITALY
Played 5   Australia won 5

1983 Rovigo **Australia** 29-7
1986 Brisbane **Australia** 39-18
1988 Rome **Australia** 55-6

1994 *1* Brisbane **Australia** 23-20
    2 Melbourne **Australia** 20-7
    Australia won series 2-0

AUSTRALIA v CANADA
Played 4   Australia won 4

1985 *1* Sydney **Australia** 59-3
    2 Brisbane **Australia** 43-15
    Australia won series 2-0

1993 Calgary **Australia** 43-16
1995 Port Elizabeth *WC* **Australia** 27-11

AUSTRALIA v KOREA
Played 1   Australia won 1

1987 Brisbane **Australia** 65-18

AUSTRALIA v ROMANIA
Played 1   Australia won 1

1995 Stellenbosch **Australia** 42-3

INTERNATIONAL HONOURS

WORLD CUP WINNERS
New Zealand once: 1987
Australia once: 1991
South Africa once: 1995

GRAND SLAM WINNERS
England 11 times: 1913, 1914, 1921, 1923, 1924, 1928, 1957, 1980, 1991, 1992, 1995.
Wales 8 times: 1908, 1909, 1911, 1950, 1952, 1971, 1976, 1978.
France 4 times: 1968, 1977, 1981, 1987.
Scotland 3 times; 1925, 1984, 1990.
Ireland once: 1948.

TRIPLE CROWN WINNERS
England 19 times: 1883, 1884, 1892, 1913, 1914, 1921, 1923, 1924, 1928, 1934, 1937, 1954, 1957, 1960, 1980, 1991, 1992, 1995, 1996. **Wales** 17 times: 1893, 1900, 1902, 1905, 1908, 1909, 1911, 1950, 1952, 1965, 1969, 1971, 1976, 1977, 1978, 1979, 1988. **Scotland** 10 times: 1891, 1895, 1901, 1903, 1907, 1925, 1933, 1938, 1984, 1990. **Ireland** 6 times: 1894, 1899, 1948, 1949, 1982, 1985.

INTERNATIONAL CHAMPIONSHIP WINNERS

Year	Winner	Year	Winner	Year	Winner	Year	Winner
1883	England	1912 {	England	1947 {	Wales	1972*	—
1884	England		Ireland		England	1973	Quintuple
1885*	—	1913	England	1948	Ireland		tie
1886 {	England	1914	England	1949	Ireland	1974	Ireland
	Scotland		England	1950	Wales	1975	Wales
1887	Scotland	1920 {	Scotland	1951	Ireland	1976	Wales
1888*	—		Wales	1952	Wales	1977	France
1889*	—	1921	England	1953	England	1978	Wales
1890 {	England	1922	Wales	1954 {	England	1979	Wales
	Scotland	1923	England		France	1980	England
1891	Scotland	1924	England		Wales	1981	France
1892	England	1925	Scotland	1955 {	France	1982	Ireland
1893	Wales	1926 {	Scotland		Wales	1983 {	France
1894	Ireland		Ireland	1956	Wales		Ireland
1895	Scotland	1927 {	Scotland	1957	England	1984	Scotland
1896	Ireland		Ireland	1958	England	1985	Ireland
1897*	—	1928	England	1959	France	1986 {	France
1898*	—	1929	Scotland	1960 {	France		Scotland
1899	Ireland	1930	England		England	1987	France
1900	Wales	1931	Wales	1961	France	1988 {	Wales
1901	Scotland	1932 {	England	1962	France		France
1902	Wales		Wales	1963	England	1989	France
1903	Scotland		Ireland	1964 {	Scotland	1990	Scotland
1904	Scotland	1933	Scotland		Wales	1991	England
1905	Wales	1934	England	1965	Wales	1992	England
1906 {	Ireland	1935	Ireland	1966	Wales	1993	France
	Wales	1936	Wales	1967	France	1994**	Wales
1907	Scotland	1937	England	1968	France	1995	England
1908	Wales	1938	Scotland	1969	Wales	1996**	England
1909	Wales	1939 {	England	1970 {	France		
1910	England		Wales		Wales		
1911	Wales		Ireland	1971	Wales		

*Matches not completed, for various reasons
** Indicates winners of the Five Nations Trophy (introduced 1993) on points difference

Wales and England have won the title outright most times, 22 each; Scotland have won it 13 times; Ireland 10 and France 10.

LATIN CUP WINNERS
France once: 1995

OTHER INTERNATIONAL MATCHES 1995-96

22 July 1995, Eden Park, Auckland **Bledisloe Cup, 1st Test**
NEW ZEALAND 28 (1G 5PG 2DG) **AUSTRALIA 16** (1G 3PG)

NEW ZEALAND: G M Osborne (North Harbour); J W Wilson (Otago), F E Bunce (North Harbour), W K Little (North Harbour), J T Lomu (Counties); A P Mehrtens (Canterbury), G T M Bachop (Otago); C W Dowd (Auckland), S B T Fitzpatrick (Auckland) (*capt*), O M Brown (Auckland), I D Jones (North Harbour), R M Brooke (Auckland), M R Brewer (Canterbury), Z V Brooke (Auckland), J A Kronfeld (Otago) *Replacement* M N Jones (Auckland) for Z Brooke (51 mins)
Scorers *Try:* Lomu *Conversion:* Mehrtens *Penalty Goals:* Mehrtens (5) *Dropped Goals:* Mehrtens (2)
AUSTRALIA: M Burke (Eastwood & NSW); D P Smith (Souths & Queensland), J S Little (Souths & Queensland), T J Horan (Souths & Queensland), J W Roff (Canberra & ACT); S Bowen (Southern Districts & NSW), S Merrick (Hunter Valley & NSW Country); D J Crowley (Souths & Queensland), P N Kearns (Randwick & NSW) (*capt*), M N Hartill (Gordon & NSW), W W Waugh (Randwick & NSW), J A Eales (Souths & Queensland), V Ofahengaue (Manly & NSW), B T Gavin (Eastern Suburbs & NSW), D T Manu (Eastwood & NSW) *Replacements* P W Howard (University & Queensland) for Burke (29 mins); T Coker (Souths & Queensland) for Gavin (73 mins)
Scorers *Try:* Ofahengaue *Conversion:* Roff *Penalty Goals:* Burke, Roff (2)
Referee R J Megson (Scotland)

29 July 1995, Sydney Football Stadium, **Bledisloe Cup, 2nd Test**
AUSTRALIA 23 (2G 3PG) **NEW ZEALAND 34** (3G 1PG 2T)

AUSTRALIA: M Burke (Eastwood & NSW); D P Smith (Souths & Queensland), J S Little (Souths & Queensland), T J Horan (Souths & Queensland), J W Roff (Canberra & ACT); S Bowen (Southern Districts & NSW), S Merrick (Hunter Valley & NSW Country); M N Hartill (Gordon & NSW), P N Kearns (Randwick & NSW) (*capt*), E J A McKenzie (Paris U & NSW), W W Waugh (Randwick & NSW), J A Eales (Souths & Queensland), V Ofahengaue (Manly & NSW), B T Gavin (Eastern Suburbs & NSW), D T Manu (Eastwood & NSW) *Replacements* D I Campese (Randwick & NSW) for Smith (41 mins); P W Howard (University & Queensland) for Burke (temp)
Scorers *Tries:* Smith, Ofahengaue *Conversions:* Burke (2) *Penalty Goals:* Burke (3)
NEW ZEALAND: G M Osborne (North Harbour); J W Wilson (Otago), F E Bunce (North Harbour), W K Little (North Harbour), J T Lomu (Counties); A P Mehrtens (Canterbury), G T M Bachop (Otago); C W Dowd (Auckland), S B T Fitzpatrick (Auckland) (*capt*), O M Brown (Auckland), I D Jones (North Harbour), R M Brooke (Auckland), M R Brewer (Canterbury), Z V Brooke (Auckland), M N Jones (Auckland) *Replacements* J A Kronfeld (Otago) for M N Jones (41 mins); R W Loe (Canterbury) for I D Jones and Brewer (temp)
Scorers *Tries:* Bunce (2), Mehrtens, Lomu, Wilson *Conversions:* Mehrtens (3) *Penalty Goal:* Mehrtens
Referee B W Stirling (Ireland)

9 September 1995, Fletcher's Field, Toronto
CANADA 14 (3PG 1T) **USA 15** (1G 1PG 1T)

CANADA: S Stewart (UBCOB); W Stanley (UBCOB), S Gray (Kats), S Lytton (Meraloma), C Smith (Meraloma); J Graf (UBCOB) (*capt*), A Tynan (UBCOB);

D Penney (Swilers), K Svoboda (Ajax Wanderers), R Snow (Dogs & Eastern Province), M James (Burnaby Lake), G Rowlands (Velox Valhallians), I Gordon (James Bay), A Charron (Ottawa Irish), J Hutchinson (UBCOB)
Replacement N Clapinson (Ste-Anne-de-Bellevue) for Svoboda (temp)
Scorers *Try:* Stanley   *Penalty Goals:* Graf (3)
USA: M Fabling (PAC); V Anitoni (San Francisco Yankees), R Green (OMBAC), M Scharrenberg (Golden Gate), J Santos (OMBAC); M Alexander (Denver Barbarians), A Bachelet (Old Blues) (*capt*); S Bracken (OMBAC), T Billups (Old Blues), R Lehner (Old Blues), A Freeman (Charlotte), R Randell (Salt Lake City U), D Lyle (OMBAC), R Tardits (Mystic River), J Holtzman (Seven River)   *Replacement* P Molloy (PAC) for Freeman (55 mins)
Scorers *Tries:* Alexander, Green   *Conversion:* Alexander   *Penalty Goal:* Alexander
Referee M Toshiyuki (Japan)

6 January 1996, Life College, Marietta, Georgia
USA 18 (1G 1PG 1DG 1T)   IRELAND 25 (1G 6PG)

USA: M Williams (Aspen); V Anitoni (San Francisco Yankees), R Green (OMBAC), M Scharrenberg (Golden Gate), M Delai (OMBAC); M Alexander (Denver Barbarians), A Bachelet (Old Blues) (*capt*); G McDonald (Washington), T Billups (Old Blues), J Rissone (Old Puget Sound Beach), L Gross (Cincinnati Wolfhounds), A Freeman (Charlotte), R Randell (Salt Lake City U), R Tardits (Mystic River & Paris U), D Lyle (OMBAC)   *Replacement* J Walker (Aspen) for Randell (40 mins)

Justin Thomas on his way to scoring his try for Wales in their 31-26 defeat of Italy in Cardiff.

Scorers *Tries:* Walker, Tardits   *Conversion:* Alexander
Penalty Goal: Alexander   *Dropped Goal:* Alexander
IRELAND: J E Staples (Harlequins) (*capt*); R M Wallace (Garryowen), J C Bell
(Northampton), K P McQuilkin (Bective Rangers), S P Geoghegan (Bath);
E P Elwood (Lansdowne), C Saverimutto (Sale); N J Popplewell (Newcastle),
T J Kingston (Dolphin), P S Wallace (Blackrock Coll), G M Fulcher (Cork Const),
N P J Francis (Old Belvedere), V C P Costello (St Mary's Coll), P S Johns
(Dungannon), D S Corkery (Cork Const)   *Replacement* P A Burke (Cork Const) for
Elwood (49 mins)
Scorers *Try:* R Wallace   *Conversion:* Elwood   *Penalty Goals:* Elwood (3), Burke (3)
Referee G Gadjovich (Canada)

16 January 1996, Cardiff Arms Park
WALES 31 (2G 4PG 1T)   ITALY 26 (2G 4PG)

WALES: W J L Thomas (Llanelli); I C Evans (Llanelli), L B Davies (Neath),
M E Wintle (Llanelli), W T Proctor (Llanelli); A C Thomas (Bristol), A P Moore
(Cardiff); A L P Lewis (Cardiff), J M Humphreys (Cardiff) (*capt*), J D Davies
(Neath), G O Llewellyn (Neath), D Jones (Cardiff), E W Lewis (Cardiff), H T Taylor
(Cardiff), R G Jones (Llanelli)
Scorers *Tries:* Evans (2), J Thomas   *Conversions:* A Thomas (2)
Penalty Goals: A Thomas (4)
ITALY: M Ravazzolo (Calvisano); P Vaccari (Calvisano), I Francescato (Treviso),
T Visentin (Treviso), F Roselli (Roma); D Dominguez (Milan), A Troncon
(Treviso); Massimo Cuttitta (Milan) (*capt*), C Orlandi (Milan), F Properzi-Curti
(Milan), M Giacheri (Treviso), P Pedroni (Milan), O Arancio (Catania),
J M Gardner (Treviso), A Sgorlon (San Dona)   *Replacements* M Bonomi (Milan) for
Visentin (64 mins); G de Carli (Roma) for Orlandi (73 mins)
Scorers *Tries:* Gardner, Properzi-Curti   *Conversions:* Dominguez (2)
Penalty Goals: Dominguez (4)
Referee G Black (Ireland)

20 April 1996, Stade Jean Alric, Aurillac
FRANCE 64 (7G 3T)   ROMANIA 12 (3PG 1DG)

FRANCE: R Dourthe (Dax); D Venditti (Bourgoin), O Campan (Agen), S Glas
(Bourgoin), P Saint-André (Montferrand) (*capt*); A Penaud (Brive), G Accoceberry
(Bègles-Bordeaux); C Califano (Toulouse), H Guiraud (Nîmes), F Tournaire
(Narbonne), O Merle (Montferrand), H Miorin (Toulouse), M Lievremont
(Perpignan), T Labrousse (Brive), C Moni (Nice)   *Replacements* J-L Jordana (Pau)
for Tournaire (70 mins); E Ntamack (Toulouse) for Venditti (73 mins);
P Carbonneau (Toulouse) for Accoceberry (74 mins); F Pelous (Dax) for Merle
(74 mins)
Scorers *Tries:* Califano (3), Glas (2), Labrousse (2), Moni, Penaud, Ntamack
Conversions: Dourthe (7)
ROMANIA: V Brici (Farul Constanta); R Fugigi (CSM Sibiu), R Gontineac (Cluj
U), T Luca (Grivita Bucharest), G Solomie (Timisoara U); V Popisteanu (Steaua
Bucharest), D Neaga (Dinamo Bucharest); G Vlad (Dinamo Bucharest), V Tufa
(Dinamo Bucharest), A Salageanu (Dinamo Bucharest), C Cojocariu (Bayonne),
S Ciorascu (Auch), O Slusariuc (Dinamo Bucharest), T Brinza (Cluj U) (*capt*),
A Gealapu (Steaua Bucharest)   *Replacements* I Rotaru (Dinamo Bucharest) for
Solomie (40 mins); A Girbu (Farul Constanta) for Cojocariu (71 mins); C Stan
(Dinamo Bucharest) for Vlad (71 mins)
Scorer *Penalty Goals:* Popisteanu (3)   *Dropped Goal:* Popisteanu
Referee J Atorasagasti (Spain)

A INTERNATIONALS 1995-96

6 January 1996, Rieti
Italy A 29 (3G 1PG 1T)   Scotland A 17 (4PG 1T)

Italy A: M Ravazzolo (Calvisano); P Vaccari (Calvisano), T Visentin (Treviso), I Francescato (Treviso), F Roselli (Roma Olimpic); D Dominguez (Milan), A Troncon (Treviso); M dal Sie (San Dona), C Orlandi (Milan), F Properzi (Milan), P Pedroni (Milan), M Giacheri (Treviso), O Arancio (Catania), J Gardner (Treviso), A Sgorlon (San Dona) *(capt)* *Replacement* R Favaro (Treviso) for Pedroni
Scorers *Tries:* Arancio, Gardner, Vaccari, Visentin *Conversions:* Dominguez (3) *Penalty Goal:* Dominguez
Scotland A: R J S Shepherd (Melrose); C A Joiner (Melrose), S Hastings (Watsonians), I C Jardine (Stirling County), K M Logan (Stirling County); G P J Townsend (Northampton), B W Redpath (Melrose); D I W Hilton (Bath), K D McKenzie (Stirling County), P H Wright (Boroughmuir), S J Campbell (Dundee HSFP), S Murray (Edinburgh Acads), S J Reid (Boroughmuir), E W Peters (Bath), R I Wainwright (West Hartlepool) *(capt)* *Replacements* G W Weir (Melrose) for Reid; C M Chalmers (Melrose) for Jardine (temp)
Scorers *Try:* Redpath *Penalty Goals:* Shepherd (3), Townsend
Referee G Simmonds (Wales)

19 January 1996, Stade Jean Bouin, Paris
France A 15 (5PG)   England A 25 (1G 5PG 1DG)

France A: O Touluze (Grenoble); D Venditti (Bourgoin), S Glas (Bourgoin), C Lamaison (Bayonne), L Arbo (Perpignan); Y Delaigue (Toulon), F Galthié (Colomiers) *(capt)*; J-J Crenca (Agen), H Guiraud (Nîmes), F Tournaire (Narbonne), Y Lemeur (RCF), J-P Versailles (Montferrand), L Malié (Grenoble), C Juillet (Montferrand), P Farner (Bègles-Bordeaux) *Replacement* F Belot (Toulouse) for Lemeur (39 mins)
Scorer *Penalty Goals:* Lamaison (5)
England A: T Stimpson (West Hartlepool); D Hopley (Wasps), P Mensah (Harlequins), W Greenwood (Harlequins), A Adebayo (Bath); A King (Bristol U), A Gomarsall (Wasps); R Hardwick (Coventry), P Greening (Gloucester), D Garforth (Leicester), G Archer (Bristol), D Sims (Gloucester), M Corry (Bristol), A Diprose (Saracens) *(capt)*, R Jenkins (Harlequins)
Scorers *Try:* Stimpson *Conversion:* Stimpson *Penalty Goals:* Stimpson (5) *Dropped Goal:* King
Referee B Smith (Ireland)

19 January 1996, Donnybrook, Dublin
Ireland A 26 (1G 3PG 2T)   Scotland A 19 (3PG 2T)

Ireland A: C M P O'Shea (London Irish); S J P Mason (Orrell), J A Gallagher (Blackheath), S A McCahill (Sunday's Well), N K P J Woods (Blackrock Coll); D G Humphreys (London Irish), A C Rolland (Blackrock Coll) *(capt)*; P Flavin (Blackrock Coll), S J Byrne (Blackrock Coll), P S Wallace (Blackrock Coll), D A Tweed (Ballymena), M E O'Kelly (St Mary's Coll), V C P Costello (St Mary's Coll), A G Foley (Shannon), E R P Miller (Leicester) *Replacement* L Toland (Old Crescent) for Miller
Scorers *Tries:* Mason, Wallace, pen try *Conversion:* Mason *Penalty Goals:* Mason (3)

Scotland A: S D Lang (Heriot's FP); I C Glasgow (Heriot's FP), A G Shiel (Melrose), B R S Eriksson (London Scottish), J A Kerr (Watsonians); W S Welsh (Hawick), G Armstrong (Newcastle) (*capt*); M G Browne (Melrose), D G Ellis (Currie), B D Stewart (Edinburgh Acads), M Norval (Stirling County), D F Cronin (Bourges), P Walton (Newcastle), B L Renwick (Hawick), J P Amos (Gala)
Scorers *Tries:* Kerr, Walton   *Penalty Goals:* Welsh (3)
Referee J Pearson (England)

31 January 1996, Welford Road, Leicester
England A 24 (1G 4PG 1T)   New South Wales 22 (1G 5PG)

England A: T Stimpson (West Hartlepool); P Hull (Bristol), A Blyth (West Hartlepool), W Greenwood (Harlequins), A Adebayo (Bath); A King (Bristol U), A Healey (Orrell); R Hardwick (Coventry), R Cockerill (Leicester), D Garforth (Leicester), G Archer (Bristol), J Fowler (Sale), M Corry (Bristol), A Diprose (Saracens) (*capt*), R Hill (Saracens)
Scorers *Tries:* Greenwood, Blyth   *Conversion:* King   *Penalty Goals:* Stimpson (2) King (2)
New South Wales: M Burke; D Campese, J Madz, R Tombs, A Murdoch; S Bowen, S Payne; R Harry, M Bell, M Hartill, W Waugh, S Domoni, W Ofahengaue, T Gavin (*capt*), D Manu *Replacement* A Blades for Harry (54 mins)
Scorers *Try:* Manu   *Conversion:* Burke   *Penalty Goals:* Burke (5)
Referee D Davies (Wales)

England A fly-half Alex King is tackled by Scott Bowen (No 10) and Sam Domoni of New South Wales in the match at Leicester. King contributed two penalty goals and a conversion to England's narrow win.

2 February 1996, Myreside, Edinburgh
Scotland A 38 (3G 4PG 1T)   France A 32 (2G 1DG 3T)

Scotland A: S D Lang (Heriot's FP); I C Glasgow (Heriot's FP), A G Shiel (Melrose), B R S Eriksson (London Scottish), D A Stark (Boroughmuir); W S Welsh (Hawick), D W Patterson (West Hartlepool); M G Browne (Melrose), D G Ellis

(Currie), B D Stewart (Edinburgh Acads), D G Burns (Boroughmuir), D F Cronin (Bourges) *(capt)*, P Walton (Newcastle), B L Renwick (Hawick), N J R Broughton (Melrose) *Replacements* S A Nichol (Selkirk) for Eriksson (temp); S R Laing (Instonians) for Welsh (72 mins)
Scorers *Tries:* Cronin (2), Renwick, Stark   *Conversions:* Welsh (3)
Penalty Goals: Welsh (4)
France A: C Lamaison (Bayonne); S Venditti (Bourgoin), Y Delaigue (Toulon), O Campan (Agen), D Berty (Toulouse); G Merceron (Montferrand), F Galthié (Colomiers) *(capt)*, F Tournaire (Narbonne), H Guiraud (Nîmes), J-L Jordana (Pau), H Miorin (Toulouse), J-P Versailles (Montferrand), C Moni (Nice), T Labrousse (Brive), S Dispagne (Toulouse)
Scorers *Tries:* Campan, Delaigue (2), Lamaison, Venditti
Conversions: Lamaison (2)   *Dropped Goal:* Merceron
Referee H Lewis (Wales), replaced by J L Bacigalupo (Scotland) at half-time

16 February 1996, St Helens, Swansea
Wales A 22 (2G 1PG 1T)   Scotland A 32 (1G 5PG 2T)

Wales A: S Cormack (Pontypridd); S D Hill (Cardiff), M Wintle (Llanelli), M Taylor (Swansea), G Evans (Llanelli); M Lewis (Bridgend), P John (Pontypridd); C Loader (Swansea), R C McBryde (Llanelli) *(capt)*, S C John (Llanelli), M Voyle (Newport), J Wakeford (Cardiff), M Workman (Newport), O Williams (Cardiff), M Williams (Pontypridd) *Replacement* A Davies (Cardiff) for Lewis (2 mins)
Scorers *Tries:* Evans, McBryde, Taylor   *Conversions:* Davies (2)
Penalty Goal: Davies
Scotland A: S D Lang (Heriot's FP); I C Glasgow (Heriot's FP), A G Shiel (Melrose), B R S Eriksson (London Scottish), D A Stark (Boroughmuir); W S Welsh (Hawick), D W Patterson (West Hartlepool); M G Browne (Melrose), D G Ellis (Currie), B D Stewart (Edinburgh Acads), D G Burns (Boroughmuir), D F Cronin (Bourges) *(capt)*, P Walton (Newcastle), B L Renwick (Hawick), N J R Broughton (Melrose)   *Replacements* G G Burns (Stewart's-Melville FP) for Patterson;
S A Nichol (Selkirk) for Eriksson (temp)
Scorers *Tries:* Broughton, Stark (2)   *Conversion:* Welsh   *Penalty Goals:* Welsh (5)
Referee S W Piercy (England)

1 March 1996, Donnybrook
Ireland A 25 (2G 2PG 1T)   Wales A 11 (2PG 1T)

Ireland A: C O'Shea (London Irish); R Wallace (Garryowen), R Henderson (London Irish), S McCahill (Sunday's Well), J Topping (Ballymena); E Elwood (Lansdowne), A Rolland (Blackrock Coll) *(capt)*; P Flavin (Blackrock Coll), P Cunningham (Garryowen), A McKeen (Lansdowne), M O'Kelly (St Mary's Coll), N Francis (Old Belvedere), A Foley (Shannon), B Walsh (London Irish), L Toland (Old Crescent)
Scorers *Tries:* Henderson, Walsh, Foley   *Conversions:* Elwood (2)
Penalty Goals: Elwood (2)
Wales A: R Jones (Neath); S D Hill (Cardiff), M Taylor (Swansea), M Wintle (Llanelli), G Evans (Llanelli); A Davies (Cardiff), P John (Pontypridd); C Loader (Swansea), R C McBryde (Llanelli) *(capt)*, S C John (Llanelli), M Voyle (Newport), P Jones (Llanelli), A Gibbs (Newbridge), S Davies (Swansea), M Williams (Pontypridd)
Scorers *Try:* S Davies   *Penalty Goals:* A Davies (2)
Referee D Gillet (France)

2 March 1996, L'Aquila, Italy
Italy A 19 (1G 4PG) England A 22 (1G 5PG)

Italy A: J Pertile (Roma); M Perziano (Treviso), T Visentin (Treviso), G Filizzola (Calvisano), P Donati (Treviso); A Scanavacca (Rovigo), A Troncon (Treviso) *(capt)*; A Castellani (L'Aquila), G de Carli (Roma), D Sie Mauro (San Dona), P Alessandro (Rovigo), D Scaglia (Treviso), M Giovanelli (Milan), J Gardner (Treviso), R Rampazzo (Padua)
Scorers *Try:* Perziano *Conversion:* Scanavacca *Penalty Goals:* Scanavacca (4)
England A: P Hull (Bristol); D O'Leary (Harlequins), A Blyth (West Hartlepool), P Mensah (Harlequins), A Adebayo (Bath); A King (Bristol U), A Gomarsall (Wasps); K Yates (Bath), P Greening (Gloucester), R Hardwick (Coventry), D Sims (Gloucester), J Fowler (Sale), C Sheasby (Harlequins), A Diprose (Saracens) *(capt)*, R Jenkins (Harlequins) *Replacement* W Greenwood (Harlequins) for Blyth (78 mins)
Scorers *Try:* Gomarsall *Conversion:* King *Penalty Goals:* King (5)
Referee H Rohr (Germany)

15 March 1996, Athletic Ground, Richmond
England A 56 (6G 2PG 1DG 1T) Ireland A 26 (2PG 4T)

England A: T Stimpson (West Hartlepool); P Hull (Bristol), W Greenwood (Harlequins), N Greenstock (Wasps), A Adebayo (Bath); A King (Bristol U), A Gomarsall (Wasps); R Hardwick (Coventry), R Cockerill (Leicester), D Garforth (Leicester), C Murphy (West Hartlepool), D Sims (Gloucester), M Corry (Bristol), A Diprose (Saracens) *(capt)*, R Jenkins (Harlequins)
Scorers *Tries:* Garforth (2), Gomarsall, Adebayo, Stimpson, King, Diprose *Conversions:* King (6) *Penalty Goals:* King (2) *Dropped Goal:* King
Ireland A: C O'Shea (London Irish); R Wallace (Garryowen), R Henderson (London Irish), S McCahill (Sunday's Well), J Topping (Ballymena); E Elwood (Lansdowne), A Rolland (Blackrock Coll) *(capt)*; P Flavin (Blackrock Coll), J S Byrne (Blackrock Coll), A McKeen (Lansdowne), M O'Kelly (St Mary's Coll), N Francis (Old Belvedere), A Foley (Shannon), B Walsh (London Irish), L Toland (Old Crescent)
Scorers *Tries:* O'Shea, Wallace (2), Francis *Penalty Goals:* Elwood (2)
Referee G Gadjovich (Canada)

15 March 1996, Rodney Parade, Newport
Wales A 13 (1G 2PG) France A 34 (4G 2PG)

Wales A: R Jones (Neath); S Hill (Cardiff), M Taylor (Swansea), J Funnell (Neath), G Evans (Llanelli); S Connor (Abertillery), P John (Pontypridd) *(capt)*; A Lewis (Cardiff), B Williams (Neath), S John (Llanelli), M Voyle (Newport), P Arnold (Swansea), A Gibbs (Newbridge), M Workman (Newport), V Davies (Cardiff)
Scorers *Try:* pen try *Conversion:* Connor *Penalty Goals:* Connor (2)
France A: S Venditti (Bourgoin); M Marfaing (Narbonne), C Paille (Pau), Y Delaigue (Toulon), D Berty (Toulouse); L Mazas (Colomiers), P Carbonneau (Toulouse) *(capt)*; C Soulette (Béziers), A Azam (Montferrand), J-L Jordana (Pau), H Miorin (Toulouse), L Bonventre (Brive), C Moni (Nice), T Labrousse (Brive), L Loppy (Toulon)
Scorers *Tries:* Delaigue, Labrousse, Venditti, Berty *Conversions:* Mazas (4) *Penalty Goals:* Mazas (2)
Referee A Lewis (Ireland)

A SUCCESS FROM THE FIRST KICK-OFF

SUPER-12 SERIES 1996

There was so much agonising in the northern hemisphere about the switch to professionalism that it was difficult at times not to absorb some of the anxieties. When that happened there was only one antidote: one look south of the equator and all the fears vanished. The Super-12 was Rugby Union's first professional competition. The announcement on the eve of the 1995 World Cup final in Johannesburg stunned everyone. The £360 million deal with Rupert Murdoch's Newscorp included a new tri-nation competition between South Africa, Australia and New Zealand and a revamped Super-10. The downside was that the Pacific Islanders were to be excluded, although no one could quibble with the product which evolved among the state and provincial sides of the respective countries. There were to be five New Zealand teams, four from South Africa and three from Australia. A draft system for each side was drawn up, enabling the international players from outside the provincial boundaries to be brought in specifically for this particular competition – Jonah Lomu, for example, was drafted from Counties to Auckland for the duration of the Super-12.

The tournament was a huge success from the very first kick-off, especially in Australia, where Rugby League usually enjoys a huge advantage in terms of spectator appeal. Games in Brisbane and Sydney regularly attracted crowds of 20,000 and even unheralded Australian Capital Territories had attendances of 15,000 and more.

The fact that Rugby League was tearing itself apart in the courtroom was one reason for the increased attendances. If the converts were only temporary at the beginning then most of them stayed after witnessing some spectacular rugby. The average of six tries a game compares rather favourably with the return of fewer than two per match for the Five Nations. The bonus-point system, whereby an extra point was awarded for scoring more than four tries, galvanised many teams, as did the bonus point for finishing within seven points of the winner.

There was controversy to go with the high scoring, and violence, too. The New Zealand and Australian teams felt hard done by in South Africa in particular, and there has been a call for neutral referees for next year. Johan le Roux, the Transvaal prop, was sent off in an early match against ACT, having only just completed an 18-month ban for biting Sean Fitzpatrick's ear. Transvaal, runners-up in the 1995 Super-10, made a dismal start, losing their opening four games on a 15-day tour of Australia and New Zealand.

ACT, with Gregan, Roff, Howard and McKenzie in their ranks, were the surprise package, defeating three of the eventual four semi-finalists, Auckland, Natal and Queensland.

The semi-finals yielded a real surprise when Queensland, thus far unbeaten in Brisbane, lost at home to Natal, 43-25. Their pack was uncharacteristically subdued and they clearly missed the influence of injured centre Jason Little. In the other semi-final the elusive running of Auckland full-back Adrian Cashmore tormented Northern Transvaal, who went down 48-11 in Auckland.

FINAL
25 May, Auckland

Auckland 45 (3G 3PG 3T)   **Natal 21** (1G 3PG 1T)

After their emphatic performance in Brisbane, Natal travelled to Auckland with few fears. Their confidence was soon shattered by the all too familiar, and still awesome, figure of Jonah Lomu. He punched through for a typical try in the opening quarter, bouncing André Joubert at the end to score in the corner. More Lomu mayhem opened up the field, from where Andrew Blowers, the new Kiwi sensation on the open side, got another. Auckland led 20-3 and the 45,000-strong crowd were already counting their chickens. A spirited riposte by Natal, during which Joubert got a touchdown, saw that lead cut to 20-16, but the chickens were duly hatched in the second half as Auckland ran in tries in quick succession. They finished with six in all. James Small scored a consolation try from a tapped penalty for Natal.

Auckland: A R Cashmore; J Vidiri, E Clarke, J F Ngauamo, J T Lomu; C J Spencer, O F J Tonu'u; C W Dowd, S B T Fitzpatrick, O M Brown, R M Brooke, C C Riechelmann, M N Jones, Z V Brooke (*capt*), A Blowers
Replacement J W Chandler for Riechelmann (55 mins)
Scorers *Tries:* Blowers (2), Lomu, Spencer, Clarke, Riechelmann   *Conversions:* Cashmore (3)   *Penalty Goals:* Cashmore (3)
Natal: A J Joubert; J T Small, J R D Thomson, R Muir, J F van der Westhuizen; H W Honiball, K B Putt; A H le Roux, J Allan, A C Garvey, S Atherton, M G Andrews, P J L van Heerden, G H Teichmann (*capt*), W Fyvie *Replacements* J Joubert for Small (72 mins); R J du Preez for Putt (53 mins); D Kriese for Van Heerden (60 mins)
Scorers *Tries:* A Joubert, Small   *Conversion:* Honiball   *Penalty Goals:* Honiball (3)
Referee W J Erickson (Australia)

SEMI-FINALS
18 May, Brisbane
Queensland 25 (2G 2PG 1T)   **Natal 43** (4G 3T)

Queensland: T Mandrusiak; B Tune, D J Herbert, T J Horan (*capt*), P V Carozza; E Flatley, B Johnstone; D J Crowley, M A Foley, A J Daly, G Morgan, J A Eales, T Kefu, M Connors, D J Wilson
Scorers *Tries:* Horan, Foley, pen try   *Conversions:* Eales (2)
Penalty Goals: Eales (2)
Natal: A J Joubert; J T Small, J R D Thomson, R Muir, J F van der Westhuizen; H W Honiball, K B Putt; A H le Roux, J Allan, A C Garvey, M G Andrews, S Atherton, P J L van Heerden, G H Teichmann (*capt*), W Fyvie

Replacements D Kriese for Van Heerden (66 mins); J Joubert for Van der Westhuizen (78 mins)
Scorers *Tries:* Van der Westhuizen (3), Joubert (2), Thomson, Van Heerden
Conversions: Joubert (2), Honiball (2)
Referee P D O'Brien (New Zealand)

19 May, Auckland
Auckland 48 (4G 4T)   **Northern Transvaal 11** (2PG 1T)

Auckland: A R Cashmore; J Vidiri, E Clarke, J F Ngauamo, J T Lomu; L Stensness,
O F J Tonu'u; C W Dowd, S B T Fitzpatrick, O M Brown, R M Brooke,
C C Riechelmann, D G Mika, Z V Brooke (*capt*), A F Blowers
Scorers *Tries:* Lomu (2), Cashmore, Vidiri, Ngauamo, Tonu'u, R Brooke,
Fitzpatrick   *Conversions:* Cashmore (4)
Northern Transvaal: J T J van Rensburg; J H van der Westhuizen, J P Claassens,
D van Schalkwyk, J Venter; J Kruger, C Breytenbach; F Bosman, J A Truscott,
M H Hurter, J Ackermann, K Otto, R J Kruger (*capt*), A Richter, S Bekker
Replacements B van Straaten for Van Schalkwyk (6 mins); R Rein for J Kruger
(74 mins); D du Toit for Van Straaten (40 mins)
Scorers *Try:* Breytenbach   *Penalty Goals:* J Kruger (2)
Referee W J Erickson (Australia)

ROUND ROBIN SUMMARY

1 Mar: Wellington 28, Auckland 36 (Palmerston North); New South Wales 32,
Transvaal 11 (Sydney)
2 Mar: Natal 28, Western Province 22 (Durban)
3 Mar: Waikato 27, Canterbury 26 (Hamilton); Otago 57, Queensland 17 (Dunedin)
5 Mar: ACT 13, Transvaal 9 (Canberra)
9 Mar: ACT 35, Wellington 28 (Canberra); Otago 29, Transvaal 15 (Dunedin);
Northern Transvaal 30, Natal 8 (Pretoria); New South Wales 30, Western Province
22 (Cape Town)
10 Mar: Canterbury 18, Auckland 49 (Christchurch); Queensland 26, Waikato 22
(Brisbane)
15 Mar: ACT 40, Auckland 34 (Canberra); Wellington 32, Transvaal 16 (Napier)
16 Mar: Western Province 25, Otago 52 (Cape Town); Northern Transvaal 32, New
South Wales 29 (Pretoria)
17 Mar: Natal 63, Waikato 25 (Durban); Queensland 52, Canterbury 16 (Brisbane)
20 Mar: Northern Transvaal 59, Otago 29 (Pretoria)
22 Mar: Canterbury 16, Western Province 16 (Christchurch)
23 Mar: Transvaal 26, Waikato 23 (Johannesburg)
24 Mar: Wellington 25, Queensland 32 (Wellington); New South Wales 44, ACT 10
(Sydney)
27 Mar: Auckland 48, Western Province 30 (Auckland)
29 Mar: Canterbury 21, New South Wales 16 (Christchurch); ACT 44, Natal 31
(Canberra); Queensland 25, Northern Transvaal 18 (Brisbane)
30 Mar: Otago 15, Wellington 44 (Dunedin); Waikato 44, Western Province 17
(Hamilton)
2 Apr: Auckland 51, Otago 29 (Pukekohe); New South Wales 6, Natal 34 (Sydney)
3 Apr: Waikato 26, ACT 18 (Whangarei); Canterbury 18, Northern Transvaal 34
(Christchurch); Queensland 36, Western Province 26 (Brisbane)
6 Apr: Wellington 27, Natal 43 (Wellington)
7 Apr: Auckland 30, Northern Transvaal 26 (Auckland)
8 Apr: Canterbury 7, ACT 29 (Christchurch)
10 Apr: Otago 33, Natal 32 (Dunedin)

11 Apr: Waikato 17, Northern Transvaal 9 (Hamilton)
13 Apr: Transvaal 23, Western Province 26 (Johannesburg)
14 Apr: Wellington 13, Canterbury 36 (New Plymouth); Queensland 15, New South Wales 13 (Brisbane)
16 Apr: Otago 5, Waikato 22 (Invercargill)
19 Apr: Northern Transvaal 25, Transvaal 15 (Pretoria)
20 Apr: ACT 21, Queensland 20 (Canberra); Auckland 39, Waikato 31 (Auckland)
21 Apr: New South Wales 29, Otago 25 (Sydney)
23 Apr: Western Province 35, Wellington 25 (Cape Town); Transvaal 55, Canterbury 23 (Johannesburg)
26 Apr: Queensland 51, Auckland 13 (Brisbane)
27 Apr: Northern Transvaal 38, Wellington 20 (Pretoria); Natal 58, Canterbury 26 (Durban); Waikato 39, New South Wales 17 (Hamilton); Western Province 25, ACT 16 (Cape Town)
1 May: Auckland 56, New South Wales 44 (Auckland); Natal 49, Transvaal 13 (Durban)
4 May: Waikato 15, Wellington 23 (Rotorua); Northern Transvaal 23, ACT 10 (Pretoria)
5 May: Canterbury 27, Otago 29 (Christchurch); Natal 20, Queensland 21 (Durban)
7 May: Transvaal 34, Auckland 22 (Johannesburg)
10 May: New South Wales 52, Wellington 25 (Sydney); Western Province 7, Northern Transvaal 35 (Cape Town)
11 May: Transvaal 16, Queensland 25 (Johannesburg); Natal 23, Auckland 30 (Durban)
12 May: ACT 70, Otago 26 (Canberra)

FINAL TABLE

	P	W	D	L	F	A	Bonus	Pts
Queensland Reds	11	9	0	2	320	247	5	41
Auckland Blues	11	8	0	3	408	354	9	41
Northern Transvaal Bulls	11	8	0	3	329	208	6	38
Natal Sharks	11	6	0	5	389	277	9	33
ACT Brumbies	11	7	0	4	306	273	4	32
Waikato Chiefs	11	6	0	5	291	269	4	28
NSW Waratahs	11	5	0	6	312	290	8	28
Otago Highlanders	11	5	0	6	329	391	6	26
Wellington Hurricanes	11	3	0	8	290	353	5	17
Transvaal Golden Lions	11	3	0	8	233	299	4	16
Western Province	11	3	1	7	251	353	1	15
Canterbury Crusaders	11	2	1	8	234	378	3	13

The League yielded 417 tries (including 14 penalty tries), 271 conversions, 344 penalty goals and 11 dropped goals
Leading point-scorers: 157 – M Burke (NSW); 145 – J Eales (Queensland); 136 – J Kruger (Northern Transvaal)
Leading try-scorers: 14 – pen tries; 12 – J Small (Natal); 9 – A Joubert (Natal), J Vidiri (Auckland)

SPECIAL BREW IS A SUCCESS

HEINEKEN EUROPEAN CUP 1995-96

The European Cup did not have the most auspicious of beginnings. A low-key opener in deepest Romania was not likely to nudge, let alone divert, the attention of the great sporting public. The organisers, though, were determined to get the competition off the ground. Their resolve and optimism are to be applauded, for by the tournament's end in Cardiff there was no one who doubted that this would rapidly become one of the most cherished fixtures in the calendar.

Much to their annoyance, the English clubs were not permitted to enter by the RFU, a state of affairs which created echoes of the situation in English soccer 40 years ago. The Scottish teams were also absent. They missed out on some great competitive rugby as well as a share of the £20 million financial spoils put up by Heineken and ITV. There were four pools of three teams, with the group winners going through to the semi-finals. The pool games threw up some terrific contests: Cardiff's 14-14 draw at Bègles-Bordeaux and Leinster's last-gasp 23-22 home win over Pontypridd were the highlights. The only unsavoury moment came after the Swansea-Castres match, when referee Charles Muir needed a police escort from the field amid protests from the French side.

The semi-finals offered two contrasting matches. Toulouse accounted comfortably for Swansea, 30-3, but Cardiff had to battle in Dublin in dreadful conditions for their final slot, finally coming through 23-14 against Leinster.

The future of the competition is assured, and all the five nations want to be involved. The only sticking point now is the precise format. There are many great European nights to come.

FINAL
7 January 1996, Cardiff Arms Park
Cardiff 18 (6PG)   Toulouse 21 (1G 2PG 1DG 1T)

Who could have scripted it better? A Deylaud penalty goal in the last minute of extra time gave Toulouse the inaugural Heineken European Cup. Thomas Castaignède showed all the flourishing skills which were soon to grace the Five Nations Championship. He scored a try, dropped a goal and delivered the critical pass for Cazalbou's try.

Even though the match could not quite sustain the thrilling brilliance of its opening quarter, there was still enough verve and crunching confrontation to satisfy the 22,000-strong crowd. Toulouse were out of the traps so quickly that Cardiff did well to even get within sight of them. Ougier created Castaignède's try in the sixth minute and Cazalbou's arrived four minutes later. Adrian Davies managed to nibble away at Toulouse's initial

117

12-point advantage with some accurate goal-kicking. Jonathan Davies was given a great reception when he came on as a replacement in the 40th minute. Davies chipped away and brought the scores level with the last kick of normal time from 43 metres. Toulouse dominated the extra period. Deylaud and Davies exchanged penalty goals to keep the scores level. The Frenchman, though, was to have the last word.

Cardiff: M Rayer; S Ford, M Hall, M Ring, S Hill; A Davies, A Moore; A Lewis, J Humphreys, L Mustoe, J Wakeford, D Jones, E Lewis, H Taylor (*capt*), O Williams *Replacements* J Davies for Ring (40 mins); N Walker for Ford (97 mins)
Scorer *Penalty Goals:* Davies (6)
Toulouse: S Ougier; E Ntamack (*capt*), P Carbonneau, T Castaignède, D Berty; C Deylaud, J Cazalbou; C Califano, P Soula, C Portolan, H Miorin, F Belot, D Lacroix, S Dispagne, H Manent *Replacements* R Castel for Lacroix (58 mins); U Mola for Berty (69 mins); E Artiguste for Carbonneau (93 mins); C Guiter for Soula (temp)
Scorers *Tries:* Castaignède, Cazalbou   *Conversion:* Deylaud
Penalty Goals: Deylaud (2)   *Dropped Goal:* Castaignède
Referee D McHugh (Ireland)

Stephane Ougier of Toulouse steams past Cardiff full-back Mike Rayer in the European Cup final.

SEMI-FINALS
30 December 1995, Les Sept-Deniers, Toulouse
Toulouse 30 (3G 3PG)   **Swansea 3** (1PG)

Toulouse: S Ougier; E Ntamack (*capt*), E Artiguste, T Castaignède, D Berty; C Deylaud, J Cazalbou; C Califano, P Soula, C Portolan, H Miorin, F Belot, D Lacroix, S Dispagne, H Manent *Replacements* R Castel for Lacroix (56 mins);

U Mola for Berty (61 mins); P Lasserre for Califano (67 mins); O Carbonneau for Castaignède (69 mins)
Scorers *Tries:* Manent, Artiguste, pen try   *Conversions:* Deylaud (3)
Penalty Goals: Deylaud (3)
Swansea: R Boobyer; A Harris, M Taylor, D Weatherley, Simon Davies; A Williams, Robert Jones; C Loader, G Jenkins, K Colclough, A Moore, S Moore, A Reynolds, Stuart Davies (*capt*), R Appleyard *Replacements* M Evans for Reynolds (29 mins); M Thomas for A Moore (37 mins)
Scorer *Penalty Goal:* Williams
Referee J M Fleming (Scotland)

30 December 1995, Lansdowne Road, Dublin
Leinster 14 (3PG 1T)   Cardiff 23 (2G 1PG 2DG)

Leinster: C Clarke; P Gavin, V Cunningham, K McQuilkin, C O'Shea; A McGowan, A Rolland; H Hurley, S Byrne, P Wallace, S Jamieson, N Francis, C Pim (*capt*), V Costello, S Rooney *Replacement* R Hennessey for Clarke (54 mins)
Scorers *Try:* Pim   *Penalty Goals:* McGowan (3)
Cardiff: M Rayer; S Ford, M Hall, M Ring, S Hill; A Davies, A Moore; A Lewis, J Humphreys, L Mustoe, J Wakeford, D Jones, E Lewis, H Taylor (*capt*), O Williams
Scorers *Tries:* Taylor, Hall   *Conversions:* Davies (2)   *Penalty Goal:* Davies
Dropped Goals: Davies, Moore
Referee B Campsall (England)

KNOCK-OUT STAGE
Pool A

	P	W	D	L	F	A	Pts
Toulouse	2	2	0	0	72	19	4
Benetton Treviso	2	1	0	1	95	26	2
Farul Constanta	2	0	0	2	18	140	0

31 October 1995, Constanta
Farul Constanta 10 (1G 1PG)   Toulouse 54 (7G 1T)

Farul Constanta: V Brici; C Sasu, A Tinca, N Fulina (*capt*), E Florea; V Besarau, M Foca; C Pingert, N Lupu, D Manole, N Branescu, N Marin, C Florea, T Oroian, A Girbu *Replacements* D Tabala for E Florea (38 mins); A Secuiu for Lupu (50 mins); E Rujada for Marin (50 mins); T Coman for Foca (75 mins)
Scorers *Try:* Foca   *Conversion:* E Florea   *Penalty Goal:* E Florea
Toulouse: S Ougier; E Ntamack (*capt*), P Carbonneau, T Castaignède, D Berty; C Deylaud, J Cazalbou; C Califano, P Soula, C Portolan, H Miorin, F Belot, J-L Cester, S Dispagne, R Castel *Replacements* O Carbonneau for Castaignède (48 mins); E Artiguste for Cazalbou (48 mins); D Lacroix for Castel (60 mins); P Lasserre for Portolan (70 mins)
Scorers *Tries:* Ntamack (2), Berty (2), Cester, Castaignède, Ougier, pen try
Conversions: Deylaud (7)
Referee R G Davies (Wales)

7 November 1995, Stadio Comunale di Monigo, Treviso
Benetton Treviso 86 (10G 2PG 2T)   Farul Constanta 8 (1PG 1T)

Benetton Treviso: P Dotto; M Perziano, I Francescato, M Visentin, L Manteri; M Lynagh, A Troncon; G Grespan (*capt*), N Giulato, G Rossi, D Scaglia, M Giacheri, S Rigo, C Checchinato, J Gardner *Replacement* L Perziano for M Perziano (59 mins)
Scorers *Tries:* Manteri (2), M Perziano (2), L Perziano (2), Dotto (2), Checchinato, Troncon, Giulato, Gardner   *Conversions:* Lynagh (10)   *Penalty Goals:* Lynagh (2)

Farul Constanta: E Florea; C Sasu, A Tinca, N Fulina (*capt*), D Talaba; V Besarau,
T Coman; C Pingert, N Lupu, D Manole, N Branescu, T Oroian, C Florea,
I Ruxanda, A Girbu *Replacements* V Dragomir for Sasu (19 mins); D Miron for
Besarau (23 mins); V Matasaru for Manole (74 mins); M Plugaro for Oroian (70
mins); D Chiriac for C Florea (47 mins)
Scorers *Try:* Talaba   *Penalty Goal:* E Florea
Referee B W Stirling (Ireland)

12 December 1995, Les Sept-Deniers, Toulouse
Toulouse 18 (5PG 1DG)   **Benetton Treviso 9** (2PG 1DG)

Toulouse: S Ougier; E Ntamack (*capt*), P Carbonneau, T Castaignède, D Berty;
C Deylaud, J Cazalbou; C Califano, P Soula, C Portolan, H Miorin, F Belot,
D Lacroix, S Dispagne, H Manent *Replacements* U Mola for Berty (77 mins);
N Bacque for Lacroix (78 mins)
Scorer *Penalty Goals:* Deylaud (5)   *Dropped Goal:* Deylaud
Benetton Treviso: P Dotto; M Perziano, I Francescato, F Mazzariol, L Manteri;
M Lynagh, A Troncon; G Grespan (*capt*), M Trevisiol, G Rossi, D Scaglia,
M Giacheri, S Rigo, C Checchinato, J Gardner *Replacement* W Cristofoletto for
Checchinato (8 mins)
Scorer *Penalty Goals:* Lynagh (2)   *Dropped Goal:* Lynagh
Referee J L Bacigalupo (Scotland)

Pool B

	P	W	D	L	F	A	Pts
Cardiff	2	1	1	0	60	20	3
Bègles-Bordeaux	2	1	1	0	43	30	3
Ulster	2	0	0	2	22	75	0

21 November 1995, Stade Andrè Moga, Bordeaux
Bègles-Bordeaux 14 (3PG 1T)   **Cardiff 14** (3PG 1T)

Bègles-Bordeaux: P Fauthoux; P Bernat-Salles, E Darritchon, L Lafforgue,
P Tauzin; V Etcheto, G Accoceberry (*capt*); L Verge, S Morizot, O Sourgens,
A Berthozat, C Mougeot, M Barrague, J-J Alibert, P Farner *Replacements* S Conchy
for Berthozat (65 mins); P Eyhartz for Barrague (76 mins)
Scorers *Try:* Bernat-Salles   *Penalty Goals:* Etcheto (3)
Cardiff: M Rayer; N Walker, M Hall, M Ring, S Hill; A Davies, A Moore; A Lewis,
J Humphreys, L Mustoe, J Wakeford, D Jones, E Lewis, H Taylor (*capt*), M Bennett
Replacement C Mills for Bennett (35 mins)
Scorers *Try:* Bennett   *Penalty Goals:* Davies (3)
Referee D McHugh (Ireland)

28 November 1995, Cardiff Arms Park
Cardiff 46 (5G 2PG 1T)   **Ulster 6** (2PG)

Cardiff: M Rayer; S Ford, M Hall, S John, N Walker; A Davies, A Moore; A Lewis,
J Humphreys, L Mustoe, J Wakeford, D Jones, E Lewis, H Taylor (*capt*), O Williams
Replacement M Bennett for E Lewis (78 mins)
Scorers *Tries:* Moore (2), John, Taylor, Davies, Hall   *Conversions:* Davies (5)
Penalty Goals: Davies (2)
Ulster: J Bell; J Topping, M Field, W Harbinson (*capt*), J Cunningham; M McCall,
N Doak; R Mackey, A Clarke, G Leslie, J Davidson, G Longwell, S Duncan,
S Erskine, D McBride *Replacement* R Wilson for McBride (78 mins)
Scorer *Penalty Goals:* McCall (2)
Referee G Borreani (France)

13 December 1995, Ravenhill, Belfast
Ulster 16 (2PG 2T)   **Bègles-Bordeaux 29** (2G 3T)

Ulster: J Bell; J Topping, W Harbinson (*capt*), M Field, A Park; M McCall,
A Matchett; R Mackey, A Clarke, G Leslie, G Longwell, D Tweed, S Duncan,
P Johns, D McBride
Scorers *Tries:* Matchett, McBride   *Penalty Goals:* McCall (2)
Bègles-Bordeaux: P Fauthoux; P Bernat-Salles, S Loubsens, E Darritchon,
P Tauzin; J Berthe, X Pierre; L Dehez, S Morizot, O Sourgens, A Berthozat (*capt*),
C Mougeot, S Conchy, J-J Alibert, P Farner *Replacements* P Eyhartz for Mougeot (18
mins); V Chambauline for Morizot (50 mins); F Garcia for Chambauline (56 mins)
Scorers *Tries:* Loubsens (2), Bernat-Salles, Fauthoux, Berthe
Conversions: Fauthoux, Berthe
Referee W D Bevan (Wales)

Pool C

	P	W	D	L	F	A	Pts
Leinster	2	2	0	0	47	43	4
Pontypridd	2	1	0	1	53	35	2
Milan	2	0	0	2	33	55	0

1 November 1995, Milan
Milan 21 (1G 3PG 1T)   **Leinster 24** (1G 4PG 1T)

Milan: F Williams; R Crotti, M Platania, M Tommasi, Marcello Cuttitta;
D Dominguez, M Bonomi; S Cerioni, C Orlandi, F Properzi, F Battista-Croci,
F Berni, T Ciccio, G Milano (*capt*), D Beretta *Replacement* M Giovanelli for Milano
(50 mins)
Scorers *Tries:* Crotti, Platania   *Conversion:* Bonomi   *Penalty Goals:* Dominguez (3)
Leinster: C O'Shea; P Gavin, V Cunningham, K McQuilkin, N Woods;
A McGowan, A Rolland; H Hurley, S Byrne, P Wallace, M O'Kelly, B Rigney, C Pim
(*capt*), V Costello, D Oswald
Scorers *Tries:* O'Shea, Woods   *Conversion:* McGowan
Penalty Goals: McGowan (4)
Referee F Maceillo (France)

22 November 1995, Sardis Road, Pontypridd
Pontypridd 31 (1G 8PG)   **Milan 12** (4PG)

Pontypridd: C Cormack; D Manley, J Lewis, S McIntosh, G Jones; N Jenkins, Paul
John; N Bezani (*capt*), Phil John, N Eynon, G Prosser, M Rowley, M Spiller,
M Lloyd, P Thomas *Replacement* R Collins for Spiller (21 mins)
Scorers *Try:* Manley   *Conversion:* Jenkins   *Penalty Goals:* Jenkins (8)
Milan: F Williams; M Platania, F Gomez, M Tommasi, Marcello Cuttitta;
D Dominguez, M Bonomi; Massimo Cuttitta (*capt*), A Marengoni, F Properzi,
P Pedroni, F Berni, D Beretta, G Milano, M Giovanelli
Scorer *Penalty Goals:* Dominguez (4)
Referee B Campsall (England)

6 December 1995, Lansdowne Road, Dublin
Leinster 23 (2G 3PG)   **Pontypridd 22** (1G 5PG)

Leinster: C O'Shea; P Gavin, V Cunningham, K McQuilkin, N Woods;
A McGowan, A Rolland; H Hurley, S Byrne, P Wallace, B Rigney, N Francis, C Pim
(*capt*), V Costello, S Rooney *Replacement* A McKeen for Wallace (temp); N Hogan for
Rolland (32 mins); E Millar for Costello (temp)

Scorers *Tries:* McGowan, O'Shea   *Conversions:* McGowan (2)
Penalty Goals: McGowan (3)
Pontypridd: C Cormack; D Manley, S McIntosh, J Lewis, S Enoch; L Jarvis, Paul
John; N Bezani (*capt*), Phil John, A Metcalfe, G Prosser, M Rowley, P Thomas,
M Lloyd, R Collins
Scorers *Try:* Cormack   *Conversion:* Jarvis   *Penalty Goals:* Jarvis (5)
Referee D Gillet (France)

Pool D

	P	W	D	L	F	A	Pts
Swansea	2	1	0	1	35	27	2
Munster	2	1	0	1	29	32	2
Castres	2	1	0	1	29	34	2

1 November 1995, Limerick
Munster 17 (2G 1PG)   **Swansea 13** (1G 2PG)

Munster: P Murray (*capt*); R Wallace, S McCahill, D Larkin, K Smith; P Burke,
D O'Mahony; J Fitzgerald, T Kingston, P Clohessy, M Galwey, G Fulcher, E Halvey,
A Foley, D Corkery *Replacements* M Fitzgerald for J Fitzgerald (temp); B Toland for
Halvey (32 mins)
Scorers *Tries:* Wallace, Murray   *Conversions:* Smith (2)   *Penalty Goal:* Smith
Swansea: G Thomas; A Harris, R Boobyer, D Weatherley, Simon Davies;
A Williams, Rhodri Jones; C Loader, G Jenkins, C Anthony, S Moore, A Moore,
A Reynolds, Stuart Davies (*capt*), R Appleyard *Replacement* Lee Davies for Harris
(temp)
Scorers *Try:* Harris   *Conversion:* Williams   *Penalty Goals:* Williams (2)
Referee E F Morrison (England)

8 November 1995, Mazamet
Castres 19 (1G 4PG)   **Munster 12** (4PG)

Castres: L Labit; C Savy, N Combes, J-M Aue, P Garrigue; F Rui, F Seguier (*capt*);
L Toussaint, C Urlos, T Lafforgue, T Bourdet, J-F Gourragne, G Pages, A Cigagna,
N Hallinger *Replacement* S Bristow for Toussaint (70 mins)
Scorers *Try:* Combes   *Conversion:* Labit   *Penalty Goals:* Labit (4)
Munster: P Murray (*capt*); R Wallace, S McCahill, D Larkin, K Smith; P Burke,
D O'Mahony; J Fitzgerald, T Kingston, P Clohessy, P O'Connor, G Fulcher,
M Galwey, A Foley, D Corkery *Replacements* B Walsh for Burke (70 mins); D Toland
for Galwey (temp); B Toland for Corkery (temp)
Scorer *Penalty Goals:* Smith (4)
Referee D R Davies (Wales)

5 December 1995, St Helens, Swansea
Swansea 22 (4PG 2T)   **Castres 10** (1G 1PG)

Swansea: A Flowers; A Harris, D Weatherley, M Taylor, Simon Davies; A Williams,
Robert Jones; K Colclough, G Jenkins, C Anthony, A Moore, S Moore, A Reynolds,
Stuart Davies (*capt*), R Appleyard
Scorers *Tries:* Harris, Jenkins   *Penalty Goals:* Williams (4)
Castres: C Savy; J-M Aue, A Hyardet, N Combes, P Garrigue; F Rui, F Seguier
(*capt*); S Bristow, C Urlos, T Lafforgue, T Bourdet, J-F Gourragne, G Pages,
A Cigagna, N Hallinger *Replacement* G Jeannard for Gourragne (66 mins)
Scorers *Try:* Rui   *Conversion:* Savy   *Penalty Goal:* Savy
Referee C B Muir (Scotland)

FIRA 1995-96

FIRA SENIOR CHAMPIONSHIP 1995-96

France and Italy won the two Group A divisions of the 1995-96 FIRA Championship, and will contest the final in autumn 1996. France, who did not have to play Italy and Romania in their group, fielded Development and Armed Forces XVs and an indication of their dominance in Group A1 was provided by an 81-9 win in Barcelona against Spain, the group runners-up. They scored 13 tries in the process.

Three points are awarded for a win, two for a draw and one for a loss. No points are given for a forfeit.

GROUP A1
1995

19 Nov	Blanc Mesnel	France	33	Russia	12
10 Dec	Msaken	Tunisia	11	Morocco	20

1996

6 Jan	Casablanca	Morocco	8	France	22
16 Mar	Albertville	France	58	Tunisia	0
16 Mar	Casablanca	Morocco	3	Spain	24
31 Mar	Barcelona	Spain	9	France	81
14 Apr	Madrid	Spain	52	Russia	6
11 May	Safi	Morocco	10	Russia	13

Tunisia forfeited matches against Spain (24 April) and Russia (9 May)

Final table

	P	W	D	L	F	A	Pts
France	4	4	0	0	194	29	12
Spain	4	3	0	1	85	90	10
Russia	4	2	0	2	31	95	8
Morocco	4	1	0	3	41	70	6
Tunisia	4	0	0	4	11	78	2

GROUP A2
1995

21 Oct	Buenos Aires*	Italy	40	Romania	3
28 Oct	Warsaw	Poland	30	Belgium	10

1996

2 Mar	Lisbon	Portugal	3	Italy	64
16 Mar	Brussels	Belgium	18	Portugal	29
13 Apr	Bucharest	Romania	92	Portugal	0
20 Apr	Bucharest	Romania	83	Belgium	5
27 Apr	Lisbon	Portugal	38	Poland	3
12 May	Sochaczew	Poland	9	Romania	40
25 May	Brussels	Belgium	10	Italy	38
25 May	Udine	Italy	107	Poland	19

Played as part of 1995 Latin Cup

Final Table

	P	W	D	L	F	A	Pts
Italy	4	4	0	0	249	35	12
Romania	4	3	0	1	218	54	10
Portugal	4	2	0	2	70	177	8
Poland	4	1	0	3	61	195	6
Belgium	4	0	0	4	43	180	4

FIRA JUNIOR CHAMPIONSHIP 1995-96

GROUP B1
1995

23 Sept	Hanover	Germany	28	Czech Republic	17
15 Oct	Tiblisi	Georgia	14	Germany	3
29 Oct	Copenhagen	Denmark	20	Holland	20
11 Nov	Aalborg	*Denmark forfeited against Georgia*			
24 Nov	Castricum	Holland	55	Georgia	3

1996

30 Mar	Prague	Czech Republic	3	Holland	26
12 Apr	Kutasi	Georgia	20	Czech Republic	3
21 Apr	Hilversum	Holland	6	Germany	5
27 Apr	Prague	Czech Republic	39	Denmark	6
12 May	Hanover	Germany	16	Denmark	11

Final Table

	P	W	D	L	F	A	Pts
Holland	4	3	1	0	107	31	11
Georgia	4	3	0	1	37	61	10
Germany	4	2	0	2	52	48	8
Czech Republic	4	1	0	3	62	80	6
Denmark	4	0	1	3	37	75	4

Further matches are to be played through summer 1996

GROUP B2
Competing nations: **Yugoslavia, Bulgaria, Andorra**
Result: Andorra 13, Bulgaria 8

GROUP B3
Competing nations: **Lithuania, Ukraine, Latvia, Moldova**
Results: Lithuania 8, Ukraine 27; Latvia 3, Ukraine 19; Latvia 13, Moldova 5;
Ukraine 38, Moldova 0
To play: Lithuania v Moldova; Latvia v Lithuania

GROUP B4
Competing nations: **Austria, Hungary, Slovenia**
Result: Austria 8, Hungary 21
To play: Slovenia v Austria; Hungary v Slovenia

SEVENS TOURNAMENTS 1995-96

Michael Austin

THE 1996 CATHAY PACIFIC-HONG KONG BANK SEVENS
29-31 March 1996, Hong Kong
NEW ZEALAND 19 (2G 1T)   FIJI 17 (2G 1PG)

Christian Cullen, the newest young talent to graduate through the Hong Kong Sevens, helped New Zealand retain their title with a 19-17 win over Fiji in a tense final watched by a crowd of 40,000. New Zealand won the world's premier annual sevens tournament for a third consecutive time by beating the same opposition they had faced in the 1995 final, though this time by a narrower margin.

Cullen, a recent New Zealand Colt, scored an astonishing 18 tries in the tournament, averaging a hat-trick per match. At 20, he had already impressed for Wellington and in Hong Kong he demonstrated his pace, tactical acumen and tackling power. He was regarded as the quickest and best-balanced runner ever to have played in the competition, and despite his tender years, he was far from overawed. Cullen created the first of two lavish tries for Waisake Masirewa in the final. Though blockaded in his own in-goal area, he somehow evaded three tacklers before straightening his run beneath his own posts, beating a fourth tackle and unleashing Masirewa to the line. New Zealand had begun with a penalty try when Cullen was tripped by Waisale Serevi, the Fijian captain, who atoned by fashioning a brilliant try for Setareki Naivaluwaqa. Serevi kicked a penalty goal and Joppe Tuikabe added another try for Fiji.

England had the distinction of being the only team to score three tries against the eventual champions. Chris Sheasby, Neil Back and Austin Healey crossed their line in the 42-19 semi-final defeat during which the remarkable Cullen ran in four himself.

Fiji's progress to the final had been impressive: they swept through their group games, scoring 40 points or more against Thailand, Hong Kong and Tonga. Australia, though beaten 24-7 by Fiji in the semi-finals, confirmed their place, alongside England, among the four leading exponents of sevens. In the quarter-final, England had outplayed Western Samoa 27-7, despite only three days' preparation for the tournament. They breezed past Singapore 52-0, offering a suggestion that the southern hemisphere countries might be challenged, before going on to beat Scotland and Argentina. England scored eight tries against Singapore, including a hat-trick from Jon Sleightholme, two tries each for Damian Hopley and Adedayo Adebayo and one from Nick Beal, who added six conversions.

Scotland made a poor start, trailing 29-7 to Argentina before staging a recovery with tries by Brian Renwick and Gregor Townsend to narrow the gap to 29-19. But despite accumulating 56 points without reply from Singapore they failed to reach the quarter-finals. Surprise qualifiers were Canada, who deserved their 19-12 victory over South Africa in a group match before their hopes of a semi-final place were dashed by Australia. The view that France, despite their flair, are under-achievers on the sevens field was not challenged here. They began with a 19-7 win over Japan and overpowered Sri Lanka, but went the way of others in a 28-14 defeat by New Zealand.

Ireland appeared in the last eight, beating Namibia and Malaysia, as well as drawing with Western Samoa along the way to a 49-point drubbing by New Zealand. Wales, too, failed to find a pathway to the semi-finals. They beat Korea, an emerging sevens nation, 29-19, with Ieuan Evans, Gareth Thomas and Neil Jenkins among the try-scorers, rattled up 52 points against Taiwan and then lost by two points to Australia and by 28-12 to Fiji in the quarter-finals.

Australia were dogged by injuries and even invited Ieuan Evans of Wales to sit on the bench for the semi-final against Fiji. Evans accepted and played for the final 20 seconds. It was an example of the bonhomie which characterises this rugby jamboree notwithstanding its deeply rooted competitive traditions. The tournament also offered a yardstick for the forthcoming World Sevens, a title held by England after their

Christian Cullen, New Zealand's latest sevens star, shows his pace in the 77-0 defeat of Japan.

remarkable triumph over Australia at Murrayfield in 1993. New Zealand emerged as distinct favourites from the 24-country Hong Kong event, having set the pattern in their first game, a 75-0 annihilation of Sri Lanka, in which Cullen romped over for seven tries.

Group A: New Zealand 75, Sri Lanka 0; France 19, Japan 7; France 56, Sri Lanka 5; New Zealand 77, Japan 0; Japan 35, Sri Lanka 0; New Zealand 28, France 14 **Group B:** England 52, Singapore 0; Argentina 57, Singapore 7; England 31, Scotland 12; Scotland 56, Singapore 0; England 24, Argentina 7 **Group C:** Western Samoa 54, Malaysia 5; Ireland 21, Namibia 15; Ireland 43, Malaysia 5; Western Samoa 49, Namibia 0; Namibia 24, Malaysia 21; Western Samoa 14, Ireland 14 **Group D:** Australia 47, Taipei 0; Wales 29, Korea 19; Wales 52, Taiwan 0; Australia 33, Korea 7; Korea 35, Taiwan 5; Australia 21, Wales 19 **Group E:** South Africa 45, Papua New Guinea 12, Canada 20, USA 19; Canada 21, Papua New Guinea 5; South Africa 38, USA 5; USA 24, Papua New Guinea 21; South Africa 12, Canada 19 **Group F:** Fiji 68, Thailand 12; Tonga 17, Hong Kong 12; Tonga 56, Thailand 5; Fiji 49, Hong Kong 0; Hong Kong 54, Thailand 5; Fiji 40, Tonga 0

PLATE FINAL: France 45, Hong Kong 12
BOWL FINAL: Japan 55, Namibia 21
CUP:
Quarter-finals: New Zealand 49, Ireland 0; England 27, Western Samoa 7; Australia 19, Canada 5; Fiji 28, Wales 12
Semi-finals: New Zealand 42, England 19; Fiji 24, Australia 7

Final: New Zealand 19, Fiji 17
New Zealand *Tries:* W Masirewa (2), pen try *Conversions:* C Cullen (2)
Fiji *Tries:* S Naivaluwaqa, J Tuikabe *Conversions:* W Serevi (2) *Penalty Goal:* W Serevi
Winning New Zealand team: C Cullen, B Fleming, J Lomu, W Masirewa; E Rush, J Tauiwi, P Woods

THE MIDDLESEX SEVENS 1996
(sponsored by Save & Prosper)

11 May 1996, Twickenham
Wigan 38 (4G 2T) Wasps 15 (3T)

Wigan, the first Rugby League team to appear at Twickenham, took the RFU's headquarters by storm by lifting the Russell Cargill Memorial Cup as winners of the Middlesex Sevens. It was not their triumph that was remarkable, for it had been anticipated by many, but the manner in which it was achieved. Wigan left Richmond, Harlequins, Leicester and fellow finalists Wasps way back in their slipstream, scoring 25 tries in all to add to the 16 they had plundered three days earlier in the Rugby League leg of the 15-a-side cross-code challenge against Bath at Maine Road in Manchester. Bath had withdrawn from this tournament because of heavy commitments and were replaced by Wakefield.

The appearance of the cherry-and-whites was a symbol of the new relationship between Rugby Union and League. It also demonstrated the extra athleticism of the established professionals. Wigan had seven players with pace, adding an extra dimension to the usual Rugby Union sevens approach of fielding merely one or two 'fliers'. The prime League pace men were Vai'aga Tuigamala, Martin Offiah, Henry Paul and captain Shaun Edwards, who also displayed skilful handling, powerful tackling and the precise timing of support running to hurtle through gaps.

Yet oddly enough, Wigan did not provide the competition's leading scorer. Offiah's 32 points were pipped by Andy Gomarsall of Wasps. Nevertheless, the former Rosslyn Park wing was quick to reacquaint himself with Twickenham, announcing his return with a 65-metre dash for a second-minute try against Richmond.

To win the title Wigan had to recover from 12- and 15-point deficits against Harlequins and Wasps respectively on a blustery afternoon in which Lawrence Dallaglio, the Wasps captain, Gomarsall, his team-mate, and Orrell's Austin Healey all produced significant performances. Leicester, the holders, who had beaten Ithuba in the previous year's final, tumbled 35-12 to Wigan in the semi-finals, having eliminated London Scottish and Sale. Orrell, whose conquests included Malaysia, narrowly missed the opportunity to meet their neighbours Wigan when they lost to Wasps in the semi-finals of an illuminating tournament watched by a crowd of 61,000. This record attendance generated more than £400,000 for rugby charities and other worthy causes.

RESULTS
Sixth round: Stirling County 29, Haywards Heath 10; Wasps 33, Bristol 12; Orrell 45, Malaysia 7; Blackheath 14, Wakefield 5; Wigan 48, Richmond 5; Harlequins 35, Gloucester 5; Sale 22, Saracens 21; Leicester 26, London Scottish 22
Seventh round: Wasps 24, Stirling County 12; Orrell 31, Blackheath 15; Wigan 36, Harlequins 24; Leicester 31, Sale 5
Semi-finals: Wasps 21, Orrell 12; Wigan 35, Leicester 12
Final: Wigan 38, Wasps 15

Teams in the final
Wigan: J Robinson, M Offiah, G Connolly, S Edwards *(capt)*; S Quinnell, A Farrell, V Tuigamala *Replacements* R Smyth for Offiah; K Radlinski for Quinnell
Scorers *Tries:* Offiah (2), Tuigamala, Connolly, Robinson, Edwards
Conversions: Farrell (3), Connolly
Wasps: S Roiser, A Thompson, N Greenstock, A Gomarsall; L Dallaglio *(capt)*, M White, P Scrivener *Replacements* L Scrase for Roiser; A James for Thompson
Scorers *Tries:* White, Gomarsall, Scrivener
Referee A Ellison (London Society)

WINNERS

1926 **Harlequins**	1929 **Harlequins**	1932 **Blackheath**
1927 **Harlequins**	1930 **London Welsh**	1933 **Harlequins**
1928 **Harlequins**	1931 **London Welsh**	1934 **Barbarians**

1935 **Harlequins**	1956 **London Welsh**	1977 **Richmond**
1936 **Sale**	1957 **St Luke's College**	1978 **Harlequins**
1937 **London Scottish**	1958 **Blackheath**	1979 **Richmond**
1938 **Metropolitan Police**	1959 **Loughborough Colls**	1980 **Richmond**
1939 **Cardiff**	1960 **London Scottish**	1981 **Rosslyn Park**
1940 **St Mary's Hospital**	1961 **London Scottish**	1982 **Stewart's-Melville FP**
1941 **Cambridge University**	1962 **London Scottish**	1983 **Richmond**
1942 **St Mary's Hospital**	1963 **London Scottish**	1984 **London Welsh**
1943 **St Mary's Hospital**	1964 **Loughborough Colls**	1985 **Wasps**
1944 **St Mary's Hospital**	1965 **London Scottish**	1986 **Harlequins**
1945 **Nottinghamshire**	1966 **Loughborough Colls**	1987 **Harlequins**
1946 **St Mary's Hospital**	1967 **Harlequins**	1988 **Harlequins**
1947 **Rosslyn Park**	1968 **London Welsh**	1989 **Harlequins**
1948 **Wasps**	1969 **St Luke's College**	1990 **Harlequins**
1949 **Heriot's FP**	1970 **Loughborough Colls**	1991 **London Scottish**
1950 **Rosslyn Park**	1971 **London Welsh**	1992 **Western Samoa**
1951 **Richmond II**	1972 **London Welsh**	1993 **Wasps**
1952 **Wasps**	1973 **London Welsh**	1994 **Bath**
1953 **Richmond**	1974 **Richmond**	1995 **Leicester**
1954 **Rosslyn Park**	1975 **Richmond**	1996 **Wigan**
1955 **Richmond**	1976 **Loughborough Colls**	

Harlequins have won the title 13 times, Richmond 9 (including one by their second VII), London Welsh 8, London Scottish 7, St Mary's Hospital and Loughborough Colleges 5 each, Rosslyn Park and Wasps 4 each, Blackheath and St Luke's College (now Exeter University) twice, Barbarians, Sale, Met Police, Cardiff, Cambridge University, Notts (now Nottingham), Heriot's FP, Stewart's-Melville FP, Western Samoa, Bath and Leicester once each

WORTHINGTON WELSH SEVENS 1995-96
(for the Snelling Trophy)

26 August 1995, Cardiff RFC Ground, Cardiff Arms Park
Swansea 29 (2G 3T)   Bridgend 28 (4G)

Swansea edged to a thrilling victory in the Worthington Welsh tournament, frustrating Bridgend's attempt to win the trophy for the 16th time and overtake Cardiff's record in the competition. Bridgend had the consolation of their captain, Robert Howley, being nominated as Player of the Tournament, and his try and four conversions in the final did much to challenge Swansea's ambitions. When Swansea were last in the final, four years earlier, they had lost a similar high-scoring match 28-24 to Pontypridd.

Teams in the final
Swansea: W Leach, R Boobyer, S Davies *(capt)*, R Jones; A Moore, C Charvis, R Appleyard
Scorers *Tries:* Davies (2), Jones, Leach, Charvis *Conversions:* Davies (2)
Bridgend: G Wilkins, D James, A Durston, R Howley *(capt)*; J Forster, I Greenslade, J Purnell *Replacement* N Thomas for Purnell
Scorers *Tries:* Wilkins (2), James, Howley *Conversions:* Howley (4)
Referee R G Davies (Dunvant)
Bill Everson Player of the Competition: R Howley (Bridgend)

CLOUDS FINALLY CLEAR TO REVEAL BRIGHT FUTURE

THE 1995-96 SEASON IN ENGLAND

There was no template available for this season. It was to be professionalism's first year, and no one had the slightest idea how it would all turn out. There was a great deal of heart-searching, no end of acrimony and many confusing, fraught months when it appeared as if there was no one in charge of rugby's runaway train. Thank goodness we still had the players themselves. When the politics got too bitter and too egotistical, we could always switch to the proper arenas of the sport. Not that it was all plain sailing there. The national team itself was 'in transition', the vogue explanation trotted out when any side gets beaten a couple of times. England argued about the way forward; about the means and the players to get them there. They will be much the better for having struggled. It is adversity which defines real character, not an easy pathway to success.

The emergence of several new faces was by far the most heartening aspect of the season. Lawrence Dallaglio had been limbering up on the sidelines for a few years but had never been given the chance to make a real mark. He came on as a replacement against South Africa and never looked back. His mature and committed leadership of his club, Wasps, in the wake of Rob Andrew's departure to Newcastle – accompanied by Dean Ryan and Steve Bates – was commendable. Jon Sleightholme, Paul Grayson, Matt Dawson, Mark Regan and Garath Archer joined Dallaglio as full debutants. Given that both Graham Rowntree and Damian Hopley were still fledgling internationals, England can look back with some satisfaction on having groomed a new generation.

That generation battled hard, were disciplined, cussed, defensively sound and occasionally bright and bubbly, but they know better than anyone that theirs was not a vintage championship side. They were long on heart and spirit; rather short of flair and thrust. Manager Jack Rowell had a tough year. From a man used to success in business and sport, he must have been taken by surprise by England's early turmoil. Some of it was self-inflicted in that the selection appeared haphazard. Andy Robinson, the Bath openside, came back after an international absence of six years for the South African match, only to promptly return to the wilderness. Mike Catt was announced as the successor to Rob Andrew. England lost to South Africa, 24-14, and Catt found himself back at full-back for the Western Samoa match, and the rest of the season thereafter. It took him all those months to rediscover his old self. He ended up playing fly-half for Bath and looked every inch an international No 10.

The England team which beat Wales at Twickenham. L-R, back row: J Rowell (manager), V E Ubogu (replacement), G C Rowntree, L B N Dallaglio, B B Clarke, T A K Rodber, M C Bayfield, M O Johnson, J Leonard, P R de Glanville (replacement), R G R Dawe (replacement), D Richards (replacement); front row: K P P Bracken (replacement), J E B Callard (replacement), M J Catt, J C Guscott, M P Regan, W D C Carling (capt), R Underwood, J M Sleightholme, M J S Dawson, P J Grayson.

Brian Moore came out of retirement but, in dodgy form and overlooked for the Springboks match, he eventually headed back to his slippers and pipe. Mark Regan, who has the looks of the pitbull, eventually began to emulate his predecessor's wonderfully committed and snarling play on the field as well. Dawson and Grayson won their spurs on the strength of an impressive display for the Midlands against the Samoans. Also on form in that match was Tim Rodber, though he too was to experience a turbulent year. He was recalled, dropped, then recalled without playing a game in between. His club colleague, Martin Bayfield, who took leave from the police force to focus on rugby, must have wondered whether it had all been worthwhile when he was dropped after the Welsh match.

One factor did stay constant – just. Will Carling took England to their fourth championship of his eight-year reign, having begun the season under ferocious media scrutiny following his alleged affair with Princess Diana. There was to be a hiccup in the captaincy stakes, too. Carling announced his captaincy in late August only for it to emerge that his candidacy had not been presented formally to the RFU. Jack Rowell and Carling did not have a warm relationship, and perhaps that was the reason why Carling finally chose to call it a day after 59 games in charge and with 44 victories to his name, a record no one else in the history of the game has come close to. He announced his decision a week before the final game of the championship, against Ireland. He wanted no special fanfares, he said. In the end that grand old dame of showbusiness, anti-climax, put in an appearance. Carling, merely following the ball, turned on his ankle after about half an hour's play and left the field to tumultuous applause. By the time he hobbled up the steps to collect the Millennium Trophy, he knew that his eight years at the helm had been rounded off in the best possible fashion with the Five Nations title as well. France had lost in Cardiff that day, so the championship went to England on points difference from Scotland.

It was only in that last match, though, that England strung together the elusive rounded game which Rowell had talked about all year. England scored only three tries in the championship, a woeful return. What did they learn about themselves? That they are heavily reliant on Dean Richards, who returned to the side at Murrayfield. He donned the hero's cape as if he'd never been away, denying Scotland a Grand Slam in the process. Bath winger John Sleightholme was an exciting addition to the ranks; Martin Johnson has no equal as a front jumper and Dallaglio looks to have captaincy credentials. England will also take hope from the fine showing of their A side, superbly coached by Richard Hill and Keith Richardson, which swept all before them, beating Western Samoa (55-0), France (15-25), New South Wales (24-22), Italy A (19-22) and Ireland A (56-26). How long before Austin Healey, Richard Cockerill, Darren Garforth and

Alex King follow Sleightholme and Archer into the senior side?

The domestic season was a pot-boiler. At the top end of Division 1 Bath and Leicester slugged it out in typically pugnacious fashion. Bath took first advantage, beating the Tigers at Welford Road 14-9 in September, but succumbed to Leicester 15-14 at home in January. Bath still had their noses in front, however, Leicester also having slipped up early on, at Saracens. In mid-April, on one of the most emotional nights many at Kingsholm can remember, Gloucester, themselves fighting relegation, beat their great rivals from Bath by 16-10. And so it all came down to the last Saturday. If Bath won against Sale they were home and dry, since they enjoyed a massive advantage in points difference over Leicester. But Sale fought back brilliantly to draw with Bath, 38-38, Rob Liley's last-minute conversion bringing the scores level. Meanwhile, many miles to the north, Rob's more famous brother, John, was lining up a 45-metre penalty kick which would have brought Leicester victory over Harlequins 22-21 and with it the Courage title. The kick missed, the match was lost by two points and Leicester's title went back to the Recreation Ground.

The Pilkington Cup followed a week later in controversial circumstances. Once again Leicester appeared to have the edge on Bath. As the seconds ticked away they led 15-10. With one minute remaining they defended their line zealously as Bath attacked. Too zealously – at the fourth infringement referee Steve Lander awarded a penalty try, Callard converted and Bath were home by 16-15. Worse was to follow. Leicester's Neil Back pushed Lander at the final whistle, causing him to fall over. Back claimed he mistook Lander for Bath's Andy Robinson. It was a feeble excuse. Back was subsequently banned for six months.

Bath, Leicester, Harlequins and Wasps qualified as England's representatives in Europe. Gloucester and Saracens had a ding-dong battle to avoid the second relegation spot, Gloucester winning through on merit only for Saracens to join them later when the RFU rescinded relegation. Northampton were outstanding winners of the Second Division, averaging close to 50 points a match. Rotherham, promoted for the sixth time in nine years, can justifiably claim to be the success story of the 1990s: from North-East 1 to National League 2 in several significant leaps.

The tenor of the season, though, was undoubtedly financial. Newcastle, Saracens, Richmond, Wasps, Harlequins and Bedford all signed million-pound deals of one sort or another. Rob Andrew, Tony Underwood, Ben Clarke, Scott Quinnell, Adrian Davies, Michael Lynagh and Philippe Sella were just some of the major players who changed either code or club. Tony Russ of Leicester and Paul Turner of Sale became the first soccer-type managerial casualties. Australia's Bob Dwyer takes over at Welford Road; Turner, along with Geoff Cooke, at Bedford. Suddenly, it's a whole new ball game.

ENGLISH INTERNATIONAL PLAYERS
(*up to 30 April 1996*)

ABBREVIATIONS

A – Australia; *Arg* – Argentina; *C* – Canada; *F* – France; *Fj* – Fiji; *I* – Ireland; *It* – Italy; *J* -Japan; *M* – Maoris; *NZ* – New Zealand; *R* – Romania; *S* – Scotland; *SA* – South Africa; *US* – United States; *W* – Wales; *WS* – Western Samoa; (C) – Centenary match v Scotland at Murrayfield, 1971 (non-championship); *P* – England v President's Overseas XV at Twickenham in RFU's Centenary season, 1970-71; (R) – Replacement; (t) – temporary replacement. Entries in square brackets [ ] indicate appearances in the World Cup.

Note: Years given for Five Nations' matches are for second half of season; eg 1972 means season 1971-72. Years for all other matches refer to the actual year of the match. When a series has taken place, figures have been used to denote the particular matches in which players have featured. Thus 1984 *SA 2* indicates that a player appeared in the second Test of the series.

Aarvold, C D (Cambridge U, W Hartlepool, Headingley, Blackheath) 1928 *A, W, I, F, S*, 1929 *W, I, F*, 1931 *W, S, F*, 1932 *SA, W, I, S*, 1933 *W*
Ackford, P J (Harlequins) 1988 *A*, 1989 *S, I, F, W, R, Fj*, 1990 *I, F, W, S, Arg* 3, 1991 *W, S, I, F, A, [NZ, It, F, S, A]*
Adams, A A (London Hospital) 1910 *F*
Adams, F R (Richmond) 1875 *I, S*, 1876 *S*, 1877 *I*, 1878 *S*, 1879 *S, I*
Adey, G J (Leicester) 1976 *I, F*
Adkins, S J (Coventry) 1950 *I, F, S*, 1953 *W, I, F, S*
Agar, A E (Harlequins) 1952 *SA, W, S, I, F*, 1953 *W, I*
Alcock, A (Guy's Hospital) 1906 *SA*
Alderson, F H R (Hartlepool R) 1891 *W, I, S*, 1892 *W, S*, 1893 *W*
Alexander, H (Richmond) 1900 *I, S*, 1901 *W, I, S*, 1902 *W, I*
Alexander, W (Northern) 1927 *F*
Allison, D F (Coventry) 1956 *W, I, S, F*, 1957 *W*, 1958 *W, S*
Allport, A (Blackheath) 1892 *W*, 1893 *I*, 1894 *W, I, S*
Anderson, S (Rockcliff) 1899 *I*
Anderson, W F (Orrell) 1973 *NZ* 1
Anderton, C (Manchester FW) 1889 *M*
Andrew, C R (Cambridge U, Nottingham, Wasps, Toulouse) 1985 *R, F, S, I, W*, 1986 *W, S, I, F*, 1987 *I, F, W*, [*J* (R), *US*], 1988 *S, I* 1,2, *A* 1,2, *Fj, A*, 1989 *S, I, F, W, R, Fj*, 1990 *I, F, W, S, Arg* 3, 1991 *W, S, I, F, Fj, A, [NZ, It, US, F, S, A]*, 1992 *S, I, F, W, C, SA*, 1993 *F, W, NZ*, 1994 *S, I, F, W, SA* 1,2, *R, C*, 1995 *I, F, W, S, [Arg, It, A, NZ, F]*
Archer, G S (Bristol, Army) 1996 *S, I*
Archer, H (Bridgwater A) 1909 *W, F, I*
Armstrong, R (Northern) 1925 *W*
Arthur, T G (Wasps) 1966 *W, I*
Ashby, R C (Wasps) 1966 *I, F*, 1967 *A*
Ashcroft, A (Waterloo) 1956 *W, I, S, F*, 1957 *W, I, F, S*, 1958 *W, A, I, F, S*, 1959 *I, F, S*
Ashcroft, A H (Birkenhead Park) 1909 *A*
Ashford, W (Richmond) 1897 *W, I*, 1898 *S, W*
Ashworth, A (Oldham) 1892 *I*
Askew, J G (Cambridge U) 1930 *W, I, F*
Aslett, A R (Richmond) 1926 *W, I, F, S*, 1929 *S, F*
Assinder, E W (O Edwardians) 1909 *A, W*
Aston, R L (Blackheath) 1890 *S, I*
Auty, J R (Headingley) 1935 *S*

Back, N A (Leicester) 1994 *S, I*, 1995 *[Arg* (t), *It, WS]*
Bailey, M D (Cambridge U, Wasps) 1984 *SA* 1,2, 1987 *[US]*, 1989 *Fj*, 1990 *I, F, S* (R)
Bainbridge, S (Gosforth, Fylde) 1982 *F, W*, 1983 *F, W, S, I, NZ*, 1984 *S, I, F, W*, 1985 *NZ* 1,2, 1987 *F, W, S, [J, US]*
Baker, D G S (OMTs) 1955 *W, I, F, S*
Baker, E M (Moseley) 1895 *W, I, S*, 1896 *W, I, S*, 1897 *W*
Baker, H C (Clifton) 1887 *W*
Bance, J P (Bedford) 1954 *S*
Barley, B (Wakefield) 1984 *I, F, W, A*, 1988 *A* 1,2, *Fj*
Barnes, S (Bristol, Bath) 1984 *A*, 1985 *R* (R), *NZ* 1,2, 1986 *S* (R), *F* (R), 1987 *I* (R), 1988 *Fj*, 1993 *S, I*
Barr, R J (Leicester) 1932 *SA, W, I*
Barrett, E I M (Lennox) 1903 *S*
Barrington, T J M (Bristol) 1931 *W, I*
Barrington-Ward, L E (Edinburgh U) 1910 *W, I, F, S*
Barron, J H (Bingley) 1896 *S*, 1897 *W, I*
Bartlett, J T (Waterloo) 1951 *W*
Bartlett, R M (Harlequins) 1957 *W, I, F, S*, 1958 *I, F, S*
Barton, J (Coventry) 1967 *I, F, W*, 1972 *F*
Batchelor, T B (Oxford U) 1907 *F*

Bates, S M (Wasps) 1989 *R*
Bateson, A H (Otley) 1930 *W, I, F, S*
Bateson, H D (Liverpool) 1879 *I*
Batson, T (Blackheath) 1872 *S*, 1874 *S*, 1875 *I*
Batten, J M (Cambridge U) 1874 *S*
Baume, J L (Northern) 1950 *S*
Baxter, J (Birkenhead Park) 1900 *W, I, S*
Bayfield, M C (Northampton) 1991 *Fj, A*, 1992 *S, I, F, W, C, SA*, 1993 *F, W, S, I*, 1994 *S, I, SA* 1,2, *R, C*, 1995 *I, F, W, S, [Arg, It, A, NZ, F]*, *SA, WS*, 1996 *F, W*
Bazley, R C (Waterloo) 1952 *I, F*, 1953 *W, I, F, S*, 1955 *W, I, F, S*
Beaumont, W B (Fylde) 1975 *I, A* 1(R),2, 1976 *A, W, S, I, F*, 1977 *S, I, F, W*, 1978 *F, W, S, I, NZ*, 1979 *S, I, F, W, NZ*, 1980 *I, F, W, S*, 1981 *W, S, I, F, Arg* 1,2, 1982 *A, S*
Bedford, H (Morley) 1889 *M*, 1890 *S, I*
Bedford, L L (Headingley) 1931 *W, I*
Beer, I D S (Harlequins) 1955 *F, S*
Beese, M C (Liverpool) 1972 *W, I, F*
Bell, F J (Northern) 1900 *W*
Bell, H (New Brighton) 1884 *I*
Bell, J L (Darlington) 1878 *I*
Bell, P J (Blackheath) 1968 *W, I, F, S*
Bell, R W (Northern) 1900 *W, I, S*
Bendon, G J (Wasps) 1959 *W, I, F, S*
Bennett, N O (St Mary's Hospital, Waterloo) 1947 *W, S, F*, 1948 *A, W, I, S*
Bennett, W N (Bedford, London Welsh) 1975 *S, A*1, 1976 *S* (R), 1979 *S, I, F, W*
Bennetts, B B (Penzance) 1909 *A, W*
Bentley, J (Sale) 1988 *I* 2, *A* 1
Bentley, J E (Gipsies) 1871 *S*, 1872 *S*
Berridge, M J (Northampton) 1949 *W, I*
Berry, H (Gloucester) 1910 *W, I, F, S*
Berry, J (Tyldesley) 1891 *W, I, S*
Berry, J T W (Leicester) 1939 *W, I, S*
Beswick, E (Swinton) 1882 *I, S*
Biggs, J M (UCH) 1878 *S*, 1879 *I*
Birkett, J G G (Harlequins) 1906 *S, F, SA*, 1907 *F, W, S*, 1908 *F, W, I, S*, 1910 *W, I, S*, 1911 *W, F, I, S*, 1912 *W, I, S, F*
Birkett, L (Clapham R) 1875 *S*, 1877 *I, S*
Birkett, R H (Clapham R) 1871 *S*, 1875 *S*, 1876 *S*, 1877 *I*
Bishop, C C (Blackheath) 1927 *F*
Black, B H (Blackheath) 1930 *W, I, F, S*, 1931 *W, I, S, F*, 1932 *S*, 1933 *W*
Blacklock, J H (Aspatria) 1898 *I*, 1899 *I*
Blakeway, P J (Gloucester) 1980 *I, F, W, S*, 1981 *W, S, I, F*, 1982 *I, F, W*, 1984 *I, F, W, SA* 1, 1985 *R, F, S, I*
Blakiston, A F (Northampton) 1920 *S*, 1921 *W, I, S, F*, 1922 *W*, 1923 *S, F*, 1924 *W, I, F, S*, 1925 *NZ, W, I, S, F*
Blatherwick, T (Manchester) 1878 *I*
Body, J A (Gipsies) 1872 *S*, 1873 *S*
Bolton, C A (United Services) 1909 *F*
Bolton, R (Harlequins) 1933 *W*, 1936 *S*, 1937 *S*, 1938 *W, I*
Bolton, W N (Blackheath) 1882 *I, S*, 1883 *W, I, S*, 1884 *W, I, S*, 1885 *I*, 1887 *I, S*
Bonaventura, M S (Blackheath) 1931 *W*
Bond, A M (Sale) 1978 *NZ*, 1979 *S, I, NZ*, 1980 *I*, 1982 *I*
Bonham-Carter, E (Oxford U) 1891 *S*
Bonsor, F (Bradford) 1886 *W, I, S*, 1887 *W, S*, 1889 *M*
Boobbyer, B (Rosslyn Park) 1950 *W, I, F, S*, 1951 *W, F*, 1952 *S, I, F*
Booth, L A (Headingley) 1933 *W, I, S*, 1934 *S*, 1935 *W, I, S*
Botting, I J (Oxford U) 1950 *W, I*
Boughton, H J (Gloucester) 1935 *W, I, S*

Boyle, C W (Oxford U) 1873 *S*
Boyle, S B (Gloucester) 1983 *W, S, I*
Boylen, F (Hartlepool R) 1908 *F, W, I, S*
Bracken, K P P (Bristol) 1993 *NZ,* 1994 *S, I, C,* 1995 *I, F, W, S, [It, WS* (t)], *SA*
Bradby, M S (United Services) 1922 *I, F*
Bradley, R (W Hartlepool) 1903 *W*
Bradshaw, H (Bramley) 1892 *S,* 1893 *W, I, S,* 1894 *W, I, S*
Brain, S E (Coventry) 1984 *SA* 2, *A* (R), 1985 *R, F, S, I, W, NZ* 1,2, 1986 *W, S, I, F*
Braithwaite, J (Leicester) 1905 *NZ*
Braithwaite-Exley, B (Headingley) 1949 *W*
Brettargh, A T (Liverpool OB) 1900 *W,* 1903 *I, S,* 1904 *W, I, S,* 1905 *I, S*
Brewer, J (Gipsies) 1876 *I*
Briggs, A (Bradford) 1892 *W, I, S*
Brinn, A (Gloucester) 1972 *W, I, S*
Broadley, T (Bingley) 1893 *W, S,* 1894 *W, I, S,* 1896 *S*
Bromet, W E (Richmond) 1891 *W, I,* 1892 *W, I, S,* 1893 *W, I, S,* 1895 *W, I, S,* 1896 *I*
Brook, P W P (Harlequins) 1930 *S,* 1931 *F,* 1936 *S*
Brooke, T J (Richmond) 1968 *F, S*
Brooks, F G (Bedford) 1906 *SA*
Brooks, M J (Oxford U) 1874 *S*
Brophy, T J (Liverpool) 1964 *I, F, S,* 1965 *W, I,* 1966 *W, I, F*
Brough, J W (Silloth) 1925 *NZ, W*
Brougham, H (Harlequins) 1912 *W, I, S, F*
Brown, A A (Exeter) 1938 *S*
Brown, L G (Oxford U, Blackheath) 1911 *W, F, I, S,* 1913 *SA, W, F, I, S,* 1914 *W, I, S, F,* 1921 *W, I, S, F,* 1922 *W*
Brown, T W (Bristol) 1928 *S,* 1929 *W, I, S, F,* 1932 *S,* 1933 *W, I, S*
Brunton, J (N Durham) 1914 *W, I, S*
Brutton, E B (Cambridge U) 1886 *S*
Bryden, C C (Clapham R) 1876 *I,* 1877 *S*
Bryden, H A (Clapham R) 1874 *S*
Buckingham, R A (Leicester) 1927 *F*
Bucknall, A L (Richmond) 1969 *SA,* 1970 *I, W, S, F,* 1971 *W, I, F, S* (2[1C])
Buckton, J R D (Saracens) 1988 *A* (R), 1990 *Arg* 1,2
Budd, A (Blackheath) 1878 *I,* 1879 *S, I,* 1881 *W, S*
Budworth, R T D (Blackheath) 1890 *W,* 1891 *W, S*
Bull, A G (Northampton) 1914 *W*
Bullough, E (Wigan) 1892 *W, I, S*
Bulpitt, M P (Blackheath) 1970 *S*
Bulteel, A J (Manchester) 1876 *I*
Bunting, W L (Moseley) 1897 *I, S,* 1898 *I, S, W,* 1899 *S,* 1900 *S,* 1901 *I, S*
Burland, D W (Bristol) 1931 *W, I, F,* 1932 *I, S,* 1933 *W, I, S*
Burns, B (Blackheath) 1871 *S*
Burton, G W (Blackheath) 1879 *S, I,* 1880 *S,* 1881 *I, W, S*
Burton, H C (Richmond) 1926 *W*
Burton, M A (Gloucester) 1972 *W, I, F, S, SA,* 1974 *F, W,* 1975 *S, A* 1,2, 1976 *A, W, S, I, F,* 1978 *F, W*
Bush, J A (Clifton) 1872 *S,* 1873 *S,* 1875 *S,* 1876 *I, S*
Butcher, C J S (Harlequins) 1984 *SA* 1,2, *A*
Butcher, W V (Streatham) 1903 *S,* 1904 *W, I, S,* 1905 *W, I, S*
Butler, A G (Harlequins) 1937 *W, I*
Butler, P E (Gloucester) 1975 *A* 1, 1976 *F*
Butterfield, J (Northampton) 1953 *F, S,* 1954 *W, NZ, I, S, F,* 1955 *W, I, F, S,* 1956 *W, I, S, F,* 1957 *W, I, F, S,* 1958 *W, A, I, F, S,* 1959 *W, I, F, S*
Byrne, F A (Moseley) 1897 *W*
Byrne, J F (Moseley) 1894 *W, I, S,* 1895 *I, S,* 1896 *I,* 1897 *W, I, S,* 1898 *I, S, W,* 1899 *I*

Cain, J J (Waterloo) 1950 *W*
Callard, J E B (Bath) 1993 *NZ,* 1994 *S, I,* 1995 *[WS], SA*
Campbell, D A (Cambridge U) 1937 *W, I*
Candler, P L (St Bart's Hospital) 1935 *W,* 1936 *NZ, W, I, S,* 1937 *W, I, S,* 1938 *W, S*
Cannell, L B (Oxford U, St Mary's Hospital) 1948 *F,* 1949 *W, I, F, S,* 1950 *W, I, F, S,* 1952 *SA, W,* 1953 *W, I, F,* 1956 *I, S, F,* 1957 *W, I*
Caplan, D W N (Headingley) 1978 *S, I*
Cardus, R M (Roundhay) 1979 *F, W*
Carey, G M (Blackheath) 1895 *W, I, S,* 1896 *W, I*
Carleton, J (Orrell) 1979 *NZ,* 1980 *I, F, W, S,* 1981 *W, S, I, F, Arg* 1,2, 1982 *A, S, I, F, W,* 1983 *F, W, S, I, NZ,* 1984 *S, I, F, W, A*

Carling, W D C (Durham U, Harlequins) 1988 *F, W, S, I* 1,2, *A2, Fj, A,* 1989 *S, I, F, W, Fj,* 1990 *I, F, W, S, Arg* 1,2,3, 1991 *W, S, I, F, Fj, A, [NZ, It, US, F, S, A],* 1992 *S, I, F, W, C, SA,* 1993 *F, W, S, I, NZ,* 1994 *S, I, F, W, SA* 1,2, *R, C,* 1995 *I, F, W, S, [Arg, WS, A, NZ, F], SA, WS,* 1996 *F, W, S, I*
Carpenter, A D (Gloucester) 1932 *SA*
Carr, R S L (Manchester) 1939 *W, I, S*
Cartwright, V H (Nottingham) 1903 *W, I, S,* 1904 *W, S,* 1905 *W, I, S, NZ,* 1906 *W, I, S, F, SA*
Catcheside, H C (Percy Park) 1924 *W, I, F, S,* 1926 *W, I,* 1927 *I, S*
Catt, M J (Bath) 1994 *W* (R), *C* (R), 1995 *I, F, W, S, [Arg, It, WS, A, NZ, F], SA, WS,* 1996 *F, W, S, I*
Cattell, R H B (Blackheath) 1895 *W, I, S,* 1896 *W, I, S,* 1900 *W*
Cave, J W (Richmond) 1889 *M*
Cave, W T C (Blackheath) 1905 *W*
Challis, R (Bristol) 1957 *I, F, S*
Chambers, E L (Bedford) 1908 *F,* 1910 *W, I*
Chantrill, B S (Bristol) 1924 *W, I, F, S*
Chapman, C E (Cambridge U) 1884 *W*
Chapman, F E (Hartlepool) 1910 *W, I, F, S,* 1912 *W,* 1914 *W, I*
Cheesman, W I (OMTs) 1913 *SA, W, F, I*
Cheston, E C (Richmond) 1873 *S,* 1874 *S,* 1875 *I, S,* 1876 *S*
Chilcott, G J (Bath) 1984 *A,* 1986 *I, F,* 1987 *F* (R), *W, [J, US, W* (R)], 1988 *I* 2 (R), *Fj,* 1989 *I* (R), *F, W, R*
Christopherson, P (Blackheath) 1891 *W, S*
Clark, C W H (Liverpool) 1876 *I*
Clarke, A J (Coventry) 1935 *W, I, S,* 1936 *NZ, W, I*
Clarke, B B (Bath) 1992 *SA,* 1993 *F, W, S, I, NZ,* 1994 *S, F, W, SA* 1,2, *R, C,* 1995 *I, F, W, S, [Arg, It, A, NZ, F], SA, WS,* 1996 *F, W, S, I*
Clarke, S J S (Cambridge U, Blackheath) 1963 *W, I, F, S, NZ* 1,2, *A,* 1964 *NZ, W, I,* 1965 *I, F, S*
Clayton, J H (Liverpool) 1871 *S*
Clements, J W (O Cranleighans) 1959 *I, F, S*
Cleveland, C R (Blackheath) 1887 *W, S*
Clibborn, W G (Richmond) 1886 *W, I, S,* 1887 *W, I, S*
Clough, F J (Cambridge U, Orrell) 1986 *I, F,* 1987 *[J* (R), *US]*
Coates, C H (Yorkshire W) 1880 *S,* 1881 *S,* 1882 *S*
Coates, V H M (Bath) 1913 *SA, W, F, I, S*
Cobby, W (Hull) 1900 *W*
Cockerham, A (Bradford Olicana) 1900 *W*
Colclough, M J (Angoulême, Wasps, Swansea) 1978 *S, I,* 1979 *NZ,* 1980 *F, W, S,* 1981 *W, S, I, F,* 1982 *A, S, I, F, W,* 1983 *F, NZ,* 1984 *S, I, F, W,* 1986 *W, S, I, F*
Coley, E (Northampton) 1929 *F,* 1932 *W*
Collins, P J (Camborne) 1952 *S, I, F*
Collins, W E (O Cheltonians) 1874 *S,* 1875 *I, S,* 1876 *I, S*
Considine, S G U (Bath) 1925 *F*
Conway, G S (Cambridge U, Rugby, Manchester) 1920 *F, I, S,* 1921 *F,* 1922 *W, I, F, S,* 1923 *W, I, S, F,* 1924 *W, I, F, S,* 1925 *NZ,* 1927 *W*
Cook, J G (Bedford) 1937 *S*
Cook, P W (Richmond) 1965 *I, F*
Cooke, D A (Harlequins) 1976 *W, S, I, F*
Cooke, D H (Harlequins) 1981 *W, S, I, F,* 1984 *I,* 1985 *R, F, S, I, W, NZ* 1,2
Cooke, P (Richmond) 1939 *W, I*
Coop, T (Leigh) 1892 *S*
Cooper, J G (Moseley) 1909 *A, W*
Cooper, M J (Moseley) 1973 *F, S, NZ* 2 (R), 1975 *F, W,* 1976 *A, W,* 1977 *S, I, F, W*
Coopper, S F (Blackheath) 1900 *W,* 1902 *W, I,* 1905 *W, I, S,* 1907 *W*
Corbett, L J (Bristol) 1921 *F,* 1923 *W, I,* 1924 *W, I, F, S,* 1925 *NZ, W, I, S, F,* 1927 *W, I, S, F*
Corless, B J (Coventry, Moseley) 1976 *A, I* (R), 1977 *S, I, F, W,* 1978 *F, S*
Cotton, F E (Loughborough Colls, Coventry, Sale) 1971 *S* (2[1C]), *P,* 1973 *W, I, F, S, NZ* 2, *A,* 1974 *S, I,* 1975 *I, F, W,* 1976 *A, W, S, I, F,* 1977 *S, I, F, W,* 1978 *S, I,* 1979 *NZ,* 1980 *I, F, W, S,* 1981 *W*
Coulman, M J (Moseley) 1967 *A, I, F, S, W,* 1968 *W, I, F, S*
Coulson, T J (Coventry) 1927 *W,* 1928 *A, W*
Court, E D (Blackheath) 1885 *W*
Coverdale, H (Blackheath) 1910 *F,* 1912 *I, F,* 1920 *W*
Cove-Smith, R (OMTs) 1921 *S, F,* 1922 *I, F, S,* 1923 *W, I, S, F,* 1924 *W, I, S, F,* 1925 *NZ, W, I, S, F,* 1927 *W, I, S, F,* 1928 *A, W, I, F, S,* 1929 *W, I*

Cowling, R J (Leicester) 1977 *S, I, F, W*, 1978 *F, NZ*, 1979 *S, I*
Cowman, A R (Loughborough Colls, Coventry) 1971 *S* (2[1C]), *P*, 1973 *W, I*
Cox, N S (Sunderland) 1901 *S*
Cranmer, P (Richmond, Moseley) 1934 *W, I, S*, 1935 *W, I, S*, 1936 *NZ, W, I, S*, 1937 *W, I, S*, 1938 *W, I, S*
Creed, R N (Coventry) 1971 *P*
Cridlan, A G (Blackheath) 1935 *W, I, S*
Crompton, C A (Blackheath) 1871 *S*
Crosse, C W (Oxford U) 1874 *S*, 1875 *I*
Cumberlege, B S (Blackheath) 1920 *W, I, S*, 1921 *W, I, S, F*, 1922 *W*
Cumming, D C (Blackheath) 1925 *S, F*
Cunliffe, F L (RMA) 1874 *S*
Currey, F I (Marlborough N) 1872 *S*
Currie, J D (Oxford U, Harlequins, Bristol) 1956 *W, I, S, F*, 1957 *W, I, F, S*, 1958 *W, A, I, F, S*, 1959 *W, I, F, S*, 1960 *W, I, F, S*, 1961 *SA*, 1962 *W, I, F*
Cusani, D A (Orrell) 1987 *I*
Cusworth, L (Leicester) 1979 *NZ*, 1982 *F, W*, 1983 *F, W, NZ*, 1984 *S, I, F, W*, 1988 *F, W*

D'Aguilar, F B G (Royal Engineers) 1872 *S*
Dallaglio, L B N (Wasps) 1995 *SA* (R), *WS*, 1996 *W, S, I*
Dalton, T J (Coventry) 1969 *S*(R)
Danby, T (Harlequins) 1949 *W*
Daniell, J (Richmond) 1899 *W*, 1900 *I, S*, 1902 *I, S*, 1904 *I, S*
Darby, A J L (Birkenhead Park) 1899 *I*
Davenport, A (Ravenscourt Park) 1871 *S*
Davey, J (Redruth) 1908 *S*, 1909 *W*
Davey, R F (Teignmouth) 1931 *W*
Davidson, Jas (Aspatria) 1897 *S*, 1898 *S, W*, 1899 *I, S*
Davidson, Jos (Aspatria) 1899 *W, S*
Davies, G H (Cambridge U, Coventry, Wasps) 1981 *S, I, F, Arg* 1,2, 1982 *A, S, I*, 1983 *F, W, S*, 1984 *S, SA* 1,2, 1985 *R* (R), *NZ* 1,2, 1986 *W, S, I, F*
Davies, P H (Sale) 1927 *I*
Davies, V G (Harlequins) 1922 *W*, 1925 *NZ*
Davies, W J A (United Services, RN) 1913 *SA, W, F, I, S*, 1914 *I, S, F*, 1920 *F, I, S*, 1921 *W, I, S, F*, 1922 *I, F, S*, 1923 *W, I, S, F*
Davies, W P C (Harlequins) 1953 *S*, 1954 *NZ, I*, 1955 *W, I, F, S*, 1956 *W*, 1957 *F, S*, 1958 *W*
Davis, A M (Torquay Ath, Harlequins) 1963 *W, I, S, NZ* 1,2, 1964 *NZ, W, I, F, S*, 1966 *W*, 1967 *A*, 1969 *SA*, 1970 *I, W, S*
Dawe, R G R (Bath) 1987 *I, F, W, [US]*, 1995 *[WS]*
Dawson, E F (RIEC) 1878 *I*
Dawson, M J S (Northampton) 1995 *WS*, 1996 *F, W, S, I*
Day, H L V (Leicester) 1920 *W*, 1922 *W, F*, 1926 *S*
Dean, G J (Harlequins) 1931 *I*
Dee, J M (Hartlepool R) 1962 *S*, 1963 *NZ* 1
Devitt, Sir T G (Blackheath) 1926 *I, F*, 1928 *A, W*
Dewhurst, J H (Richmond) 1887 *W, I, S*, 1890 *W*
De Glanville, P R (Bath) 1992 *SA* (R), 1993 *W* (R), *NZ*, 1994 *S, I, F, W, SA* 1,2, *C* (R), 1995 *[Arg* (R), *It, WS], SA* (R), 1996 *W* (R), *I* (R)
De Winton, R F C (Marlborough N) 1893 *W*
Dibble, R (Bridgwater A) 1906 *S, F, SA*, 1908 *F, W, I, S*, 1909 *A, W, F, I, S*, 1910 *S*, 1911 *W, F, S*, 1912 *W, I, S*
Dicks, J (Northampton) 1934 *W, I, S*, 1935 *W, I, S*, 1936 *S*, 1937 *I*
Dillon, E W (Blackheath) 1904 *W, I, S*, 1905 *W*
Dingle, A J (Hartlepool R) 1913 *I*, 1914 *S, F*
Dixon, P J (Harlequins, Gosforth) 1971 *P*, 1972 *W, I, F, S*, 1973 *I, F, S*, 1974 *S, I, F, W*, 1975 *I*, 1976 *F*, 1977 *S, I, F, W*, 1978 *F, S, I, NZ*
Dobbs, G E B (Devonport A) 1906 *W, I*
Doble, S A (Moseley) 1972 *SA*, 1973 *NZ* 1, *W*
Dobson, D D (Newton Abbot) 1902 *W, I, S*, 1903 *W, I, S*
Dobson, T H (Bradford) 1895 *S*
Dodge, P W (Leicester) 1978 *W, S, I, NZ*, 1979 *S, I, F, W*, 1980 *W, S*, 1981 *W, S, I, F, Arg* 1,2, 1982 *A, S, F, W*, 1983 *F, W, S, I, NZ*, 1985 *R, F, S, I, W, NZ* 1,2
Donnelly, M P (Oxford U) 1947 *I*
Dooley, W A (Preston Grasshoppers, Fylde) 1985 *R, F, S, I, W, NZ* 2 (R), 1986 *W, S, I, F*, 1987 *F, W, [A, US, W]*, 1988 *F, W, S, I* 1,2, *A* 1,2, *Fj, A*, 1989 *S, I, F, W, R, Fj*, 1990 *I, F, W, S, Arg* 1,2,3, 1991 *W, S, I, F, [NZ, US, F, S, A]*, 1992 *S, I, F, W, C, SA*, 1993 *W, S, I*
Dovey, B A (Rosslyn Park) 1963 *W, I*
Down, P J (Bristol) 1909 *A*

Dowson, A O (Moseley) 1899 *S*
Drake-Lee, N J (Cambridge U, Leicester) 1963 *W, I, F, S*, 1964 *NZ, W, I*, 1965 *W*
Duckett, H (Bradford) 1893 *I, S*
Duckham, D J (Coventry) 1969 *I, F, S, W, SA*, 1970 *I, W, S, F*, 1971 *W, I, F, S* (2[1C]), *P*, 1972 *W, I, F, S*, 1973 *NZ* 1, *W, I, F, S, NZ* 2, *A*, 1974 *S, I, F, W*, 1975 *I, F, W*, 1976 *A, W, S*
Dudgeon, H W (Richmond) 1897 *S*, 1898 *I, S, W*, 1899 *W, I, S*
Dugdale, J M (Ravenscourt Park) 1871 *S*
Dun, A F (Wasps) 1984 *W*
Duncan, R F H (Guy's Hospital) 1922 *I, F, S*
Dunkley, P E (Harlequins) 1931 *I, S*, 1936 *NZ, W, I, S*
Duthie, J (W Hartlepool) 1903 *W*
Dyson, J W (Huddersfield) 1890 *S*, 1892 *S*, 1893 *I, S*

Ebdon, P J (Wellington) 1897 *W, I*
Eddison, J H (Headingley) 1912 *W, I, S, F*
Edgar, C S (Birkenhead Park) 1901 *S*
Edwards, R (Newport) 1921 *W, I, S, F*, 1922 *W, F*, 1923 *W*, 1924 *W, F, S*, 1925 *NZ*
Egerton, D W (Bath) 1988 *I* 2, *A* 1, *Fj* (R), *A*, 1989 *Fj*, 1990 *I, Arg* 2 (R)
Elliot, C H (Sunderland) 1886 *W*
Elliot, E W (Sunderland) 1901 *W, I, S*, 1904 *W*
Elliot, W (United Services, RN) 1932 *I, S*, 1933 *W, I, S*, 1934 *W, I*
Elliott, A E (St Thomas's Hospital) 1894 *S*
Ellis, J (Wakefield) 1939 *S*
Ellis, S S (Queen's House) 1880 *I*
Emmott, C (Bradford) 1892 *W*
Enthoven, H J (Richmond) 1878 *I*
Estcourt, N S D (Blackheath) 1955 *S*
Evans, B J (Leicester) 1988 *A* 2, *Fj*
Evans, E (Sale) 1948 *A*, 1950 *W*, 1951 *I, F, S*, 1952 *SA, W, S, I, F*, 1953 *I, F, S*, 1954 *W, NZ, I, F*, 1956 *W, I, S, F*, 1957 *W, I, F, S*, 1958 *W, A, I, F, S*
Evans, G W (Coventry) 1972 *S*, 1973 *W* (R), *F, S, NZ* 2, 1974 *S, I, F, W*
Evans, N L (RNEC) 1932 *W, I, S*, 1933 *W, I*
Evanson, A M (Richmond) 1883 *W, I, S*, 1884 *S*
Evanson, W A D (Richmond) 1875 *S*, 1877 *S*, 1878 *S*, 1879 *S, I*
Evershed, F (Blackheath) 1889 *M*, 1890 *W, S, I*, 1892 *W, I, S*, 1893 *W, I, S*
Eyres, W C T (Richmond) 1927 *I*

Fagan, A R St L (Richmond) 1887 *I*
Fairbrother, K E (Coventry) 1969 *I, F, S, W, SA*, 1970 *I, W, S, F*, 1971 *W, I, F*
Faithfull, C K T (Harlequins) 1924 *I*, 1926 *F, S*
Fallas, H (Wakefield T) 1884 *I*
Fegan, J H C (Blackheath) 1895 *W, I, S*
Fernandes, C W L (Leeds) 1881 *I, W, S*
Fidler, J H (Gloucester) 1981 *Arg* 1,2, 1984 *SA* 1,2
Field, E (Middlesex W) 1893 *W, I*
Fielding, K J (Moseley, Loughborough Colls) 1969 *I, F, S, SA*, 1970 *I, F*, 1972 *W, I, F, S*
Finch, R T (Cambridge U) 1880 *S*
Finlan, J F (Moseley) 1967 *I, F, S, W, NZ*, 1968 *W, I*, 1969 *I, F, S, W*, 1970 *F*, 1973 *NZ* 1
Finlinson, H W (Blackheath) 1895 *W, I, S*
Finney, S (RIE Coll) 1872 *S*, 1873 *S*
Firth, F (Halifax) 1894 *W, I, S*
Fletcher, N C (OMTs) 1901 *W, I, S*, 1903 *S*
Fletcher, T (Seaton) 1897 *W*
Fletcher, W R B (Marlborough N) 1873 *S*, 1875 *S*
Fookes, E F (Sowerby Bridge) 1896 *W, I, S*, 1897 *W, I, S*, 1898 *I, W*, 1899 *I, S*
Ford, P J (Gloucester) 1964 *W, I, F, S*
Forrest, J W (United Services, RN) 1930 *W, I, F, S*, 1931 *W, I, S, F*, 1934 *I, S*
Forrest, R (Wellington) 1899 *W*, 1900 *S*, 1902 *I, S*, 1903 *I, S*
Foulds, R T (Waterloo) 1929 *W, I*
Fowler, F D (Manchester) 1878 *S*, 1879 *S*
Fowler, H (Oxford U) 1878 *S*, 1881 *W, S*
Fowler, R H (Leeds) 1877 *I*
Fox, F H (Wellington) 1890 *W, S*
Francis, T E S (Cambridge U) 1926 *W, I, F, S*
Frankcom, G P (Cambridge U, Bedford) 1965 *W, I, F, S*
Fraser, E C (Blackheath) 1875 *I*
Fraser, G (Richmond) 1902 *W, I, S*, 1903 *W, I*
Freakes, H D (Oxford U) 1938 *W*, 1939 *W, I*

Freeman, H (Marlborough N) 1872 *S*, 1873 *S*, 1874 *S*
French, R J (St Helens) 1961 *W, I, F, S*
Fry, H A (Liverpool) 1934 *W, I, S*
Fry, T W (Queen's House) 1880 *I, S*, 1881 *W*
Fuller, H G (Cambridge U) 1882 *I, S*, 1883 *W, I, S*, 1884 *W*

Gadney, B C (Leicester, Headingley) 1932 *I, S*, 1933 *I, S*, 1934 *W, I, S*, 1935 *S*, 1936 *NZ, W, I, S*, 1937 *S*, 1938 *W*
Gamlin, H T (Blackheath) 1899 *W, S*, 1900 *W, I, S*, 1901 *S*, 1902 *W, I, S*, 1903 *W, I, S*, 1904 *W, I, S*
Gardner, E R (Devonport Services) 1921 *W, I, S*, 1922 *W, I, F*, 1923 *W, I, S, F*
Gardner, H P (Richmond) 1878 *I*
Garnett, H W T (Bradford) 1877 *S*
Gavins, M N (Leicester) 1961 *W*
Gay, D J (Bath) 1968 *W, I, F, S*
Gent, D R (Gloucester) 1905 *NZ*, 1906 *W, I*, 1910 *W, I*
Genth, J S M (Manchester) 1874 *S*, 1875 *S*
George, J T (Falmouth) 1947 *S, F*, 1949 *I*
Gerrard, R A (Bath) 1932 *SA, W, I, S*, 1933 *W, I, S*, 1934 *W, I, S*, 1936 *NZ, W, I, S*
Gibbs, G A (Bristol) 1947 *F*, 1948 *I*
Gibbs, J C (Harlequins) 1925 *NZ, W*, 1926 *F*, 1927 *W, I, S, F*
Gibbs, N (Harlequins) 1954 *S, F*
Giblin, L F (Blackheath) 1896 *W, I*, 1897 *S*
Gibson, A S (Manchester) 1871 *S*
Gibson, C O P (Northern) 1901 *W*
Gibson, G R (Northern) 1899 *W*, 1901 *S*
Gibson, T A (Northern) 1905 *W, S*
Gilbert, F G (Devonport Services) 1923 *W, I*
Gilbert, R (Devonport A) 1908 *W, I, S*
Giles, J L (Coventry) 1935 *W, I*, 1937 *W, I*, 1938 *I, S*
Gittings, W J (Coventry) 1967 *NZ*
Glover, P B (Bath) 1967 *A*, 1971 *F, P*
Godfray, R E (Richmond) 1905 *NZ*
Godwin, H O (Coventry) 1959 *F, S*, 1963 *S, NZ* 1,2, *A*, 1964 *NZ, I, F, S*, 1967 *NZ*
Gordon-Smith, G W (Blackheath) 1900 *W, I, S*
Gotley, A L H (Oxford U) 1910 *F, S*, 1911 *W, F, I, S*
Graham, D (Aspatria) 1901 *W*
Graham, H J (Wimbledon H) 1875 *I, S*, 1876 *I, S*
Graham, J D G (Wimbledon H) 1876 *I*
Gray, A (Otley) 1947 *W, I, S*
Grayson, P J (Northampton) 1995 *WS*, 1996 *F, W, S, I*
Green, J (Skipton) 1905 *I*, 1906 *S, F, SA*, 1907 *F, W, I, S*
Green, J F (West Kent) 1871 *S*
Greenwell, J H (Rockcliff) 1893 *W, I*
Greenwood, J E (Cambridge U, Leicester) 1912 *F*, 1913 *SA, W, F, I, S*, 1914 *W, S, F*, 1920 *W, F, I, S*
Greenwood, J R H (Waterloo) 1966 *I, F, S*, 1967 *A*, 1969 *I*
Greg, W (Manchester) 1876 *I, S*
Gregory, G G (Bristol) 1931 *I, S, F*, 1932 *SA, W, I, S*, 1933 *W, I, S*, 1934 *W, I, S*
Gregory, J A (Blackheath) 1949 *W*
Grylls, W M (Redruth) 1905 *I*
Guest, R H (Waterloo) 1939 *W, I, S*, 1947 *W, I, S, F*, 1948 *A, W, I, S*, 1949 *F, S*
Guillemard, A G (West Kent) 1871 *S*, 1872 *S*
Gummer, C H A (Plymouth A) 1929 *F*
Gunner, C R (Marlborough N) 1876 *I*
Gurdon, C (Richmond) 1880 *I, S*, 1881 *I, W, S*, 1882 *I, S*, 1883 *S*, 1884 *W, S*, 1885 *I*, 1886 *W, I, S*
Gurdon, E T (Richmond) 1878 *S*, 1879 *I*, 1880 *S*, 1881 *I, W, S*, 1882 *S*, 1883 *W, I, S*, 1884 *W, I, S*, 1885 *W, I*, 1886 *S*
Guscott, J C (Bath) 1989 *R, Fj*, 1990 *I, F, W, S, Arg* 3, 1991 *W, S, I, F, Fj, A, [NZ, It, F, S, A]*, 1992 *S, I, F, W, C, SA*, 1993 *F, W, S, I*, 1994 *R, C*, 1995 *I, F, W, S, [Arg, It, A, NZ, F]*, *SA, WS*, 1996 *F, W, S, I*

Haigh, L (Manchester) 1910 *W, I, S*, 1911 *W, F, I, S*
Hale, P M (Moseley) 1969 *SA*, 1970 *I, W*
Hall, C (Gloucester) 1901 *I, S*
Hall, J (N Durham) 1894 *W, I, S*
Hall, J P (Bath) 1984 *S* (R), *I, F, SA* 1,2, *A*, 1985 *R, F, S, I, W, NZ* 1,2, 1986 *W, S*, 1987 *I, F, W, S*, 1990 *Arg* 3, 1994 *S*
Hall, N M (Richmond) 1947 *W, I, S, F*, 1949 *W, I*, 1952 *SA, W, S, I, F*, 1953 *W, I, F, S*, 1955 *W, I*
Halliday, S J (Bath, Harlequins) 1986 *W, S*, 1987 *S*, 1988 *S, I* 1,2, *A* 1, 1989 *S, I, F, W, R, Fj* (R), 1990 *W, S*, 1991 *[US, S, A]*, 1992 *S, I, F, W*
Hamersley, A St G (Marlborough N) 1871 *S*, 1872 *S*, 1873 *S*, 1874 *S*
Hamilton-Hill, E A (Harlequins) 1936 *NZ, W, I*

Hamilton-Wickes, R H (Cambridge U) 1924 *I*, 1925 *NZ, W, I, S, F*, 1926 *W, I, S*, 1927 *W*
Hammett, E D G (Newport) 1920 *W, F, S*, 1921 *W, I, S, F*, 1922 *W*
Hammond, C E L (Harlequins) 1905 *S, NZ*, 1906 *W, I, S, F*, 1908 *W, I*
Hancock, A W (Northampton) 1965 *F, S*, 1966 *F*
Hancock, G E (Birkenhead Park) 1939 *W, I, S*
Hancock, J H (Newport) 1955 *W, I*
Hancock, P F (Blackheath) 1886 *W, I*, 1890 *W*
Hancock, P S (Richmond) 1904 *W, I, S*
Handford, F G (Manchester) 1909 *W, F, I, S*
Hands, R H M (Blackheath) 1910 *F, S*
Hanley, J (Plymouth A) 1927 *W, S, F*, 1928 *W, I, F, S*
Hannaford, R C (Bristol) 1971 *W, I, F*
Hanvey, R J (Aspatria) 1926 *W, I, F, S*
Harding, E H (Devonport Services) 1931 *I*
Harding, R M (Bristol) 1985 *R, F, S*, 1987 *S, [A, J, W]*, 1988 *I* 1 (R),2, *A* 1,2, *Fj*
Harding, V S J (Saracens) 1961 *F, S*, 1962 *W, I, F, S*
Hardwick, P F (Percy Park) 1902 *I, S*, 1903 *W, I, S*, 1904 *W, I, S*
Hardy, E M P (Blackheath) 1951 *I, F, S*
Hare, W H (Nottingham, Leicester) 1974 *W*, 1978 *F, NZ*, 1979 *NZ*, 1980 *I, F, W, S*, 1981 *W, S, Arg* 1,2, 1982 *F, W*, 1983 *F, W, S, I, NZ*, 1984 *S, I, F, W, SA* 1,2
Harper, C H (Exeter) 1899 *W*
Harriman, A T (Harlequins) 1988 *A*
Harris, S W (Blackheath) 1920 *I, S*
Harris, T W (Northampton) 1929 *S*, 1932 *I*
Harrison, A C (Hartlepool R) 1931 *I, S*
Harrison, A L (United Services, RN) 1914 *I, F*
Harrison, G (Hull) 1877 *I, S*, 1879 *S, I*, 1880 *S*, 1885 *W, I*
Harrison, H C (United Services, RN) 1909 *S*, 1914 *I, S, F*
Harrison, M E (Wakefield) 1985 *NZ* 1,2, 1986 *S, I, F*, 1987 *I, F, W, S, [A, J, US, W]*, 1988 *F, W*
Hartley, B C (Blackheath) 1901 *S*, 1902 *S*
Haslett, L W (Birkenhead Park) 1926 *I, F*
Hastings, G W D (Gloucester) 1955 *W, I, F, S*, 1957 *W, I, F, S*, 1958 *W, A, I, F, S*
Havelock, H (Hartlepool R) 1908 *F, W, I*
Hawcridge, J J (Bradford) 1885 *W, I*
Hayward, L W (Cheltenham) 1910 *I*
Hazell, D St G (Leicester) 1955 *W, I, F, S*
Hearn, R D (Bedford) 1966 *F, S*, 1967 *I, F, S, W*
Heath, A H (Oxford U) 1876 *S*
Heaton, J (Waterloo) 1935 *W, I, S*, 1939 *W, I, S*, 1947 *I, S, F*
Henderson, A P (Edinburgh Wands) 1947 *W, I, S, F*, 1948 *I, S, F*, 1949 *W, I*
Henderson, R S F (Blackheath) 1883 *W, S*, 1884 *W, S*, 1885 *W*
Heppell, W G (Devonport A) 1903 *I*
Herbert, A J (Wasps) 1958 *F, S*, 1959 *W, I, F, S*
Hesford, R (Bristol) 1981 *S* (R), 1982 *A, S, F* (R), 1983 *F* (R), 1985 *R, F, S, I, W*
Heslop, N J (Orrell) 1990 *Arg* 1,2,3, 1991 *W, S, I, F*, *[US, F]*, 1992 *W* (R)
Hetherington, J G G (Northampton) 1958 *A, I*, 1959 *W, I, F, S*
Hewitt, E N (Coventry) 1951 *W, I, F*
Hewitt, W W (Queen's House) 1881 *I, W, S*, 1882 *I*
Hickson, J L (Bradford) 1887 *W, I, S*, 1890 *W, S, I*
Higgins, R (Liverpool) 1954 *W, NZ, I, S*, 1955 *W, I, F, S*, 1957 *W, I, F, S*, 1959 *W*
Hignell, A J (Cambridge U, Bristol) 1975 *A* 2, 1976 *A, W, S, I*, 1977 *S, I, F, W*, 1978 *W*, 1979 *S, I, F, W*
Hill, B A (Blackheath) 1903 *I, S*, 1904 *W, I*, 1905 *W, NZ*, 1906 *SA*, 1907 *F, W*
Hill, R J (Bath) 1984 *SA* 1,2, 1985 *I* (R), *NZ* 2 (R), 1986 *F* (R), 1987 *I, F, W, [US]*, 1989 *Fj*, 1990 *I, F, W, S, Arg* 1,2,3, 1991 *W, S, I, F, Fj, A, [NZ, It, US, F, S, A]*
Hillard, R J (Oxford U) 1925 *NZ*
Hiller, R (Harlequins) 1968 *W, I, F, S*, 1969 *I, F, S, W, SA*, 1970 *I, W, S*, 1971 *I, F, S* (2[1C]), *P*, 1972 *W, I*
Hind, A E (Leicester) 1905 *NZ*, 1906 *W*
Hind, G R (Blackheath) 1910 *S*, 1911 *I*
Hobbs, R F A (Blackheath) 1899 *S*, 1903 *W*
Hobbs, R G S (Richmond) 1932 *SA, W, I, S*
Hodges, H A (Nottingham) 1906 *W, I*
Hodgkinson, S D (Nottingham) 1989 *R, Fj*, 1990 *I, F, W, S, Arg* 1,2,3, 1991 *W, S, I, F, [US]*
Hodgson, J McD (Northern) 1932 *SA, W, I, S*, 1934 *W, I*, 1936 *I*

Hodgson, S A M (Durham City) 1960 *W, I, F, S,* 1961 *SA, W,* 1962 *W, I, F, S,* 1964 *W*
Hofmeyr, M B (Oxford U) 1950 *W, F, S*
Hogarth, T B (Hartlepool R) 1906 *F*
Holford, G (Gloucester) 1920 *W, F*
Holland, D (Devonport A) 1912 *W, I, S*
Holliday, T E (Aspatria) 1923 *S, F,* 1925 *I, S, F,* 1926 *F, S*
Holmes, C B (Manchester) 1947 *S,* 1948 *I, F*
Holmes, E (Manningham) 1890 *S, I*
Holmes, W A (Nuneaton) 1950 *W, I, F, S,* 1951 *W, I, F, S,* 1952 *SA, S, I, F,* 1953 *W, I, F, S*
Holmes, W B (Cambridge U) 1949 *W, I, F, S*
Hook, W G (Gloucester) 1951 *S,* 1952 *SA, W*
Hooper, C A (Middlesex W) 1894 *W, I, S*
Hopley, D P (Wasps) 1995 *[WS (R)], SA, WS*
Hopley, F J V (Blackheath) 1907 *F, W,* 1908 *I*
Hordern, P C (Gloucester) 1931 *I, S, F,* 1934 *W*
Horley, C H (Swinton) 1885 *I*
Hornby, A N (Manchester) 1877 *I, S,* 1878 *S, I,* 1880 *I,* 1881 *I, S,* 1882 *I, S*
Horrocks-Taylor, J P (Cambridge U, Leicester, Middlesbrough) 1958 *W, A,* 1961 *S,* 1962 *S,* 1963 *NZ* 1,2, *A,* 1964 *NZ, W*
Horsfall, E L (Harlequins) 1949 *W*
Horton, A L (Blackheath) 1965 *W, I, F, S,* 1966 *F, S,* 1967 *NZ*
Horton, J P (Bath) 1978 *W, S, I, NZ,* 1980 *I, F, W, S,* 1981 *W,* 1983 *S, I,* 1984 *SA* 1,2
Horton, N E (Moseley, Toulouse) 1969 *I, F, S, W,* 1971 *I, F, S,* 1974 *S,* 1975 *W,* 1977 *S, I, F, W,* 1978 *F, W,* 1979 *S, I, F, W,* 1980 *I*
Hosen, R W (Bristol, Northampton) 1963 *NZ* 1,2, *A,* 1964 *F, S,* 1967 *A, I, F, S, W*
Hosking, G R d'A (Devonport Services) 1949 *W, I, F, S,* 1950 *W*
Houghton, S (Runcorn) 1892 *I,* 1896 *W*
Howard, P D (O Millhillians) 1930 *W, I, F, S,* 1931 *W, I, S, F*
Hubbard, G C (Blackheath) 1892 *W, I*
Hubbard, J C (Harlequins) 1930 *S*
Hudson, A (Gloucester) 1906 *W, I, F,* 1908 *F, W, I, S,* 1910 *F*
Hughes, G E (Barrow) 1896 *S*
Hull, P A (Bristol, RAF) 1994 *SA* 1,2, *R, C*
Hulme, F C (Birkenhead Park) 1903 *W, I,* 1905 *W, I*
Hunt, J T (Manchester) 1882 *I, S,* 1884 *W*
Hunt, R (Manchester) 1880 *I,* 1881 *W, S,* 1882 *I*
Hunt, W H (Manchester) 1876 *S,* 1877 *I, S,* 1878 *I*
Hunter, I (Northampton) 1992 *C,* 1993 *F, W,* 1994 *F, W,* 1995 *[WS, F]*
Huntsman, R P (Headingley) 1985 *NZ* 1,2
Hurst, A C B (Wasps) 1962 *S*
Huskisson, T F (OMTs) 1937 *W, I, S,* 1938 *W, I,* 1939 *W, I, S*
Hutchinson, F (Headingley) 1909 *F, I, S*
Hutchinson, J E (Durham City) 1906 *I*
Hutchinson, W C (RIE Coll) 1876 *S,* 1877 *I*
Hutchinson, W H H (Hull) 1875 *I,* 1876 *I*
Huth, H (Huddersfield) 1879 *S*
Hyde, J P (Northampton) 1950 *F, S*
Hynes, W B (United Services, RN) 1912 *F*

Ibbitson, E D (Headingley) 1909 *W, F, I, S*
Imrie, H M (Durham City) 1906 *NZ,* 1907 *I*
Inglis, R E (Blackheath) 1886 *W, I, S*
Irvin, S H (Devonport A) 1905 *W*
Isherwood, F W (Ravenscourt Park) 1872 *S*

Jackett, E J (Leicester, Falmouth) 1905 *NZ,* 1906 *W, I, S, F, SA,* 1907 *W, I, S,* 1909 *W, F, I, S*
Jackson, A H (Blackheath) 1878 *I,* 1880 *I*
Jackson, B S (Broughton Park) 1970 *S* (R), *F*
Jackson, P B (Coventry) 1956 *W, I, F,* 1957 *W, I, F, S,* 1958 *W, A, F, S,* 1959 *W, I, F, S,* 1961 *S,* 1963 *W, I, F, S*
Jackson, W J (Halifax) 1894 *S*
Jacob, F (Cambridge U) 1897 *W, I, S,* 1898 *I, S, W,* 1899 *W, I*
Jacob, H P (Blackheath) 1924 *W, I, F, S,* 1930 *F*
Jacob, P G (Blackheath) 1898 *I*
Jacobs, C R (Northampton) 1956 *W, I, S, F,* 1957 *W, I, F, S,* 1958 *W, A, I, F, S,* 1960 *W, I, F, S,* 1961 *SA, W, I, F, S,* 1963 *NZ* 1,2, *A,* 1964 *W, I, F, S*
Jago, R A (Devonport A) 1906 *W, I, SA,* 1907 *W, I*

Janion, J P A G (Bedford) 1971 *W, I, F, S* (2[1C]), *P,* 1972 *W, S, SA,* 1973 *A,* 1975 *A* 1,2
Jarman, J W (Bristol) 1900 *W*
Jeavons, N C (Moseley) 1981 *S, I, F, Arg* 1,2, 1982 *A, S, I, F, W,* 1983 *F, W, S, I*
Jeeps, R E G (Northampton) 1956 *W,* 1957 *W, I, F, S,* 1958 *W, A, I, F, S,* 1959 *I,* 1960 *W, I, F, S,* 1961 *SA, W, I, F, S,* 1962 *W, I, F, S*
Jeffery, G L (Blackheath) 1886 *W, I, S,* 1887 *W, I, S*
Jennins, C R (Waterloo) 1967 *A, I, F*
Jewitt, J (Hartlepool R) 1902 *W*
Johns, W A (Gloucester) 1909 *W, F, I, S,* 1910 *W, I, F*
Johnson, M O (Leicester) 1993 *F, NZ,* 1994 *S, I, F, W, R, C,* 1995 *I, F, W, S, [Arg, It, WS, A, NZ, F], SA, WS,* 1996 *F, W, S, I*
Johnston, W R (Bristol) 1910 *W, I, S,* 1912 *W, I, S, F,* 1913 *SA, W, F, I, S,* 1914 *W, I, S, F*
Jones, F P (New Brighton) 1893 *S*
Jones, H A (Barnstaple) 1950 *W, I, F*
Jorden, A M (Cambridge U, Blackheath, Bedford) 1970 *F,* 1973 *I, F, S,* 1974 *F,* 1975 *W, S*
Jowett, D (Heckmondwike) 1889 *M,* 1890 *S, I,* 1891 *W, I, S*
Judd, P E (Coventry) 1962 *W, I, F, S,* 1963 *S, NZ* 1,2, *A,* 1964 *NZ,* 1965 *I, F, S,* 1966 *W, I, F, S,* 1967 *A, I, F, S, W, NZ*

Kayll, H E (Sunderland) 1878 *S*
Keeling, J H (Guy's Hospital) 1948 *A, W*
Keen, B W (Newcastle U) 1968 *W, I, F, S*
Keeton, G H (Leicester) 1904 *W, I, S*
Kelly, G A (Bedford) 1947 *W, I, S,* 1948 *W*
Kelly, T S (London Devonians) 1906 *W, I, S, F, SA,* 1907 *F, W, I, S,* 1908 *F, I, S*
Kemble, A T (Liverpool) 1885 *W, I,* 1887 *I*
Kemp, D T (Blackheath) 1935 *W*
Kemp, T A (Richmond) 1937 *W, I,* 1939 *S,* 1948 *A, W*
Kendall, P D (Birkenhead Park) 1901 *S,* 1902 *W,* 1903 *S*
Kendall-Carpenter, J MacG K (Oxford U, Bath) 1949 *I, F, S,* 1950 *W, I, F, S,* 1951 *I, F, S,* 1952 *SA, W, S, F,* 1953 *W, I, F, S,* 1954 *W, NZ, I, F*
Kendrew, D A (Leicester) 1930 *W, I,* 1933 *I, S,* 1934 *S,* 1935 *W, I,* 1936 *NZ, W, I*
Kennedy, R D (Camborne S of M) 1949 *I, F, S*
Kent, C P (Rosslyn Park) 1977 *S, I, F, W,* 1978 *F* (R)
Kent, T (Salford) 1891 *W, I, S,* 1892 *W, I, S*
Kershaw, C A (United Services, RN) 1920 *W, F, I, S,* 1921 *W, I, S, F,* 1922 *W, I, F, S,* 1923 *W, I, S, F*
Kewley, E (Liverpool) 1874 *S,* 1875 *S,* 1876 *I, S,* 1877 *I, S,* 1878 *S*
Kewney, A L (Leicester) 1906 *W, I, S, F,* 1909 *A, W, F, I, S,* 1911 *W, F, I, S,* 1912 *I, S,* 1913 *SA*
Key, A (O Cranleighans) 1930 *I,* 1933 *W*
Keyworth, M (Swansea) 1976 *A, W, S, I*
Kilner, B (Wakefield T) 1880 *I*
Kindersley, R S (Exeter) 1883 *W,* 1884 *S,* 1885 *W*
King, I (Harrogate) 1954 *W, NZ, I*
King, J A (Headingley) 1911 *W, F, I, S,* 1912 *W, I, S,* 1913 *SA, W, F, I, S*
King, Q E M A (Army) 1921 *S*
Kingston, P (Gloucester) 1975 *A* 1,2, 1979 *I, F, W*
Kitching, A E (Blackheath) 1913 *I*
Kittermaster, H J (Harlequins) 1925 *NZ, W, I,* 1926 *W, I, F, S*
Knight, F (Plymouth) 1909 *A*
Knight, P M (Bristol) 1972 *F, S, SA*
Knowles, E (Millom) 1896 *S,* 1897 *S*
Knowles, T C (Birkenhead Park) 1931 *S*
Krige, J A (Guy's Hospital) 1920 *W*

Labuschagne, N A (Harlequins, Guy's Hospital) 1953 *W,* 1955 *W, I, F, S*
Lagden, R O (Richmond) 1911 *S*
Laird, H C C (Harlequins) 1927 *W, I, S,* 1928 *A, W, I, F, S,* 1929 *W, I*
Lambert, D (Harlequins) 1907 *F,* 1908 *F, W, S,* 1911 *W, F, I*
Lampkowski, M S (Headingley) 1976 *A, W, S, I*
Lapage, W N (United Services, RN) 1908 *F, W, I, S*
Larter, P J (Northampton, RAF) 1967 *A, NZ,* 1968 *W, I, F, S,* 1969 *I, F, S, W, SA,* 1970 *I, W, F, S,* 1971 *W, I, F, S* (2[1C]), *P,* 1972 *SA,* 1973 *NZ* 1, *W*
Law, A F (Richmond) 1877 *S*
Law, D E (Birkenhead Park) 1927 *I*
Lawrence, Hon H A (Richmond) 1873 *S,* 1874 *S,* 1875 *I, S*

Lawrie, P W (Leicester) 1910 *S*, 1911 *S*
Lawson, R G (Workington) 1925 *I*
Lawson, T M (Workington) 1928 *A, W*
Leadbetter, M M (Broughton Park) 1970 *F*
Leadbetter, V H (Edinburgh Wands) 1954 *S, F*
Leake, W R M (Harlequins) 1891 *W, I, S*
Leather, G (Liverpool) 1907 *I*
Lee, F H (Marlborough N) 1876 *S*, 1877 *I*
Lee, H (Blackheath) 1907 *F*
Le Fleming, J (Blackheath) 1887 *W*
Leonard, J (Saracens, Harlequins) 1990 *Arg* 1,2,3, 1991 *W, S, I, F, Fj, A, [NZ, It, US, F, S, A]*, 1992 *S, I, F, W, C, SA*, 1993 *F, W, S, I, NZ*, 1994 *S, I, F, W, SA* 1,2, *R, C*, 1995 *I, F, W, S, [Arg, It, A, NZ, F]*, *SA, WS*, 1996 *F, W, S, I*
Leslie-Jones, F A (Richmond) 1895 *W, I*
Lewis, A O (Bath) 1952 *SA, W, S, I, F*, 1953 *W, I, F, S*, 1954 *F*
Leyland, R (Waterloo) 1935 *W, I, S*
Linnett, M S (Moseley) 1989 *Fj*
Livesay, R O'H (Blackheath) 1898 *W*, 1899 *W*
Lloyd, R H (Harlequins) 1967 *NZ*, 1968 *W, I, F, S*
Locke, H M (Birkenhead Park) 1923 *S, F*, 1924 *W, F, S*, 1925 *W, I, S, F*, 1927 *W, I, S*
Lockwood, R E (Heckmondwike) 1887 *W, I, S*, 1889 *M*, 1891 *W, I, S*, 1892 *W, I, S*, 1893 *W, I*, 1894 *W, I*
Login, S H M (RN Coll) 1876 *I*
Lohden, F C (Blackheath) 1893 *W*
Longland, R J (Northampton) 1932 *S*, 1933 *W, S*, 1934 *W, I, S*, 1935 *W, I, S*, 1936 *NZ, W, I, S*, 1937 *W, I, S*, 1938 *W, I, S*
Lowe, C N (Cambridge U, Blackheath) 1913 *SA, W, F, I, S*, 1914 *W, I, S, F*, 1920 *W, F, I, S*, 1921 *W, I, S, F*, 1922 *W, I, F, S*, 1923 *W, I, S, F*
Lowrie, F (Wakefield T) 1889 *M*, 1890 *W*
Lowry, W M (Birkenhead Park) 1920 *F*
Lozowski, R A P (Wasps) 1984 *A*
Luddington, W G E (Devonport Services) 1923 *W, I, S, F*, 1924 *W, I, F, S*, 1925 *W, I, S, F*, 1926 *W*
Luscombe, F (Gipsies) 1872 *S*, 1873 *S*, 1875 *I, S*, 1876 *I, S*
Luscombe, J H (Gipsies) 1871 *S*
Luxmoore, A F C C (Richmond) 1900 *S*, 1901 *W*
Luya, H F (Waterloo, Headingley) 1948 *W, I, S, F*, 1949 *W*
Lyon, A (Liverpool) 1871 *S*
Lyon, G H d'O (United Services, RN) 1908 *S*, 1909 *A*

McCanlis, M A (Gloucester) 1931 *W, I*
McFadyean, C W (Moseley) 1966 *I, F, S*, 1967 *A, I, F, S, W, NZ*, 1968 *W, I*
MacIlwaine, A H (United Services, Hull & E Riding) 1912 *W, I, S, F*, 1920 *I*
Mackie, O G (Wakefield T, Cambridge U) 1897 *S*, 1898 *I*
Mackinlay, J E H (St George's Hospital) 1872 *S*, 1873 *S*, 1875 *I*
MacLaren, W (Manchester) 1871 *S*
MacLennan, R R F (OMTs) 1925 *I, S, F*
McLeod, N F (RIE Coll) 1879 *S, I*
Madge, R J P (Exeter) 1948 *A, W, I, S*
Malir, F W S (Otley) 1930 *W, I, S*
Mallett, J A (Bath) 1995 *[WS (R)]*
Mangles, R H (Richmond) 1897 *W, I*
Manley, D C (Exeter) 1963 *W, I, F, S*
Mann, W E (United Services, Army) 1911 *W, F, I*
Mantell, N D (Rosslyn Park) 1975 *A* 1
Markendale, E T (Manchester R) 1880 *I*
Marques, R W D (Cambridge U, Harlequins) 1956 *W, I, S, F*, 1957 *W, I, F, S*, 1958 *W, A, I, F, S*, 1959 *W, I, F, S*, 1960 *W, I, F, S*, 1961 *SA, W*
Marquis, J C (Birkenhead Park) 1900 *I, S*
Marriott, C J B (Blackheath) 1884 *W, I, S*, 1886 *W, I, S*, 1887 *I*
Marriott, E E (Manchester) 1876 *I*
Marriott, V R (Harlequins) 1963 *NZ* 1,2, *A*, 1964 *NZ*
Marsden, G H (Morley) 1900 *W, I, S*
Marsh, H (RIE Coll) 1873 *S*
Marsh, J (Swinton) 1892 *I*
Marshall, H (Blackheath) 1893 *W*
Marshall, M W (Blackheath) 1873 *S*, 1874 *S*, 1875 *I, S*, 1876 *I, S*, 1877 *I, S*, 1878 *S, I*
Marshall, R M (Oxford U) 1938 *I, S*, 1939 *W, I, S*
Martin, C R (Bath) 1985 *F, S, I, W*
Martin, N O (Harlequins) 1972 *F* (R)
Martindale, S A (Kendal) 1929 *F*
Massey, E J (Leicester) 1925 *W, I, S*
Mathias, J L (Bristol) 1905 *W, I, S, NZ*
Matters, J C (RNE Coll) 1899 *S*

Matthews, J R C (Harlequins) 1949 *F, S*, 1950 *I, F, S*, 1952 *SA, W, S, I, F*
Maud, P (Blackheath) 1893 *W, I*
Maxwell, A W (New Brighton, Headingley) 1975 *A* 1, 1976 *A, W, S, I, F*, 1978 *F*
Maxwell-Hyslop, J E (Oxford U) 1922 *I, F, S*
Maynard, A F (Cambridge U) 1914 *W, I, S*
Meikle, G W C (Waterloo) 1934 *W, I, S*
Meikle, S S C (Waterloo) 1929 *S*
Mellish, F W (Blackheath) 1920 *W, F, I, S*, 1921 *W, I*
Melville, N D (Wasps) 1984 *A*, 1985 *I, W, NZ* 1,2, 1986 *W, S, I, F*, 1988 *F, W, S, I* 1
Merriam, L P B (Blackheath) 1920 *W, F*
Michell, A T (Oxford U) 1875 *I, S*, 1876 *I*
Middleton, B B (Birkenhead Park) 1882 *I*, 1883 *I*
Middleton, J A (Richmond) 1922 *S*
Miles, J H (Leicester) 1903 *W*
Millett, H (Richmond) 1920 *F*
Mills, F W (Marlborough N) 1872 *S*, 1873 *S*
Mills, S G F (Gloucester) 1981 *Arg* 1,2, 1983 *W*, 1984 *SA* 1, *A*
Mills, W A (Devonport A) 1906 *W, I, S, F, SA*, 1907 *F, W, I, S*, 1908 *F, W*
Milman, D L K (Bedford) 1937 *W*, 1938 *W, I, S*
Milton, C H (Camborne S of M) 1906 *I*
Milton, J G (Camborne S of M) 1904 *W, I, S*, 1905 *S*, 1907 *I*
Milton, W H (Marlborough N) 1874 *S*, 1875 *I*
Mitchell, F (Blackheath) 1895 *W, I, S*, 1896 *W, I, S*
Mitchell, W G (Richmond) 1890 *W, S, I*, 1891 *W, I, S*, 1893 *S*
Mobbs, E R (Northampton) 1909 *A, W, F, I, S*, 1910 *I, F*
Moberley, W O (Ravenscourt Park) 1872 *S*
Moore, B C (Nottingham, Harlequins) 1987 *S, [A, J, W]*, 1988 *F, W, S, I* 1,2, *A* 1, 2, *Fj, A*, 1989 *S, I, F, W, R, Fj*, 1990 *I, F, W, S, Arg* 1,2, 1991 *W, S, I, F, Fj, A, [NZ, It, F, S, A]*, 1992 *S, I, F, W, SA*, 1993 *F, W, S, I, NZ*, 1994 *S, I, F, W, SA* 1,2, *R, C*, 1995 *I, F, W, S, [Arg, It, WS (R), A, NZ, F]*
Moore, E J (Blackheath) 1883 *I, S*
Moore, N J N H (Bristol) 1904 *W, I, S*
Moore, P B C (Blackheath) 1951 *W*
Moore, W K T (Leicester) 1947 *W, I*, 1949 *F, S*, 1950 *I, F, S*
Mordell, R J (Rosslyn Park) 1978 *W*
Morfitt, S (W Hartlepool) 1894 *W, I, S*, 1896 *W, I, S*
Morgan, J R (Hawick) 1920 *W*
Morgan, W G D (Medicals, Newcastle) 1960 *W, I, F, S*, 1961 *SA, W, I, F, S*
Morley, A J (Bristol) 1972 *SA*, 1973 *NZ* 1, *W, I*, 1975 *S, A* 1,2
Morris, A D W (United Services, RN) 1909 *A, W, F*
Morris, C D (Liverpool St Helens, Orrell) 1988 *A*, 1989 *S, I, F, W*, 1992 *S, I, F, W, C, SA*, 1993 *F, W, S, I*, 1994 *F, W, SA* 1,2, *R*, 1995 *S* (t), *[Arg, WS, A, NZ, F]*
Morrison, P H (Cambridge U) 1890 *W, S, I*, 1891 *I*
Morse, S (Marlborough N) 1873 *S*, 1874 *S*, 1875 *S*
Mortimer, W (Marlborough N) 1899 *W*
Morton, H J S (Blackheath) 1909 *I, S*, 1910 *W, I*
Moss, F (Broughton) 1885 *W, I*, 1886 *W*
Mullins, A R (Harlequins) 1989 *Fj*
Mycock, J (Sale) 1947 *W, I, S, F*, 1948 *A*
Myers, E (Bradford) 1920 *I, S*, 1921 *W, I*, 1922 *W, I, F, S*, 1923 *W, I, S, F*, 1924 *W, I, F, S*, 1925 *S, F*
Myers, H (Keighley) 1898 *I*

Nanson, W M B (Carlisle) 1907 *F, W*
Nash, E H (Richmond) 1875 *I*
Neale, B A (Rosslyn Park) 1951 *I, F, S*
Neale, M E (Blackheath) 1912 *F*
Neame, S (O Cheltonians) 1879 *S, I*, 1880 *I, S*
Neary, A (Broughton Park) 1971 *W, I, F, S* (2[1C]), *P*, 1972 *W, I, F, S, SA*, 1973 *NZ* 1, *W, I, F, S, NZ* 2, *A*, 1974 *S, I, F, W*, 1975 *I, F, W, NZ, S, A* 1, 1976 *A, W, S, I, F*, 1977 *I*, 1978 *F* (R), 1979 *S, I, F, W, NZ*, 1980 *I, F, W, S*
Nelmes, B G (Cardiff) 1975 *A* 1,2, 1978 *W, S, I, NZ*
Newbold, C J (Blackheath) 1904 *W, I, S*, 1905 *W, I, S*
Newman, S C (Oxford U) 1947 *F, I*, 1948 *A, W*
Newton, A W (Blackheath) 1907 *S*
Newton, P A (Blackheath) 1882 *S*
Newton-Thompson, J O (Oxford U) 1947 *S, F*
Nichol, W (Brighouse R) 1892 *W, S*
Nicholas, P L (Exeter) 1902 *W*
Nicholson, B E (Harlequins) 1938 *W, I*
Nicholson, E S (Leicester) 1935 *W, I, S*, 1936 *NZ, W, I*
Nicholson, E T (Birkenhead Park) 1900 *W, I*

Richardson, J V (Birkenhead Park) 1928 *A, W, I, F, S*
Richardson, W R (Manchester) 1881 *I*
Rickards, C H (Gipsies) 1873 *S*
Rimmer, G (Waterloo) 1949 *W, I*, 1950 *W*, 1951 *W, I, F*, 1952 *SA, W*, 1954 *W, NZ, I, S*
Rimmer, L I (Bath) 1961 *SA, W, I, F, S*
Ripley, A G (Rosslyn Park) 1972 *W, I, F, S, SA*, 1973 *NZ* 1, *W, I, F, S, NZ* 2, *A*, 1974 *S, I, F, W*, 1975 *I, F, S, A* 1,2, 1976 *A, W, S*
Risman, A B W (Loughborough Coll) 1959 *W, I, F, S*, 1961 *SA, W, I, F*
Ritson, J A S (Northern) 1910 *F, S*, 1912 *F*, 1913 *SA, W, F, I, S*
Rittson-Thomas, G C (Oxford U) 1951 *W, I, F*
Robbins, G L (Coventry) 1986 *W, S*
Robbins, P G D (Oxford U, Moseley, Coventry) 1956 *W, I, S, F*, 1957 *W, I, F, S*, 1958 *W, A, I, S*, 1960 *W, I, F, S*, 1961 *SA, W*, 1962 *S*
Roberts, A D (Northern) 1911 *W, F, I, S*, 1912 *I, S, F*, 1914 *I*
Roberts, E W (RNE Coll) 1901 *W, I*, 1905 *NZ*, 1906 *W, I*, 1907 *S*
Roberts, G D (Harlequins) 1907 *S*, 1908 *F, W*
Roberts, J (Sale) 1960 *W, I, F, S*, 1961 *SA, W, I, F, S*, 1962 *W, I, F, S*, 1963 *W, I, F, S*, 1964 *NZ*
Roberts, R S (Coventry) 1932 *I*
Roberts, S (Swinton) 1887 *W, I*
Roberts, V G (Penryn, Harlequins) 1947 *F*, 1949 *W, I, F, S*, 1950 *I, F, S*, 1951 *W, I, F, S*, 1956 *W, I, S, F*
Robertshaw, A R (Bradford) 1886 *W, I, S*, 1887 *W, S*
Robinson, A (Blackheath) 1889 *M*, 1890 *W, S, I*
Robinson, E T (Coventry) 1954 *S*, 1961 *I, F, S*
Robinson, G C (Percy Park) 1897 *I, S*, 1898 *I*, 1899 *W*, 1900 *I, S*, 1901 *I, S*
Robinson, J J (Headingley) 1893 *S*, 1902 *W, I, S*
Robinson, R A (Bath) 1988 *A* 2, *Fj, A*, 1989 *S, I, F, W*, 1995 *SA*
Robson, A (Northern) 1924 *W, I, F, S*, 1926 *W*
Robson, M (Oxford U) 1930 *W, I, F, S*
Rodber, T A K (Army, Northampton) 1992 *S, I*, 1993 *NZ*, 1994 *I, F, W, SA* 1,2, *R, C*, 1995 *I, F, W, S, [Arg, It, WS* (R), *A, NZ, F], SA, WS*, 1996 *W, S* (R), *I* (t)
Rogers, D P (Bedford) 1961 *I, F, S*, 1962 *W, I, F*, 1963 *W, I, F, S, NZ* 1,2, *A*, 1964 *NZ, W, I, F, S*, 1965 *W, I, F, S*, 1966 *W, I, F, S*, 1967 *A, S, W, NZ*, 1969 *I, F, S, W*
Rogers, J H (Moseley) 1890 *W, S, I*, 1891 *S*
Rogers, W L Y (Blackheath) 1905 *W, I*
Rollitt, D M (Bristol) 1967 *I, F, S, W*, 1969 *I, F, S, W*, 1975 *S, A* 1,2
Roncoroni, A D S (West Herts, Richmond) 1933 *W, I, S*
Rose, W M H (Cambridge U, Coventry, Harlequins) 1981 *I, F*, 1982 *A, S, I*, 1987 *I, F, W, S, [A]*
Rossborough, P A (Coventry) 1971 *W*, 1973 *NZ* 2, *A*, 1974 *S, I*, 1975 *I, F*
Rosser, D W A (Wasps) 1965 *W, I, F, S*, 1966 *W*
Rotherham, Alan (Richmond) 1883 *W, S*, 1884 *W, S*, 1885 *W, I*, 1886 *W, I, S*, 1887 *W, I, S*
Rotherham, Arthur (Richmond) 1898 *S, W*, 1899 *W, I, S*
Roughley, D (Liverpool) 1973 *A*, 1974 *S, I*
Rowell, R E (Leicester) 1964 *W*, 1965 *W*
Rowley, A J (Coventry) 1932 *SA*
Rowley, H C (Manchester) 1879 *S, I*, 1880 *I, S*, 1881 *I, W, S*, 1882 *I, S*
Rowntree, G C (Leicester) 1995 *S* (t), *[It, WS], WS*, 1996 *F, W, S, I*
Royds, P M R (Blackheath) 1898 *S, W*, 1899 *W*
Royle, A V (Broughton R) 1889 *M*
Rudd, E L (Liverpool) 1965 *W, I, S*, 1966 *W, I, S*
Russell, R F (Leicester) 1905 *NZ*
Rutherford, D (Percy Park, Gloucester) 1960 *W, I, F, S*, 1961 *SA*, 1965 *W, I, F, S*, 1966 *W, I, F, S*, 1967 *NZ*
Ryalls, H J (New Brighton) 1885 *W, I*
Ryan, D (Wasps) 1990 *Arg* 1,2, 1992 *C*
Ryan, P H (Richmond) 1955 *W, I*

Sadler, E H (Army) 1933 *I, S*
Sagar, J W (Cambridge U) 1901 *W, I*
Salmon, J L B (Harlequins) 1985 *NZ* 1,2, 1986 *W, S*, 1987 *I, F, W, S, [A, J, US, W]*
Sample, C H (Cambridge U) 1884 *I*, 1885 *I*, 1886 *S*
Sanders, D L (Harlequins) 1954 *W, NZ, I, S, F*, 1956 *W, I, S, F*
Sanders, F W (Plymouth A) 1923 *I, S, F*
Sandford, J R P (Marlborough N) 1906 *I*

Sangwin, R D (Hull and E Riding) 1964 *NZ, W*
Sargent, G A F (Gloucester) 1981 *I* (R)
Savage, K F (Northampton) 1966 *W, I, F, S*, 1967 *A, I, F, S, W, NZ*, 1968 *W, F, S*
Sawyer, C M (Broughton) 1880 *S*, 1881 *I*
Saxby, L E (Gloucester) 1932 *SA, W*
Schofield, J W (Manchester) 1880 *I*
Scholfield, J A (Preston Grasshoppers) 1911 *W*
Schwarz, R O (Richmond) 1899 *S*, 1901 *W, I*
Scorfield, E S (Percy Park) 1910 *F*
Scott, C T (Blackheath) 1900 *W, I*, 1901 *W, I*
Scott, E K (St Mary's Hospital, Redruth) 1947 *W*, 1948 *A, W, I, S*
Scott, F S (Bristol) 1907 *W*
Scott, H (Manchester) 1955 *F*
Scott, J P (Rosslyn Park, Cardiff) 1978 *F, W, S, I, NZ*, 1979 *S* (R), *I, F, W, NZ*, 1980 *I, F, W, S*, 1981 *W, S, I, F, Arg* 1,2, 1982 *I, F, W*, 1983 *F, W, S, I, NZ*, 1984 *S, I, F, W, SA* 1,2
Scott, J S M (Oxford U) 1958 *F*
Scott, M T (Cambridge U) 1887 *I*, 1890 *S, I*
Scott, W M (Cambridge U) 1889 *M*
Seddon, R L (Broughton R) 1887 *W, I, S*
Sellar, K A (United Services, RN) 1927 *W, I, S*, 1928 *A, W, I, F*
Sever, H S (Sale) 1936 *NZ, W, I, S*, 1937 *W, I, S*, 1938 *W, I, S*
Shackleton, I R (Cambridge U) 1969 *SA*, 1970 *I, W, S*
Sharp, R A W (Oxford U, Wasps, Redruth) 1960 *W, I, F, S*, 1961 *I, F*, 1962 *W, I, F*, 1963 *W, I, F, S*, 1967 *A*
Shaw, C H (Moseley) 1906 *S, SA*, 1907 *F, W, I, S*
Shaw, F (Cleckheaton) 1898 *I*
Shaw, J F (RNE Coll) 1898 *S, W*
Sheppard, A (Bristol) 1981 *W* (R), 1985 *W*
Sherrard, C W (Blackheath) 1871 *S*, 1872 *S*
Sherriff, G A (Saracens) 1966 *S*, 1967 *A, NZ*
Shewring, H E (Bristol) 1905 *I, NZ*, 1906 *W, S, F, SA*, 1907 *F, W, I, S*
Shooter, J H (Morley) 1899 *I, S*, 1900 *I, S*
Shuttleworth, D W (Headingley) 1951 *S*, 1953 *S*
Sibree, H J H (Harlequins) 1908 *F*, 1909 *I, S*
Silk, N (Harlequins) 1965 *W, I, F, S*
Simms, K G (Cambridge U, Liverpool, Wasps) 1985 *R, F, S, I, W*, 1986 *I, F*, 1987 *I, F, W, [A, J, W]*, 1988 *F, W*
Simpson, C P (Harlequins) 1965 *W*
Simpson, P D (Bath) 1983 *NZ*, 1984 *S*, 1987 *I*
Simpson, T (Rockcliff) 1902 *S*, 1903 *W, I, S*, 1904 *I, S*, 1905 *I, S*, 1906 *S, SA*, 1909 *F*
Skinner, M G (Harlequins) 1988 *F, W, S, I* 1,2, 1989 *Fj*, 1990 *I, F, W, S, Arg* 1,2, 1991 *Fj* (R), *[US, F, S, A]*, 1992 *S, I, F, W*
Sladen, G M (United Services, RN) 1929 *W, I, S*
Sleightholme, J M (Bath) 1996 *F, W, S, I*
Slemen, M A C (Liverpool) 1976 *I, F*, 1977 *S, I, F, W*, 1978 *F, W, S, I, NZ*, 1979 *S, I, F, W, NZ*, 1980 *I, F, W, S*, 1981 *W, S, I, F*, 1982 *A, S, I, F, W*, 1983 *NZ*, 1984 *S*
Slocock, L A N (Liverpool) 1907 *F, W, I, S*, 1908 *F, W, I, S*
Slow, C F (Leicester) 1934 *S*
Small, H D (Oxford U) 1950 *W, I, F, S*
Smallwood, A M (Leicester) 1920 *F, I*, 1921 *W, I, S, F*, 1922 *I, S*, 1923 *W, I, S, F*, 1925 *I, S*
Smart, C E (Newport) 1979 *F, W, NZ*, 1981 *S, I, F, Arg* 1,2, 1982 *A, S, I, F, W*, 1983 *F, W, S, I*
Smart, S E J (Gloucester) 1913 *SA, W, F, I, S*, 1914 *W, I, S, F*, 1920 *W, I, S*
Smeddle, R W (Cambridge U) 1929 *W, I, S*, 1931 *F*
Smith, C C (Gloucester) 1901 *W*
Smith, D F (Richmond) 1910 *W, I*
Smith, J V (Cambridge U, Rosslyn Park) 1950 *W, I, F, S*
Smith, K (Roundhay) 1974 *F, W*, 1975 *W, S*
Smith, M J K (Oxford U) 1956 *W*
Smith, S J (Sale) 1973 *I, F, S, A*, 1974 *I, F*, 1975 *W* (R), 1976 *F*, 1977 *F* (R), 1979 *NZ*, 1980 *I, F, W, S*, 1981 *W, S, I, F, Arg* 1,2, 1982 *A, S, I, F, W*, 1983 *F, W, S*
Smith, S R (Richmond) 1959 *W, F, S*, 1964 *F, S*
Smith, S T (Wasps) 1985 *R, F, S, I, W, NZ* 1,2, 1986 *W, S*
Smith, T H (Northampton) 1951 *W*
Soane, F (Bath) 1893 *S*, 1894 *W, I, S*
Sobey, W H (O Millhillians) 1930 *W, F, S*, 1932 *SA, W*
Solomon, B (Redruth) 1910 *W*
Sparks, R H W (Plymouth A) 1928 *I, F, S*, 1929 *W, I, S*, 1931 *I, S, F*
Speed, H (Castleford) 1894 *W, I, S*, 1896 *S*
Spence, F W (Birkenhead Park) 1890 *I*
Spencer, J (Harlequins) 1966 *W*

Spencer, J S (Cambridge U, Headingley) 1969 *I, F, S, W, SA,* 1970 *I, W, S, F,* 1971 *W, I, S* (2[1C]), *P*
Spong, R S (O Millhilians) 1929 *F,* 1930 *W, I, F, S,* 1931 *F,* 1932 *SA, W*
Spooner, R H (Liverpool) 1903 *W*
Springman, H H (Liverpool) 1879 *S,* 1887 *S*
Spurling, A (Blackheath) 1882 *I*
Spurling, N (Blackheath) 1886 *I, S,* 1887 *W*
Squires, P J (Harrogate) 1973 *F, S, NZ* 2, A, 1974 *S, I, F, W,* 1975 *I, F, W, S, A* 1,2, 1976 *A, W,* 1977 *S, I, F, W,* 1978 *F, W, S, I, NZ,* 1979 *S, I, F, W*
Stafford R C (Bedford) 1912 *W, I, S, F*
Stafford, W F H (RE) 1874 *S*
Stanbury, E (Plymouth A) 1926 *W, I, S,* 1927 *W, I, S, F,* 1928 *A, W, I, F, S,* 1929 *W, I, S, F*
Standing, G (Blackheath) 1883 *W, I*
Stanger-Leathes, C F (Northern) 1905 *I*
Stark, K J (O Alleynians) 1927 *W, I, S, F,* 1928 *A, W, I, F, S*
Starks, A (Castleford) 1896 *W, I*
Starmer-Smith, N C (Harlequins) 1969 *SA,* 1970 *I, W, S, F,* 1971 *S* (C), *P*
Start, S P (United Services, RN) 1907 *S*
Steeds, J H (Saracens) 1949 *F, S,* 1950 *I, F, S*
Steele-Bodger, M R (Cambridge U) 1947 *W, I, S, F,* 1948 *A, W, I, S, F*
Steinthal, F E (Ilkley) 1913 *W, F*
Stevens, C B (Penzance-Newlyn, Harlequins) 1969 *SA,* 1970 *I, W, S,* 1971 *P,* 1972 *W, I, F, S, SA,* 1973 *NZ* 1, *W, I, F, S, NZ* 2, A, 1974 *S, I, F, W,* 1975 *I, F, W, S*
Still, E R (Oxford U, Ravenscourt P) 1873 *S*
Stirling, R V (Leicester, RAF, Wasps) 1951 *W, I, F, S,* 1952 *SA, W, S, I, F,* 1953 *W, I, F, S,* 1954 *W, NZ, I, S, F*
Stoddart, A E (Blackheath) 1885 *W, I,* 1886 *W, I, S,* 1889 *M,* 1890 *W, I,* 1893 *W, S*
Stoddart, W B (Liverpool) 1897 *W, I, S*
Stokes, F (Blackheath) 1871 *S,* 1872 *S,* 1873 *S*
Stokes, L (Blackheath) 1875 *I,* 1876 *S,* 1877 *I, S,* 1878 *S,* 1879 *S, I,* 1880 *I, S,* 1881 *I, W, S*
Stone, F le S (Blackheath) 1914 *F*
Stoop, A D (Harlequins) 1905 *S,* 1906 *S, F, SA,* 1907 *F, W,* 1910 *W, I, S,* 1911 *W, F, I, S,* 1912 *W, S*
Stoop, F M (Harlequins) 1910 *S,* 1911 *F, I,* 1913 *SA*
Stout, F M (Richmond) 1897 *W, I,* 1898 *I, S, W,* 1899 *I, S,* 1903 *S,* 1904 *W, I, S,* 1905 *W, I, S*
Stout, P W (Richmond) 1898 *S, W,* 1899 *W, I, S*
Stringer, N C (Wasps) 1982 *A* (R), 1983 *NZ* (R), 1984 *SA* 1 (R), *A,* 1985 *R*
Strong, E L (Oxford U) 1884 *W, I, S*
Summerscales, G E (Durham City) 1905 *NZ*
Sutcliffe, J W (Heckmondwike) 1889 *M*
Swarbrick, D W (Oxford U) 1947 *W, I, F,* 1948 *A, W,* 1949 *I*
Swayne, D H (Oxford U) 1931 *W*
Swayne, J W R (Bridgwater) 1929 *W*
Swift, A H (Swansea) 1981 *Arg* 1,2, 1983 *F, W, S,* 1984 *SA* 2
Syddall, J P (Waterloo) 1982 *I,* 1984 *A*
Sykes, A R V (Blackheath) 1914 *F*
Sykes, F D (Northampton) 1955 *F, S,* 1963 *NZ* 2, A
Sykes, P W (Wasps) 1948 *F,* 1952 *S, I, F,* 1953 *W, I, F*
Syrett, R E (Wasps) 1958 *W, A, I, F,* 1960 *W, I, F, S,* 1962 *W, I, F*

Tallent, J A (Cambridge U, Blackheath) 1931 *S, F,* 1932 *SA, W,* 1935 *I*
Tanner, C C (Cambridge U, Gloucester) 1930 *S,* 1932 *SA, W, I, S*
Tarr, F N (Leicester) 1909 *A, W, F,* 1913 *S*
Tatham, W M (Oxford U) 1882 *S,* 1883 *W, I, S,* 1884 *W, I, S*
Taylor, A S (Blackheath) 1883 *W, I,* 1886 *W, I*
Taylor, E W (Rockcliff) 1892 *I,* 1893 *I,* 1894 *W, I, S,* 1895 *W, I, S,* 1896 *W, I,* 1897 *W, I, S,* 1899 *I*
Taylor, F (Leicester) 1920 *F, I*
Taylor, F M (Leicester) 1914 *W*
Taylor, H H (Blackheath) 1879 *S,* 1880 *S,* 1881 *I, W,* 1882 *S*
Taylor, J T (W Hartlepool) 1897 *I,* 1899 *I,* 1900 *I,* 1901 *W, I,* 1902 *W, I, S,* 1903 *W, I,* 1905 *S*
Taylor, P J (Northampton) 1955 *W, I,* 1962 *W, I, F, S*
Taylor, R B (Northampton) 1966 *W,* 1967 *I, F, S, W, NZ,* 1969 *F, S, W, SA,* 1970 *I, W, S, F,* 1971 *S* (2[1C])
Taylor, W J (Blackheath) 1928 *A, W, I, F, S*

Teague, M C (Gloucester, Moseley) 1985 *F* (R), *NZ* 1, 2, 1989 *S, I, F, W, R,* 1990 *F, W, S,* 1991 *W, S, I, F, Fj, A,* [*NZ, It, F, S, A*], 1992 *SA,* 1993 *F, W, S, I*
Teden, D E (Richmond) 1939 *W, I, S*
Teggin, A (Broughton R) 1884 *I,* 1885 *W,* 1886 *I, S,* 1887 *I, S*
Tetley, T S (Bradford) 1876 *S*
Thomas, C (Barnstaple) 1895 *W, I, S,* 1899 *I*
Thompson, P H (Headingley, Waterloo) 1956 *W, I, S, F,* 1957 *W, I, F, S,* 1958 *W, A, I, F, S,* 1959 *W, I, F, S*
Thomson, G T (Halifax) 1878 *S,* 1882 *I, S,* 1883 *W, I, S,* 1884 *I, S,* 1885 *I*
Thomson, W B (Blackheath) 1892 *W,* 1895 *W, I, S*
Thorne, J D (Bristol) 1963 *W, I, F*
Tindall, V R (Liverpool U) 1951 *W, I, F, S*
Tobin, F (Liverpool) 1871 *S*
Todd, A F (Blackheath) 1900 *I, S*
Todd, R (Manchester) 1877 *S*
Toft, H B (Waterloo) 1936 *S,* 1937 *W, I, S,* 1938 *W, I, S,* 1939 *W, I, S*
Toothill, J T (Bradford) 1890 *S, I,* 1891 *W, I,* 1892 *W, I, S,* 1893 *W, I, S,* 1894 *W, I*
Tosswill, L R (Exeter) 1902 *W, I, S*
Touzel, C J C (Liverpool) 1877 *I, S*
Towell, A C (Bedford) 1948 *F,* 1951 *S*
Travers, B H (Harlequins) 1947 *W, I,* 1948 *A, W,* 1949 *F, S*
Treadwell, W T (Wasps) 1966 *I, F, S*
Trick, D M (Bath) 1983 *I,* 1984 *SA* 1
Tristram, H B (Oxford U) 1883 *S,* 1884 *W, S,* 1885 *W,* 1887 *S*
Troop, C L (Aldershot S) 1933 *I, S*
Tucker, J S (Bristol) 1922 *W,* 1925 *NZ, W, I, S, F,* 1926 *W, I, F, S,* 1927 *W, I, S, F,* 1928 *A, W, I, F, S,* 1929 *W, I, F,* 1930 *W, I, F, S,* 1931 *W*
Tucker, W E (Blackheath) 1894 *W, I,* 1895 *W, I, S*
Tucker, W E (Blackheath) 1926 *I,* 1930 *W, I*
Turner, D P (Richmond) 1871 *S,* 1872 *S,* 1873 *S,* 1874 *S,* 1875 *I, S*
Turner, E B (St George's Hospital) 1876 *I,* 1877 *I,* 1878 *I*
Turner, G R (St George's Hospital) 1876 *S*
Turner, H J C (Manchester) 1871 *S*
Turner, M F (Blackheath) 1948 *S, F*
Turquand-Young, D (Richmond) 1928 *A, W,* 1929 *I, S, F*
Twynam, H T (Richmond) 1879 *I,* 1880 *I,* 1881 *W,* 1882 *I,* 1883 *I,* 1884 *W, I, S*

Ubogu, V E (Bath) 1992 *C, SA,* 1993 *NZ,* 1994 *S, I, F, W, SA* 1,2, *R, C,* 1995 *I, F, W, S,* [*Arg, WS, A, NZ, F*], *SA*
Underwood, A M (Exeter) 1962 *W, I, F, S,* 1964 *I*
Underwood, R (Leicester, RAF) 1984 *I, F, W, A,* 1985 *R, F, S, I, W,* 1986 *W, I, F,* 1987 *I, F, W, S,* [*A, J, W*], 1988 *F, W, S, I* 1,2, *A* 1,2, *Fj, A,* 1989 *S, I, F, W, R, Fj,* 1990 *I, F, W, S, Arg* 3, 1991 *W, S, I, F, Fj, A,* [*NZ, It, US, F, S, A*], 1992 *S, I, F, W, SA,* 1993 *F, W, S, I, NZ,* 1994 *S, I, F, W, SA* 1,2, *R, C,* 1995 *I, F, W, S,* [*Arg, It, WS, A, NZ, F*], *SA, WS,* 1996 *F, W, S, I*
Underwood, T (Leicester) 1992 *C, SA,* 1993 *S, I, NZ,* 1994 *S, I, W, SA* 1,2, *R, C,* 1995 *I, W, S,* [*Arg, It, A, NZ*]
Unwin, E J (Rosslyn Park, Army) 1937 *S,* 1938 *W, I, S*
Unwin, G T (Blackheath) 1898 *S*
Uren, R (Waterloo) 1948 *I, S, F,* 1950 *I*
Uttley, R M (Gosforth) 1973 *I, F, S, NZ* 2, A, 1974 *I, F, W,* 1975 *F, W, S, A* 1,2, 1977 *S, I, F, W,* 1978 *NZ* 1979 *S,* 1980 *I, F, W, S*

Valentine J (Swinton) 1890 *W,* 1896 *W, I, S*
Vanderspar, C H R (Richmond) 1873 *S*
Van Ryneveld, C B (Oxford U) 1949 *W, I, F, S*
Varley, H (Liversedge) 1892 *S*
Vassall, H (Blackheath) 1881 *W, S,* 1882 *I, S,* 1883 *W*
Vassall, H H (Blackheath) 1908 *I*
Vaughan, D B (Headingley) 1948 *A, W, I, S,* 1949 *I, F, S,* 1950 *W*
Vaughan-Jones, A (Army) 1932 *I, S,* 1933 *W*
Verelst, C L (Liverpool) 1876 *I,* 1878 *I*
Vernon, G F (Blackheath) 1878 *S, I,* 1880 *I, S,* 1881 *I*
Vickery, G (Aberavon) 1905 *I*
Vivyan, E J (Devonport A) 1901 *W,* 1904 *W, I, S*
Voyce, A T (Gloucester) 1920 *I, S,* 1921 *W, I, S, F,* 1922 *W, I, F, S,* 1923 *W, I, S, F,* 1924 *W, I, F, S,* 1925 *NZ, W, I, S, F,* 1926 *W, I, F, S*

Wackett, J A S (Rosslyn Park) 1959 *W, I*

Wade, C G (Richmond) 1883 *W, I, S*, 1884 *W, S*, 1885 *W*, 1886 *W, I*
Wade, M R (Cambridge U) 1962 *W, I, F*
Wakefield, W W (Harlequins) 1920 *W, F, I, S*, 1921 *W, I, S, F*, 1922 *W, I, F, S*, 1923 *W, I, S, F*, 1924 *W, I, F, S*, 1925 *NZ, W, I, S, F*, 1926 *W, I, F, S*, 1927 *S, F*
Walker, G A (Blackheath) 1939 *W, I*
Walker, H W (Coventry) 1947 *W, I, S, F*, 1948 *A, W, I, S, F*
Walker, R (Manchester) 1874 *S*, 1875 *I*, 1876 *S*, 1879 *S*, 1880 *S*
Wallens, J N S (Waterloo) 1927 *F*
Walton, E J (Castleford) 1901 *W, I*, 1902 *I, S*
Walton, W (Castleford) 1894 *S*
Ward, G (Leicester) 1913 *W, F, S*, 1914 *W, I, S*
Ward, H (Bradford) 1895 *W*
Ward, J I (Richmond) 1881 *I*, 1882 *I*
Ward, J W (Castleford) 1896 *W, I, S*
Wardlow, C S (Northampton) 1969 *SA* (R), 1971 *W, I, F, S* (2[1C])
Warfield, P J (Rosslyn Park, Durham U) 1973 *NZ* 1, *W, I*, 1975 *I, F, S*
Warr, A L (Oxford OB) 1934 *W, I*
Watkins, J A (Gloucester) 1972 *SA*, 1973 *NZ* 1, *W, NZ* 2, *A*, 1975 *F, W*
Watkins, J K (United Services, RN) 1939 *W, I, S*
Watson, F B (United Services, RN) 1908 *S*, 1909 *S*
Watson, J H D (Blackheath) 1914 *W, S, F*
Watt, D E J (Bristol) 1967 *I, F, S, W*
Webb, C S H (Devonport Services, RN) 1932 *SA, W, I, S*, 1933 *W, I, S*, 1935 *S*, 1936 *NZ, W, I, S*
Webb, J M (Bristol, Bath) 1987 [*A* (R), *J, US, W*], 1988 *F, W, S, I* 1,2, *A* 1,2, *A*, 1989 *S, I, F, W*, 1991 *Fj, A, [NZ, It, F, S, A]*, 1992 *S, I, F, W, C, SA*, 1993 *F, W, S, I*
Webb, J W G (Northampton) 1926 *F, S*, 1929 *S*
Webb, R E (Coventry) 1967 *S, W, NZ*, 1968 *I, F, S*, 1969 *I, F, S, W*, 1972 *I, F*
Webb, St L H (Bedford) 1959 *W, I, F, S*
Webster, J G (Moseley) 1972 *W, I, SA*, 1973 *NZ* 1, *W, NZ* 2, 1974 *S, W*, 1975 *I, F, W*
Wedge, T G (St Ives) 1907 *F*, 1909 *W*
Weighill, R H G (RAF, Harlequins) 1947 *S, F*, 1948 *S, F*
Wells, C M (Cambridge U, Harlequins) 1893 *S*, 1894 *W, S*, 1896 *S*, 1897 *W, S*
West, B R (Loughborough Colls, Northampton) 1968 *W, I, F, S*, 1969 *SA*, 1970 *I, W, S*
West, R (Gloucester) 1995 [*WS*]
Weston, H T F (Northampton) 1901 *S*
Weston, L E (W of Scotland) 1972 *F, S*
Weston, M P (Richmond, Durham City) 1960 *W, I, F, S*, 1961 *SA, W, I, F, S*, 1962 *W, I, F*, 1963 *W, I, F, S, NZ* 1,2, *A*, 1964 *NZ, W, I, F, S*, 1965 *F, S*, 1966 *S*, 1968 *F, S*
Weston, W H (Northampton) 1933 *I, S*, 1934 *I, S*, 1935 *W, I, S*, 1936 *NZ, W, S*, 1937 *W, I, S*, 1938 *W, I, S*
Wheatley, A A (Coventry) 1937 *W, I, S*, 1938 *W, S*
Wheatley, H F (Coventry) 1936 *I*, 1937 *S*, 1938 *W, S*, 1939 *W, I, S*
Wheeler, P J (Leicester) 1975 *F, W*, 1976 *A, W, S, I*, 1977 *S, I, F, W*, 1978 *F, W, S, I, NZ*, 1979 *S, I, F, W, NZ*, 1980 *I, F, W, S*, 1981 *W, S, I, F*, 1982 *A, S, I, F, W*, 1983 *F, S, I, NZ*, 1984 *S, I, F, W*
White, C (Gosforth) 1983 *NZ*, 1984 *S, I, F*
White, D F (Northampton) 1947 *W, I, S*, 1948 *I, F*, 1951 *S*, 1952 *SA, W, S, I, F*, 1953 *W, I, S*
Whiteley, E C P (O Alleynians) 1931 *S, F*
Whiteley, W (Bramley) 1896 *W*
Whitely, H (Northern) 1929 *W*
Wightman, B J (Moseley, Coventry) 1959 *W*, 1963 *W, I, NZ* 2, *A*
Wigglesworth, H J (Thornes) 1884 *I*
Wilkins, D T (United Services, RN, Roundhay) 1951 *W, I, F, S*, 1952 *SA, W, S, I, F*, 1953 *W, I, F, S*
Wilkinson, E (Bradford) 1886 *W, I, S*, 1887 *W, S*
Wilkinson, H (Halifax) 1929 *W, I, S*, 1930 *F*
Wilkinson, H J (Halifax) 1889 *M*
Wilkinson, P (Law Club) 1872 *S*
Wilkinson, R M (Bedford) 1975 *A* 2, 1976 *A, W, S, I, F*

Willcocks, T J (Plymouth) 1902 *W*
Willcox, J G (Oxford U, Harlequins) 1961 *I, F, S*, 1962 *W, I, F, S*, 1963 *W, I, F, S*, 1964 *NZ, W, I, F, S*
William-Powlett, P B R W (United Services, RN) 1922 *S*
Williams, C G (Gloucester, RAF) 1976 *F*
Williams, C S (Manchester) 1910 *F*
Williams, J E (O Millhillians, Sale) 1954 *F*, 1955 *W, I, F, S*, 1956 *I, S, F*, 1965 *W*
Williams, J M (Penzance-Newlyn) 1951 *I, S*
Williams, P N (Orrell) 1987 *S, [A, J, W]*
Williams, S G (Devonport A) 1902 *W, I, S*, 1903 *I, S*, 1907 *I, S*
Williams, S H (Newport) 1911 *W, F, I, S*
Williamson, R H (Oxford U) 1908 *W, I, S*, 1909 *A, F*
Wilson, A J (Camborne S of M) 1909 *I*
Wilson, C E (Blackheath) 1898 *I*
Wilson, C P (Cambridge U, Marlborough N) 1881 *W*
Wilson, D S (Met Police, Harlequins) 1953 *F*, 1954 *W, NZ, I, S, F*, 1955 *F, S*
Wilson, G S (Tyldesley) 1929 *W, I*
Wilson, K J (Gloucester) 1963 *F*
Wilson, R P (Liverpool OB) 1891 *W, I, S*
Wilson, W C (Richmond) 1907 *I, S*
Winn, C E (Rosslyn Park) 1952 *SA, W, S, I, F*, 1954 *W, S, F*
Winterbottom, P J (Headingley, Harlequins) 1982 *A, S, I, F, W*, 1983 *F, W, S, I, NZ*, 1984 *S, F, W, SA* 1,2, 1986 *W, S, I, F*, 1987 *I, F, W, [A, J, US, W]*, 1988 *F, W, S*, 1989 *R, Fj*, 1990 *I, F, W, S, Arg* 1,2,3, 1991 *W, S, I, F, A, [NZ, It, F, S, A]*, 1992 *S, I, F, W, C, SA*, 1993 *F, W, S, I*
Wintle, T C (Northampton) 1966 *S*, 1969 *I, F, S, W*
Wodehouse, N A (United Services, RN) 1910 *F*, 1911 *W, F, I, S*, 1912 *W, I, S, F*, 1913 *SA, W, F, I, S*
Wood, A (Halifax) 1884 *I*
Wood, A E (Gloucester, Cheltenham) 1908 *F, W, I*
Wood, G W (Leicester) 1914 *W*
Wood, R (Liversedge) 1894 *I*
Wood, R D (Liverpool OB) 1901 *I*, 1903 *W, I*
Woodgate, E E (Paignton) 1952 *W*
Woodhead, E (Huddersfield) 1880 *I*
Woodruff, C G (Harlequins) 1951 *W, I, F, S*
Woods, S M J (Cambridge U, Wellington) 1890 *W, S, I*, 1891 *W, I, S*, 1892 *I, S*, 1893 *W, I*, 1895 *W, I, S*
Woods, T (Bridgwater) 1908 *S*
Woods, T (United Services, RN) 1920 *S*, 1921 *W, I, S, F*
Woodward, C R (Leicester) 1980 *I* (R), *F, W, S*, 1981 *W, S, I, F, Arg* 1,2, 1982 *A, S, I, F, W*, 1983 *I, NZ*, 1984 *S, I, F, W*
Woodward, J E (Wasps) 1952 *SA, W, S*, 1953 *W, I, F, S*, 1954 *W, NZ, I, S, F*, 1956 *W, I, S*
Wooldridge, C S (Oxford U, Blackheath) 1883 *W, I, S*, 1884 *W, I, S*, 1885 *I*
Wordsworth, A J (Cambridge U) 1975 *A* 1 (R)
Worton, J R B (Harlequins, Army) 1926 *W*, 1927 *W*
Wrench, D F B (Harlequins) 1964 *F, S*
Wright, C C G (Cambridge U, Blackheath) 1909 *I, S*
Wright, F T (Edinburgh Acady, Manchester) 1881 *S*
Wright, I D (Northampton) 1971 *W, I, F, S* (R)
Wright, J C (Met Police) 1934 *W*
Wright, J F (Bradford) 1890 *W*
Wright, T P (Blackheath) 1960 *W, I, F, S*, 1961 *SA, W, I, F, S*, 1962 *W, I, F, S*
Wright, W H G (Plymouth) 1920 *W, F*
Wyatt, D M (Bedford) 1976 *S* (R)

Yarranton, P G (RAF, Wasps) 1954 *W, NZ, I*, 1955 *F, S*
Yiend, W (Hartlepool R, Gloucester) 1889 *M*, 1892 *W, I, S*, 1893 *I, S*
Young, A T (Cambridge U, Blackheath, Army) 1924 *W, I, F, S*, 1925 *NZ, F*, 1926 *I, F, S*, 1927 *I, S, F*, 1928 *A, W, I, F, S*, 1929 *I*
Young, J R C (Oxford U, Harlequins) 1958 *I*, 1960 *W, I, F, S*, 1961 *SA, W, I, F*
Young, M (Gosforth) 1977 *S, I, F, W*, 1978 *F, W, S, I, NZ*, 1979 *S*
Young, P D (Dublin Wands) 1954 *W, NZ, I, S, F*, 1955 *W, I, F, S*
Youngs, N G (Leicester) 1983 *I, NZ*, 1984 *S, I, F, W*

143

ENGLISH INTERNATIONAL RECORDS

Both team and individual records are for official England international matches up to 30 April 1996.

TEAM RECORDS

Highest score

60 $\begin{cases} \text{v Japan (60-7) 1987 Sydney} \\ \text{v Canada (60-19) 1994 Twickenham} \end{cases}$

v individual countries
51 v Argentina (51-0) 1990 Twickenham
28 v Australia (28-19) 1988 Twickenham
60 v Canada (60-19) 1994 Twickenham
58 v Fiji (58-23) 1989 Twickenham
41 v France (41-13) 1907 Richmond
38 v Ireland (38-9) 1992 Twickenham
36 v Italy (36-6) 1991 Twickenham
60 v Japan (60-7) 1987 Sydney
29 v N Zealand (29-45) 1995 Cape Town
58 v Romania (58-3) 1989 Bucharest
30 v Scotland (30-18) 1980 Murrayfield
33 v S Africa (33-16) 1992 Twickenham
37 v US (37-9) 1991 Twickenham
34 v Wales (34-6) 1990 Twickenham
44 v W Samoa (44-22) 1995 Durban

Biggest winning points margin

55 v Romania (58-3) 1989 Bucharest
v individual countries
51 v Argentina (51-0) 1990 Twickenham
17 v Australia $\begin{cases} \text{(20-3) 1973 Twickenham} \\ \text{(23-6) 1976 Twickenham} \end{cases}$
41 v Canada (60-19) 1994 Twickenham
35 v Fiji (58-23) 1989 Twickenham
37 v France (37-0) 1911 Twickenham
32 v Ireland (35-3) 1988 Twickenham
30 v Italy (36-6) 1991 Twickenham
53 v Japan (60-7) 1987 Sydney
13 v N Zealand (13-0) 1936 Twickenham
55 v Romania (58-3) 1989 Bucharest
20 v Scotland (26-6) 1977 Twickenham
17 v S Africa $\begin{cases} \text{(33-16) 1992 Twickenham} \\ \text{(32-15) 1994 Pretoria} \end{cases}$
28 v US $\begin{cases} \text{(34-6) 1987 Sydney} \\ \text{(37-9) 1991 Twickenham} \end{cases}$
28 v Wales (34-6) 1990 Twickenham
22 v W Samoa (44-22) 1995 Durban

Longest winning sequence
10 matches – 1882-86 and 1994-95

Highest score by opposing team
45 N Zealand (29-45) 1995 Cape Town
by individual countries
19 Argentina (19-19) 1981 Buenos Aires
40 Australia (15-40) 1991 Sydney
19 Canada (60-19) 1994 Twickenham
23 Fiji (58-23) 1989 Twickenham
37 France (12-37) 1972 Colombes
26 Ireland (21-26) 1974 Twickenham

20 Italy (27-20) 1995 Durban
7 Japan (60-7) 1987 Sydney
45 N Zealand (29-45) 1995 Cape Town
15 Romania (22-15) 1985 Twickenham
33 Scotland (6-33) 1986 Murrayfield
35 S Africa (9-35) 1984 Johannesburg
9 United States (37-9) 1991 Twickenham
34 Wales (21-34) 1967 Cardiff
22 W Samoa (44-22) 1995 Durban

Biggest losing points margin

27 v N Zealand (15-42) 1985 Wellington
27 v Scotland (6-33) 1986 Murrayfield
v individual countries
2 v Argentina (13-15) 1990 Buenos Aires
25 v Australia (15-40) 1991 Sydney
25 v France (12-37) 1972 Colombes
22 v Ireland (0-22) 1947 Dublin
27 v N Zealand (15-42) 1985 Wellington
27 v Scotland (6-33) 1986 Murrayfield
26 v S Africa (9-35) 1984 Johannesburg
25 v Wales (0-25) 1905 Cardiff
No defeats v Canada, Fiji, Italy, Japan, Romania, United States or W Samoa

Longest losing sequence
7 matches – 1904-06 and 1971-72

Most tries by England in an international
13 v Wales 1881 Blackheath

Most tries against England in an international
8 by Wales (6-28) 1922 Cardiff

Most points by England in International Championship in a season – 118
in season 1991-92

Most tries by England in International Championship in a season – 20
in season 1913-14

INDIVIDUAL RECORDS

Most capped player
R Underwood   85   1984-96
in individual positions
Full-back
J M Webb   33   1987-93

Wing
R Underwood   85   1984-96
Centre
W D C Carling   66   1988-96
Fly-half
C R Andrew   69(70)[1]   1985-95
Scrum-half
R J Hill   29   1984-91
Prop
J Leonard   49   1990-96
Hooker
B C Moore   63(64)[2]   1987-95
Lock
W A Dooley   55   1985-93
Flanker
P J Winterbottom   58   1982-93
No 8
D Richards   47(48)[3]   1986-96
[1] *Andrew has played once as a full-back*
[2] *Moore was capped once as a replacement forward*
[3] *Excludes 1 appearance as a temporary replacement*

Longest international career
G S Pearce 14 seasons 1978-79 to 1991-92

Most consecutive internationals – 44
W D C Carling 1989-95

Most internationals as captain – 59
W D C Carling 1988-96

Most points in internationals – 396
C R Andrew (70 matches) 1985-95

Most points in International Championship in a season – 67
J M Webb (4 matches) 1991-92

Most points in an international – 30
C R Andrew v Canada 1994 Twickenham

Most tries in internationals – 49
R Underwood (85 matches) 1984-96

Most tries in International Championship in a season – 8
C N Lowe (4 matches) 1913-14

Most tries in an international – 5
D Lambert v France 1907 Richmond
R Underwood v Fiji 1989 Twickenham

Most conversions in internationals – 41

J M Webb (33 matches) 1987-93

Most conversions in International Championship in a season – 11
J M Webb (4 matches) 1991-92

Most conversions in an international – 8
S D Hodgkinson v Romania 1989 Bucharest

Most dropped goals in internationals – 21
C R Andrew (70 matches) 1985-95

Most dropped goals in an international – 2
R Hiller v Ireland 1970 Twickenham
A G B Old v France 1978 Paris
A G B Old v France 1980 Paris
C R Andrew v Romania 1985 Twickenham
C R Andrew v Fiji 1991 Suva
C R Andrew v Argentina 1995 Durban
P J Grayson v France 1996 Paris

Most penalty goals in internationals – 86
C R Andrew (70 matches) 1985-95

Most penalty goals in International Championship in a season – 18
S D Hodgkinson (4 matches) 1990-91

Most penalty goals in an international – 7
S D Hodgkinson v Wales 1991 Cardiff
C R Andrew v Scotland 1995 Twickenham

Most points on major tour – 58
C R Andrew (4 matches) South Africa 1994
W H Hare scored 79 points on the N American tour of 1982, but this was not a major tour

Most points in a tour match – 36
W N Bennett v Western Australia 1975 Perth

Most tries in a tour match – 4
A J Morley v Western Australia 1975 Perth
P S Preece v New South Wales 1975 Sydney
R E Webb scored 4 tries v Canada in 1967, and J Carleton scored 4 against Mid-West at Cleveland in 1982, but these were not on major tours

FIFTH AND FINAL TITLE FOR THE NORTH

CIS INSURANCE DIVISIONAL CHAMPIONSHIP 1995
Michael Austin

The North, heartland of the game at divisional level, appropriately won the final championship title before this competition was discontinued, beating the Midlands, the holders, 45-42 at Nottingham. Just as the Midlands had defeated London the previous year at Sudbury, the North, led by Paul Johnson of Orrell, won the decisive away match, which yielded 12 tries.

Whatever the many and ongoing criticisms levelled at the competition, which began in 1977, it did serve as a development tournament and provide a shop window for young players to display their potential. It would be difficult to imagine, for example, Jack Rowell, the England manager, being able to see 20-year-old Alex King, the Bristol University fly-half without a senior club to his name, playing in any other circumstances. The South & South-West selectors, chaired by John Lockyer, had identified King as a player of burgeoning skill; Rowell watched him against the Midlands at Gloucester and King went on to play with distinction for England A and later to sign a contract with Wasps. His exploits included landing the match-winning penalty goal for England A against New South Wales and amassing 17 points in another victory against Italy A. Phil Greening, the Gloucester and South & South-West hooker, and Chris Murphy, the West Hartlepool and North lock, were among other hitherto 'unknowns' who rose to A team prominence through the divisional system.

The competition did other players such as Austin Healey, the Orrell scrum-half bound for Leicester, far more good than harm. Richard West, the Gloucester lock, capped once by England in the 1995 World Cup, rehabilitated his career through the competition on his way to a contract with Richmond. Even Brian Moore, the newly retired England hooker, captained London against the North. Three players destined for an England debut in the Five Nations Championship also emerged. Jon Sleightholme, the Bath wing often consigned to second-team club rugby, used the competition as a platform to display his skills, as did Garath Archer, the Bristol lock, and Paul Grayson, who was playing in Courage League 2 for Northampton. Indeed, the performances of Grayson and his club-mate Matt Dawson for the Midlands in the match against Western Samoa launched them to full caps. It would have been harder to judge their international credentials at a club level lower than the top league.

The North, with Fran Cotton, the former England prop, in charge, remained the staunchest supporters of divisional games. With justification, they wanted to retain the system, partly to keep their own identity. Of 14 Yorkshiremen in a training squad of 36 during October, only one, Wakefield scrum-half David Scully, was still with a Yorkshire club. Their community spirit did much to win them the title for a record fifth time, although the Midlands, coached by England A manager Peter Rossborough, had also begun to develop their own identity as a unit, a point which was illustrated by a fierce rally when they were trailing 21-6 to the eventual champions. The superior goal-kicking of the North's Rob Liley, younger brother of John, the Leicester full-back, made the critical difference. Liley landed seven of his eight kicks while the Midlands' Jim Quantrill, who otherwise had an excellent championship, kicked only five of ten, missing his last four at the height of the Midlands' challenge.

A 38-15 win over the South & South-West at Bridgwater's admirable new ground had signalled the North's intent. But on the opening Sunday of the competition – both matches had to be rearranged to avoid a clash with the televised England-South Africa game – the Midlands, with ten newcomers in a team drawn mostly from League 2 clubs, were also victorious, beating London 36-34 in a tense match at Northampton. London trailed 23-5 after 35 minutes, but Nick Greenstock's two tries and others from O'Leary and Mensah rewarded their extra pace in the backs. The Midlands pack, though, was indomitable and Quantrill kicked 16 points to impress alongside John Farr, the former Bedford scrum-half, plucked from the backwaters of Winnington Park.

The North, fortified by full-back Tim Stimpson, went on to beat London, for whom Tony Diprose excelled along the way to becoming England A captain, and the Midlands defeated the South & South-West, despite the poise, running freedom and tackling aptitude of King, a former England Colt who had been an England Under-21 bench reserve earlier in the month.

Richard Hill of Saracens increased his try total for the South & South-West to seven in two seasons as London were beaten 26-11 at Sunbury, the home of London Irish, and consigned to the wooden spoon. Prop Darren Crompton, mostly denied first-team games at Bath, produced an authoritative display and later became one of five leading players to join Richmond as the professional rugby revolution took hold. The North's title-clinching game on the same day completed the three-year involvement of CIS Insurance with the Divisional Championship. Their sponsorship, which also covered the County Championship and the Under-21 Divisional Championship, had been worth £750,000 during that period. Moreover, CIS had actively promoted the competitions alongside their own name in an energetic and unstinting way which earned the company a well-deserved reputation as one of the game's best sponsors for many years.

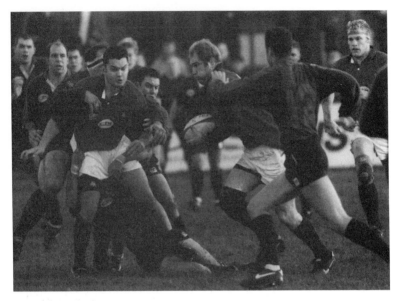

Matt Greenwood, one of the try-scorers in the North's 45-42 victory over the Midlands in the deciding match, on the attack.

FINAL TABLE

	P	W	D	L	F	A	Pts
North	3	3	0	0	101	66	6
Midlands	3	2	0	1	94	90	4
South & South-West	3	1	0	2	52	65	2
London	3	0	0	3	54	80	0

The North have won the Divisional Championship 5 times (1977, 1980, 1986, 1987, 1995); London (1988, 1989, 1990) and the Midlands (1985, 1991, 1994) 3 times each and the South & South-West twice (1992, 1993). The championship was not played between 1977 and 1980 or 1980 and 1985.

19 November, Northampton RFC

Midlands Division 36 (2G 4PG 2T)   **London Division 34** (3G 1PG 2T)
Midlands Division: J Quantrill (Rugby Lions); R Subbiani (Bedford), A Kerr (Moseley), B Whetstone (Bedford), H Thorneycroft (Northampton); P Grayson (Northampton), J Farr (Winnington Park); M Volland (Northampton), T Beddow (Northampton), N Webber (Moseley), D Grewcock (Coventry), R West (Gloucester), I Skingsley (Bedford), C Tarbuck (Leicester) (*capt*), B Pountney (Northampton)
Scorers *Tries:* Pountney, Grewcock, Skingsley, Farr   *Conversions:* Quantrill (2)   *Penalty Goals:* Quantrill (4)
London Division: J Ufton (Wasps); D O'Leary (Harlequins), N Greenstock (Wasps), P Mensah (Harlequins), S Roiser (Wasps); G Gregory (Wasps), S Bates (Wasps) (*capt*); G Holmes (Saracens), G Botterman (Saracens), A Mullins (Harlequins), R Kinsey (Wasps), A Snow (Harlequins), M White (Wasps), A Diprose (Saracens), R Jenkins (Harlequins)
Scorers *Tries:* Greenstock (2), O'Leary, Mensah, pen try   *Conversions:* Gregory (3)   *Penalty Goal:* Gregory
Referee A Watson (Ireland)

19 November, Bridgwater RFC

South & South-West Division 15 (1G 1PG 1T)   **Northern Division 38** (4G 2T)
South & South-West Division: G Way (Reading); P Holford (Gloucester), N Beal (Northampton), M Denney (Bristol), J Sleightholme (Bath); A King (Bristol U), R Kitchin (Bristol) (*capt*); K Yates (Bath), P Greening (Gloucester), D Hinkins (Bristol), G Archer (Bristol), D Sims (Gloucester), P Glanville (Gloucester), C Yandell (Saracens), R Hill (Saracens) *Replacement* E Pearce (Bath) for Hill (64 mins)
Scorers *Tries:* Glanville, Kitchin   *Conversion:* King   *Penalty Goal:* King

Northern Division: T Stimpson (West Hartlepool); J Naylor (Orrell), P Johnson (Orrell) (*capt*), W Greenwood (Harlequins), J Mallinder (Sale); R Liley (Sale), A Healey (Orrell); P Winstanley (Orrell), T Herbert (West Hartlepool), A Smith (Sale), J Fowler (Sale), C Murphy (West Hartlepool), M Greenwood (Wasps), C Vyvyan (Sale), N Ashurst (Orrell) *Replacements* R Arnold (Newcastle) for Ashurst (8 mins); G Baldwin (Wakefield) for Smith (73 mins)
Scorers *Tries:* Liley, Stimpson, W Greenwood, Ashurst, Vyvyan, Naylor *Conversions:* Liley (4)
Referee H Lewis (Wales)

25 November, Wakefield RFC

Northern Division 18 (1G 2PG 1T) **London Division 9** (3PG)
Northern Division: T Stimpson (West Hartlepool); J Naylor (Orrell), W Greenwood (Harlequins), P Johnson (Orrell) (*capt*), J Mallinder (Sale); R Liley (Sale), A Healey (Orrell); P Winstanley (Orrell), S Diamond (Sale), M Shelley (West Hartlepool), J Fowler (Sale), M Greenwood (Wasps), R Arnold (Newcastle), C Vyvyan (Sale), N Ashurst (Sale) *Replacements* G Baldwin (Wakefield) for Winstanley (2 mins); P Stewart (Wakefield) for Vyvyan (48 mins)
Scorers *Tries:* Mallinder, W Greenwood *Conversion:* Liley *Penalty Goals:* Liley (2)
London Division: A Tunningley (Saracens); M Griffiths (Wasps), P Mensah (Harlequins), N Greenstock (Wasps), S Roiser (Wasps); G Gregory (Wasps), A Gomarsall (Wasps); S Brown (Harlequins), B Moore (Harlequins) (*capt*), I Dunston (Wasps), A Snow (Harlequins), M Watson (Harlequins), M White (Wasps), A Diprose (Saracens), R Jenkins (Harlequins)
Scorer *Penalty Goals:* Gregory (3)
Referee A Spreadbury (Somerset Society)

25 November, Gloucester RFC

South & South-West Division 11 (1PG 1DG 1T) **Midlands Division 16** (2PG 2T)
South & South-West Division: P Hull (Bristol) (*capt*); P Holford (Gloucester), S Enoch (Pontypridd), M Denney (Bristol), J Sleightholme (Bath); A King (Bristol U), B Fenley (Gloucester); K Yates (Bath), P Greening (Gloucester), D Crompton (Bath), G Archer (Bristol), C Yandell (Saracens), P Glanville (Gloucester), E Rollitt (Bristol), J Pearson (Bristol) *Replacement* R Fidler (Gloucester) for Yandell (42 mins)
Scorers *Try:* Fenley *Penalty Goal:* King *Dropped Goal:* King
Midlands Division: J Quantrill (Rugby Lions); R Subbiani (Bedford), A Kerr (Moseley), B Whetstone (Bedford), H Thorneycroft (Northampton); P Grayson (Northampton) (*capt*), J Farr (Winnington Park); M Volland (Northampton), T Beddow (Northampton), N Webber (Moseley), D Grewcock (Coventry), R West (Gloucester), I Skingsley (Bedford), G Seely (Northampton), B Pountney (Northampton)
Scorers *Tries:* Pountney, Skingsley *Penalty Goals:* Quantrill (2)
Referee J Pearson (Durham Society)

2 December, London Irish RFC

London Division 11 (2PG 1T) **South & South-West Division 26** (1G 3PG 2T)
London Division: J Ufton (Wasps); D O'Leary (Harlequins), N Greenstock (Wasps), L Scrase (Wasps), S Roiser (Wasps); G Gregory (Wasps), A Gomarsall (Wasps); S Brown (Harlequins), S Mitchell (Harlequins), G Holmes (Saracens), M Watson (Harlequins), M Langley (Saracens), G Allison (Harlequins), A Diprose (Saracens) (*capt*), M White (Wasps) *Replacement* S Ravenscroft (Saracens) for Greenstock (50 mins)
Scorers *Try:* Allison *Penalty Goals:* Gregory (2)
South & South-West Division: P Hull (Bristol) (*capt*); N Beal (Northampton), S Enoch (Pontypridd), F Waters (Bristol U), P Holford (Gloucester); A King (Bristol U), B Fenley (Gloucester); T Windo (Gloucester), P Greening (Gloucester), D Crompton (Bath), G Archer (Bristol), C Yandell (Saracens), P Glanville (Gloucester), E Rollitt (Bristol), R Hill (Saracens)
Scorers *Tries:* Hill (2), Hull *Conversion:* Hull *Penalty Goals:* Hull (2), King
Referee I Ramage (Scotland)

2 December, Nottingham RFC

Midlands Division 42 (3G 2PG 3T) **Northern Division 45** (6G 1PG)
Midlands Division: J Quantrill (Rugby Lions); A Smallwood (Nottingham), B Whetstone (Bedford), A Kerr (Moseley), H Thorneycroft (Northampton); P Challinor (Harlequins), J Farr (Winnington Park); M Volland (Northampton), R Cockerill (Leicester), N Webber (Moseley), J-L Phillips (Northampton), D Grewcock (Coventry), I Skingsley (Bedford), C Tarbuck (Leicester) (*capt*), B Pountney (Northampton) *Replacement* M Freer (Nottingham) for Volland (42 mins)
Scorers *Tries:* Challinor (2), Grewcock, Pountney, Farr, Whetstone *Conversions:* Quantrill (3) *Penalty Goals:* Quantrill (2)
Northern Division: J Mallinder (Sale); A Healey (Orrell), J Baxendell (Sale), P Johnson (Orrell) (*capt*), C Yates (Sale); R Liley (Sale), D Scully (Wakefield); G Baldwin (Wakefield), G French (Bath), M Shelley (West Hartlepool), K Westgarth (West Hartlepool), P Stewart (Wakefield), R Arnold (Newcastle), M Greenwood (Wasps), A Brown (West Hartlepool) *Replacement* S Cook (West Hartlepool) for Yates (60 mins)
Scorers *Tries:* Baxendell (2), Healey (2), Greenwood, pen try *Conversions:* Liley (6) *Penalty Goal:* Liley
Referee I Rogers (South Africa)

ALL-ACTION SEASON IN THE COMMITTEE ROOMS

THE COURAGE LEAGUES 1995-96

There was as much decisive action in the committee rooms as there was on the field of play last season. Sweeping changes were made to the structure and composition of the Leagues, and not all of them for better. In a move which had nothing to do with competitive logic and everything to do with collective solidarity, the First Division clubs insisted that there should be no relegation from the top division. In their protracted negotiations with the RFU over money and power, the clubs had agreed to stick together come what may. They cited the RFU's generous attitude in sanctioning no relegation from the Second Division during the season as a notable precedent. As a trade-off, the RFU gave in to their demand for one season only. The ruling made a mockery of sport.

So, after the final whistle had been blown on the season, during which they had lost all 18 matches, West Hartlepool were granted a stay of execution and we are left with expanded top divisions for 1996-97. The First and Second will be 12 strong, with teams playing home and away; National League 3 will have 16 teams. Four were promoted to Division 2 – Coventry, Richmond, Rotherham and Rugby – leaving six clubs behind. Eight came up from the old Fourth Division while one from each of the old Five North and South – namely Wharfedale and Lydney – were also promoted. There was no relegation, either, from the old League 3. The new national Leagues 4 North and 3 South will have 14 teams, Hereford and Manchester joining the northern section, Charlton Park and Newbury the southern.

Matters on the field were far less confusing and infinitely more dramatic. Bath won their sixth Courage title by the skin of their teeth. The outcome of the final Saturday had seemed a foregone conclusion: Bath would defeat Sale at home, while Leicester would see off Harlequins at Welford Road, giving Bath the title on points difference. With Bath leading 32-12 at half-time no one had any reason to suspect otherwise. But Sale came back to snatch a draw, Rob Liley's conversion in the last minute bringing the scores level at 38-38. Meanwhile, a couple of hundred miles away, brother John was missing a 45th-minute penalty which would have given Leicester the title. On such small margins are championships won and lost.

Big-money spenders Saracens were given a reprieve from relegation while Northampton romped through the Second Division, averaging almost 50 points a match. Rotherham continued their remarkable rise with their sixth promotion in nine seasons.

Bath show their delight at taking the Courage Leagues title for the sixth time in the nine years of the competition after a dramatic last Saturday.

PREVIOUS WINNERS OF THE COURAGE TROPHY

1987-88: **Leicester** (runners-up: Wasps); 1988-89: **Bath** (runners-up: Gloucester);
1989-90: **Wasps** (runners-up: Gloucester); 1990-91: **Bath** (runners-up: Wasps);
1991-92: **Bath** (runners-up: Orrell); 1992-93: **Bath** (runners-up: Wasps); 1993-94:
Bath (runners-up: Leicester); 1995-96: **Leicester** (runners-up: Bath)

*Due to extensive restructuring throughout the Leagues, no promotion or relegation can be shown on the tables this
year. *Points deducted for various reasons*

NATIONAL DIVISION

National 1

	P	W	D	L	F	A	Pts
Bath	18	15	1	2	575	276	31
Leicester	18	15	0	3	476	242	30
Harlequins	18	13	0	5	524	314	26
Wasps	18	11	0	7	439	322	22
Sale	18	9	1	8	365	371	19
Bristol	18	8	0	10	329	421	16
Orrell	18	7	0	11	323	477	14
Gloucester	18	6	0	12	275	370	12
Saracens	18	5	0	13	284	451	10
W Hartlepool	18	0	0	18	288	634	0

National 2

	P	W	D	L	F	A	Pts
Northampton	18	18	0	0	867	203	36
L Irish	18	15	0	3	584	405	30
L Scottish	18	10	2	6	361	389	22
Wakefield	18	8	0	10	328	331	16
Waterloo	18	7	2	9	309	483	16
Moseley	18	7	0	11	327	447	14
Blackheath	18	6	1	11	341	469	13
Newcastle	18	5	1	12	348	405	11
Nottingham	18	5	1	12	333	433	11
Bedford	18	5	1	12	287	520	11

National 3

	P	W	D	L	F	A	Pts
Coventry	18	15	0	3	524	264	30
Richmond	18	13	1	4	476	266	27
Rugby	18	12	1	5	395	284	25
Rotherham	18	12	0	6	384	368	24
Morley	18	9	2	7	336	328	20
Harrogate	18	6	3	9	333	387	15
Otley	18	6	1	11	278	441	13
Reading	18	5	1	12	397	484	11
Rosslyn Pk	18	3	2	13	290	426	8
Fylde	18	3	1	14	283	448	7

National 4

	P	W	D	L	F	A	Pts
Exeter	18	14	0	4	448	230	28
L Welsh	18	12	0	6	424	269	24
Liverpool St H	18	11	1	6	471	343	23
Walsall	18	10	0	8	406	324	20
Leeds	18	9	1	8	311	345	19
Clifton	18	7	2	9	283	298	16
Redruth	18	7	2	9	358	391	16
Havant	18	7	1	10	287	368	15
Aspatria	18	5	1	12	356	497	11
Plymouth Alb	18	4	0	14	266	545	8

National 5 North

	P	W	D	L	F	A	Pts
Wharfedale	12	12	0	0	331	146	24
Worcester	12	9	0	3	317	187	18
B'ham S'hull	12	8	1	3	202	160	17
Winnington Pk	12	8	0	4	225	215	16
Sheffield	12	7	0	5	205	190	14
Sandal	12	6	0	6	244	198	12
Stourbridge	12	6	0	6	200	177	12
Preston Grass	12	5	1	6	167	209	11
Kendal	12	5	0	7	215	227	10
Nuneaton	12	4	1	7	178	329	9
Stoke-on-Trent	12	3	0	9	184	204	6
Lichfield	12	3	0	9	165	284	6
Broughton Pk	12	0	1	11	127	234	1

National 5 South

	P	W	D	L	F	A	Pts
Lydney	12	11	1	0	320	132	23
Weston-s-Mare	12	10	0	2	207	123	20
Henley	12	8	0	4	349	192	16
Barking	12	8	0	4	243	187	16
Berry Hill	12	7	0	5	203	195	14
Cheltenham	12	6	0	6	194	173	12
Camberley	12	5	1	6	151	212	11
Askeans	12	5	0	7	186	275	10
Tabard	12	4	1	7	195	244	9
High Wycombe	12	4	1	7	161	244	9
North Walsham	12	3	1	8	149	212	7
Met Police	12	2	1	9	130	204	5
Camborne	12	2	0	10	146	241	4

LONDON DIVISION

London 1

	P	W	D	L	F	A	Pts
Charlton Pk	12	10	0	2	338	131	20
Southend	12	10	0	2	268	155	20
Esher	12	9	0	3	280	159	18
Staines	12	8	0	4	217	197	16
Harlow	12	6	2	4	263	191	14
Sutton & Epsom	12	6	1	5	196	223	13
Sudbury	12	6	0	6	218	217	12
O Mid-Whitgift	12	5	0	7	210	199	10
Ruislip	12	5	0	7	170	214	10
O Colfeians	12	4	0	8	138	241	8
Basingstoke	12	3	1	8	179	210	7
G'ford & God	12	2	0	10	159	310	4
Ealing	12	2	0	10	144	333	4

London 2 North

	P	W	D	L	F	A	Pts
Norwich	12	10	0	2	250	72	20
Thurrock	12	9	2	1	307	165	20
Cambridge	12	8	0	4	251	177	16
B'p's Stortford	12	8	0	4	216	210	16
Cheshunt	12	7	2	3	214	217	16
Brentwood	12	5	1	6	140	150	11
Finchley	12	5	0	7	227	157	10
Colchester	12	5	0	7	177	178	10
R'ford & Gidea Pk	12	5	0	7	185	206	10
O Verulamians	12	5	0	7	179	204	10
Woodford	12	4	1	7	186	297	9
Hertford	12	4	0	8	173	187	8
Eton Manor	12	0	0	12	97	382	0

London 2 South

	P	W	D	L	F	A	Pts
Wimbledon	12	11	0	1	303	86	22
Thanet Wands	12	10	0	2	346	142	20
O Wimbledonians	12	9	1	2	240	128	19
O Blues	12	8	0	4	302	158	16
Westcombe Pk	12	7	0	5	317	196	14
Horsham	12	6	1	5	243	217	13
Dorking	12	6	0	6	233	181	12
Brockleians	12	6	0	6	207	207	12
O Juddian	12	6	0	6	143	296	12
S'ham-Croydon	12	4	0	8	153	291	8
Gravesend	12	2	0	10	169	268	4
O Reigatian	12	1	1	10	186	291	3
Maidstone	12	0	1	11	95	476	1

London 3 North-East

	P	W	D	L	F	A	Pts
Ipswich	12	11	0	1	410	132	22
Lowestoft & Yar	12	11	0	1	323	139	22
Chingford	12	10	0	2	265	153	20
Bury St Eds	12	6	0	6	170	161	12
Braintree	12	6	0	6	199	213	12
O Edwardians	12	5	0	7	165	172	10
Rochford	12	5	0	7	119	177	10
Canvey I	12	5	0	7	169	240	10
Chelmsford*	12	6	0	6	185	196	8
W Norfolk*	12	5	0	7	179	217	8
Maldon	12	3	0	9	118	231	6
Campion	12	3	0	9	200	325	6
Shelford	12	2	0	10	150	296	4

London 3 North-West

	P	W	D	L	F	A	Pts
O Albanians	12	12	0	0	294	106	24
O Gaytonians	12	9	2	1	257	125	20
O M Taylors	12	7	1	4	268	165	15
Old Millhillians	12	7	1	4	221	156	15
Lensbury	12	6	1	5	231	206	13
Letchworth	12	6	0	6	243	241	12
Welwyn	12	5	1	6	170	219	11
Barnet	12	5	0	7	195	210	10
Grasshoppers	12	5	0	7	166	240	10
Fullerians	12	4	1	7	206	197	9
Kingsburians	12	4	1	7	118	200	9
O Elizabethans	12	3	2	7	133	220	8
Mill Hill	12	0	0	12	146	363	0

London 3 South-East

	P	W	D	L	F	A	Pts
Beckenham	12	9	1	2	267	131	19
Brighton	12	9	1	2	230	136	19
Haywards Hth	12	8	1	3	249	153	17
Sidcup	12	7	1	4	206	139	15
Canterbury	12	7	0	5	181	176	14
Worthing	12	6	1	5	218	177	13
Sevenoaks	12	6	1	5	264	228	13
Park House	12	6	1	5	205	178	13
Chichester	12	5	1	6	172	238	11
Lewes	12	5	0	7	144	147	10
O Beccehamian	12	3	2	7	156	201	8
Uckfield	12	1	0	11	116	236	2
H'field & Waldron	12	1	0	11	71	339	2

London 3 South-West

	P	W	D	L	F	A	Pts
O Guildfordians	12	9	1	2	328	157	19
Portsmouth	12	9	0	3	287	137	18
Warlingham	12	8	0	4	286	145	16
Purley	12	6	2	4	126	121	14
Guy's Hosp	12	7	0	5	199	264	14
Alton	12	6	0	6	187	169	12
Jersey	12	6	0	6	131	131	12
O Emanuel	12	6	0	6	147	197	12
Gosport	12	5	0	7	152	194	10
O Walcountians	12	4	2	6	192	244	10
O Whitgiftians	12	4	1	7	209	234	9
O Alleynian	12	3	0	9	137	280	6
Cranleigh*	12	2	0	10	147	255	-2

Eastern Counties 1

	P	W	D	L	F	A	Pts
Diss	12	12	0	0	362	89	24
Woodbridge	12	8	0	4	230	200	16
Holt	12	6	2	4	167	138	14
Ilford Wands	12	7	0	5	163	150	14
Wymondham	12	6	1	5	223	207	13
Ely	12	6	0	6	205	176	12
Basildon	12	6	0	6	184	165	12
S Walden	12	5	1	6	165	158	11
Harwich & D'ct	12	5	1	6	196	198	11
Newmarket	12	5	0	7	181	303	10
Upminster	12	4	0	8	154	190	8
Bancroft	12	3	1	8	140	218	7
Loughton	12	2	0	10	141	319	4

Eastern Counties 2

	P	W	D	L	F	A	Pts
Cantabrigian	12	11	1	0	200	85	23
Wanstead	12	8	1	3	203	117	17
Met Pol Chigwell	12	8	0	4	216	149	16
O Palmerians	12	8	0	4	195	128	16
Thetford	12	8	0	4	206	143	16
Fakenham	12	7	1	4	257	117	15
O Cooperians	12	7	0	5	212	134	14
Westcliff	12	5	1	6	136	193	11
Thames	12	3	1	8	111	186	7
Ravens	12	3	0	9	158	278	6
Southwold*	12	3	1	8	104	200	5
Lakenham H*	12	3	0	9	230	173	4
O Bealonians	12	1	0	11	94	419	2

Eastern Counties 3

	P	W	D	L	F	A	Pts
Hadleigh	12	10	1	1	464	102	21
Felixstowe	12	10	1	1	376	80	21
Billericay	12	9	1	2	354	105	19
S Woodham F	12	8	1	3	260	112	17
Crusaders	12	7	0	5	223	158	14
E London	12	7	0	5	204	193	14
Ipswich YM	12	6	0	6	230	226	12
Stowmarket	12	6	0	6	173	195	12
Wisbech	12	4	0	8	167	176	8
Thurston	12	3	0	9	236	240	6
Broadland	12	3	0	9	233	276	6
Haverhill	12	3	0	9	170	339	6
Clacton	12	0	0	12	65	953	0

Eastern Counties 4

	P	W	D	L	F	A	Pts
Beccles*	9	8	0	1	280	95	14
Mersea I	9	7	0	2	238	89	14
Burnham-on-C	9	7	0	2	199	77	14
March	9	6	0	3	253	99	12
Brightlingsea*	9	6	0	3	161	95	10
Witham	9	5	0	4	166	103	10
Ongar	9	2	0	7	81	201	4
Sawston	9	2	0	7	83	214	4
Rayleigh	9	2	0	7	74	250	4
May & Baker	9	0	0	9	45	357	0

Eastern Counties 5

	P	W	D	L	F	A	Pts
Norwich U	10	9	0	1	273	71	18
Stanford	10	6	1	3	210	89	13
Swaffham*	10	6	1	3	275	119	9
Essex CC	10	4	0	6	127	136	8
Dagenham	10	4	0	6	137	196	8
Orwell*	10	0	0	10	45	346	-4

Hampshire 1

	P	W	D	L	F	A	Pts
Winchester	12	12	0	0	284	78	24
US Portsmouth	12	9	1	2	312	115	19
Farnborough	12	8	1	3	214	132	17
Petersfield	12	7	2	3	209	157	16
Millbrook	12	6	1	5	280	195	13
Andover	12	6	1	5	173	213	13
Tottonians	12	5	1	6	145	227	11
Eastleigh	12	5	1	6	142	235	11
Southampton	12	4	2	6	188	181	10
Guernsey	12	4	0	8	269	292	8
Fordingbridge	12	3	1	8	87	270	7
Esso	12	2	2	8	127	143	6
Trojans	12	0	1	11	124	316	1

Hampshire 2

	P	W	D	L	F	A	Pts
Ventnor	12	12	0	0	233	85	24
Isle of Wight	12	10	0	2	282	84	20
Fareham Heathens	12	5	1	6	211	231	11
Romsey	12	5	0	7	138	221	10
S'down & Shank*	12	5	1	6	179	140	9
New Milton	12	3	0	9	171	285	6
Fleet*	12	1	0	11	88	256	0

Hampshire 3

	P	W	D	L	F	A	Pts
Overton	12	12	0	0	624	65	24
Alresford	12	7	0	5	196	121	14
Nomads	12	7	0	5	164	172	14
B'stoke Wombats*	12	7	0	5	187	160	10
AC Delco	12	5	0	7	164	277	10
Ellingham	12	3	0	9	107	244	6
Waterlooville	12	1	0	11	100	503	2

Hertfordshire 1

	P	W	D	L	F	A	Pts
Harpenden	10	8	1	1	353	94	17
Stevenage T	10	8	1	1	227	80	17
Datchworth	10	8	0	2	200	104	16
Watford	10	7	0	3	132	119	14
Hitchin	10	6	0	4	158	129	12
O Standfordians	10	5	0	5	137	90	10
Royston	10	4	1	5	231	148	9
O Ashmoleans	10	4	1	5	180	163	9
Cuffley	10	2	0	8	95	171	4
QE II Hosp	10	1	0	9	38	394	2
Hatfield	10	0	0	10	56	315	0

Herts/Middlesex 1

	P	W	D	L	F	A	Pts
Hampstead	12	11	0	1	304	182	22
Haringey	12	10	0	2	265	109	20
O Hamptonians	12	10	0	2	263	126	20
St Albans	12	7	1	4	265	141	15
Hemel Hempstead	12	7	0	5	168	150	14
O Meadonians	12	6	0	6	190	154	12
Tring	12	5	2	5	185	179	12
Hendon	12	6	0	6	151	174	12
Uxbridge	12	4	1	7	125	171	9
St Mary's Hosp	12	4	1	7	217	278	9
Centaurs	12	3	1	8	138	237	7
Upper Clapton	12	2	0	10	125	243	4
L New Zealand	12	0	0	12	91	343	0

Kent 1

	P	W	D	L	F	A	Pts
Tunbridge Wells	12	10	0	2	330	81	20
Gillingham Anch	12	10	0	2	363	129	20
O Dunstonians	12	9	2	1	285	170	20
Sheppey*	12	9	0	3	246	139	16
Met Pol Hayes*	12	8	1	3	185	161	15
O Shootershillians	12	5	2	5	228	201	12
Ashford	12	5	1	6	186	209	11
Dover	12	5	0	7	135	177	10
Dartfordians	12	3	0	9	170	302	6
Bromley*	12	2	1	9	175	225	3
Erith	12	1	1	10	87	328	3
Medway*	12	6	0	6	211	179	2
O Elthamians	12	1	0	11	98	388	2

Kent 2

	P	W	D	L	F	A	Pts
Betteshanger	12	12	0	0	284	80	24
Cranbrook	12	11	0	1	314	96	22
Folkestone	12	9	0	3	279	97	18
Snowdon CW	12	7	1	4	233	181	15
Whitstable	12	7	0	5	176	149	14

	P	W	D	L	F	A	Pts
O Williamsonians	12	6	1	5	187	198	13
Nat West Bank	12	6	0	6	197	100	12
Deal	12	6	0	6	205	166	12
Sittingbourne	12	4	0	8	110	286	8
O Gravesendians	12	2	2	8	164	248	6
Lordswood★	12	3	1	8	143	212	5
Greenwich Acad	12	2	0	10	94	361	4
Vigo	12	0	1	11	48	260	1

Kent 3

	P	W	D	L	F	A	Pts
Tonbridge	9	8	0	1	306	86	16
New Ash Green★	9	8	0	1	242	46	14
Aylesford★	9	8	0	1	241	45	14
Midland Bank★	9	5	0	4	96	138	8
O Olavians	9	3	1	5	94	100	7
Citizens	9	3	1	5	55	189	7
STC Footscray★	9	4	0	5	76	138	6
Bexley	9	2	1	6	64	146	5
Orpington	9	2	0	7	82	201	4
Darenth Valley★	9	0	1	8	49	216	-1

Kent 4

	P	W	D	L	F	A	Pts
Edenbridge	8	7	0	1	159	61	14
Canterbury Ex	8	6	1	1	131	89	13
Faversham	8	3	2	3	71	52	8
Westerham	8	2	1	5	86	101	5
Greenwich	8	0	0	8	44	188	0
Lloyds Bank★							−2

Middlesex 1

	P	W	D	L	F	A	Pts
Hackney	12	10	0	2	299	150	20
L Nigerians	12	9	0	3	317	130	18
Civil Service	12	9	0	3	230	121	18
Harrow	12	9	0	3	229	131	18
O Haberdashers	12	9	0	3	198	111	18
HAC	12	7	0	5	255	236	14
O Paulines	12	6	0	6	229	148	12
Wembley	12	5	0	7	261	127	10
Twickenham★	12	5	0	7	173	187	8
O Actonians	12	4	0	8	173	271	8
Roxeth Manor OB	12	3	1	8	163	256	7
Sudbury C	12	1	1	10	103	378	3
Belsize Pk	12	0	0	12	86	470	0

Middlesex 2

	P	W	D	L	F	A	Pts
Enfield Ignats	12	11	0	1	237	68	22
O Abbotstonians	12	9	0	3	193	122	18
Barclays Bank	12	8	1	3	273	135	17
Antlers	12	8	0	4	174	158	16
L French	12	7	0	5	222	172	14
Bank of England	12	7	0	5	174	159	14
London Exiles	12	6	1	5	257	153	13
Feltham	12	6	0	6	240	209	12
H'smith & Fulham	12	5	0	7	141	179	10
O Isleworthians	12	4	0	8	156	243	8
Thamesians	12	2	0	10	130	213	4
Pinner & Gramms	12	2	0	10	124	303	4
Hayes	12	2	0	10	123	330	4

Middlesex 3

	P	W	D	L	F	A	Pts
UCS OB	9	8	0	1	266	54	16
L Cornish★	9	6	2	1	227	101	12
Southgate	9	6	0	3	225	118	12
O Grammarians	9	5	1	3	130	104	11
St Nicholas OB	9	5	0	4	181	75	10
O Tottonians★	9	5	1	3	91	93	9
Northolt	9	4	0	5	164	130	8
Quintin	9	3	0	6	84	152	6
Orleans FP	9	1	0	8	72	262	2
BA	9	0	0	9	20	371	0

Middlesex 4

	P	W	D	L	F	A	Pts
Royal Hosps	4	3	0	1	132	28	6
Middlesex Hosp	5	3	0	2	83	39	6
Kodak	5	3	0	2	112	71	6
Meadhurst	5	3	0	2	64	100	6
GWR	5	2	0	3	54	165	4
Osterley	4	0	0	4	33	75	0

Surrey 1

	P	W	D	L	F	A	Pts
Barnes	12	10	0	2	363	153	20
O Reedonians	12	9	0	3	279	146	18
Chobham	12	8	0	4	196	115	16
O Caterhamians	12	8	0	4	219	150	16
John Fisher OB★	12	7	0	5	177	166	12
Kingston	12	6	0	6	168	182	12
Effingham	12	5	0	7	197	208	10
KCS OB	12	5	0	7	121	170	10
U Vandals	12	4	1	7	187	194	9
Woking★	12	5	1	6	139	190	9
O Cranleighans	12	3	2	7	135	235	8
Shirley Wands	12	3	0	9	111	217	6
Farnham	12	3	0	9	120	286	6

Surrey 2

	P	W	D	L	F	A	Pts
Chipstead	12	11	0	1	246	99	22
Battersea Irons	12	10	0	2	253	64	20
Wandsworthians	12	7	1	4	196	158	15
Raynes Pk	12	7	0	5	186	117	14
O Haileyburians	12	7	0	5	212	188	14
O Rutlishians	12	6	0	6	205	169	12
Cobham	12	6	0	6	183	172	12
O Tiffinians	12	5	1	6	183	213	11
Merton	12	5	0	7	130	187	10
Law Soc	12	5	0	7	195	316	10
O Suttonians	12	4	0	8	167	194	8
Bec OB	12	4	0	8	157	282	8
Mitcham	12	0	0	12	97	251	0

Surrey 3

	P	W	D	L	F	A	Pts
O Freemans	9	8	0	1	278	72	16
L Media	9	8	0	1	271	88	16
O Wellingtonian	9	7	0	2	339	77	14
O Bevonians	9	6	0	3	208	114	12
L Fire Brigade	9	5	0	4	113	216	10
Kew Occasionals	9	3	0	6	137	241	6
Egham	9	3	0	6	93	207	6

	P	W	D	L	F	A	Pts
Lightwater*	9	3	0	6	112	137	4
Reigate & Redhill	9	2	0	7	73	196	4
Croydon	9	0	0	9	51	327	0
O Johnians*							−1

Surrey 4

	P	W	D	L	F	A	Pts
King's Coll Hosp	7	6	0	1	148	33	12
Worth OB	7	5	0	2	179	66	10
Surrey U	7	5	0	2	183	91	10
Economicals	7	5	0	2	147	85	10
Haslemere	7	3	0	4	138	89	6
St George's Hosp	7	3	0	4	96	84	6
Oxted	7	1	0	6	55	272	2
Racal-Decca	7	0	0	7	41	267	0
Surrey Pol*							−1
O Epsomians*							−1
Charing X/West*							−1

Sussex 1

	P	W	D	L	F	A	Pts
Bognor	12	12	0	0	332	86	24
Crawley	12	9	1	2	297	126	19
E Grinstead	12	9	0	3	317	115	18
Hastings & B'hill	12	9	0	3	249	151	18
Hove	12	8	1	3	195	112	17
Eastbourne	12	7	0	5	205	211	14
Seaford	12	5	0	7	204	236	10
Pulborough	12	4	1	7	125	266	9
Burgess Hill	12	4	0	8	182	253	8
O Brightonians	12	4	0	8	189	269	8
BA Wingspan	12	1	2	9	137	190	4
Hellingly	12	2	0	10	90	345	4
SA Horsham	12	1	1	10	104	266	3

Sussex 2

	P	W	D	L	F	A	Pts
Ditchling	10	8	2	0	206	85	18
Crowborough	10	8	1	1	314	76	17
St Francis	10	4	2	4	143	169	10
Newick	10	3	0	7	96	131	6
Shoreham	10	2	1	7	114	245	5
Rye	10	2	0	8	104	271	4

Sussex 3

	P	W	D	L	F	A	Pts
Sussex Pol	10	8	0	2	265	100	16
Plumpton	10	6	2	2	118	93	14
Barns Green	10	6	0	4	169	160	12
Midhurst	10	5	1	4	146	125	11
Robertsbridge	10	2	0	8	96	140	4
Arun	10	1	1	8	59	235	3

MIDLANDS DIVISION

Midlands 1

	P	W	D	L	F	A	Pts
Hereford	12	9	1	2	229	145	19
Burton	12	9	0	3	260	146	18
Barker's Butts	12	9	0	3	226	138	18
Camp Hill	12	7	2	3	216	155	16
Broadstreet	12	6	2	4	242	199	14

	P	W	D	L	F	A	Pts
Wolverhampton*	12	7	0	5	249	219	12
Westleigh	12	5	1	6	263	226	11
Whitchurch	12	5	1	6	197	171	11
Syston*	12	6	0	6	203	207	10
Leighton Buzzard	12	4	0	8	135	233	8
Leamington	12	3	1	8	147	217	7
Mansfield*	12	2	2	8	144	208	4
Stafford	12	1	0	11	113	360	2

Midlands 2

	P	W	D	L	F	A	Pts
Scunthorpe	12	10	0	2	303	118	20
Hinckley	12	10	0	2	278	129	20
Derby	12	8	0	4	237	186	16
Stockwood Pk	12	8	0	4	180	142	16
Belgrave	12	7	1	4	205	131	15
Keresley	12	6	1	5	154	127	13
Newport	12	6	0	6	179	161	12
Bedworth	12	4	3	5	133	158	11
Sutton Cold	12	5	0	7	177	166	10
Bedford Ath	12	3	2	7	150	163	8
Paviors	12	3	2	7	180	213	8
Towcestrians	12	3	1	8	126	285	7
Matlock	12	0	0	12	87	410	0

Midlands East 1

	P	W	D	L	F	A	Pts
Kettering	12	9	0	3	246	152	18
Huntingdon	12	9	0	3	198	123	18
Ampthill	12	8	0	4	250	168	16
Long Buckby	12	8	0	4	211	131	16
Newark	12	6	1	5	140	119	13
Stoneygate	12	6	0	6	163	139	12
Ilkeston	12	6	0	6	151	140	12
Peterborough	12	6	0	6	178	223	12
Spalding	12	5	1	6	174	219	11
Vipers	12	3	2	7	113	150	8
Stew & Lloyds*	12	4	1	7	104	145	7
Amber Valley	12	3	0	9	101	196	6
Biggleswade	12	2	1	9	127	251	5

Midlands West 1

	P	W	D	L	F	A	Pts
Luctonians	12	12	0	0	458	126	24
Dudley	12	9	0	3	202	181	18
Kenilworth	12	8	1	3	285	125	17
Bromsgrove	12	8	1	3	303	152	17
O Laurentians	12	8	1	3	255	175	17
Longton	12	7	0	5	219	176	14
Newbold	12	6	0	6	215	193	12
O Halesonians	12	6	0	6	218	267	12
Kings Norton	12	3	1	8	157	266	7
O Leamingtons	12	3	1	8	124	311	7
Leek	12	3	0	9	137	311	6
Aston O Ed	12	1	1	10	142	334	3
Willenhall	12	1	0	11	120	218	2

Midlands East 2

	P	W	D	L	F	A	Pts
Lutterworth	12	12	0	0	315	70	24
O N'ptonians	12	10	0	2	270	122	20
Lincoln	12	8	2	2	229	112	18

	P	W	D	L	F	A	Pts
Wellingborough	12	8	0	4	187	147	16
Moderns*	12	7	0	5	329	185	12
Ashbourne	12	6	0	6	175	193	12
N'pton BB	12	5	1	6	197	222	11
Coalville	12	4	1	7	113	181	9
Kibworth*	12	4	1	7	155	196	7
Mellish	12	3	1	8	60	240	7
W Bridgford	12	3	0	9	172	264	6
S Leicester*	12	4	0	8	210	211	4
Chesterfield	12	1	0	11	80	349	2

Midlands West 2

	P	W	D	L	F	A	Pts
Selly Oak	12	11	1	0	316	113	23
Malvern	12	9	0	3	203	108	18
O Coventrians	12	8	0	4	260	134	16
Ludlow*	12	8	1	3	199	141	15
Stratford-upon-A	12	7	0	5	211	175	14
Nuneaton O Eds	12	7	0	5	195	167	14
Tamworth	12	6	1	5	133	136	13
Stoke OB	12	5	2	5	180	153	12
Dixonians	12	4	2	6	170	223	10
O Yardleians	12	4	0	8	153	181	8
Shrewsbury	12	3	0	9	126	179	6
Woodrush	12	1	1	10	123	333	3
Newcastle (Staffs)*	12	1	0	11	87	313	0

East Midlands/Leicestershire 1

	P	W	D	L	F	A	Pts
N'pton MO	12	11	0	1	281	107	22
Bedford Queens	12	10	0	2	228	125	20
N'pton OS	12	9	1	2	309	165	19
Oadby Wygges	12	9	1	2	197	144	19
Dunstablians	12	8	1	3	266	159	17
Loughborough	12	7	0	5	208	142	14
Market Bosworth	12	5	0	7	150	158	10
Oakham	12	5	0	7	147	207	10
Luton	12	4	1	7	145	159	9
St Neots	12	3	1	8	162	216	7
Rushden & Higham	12	2	1	9	153	218	5
Aylestone St James	12	1	1	10	49	330	3
Melton Mowbray	12	0	1	11	96	261	1

East Midlands/Leicestershire 2

	P	W	D	L	F	A	Pts
Bedford Swifts*	12	12	0	0	345	66	22
O Bosworthians	12	9	2	1	245	87	20
Bugbrooke	12	9	0	3	238	165	18
St Ives	12	8	0	4	222	134	16
Wellingborough OG	12	6	1	5	202	128	13
Brackley	12	6	1	5	148	141	13
Colworth House	12	6	0	6	142	192	12
Daventry	12	5	0	7	154	155	10
Old Ashbeians	12	4	0	8	142	259	8
Birstall	12	4	0	8	134	261	8
Kempston	12	3	0	9	104	251	6
N'pton Cas	12	2	0	10	77	147	4
New Pks.	12	2	0	10	89	256	4

East Midlands/Leicestershire 3

	P	W	D	L	F	A	Pts
Oundle	12	11	1	0	271	67	23
Deepings	12	11	1	0	269	108	23
Vauxhall Motors	12	9	1	2	342	111	19
Corby	12	7	1	4	238	127	15
O Newtonians	12	5	2	5	186	127	12
Wigston	12	4	2	6	132	154	10
Westwood	12	4	1	7	120	167	9
N'pton Heaths	12	4	1	7	107	193	9
W Leicester	12	4	1	7	153	294	9
Anstey*	12	5	0	7	96	168	8
Thorney	12	4	0	8	129	242	8
Aylestonians	12	3	0	9	104	251	6
Burbage*	12	1	1	10	101	239	1

East Midlands/Leicestershire 4

	P	W	D	L	F	A	Pts
Loughborough S	12	12	0	0	599	52	22
Cosby	12	7	1	4	143	138	15
Braunstone T	12	7	0	5	265	133	14
O Wellingburians	12	6	0	6	183	284	12
Clapham T	12	5	0	7	115	158	10
Shepshed	12	3	0	9	84	320	6
Biddenham	12	1	1	10	105	409	3

North Midlands 1

	P	W	D	L	F	A	Pts
Evesham	12	11	0	1	247	100	22
Telford	12	9	1	2	306	147	19
O Griffinians	12	8	1	3	243	161	17
Edwardians	12	8	1	3	233	152	17
Warley	12	8	1	3	218	173	17
Pershore	12	7	0	5	239	149	14
Erdington	12	7	0	5	253	175	14
Five Ways OE	12	5	0	7	136	198	10
Kidderminster	12	4	0	8	178	221	8
Bromyard	12	4	0	8	122	214	8
Veseyans	12	3	0	9	133	256	6
Bridgnorth	12	2	0	10	125	305	4
O Centrals	12	0	0	12	111	293	0

North Midlands 2

	P	W	D	L	F	A	Pts
Birmingham CO	12	12	0	0	316	96	24
O Saltleians	12	8	1	3	159	163	17
Kynoch	12	8	0	4	138	151	16
Droitwich	12	7	1	4	257	139	15
Redditch	12	7	0	5	173	125	14
Upton-on-Severn	12	6	1	5	187	125	13
Ross-on-Wye	12	6	1	5	158	105	13
Birmingham CS	12	6	1	5	86	114	13
Wulfrun	12	6	1	5	94	128	13
Tenbury	12	5	0	7	117	187	10
B'ham Welsh	12	3	0	9	120	236	6
Stourport	12	1	0	11	99	223	2
Bournville	12	0	0	12	95	207	0

North Midlands 3

	P	W	D	L	F	A	Pts
Ledbury	10	10	0	0	410	50	20
Cleobury Mort	10	8	0	2	174	102	16
Bishops Castle	10	6	0	4	254	66	12
Oswestry	10	6	0	4	191	99	12
Yardley & Dist★	10	7	0	3	188	102	12
Birchfield	10	5	1	4	157	187	11
Harborne★	10	3	1	6	178	290	5
Witton★	10	4	0	6	152	232	2
Market Drayton	10	1	0	9	87	266	2
Bredon Star	10	1	0	9	81	411	2
O Moseleians★	10	3	0	7	85	152	0

Notts, Lincs & Derbys 1

	P	W	D	L	F	A	Pts
Long Eaton	12	10	0	2	291	105	20
Stamford	12	9	0	3	250	106	18
East Retford	12	9	0	3	223	143	18
Grimsby	12	8	1	3	276	109	17
Kesteven	12	8	1	3	202	116	17
Nottingham Cas	12	7	0	5	184	149	14
Buxton	12	5	2	5	193	231	12
Southwell	12	4	2	6	166	199	10
Glossop	12	4	0	8	102	139	8
Sleaford	12	4	0	8	146	187	8
Worksop★	12	3	1	8	106	214	5
Melbourne	12	2	0	10	78	241	4
E Leake	12	1	1	10	68	346	3

Notts, Lincs & Derbys 2

	P	W	D	L	F	A	Pts
Bakewell Manns	12	10	1	1	269	150	21
Keyworth	12	10	0	2	213	118	20
M Rasen & Louth	12	9	0	3	187	113	18
Leesbrook★	12	9	0	3	285	101	16
Dronfield	12	7	0	5	141	80	14
Castle D'ton	12	7	0	5	143	125	14
Ashfield Swans	12	6	0	6	139	123	12
All Spartans★	12	5	0	7	140	175	8
Boston	12	4	0	8	143	326	8
N Kesteven	12	3	1	8	155	219	7
Rolls-Royce	12	3	0	9	133	214	6
Notts Cons	12	3	0	9	96	187	6
Boots Ath★	12	1	0	11	143	256	0

Notts, Lincs & Derbys 3

	P	W	D	L	F	A	Pts
Stamford Coll	11	10	0	1	274	83	20
Cotgrave	11	8	1	2	263	78	17
Nottinghamians	11	8	1	2	203	117	17
Belper	11	7	0	4	200	95	14
Meden Vale	11	6	1	4	155	118	13
Barton & Dist	11	5	0	6	221	128	10
Cleethorpes	11	4	0	7	131	207	8
U of Derby	11	4	0	7	118	198	8
Ollerton	11	4	0	7	114	269	8
Yarborough Bees	11	3	1	7	148	274	7
Bingham	11	3	0	8	102	213	6
Tupton	11	2	0	9	126	275	4

Notts, Lincs & Derbys 4

	P	W	D	L	F	A	Pts
Bourne	8	6	0	2	157	84	12
Bolsover	7	5	0	2	223	71	10
Sutton B'ton Sc	8	5	0	3	204	83	10
Hope Valley★	7	6	0	1	236	53	8
Skegness	7	4	0	3	208	59	8
Gainsborough	8	4	0	4	186	130	8
Whitwell	7	3	0	4	118	172	6
Bilsthorpe	6	2	0	4	71	86	4
RAF Waddington	7	1	0	6	109	174	2
Metheringham	7	0	0	7	0	600	0

Staffordshire/Warwickshire 1

	P	W	D	L	F	A	Pts
Manor Pk	12	12	0	0	410	91	24
Southam	12	10	0	2	376	107	20
Coventry Saras	12	9	1	2	245	130	19
Rugby St Andrews	12	6	2	4	178	171	14
Trinity Guild	12	6	0	6	242	142	12
GPT Coventry★	12	7	0	5	180	153	12
Silhillians	12	6	0	6	199	182	12
Cov Welsh	12	4	1	7	146	188	9
Dunlop	12	4	0	8	127	184	8
Coventrians	12	4	0	8	95	214	8
GEC St Leonards	12	4	0	8	94	239	8
Atherstone★	12	4	0	8	143	203	6
Eccleshall	12	0	0	12	34	465	0

Staffordshire/Warwickshire 2

	P	W	D	L	F	A	Pts
Berkswell & Bals	12	11	0	1	206	54	22
Earlsdon	12	8	1	3	247	108	17
Alcester	12	8	1	3	175	137	17
Trentham	12	8	0	4	171	122	16
O Wheatleyans	12	6	1	5	210	174	13
Spartans★	12	7	0	5	221	164	12
Pinley	12	6	0	6	148	152	12
Shipston-on-S	12	5	0	7	135	157	10
Handsworth	12	5	0	7	136	168	10
O Warwickians	12	4	1	7	115	211	9
Cannock	12	4	0	8	189	249	8
Uttoxeter	12	1	2	9	113	216	4
Wednesbury	12	2	0	10	80	234	4

Staffordshire/Warwickshire 3

	P	W	D	L	F	A	Pts
Burntwood	11	10	0	1	261	60	20
Linley	11	10	0	1	247	94	20
Claverdon	11	9	0	2	241	106	18
Rubery Owen	11	7	1	3	172	120	15
Rugeley	11	6	1	4	154	197	13
Bloxwich	11	6	0	5	166	112	12
Wheaton Aston	11	6	0	5	220	168	12
Shottery	11	4	0	7	136	216	8
Standard	11	3	0	8	137	129	6
Rugby Welsh	11	2	0	9	98	162	4
Harbury★	11	2	0	9	63	288	2
Coventry Tech★	11	0	0	11	99	342	-2

Staffordshire/Warwickshire 4

	P	W	D	L	F	A	Pts
Ford	8	6	1	1	140	29	13
Warwick	8	5	2	1	138	120	12
Michelin*	8	4	2	2	102	76	8
Stone	8	2	0	6	49	109	4
Jaguar (Cov)*	8	0	1	7	50	145	-5

NORTH DIVISION

North 1

	P	W	D	L	F	A	Pts
Manchester	12	10	1	1	362	124	21
Macclesfield	12	10	1	1	301	159	21
Hull Ionians	12	10	0	2	294	133	20
Bridlington	12	7	1	4	212	148	15
Tynedale	12	7	1	4	212	163	15
Widnes	12	5	2	5	159	220	12
Wigton	12	5	1	6	194	219	11
Bradford & Bing*	12	6	0	6	163	218	10
Stockton	12	5	0	7	165	222	10
West Pk Bramhope	12	3	0	9	127	181	6
Huddersfield	12	2	1	9	159	223	5
Middlesbrough	12	2	1	9	157	260	5
York	12	1	1	10	127	362	3

North 2

	P	W	D	L	F	A	Pts
N Brighton	12	10	1	1	232	105	21
Sedgley Pk	12	10	0	2	257	141	20
Blaydon	12	9	1	2	247	80	19
Northern	12	8	0	4	249	188	16
Alnwick	12	6	1	5	190	202	13
Vale of Lune	12	6	0	6	183	183	12
Durham City	12	6	0	6	195	204	12
Halifax	12	6	0	6	175	209	12
Doncaster	12	4	2	6	183	168	10
H'pool Rovers	12	4	0	8	164	208	8
O Crossleyans	12	3	2	7	140	189	8
West Pk St Helens	12	1	1	10	144	275	3
Birkenhead Pk	12	1	0	11	112	319	2

North-West 1

	P	W	D	L	F	A	Pts
Lymm	12	10	0	2	233	128	20
Penrith	12	9	0	3	276	182	18
Wilmslow	12	8	1	3	247	148	17
Blackburn	12	8	1	3	200	126	17
Oldershaw	12	7	1	4	272	154	15
Chester	12	6	1	5	296	199	13
Netherhall	12	6	1	5	190	185	13
Leigh	12	6	0	6	276	209	12
Ashton on Mersey*	12	6	0	6	173	183	10
Carlisle	12	4	0	8	187	319	8
Northwich	12	1	0	11	86	301	2
Sandbach	12	1	0	11	135	366	2
Cockermouth*	12	3	1	8	137	208	-3

North-West 2

	P	W	D	L	F	A	Pts
Vagabonds (IoM)	12	9	0	3	291	133	18
Aspull	12	9	0	3	258	107	18
O Salians	12	7	3	2	228	129	17
O Aldwinians	12	6	2	4	201	164	14
Kirkby Lonsdale	12	6	1	5	225	203	13

	P	W	D	L	F	A	Pts
Fleetwood	12	6	1	5	184	213	13
Egremont	12	6	0	6	183	264	12
Windermere*	12	6	1	5	184	181	11
Merseyside Pol	12	5	0	7	142	207	10
Rossendale	12	4	0	8	136	187	8
Caldy	12	3	1	8	192	265	7
Wigan	12	3	1	8	162	246	7
Stockport	12	3	0	9	175	262	6

Cumbria/Lancashire North

	P	W	D	L	F	A	Pts
Workington	12	11	0	1	398	102	22
Calder Vale	12	10	1	1	267	161	21
Metrovick	12	8	1	3	279	148	17
St Benedicts	12	8	0	4	218	148	16
Vickers	12	8	0	4	210	147	16
Ormskirk	12	6	0	6	202	190	12
Tyldesley	12	5	0	7	210	186	10
Keswick	12	5	0	7	183	227	10
Rochdale	12	5	0	7	179	227	10
Upper Eden	12	4	1	7	177	234	9
Furness	12	3	0	9	142	238	6
Carnforth	12	3	0	9	82	345	6
Moresby	12	0	1	11	91	285	1

Cumbria

	P	W	D	L	F	A	Pts
Ambleside	8	7	0	1	247	77	14
Whitehaven	8	7	0	1	235	67	14
Creighton	7	6	0	1	128	91	12
Green Garth	7	3	0	4	129	100	6
Cumbria Const	7	2	1	4	97	151	5
Smith Bros	5	2	0	3	86	82	4
Millom	7	2	0	5	66	125	4
Silloth	8	1	1	6	65	182	3
British Steel	5	0	0	5	14	192	0

Lancashire North 1

	P	W	D	L	F	A	Pts
Ashton-under-Lyne	12	9	1	2	221	96	19
Blackpool	12	9	0	3	173	68	18
Heaton Moor	12	9	0	3	138	100	18
Bolton	12	6	2	4	212	120	14
Thornton Cleveleys	12	7	0	5	218	150	14
Littleborough	12	6	0	6	154	163	12
Bury	12	6	0	6	140	150	12
Dukinfield	12	5	1	6	105	147	11
Colne & Nelson	12	5	0	7	187	177	10
De La Salle (Salford)	12	5	0	7	171	169	10
Oldham	12	5	0	7	149	196	10
Eccles	12	4	0	8	143	177	8
N Manchester	12	0	0	12	82	380	0

Lancashire North 2

	P	W	D	L	F	A	Pts
O Bedians	8	8	0	0	233	37	16
Broughton	8	7	0	1	248	78	14
Marple	7	5	0	2	242	29	10
Chorley	7	4	0	3	137	89	8
Burnage	8	4	0	4	109	132	8
Clitheroe*	8	4	0	4	163	159	6
Shell Carrington	8	2	0	6	27	188	4
Lostock	8	1	0	7	48	214	2
B Aerospace	8	0	0	8	32	313	0

Cheshire/Lancashire South

	P	W	D	L	F	A	Pts
Ruskin Pk	12	11	1	0	317	153	23
Newton-le-W	10	8	2	0	355	92	18
St Edwards OB	11	9	0	2	241	135	18
Warrington	12	7	1	4	268	136	15
Wirral	10	6	1	3	252	119	13
Eagle	12	6	0	6	212	178	12
O Parkonians	12	5	1	6	145	176	11
Altrincham Kersal	12	5	0	7	164	292	10
S Liverpool	11	4	0	7	221	191	8
Crewe & Nantwich	12	4	0	8	234	236	8
Congleton	12	4	0	8	111	243	8
Sefton	12	3	0	9	138	235	6
Port Sunlight	12	0	0	12	52	525	0

Cheshire

	P	W	D	L	F	A	Pts
O Anselmians	9	8	0	1	369	99	16
Wallasey	9	8	0	1	174	57	16
Bowdon	9	8	0	1	188	108	16
Hoylake	9	5	0	4	182	102	10
Helsby	9	4	0	5	163	189	8
Prenton	9	3	0	6	92	157	6
Shell Stanlow★	9	4	0	5	196	153	4
Moore★	9	3	0	6	136	228	2
Holmes Chapel	9	1	0	8	109	207	2
Whitehouse Pk★	9	1	0	8	51	360	0

Lancashire South

	P	W	D	L	F	A	Pts
Birchfield	9	9	0	0	289	82	18
Southport	9	8	0	1	317	54	16
Didsbury Toc H	9	5	2	2	138	109	12
Mossley Hill	9	4	0	5	87	213	8
Liverpool Coll	9	3	1	5	115	121	7
Douglas (IoM)	9	3	1	5	147	218	7
St Mary's OB★	9	4	0	5	119	95	6
Vulcan★	9	4	1	4	206	131	5
Halton	9	1	1	7	94	228	3
Hightown★	9	1	0	8	45	306	-4

North-East 1

	P	W	D	L	F	A	Pts
Driffield	12	10	1	1	244	100	21
O Brodleians	12	10	1	1	262	136	21
Gateshead Fell	12	8	0	4	221	241	16
Morpeth	12	7	0	5	268	145	14
Keighley	12	7	0	5	233	189	14
Pontefract	12	7	0	5	231	198	14
Horden	12	7	0	5	194	172	14
Ashington	12	6	0	6	206	199	12
Cleckheaton	12	6	0	6	223	245	12
Selby	12	4	1	7	171	198	9
N Ribblesdale	12	2	0	10	166	290	4
Roundhegians	12	1	1	10	117	231	3
Redcar	12	1	0	11	109	301	2

North-East 2

	P	W	D	L	F	A	Pts
Wheatley Hills	12	10	0	2	285	105	20
Percy Pk	12	10	0	2	252	111	20
Darl'ton Mowden PA	12	9	0	3	272	133	18
Goole	12	9	0	3	189	99	18

Beverley

Beverley	12	8	0	4	191	107	16
Westoe	12	8	0	4	190	110	16
Whitby	12	6	0	6	218	153	12
Blyth	12	6	0	6	188	187	12
Hull★	12	5	0	7	132	182	8
Whitley Bay R'cliff	12	3	0	9	91	237	6
Thornesians	12	2	0	10	86	201	4
Ripon	12	2	0	10	119	255	4
Bramley	12	0	0	12	80	413	0

Durham & Northumberland 1

	P	W	D	L	F	A	Pts
Darlington	11	10	0	1	422	128	20
Sunderland	11	8	1	2	237	145	17
Acklam	11	8	0	3	226	106	16
Ryton	11	7	1	3	270	169	15
W Hartlepool TDSOB	11	7	0	4	360	140	14
Winlaton Vulcans	11	6	0	5	171	181	12
Novocastrians	11	6	0	5	196	271	12
Medicals★	11	5	0	6	184	166	8
N Shields	11	3	1	7	123	218	7
Bishop Auckland	11	3	1	7	136	281	7
Ponteland	11	0	0	11	81	309	0
N Durham★	11	1	0	10	101	383	0

Durham & Northumberland 2

	P	W	D	L	F	A	Pts
Hartlepool	12	11	1	0	311	116	23
Guisborough	12	10	0	2	211	62	20
Chester-le-Street	12	8	2	2	102	121	18
Wallsend	12	8	0	4	235	130	16
Barnard Castle	12	7	0	5	212	203	14
Consett	12	5	0	7	261	176	10
Wensleydale	12	5	0	7	125	119	10
Billingham★	12	6	0	6	189	200	10
Richmondshire	12	4	1	7	131	126	9
Houghton	12	4	0	8	142	218	8
Hartlepool BBOB	12	1	1	10	93	295	3
Seaham★	12	6	0	6	211	165	2
Sedgefield★	12	0	1	11	103	395	-1

Durham & Northumberland 3

	P	W	D	L	F	A	Pts
S Tyneside Coll	11	10	1	0	477	58	21
Seaton Carew	11	10	0	1	275	84	20
Seghill	11	9	1	1	429	42	19
Benton	11	5	2	4	104	205	12
Wearside	10	5	1	4	135	107	11
Jarrovians★	11	5	2	4	128	119	10
Newton Aycliffe	11	3	2	6	75	258	8
Hartlepool Ath	10	3	1	6	59	169	7
Washington★	11	4	0	7	77	233	6
Alston Moor	10	2	1	7	54	153	5
Durham Const	10	1	1	8	51	276	3
Prudhoe Hosp★	11	1	0	10	84	244	0

Yorkshire 1

	P	W	D	L	F	A	Pts
Pocklington	12	11	0	1	253	119	22
O Otliensians	12	9	1	2	220	144	19
Ilkley	12	7	4	1	192	118	18
Wath	12	8	1	3	214	159	17
Yarnbury	12	7	0	5	201	154	14
Leodiensians	12	6	1	5	205	163	13

	P	W	D	L	F	A	Pts
Malton & Norton	12	6	0	6	237	166	12
Wibsey	12	6	0	6	162	206	12
Bradford Salem	12	4	0	8	172	241	8
Castleford*	12	4	0	8	163	240	6
Barnsley*	12	3	1	8	179	208	5
Halifax Vands	12	2	0	10	104	253	4
Sheffield Oaks*	12	1	0	11	112	243	0

Yorkshire 2

	P	W	D	L	F	A	Pts
Northallerton	12	11	0	1	288	84	22
Moortown	12	9	0	3	209	151	18
Sheffield Tigers	12	8	0	4	165	133	16
O Modernians	12	8	0	4	149	117	16
Dinnington	12	7	0	5	199	123	14
Scarborough	12	7	0	5	157	110	14
H'field YMCA	12	6	0	6	167	118	12
Wetherby	12	6	0	6	185	190	12
Hessle	12	5	1	6	182	196	11
Hemsworth	12	4	0	8	157	225	8
Aireborough	12	3	0	9	120	244	6
W Leeds	12	2	0	10	124	239	4
Skipton	12	1	1	10	95	267	3

Yorkshire 3

	P	W	D	L	F	A	Pts
Hullensians	12	11	0	1	194	77	22
Phoenix Pk	12	10	0	2	189	99	20
Lawnswood	12	8	0	4	210	163	16
Baildon	12	8	0	4	154	139	16
Leeds Corinths	12	7	0	5	216	146	14
Heath	12	7	0	5	185	134	14
Mosborough	12	6	0	6	132	150	12
O Rishworthians	12	6	0	6	107	152	12
Knottingley	12	5	0	7	142	120	10
York RI	12	4	0	8	131	161	8
Stanley Rodillians	12	4	0	8	120	171	8
Marist	12	2	0	10	94	165	4
Ossett*	12	0	0	12	75	272	-4

Yorkshire 4

	P	W	D	L	F	A	Pts
Stocksbridge*	12	12	0	0	329	57	22
Burley	12	9	1	2	240	110	19
Hornsea	11	9	0	2	266	98	18
Edlington & W	12	8	2	2	145	118	18
Garforth	11	6	1	4	163	148	13
Danum Phoenix	12	6	1	5	141	166	13
Rowntrees	12	5	0	7	151	196	10
BP Chemicals	12	4	1	7	169	202	9
De la Salle (Sheff)	12	4	1	7	135	199	9
Adwick le Street*	12	4	0	8	130	164	6
Withersea*	12	3	0	9	121	256	4
Rawmarsh	12	1	1	10	87	178	3
N Earswick*	12	2	0	10	93	278	2

Yorkshire 5

	P	W	D	L	F	A	Pts
Knaresborough	8	7	0	1	180	79	14
Pudsey	8	7	0	1	171	89	14
Menwith Hill Qs	7	2	0	5	100	110	4
Harlow Nomads	7	2	0	5	93	130	4
Yorkshire CW*	6	0	0	6	49	185	-2

SOUTH-WEST DIVISION

South-West 1

	P	W	D	L	F	A	Pts
Newbury	12	11	0	1	364	169	22
Gloucester OB	12	11	0	1	272	127	22
Maidenhead	12	10	0	2	301	135	20
Bridgwater	12	8	0	4	241	195	16
St Ives	12	7	0	5	178	212	14
Matson	12	6	0	6	241	186	12
Salisbury	12	6	0	6	232	198	12
Barnstaple	12	4	2	6	228	188	10
Brixham	12	4	1	7	214	244	9
Torquay	12	2	2	8	139	252	6
Taunton	12	3	0	9	169	317	6
Sherborne	12	2	1	9	187	271	5
Cinderford	12	1	0	11	110	382	2

South-West 2

	P	W	D	L	F	A	Pts
Launceston	12	11	1	0	490	107	23
Stroud	12	10	0	2	305	156	20
Gordon League	12	10	0	2	292	156	20
Penryn	12	7	0	5	196	185	14
Swanage	12	6	0	6	208	172	12
Combe Down	12	6	0	6	228	217	12
Dorchester	12	5	1	6	221	242	11
Bournemouth	12	4	0	8	253	214	8
Clevedon	12	4	0	8	166	201	8
O Patesians	12	4	0	8	167	231	8
Banbury	12	4	0	8	127	421	8
Aylesbury*	12	5	0	7	153	201	6
Oxford	12	1	0	11	123	426	2

Southern Counties

	P	W	D	L	F	A	Pts
Amersham & Chilt	12	12	0	0	286	111	24
Bracknell	12	11	0	1	409	76	22
Chinnor	12	7	1	4	268	144	15
Chippenham	12	7	1	4	144	187	15
Marlow	12	7	0	5	202	172	14
Swindon	12	6	1	5	234	154	13
Abbey	12	6	1	5	186	179	13
Wimborne	12	6	1	5	145	172	13
Devizes	12	4	0	8	150	275	8
Olney*	12	4	1	7	160	202	7
Bicester	12	3	1	8	180	223	7
Windsor	12	1	1	10	121	220	3
Bletchley*	12	0	0	12	58	428	-2

Western Counties

	P	W	D	L	F	A	Pts
Dings Crusaders	11	10	0	1	232	87	20
Spartans	11	7	0	4	272	121	14
Penzance	11	7	0	4	202	150	14
Devonport Servs	11	6	2	3	227	192	14
Tiverton	11	6	1	4	160	153	13
Keynsham*	11	9	1	1	304	108	9
Okehampton	11	4	1	6	145	164	9
O Culverhaysians	11	3	0	8	187	271	6
Paignton	11	3	0	8	159	257	6
Bideford*	11	4	0	7	132	288	6
Drybrook*	11	3	1	7	147	236	5
Crediton*	11	1	0	10	137	277	0

Cornwall & Devon

	P	W	D	L	F	A	Pts
Sidmouth*	12	11	0	1	395	81	20
St Austell	12	9	0	3	287	141	18
O Plymothian	12	8	0	4	249	168	16
Saltash	12	8	0	4	193	122	16
Hayle	12	8	0	4	214	152	16
Ivybridge	12	8	0	4	231	186	16
Teignmouth	12	7	0	5	353	181	14
Exmouth	12	4	0	8	277	151	8
S Molton*	12	6	0	6	232	208	8
Honiton*	12	4	0	8	162	206	6
Plymouth CS	12	3	0	9	91	552	6
Truro	12	2	0	10	146	252	4
Veor	12	0	0	12	103	533	0

Gloucestershire & Somerset

	P	W	D	L	F	A	Pts
St Mary's OB	12	11	0	1	231	79	22
Cleve	12	10	1	1	235	116	21
Hornets	12	10	0	2	301	107	20
Oldfield OB	12	7	0	5	165	145	14
Thornbury	12	7	0	5	204	188	14
Avonmouth	12	6	0	6	185	161	12
Wellington	12	6	0	6	129	179	12
Stow-on-the-Wold	12	5	0	7	193	174	10
N Bristol	12	4	1	7	162	210	9
Whitehall	12	4	0	8	167	270	8
Bristol Quins	12	3	0	9	138	215	6
Cirencester	12	3	0	9	120	247	6
O Redcliffians	12	1	0	11	82	221	2

Cornwall 1

	P	W	D	L	F	A	Pts
Bude	10	10	0	0	376	59	20
Falmouth	10	8	0	2	328	117	16
Perranporth	10	8	0	2	198	109	16
Liskeard-Looe	10	8	0	2	159	107	16
Redruth Albany	10	6	0	4	212	161	12
Helston	10	4	1	5	269	151	9
Newquay	10	4	1	5	176	123	9
Stithians	10	2	1	7	97	189	5
St Agnes	10	2	1	7	110	283	5
St Day	10	1	0	9	50	393	2
Wadenbridge	10	0	0	10	70	353	0

Cornwall 2

	P	W	D	L	F	A	Pts
Illogan Park	10	8	0	2	319	81	16
St Just	10	7	0	3	246	95	14
Camborne SoM	10	6	0	4	194	218	12
Bodmin*	10	6	0	4	242	89	10
Roseland	10	2	0	8	121	259	4
Lankelly Fowey	10	1	0	9	81	461	2

Devon 1

	P	W	D	L	F	A	Pts
Kingsbridge	12	11	0	1	496	86	22
Withycombe	12	10	1	1	208	89	21
Newton Abbot	12	9	0	3	330	160	18
Old Technicians	12	8	0	4	210	111	16
Tavistock	12	7	0	5	234	126	14
O Public Oaks	12	7	0	5	183	194	14
Exeter Saracens	12	6	0	6	172	148	12
Totnes	12	6	0	6	185	244	12
Topsham	12	3	2	7	176	218	8
Ilfracombe*	12	3	1	8	143	219	5
Salcombe	12	2	1	9	90	290	5
Dartmouth	12	2	0	10	85	304	4
Cullompton	12	1	1	10	101	424	3

Devon 2

	P	W	D	L	F	A	Pts
Tamar Saracens	11	11	0	0	272	56	22
Torrington	11	10	0	1	424	75	20
Bovey Tracey	11	9	0	2	257	118	18
Plymouth Argaum	11	6	1	4	196	144	13
Prince Rock*	11	7	0	4	232	91	12
N Tawton	11	6	0	5	204	213	12
Plymstock	11	5	0	6	168	146	10
St Columba	11	2	2	7	87	242	6
Axminster	11	1	1	9	108	280	3
Jesters*	11	5	0	6	137	168	0
Plympton-Vic*	11	1	0	10	85	377	0
Plym YMCA*	11	1	0	10	90	350	-2

Gloucester 1

	P	W	D	L	F	A	Pts
Cheltenham N	12	12	0	0	559	104	24
Barton Hill	12	10	0	2	237	126	20
Coney Hill*	12	9	0	3	308	119	16
Longlevens	12	8	0	4	221	167	16
Frampton Cotterell	12	7	1	4	239	153	15
O Richians	12	6	0	6	136	140	12
Bream	12	5	0	7	192	215	10
Brockworth	12	5	0	7	212	282	10
O Cryptians	12	4	1	7	177	253	9
Hucclecote	12	4	0	8	155	243	8
Bristol Saracens	12	4	0	8	151	279	8
Tredworth	12	3	0	9	147	368	6
Widden OB	12	0	0	12	93	378	0

Gloucester 2

	P	W	D	L	F	A	Pts
O Centralians	12	11	0	1	263	118	22
Cheltenham Saras	12	11	0	1	212	123	22
Cainscross	12	8	0	4	208	148	16
Cheltenham CS	12	7	0	5	215	134	14
Bristol Tele	12	6	0	6	128	133	12
Bishopston	12	6	0	6	154	161	12
O Bristolians	12	5	1	6	207	180	11
Painswick	12	5	0	7	188	164	10
Ashley Down OB	12	5	0	7	145	194	10
Tetbury	12	4	2	6	144	200	10
Chosen Hill FP	12	4	0	8	159	171	8
Cotham Park	12	3	0	9	129	172	6
Broad Plain	12	1	1	10	73	327	3

Gloucester 3

	P	W	D	L	F	A	Pts
Southmead	12	11	0	1	282	102	22
Westbury-on-S	12	9	1	2	238	118	19
Kingswood	12	8	1	3	270	137	17
Smiths (Industries)	12	7	0	5	201	195	14
Aretians	12	6	0	6	208	112	12
Gloucester CS	12	6	0	6	218	170	12
O Colstonians	12	6	0	6	202	177	12
Chipping Sodbury*	12	7	0	5	151	142	12

	P	W	D	L	F	A	Pts
Tewkesbury	12	4	0	8	129	152	8
Dursley	12	4	0	8	175	230	8
Bristol Aero	12	4	0	8	115	231	8
Glos Pol	12	3	0	9	104	222	6
O Elizabethians*	12	2	0	10	83	388	2

Gloucester 4

	P	W	D	L	F	A	Pts
Minchinhampton	12	10	1	1	243	81	21
Pilning	12	9	2	1	200	89	20
Gloucester AB	12	7	1	4	199	126	15
Newent*	12	5	2	5	141	123	10
Wotton-u-Edge	12	2	3	7	93	196	7
Tudorville	12	1	0	11	50	242	2
Dowty*	12	3	1	8	121	190	-1

Somerset 1

	P	W	D	L	F	A	Pts
Chard	12	9	0	3	326	189	18
Wiveliscombe	12	9	0	3	275	157	18
Tor*	12	9	0	3	224	126	16
Yatton	12	8	0	4	256	166	16
O Sulians	12	7	0	5	237	181	14
St Bernadettes OB	12	7	0	5	228	182	14
Midsomer N*	12	7	0	5	193	174	12
Walcot OB	12	6	0	6	146	142	12
Gordano	12	5	0	7	189	207	10
Frome	12	4	0	8	185	232	8
Minehead Barbs	12	4	0	8	185	273	8
Imperial*	12	2	0	10	89	291	2
Stothert & Pitt	12	1	0	11	82	295	2

Somerset 2

	P	W	D	L	F	A	Pts
Wells	12	12	0	0	306	100	24
N Petherton	12	10	0	2	263	71	20
Nailsea & Backwell	12	7	1	4	152	144	15
Avonvale	12	7	0	5	224	146	14
Chew Valley	12	7	0	5	219	203	14
Crewkerne	12	6	0	6	201	157	12
Winscombe	12	6	0	6	247	229	12
Yeovil*	12	6	1	5	151	122	11
Avon	12	4	0	8	152	172	8
Bath Saracens	12	3	0	9	142	231	6
O Ashtonians	12	3	0	9	88	183	6
Blagdon*	12	5	0	7	122	210	4
Bath O Eds*	12	1	0	11	103	402	0

Somerset 3

	P	W	D	L	F	A	Pts
St Brendans OB	14	13	0	1	651	99	26
Cheddar Valley*	14	13	0	1	467	76	24
Castle Cary	14	9	1	4	360	113	19
British Gas*	14	6	0	8	209	293	10
Burnham-on-Sea*	14	5	0	9	214	258	8
Wincanton*	14	5	0	9	213	273	8
Morganians*	14	4	1	9	145	372	7
Martock	14	0	0	14	49	824	0

Berks/Dorset/Wilts 1

	P	W	D	L	F	A	Pts
Blandford	12	12	0	0	310	53	24
Wootton Bassett	12	11	0	1	360	70	22
Marlborough	12	9	0	3	311	104	18
Corsham	12	9	0	3	240	131	18
N Dorset	12	8	0	4	288	174	16
Redingensians	12	6	0	6	203	168	12
Aldermaston*	12	6	1	5	160	171	11
Thatcham	12	4	2	6	137	183	10
Melksham	12	5	0	7	115	196	10
Weymouth	11	3	1	8	100	268	7
Supermarine	12	2	0	10	81	294	4
Bridport	12	1	0	11	148	262	2
Lytchett Minster	12	0	0	12	71	450	0

Berks/Dorset/Wilts 2

	P	W	D	L	F	A	Pts
Trowbridge	12	11	0	1	245	97	22
Westbury	12	10	0	2	231	89	20
Calne	12	9	0	3	276	104	18
Swindon Coll	12	9	0	3	285	128	18
Tadley	12	7	0	5	246	179	14
Portcastrians	12	7	0	5	216	156	14
Oakmedians*	12	6	1	5	164	159	11
Bradford-on-A	12	4	1	7	210	163	9
Berkshire SH	12	4	0	8	144	188	8
Pewsey Vale	12	2	0	10	103	275	4
Warminster*	12	3	0	9	106	285	4
Puddletown	12	2	0	10	110	382	4
Bournemouth U*	12	3	0	9	146	277	0

Berks/Dorset/Wilts 3

	P	W	D	L	F	A	Pts
Dorset Pol	10	9	0	1	176	63	18
Colerne	10	7	0	3	163	93	14
Minety	10	6	0	4	111	74	12
Christchurch	10	4	0	6	108	172	8
Poole	10	2	0	8	116	155	4
Hungerford	10	2	0	8	83	200	4

Bucks/Oxon 1

	P	W	D	L	F	A	Pts
Oxford OB	12	10	1	1	226	115	21
Witney	12	10	0	2	292	114	20
Slough	12	9	0	3	182	108	18
Buckingham	12	8	0	4	254	138	16
Oxford Marathon	12	8	0	4	271	178	16
Grove*	12	7	0	5	187	137	12
Milton K	12	6	0	6	182	182	12
Phoenix*	12	5	0	7	145	174	8
Pennanians	12	4	0	8	115	206	8
Beaconsfield	12	3	1	8	194	232	7
Wheatley	12	3	0	9	105	215	6
Chipping Norton	12	2	0	10	82	218	4
Chesham	12	2	0	10	112	330	4

Bucks/Oxon 2

	P	W	D	L	F	A	Pts
Drifters	14	12	0	2	434	87	24
Littlemore	14	12	0	2	426	88	24
Gosford AB	14	9	0	5	247	172	18
Cholsey	14	9	0	5	179	187	18
Abingdon*	14	7	0	7	246	210	12
Winslow	14	3	0	11	107	386	6
Harwell	14	2	0	12	121	358	4
Didcot	14	2	0	12	91	363	4

TIGERS REACT FURIOUSLY TO STING IN THE TAIL

PILKINGTON CUP 1995-96

4 May 1996, Twickenham
Bath 16 (1G 2PG 1DG)   **Leicester 15** (1G 1PG 1T)

The season finished, as it had begun, in quite dramatic circumstances. With just one minute of normal time remaining in the Cup final, referee Steve Lander awarded a penalty try against Leicester for persistent infringement. The Tigers were mortified as they watched the Cup slip from their grasp. One of their players, Neil Back, chose to show it by first pushing the referee over at the final whistle and then failing to go up the steps to collect his runners-up medal.

As so often, the great expectations of meetings between these two sides were not fulfilled. There was the occasional touch of glitter to admire in Catt's play, Johnson's line-out work and the running of the irrepressible Garforth, but even these were intermittent offerings. The overall impression was one of disappointment. Certainly, Leicester had so much more of the game, so much more of a stable platform, that they ought to have wrapped up the game long before Lander's intervention.

Was he right to award the penalty try? Certainly it is a rare use of the law, one seen publicly only once on a major occasion in these isles when Tony Spreadbury awarded a try against Oxford in this season's Varsity Match for the same reason. Then it was hard to sympathise with his view, since no warning had been given. As a result of that decision, however, there had been statements that referees would take such action if necessary. Here Lander had briefed the teams beforehand and then gave Leicester two verbal warnings in the build-up to the final try. Four times the referee deemed Leicester to have deliberately killed the ball and so the penalty try was given. If justice is to be done then this law must now be highlighted by the authorities and applied consistently.

No matter how aggrieved Leicester might have felt, there was simply no excusing Back's actions. There was little merit, either, in the hastily cobbled together cover story. Back claimed that he mistook Lander for Bath's Andy Robinson. As the referee was wearing a distinctive black and white checked shirt and has brown hair and a moustache, while Robinson is blond and was in a hooped jersey, the excuse beggared belief. 'Neil was horrified when he was told he had jostled the referee,' said Tigers captain Dean Richards. RFU spokesman Steve Griffiths was anxious to play down the incident. 'A Leicester player knocked into Steve Lander thinking he

The faces of Leicester's Dean Richards and Martin Johnson say it all as referee Steve Lander awards Bath the penalty try which cost the Tigers the Pilkington Cup in the dying moments of the final.

was a Bath player,' he said. 'That player has since apologised. I suspect no further action will be taken.'

How wrong he was. There was an outcry over Back's actions. A week later an RFU disciplinary hearing banned him for six months, although they did undermine their own judgement by adding that they accepted his plea of mistaken identity.

So much for the last minute of the game and the ensuing row. The match itself was cramped and crabby. Bath were short of four international players – Geoghegan, Guscott, Clarke and Ubogu. They struggled for primary possession, but how often have they ridden those odds? Leicester really need to look to their own game. Their pack is magnificent, and not just in performing the menial chores. The front row of Rowntree, Cockerill and Garforth are all superb footballers, while Back is the best creative openside in the country. Leicester's first try in the eighth minute owed much to the fancy footwork of the front row. Cockerill cleared up from a line-out near halfway. The ball found its way to his mate, Garforth, who galloped through the Bath defence. Malone was up in support and cut inside the outside tacklers to score.

Bath came back to lead 9-7 at half-time, Callard knocking over a penalty goal to add to his other success in the sixth minute. Catt added a dropped goal in the 40th minute. Liley, who had a wayward day with the boot, missing five from seven attempts, restored Leicester's lead early in the second half with a penalty goal. When Poole snatched a loose ball from a line-out to plunge over for a try for the Tigers five minutes from time, it looked all over. Steve Lander had other ideas, however, and Bath were home for their tenth Cup and their fourth double.

Bath: J E B Callard; A Lumsden, P R de Glanville (*capt*), A A Adebayo, J M Sleightholme; M J Catt, A D Nicol; D I W Hilton, R G R Dawe, J Mallett, M Haag, N C Redman, S O Ojomoh, E W Peters, R A Robinson
Scorers *Try:* pen try   *Conversion:* Callard   *Penalty Goals:* Callard (2)
Dropped Goal: Catt
Leicester: J G Liley; S Hackney, S Potter, R P Robinson, R Underwood; N G Malone, A Kardooni; G C Rowntree, R Cockerill, D J Garforth, M O Johnson, M D Poole, M J Wells, D Richards (*capt*), N A Back
Scorers *Tries:* Malone, Poole   *Conversion:* Liley   *Penalty Goal:* Liley
Referee S Lander (Liverpool Society)

How do they do it, those men with the delicate fingers who dip into the bags of balls every fourth Monday or so throughout the year? Once again they managed to keep apart the top two teams in the land until the final itself.

Once Winnington Park of Division 5 had perished, 57-0, to Wasps in the fifth round, the romantics' money was left to ride on London Irish. They saw off one of their old rivals and Celtic neighbours in exile, London Welsh, by 21-3 in the fourth round before accounting for Leeds 29-13 in the following round. A narrow 11-10 squeeze at home against West Hartlepool and the Irish were through to the semi-final for the first time in 16 years. In 1980 they went on to the final, where their opponents were Leicester, who took the Cup by 21-9. There was an equally emphatic result in this semi-final – 46-21 – but a different tale to tell. At a packed Sunbury, which was in danger of sinking under a sea of Guinness, Leicester built up a seemingly convincing lead of 22-8 with tries from Underwood, Wells and Johnson. But the Exiles were bent on keeping the ball alive, and no one more so than centre Rob Henderson. His surging run created an opening for Humphreys to score a try before he put his own name on the scoresheet. Corcoran's kicking closed the gap to 21-22. Leicester, though, had too much experience and too much power up front to succumb. In chasing the game London Irish made mistakes, allowing Delaney, Harris and Poole to cross for tries.

Leicester earned their place in the final, having seen off two First Division sides en route to Twickenham. They comfortably beat Saracens, 40-16, in the fifth round before accounting for the Harlequins challenge by 24-9 in the quarter-final. Bath, too, were made to work for their day out at Twickenham. Their 12-3 fourth-round win over Northampton in the December mud was a classic Cup tie. There were no tries, but enough commitment, ingenuity and courage to keep everyone happy. Second Division Wakefield almost pulled off the big shock, leading Bath until late in the game in the next round. Tries by Guscott and Butland, and two penalty goals from Callard, saw Bath through. Bristol were beaten 19-12 in the quarter-final to send Bath into the semi-final. For the first time in ten starts they were drawn at home, an advantage which helped them to resist Gloucester's spirited challenge by 19-10. A touch more self-belief and Gloucester might have managed it. How often have we said that about Bath's opponents?

RESULTS

First round

Askeans 30, Brixham 18; Basingstoke 20, Berry Hill 11; Bridlington 34, Syston 10; Broadstreet 26, Wharfedale 21; Camberley 26, Barking 24; Ealing 8, Weston-super-Mare 26; Gloucester OB 25, Camborne 8; Harlow 41, Abbey 6; Henley 30, Ruislip 8; High Wycombe 0, Cheltenham 15; Hornets 34, Bournemouth 23; Hull Ionians 52, Selly Oak 8; Launceston 10, Metropolitan Police 16; Leighton Buzzard 11, Birmingham & Solihull 29; Lewes 24, Oxford 17; Macclesfield 47, Sandal 17; Manchester 15, Scunthorpe 22; North Walsham 23, Letchworth 12; Northern 22, Sheffield 10; Nuneaton 26, Winnington Park 32; Old Blues 5, Tabard 11; Olney 0, Westcombe Park 23; Preston Grasshoppers 19, Stourbridge 44; Stafford 13, Netherall 18; Stockton 13, Broughton Park 11; Stoke-on-Trent 13, Lichfield 11; Sudbury 6, Lydney 28; Worcester 30, Kendal 17

Second round

Basingstone 19, Lewes 28; Birmingham & Solihull 14, Worcester 19; Bridlington 50, Aspatria 10; Cheltenham 11, Weston-super-Mare 13; Clifton 11, Metropolitan Police 12; Gloucester OB 7, London Welsh 16; Harrogate 6, Fylde 23; Havant 11, Exeter 20; Henley 33, Hornets 8; Liverpool St Helens 15, Hull Ionians 8;

167

Lydney 37, Harlow 7; Macclesfield 18, Morley 6; Netherall 7, Winnington Park 17; Northern 21, Stourbridge 22; Otley 16, Stoke-on-Trent 11; Plymouth Albion 18, Camberley 39; Redruth 19, North Walsham 15; Rosslyn Park 14, Richmond 22; Rotherham 15, Coventry 24; Scunthorpe 18, Walsall 49; Stockton 8, Leeds 27; Tabard 28, Askeans 15; Westcombe Park 9, Reading 32

Third round
Bridlington 13, Winnington Park 17; Coventry 78, Stourbridge 20; Exeter 17, Redruth 15; Leeds 12, Fylde 6; Lewes 10, Camberley 40; London Welsh 27, Richmond 12; Macclesfield 35, Walsall 36; Metropolitan Police 10, Reading 27; Otley 31, Rugby 40; Tabard 17, Lydney 19; Weston-super-Mare 19, Henley 18; Worcester 28, Liverpool St Helens 8

Fourth round
Nottingham 32, London Scottish 16; Camberley 0, Wakefield 18; Gloucester 47, Walsall 0; Newcastle Gosforth 26, Moseley 5; Orrell 17, Harlequins 19; Winnington Park 26, Lydney 11; Bedford 27, Worcester 12; Weston-super-Mare 9, West Hartlepool 25; Sale 9, Wasps 18; Reading 7, Bristol 44; Exeter 0, Leicester 27; Bath 12, Northampton 3; Blackheath 9, Coventry 19; Leeds 20, Waterloo 15; London Irish 21, London Welsh 3; Saracens 27, Rugby 7

Fifth round
Bedford 0, Bristol 37; Leeds 13, London Irish 29; Leicester 40, Saracens 16; Newcastle Gosforth 22, Harlequins 44; Nottingham 10, Gloucester 36; Wakefield 12, Bath 16; West Hartlepool 16, Coventry 6; Winnington Park 0, Wasps 57

Quarter-finals
Bristol 12, Bath 19; Gloucester 22, Wasps 9; Leicester 24, Harlequins 9; London Irish 11, West Hartlepool 10

Semi-finals
London Irish 21, Leicester 46; Bath 19, Gloucester 10

Previous finals (*all at Twickenham*)
1972 Gloucester 17, Moseley 6
1973 Coventry 27, Bristol 15
1974 Coventry 26, London Scottish 6
1975 Bedford 28, Rosslyn Park 12
1976 Gosforth 23, Rosslyn Park 14
1977 Gosforth 27, Waterloo 11
1978 Gloucester 6, Leicester 3
1979 Leicester 15, Moseley 12
1980 Leicester 21, London Irish 9
1981 Leicester 22, Gosforth 15
1982 Gloucester 12, Moseley 12
     (*title shared*)
1983 Bristol 28, Leicester 22
1984 Bath 10, Bristol 9
1985 Bath 24, London Welsh 15
1986 Bath 25, Wasps 17
1987 Bath 19, Wasps 12
1988 Harlequins 28, Bristol 22
1989 Bath 10, Leicester 6
1990 Bath 48, Gloucester 6
1991 Harlequins 25, Northampton 13
     (*aet*)
1992 Bath 15, Harlequins 12 (*aet*)
1993 Leicester 23, Harlequins 16
1994 Bath 21, Leicester 9
1995 Bath 36, Wasps 16

COUNTY CUP WINNERS 1995-96

Berkshire	**Bracknell**
Buckinghamshire	**Marlow**
Cheshire	**New Brighton**
Cornwall	**Launceston**
Cumbria	**Aspatria**
Devon	**Exeter**
Dorset/Wilts	**Swanage & Wareham**
Durham	**Blaydon**
Eastern Counties	**Norwich**
East Midlands	**Ampthill**
Gloucestershire	**Gloucester OB/ Berry Hill**
Hampshire	**Havant**
Hertfordshire	**Bishop's Stortford**
Kent	**Blackheath**
Lancashire	**Liverpool St Helens**
Leicestershire	**West Leigh**
Middlesex	**Staines**
North Midlands	**Worcester**
Northumberland	**Tynedale**
Notts, Lincs & Derbys	**Derby**
Oxfordshire	**Bicester**
Somerset	**Bridgwater & Albion**
Staffordshire	**Stoke-on-Trent**
Surrey	**Esher**
Sussex	**Haywards Heath**
Warwickshire	**Sutton Coldfield**
Yorkshire	**Morley**

THE END OF AN ERA

CIS INSURANCE COUNTY CHAMPIONSHIP 1995-96
Michael Austin

20 April 1996, Twickenham
Gloucestershire 17 (2G 1PG)   **Warwickshire 13** (1G 2PG)

The last championship in its traditional format brought Gloucestershire their first title since 1984 and a 16th overall to equal Lancashire's record. Warwickshire, the holders and ten times champions, lost because they failed to reproduce the forward power that had yielded 11 consecutive wins in the competition, dating back two seasons to when they rallied after losing all three matches in Area North League 2.

It was a triumphant farewell for Gloucester full-back Tim Smith, 33, and Cheltenham lock John Brain, 35, who marked their final appearances before retirement with significant performances, watched by a crowd of 7,750. The Warwickshire forwards, beset with fitness doubts in the week leading up to the match, produced an uncharacteristically limp display. They tapped loosely from the line-out for Andrew Stanley and the Gloucestershire pack to plunder possession and disrupt their half-backs.

Smith, making his fourth Twickenham appearance, landed a penalty goal and converted tries by Stanley, the captain, and Julian Davis, while Warwickshire's belated response was a try from Mark Warr, the Sale scrum-half, who learned the game at the Barker's Butts club. Matt Gallagher, the Nottingham fly-half bound for Coventry, kicked a conversion and put over two penalty goals. Warwickshire centre Mick Curtis emerged with credit.

The match, watched by the Princess Royal, the Gloucestershire patron, signalled the end of an era in sponsorship terms, too. CIS, also fervent supporters of the Under-21 County Championship, stepped down after three years. In 1996-97, the competition will be restricted to players below Courage League 4 because of increased club commitments. The North and Midlands will combine for the first time in groups to produce two semi-finalists rather than one each, following a format London and the South-West have already adopted.

Gloucestershire emerged successfully from matches against Hertfordshire, Oxfordshire, Devon and Berkshire before edging out Surrey 16-13 at Imber Court. That win expunged the memory of two successive defeats in the semi-finals, by Yorkshire and Northumberland, both by a single point. They accumulated 116 points in five games, compared with Warwickshire's 206.

Warwickshire's comprehensive semi-final win on their first visit to

Preston Grasshoppers, against Lancashire, pointed deceptively to a repeat success at Twickenham. With unerring consistency, they had scored more than 30 points in each of the five matches leading to the final. But they had not beaten Gloucestershire for 28 years, a record which included defeats in the 1972 final and the semi-finals of 1974, 1975 and 1981.

In the Under-21s final, played as a curtain-raiser to the senior match, Yorkshire beat East Midlands 20-13.

Gloucestershire: T Smith (Gloucester); J Perrins (Gloucester), D Edwards (Berry Hill), L Osborne (Gloucester), D Morgan (Cheltenham); R Mills (Lydney), J Davis (Lydney); R Phillips (Cheltenham), N Nelmes (Lydney), S Baldwin (Gloucester OB), T Clink (Cheltenham), J Brain (Cheltenham), A Knox (Lydney), I Patten (Coventry), A Stanley (Gloucester) (*capt*)
Scorers *Tries:* Stanley, Davis *Conversions:* Smith (2) *Penalty Goal:* Smith
Warwickshire: A Parton (Henley); J Minshull (Kenilworth), M Curtis (Coventry), M Palmer (Rugby Lions), D Watson (Rugby Lions); M Gallagher (Nottingham), M Warr (Sale); G Tregilgas (Coventry) (*capt*), R Burdett (Rugby Lions), T Revan (Rugby Lions), S Smith (Rugby Lions), P Bowman (Rugby Lions), M Ellis (Rugby Lions), M Fountaine (Bristol), S Carter (Rugby Lions) *Replacement* A Ruddlesdin (Long Buckby) for Ellis (66 mins)
Scorers *Try:* Warr *Conversion:* Gallagher *Penalty Goals:* Gallagher (2)
Referee B Campsall (Yorkshire Society)

SEMI-FINALS

9 March, Preston Grasshoppers RFC
Lancashire 16 (1G 3PG) **Warwickshire 36** (2G 4PG 2T)

Lancashire: J Chesworth (Preston Grasshoppers); I Bruce (Waterloo), I Wynn (Orrell), S Gough (Fylde), G Monaghan (Leigh); A Handley (Waterloo), C O'Toole (Fylde); C King (Liverpool St Helens), C Webster (Loughborough U), P Dunbavand (Sedgley Park), B Kay (Waterloo), N Allott (Waterloo), D Blyth (Waterloo), M Kenrick (Old Aldwinians) (*capt*), A Morris (Sale) *Replacements* H Parr (Waterloo) for Kenrick (52 mins); B Pilecki (Waterloo) for Dunbavand (65 mins)
Scorers *Try:* Parr *Conversion:* Gough *Penalty Goals:* Gough (3)
Warwickshire: A Parton (Henley); J Minshull (Kenilworth), M Palmer (Rugby Lions), M Curtis (Coventry), D Watson (Rugby Lions); M Gallagher (Nottingham), M Warr (Sale); G Tregilgas (Coventry) (*capt*), R Burdett (Rugby Lions), T Revan (Rugby Lions), P Bowman (Rugby Lions), S Smith (Rugby Lions), M Ellis (Rugby Lions), M Fountaine (Bristol), S Carter (Rugby Lions)
Scorers *Tries:* Fountaine, Minshull, Parton, Smith *Conversions:* Gallagher (2) *Penalty Goals:* Gallagher (4)
Referee G Gadjovich (Canada)

10 March, Metropolitan Police RFC
Surrey 13 (1G 2PG) **Gloucester 16** (2PG 2T)

Surrey: S Pilgrim (Camberley); P Greenwood (Richmond), A Holder (Rosslyn Park), R Brosch (Old Wimbledonians), N Walshe (Harlequins); J Hoad (Camberley), C Greville (Dorking); D Perrett (Rosslyn Park), M Pepper (Harlequins), J Davies (Esher) (*capt*), D Ball (Camberley), D Milward (Brunel U), I Pickup (Harlequins), W Murphy (Warlingham), P Brady (Esher) *Replacement* G Allison (Harlequins) for Holder (42 mins)

Scorers *Try:* Davies   *Conversion:* Pilgrim   *Penalty Goals:* Pilgrim (2)
Gloucestershire: T Smith (Gloucester); J Perrins (Gloucester), D Edwards (Berry Hill), L Osborne (Gloucester), D Morgan (Cheltenham); R Mills (Lydney), Julian Davis (Lydney); R Phillips (Cheltenham), N Nelmes (Lydney), S Baldwin (Gloucester OB), T Clink (Cheltenham), J Brain (Cheltenham), A Knox (Lydney), I Patten (Coventry), A Stanley (Gloucester) *(capt)* *Replacement* John Davies (Cheltenham) for Edwards (65 mins)
Scorers *Tries:* Nelmes, Clink   *Penalty Goals:* Smith (2)
Referee C Harrison (East Midlands Society)

DIVISIONAL ROUNDS

North Division

Durham 29, Cumbria 14;
Northumberland 24, Cheshire 22;
Lancashire 20, Yorkshire 14; Cheshire 26, Yorkshire 22; Durham 30, Northumberland 16; Lancashire 27, Cumbria 20; Cheshire 33, Durham 31; Cumbria 14, Yorkshire 30; Northumberland 9, Lancashire 11; Cumbria 18, Cheshire 22; Durham 16, Lancashire 19; Yorkshire 28, Northumberland 19; Lancashire 23, Cheshire 22; Northumberland 23, Cumbria 13; Yorkshire 27, Durham 22

	P	W	D	L	F	A	Pts
Lancashire	5	5	0	0	100	81	10
Cheshire	5	3	0	2	125	118	6
Yorkshire	5	3	0	2	121	101	6
Durham	5	2	0	3	128	109	4
Northumberland	5	2	0	3	91	104	4
Cumbria	5	0	0	5	79	131	0

Midlands Division

Group A
Leicestershire 6, Warwickshire 37;
Warwickshire 37, Notts, Lincs & Derbys 3;
Notts, Lincs & Derbys 8, Leicestershire 34

	P	W	D	L	F	A	Pts
Warwickshire	2	2	0	0	74	9	4
Leicestershire	2	1	0	1	40	45	2
Notts, Lincs & Derbys	2	0	0	2	11	71	0

Group B
Staffordshire 55, East Midlands 29; East Midlands 7, North Midlands 39; North Midlands 33, Staffordshire 16

	P	W	D	L	F	A	Pts
North Midlands	2	2	0	0	72	23	4
Staffordshire	2	1	0	1	71	62	2
East Midlands	2	1	0	1	36	94	2

Play-off Matches
Semi-finals: Warwickshire 57, Staffordshire 7; North Midlands 38, Leicestershire 28
Divisional final: Warwickshire 39, North Midlands 5

London & South-West

Group 1
Dorset & Wilts 12, Berkshire 13; Berkshire 22, Buckinghamshire 0; Buckinghamshire 13, Dorset & Wilts 42

	P	W	L	F	A	Pts
Berkshire	2	2	0	35	12	4
Dorset & Wilts	2	1	1	54	26	2
Buckinghamshire	2	0	2	13	64	0

Group 2
Devon 14, Oxfordshire 20; Hertfordshire 6, Gloucestershire 21; Devon 26, Hertfordshire 28; Oxfordshire 10, Gloucestershire 34; Gloucestershire 19, Devon 0; Hertfordshire 37, Oxfordshire 13

	P	W	D	L	F	A	Pts
Gloucestershire	3	3	0	0	74	16	6
Hertfordshire	3	2	0	1	71	60	4
Oxfordshire	3	1	0	2	43	85	2
Devon	3	0	0	3	40	67	0

Group 3
Middlesex 33, Hampshire 10; Sussex 15, Kent 22; Kent 27, Hampshire 31; Sussex 17, Middlesex 25; Hampshire 20, Sussex 3; Middlesex 10, Kent 10

	P	W	D	L	F	A	Pts
Middlesex	3	2	1	0	68	37	5
Hampshire	3	2	0	1	61	63	4
Kent	3	1	1	1	59	56	3
Sussex	3	0	0	3	35	67	0

Group 4
Somerset 19, Eastern Counties 12; Surrey 17, Cornwall 11; Cornwall 44, Eastern Counties 6; Surrey 25, Somerset 22; Eastern Counties 13, Surrey 32; Somerset 42, Cornwall 22

	P	W	D	L	F	A	Pts
Surrey	3	3	0	0	74	46	6
Somerset	3	2	0	1	83	59	4
Cornwall	3	1	0	2	77	65	2
Eastern Counties	3	0	0	3	31	95	0

Quarter-finals   Middlesex 14, Surrey 18; Berkshire 20,
                                      Gloucester 26

ENGLISH COUNTY CHAMPIONS 1889-96

1889	**Yorkshire**	1926	**Yorkshire**	1965	**Warwickshire**
1890	**Yorkshire**	1927	**Kent**	1966	**Middlesex**
1891	**Lancashire**	1928	**Yorkshire**	1967	***Surrey** and **Durham**
1892	**Yorkshire**	1929	***Middlesex**	1968	**Middlesex**
1893	**Yorkshire**	1930	**Gloucestershire**	1969	**Lancashire**
1894	**Yorkshire**	1931	**Gloucestershire**	1970	**Staffordshire**
1895	**Yorkshire**	1932	**Gloucestershire**	1971	**Surrey**
1896	**Yorkshire**	1933	**Hampshire**	1972	**Gloucestershire**
1897	**Kent**	1934	**E Midlands**	1973	**Lancashire**
1898	**Northumberland**	1935	**Lancashire**	1974	**Gloucestershire**
1899	**Devon**	1936	**Hampshire**	1975	**Gloucestershire**
1900	**Durham**	1937	**Gloucestershire**	1976	**Gloucestershire**
1901	**Devon**	1938	**Lancashire**	1977	**Lancashire**
1902	**Durham**	1939	**Warwickshire**	1978	**N Midlands**
1903	**Durham**	1947	***Lancashire**	1979	**Middlesex**
1904	**Kent**	1948	**Lancashire**	1980	**Lancashire**
1905	**Durham**	1949	**Lancashire**	1981	**Northumberland**
1906	**Devon**	1950	**Cheshire**	1982	**Lancashire**
1907	**Devon** and **Durham**	1951	**E Midlands**	1983	**Gloucestershire**
1908	**Cornwall**	1952	**Middlesex**	1984	**Gloucestershire**
1909	**Durham**	1953	**Yorkshire**	1985	**Middlesex**
1910	**Gloucestershire**	1954	**Middlesex**	1986	**Warwickshire**
1911	**Devon**	1955	**Lancashire**	1987	**Yorkshire**
1912	**Devon**	1956	**Middlesex**	1988	**Lancashire**
1913	**Gloucestershire**	1957	**Devon**	1989	**Durham**
1914	**Midlands**	1958	**Warwickshire**	1990	**Lancashire**
1920	**Gloucestershire**	1959	**Warwickshire**	1991	**Cornwall**
1921	**Gloucestershire**	1960	**Warwickshire**	1992	**Lancashire**
1922	**Gloucestershire**	1961	***Cheshire**	1993	**Lancashire**
1923	**Somerset**	1962	**Warwickshire**	1994	**Yorkshire**
1924	**Cumberland**	1963	**Warwickshire**	1995	**Warwickshire**
1925	**Leicestershire**	1964	**Warwickshire**	1996	**Gloucestershire**

After a draw. Lancashire and Gloucestershire have won the title 16 times each, Yorkshire 12, Warwickshire 10, Middlesex 8, Durham 8 (twice jointly), Devon 7 (once jointly), Kent 3 times, Hampshire, East Midlands, Cheshire, Northumberland and Cornwall twice each, Surrey twice (once jointly), and Midlands, Somerset, Cumberland, Leicestershire, Staffordshire and North Midlands once each.

FITNESS TELLS FOR MEDICALS

PILKINGTON SHIELD 1995-96
Michael Austin

4 May 1996, Twickenham
Helston 6 (2PG)   **Medicals 16** (1G 3DG)

Three dropped goals from Matt Bonner, a dental student, helped Newcastle-based Medicals to win the Pilkington Shield, contested for the final time under the glass company's sponsorship.

Medicals, founded in 1898 at the Durham University College of Medicine, boasted eight students and three dentists. Their former players include Derek Morgan, the international No 8 who became chairman of England's selectors in the 1980s. Extensive preparations for the final featured an hour's kicking tuition for 23-year-old Bonner from Rob Andrew and David Alred at Newcastle. The scheme worked to perfection as Bonner's dropped goals and his conversion of the game's only try, by wing Rory Fretwell, won the match for Medicals. The essence of the sixth junior clubs' final was their ability to absorb a vigorous 20-minute challenge from the Helston pack, who lacked their opponents' fitness and struggled to contain David Booth, an inspirational captain, in the line-outs.

Medicals, from Durham & Northumberland 1, had reached the final by beating Newton-le-Willows in the quarter-finals and Old Centralians (previously Saintbridge Former Pupils), of Gloucester, in the semi-finals. Stuart Bagnall, the chief executive of Hartlepool Football Club, contributed to the side's success in a coaching capacity and they conceded only one try in the first seven rounds.

Helston, a 31-year-old club, maintained Cornwall's Twickenham traditions, having battled through this competition involving the lowest-placed 512 clubs in England. They beat Old Ashmoleans of Southgate, north London, at the quarter-final stage in front of a crowd of 2,000 before squeezing out Wellingborough Old Grammarians at Bridgwater. Beverley Davis, their club secretary, finished a worthy runner-up for a second time: she had attempted to become the first woman on the RFU committee but had been beaten into second place in the election for Cornwall's representative.

Other clubs added to the competition's folklore. London Nigerians, coached by former England wing Chris Oti, overwhelmed Crusaders, of Norwich, by 113-0, while Old Bosworthians, who had dropped into East Midlands & Leicestershire 2, amassed 104 points without reply from Biddenham, No 8 Stuart Driver scoring six tries. Two of the longer journeys prompted Folkestone and Ledbury to trek a combined total of 1,200 miles to lose in the sixth round to Helston and North Shields respectively.

Looking ahead, the RFU were planning a third competition for 1996-97, designed to bridge the gap for intermediate clubs which qualify for neither the Cup nor the Shield.

Medicals scrum-half Peach sets up an attack in the 1996 Pilkington Shield final at Twickenham.

Helston: M Hocking (*capt*); M Busby, M Laity, D Savage, S Pollard; D Lockwood, D Knox; S Savvas, R Eagle, T Blandford, P Elliott, C Johns, A Punter, S Tregonning, G Hannaford
Scorer *Penalty Goals:* Lockwood (2)
Medicals: M Marriott; A Cragg, G Davies, D Melville, R Fretwell; M Bonner, T Peach; D Burrows, S Atkinson, H Cave, D Reeve, D Booth (*capt*), R Kozlowski, P Tinkler, A Greenwood *Replacement* J Banks for Greenwood (42 mins)
Scorers *Try:* Fretwell   *Conversion:* Bonner   *Dropped Goals:* Bonner (3)
Referee J Pearson (Durham Society)

Third Round

London Division: Region 1 – Eastern Counties, Hertfordshire, Middlesex Billericay 32, Feltham 10; Barclays Bank 36, Wisbech 6; Haverhill & District 20, Thames 25; Harpenden 18, Enfield Ignatians 21; Old Abbotstonians 3, Hayes 12; Fakenham 12, Hadleigh 23; London Nigerians 113, Crusaders 0; London Exiles 17, Old Tottonians 15; London French 18, St Nicholas OB 14; Old Ashmoleans 30, Cantabrigian 19 *Region 2 – Hampshire, Surrey, Kent, Sussex* Sittingbourne 48, Arun 0; Edenbridge 0, Deal Wanderers 41; Crowborough 10, Whitstable 10*; Lordswood 10, Aylesford 14; Old Wellingtonian 11, Dover 12; Battersea Ironsides 14, Andover 11; Tonbridge 34, BA Wingspan 6; Cranbrook 0, Folkestone 9; Old Gravesendians 16,

Old Haileyburians 0; Old Williamsonian 37, Wandsworthians 14

Midland Division: Region 1 – North Midlands, Staffordshire, Warwickshire Berkswell & Balsall 16, Kidderminster Carolians 6; Bloxwich 6, Yardley & District 17; Cannock 6, Upton-upon-Severn 19; Coventrians 10, Wednesbury 17; Erdington 14, Oakham 8; Oswestry 3, Ledbury 18; Spartans 15, Birmingham City Officials 11; Tenbury 10, Linley 16

Region 2 – East Midlands, Leicestershire, Notts, Lincs, & Derbys Bugbrooke 10, Wellingborough OG 12; Castle Donington 16, North Kesteven 7; Hope Valley 19, Northampton Casuals 11; Notts Constabulary 37, Kempston 8; Old Ashbeians 19, Old Spartans 10; St Ivans 8, Old Bosworthians 5; Vauxhall Motors 12, Bedford Swifts 21

South-West Division: Region 1 – Berkshire, Buckinghamshire, Dorset & Wilts, Oxfordshire Milton Keynes 20, Westbury 25; Beaconsfield 14, Oakmeadians 15; Tadley 52, Pewsey Vale 5; Trowbridge 23, Colerne 10

Region 2 – Cornwall, Gloucestershire, Devon, Somerset Torrington 8, Bodmin 9; Exeter Saracens 6, Perranporth 9; St Columba Torpoint 0, Topsham 24; Helston 39, Tavistock 22; Old Bristolians 33, Bishopston 14; Broad Plain 19, Chipping Sodbury 17; Gloucestershire Police 22, Cotham Park 12; Aretians 7, Old Centralians 41; Avon 15, Nailsea & Backwell 6; Cainscross 14, Tewkesbury 5

North Division: Region 1 – East of Pennines Billingham 0, Hullensians 18; Leeds Corinthians 13, Consett & District 9; Dinnington 5, Mosborough 6; Hessle 15, Huddersfield YMCA 25; Wensleydale 0, Medicals 30; Sheffield Tigers 18, Wetherby 3; Old Rishworthian 53, Hartlepool BBOB 3; Scarborough 3, North Shields 12

Region 2 – West of Pennines Ambleside 18, Wallasey 11; Didsbury Toc H 21, Old Anselmians 44; Littleborough 3, Marple 6; Newton-le-Willows 51, Old Bedians 10; Eccles 6, Ashton-under-Lyne 3; Carnforth 0, Shell Stanlow 10; Birchfield 30, Bolton 13

Fourth Round

London Division: Battersea Ironsides 25, Barclays Bank 22; Deal Wanderers 31, Aylesford 0; Enfield Ignatians 17, London Nigerians 0; Folkestone 39, Tonbridge 34; Hadleigh 39, Thames 3; London French 19, Hayes 6; Old Ashmoleans 20, Old Haileyburian 11; Old Williamsonian 15, Dover 25; Sittingbourne 3, London Exiles 29; Whitstable 16, Billericay 16*

Midlands Division: Berkswell & Balsall 14,

Spartans 12; Bedford Swifts 21, Hope Valley 9; Castle Donington 7, Wellingborough OG 10; Erdington 23, Linley 0; Ledbury 17, Old Ashbeians 14; Notts Constabulary 13, Yardley & District 18; Old Anselmians 51, Wednesbury 0; St Ives 8, Upton-upon-Severn 9

South-West Division: Bodmin 3, Tadley 0; Gloucestershire Police 6, Old Centralians 19; Helston 21, Avon 0; Old Bristolians 25, Cainscross 22; Topsham 57, Broad Plain 10; Trowbridge 16, Perranporth 12; Westbury 13, Oakmeadians 3

North Division: Ambleside 5, Shell Stanlow 5*; Birchfield 5, Hullensians 16; Eccles 11, Marple 13; Huddersfield YMCA 26, Mosborough 3; Medicals 15, Leeds Corinthians 9; Old Rishworthian 5, North Shields 13; Sheffield Tigers 9, Newton-le-Willows 10

Fifth Round

London Division: Billericay 8, Hadleigh 22; Enfield Ignatians 21, Deal Wanderers 10; Folkestone 19, Dover 3; London French 16, Battersea Ironsides 7†; London Exiles 7, Old Ashmoleans 10

South-West Division: Helston 29, Bodmin 12; Old Bristolians 18, Topsham 15; Trowbridge 8, Yardley & District 11; Westbury 0, Old Centralians 13

Midlands Division: Berkswell & Balsall 6, Ledbury 6*; Upton-upon-Severn 16, Erdington 4; Bedford Swifts 8, Wellingborough OG 13

Northern Division: Huddersfield YMCA 19, Newton-le-Willows 19*; Hullensians 0, Medicals 9; Marple 3, Old Anselmians 12; Shell Stanlow 5, North Shields 13

Sixth Round

North & Midlands: Old Anselmians 13, Newton-le-Willows 22; Yardley & District 6, Medicals 30; Upton-upon-Severn 11, Wellingborough OG 14; North Shields 5, Ledbury 0

London & South-West: Hadleigh 21, Enfield Ignatians 22; Helston 20, Folkestone 18; Old Centralians 13, Battersea Ironsides 3; Old Bristolians 19, Old Ashmoleans 20

Quarter-finals

North & Midlands: Newton-le-Willows 7, Medicals 24; Wellingborough OG 3, North Shields 0

London & South-West: Helston 27, Old Ashmoleans 23; Old Centralians 15, Enfield Ignatians 0

Semi-finals

Helston 20, Wellingborough OG 13 (*at Bridgwater*); Medicals 13, Old Centralians 10 (at *Wakefield*)

**Away team qualified* †*L French disqualified*

BARBARIANS RESPOND TO PEACE INITIATIVE

THE BARBARIANS 1995-96
Geoff Windsor-Lewis

For the second time in 18 months Lansdowne Road proved a happy hunting ground for the Barbarians when, following their victory over South Africa, the club responded to an invitation to play Ireland and produced a glittering display of attractive rugby. The match, dedicated to the restoration of peace in Ireland, was the brainchild of former Ireland internationals Hugo MacNeill and Trevor Ringland. In a short space of time the Barbarians assembled a star-studded side from all over the world. David Campese and François Pienaar, who had agreed to captain the team, were unfortunately injured and unable to take part, but they added to the occasion by turning up anyway.

Nonetheless the Barbarians were able to field a truly representative team, which included Philippe Sella, Dean Richards, Rory Underwood and Phil de Glanville, and a crowd of over 35,000 witnessed a match in which their individual and collective skills gave Ireland no respite. Half-backs Bachop and Roux continually tested the Irish defence. For their first try, Cabannes beat the first tackle and handed on to Rush, who found Bachop 15 metres inside with a fine pass, and the New Zealander put Underwood away. The Barbarians' ability to pass with such accuracy that the momentum never faltered was one of the best features of the match. Three more tries followed in quick succession and stunned the Irish crowd. At half-time they led by 35-14, with tries from Redman, Roux, De Glanville and Sella. Ireland battled bravely, Henderson shooting under the posts after good work by McBride, and Costello scored a try in the corner.

Eric Rush had a magnificent day for the Barbarians. After streaking away for one try he created another for Cockerill. Jonathan Callard kicked all ten conversions in the 70-38 win. All in all, the peace initiative was a marvellous idea and proved a great success, providing once again an illustration of the power of rugby to create goodwill wherever it is played.

In response to an invitation the Barbarians made a short tour to the province of Kansai in Japan in aid of the Kobe Earthquake Fund, playing the Kansai President's XV and Kobe Steel, the champion club for the last six years. The first match took place in Kyoto in front of a crowd of 20,000 in temperatures of 31 degrees. The President's XV was made up of two Japanese players, one Canadian and 12 New Zealanders, and from the outset All Blacks Jamie Joseph and Arran

Pene proved a huge handful. It took the visitors some time to get over their jet lag and grasp the fact that they were in a serious match. Healey and Sleightholme on the wings produced some fine attacking runs and Halpin thrilled the crowd with his ferocious charging breaks. A late flourish brought the visitors to within two scores of the home team in a high-scoring game that finished 76-66.

Moving on to Kobe, the team witnessed at first hand the devastating effects of the earthquake which killed more than 6,500 people and demolished over 100,000 buildings. The Barbarians were the first rugby visitors from outside Japan since the disaster, and their much-appreciated trip became a significant emblem of friendship. Japanese champions Kobe Steel were fired up for the match, attended by some 28,000 people, and their turn of pace and ability surprised the Baa-Baas, and indeed their own supporters. Yamanaka, an elusive side-stepping wing, scored five tries for the home side. Halpin led the way for the Barbarians with two tries, and Hall, Healey, Sleightholme, Jarvis and Gomarsall all put their names on the scoreboard. In the end, though, Kobe were the clear winners. The tour once again highlighted to many Barbarian players the different style of play and techniques in the southern hemisphere.

At home, a runaway victory at Newport began the season in fine style. Games at Leicester and Cardiff produced some spectacular play, and the East Midlands fielded a full Northampton side to defeat the Barbarians narrowly in an exciting match.

The Barbarians are now looking forward to playing Scotland in aid of the Dunblane Fund; Wales, to mark the swansong of the National Stadium, due to be replaced in time for the 1999 World Cup finals, and Australia at Twickenham in the autumn. In these changing times the Barbarians are confident that they will adapt to meet the current needs of players, and that players will be keen to participate in Barbarian rugby as a respite from their increasing club and international commitments.

RESULTS 1995-96

Played 8   Won 3   Lost 5   Drawn 0   Points for 382 (43G 2PG 15T)
Against 386 (42G 3PG 1DG 16T)

1995

26 Sept	**Beat Stirling County** at Forthbank Stadium
	57 (6G 3T) to 34 (3G 1DG 2T)
3 Oct	**Beat Newport** at Rodney Parade
	59 (7G 2T) to 28 (4G)
27 Dec	**Lost to Leicester** at Welford Road
	25 (2G 2PG 1T) to 51 (5G 2PG 2T)
1996	
6 Mar	**Lost to East Midlands** at Franklins Gardens
	19 (2G 1T) to 47 (6G 1T)

6 Apr	**Lost to Cardiff** at Cardiff Arms Park
	43 (4G 3T) to 49 (7G)
18 May	**Beat Ireland** at Lansdowne Road (The Peace International)
	70 (10G) to 38 (4G 2T)
2 June	**Lost to Kansai RFU President's XV** at Nishi Kyogoku Stadium
	66 (8G 2T) to 76 (8G 4T)
5 June	**Lost to Kobe Steel RFC** at Kobe Universiade Stadium
	43 (4G 3T) to 63 (5G 1PG 5T)

PLAYERS 1995-96

Abbreviations: *SC* – Stirling County; *N* – Newport; *L* – Leicester; *EM* – East Midlands; *C* – Cardiff; *I* – Ireland (The Peace International); *J1* – Kansai President's Invitation XV; *J2* – Kobe Steel; (R) – Replacement; * – New Barbarian

Full-backs: A G Hastings (Watsonians & Scotland) *SC*; *J Quantrill (Rugby) *N*; *W J L Thomas (Llanelli & Wales) *L*; P A Hull (Bristol & England) *EM*; *J A Gallagher (Blackheath & New Zealand) *C*; J E B Callard (Bath & England) *I, J1*; I C Glasgow (Heriot's FP) *J1* (R), *J2*

Wings: *R Subbiani (Bedford) *SC*, *N*; N K P J Woods (Blackrock Coll & Ireland) *SC*; *R Mailer (Stirling County) *SC* (R); D S Thorneycroft (Northampton) *N*; *D C Lougheed (Toronto Welsh & Canada) *L*; *W Proctor (Llanelli & Wales) *L*; *A S Healey (Orrell) *EM*, *J1*, *J2*; *J Topping (Ballymena) *EM*; *E Saunders (Rugby) *C*; D Stark (Boroughmuir & Scotland) *C*; R Underwood (Leicester & England) *I*; E J Rush (North Harbour & New Zealand) *I*; *L Jarvis (Pontypridd) *I, J1, J2*; J M Sleightholme (Bath & England) *J1, J2*; *A A Adebayo (Bath & England) *J2*

Centres: J Bell (Northampton & Ireland) *SC, N*; *C Little (Glasgow HK) *SC*; *I C Jardine (Stirling County & Scotland) *N*; *D Llewellyn (Neath) *N* (R); *L B Davies (Neath) *L*; A G Shiel (Melrose & Scotland) *L*; *K P McQuilkin (Bective Rangers & Ireland) *EM*; *G Evans (Neath) *EM*; *J C Harris (Leicester) *EM* (R); S R Cottrell (Cambridge U) *C*; *S Salvat (Alumni BA & Argentina) *C*; I L Evans (Cardiff Medical School) *C* (R); P R de Glanville (Bath & England) *I*; P Sella (Agen & France) *I*; *W I R Greenwood (Harlequins) *I*; M R Hall (Cardiff & Wales) *J1, J2*

Fly-halves: G P J Townsend (Northampton & Scotland) *SC*; *N R Jenkins (Pontypridd & Wales) *N*; *A King (Bristol University) *L*; J Davies (Cardiff & Wales) *EM*; R H Q B Moon (Walsall) *EM* (R); D Charvet (Agen & France) *C*; * S J Bachop (Otago & New Zealand) *I*; A Davies (Cardiff & Wales) *J1*, *J2* (R); D A Williams (Swansea & Wales) *J2*

Scrum-halves: *B W Redpath (Melrose & Scotland) *SC*; P John (Pontypridd) *N*; A C T Gomarsall (Wasps) *L*, *J1, J2*; R N Jones (Swansea & Wales) *EM*; *A Pichot (CA Isidro BA & Argentina) *C*; *J P Roux (Transvaal & South Africa) *I*

Forwards: K Colclough (Swansea) *SC*; T J Kingston (Dolphin & Ireland) *SC*; G F Halpin (London Irish & Ireland) *SC, J1, J2*; *S Paul (Heriot's FP) *SC* (R); *G Prosser (Pontypridd) *SC, L, J1*; S D Shaw (Bristol) *SC*; A J Charron (Ottawa Irish & Canada) *SC*; E W Peters (Bath & Scotland) *SC*, *N*; *I R Morrison (London Scottish & Scotland) *SC, L, C*; *R A Pask (Abertillery) *SC* (R), *N* (R); R C McBryde (Llanelli) *SC* (R); *L Bénézech (RCF & France) *N*; *K D McKenzie (Stirling County & Scotland) *N, C*; D I W Hilton (Bath & Scotland) *N*; *D Sims (Gloucester) *N*; *S J Campbell (Dundee HSFP & Scotland) *N*; *R Greenwood (Dunvant) *N*; D K Eves (Coventry) *N*; *M A Mika (Otago & Western Samoa) *L*; *B P Reidy (Marists & Western Samoa) *L*; *D la Perne (Dax) *L*; *P Berek (Dax) *L*; *P Walton (Newcastle & Scotland) *L*; *R A W Straeuli (Transvaal & South Africa) *L*; G C Rowntree (Leicester & England) *EM*, *I*; R Cockerill (Leicester) *EM*, *I*; D J Garforth (Leicester) *EM*, *I*; *C Johnson (Bishop's Stortford) *EM*; *S Murray (Edinburgh Academicals) *EM*, *C*; *C Pim (Old Wesley) *EM*; B B Clarke (Bath & England) *EM*; * L B N Dallaglio (Wasps & England) *EM*; *A Watt (Glasgow HK & Scotland) *C*; P H Wright (Boroughmuir & Scotland) *C*; (M Giacheri (Benetton Treviso & Italy) *C*; *X Blond (Racing Club & France) *C*; * J S Gardner (Benetton Treviso & Italy) *C*; M S Linnett (Worcester) *C* (R); *J A Hay (Hawick & Scotland) *C* (R), *J2*; *B Cripps (Abertillery) *C* (R); *O Brouzet (Grenoble & France) *I*; S O Ojomoh (Bath & England) *I*; L Cabannes (RCF & France) *I*; *M R Brewer (Canterbury & New Zealand) *I, J1, J2* (R); D Richards (Leicester & England) *I*; N C Redman (Bath & England) *I, J1, J2*; R G R Dawe (Bath & England) *J1*; *J Leonard (Harlequins & England) *J1*; *H E Stone (Cardiff) *J1, J2*; R A Robinson (Bath & England) *J1, J2*; *J W Davidson (Dungannon & Ireland) *J1* (R), *J2*; A P Burnell (London Scottish & Scotland) *J2*; D S Munro (Glasgow HK & Scotland) *J2*

DRAMATIC FINALE FIRES CAMBRIDGE

THE VARSITY MATCH 1995 (*for the Bowring Bowl*)

12 December, Twickenham
Cambridge University 21 (1G 3PG 1T)
Oxford University 19 (1G 3PG 1DG)

Varsity day is never a quiet occasion. In this 114th University Match, there were floodlights for the first time, a full house at the newly completed 78,000-capacity Twickenham and a controversial penalty try to effectively decide proceedings. (There was also a Viking-clad intruder who tackled Cambridge's replacement scrum-half, Ben Ryan, and was promptly set upon by both packs of forwards. The Viking beat a hasty retreat.)

Referee Tony Spreadbury was given the kind of hostile treatment he might have expected if he'd been officiating in a round-ball arena. He awarded a penalty try to Cambridge four minutes from time for 'persistent offside', which the letter of the law perfectly entitles him to do. However, if a side persistently offends in the middle of the pitch, do you award a penalty try? No, you don't. The only relevant criterion, therefore, is the concept of probability of score. As Cambridge had handled poorly throughout, there was certainly no guarantee of a try. Oxford, at best, were very hard done by.

There was still time for them to edge their noses in front, and fly-half David Humphreys did slot his third penalty goal of the afternoon. But Cambridge had been fired by their unexpected bonus. Casado, the Light Blues' right wing, kicked high downfield; Du Preez, the Oxford full-back, went up but was swamped. The ball was recycled. It flashed along the line and there, in glorious flight, was no sleek threequarter, but Jonathan Evans, the Cambridge hooker. Two defenders stood in his way, but it was no contest. Evans was home, and so were Cambridge, for their third win in succession.

The dramatic finale was all the more remarkable in that the build-up had been lively but error-strewn. There was some strong running from both camps and spirit in abundance. As ever, the form book proved to be a waste of good paper. Cambridge, who had won eight of their 15 matches, including a momentous victory over Western Samoa, began as firm favourites, Oxford having lost 12 of their 17 games. There were five Blues on show: Howe, Coveney and Yeabsley for Oxford, and Mooney and Bramley in opposition. For the first time a Frenchman, Oxford's Jerome Riondet, took the field. There was a rare sighting, too, of a freshman in Richard Ashforth and the Cambridge fly-half did reasonably well for his 11 points. The star

179

of the day, though, was his opposite number, David Humphreys, who finished with a record 19 points. He was impressive all round the field and his virtuoso try in the 23rd minute was wonderfully executed. The memory of it might be some small consolation to Oxford supporters.

Cambridge captain Richard Bramley and team-mates show off the Bowring Bowl, which they won in 1995 for the third year in succession.

Cambridge University: M J Singer (Wycliffe College & Homerton); D M Casado (Ampleforth & St Edmund's), T A Q Whitford (The Leys & Homerton), S R Cottrell (Christ's College, Christchurch & St Edmund's) *(capt)*, S P Sexton (Dublin HS & Hughes Hall); R W Ashforth (Bradford GS & Peterhouse), D M Maslen (Rendcomb College & St Edmund's); L T Mooney (St Boniface & Hughes Hall), J W Evans (Emmanuel GS & Homerton), N J Holgate (Armthorpe CS & Robinson), R A Bramley (Queen Elizabeth GS & St Edmund's), C R A Simpson (Hills Rd VIth Form College & Homerton), M J Hyde (St Ignatius, Sydney & St Edmund's), S D Surridge (St Kentigern, Auckland & Wolfson), R D Earnshaw (Yarm School & St John's) *Replacement* B C I Ryan (St Benedict's & Homerton) for Maslen (34 mins)
Scorers *Tries:* pen try, Evans *Conversion:* Ashforth *Penalty Goals:* Ashforth (3)
Oxford University: S P du Preez (Queen's College, Queenstown SA & Keble); S J Rush (Harrow & Mansfield), Q A de Bruyn (Diocesan College, Cape Town & Keble), J M D Riondet (Lycée La Kanal, Paris & Mansfield), T G Howe (Banbridge Academy & Keble) *(capt)*; D G Humphreys (Ballymena Academy & St Cross), M P Butler (King Edward VI, Lichfield); C G B Norton (St Andrew's College, Grahamstown, SA & Keble), K F Svoboda (Centennial School, Belleville, Ontario & Templeton), D N Penney (Mount Pearl HS, Newfoundland & Wolfson), N J Basson (Diocesan College, Cape Town & St Cross), P F Coveney (Clongowes Wood College, Kildare & New), M P A Reilly (St Gerard's, Bray & St Anne's), R S Yeabsley (Haberdashers' Aske's & Keble), M G P S Orsler (King's, Canterbury & Christ Church) *Replacement* M R P Mermagen (St Bartholomew's, Newbury & Keble) for Riondet (temp & 48 mins)
Scorer *Try:* Humphreys *Conversion:* Humphreys *Penalty Goals:* Humphreys (3) *Dropped Goal:* Humphreys
Referee A J Spreadbury (Somerset)

---

12 December, Stoop Memorial Ground

Oxford University Under-21s 13 (1G 2PG)   **Cambridge University U-21s 3** (1PG)
Oxford University Under-21s: M Dumbell (Brasenose); P Hallett (Jesus), J Wyatt (Worcester), N West (Worcester), C Smart (Trinity); S Ure (Keble), E Simons (Jesus); N Sharp (Brasenose), M Case (Worcester), D Grant (Worcester), S Mathieson (Keble), M Fanning (Exeter), J Bevan (St John's) *(capt)*, B Dell (St Peter's), P Prichard-Jones (St Edmund's Hall)
Scorers *Try:* West *Conversion:* Ure *Penalty Goals:* Ure (2)
Cambridge University Under-21s: A Janisch (Trinity); M Garfield (Fitzwilliam), I Higgins (Emanuel), B Cheetham (St Catharine's), S Lippiett (Corpus Christi); O Clayton (Magdalene), S Young (Pembroke); J Stacey (Trinity), R Sugden (St Catharine's) *(capt)*, P Godfrey (St John's), C Courtenay (St John's), M Bush (St Catharine's), A Browne (Downing), J Gulliford (Gonville & Caius), A Foole (Christ's) *Replacements* O Jones (St John's) for Clayton; J Gilbert (St Catharine's) for Stacey
Scorer *Penalty Goal:* Lippiett
Referee A Ellison (London)

---

7 December, Iffley Road, Oxford

Oxford University Greyhounds 7 (1G)   **Cambridge University LX Club 8** (1PG 1T)
Oxford University Greyhounds: J Sackree (St Edmund's Hall) *(capt)*; N Booth (Worcester), J Wyatt (Worcester), D Magee (Trinity), J Tilley (Pembroke); M Mermagen (Keble), C Jones (University); J Bothwell (Merton), M Case (Worcester), D Grant (Worcester), C McCarthy (Templeton), R Elliott (Oriel), C Smith (Keble), J Britton (New College), J Kindon (Queen's)
Scorers *Try:* Jones *Conversion:* Sackree
Cambridge University LX Club: J Rutter (St John's); B Sexton (Hughes Hall), D Moore (Trinity Hall), A Spencer (St John's), M Garfield (Fitzwilliam); A Kennedy (St John's), B Ryan (Homerton); D Brandt (Downing), J Edwards (St Catharine's), H Thomas (St Catharine's), A Nelstrop (Girton), G Fury (Hughes Hall) *(capt)*, D Ruffell (Homerton), M Holmes (Peterhouse), J Cocks (St Edmund's)
Scorers *Try:* Garfield *Penalty Goal:* Kennedy
Referee K Roberts (North Midlands)

VARSITY MATCH RESULTS

114 Matches played   Oxford 48 wins   Cambridge 53 wins   13 Draws

*Match played at Oxford 1871-72; Cambridge 1872-73; The Oval 1873-74 to 1879-80; Blackheath 1880-81 to 1886-87; Queen's Club 1887-88 to 1920-21; then Twickenham. *At this date no match could be won unless a goal was scored. † Penalty try.*

1871-72	**Oxford**	1G 1T to 0
1872-73	**Cambridge**	1G 2T to 0
1873-74	Drawn	1T each
1874-75*	Drawn	Oxford 2T to 0
1875-76	**Oxford**	1T to 0
1876-77	**Cambridge**	1G 2T to 0
1877-78	**Oxford**	2T to 0
1878-79	Drawn	No score
1879-80	**Cambridge**	1G 1DG to 1DG
1880-81	Drawn	1T each
1881-82	**Oxford**	2G 1T to 1G
1882-83	**Oxford**	1T to 0
1883-84	**Oxford**	3G 4T to 1G
1884-85	**Oxford**	3G 1T to 1T
1885-86	**Cambridge**	2T to 0
1886-87	**Cambridge**	3T to 0
1887-88	**Cambridge**	1DG 2T to 0
1888-89	**Cambridge**	1G 2T to 0
1889-90	**Oxford**	1G 1T to 0
1890-91	Drawn	1G each
1891-92	**Cambridge**	2T to 0
1892-93	Drawn	No score
1893-94	**Oxford**	1T to 0
1894-95	Drawn	1G each
1895-96	**Cambridge**	1G to 0
1896-97	**Oxford**	1G 1DG to 1G 1T
1897-98	**Oxford**	2T to 0
1898-99	**Cambridge**	1G 2T to 0
1899-1900	**Cambridge**	2G 4T to 0
1900-01	**Oxford**	2G to 1G 1T
1901-02	**Oxford**	1G 1T to 0
1902-03	Drawn	1G 1T each
1903-04	**Oxford**	3G 1T to 2G 1T
1904-05	**Oxford**	3G to 2G
1905-06	**Cambridge**	3G (15) to 2G 1T (13)
1906-07	**Oxford**	4T (12) to 1G 1T (8)
1907-08	**Oxford**	1G 4T (17) to 0
1908-09	Drawn	1G (5) each
1909-10	**Oxford**	4G 5T (35) to 1T (3)
1910-11	**Oxford**	4G 1T (23) to 3G 1T (18)
1911-12	**Oxford**	2G 3T (19) to 0
1912-13	**Cambridge**	2G (10) to 1T (3)
1913-14	**Cambridge**	1DG 3T (13) to 1T (3)
1914-18	*No matches*	
1919-20	**Cambridge**	1PG 1DG (7) to 1G (5)
1920-21	**Oxford**	1G 4T (17) to 1G 3T (14)
1921-22	**Oxford**	1G 2T (11) to 1G (5)
1922-23	**Cambridge**	3G 2T (21) to 1G 1T (8)
1923-24	**Oxford**	3G 2T (21) to 1G 1PG 2T (14)
1924-25	**Oxford**	1G 2T (11) to 2T (6)
1925-26	**Cambridge**	3G 6T (33) to 1T (3)
1926-27	**Cambridge**	3G 5T (30) to 1G (5)
1927-28	**Cambridge**	2G 2PG 2T (22) to 1G 3T (14)
1928-29	**Cambridge**	1G 3T (14) to 1PG 1DG 1T (10)
1929-30	**Oxford**	1G 1DG (9) to 0
1930-31	Drawn	Oxford 1PG (3) Cambridge 1T (3)
1931-32	**Oxford**	1DG 2T (10) to 1T (3)
1932-33	**Oxford**	1G 1T (8) to 1T (3)
1933-34	**Oxford**	1G (5) to 1T (3)
1934-35	**Cambridge**	2G 1PG 1DG 4T (29) to 1DG (4)
1935-36	Drawn	No score
1936-37	**Cambridge**	2T (6) to 1G (5)
1937-38	**Oxford**	1G 4T (17) to 1DG (4)
1938-39	**Cambridge**	1G 1PG (8) to 2PG (6)
1939-45	*War-time series*	
1945-46	**Cambridge**	1G 2T (11) to 1G 1PG (8)
1946-47	**Oxford**	1G 1DG 2T (15) to 1G (5)
1947-48	**Cambridge**	2PG (6) to 0
1948-49	**Oxford**	1G 1DG 2T (14) to 1G 1PG (8)

1949-50	**Oxford**	1T (3) to 0
1950-51	**Oxford**	1G 1PG (8) to 0
1951-52	**Oxford**	2G 1T (13) to 0
1952-53	**Cambridge**	1PG 1T (6) to 1G (5)
1953-54	Drawn	Oxford 1PG 1T (6) Cambridge 2PG (6)
1954-55	**Cambridge**	1PG (3) to 0
1955-56	**Oxford**	1PG 2T (9) to 1G (5)
1956-57	**Cambridge**	1G 1PG 1DG 1T (14) to 2PG 1T (9)
1957-58	**Oxford**	1T (3) to 0
1958-59	**Cambridge**	1G 1PG 3T (17) to 1PG 1T (6)
1959-60	**Oxford**	3PG (9) to 1PG (3)
1960-61	**Cambridge**	2G 1T (13) to 0
1961-62	**Cambridge**	1DG 2T (9) to 1DG (3)
1962-63	**Cambridge**	1G 1PG 1DG 1T (14) to 0
1963-64	**Cambridge**	2G 1PG 2T (19) to 1G 1PG 1DG (11)
1964-65	**Oxford**	2G 1PG 2T (19) to 1PG 1GM (6)
1965-66	Drawn	1G (5) each
1966-67	**Oxford**	1G 1T (8) to 1DG 1T (6)
1967-68	**Cambridge**	1T 1PG (6) to 0
1968-69	**Cambridge**	1T 1PG 1DG (9) to 2T (6)
1969-70	**Oxford**	3PG (9) to 2PG (6)
1970-71	**Oxford**	1G 1DG 2T (14) to 1PG (3)
1971-72	**Oxford**	3PG 3T (21) to 1PG (3)
1972-73	**Cambridge**	1G 1PG 1DG 1T (16) to 2PG (6)
1973-74	**Cambridge**	1PG 1DG 2T (14) to 1G 2PG (12)
1974-75	**Cambridge**	1G 2PG 1T (16) to 5PG (15)
1975-76	**Cambridge**	2G 5PG 1DG 1T (34) to 3PG 1DG (12)
1976-77	**Cambridge**	1G 3PG (15) to 0
1977-78	**Oxford**	4PG 1T (16) to 2PG 1T (10)
1978-79	**Cambridge**	2G 3PG 1T (25) to 1PG 1T (7)
1979-80	**Oxford**	2PG 1DG (9) to 1PG (3)
1980-81	**Cambridge**	3PG 1T (13) to 3PG (9)
1981-82	**Cambridge**	3PG (9) to 2PG (6)
1982-83	**Cambridge**	3PG 1DG 2T (20) to 1G 1PG 1T (13)
1983-84	**Cambridge**	4PG 2T (20) to 3PG (9)
1984-85	**Cambridge**	4G 2T (32) to 2PG (6)
1985-86	**Oxford**	1PG 1T (7) to 2PG (6)
1986-87	**Oxford**	3PG 2DG (15) to 1PG 1DG 1T (10)
1987-88	**Cambridge**	1DG 3T (15) to 2PG 1T (10)
1988-89	**Oxford**	2G 1DG 3T (27) to 1DG 1T (7)
1989-90	**Cambridge**	2G 2PG 1T (22) to 1G 1PG 1T (13)
1990-91	**Oxford**	2G 2PG 1DG (21) to 1G 2PG (12)
1991-92	**Cambridge**	2PG 1DG 2T (17) to 1DG 2T (11)
1992-93	**Cambridge**	1G 2PG 2DG (19) to 1PG 1DG 1T (11)
1993-94	**Oxford**	3PG 2DG 1T (20) to 1DG 1T (8)
1994-95	**Cambridge**	1G 1PG 2DG 2T (26) to 1G 2PG 1DG 1T (21)
1995-96	**Cambridge**	1G† 3PG 1T (21) to 1G 3PG 1DG (19)

THE WAR-TIME MATCHES

1939-40	**Oxford**	1G 1DG 2T (15) to	1942-43	**Cambridge**	1G 1DG (9) to 0 (at Oxford)
		1T (3) (at Cambridge)		**Cambridge**	2G 2T (16) to
	Cambridge	1G 3T (14) to			1T (3) (at Cambridge)
		2G 1T (13) (at Oxford)	1943-44	**Cambridge**	2G 1T (13) to
1940-41	**Cambridge**	1G 2T (11) to			1DG (4) (at Cambridge)
		1G 1DG (9) (at Oxford		**Oxford**	2T (6) to 1G (5) (at Oxford)
	Cambridge	2G 1T (13) to	1944-45	Drawn	1T (3) each (at Oxford)
		0 (at Cambridge)		**Cambridge**	2G 2T (16) to
1941-42	**Cambridge**	1PG 2T (9) to			1DG (4) (at Cambridge)
		1PG 1T (6) (at Cambridge)			
	Cambridge	1G 2PG 2T (17) to			
		1G 1T (8) (at Oxford)			

OXFORD and CAMBRIDGE BLUES 1872-1995

(Each year indicates a separate appearance, and refers to the first half of the season. Thus 1879 refers to the match played in the 1879-80 season. (R) indicates an appearance as a replacement; (t) denotes an appearance as a temporary replacement.)

OXFORD

Abbott, J S	1954-55	Bibby, A J	1980-81	Bullock, H	1910-11
Abell, G E B	1923-24-25-26	Binham, P A	1971	Bulpett, C W L	1871
Adamson, J A	1928-29-31	Birrell, H B	1953	Burnet, P J	1960
Adcock, J R L	1961	Black, B H	1929	Burrow, K C	1933
Aitken, A D	1993	Blair, A S	1884	Burse, R M	1974
Aitken, G G	1922-24	Blencowe, L C	1907-08	Bush, A	1934
Aldridge, J E	1888	Bloxham, C T	1834-35-36-37	Bussell, J G	1903-04
Alexander, H	1897-98	Blyth, P H	1885-86	Butcher, W M	1954
Alexander, P C	1930	Bolton, W H	1873-74-75	Butler, F E R	1959-60
Allaway, R C P	1953-54-55	Bonham-Carter, C R	1990	Butler, M P	1995
Allen, C P	1881-82-83	Bonham-Carter, E	1890-91	Button, E L	1936
Allen, T	1909	Boobbyer, B	1949-50-51	Byers, R M	1926
Allen, W C	1910	Booker, J L	1880		
Allison, G V	1994	Booth, J L	1956	Caccia, H A	1926
Allison, M G	1955	Bos, F H ten	1958-59-60	Cadell, P R	1890
Almond, R G P	1937	Boswell, J D	1885-86-87	Cairns, A G	1899-1900-01
Ashby, C J	1973	Botfield, A S G	1871	Calcraft, W J	1986-87
Asher, A G G	1881-82-83-84	Botting, I J	1949-50	Cameron, A J	1988
Asquith, P R	1974	Bourdillon, H	1873-74-75	Campbell, E	1919-20-21
Atkinson, C C	1876	Bourns, C	1903	Campbell, W	1987
		Bowers, J B	1932-34	Cannell, L B	1948-49-50
Back, A	1878	Boyce, A W	1952-53	Cardale, C F	1929-30
Badenoch, D F	1971	Boyd, A de H	1924	Carey, G M	1891-92-94
Baden-Powell, F S	1873	Boyd, E F	1912	Carey, W J	1894-95-96-97
Baggaley, J C	1953-54	Boyle, D S	1967-68-69	Carlyon, H B	1871
Bain, D McL	1910-11-12-13	Boyle, L S	1993	Carroll, B M	1970-71
Bainbrigge, J H	1874-76-77	Brace, D O	1955-56	Carroll, P R	1968-69-70
Baird, J S	1966-67	Bradby, G F	1882-85	Carter, C R	1885
Baiss, R S H	1894-95	Bradford, C C	1887	Cartwright, V H	1901-02-03-04
Baker, C D	1891-93	Branfoot, E P	1878-79	Cass, T	1961
Baker, D G S	1951-52	Bray, C N	1979	Castens, H H	1886-87
Baker, E M	1893-94-95-96	Bray, K A	1989	Cattell, R H B	1893
Baker, P	1980(R)	Bremridge, H	1876-77	Cave, H W	1881
Baker, R T	1968	Brett, J A	1935-36-37	Cawkwell, G L	1946-47
Balfour, E R	1893-94-95	Brett, P V	1978	Chadwick, A J	1898-99
Bannerman, J MacD	1927-28	Brewer, R J	1965	Chambers, J C	1921
Barclay, S L	1990-91	Brewer, T J	1951	Champain, F H B	1897-98-99
Barker, A C	1966-67	Bridge, D J W	1946-47-48	Champneys, F W	1874-75-76
Barnes, S	1981-82-83	Brierley, H	1871	Charles, A E S	1932
Barr, D C A	1980	Britton, R B	1963-64	Cheesman, W I	1910-11
Barry, C E	1897-98-99	Bromet, W E	1889	Cheyne, H	1903-04
Barry, D M	1968-69-70	Bromley, S P	1994	Chislett, J	1986-87
Barwick, W M	1880-81	Brooks, A W	1980-81-82	Cholmondeley, F G	1871-73
Bass, R G	1961	Brooks, M J	1873	Christopherson, P	1886-87-88
Basson, N J	1995	Brooks, W	1872	Clark, C J	1993
Batchelor, T B	1906	Broster, L R	1912	Clark, R B	1978-79
Bateson, H D	1874-75-77	Broughton, R C	1965	Clarke, E J D	1973
Baxter, T J	1958-59	Brown, L G	1910-11-12	Clarke, I A	1913
Beamish, S H	1971	Brown, M E O	1988	Clauss, P R	1889-90-91
Beare, A	1982	Brunskill, R F	1873-74	Clements, B S	1975
Bedford, T P	1965-66-67	Bryan, T A	1975-76-77	Cleveland, C R	1885-86
Behn, A R	1968-69	Bryce, A N S	1994	Cochran, P C	1889-91
Bell, D L	1970	Bryer, L W	1953	Cohen, B A	1884
Benson, E T	1928	Buchanan, F G	1909-10	Coker, J B H	1965
Bentley, P J	1960	Buckett, I M	1992	Coker, T	1988-89
Berkeley, W V	1924-25-26	Bucknall, A L	1965-66	Cole, B W	1945
Berry, C W	1883-84	Budge, K J	1977-78-79	Coleman, D J	1982-83
Bettington, R H B	1920-22	Budworth, R T D	1887-88-89	Coles, D G G	1937-38
Bevan, J H	1946	Bullard, G L	1950-51	Coles, P	1884-85-86

CAMBRIDGE

Todd, T	1888	Walker, D R	1980-81	Williams, H A	1876
Topping, N P	1986-87	Walker, E E	1899-1900	Williams, J M	1949
Touzel, C J C	1874-75-76	Walker, R M	1963	Williams, L T	1874-75
Tredwell, J R	1968	Walkey, J R	1902	Williams, N E	1950
Trethewy, A	1888	Wallace, W M	1912-13	Williams, P T	1888-89
Trubshaw, A R	1919	Waller, G S	1932	Williamson, I S	1972
Tucker, W E	1892-93-94	Wallis, H T	1895-96	Williamson, P R	1984
Tucker, W E	1922-23-24-25	Walne, N J	1994	Willis, H	1949-50-51
Tudsbery, F C T	1907-08	Ward, R O C	1903	Wilson, A H	1911-12-13
Tunningley, A J	1988(R)	Ware, C H	1882	Wilson, C P	1877-78-79-80
Turnbull, B R	1924-25	Warfield, P J	1974	Wilton, C W	1936
Turner, J A	1956	Warlow, S	1972-74	Winthrop, W Y	1871
Turner, J M P C	1985	Waters, F H	1927-28-29	Wintle, T C	1960-61
Turner, M F	1946	Waters, J B	1902-03-04	Withyman, T A	1985-86
Tyler, R H	1978-79-80	Watherston, J G	1931	Wood, G E	1974-75-76
Tynan, C J C	1993	Watson, C F K	1919-20	Wood, G E C	1919
		Watt, J R	1970	Woodall, B J C	1951
Umbers, R H	1954	Webb, G K M	1964-65	Woodroffe, O P	1952
Underwood, T	1990-91	Webster, A P	1971	Woods, S M J	1888-89-90
Ure, C McG	1911	Wells, C M	1891-92	Wooller, W	1933-34-35
		Wells, T U	1951	Wordley, S A	1988-89
Valentine, G E	1930	Weston, M T	1958-59-60	Wordsworth, A J	1973-75
Van Schalkwijk, J	1906	Wheeler, P J F	1951-52-53	Wotherspoon, W	1888-89
Vaughan, G P	1949	White, J B	1922	Wrench, D F B	1960
Vaux, J G	1957	White, W N	1947	Wright, C C G	1907-08
Vickerstaff, M	1988	Whiteway, S E A	1893	Wrigley, P T	1877-78-79-80
Vincent, C A	1913	Whitford, T A Q	1995	Wyles, K T	1985-86
Vivian, J M	1976	Wiggins, C E M	1928	Wynne, E H	1887
Vyvyan, C B	1987-88	Wiggins, C M	1964		
		Wilby, J B	1989		
Wace, R	1873-74	Wilkinson, R M	1971-72-73	Yetts, R M	1879-80-81
Waddell, G H	1958-60-61	Will, J G	1911-12-13	Young, A B S	1919-20
Wade, M R	1958-59-60-61	Williams, A G	1926-27	Young, A T	1922-23-24
Wainwright, J F	1956	Williams, C C U	1950	Young, J S	1935
Wainwright, M A	1980	Williams, C H	1930	Young, J V	1906
Wainwright, R I	1986-87-88	Williams, C R	1971-72-73	Young, P D	1949
Wakefield, W W	1921-22	Williams, D B	1973	Young, S K	1974
Walker, A W	1929-30	Williams, E J H	1946	Young, W B	1935-36-37

VARSITY MATCH REFEREES

(From 1881, when referees first officiated at the match. Prior to this date, the match was controlled by a pair of umpires elected by the universities.) Each year indicates a separate appearance, and refers to the first half of the season. Thus 1881 refers to the match played in the 1881-82 season.

Allan, M A	1933-34	Freethy, A E		Marsh, F W	1906
Ashmore, H L			1923-25-27-29-31-32	Morrison, E F	1992
	1891-92-93-95-96	Gadney, C H		Murdoch, W C W	1952
Bean, A S	1948-49		1935-36-37-38-45-47	Norling, C	1977-78-81-88-89
Bevan, W D	1993	Gillespie, J I	1905	Pattinson, K A	1974
Bolton, W N	1882	Harnett, G H		Potter-Irwin, F C	1909-11-13-19
Boundy, L M	1958		1897-98-99-1900-01-02	Prideaux, L	1984
Burnett, D I H	1980-82	Hilditch, S R	1994	Quittenton, R C	1985-87
Burrell, R P	1963	Hill, G R		Sanson, N R	1976
Clark, K H	1973		1883-84-86-87-88-89-90	Spreadbury, A J	1995
Cooper, Dr P F	1951-53	Hosie, A M	1979	Sturrock, J C	1921
Crawford, S H	1920	Howard, F A	1986	Taylor, H H	1881
Currey, F I	1885	Jeffares, R W	1930	Titcomb, M H	1969
Dallas, J D	1910-12	John, K S	1956-67	Trigg, J A F	1983
D'Arcy, D P	1968	Johnson, R F	1972	Vile, T H	1922-24-26-28
David, I	1954-55	Jones, T	1950	Walters, D G	
Doyle, O E	1990	Lamb, Air Cdre G C	1970		1957-60-61-62-64-65-66
Evans, G	1907	Lambert, N H	1946	Welsby, A	1975
Findlay, J C	1904-08	Lawrence, Capt H D	1894	Williams, R C	1959
Fleming, J M	1991	Lewis, R	1971	Williams, T	1903

SERVICES ALL TIED UP

THE SERVICES 1995-96
John Mace   *Daily Telegraph*

Inter-Services Tournament
The Inter-Services tournament finished in its tenth triple tie and the Willis Corroon Bowl was shared for the first time. The Royal Navy just got the better of the Army in a bruising match watched by 18,500 spectators but then, surprisingly, lost to the RAF, who emerged as worthy winners even though they were undergoing a period of team rebuilding. In the critical final game the Army, bolstered by the presence of Tim Rodber and Rob Wainwright, proved too strong for the airmen in an exciting encounter.

Two well-matched packs and committed defences ensured that the Navy v Army game was a close affair. The Army enjoyed a territorial advantage throughout and their inventive backs made consistent attempts to run the ball, but the Navy absorbed all the pressure and still came back. Neither side was able to score a try.

The RAF's respect for the perceived power of the Navy's forwards shaped their game plan to win quick rucked ball and spread it wide. As it transpired, their pack matched the Navy's and an early onslaught by their backs should have yielded several tries. Such was the intensity of the match that the first time the sailors crossed the halfway line was in the 25th minute, when they kicked off following the first of Steve Lazenby's three penalty goals. The Navy forwards were more influential in the second half and launched some impressive drives, two of which produced tries for Craig White and Derek Cross. Yet the RAF continued to run their dwindling possession and in the 70th minute Rory Underwood stepped out of two tackles and split the Navy's hitherto impregnable defence.

For their match against the Navy the Army had been unable to select Tim Rodber and Rob Wainwright, who were representing their respective countries in the Hong Kong Sevens. Given their significant contribution to the Army's victory over the RAF, one can only conclude that it was their absence from the first game that prevented the soldiers from winning this year's title outright. The Army enjoyed a distinct advantage up front but, even though they ran the ball eagerly, they were unable to break the RAF's determined defence until the second half. Under continual pressure, and existing on scraps of possession, the airmen never gave up and matched the Army's three tries.

After the final match the RAF's Steve Worrall and Steve Lazenby announced their retirement from representative rugby. Barbarians scrum-half Worrall has played in a record 28 inter-service matches.

30 March, Twickenham
Royal Navy 9 (3PG)   **Army 6** (2PG)
For the Willis Corroon Trophy

Royal Navy: Lt K B Eyre RM (CTCRM); LPT R Williams (HMS Raleigh), Mne C White (RM Deal), LS(R) D Sibson (HMS Richmond), Mne Musn S Brown (RM Deal); CPO I Fletcher (HMS Neptune), Cpl P Livingstone (RM Stonehouse); LS(R) N D Bartlett (HMS Osprey), Cpl M J Wooltorton (CTCRM), WEM(R) D Parkes (HMS Montrose), LRO G Harrison (HMS Warrior), Lcpl D Cross (RM Stonehouse), Cpl R W Armstrong (CTCRM), Capt C B Palmer RM (HMS Warrior) (*capt*), CSgt H Hewitt (RM Deal) *Replacement* S/Lt R Readwin (HMS Dryad) for Hewitt (76 mins)
Scorer *Penalty Goals:* Eyre (3)
Army: Lt M Abernethy (RGR); Capt H G Graham (RHA), Cpl A Sanger (RE), Sgt L Douglas (APTC), Lt B G W Johnson (R Sigs); Lt P Knowles (RRF), Capt S Pinder (DWR); Sgt D Coghlan (RHA), Capt J S Brammer (RE) (*capt*), LCpl M Stewart (PWRR), Capt D Dahinten (RHA), Lt A Newsham (RHA), Spr R S Hunter (RE), OCdt N Richardson (RMA Sandhurst), Cpl G Powell (GDG)
Scorer *Penalty Goals:* Knowles (2)
Referee S Piercy (Yorkshire Society)

10 April, Twickenham
Royal Navy 12 (1G 1T)   **Royal Air Force 14** (3PG 1T)
For the Willis Corroon Hibernia Cup

Royal Navy: Lt K B Eyre RM (CTCRM); LPT R Williams (HMS Raleigh), Mne C White (RM Deal), LS(R) D Sibson (HMS Richmond), Mne Musn S Brown (RM Deal); CPO I Fletcher (HMS Neptune), Cpl P Livingstone (RM Stonehouse); LS(R) N D Bartlett (HMS Osprey), Cpl M J Wooltorton (CTCRM), WEM(R) D Parkes (HMS Montrose), LRO G Harrison (HMS Warrior), LCpl D Cross (RM Stonehouse), Cpl R W Armstrong (CTCRM), Capt C B Palmer RM (HMS Warrior) (*capt*), CSgt H Hewitt (RM Deal)
Scorers *Tries:* White, Cross   *Conversion:* Eyre
Royal Air Force: Sgt S Lazenby (Cosford); SAC G Sharp (Rudloe Manor), Cpl S Roke (Wyton), Cpl D Morgan (Sealand), Flt Lt R Underwood (Cranwell); Cpl N James (Cranwell), Sgt S Worrall (Cottesmore) (*capt*); A/PO J Thorpe (Yorkshire UAS), Sqn Ldr R Miller (Wyton), JT B Williams (Brize Norton), SAC L Oakey (Brize Norton), Cpl P Taylor (Northolt), Sgt C Morgan (Brize Norton), JT S Boote (Cosford), Flt Lt C Moore (Rudloe Manor) *Replacements* SAC A George (St Athan) for Roke (40 mins); Cpl A Nisbet (Halton) for Oakey (61 mins)
Scorers *Try:* Underwood   *Penalty Goals:* Lazenby (3)

17 April, Twickenham
Army 31 (2G 4PG 1T)   **Royal Air Force 23** (1G 2PG 2T)
For the Willis Corroon Shield

Army: Lt M Abernethy (RGR); Capt H G Graham (RHA), Cpl A Sanger (RE), Sgt L Douglas (APTC), Lt B G W Johnson (R Sigs); Lt P Knowles (RRF), Capt S Pinder (DWR); LCpl M Stewart (PWRR), Capt J S Brammer (RE) (*capt*), Sgt J Fowers (RHA), Capt D Dahinten (RHA), Lt A Newsham (RHA), Spr R S Hunter (RE), Capt R Wainwright (RAMC), Capt T Rodber (GH) *Replacements* Lt C Waggett (QDG) for Sanger (78 mins); Capt M D Watters (RWF) for Graham (79 mins); SSgt D J Coghlan (RHA) for Fowers (79 mins)
Scorers *Tries:* Johnson (2), Sanger   *Conversions:* Knowles (2)   *Penalty Goals:* Knowles (4)
Royal Air Force: SAC A George (St Athan); SAC G Sharp (Rudloe Manor), Cpl S Roke (Wyton), Sgt S Lazenby (Cosford), Flt Lt R Underwood (Cranwell); Cpl N

James (Cranwell), Sgt S Worrall (Cottesmore) (*capt*); A/PO J Thorpe (Yorkshire UAS), Sqn Ldr R Miller (Wyton), JT B Williams (Brize Norton), SAC L Oakey (Brize Norton), Cpl P Taylor (Northolt), Sgt C Morgan (Brize Norton), JT S Boote (Cosford), Flt Lt C Moore (Rudloe Manor) *Replacements* CT D Robson (Odiham) for Thorpe (35 mins); Cpl R Alexander (Boulmer) for Roke (67 mins); SAC B Wakfer (Lyneham) for Worrall (79 mins)
Scorers *Tries:* Morgan (2), Sharp   *Conversion:* Lazenby   *Penalty Goals:* Lazenby (2)
Referee C Rees (London Society)

Inter-Services Tournament Champions

The Army have won the Tournament outright 28 times, the Royal Navy 17 times and the Royal Air Force 14 times. The Army and the Royal Air Force have shared it on 2 occasions and there have been 10 triple ties.

1920 **RN**	1950 **Army**	1974 **RN**
1921 **RN**	1951 **RN**	1975 Triple Tie
1922 **RN**	1952 **Army**	1976 **Army**
1923 **RAF**	1953 **Army**	1977 **RN**
1924 Triple Tie	1954 Triple Tie	1978 Triple Tie
1925 **Army & RAF**	1955 **RAF**	1979 **RAF**
1926 **Army**	1956 Triple Tie	1980 **Army**
1927 **RN**	1957 **Army**	1981 **RN**
1928 **Army**	1958 **RAF**	1982 **RAF**
1929 **Army**	1959 **RAF**	1983 **Army**
1930 **Army**	1960 **Army**	1984 Triple Tie
1931 **RN**	1961 **RN**	1985 **RAF**
1932 **Army**	1962 **RAF**	1986 **RAF**
1933 **Army**	1963 **Army**	1987 **RN**
1934 **Army**	1964 **Army**	1988 **Army**
1935 Triple Tie	1965 **Army**	1989 **Army**
1936 **Army**	1966 **RN**	1990 **Army**
1937 **Army**	1967 **Army**	1991 **RAF**
1938 **RN**	1968 **Army**	1992 Triple Tie
1939 **RN**	1969 **Army**	1993 **RAF**
1946 **Army**	1970 **RN**	1994 **RAF**
1947 **RAF**	1971 **RAF**	1995 **RN**
1948 Triple Tie	1972 **Army**	1996 Triple Tie
1949 **Army & RAF**	1973 **RN**	

Royal Navy v Army: The Royal Navy have won 33, the Army 43, and 3 matches have been drawn (including matches before 1920) **Royal Navy v RAF:** The Royal Navy have won 38, the RAF 29, and 4 matches have been drawn **Army v RAF:** The Army have won 40, the RAF 23, and 8 matches have been drawn.

Other Fixtures, Competitions and Tours

The Combined Services again fielded a weakened team against the British Police, who retained the Securicor Trophy by beating them 28-15, but they did beat Ulster, 30-20, in the first game between the sides for 27 years.

The Royal Navy were awarded the Inter-Services Under-21 title – having beaten the Army, who then beat the Royal Air Force – when the airmen were unable to raise a side against them. The Royal Navy also won the first Over-35 inter-services tournament. Portsmouth won the Royal Navy's newly instituted inter-command competition and HMS Heron won the Navy Cup.

The Royal Artillery headed Division 1 of the Army Inter-Corps

Merit Table and the Infantry won Division 2. The 7th Parachute Regiment Royal Horse Artillery recorded their eighth win in ten seasons in the final of the Army Major Units Cup competition as well as capturing the Army Sevens title for the second year running. The 9th Parachute Squadron Royal Engineers won the Minor Units Cup.

In November and December the New Zealand Army played six matches in England, Wales and Germany to commemorate the tour made by the legendary Kiwis in 1946. Twelve of the original tourists accompanied the side and watched them win all but their final game against the British Army.

Inter-Services Over-35 Tournament
Royal Navy 25, RAF 17; Royal Navy 75, Army 5; Army 34, RAF 24
Winners: Royal Navy

Inter-Services Under-21 Tournament
Royal Navy 19, Army 11; Army 27, RAF 10 (*RAF v Royal Navy not played*)
Winners: Royal Navy

Combined Services Matches
Senior: Combined Services 15, British Police 28 (*for the Securicor Trophy*); Combined Services 30, Ulster 20
Under-21: Combined Services 11, Irish Exiles 40; Combined Services 25, Middlesex 12; Combined Services 73, Millfield OB 10; Combined Services 25, Loughborough Freshmen 10; Combined Services 29, England Students 25
Under-20: Combined Services 21, Mountain Ash and District 13; Combined Services 26, Ogmore and District 37

Individual Service Competitions
ROYAL NAVY
Inter-Command Competition: Plymouth Command 0, Royal Marines 20; Scottish Command 15, Portsmouth Command 28; Plymouth Command 8, Scottish Command 16; Royal Marines 59, Air Command 17; Air Command 26, Plymouth Command 6; Portsmouth Command 31, Royal Marines 5; Royal Marines 27, Scottish Command 7; Air Command 11, Portsmouth 42; Scottish Command 62, Air Command 0; Portsmouth Command 27, Plymouth Command 0 **Winners:** Portsmouth Command **Inter-Unit Cup:** Royal Marines Stonehouse 6, HMS Heron 13 **Inter-Unit Sevens:** BRNC Dartmouth 35, HMS Daedalus 24
ARMY
Inter-Corps Merit Table: Division 1 winners: Royal Artillery **Division 2 winners:** Infantry
Major Units Cup: 7th Parachute Regiment Royal Horse Artillery 27, 4th General Support Regiment Royal Logistics Corps 11
Minor Units Cup: 9th Parachute Squadron Royal Engineers 25, 15th Regiment Royal Logistics Corps 9 **Inter-Unit Sevens:** 7th Parachute Regiment Royal Horse Artillery 22, 2nd Signals Regiment 17
ROYAL AIR FORCE
Inter-Command Competition: Logistics Command 28, Strike Command 27; Personnel and Training Command 15, Logistics Command 19; Strike Command 13, Personnel and Training Command 17 **Winners:** Logistics Command **Inter-Station Cup:** RAF St Athan 17, RAF Marham 13 **Inter-Station Shield:** RAF Honington 43, RAF Brampton 0 **Inter-Station Sevens:** RAF Laarbruch 14, RAF Locking 5

UNDER-21 INTERNATIONALS

Brendan Gallagher *Daily Telegraph*

15 November 1995, Franklins Gardens, Northampton
ENGLAND U21 10 (1G 1PG)   **IRELAND U21 23** (2G 2PG 1DG)

England U21: P Massey (Morley); A Blyth (West Hartlepool), M Denney (Bristol) (*capt*),
J Overend (Leicester), S Jones (West Hartlepool); S Binns (Leicester), A Gomarsall (Wasps);
M Volland (Northampton), N McCarthy (Bath), P Vickery (Gloucester), C Murphy (West
Hartlepool), D Zaltzman (Saracens), J Ions (West Hartlepool), A Bennett (Orrell), B Kay (Waterloo)
Scorers *Try:* Gomarsall   *Conversion:* Binns   *Penalty Goal:* Binns
Ireland U21: D Crotty (UCC); J Topping (Ballymena), R McIlreavy (Dublin U), J Bishop
(London Irish), J Cunningham (Dublin U); F Campion (St Mary's Coll), C McGuinness
(St Mary's Coll); B McConnell (Bristol U), C Egan (Terenure Coll), P Coyle (UCD),
T McWhirter (Dundee HSFP) (*capt*), M O'Kelly (St Mary's Coll), C McEntee (Lansdowne),
K Dawson (Bangor), E Miller (Leicester)
Scorers *Tries:* Topping (2)   *Conversions:* Campion (2)   *Penalty Goals:* Campion (2)
Dropped Goal: Campion

12 December 1995, Gateshead Stadium
ENGLAND U21 21 (1G 2PG 1DG 1T)   **SCOTLAND U21 18** (1G 1PG 1DG 1T)

England U21: C Catling (Exeter U); N Shaw (Durham U), J Overend (Leicester), M Denney
(Bristol) (*capt*), A Sleightholme (Wakefield); S Binns (Leicester), S Benton (Gloucester);
A Ozdemir (Harlequins), N McCarthy (Bath), M Fitzgerald (Durham U), B Kay (Waterloo),
R Fidler (Gloucester), A Bennett (Orrell), E Pearce (Bath), J Worsley (Wasps)
Replacement P Harvey (Brunel U) for Benton
Scorers *Tries:* Benton, Catling   *Conversion:* Binns   *Penalty Goals:* Binns (2)   *Dropped Goal:* Binns
Scotland U21: M Sangster (Stirling County); C MacRobert (Stirling County), C Murray
(Hawick), G Smith (Orrell) S Reed (Nottingham); M Duncan (Edinburgh Acads), G Beveridge
(Boroughmuir); D Massey (Currie), G Bulloch (West of Scotland), B Stewart (Edinburgh
Acads), G Perrett (West of Scotland), S Murray (Edinburgh Acads), D McLeish (West of
Scotland), F Dall (Heriot's FP) (*capt*), T McVie (Heriot's FP) *Replacement* C Cottrill (Langholm)
for McLeish
Scorers *Tries:* Bulloch, McLeish   *Conversion:* Duncan   *Penalty Goal:* Duncan
Dropped Goal: Duncan
Referee D McHugh (Ireland)

19 January 1996, Stradbrook, Blackrock, Dublin
IRELAND U21 21 (1G 2PG 1DG 1T)   **SCOTLAND U21 9** (3PG)

Ireland U21: D Crotty (UC Cork); N Carolan (Corinthians), R McIlreavy (Dublin U), J Bishop
(London Irish), I Cunningham (Dublin U); F Campion (St Mary's Coll), B O'Meara (Cork Const);
B McConnell (Bristol U), C Egan (Terenure Coll), G Cully (Bangor), J Ryan (UC Dublin),
A McWhirter (Dundee HSFP), C McEntee (Lansdowne), K Dawson (Bangor), D Evans (Orrell)
Scorers *Tries:* McIlreavy, Egan   *Conversion:* Campion   *Penalty Goals:* Campion (2)
Dropped Goal: Campion
Scotland U21: C Sangster (Stirling County); G Smith (Orrell), C Murray (Hawick), M Duncan
(Edinburgh Acads), S Reed (Nottingham); J McKee (Cardiff Inst), G Beveridge (Boroughmuir);
D Massey (Currie), G Bulloch (West of Scotland), D Jamieson (West of Scotland), S Begley
(Glasgow Acads), G Perrett (West of Scotland), T McVie (Heriot's FP), G Hayter (Dundee
HSFP), G Dall (Heriot's FP) (*capt*) *Replacements* E Weston (Watsonians) for Beveridge; A Bulloch
(West of Scotland) for Murray
Scorer *Penalty Goals:* McKee (3)
Referee R Davies (Wales)

2 February 1996, Myreside, Edinburgh
SCOTLAND U21 3 (1DG)   **FRANCE U21 29** (3G 1DG 1T)

Scotland U21: C Sangster (Stirling County), S Reed (Nottingham), C Murray (Hawick),
A Bulloch (West of Scotland), G Smith (Orrell); C Richards (Jedforest), E Weston (Watsonians);
D Massey (Currie), G Bulloch (West of Scotland), D Jamieson (West of Scotland), R Hogg
(Gala), G Perrett (West of Scotland), T McVie (Heriot's FP), G Dall (Heriot's FP) (*capt*),

I Sinclair (Watsonians) *Replacement* M Duncan (Edinburgh Acads) for Sangster
Scorer *Dropped Goal:* Richards
France U21: N Nadau (PUC); T Lombard (Racing), J Mazille (Grenoble), S Roque (Colomiers), D Bory (Montferrand); N Bruzy (Perpignan), G Sudrre (Agen); X Audu (Toulouse), J-Y Duhart (Lourdes), W Begarry (Toulouse), D Barrier (Montferrand), A Bonnet (Lourdes), T Lievremont (Argeles-sur-Mer), D Gabin (Montferrand), R Jechoux (Racing)
Scorers *Tries:* Nadau, Lombard, Lievremont, Gabin *Conversions:* Bruzy (3)
Dropped Goal: Bruzy
Referee H Lewis (Wales)

16 February 1996, St Helens, Swansea
WALES U21 25 (2G 2PG 1T) **SCOTLAND U21 21** (1G 2PG 1DG 1T)

Wales U21: A Jones (Harlequins); N Walne (Cambridge U), G Jones (Cardiff), J Funnell (Neath), D James (Bridgend); S Connor (Abertillery), D Hawkins (Swansea); L Manning (Bridgend), R Campbell (Cardiff Inst), C Anthony (Swansea), S Ford (Bridgend), N Watkins (Cardiff Inst), H Jenkins (Bedwas), J Ringer (Cardiff), Nathan Thomas (Maesteg) *Replacements* R Sadler (Newport) for James; Noel Thomas (Maesteg) for Ringer (temp) & for Ford; D Morris (Maesteg) for A Jones
Scorers *Tries:* Funnell, G Jones, Hawkins *Conversions:* Connor (2) *Penalty Goals:* Connor (2)
Scotland U21: C Aitken (Heriot's FP); J Goldie (Glenrothes), C Murray (Hawick), A Bulloch (West of Scotland), S Reed (Nottingham); C Richards (Jedforest), E Weston (Watsonians); S Lithgow (Dundee HSFP), G Bulloch (West of Scotland), J Kelly (London Scottish), R Hogg (Gala), G Perrett (West of Scotland), C Cottrill (Langholm), G Dall (Heriot's FP) *(capt)*, I Sinclair (Watsonians) *Replacement* G Dalgleish (Gala) for Richards
Scorers *Tries:* Goldie, A Bulloch *Conversion:* Richards *Penalty Goals:* Richards, Dalgleish
Dropped Goal: Dalgleish
Referee J Wallis (England)

1 March 1996, Wicklow
IRELAND U21 20 (2G 1PG 1DG) **WALES U21 12** (1G 1T)

Ireland U21: D Crotty (UCC); D Hickie (St Mary's Coll), R McIlreavy (Dublin U), J Bishop (London Irish), J Cunningham (Dublin U); F Campion (St Mary's Coll), B O'Meara (Cork Const); B McConnell (Bristol U), C Egan (Terenure Coll), G Cully (Bangor), T McWhirter (Dundee HSFP) *(capt)*, A Robinson (Ballymena), C McEntee (Lansdowne), K Dawson (Bangor), E Miller (Leicester)
Scorers *Tries:* Cunningham, McConnell *Conversions:* Campion (2) *Penalty Goal:* Campion
Dropped Goal: Campion
Wales U21: A Durston (Bridgend); N Walne (Cambridge U), G Jones (Cardiff), J Funnell (Neath), D James (Bridgend); S Connor (Abertillery), D Hawkins (Swansea U) *(capt)*; L Manning (Bridgend), R Campbell (Cardiff Inst), C Anthony (Swansea), S Ford (Bridgend), N Watkins (Cardiff Inst), C Quinnell (Llanelli), N Thomas (Bridgend), J Ringer (Cardiff)
Scorers *Tries:* Manning, Connor *Conversion:* Connor
Referee E Murray (Scotland)

6 January 1996, Rieti
ITALY U21 10 (1G 1PG) **SCOTLAND U21 31** (4G 1PG)

Italy U21: *Try:* Piovan *Conversion:* Mazzariol *Penalty Goal:* Mazzariol
Scotland U21: *Tries:* Reed (2), Murray, pen try *Conversions:* McKee (4) *Penalty Goal:* McKee
Referee J Pearson (England)

19 April 1996, Recreation Ground, Bath
ENGLAND U21 3 (1PG) **FRANCE U21 40** (2G 2PG 4T)

England U21: *Penalty Goal:* Jones
France U21: *Tries:* Gabin (2), Lazerges, Nadau, Bory, Sanurer *Conversions:* Bruzy (2)
Penalty Goals: Bruzy (2)

11 May 1996, Milan
ITALY U21 8 **ENGLAND U21 39** (4G 1PG 1DG 1T)

England *Tries:* Rees (2), Luger, Benton, Sampson *Conversions:* Sampson, Jones (3)
Penalty Goal: Jones *Dropped Goal:* Jones

SENSIBLE SPENDING NEEDED

STUDENT RUGBY 1995-96
Harry Townsend

In the new era of professionalism, promising players are being put under contract by clubs, and short-term ambition takes over from long-term career prospects. Never again, one suspects, will a Jon Webb play international rugby while working as a consultant surgeon.

Many clubs, including Newcastle, Bath, Harlequins and Worcester, now offer sports scholarships which ease the financial problems of gifted students, but excessive altruism would be needed for all such players to be released for student rugby, even at the highest level. The original 26-man England squad for the Student World Cup in South Africa did not contain Dallaglio, nor the England A players Stimpson, Naylor, Blyth, Greenstock, King, Healey or Corry, and by the eve of departure, there had been 19 changes. How many of them were due to club pressures? South Africa will doubtless field a top-class squad; France has announced the inclusion of six players with senior international experience, omitted from their senior tour to Argentina. It is a question of priorities, and of where money is allocated.

Among the major problems addressed by the Student Rugby Conference at Cambridge were the development of talent and the encouragement of all students as players, administrators and referees at every level. There are more than 10,000 students in higher education with rugby-playing experience: without support, many will join the swelling ranks of couch potatoes. The most perceptive proposal at Cambridge – the appointment of Rugby Union student liaison officers – merits RFU money far more than the coffers of the senior clubs.

A pilot scheme will appoint four officers, one in each division, attached to an IHE. They will be paid expenses and a low salary, and work with students on player development, coaching, organisation and administration, arranging courses and acting as a catalyst to help students run the game within their IHE. The ultimate aim is to have 30 or more RUSLOs, and the sooner the better. Sponsorship is needed urgently: there are an infinite number of students out there who should be the lifeblood of the game.

Representative matches: Ireland Students 8, Natal Duikers 12 (Cork); France Students 42, Ireland Students 11 (Clermont Ferrand); France Students 33, England Students 14 (Paris); England Students 33, Wales Students 17 (Rosslyn Park); Scotland Students 9, England Students 44 (Stewart's Melville, Inverleith); England Students 19, Ireland Students 24 (Iffley Road, Oxford); Wales Students 15, France Students 41 (Cardiff Arms Park); English Universities 23, Irish Universities 30 (Sale); Irish Universities 43, Scottish Universities 9 (Dublin); English Universities 8, Welsh Universities 35 (Richmond); Welsh Universities 21, Scottish Universities 12 (Pontypool); Scottish Universities 10, English Universities 34 (Peffermill); Irish

Universities 21, Welsh Universities 22 (Trinity College, Dublin); Irish Colleges 22, Connacht Development XV 18 (Athlone); Irish Colleges 22, Irish Universities 15 (Dublin); Irish Colleges 29, Exiles Students 17; Irish Colleges 83, Netherlands Under-21s 5; Scottish Universities 30, South Under-21s 3; Scottish Universities 20, Glasgow Under-21s 21 (Braidholm, Glasgow); England Students Under-21s 42, Irish Exiles Under-21s 14 (St Mary's); England Students Under-21s 25, Combined Services Under-21s 29 (Twickenham); Nottinghamshire 34, Midlands Universities 25 (Newark RFC); South Yorkshire 25, Midlands Universities 16 (Sheffield RFC); Gloucester Invitation XV 20, London Universities 19 (Kingsholm)

BRITISH UNIVERSITIES SPORTS ASSOCIATION CHAMPIONSHIP 1995-96
Sponsored by Vaseline

20 March, Twickenham
Cardiff Institute 6 (2PG)   Loughborough 3 (1PG)

Cardiff Institute, denied their chance of glory last season for not completing their group fixtures, made no such mistake this year as they brushed aside their six Welsh opponents. Promoted for the fourth time in recent years in the regular Heineken Leagues in Wales, they join League 2 next season, and their insistence on all players putting the student club first has paid off in team-work.

Loughborough, 25 times champions, had not won the Student title for two years after nine successes in the previous 11. Although they were defeated by Sheffield Hallam they still went through as leaders, and progressed more easily thereafter.

The final was played in swirling wind and driving rain, a contrast to the sun-baked high-scoring match of the previous year. Both teams nevertheless set out to play a typically exuberant open game, although handling errors abounded with a greasy ball. The two teams had vast representative experience, with Loughborough fly-half Alan Buzza, a former England reserve, the elder statesman. Cardiff No 8 James Savastano, one of ten Wales Under-21 caps in the Cardiff squad, opened the scoring with a 35-yard penalty from near the right touchline and struck again ten minutes later before Buzza reduced the arrears a minute before half-time. That was the end of the scoring, but not of the entertainment, as both teams battled it out in deteriorating conditions. Loughborough worked tirelessly and their pressure was almost rewarded, but lock Steve Martin saved the day for Cardiff by snapping up a crucial last-minute Loughborough line-out a metre from the line.

Cardiff Institute: M Evans; J Dodd, G Eastment, R Sheppeard, G Stiff; G Vobe, D Edwards; J Evans (*capt*), R Campbell, A Millward, S Martin, N Watkins, A Davies, S Gardner, J Savastano *Replacement* M Sage for Edwards (39 mins)
Scorer *Penalty Goals:* Savastano (2)
Loughborough University: S Jones; R O'Neill, N Propper, N Osman, N Miller; A Buzza, J Daniels; S Beaufoy, C Johnson, A Kelly, G Webster, R White, J Powell,

C Davis (*capt*), R Winters *Replacements* A Poole for Beaufoy (38 mins); D Nunn for Johnson (45 mins); C Leslie for Daniels (69 mins)
Scorer *Penalty Goal:* Buzza
Referee G Gadjovich (Canada)
Loughborough have won the title 25 times, Durham 8, Liverpool and Swansea 7, Bristol 5, Cardiff and Manchester 4, Bangor and UWIST 2, Aberystwyth, Birmingham, Leeds, Newcastle, Northumbria, West London Institute (Brunel University College) and Cardiff Institute once each.
Second XV final: Cardiff Institute 22, Edinburgh 17
Third XV final: Durham 34, Swansea 22

Buckinghamshire College, the only new entrant to the 130-team BUSA Championships, narrowly failed to qualify for the play-off rounds despite an 83-10 defeat by current BUSA champions Brunel UC, who went out in the third round to Cardiff University 25-17.

Loughborough, who had defeated both Oxford and Cambridge, tottered a little in their group but got better as the competition progressed before crashing at the final hurdle. Chichester again did well, losing only 19-0 to Cardiff Institute and winning their group undefeated.

Edinburgh easily won the Scottish Championship, defeating St Andrews in the Scottish final by 45-0. Cardiff University were beaten 44-7 and only Cardiff Institute prevented them from becoming the first Scottish team in the final by winning 25-19 in Cardiff, where they had also beaten Exeter and well-favoured Durham.

GROUP TABLES

An agreed number of places in the first play-off round are allocated to each division, which decides the number of teams to progress from each group within the division.
The qualifier from Scotland, who entered the competition in the third round, was the winner of a play-off between the winners of two groups played on a league basis.

LONDON DIVISION: Group A

	P	W	D	L	F	A	Pts
UCL	5	4	0	1	134	62	8
King's College	5	3	1	1	73	37	7
RHBNC	5	2	1	2	68	50	5
LSE	5	2	0	3	81	86	4
Queen Mary Westfield	5	2	0	3	76	114	4
Imperial College	5	1	0	4	38	121	2

LONDON DIVISION: Group B

	P	W	D	L	F	A	Pts
UMDS	4	3	0	1	137	38	6
St George's Hosp	4	2	0	2	70	65	4
R London/St Bart's Hosp	4	2	0	2	36	58	4
Charing X/West Hosp	4	2	0	2	23	80	4
St Mary's Hosp	4	1	0	3	63	88	2

LONDON DIVISION: Group C

	P	W	D	L	F	A	Pts
UCHMS	3	2	0	1	53	32	4
Royal Free Hosp	3	2	0	1	23	32	4
Goldsmiths	3	1	0	2	50	38	2
Wye	3	1	0	2	13	37	2

SOUTH-EAST DIVISION: Group A

	P	W	D	L	F	A	Pts
Brunel UC	5	5	0	0	490	52	10
Reading	5	4	0	1	141	67	8
Portsmouth	5	3	0	2	131	158	6
Buckinghamshire Coll	5	1	0	4	76	149	2
Surrey	5	1	0	4	62	208	2
Brunel	5	1	0	4	25	291	2

SOUTH-EAST DIVISION: Group B

	P	W	D	L	F	A	Pts
Chichester Inst	5	5	9	0	199	33	10
Canterbury Christchurch	5	4	0	1	150	37	8
Brighton	5	3	0	2	130	88	6
Kent	5	2	0	3	83	104	4
Sussex	5	1	0	4	51	238	2
Greenwich	5	0	0	5	51	164	0

SOUTH-EAST DIVISION: Group C

	P	W	D	L	F	A	Pts
Luton	5	5	0	0	162	48	10
North London	5	3	0	2	111	86	6
Hertfordshire	5	3	0	2	101	115	6

	P	W	D	L	F	A	Pts
Essex	5	2	0	3	129	99	4
East Anglia	5	2	0	3	70	107	4
Cranfield (Beds)	5	0	0	5	7	145	0

SOUTH-EAST DIVISION: Group D

	P	W	D	L	F	A	Pts
St Mary's UC	6	5	0	1	234	48	10
Roehampton	6	5	0	1	227	48	10
Kingston	6	4	0	2	114	86	8
South Bank	6	3	0	3	107	139	6
Thames Valley	6	2	0	4	93	140	4
Westminster	6	2	0	4	77	258	4
City	6	0	0	6	77	210	0

SOUTH-WEST DIVISION: Group A

	P	W	D	L	F	A	Pts
Bristol	6	6	0	0	277	59	12
Exeter	6	4	0	2	244	66	8
Bath	6	3	1	2	134	87	7
Southampton Inst	6	3	1	2	113	146	7
UWE	6	3	0	3	67	144	6
Southampton	6	1	0	5	106	161	2
Plymouth	6	0	0	6	33	311	0

SOUTH-WEST DIVISION: Group B

	P	W	D	L	F	A	Pts
Marjons	3	3	0	0	117	17	6
Seal Hayne	3	2	0	1	44	67	4
Royal Ag Coll	3	1	0	0	28	78	2
Cranfield	3	0	0	3	42	69	0

MIDLANDS DIVISION: Group A

	P	W	D	L	F	A	Pts
Loughborough	6	5	0	1	226	53	10
Birmingham	6	4	0	2	210	88	8
Sheffield Hallam	6	4	0	2	159	76	8
Nottingham	6	4	0	2	175	119	8
Harper Adams	6	2	0	4	120	128	4
Warwick	6	2	0	4	70	182	4
Leicester	6	0	0	6	21	335	0

MIDLANDS DIVISION: Group B

	P	W	D	L	F	A	Pts
Sheffield	5	4	0	1	185	66	8
Coventry	5	4	0	1	120	66	8
Cheltenham & Glos	5	3	0	2	166	72	6
Wolverhampton	5	3	0	2	108	76	6
De Montfort (Beds)	5	1	0	4	11	70	2
Aston	5	0	0	5	27	267	0

MIDLANDS DIVISION: Group C

	P	W	D	L	F	A	Pts
Oxford Brookes	5	4	0	1	181	30	8
Nene	5	4	0	1	145	30	8
Central England	5	4	0	1	69	37	8
Nottingham Trent	5	2	0	3	117	117	4
Newman College	4	1	0	3	29	132	2
Derby	4	0	0	4	22	217	0

Newman College v Derby void

MIDLANDS DIVISION: Group D

	P	W	D	L	F	A	Pts
Worcester	5	5	0	0	208	63	10
Staffs (Stoke)	5	4	0	1	174	40	8
Staffs (Stafford)	5	3	0	2	105	66	6
Birmingham FTC	5	2	0	3	59	67	4
Buckingham	5	1	0	4	35	48	2
De Montfort (MK)	5	0	0	5	29	326	0

NORTH-EAST DIVISION: Group A

	P	W	D	L	F	A	Pts
Durham	6	6	0	0	132	46	12
Northumbria	6	4	0	2	148	109	8
Newcastle	6	2	0	4	99	119	4
Leeds	6	0	0	6	64	169	0

NORTH-EAST DIVISION: Group B1

	P	W	D	L	F	A	Pts
Hull	4	3	0	1	116	57	6
Leeds Met	4	3	0	1	85	72	6
Humberside	4	0	0	4	25	97	0

NORTH-EAST DIVISION: Group B2

	P	W	D	L	F	A	Pts
Ripon and York	6	4	1	1	152	75	9
Teesside	6	4	0	2	123	68	8
York	6	3	1	2	67	122	7
Sunderland	6	0	0	6	66	143	0

NORTH-EAST DIVISION: Group C

	P	W	D	L	F	A	Pts
Bradford and Ilkley	2	1	0	1	45	15	2
New College Durham	2	1	0	1	15	45	2

NORTH-WEST DIVISION: Group A

	P	W	D	L	F	A	Pts
Manchester	5	5	0	0	130	46	10
Keele	5	4	0	1	84	52	8
Manchester Met	5	3	0	2	111	85	6
Liverpool	5	2	0	3	165	107	4
Salford	5	1	0	4	72	172	2
Lancaster	5	0	0	5	63	163	0

NORTH-WEST DIVISION: Group B

	P	W	D	L	F	A	Pts
Chester	5	5	0	0	151	51	10
Crewe & Alsager	5	4	0	1	146	65	8
Bradford	5	3	0	2	72	100	6
Liverpool JM	5	2	0	3	91	90	4
Central Lancs	5	1	0	4	90	106	2
UMIST	5	0	0	5	50	188	0

NORTH-WEST DIVISION: Group C

	P	W	D	L	F	A	Pts
Edge Hill	4	3	1	0	166	41	7
Bolton	4	3	0	1	63	71	6
St Martins	4	2	1	1	60	39	5
Warrington	4	1	0	3	46	92	2
Carlisle	4	0	0	4	24	116	0

WALES DIVISION: Group A

	P	W	D	L	F	A	Pts
Cardiff Inst	6	6	0	0	365	55	12
Swansea	6	4	1	1	175	136	9
Cardiff Medics	6	4	1	1	167	164	9
Cardiff	6	3	0	3	122	60	6
Glamorgan	6	1	0	5	97	212	2
Bangor	6	1	0	5	110	250	2
Aberystwyth	6	0	0	6	85	244	0

WALES DIVISION: Group B

	P	W	D	L	F	A	Pts
Trinity	4	4	0	0	188	40	8
Swansea Inst	4	3	0	1	122	58	6
Gwent	4	2	0	2	102	81	4
Lampeter	4	1	0	3	28	186	2
Bangor Normal Coll	4	0	0	4	59	134	0

SCOTTISH CHAMPIONSHIP
SCOTLAND: Group A

	P	W	D	L	F	A	Pts
St Andrews	5	5	0	0	176	104	10
Dundee	5	3	0	2	152	72	6
Glasgow	4	2	0	2	102	71	4
Strathclyde	4	1	0	3	62	101	2
Napier	4	1	0	3	58	118	2
Robert Gordon	2	0	0	2	31	115	0

SCOTLAND: Group B

	P	W	D	L	F	A	Pts
Edinburgh	4	4	0	0	176	25	8
Aberdeen	4	3	0	1	157	31	6
Heriot-Watt	4	2	0	2	53	106	4
Stirling	4	1	0	3	49	88	2
Glasgow Cal	4	1	0	3	27	212	2

Scotland Final: Edinburgh 45, St Andrews 0
Winner qualified for third play-off round

BUSA CHAMPIONSHIPS
Sponsored by Vaseline
Knock-out rounds
1st play-off round: Warwick 0, Oxford Brookes 21; Hull 17, Newcastle 27; Birmingham w/o Bolton; Nottingham 6, Manchester 22; Sheffield 10, Manchester Metropolitan 13; Crewe and Alsager 22, Keele 12; Worcester 29, Loughborough 49; Durham w/o Cheltenham and Gloucester; Nene w/o Bradford; Leeds Metropolitan 53, Edge Hill 5; Coventry 9, Ripon and York 16; Northumbria 20, Chester 17; TASC 3, Sheffield Hallam 68; Harper Adams 28, Teesside 0; Marjons w/o Royal Free Hospital; St Mary's Coll w/o St George's Hospital; West of England 17, Luton 19; Hertfordshire 5, UW Swansea 43; UCL 19, UW Cardiff 53; Swansea Inst. 13, Exeter 72; Seale Hayne 3, Trinity College 34; Cardiff Institute 50, Bath 0; Brunel UC w/o Cardiff Medics; North London 9, Roehampton Institute 17; Kings 12, Brighton 6; Bristol w/o Canterbury Christchurch; Chichester w/o Goldsmiths; RHBNC 5, Portsmouth 33; Kingston 20, Reading 5; RAC 8, UMDS 10
2nd play-off round: Manchester 25, Oxford Brookes 12; Keele 12, Loughborough 42; Newcastle 7, Birmingham 15; Ripon and York 27, Leeds Metropolitan 33; Sheffield Hallam 7, Durham 27; Manchester Metropolitan 19, Northumbria 17; Harper Adams 11, Nene 10; Kingston 27, Exeter 30; UMDS 3, Bristol 36; UW Swansea 25, Trinity College 15; St Mary's College 45, Kings 12; Chichester 0, Cardiff Institute 19; UW Cardiff 15, Roehampton Institute 10; Portsmouth 22, Marjons 36; Brunel UC 49, Luton 7
3rd play-off round: Birmingham 12, Loughborough 47; Exeter 36, St Mary's College 17; Leeds Metropolitan 23, Manchester Metropolitan 17; Cardiff Institute 25, Durham 21; UW Cardiff 25, Brunel UC 17; Edinburgh 12, Harper Adams 0; Bristol w/o Marjons; UW Swansea 31, Manchester 3
Quarter-finals: Cardiff Institute 28, Exeter 16; Loughborough 62, Leeds Metropolitan 7; Edinburgh 44, UW Cardiff 7; Bristol 0, UW Swansea 10
Semi-finals: Cardiff Institute 25, Edinburgh 10; UW Swansea 10, Loughborough 25

ENGLISH UNIVERSITIES INTER-DIVISIONAL TOURNAMENT
20 December 1995, Nottingham RUFC
Final: Midlands 32, South-West 13 **3rd and 4th Place:** London and South-East 29, North 10
BUSA SEVEN-A-SIDE TOURNAMENT
24 March 1995, Bristol University
Semi-finals: Brunel UC 25, Exeter 19; Bristol 1st 24, Bristol 2nd 17
Final: Bristol 33, Brunel UC 22
YORKSHIRE UNIVERSITIES CUP
1st XV Final (6 May 1996, Pontefract RFC): Sheffield Hallam 36, Huddersfield 6
2nd XV Final (30 April 1996, Sandal RFC): Leeds Metropolitan 25, Sheffield Hallam 10

IRELAND CLAIM TRIPLE CROWN

SCHOOLS RUGBY 1995-96
Brendan Gallagher *Daily Telegraph*

Ireland, calling on no fewer than six members of the exceptional Blackrock College team, deservedly took the Schools Triple Crown, although the decisive game, against Wales at Ravenhill, was a 13-12 cliffhanger. Fittingly, it was their outstanding captain, Barry Gibney, who scored the decisive try. Ireland had started their campaign with an emphatic 37-12 victory over Scotland in Cork, wing Cormac Dowling showing his pace to score two tries, while four days later in Hull a huge team effort was needed to end England's three-season unbeaten run against Five Nations opposition. Fly-half Brian O'Mahony kicked four penalties in Ireland's priceless 12-9 triumph. Ireland's continued excellence at this level gives hope for the future.

England were not helped by an exhausting schedule, and only against Scotland and France did they perform to their true potential. Lacking the bulk up front of previous years, they were much more vulnerable. Scotland did not enjoy a vintage year and used 32 players in four games, including flanker Peter Phillips, son of the Princess Royal and Mark Phillips, who played against France and Wales and appeared as a replacement against Ireland. Wales, with Lampeter full-back Daniel Jones impressing, played attractive rugby, holding England to a 7-7 draw and forcing Ireland to work hard for victory.

Colston's Collegiate, who said farewell to coach Andy Robinson in the summer, were again the top school in England. Only Millfield posed a serious threat to their unbeaten record. Centres Joe Ewens and Paul Pritchard, scrum-half Ricky Pellow and wing Nathan Millett were all capped by England 18 Group and Colston's retained the *Daily Mail* Under-18 Cup at Twickenham by again defeating QEGS, Wakefield in a repeat of the 1995 final. This time the score was 20-0, Millett scoring two tries and lock Alex Brown adding a third. The *Daily Mail* Under-15 tournament was won by RGS, High Wycombe, who beat Wellington 17-13 in an entertaining final. Wings Nick Duncombe and Ross Deering scored tries for the winners.

John Fisher School, Purley, were probably the best team in the south-east, winning all 18 of their games for the first time since rugby was introduced at the school 35 years ago. Particularly memorable was their emphatic 47-11 victory over Reigate, who themselves enjoyed a useful season. Wins against local rivals Whitgift (28-5) and Trinity Croydon (18-0) were also satisfying. The team was well captained by prop Ricky Nebbett, who subsequently appeared later for Harlequins second XV, while vice-captain Duncan Godfrey was capped by Scotland Youth.

Millfield's record was unblemished save for an 18-13 defeat against Colston's. A thumping 68-0 against Monmouth was their best performance along with a tough 15-0 win over St Joseph's, Ipswich. Full-back Daley Thompson and fly-half James Brown both played for England 18 Group with distinction, captain Geraint Thomas was a Welsh Schools cap and Dinos Alexopolous and wing Jerry Cook appeared in the England Colts squad. During one week in April the school's last three fly-halves – Brown, Matt Perry and Matt Jones – played for England 18 Group, England Colts and England Under-21s respectively. Sedbergh came tantalisingly close to an unbeaten season before losing their last game to Hymer's. A large pack, with Alastair Raman and Tom Fleming to the fore, was never matched, though the backs lost some of their potency after scrum-half Chris Simpson-Daniel was injured at half-term. QEGS, Wakefield were again one of the country's strongest sides. Their only defeat, apart from in the *Daily Mail* Cup final, was away at King's, Macclesfield. Altogether they scored 542 points and conceded just 81 in 17 games, and 16 boys played age-group county rugby.

Ampleforth's impressive season was marred slightly by the two below-par performances on their Christmas tour of London: defeats by 19-12 by Dulwich and 14-9 by Whitgift. Previously only narrow defeats against Hymer's and Sedbergh had hindered their progress. Centre Stephan Banna was a tower of strength, as was No 8 Ben Pennington. Bradford GS have been so dominant for so long that when their very young side lost eight of their first twelve games everybody was aghast. Needless to say, they recovered to win their next ten matches, and after a squad-building tour to South Africa will return this autumn to challenge the likes of Colston's. Wing Chris Armitage and lock Jonathan Marston both won England 18 Group honours. Hymer's College, Hull remain a force in the north. Six boys gained Yorkshire honours and victories over Ampleforth, Mount St Mary's and the previously unbeaten Sedbergh were the season's highlights. Narrow defeats against Durham and Stonyhurst and a 43-10 reverse against the superb Blackrock College XV gave food for thought.

Mount St Mary's produced their traditional free-running game and enjoyed their first win over Bradford GS for 14 years. Reaching the *Daily Mail* quarter-finals, where they lost 18-9 to QEGS, Wakefield, was also a fine achievement. Clifton lacked bulk up front but compensated with mobility in a season that saw just two defeats, against Sherborne and Cheltenham. Bedford's young team notched up 11 wins in 15 games, fly-half Richard Jackson and centre Simon Lincoln both earning selection for the Midlands.

Although hampered by injuries, RGS, Lancaster suffered only seven defeats in 20 games. Fly-half Andrew Miller was their main threat. Lord Wandsworth School from Hook in Hampshire enjoyed their best-ever season, losing only to QEGS, Wakefield in the *Daily Mail* semi-final.

A successful summer tour of South Africa paved the way for Radley's second undefeated season in their history. Outstanding victories were recorded over Harrow, Rugby, Sherborne and Wellington while only St Edward's, Oxford and Cheltenham provided really testing opposition. The pack was immense with a powerful front row and two line-out experts in lock Ben Spiegelberg and No 8 James Johnson. Yarm School in Cleveland have made tremendous progress recently and celebrated their most successful season to date with 11 victories in 13 games. Hymer's College were defeated in the schools' first meeting, while their derby against Durham resulted in a narrow 10-8 loss. Six of the pack won Durham county honours and Gareth Blades became the first pupil from the school to win England recognition when he played for England A against Japan. Caterham, King's, Macclesfield, King's, Bruton and Tonbridge all enjoyed fine seasons, too.

In Wales, Llandovery recovered from three early defeats, against Millfield, St Joseph's and Cowbridge, to impress with their entertaining style of rugby. They won 16 of their remaining games, notably against Glantaf, Monmouth, Rydal and their annual encounter with Christ College, Brecon. Lock Gareth Phillips was capped by Wales Youth, scrum-half James Roberts earned Wales Under-18 honours and fly-half Cerith Rees broke the schools points-scoring record with 206. Ysgol Glantaf became the first school, as opposed to sixth-form college, to win the Welsh Schools Cup, defeating Gowerton 10-8.

In Northern Ireland the Ulster Bank Schools Cup was shared for the first time since 1964 when Regent House, for whom fly-half John Anderson impressed, drew 9-9 with Methodist College, Belfast in front of the usual capacity crowd at Ravenhill on St Patrick's Day. In Scotland St Aloysius College defeated Peebles HS 13-12 to win the Schools Cup for a record fifth time.

On the Sevens circuit, Stonyhurst emerged as the most outstanding side since the famous Ampleforth VII won the double at Rosslyn Park, beating no longer possible but the Lancashire side were convincing 29-10 winners over Glantaf in the open competition. They arrived at Rosslyn Park with six consecutive tournament victories under their belts, having won the North of England Invitation Sevens and competitions at Hulme GS, Christ College, Brecon, Mount St Mary's, Birkenhead and Stonyhurst itself. Their squad of ten, led by Paul Howard, remained unchanged. The Festival at Rosslyn Park was won by Bryanston, who survived a thrilling semi-final against Wellington (27-26), Ed Hallett, son of RFU secretary Tony, scoring the vital late try. In the final they accounted for Cheltenham, 26-14. GRS Guildford took the junior tournament and St Olave's the prep-school title.

MATCH DETAILS

22 December 1995, Murrayfield

SCOTLAND 12 (4PG)   **FRANCE 18** (1PG 3T)
SCOTLAND *Penalty Goals:* G Ross (4)
FRANCE *Tries:* Jezequel, Heymans, Kuzdik   *Penalty Goals:* Teulet

5 January 1996, Brewery Field, Bridgend

WALES 30 (1G 1PG 4T)   **SCOTLAND 3** (1DG)
WALES *Tries:* Jones (2), Hawkins, Young, Thomas   *Conversion:* Jones   *Penalty Goal:* Jones
SCOTLAND *Dropped Goal:* G Ross

24 February 1996, Mountain Ash

WALES 16 (1G 3PG)   **FRANCE 7** (1G)
WALES *Try:* G Thomas   *Conversion:* S Jones   *Penalty Goals:* S Jones (3)
FRANCE *Try:* Kuzbick   *Conversion:* Teulet

27 March 1996, Hawick

SCOTLAND 7 (1G)   **ENGLAND 50** (3G 2PG 1DG 4T)
SCOTLAND *Try:* M Dirollo   *Conversion:* C Paterson
ENGLAND *Tries:* Hartley (3), Thompson (2), Ogilvie (2)   *Conversions:* Thompson (3)   *Penalty Goals:* Thompson (2)   *Dropped Goal:* J Brown

30 March 1996, Bridgwater & Albion RFC

ENGLAND 7(1G)   **WALES 7** (1G)
ENGLAND *Try:* Ewens   *Conversion:* Thompson
WALES *Try:* Greenaway   *Conversion:* Jones

6 April 1996, Vannes Stade Jo Courtel

FRANCE 11 (2PG 1T)   **ENGLAND 14** (3PG 1T)
FRANCE *Try:* Heymans   *Penalty Goals:* Teulet (2)
ENGLAND *Try:* Thompson   *Penalty Goals:* Brown (3)

6 April 1996, The Mardyke, Cork

IRELAND 37 (3G 2PG 2T)   **SCOTLAND 12** (4PG)
IRELAND *Tries:* Dowling (2), Davis, Travers, O'Mahony   *Conversions:* O'Mahony (3)   *Penalty Goals:* O'Mahony (2)
SCOTLAND *Penalty Goals:* Paterson (4)

10 April 1996, Hull Ionians RFC

ENGLAND 9 (3PG)   **IRELAND 12** (4PG)
ENGLAND *Penalty Goals:* Brown (3)
IRELAND *Penalty Goals:* O'Mahony (4)

17 April 1996, Ravenhill, Belfast

IRELAND 13 (1G 2PG)   **WALES 12** (1G 1T)
IRELAND *Try:* Gibney   *Conversion:* O'Mahony   *Penalty Goals:* O'Mahony (2)
WALES *Tries:* Price, Thomas   *Conversion:* Jones

ENGLAND

Full-back: D Thompson (Millfield) *S, W, F, I*
Threequarters: C Armitage (Bradford GS) *S, F, I*; N Millett (Colston's Collegiate) *W*;
J Ewens (Colston's Collegiate) *S, W, F, I*; J Pritchard (Colston's Collegiate) *S, W, F, I*;
R Hartley (King's, Macclesfield) *S, W, F, I*; S Banna (Ampleforth) *S* (R), *W* (R);
P Richards (Lord Wandsworth) *W* (R)
Half-backs: J Brown (Millfield) *S, W, F, I*; R Pellow (Colston's Collegiate) *S, W, F, I*
Forwards: S Trethewey (Estover Community Coll) *S, W, F, I*; A Long (St Peter's
Bournemouth), *S, W, F, I*; J McCormick (St Joseph's, Ipswich) *S, W, F, I*; J Marston
(Bradford GS) *S, W, F, I*; J Winterbottom (Diss HS) *S, W, F, I*; P Buxton (Cleeve Coll) *S,
W, F, I*; L Moody (Oakham School) *S, W, F, I*; P Ogilvie (Tonbridge) *S, W, F*; R Beattie
(Hymer's Coll, Hull) *I*; A Kershaw (QE Barnet) *W* (R), *I* (R); M Swift (London Oratory) *F*
(R), R Lloyd (Solihull) *I* (R)
J Ewens was captain in all four games

SCOTLAND

Full-backs: S Connell (Strathallan School) *F*; T Lightoller (Gordonstoun) *W, E, I*
Threequarters: S Walker (Dollar Acad) *F, W, E, I*; G Hood (George Heriot's) *F, W, E, I*;
J Mackley (Merchiston Castle) *W* (R); T Lightoller (Gordonstoun) *F*; C Carnochan
(Dollar) *E*; D Affleck (Berwickshire HS) *F* (R), *W*; A Raistrick (George Watson's) *F*;
S Connell (Strathallan) *W*; M Dirollo (George Watson's Coll) *E, I*; G Lawson (Dollar
Acad) *I, E* (R)
Half-backs: G Ross (George Heriot's) *F, W*; C Paterson (Galashiels Acad) *E, I*;
R Chrystie (Hawick HS) *F, W, E, I*
Forwards: T Gordon-Duff (Gordonstoun) *E, I*; M Welch (Dunfermline HS) *F, W*;
R Spernagel (Douglas Ewart HS) *W* (R); S Mackinnon (Queen Victoria) *F, W, E*;
S Linden (Gordonstoun) *F* (R); J Nelson (Queen Victoria's School) *E*; A Lawson
(Eastwood HS) *E* (R), *I*; C Buchanan (George Watson's) *F, E* (R), *I*; E Mackay
(Strathallan) *F* (R), *W*; J White (George Watson's) *F, W, E, I*; T Boyd (Hutchesons' GS) *F,
W, E, I*; S Taylor (Morrison's Acad) *E, I*; P Phillips (Gordonstoun) *F, W, I* (R); G
Howieson (Hutchesons' GS) *F, E, I*; R Muir (Fettes) *F, W*; A Ness (Edinburgh Acad) *W*
(R), *I* (R); H Calder (George Watson's Coll) *W*; F Gladstone (Gordonstoun) *E, I*
G Ross was captained against France and Wales; R Chrystie against England and Ireland

IRELAND

Full-back: T Keating (Blackrock Coll) *S, E, W*
Threequarters: J Davis (Belfast HS) *S, E, W*; E Travers (Terenure Coll) *S, E, W*;
K Hartigan (St Munchin's College) *S, E, W*; C Dowling (PBC Bray) *S, E, W*
Half-backs: B O'Mahony (CBC Cork) *S, E, W*; C Scally (Blackrock Coll) *S, E, W*
Forwards: S McConnell (Coleraine AI) *S, E, W*; P Smyth (Blackrock Coll) *S, E, W*; S Best
(Portadown College) *S, E*; J Campbell (Terenure Coll) *E* (R), *W*; P Bracken (St Andrew's
Coll) *S, E, W*; R Casey (Blackrock Coll) *S, E, W*; T Cahill (PBC Cork) *S, E, W*, B Gibney
(Blackrock Coll) *S, E, W*; J Fogarty (Rockwell Coll) *S* (R); S Kennedy (Regent House) *W* (R)
B Gibney was captain in all three games

WALES

Full-backs: D Jones (Lampeter) *S, F, E, I*; D Jones (St Cyres) *I* (R)
Threequarters: J Young (Neath Coll) *S, E, I*; S Greenaway (St Cyres) *F*; D Hawkins
(Neath College) *S, F, E*; S Jones (Bro Myrddin) *S, F, E, I*; G Thomas (Tregib) *S, F, E, I*;
S Ward (Brynteg) *F*
Half-backs: T Price (Coedylan) *S, F, E, I*; B Treharne (Radyr) *S, F, E, I*
Forwards: I Poley (Brecon) *S, F, E, I*; M Davies (Aberdare) *S, F, I*; G Williams (Brynteg)
E; D Sweet (Hawthorn) *S, F, E, I*; R Edwards (Tregaron) *S, F, E, I*; D Jones (Dyffrin Teifi)
S, F, E, I; C Hughes (Aman Valley) *S, F, I*; P Morgan (QE Maridinum) *S, F, E, I*;
G Thomas (Millfield) *S, F, E, I*; G Bennett (QE Maridinum) *E*; G Groves (Y Pant) *I* (R)
S Jones was captain in all four games

WALES POINT THE WAY

COLTS AND YOUTH RUGBY 1995-96
Harry Townsend

Wales Youth, after their shock introduction to the FIRA tournament in Romania last year, proved they had been quick learners in Italy this time around. They had already won their second successive junior Grand Slam, beating Italy (34-8), France (21-8), England (9-3) and Scotland (18-11), and although they had to combine the Under-18 and Under-19 age groups to meet the FIRA deadline, they defeated defending champions France and Uruguay in their pool. A last-second try, completing a hat-trick for Martin Giraud of London Welsh, overcame Romania 21-17 in the semi-final. Favourites Argentina, champions five times in ten years, had prepared meticulously with a two-week tour in France and Italy, and dynamic rugby took them to a 29-0 half-time lead and eventual 34-7 victory over Wales in the final. Scotland, after a 17-17 draw with surprise packet Uruguay, beat South Africa 18-15 and lost in their semi-final to Argentina, 41-20.

England nearly had a very good season. They beat Italy (60-3) and Scotland (36-13), but after losing a battle of penalties with Wales they went down to a scrambled last-minute try by France, 22-18. Full-back Paul Sampson, called up for training with the England senior squad, scored 47 of the England Colts' points.

It is to be hoped that England and Ireland will realise the benefits of the FIRA competition and join the ranks in Argentina in 1997. Much will depend on the Horner Report, widely condemned at club level for recommendations that youth rugby should be restricted to under-18s, and under-21 rugby replaced by under-20. This could be a drastic blow to many smaller clubs. The advantage at representative level (the tip of the iceberg) would be schools and Colts teams run in tandem, providing an international stage for more young players. Most representative Colts teams currently duplicate a high proportion of the Schools 18 Group team of the previous season – indeed, 12 of the present England Colts squad have taken this route. Six already play for Bath; five are students at Loughborough University. National (fast-track) Under-19 and Under-20 teams would combine the best of both Under-18 squads, and mitigate the reluctance of clubs to release the players.

East Midlands, drawn in equal numbers from Bedford and Northampton, beat Hertfordshire 13-8 to win the Sun Alliance Colts County Championship at Twickenham, while the South-West defeated London and the South-East 22-16 to win the Sun Alliance Colts Divisional Championship at Castlecroft. Preston Lodge beat

Langholm 15-8 for the Scottish Youth Cup, and Neath and Rhondda drew 3-3 in the final of the Welsh District Cup. As ever, there were many excellent teams at every age level, but team of the year must be Swansea, who beat Newport 10-9 in the Welsh Youth Cup final. They won all of their 29 matches and ten of their players (including FIRA captain Chris Wells) represented Wales Schools or Youth. Bristol, National Colts Sevens winners against Hinckley by 51-0, lost only three of 33 games, one of which was against Swansea, when Bristol were without 11 divisional players. Cheltenham, Gloucestershire Colts Cup winners for the third year, lost only to Leicester and Swansea. Unbeaten teams included Maidstone and Fylde Under-13s, Haywards Heath Under-14s, Torquay Athletic Under-15s and Middlesbrough Under-16s.

The following players took part in the Youth/Colts international matches. Countries played against are shown in square brackets.
Abbreviations: *A* – Argentina, *C* – Chile, *E* – England, *F* – France, *I* – Ireland, *It* – Italy, *R* – Romania, *S* – Scotland, *SA* – South Africa, *Sp* – Spain, *SS* – Scottish Schools, *U* – Uruguay, *W* – Wales, *WS* – Welsh Schools, (R) – Replacement.

ENGLAND

Colts

Full-back: P Sampson (Woodhouse Grove School & Otley) *It, S, W, F*
Threequarters: T Barlow (Leicester) *It, S, W, F*; C Pawson (Tunbridge Wells & Exeter U) *It, S, F*; K Sorrell (Saracens) *It, S, W, F*; M Horne (Harlequins) *It, S, W, F*; J Cook (Millfield School & Bath) *S* (R); J Storey (Harlequins & Loughborough U) *W* (R)
Half-backs: J Lewsey (Wasps & Bristol U) *It, S, W, F* (R); M Wood (Harrogate) *It, S, W, F*; M Perry (Bath) *It* (R), *S* (R), *W, F*; R Sharples (Harlequins & Loughborough U) *It* (R)
Forwards: V Hartland (Gloucester) *It, S, W, F*; R Protherough (Worcester & Loughborough U) *It, S, W, F*; C Horsman (Bath) *It, S, W, F*; A Bell (Bristol) *It, S, W, F*; W James (Bath) *It*; R Bryan (Bath) *It*; J Worsley (Wasps) *It, S, W, F*; J Cockle (Bath) *It, S, W, F*; D Alexopoulos (Harlequins) *It* (R); W Fuller (Leicester & Loughborough U) *It* (R), *S, W, F*; M Cornish (Leicester & Loughborough U) *S, W, F*; J Clark (Bristol) *S* (R)
Pawson was captain against Italy, Scotland and France; Worsley against Wales.

IRELAND

Under-18s

Full-back: A Poniard (Monivea) *Sp, S, W*
Threequarters: R Hartman (Corinthians) *Sp, S, W*; O Geoghegan (Thurles) *Sp, S, W*; S Horgan (Drogheda) *Sp, S, W*; M Crothers (Dromore) *Sp, S, W*; A Morrissey (Highfield) *S* (R)
Half-backs: M Maguire (Banbridge) *Sp, S, W*; J Aiken (Dromore) *Sp*; I O'Gorman (Old Crescent) *S, W*
Forwards: R Bolger (New Ross) *Sp, S, W*; A Keaveney (Ballina) *Sp, S, W*; E Scullion (Ballymena) *Sp, S, W*; D O'Kane (Ballymena) *Sp, S, W*; B O'Connor (Skerries) *Sp, S, W*; A O'Gorman (Newport) *Sp, S, W*; K McKinley (Mullingar) *Sp, S, W*; J Shanks (Ballynahinch) *Sp*; B Kelleher (Dolphin) *S, W*; D Quinlan (Clanwilliam) *W* (R); D Lillis (Corinthians) *W* (R); C Lyons (Clogher Valley) *W* (R); S Keane (Highfield) *W* (R)
Maguire was captain against Spain; Geoghegan against Scotland and Wales.

SCOTLAND
Under-18s
Full-backs: R Chassels (Aberdeen U) *S*; I McKerrow (Sedbergh) *SS*(2), *It, I, W*
Threequarters: R Lothian (Melrose) *SS*(2), *It, I, W*; G Kiddie (Edinburgh Acads)
SS, It, W; J Philip (Aberdeen GSFP) *SS*(2), *It, I*; A Dickson (Walkerburn) *SS, I, W*;
A Pollock (Glasgow Southern) *SS, It, I, W*
Half-backs: S Ruthven (Melrose) *SS*; J Sim (Heriot's FP) *SS, It, I, W*; C Black
(Watsonians) *SS, It, W*; G Thomson (Selkirk) *SS*; F Kennedy (Stirling County)
SS (R), *I*
Forwards: A Milne (King's School) *SS*(2), *It, I, W*; G McLeod (Hawick Wands)
SS(2), It; D Harley (Heriot's FP) *I, W*; G Hoyle (Stewart's-Melville FP) *SS*(2), *It, I,
W*; A Green (Heriot's FP) *I* (R); R Tod (Langholm) *SS*(2), *It* (R); D Sumner (Preston
Lodge FP) *SS, It*; J Mavor (London Scottish) *W*; S Tait (Penicuik) *SS, It, I, W*;
J Henderson (Jed Thistle) *SS*(2), *It* (R), *I, W* (R); D Wilson (Dumfries) *SS, It*;
S Pearman (London Scottish) *SS*(2), *It, I, W*; J Officer (Edinburgh U) *SS, I*; A Lees
(Ayr) *I*; R Beattie (Hymer's College) *W*
*Black was captain against Scottish Schools and Italy; Milne against Scottish Schools,
Ireland and Wales.*

Under-19s
Full-backs: P Thomson (Birmingham & Solihull) *Sp*; S Tomlinson (Selkirk) *E, W*
Threequarters: G Kiddie (Edinburgh Acads) *Sp* (R), *E* (R); J Craig (West of
Scotland) *Sp*; G Caldwell (GHK) *E, W*; A Bulloch (West of Scotland) *Sp*; M Mayer
(Watsonians) *Sp, E, W*; M Tweedie (Stewart's-Melville FP) *Sp*; J Melvin (Preston
Lodge FP) *E, W*; J Millard (Dundee U) *Sp* (R); D Bull (Stewart's-Melville FP) *E, W*
Half-backs: S Ruthven (Melrose) *Sp, E* (R), *W* (R); S Ure (Otley) *E, W*; C Laidlaw
(Jedforest) *Sp, W*; D Short (Heriot's FP) *E*
Forwards: S Paris (Livingston) *Sp, E, W*; P Fitzgerald (Watsonians) *Sp* (R), *W* (R);
D Bishop (Newport) *Sp*; M Landale (Heriot's FP) *E, W*; G Kerr (Jedforest) *Sp, E, W*;
E Webb (Eltham College) *Sp* (R); D Paton (Heriot's FP) *Sp, E*; D Whitehead
(Newcastle) *Sp*; E Emerson (Boroughmuir) *Sp* (R); G McCallum (Boroughmuir) *E,
W*; J White (Watson's College) *E* (R), *W*; P Simpson (Currie) *Sp, E, W*; A Dall
(Heriot's FP) *Sp, E, W*; G Inglis (Hutcheson's/Aloysians) *Sp*; I Sinclair (Watsonians)
E, W
Bulloch was captain against Spain; Sinclair against England and Wales.

FIRA Tournament
Full-backs: P Thomson (Birmingham & Solihull) *SA, A, R*; C Keenan (Heriot's FP)
C, SA (R)
Threequarters: J Craig (West of Scotland) *C, SA, A, R*; A Bulloch (West of
Scotland) *C, SA, A*; M Mayer (Watsonians) *SA, A, R*; M Tweedie (Stewart's-Melville
FP) *SA*; R Steel (Stewart's-Melville FP) *C, A* (R), *R*; J Millard (Dundee U) *C, A, R*
Half-backs: G Kiddie (Edinburgh Acads) *C, SA* (R); S Ruthven (Melrose) *SA, A, R*;
C Laidlaw (Jedforest) *C, A*; C Black (Watsonians) *SA*
Forwards: S Paris (Livingston) *SA, A*; P Fitzgerald (Watsonians) *C, R*; D Bishop
(Newport) *SA, A*; M Landels (Hawick Linden) *C, A* (R), *R*; G Kerr (Jedforest) *C,
SA, A*; E Webb (Eltham College) *C* (R), *R*; D Paton (Heriot's FP) *SA, A*; D
Whitehead (Newcastle) *C, A*; E Emerson (Boroughmuir) *C* (R), *R*; A Barnes
(Hawick) *C, SA, R*; P Simpson (Currie) *C, SA, A, R*; A Dall (Heriot's FP) *C, SA, A,
R*; G Inglis (Hutcheson's/Aloysians) *C, SA, A*; A Hotson (Langholm) *SA* (R),
A (R), *R*
Bulloch was captain against Chile, South Africa and Argentina; Dall against Romania.

WALES
Under-18s
Full-back: J Adams (Llanelli Wanderers) *WS, S, I*

Threequarters: I Farr (Pontypool) *WS, I*; S Winn (Maesteg Celtic) *WS, S, I*; M Watkins (Pontllanfraith) *WS, S, I*; M Giraud (London Welsh) *WS, I*; C Williams (Crynant) *S*
Half-backs: M Davies (Newport) *WS*; M Kehoe (Bridgend) *WS, S, I*; J Davies (Aberavon Quins) *S, I*; P Davies (Pontyberem) *S* (R), *I* (R); M Harris (Waunarlwydd) *I* (R)
Forwards: D Hurford (Cardiff) *WS*; S Delaney (Felinfoel) *WS, S, I*; G Bayliss (Bridgend) *WS*; D Morris-Falconer (Blaydon) *WS, S, I*; P Griffiths (Loughor) *WS, I* (R); G Lucas (Cardiff) *WS*; G Thomas (Bridgend) *WS*; I McQueen (Pontypridd) *WS, S, I*; D Perry (Pontypridd) *S, I*; D Jones (Llanelli Wanderers) *S, I*; N Bonner-Evans (Llanelli Wanderers) *S, I*; D Gibbs (Crumlin) *S, I*; M Ryce (Cardiff) *S, I*; D Williams (Llandovery) *I* (R); C O'Donoghue (Rumney) *I* (R); J Bonner (Pontyberem) *I* (R)
Winn was captain against Welsh Schools; Kehoe against Scotland and Ireland.

Under-19s
Full-back: K Morgan (Pontypridd) *It, F, E, S*
Threequarters: G Wyatt (Pontypridd) *It, F, E, S*; T Davies (Ystradgynlais) *It, F, E, S*; P Matthews (Pontypridd) *It, F, E, S*; R Shorney (Senghenydd) *It, F, E, S*; G Roberts (Treorchy) *F* (R)
Half-backs: L Jarvis (Pontypridd) *It, F, E, S*; G Downes (Pontypridd) *It, F, E, S*; D Cambourne (Treherbert) *E* (R)
Forwards: I Thomas (Pontypool) *It, F, E, S*; G Thomas (Bridgend) *It, F, E, S*; S Lee (Bridgend) *It, F, E, S*; A Grabham (Cardiff) *It, F, E, S*; J Griffiths (Swansea) *It, F, E, S*; G Newman (Cwmavon) *It, F, E, S*; M Cook (Resolven) *It, F*; A Lloyd (Pontypridd) *It, F, E, S*; M Davey (Cardiff) *It* (R); I Gough (Newport) *It* (R); C Wells (Swansea) *F* (R); K Evans (Carmarthen Quins) *F* (R), *E, S*; E Fear (Bridgend) *F* (R)
Downes was captain in all four matches.

FIRA Tournament
Full-backs: K Morgan (Pontypridd) *F, U, R, A*; G Tremain (Crynant) *U* (R)
Threequarters: R Shorney (Senghenydd) *F, U, R, A*; P Matthews (Pontypridd) *F, U, R, A*; C Murphy (Pontypridd) *F, U, R, A*; M Giraud (London Welsh) *F, U, R, A*; D Simpson (Carmarthen Ath) *A* (R)
Half-backs: G Wyatt (Pontypridd) *F, U, R, A*; M Kehoe (Bridgend) *F, U, R, A*; M Harris (Waunarlwydd) *A* (R)
Forwards: K Jones (Ystradgynlais) *F, U, R, A*; C Wells (Swansea) *F, U* (R), *R, A*; C Howells (Pontypridd) *F, A*; V Cooper (Ystradgynlais) *F, U, R*; J Griffiths (Swansea) *F, U, R, A*; N Kelly (Cardiff) *F, U* (R), *R, A*; A Lewis (Ystradgynlais) *F, R, A*; L Griffiths (Swansea) *F, U, R, A*; W Williams (Cardiff) *U*; J Scott (Crumlin and Cross Keys Coll) *U, R, A* (R); G Phillips (Llandovery Coll) *U, A* (R); A McDonagh (Cardiff and Ysgol Glantaf) *U*; J Grabham (Pembroke) *U* (R); P Savage (Cardiff) *A*; S Mason (Cardiff and Pontypool Coll) *A* (R)
Wells was captain against France, Romania and Argentina; Matthews against Uruguay.

MATCH DETAILS 1995-96

17 November 1995, Meggetland

SCOTTISH SCHOOLS 8 (1PG 1T)   **SCOTLAND UNDER-18 YOUTH 23** (1G 2PG 2T)
SCOTLAND *Tries:* Lothian, McKerrow, Milne   *Conversion:* Ruthven
Penalty Goals: Ruthven, Kiddie

14 February 1996, The Gnoll, Neath

WELSH SCHOOLS 51 (4G 1PG 4T)   **WALES U18 YOUTH 12** (1G 1T)
WELSH SCHOOLS *Tries:* Greenway (2), Graham Thomas (2), Geraint Thomas, Edwards, Hughes, Groves   *Conversions:* S Jones (4)   *Penalty Goal:* S Jones
WALES *Tries:* Giraud, Watkins   *Conversion:* M Davies
Referee C Thomas (Wales)

18 February 1996, Aberavon

WALES U19 YOUTH 34 (3G 1PG 2T)   **ITALY YOUTH 8** (1PG 1T)
WALES *Tries:* Morgan (3), Matthews, Jarvis   *Conversions:* Jarvis (3)
Penalty Goal: Jarvis
ITALY *Try:* Zaffiri   *Penalty Goal:* Ribola
Referee N Cousins (England)

2 March 1996, Rovato

ITALY YOUTH 3 (1PG)   **ENGLAND COLTS 60** (6G 1PG 3T)
ENGLAND *Tries:* Lewsey (3), Barlow, Pawson, Worsley, Sorrell, Bryan, Sampson   *Conversions:* Sampson (6)   *Penalty Goal:* Sampson
Referee G Borreani (France)

9 March 1996, Soustons

FRANCE JUNIORS 8 (1PG 1T)   **WALES U19 YOUTH 21** (1G 2PG 1DG 1T)
FRANCE *Try:* Leite   *Penalty Goal:* Bonetti
WALES *Tries:* Matthews, T Davies   *Conversion:* Jarvis   *Penalty Goals:* Jarvis (2)
Dropped Goal: Jarvis
Referee C White (England)

10 March 1996, Valladolid

SPAIN U19 YOUTH 23   **IRELAND U18 YOUTH 6** (2PG)
IRELAND *Penalty Goals:* Maguire (2)
Referee D Irazoqui (France)

13 March 1996, Mirano

ITALY YOUTH 8 (1PG 1T)   **SCOTLAND U18 YOUTH 26** (3G 1T)
SCOTLAND *Tries:* Lothian, Pollock, Tod, Henderson   *Conversions:* Sim (3)

22 March 1996, Penicuik

SCOTLAND U18 YOUTH 8 (1DG 1T)   **SCOTTISH SCHOOLS 6** (2PG)
SCOTLAND *Try:* Milne   *Dropped Goal:* Sim

22 March 1996, Myreside

SCOTLAND U19 YOUTH 63 (7G 3PG 1T)   **SPAIN 17**
SCOTLAND *Tries:* Craig (4), Thomson, Kiddie, Tweedie, Inglis
Conversions: Ruthven (7)   *Penalty Goals:* Ruthven (3)

24 March 1996, St Helens, Swansea

WALES U19 YOUTH 9 (3PG)   **ENGLAND COLTS 3** (1PG)
WALES *Penalty Goals:* Jarvis (3)
ENGLAND *Penalty Goal:* Sampson
Referee J Cole (Ireland)

30 March 1996, Galway

IRELAND U18 YOUTH 17 (2G 1PG) **SCOTLAND U19 YOUTH 18** (1G 2PG 1T)
IRELAND *Tries:* Horgan, O'Kane   *Conversions:* Maguire (2)
Penalty Goal: Maguire
SCOTLAND *Tries:* Lothian, Milne   *Conversion:* Sim   *Penalty Goals:* Sim (2)
Referee T Rowlands (Wales)

13 April 1996, Coventry

ENGLAND COLTS 36 (1G 3PG 4T)   **SCOTLAND U19 13** (1PG 2T)
ENGLAND *Tries:* Horne, Bell, Worsley, Barlow, Sampson
Conversion: Sampson   *Penalty Goals:* Sampson (3)
SCOTLAND *Tries:* Caldwell (2)   *Penalty Goal:* Ure
Referee C Giacomel (Italy)

13 April 1996, Galway

IRELAND U18 YOUTH 17 (2G 1PG) **SCOTLAND U18 YOUTH 18** (1G 2PG 1T)
IRELAND *Tries:* Horgan, O'Kane   *Conversions:* Maguire (2)
Penalty Goal: Maguire
SCOTLAND *Tries:* Lothian, Milne   *Conversion:* Sim   *Penalty Goals:* Sim (2)
Referee T Rowlands (Wales)

20 April 1996, Chester

ENGLAND COLTS 18 (1G 2PG 1T)   **FRANCE JUNIORS 22** (2G 1PG 1T)
ENGLAND *Tries:* Perry, Pawson   *Conversion:* Sampson
Penalty Goals: Sampson (2)
Referee S Buggy (Ireland)

20 April 1996, Ayr

SCOTLAND U18 YOUTH 19 (2PG 1DG 2T)   **WALES U18 YOUTH 11** (2PG 1T)
SCOTLAND *Tries:* Milne, Tait   *Penalty Goals:* Sim, Kiddie   *Dropped Goal:* Kiddie
WALES *Try:* Ryce   *Penalty Goals:* J Davies (2)
Referee D Tyndall (Ireland)

20 April 1996, Ayr

SCOTLAND U19 YOUTH 11 (1PG 1DG 1T)   **WALES U19 YOUTH 18**
(1G 2PG 1T)
SCOTLAND *Try:* Bull   *Penalty Goal:* Ure   *Dropped Goal:* Ure
WALES *Tries:* Newman, G Thomas   *Conversion:* Jarvis   *Penalty Goals:* Jarvis (2)
Referee L Mayne (Ireland)

27 April 1996, Cardiff Arms Park

WALES U18 YOUTH 21 (1G 3PG 1T)   **IRELAND U18 YOUTH 16** (1G 3PG)
WALES *Tries:* Ryce, Watkins   *Conversion:* Watkins   *Penalty Goals:* Watkins (2), J Davies
IRELAND *Try:* O'Gorman   *Conversion:* Maguire   *Penalty Goals:* Maguire (3)
Referee J Steele (Scotland)

FIRA YOUTH TOURNAMENT, ITALY

1 April 1996, Ghedi
SCOTLAND 17 (2G 1PG)   **CHILE 17**
SCOTLAND *Tries:* Steel, Millard   *Conversions:* Kiddie (2)   *Penalty Goal:* Kiddie

April 3 1996, Mantova

SCOTLAND 18 (1G 2PG 1T)   **SOUTH AFRICA 15**
SCOTLAND *Tries:* Simpson, Inglis   *Conversion:* Kiddie   *Penalty Goals:* Kiddie (2)

5 April 1996, Viadona

SCOTLAND 20 (2G 2PG)   **ARGENTINA 41**
SCOTLAND *Tries:* Craig (2)   *Conversions:* Ruthven (2)   *Penalty Goals:* Ruthven (2)

7 April 1996, Calvisano

SCOTLAND 6 (2PG)   **ROMANIA 32**
SCOTLAND *Penalty Goals:* Ruthven (2)

30 March 1996, Brescia

WALES 20 (2G 2PG)   **FRANCE 11** (2PG 1T)
WALES *Tries:* Murphy, pen try   *Conversions:* Wyatt (2)   *Penalty Goals:* Wyatt (2)
Referee M Schiavo (Italy)

1 April 1996, Mantova

WALES 17 (3PG 1DG 1T)   **URUGUAY 3** (1PG)
WALES *Try:* Wyatt   *Penalty Goals:* Wyatt (3)   *Dropped Goal:* Wyatt
Referee M Paraschivescu (Romania)

5 April 1996, Brescia

WALES 21 (3G)   **ROMANIA 17** (4PG 1T)
WALES *Tries:* Giraud (3)   *Conversions:* Wyatt (3)
Referee V Rabuffetti (Argentina)

Final: 7 April 1996, Calvisano

WALES 7 (1G)   **ARGENTINA** (3G 1PG 2T)
WALES *Try:* Kehoe   *Conversion:* Wyatt
Referee J Gastou (France)

RETURN OF THE WRITE–OFFS

THE 1995-96 SEASON IN SCOTLAND
Bill McMurtrie

After an uninspiring 15-15 draw with Western Samoa at Murrayfield, yet another sobering November result after hefty defeats by New Zealand and South Africa in successive seasons, Scotland were all but written off. Yet for the second year running they came within one game of a Grand Slam, only to be denied by England.

Scotland, beaten by the All Blacks in the 1995 World Cup quarter-final, went into the season under completely new management. Jim Telfer, the Scottish Rugby Union's director of rugby, assumed the additional duty of team manager, taking over from Duncan Paterson. Richie Dixon stepped up from assistant coach to replace Douglas Morgan, and Rob Wainwright succeeded Gavin Hastings as captain. Their opening gambit, however, was far from being the ideal launch pad for the international season. Worse was to follow when Scotland A – the full national team in all but name – were beaten 29-17 by Italy on a January visit to Rieti.

Yet only two weeks later, with only three changes from the team humbled in Italy, Scotland opened their Five Nations Championship campaign with victory against Ireland at Lansdowne Road. The Scots garnered a 16-10 lead from the first half and held on to that unchanging score. A fortnight later, back home at Murrayfield, they turned in their best performance of the season. Their 'total' rugby subdued France, and Scotland, avenging their World Cup defeat, won more comfortably than the 19-14 result suggests. Dods scored all of Scotland's points, and his three penalty goals surpassed Gavin Hastings' haul in the 18-17 victory in 1986. In their next match the Scots slipped into a nervous game in Cardiff. Too much of the rugby on both sides, especially Scotland's, was uncertain and loose, and for more than an hour the only scores were penalty goals – three apiece. Then came tries for Townsend for Scotland and Proctor for Wales, but Dods' conversion left Scotland with a 16-14 victory and the prospect of a Murrayfield match against England for the Grand Slam. It was not to be. England ground out an 18-9 victory in a match dominated by the wily Dean Richards.

Scotland's A team had a mixed season. After successive defeats by Western Samoa, Italy and Ireland they turned in two satisfying wins – 38-32 against France at Myreside, and 32-22 against Wales at St Helens, Swansea. Damian Cronin, veteran of 35 internationals, not only led the Scots to those two victories but also scored a pair of tries against the French.

The Scotland team which beat Wales in Cardiff. L-R, back row: A P Burnell (replacement), K M Logan (replacement), M Dods, S J Campbell, G W Weir, E W Peters, D I W Hilton, P H Wright, C M Chalmers (replacement), J A Hay (replacement), G Armstrong (replacement); front row: G P J Townsend, B W Redpath, R J S Shepherd, S Hastings, R I Wainwright (capt), K D McKenzie, I R Smith, C A Joiner, I C Jardine.

Scotland's Under-21 XV also played in Rieti, recording a 31-10 win against their contemporaries. Disappointingly, however, they lost all of their other Under-21 internationals, against England, Ireland, France and Wales. Scotland had a runaway win against Spain by 63-17 in their opening Under-19 international of the season, James Craig running in four of the ten tries on the right wing, and they also had a notable 18-15 win over the South Africans in the FIRA junior tournament in Italy. It was their only win in the competition, though they finished in fourth place. It was the Under-18 team which had the best results of all Scotland's national age-group XVs, winning all six matches they played.

In domestic rugby the Scottish Exiles recorded their second clean sweep in the championship. Debate raged as to whether districts or clubs should represent Scotland in the European Cup, and discussion went as far as an SRU special general meeting. The vast majority of clubs supported the SRU's proposal for districts in Europe. Edinburgh and the South were nominated for two of the three places, and North & Midlands gained the third spot by beating Glasgow 21-13 in a play-off for the privilege. It was an unhappy season for Glasgow, who also lost all four District Championship matches, though they took the Under-21 title on points difference from the Exiles.

Melrose took the club title, the SRU Tennents Championship, for the fifth time in seven seasons, but it was their fellow Borderers, Hawick, who claimed pride of place by returning to the top of the honours list, a place that has been theirs by right for so long. Not only did Hawick lift the Border League trophy for the first time since 1989 but they won the inaugural SRU Tennents Cup competition, recovering from an inauspicious start to beat Watsonians 17-15 before a crowd of almost 23,000 at Murrayfield.

SRU TENNENTS CHAMPIONSHIP REVIEW

Scottish rugby's club league competition had new sponsors and a new format, contested home and away, but the winners were familiar. Melrose won title for the fifth time in seven seasons, though they had to come from behind to take the SRU Tennents Championship on points difference from Stirling County, the previous season's winners. With four defeats against them, Melrose were trailing Boroughmuir by three points just after the midway stage. Boroughmuir had achieved the double against Melrose, and Stirling had also won at the Greenyards, holding off a Melrose fightback to win by 27-26. Melrose then slipped twice in successive matches, both away: 15-31 against Boroughmuir and then 9-10 at Hawick.

However, Melrose did not lose again in the League. Their surge started with a 25-20 victory against Watsonians at Myreside on the day that Hawick beat Boroughmuir 19-18 less than a mile away at

Meggetland. Melrose then scraped an 18-15 win over Edinburgh Academicals with a Bryan Redpath try long into added time at Raeburn Place, and a 15-15 draw at Bridgehaugh was followed by a 31-11 victory against Gala at the Greenyards, a result that left Stirling County needing to beat Heriot's by 43 clear points at Bridgehaugh to retain the title. County won that final game 34-14. It was not enough.

Stirling had a horrid start to their title defence, losing three of their first four matches – against Hawick, Watsonians and Gala. The champions swept back with eight wins in their remaining ten games, but the point dropped against the Greenyards club proved crucial.

Boroughmuir were three points clear after their double against Melrose and an away victory against Gala, but failed to win any of their last four matches, a rot interrupted only by a 40-40 draw with Heriot's at home.

It was not the happiest of seasons for Academicals. They were relegated, along with Gala, from the First Division, giving way to Currie and Jedforest, and their coach, David Sole, Scotland's 1990 Grand Slam captain, was suspended by the Scottish Rugby Union until the end of the season because of comments he made about the referee of the match in which Melrose sneaked a very late victory.

SRU TENNENT'S PREMIERSHIP

Division 1	P	W	D	L	F	A	Pts
Melrose	14	9	1	4	326	199	19
Stirling County	14	9	1	4	320	215	19
Watsonians	14	8	1	5	393	270	17
Boroughmuir	14	7	2	5	327	301	16
Hawick	14	7	0	7	243	288	14
Heriot's FP	13	5	1	7	278	360	11
Edinburgh Acads	14	4	1	9	243	282	9
Gala	13	2	1	10	179	394	5

Previous champions: Hawick 10 times, 1973-74 to 1977-78, 1981-82, 1983-84 to 1986-87; Gala 3 times, 1979-80, 1980-81, 1982-83; Melrose 4 times, 1989-90, 1991-92 to 1993-94; Kelso twice, 1987-88, 1988-89; Heriot's FP 1979-80; Boroughmuir 1990-91; Stirling County 1994-95

Division 2	P	W	D	L	F	A	Pts
Currie	14	11	0	3	357	266	22
Jedforest	14	10	0	4	302	185	20
GHK	14	8	0	6	377	239	16
West of Scotland	14	7	0	7	268	258	14
Dundee HSFP	14	6	0	8	259	239	12
Kelso	14	6	0	8	275	260	12
Selkirk	14	5	0	9	215	307	10
Stewart's-Melville FP	14	3	0	11	193	492	6

Division 3	P	W	D	L	F	A	Pts
Glasgow Acads	14	12	0	2	461	132	24
Biggar	14	11	0	3	324	181	22
Kirkcaldy	14	10	0	4	316	182	20
Preston Lodge FP	14	6	0	8	243	246	12
Peebles	14	6	0	8	200	237	12
Musselburgh	14	6	0	8	229	336	12
Grangemouth	14	5	0	9	201	273	10
Corstorphine	14	0	0	14	154	541	0

Division 4	P	W	D	L	F	A	Pts
Kilmarnock	14	12	1	1	418	130	25
Glasgow Southern	14	10	1	3	415	174	21
Gordonians	14	10	0	4	383	163	20
Ayr	14	7	1	6	343	218	15
Langholm	14	6	1	7	183	217	13
Haddington	14	5	0	9	263	471	10
Edinburgh Wands	14	4	0	10	252	349	8
Wigtownshire	14	0	0	14	123	658	0

SRU TENNENT'S NATIONAL LEAGUE

Division 1	P	W	D	L	F	A	Pts
Glenrothes	17	15	0	2	454	203	30
Hillhead/J'hill	18	14	0	4	619	164	28
Stewartry	16	11	0	5	294	190	22
Portobello FP	18	10	1	7	290	281	21
Duns	18	10	0	8	411	328	20
Trinity Acads	18	9	0	9	365	413	18
Dunfermline	18	7	0	11	329	378	14
Edinburgh U	18	6	0	12	301	351	12
Dumfries	17	4	1	12	208	423	9
Royal High	18	1	0	17	132	672	2

Division 2	P	W	D	L	F	A	Pts
East Kilbride	17	15	1	1	420	179	31
Aberdeen GSFP	17	12	0	5	419	254	24
Livingston	18	10	2	6	318	227	22
Hutchesons'/Aloysians	17	7	2	8	263	253	16
St Boswells	17	8	0	9	242	336	16
Dalziel	18	8	0	10	242	395	16
Ardrossan Acads	18	7	1	10	295	304	15
Cambuslang	18	7	1	10	226	281	15
Perthshire	17	6	0	11	245	235	12
Howe of Fife	17	3	1	13	202	408	7

Division 3	P	W	D	L	F	A	Pts
Berwick	17	17	0	0	656	118	34
Allan Glen's	18	12	2	4	468	197	26
Leith Acads	18	10	3	5	339	257	23
Linlithgow	18	9	2	7	483	267	20
Cartha Queen's Pk	18	9	2	7	360	335	20
Morgan Acad FP	17	7	1	9	295	304	15
Alloa	18	7	1	10	346	412	15
Cumbernauld	18	7	0	11	366	361	14
Highland	17	3	1	13	196	506	7
N Berwick	17	1	0	16	137	889	2

Division 4	P	W	D	L	F	A	Pts
Annan	18	16	0	2	872	178	32
Lismore	18	14	1	3	439	245	29
Clydebank	18	13	2	3	399	171	28
Madras Coll FP	18	10	1	7	398	313	21
Penicuik	18	8	3	7	284	237	19
Paisley	18	6	1	11	212	326	13
Hillfoots	18	6	1	11	201	362	13
Waysiders/D'pellier	18	6	0	12	279	414	12
Falkirk	18	4	1	13	216	571	9
Irvine	18	2	0	16	175	658	4

Division 5	P	W	D	L	F	A	Pts
Ross High	18	16	0	2	600	110	32
Aberdeenshire	18	14	0	4	368	174	28
Aberdeen U	18	11	0	7	452	278	22
Dunbar	18	10	0	8	358	254	20
Forrester FP	18	9	0	9	312	301	18
Greenock Wands	18	8	0	10	278	390	16
Lenzie	18	7	0	11	382	438	14
Murrayfield	18	6	0	12	261	377	12
Earlston	18	6	0	12	260	463	12
Marr	18	3	0	15	209	695	6

Division 6	P	W	D	L	F	A	Pts
Garnock	18	17	0	1	715	104	34
Lochaber	18	12	0	6	462	174	24
Walkerburn	17	9	1	7	303	321	19
St Andrews U	18	9	0	9	391	369	18
RAF Kinloss	18	8	1	9	247	296	17
Cumnock	18	8	0	10	322	355	16
Holy Cross	18	8	0	10	246	425	16
Whitecraigs	17	7	1	9	298	217	15
Broughton FP	18	6	0	12	166	504	12
Harris Acad FP	18	3	1	14	182	567	7

Division 7	P	W	D	L	F	A	Pts
Lasswade	18	14	0	4	405	160	28
Moray	18	12	1	5	359	193	25
Hamilton Acads	18	12	0	6	367	217	24
Panmure	18	9	0	9	347	251	18
RAF Lossiemouth	18	9	0	9	432	269	18
Rosyth & Dist	18	8	0	10	290	321	16
Dalkeith	18	7	1	10	344	339	15
Waid Acad FP	18	7	0	11	324	412	14
Edinburgh N	18	7	0	11	188	321	14
Hyndland FP	18	4	0	14	211	784	8

District League Champions
Edinburgh: Heriot-Watt University
Glasgow: Helensburgh
Midlands: Carnoustie High School FP
North: Orkney

Carnoustie won all three matches in the District Champions' round-robin play-offs to decide the two clubs to be promoted to the National League's seventh division. Helensburg also won through, beating Heriot-Watt and Orkney.

BANK OF SCOTLAND BORDER LEAGUE

	P	W	D	L	F	A	Pts
Hawick	11	9	0	2	338	133	18
Melrose	10	6	1	3	288	153	13
Jedforest	10	6	1	3	248	166	13
Kelso	11	5	0	6	271	235	10
Gala	9	5	0	4	183	209	10
Selkirk	10	4	0	6	159	199	8
Langholm	11	0	0	11	77	469	0

SCOTTISH INTER-DISTRICT CHAMPIONSHIP

	P	W	D	L	F	A	Pts
Scottish Exiles	4	4	0	0	100	50	8
Edinburgh	4	2	0	2	109	82	4
North & Midlands	4	2	0	2	95	72	4
South	4	2	0	2	80	82	4
Glasgow	4	0	0	4	63	161	0

SCOTTISH INTER-DISTRICT CHAMPIONSHIP 1995-96

6 December 1995, Richmond

Exiles 17 (4PG 1T) **Edinburgh 6** (2PG)
Exiles: G Fraser (London Scottish); M Dods (Northampton), A James (Wasps), B R S Eriksson (London Scottish), G M O Smith (Orrell); S R Laing (Instonians), D W Patterson (West Hartlepool); D I W Hilton (Bath), M W Scott (Orrell), A P Burnell (London Scottish), A Nisbett (London Scottish), K Stewart (Cardiff), D Blyth (Waterloo), E W Peters (Bath) *(capt)*, S D Holmes (London Scottish) *Replacements* M P Craig (Leicester) for Eriksson; G Thompson (London Scottish) for Dods
Scorers *Try:* Smith *Penalty Goals:* Laing (4)

Edinburgh: S D Lang (Heriot's FP); D Macrae (Boroughmuir), S Hastings (Watsonians), D S Wyllie (Stewart's-Melville FP), I C Glasgow (Heriot's FP); A Donaldson (Currie) (*capt*), G G Burns (Stewart's-Melville FP); R B McNulty (Stewart's-Melville FP), G McKelvie (Watsonians), S W Paul (Heriot's FP), D G Burns (Boroughmuir), S Murray (Edinburgh Acads), D G Clark (Stewart's-Melville FP), S J Reid (Boroughmuir), G F Hall (Heriot's FP) *Replacement* D Lindsay (Musselburgh) for McKelvie
Scorer *Penalty Goals:* Donaldson (2)
Referee I C Henderson (Kelso)

6 December, Beveridge Park, Kirkcaldy

North & Midlands 53 (5G 1DG 3T)   **Glasgow 18** (1G 2PG 1T)
North & Midlands: R J S Shepherd (Melrose); S A D Burns (Edinburgh Acads), A K Carruthers (Kirkcaldy), P R Rouse (Dundee HSFP), J A Kerr (Watsonians); M McKenzie (Stirling County), K G M Harper (Stirling County); J J Manson (Stirling County), R Cairney (Stirling County), D J Herrington (Kirkcaldy), S J Campbell (Dundee HSFP), J S Hamilton (Stirling County), D J McIvor (Edinburgh Acads) (*capt*), M Waite (Edinburgh Acads), G N Flockhart (Stirling County) *Replacements* B Ireland (Stirling County) for Campbell; J R Mitchell (Kirkcaldy) for McKenzie
Scorers *Tries:* Burns (2), Carruthers, Flockhart, Kerr, Shepherd, Waite (2)   *Conversions:* Shepherd (5)
Dropped Goal: Mitchell
Glasgow: C M Sangster (Stirling County); T G R Mathewson (Glasgow Acads), A R Garry (Watsonians), T J Sanderson (GHK), A S M Turner (Stirling County) (*capt*); C G MacGregor (Glasgow Acads), C E Little (GHK); J T Gibson (Stirling County), G C Bulloch (West of Scotland), G R McIlwham (GHK), M Norval (Stirling County), G C Perrett (West of Scotland), J Brough (Stirling County), M F Begley (Glasgow Acads), I W Sinclair (Watsonians) *Replacements* G M Breckenridge (GHK) for Turner; H S Bassi (GHK) for Garry
Scorers *Tries:* Breckenridge, Little   *Conversion:* MacGregor   *Penalty Goals:* MacGregor (2)
Referee R J Megson (Edinburgh Wands)

10 December, Burnbrae, Milngavie

Glasgow 27 (3G 2PG)   **Exiles 28** (1G 2PG 3T)
Glasgow: G M Breckenridge (GHK); T G R Mathewson (Glasgow Acads), A R Garry (Watsonians), I C Jardine (Stirling County) (*capt*), G F Hawkes (GHK); C G MacGregor (Glasgow Acads), C E Little (GHK); J T Gibson (Stirling County), C P Docherty (GHK), G R McIlwham (GHK), M F Begley (Glasgow Acads), M Norval (Stirling County), D A McVey (Ayr), G T Mackay (Stirling County), I W Sinclair (Watsonians)
Scorers *Tries:* Little, McIlwham, Sinclair   *Conversions:* MacGregor (3)   *Penalty Goals:* MacGregor (2)
Exiles: G Fraser (London Scottish); G Thompson (London Scottish), A James (Wasps), B R S Eriksson (London Scottish), M P Craig (Leicester); S R Laing (Instonians), A D Nicol (Bath); D I W Hilton (Bath), M W Scott (Orrell), A P Burnell (London Scottish), A Nisbett (London Scottish), J J Whittaker (West Hartlepool), D Blyth (Waterloo), E W Peters (Bath) (*capt*), S D Holmes (London Scottish) *Replacements* D W Patterson (West Hartlepool) for Nicol; N Mitchell (Stourbridge) for Peters (temp)
Scorers *Tries:* Craig, James, Patterson, Thompson   *Conversion:* Laing   *Penalty Goals:* Laing (2)
Referee D I Ramage (Berwick) replaced by I C Henderson (Kelso) (half-time)

10 December, Murrayfield

South 18 (6PG)   **North & Midlands 12** (4PG)
South: W S Welsh (Hawick); C A Joiner (Melrose), D Grant (Hawick), S A Nichol (Selkirk), K L Suddon (Hawick); C M Chalmers (Melrose) (*capt*), B W Redpath (Melrose); G R Isaac (Gala), J A Hay (Hawick), J R S McColm (Selkirk), R R Brown (Melrose), I Elliot (Hawick), S Bennet (Kelso), B L Renwick (Hawick), J P Amos (Gala) *Replacement* H A Hunter (Gala) for Isaac (temp)
Scorer *Penalty Goals:* Welsh (6)
North & Midlands: R J S Shepherd (Melrose); S A D Burns (Edinburgh Acads), A K Carruthers (Kirkcaldy), P R Rouse (Dundee HSFP), J A Kerr (Watsonians); M McKenzie (Stirling County), K G M Harper (Stirling County); J J Manson (Stirling County), R Cairney (Stirling County), D J Herrington (Kirkcaldy), J S Hamilton (Stirling County), S D Grimes (Watsonians), D J McIvor (Edinburgh Acads) (*capt*), G N Flockhart (Stirling County), B Ireland (Stirling County) *Replacements* W D Anderson (Kirkcaldy) for Ireland; R R Dewar (Kirkcaldy) for Harper (temp)
Scorer   *Penalty Goals:* McKenzie (4)
Referee J L Bacigalupo (Edinburgh Wands)

17 December, Meggetland

Edinburgh 31 (2G 3PG 1DG 1T)   **South 30** (1G 6PG 1T)
Edinburgh: C T Simmers (Edinburgh Acads); F M Henderson (Watsonians), S Hastings (Watsonians), D S Wyllie (Stewart's-Melville FP), N Penny (Stewart's-Melville FP); A Donaldson (Currie) (*capt*), G G Burns (Stewart's-Melville FP); G D Wilson (Boroughmuir), G McKelvie (Watsonians), P H Wright (Boroughmuir), D G Burns (Boroughmuir), S Murray (Edinburgh Acads), B W Ward (Currie), D G Clark (Stewart's-Melville FP), R Hoole (Edinburgh Acads) *Replacement* C K Aitken (Heriot's FP) for Simmers
Scorers *Tries:* D G Burns, Hastings, Henderson   *Conversions:* Donaldson (2)   *Penalty Goals:* Donaldson (3)
Dropped Goal: Donaldson
South: W S Welsh (Hawick); C A Joiner (Melrose), D Grant (Hawick), S A Nichol (Selkirk), K L Suddon (Hawick); C M Chalmers (Melrose) (*capt*), G Armstrong (Jedforest); M G Browne (Melrose), J A Hay (Hawick),

J R S McColm (Selkirk), R R Brown (Melrose), I Elliot (Hawick), B L Renwick (Hawick), G W Weir (Melrose), S Bennet (Kelso) *Replacement* G R Isaac (Gala) for Browne
Scorers *Tries:* Elliot, Isaac *Conversion:* Welsh *Penalty Goals:* Welsh (6)
Referee S Lander (England)

17 December, Rubislaw, Aberdeen

North & Midlands 8 (1PG 1T) **Exiles 21** (2PG 3T)
North & Midlands: R J S Shepherd (Melrose); S A D Burns (Edinburgh Acads), A K Carruthers (Kirkcaldy), P R Rouse (Dundee HSFP), J A Kerr (Watsonians); B R Easson (Boroughmuir), A M Fraser (Stirling County); W D Anderson (Kirkcaldy), R Cairney (Stirling County), D J Herrington (Kirkcaldy), S D Grimes (Watsonians), R J Gray (Dundee HSFP), D J McIvor (Edinburgh Acads) (*capt*), M Waite (Edinburgh Acads), R I Wainwright (Edinburgh Acads) *Replacement* S D Brown (Kirkcaldy) for Cairney
Scorer *Try:* Easson *Penalty Goal:* Easson
Exiles: G Fraser (London Scottish); M Dods (Northampton), A James (Wasps), B R S Eriksson (London Scottish), G Thompson (London Scottish); S R Laing (Instonians), A Withers-Green (London Scottish); D I W Hilton (Bath), M W Scott (Orrell), M Stewart (Blackheath), A Nisbett (London Scottish), K Stewart (Cardiff), D Blyth (Waterloo), E W Peters (Bath) (*capt*), S D Holmes (London Scottish)
Scorers *Tries:* Thompson (2), Peters *Penalty Goals:* Laing (2)
Referee K W McCartney (Hawick)

24 December, Murrayfield

South 23 (2G 3PG) **Glasgow 5** (1T)
South: W S Welsh (Hawick); C A Joiner (Melrose), S A Nichol (Selkirk), A G Shiel (Melrose), K L Suddon (Hawick); C M Chalmers (Melrose) (*capt*), B W Redpath (Melrose); G R Isaac (Gala), J A Hay (Hawick), J R S McColm (Selkirk), R R Brown (Melrose), G W Weir (Melrose), S Bennet (Kelso), B L Renwick (Hawick), R M Kirkpatrick (Jedforest) *Replacements* J P Amos (Gala) for Bennet; H A Hunter (Gala) for Isaac (temp)
Scorers *Tries:* Joiner (2) *Conversions:* Welsh (2) *Penalty Goals:* Welsh (3)
Glasgow: G M Breckenridge (GHK); T G R Mathewson (Glasgow Acads), A R Garry (Watsonians), I C Jardine (Stirling County), A S M Turner (Stirling County); C G MacGregor (Glasgow Acads), C E Little (GHK); J T Gibson (Stirling County), C G Bulloch (West of Scotland), G B Robertson (Stirling County), M Norval (Stirling County), G C Perrett (West of Scotland), F D Wallace (Boroughmuir) (*capt*), G T Mackay (Stirling County), I W Sinclair (Watsonians) *Replacement* A J Bulloch (West of Scotland) for Jardine (temp)
Scorer *Try:* Mathewson
Referee R J Megson (Edinburgh Wands)

31 December, Murrayfield

Edinburgh 57 (5G 4PG 2T) **Glasgow 13** (1G 2PG)
Edinburgh: C T Simmers (Edinburgh Acads); F M Henderson (Watsonians), S Hastings (Watsonians), D S Wyllie (Stewart's-Melville FP), N Penny (Stewart's-Melville FP); A Donaldson (Currie) (*capt*), G G Burns (Stewart's-Melville FP); G D Wilson (Boroughmuir), G McKelvie (Watsonians), P H Wright (Boroughmuir), D G Burns (Boroughmuir), M J McVie (Edinburgh Acads), B W Ward (Currie), S J Reid (Boroughmuir), R Hoole (Edinburgh Acads) *Replacements* S D Lang (Heriot's FP) for Hoole; C Mather (Watsonians) for Ward
Scorers *Tries:* Donaldson (2), Hastings, Penny, Reid, Ward *Conversions:* Donaldson (5) *Penalty Goals:* Donaldson (4)
Glasgow: G M Breckenridge (GHK); T G R Mathewson (Glasgow Acads), A R Garry (Watsonians), I C Jardine (Stirling County), K M Logan (Stirling County); C G MacGregor (Glasgow Acads), C E Little (GHK); S McGregor (West of Scotland), G C Bulloch (West of Scotland), G Doran (Glasgow Acads), M Norval (Stirling County), G C Perrett (West of Scotland), F D Wallace (Boroughmuir) (*capt*), G T Mackay (Stirling County), I W Sinclair (Watsonians) *Replacement* C M Sangster (Stirling County) for Jardine
Scorers *Try:* S McGregor *Conversion:* C G MacGregor *Penalty Goals:* C G MacGregor (2)
Referee C B Muir (Langholm)

10 January 1996, Richmond

Exiles 34 (4G 2PG) **South 9** (3PG)
Exiles: A Kerr (Moseley); M Kemp (London Scottish), I Wynn (Orrell), A James (Wasps), G M O Smith (Orrell); S R Laing (Instonians), D W Patterson (West Hartlepool); D I W Hilton (Bath), L M Mair (London Scottish), M Stewart (Blackheath), D F Cronin (Bourges), K Stewart (Cardiff), P Walton (Newcastle), E W Peters (Bath) (*capt*), C I M Dixon (Bristol) *Replacement* D C M McGavin (London Scottish) for Mair
Scorers *Tries:* Dixon (2), James, Patterson *Conversions:* Laing (4) *Penalty Goals:* Laing (2)
South: G J Aitchison (Kelso); C A Joiner (Melrose), S A Nichol (Selkirk), D Grant (Hawick), K L Suddon (Hawick); W S Welsh (Hawick), K W Reid (Hawick); G R Isaac (Gala), J A Hay (Hawick), J R S McColm (Selkirk), R R Brown (Melrose), G W Weir (Melrose), S Bennet (Kelso), R M Kirkpatrick (Jedforest) (*capt*), K Armstrong (Jedforest) *Replacement* I Elliot (Hawick) for Brown
Scorer *Penalty Goals:* Welsh (3)
Referee J M Fleming (Boroughmuir)

10 January, Meggetland

Edinburgh 15 (5PG) **North & Midlands 22** (3PG 1DG 2T)

Edinburgh: S D Lang (Heriot's FP); F M Henderson (Watsonians), S Hastings (Watsonians), D S Wyllie (Stewart's-Melville FP), I C Glasgow (Heriot's FP); A Donaldson (Currie) (*capt*), G G Burns (Stewart's-Melville FP); G D Wilson (Boroughmuir), D G Ellis (Currie), B D Stewart (Edinburgh Acads), D G Burns (Boroughmuir), M J McVie (Edinburgh Acads), B W Ward (Currie), D G Clark (Stewart's-Melville FP), R Hoole (Edinburgh Acads)

Scorer *Penalty Goals:* Donaldson (5)

North & Midlands: R J S Shepherd (Melrose); N C Renton (Kirkcaldy), P R Rouse (Dundee HSFP), D R Hamilton (Dundee HSFP), J A Kerr (Watsonians); M McKenzie (Stirling County), K G M Harper (Stirling County); W D Anderson (Kirkcaldy), K D McKenzie (Stirling County), D J Herrington (Kirkcaldy), S J Campbell (Dundee HSFP), J S Hamilton (Stirling County), D J McIvor (Edinburgh Acads) (*capt*), M Waite (Edinburgh Acads), G N Flockhart (Stirling County) *Replacements* S A D Burns (Edinburgh Acads) for Shepherd; A K Penman (Grangemouth) for Herrington; A M Fraser (Stirling County) for Harper

Scorers *Tries:* Hamilton, Harper *Penalty Goals:* M McKenzie (3) *Dropped Goal:* M McKenzie

Referee K W McCarthy (Hawick)

SRU TENNENTS CUP 1995-96

11 May 1996, Murrayfield
Hawick 17 (1G 2T) Watsonians 15 (1G 1PG 1T)

Hawick battled back from a 15-point deficit to beat Watsonians in the final of Scottish rugby's first national cup competition. In doing so, they achieved a unique treble: Hawick had also been the first winners of the Border League in 1902 and the National League in 1974. No one did more than Brian Renwick, Hawick's captain and No 8, to spur the Borderers' fightback. He led from the front with his driving play and was a vital link with the scoring pass for a timely try by lock forward Alistair Imray. The captain also played a notable role in turning the line-out game away from Stuart Grimes, who had threatened to dominate for Watsonians.

The Edinburgh club were 15 points clear within the first quarter, with three scores that all had the touch of Duncan Hodge in them. The young fly-half followed his opening penalty goal by slipping out the short pass that released Scott Hastings for a slicing try. Hodge converted, and soon added a try of his own from a tapped-penalty assault.

It was late in the second half before Hawick made their winning surge with two tries that originated in short penalties. Full-back Colin Turnbull cut in for one, a score as vital to Hawick's cause as his try in the semi-final against Melrose. Scott Welsh converted, and Hawick's enterprise in running another penalty paid off when Welsh slipped in close enough to plant the ball on the line.

Hawick: C W Turnbull; G W J Sharp, C A Murray, A G Stanger, K L Suddon; W S Welsh, K W Reid; B J McDonnell, J A Hay, A Johnstone, A Imray, I Elliot, J Graham, B L Renwick (*capt*), G L Harris *Replacement* A Barnes for Graham

Scorers *Tries:* Imray, Turnbull, Welsh *Conversion:* Welsh

Watsonians: D J Lee; F M Henderson (*capt*), S Hastings, A R Garry, J A Kerr; D W Hodge, E J W Weston; T J Smith, G McKelvie, J Waddell, S D Grimes, C M Mather, G J Hannah, C Browne, I W Sinclair

Scorers *Tries:* Hastings, Hodge *Conversion:* Hodge *Penalty Goal:* Hodge

Referee J M Fleming (Boroughmuir)

A field of 102 clubs contested the Scottish Cup, beginning with a preliminary round for 12 National League clubs in September, but when the big guns fired their first shots in the third round in February it was Premier League champions Melrose who set the pace as obvious favourites. They opened with a 72-5 win at Dunfermline, thrashed West of Scotland 89-12 at the Greenyards, and, even more significantly, again at home, saw off Boroughmuir by 50-22. Only then did they run into a close encounter, beating Glasgow Academicals by 14-8 at New Anniesland, each side scoring one try.

By then, Stirling County, the 1994-95 national champions, had gone, beaten 5-3 at Dundee. Watsonians, however, had emerged as an obvious threat to Melrose after successive victories against Edinburgh Academicals, Stewartry and Langholm. A 23-6 win against Heriot's at Myreside put them through to the semi-finals.

Hawick had come through to the same stage with successive wins against East Kilbride, Duns, Biggar and Preston Lodge. They rose to the occasion when they met Melrose on Gala's ground at Netherdale. Graham Shiel gave Melrose an early try, and when Derek Bain intercepted within his own 22 he ran all the way to overturn Hawick's 9-5 half-time lead. Hawick, however, persevered with the spirit that lifted them to victory in the final, and they had due reward in a 28-15 win. In the other semi-final Watsonians overwhelmed Dundee High School FP by 57-7 at Meggetland.

Edinburgh clubs took the two minor trophies. Currie beat Stirling County 75-20 in the final of the SRU Tennents Shield (contested by fourth-round losers), and Edinburgh Academicals won the bowl with a 28-21 win over Selkirk.

RESULTS

Third round
Aberdeen GSFP 11, Dundee HSFP 12; Biggar 14, Ayr 6; Cambuslang 19, Glenrothes 28; Dumfermline 5, Melrose 72; Duns 30, Peebles 19; GHK 59, Annan 15; Glasgow Academicals 44, Cartha Queen's Park 10; Hawick 46, East Kilbride 6; Hillhead/Jordanhill 20, Gordonians 25 (*aet*); Kirkcaldy 54, Edinburgh Wanderers 0; Portobello FP 32, Haddington 10; Selkirk 10, Gala 21; Stewartry 18, Livingston 10; Trinity Academicals 57, Perthshire 22; Watsonians 33, Edinburgh Academicals 6; Waysiders/Drumpellier 8, Hutchesons'/Aloysians 21

Fourth Round
Boroughmuir 25, GHK 15; Corstorphine 23, Trinity Academicals 8; Dundee HSFP 5, Stirling County 3; Duns 3, Hawick 22; Glasgow Academicals 17, Currie 12; Glasgow Southern 8, Jedforest 25; Glenrothes 10, Musselburgh 20; Gordonians 16, Gala 18; Grangemouth

16, Kilmarnock 22; Heriot's FP 18, Kirkcaldy 12; Langholm 20, Portobello FP 16; Melrose 89, West of Scotland 12; Preston Lodge FP 29, Kelso 26; Stewartry 3, Watsonians 62; Stewart's-Melville FP 70, Hutchesons'/Aloysians 0; Wigtownshire 9, Biggar 21

Fifth round
Dundee HSFP 17, Jedforest 6; Glasgow Academicals 29, Gala 6; Hawick 52, Biggar 17; Kilmarnock 27, Corstorphine 8; Melrose 50, Boroughmuir 22; Musselburgh 17, Preston Lodge FP 20; Stewart's-Melville FP 20, Heriot's FP 25; Watsonians 98, Langholm 3

Quarter-finals
Glasgow Academicals 8, Melrose 14; Hawick 26, Preston Lodge FP 11; Heriot's FP 6, Watsonians 23; Kilmarnock 13, Dundee HSFP 37

Semi-finals
Dundee HSFP 7, Watsonians 57 (*at Myreside*); Hawick 28, Melrose 15 (*at Netherdale*)

SCOTTISH INTERNATIONAL PLAYERS
(*up to 30 April 1996*)

ABBREVIATIONS

A – Australia; *Arg* – Argentina; *C* – Canada; *E* – England; *F* – France; *Fj* – Fiji; *I* – Ireland; *Iv* – Ivory Coast; *J* – Japan; *NZ* – New Zealand; *R* – Romania; *SA* – South Africa; *Tg* – Tonga; *W* – Wales; *WS* – Western Samoa; *Z* – Zimbabwe; (C) – Centenary match v England at Murrayfield, 1971 (non-championship); P – Scotland v President's Overseas XV at Murrayfield in SRU's Centenary season, 1972-73; (R) Replacement; (t) – temporary replacement. Entries in square brackets [ ] indicate appearances in the World Cup.

Note: Years given for Five Nations' matches are for second half of season; eg 1972 means season 1971-72. Years for all other matches refer to the actual year of the match. When a series has taken place, figures have been used to denote the particular matches in which players have featured. Thus 1981 *NZ* 1,2 indicates that a player appeared in the first and second Tests of the series. The abandoned game with Ireland at Belfast in 1885 is now included as a cap-match.

Abercrombie, C H (United Services) 1910 *I, E,* 1911 *F, W,* 1913 *F, W*

Abercrombie, J G (Edinburgh U) 1949 *F, W, I,* 1950 *F, W, I, E*

Agnew, W C C (Stewart's Coll FP) 1930 *W, I*

Ainslie, R (Edinburgh Inst FP) 1879 *I, E,* 1880 *I, E,* 1881 *E,* 1882 *I, E*

Ainslie, T (Edinburgh Inst FP) 1881 *E,* 1882 *I, E,* 1883 *W, I, E,* 1884 *W, I, E,* 1885 *W, I* 1,2

Aitchison, G R (Edinburgh Wands) 1883 *I*

Aitchison, T G (Gala) 1929 *W, I, E*

Aitken, A I (Edinburgh Inst FP) 1889 *I*

Aitken, G G (Oxford U) 1924 *W, I, E,* 1925 *F, W, I, E,* 1929 *F*

Aitken, J (Gala) 1977 *E, I, F,* 1981 *F, W, E, I, NZ* 1,2, *R, A,* 1982 *E, I, F, W,* 1983 *F, W, E, NZ,* 1984 *W, E, I, F, R*

Aitken, R (London Scottish) 1947 *W*

Allan, B (Glasgow Acads) 1881 *I*

Allan, J (Edinburgh Acads) 1990 *NZ* 1, 1991, *W, I, R,* [*J, I, WS, I, NZ*]

Allan, J L (Melrose) 1952 *F, W, I,* 1953 *W*

Allan, J L F (Cambridge U) 1957 *I, E*

Allan, J W (Melrose) 1927 *F,* 1928 *I,* 1929 *F, W, I, E,* 1930 *F, E,* 1931 *F, W, I, E,* 1932 *SA, W, I,* 1934 *I, E*

Allan, R C (Hutchesons' GSFP) 1969 *I*

Allardice, W D (Aberdeen GSFP) 1947 *A,* 1948 *F, W, I,* 1949 *F, W, I, E*

Allen, H W (Glasgow Acads) 1873 *E*

Anderson, A H (Glasgow Acads) 1894 *I*

Anderson, D G (London Scottish) 1889 *I,* 1890 *W, I, E,* 1891 *W, E,* 1892 *W, E*

Anderson, E (Stewart's Coll FP) 1947 *I, E*

Anderson, J W (W of Scotland) 1872 *E*

Anderson, T (Merchiston) 1882 *I*

Angus, A W (Watsonians) 1909 *W,* 1910 *F, W, E,* 1911 *W, I,* 1912 *F, W, I, E, SA,* 1913 *F, W,* 1914 *E,* 1920 *F, W, I, E*

Anton, P A (St Andrew's U) 1873 *E*

Armstrong, G (Jedforest) 1988 *A,* 1989 *W, E, I, F, Fj, R,* 1990 *I, F, W, E, NZ* 1,2, *Arg,* 1991 *F, W, E, I, R,* [*J, I, WS, E, NZ*], 1993 *I, F, W, E,* 1994 *E, I*

Arneil, R J (Edinburgh Acads, Leicester and Northampton) 1968 *I, E, A,* 1969 *F, W, I, E, SA,* 1970 *W, I, E, A,* 1971 *F, W, I, E* (2[1C]), 1972 *F, W, E, NZ*

Arthur, A (Glasgow Acads) 1875 *E,* 1876 *E*

Arthur, J W (Glasgow Acads) 1871 *E,* 1872 *E*

Asher, A G G (Oxford U) 1882 *I,* 1884 *W, I, E,* 1885 *W,* 1886 *I, E*

Auld, W (W of Scotland) 1889 *W,* 1890 *W*

Auldjo, L J (Abertay) 1878 *E*

Bain, D McL (Oxford U) 1911 *E,* 1912 *F, W, E, SA,* 1913 *F, W, I, E,* 1914 *W, I*

Baird, G R T (Kelso) 1981 *A,* 1982 *E, I, F, W, A* 1,2, 1983 *I, F, W, E, NZ,* 1984 *W, E, I, F, A,* 1985 *I, W, E,* 1986 *F, W, E, I, R,* 1987 *E,* 1988 *I*

Balfour, A (Watsonians) 1896 *W, I, E,* 1897 *E*

Balfour, L M (Edinburgh Acads) 1872 *E*

Bannerman, E M (Edinburgh Acads) 1872 *E,* 1873 *E*

Bannerman, J M (Glasgow HSFP) 1921 *F, W, I, E,* 1922 *F, W, I, E,* 1923 *F, W, I, E,* 1924 *F, W, I, E,* 1925 *F, W, I, E,* 1926 *F, W, I, E,* 1927 *F, W, I, E, A,* 1928 *F, W, I, E,* 1929 *F, W, I, E*

Barnes, I A (Hawick) 1972 *W,* 1974 *F* (R), 1975 *E* (R), *NZ,* 1977 *I, F, W*

Barrie, R W (Hawick) 1936 *E*

Bearne, K R F (Cambridge U, London Scottish) 1960 *F, W*

Beattie, J A (Hawick) 1929 *F, W,* 1930 *W,* 1931 *F, W, I, E,* 1932 *SA, W, I, E,* 1933 *W, E, I,* 1934 *I, E,* 1935 *W, I, E, NZ,* 1936 *W, I, E*

Beattie, J R (Glasgow Acads) 1980 *I, F, W, E,* 1981 *F, W, E, I,* 1983 *F, W, E, NZ,* 1984 *E* (R), *R, A,* 1985 *I,* 1986 *F, W, E, I, R,* 1987 *I, F, W, E*

Bedell-Sivright, D R (Cambridge U, Edinburgh U) 1900 *W,* 1901 *W, I, E,* 1902 *W, I, E,* 1903 *W, I,* 1904 *W, I, E,* 1905 *NZ,* 1906 *W, I, E, SA,* 1907 *W, I, E,* 1908 *W, I*

Bedell-Sivright, J V (Cambridge U) 1902 *W*

Begbie, T A (Edinburgh Wands) 1881 *I, E*

Bell, D L (Watsonians) 1975 *I, F, W, E*

Bell, J A (Clydesdale) 1901 *W, I, E,* 1902 *W, I, E*

Bell, L H I (Edinburgh Acads) 1900 *E,* 1904 *W, I*

Berkeley, W V (Oxford U) 1926 *F,* 1929 *F, W, I*

Berry, C W (Fettesian-Lorettonians) 1884 *I, E,* 1885 *W, I,* 1887 *I, W, E,* 1888 *W, I*

Bertram, D M (Watsonians) 1922 *F, W, I, E,* 1923 *F, W, I, E,* 1924 *I, E*

Biggar, A G (London Scottish) 1969 *SA,* 1970 *F, I, E, A,* 1971 *F, W, I, E* (2[1C]), 1972 *F, W*

Biggar, M A (London Scottish) 1975 *I, F, W, E,* 1976 *W, E, I,* 1977 *I, F, W,* 1978 *I, F, W, E, NZ,* 1979 *W, E, I, F, NZ,* 1980 *I, F, W, E*

Birkett, G A (Harlequins, London Scottish) 1975 *NZ*

Bishop, J M (Glasgow Acads) 1893 *I*

Bisset, A A (RIE Coll) 1904 *W*

Black, A W (Edinburgh U) 1947 *F, W,* 1948 *E,* 1950 *W, I, E*

Black, W P (Glasgow HSFP) 1948 *F, W, I, E,* 1951 *E*

Blackadder, W F (W of Scotland) 1938 *E*

Blaikie, C F (Heriot's FP) 1963 *I, E,* 1966 *E,* 1968 *A,* 1969 *F, W, I, E*

Blair, P C B (Cambridge U) 1912 *SA,* 1913 *F, W, I, E*

Bolton, W H (W of Scotland) 1876 *E*

Borthwick, J B (Stewart's Coll FP) 1938 *W, I*

Bos, F H ten (Oxford U, London Scottish) 1959 *E,* 1960 *F, W, SA,* 1961 *F, SA, W, I, E,* 1962 *F, W, I, E,* 1963 *F, W, I, E*

Boswell, J D (W of Scotland) 1889 *W, I,* 1890 *W, I, E,* 1891 *W, I, E,* 1892 *W, I, E,* 1893 *I, E,* 1894 *I, E*

Bowie, T C (Watsonians) 1913 *I,* 1914 *I, E*

Boyd, G M (Glasgow HSFP) 1926 *E*

Boyd, J L (United Services) 1912 *E, SA*

Boyle, A C W (London Scottish) 1963 *F, W, I*

Boyle, A H W (St Thomas's Hospital, London Scottish) 1966 *A,* 1967 *F, NZ,* 1968 *F, W, I*

Brash, J C (Cambridge U) 1961 *E*

Breakey, R W (Gosforth) 1978 *E*

Brewis, N T (Edinburgh Inst FP) 1876 *E,* 1878 *E,* 1879 *I, E,* 1880 *I, E*

Brewster, A K (Stewart's-Melville FP) 1977 *E,* 1980 *I, F,* 1986 *E, I, R*

Brown, A H (Heriot's FP) 1928 *E,* 1929 *F, W*

Brown, A R (Gala) 1971 *E* (2[1C]), 1972 *F, W, E*

Brown, C H C (Dunfermline) 1929 *E*

Brown, D I (Cambridge U) 1933 *W, E, I*

Brown, G L (W of Scotland) 1969 *SA,* 1970 *F, W* (R), *I, E, A,* 1971 *F, W, I, E* (2[1C]), 1972 *F, W, E, NZ,* 1973 *E* (R), *P,* 1974 *W, E, I, F,* 1975 *I, F, W, E, A,* 1976 *F, W, E, I*

Brown, J A (Glasgow Acads) 1908 *W, I*

Brown, J B (Glasgow Acads) 1879 *I, E,* 1880 *I, E,* 1881 *I, E,* 1882 *I, E,* 1883 *W, I, E,* 1884 *W, I, E,* 1885 *I* 1,2, 1886 *W, I, E*

Brown, P C (W of Scotland, Gala) 1964 *F, NZ, W, I, E,* 1965 *I, E, SA,* 1966 *A,* 1969 *I, E,* 1970 *W, E,* 1971 *F, W, I, E* (2[1C]), 1972 *F, W, E, NZ,* 1973 *F, W, I, E, P*
Brown, T G (Heriot's FP) 1929 *W*
Brown, W D (Glasgow Acads) 1871 *E,* 1872 *E,* 1873 *E,* 1874 *E,* 1875 *E*
Brown, W S (Edinburgh Inst FP) 1880 *I, E,* 1882 *I, E,* 1883 *W, E*
Browning, A (Glasgow HSFP) 1920 *I,* 1922 *F, W, I,* 1923 *W, I, E*
Bruce, C R (Glasgow Acads) 1947 *F, W, I, E,* 1949 *F, W, I, E*
Bruce, N S (Blackheath, Army and London Scottish) 1958 *F, A, I, E,* 1959 *F, W, I, E,* 1960 *F, W, I, E, SA,* 1961 *F, SA, W, I, E,* 1962 *F, W, I, E,* 1963 *F, W, I, E,* 1964 *F, NZ, W, I, E*
Bruce, R M (Gordonians) 1947 *A,* 1948 *F, W, I*
Bruce-Lockhart, J H (London Scottish) 1913 *W,* 1920 *E*
Bruce-Lockhart, L (London Scottish) 1948 *E,* 1950 *F, W,* 1953 *I, E*
Bruce-Lockhart, R B (Cambridge U and London Scottish) 1937 *I,* 1939 *I, E*
Bryce, C C (Glasgow Acads) 1873 *E,* 1874 *E*
Bryce, R D H (W of Scotland) 1973 *I* (R)
Bryce, W E (Selkirk) 1922 *W, I, E,* 1923 *F, W, I, E,* 1924 *F, W, I, E*
Brydon, W R C (Heriot's FP) 1939 *W*
Buchanan, A (Royal HSFP) 1871 *E*
Buchanan, F G (Kelvinside Acads and Oxford U) 1910 *F,* 1911 *F, W*
Buchanan, J C R (Stewart's Coll FP) 1921 *W, I, E,* 1922 *W, I, E,* 1923 *F, W, I, E,* 1924 *F, W, I, E,* 1925 *F, I*
Buchanan-Smith, G A E (London Scottish, Heriot's FP) 1989 *Fj* (R), 1990 *Arg*
Bucher, A M (Edinburgh Acads) 1897 *E*
Budge, G M (Edinburgh Wands) 1950 *F, W, I, E*
Bullmore, H H (Edinburgh U) 1902 *I*
Burnell, A P (London Scottish) 1989 *E, I, F, Fj, R,* 1990 *I, F, W, E, Arg,* 1991 *F, W, E, I, R, [J, Z, I, WS, E, NZ],* 1992 *E, I, F, W,* 1993 *I, F, W, E, NZ,* 1994 *W, E, I, F, Arg* 1,2, *SA,* 1995 *[Iv, Tg* (R), *F* (R)], *WS*
Burnet, P J (London Scottish and Edinburgh Acads) 1960 *SA*
Burnet, W (Hawick) 1912 *E*
Burnet, W A (W of Scotland) 1934 *W,* 1935 *W, I, E, NZ,* 1936 *W, I, E*
Burnett, J N (Heriot's FP) 1980 *I, F, W, E*
Burrell, G (Gala) 1950 *F, W, I,* 1951 *SA*

Cairns, A G (Watsonians) 1903 *W, I, E,* 1904 *W, I, E,* 1905 *W, I, E,* 1906 *W, I, E*
Calder, F (Stewart's-Melville FP) 1986 *F, W, E, I, R,* 1987 *I, F, W, E,* [*F, Z, R, NZ*], 1988 *I, F, W, E,* 1989 *W, E, I, F, R,* 1990 *I, F, W, E, NZ* 1,2, 1991 *R,* [*J, I, WS, E, NZ*]
Calder, J H (Stewart's-Melville FP) 1981 *F, W, E, I, NZ* 1,2, *R, A,* 1982 *E, I, F, W, A* 1,2, 1983 *I, F, W, E, NZ,* 1984 *W, E, I, F, A,* 1985 *I, F, W*
Callander, G J (Kelso) 1984 *R,* 1988 *I, F, W, E, A*
Cameron, A (Glasgow HSFP) 1948 *W,* 1950 *I, E,* 1951 *F, W, I, E, SA,* 1953 *I, E,* 1955 *F, W, I, E,* 1956 *F, W, I*
Cameron, A D (Hillhead HSFP) 1951 *F,* 1954 *F, W*
Cameron, A W (Watsonians) 1887 *W,* 1893 *W,* 1894 *I*
Cameron, D (Glasgow HSFP) 1953 *I, E,* 1954 *F, NZ, I, E*
Cameron, N W (Glasgow U) 1952 *E,* 1953 *F, W*
Campbell, A J (Hawick) 1984 *I, F, R,* 1985 *I, F, W, E,* 1986 *F, W, E, I, R,* 1988 *F, W, A*
Campbell, G T (London Scottish) 1892 *W, I, E,* 1893 *I, E,* 1894 *W, I, E,* 1895 *W, I, E,* 1896 *W, I, E,* 1897 *I,* 1899 *I,* 1900 *E*
Campbell, H H (Cambridge U, London Scottish) 1947 *I, E,* 1948 *I, E*
Campbell, J A (W of Scotland) 1878 *E,* 1879 *I, E,* 1881 *I, E*
Campbell, J A (Cambridge U) 1900 *I*
Campbell, N M (London Scottish) 1956 *F, W*
Campbell, S J (Dundee HSFP) 1995 *C, I, F, W, E, R,* [*Iv, NZ* (R)], WS (t), 1996 *I, F, W, E*
Campbell-Lamerton, J R E (London Scottish) 1986 *F,* 1987 [*Z, R*(R)]
Campbell-Lamerton, M J (Halifax, Army, London Scottish) 1961 *F, SA, W, I,* 1962 *F, W, I, E,* 1963 *F, W, I, E,* 1964 *I, E,* 1965 *F, W, I, E, SA,* 1966 *F, W, I, E*
Carmichael, A B (W of Scotland) 1967 *I, NZ,* 1968 *F, W, I, E, A,* 1969 *F, W, I, E, SA,* 1970 *F, W, I, E, A,* 1971 *F, W, I, E* (2[1C]), 1972 *F, W, E, NZ,* 1973 *F, W, I, E, P,* 1974 *W, E, I, F,* 1975 *I, F, W, E, NZ, A,* 1976 *F, W, E, I,* 1977 *E, I* (R), *F, W,* 1978 *I*

Carmichael, J H (Watsonians) 1921 *F, W, I*
Carrick, J S (Glasgow Acads) 1876 *E,* 1877 *E*
Cassels, D Y (W of Scotland) 1880 *E,* 1881 *I,* 1882 *I, E,* 1883 *W, I, E*
Cathcart, C W (Edinburgh U) 1872 *E,* 1873 *E,* 1876 *E*
Cawkwell, G L (Oxford U) 1947 *F*
Chalmers, C M (Melrose) 1989 *W, E, I, F, Fj,* 1990 *I, F, W, E, NZ* 1,2, *Arg,* 1991 *F, W, E, I, R,* [*J, Z*(R), *I, WS, E, NZ*], 1992 *E, I, F, W, A* 1,2, 1993 *I, F, W, E, NZ,* 1994 *W, SA,* 1995 *C, I, F, W, E, R,* [*Iv, Tg, F, NZ*], *WS*
Chalmers, T (Glasgow Acads) 1871 *E,* 1872 *E,* 1873 *E,* 1874 *E,* 1875 *E,* 1876 *E*
Chambers, H F T (Edinburgh U) 1888 *W, I,* 1889 *W, I*
Charters, R G (Hawick) 1955 *W, I, E*
Chisholm, D H (Melrose) 1964 *I, E,* 1965 *E, SA,* 1966 *F, I, E, A,* 1967 *F, W, NZ,* 1968 *F, W, I*
Chisholm, R W T (Melrose) 1955 *I, E,* 1956 *F, W, I, E,* 1958 *F, W, A, I,* 1960 *SA*
Church, W C (Glasgow Acads) 1906 *W*
Clark, R L (Edinburgh Wands, Royal Navy) 1972 *F, W, E, NZ,* 1973 *F, W, I, E, P*
Clauss, P R A (Oxford U) 1891 *W, I, E,* 1892 *W, E,* 1895 *I*
Clay, A T (Edinburgh Acads) 1886 *W, I, E,* 1887 *I, W, E,* 1888 *W*
Clunies-Ross, A (St Andrew's U) 1871 *E*
Coltman, S (Hawick) 1948 *I,* 1949 *F, W, I, E*
Colville, A G (Merchistonians, Blackheath) 1871 *E,* 1872 *E*
Connell, G C (Trinity Acads and London Scottish) 1968 *E, A,* 1969 *F, E,* 1970 *F*
Cooper, M McG (Oxford U) 1936 *W, I*
Corcoran, I (Gala) 1992 *A* 1(R)
Cordial, I F (Edinburgh Wands) 1952 *F, W, I, E*
Cotter, J L (Hillhead HSFP) 1934 *I, E*
Cottington, G S (Kelso) 1934 *I, E,* 1935 *W, I,* 1936 *E*
Coughtrie, S (Edinburgh Acads) 1959 *F, W, I, E,* 1962 *W, I, E,* 1963 *F, W, I, E*
Couper, J H (W of Scotland) 1896 *W, I,* 1899 *I*
Coutts, F H (Melrose, Army) 1947 *W, I, E*
Coutts, I D F (Old Alleynians) 1951 *F,* 1952 *E*
Cowan, R C (Selkirk) 1961 *F,* 1962 *F, W, I, E*
Cowie, W L K (Edinburgh Wands) 1953 *E*
Cownie, W B (Watsonians) 1893 *W, I, E,* 1894 *W, I, E,* 1895 *W, I, E*
Crabbie, G E (Edinburgh Acads) 1904 *W*
Crabbie, J E (Edinburgh Acads, Oxford U) 1900 *W,* 1902 *I,* 1903 *W, I,* 1904 *E,* 1905 *W*
Craig, J B (Heriot's FP) 1939 *W*
Cramb, R I (Harlequins) 1987 [*R*(R)], 1988 *I, F, A*
Cranston, A G (Hawick) 1976 *W, E, I,* 1977 *E, W,* 1978 *F* (R), *W, E, NZ,* 1981 *NZ* 1,2
Crawford, J A (Army, London Scottish) 1934 *I*
Crawford, W H (United Services, RN) 1938 *W, I, E,* 1939 *W, E*
Crichton-Miller, D (Gloucester) 1931 *W, I, E*
Crole, G B (Oxford U) 1920 *F, W, I, E*
Cronin, D F (Bath, London Scottish, Bourges) 1988 *I, F, W, E, A,* 1989 *W, E, I, F, Fj, R,* 1990 *I, F, W, E, NZ* 1,2, 1991 *F, W, E, I, R,* [Z], 1992 *A* 2, 1993 *I, F, W, E, NZ,* 1995 *C, I, F, [Tg, F, NZ], WS*
Cross, M (Merchistonians) 1875 *E,* 1876 *E,* 1877 *I, E,* 1878 *E,* 1879 *I, E,* 1880 *I, E*
Cross, W (Merchistonians) 1871 *E,* 1872 *E*
Cumming, R S (Aberdeen U) 1921 *F, W*
Cunningham, G (Oxford U) 1908 *W, I,* 1909 *W, E,* 1910 *F, I, E,* 1911 *E*
Cunningham, R F (Gala) 1978 *NZ,* 1979 *W, E*
Currie, L R (Dunfermline) 1947 *A,* 1948 *F, W, I,* 1949 *F, W, I, E*
Cuthbertson, W (Kilmarnock, Harlequins) 1980 *I,* 1981 *W, E, I, NZ* 1,2, *R, A,* 1982 *E, I, F, W, A* 1,2, 1983 *I, F, W, NZ,* 1984 *W, E, A*

Dalgleish, A (Gala) 1890 *W, E,* 1891 *W, I,* 1892 *W,* 1893 *W,* 1894 *W, I*
Dalgleish, K J (Edinburgh Wands, Cambridge U) 1951 *I, E,* 1953 *F, W*
Dallas, J D (Watsonians) 1903 *E*
Davidson, J A (London Scottish, Edinburgh Wands) 1959 *E,* 1960 *I, E*
Davidson, J N G (Edinburgh U) 1952 *F, W, I, E,* 1953 *F, W,* 1954 *F*
Davidson, J P (RIE Coll) 1873 *E,* 1874 *E*
Davidson, R S (Royal HSFP) 1893 *E*

Gillies, A C (Watsonians) 1924 *W, I, E*, 1925 *F, W, E*, 1926 *F, W*, 1927 *F, W, I, E*
Gilray, C M (Oxford U, London Scottish) 1908 *E*, 1909 *W, E*, 1912 *I*
Glasgow, R J C (Dunfermline) 1962 *F, W, I, E*, 1963 *I, E*, 1964 *I, E*, 1965 *W, I*
Glen, W S (Edinburgh Wands) 1955 *W*
Gloag, L G (Cambridge U) 1949 *F, W, I, E*
Goodfellow, J (Langholm) 1928 *W, I, E*
Goodhue, F W J (London Scottish) 1890 *W, I, E*, 1891 *W, I, E*, 1892 *W, I, E*
Gordon, R (Edinburgh Wands) 1951 *W*, 1952 *F, W, I, E*, 1953 *W*
Gordon, R E (Royal Artillery) 1913 *F, W, I*
Gordon, R J (London Scottish) 1982 *A 1,2*
Gore, A C (London Scottish) 1882 *I*
Gossman, B M (W of Scotland) 1980 *W*, 1983 *F, W*
Gossman, J S (W of Scotland) 1980 *E* (R)
Gowans, J J (Cambridge U, London Scottish) 1893 *W*, 1894 *W, E*, 1895 *W, I, E*, 1896 *I, E*
Gowland, G C (London Scottish) 1908 *W*, 1909 *W, E*, 1910 *F, W, I, E*
Gracie, A L (Harlequins) 1921 *F, W, I, E*, 1922 *F, W, I, E*, 1923 *F, W, I, E*, 1924 *F*
Graham, I N (Edinburgh Acads) 1939 *I, E*
Graham, J (Kelso) 1926 *I, E*, 1927 *F, W, I, E, A*, 1928 *F, W, I, E*, 1930 *I, E*, 1932 *SA, W*
Graham, J H S (Edinburgh Acads) 1876 *E*, 1877 *I, E*, 1878 *E*, 1879 *I, E*, 1880 *I, E*, 1881 *I, E*
Grant, D (Hawick) 1965 *F, E, SA*, 1966 *F, W, I, E, A*, 1967 *F, W, I, E, NZ*, 1968 *F*
Grant, D M (East Midlands) 1911 *W, I*
Grant, M L (Harlequins) 1955 *F*, 1956 *F, W*, 1957 *F*
Grant, T O (Hawick) 1960 *I, E, SA*, 1964 *F, NZ, W*
Grant, W St C (Craigmount) 1873 *E*, 1874 *E*
Gray, C A (Nottingham) 1989 *W, E, I, F, Fj, R*, 1990 *I, F, W, E, NZ 1,2, Arg*, 1991 *F, W, E, I, [J, I, WS, E, NZ]*
Gray, D (W of Scotland) 1978 *E*, 1979 *I, F, NZ*, 1980 *I, F, W, E*, 1981 *F*
Gray, G L (Gala) 1935 *NZ*, 1937 *W, I, E*
Gray, T (Northampton, Heriot's FP) 1950 *E*, 1951 *F, E*
Greenlees, H D (Leicester) 1927 *A*, 1928 *F, W*, 1929 *I, E*, 1930 *E*
Greenlees, J R C (Cambridge U, Kelvinside Acads) 1900 *I*, 1902 *W, I, E*, 1903 *W, I, E*
Greenwood, J T (Dunfermline and Perthshire Acads) 1952 *F*, 1955 *F, W, I, E*, 1956 *F, W, I, E*, 1957 *F, W, E*, 1958 *F, W, A, I, E*, 1959 *F, W, I*
Greig, A (Glasgow HSFP) 1911 *I*
Greig, L L (Glasgow Acads, United Services) 1905 *NZ*, 1906 *SA*, 1907 *W*, 1908 *W, I*
Greig, R C (Glasgow Acads) 1893 *W*, 1897 *I*
Grieve, C F (Oxford U) 1935 *W*, 1936 *E*
Grieve, R M (Kelso) 1935 *W, I, E, NZ*, 1936 *W, I, E*
Gunn, A W (Royal HSFP) 1912 *F, W, I, SA*, 1913 *F*

Hamilton, A S (Headingley) 1914 *W*, 1920 *F*
Hamilton, H M (W of Scotland) 1874 *E*, 1875 *E*
Hannah, R S M (W of Scotland) 1971 *I*
Harrower, P R (London Scottish) 1885 *W*
Hart, J G M (London Scottish) 1951 *SA*
Hart, T M (Glasgow U) 1930 *W, I*
Hart, W (Melrose) 1960 *SA*
Harvey, L (Greenock Wands) 1899 *I*
Hastie, A J (Melrose) 1961 *W, I, E*, 1964 *I, E*, 1965 *E, SA*, 1966 *F, W, I, E, A*, 1967 *F, W, I, NZ*, 1968 *F, W*
Hastie, I R (Kelso) 1955 *F*, 1958 *F, E*, 1959 *F, W, I*
Hastie, J D H (Melrose) 1938 *W, I, E*
Hastings, A G (Cambridge U, Watsonians, London Scottish) 1986 *F, W, E, I, R*, 1987 *I, F, W, E, [F, Z, R, NZ]*, 1988 *I, F, W, E, A*, 1989 *Fj, R*, 1990 *I, F, W, E, NZ 1,2, Arg*, 1991 *F, W, E, I, [J, I, WS, E, NZ]*, 1992 *E, I, F, W, A 1,2*, 1993 *I, F, W, E, NZ*, 1994 *W, E, I, F, SA*, 1995 *C, I, F, W, E, R, [Iv, Tg, F, NZ]*
Hastings, S (Watsonians) 1986 *F, W, E, I, R*, 1987 *I, F, W, [R]*, 1988 *I, F, W, A*, 1989 *W, E, I, F, Fj, R*, 1990 *I, F, W, E, NZ 1,2, Arg*, 1991 *F, W, E, I, [J, Z, I, WS, E, NZ]*, 1992 *E, I, F, W, A 1,2*, 1993 *I, F, W, E, NZ*, 1994 *E, I, F, SA*, 1995 *W, E, R (R), [Tg, F, NZ]*, 1996 *I, F, W, E*
Hay, B H (Boroughmuir) 1975 *NZ, A*, 1976 *F*, 1978 *I, F, W, E, NZ*, 1979 *W, E, I, F, NZ*, 1980 *I, F, W, E*, 1981 *F, W, E, I, NZ 1,2*
Hay, J A (Hawick) 1995 *WS*
Hay-Gordon, J R (Edinburgh Acads) 1875 *E*, 1877 *I, E*

Hegarty, C B (Hawick) 1978 *I, F, W, E*
Hegarty, J J (Hawick) 1951 *F*, 1953 *F, W, I, E*, 1955 *F*
Henderson, B C (Edinburgh Wands) 1963 *E*, 1964 *F, I, E*, 1965 *F, W, I, E*, 1966 *F, W, I, E*
Henderson, F W (London Scottish) 1900 *W, I*
Henderson, I C (Edinburgh Acads) 1939 *I, E*, 1947 *F, W, E, A*, 1948 *I, E*
Henderson, J H (Oxford U, Richmond) 1953 *F, W, I, E*, 1954 *F, NZ, I, E, W*
Henderson, J M (Edinburgh Acads) 1933 *W, E, I*
Henderson, J Y M (Watsonians) 1911 *E*
Henderson, M M (Dunfermline) 1937 *W, I, E*
Henderson, N F (London Scottish) 1892 *I*
Henderson, R G (Newcastle Northern) 1924 *I, E*
Hendrie, K G P (Heriot's FP) 1924 *F, W, I*
Hendry, T L (Clydesdale) 1893 *W, I, E*, 1895 *I*
Henriksen, E H (Royal HSFP) 1953 *I*
Hepburn, D P (Woodford) 1947 *A*, 1948 *F, W, I, E*, 1949 *F, W, I, E*
Heron, G (Glasgow Acads) 1874 *E*, 1875 *E*
Hill, C C P (St Andrew's U) 1912 *F, I*
Hilton, D I W (Bath) 1995 *C, I, F, W, E, R, [Tg, F, NZ]*, WS, 1996 *I, F, W, E*
Hinshelwood, A J W (London Scottish) 1966 *F, W, I, E, A*, 1967 *F, W, I, E, NZ*, 1968 *F, W, I, E, A*, 1969 *F, W, I, SA*, 1970 *F, W*
Hodgson, C G (London Scottish) 1968 *I, E*
Hogg, C D (Melrose) 1992 *A 1,2*, 1993 *NZ* (R), 1994 *Arg 1,2*
Hogg, C G (Boroughmuir) 1978 *F* (R), *W* (R)
Holms, W F (RIE Coll) 1886 *W, E*, 1887 *I, E*, 1889 *W, I*
Horsburgh, G B (London Scottish) 1937 *W, I, E*, 1938 *W, I, E*, 1939 *W, I, E*
Howie, D D (Kirkcaldy) 1912 *F, W, I, E, SA*, 1913 *F, W*
Howie, R A (Kirkcaldy) 1924 *F, W, I, E*, 1925 *W, I, E*
Hoyer-Millar, G C (Oxford U) 1953 *I*
Huggan, J L (London Scottish) 1914 *E*
Hume, J (Royal HSFP) 1912 *F*, 1920 *F*, 1921 *F, W, I, E*, 1922 *F*
Hume, J W G (Oxford U, Edinburgh Wands) 1928 *I*, 1930 *F*
Hunter, F (Edinburgh U) 1882 *I*
Hunter, I G (Selkirk) 1984 *I* (R), 1985 *F* (R), *W, E*
Hunter, J M (Cambridge U) 1947 *F*
Hunter, M D (Glasgow High) 1974 *F*
Hunter, W J (Hawick) 1964 *F, NZ, W*, 1967 *F, W, I, E*
Hutchison, W R (Glasgow HSFP) 1911 *E*
Hutton, A H M (Dunfermline) 1932 *I*
Hutton, J E (Harlequins) 1930 *E*, 1931 *F*

Inglis, H M (Edinburgh Acads) 1951 *F, W, I, E, SA*, 1952 *W, I*
Inglis, J M (Selkirk) 1952 *E*
Inglis, W M (Cambridge U, Royal Engineers) 1937 *W, I, E*, 1938 *W, I, E*
Innes, J R S (Aberdeen GSFP) 1939 *W, I, E*, 1947 *A*, 1948 *F, W, I, E*
Ireland, J C H (Glasgow HSFP) 1925 *W, I, E*, 1926 *F, W, I, E*, 1927 *F, W, I, E*
Irvine, A R (Heriot's FP) 1972 *NZ*, 1973 *F, W, I, E, P*, 1974 *W, E, I, F*, 1975 *I, F, W, E, NZ, A*, 1976 *F, W, E, I*, 1977 *E, I, F, W*, 1978 *I, F, E, NZ*, 1979 *W, E, I, F, NZ*, 1980 *I, F, W, E*, 1981 *F, W, E, I, NZ 1,2, R, A*, 1982 *E, I, F, W, A 1,2*
Irvine, D R (Edinburgh Acads) 1878 *E*, 1879 *I, E*
Irvine, R W (Edinburgh Acads) 1871 *E*, 1872 *E*, 1873 *E*, 1874 *E*, 1875 *E*, 1876 *E*, 1877 *I, E*, 1878 *E*, 1879 *I, E*, 1880 *I, E*
Irvine T W (Edinburgh Acads) 1885 *I* 1,2, 1886 *W, I, E*, 1887 *I, W, E*, 1888 *W, I*, 1889 *I*

Jackson, K L T (Oxford U) 1933 *W, E, I*, 1934 *W*
Jackson, T G H (Army) 1947 *F, W, E, A*, 1948 *F, W, I, E*, 1949 *F, W, I, E*
Jackson, W D (Hawick) 1964 *I*, 1965 *E, SA*, 1968 *A*, 1969 *F, W, I, E*
Jamieson, J (W of Scotland) 1883 *W, I, E*, 1884 *W, I, E*, 1885 *W, I* 1,2
Jardine, I C (Stirling County) 1993 *NZ*, 1994 *W, E* (R), *Arg* 1,2, 1995 *C, I, F, [Tg, F (t & R), NZ (R)]*, 1996 *I, F, W, E*
Jeffrey, J (Kelso) 1984 *A*, 1985 *I, E*, 1986 *F, W, E, I, R*, 1987 *I, F, W, E, [F, Z, R]*, 1988 *I, W, A*, 1989 *W, E, I, F, Fj, R*, 1990 *I, F, W, E, NZ 1,2, Arg*, 1991 *F, W, E, I, [J, I, WS, E, NZ]*

Johnston, D I (Watsonians) 1979 *NZ*, 1980 *I, F, W, E*, 1981 *R, A*, 1982 *E, I, F, W, A* 1,2, 1983 *I, F, W, NZ*, 1984 *W, E, I, F, R*, 1986 *F, W, E, I, R*
Johnston, H H (Edinburgh Collegian FP) 1877 *I, E*
Johnston, J (Melrose) 1951 *SA*, 1952 *F, W, I, E*
Johnston, W C (Glasgow HSFP) 1922 *F*
Johnston, W G S (Cambridge U) 1935 *W, I*, 1937 *W, I, E*
Joiner, C A (Melrose) 1994 *Arg* 1,2, 1995 *C, I, F, W, E, R*, [*Iv, Tg, F, NZ*], 1996 *I, F, W, E*
Jones, P M (Gloucester) 1992 *W* (R)
Junor, J E (Glasgow Acads) 1876 *E*, 1877 *I, E*, 1878 *E*, 1879 *E*, 1881 *I*

Keddie, R R (Watsonians) 1967 *NZ*
Keith, G J (Wasps) 1968 *F, W*
Keller, D H (London Scottish) 1949 *F, W, I, E*, 1950 *F, W, I*
Kelly, R F (Watsonians) 1927 *A*, 1928 *F, W, E*
Kemp, J W Y (Glasgow HSFP) 1954 *W*, 1955 *F, W, I, E*, 1956 *W, I, E*, 1957 *F, W, I, E*, 1958 *F, W, A, I, E*, 1959 *F, W, I, E*, 1960 *F, W, I, E, SA*
Kennedy, A E (Watsonians) 1983 *NZ*, 1984 *W, E, A*
Kennedy, F (Stewart's Coll FP) 1920 *F, W, I, E*, 1921 *E*
Kennedy, N (W of Scotland) 1903 *W, I, E*
Ker, A B M (Kelso) 1988 *W, E*
Ker, H T (Glasgow Acads) 1887 *I, W, E*, 1888 *I*, 1889 *W*, 1890 *I, E*
Kerr, D S (Heriot's FP) 1923 *F, W*, 1924 *F*, 1926 *I, E*, 1927 *W, I, E*, 1928 *I, E*
Kerr, G C (Old Dunelmians, Edinburgh Wands) 1898 *I, E*, 1899 *I, W, E*, 1900 *W, I, E*
Kerr, J M (Heriot's FP) 1935 *NZ*, 1936 *I, E*, 1937 *W, I*
Kerr, W (London Scottish) 1953 *E*
Kidston, D W (Glasgow Acads) 1883 *W, E*
Kidston, W H (W of Scotland) 1874 *E*
Kilgour, I J (RMC Sandhurst) 1921 *F*
King, J H F (Selkirk) 1953 *F, W, E*, 1954 *E*
Kininmonth, P W (Oxford U, Richmond) 1949 *F, W, I, E*, 1950 *F, W, I, E*, 1951 *F, W, I, E, SA*, 1952 *F, W, I*, 1954 *F, NZ, I, E, W*
Kinnear, R M (Heriot's FP) 1926 *F, W, I*
Knox, J (Kelvinside Acads) 1903 *W, I, E*
Kyle, W E (Hawick) 1902 *W, I, E*, 1903 *W, I, E*, 1904 *W, I, E*, 1905 *W, I, E, NZ*, 1906 *W, I, E*, 1908 *W, I, E*, 1909 *W, I, E*, 1910 *W*

Laidlaw, A S (Hawick) 1897 *I*
Laidlaw, F A L (Melrose) 1965 *F, W, I, E, SA*, 1966 *F, W, I, E, A*, 1967 *F, W, I, E, NZ*, 1968 *F, W, I, A*, 1969 *F, W, I, E, SA*, 1970 *F, W, I, E, A*, 1971 *F, W, I*
Laidlaw, R J (Jedforest) 1980 *I, F, W, E*, 1981 *F, W, E, I, NZ* 1,2, *R, A*, 1982 *E, I, F, W, A* 1,2, 1983 *I, F, W, E, NZ*, 1984 *W, E, I, F, R, A*, 1985 *I, F*, 1986 *F, W, E, I, R*, 1987 *I, F, W, E*, [*F, R, NZ*], 1988 *I, F, W, E*
Laing, A D (Royal HSFP) 1914 *W, I, E*, 1920 *F, W, I*, 1921 *F*
Lambie, I K (Watsonians) 1978 *NZ* (R), 1979 *W, E, NZ*
Lambie, L B (Glasgow HSFP) 1934 *W, I, E*, 1935 *W, I, E, NZ*
Lamond, G A W (Kelvinside Acads) 1899 *W, E*, 1905 *E*
Lang, D (Paisley) 1876 *E*, 1877 *I*
Langrish, R W (London Scottish) 1930 *F*, 1931 *F, W, I*
Lauder, W (Neath) 1969 *I, E, SA*, 1970 *F, W, I, A*, 1973 *F*, 1974 *W, E, I, F*, 1975 *I, F, NZ, A*, 1976 *F*, 1977 *E*
Laughland, I H P (London Scottish) 1959 *F*, 1960 *F, W, I, E*, 1961 *SA, W, I, E*, 1962 *F, W, I, E*, 1963 *F, W, I*, 1964 *F, NZ, W, I, E*, 1965 *F, W, I, E, SA*, 1966 *F, W, I, E*, 1967 *E*
Lawrie, J R (Melrose) 1922 *F, W, I, E*, 1923 *F, W, I, E*, 1924 *W, I, E*
Lawrie, K G (Gala) 1980 *F* (R), *W, E*
Lawson, A J M (Edinburgh Wands, London Scottish) 1972 *F* (R), 1973 *F*, 1974 *W, E*, 1976 *E, I*, 1977 *E*, 1978 *NZ*, 1979 *W, E, I, F, NZ*, 1980 *W* (R)
Lawther, T H B (Old Millhillians) 1932 *SA, W*
Ledingham, G A (Aberdeen GSFP) 1913 *F*
Lees, J B (Gala) 1947 *I, A*, 1948 *F, W, E*
Leggatt, H T O (Watsonians) 1891 *W, I, E*, 1892 *W, I*, 1893 *W, E*, 1894 *I, E*
Lely, W G (Cambridge U, London Scottish) 1909 *I*
Leslie, D G (Dundee HSFP, W of Scotland, Gala) 1975 *I, F, W, E, NZ, A*, 1976 *F, W, E, I*, 1978 *NZ*, 1980 *E, I, W, E*, *I, NZ* 1,2, *R, A*, 1982 *E*, 1983 *I, F, W, E*, 1984 *W, E, I, F, R*, 1985 *F, W, E*
Liddell, E H (Edinburgh U) 1922 *F, W, I*, 1923 *F, W, I, E*
Lind, H (Dunfermline) 1928 *I*, 1931 *F, W, I, E*, 1932 *SA, W, E*, 1933 *W, E, I*, 1934 *W, I, E*, 1935 *I*, 1936 *E*

Lindsay, A B (London Hospital) 1910 *I*, 1911 *I*
Lindsay, G C (London Scottish) 1884 *W*, 1885 *I* 1, 1887 *W, E*
Lindsay-Watson, R H (Hawick) 1909 *I*
Lineen, S R P (Boroughmuir) 1989 *W, E, I, F, Fj, R*, 1990 *I, F, W, E, NZ* 1,2, *Arg*, 1991 *F, W, E, I, R*, [*J, Z, I, E, NZ*], 1992 *E, I, F, W, A* 1,2
Little, A W (Hawick) 1905 *W*
Logan, K M (Stirling County) 1992 *A* 2, 1993 *E* (R), *NZ* (t), 1994 *W, E, I, F, Arg* 1,2, *SA*, 1995 *C, I, F, W, E, R*, [*Iv, Tg, F, NZ*], *WS*, 1996 *W* (R)
Logan, W R (Edinburgh U, Edinburgh Wands) 1931 *E*, 1932 *SA, W, I*, 1933 *W, E, I*, 1934 *W, I, E*, 1935 *W, I, E, NZ*, 1936 *W, I, E*, 1937 *W, I, E*
Lorraine, H D B (Oxford U) 1933 *W, E, I*
Loudoun-Shand, E G (Oxford U) 1913 *E*
Lowe, J D (Heriot's FP) 1934 *W*
Lumsden, I J M (Bath, Watsonians) 1947 *F, W, A*, 1949 *F, W, I, E*
Lyall, G G (Gala) 1947 *A*, 1948 *F, W, I, E*
Lyall, W J C (Edinburgh Acads) 1871 *E*

Mabon, J T (Jedforest) 1898 *I, E*, 1899 *I*, 1900 *I*
Macarthur, J P (Waterloo) 1932 *E*
MacCallum, J C (Watsonians) 1905 *E, NZ*, 1906 *W, I, E, SA*, 1907 *W, I, E*, 1908 *W, I, E*, 1909 *W, I, E*, 1910 *F, W, I, E*, 1911 *F, I, E*, 1912 *F, W, I, E*
McClung, T (Edinburgh Acads) 1956 *I, E*, 1957 *W, I, E*, 1959 *F, W, I*, 1960 *W*
McClure, G B (W of Scotland) 1873 *E*
McClure, J H (W of Scotland) 1872 *E*
McCowan, D (W of Scotland) 1880 *I, E*, 1881 *I, E*, 1882 *I, E*, 1883 *I, E*, 1884 *I, E*
McCowat, R H (Glasgow Acads) 1905 *I*
McCrae, I G (Gordonians) 1967 *E*, 1968 *I*, 1969 *F* (R), *W*, 1972 *F, NZ*
McCrow, J W S (Edinburgh Acads) 1921 *I*
Macdonald, A E D (Heriot's FP) 1993 *NZ*
McDonald, C (Jedforest) 1947 *A*
Macdonald, D C (Edinburgh U) 1953 *F, W*, 1958 *I, E*
Macdonald, D S M (Oxford U, London Scottish, W of Scotland) 1977 *E, I, F, W*, 1978 *I, W, E*
Macdonald, J D (London Scottish, Army) 1966 *F, W, I, E*, 1967 *F, W, I, E*
Macdonald, J M (Edinburgh Wands) 1911 *W*
Macdonald, J S (Edinburgh U) 1903 *E*, 1904 *W, I, E*, 1905 *W*
Macdonald, K R (Stewart's Coll FP) 1956 *F, W, I*, 1957 *W, I, E*
Macdonald, R (Edinburgh U) 1950 *F, W, I, E*
McDonald, W A (Glasgow U) 1889 *W*, 1892 *I, E*
Macdonald, W G (London Scottish) 1969 *I* (R)
Macdougall, J B (Greenock Wands, Wakefield) 1913 *F*, 1914 *I*, 1921 *F, I, E*
McEwan, M C (Edinburgh Acads) 1886 *E*, 1887 *I, W, E*, 1888 *W, I*, 1889 *W, I*, 1890 *W, I, E*, 1891 *W, I, E*, 1892 *E*
MacEwan, N A (Gala, Highland) 1971 *F, W, I, E* (2[1C]), 1972 *F, W, E, NZ*, 1973 *F, W, I, E, P*, 1974 *W, E, I, F*, 1975 *W, E*
McEwan, W M C (Edinburgh Acads) 1894 *W, E*, 1895 *W, E*, 1896 *W, I, E*, 1897 *I, E*, 1898 *I, E*, 1899 *I, W, E*, 1900 *W, E*
MacEwen, R K G (Cambridge U, London Scottish) 1954 *F, NZ, I, W*, 1956 *F, W, I, E*, 1957 *F, W, I, E*, 1958 *W*
Macfarlan, D J (London Scottish) 1883 *W*, 1884 *W, I, E*, 1886 *W, I*, 1887 *I*, 1888 *I*
McFarlane, J L H (Edinburgh U) 1871 *E*, 1872 *E*, 1873 *E*
McGaughey, S K (Hawick) 1984 *R*
McGeechan, I R (Headingley) 1972 *NZ*, 1973 *F, W, I, E, P*, 1974 *W, E, I, F*, 1975 *I, F, W, E, NZ, A*, 1976 *F, W, E, I*, 1977 *E, I, F, W*, 1978 *I, F, W, NZ*, 1979 *W, E, I, F*
McGlashan, T P L (Royal HSFP) 1947 *F, I, E*, 1954 *F, NZ, I, E, W*
MacGregor, D G (Watsonians, Pontypridd) 1907 *W, I, E*
MacGregor, G (Cambridge U) 1890 *W, I, E*, 1891 *W, I, E*, 1893 *W, I, E*, 1894 *W, I, E*, 1896 *E*
MacGregor, I A A (Hillhead HSFP, Llanelli) 1955 *I, E*, 1956 *F, W, I, E*, 1957 *F, W, I*
MacGregor, J R (Edinburgh U) 1909 *I*
McGuinness, G M (W of Scotland) 1982 *A* 1,2, 1983 *I*, 1985 *I, F, W, E*
McHarg, A F (W of Scotland, London Scottish) 1968 *I, E, A*, 1969 *F, W, I, E*, 1971 *F, W, I, E* (2[1C]), 1972 *F, E, NZ*, 1973 *F, W, I, E, P*, 1974 *W, E, I, F*, 1975 *I, F, W, E, NZ, A*, 1976 *F, W, E, I*, 1977 *E, I, F, W*, 1978 *I, F, W, NZ*, 1979 *W, E*

McIndoe, F (Glasgow Acads) 1886 *W, I*
MacIntyre, I (Edinburgh Wands) 1890 *W, I, E*, 1891 *W, I, E*
McIvor, D J (Edinburgh Acads) 1992 *E, I, F, W*, 1993 *NZ*, 1994 *SA*
Mackay, E B (Glasgow Acads) 1920 *W*, 1922 *E*
McKeating, E (Heriot's FP) 1957 *F, W*, 1961 *SA, W, I, E*
McKendrick, J G (W of Scotland) 1889 *I*
Mackenzie, A D G (Selkirk) 1984 *A*
Mackenzie, C J G (United Services) 1921 *E*
Mackenzie, D D (Edinburgh U) 1947 *W, I, E*, 1948 *F, W, I*
Mackenzie, D K A (Edinburgh Wands) 1939 *I, E*
Mackenzie, J M (Edinburgh U) 1905 *NZ*, 1909 *W, I, E*, 1910 *W, I, E*, 1911 *W, I*
McKenzie, K D (Stirling County) 1994 *Arg* 1,2, 1995 *R, [Iv]*, 1996 *I, F, W, E*
Mackenzie, R C (Glasgow Acads) 1877 *I, E*, 1881 *I, E*
Mackie, G Y (Highland) 1975 *A*, 1976 *F, W*, 1978 *F*
MacKinnon, A (London Scottish) 1898 *I, E*, 1899 *I, W, E*, 1900 *E*
Mackintosh, C E W C (London Scottish) 1924 *F*
Mackintosh, H S (Glasgow U, W of Scotland) 1929 *F, W, I, E*, 1930 *F, W, I, E*, 1931 *F, W, I, E*, 1932 *SA, W, I, E*
MacLachlan, L P (Oxford U, London Scottish) 1954 *NZ, I, E, W*
Maclagan, W E (Edinburgh Acads) 1878 *E*, 1879 *I, E*, 1880 *I, E*, 1881 *I, E*, 1882 *I, E*, 1883 *W, I, E*, 1884 *W, I, E*, 1885 *W, I* 1,2, 1887 *I, W, E*, 1888 *W, I*, 1890 *W, I, E*
McLaren, A (Durham County) 1931 *F*
McLaren, E (London Scottish, Royal HSFP) 1923 *F, W, I, E*, 1924 *F*
McLauchlan, J (Jordanhill) 1969 *E, SA*, 1970 *F, W*, 1971 *F, W, I, E* (2[1C]), 1972 *F, W, E, NZ*, 1973 *F, W, I, E, P*, 1974 *W, E, I, F*, 1975 *I, F, W, E, NZ, A*, 1976 *F, W, E, I*, 1977 *W*, 1978 *I, F, W, E, NZ*, 1979 *W, E, I, F, NZ*
McLean, D I (Royal HSFP) 1947 *I, E*
Maclennan, W D (Watsonians) 1947 *F, I*
MacLeod, D A (Glasgow U) 1886 *I, E*
MacLeod, G (Edinburgh Acads) 1878 *E*, 1882 *I*
McLeod, H F (Hawick) 1954 *F, NZ, I, E, W*, 1955 *F, W, I, E*, 1956 *F, W, I, E*, 1957 *F, W, I, E*, 1958 *F, W, A, I, E*, 1959 *F, W, I, E*, 1960 *F, W, I, E, SA*, 1961 *F, SA, W, I, E*, 1962 *F, W, I, E*
MacLeod, K G (Cambridge U) 1905 *NZ*, 1906 *W, I, E, SA*, 1907 *W, I, E*, 1908 *I, E*
MacLeod, L M (Cambridge U) 1904 *W, I, E*, 1905 *W, I, NZ*
Macleod, W M (Fettesian-Lorettonians, Edinburgh Wands) 1886 *W, I*
McMillan, K H D (Sale) 1953 *F, W, I, E*
MacMillan, R G (London Scottish) 1887 *W, I, E*, 1890 *W, I, E*, 1891 *W, E*, 1892 *W, I, E*, 1893 *W, E*, 1894 *W, I, E*, 1895 *W, I, E*, 1897 *I, E*
MacMyn, D J (Cambridge U, London Scottish) 1925 *F, W, I, E*, 1926 *F, W, I, E*, 1927 *E, A*, 1928 *F*
McNeil, A S B (Watsonians) 1935 *I*
McPartlin, J J (Harlequins, Oxford U) 1960 *F, W*, 1962 *F, W, I, E*
Macphail, J A R (Edinburgh Acads) 1949 *E*, 1951 *SA*
Macpherson, D G (London Hospital) 1910 *I, E*
Macpherson, G P S (Oxford U, Edinburgh Acads) 1922 *F, W, I, E*, 1924 *W, E*, 1925 *F, W, E*, 1927 *F, W, I, E*, 1928 *F, W, E*, 1929 *I, E*, 1930 *F, W, I, E*, 1931 *W, E*, 1932 *SA, E*
Macpherson, N C (Newport) 1920 *W, I, E*, 1921 *F, E*, 1923 *I, E*
McQueen, S B (Waterloo) 1923 *F, W, I, E*
Macrae, D J (St Andrew's U) 1937 *W, I, E*, 1938 *W, I, E*, 1939 *W, I, E*
Madsen, D F (Gosforth) 1974 *W, E, I, F*, 1975 *I, F, W, E*, 1976 *F*, 1977 *E, I, F, W*, 1978 *I*
Mair, N G R (Edinburgh U) 1951 *F, W, I, E*
Maitland, G (Edinburgh Inst FP) 1885 *W, I* 2
Maitland, R (Edinburgh Inst FP) 1881 *E*, 1882 *I, E*, 1884 *W*, 1885 *W*
Maitland, R P (Royal Artillery) 1872 *E*
Malcolm, A G (Glasgow U) 1888 *I*
Manson, J J (Dundee HSFP) 1995 *E* (R)
Marsh, J (Edinburgh Inst FP) 1889 *W, I*
Marshall, A (Edinburgh Acads) 1875 *E*
Marshall, G R (Selkirk) 1988 *A* (R), 1989 *Fj*, 1990 *Arg*, 1991 *[Z]*
Marshall, J C (London Scottish) 1954 *F, NZ, I, E, W*
Marshall, K W (Edinburgh Acads) 1934 *W, I, E*, 1935 *W, I, E*, 1936 *W*, 1937 *E*

Marshall, T R (Edinburgh Acads) 1871 *E*, 1872 *E*, 1873 *E*, 1874 *E*
Marshall, W (Edinburgh Acads) 1872 *E*
Martin, H (Edinburgh Acads, Oxford U) 1908 *W, I, E*, 1909 *W, E*
Masters, W H (Edinburgh Inst FP) 1879 *I*, 1880 *I, E*
Maxwell, F T (Royal Engineers) 1872 *E*
Maxwell, G H H P (Edinburgh Acads, RAF, London Scottish) 1913 *I, E*, 1914 *W, I, E*, 1920 *W, E*, 1921 *F, W, I, E*, 1922 *F, E*
Maxwell, J M (Langholm) 1957 *I*
Mein, J (Edinburgh Acads) 1871 *E*, 1872 *E*, 1873 *E*, 1874 *E*, 1875 *E*
Melville, C L (Army) 1937 *W, I, E*
Menzies, H F (W of Scotland) 1893 *W, I*, 1894 *W, E*
Methuen, A (London Scottish) 1889 *W, I*
Michie, E J S (Aberdeen U, Aberdeen GSFP) 1954 *F, NZ, I, E*, 1955 *W, I, E*, 1956 *F, W, I, E*, 1957 *F, W, I, E*
Millar, J N (W of Scotland) 1892 *W, I, E*, 1893 *W*, 1895 *I, E*
Millar, R K (London Scottish) 1924 *I*
Millican, J G (Edinburgh U) 1973 *W, I, E*
Milne, C J B (Fettesian-Lorettonians, W of Scotland) 1886 *W, I, E*
Milne, D F (Heriot's FP) 1991 *[J(R)]*
Milne, I G (Heriot's FP, Harlequins) 1979 *I, F, NZ*, 1980 *I, F*, 1981 *NZ* 1,2, *R, A*, 1982 *E, I, F, W, A* 1,2, 1983 *I, F, W, E, NZ*, 1984 *W, E, I, F, A*, 1985 *F, W, E*, 1986 *F, W, E, I, R*, 1987 *I, F, W, E, [F, Z, NZ]*, 1988 *A*, 1989 *W*, 1990 *NZ* 1,2
Milne, K S (Heriot's FP) 1989 *W, E, I, F, Fj, R*, 1990 *I, F, W, E, NZ* 2, *Arg*, 1991 *F, W* (R), *E, [Z]*, 1992 *E, I, F, W, A* 1, 1993 *I, F, W, E, NZ*, 1994 *W, E, I, F, SA*, 1995 *C, I, F, W, E, [Tg, F, NZ]*
Milne, W M (Glasgow Acads) 1904 *I, E*, 1905 *W, I*
Milroy, E (Watsonians) 1910 *W*, 1911 *E*, 1912 *W, I, E, SA*, 1913 *F, W, I, E*, 1914 *I, E*
Mitchell, G W E (Edinburgh Wands) 1967 *NZ*, 1968 *F, W*
Mitchell, J G (W of Scotland) 1885 *W, I* 1,2
Moncreiff, F J (Edinburgh Acads) 1871 *E*, 1872 *E*, 1873 *E*
Monteith, H G (Cambridge U, London Scottish) 1905 *E*, 1906 *W, I, E, SA*, 1907 *W, I*, 1908 *E*
Monypenny, D B (London Scottish) 1899 *I, W, E*
Moodie, A R (St Andrew's U) 1909 *E*, 1910 *F*, 1911 *F*
Moore, A (Edinburgh Acads) 1990 *NZ* 2, *Arg*, 1991 *F, W, E*
Morgan, D W (Stewart's-Melville FP) 1973 *W, I, E, P*, 1974 *I, F*, 1975 *I, F, W, E, NZ, A*, 1976 *F, W*, 1977 *I, F, W*, 1978 *I, F, W, E*
Morrison, I R (London Scottish) 1993 *I, F, W, E*, 1994 *W, SA*, 1995 *C, I, F, W, E, R, [Tg, F, NZ]*
Morrison, M C (Royal HSFP) 1896 *W, I, E*, 1897 *I, E*, 1898 *I, E*, 1899 *I, W, E*, 1900 *W, E*, 1901 *W, I, E*, 1902 *W, I, E*, 1903 *W, I*, 1904 *W, I, E*
Morrison, R H (Edinburgh U) 1886 *W, I, E*
Morrison, W H (Edinburgh Acads) 1900 *W*
Morton, D S (W of Scotland) 1887 *I, W, E*, 1888 *W, I*, 1889 *W, I*, 1890 *I, E*
Mowat, J G (Glasgow Acads) 1883 *W, E*
Muir, D E (Heriot's FP) 1950 *F, W, I, E*, 1952 *W, I, E*
Munnoch, N M (Watsonians) 1952 *F, W, I*
Munro, D S (Glasgow High Kelvinside) 1994 *W, E, I, F, Arg* 1,2
Munro, P (Oxford U, London Scottish) 1905 *W, I, E, NZ*, 1906 *W, I, E, SA*, 1907 *I, E*, 1911 *F, W, I*
Munro, R (St Andrew's U) 1871 *E*
Munro, S (Ayr, W of Scotland) 1980 *I, F*, 1981 *F, W, E, I, NZ* 1,2, *R*, 1984 *W*
Munro, W H (Glasgow HSFP) 1947 *I, E*
Murdoch, W C W (Hillhead HSFP) 1935 *E, NZ*, 1936 *W, I*, 1939 *E*, 1948 *F, W, I, E*
Murray, G M (Glasgow Acads) 1921 *I*, 1926 *W*
Murray, H M (Glasgow U) 1936 *W, I*
Murray, K T (Hawick) 1985 *I, F, W*
Murray, R O (Cambridge U) 1935 *W, E*
Murray, W A K (London Scottish) 1920 *F, I*, 1921 *F*

Napier, H M (W of Scotland) 1877 *I, E*, 1878 *E*, 1879 *I, E*
Neill, J B (Edinburgh Acads) 1963 *E*, 1964 *F, NZ, W, I, E*, 1965 *F*
Neill, R M (Edinburgh Acads) 1901 *E*, 1902 *I*
Neilson, G T (W of Scotland) 1891 *W, I, E*, 1892 *W, E*, 1893 *W*, 1894 *W, I*, 1895 *W, I, E*, 1896 *W, I, E*
Neilson, J A (Glasgow Acads) 1878 *E*, 1879 *E*
Neilson, R T (W of Scotland) 1898 *I, E*, 1899 *I, W*, 1900 *I, E*

229

Neilson, T (W of Scotland) 1874 *E*
Neilson, W (Merchiston, Cambridge U, London Scottish) 1891 *W, E,* 1892 *W, I, E,* 1893 *I, E,* 1894 *E,* 1895 *W, I, E,* 1896 *I,* 1897 *I, E*
Neilson, W G (Merchistonians) 1894 *E*
Nelson, J B (Glasgow Acads) 1925 *F, W, I, E,* 1926 *F, W, I, E,* 1927 *F, W, I, E,* 1928 *I, E,* 1929 *F, W, I, E,* 1930 *F, W, I, E,* 1931 *F, W, I*
Nelson, T A (Oxford U) 1898 *E*
Nichol, J A (Royal HSFP) 1955 *W, I, E*
Nichol, S A (Selkirk) 1994 *Arg* 2 (R)
Nicol, A D (Dundee HSFP) 1992 *E, I, F, W, A* 1,2, 1993 *NZ,* 1994 *W*
Nimmo, C S (Watsonians) 1920 *E*

Ogilvy, C (Hawick) 1911 *I, E,* 1912 *I*
Oliver, G H (Hawick) 1987 [Z], 1990 *NZ* 2 (R), 1991 [Z]
Oliver, G K (Gala) 1970 *A*
Orr, C E (W of Scotland) 1887 *I, E, W,* 1888 *W, I,* 1889 *W, I,* 1890 *W, I, E,* 1891 *W, I, E,* 1892 *W, I, E*
Orr, H J (London Scottish) 1903 *W, I, E,* 1904 *W, I*
Orr, J E (W of Scotland) 1889 *I,* 1890 *W, I, E,* 1891 *W, I, E,* 1892 *W, I, E,* 1893 *I, E*
Orr, J H (Edinburgh City Police) 1947 *F, W*
Osler, F L (Edinburgh U) 1911 *F, W*

Park, J (Royal HSFP) 1934 *W*
Paterson, D S (Gala) 1969 *SA,* 1970 *I, E, A,* 1971 *F, W, I, E* (2[1C]), 1972 *W*
Paterson, G Q (Edinburgh Acads) 1876 *E*
Paterson, J R (Birkenhead Park) 1925 *F, W, I, E,* 1926 *F, W, I, E,* 1927 *F, W, I, E, A,* 1928 *F, W, I, E,* 1929 *F, W, I, E*
Patterson, D (Hawick) 1896 *W*
Patterson, D W (West Hartlepool) 1994 *SA,* 1995 [Tg]
Pattullo, G L (Panmure) 1920 *F, W, I, E*
Paxton, I A M (Selkirk) 1981 *NZ* 1,2, *R, A,* 1982 *E, I, F, W, A* 1,2, 1983 *I, E, NZ,* 1984 *W, E, I, F,* 1985 *I* (R), *F, W, E,* 1986 *W, E, I, R,* 1987 *I, F, W, E,* [*F, Z, R, NZ*], 1988 *I, E, A*
Paxton, R E (Kelso) 1982 *I, A* 2 (R)
Pearson, J (Watsonians) 1909 *I, E,* 1910 *F, W, I, E,* 1911 *F,* 1912 *F, W, SA,* 1913 *I, E*
Pender, I M (London Scottish) 1914 *E*
Pender, N E K (Hawick) 1977 *I,* 1978 *F, W, E*
Penman, W M (RAF) 1939 *I*
Peterkin, W A (Edinburgh U) 1881 *E,* 1883 *I,* 1884 *W, I, E,* 1885 *W, I* 1,2
Peters, E W (Bath) 1995 *C, I, F, W, E, R,* [*Tg, F, NZ*], 1996 *I, F, W, E*
Petrie, A G (Royal HSFP) 1873 *E,* 1874 *E,* 1875 *E,* 1876 *E,* 1877 *I, E,* 1878 *E,* 1879 *I, E,* 1880 *I, E*
Philp, A (Edinburgh Inst FP) 1882 *E*
Pocock, E I (Edinburgh Wands) 1877 *I, E*
Pollock, J A (Gosforth) 1982 *W,* 1983 *E, NZ,* 1984 *E* (R), *I, F, R,* 1985 *F*
Polson, A H (Gala) 1930 *E*
Purdie, W (Jedforest) 1939 *W, I, E*
Purves, A B H L (London Scottish) 1906 *W, I, E, SA,* 1907 *W, I, E,* 1908 *W, I, E*
Purves, W D C L (London Scottish) 1912 *F, W, I, SA,* 1913 *I, E*

Rea, C W W (W of Scotland, Headingley) 1968 *A,* 1969 *F, W, I, SA,* 1970 *F, W, I, A,* 1971 *F, W, E* (2[1C])
Redpath, B W (Melrose) 1993 *NZ* (t), 1994 *E* (t), *F, Arg* 1,2, 1995 *C, I, F, W, E, R,* [*Iv, F, NZ*], WS, 1996 *I, F, W, E*
Reed, A I (Bath) 1993 *I, F, W, E,* 1994 *E, I, F, Arg* 1,2, *SA*
Reid, C (Edinburgh Acads) 1881 *I, E,* 1882 *I, E,* 1883 *W, I, E,* 1884 *W, I, E,* 1885 *W, I* 1,2, 1886 *W, I, E,* 1887 *I, W, E,* 1888 *W, I*
Reid, J (Edinburgh Wands) 1874 *E,* 1875 *E,* 1876 *E,* 1877 *I, E*
Reid, J M (Edinburgh Acads) 1898 *I, E,* 1899 *I*
Reid, M F (Loretto) 1883 *I, E*
Reid, S J (Boroughmuir) 1995 *WS*
Reid-Kerr, J (Greenock Wand) 1909 *E*
Relph, W K L (Stewart's Coll FP) 1955 *F, W, I, E*
Renny-Tailyour, H W (Royal Engineers) 1872 *E*
Renwick, J M (Hawick) 1972 *F, W, E, NZ,* 1973 *F,* 1974 *W, E, I, F,* 1975 *I, F, W, E, NZ, A,* 1976 *W, E* (R), 1977 *I, F, W,* 1978 *I, F, W, E, NZ,* 1979 *W, E, I, F, NZ,* 1980 *I, F, W, E,* 1981 *F, W, E, I, NZ* 1,2, *R, A,* 1982 *E, I, F, W,* 1983 *I, F, W, E,* 1984 *R*
Renwick, W L (London Scottish) 1989 *R*

Renwick, W N (London Scottish, Edinburgh Wands) 1938 *E,* 1939 *W*
Richardson, J F (Edinburgh Acads) 1994 *SA*
Ritchie, G (Merchistonians) 1871 *E*
Ritchie, G F (Dundee HSFP) 1932 *E*
Ritchie, J M (Watsonians) 1933 *W, E, I,* 1934 *W, I, E*
Ritchie, W T (Cambridge U) 1905 *I, E*
Robb, G H (Glasgow U) 1881 *I,* 1885 *W*
Roberts, G (Watsonians) 1938 *W, I, E,* 1939 *W, E*
Robertson, A H (W of Scotland) 1871 *E*
Robertson, A W (Edinburgh Acads) 1897 *E*
Robertson, D (Edinburgh Acads) 1875 *E*
Robertson, D D (Cambridge U) 1893 *W*
Robertson, I (London Scottish, Watsonians) 1968 *E,* 1969 *E, SA,* 1970 *F, W, I, E, A*
Robertson, I P M (Watsonians) 1910 *F*
Robertson, J (Clydesdale) 1908 *E*
Robertson, K W (Melrose) 1978 *NZ,* 1979 *W, E, I, F, NZ,* 1980 *W, E,* 1981 *F, W, E, I, R, A,* 1982 *E, I, F, A* 1,2, 1983 *I, F, W, E,* 1984 *E, I, F, R, A,* 1985 *I, F, W, E,* 1986 *I,* 1987 *F* (R), *W, E,* [*F, Z, NZ*], 1988 *E, A,* 1989 *E, I, F*
Robertson, L (London Scottish United Services) 1908 *E,* 1911 *W,* 1912 *W, I, E, SA,* 1913 *W, I, E*
Robertson, M A (Gala) 1958 *F*
Robertson, R D (London Scottish) 1912 *F*
Robson, A (Hawick) 1954 *F,* 1955 *F, W, I, E,* 1956 *F, W, I, E,* 1957 *F, W, I, E,* 1958 *W, A, I, E,* 1959 *F, W, I, E,* 1960 *F*
Rodd, J A T (United Services, RN, London Scottish) 1958 *F, W, A, I, E,* 1960 *F, W,* 1962 *F,* 1964 *F, NZ, W,* 1965 *F, W, I*
Rogerson, J (Kelvinside Acads) 1894 *W*
Roland, E T (Edinburgh Acads) 1884 *I, E*
Rollo, D M D (Howe of Fife) 1959 *E,* 1960 *F, W, I, E, SA,* 1961 *F, S, I, E, W,* 1962 *F, W, E,* 1963 *F, W, I, E,* 1964 *F, NZ, W, I, E,* 1965 *F, W, I, E, SA,* 1966 *F, W, I, E, A,* 1967 *F, W, E, NZ,* 1968 *F, W, I*
Rose, D M (Jedforest) 1951 *F, W, I, E, SA,* 1953 *F, W*
Ross, A (Kilmarnock) 1924 *F, W*
Ross, A (Royal HSFP) 1905 *W, I, E,* 1909 *W, I*
Ross, A R (Edinburgh U) 1911 *W,* 1914 *W, I, E*
Ross, E J (London Scottish) 1904 *W*
Ross, G T (Watsonians) 1954 *NZ, I, E, W*
Ross, I A (Hillhead HSFP) 1951 *F, W, I, E*
Ross, J (London Scottish) 1901 *W, I, E,* 1902 *W,* 1903 *E*
Ross, K I (Boroughmuir FP) 1961 *SA, W, I, E,* 1962 *F, W, I, E,* 1963 *F, W, E*
Ross, W A (Hillhead HSFP) 1937 *W, E*
Rottenburg, H (Cambridge U, London Scottish) 1899 *W, E,* 1900 *W, I, E*
Roughead, W N (Edinburgh Acads, London Scottish) 1927 *A,* 1928 *F, W, I, E,* 1930 *I, E,* 1931 *F, W, I, E,* 1932 *W*
Rowan, N A (Boroughmuir) 1980 *W, E,* 1981 *F, W, E, I,* 1984 *R,* 1985 *I,* 1987 [*R*], 1988 *I, F, W, E*
Rowand, R (Glasgow HSFP) 1930 *F, W,* 1932 *E,* 1933 *W, E, I,* 1934 *W*
Roy, A (Waterloo) 1938 *W, I, E,* 1939 *W, I, E*
Russell, W L (Glasgow Acads) 1905 *NZ,* 1906 *W, I, E*
Rutherford, J Y (Selkirk) 1979 *W, E, I, F, NZ,* 1980 *I, F, E,* 1981 *F, W, E, I, NZ* 1,2, *A,* 1982 *E, I, F, W, A* 1,2, 1983 *E, NZ,* 1984 *W, E, I, F, R,* 1985 *I, F, W, E,* 1986 *F, W, E, I, R,* 1987 *I, F, W, E,* [*F*]

Sampson, R W F (London Scottish) 1939 *W,* 1947 *W*
Sanderson, G A (Royal HSFP) 1907 *W, I, E,* 1908 *I*
Sanderson, J L P (Edinburgh Acads) 1873 *E*
Schulze, D G (London Scottish) 1905 *E,* 1907 *I, E,* 1908 *W, I, E,* 1909 *W, I, E,* 1910 *W, I, E,* 1911 *W*
Scobie, R M (Royal Military Coll) 1914 *W, I, E*
Scotland, K J F (Heriot's FP, Cambridge U, Leicester) 1957 *F, W, I, E,* 1958 *E,* 1959 *F, W, I, E,* 1960 *F, W, I, E,* 1961 *F, SA, W, I, E,* 1962 *F, W, I, E,* 1963 *F, W, I, E,* 1965 *F*
Scott, D M (Langholm, Watsonians) 1950 *I, E,* 1951 *W, I, E, SA,* 1952 *F, W, I,* 1953 *F*
Scott, J M B (Edinburgh Acads) 1907 *E,* 1908 *W, I, E,* 1909 *W, I, E,* 1910 *F, W, I, E,* 1911 *F, W, I,* 1912 *W, I, E, SA,* 1913 *W, I, E*
Scott, J S (St Andrew's U) 1950 *E*
Scott, J W (Stewart's Coll FP) 1925 *F, W, I, E,* 1926 *F, W, I, E,* 1927 *F, W, I, E, A,* 1928 *F, W, E,* 1929 *E,* 1930 *F*
Scott, M (Dunfermline) 1992 *A* 2
Scott, R (Hawick) 1898 *I,* 1900 *I, E*
Scott, T (Langholm, Hawick) 1896 *W,* 1897 *I, E,* 1898 *I, E,* 1899 *I, W, E,* 1900 *W, I, E*
Scott, T M (Hawick) 1893 *E,* 1895 *W, I, E,* 1896 *W, E,* 1897 *I, E,* 1898 *I, E,* 1900 *W, I*

Rowen Shepherd beats Olivier Merle, but Philippe Carbonneau is moving in to tackle. Shepherd, of Melrose, won his first cap against Western Samoa, and went on to play in all four of Scotland's Five Nations matches.

231

Scott, W P (W of Scotland) 1900 *I, E*, 1902 *I, E*, 1903 *W, I, E*, 1904 *W, I, E*, 1905 *W, I, E, NZ*, 1906 *W, I, E, SA*, 1907 *W, I, E*
Scoular, J G (Cambridge U) 1905 *NZ*, 1906 *W, I, E, SA*
Selby, J A R (Watsonians) 1920 *W, I*
Shackleton, J A P (London Scottish) 1959 *E*, 1963 *F, W*, 1964 *NZ, W*, 1965 *I, SA*
Sharp, A V (Bristol) 1994 *E, I, F, Arg* 1,2 *SA*
Sharp, G (Stewart's FP, Army) 1960 *F*, 1964 *F, NZ, W*
Shaw, G D (Sale) 1935 *NZ*, 1936 *W*, 1937 *W, I, E*, 1939 *I*
Shaw, I (Glasgow HSFP) 1937 *I*
Shaw, J N (Edinburgh Acads) 1921 *W, I*
Shaw, R W (Glasgow HSFP) 1934 *W, I, E*, 1935 *W, I, E, NZ*, 1936 *W, I, E*, 1937 *W, I, E*, 1938 *W, I, E*, 1939 *W, I, E*
Shedden, D (W of Scotland) 1972 *NZ*, 1973 *F, W, I, E, P*, 1976 *W, E, I*, 1977 *I, F, W*, 1978 *I, F, W*
Shepherd, R J S (Melrose) 1995 *WS*, 1996 *I, F, W, E*
Shiel, A G (Melrose) 1991 [*I* (R), *WS*], 1993 *I, F, W, E, NZ*, 1994 *Arg* 1,2, *SA*, 1995 *R*, [*Iv, F, NZ*], *WS*
Shillinglaw, R B (Gala, Army) 1960 *I, E, SA*, 1961 *F, SA*
Simmers, B M (Glasgow Acads) 1965 *F, W*, 1966 *A*, 1967 *F, W, I*, 1971 *F* (R)
Simmers, W M (Glasgow Acads) 1926 *W, I, E*, 1927 *F, W, I, E, A*, 1928 *F, W, I, E*, 1929 *F, W, I, E*, 1930 *F, W, I, E*, 1931 *F, W, I, E*, 1932 *SA, W, I, E*
Simpson, J W (Royal HSFP) 1893 *I, E*, 1894 *W, I, E*, 1895 *W, I, E*, 1896 *W, I*, 1897 *E*, 1899 *W, E*
Simpson, R S (Glasgow Acads) 1923 *I*
Simson, E D (Edinburgh U, London Scottish) 1902 *E*, 1903 *W, I, E*, 1904 *W, I, E*, 1905 *W, I, E, NZ*, 1906 *W, I, E*, 1907 *W, I, E*
Simson, J T (Watsonians) 1905 *NZ*, 1909 *W, I, E*, 1910 *F, W*, 1911 *I*
Simson, R F (London Scottish) 1911 *E*
Sloan, A T (Edinburgh Acads) 1914 *W*, 1920 *F, W, I, E*, 1921 *F, W, I, E*
Sloan, D A (Edinburgh Acads, London Scottish) 1950 *F, W, E*, 1951 *W, I, E*, 1953 *F*
Sloan, T (Glasgow Acads, Oxford U) 1905 *NZ*, 1906 *W, SA*, 1907 *W, E*, 1908 *W*, 1909 *I*
Smeaton, P W (Edinburgh Acads) 1881 *I*, 1883 *I, E*
Smith, A R (Oxford U) 1895 *W, I, E*, 1896 *W, I*, 1897 *I, E*, 1898 *I, E*, 1900 *I, E*
Smith, A R (Cambridge U, Gosforth, Ebbw Vale, Edinburgh Wands) 1955 *W, I, E*, 1956 *F, W, I, E*, 1957 *F, W, I, E*, 1958 *F, W, A, I*, 1959 *F, W, I, E*, 1960 *F, W, I, E, SA*, 1961 *F, SA, W, I, E*, 1962 *F, W, I, E*
Smith, D W C (London Scottish) 1949 *F, W, I, E*, 1950 *F, W, I*, 1953 *I*
Smith, E R (Edinburgh Acads) 1879 *I*
Smith, G K (Kelso) 1957 *I, E*, 1958 *F, W, A*, 1959 *F, W, I, E*, 1960 *F, W, I, E*, 1961 *F, SA, W, I, E*
Smith, H O (Watsonians) 1895 *W*, 1896 *W, I, E*, 1898 *I, E*, 1899 *W, I, E*, 1900 *E*, 1902 *E*
Smith, I R (Gloucester) 1992 *E, I, W, A* 1,2, 1994 *E* (R), *I, F, Arg* 1,2, 1995 [*Iv*], *WS*, 1996 *I, F, W, E*
Smith, I S (Oxford U, Edinburgh U) 1924 *W, I, E*, 1925 *F, W, I, E*, 1926 *F, W, I, E*, 1927 *F, I, E*, 1929 *F, W, I, E*, 1930 *F, W, I*, 1931 *F, W, I, E*, 1932 *SA, W, I, E*, 1933 *W, E, I*
Smith I S G (London Scottish) 1969 *SA*, 1970 *F, W, I, E*, 1971 *F, W, I*
Smith, M A (London Scottish) 1970 *W, I, E, A*
Smith, R T (Kelso) 1929 *F, W, I, E*, 1930 *F, W, I*
Smith, S H (Glasgow Acads) 1877 *I*, 1878 *E*
Smith, T J (Gala) 1983 *E, NZ*, 1985 *I, F*
Sole, D M B (Bath, Edinburgh Acads) 1986 *F, W*, 1987 *I, F, W, E*, [*F, Z, R, NZ*], 1988 *I, F, W, E, A*, 1989 *W, E, I, F, Fj, R*, 1990 *I, F, W, E, NZ* 1,2, *Arg*, 1991 *F, W, E, I, R*, [*J, I, WS, E, NZ*], 1992 *E, I, F, W, A* 1,2
Somerville, D (Edinburgh Inst FP) 1879 *I*, 1882 *I*, 1883 *W, I, E*, 1884 *W*
Speirs, L M (Watsonians) 1906 *SA*, 1907 *W, I, E*, 1908 *W, I, E*, 1910 *F, W, E*
Spence, K M (Oxford U) 1953 *I*
Spencer, E (Clydesdale) 1898 *I*
Stagg, P K (Sale) 1965 *F, W, E, SA*, 1966 *F, W, I, E, A*, 1967 *F, W, I, E, NZ*, 1968 *F, W, I, E, A*, 1969 *F, W, I* (R), *SA*, 1970 *F, W, I, E, A*
Stanger, A G (Hawick) 1989 *Fj, R*, 1990 *I, F, W, E, NZ* 1,2, *Arg*, 1991 *F, W, E, I, R*, [*J, Z, I, WS, E, NZ*], 1992 *E, I, F, W, A* 1,2, 1993 *I, F, W, E, NZ*, 1994 *W, E, I, F, SA*, 1995 *R*, [*Iv*]
Stark, D A (Boroughmuir) 1993 *I, F, W, E*
Steele, W C C (Langholm, Bedford, RAF, London Scottish) 1969 *E*, 1971 *F, W, I, E* (2[1C]), 1972 *F, W, E, NZ*, 1973 *F, W, I, E*, 1975 *I, F, W, E, NZ* (R), 1976 *W, E, I*, 1977 *E*

Stephen, A E (W of Scotland) 1885 *W*, 1886 *I*
Steven, P D (Heriot's FP) 1984 *A*, 1985 *F, W, E*
Steven, R (Edinburgh Wands) 1962 *I*
Stevenson, A K (Glasgow Acads) 1922 *F*, 1923 *F, W, E*
Stevenson, A M (Glasgow U) 1911 *F*
Stevenson, G D (Hawick) 1956 *E*, 1957 *F*, 1958 *F, W, A, I, E*, 1959 *W, I, E*, 1960 *W, I, E, SA*, 1961 *F, SA, W, I, E*, 1963 *F, W, I*, 1964 *E*, 1965 *F*
Stevenson, H J (Edinburgh Acads) 1888 *W, I*, 1889 *W, I*, 1890 *W, I, E*, 1891 *W, I, E*, 1892 *W, I, E*, 1893 *I, E*
Stevenson, L E (Edinburgh U) 1888 *W*
Stevenson, R C (London Scottish) 1897 *I, E*, 1898 *E*, 1899 *I, W, E*
Stevenson, R C (St Andrew's U) 1910 *F, I, E*, 1911 *F, W, I*
Stevenson, W H (Glasgow Acads) 1925 *F*
Stewart, A K (Edinburgh U) 1874 *E*, 1876 *E*
Stewart, A M (Edinburgh Acads) 1914 *W*
Stewart, C A R (W of Scotland) 1880 *I, E*
Stewart, C E B (Kelso) 1960 *W*, 1961 *F*
Stewart, J (Glasgow HSFP) 1930 *F*
Stewart, J L (Edinburgh Acads) 1921 *I*
Stewart, M S (Stewart's Coll FP) 1932 *SA, W, I*, 1933 *W, E, I*, 1934 *W, I, E*
Stewart, W A (London Hospital) 1913 *F, W, I*, 1914 *W*
Steyn, S S L (Oxford U) 1911 *E*, 1912 *I*
Strachan, G M (Jordanhill) 1971 *E* (C) (R), 1973 *W, I, E, P*
Stronach, R S (Glasgow Acads) 1901 *W, E*, 1905 *W, I, E*
Stuart, C D (W of Scotland) 1909 *I*, 1910 *F, W, I, E*, 1911 *I, E*
Stuart, L M (Glasgow HSFP) 1923 *F, W, I, E*, 1924 *F*, 1928 *E*, 1930 *I, E*
Suddon, N (Hawick) 1965 *W, I, E, SA*, 1966 *A*, 1968 *E, A*, 1969 *F, W, I*, 1970 *I, E, A*
Sutherland, W R (Hawick) 1910 *W, E*, 1911 *F, E*, 1912 *F, W, E, SA*, 1913 *F, W, I, E*, 1914 *W*
Swan, J S (Army, London Scottish, Leicester) 1953 *E*, 1954 *F, NZ, I, E, W*, 1955 *F, W, I, E*, 1956 *F, W, I, E*, 1957 *F, W*, 1958 *F*
Swan, M W (Oxford U, London Scottish) 1958 *F, W, A, I, E*, 1959 *F, W, I*
Sweet, J B (Glasgow HSFP) 1913 *E*, 1914 *I*
Symington, A W (Cambridge U) 1914 *W, E*

Tait, A V (Kelso) 1987 [*F*(R), *Z, R, NZ*], 1988 *I, F, W, E*
Tait, J G (Edinburgh Acads) 1880 *I*, 1885 *I* 2
Tait, P W (Royal HSFP) 1935 *E*
Taylor, E G (Oxford U) 1927 *W, A*
Taylor, R C (Kelvinside-West) 1951 *W, I, E, SA*
Telfer, C M (Hawick) 1968 *A*, 1969 *F, W, I, E*, 1972 *F, W, E*, 1973 *W, I, E, P*, 1974 *W, E, I*, 1975 *A*, 1976 *F*
Telfer, J W (Melrose) 1964 *F, NZ, W, I, E*, 1965 *F, W, I*, 1966 *F, W, I, E*, 1967 *W, I, E*, 1968 *E, A*, 1969 *F, W, I, E, SA*, 1970 *F, W, I*
Tennent, J M (W of Scotland) 1909 *W, I, E*, 1910 *F, W, E*
Thom, D A (London Scottish) 1934 *W*, 1935 *W, I, E, NZ*
Thom, G (Kirkcaldy) 1920 *F, W, I, E*
Thom, J R (Watsonians) 1933 *W, E, I*
Thomson, A E (United Services) 1921 *F, W, E*
Thomson, A M (St Andrew's U) 1949 *I*
Thomson, B E (Oxford U) 1953 *F, W, I*
Thomson, I H M (Heriot's FP, Army) 1951 *W, I*, 1952 *F, W, I*, 1953 *I, E*
Thomson, J S (Glasgow Acads) 1871 *E*
Thomson, R H (London Scottish, PUC) 1960 *I, E, SA*, 1961 *F, SA, W, I, E*, 1963 *F, W, I, E*, 1964 *NZ, W*
Thomson, W H (W of Scotland) 1906 *SA*
Thomson, W J (W of Scotland) 1899 *W, E*, 1900 *W*
Timms, A B (Edinburgh U, Edinburgh Wands) 1896 *W*, 1900 *W, I*, 1901 *W, I, E*, 1902 *W, E*, 1903 *W, E*, 1904 *I, E*, 1905 *I, E*
Tod, H B (Gala) 1911 *F*
Tod, J (Watsonians) 1884 *W, I, E*, 1885 *W, I* 1,2, 1886 *W, I, E*
Todd, J K (Glasgow Acads) 1874 *E*, 1875 *E*
Tolmie, J M (Glasgow HSFP) 1922 *E*
Tomes, A J (Hawick) 1976 *E, I*, 1977 *E, I, F, W, E, NZ*, 1979 *W, E, I, F, NZ*, 1980 *F, W, E*, 1981 *F, W, E, I, NZ* 1,2, *R, A*, 1982 *E, I, F, W, A* 1,2, 1983 *I, F, W*, 1984 *W, E, I, F, R, A*, 1985 *W, E*, 1987 *I, F, E* (R), [*F, Z, R, NZ*]
Torrie, T J (Edinburgh Acads) 1877 *E*
Townsend, G P J (Gala, Northampton) 1993 *E* (R), 1994 *W, E, I, F, Arg* 1,2, 1995 *C, I, F, W, E, WS*, 1996 *I, F, W, E*

Tukalo, I (Selkirk) 1985 *I*, 1987 *I, F, W, E, [F, Z, R, NZ]*, 1988 *F, W, E, A*, 1989 *W, E, I, F, Fj*, 1990 *I, F, W, E, NZ* 1, 1991 *I, R, [J, Z, I, WS, E, NZ]*, 1992 *E, I, F, W, A* 1,2
Turk, A S (Langholm) 1971 *E* (R)
Turnbull, D J (Hawick) 1987 *[NZ]*, 1988 *F, E*, 1990 *E* (R), 1991 *F, W, E, I, R, [Z]*, 1993 *I, F, W, E*, 1994 *W*
Turnbull, F O (Kelso) 1951 *F, SA*
Turnbull, G O (W of Scotland) 1896 *I, E*, 1897 *I, E*, 1904 *W*
Turnbull, P (Edinburgh Acads) 1901 *W, I, E*, 1902 *W, I, E*
Turner, F H (Oxford U, Liverpool) 1911 *F, W, I, E*, 1912 *F, W, I, E, SA*, 1913 *F, W, I, E*, 1914 *I, E*
Turner, J W C (Gala) 1966 *W, A*, 1967 *F, W, I, E, NZ*, 1968 *F, W, I, E, A*, 1969 *F*, 1970 *E, A*, 1971 *F, W, I, E* (2[1C])

Usher, C M (United Services, Edinburgh Wands) 1912 *E*, 1913 *F, W, I, E*, 1914 *E*, 1920 *F, W, I, E*, 1921 *W, E*, 1922 *F, W, I, E*

Valentine, A R (RNAS, Anthorn) 1953 *F, W, I*
Valentine, D D (Hawick) 1947 *I, E*
Veitch, J P (Royal HSFP) 1882 *E*, 1883 *I*, 1884 *W, I, E*, 1885 *I* 1,2, 1886 *E*
Villar, C (Edinburgh Wands) 1876 *E*, 1877 *I, E*

Waddell, G H (London Scottish, Cambridge U) 1957 *E*, 1958 *F, W, A, I, E*, 1959 *F, W, I, E*, 1960 *I, E, SA*, 1961 *F*, 1962 *F, W, I, E*
Waddell, H (Glasgow Acads) 1924 *F, W, I, E*, 1925 *I, E*, 1926 *F, W, I, E*, 1927 *F, W, I, E*, 1930 *W*
Wade, A L (London Scottish) 1908 *E*
Wainwright, R I (Edinburgh Acads, West Hartlepool, Watsonians, Army) 1992 *I* (R), *F, A* 1,2, 1993 *NZ*, 1994 *W, E*, 1995 *C, I, F, W, E, R, [Iv, Tg, F, NZ]*, WS, 1996 *I, F, W, E*
Walker, A (W of Scotland) 1881 *I*, 1882 *E*, 1883 *W, I, E*
Walker, A W (Cambridge U, Birkenhead Park) 1931 *F, W, I, E*, 1932 *I*
Walker, J G (W of Scotland) 1882 *E*, 1883 *W*
Walker, M (Oxford U) 1952 *F*
Wallace, A C (Oxford U) 1923 *F*, 1924 *F, W, E*, 1925 *F, W, I, E*, 1926 *F*
Wallace, W M (Cambridge U) 1913 *E*, 1914 *W, I, E*
Walls, W A (Glasgow Acads) 1882 *E*, 1883 *W, I, E*, 1884 *W, I, E*, 1886 *W, I, E*
Walter, M W (London Scottish) 1906 *I, E, SA*, 1907 *W, I*, 1908 *W, I*, 1910 *I*
Walton, P (Northampton) 1994 *E, I, F, Arg* 1,2, 1995 *[Iv]*
Warren, J R (Glasgow Acads) 1914 *I*
Warren, R C (Glasgow Acads) 1922 *W, I*, 1930 *W, I, E*
Waters, F H (Cambridge U, London Scottish) 1930 *F, W, I, E*, 1932 *SA, W, I*
Waters, J A (Selkirk) 1933 *W, E, I*, 1934 *W, I, E*, 1935 *W, I, E, NZ*, 1936 *W, I, E*, 1937 *W, I, E*
Waters, J B (Cambridge U) 1904 *I, E*
Watherston, J G (Edinburgh Wands) 1934 *I, E*
Watherston, W R A (London Scottish) 1963 *F, W, I*
Watson, D H (Glasgow Acads) 1876 *E*, 1877 *I, E*
Watson, W S (Boroughmuir) 1974 *W, E, I, F*, 1975 *NZ*, 1977 *I, F, W*, 1979 *I, F*
Watt, A G J (Glasgow High Kelvinside) 1991 *[Z]*, 1993 *I*, *NZ*, 1994 *Arg* 2 (t & R)
Watt, A G M (Edinburgh Acads) 1947 *F, W, I, A*, 1948 *F, W*
Weatherstone, T G (Stewart's Coll FP) 1952 *E*, 1953 *I, E*, 1954 *F, NZ, I, E, W*, 1955 *F*, 1958 *W, A, I, E*, 1959 *W, I, E*

Weir, G W (Melrose, Newcastle) 1990 *Arg*, 1991 *R*, *[J, Z, I, WS, E, NZ]*, 1992 *E, I, F, W, A* 1,2, 1993 *I, F, W, E, NZ*, 1994 *W* (R), *E, I, F, SA*, 1995 *F* (R), *W, E, R*, *[Iv, Tg, F, NZ]*, *WS*, 1996 *I, F, W, E*
Welsh, R (Watsonians) 1895 *W, I, E*, 1896 *W*
Welsh, R B (Hawick) 1967 *I, E*
Welsh, W B (Hawick) 1927 *A*, 1928 *F, W, I*, 1929 *I, E*, 1930 *F, W, I, E*, 1931 *F, W, I, E*, 1932 *SA, W, I, E*, 1933 *W, E, I*
Welsh, W H (Edinburgh U) 1900 *I, E*, 1901 *W, I, E*, 1902 *W, I, E*
Wemyss, A (Gala, Edinburgh Wands) 1914 *W, I*, 1920 *F, E*, 1922 *F, W, I, E*
West, L (Edinburgh U, West Hartlepool) 1903 *W, I, E*, 1905 *I, E, NZ*, 1906 *W, I, E*
Weston, V G (Kelvinside Acads) 1936 *I, E*
White, D B (Gala, London Scottish) 1982 *F, W, A* 1,2, 1987 *W, E, [F, R, NZ]*, 1988 *I, F, W, E, A*, 1989 *W, E, I, F, Fj*, *R*, 1990 *I, F, W, E, NZ* 1,2, 1991 *W, E, I, R, [J, Z, I, WS, E, NZ]*, 1992 *E, I, F, W*
White, D M (Kelvinside Acads) 1963 *F, W, I, E*
White, T B (Edinburgh Acads) 1888 *W, I*, 1889 *W*
Whittington, T P (Merchistonians) 1873 *E*
Whitworth, R J E (London Scottish) 1936 *I*
Whyte, D J (Edinburgh Wands) 1965 *W, I, E, SA*, 1966 *F, W, I, E, A*, 1967 *F, W, I, E*
Will, J G (Cambridge U) 1912 *F, W, I, E*, 1914 *W, I, E*
Wilson, A W (Dunfermline) 1931 *F, I, E*
Wilson, G A (Oxford U) 1949 *F, W, E*
Wilson, G R (Royal HSFP) 1886 *E*, 1890 *W, I, E*, 1891 *I*
Wilson, J H (Watsonians) 1953 *I*
Wilson, J S (St Andrew's U) 1931 *F, W, I, E*, 1932 *E*
Wilson, J S (United Services, London Scottish) 1908 *I*, 1909 *W*
Wilson, R (London Scottish) 1976 *E, I*, 1977 *E, I, F*, 1978 *I, F*, 1981 *R*, 1983 *I*
Wilson, R L (Gala) 1951 *F, W, I, E, SA*, 1953 *F, W, E*
Wilson, R W (W of Scotland) 1873 *E*, 1874 *E*
Wilson, S (Oxford U, London Scottish) 1964 *F, NZ, W, I, E*, 1965 *W, I, E, SA*, 1966 *F, W, I, A*, 1967 *W, I, E, NZ*, 1968 *F, W, I, E*
Wood, A (Royal HSFP) 1873 *E*, 1874 *E*, 1875 *E*
Wood, G (Gala) 1931 *W, I*, 1932 *W, I, E*
Woodburn, J C (Kelvinside Acads) 1892 *I*
Woodrow, A N (Glasgow Acads) 1887 *I, W, E*
Wotherspoon, W (W of Scotland) 1891 *I*, 1892 *I*, 1893 *W, E*, 1894 *W, I, E*
Wright, F A (Edinburgh Acads) 1932 *E*
Wright, H B (Watsonians) 1894 *W*
Wright, K M (London Scottish) 1929 *F, W, I, E*
Wright, P H (Boroughmuir) 1992 *A* 1,2, 1993 *F, W, E*, 1994 *W*, 1995 *C, I, F, W, E, R*, *[Iv, Tg, F, NZ]*, 1996 *W, E*
Wright, R W J (Edinburgh Wands) 1973 *F*
Wright, S T H (Stewart's Coll FP) 1949 *E*
Wright, T (Hawick) 1947 *A*
Wyllie, D S (Stewart's-Melville FP) 1984 *A*, 1985 *W* (R), *E*, 1987 *I, F, [F, Z, R, NZ]*, 1989 *R*, 1991 *R*, *[J* (R), *Z]*, 1993 *NZ* (R), 1994 *W* (R), *E, I, F*

Young, A H (Edinburgh Acads) 1874 *E*
Young, E T (Glasgow Acads) 1914 *E*
Young, R G (Watsonians) 1970 *W*
Young, T E B (Durham) 1911 *F*
Young, W B (Cambridge U, London Scottish) 1937 *W, I, E*, 1938 *W, I, E*, 1939 *W, I, E*, 1948 *E*

SCOTTISH INTERNATIONAL RECORDS

Both team and individual records are for official Scotland international matches, up to 30 April 1996.

TEAM RECORDS

Highest score
89 v Ivory Coast (89-0) 1995 Rustenburg

v individual countries
49 v Argentina (49-3) 1990 Murrayfield
24 v Australia (24-15) 1981 Murrayfield
22 v Canada (22-6) 1995 Murrayfield
33 v England (33-6) 1986 Murrayfield
38 v Fiji (38-17) 1989 Murrayfield
31 v France (31-3) 1912 Inverleith
37 v Ireland (37-21) 1989 Murrayfield
89 v Ivory Coast (89-0) 1995 Rustenburg

47 v Japan (47-9) 1991 Murrayfield
30 v N Zealand (30-48) 1995 Pretoria
55 v Romania (55-28) 1987 Dunedin
10 v S Africa { (10-18) 1960 Port Elizabeth
            { (10-34) 1994 Murrayfield
41 v Tonga (41-5) 1995 Pretoria
35 v Wales (35-10) 1924 Inverleith
28 v W Samoa (28-6) 1991 Murrayfield
60 v Zimbabwe (60-21) 1987 Wellington

Biggest winning points margin
89 v Ivory Coast (89-0) 1995 Rustenburg

v individual countries
46 v Argentina (49-3) 1990 Murrayfield
 9 v Australia (24-15) 1981 Murrayfield
16 v Canada (22-6) 1995 Murrayfield
27 v England (33-6) 1986 Murrayfield
21 v Fiji (38-17) 1989 Murrayfield
28 v France (31-3) 1912 Inverleith
23 v Ireland (32-9) 1984 Dublin
89 v Ivory Coast (89-0) 1995 Rustenburg
38 v Japan (47-9) 1991 Murrayfield
No win v N Zealand
33 v Romania (49-16) 1995 Murrayfield
 6 v S Africa (6-0) 1906 Glasgow
36 v Tonga (41-5) 1995 Pretoria
25 v Wales (35-10) 1924 Inverleith
22 v W Samoa (28-6) 1991 Murrayfield
39 v Zimbabwe { (60-21) 1987 Wellington
             { (51-12) 1991 Murrayfield

Longest winning sequence
6 matches – 1925-26 and 1989-90

Highest score by opposing team
51 N Zealand (15-51) 1993 Murrayfield

by individual countries
19 Argentina (17-19) 1994 Buenos Aires
37 Australia { (12-37) 1984 Murrayfield
            { (13-37) 1992 Brisbane
 6 Canada (22-6) 1995 Murrayfield
30 England (18-30) 1980 Murrayfield
17 Fiji (38-17) 1989 Murrayfield
28 France (22-28) 1987 Parc des Princes
26 Ireland (8-26) 1953 Murrayfield
 0 Ivory Coast (89-0) 1995 Rustenburg
 9 Japan (47-9) 1991 Murrayfield
51 N Zealand (15-51) 1993 Murrayfield
28 Romania { (22-28) 1984 Bucharest
           { (55-28) 1987 Dunedin
44 S Africa (0-44) 1951 Murrayfield
 5 Tonga (41-5) 1995 Pretoria
35 Wales (12-35) 1972 Cardiff
15 W Samoa (15-15) 1995 Murrayfield
21 Zimbabwe (60-21) 1987 Wellington

Biggest losing points margin
44 v S Africa (0-44) 1951 Murrayfield

234

v individual countries
 2 v Argentina (17-19) 1994 Buenos Aires
25 v Australia (12-37) 1984 Murrayfield
20 v England (6-26) 1977 Twickenham
20 v France (3-23) 1977 Parc des Princes
21 v Ireland (0-21) 1950 Dublin
36 v N Zealand (15-51) 1993 Murrayfield
 6 v Romania { (22-28) 1984 Bucharest
            { (12-18) 1991 Bucharest
44 v S Africa (0-44) 1951 Murrayfield
23 v Wales { (12-35) 1972 Cardiff
           { (6-29) 1994 Cardiff
*No defeats v Canada, Fiji, Ivory Coast, Japan, Tonga,
Western Samoa or Zimbabwe*

Longest losing sequence
17 matches – 1951-55

**Most tries by Scotland in an
international**
13 v Ivory Coast (89-0) 1995 Rustenburg

**Most tries against Scotland in an
international**
9 by S Africa (0-44) 1951 Murrayfield

**Most points by Scotland in
International Championship in a
season – 87**
in season 1994-95

**Most tries by Scotland in
International Championship in a
season – 17**
in season 1924-25

INDIVIDUAL RECORDS

Most capped player
A G Hastings   61   1986-95
S Hastings   61   1986-96
in individual positions
Full-back
A G Hastings   56   1986-95
Wing
I Tukalo   37[1]   1985-92
Centre
S Hastings   59(61)[2]   1986-96
Fly-half
C M Chalmers   46(47)[3]   1989-95
Scrum-half
R J Laidlaw   47   1980-88
Prop
A B Carmichael   50   1967-78
Hooker
C T Deans   52   1978-87
Lock
A J Tomes   48   1976-87

Flanker
J Jeffrey   40   1984-91
No 8
D B White   29(41)[4]   1982-92
[1] *A G Stanger, 38 caps, won 36 as a wing and 2 in the centre*
[2] *S Hastings won 1 cap as a wing and 1 as a replacement full-back*
[3] *C M Chalmers won 1 cap as a replacement wing*
[4] *White won 5 caps as a flanker and 7 as a lock*

Longest international career
W C W Murdoch 14 seasons 1935-48

Most consecutive internationals – 49
A B Carmichael 1967-78

Most internationals as captain – 25
D M B Sole 1989-92

Most points in internationals – 667
A G Hastings (61 matches) 1986-95

Most points in International Championship in a season – 56
A G Hastings (4 matches) 1994-95

Most points in an international – 44
A G Hastings v Ivory Coast 1995 Rustenburg

Most tries in internationals – 24
I S Smith (32 matches) 1924-33

Most tries in International Championship in a season – 8
I S Smith (4 matches) 1924-25

Most tries in an international – 5
G C Lindsay v Wales 1887 Raeburn Place (Edinburgh)

Most conversions in internationals – 86
A G Hastings (61 matches) 1986-95

Most conversions in International Championship in a season – 8
P W Dods (4 matches) 1983-84

Most conversions in an international – 9
A G Hastings v Ivory Coast 1995 Rustenburg

Most dropped goals in internationals – 12
J Y Rutherford (42 matches) 1979-87

Most dropped goals in an international – 2
R C MacKenzie v Ireland 1877 Belfast
N J Finlay v Ireland 1880 Glasgow
B M Simmers v Wales 1965 Murrayfield
D W Morgan v Ireland 1973 Murrayfield
B M Gossman v France 1983 Paris
J Y Rutherford v N Zealand 1983 Murrayfield
J Y Rutherford v Wales 1985 Murrayfield
J Y Rutherford v Ireland 1987 Murrayfield
C M Chalmers v England 1995 Twickenham

Most penalty goals in internationals – 140
A G Hastings (61 matches) 1986-95

Most penalty goals in International Championship in a season – 14
A G Hastings (4 matches) 1985-86

Most penalty goals in an international – 8
A G Hastings v Tonga 1995 Pretoria

Most points on major tour – 58
P W Dods (4 matches) N Zealand 1990
C D R Mair scored 100 points in the Far East in 1977, but this was not on a major tour

---

Most points in a tour match – 24
D W Morgan v Wellington 1975 Wellington, NZ
A R Irvine v King Country 1981 Taumarunui, NZ
A R Irvine v Wairarapa-Bush 1981 Masterton, NZ
P W Dods scored 43 points v Alberta in 1985, but this was not on a major tour

---

Most tries in a tour match – 3
A R Smith v Eastern Transvaal 1960 Springs, SA
K R F Bearne scored 5 tries v Ontario U in 1964, A J W Hinshelwood scored 5 v Quebec in 1964, and D E W Leckie scored 5 v Goshawks (Zimbabwe) in 1988, but these were not on a major tour

IRISH RUGBY SOLID AT HEART

THE 1995-96 SEASON IN IRELAND
Sean Diffley *Irish Independent*

Whatever else occurred in this creaky season of transition from amateurism to professionalism, the Irish did somewhat better in the Five Nations than they had in the previous year. This statement may be perceived as a mild classic of the clutching-at-straws variety; certainly, Ireland started badly. Scotland rocked them to their heels and they were devastated in Paris. Here we go again, we thought. But in their other match at Lansdowne Road the Irish scored 30 points, their highest-ever score against Wales in some 110 years of confrontation. In fact, Ireland had a clean sweep over the Welsh last season, winning at A level, under-21 and schools as well.

And though beaten by the sheer bulk of England, the senior Irish side did emerge with some credit. Indeed, had the opposition emulated their ancestor, William Webb Ellis, to even the slightest degree and run with the ball, Ireland could even have stolen it. So the season ended on a hopeful note. New coach Murray Kidd, from New Zealand, felt that he had talent to work with and that by the time of the next World Cup, he will have a mature side capable of giving a good account of itself. The 70-38 defeat by the Barbarians in the Peace International will have given Kidd something to chew over.

There are only 14,000 officially confirmed adult players in Ireland, which poses obvious problems against the bigger countries with greater resources of *avoirdupois* and height. But at a lower level Ireland's returns in recent times have been quite good: triple crowns at schools and under-21s this season and victories over Scotland and Wales at A level. So, at heart, the game is solid in Ireland, although the threat of so many bulging purses in English clubs enticing the best Irish players across the Channel has left the domestic game feeling desperately insecure. In a bid to counteract the menace the IRFU are putting more than 40 players on contract, and this paid pool could earn a minimum of £30,000 per annum. Twenty-five or so will be members of the national squad, and, with bonuses and match fees, a home-based international player could earn a basic of £45,000.

Those who play their club rugby away from home – even the Simon Geoghegans and Jim Staples – are not included (the feeling in the IRFU is that they will be well paid by their clubs), though they will, of course, qualify for international match fees and bonuses.

Leinster, who have not won the Irish Inter-Provincial Championship for more than a decade, since the days of Mick Doyle's coaching, took provincial honours. They were supreme last season: they had ten victories before going under to Cardiff in the Heineken European

The Ireland team which met England at Twickenham. L–R, back row: N K P J Woods, S P Geoghegan, P S Wallace, G M Fulcher, J W Davidson, V C P Costello, D S Corkery, S J P Mason, J C Bell, D G Humphreys; front row: N J Popplewell, W D McBride, N A Hogan (capt), A T H Clarke, M J Field.

Cup. In quick succession they beat South African touring sides Natal Duikers, Griqualand West and Transvaal. A narrow win over Swansea was followed by a clean sweep through the Irish teams – the Irish Exiles, Connacht, reigning champions Munster and finally a record score over Ulster. Then came wins in the European competition over Milan and Pontypridd, and to round off a most exciting semi-final at Lansdowne Road and the defeat by Cardiff.

Yet the most incredible story to emerge from Irish rugby in 1995-96 was that of Limerick, who remain the dominant area in club rugby. In its first year, the Insurance Corporation All-Ireland League was won by Cork Constitution. After that, the city of Limerick took over: first came Garryowen, then Young Munster, then Garryowen again, then Shannon. This season Shannon won the League again, the first club to take the title back to back. Dublin, with its bigger rugby population and 15 senior clubs, has never won the All-Ireland, nor has any Ulster side really challenged for it.

In the coming season, Limerick City, population approximately 70,000, will boast four clubs in the First Division of the League: Shannon, the champions; Young Munster, Garryowen and Old Crescent, who have won promotion to the top division. And it was Young Munster's defeat of Garryowen which deprived their neighbours of a fourth title on the last Saturday of April in what was effectively a private Limerick championship rather than an All-Ireland one. What is it that makes the clubs outside Limerick almost irrelevant? Is it because rugby in Limerick is played in a classless rugby society, comparable to that of a typical Welsh town? More to the point, is there any club out there capable of putting a stop to the Limerick monopoly?

INSURANCE CORPORATION ALL-IRELAND LEAGUE 1995-96

Division 1	P	W	D	L	F	A	Pts
Shannon	10	8	0	2	156	78	16
Garryowen	10	8	0	2	171	165	16
Cork Const	10	7	0	3	208	149	14
Young Munster	10	7	0	3	170	127	14
St Mary's Coll	10	5	1	4	147	119	11
Lansdowne	10	4	1	5	180	172	9
Ballymena	10	4	1	5	157	181	9
Old Wesley	10	3	1	6	156	164	7
Blackrock Coll	10	3	0	7	160	208	6
Old Belvedere	10	3	0	7	135	189	6
Instonians	10	1	0	9	145	233	2

Division 2	P	W	D	L	F	A	Pts
Old Crescent	10	9	1	0	246	103	19
Dungannon	10	7	1	2	254	171	15
Terenure Coll	10	7	1	2	191	118	15
Bective Rangers	10	6	0	4	186	147	12
Greystones	10	5	1	4	164	173	11
Sunday's Well	10	4	2	4	223	194	10
Malone	10	5	0	5	205	220	10
Wanderers	10	4	0	6	167	206	8

	P	W	D	L	F	A	Pts
Clontarf	10	3	0	7	130	212	6
Dolphin	10	1	0	9	165	245	2
NIFC	10	1	0	9	157	299	2

Division 3	P	W	D	L	F	A	Pts
Monkstown	11	9	1	1	186	137	19
City of Derry	11	8	1	2	169	117	17
Highfield	11	6	3	2	182	163	15
DLS Palmerston	11	6	1	4	177	108	13
Skerries	11	5	3	3	169	153	13
UC, Cork	11	5	2	4	211	130	12
Bohemians	11	5	1	5	139	149	11
Buccaneers	11	4	1	6	148	129	9
Waterpark	11	3	2	6	121	252	8
Bangor	11	3	0	8	153	185	6
UC, Dublin	11	3	0	8	145	197	6
Galwegians	11	1	1	9	127	207	3

Division 4	P	W	D	L	F	A	Pts
Portadown	9	8	0	1	211	81	16
Dublin U	9	7	0	2	254	105	14
Collegians	9	7	0	2	183	101	14

Queens U	9	6	0	3	176	92	12	Ballina	9	2	1	6	129 178	4
Galway Corin	9	6	0	3	127	81	12	Sligo	9	1	1	7	79 211	3
CIYMS	9	3	0	6	145	203	6	City of Armagh	9	1	0	8	86 233	2
Ards	9	3	0	6	139	244	6							

No relegation from Divisions 1, 2 or 3. Six teams promoted from Division 3. Four provincial junior sides have accepted invitations to join Division 4. They are Suttonians (Leinster), Ballynahinch (Ulster), Richmond (Munster) and Creggs (Connacht).

SMITHWICK'S INTER-PROVINCIAL TOURNAMENT 1995

25 November, Ravenhill, Belfast

Ulster 14 (3PG 1T) **Munster 10** (1G 1PG)
Ulster: J Bell (Northampton); J Topping (Ballymena), M Field (Malone), B Harbinson (Malone), J Cunningham (Dublin U); M McCall (Bangor), N Doak (NIFC); R Mackey (Malone), A Clarke (Northampton), G Leslie (Dungannon), J Davidson (Dungannon), D Tweed (Ballymena), S Duncan (Malone), P Johns (Dungannon), D McBride (Malone)
Scorers *Try:* Mackey *Penalty Goals:* McCall (3)
Munster: P Murray (Shannon); R Wallace (Garryowen), R Walsh (Cork Const), S McCahill (Sunday's Well), K Smith (Garryowen); P Burke (Cork Const), D O'Mahony (Cork Const); J Fitzgerald (Young Munster), P Cunningham (Garryowen), P Clohessy (Young Munster), G Fulcher (Cork Const), P O'Connor (Lansdowne), M Galwey (Shannon), A Foley (Shannon), D Corkery (Terenure Coll)
Scorers *Try:* Walsh *Conversion:* Smith *Penalty Goal:* Smith
Referee A Lewis

25 November, Sunbury, London

Exiles 28 (1G 2PG 3T) **Connacht 22** (1G 5PG)
Exiles: J Staples (Harlequins); M Corcoran (London Irish), R Henderson (London Irish), P Flood (London Irish), S Geoghegan (Bath); N Malone (Leicester), C Saverimutto (Sale); N Donovan (Clontarf), D Addleton (Coventry), G Halpin (London Irish), J Etheridge (Northampton), S Smith (Rugby), J Green (Saracens), D O'Grady (Sale), D Adams (Racing)
Scorers *Tries:* Staples (2), Henderson, Halpin *Conversion:* Corcoran *Penalty Goals:* Corcoran (2)
Connacht: A White (Corinthians); M Devine (Buccaneers), R Corrigan (Lansdowne), B Carey (UCD), M O'Reilly (Old Belvedere); E Elwood (Lansdowne), D Reddan (Old Crescent); D Kavanagh (Blackrock Coll), W Mulcahy (Skerries), C Shanley (DLSP), G Heaslip (Galwegians), J O'Callaghan (Wanderers), R Rogers (Blackrock Coll), K Devlin (St Mary's Coll), N Mannion (Buccaneers)
Scorers *Try:* Mannion *Conversion:* Elwood *Penalty Goals:* Elwood (5)
Referee L Mayne

2 December, Sportsground, Galway

Ulster 27 (1G 5PG 1T) **Connacht 9** (3PG)
Ulster: J Bell (Northampton); J Topping (Ballymena), M Field (Malone), B Harbinson (Malone), J Cunningham (Dublin U); M McCall (Bangor), N Doak (NIFC); R Mackey (Malone), A Clarke (Northampton), G Leslie (Dungannon), J Davidson (Dungannon), D Tweed (Ballymena), S Duncan (Malone), P Johns (Dungannon), D McBride (Malone)
Scorers *Tries:* Topping, Field *Conversion:* McCall *Penalty Goals:* McCall (5)
Connacht: P Boland (Young Munster); M Devine (Buccaneers), R Corrigan (Lansdowne), B Carey (UCD), M O'Reilly (Old Belvedere); E Elwood (Lansdowne), D Reddan (Old Crescent); D Kavanagh (Blackrock Coll), W Mulcahy (Skerries), C Shanley (DLSP), G Heaslip (Galwegians), J O'Callaghan (Wanderers), R Rogers (Blackrock Coll), N Mannion (Buccaneers), K Devlin (St Mary's Coll)
Scorer *Penalty Goals:* Elwood (3)
Referee D McHugh

2 December, Sale

Leinster 42 (3G 2PG 3T) **Exiles 26** (3G 1T)
Leinster: C O'Shea (London Irish); P Gavin (Old Belvedere), V Cunningham (St Mary's Coll), K McQuilkin (Bective Rangers), N Woods (Blackrock Coll); A McGowan (Blackrock Coll), A Rolland (Blackrock Coll); H Hurley (Old Wesley), S Byrne (Blackrock Coll), P Wallace (Blackrock Coll), B Rigney (Shannon), N Francis (Old Belvedere), C Pim (Old Wesley), V Costello (St Mary's Coll), S Rooney (Lansdowne) *Replacements* C Clarke (Terenure Coll) for McQuilkin; N Hogan (Terenure Coll) for Rolland
Scorers *Tries:* McQuilkin (3), Costello, O'Shea, Gavin *Conversions:* McGowan (3) *Penalty Goals:* O'Shea, McGowan
Exiles: S Mason (Orrell); M Corcoran (London Irish), R Henderson (London Irish), P Flood (London Irish), J Staples (Harlequins); N Malone (Leicester), C Saverimutto (Sale); N Donovan (Clontarf), D Addleton

(Coventry), G Halpin (London Irish), J Etheridge (Northampton), S Smith (Rugby), J Green (Saracens), D Adams (Racing), D O'Grady (Sale) *Replacement* B Walsh (London Irish) for O'Grady
Scorers *Tries:* Henderson, Saverimutto, Corcoran, Malone *Conversions:* Corcoran (3)
Referee J Cole

9 December, Donnybrook

Leinster 41 (3G 5PG 1T) **Connacht 9** (3PG)
Leinster: C O'Shea (London Irish); P Gavin (Old Belvedere), V Cunningham (St Mary's Coll), K McQuilkin (Bective Rangers), N Woods (Blackrock Coll); A McGowan (Blackrock Coll), N Hogan (Terenure Coll); P Flavin (Blackrock Coll), S Byrne (Blackrock Coll), P Wallace (Blackrock Coll), M O'Kelly (St Mary's Coll), N Francis (Old Belvedere), C Pim (Old Wesley), V Costello (St Mary's Coll), E Miller (Leicester)
Scorers *Tries:* C O'Shea (2), Hogan, Gavin *Conversions:* McGowan (3) *Penalty Goals:* McGowan (4), O'Shea
Connacht: P Boland (Young Munster); M Devine (Buccaneers), R Corrigan (Lansdowne), B Carey (UCD), M O'Reilly (Old Belvedere); E Elwood (Lansdowne), D Reddan (Old Crescent); D Kavanagh (Blackrock Coll), W Mulcahy (Skerries), C Shanley (DLSP), G Heaslip (Galwegians), J O'Callaghan (Wanderers), R Rogers (Blackrock Coll), N Mannion (Buccaneers), K Devlin (St Mary's Coll) *Replacements* M Murphy (Galwegians) for Carey; D Henshaw (Buccaneers) for Kavanagh
Scorer *Penalty Goals:* Elwood (3)
Referee B Smith

9 December, Musgrave Park, Cork

Munster 20 (2G 1PG 1DG) **Exiles 14** (2G)
Munster: S McCahill (Sunday's Well); R Wallace (Garryowen), B Walsh (Cork Const), P Murray (Shannon), J Lacey (Sunday's Well); P Burke (Cork Const), P McIvor (Garryowen); P Spain (Garryowen), P Cunningham (Garryowen), P Clohessy (Young Munster), G Fulcher (Cork Const), M Galwey (Shannon), D Corkery (Terenure Coll), B Toland (Old Crescent), L Toland (Old Crescent) *Replacements* D Crotty (UCC) for Lacey; S Tuohy (Old Crescent) for Burke
Scorers *Tries:* L Toland (2) *Conversions:* Burke (2) *Penalty Goal:* Burke *Dropped Goal:* Tuohy
Exiles: J Staples (Harlequins); M Corcoran (London Irish), N Malone (Leicester), C Saverimutto (Sale); N Donovan (Clontarf), D Addleton (Coventry), C Boyd (Currie); J Etheridge (Northampton), S Smith (Rugby), J Green (Saracens), B Walsh (London Irish), D Adams (Racing)
Scorers *Tries:* Henderson, Malone *Conversions:* Corcoran (2)
Referee B Stirling

16 December, Ravenhill

Ulster 29 (1G 4PG 2T) **Exiles 3** (1PG)
Ulster: J Bell (Northampton); J Topping (Ballymena), B Harbinson (Malone), M Field (Malone), J Cunningham (Dublin U); M McCall (Bangor), A Matchett (Ballymena); R Mackey (Malone), A Clarke (Northampton), G Leslie (Dungannon), D Tweed (Ballymena), J Davidson (Dungannon), S Duncan (Malone), P Johns (Dungannon), D McBride (Malone) *Replacement* S Booth (Ballymena) for Mackey
Scorers *Tries:* Cunningham, Tweed, Harbinson *Conversion:* McCall *Penalty Goals:* McCall (4)
Exiles: J Staples (Harlequins); M Corcoran (London Irish), R Henderson (London Irish), P Flood (London Irish), J Gallagher (Harlequins); N Malone (Leicester), C Saverimutto (Sale); G Halpin (London Irish), D Addleton (Coventry), C Boyd (Currie), J Etheridge (Northampton), S Smith (Rugby), J Green (Saracens), B Walsh (London Irish), D Adams (Racing) *Replacements* B Wellens (Liverpool St Helens) for Flood; S Mason (Orrell) for Staples; R Saverimutto (Coventry) for Saverimutto; D O'Grady (Sale) for Green
Scorer *Penalty Goal:* Corcoran
Referee R McDowell

16 December, Thomond Park, Limerick

Leinster 19 (1G 4PG) **Munster 15** (1G 1PG 1T)
Leinster: C O'Shea (London Irish); P Gavin (Old Belvedere), V Cunningham (St Mary's Coll), K McQuilkin (Bective Rangers), N Woods (Blackrock Coll); A McGowan (Blackrock Coll), A Rolland (Blackrock Coll); H Hurley (Old Wesley), S Byrne (Blackrock Coll), P Wallace (Blackrock Coll), S Jameson (St Mary's Coll), N Francis (Old Belvedere), C Pim (Old Wesley), V Costello (St Mary's Coll), S Rooney (Lansdowne)
Scorers *Tries:* Rolland *Conversion:* McGowan *Penalty Goals:* McGowan (4)
Munster: P Murray (Shannon); R Wallace (Garryowen), B Walsh (Cork Const), S McCahill (Sunday's Well), D Crotty (UCC); P Burke (Cork Const), S McIvor (Garryowen); P McCarthy (Cork Const), P Cunningham (Garryowen), P Clohessy (Young Munster), M Galwey (Shannon), G Fulcher (Cork Const), D Corkery (Terenure Coll), B Toland (Old Crescent), L Toland (Old Crescent)
Scorers *Tries:* Wallace (2) *Conversion:* Murray *Penalty Goal:* Burke
Referee A Watson

23 December, Donnybrook

Leinster 31 (2G 4PG 1T) **Ulster 3** (1PG)
Leinster: C O'Shea (London Irish); P Gavin (Old Belvedere), V Cunningham (St Mary's Coll), K McQuilkin (Bective Rangers), N Woods (Blackrock Coll); A McGowan (Blackrock Coll), A Rolland (Blackrock Coll); H Hurley (Old Wesley), S Byrne (Blackrock Coll), P Wallace (Blackrock Coll), S Jameson (St Mary's Coll), N Francis (Old Belvedere), C Pim (Old Wesley), V Costello (St Mary's Coll), S Rooney (Lansdowne) *Replacement* C Clarke (Terenure Coll) for Woods
Scorers *Tries:* Wallace, Jameson, Gavin *Conversions:* McGowan (2) *Penalty Goals:* McGowan (4)
Ulster: J Bell (Northampton); J Topping (Ballymena), B Harbinson (Malone), M Field (Malone), J Cunningham (Dublin U); M McCall (Bangor), A Matchett (Ballymena); R Mackey (Malone), A Clarke (Northampton), G Leslie (Dungannon), D Tweed (Ballymena), J Davidson (Dungannon), S Duncan (Malone), P Johns (Dungannon), D McBride (Malone)
Scorer *Penalty Goal:* McCall
Referee C White (RFU)

23 December, Sportsground, Galway

Munster 46 (5G 2PG 1T) **Connacht 11** (2PG 1T)
Munster: D Crotty (UCC); R Wallace (Garryowen), B Walsh (Cork Const), S McCahill (Sunday's Well), K Smith (Garryowen); P Burke (Cork Const), S McIvor (Garryowen); P Spain (Garryowen), P Cunningham (Garryowen), P Clohessy (Young Munster), M Galwey (Shannon), G Fulcher (Cork Const), D Clohessy (Young Munster), L Toland (Old Crescent), B Toland (Old Crescent) *Replacements* F Aherne (Lansdowne) for McIvor; C Twomey (Cork Const) for Cunningham; S Tuohy (Old Crescent) for Burke
Scorers *Tries:* McIvor, P Clohessy, D Clohessy, Crotty, Walsh, L Toland *Conversions:* Smith (5) *Penalty Goals:* Smith (2)
Connacht: A White (Buccaneers); N Carolan (Buccaneers), B Carey (UCD), R Corrigan (Lansdowne), M O'Reilly (Old Belvedere); E Elwood (Lansdowne), D Reddan (Old Crescent); D Kavanagh (Blackrock Coll), W Mulcahy (Skerries), C Shanley (DLSP), G Heaslip (Galwegians), J O'Callaghan (Wanderers), R Rogers (Blackrock Coll), K Devlin (St Mary's Coll), N Mannion (Buccaneers) *Replacement* M Murphy (Galwegians) for Carey
Scorers *Try:* Heaslip *Penalty Goals:* Elwood (2)
Referee A Lewis

FINAL TABLE

	P	W	D	L	F	A	Pts
Leinster	4	4	0	0	133	53	8
Ulster	4	3	0	1	73	53	6
Munster	4	2	0	2	91	58	4
Exiles	4	1	0	3	71	113	2
Connacht	4	0	0	4	51	132	0

IRISH INTERNATIONAL PLAYERS
(*up to 30 April 1996*)

ABBREVIATIONS

A – Australia; *Arg* – Argentina; *C* – Canada; *E* – England; *Fj* – Fiji; *F* – France; *It* – Italy; *J* – Japan; *M* – Maoris; *Nm* – Namibia; *NZ* – New Zealand; *R* – Romania; *S* – Scotland; *SA* – South Africa; *Tg* – Tonga; *US* – United States; *W* – Wales; *WS* – Western Samoa; *Z* – Zimbabwe; *P* – Ireland v IRFU President's XV at Lansdowne Road in IRFU centenary season, 1974-75; (R) – Replacement; (t) – temporary replacement. Entries in square brackets [ ] indicate appearances in the World Cup. NIFC – North of Ireland Football Club, CIYMS – Church of Ireland Young Men's Society; KCH – King's College Hospital

Note: Years given for Five Nations' matches are for second half of season; eg 1972 means season 1971-72. Years for all other matches refer to the actual year of the match. When a series has taken place, figures have been used to denote the particular matches in which players have featured. Thus 1981 *SA* 2 indicates that a player appeared in the second Test of the series. The abandoned game with Scotland at Belfast in 1885 is now included as a cap match.

NB – The second of Ireland's two matches against France in 1972 was a non-championship match.

Abraham, M (Bective Rangers) 1912 *E, S, W, SA*, 1914 *W*

Adams, C (Old Wesley) 1908 *E*, 1909 *E, F*, 1910 *F*, 1911 *E, S, W, F*, 1912 *S, W, SA*, 1913 *W, F*, 1914 *F, E, S*

Agar, R D (Malone) 1947 *F, E, S, W*, 1948 *F*, 1949 *S, W*, 1950 *F, E, W*

Agnew, P J (CIYMS) 1974 *F* (R), 1976 *A*

Ahearne, T (Queen's Coll, Cork) 1899 *E*

Aherne, L F P (Dolphin, Lansdowne) 1988 *E* 2, *WS, It*, 1989 *F, W, E, S, NZ*, 1990 *E, S, F, W* (R), 1992 *E, S, F, A*

Alexander, R (NIFC, Police Union) 1936 *E, S, W*, 1937 *E, S, W*, 1938 *E, S*, 1939 *E, S, W*

Allen, C E (Derry, Liverpool) 1900 *E, S, W*, 1901 *E, S, W*, 1903 *S, W*, 1904 *E, S, W*, 1905 *E, S, W, NZ*, 1906 *E, S, W, SA*, 1907 *S, W*

Allen, G G (Derry, Liverpool) 1896 *E, S, W*, 1897 *E, S*, 1898 *E, S*, 1899 *E, W*

Allen, T C (NIFC) 1885 *E, S* 1

Allen, W S (Wanderers) 1875 *E*

Allison, J B (Edinburgh U) 1899 *E, S*, 1900 *E, S, W*, 1901 *E, S, W*, 1902 *E, S, W*, 1903 *S*

Anderson, F E (Queen's U, Belfast, NIFC) 1953 *F, E, S, W*, 1954 *NZ, F, E, S, W*, 1955 *F, E, S, W*

Anderson, H J (Old Wesley) 1903 *E, S*, 1906 *E, S*

Anderson, W A (Dungannon) 1984 *A*, 1985 *S, F, W, E*, 1986 *F, S, R*, 1987 *E, S, F, W*, [*W, C, Tg, A*], 1988 *S, F, W, E* 1,2, 1989 *F, W, E, NZ*, 1990 *E, S*

Andrews, G (NIFC) 1875 *E*, 1876 *E*

Andrews, H W (NIFC) 1888 *M*, 1889 *S, W*

Archer, A M (Dublin U, NIFC) 1879 *S*

Arigho, J E (Lansdowne) 1928 *F, E, W*, 1929 *F, E, S, W*, 1930 *F, E, S, W*, 1931 *F, E, S, W, SA*

Armstrong, W K (NIFC) 1960 *SA*, 1961 *E*

Arnott, D T (Lansdowne) 1876 *E*

Ash, W H (NIFC) 1875 *E*, 1876 *E*, 1877 *S*

Aston, H R (Dublin U) 1908 *E, W*

Atkins, A P (Bective Rangers) 1924 *F*

Atkinson, J M (NIFC) 1927 *F, A*

Atkinson, J R (Dublin U) 1882 *W, S*

Bagot, J C (Dublin U, Lansdowne) 1879 *S, E*, 1880 *E, S*, 1881 *S*

Bailey, A H (UC Dublin, Lansdowne) 1934 *W*, 1935 *E, S, W, NZ*, 1936 *E, S, W*, 1937 *E, S, W*, 1938 *E, S*

Bailey, N (Northampton) 1952 *E*

Bardon, M E (Bohemians) 1934 *E*

Barlow, M (Wanderers) 1875 *E*

Barnes, R J (Dublin U, Armagh) 1933 *W*

Barr, A (Methodist Coll, Belfast) 1898 *W*, 1899 *S*, 1901 *E, S*

Barry, N J (Garryowen) 1991 *Nm* 2 (R)

Beamish, C E St J (RAF, Leicester) 1933 *W, S*, 1934 *S, W*, 1935 *E, S, W, NZ*, 1936 *E, S, W*, 1938 *W*

Beamish, G R (RAF, Leicester) 1925 *E, S, W*, 1928 *F, E, S, W*, 1929 *F, E, S, W*, 1930 *F, S, W*, 1931 *F, E, S, W, SA*, 1932 *E, S, W*, 1933 *E, W, S*

Beatty, W J (NIFC, Richmond) 1910 *F*, 1912 *F, W*

Becker, V A (Lansdowne) 1974 *F, W*

Beckett, G G P (Dublin U) 1908 *E, S, W*

Bell, J C (Ballymena, Northampton) 1994 *A* 1,2, *US*, 1995 *S, It*, [*NZ, W, F*], *Fj*, 1996 *US, S, F, W, E*

Bell, R J (NIFC) 1875 *E*, 1876 *E*

Bell, W E (Belfast Collegians) 1953 *F, E, S, W*

Bennett, F (Belfast Collegians) 1913 *S*

Bent, G C (Dublin U) 1882 *W, E*

Berkery, P J (Lansdowne) 1954 *W*, 1955 *W*, 1956 *S, W*, 1957 *F, E, S, W*, 1958 *A, E, S*

Bermingham, J J C (Blackrock Coll) 1921 *E, S, W, F*

Blackham, J C (Queen's Coll, Cork) 1909 *S, W, F*, 1910 *E, S, W*

Blake-Knox, S E F (NIFC) 1976 *E, S*, 1977 *F* (R)

Blayney, J J (Wanderers) 1950 *S*

Bond, A T W (Derry) 1894 *S, W*

Bornemann, W W (Wanderers) 1960 *E, S, W, SA*

Bowen, D St J (Cork Const) 1977 *W, E, S*

Boyd, C A (Dublin U) 1900 *S*, 1901 *S, W*

Boyle, C V (Dublin U) 1935 *NZ*, 1936 *E, S, W*, 1937 *E, S, W*, 1938 *W*, 1939 *W*

Brabazon, H M (Dublin U) 1884 *E*, 1885 *S* 1, 1886 *E*

Bradley, M J (Dolphin) 1920 *W, F*, 1922 *E, S, W, F*, 1923 *E, S, W, F*, 1925 *F, S, W*, 1926 *F, E, S, W*, 1927 *F, W*

Bradley, M T (Cork Constitution) 1984 *A*, 1985 *S, F, W, E*, 1986 *F, W, E, S, R*, 1987 *E, S, F, W*, [*W, C, Tg, A*], 1988 *S, F, W, E* 1 1, 1990 *W*, 1992 *NZ* 1,2, 1993 *S, F, W, E, R*, 1994 *F, W, E, S, A* 1,2, *US*, 1995 *S, F*, [*NZ*]

Bradshaw, G (Belfast Collegians) 1903 *W*

Bradshaw, R M (Wanderers) 1885 *E, S* 1,2

Brady, A M (UC Dublin, Malone) 1966 *S*, 1968 *E, S, W*

Brady, J A (Wanderers) 1976 *E, S*

Brady, J R (CIYMS) 1951 *S, W*, 1953 *F, E, S, W*, 1954 *W*, 1956 *W*, 1957 *E, S, W*

Bramwell, T (NIFC) 1928 *F*

Brand, T N (NIFC) 1924 *NZ*

Brennan, J I (CIYMS) 1957 *S, W*

Bresnihan, F P K (UC Dublin, Lansdowne, London Irish) 1966 *E, W*, 1967 *A* 1, *E, S, W, F*, 1968 *F, E, S, W, A*, 1969 *F, E, S, W*, 1970 *SA, F, E, S, W*, 1971 *F, E, S, W*

Brett, J T (Monkstown) 1914 *W*

Bristow, J R (NIFC) 1879 *E*

Brophy, N H (Blackrock Coll, UC Dublin, London Irish) 1957 *F, E*, 1959 *E, S, W, F*, 1960 *F, SA*, 1961 *S, W*, 1962 *E, S, W*, 1963 *E, S, W*, 1967 *E, S, W, F, A* 2

Brown, E L (Instonians) 1958 *F*

Brown, G S (Monkstown, United Services) 1912 *S, W, SA*

Brown, H (Windsor) 1877 *E*

Brown, T (Windsor) 1877 *E, S*

Brown, W H (Dublin U) 1899 *E*

Brown, W (Malone) 1970 *SA, F, S, W*

Brown, W S (Dublin U) 1893 *S, W*, 1894 *E, S, W*

Browne, A W (Dublin U) 1951 *SA*

Browne, D (Blackrock Coll) 1920 *F*

Browne, H C (United Services and RN) 1929 *E, S, W*

Browne, W F (United Services and Army) 1925 *E, S, W*, 1926 *S, W*, 1927 *F, E, S, W, A*, 1928 *E, S*

Browning, D R (Wanderers) 1881 *E, S*

Bruce, S A M (NIFC) 1883 *E, S*, 1884 *E*

Brunker, A A (Lansdowne) 1895 *E, W*

Bryant, C H (Cardiff) 1920 *E, S*

Buchanan, A McM (Dublin U) 1926 *E, S, W*, 1927 *S, W, A*

Buchanan, J W B (Dublin U) 1882 *S*, 1884 *E, S*

Buckley, J H (Sunday's Well) 1973 *E, S*

Bulger, L Q (Lansdowne) 1896 *E, S, W*, 1897 *E, S*, 1898 *E, S, W*

Bulger, M J (Dublin U) 1888 *M*

Burges, J H (Rosslyn Park) 1950 *F, E*

Burgess, R B (Dublin U) 1912 *SA*
Burke, P A (Cork Constitution) 1995 *E, S, W* (R), *It, [J], Fj*, 1996 *US* (R)
Burkitt, J C S (Queen's Coll, Cork) 1881 *E*
Burns, I J (Wanderers) 1980 *E* (R)
Butler, L G (Blackrock Coll) 1960 *W*
Butler, N (Bective Rangers) 1920 *E*
Byers, R M (NIFC) 1928 *S, W*, 1929 *E, S, W*
Byrne, E M J (Blackrock Coll) 1977 *S, F*, 1978 *F, W, E, NZ*
Byrne, N F (UC Dublin) 1962 *F*
Byrne, S J (UC Dublin, Lansdowne) 1953 *S, W*, 1955 *F*
Byron, W G (NIFC) 1896 *E, S, W*, 1897 *E, S*, 1898 *E, S, W*, 1899 *E, S, W*

Caddell, E D (Dublin U, Wanderers) 1904 *S*, 1905 *E, S, W, NZ*, 1906 *E, S, W, SA*, 1907 *E, S*, 1908 *S, W*
Cagney, S J (London Irish) 1925 *W*, 1926 *F, E, S, W*, 1927 *F*, 1928 *E, S, W*, 1929 *F, E, S, W*
Callan, C P (Lansdowne) 1947 *F, E, S, W*, 1948 *F, E, S, W*, 1949 *F, E*
Cameron, E D (Bective Rangers) 1891 *S, W*
Campbell, C E (Old Wesley) 1970 *SA*
Campbell, E F (Monkstown) 1899 *S, W*, 1900 *E, W*
Campbell, S B B (Derry) 1911 *E, S, W, F*, 1912 *F, E, S, W, SA*, 1913 *E, S, F*
Campbell, S O (Old Belvedere) 1976 *A*, 1979 *A 1,2*, 1980 *E, S, F, W*, 1981 *F, W, E, S, SA 1*, 1982 *W, E, S, F*, 1983 *S, F, W, E*, 1984 *F, W*
Canniffe, D M (Lansdowne) 1976 *W, E*
Cantrell, J L (UC Dublin, Blackrock Coll) 1976 *A, F, W, E, S*, 1981 *S, SA 1,2, A*
Carey, R W (Dungannon) 1992 *NZ 1,2*
Carpendale, M J (Monkstown) 1886 *S*, 1887 *W*, 1888 *W, S*
Carr, N J (Ards) 1985 *S, F, W, E*, 1986 *W, E, S, R*, 1987 *E, S, W*
Carroll, C (Bective Rangers) 1930 *F*
Carroll, R (Lansdowne) 1947 *F*, 1950 *S, W*
Casement, B N (Dublin U) 1875 *E*, 1876 *E*, 1879 *E*
Casement, F (Dublin U) 1906 *E, S, W*
Casey, J C (Young Munster) 1930 *S*, 1932 *E*
Casey, P J (UC Dublin, Lansdowne) 1963 *F, E, S, W, NZ*, 1964 *F, E, S, W, F*, 1965 *F, E, S*
Chambers, J (Dublin U) 1886 *E, S*, 1887 *E, S, W*
Chambers, R R (Instonians) 1951 *F, E, S, W*, 1952 *F, W*
Clancy, T P J (Lansdowne) 1988 *W, E 1,2, WS, It*, 1989 *F, W, E, S*
Clarke, A T H (Northampton) 1995 *Fj* (R), 1996 *W, E*
Clarke, C P (Terenure Coll) 1993 *F, W, E*
Clarke, D J (Dolphin) 1991 *W, Nm 1,2, [J, A]*, 1992 *NZ 2*(R)
Clarke, J A B (Bective Rangers) 1922 *S, W, F*, 1923 *F*, 1924 *E, S, W*
Clegg, R J (Bangor) 1973 *F*, 1975 *E, S, F, W*
Clifford, J T (Young Munster) 1949 *F, E, S, W*, 1950 *F, E, S, W*, 1951 *F, E, SA*, 1952 *F, S, W*
Clinch, A D (Dublin U, Wanderers) 1892 *S*, 1893 *W*, 1895 *E, S, W*, 1896 *E, S, W*, 1897 *E, S*
Clinch, J D (Wanderers, Dublin U) 1923 *W*, 1924 *F, E, S, W, NZ*, 1925 *F, E, S*, 1926 *E, S, W*, 1927 *F*, 1928 *F, E, S, W*, 1929 *F, E, S, W*, 1930 *F, E, S, W*, 1931 *F, E, S, W*
Clohessy, P M (Young Munster) 1993 *F, W, E*, 1994 *F, W, E, S, A 1,2, US*, 1995 *E, S, F, W*, 1996 *S, F*
Clune, J J (Blackrock Coll) 1912 *SA*, 1913 *W, F*, 1914 *F, E, W*
Coffey, J J (Lansdowne) 1900 *E*, 1901 *W*, 1902 *E, S, W*, 1903 *E, S, W*, 1905 *E, S, W, NZ*, 1906 *E, S, W, SA*, 1907 *F*, 1908 *W*, 1910 *F*
Cogan, W St J (Queen's Coll, Cork) 1907 *E, S*
Collier, S R (Queen's Coll, Belfast) 1883 *S*
Collins, P C (Lansdowne, London Irish) 1987 *[C]*, 1990 *S*(R)
Collis, W R F (KCH, Harlequins) 1924 *F, W, NZ*, 1925 *F, E, S*, 1926 *F*
Collis, W S (Wanderers) 1884 *W*
Collopy, G (Bective Rangers) 1891 *S*, 1892 *S*
Collopy, R (Bective Rangers) 1923 *E, S, W, F*, 1924 *F, E, S, W, NZ*, 1925 *F, E, S, W*
Collopy, W P (Bective Rangers) 1914 *F, E, S, W*, 1921 *E, S, W, F*, 1922 *E, S, W, F*, 1923 *S, W, F*, 1924 *F, E, S, W*
Combe, A (NIFC) 1875 *E*
Condon, H C (London Irish) 1984 *S* (R)
Cook, H G (Lansdowne) 1884 *W*

Coote, P B (RAF, Leicester) 1933 *S*
Corcoran, J C (London Irish) 1947 *A*, 1948 *F*
Corken, T S (Belfast Collegians) 1937 *E, S, W*
Corkery, D S (Cork Constitution) 1994 *A 1,2, US*, 1995 *E, [NZ, J, W, F], Fj*, 1996 *US, S, F, W, E*
Corley, H H (Dublin U, Wanderers) 1902 *E, S, W*, 1903 *E, S, W*, 1904 *E, S*
Cormac, H S T (Clontarf) 1921 *E, S, W*
Costello, P (Bective Rangers) 1960 *F*
Costello, R A (Garryowen) 1993 *S*
Costello, V C P (St Mary's Coll) 1996 *US, F, W, E*
Cotton, J (Wanderers) 1889 *W*
Coulter, H H (Queen's U, Belfast) 1920 *E, S, W*
Courtney, A W (UC Dublin) 1920 *S, W, F*, 1921 *E, S, W, F*
Cox, H L (Dublin U) 1875 *E*, 1876 *E*, 1877 *E, S*
Craig, R G (Queen's U, Belfast) 1938 *S, W*
Crawford, E C (Dublin U) 1885 *E, S 1*
Crawford, W E (Lansdowne) 1920 *E, S, W, F*, 1921 *E, S, W, F*, 1922 *E, S*, 1923 *E, S, W, F*, 1924 *F, E, W, NZ*, 1925 *F, E, S, W*, 1926 *F, E, S, W*, 1927 *F, E, S, W*
Crean, T J (Wanderers) 1894 *E, S, W*, 1895 *E, S, W*, 1896 *E, S, W*
Crichton, R Y (Dublin U) 1920 *E, S, W, F*, 1921 *F*, 1922 *E*, 1923 *W, F*, 1924 *F, E, S, W, NZ*, 1925 *E, S*
Croker, E W D (Limerick) 1878 *E*
Cromey, G E (Queen's U, Belfast) 1937 *E, S, W*, 1938 *E, S, W*, 1939 *E, S, W*
Cronin, B M (Garryowen) 1995 *S*
Cronyn, A P (Dublin U, Lansdowne) 1875 *E*, 1876 *E*, 1880 *S*
Crossan, K D (Instonians) 1982 *S*, 1984 *F, W, E, S*, 1985 *S, F, W, E*, 1986 *E, S, R*, 1987 *E, S, F, W, [W, C, Tg, A]*, 1988 *S, F, W, E 1, WS, It*, 1989 *W, S, NZ*, 1990 *E, S, F, W, Arg*, 1991 *E, S, Nm 2 [Z, J, S]*, 1992 *W*
Crowe, J F (UC Dublin) 1974 *NZ*
Crowe, L (Old Belvedere) 1950 *E, S, W*
Crowe, M P (Lansdowne) 1929 *W*, 1930 *E, S, W*, 1931 *F, S, W, SA*, 1932 *S, W*, 1933 *W, S*, 1934 *E*
Crowe, P M (Blackrock Coll) 1935 *E*, 1938 *E*
Cullen, T J (UC Dublin) 1949 *F*
Cullen, W J (Monkstown and Manchester) 1920 *E*
Culliton, M G (Wanderers) 1959 *E, S, W, F*, 1960 *E, S, W, F, SA*, 1961 *E, S, W, F*, 1962 *S, F*, 1964 *E, S, W, F*
Cummins, W E A (Queen's Coll, Cork) 1879 *S*, 1881 *E*, 1882 *E*
Cunningham, D McC (NIFC) 1923 *E, S, W*, 1925 *F, E, W*
Cunningham, M J (UC Cork) 1955 *F, E, S, W*, 1956 *F, S, W*
Cunningham, V J G (St Mary's Coll) 1988 *E 2, It*, 1990 *Arg* (R), 1991 *Nm 1,2, [Z, J,(R)]*, 1992 *NZ 1,2, A*, 1993 *S, F, W, E, R*, 1994 *F*
Cunningham, W A (Lansdowne) 1920 *W*, 1921 *E, S, W, F*, 1922 *E*, 1923 *S, W*
Cuppaidge, J L (Dublin U) 1879 *E*, 1880 *E, S*
Currell, J (NIFC) 1877 *S*
Curtis, A B (Oxford U) 1950 *F, E, S*
Curtis, D M (London Irish) 1991 *W, E, S, Nm 1,2, [Z, J, S, A]*, 1992 *W, E, S* (R), *F*
Cuscaden, W A (Dublin U, Bray) 1876 *E*
Cussen, D J (Dublin U) 1921 *E, S, W, F*, 1922 *E*, 1923 *E, S, W, F*, 1926 *F, E, S, W*, 1927 *F, E*

Daly, J C (London Irish) 1947 *F, E, S, W*, 1948 *E, S, W*
Daly, M J (Harlequins) 1938 *E*
Danaher, P P A (Lansdowne, Garryowen) 1988 *S, F, W, WS, It*, 1989 *F, NZ* (R), 1990 *F*, 1992 *S, F, NZ 1, A*, 1993 *S, F, W, E, R*, 1994 *F, W, E, S, A 1,2, US*, 1995 *E, S, F, W*
Dargan, M J (Old Belvedere) 1952 *S, W*
Davidson, C T (NIFC) 1921 *F*
Davidson, I G (NIFC) 1899 *E*, 1900 *S, W*, 1901 *E, S, W*, 1902 *E, S, W*
Davidson, J C (Dungannon) 1969 *F, E, S, W*, 1973 *NZ*, 1976 *NZ*
Davidson, J W (Dungannon) 1995 *Fj*, 1996 *S, F, W, E*
Davies, F E (Lansdowne) 1892 *S, W*, 1893 *E, S, W*
Davis, J L (Monkstown) 1898 *E, S*
Davis, W J N (Edinburgh U, Bessbrook) 1890 *S, W, E*, 1891 *E, S, W*, 1892 *E, S*, 1895 *S*
Davison, W (Belfast Academy) 1887 *W*
Davy, E O'D (UC Dublin, Lansdowne) 1925 *W*, 1926 *F, E, S, W*, 1927 *F, E, S, W, A*, 1928 *F, E, S, W*, 1929 *F, E, S, W*, 1930 *F, E, S, W*, 1931 *F, E, S, W, SA*, 1932 *E, S, W*, 1933 *E, W, S*, 1934 *E*

Gaston, J T (Dublin U) 1954 *NZ, F, E, S, W*, 1955 *W* 1956 *F, E*
Gavin, T J (Moseley, London Irish) 1949 *F, E*
Geoghegan, S P (London Irish, Bath) 1991 *F, W, E, S, Nm* 1, [*Z, S, A*], 1992 *E, S, F, A*, 1993 *S, F, W, E, R*, 1994 *F, W, E, S, A* 1,2, *US*, 1995 *E, S, F, W,* [*NZ, J, W, F*], *Fj*, 1996 *US, S, W, E*
Gibson, C M H (Cambridge U, NIFC) 1964 *E, S, W, F,* 1965 *F, E, S, W, SA,* 1966 *F, E, S, W,* 1967 *A* 1, *E, S, W, F, A* 2, 1968 *E, S, W, A,* 1969 *E, S, W,* 1970 *SA, F, E, S, W,* 1971 *F, E, S, W,* 1972 *F* 1, *E, F* 2, 1973 *NZ, E, S, W, F,* 1974 *F, W, E, S, P,* 1975 *E, S, F, W,* 1976 *A, F, W, E, S, NZ,* 1977 *W, E, S, F,* 1978 *F, W, E, NZ,* 1979 *S, A* 1,2
Gibson, M E (Lansdowne, London Irish) 1979 *F, W, E, S,* 1981 *W* (R), 1986 *R,* 1988 *S, F, W, E* 2
Gifford, H P (Wanderers) 1890 *S*
Gillespie, J C (Dublin U) 1922 *W, F*
Gilpin, F G (Queen's U, Belfast) 1962 *E, S, F*
Glass, D C (Belfast Collegians) 1958 *F,* 1960 *W,* 1961 *W, SA*
Glennon, B T (Lansdowne) 1993 *F* (R)
Glennon, J J (Skerries) 1980 *E, S,* 1987 *E, S, F,* [*W* (R)]
Godfrey, R P (UC Dublin) 1954 *S, W*
Goodall, K G (City of Derry, Newcastle U) 1967 *A* 1, *E, S, W, F, A* 2, 1968 *F, E, S, W, A,* 1969 *F, E, S,* 1970 *SA, F, E, S, W*
Gordon, A (Dublin U) 1884 *S*
Gordon, T G (NIFC) 1877 *E, S,* 1878 *E*
Gotto, R P C (NIFC) 1906 *SA*
Goulding, W J (Cork) 1879 *S*
Grace, T O (UC Dublin, St Mary's Coll) 1972 *F* 1, *E,* 1973 *NZ, E, S, W,* 1974 *E, S, P, NZ,* 1975 *E, S, F, W,* 1976 *A, F, W, E, S, NZ,* 1977 *W, E, S,* 1978 *S*
Graham, R I (Dublin U) 1911 *F*
Grant, E L (CIYMS) 1971 *F, E, S*
Grant, P J (Bective Rangers) 1894 *S, W*
Graves, C R A (Wanderers) 1934 *E, S, W,* 1935 *E, S, W, NZ,* 1936 *E, S, W,* 1937 *E, S,* 1938 *E, S, W*
Gray, R D (Old Wesley) 1923 *E, S,* 1925 *F,* 1926 *F*
Greene, E H (Dublin U, Kingstown) 1882 *W,* 1884 *W,* 1885 *E, S* 2, 1886 *E*
Greer, R (Kingstown) 1876 *E*
Greeves, T J (NIFC) 1907 *E, S, W,* 1909 *W, F*
Gregg, R J (Queen's U, Belfast) 1953 *F, E, S, W,* 1954 *F, E, S*
Griffin, C S (London Irish) 1951 *F, E*
Griffin, J L (Wanderers) 1949 *S, W*
Griffiths, W (Limerick) 1878 *E*
Grimshaw, C (Queen's U, Belfast) 1969 *E* (R)
Guerin, B N (Galwegians) 1956 *S*
Gwynn, A P (Dublin U) 1895 *W*
Gwynn, L H (Dublin U) 1893 *S,* 1894 *E, S, W,* 1897 *S,* 1898 *E, S*

Hakin, R F (CIYMS) 1976 *W, S, NZ,* 1977 *W, E, F*
Hall, R O N (Dublin U) 1884 *W*
Hall, W H (Instonians) 1923 *E, S, W, F,* 1924 *F, S*
Hallaran, C F G T (Royal Navy) 1921 *E, S, W,* 1922 *E, S, W,* 1923 *E, F,* 1924 *F, E, S, W,* 1925 *F,* 1926 *F, E*
Halpin, G F (Wanderers, London Irish) 1990 *E,* 1991 [*J*], 1992 *E, S, F,* 1993 *A,* 1994 *F* (R), 1995 *It,* [*NZ, W, F*]
Halpin, T (Garryowen) 1909 *S, W, F,* 1910 *E, S, W,* 1911 *E, S, W, F,* 1912 *F, E, S*
Halvey, E O (Shannon) 1995 *F, W, It,* [*J, W* (t), *F* (R)]
Hamilton, A J (Lansdowne) 1884 *W*
Hamilton, G F (NIFC) 1991 *F, W, E, S, Nm* 2, [*Z, J, S, A*], 1992 *A*
Hamilton, R L (NIFC) 1926 *F*
Hamilton, R W (Wanderers) 1893 *W*
Hamilton, W J (Dublin U) 1877 *E*
Hamlet, G T (Old Wesley) 1902 *E, S, W,* 1903 *E, S, W,* 1904 *S, W,* 1905 *E, S, W, NZ,* 1906 *SA,* 1907 *E, S, W,* 1908 *E, S, W,* 1909 *E, S, W, F,* 1910 *E, S, F,* 1911 *E, S, W, F*
Hanrahan, C J (Dolphin) 1926 *S, W,* 1927 *E, S, W, A,* 1928 *F, E, S,* 1929 *F, E, S, W,* 1930 *F, E, S, W,* 1931 *F,* 1932 *S, W*
Harbison, H T (Bective Rangers) 1984 *W* (R), *E, S,* 1986 *R,* 1987 *E, S, F, W*
Hardy, G G (Bective Rangers) 1962 *S*
Harman, G R A (Dublin U) 1899 *E, W*
Harper, J (Instonians) 1947 *F, E, S*
Harpur, T G (Dublin U) 1908 *E, S, W*
Harrison, T (Cork) 1879 *S,* 1880 *S,* 1881 *E*
Harvey, F M W (Wanderers) 1907 *W,* 1911 *F*

Harvey, G A D (Wanderers) 1903 *E, S,* 1904 *W,* 1905 *E, S*
Harvey, T A (Dublin U) 1900 *W,* 1901 *S, W,* 1902 *E, S, W,* 1903 *E, W*
Haycock, P P (Terenure Coll) 1989 *E*
Headon, T A (UC Dublin) 1939 *S, W*
Healey, P (Limerick) 1901 *E, S, W,* 1902 *E, S, W,* 1903 *E, S, W,* 1904 *S*
Heffernan, M R (Cork Constitution) 1911 *E, S, W, F*
Hemphill, R (Dublin U) 1912 *F, E, S, W*
Henderson, N J (Queen's U, Belfast, NIFC) 1949 *S, W,* 1950 *F,* 1951 *F, E, S, W, SA,* 1952 *F, S, W, E,* 1953 *F, E, S, W,* 1954 *NZ, F, E, S, W,* 1955 *F, E, S, W,* 1956 *S, W,* 1957 *F, E, S, W,* 1958 *A, E, S, W, F,* 1959 *E, S, W, F*
Henebrey, G J (Garryowen) 1906 *E, S, W, SA,* 1909 *W, F*
Heron, A G (Queen's Coll, Belfast) 1901 *E*
Heron, J (NIFC) 1877 *S,* 1879 *E*
Heron, W T (NIFC) 1880 *E, S*
Herrick, R W (Dublin U) 1886 *S*
Heuston, F S (Kingstown) 1882 *W,* 1883 *E, S*
Hewitt, D (Queen's U, Belfast, Instonians) 1958 *A, E, S, F,* 1959 *S, W, F,* 1960 *E, S, W, F,* 1961 *E, S, W, F,* 1962 *S, F,* 1965 *W*
Hewitt, F S (Instonians) 1924 *W, NZ,* 1925 *F, E, S,* 1926 *F,* 1927 *E, S, W*
Hewitt, J A (NIFC) 1981 *SA* 1 (R), 2 (R)
Hewitt, T R (Queen's U, Belfast) 1924 *W, NZ,* 1925 *F, E, S,* 1926 *F, E, S, W*
Hewitt, V A (Instonians) 1935 *S, W, NZ,* 1936 *E, S, W*
Hewitt, W J (Instonians) 1954 *E,* 1956 *S,* 1959 *W,* 1961 *SA*
Hewson, F T (Wanderers) 1875 *E*
Hickie, D J (St Mary's Coll) 1971 *F, E, S, W,* 1972 *F* 1, *E,* 1973 *F, E, S, W*
Higgins, J A D (Civil Service) 1947 *S, W, A,* 1948 *F, S, W*
Higgins, W W (NIFC) 1884 *E, S*
Hillary, M F (UC Dublin) 1952 *E*
Hingerty, D J (UC Dublin) 1947 *F, E, S, W*
Hinton, W P (Old Wesley) 1907 *W,* 1908 *E, S, W,* 1909 *E, S,* 1910 *E, S, W, F,* 1911 *E, S, W,* 1912 *F, E, W*
Hipwell, M L (Terenure Coll) 1962 *E, S,* 1968 *F, A,* 1969 *F* (R), *S* (R), *W,* 1971 *F, E, S, W,* 1972 *F* 2
Hobbs, T H M (Dublin U) 1884 *S,* 1885 *F*
Hobson, E W (Dublin U) 1876 *E*
Hogan, N A (Terenure Coll) 1995 *E, W,* [*J, W, F*], 1996 *F, W, E*
Hogan, P (Garryowen) 1992 *F*
Hogg, W (Dublin U) 1885 *S* 2
Holland, J J (Wanderers) 1981 *SA* 1,2, 1986 *W*
Holmes, G W (Dublin U) 1912 *SA,* 1913 *E, S*
Holmes, L J (Lisburn) 1889 *S, W*
Hooks, K J (Queen's U, Belfast, Ards, Bangor) 1981 *S,* 1989 *NZ,* 1990 *F, W, Arg,* 1991 *F*
Horan, A K (Blackheath) 1920 *E, W*
Houston, K J (Oxford U, London Irish) 1961 *SA,* 1964 *S, W,* 1965 *F, E, SA*
Hughes, R W (NIFC) 1878 *E,* 1880 *E, S,* 1881 *S,* 1882 *E, S,* 1883 *E, S,* 1884 *E, S,* 1885 *E,* 1886 *E*
Humphreys, D G (London Irish) 1996 *F, W, E*
Hunt, E W F de Vere (Army, Rosslyn Park) 1930 *F,* 1932 *E, S, W,* 1933 *E*
Hunter, D V (Dublin U) 1885 *S* 2
Hunter, L (Civil Service) 1968 *W, A*
Hunter, W R (CIYMS) 1962 *E, S, W, F,* 1963 *F, E, S,* 1966 *F, E, S*
Hurley, H D (Old Wesley) 1995 *Fj* (t)
Hutton, S A (Malone) 1967 *S, W, F, A* 2

Ireland J (Windsor) 1876 *E,* 1877 *F*
Irvine, H A S (Collegians) 1901 *S*
Irwin, D G (Queen's U, Belfast, Instonians) 1980 *F, W,* 1981 *F, W, E, S, SA* 1,2, *A,* 1982 *W,* 1983 *S, F, W, E,* 1984 *F, W,* 1987 [*Tg, A* (R)], 1989 *F, W, E, S, NZ,* 1990 *E, S*
Irwin, J W S (NIFC) 1938 *E, S,* 1939 *E, S, W*
Irwin, S T (Queen's Coll, Belfast) 1900 *E, S, W,* 1901 *E, W,* 1902 *E, S, W,* 1903 *S*

Jack, H W (UC Cork) 1914 *S, W,* 1921 *W*
Jackson, A R V (Wanderers) 1911 *E, S, W, F,* 1913 *W, F,* 1914 *F, E, S, W*
Jackson, F (NIFC) 1923 *E*
Jackson, H W (Dublin U) 1877 *E*
Jameson, J S (Lansdowne) 1888 *M,* 1889 *S, W,* 1891 *W,* 1892 *E, W,* 1893 *S*
Jeffares, E W (Wanderers) 1913 *E, S*

245

Johns, P S (Dublin U, Dungannon) 1990 *Arg*, 1992 *NZ* 1,2, *A*, 1993 *S, F, W, E, R*, 1994 *F, W, E, S, A* 1,2, *US*, 1995 *E, S, W, It*, [*NZ, J, W, F*], *Fj*, 1996 *US, S, F*
Johnston, J (Belfast Acad) 1881 *S*, 1882 *S*, 1884 *S*, 1885 *S* 1,2, 1886 *E*, 1887 *E, S, W*
Johnston, M (Dublin U) 1880 *E, S*, 1881 *E, S*, 1882 *E*, 1884 *E, S*, 1886 *E*
Johnston, R (Wanderers) 1893 *E, W*
Johnston, R W (Dublin U) 1890 *S, W, E*
Johnston, T J (Queen's Coll, Belfast) 1892 *E, S, W*, 1893 *E, S*, 1895 *E*
Johnstone, W E (Dublin U) 1884 *W*
Johnstone-Smyth, T R (Lansdowne) 1882 *E*

Kavanagh, J R (UC Dublin, Wanderers) 1953 *F, E, S, W*, 1954 *NZ, S, W*, 1955 *F, E*, 1956 *E, S, W*, 1957 *F, E, S, W*, 1958 *A, E, S, W*, 1959 *E, S, W, F*, 1960 *E, S, W, F, SA*, 1961 *E, S, W, F, SA*, 1962 *F*
Kavanagh, P J (UC Dublin, Wanderers) 1952 *E*, 1955 *W*
Keane, M I (Lansdowne) 1974 *F, W, E, S, P, NZ*, 1975 *E, S, F, W*, 1976 *A, F, W, E, S, NZ*, 1977 *W, E, S, F*, 1978 *S, F, W, E, NZ*, 1979 *F, W, E, S, A* 1,2, 1980 *E, S, F, W*, 1981 *F, W, E, S*, 1982 *W, E, S, F*, 1983 *S, F, W, E*, 1984 *F, W, E, S*
Kearney, R K (Wanderers) 1982 *F*, 1984 *A*, 1986 *F, W*
Keeffe, E (Sunday's Well) 1947 *F, E, S, W, A*, 1948 *F*
Kelly, H C (NIFC) 1877 *E, S*, 1878 *E*, 1879 *S*, 1880 *E, S*
Kelly, J C (UC Dublin) 1962 *F, W*, 1963 *F, E, S, W, NZ*, 1964 *E, S, W, F*
Kelly, S (Lansdowne) 1954 *S, W*, 1955 *S*, 1960 *W, F*
Kelly, W (Wanderers) 1884 *S*
Kennedy, A G (Belfast Collegians) 1956 *F*
Kennedy, A P (London Irish) 1986 *W, E*
Kennedy, F (Wanderers) 1880 *E*, 1881 *E*, 1882 *W*
Kennedy, F A (Wanderers) 1904 *E, W*
Kennedy, H (Bradford) 1938 *S, W*
Kennedy, J M (Wanderers) 1882 *W*, 1884 *W*
Kennedy, K W (Queen's U, Belfast, London Irish) 1965 *F, E, S, W, SA*, 1966 *F, E, W*, 1967 *A* 1, *E, S, W, F, A* 2, 1968 *F, A*, 1969 *F, E, S, W*, 1970 *SA, F, E, S, W*, 1971 *F, E, S, W*, 1972 *F* 1, *E, F* 2, 1973 *NZ, E, S, W, F*, 1974 *F, W, E, S, P, NZ*, 1975 *F, W*
Kennedy, T J (St Mary's Coll) 1978 *NZ*, 1979 *F, W, E* (R), *A* 1,2, 1980 *E, S, F, W*, 1981 *SA* 1,2, *A*
Kenny, P (Wanderers) 1992 *NZ* 2 (R)
Keogh, F S (Bective Rangers) 1964 *W, F*
Keon, J J (Limerick) 1879 *E*
Keyes, R P (Cork Constitution) 1986 *E*, 1991 [*Z, J, S, A*], 1992 *W, E, S*
Kidd, F W (Dublin U, Lansdowne) 1877 *E, S*, 1878 *E*
Kiely, M D (Lansdowne) 1962 *W*, 1963 *F, E, S, W*
Kiernan, M J (Dolphin, Lansdowne) 1982 *W* (R), *E, S, F*, 1983 *S, F, W, E*, 1984 *E, S, A*, 1985 *S, F, W, E*, 1986 *F, W, E, S, R*, 1987 *E, S, F, W*, [*W, C, A*], 1988 *S, F, W, E* 1,2, *WS*, 1989 *F, W, E, S*, 1990 *E, S, F, W, Arg*, 1991 *F*
Kiernan, T J (UC Cork, Cork Const) 1960 *E, S, W, F, SA*, 1961 *E, S, W, F, SA*, 1962 *E, W*, 1963 *F, S, W, NZ*, 1964 *E, S*, 1965 *F, E, S, W, SA*, 1966 *F, E, S, W*, 1967 *A* 1, *E, S, W, F, A* 2, 1968 *F, E, S, W, A*, 1969 *F, E, S, W*, 1970 *SA, F, E, S, W*, 1971 *F*, 1972 *F* 1, *E, F* 2, 1973 *NZ, E, S*
Killeen, G V (Garryowen) 1912 *E, S, W*, 1913 *E, S, W, F*, 1914 *E, S, W*
King, H (Dublin U) 1883 *E, S*
Kingston, T J (Dolphin) 1987 [*W, Tg, A*], 1988 *S, F, W, E* 1, 1990 *F, W*, 1991 [*J*], 1993 *F, W, E, R*, 1994 *F, W, E, S*, 1995 *F, W, It*, [*NZ, J* (R), *W, F*], *Fj*, 1996 *US, S, F*
Knox, J H (Dublin U, Lansdowne) 1904 *W*, 1905 *E, S, W, NZ*, 1906 *E, S, W*, 1907 *W*, 1908 *S*
Kyle, J W (Queen's U, Belfast, NIFC) 1947 *F, E, S, W, A*, 1948 *F, E, S, W*, 1949 *F, E, S, W*, 1950 *F, E, S, W*, 1951 *F, E, S, W, SA*, 1952 *F, S, W, E*, 1953 *F, E, S, W*, 1954 *NZ, F*, 1955 *F, E, W, S*, 1956 *F, E, S, W*, 1957 *F, E, S, W*, 1958 *A, E, S*

Lambert, N H (Lansdowne) 1934 *S, W*
Lamont, R A (Instonians) 1965 *F, E, SA*, 1966 *F, E, S, W*, 1970 *SA, F, E, S, W*
Landers, M F (Cork Const) 1904 *W*, 1905 *E, S, W, NZ*
Lane, D (UC Cork) 1934 *S, W*, 1935 *E, S*
Lane, M F (UC Cork) 1947 *W*, 1949 *F, E, S, W*, 1950 *F, E, S, W*, 1951 *F, S, W, SA*, 1952 *F, S*, 1953 *F, E*
Lane, P (Old Crescent) 1964 *W*
Langan, D J (Clontarf) 1934 *W*
Langbroek, J A (Blackrock Coll) 1987 [*Tg*]
Lavery, P (London Irish) 1974 *W*, 1976 *W*

Lawlor, P J (Clontarf) 1951 *S, SA*, 1952 *F, S, W, E*, 1953 *F*, 1954 *NZ, E, S*, 1956 *F, E*
Lawlor, P J (Bective Rangers) 1935 *E, S, W*, 1937 *E, S, W*
Lawlor, P J (Bective Rangers) 1990 *Arg*, 1992 *A*, 1993 *S*
Leahy, K T (Wanderers) 1992 *NZ* 1
Leahy, M W (UC Cork) 1964 *W*
Lee, S (NIFC) 1891 *E, S, W*, 1892 *E, S, W*, 1893 *E, S, W*, 1894 *E, S, W*, 1895 *E, W*, 1896 *E, S, W*, 1897 *E*, 1898 *E*
Le Fanu, V C (Cambridge U, Lansdowne) 1886 *E, S*, 1887 *E, W*, 1888 *S*, 1889 *W*, 1890 *E*, 1891 *E*, 1892 *E, S, W*
Lenihan, D G (UC Cork, Cork Const) 1981 *A*, 1982 *W, E, S, F*, 1983 *S, F, W, E*, 1984 *F, W, E, S, A*, 1985 *S, F, W, E*, 1986 *F, W, E, S, R*, 1987 *E, S, F, W*, [*W, C, Tg, A*], 1988 *S, F, W, E* 1,2, *WS, It*, 1989 *F, W, E, S, NZ*, 1990 *S, F, W, Arg*, 1991 *Nm* 2, [*Z, S, A*], 1992 *W*
L'Estrange, L P F (Dublin U) 1962 *E*
Levis, F H (Wanderers) 1884 *E*
Lightfoot, E J (Lansdowne) 1931 *F, E, S, W, SA*, 1932 *E, S, W*, 1933 *E, W, S*
Lindsay, H (Dublin U, Armagh) 1893 *E, S, W*, 1894 *E, S, W*, 1895 *E*, 1896 *E, S, W*, 1898 *E, S, W*
Little, T J (Bective Rangers) 1898 *W*, 1899 *S, W*, 1900 *S, W*, 1901 *E, S*
Lloyd, R A (Dublin U, Liverpool) 1910 *E, S, W*, 1912 *F, E, S, W, SA*, 1913 *E, S, W, F*, 1914 *F, E*, 1920 *E, F*
Lydon, C T J (Galwegians) 1956 *S*
Lyle, R K (Dublin U) 1910 *W, F*
Lyle, T R (Dublin U) 1885 *E, S* 1,2, 1886 *E*, 1887 *E, S*
Lynch, J F (St Mary's Coll) 1971 *F, E, S, W*, 1972 *F* 1, *E, F* 2, 1973 *NZ, E, S, W*, 1974 *F, W, E, S, P, NZ*
Lynch, L (Lansdowne) 1956 *S*
Lytle, J H (NIFC) 1894 *E, S, W*, 1895 *W*, 1896 *E, S, W*, 1897 *E, S*, 1898 *E, S*, 1899 *S*
Lytle, J N (NIFC) 1888 *M*, 1889 *W*, 1890 *E*, 1891 *E, S*, 1894 *E, S, W*
Lyttle, V J (Collegians, Bedford) 1938 *E*, 1939 *E, S*

McAleese, D R (Ballymena) 1992 *F*
McAllan, G H (Dungannon) 1896 *S, W*
Macauley, J (Limerick) 1887 *E, S*
McBride, W D (Malone) 1988 *W, E* 1, *WS, It*, 1989 *S*, 1990 *F, W, Arg*, 1993 *S, F, W, E, R*, 1994 *W, E, S, A* 1 (R), 1995 *S, F*, [*NZ, W, F*], *Fj* (R), 1996 *W, E*
McBride, W J (Ballymena) 1962 *E, S, F, W*, 1963 *F, E, S, W, NZ*, 1964 *E, S, F*, 1965 *F, E, S, W, SA*, 1966 *F, E, S, W*, 1967 *A* 1, *E, S, W, F, A* 2, 1968 *F, E, S, W, A*, 1969 *F, E, S, W*, 1970 *SA, F, E, S, W*, 1971 *F, E, S, W*, 1972 *F* 1, *E, F* 2, 1973 *NZ, E, S, W, F*, 1974 *F, W, E, S, P, NZ*, 1975 *E, S, F, W*
McCahill, S A (Sunday's Well) 1995 *Fj* (t)
McCall, B W (London Irish) 1985 *F* (R), 1986 *E, S*
McCall, C M (Bangor) 1992 *NZ* 1 (R), 2, 1994 *W*, 1996 *E* (R)
McCallan, B (Ballymena) 1960 *E, S*
McCarten, R J (London Irish) 1961 *E, W, F*
McCarthy, E A (Kingstown) 1882 *W*
McCarthy, J S (Dolphin) 1948 *F, E, S, W*, 1949 *F, E, S, W*, 1950 *W*, 1951 *F, E, S, W, SA*, 1952 *F, S, W, E*, 1953 *F, E, S*, 1954 *NZ, F, E, S, W*, 1955 *F, E*
McCarthy, P D (Cork Const) 1992 *NZ* 1,2, *A*, 1993 *S, R* (R)
MacCarthy, St G (Dublin U) 1882 *W*
McCarthy, T (Cork) 1898 *W*
McClelland, T A (Queen's U, Belfast) 1921 *E, S, W, F*, 1922 *E, W, F*, 1923 *E, S, W, F*, 1924 *F, E, S, W, NZ*
McClenahan, R O (Instonians) 1923 *E, S, W*
McClinton, A N (NIFC) 1910 *W, F*
McCombe, W McM (Dublin U, Bangor) 1968 *F*, 1975 *E, S, F, W*
McConnell, A A (Collegians) 1947 *A*, 1948 *F, E, S, W*, 1949 *F, E*
McConnell, G (Derry, Edinburgh U) 1912 *F, E*, 1913 *W, F*
McConnell, J W (Lansdowne) 1913 *S*
McCormac, F M (Wanderers) 1909 *W*, 1910 *W, F*
McCormick, W J (Wanderers) 1930 *E*
McCoull, H C (Belfast Albion) 1895 *E, S, W*, 1899 *E*
McCourt, D (Queen's U, Belfast) 1947 *A*
McCoy, J J (Dungannon, Bangor, Ballymena) 1984 *W, A*, 1985 *S, F, W, E*, 1986 *F*, 1987 [*Tg*], 1988 *E* 2, *WS, It*, 1989 *F, W, E, S, NZ*
McCracken, H (NIFC) 1954 *W*
McDermott, S J (London Irish) 1955 *S, W*
Macdonald, J A (Methodist Coll, Belfast) 1875 *E*, 1876 *E*, 1877 *S*, 1878 *E*, 1879 *S*, 1880 *E*, 1881 *S*, 1882 *E, S*, 1883 *E, S*, 1884 *E, S*

McDonald, J P (Malone) 1987 [C], 1990 E (R), S, Arg
McDonnell, A C (Dublin U) 1889 W, 1890 S, W, 1891 E
McDowell, J C (Instonians) 1924 F, NZ
McFarland, B A T (Derry) 1920 S, W, F, 1922 W
McGann, B J (Lansdowne) 1969 F, E, S, W, 1970 SA, F, E, S, W, 1971 F, E, S, W, 1972 F 1, E, F 2, 1973 NZ, E, S, W, 1976 F, W, E, S, NZ
McGowan, A N (Blackrock Coll) 1994 US
McGown, T M W (NIFC) 1899 E, S, 1901 S
McGrath, D G (UC Dublin, Cork Const) 1984 S, 1987 [W, C, Tg, A]
McGrath, N F (Oxford U, London Irish) 1934 W
McGrath, P J (UC Cork) 1965 E, S, W, SA, 1966 F, E, S, W, 1967 A 1, A 2
McGrath, R J M (Wanderers) 1977 W, E, F (R), 1981 SA 1,2, A, 1982 W, E, S, F, 1983 S, F, W, E, 1984 F, W
McGrath, T (Garryowen) 1956 W, 1958 F, 1960 E, S, W, F, 1961 SA
McGuire, E P (UC Galway) 1963 E, S, W, NZ, 1964 E, S, W, F
MacHale, S (Lansdowne) 1965 F, E, S, W, SA, 1966 F, E, S, W, 1967 S, W, F
McIldowie, G (Malone) 1906 SA, 1910 E, S, W
McIlrath, J A (Ballymena) 1976 A, F, NZ, 1977 W, E
McIlwaine, E H (NIFC) 1895 S, W
McIlwaine, E N (NIFC) 1875 E, 1876 E
McIlwaine, J E (NIFC) 1897 E, S, 1898 E, S, W, 1899 E, W
McIntosh, L M (Dublin U) 1884 S
MacIvor, C V (Dublin U) 1912 F, E, S, W, 1913 E, S, F
McKay, J W (Queen's U, Belfast) 1947 F, E, S, W, A, 1948 F, E, S, W, 1949 F, E, S, W, 1950 F, E, S, W, 1951 F, E, S, W, SA, 1952 F
McKee, W D (NIFC) 1947 A, 1948 F, E, S, W, 1949 F, E, S, W, 1950 F, E, 1951 SA
McKelvey, J M (Queen's U, Belfast) 1956 F, E
McKibbin, A R (Instonians, London Irish) 1977 W, E, S, 1978 S, F, W, E, NZ, 1979 F, W, E, S, 1980 E, S
McKibbin, C H (Instonians) 1976 S (R)
McKibbin, D (Instonians) 1950 F, E, S, W, 1951 F, E, S, W
McKibbin, H R (Queen's U, Belfast) 1938 W, 1939 E, S, W
McKinney, S A (Dungannon) 1972 F 1, E, F 2, 1973 W, F, 1974 F, E, S, P, NZ, 1975 E, S, 1976 A, F, W, E, S, NZ, 1977 W, E, S, 1978 S (R), F, W, E
McLaughlin, J H (Derry) 1887 E, S, 1888 W, S
McLean, R E (Dublin U) 1881 S, 1882 W, E, S, 1883 E, S, 1884 E, S, 1885 E, S 1
Maclear, B (Cork County, Monkstown) 1905 E, S, W, NZ, 1906 E, S, W, SA, 1907 E, S, W
McLennan, A C (Wanderers) 1977 F, 1978 S, F, W, E, NZ, 1979 F, W, E, S, 1980 E, F, 1981 F, W, E, S, SA 1,2
McLoughlin, F M (Northern) 1976 A
McLoughlin, G A J (Shannon) 1979 F, W, E, S, A 1,2, 1980 E, 1981 SA 1,2, 1982 W, E, S, F, 1983 S, F, W, E, 1984 F
McLoughlin, R J (UC Dublin, Blackrock Coll, Gosforth) 1962 E, S, F, 1963 E, S, W, NZ, 1964 E, S, 1965 F, E, S, W, SA, 1966 F, E, S, W, 1971 F, E, S, W, 1972 F 1, E, F 2, 1973 NZ, E, S, W, F, 1974 F, W, E, S, P, NZ, 1975 E, S, F, W
McMahon, L B (Blackrock Coll, UC Dublin) 1931 E, SA, 1933 E, 1934 E, 1936 E, S, W, 1937 E, S, W, 1938 E, S
McMaster, A W (Ballymena) 1972 F 1, E, F 2, 1973 NZ, E, S, W, F, 1974 F, E, S, P, 1975 F, W, 1976 A, F, W, NZ
McMordie, J (Queen's Coll, Belfast) 1886 S
McMorrow, A (Garryowen) 1951 W
McMullen, A R (Cork) 1881 E, S
McNamara, V (UC Cork) 1914 E, S, W
McNaughton, P P (Greystones) 1978 S, F, W, E, 1979 F, W, E, S, A 1,2, 1980 E, S, F, W, 1981 F
MacNeill, H P (Dublin U, Oxford U, Blackrock Coll, London Irish) 1981 F, W, E, S, A, 1982 W, E, S, F, 1983 S, F, W, E, 1984 F, W, E, A, 1985 S, F, W, E, 1986 F, W, E, S, R, 1987 E, S, F, W, [W, C, Tg, A], 1988 S (R), E 1,2
McQuilkin, K P (Bective Rangers) 1996 US, S, F
MacSweeney, D A (Blackrock Coll) 1955 S
McVicker, H (Army, Richmond) 1927 E, S, W, A, 1928 F
McVicker, J (Collegians) 1924 F, E, S, W, NZ, 1925 F, E, S, W, 1926 F, E, S, W, 1927 F, E, S, W, A, 1928 W, 1930 F
McVicker, S (Queen's U, Belfast) 1922 E, S, W, F
Madden, M N (Sunday's Well) 1955 E, S, W
Magee, J T (Bective Rangers) 1895 E, S
Magee, A M (**Louis**) (Bective Rangers, London Irish) 1895 E, S, W, 1896 E, S, W, 1897 E, S, 1898 E, S, W, 1899 E, S, W, 1900 E, S, W, 1901 E, S, W, 1902 E, S, W, 1903 E, S, W, 1904 W

Maginiss, R M (Dublin U) 1875 E, 1876 E
Magrath, R M (Cork Constitution) 1909 S
Maguire, J F (Cork) 1884 S
Mahoney, J (Dolphin) 1923 E
Malcolmson, G L (RAF, NIFC) 1935 NZ, 1936 E, S, W, 1937 E, S, W
Malone, N G (Oxford U, Leicester) 1993 S, F, 1994 US (R)
Mannion, N P (Corinthians, Lansdowne, Wanderers) 1988 WS, It, 1989 F, W, E, S, NZ, 1990 E, S, F, W, Arg, 1991 Nm 1 (R), 2, [J], 1993 S
Marshall, B D E (Queen's U, Belfast) 1963 E
Mason, S J P (Orrell) 1996 W, E
Massey-Westropp, R H (Limerick, Monkstown) 1886 E
Matier, R N (NIFC) 1878 E, 1879 S
Matthews, P M (Ards, Wanderers) 1984 A, 1985 S, F, W, E, 1986 R, 1987 E, S, F, W, [W, Tg, A], 1988 S, F, W, E 1,2, WS, It, 1989 F, W, E, S, NZ, 1990 E, S, 1991 F, W, E, S, Nm 1 [Z, S, A], 1992 W, E, S
Mattsson, J (Wanderers) 1948 E
Mayne, R B (Queen's U, Belfast) 1937 W, 1938 E, W, 1939 E, S, W
Mayne, R H (Belfast Academy) 1888 W, S
Mayne, T (NIFC) 1921 E, S, F
Mays, K M A (UC Dublin) 1973 NZ, E, S, W
Meares, A W D (Dublin U) 1899 S, W, 1900 E, W
Megaw, J (Richmond, Instonians) 1934 W, 1938 E
Millar, A (Kingstown) 1880 E, S, 1883 E
Millar, H J (Monkstown) 1904 W, 1905 E, S, W
Millar, S (Ballymena) 1958 F, 1959 E, S, W, F, 1960 E, S, W, F, SA, 1961 E, S, W, F, SA, 1962 E, S, F, 1963 E, S, W, 1964 F, 1968 F, E, S, W, A, 1969 F, E, S, W, 1970 SA, F, E, S, W
Millar, W H J (Queen's U, Belfast) 1951 E, S, W, 1952 S, W
Miller, F H (Wanderers) 1886 S
Milliken, R A (Bangor) 1973 E, S, W, F, 1974 F, W, E, S, P, NZ, 1975 E, S, F, W
Millin, T J (Dublin U) 1925 W
Minch, J B (Bective Rangers) 1912 SA, 1913 E, S, 1914 E, S
Moffat, J (Belfast Academy) 1888 W, S, M, 1889 S, 1890 S, W, 1891 S
Moffatt, J E (Old Wesley) 1904 S, 1905 E, S, W
Moffett, J W (Ballymena) 1961 E, S
Molloy, M G (UC Galway, London Irish) 1966 F, E, 1967 A 1, E, S, W, F, A 2, 1968 F, E, S, W, A, 1969 F, E, S, W, 1970 F, E, S, W, 1971 F, E, S, W, 1973 F, W, 1976 A
Moloney, J J (St Mary's Coll) 1972 F 1, E, F 2, 1973 NZ, E, S, W, F, 1974 F, W, E, S, P, NZ, 1975 E, S, F, W, 1976 S, 1978 S, F, W, E, 1979 A 1,2, 1980 S, W
Moloney, L A (Garryowen) 1976 W (R), S, 1978 S (R), NZ
Molony, J C (UC Dublin) 1950 S
Monteith, J D E (Queen's U, Belfast) 1947 E, S, W
Montgomery, A (NIFC) 1895 S
Montgomery, F P (Queen's U, Belfast) 1914 E, S, W
Montgomery, R (Cambridge U) 1887 E, S, W, 1891 E, 1892 W
Moore, C M (Dublin U) 1887 S, 1888 W, S
Moore, D F (Wanderers) 1883 E, S, 1884 E, W
Moore, F W (Wanderers) 1884 W, 1885 E, S 2, 1886 S
Moore, H (Windsor) 1876 E, 1877 S
Moore, H (Queen's U, Belfast) 1910 S, 1911 W, F, 1912 F, E, S, W, SA
Moore, T A P (Highfield) 1967 A 2, 1973 NZ, E, S, W, F, 1974 F, W, E, S, P, NZ
Moore, W D (Queen's Coll, Belfast) 1878 E
Moran, F G (Clontarf) 1936 E, 1937 E, S, W, 1938 S, W, 1939 E, S, W
Morell, H B (Dublin U) 1881 E, S, 1882 W, E
Morgan, G J (Clontarf) 1934 E, S, W, 1935 E, S, W, NZ, 1936 E, S, W, 1937 E, S, W, 1938 E, S, W, 1939 E, S, W
Moriarty, C C H (Monkstown) 1899 W
Moroney, J C M (Garryowen) 1968 W, A, 1969 F, E, S, W
Moroney, R J M (Lansdowne) 1984 F, W, 1985 F
Moroney, T A (UC Dublin) 1964 W, 1967 A 1, E
Morphy, E McG (Dublin U) 1908 E
Morris, D P (Bective Rangers) 1931 W, 1932 E, 1935 E, S, W, NZ
Morrow, J W R (Queen's Coll, Belfast) 1882 S, 1883 E, S, 1884 E, W, 1885 S 1,2, 1886 E, S, 1888 S
Morrow, R D (Bangor) 1986 F, E, S
Mortell, M (Bective Rangers, Dolphin) 1953 F, E, S, W, 1954 NZ, F, E, S, W

Newcomer Simon Mason of Orrell, who won his first cap against Wales in the 1996 Five Nations Championship.

248

Morton, W A (Dublin U) 1888 *S*
Moyers, L W (Dublin U) 1884 *W*
Moylett, M M F (Shannon) 1988 *E* 1
Mulcahy, W A (UC Dublin, Bective Rangers, Bohemians) 1958 *A, E, S, W, F,* 1959 *E, S, W, F,* 1960 *E, S, W, SA,* 1961 *E, S, W, SA,* 1962 *E, S, F, W,* 1963 *F, E, S, W, NZ,* 1964 *E, S, W, F,* 1965 *F, E, S, W, SA*
Mullan, B (Clontarf) 1947 *F, E, S, W,* 1948 *F, E, S, W*
Mullane, J P (Limerick Bohemians) 1928 *W,* 1929 *F*
Mullen, K D (Old Belvedere) 1947 *F, E, S, W, A,* 1948 *F, E, S, W,* 1949 *F, E, S, W,* 1950 *F, E, S, W,* 1951 *F, E, S, W, SA,* 1952 *F, S, W*
Mulligan, A A (Wanderers) 1956 *F, E,* 1957 *F, E, S, W,* 1958 *A, E, S, F,* 1959 *E, S, W, F,* 1960 *E, S, W, F, SA,* 1961 *W, F, SA*
Mullin, B J (Dublin U, Oxford U, Blackrock Coll, London Irish) 1984 *A,* 1985 *S, W, E,* 1986 *F, W, E, S, R,* 1987 *E, S, F, W,* [*W, C, Tg, A*]*,* 1988 *S, F, W, E* 1,2, *WS, It,* 1989 *F, W, E, S, NZ,* 1990 *E, S, W, Arg,* 1991 *F, W, E, S, Nm* 1,2, [*J, S, A*]*,* 1992 *W, E, S,* 1994 *US,* 1995 *E, S, F, W, It,* [*NZ, J, W, F*]
Murphy, C J (Lansdowne) 1939 *E, S, W,* 1947 *F, E*
Murphy, J G M W (London Irish) 1951 *SA,* 1952 *S, W, E,* 1954 *NZ,* 1958 *W*
Murphy, J J (Greystones) 1981 *SA* 1, 1982 *W* (R), 1984 *S*
Murphy, J N (Greystones) 1992 *A*
Murphy, K J (Cork Constitution) 1990 *E, S, F, W, Arg,* 1991 *F, W* (R), *S* (R), 1992 *S, F, NZ* 2 (R)
Murphy, N A A (Cork Constitution) 1958 *A, E, S, W, F,* 1959 *E, S, W, F,* 1960 *E, S, W, F, SA,* 1961 *E, S, W,* 1962 *E, W,* 1963 *NZ,* 1964 *E, S, W, F,* 1965 *F, E, S, W, SA,* 1966 *F, E, S, W,* 1967 *A* 1, *E, S, W, F,* 1969 *F, E, S, W*
Murphy, N F (Cork Constitution) 1930 *E, W,* 1931 *F, E, S, W, SA,* 1932 *E, S, W,* 1933 *E*
Murphy-O'Connor, J (Bective Rangers) 1954 *E*
Murray, H W (Dublin U) 1877 *S,* 1878 *E,* 1879 *E*
Murray, J B (UC Dublin) 1963 *F*
Murray, P F (Wanderers) 1927 *F,* 1929 *F, E, S,* 1930 *F, E, S, W,* 1931 *F, E, S, W, SA,* 1932 *E, S, W,* 1933 *E, W, S*
Murtagh, C W (Portadown) 1977 *S*
Myles, J (Dublin U) 1875 *E*

Nash, L C (Queen's Coll, Cork) 1889 *S,* 1890 *W, E,* 1891 *E, S, W*
Neely, M R (Collegians) 1947 *F, E, S, W*
Neill, H J (NIFC) 1885 *E, S* 1,2, 1886 *S,* 1887 *E, S, W,* 1888 *W, S*
Neill, J McF (Instonians) 1926 *F*
Nelson, J E (Malone) 1947 *A,* 1948 *E, S, W,* 1949 *F, E, S, W,* 1950 *F, E, S, W,* 1951 *F, E, S, W,* 1954 *F*
Nelson, R (Queen's Coll, Belfast) 1882 *E, S,* 1883 *S,* 1886 *S*
Nesdale, T J (Garryowen) 1961 *F*
Neville, W C (Dublin U) 1879 *S, E*
Nicholson, P C (Dublin U) 1900 *E, S, W*
Norton, G W (Bective Rangers) 1949 *F, E, S, W,* 1950 *F, E, S, W,* 1951 *F, E, S*
Notley, J R (Wanderers) 1952 *F, S*

O'Brien, B (Derry) 1893 *S, W*
O'Brien, B A P (Shannon) 1968 *F, E, S*
O'Brien, D J (London Irish, Cardiff, Old Belvedere) 1948 *E, S, W,* 1949 *F, E, S, W,* 1950 *F, E, S, W,* 1951 *F, E, S, W, SA,* 1952 *F, S, W, E*
O'Brien, K A (Broughton Park) 1980 *E,* 1981 *SA* 1 (R), 2
O'Brien-Butler, P E (Monkstown) 1897 *S,* 1898 *E, S,* 1899 *W,* 1900 *E*
O'Callaghan, C T (Carlow) 1910 *W, F,* 1911 *E, S, W, F,* 1912 *F*
O'Callaghan, M P (Sunday's Well) 1962 *W,* 1964 *E, F*
O'Callaghan, P (Dolphin) 1967 *A* 1, *E, A* 2, 1968 *F, E, S, W,* 1969 *F, E, S, W,* 1970 *SA, F, E, S, W,* 1976 *F, W, E, S, NZ*
O'Connell, K D (Sunday's Well) 1994 *F, E* (t)
O'Connell, P (Bective Rangers) 1913 *W, F,* 1914 *F, E, S, W*
O'Connell, W J (Lansdowne) 1955 *F*
O'Connor, H S (Dublin U) 1957 *F, E, S, W*
O'Connor, J (Garryowen) 1895 *S*
O'Connor, J H (Bective Rangers) 1888 *M,* 1890 *S, W, E,* 1891 *E, S,* 1892 *E, W,* 1893 *E, S,* 1894 *E, S, W,* 1895 *E,* 1896 *E, S, W*
O'Connor, J J (Garryowen) 1909 *F*
O'Connor, J J (UC Cork) 1933 *S,* 1934 *E, S, W,* 1935 *E, S, W, NZ,* 1936 *S, W,* 1938 *S*
O'Connor, P J (Lansdowne) 1887 *W*

Odbert, R V M (RAF) 1928 *F*
O'Donnell, R C (St Mary's Coll) 1979 *A* 1,2, 1980 *S, F, W*
O'Donoghue, P J (Bective Rangers) 1955 *F, E, S, W,* 1956 *W,* 1957 *F, E,* 1958 *A, E, S, W*
O'Driscoll, B J (Manchester) 1971 *F* (R), *E, S, W*
O'Driscoll, J B (London Irish, Manchester) 1978 *S,* 1979 *A* 1,2, 1980 *E, S, F, W,* 1981 *F, W, E, S, SA* 1,2, *A,* 1982 *W, E, S, F,* 1983 *S, F, W, E,* 1984 *F, W, E, S*
O'Flanagan, K P (London Irish) 1947 *A*
O'Flanagan, M (Lansdowne) 1948 *S*
O'Hanlon, B (Dolphin) 1947 *E, S, W,* 1948 *F, E, S, W,* 1949 *F, E, S, W,* 1950 *F*
O'Hara, P T J (Sunday's Well, Cork Const) 1988 *WS* (R), 1989 *F, W, E, NZ,* 1990 *E, S, F, W,* 1991 *Nm* 1, [*J*], 1993 *F, W, E,* 1994 *US*
O'Leary, A (Cork Constitution) 1952 *S, W, E*
O'Loughlin, D B (UC Cork) 1938 *E, S, W,* 1939 *E, S, W*
O'Mahony, Darragh (UC Dublin) 1995 *It,* [*F*]
O'Mahony, David (Cork Constitution) 1995 *It*
O'Meara, J A (UC Cork, Dolphin) 1951 *F, E, S, W, SA,* 1952 *F, S, W, E,* 1953 *F, E, S, W,* 1954 *NZ, F, E, S,* 1955 *F, E,* 1956 *S, W,* 1958 *W*
O'Neill, H O'H (Queen's U, Belfast, UC Cork) 1930 *E, S, W,* 1933 *E, S, W*
O'Neill, J B (Queen's U, Belfast) 1920 *S*
O'Neill, W A (UC Dublin, Wanderers) 1952 *E,* 1953 *F, E, S, W,* 1954 *NZ*
O'Reilly, A J F (Old Belvedere, Leicester) 1955 *F, E, S, W,* 1956 *F, E, S, W,* 1957 *F, E, S, W,* 1958 *A, E, S, W, F,* 1959 *E, S, W, F,* 1960 *E,* 1961 *E, F, SA,* 1963 *F, S, W,* 1970 *E*
Orr, P A (Old Wesley) 1976 *F, W, E, S, NZ,* 1977 *W, E, S, F,* 1978 *S, F, W, E, NZ,* 1979 *F, W, E, S, A* 1,2, 1980 *E, S, F, W,* 1981 *F, W, E, S, SA* 1,2, *A,* 1982 *W, E, S, F,* 1983 *S, F, W, E,* 1984 *F, W, E, S, A,* 1985 *S, F, W, E,* 1986 *F, S, R,* 1987 *E, S, F, W,* [*W, C, A*]
O'Shea, C M P (Lansdowne) 1993 *R,* 1994 *F, W, E, S, A* 1,2, *US,* 1995 *E, S,* [*J, W, F*]
O'Sullivan, A C (Dublin U) 1882 *S*
O'Sullivan, J M (Limerick) 1884 *S,* 1887 *S*
O'Sullivan, P J A (Galwegians) 1957 *F, E, S, W,* 1959 *E, S, W, F,* 1960 *SA,* 1961 *E, S,* 1962 *F, W,* 1963 *F, NZ*
O'Sullivan, W (Queen's Coll, Cork) 1895 *S*
Owens, R H (Dublin U) 1922 *E, S*

Parfrey, P (UC Cork) 1974 *NZ*
Parke, J C (Monkstown) 1903 *W,* 1904 *E, S, W,* 1905 *W, NZ,* 1906 *E, S, W, SA,* 1907 *E, S, W,* 1908 *E, S, W,* 1909 *E, S, W, F*
Parr, J S (Wanderers) 1914 *F, E, S, W*
Patterson, C S (Instonians) 1978 *NZ,* 1979 *F, W, E, S, A* 1,2, 1980 *E, S, F, W*
Patterson, R d'A (Wanderers) 1912 *F, S, W, SA,* 1913 *E, S, W, F*
Payne, C T (NIFC) 1926 *E,* 1927 *F, E, S, A,* 1928 *F, E, S, W,* 1929 *F, E, W,* 1930 *F, E, S, W*
Pedlow, A C (CIYMS) 1953 *W,* 1954 *NZ, F, E,* 1955 *F, E, S, W,* 1956 *F, E, S, W,* 1957 *F, E, S, W,* 1958 *A, E, S, W, F,* 1959 *E,* 1960 *E, S, W, F, SA,* 1961 *S,* 1962 *W,* 1963 *F*
Pedlow, J (Bessbrook) 1882 *S,* 1884 *W*
Pedlow, R (Bessbrook) 1891 *W*
Pedlow, T B (Queen's Coll, Belfast) 1889 *S, W*
Peel, T (Limerick) 1892 *E, S, W*
Peirce, W (Cork) 1881 *E*
Phipps, G C (Army) 1950 *E, W,* 1952 *F, W, E*
Pike, T O (Lansdowne) 1927 *E, S, W, A,* 1928 *F, E, S, W*
Pike, V J (Lansdowne) 1931 *E, S, W, SA,* 1932 *E, S, W,* 1933 *E, W, S,* 1934 *E, S, W*
Pike, W W (Kingstown) 1879 *E,* 1881 *E, S,* 1882 *E, S,* 1883 *S*
Pinion, G (Belfast Collegians) 1909 *E, S, W, F*
Piper, O J S (Cork Constitution) 1909 *E, S, W, F,* 1910 *E, S, W, F*
Polden, S E (Clontarf) 1913 *W, F,* 1914 *F,* 1920 *F*
Popham, I (Cork Constitution) 1922 *S, W, F,* 1923 *F*
Popplewell, N J (Greystones, Wasps, Newcastle) 1989 *NZ,* 1990 *Arg,* 1991 *Nm* 1,2, [*Z, S, A*], 1992 *W, E, S, F, NZ* 1,2, *A,* 1993 *S, F, W, E,* 1994 *F, W, E, S, US,* 1995 *E, S, F, W, It,* [*NZ, J, W, F*], *Fj,* 1996 *US, S, F, W, E*
Potterton, H N (Wanderers) 1920 *W*
Pratt, R H (Dublin U) 1933 *E, W, S,* 1934 *E, S*
Price, A H (Dublin U) 1920 *S, F*
Pringle, J C (NIFC) 1902 *S, W*
Purcell, N M (Lansdowne) 1921 *E, S, W, F*
Purdon, H (NIFC) 1879 *S, E,* 1880 *E, S,* 1881 *E, S*
Purdon, W B (Queen's Coll, Belfast) 1906 *E, S, W*

Sugden, M (Wanderers) 1925 *F, E, S, W,* 1926 *F, E, S, W,* 1927 *E, S, W, A,* 1928 *F, E, S, W,* 1929 *F, E, S, W,* 1930 *F, E, S, W,* 1931 *F, E, S, W*
Sullivan, D B (UC Dublin) 1922 *E, S, W, F*
Sweeney, J A (Blackrock Coll) 1907 *E, S, W*
Symes, G R (Monkstown) 1895 *E*
Synge, J S (Lansdowne) 1929 *S*

Taggart, T (Dublin U) 1887 *W*
Taylor, A S (Queen's Coll, Belfast) 1910 *E, S, W,* 1912 *F*
Taylor, D R (Queen's Coll, Belfast) 1903 *E*
Taylor, J (Belfast Collegians) 1914 *E, S, W*
Taylor, J W (NIFC) 1879 *S,* 1880 *E, S,* 1881 *S,* 1882 *E, S,* 1883 *E, S*
Tector, W R (Wanderers) 1955 *F, E, S*
Tedford, A (Malone) 1902 *E, S, W,* 1903 *E, S, W,* 1904 *E, S, W,* 1905 *E, S, W, NZ,* 1906 *E, S, W, SA,* 1907 *E, S, W,* 1908 *E, S, W*
Teehan, C (UC Cork) 1939 *E, S, W*
Thompson, C (Belfast Collegians) 1907 *E, S,* 1908 *E, S, W,* 1909 *E, S, W, F,* 1910 *E, S, W, F*
Thompson, J A (Queen's Coll, Belfast) 1885 *S* 1,2
Thompson, J K S (Dublin U) 1921 *W,* 1922 *E, S, F,* 1923 *E, S, W, F*
Thompson, R G (Lansdowne) 1882 *W*
Thompson, R H (Instonians) 1951 *SA,* 1952 *F,* 1954 *NZ, F, E, S, W,* 1955 *F, S, W,* 1956 *W*
Thornhill, T (Wanderers) 1892 *E, S, W,* 1893 *E*
Thrift, H (Dublin U) 1904 *W,* 1905 *E, S, W, NZ,* 1906 *E, W, SA,* 1907 *E, S, W,* 1908 *E, S, W,* 1909 *E, S, W, F*
Tierney, D (UC Cork) 1938 *S, W,* 1939 *E*
Tillie, C R (Dublin U) 1887 *E, S,* 1888 *W, S*
Todd, A W P (Dublin U) 1913 *W, F,* 1914 *F*
Torrens, J D (Bohemians) 1938 *W,* 1939 *E, S, W*
Tucker, C C (Shannon) 1979 *F, W,* 1980 *F* (R)
Tuke, B B (Bective Rangers) 1890 *E,* 1891 *E, S,* 1892 *E,* 1894 *E, S, W,* 1895 *E, S*
Turley, N (Blackrock Coll) 1962 *E*
Tweed, D A (Ballymena) 1995 *F, W, It,* [*J*]
Tydings, J J (Young Munster) 1968 *A*
Tyrrell, W (Queen's U, Belfast) 1910 *F,* 1913 *E, S, W, F,* 1914 *F, E, S, W*

Uprichard, R J H (Harlequins, RAF) 1950 *S, W*

Waide, S L (Oxford U, NIFC) 1932 *E, S, W,* 1933 *E, W*
Waites, J (Bective Rangers) 1886 *S,* 1888 *M,* 1889 *W,* 1890 *S, W, E,* 1891 *E*
Waldron, O C (Oxford U, London Irish) 1966 *S, W,* 1968 *A*
Walker, S (Instonians) 1934 *E, S,* 1935 *E, S, W, NZ,* 1936 *E, S, W,* 1937 *E, S, W,* 1938 *E, S, W*
Walkington, D B (NIFC) 1887 *E, W,* 1888 *W, E,* 1890 *W, E,* 1891 *E, S, W*
Walkington, R B (NIFC) 1875 *E,* 1876 *E,* 1877 *E, S,* 1878 *E,* 1879 *S,* 1880 *E, S,* 1882 *E, S*
Wall, H (Dolphin) 1965 *S, W*
Wallace, Jas (Wanderers) 1904 *E, S*
Wallace, Jos (Wanderers) 1903 *S, W,* 1904 *E, S, W,* 1905 *E, S, W, NZ,* 1906 *W*
Wallace, P S (Blackrock Coll) 1995 [*J*], *Fj,* 1996 *US, W, E*

Wallace, R M (Garryowen) 1991 *Nm* 1 (R), 1992 *W, E, S, F, A,* 1993 *S, F, W, E, R,* 1994 *F, W, E, S,* 1995 *W, It,* [*NZ, J, W*], *Fj,* 1996 *US, S, F*
Wallace, T H (Cardiff) 1920 *E, S, W*
Wallis, A K (Wanderers) 1892 *E, S, W,* 1893 *E, W*
Wallis, C O'N (Old Cranleighans, Wanderers) 1935 *NZ*
Wallis, T G (Wanderers) 1921 *F,* 1922 *E, S, W, F*
Wallis, W A (Wanderers) 1880 *S,* 1881 *E, S,* 1882 *W,* 1883 *S*
Walmsley, G (Bective Rangers) 1894 *E*
Walpole, A (Dublin U) 1888 *S, M*
Walsh, E J (Lansdowne) 1887 *E, S, W,* 1892 *E, S, W,* 1893 *E*
Walsh, H D (Dublin U) 1875 *E,* 1876 *E*
Walsh, J C (UC Cork, Sunday's Well) 1960 *S, SA,* 1961 *E, S, F, SA,* 1963 *E, S, W, NZ,* 1964 *E, S, W, F,* 1965 *F, S, W, SA,* 1966 *F, S, W,* 1967 *E, S, W, F, A* 2
Ward, A J P (Garryowen, St Mary's Coll, Greystones) 1978 *S, F, W, E, NZ,* 1979 *F, W, E, S,* 1981 *W, E, S, A,* 1983 *E* (R), 1984 *E, S,* 1986 *S,* 1987 [*C, Tg*]
Warren, J P (Kingstown) 1883 *E*
Warren, R G (Lansdowne) 1884 *W,* 1885 *E, S* 1,2, 1886 *E,* 1887 *E, S, W,* 1888 *W, S, M,* 1889 *S, W,* 1890 *S, W, E*
Watson, R (Wanderers) 1912 *SA*
Wells, H G (Bective Rangers) 1891 *S, W,* 1894 *E, S*
Westby, A J (Dublin U) 1876 *E*
Wheeler, G H (Queen's Coll, Belfast) 1884 *S,* 1885 *E*
Wheeler, J R (Queen's U, Belfast) 1922 *E, S, W, F,* 1924 *E*
Whelan, P C (Garryowen) 1975 *E, S,* 1976 *NZ,* 1977 *W, E, S, F,* 1978 *S, F, W, E, NZ,* 1979 *F, W, E, S,* 1981 *F, W, E*
White, M (Queen's Coll, Cork) 1906 *E, S, W, SA,* 1907 *E, W*
Whitestone, A M (Dublin U) 1877 *E,* 1879 *S, E,* 1880 *E,* 1883 *S*
Whittle, D (Bangor) 1988 *F*
Wilkinson, C R (Malone) 1993 *S*
Wilkinson, R W (Wanderers) 1947 *A*
Williamson, F W (Dolphin) 1930 *E, S, W*
Willis, W J (Lansdowne) 1879 *E*
Wilson, F (CIYMS) 1977 *W, E, S*
Wilson, H G (Glasgow U, Malone) 1905 *E, S, W, NZ,* 1906 *E, S, W, SA,* 1907 *E, S, W,* 1908 *E, S, W,* 1909 *E, S, W,* 1910 *W*
Wilson, W H (Bray) 1877 *E, S*
Withers, H H C (Army, Blackheath) 1931 *F, E, S, W, SA*
Wolfe, E J (Armagh) 1882 *E*
Wood, G H (Dublin U) 1913 *W,* 1914 *F*
Wood, B G M (Garryowen) 1954 *E, S,* 1956 *F, E, S, W,* 1957 *F, E, S, W,* 1958 *A, E, S, W, F,* 1959 *E, S, W, F,* 1960 *E, S, W, F, SA,* 1961 *E, S, W, F, SA*
Wood, K G M (Garryowen) 1994 *A* 1,2, *US,* 1995 *E, S,* [*J*]
Woods, D C (Bessbrook) 1888 *M,* 1889 *S*
Woods, N K P J (Blackrock Coll) 1994 *A* 1,2, 1995 *E, F,* 1996 *F, W, E*
Wright, R A (Monkstown) 1912 *S*

Yeates, R A (Dublin U) 1889 *S, W*
Young, G (UC Cork) 1913 *E*
Young, R M (Collegians) 1965 *F, E, S, W, SA,* 1966 *F, E, S, W,* 1967 *W, F,* 1968 *W, A,* 1969 *F, E, S, W,* 1970 *SA, F, E, S, W,* 1971 *F, E, S, W*

IRISH INTERNATIONAL RECORDS

Both team and individual records are for official Ireland international matches up to 30 April 1996.

TEAM RECORDS

Highest score
60 v Romania (60-0) 1986 Dublin

v individual countries
20 v Argentina (20-18) 1990 Dublin
27 v Australia (27-12) 1979 Brisbane
46 v Canada (46-19) 1987 Dunedin
26 v England (26-21) 1974 Twickenham
44 v Fiji (44-8) 1995 Dublin
25 v France {(25-5) 1911 Cork / (25-6) 1975 Dublin}
31 v Italy (31-15) 1988 Dublin
50 v Japan (50-28) 1995 Bloemfontein
15 v Namibia (15-26) 1991 Windhoek
21 v N Zealand (21-24) 1992 Dunedin
60 v Romania (60-0) 1986 Dublin
15 v S Africa (15-23) 1981 Cape Town
26 v Scotland (26-8) 1953 Murrayfield
32 v Tonga (32-9) 1987 Brisbane
26 v United States (26-15) 1994 Dublin

30 v Wales (30-17) 1996 Dublin
49 v W Samoa (49-22) 1988 Dublin
55 v Zimbabwe (55-11) 1991 Dublin

Biggest winning points margin
60 v Romania (60-0) 1986 Dublin

v individual countries
 2 v Argentina (20-18) 1990 Dublin
15 v Australia (27-12) 1979 Brisbane
27 v Canada (46-19) 1987 Dunedin
22 v England (22-0) 1947 Dublin
36 v Fiji (44-8) 1995 Dublin
24 v France (24-0) 1913 Cork
16 v Italy (31-15) 1988 Dublin
22 v Japan (50-28) 1995 Bloemfontein
60 v Romania (60-0) 1986 Dublin
 3 v S Africa (9-6) 1965 Dublin
21 v Scotland (21-0) 1950 Dublin
23 v Tonga (32-9) 1987 Brisbane
11 v United States (26-15) 1994 Dublin
16 v Wales (19-3) 1925 Belfast
27 v W Samoa (49-22) 1988 Dublin
44 v Zimbabwe (55-11) 1991 Dublin
No wins v Namibia or New Zealand

Longest winning sequence
6 matches 1968-69

Highest score by opposing team
59 N Zealand (6-59) 1992 Wellington

by individual countries
18 Argentina (20-18) 1990 Dublin
42 Australia (17-42) 1992 Dublin
19 Canada (46-19) 1987 Dunedin
38 England (9-38) 1992 Twickenham
 8 Fiji (44-8) 1995 Dublin
45 France (10-45) 1996 Paris
22 Italy (12-22) 1995 Treviso
28 Japan (50-28) 1995 Bloemfontein
26 Namibia (15-26) 1991 Windhoek
59 N Zealand (6-59) 1992 Wellington
 3 Romania (25-3) 1993 Dublin
38 S Africa (0-38) 1912 Dublin
37 Scotland (21-37) 1989 Murrayfield
 9 Tonga (32-9) 1987 Brisbane
18 United States (25-18) 1996 Atlanta
34 Wales (9-34) 1976 Dublin
22 W Samoa (49-22) 1988 Dublin
11 Zimbabwe (55-11) 1991 Dublin

Biggest losing points margin
53 v N Zealand (6-59) 1992 Wellington

v individual countries
25 v Australia (17-42) 1992 Dublin
32 v England (3-35) 1988 Twickenham
35 v France (10-45) 1996 Paris
10 v Italy (12-22) 1995 Treviso

11 v Namibia (15-26) 1991 Windhoek
53 v N Zealand(6-59) 1992 Wellington
38 v S Africa (0-38) 1912 Dublin
23 v Scotland (9-32) 1984 Dublin
29 v Wales (0-29) 1907 Cardiff
No defeats v Argentina, Canada, Fiji, Japan, Romania, Tonga, United States, W Samoa or Zimbabwe

Longest losing sequence
11 matches 1991-93

Most tries by Ireland in an international
10 v Romania (60-0) 1986 Dublin

Most tries against Ireland in an international
10 by S Africa (0-38) 1912 Dublin

Most points by Ireland in International Championship in a season – 71
in season 1982-83

Most tries by Ireland in International Championship in a season – 12
in seasons 1927-28 and 1952-53

INDIVIDUAL RECORDS

Most capped player
C M H Gibson   69   1964-79
in individual positions

Full-back
T J Kiernan   54   1960-73
Wing
K D Crossan   41   1982-92
Centre
B J Mullin   55[1]   1984-95
Fly-half
J W Kyle   46   1947-58
Scrum-half
M T Bradley   40   1984-95
Prop
P A Orr   58   1976-87
Hooker
K W Kennedy   45   1965-75
Lock
W J McBride   63   1962-75
Flanker
J F Slattery   61   1970-84
No 8
W P Duggan   39(41)[2]   1975-84
[1] *C M H Gibson won 40 caps as a centre, 25 at fly-half and 4 as a wing*
[2] *Duggan won 39 caps at No 8 and 2 as a flanker*

Longest international career
A J F O'Reilly 16 seasons 1955-70
C M H Gibson 16 seasons 1964-79
Gibson's career ended during a southern hemisphere season

Most consecutive Tests – 52
W J McBride 1964-75

Most internationals as captain – 24
T J Kiernan 1963-73

Most points in internationals – 308
M J Kiernan (43 matches) 1982-91

Most points in International Championship in a season – 52
S O Campbell (4 matches) 1982-83

Most points in an international – 23
R P Keyes v Zimbabwe 1991 Dublin

Most tries in internationals – 17
B J Mullin (55 matches) 1984-95

Most tries in International Championship in a season – 5
J E Arigho (3 matches) 1927-28

Most tries in an international – 4
B F Robinson v Zimbabwe 1991 Dublin

Most conversions in internationals – 40
M J Kiernan (43 matches) 1982-91

Most conversions in International Championship in a season – 7
R A Lloyd (4 matches) 1912-13

Most conversions in an international – 7
M J Kiernan v Romania 1986 Dublin

Most dropped goals in internationals – 7
R A Lloyd (19 matches) 1910-20
S O Campbell (22 matches) 1976-84

Most dropped goals in an international – 2
C M H Gibson v Australia 1967 Dublin
W M McCombe v France 1975 Dublin
S O Campbell v Australia 1979 Sydney
E P Elwood v England 1993 Dublin

Most penalty goals in internationals – 62
M J Kiernan (43 matches) 1982-91

Most penalty goals in International Championship in a season – 14
S O Campbell (4 matches) 1982-83
E P Elwood (4 matches) 1993-94

Most penalty goals in an international – 6
S O Campbell v Scotland 1982 Dublin
E P Elwood v Romania 1993 Dublin

Most points for Ireland on overseas tour – 60
S O Campbell (5 appearances) 1979 Australia
M J Kiernan scored 65 points in Japan 1985, but this was not on a major tour

Most points in any match on tour – 19
A J P Ward v Australian Capital Territory 1979 Canberra
S O Campbell v Australia 1979 Brisbane
E P Elwood v Western Australia 1994 Perth
M J Kiernan scored 25 points in the second match against Japan 1985, but this was not on a major tour

Most tries in any match on tour – 3
A T A Duggan v Victoria 1967 Melbourne
J F Slattery v SA President's XV 1981 East London
M J Kiernan v Gold Cup XV 1981 Oudtshoorn, SA
M J Field v Western Australia 1994 Perth
T M Ringland scored 3 tries v Japan at Osaka 1985, but this was not on a major tour

CLUBS DREAD THIS NEW SCOURGE

THE 1995-96 SEASON IN WALES
John Billot *Western Mail*

'From the fury of the northmen, O Lord, deliver us!' was the solemn chant of ninth-century monks of Western Europe. But it is no longer the northerners of the Rugby League who come to plunder: the new scourge is England's millionaire clubs, capable of outbidding all others, which have instilled into Welsh clubs the abiding fear that the majority of them will be left on Poverty Row. Already, significant numbers of the nation's rugby treasures have been stolen away.

Clubs who had big deals cooking to sign important players suddenly found they were being gazumped. Cardiff signed Jonathan Davies from Warrington for a negotiated fee of some £70,000, but at the end of the season found themselves relieved of their half-back pairing of Adrian Davies and Andy Moore by Richmond on contracts said to be worth £65,000 per annum. Wasps signed Cardiff prop Mike Griffiths in a three-year deal worth more than £200,000, having already secured Matthew Lewis, the Bridgend fly-half, and Neath jumper Glyn Llewellyn. Big money attracted Phil Davies, the Llanelli captain, to Leeds and Gareth Llewellyn, the Neath captain, to Harlequins. The list was growing longer by the week.

Russell Jenkins, a solicitor and respected WRU committeeman, painted a dark vision of the future: 'I suspect, because of the lack of corporate money in Wales, the future stars of rugby are likely to play outside the country. From the Welsh clubs' point of view, I think there is a major danger we will not have as strong a club scene as we have now. I think there is a distinct danger that our national team will be like our soccer side: made up of players playing in other countries.'

The WRU applied themselves diligently to restructuring national coaching. Neath-born Kevin Bowring became their first professional coaching chief in November 1995 on a four-year contract and a salary of around £50,000. The 41-year-old had played more than 350 games for London Welsh, mainly at No 8, between 1977 and 1986, and coached Wales A to nine victories in 13 matches. Allan Lewis (Llanelli) was appointed national assistant coach and Terry Cobner was headhunted from teaching at Oundle School to take up the role of first WRU director of rugby in January 1996 at around £50,000 per annum. Cobner, who captained Pontypool for ten seasons and won 19 caps, was a British Lion in New Zealand in 1977 and led Wales in 1978 in Australia. As the inspiration of Pontypool's fearsome pack, he has a proven record as a dynamic motivator.

Welsh tactics had been prisoner to lack of confidence and a reliance on kicking with little tactical response. They desperately needed to

The Wales team which beat France at Cardiff. L-R, back row: W T Proctor (replacement), N R Jenkins (replacement), S Williams (replacement), R G Jones, N G Davies, G Thomas, G O Llewellyn, D Jones, E W Lewis, H T Taylor, L Mustoe (replacement), A P Moore (replacement), G R Jenkins (replacement); front row: A C Thomas (replacement), L B Davies, I C Evans, C D Loader, J M Humphreys (capt), R Howley, W J L Thomas, J D Davies.

escape from the claustrophobia of the tight game, and Bowring pledged a change of style: 'When you play a more mobile game, you make more mistakes,' he admitted, 'but we have tried to take away the fear of making mistakes.' Such errors were evident at Twickenham, where a dramatic blunder by Justin Thomas cost Wales dear, and then Arwel Thomas, chosen ahead of Neil Jenkins, endured a nightmare match in Ireland. Jenkins was obviously the steadiest fly-half in Wales and his omission was another example of faulty selection. He was sacrificed to the running style, but the experiment foundered.

Bowring reflected: 'We could have beaten England, we should have beaten Scotland and we expected to beat Ireland.' Instead, Wales faced the chilling prospect of a second successive Five Nations whitewash. However, with Jenkins restored as the pivot, the team responded magnificently. Victory by a whisker (16-15) against France ended a record sequence of eight championship matches without success. 'We needed to prove to everyone that the style of rugby we are trying to play is a winning style,' stressed Jonathan Humphreys, the Welsh captain. Actually, it was a meld of open and tight rugby that brought belated cheer to a nation on its rugby knees.

A coach who repudiates negative methods and excessive kicking has been found; also a scrum-half whose talents had been ignored by previous coaches was brought in to score a debut try at Twickenham and cross again in the victory over France. Robert Howley, the Bridgend captain, was voted Welsh Player of the Year ahead of two other outstanding newcomers, Gwyn Jones, the Llanelli openside, and Leigh Davies, of Neath, in the centre.

The most exciting news of the season came in February, when the Millennium Commission awarded £46 million towards the £106 million cost of rebuilding the Arms Park National Stadium, to be completed in time to stage the 1999 World Cup finals. The ground will have a capacity of 75,000 and a retractable roof, the first of its kind in Britain. Around £60 million will be contributed by the WRU, debenture sales and the private sector. We can but hope that playing fortunes will revive to end the jibe that Wales possess a multi-million-pound ground and a tuppenny-ha'penny team.

NEATH BY A TWO-TRY MARGIN

THE HEINEKEN LEAGUES 1995-96

A try by Steve Williams, the Neath No 8, holding a tackler at arm's length for the last 15 yards, brought the Gnoll team their seventh try against Pontypridd, five minutes from the end, and a maximum three bonus points to reclaim the League title they last won in its inaugural season of 1990-91. Never before had the championship been decided on the final day of the season (extended to 14 May because of an icy winter), and the new scoring system was responsible for the high drama that accompanied the two decisive fixtures.

Neath were in pole position on the try count, six ahead of their rivals, so, while Gareth Llewellyn's team had to wring maximum points out of Ponty (the only club to have defeated Neath during the second half of the season, and that in the SWALEC Cup final ten days earlier), Cardiff not only required maximum points against Llanelli at the Arms Park, but had to score 13 tries to boot. In the event, Cardiff did collect 11 in their record 65-13 victory over the Scarlets, which provided some solace for Steve Ford, whose brace made him the League's record-holder with 21 in a season.

But Neath's 45-25 success brought them the title by a two-try margin in front of a packed and vibrant Gnoll. They had suffered their worst try aggregate (33) for five years during the previous season: now they had 121. The recruitment of Darryl Jones from Aberavon and the return of Lyn Jones from Treorchy to front their new coaching operation produced exciting results. It was a mixture of joy and sadness for skipper Llewellyn, playing his final game before joining Harlequins. Ponty, too, experienced mixed emotions. Neil Jenkins scored ten points to overtake Newport's Gareth Rees as League top scorer for the season with 285, equalling his own record, while veteran captain Nigel Bezani played his last game before bowing out. Steele Lewis suffered one of those mad flushes and was sent off for butting. A case of the good, the old and the ugly.

It was a bitter twist for Cardiff that they had defeated Neath twice and would have retained the title but for the new bonus system – they won 18 matches to Neath's 17. In addition to two points for a win or one for a draw, there was one point for three tries, a second point for a fifth and a final point for seven tries or more. Undeniably, the bonus points added zest to the tournament for both players and spectators. Bridgend (twice) and Newport were the only teams to defeat Cardiff; Neath lost to Cardiff (twice) and at Pontypridd and Llanelli. Cardiff could have kept the title had they won at Pontypridd four days earlier, but they were thankful enough to scrape a 27-27 draw through Nigel Walker's second try (his first, for which he ran from his own goal-line, was the most amazing try of the season), from the last move of the game. Mike Rayer converted to stun Sardis Road.

Swansea, twice League winners, suffered horrendously from injuries and lost eight of their 11 away games. Llanelli faded after a promising start and found themselves on the wrong end of a 41-0 result at the Gnoll in late April which proved the springboard for Neath's race to the top. Llanelli had to compensate Mike Hall for 'loss of earnings' when Tony Copsey broke the Cardiff centre's jaw with a punch. Hall received about £1,000 for having to miss four League games and his club's match against the Fijians. Dunvant returned to the top division after a season's absence.

HEINEKEN LEAGUES

Division 1

	P	W	D	L	Bon	T	Pts
Neath	22	17	1	4	37	121	72
Cardiff	22	18	1	3	35	119	72
Pontypridd	22	16	1	5	28	98	61
Llanelli	22	15	0	7	29	88	59
Bridgend	22	12	1	9	22	73	47
Swansea	22	11	0	11	22	83	44
Ebbw Vale	22	11	0	11	8	44	30
Newport	22	10	1	11	9	43	30
Newbridge	22	9	0	13	11	47	29
Treorchy	22	5	1	16	10	45	21
Aberavon	22	3	0	19	8	38	14
Abertillery	22	2	0	20	8	43	12

Division 2

	P	W	D	L	Bon	T	Pts
Dunvant	22	18	0	4	24	78	60
Caerphilly	22	18	0	4	14	57	50
Cross Keys	22	11	0	11	18	68	40
Pontypool	22	12	0	10	15	63	39
Bonymaen	22	10	0	12	14	55	34
Llandovery	22	11	2	9	5	37	29
Maesteg	22	10	1	11	7	38	28
Abercynon	22	10	0	12	6	39	26
Ystradgynlais	22	10	1	11	5	38	26
SW Police	22	7	0	15	11	49	25
Llanharan	22	9	0	13	6	41	24
Tenby Utd	22	4	0	18	4	33	12

Division 3

	P	W	D	L	Bon	T	Pts
Blackwood	22	18	2	2	23	78	61
Cardiff Inst	22	14	1	7	15	60	44
Kenfig Hill	22	13	0	9	13	58	39
Tondu	22	14	0	8	11	48	39
Penarth	22	10	1	11	9	47	30
Tredegar	22	10	0	12	7	47	27
Narberth	22	9	1	12	8	45	27
Builth Wells	22	9	2	11	6	41	26
Pyle	22	9	1	12	7	35	26
Mountain Ash	22	9	2	11	5	30	25
Blaina	22	8	2	12	6	35	24
Glamorgan W	22	3	0	19	5	35	11

Division 4

	P	W	D	L	Bon	T	Pts
Merthyr	22	17	0	5	25	85	59
Rumney	22	15	1	6	21	79	52
Carmarthen Qs	22	15	1	6	20	69	51
Tumble	22	18	0	4	12	51	48
Llantrisant	22	16	1	5	11	48	44
Whitland	22	11	1	10	17	57	40
Glynneath	22	12	0	10	11	48	35
Rhymney	22	8	0	14	11	54	27
Vardre	22	7	1	14	6	42	21
St Peter's	22	5	0	17	9	39	19
Aberavon Quins	22	4	1	17	5	34	14
Pontypool Utd	22	1	0	21	4	25	6

Division 5

	P	W	D	L	Bon	T	Pts
Kidwelly	22	18	0	4	29	94	65
Oakdale	22	15	1	6	21	69	52
Ystrad Rhondda	22	15	0	7	17	71	47
Seven Sisters	22	14	0	8	18	64	46
Abergavenny	22	13	0	9	14	52	40
Felinfoel	22	13	0	9	11	49	37
Tonmawr	22	10	1	11	4	30	25
Garndiffaith	22	7	0	15	10	47	24
Cardiff Quins	22	7	0	15	8	42	22
Abercarn	22	6	1	15	9	41	22
Pontyberem*	22	7	0	15	5	36	17
Hendy	22	5	1	16	5	29	16

NATIONAL LEAGUES

Division 6 East

	P	W	D	L	T	Pts
Bedwas	22	19	2	1	98	71
Brynmawr	22	16	1	5	71	52
Dinas Powys	22	12	1	9	63	43
Croesyceiliog	22	12	3	7	41	34
O Penarthians	22	12	0	10	43	34
Wrexham*	22	13	1	8	40	34
Mold	22	9	1	12	61	33
Pencoed	22	11	1	10	52	37
O Illtydians	22	8	1	13	34	22
Talywain	22	6	1	15	41	20
Rhiwbina	22	6	0	16	27	16
Blaenau Gwent*	22	2	0	20	23	6

Division 6 Central	P	W	D	L	T	Pts
Resolven	22	18	1	3	109	68
Gilfach Goch	22	16	2	4	85	61
Beddau	22	16	1	5	88	60
Hirwaun	22	14	0	8	49	41
Morriston	22	13	1	8	42	37
Tonyrefail*	22	10	2	10	56	33
Nelson	22	8	2	12	60	32
Abercrave	22	9	2	11	49	32
Ynysybwl	22	7	0	15	50	26
Maesteg Celtic*	22	8	1	13	44	24
Cwmgwrach*	22	7	0	15	43	22
Nantymoel	22	0	0	22	16	1

Division 6 West	P	W	D	L	T	Pts
Waunarlwydd	22	19	1	2	90	66
Carmarthen Ath	22	14	0	8	76	52
Cardigan	22	14	0	8	74	52
Pembroke	22	14	1	7	55	45
Llandeilo	22	13	0	9	54	40
Ammanford	22	12	0	10	45	35
Pwllheli	22	11	1	10	54	33
Brynamman	22	11	0	11	45	31
Penygroes	22	9	1	12	48	29
New Dock Stars*	22	5	0	17	24	11
Pembroke DQ	22	5	0	17	23	11
Llandybie	22	3	0	19	26	8

Division 7A East	P	W	D	L	T	Pts
Fleur-de-Lys	18	14	2	2	48	41
Newport Saras	18	10	2	6	41	30
Risca	18	11	1	6	30	29
Ruthin	18	9	1	8	31	24
Rhyl	18	8	0	10	34	22
Monmouth	18	10	0	8	22	22
Newport HSOB	18	7	2	9	32	21
Cwmbran	18	7	2	9	31	21
Chepstow	18	7	1	10	30	19
Pill Harriers	18	1	1	16	18	4

Division 7A Central	P	W	D	L	T	Pts
Penygraig	18	18	0	0	89	69
Skewen	18	15	0	3	83	53
Senghenydd	18	14	0	4	79	52
Treherbert	18	10	0	8	58	38
Neath Ath	18	7	0	11	38	24

	P	W	D	L	T	Pts
Rhydyfelin	18	8	0	10	34	24
Blaengarw	18	7	0	11	30	22
Bridgend Ath	18	8	0	10	29	21
Bridgend Sports	18	3	0	15	29	12
Aberavon GS*	18	0	0	18	6	2

Division 7A West	P	W	D	L	T	Pts
Newcastle E	18	17	0	1	84	62
Gowerton	18	12	0	6	62	42
Aberystwyth	18	13	0	5	48	41
Gorseinon	18	9	0	9	54	32
Pontarddulais	18	8	1	9	31	24
Neyland	18	7	1	10	36	23
Loughor	18	6	1	11	23	17
Mumbles	18	6	1	11	28	16
Milford Haven*	18	5	1	12	33	15
Haverfordwest	18	4	1	13	32	14

Division 7B East finishing order:
Llanhilleth, St Joseph's, RTB (Ebbw Vale), Llanishen, Cowbridge, Pentyrch, Llandaff North, Llandaff, Blaenavon, Tredegar Irons

Division 7B Central finishing order:
Llantwit Fardre, Heol-y-Cyw, Bargoed, Nantyffyllon, Dolgellau, Newtown, Aberdare, Cefn Coed, Cilfynydd, Porthcawl

Division 7B West finishing order:
Cwmgors, Trimsaran, Glais, Llangennech, Bynea, Trebanos, Amman Utd, Laugharne, Lampeter, Furnace Utd

Division 8A East finishing order:
New Tredegar, Ynysddu, Barry, Canton, Machen, Trinant, Pontyclun, Colwyn Bay, Nantyglo, Caernarfon

Division 8A Central finishing order:
Tonna, Pontycymmer, Taibach, Baglan, Cefn Cribbwr, Cwmavon, Maesteg Quins, Ogmore Vale, British Steel

Division 8A West finishing order:
Fishguard, Aberaeron, Llanelli Wands, St Davids, Burry Port, Crymych, Pontyates, Llanybydder, Llangwm

Division 8B East finishing order:
Crumlin, Taffs Well, Caldicot, Usk, Bethesda, Llandudno, Cardiff U, Llantwit Major, Denbigh

Division 8B Central finishing order:
Tylorstown, Banwen, Briton Ferry, Ystalyfera, Gwernyfed, Bangor, Brynchoch, Brecon, Crynant, Welshpool

259

Division 8B West finishing order:
Birchgrove, Cwmllynfell, Tycroes,
Cwmtwrch, Alltwen, BP Llandarcy,

Penclawdd, Cefneithin, Pontardawe,
Swansea Uplands
★ 2 points deducted

A FANTASTIC FIGHTBACK

THE SWALEC CUP 1995-96
4 May, Cardiff Arms Park

Pontypridd 29 (1G 3PG 1DG 2T)　Neath 22 (1G 3T)

Pontypridd call it risk rugby. It involves passing under pressure at 100 mph, and mistakes are inevitable. They handed Neath two gift tries and a 22-9 lead. No team should expect to win after that. Ponty did. They were determined not to finish as nearly men and losers of the final for a second successive year. Gareth Llewellyn, the Neath captain, reflected sombrely, 'We won it – and we blew it!'

This was an epic final: the best of them all. It had a full house of 53,000 pinned by the tension of the seemingly impossible fightback. Neil Jenkins began to atone for his missed kicks of a year earlier with a sweet drop-shot. Although a ghastly blunder then let Leigh Davies in for a try, Neil Jenkins kept Ponty ahead by 9-5 with two penalty goals. Neath's response was a try by Richard Jones, the burly full-back, for Horgan to convert. They went further in front when Horgan intercepted a McIntosh pass. Disasters were crowding in thick and fast for Nigel Bezani's team. In his 40th year, the Ponty captain dearly wanted the cup to end his career.

Within the first five minutes of the second half, Bezani's dream became a nightmare as Horgan went over for his second try. Cometh the hour, cometh the man: he was Paul John, the Ponty scrum-half. He burrowed across, Jenkins converted and they were back in business. Another Jenkins penalty shot shaved the deficit to 22-19; then the magnetic Manley drew the Neath defence and freed Geraint Lewis for a try and a 23-22 lead. Three minutes later, the wing chased a push-through by Steele Lewis for his second try, and the stadium erupted like Krakatoa.

The loss of Paul Williams, their fly-half, with a dislocated elbow after 30 minutes was a major disruption for Neath, who switched Geraint Evans in from the wing to deputise. Mark Rowley's line-out domination was another problem for them, but it was Paul John's probing and decision-making that brought about the downfall of opponents who were persuaded to kick too often and were almost too dazed to realise that the game had been stolen from them. Pontypridd's first Cup triumph will be remembered as the greatest heart-stopper of the tournament.

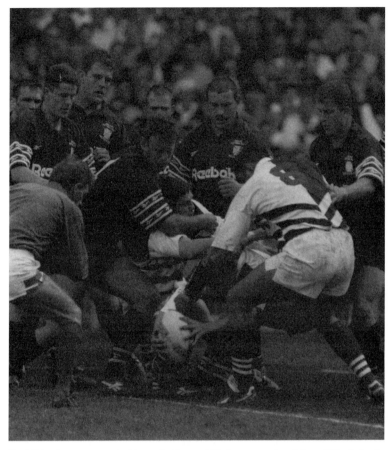

Paul John burrows over for his try in Pontypridd's heart-stopping defeat of Neath in the SWALEC Cup final.

Pontypridd: C Cormack; D Manley, J Lewis, S Lewis, G Lewis; N R Jenkins, Paul John; N Bezani (*capt*), Phil John, N Eynon, G Prosser, M Rowley, M Lloyd, D McIntosh, R G Collins *Replacement* M Spiller for McIntosh (75 mins)
Scorers *Tries:* G Lewis (2), Paul John *Conversion:* Jenkins
Penalty Goals: Jenkins (3) *Dropped Goal:* Jenkins
Neath: Richard Jones; C Higgs, L B Davies, J Funnell, G Evans; P Williams, P Horgan; D Morris, B Williams, J D Davies, G D Llewellyn, G O Llewellyn (*capt*), Robin Jones, S Williams, I Boobyer *Replacement* H Woodland for P Williams (30 mins)
Scorers *Tries:* Horgan (2), L B Davies, Richard Jones *Conversion:* Horgan
Referee W D Bevan (Clydach)

Pontypridd's trail to the final began in the fourth round with a 102-5 win at Llanharan after the draw had to be made afresh because of a mix-up over seeded teams. The same error had occurred in October 1973. Geraint Lewis scored three of Ponty's 15 tries and Neil Jenkins provided 37 points. Then they avenged a League defeat against Treorchy with 19-year-old Lee Jarvis (later signed by Cardiff for £30,000 per annum) scoring 21 goal points in a 41-5 success while deputising for Jenkins (broken collarbone). Jenkins was back to pounce over for three tries in the sixth round as Ponty saw off Maesteg by 41-13. He fired in five penalty goals at Newbridge in the quarter-final to squeeze a tense 20-15 verdict, and another five found the target to knock out nine-times winners Llanelli by 35-17 in the semi-final at Bridgend. Jenkins also cut inside the drifting Gwyn Jones with an explosive burst to set up a dazzling try for Manley.

Neath launched their Cup quest in the fourth round with five tries from Chris Higgs to win 48-3 at Cardigan. Huw Woodland collected three of the 12 scored when Neath toppled Heol-y-Cyw 76-8. Horgan's eight conversions and a penalty goal brought a 64-17 success against Whitland before Dunvant became Neath's 44-17 victims in the quarter-finals. Neath's only problem was a near-fatal one in the semi-final at Cardiff, when they found themselves trailing 7-0 after just 15 seconds of play. Newport wing Richard Rees caught the wide 'wrong-way' kick-off in the deep and raced 70 yards to cross the line. Gareth Rees converted. Two weeks earlier, Neath had shattered Newport 65-23 in a League match: now it was the Gnoll club's turn to suffer trauma. Newport looked sure to win, leading 22-21 with little time remaining after Gareth Rees's fourth penalty goal. Alas for them, there was just enough for Horgan to steal the game by 24-22 with a penalty shot from just over 40 yards.

Llanelli entertained prospects of a 13th final as they disposed of such formidable opponents as Bridgend and Cardiff. Justin Thomas missed five penalty attempts against Cardiff in the quarter-final tie, but the Wales full-back was given another chance in the 74th minute and his kick lifted Stradey hearts with an 11-10 triumph.

Swansea, the holders, suffered a double disappointment. Having been savaged 30-3 by Toulouse in the European Cup semi-final, they then went out of the SWALEC Cup 20-9 to Cardiff in the sixth round. It was only the fifth home defeat for Swansea in 25 Cup years, and avenged Cardiff's semi-final exit the previous year.

Among the inevitable shocks was Aberavon's first home defeat by a small club. Caerphilly put the Wizards out by an impressive 27-0 margin. Pontypool also had some close shaves against the minnows, but never allowed any more than a glimpse of the promised land until Fourth Division Rumney took them by 22-12. Keith Lee, the home captain and scrum-half, swooped in for three famous tries.

A WRU referees' strike during the quarter-finals was averted in March. Their demand was an increase in petrol expenses for matches from 27p to 40p. A compromise was reached at 32p with immediate effect, to be increased to 38p from the start of the 1996-97 season. These refs are not whistling in the dark: they deserve a top-up, however meagre, in this new age of lotsacash.

RESULTS

Third Round

Aberavon Quins 8, Oakdale 16; Abergavenny 8, Llantrisant 3; Bargoed 14, Tumble 21; Blaina 23, Narberth 22; Cefn Cribbwr 11, Aberdare 10; Cowbridge 17, Usk 0; Cwmgwrach 5, Fleur-de-Lys 18; Garndiffaith 33, Llandaff North 8; Glamorgan Wanderers 25, Blaengarw 16; Hendy 38, Bedwas 27; Kenfig Hill 13, Resolven 21; Llangennech 25, Cwmavon 17; Llantwit Fardre 3, Heol-y-Cyw 8; Maesteg Celtic 14, Baglan 5; Merthyr 32, Aberystwyth 0; Nelson 23, Tondu 7; Newcastle Emlyn 18, Pontycymmer 0; Penarth 58, Felinfoel 17; Pontyberem 13, Talywain 18; Pontypool Utd 19, Abercrave 26; Rhiwbina 0, Cardigan 10; Ruthin 9, Gilfach Goch 13; St Peter's 20, Glynneath 25; Taibach 3, Carmarthen Quins 66; Tonmawr 25, Croesyceiliog 5; Treherbert 11, Kidwelly 43; Trimsaran 12, Newport Saracens 22; Vardre 25, Pwllheli 17; Waunarlwydd 11, Rhymney 15; Whitland 15, Pyle 11; Wrexham 13, Rumney 28; Ynysddu 16, Pembroke 3; Ystrad Rhondda 20, Tredegar 8

Fourth Round

Aberavon 0, Caerphilly 27; Abercrave 11, Blackwood 16; Abertillery 46, Hendy 0; Blaina 6, Abercynon 23; Builth Wells 16, Fleur-de-Lys 9; Cardiff 26, Oakdale 7; Cardiff Institute 22, Maesteg Celtic 16; Cardigan 3, Neath 48; Carmarthen Quins 25, Bridgend 28; Cefn Cribbwr 6, Whitland 24; Garndiffaith 0, Newbridge 41; Gilfach Goch 7, Cross Keys 31; Heol-y-Cyw 10, Cowbridge 3; Llangennech 19, Abergavenny 52; Llanharan 5, Pontypridd 102; Maesteg 26, Bonymaen 24; Mountain Ash 14, Ystradgynlais 29; Newcastle Emlyn 10, Merthyr 17; Newport 62, Tumble 0; Newport Saracens 0, Tonmawr 5; Penarth 30, Ebbw Vale 11; Penygraig 22, Glynneath 14; Resolven 0, Llanelli 27; Rhymney 13, Nelson 3; Rumney 22, Pontypool 12; SW Police 44, Old Illtydians 12; Swansea 46, Tenby Utd 9; Talywain 0, Dunvant 39; Treorchy 37, Kidwelly 17; Vardre 3, Glamorgan Wanderers 13; Ynysddu 10, Old Penarthians 7; Ystrad Rhondda 3, Llandovery 17

Fifth Round

Abergavenny 8, Cardiff Institute 23; Abertillery 3, Bridgend 32; Builth Wells 7, Rumney 25; Caerphilly 32, Rhymney 5; Dunvant 16, Glamorgan Wanderers 8; Merthyr 17, Llanelli 30; Neath 76, Heol-y-Cyw 8; Newbridge 24, Cross Keys 8; Newport 49, Ystradgynlais 5; Penarth 6, Cardiff 62; Penygraig 9, Llandovery 10; Pontypridd 41, Treorchy 5; SW Police 26, Abercynon 16; Swansea 27, Tonmawr 8; Whitland 19, Blackwood 17; Ynysddu 15, Maesteg 36

Sixth Round

Caerphilly 29, SW Police 13; Cardiff Institute 13, Dunvant 41; Llandovery 5, Newport 25; Llanelli 18, Bridgend 15; Pontypridd 41, Maesteg 13; Neath 64, Whitland 17; Newbridge 13, Rumney 10; Swansea 9, Cardiff 20

Quarter-finals

Llanelli 11, Cardiff 10; Neath 44, Dunvant 17; Newbridge 15, Pontypridd 20; Newport 16, Caerphilly 10

Semi-finals

Neath 24, Newport 22 (*at Cardiff RFC*); Pontypridd 35, Llanelli 17 (*at Bridgend*)

FINAL (*at Cardiff Arms Park*)

Pontypridd 29, Neath 22

Previous finals

(all at Cardiff Arms Park)

1972	Neath 15 Llanelli 9
1973	Llanelli 30 Cardiff 7
1974	Llanelli 12 Aberavon 10
1975	Llanelli 16 Aberavon 6
1976	Llanelli 16 Swansea 4
1977	Newport 16 Cardiff 15
1978	Swansea 13 Newport 9
1979	Bridgend 18 Pontypridd 12
1980	Bridgend 15 Swansea 9
1981	Cardiff 14 Bridgend 6
1982*	Cardiff 12 Bridgend 12
1983	Pontypool 18 Swansea 6
1984	Cardiff 24 Neath 19
1985	Llanelli 15 Cardiff 14
1986	Cardiff 28 Newport 21
1987	Cardiff 16 Swansea 15
1988	Llanelli 28 Neath 13
1989	Neath 14 Llanelli 13
1990	Neath 16 Bridgend 10
1991	Llanelli 24 Pontypool 9
1992	Llanelli 16 Swansea 7
1993	Llanelli 21 Neath 18
1994	Cardiff 15 Llanelli 8
1995	Swansea 17 Pontypridd 12

Winners on 'most tries' rule

WELSH INTERNATIONAL PLAYERS
(*up to 30 April 1996*)

ABBREVIATIONS

A – Australia; *Arg* – Argentina; *Bb* – Barbarians; *C* – Canada; *E* – England; *F* – France; *Fj* – Fiji; *I* – Ireland; *It* – Italy; *J* – Japan; *M* – Maoris; *Nm* – Namibia; *NZ* – New Zealand; *NZA* – New Zealand Army; *Pt* – Portugal; *R* – Romania; *S* – Scotland; *SA* – South Africa; *Sp* – Spain; *Tg* – Tonga; *US* – United States; *WS* – Western Samoa; *Z* – Zimbabwe; (R) – Replacement; (t) – temporary replacement. Entries in square brackets [ ] indicate appearances in the World Cup.

Note: Years given for Five Nations' matches are for second half of season; eg 1972 means season 1971-72. Years for all other matches refer to the actual year of the match. When a series has taken place, figures have been used to denote the particular matches in which players have featured. Thus 1969 *NZ* 2 indicates that a player appeared in the second Test of the series.

Ackerman, R A (Newport, London Welsh) 1980 *NZ*, 1981 *E, S, A*, 1982 *I, F, E, S*, 1983 *S, I, F, R*, 1984 *S, I, F, E, A*, 1985 *S, I, F, E, Fj*
Alexander, E P (Llandovery Coll, Cambridge U) 1885 *S*, 1886 *E, S*, 1887 *E, I*
Alexander, W H (Llwynypia) 1898 *I, E*, 1899 *E, S, I*, 1901 *S, I*
Allen, A G (Newbridge) 1990 *F, E, I*
Allen, C P (Oxford U, Beaumaris) 1884 *E, S*
Andrews, F (Pontypool) 1912 *SA*, 1913 *E, S, I*
Andrews, F G (Swansea) 1884 *E, S*
Andrews, G E (Newport) 1926 *E, S*, 1927 *E, F, I*
Anthony, L (Neath) 1948 *E, S, F*
Arnold, P (Swansea) 1990 *Nm* 1, 2, *Bb*, 1991 *E, S, I, F* 1, *A*, [*Arg*, *A*], 1993 *F* (R), *Z* 2, 1994 *Sp, Fj*, 1995 *SA*
Arnold, W R (Swansea) 1903 *S*
Arthur, C S (Cardiff) 1888 *I, M*, 1891 *E*
Arthur, T (Neath) 1927 *S, F, I*, 1929 *E, S, F, I*, 1930 *E, S, I, F*, 1931 *E, S, F, I, SA*, 1933 *E, S*
Ashton, C (Aberavon) 1959 *E, S, I*, 1960 *E, S, I*, 1962 *I*
Attewell, S L (Newport) 1921 *E, S, F*

Back, M J (Bridgend) 1995 *F* (R), *E* (R), *S, I*
Badger, O (Llanelli) 1895 *E, S, I*, 1896 *E*
Baker, A (Neath) 1921 *I*, 1923 *E, S, F, I*
Baker, A M (Newport) 1909 *S, F*, 1910 *S*
Bancroft, J (Swansea) 1909 *E, S, F, I*, 1910 *F, E, S, I*, 1911 *E, F, I*, 1912 *E, S, I*, 1913 *I*, 1914 *E, S, F*
Bancroft, W J (Swansea) 1890 *S, E, I*, 1891 *E, S, I*, 1892 *E, S, I*, 1893 *E, S, I*, 1894 *E, S, I*, 1895 *E, S, I*, 1896 *E, S, I*, 1897 *E*, 1898 *I, E*, 1899 *E, S, I*, 1900 *E, S, I*, 1901 *E, S, I*
Barlow, T M (Cardiff) 1884 *I*
Barrell, R J (Cardiff) 1929 *S, F, I*, 1933 *I*
Bartlett, J D (Llanelli) 1927 *S*, 1928 *E, S*
Bassett, A (Cardiff) 1934 *I*, 1935 *E, S, I*, 1938 *E, S*
Bassett, J A (Penarth) 1929 *E, S, F, I*, 1930 *E, S, I*, 1931 *E, S, F, I, SA*, 1932 *E, S, I*
Bateman, A G (Neath) 1990 *S, I, Nm* 1,2
Bayliss, G (Pontypool) 1933 *S*
Bebb, D I E (Carmarthen TC, Swansea) 1959 *E, S, I, F*, 1960 *E, S, I, F, SA*, 1961 *E, S, I, F*, 1962 *E, S, F, I*, 1963 *E, F*, *NZ*, 1964 *E, S, F, SA*, 1965 *E, S, I, F*, 1966 *F, A*, 1967 *S, I, F, E*
Beckingham, G (Cardiff) 1953 *E, S*, 1958 *F*
Bennett, A M (Cardiff) 1995 [*NZ*] *SA, Fj*
Bennett, I (Aberavon) 1937 *I*
Bennett, P (Cardiff Harlequins) 1891 *E, S*, 1892 *S, I*
Bennett, P (Llanelli) 1969 *F* (R), 1970 *SA, S, F*, 1972 *S* (R), *NZ*, 1973 *E, S, I, F, A*, 1974 *S, I, F, E*, 1975 *S* (R), *I*, 1976 *E, S, I, F*, 1977 *I, F, E, S*, 1978 *E, S, I, F*
Bergiers, R T E (Cardiff Coll of Ed, Llanelli) 1972 *E, S, F, NZ*, 1973 *E, S, I, F, A*, 1974 *E*, 1975 *I*
Bevan, G W (Llanelli) 1947 *E*
Bevan, J A (Cambridge U) 1881 *E*
Bevan, J C (Cardiff, Cardiff Coll of Ed) 1971 *E, S, I, F*, 1972 *E, S, F, NZ*, 1973 *E, S*
Bevan, J D (Aberavon) 1975 *F, E, S, A*
Bevan, J (Swansea) 1904 *I*
Beynon, B (Swansea) 1920 *E, S*
Beynon, G E (Swansea) 1925 *F, I*
Bidgood, R A (Newport) 1992 *S*, 1993 *Z* 1,2, *Nm, J* (R)
Biggs, N W (Cardiff) 1888 *M*, 1889 *I*, 1892 *I*, 1893 *E, S, I*, 1894 *E, I*
Biggs, S H (Cardiff) 1895 *E, S*, 1896 *S*, 1897 *E*, 1898 *I, E*, 1899 *S, I*, 1900 *I*

Birch, J (Neath) 1911 *S, F*
Birt, F W (Newport) 1911 *E, S*, 1912 *E, S, I, SA*, 1913 *E*
Bishop, D J (Pontypool) 1984 *A*
Bishop, E H (Swansea) 1889 *S*
Blackmore, J H (Abertillery) 1909 *E*
Blackmore, S W (Cardiff) 1987 *I*, [*Tg* (R), *C, A*]
Blake, J (Cardiff) 1899 *E, S, I*, 1900 *E, S, I*, 1901 *E, S, I*
Blakemore, R E (Newport) 1947 *E*
Bland, A F (Cardiff) 1887 *E, S, I*, 1888 *S, I, M*, 1890 *S, E, I*
Blyth, L (Swansea) 1951 *SA*, 1952 *E, S*
Blyth, W R (Swansea) 1974 *E*, 1975 *S* (R), 1980 *F, E, S, I*
Boobyer, N (Llanelli) 1993 *Z* 1 (R), 2, *Nm*, 1994 *Fj, Tg*
Boon, R W (Cardiff) 1930 *S, F*, 1931 *E, S, F, I, SA*, 1932 *E, S, I*, 1933 *E, I*
Booth, J (Pontymister) 1898 *I*
Boots, J G (Newport) 1898 *I, E*, 1899 *I*, 1900 *E, S, I*, 1901 *E, S, I*, 1902 *E, S, I*, 1903 *E, S, I*, 1904 *E*
Boucher, A W (Newport) 1892 *E, S, I*, 1893 *E, S, I*, 1894 *E*, 1895 *E, S, I*, 1896 *E, I*, 1897 *E*
Bowcott, H M (Cardiff, Cambridge U) 1929 *S, F, I*, 1930 *E, I*, 1931 *E, S, I*, 1933 *E, I*
Bowdler, F A (Cross Keys) 1927 *A*, 1928 *E, S, I, F*, 1929 *E, S, F, I*, 1930 *E, I*, 1931 *SA*, 1932 *E, S, I*, 1933 *I*
Bowen, B (S Wales Police, Swansea) 1983 *R*, 1984 *S, I, F, E*, 1985 *Fj*, 1986 *E, S, I, F, Fj, Tg, WS*, 1987 [*C, E, NZ*], *US*, 1988 *E, S, I, F, WS*, 1989 *S, I*
Bowen, C A (Llanelli) 1896 *E, S, I*, 1897 *E*
Bowen, D H (Llanelli) 1883 *E*, 1886 *E, S*, 1887 *E*
Bowen, G E (Swansea) 1887 *S, I*, 1888 *S, I*
Bowen, W (Swansea) 1921 *S, F*, 1922 *E, S, I, F*
Bowen, Wm A (Swansea) 1886 *E, S*, 1887 *E, S, I*, 1888 *M*, 1889 *S, I*, 1890 *S, E, I*, 1891 *E, S*
Brace, D O (Llanelli, Oxford U) 1956 *E, S, I, F*, 1957 *E*, 1960 *S, I, F*, 1961 *I*
Braddock, K J (Newbridge) 1966 *A*, 1967 *S, I*
Bradshaw, K (Bridgend) 1964 *E, S, I, F, SA*, 1966 *E, S, I, F*
Brewer, T J (Newport) 1950 *E*, 1955 *E, S*
Brice, A B (Aberavon) 1899 *E, S, I*, 1900 *E, S, I*, 1901 *E, S, I*, 1902 *E, S, I*, 1903 *S*, 1904 *E, S, I*
Bridges, C J (Neath) 1990 *Nm* 1,2, *Bb*, 1991 *E* (R), *I, F* 1, *A*
Bridie, R H (Newport) 1882 *I*
Britton, G R (Newport) 1961 *S*
Broughton, A S (Treorchy) 1927 *A*, 1929 *S*
Brown, A (Newport) 1921 *I*
Brown, J (Cardiff) 1925 *I*
Brown, J A (Cardiff) 1907 *E, S, I*, 1908 *E, S, F*, 1909 *E*
Brown, M (Pontypool) 1983 *R*, 1986 *E, S, Fj* (R), *Tg, WS*
Bryant, D J (Bridgend) 1988 *NZ* 1,2, *WS, R*, 1989 *S, I, F, E*
Buchanan, A (Llanelli) 1987 [*Tg, E, NZ, A*], 1988 *I*
Buckett, I M (Swansea) 1994 *Tg*
Burcher, D H (Newport) 1977 *I, F, E, S*
Burgess, R C (Ebbw Vale) 1977 *I, F, E, S*, 1981 *I, F*, 1982 *F, E, S*
Burnett, R (Newport) 1953 *E*
Burns, J (Cardiff) 1927 *F, I*
Bush, P F (Cardiff) 1905 *NZ*, 1906 *E, SA*, 1907 *I*, 1908 *E, S*, 1910 *S, I*
Butler, E T (Pontypool) 1980 *F, E, S, I, NZ* (R), 1982 *S*, 1983 *E, S, I, F, R*, 1984 *S, I, F, E, A*
Cale, W R (Newbridge, Pontypool) 1949 *E, S, I*, 1950 *E, S, I, F*
Carter, A J (Newport) 1991 *E, S*
Cattell, A (Llanelli) 1883 *E, S*

Challinor, C (Neath) 1939 *E*
Clapp, T J S (Newport) 1882 *I*, 1883 *E, S*, 1884 *E, S, I*, 1885 *E, S*, 1886 *S*, 1887 *E, S, I*, 1888 *S, I*
Clare, J (Cardiff) 1883 *E*
Clark, S S (Neath) 1882 *I*, 1887 *I*
Cleaver, W B (Cardiff) 1947 *E, S, F, I, A*, 1948 *E, S, F, I*, 1949 *I*, 1950 *E, S, I, F*
Clegg, B G (Swansea) 1979 *F*
Clement, A (Swansea) 1987 *US* (R), 1988 *E, NZ* 1, *WS* (R), *R*, 1989 *NZ*, 1990 *S* (R), *I* (R), *Nm* 1,2, 1991 *S* (R), *A* (R), *F* 2, [*WS, A*], 1992 *I, F, E, S*, 1993 *I* (R), *F, J, C*, 1994 *S, I, F, Sp, C* (R), *Tg, WS, It, SA*, 1995 *F, E*, [*J, NZ, I*]
Clement, W H (Llanelli) 1937 *E, S, I*, 1938 *E, S, I*
Cobner, T J (Pontypool) 1974 *S, I, F, E*, 1975 *F, E, S, I, A*, 1976 *E, S*, 1977 *F, E, S*, 1978 *E, S, I, F, A* 1
Coldrick, A P (Newport) 1911 *E, S, I*, 1912 *E, S, F*
Coleman, E (Newport) 1949 *E, S, I*
Coles, F C (Pontypool) 1960 *S, I, F*
Collins, J (Aberavon) 1958 *A, E, S, F*, 1959 *E, S, I, F*, 1960 *E*, 1961 *F*
Collins, R G (S Wales Police, Cardiff, Pontypridd) 1987 *E* (R), *I*, [*I, E, NZ*], *US*, 1988 *E, S, I, F, R*, 1990 *E, S, I*, 1991 *A, F* 2, [*WS*], 1994 *C, Fj, Tg, WS, R, It, SA*, 1995 *F, E, S, I*
Collins, T (Mountain Ash) 1923 *I*
Conway-Rees, J (Llanelli) 1892 *S*, 1893 *E*, 1894 *E*
Cook, T (Cardiff) 1949 *S, I*
Cope, W (Cardiff, Blackheath) 1896 *S*
Copsey, A H (Llanelli) 1992 *I, F, E, S, A*, 1993 *E, S, I, J, C*, 1994 *E* (R), *Pt, Sp* (R), *Fj, Tg, WS* (R)
Cornish, F H (Cardiff) 1897 *E*, 1898 *I, E*, 1899 *I*
Cornish, R A (Cardiff) 1923 *E, S*, 1924 *E*, 1925 *E, S, F*, 1926 *E, S, I, F*
Coslett, K (Aberavon) 1962 *E, S, F*
Cowey, B T V (Welch Regt, Newport) 1934 *E, S, I*, 1935 *E*
Cresswell, B (Newport) 1960 *E, S, I, F*
Cummins, W (Treorchy) 1922 *E, S, I, F*
Cunningham, L J (Aberavon) 1960 *E, S, I, F*, 1962 *E, S, F, I*, 1963 *NZ*, 1964 *E, S, I, F, SA*

Dacey, M (Swansea) 1983 *E, S, I, F, R*, 1984 *S, I, F, E, A*, 1986 *Fj, Tg, WS*, 1987 *F* (R), [*Tg*]
Daniel, D J (Llanelli) 1891 *S*, 1894 *E, S, I*, 1898 *I, E*, 1899 *E, I*
Daniel, L T D (Newport) 1970 *S*
Daniels, P C T (Cardiff) 1981 *A*, 1982 *I*
Darbishire, G (Bangor) 1881 *E*
Dauncey, F H (Newport) 1896 *E, S, I*
Davey, C (Swansea) 1930 *F*, 1931 *E, S, F, I, SA*, 1932 *E, S, I*, 1933 *E, S*, 1934 *E, S, I*, 1935 *E, S, I, NZ*, 1936 *S*, 1937 *E, I*, 1938 *E, I*
David, R J (Cardiff) 1907 *I*
David, T P (Llanelli, Pontypridd) 1973 *F, A*, 1976 *I, F*
Davidge, G D (Newport) 1959 *F*, 1960 *S, I, F, SA*, 1961 *E, S, I*, 1962 *F*
Davies, A (Cambridge U, Neath, Cardiff) 1990 *Bb* (R), 1991 *A*, 1993 *Z* 1,2, *J, C*, 1994 *Fj*, 1995 [*J, I*]
Davies, A C (London Welsh) 1889 *I*
Davies, A E (Llanelli) 1984 *A*
Davies, B (Llanelli) 1895 *E*, 1896 *E*
Davies, C (Cardiff) 1947 *S, F, I, A*, 1948 *E, S, F, I*, 1949 *F*, 1950 *E, S, I, F*, 1951 *E, S, I*
Davies, C (Llanelli) 1988 *WS*, 1989 *S, I* (R), *F*
Davies, C H A (Llanelli, Cardiff) 1957 *I*, 1958 *A, E, S, I*, 1960 *SA*, 1961 *E*
Davies, C L (Cardiff) 1956 *E, S, I*
Davies, C R (Bedford, RAF) 1934 *E*
Davies, D (Bridgend) 1921 *I*, 1925 *I*
Davies, D B (Llanelli) 1907 *E*
Davies, D B (Llanelli) 1962 *I*, 1963 *E, S*
Davies, D G (Cardiff) 1923 *E, S*
Davies, D H (Neath) 1904 *S*
Davies, D H (Aberavon) 1924 *E*
Davies, D I (Swansea) 1939 *E*
Davies, D J (Neath) 1962 *I*
Davies, D M (Somerset Police) 1950 *E, S, I, F*, 1951 *E, S, I, F, SA*, 1952 *E, S, I, F*, 1953 *I, F, NZ*, 1954 *E*
Davies, E (Aberavon) 1947 *A*, 1948 *I*
Davies, E (Maesteg) 1919 *NZA*
Davies, E G (Cardiff) 1912 *E, F*
Davies, E G (Cardiff) 1928 *F*, 1929 *E*, 1930 *S*
Davies, G (Swansea) 1900 *E, S, I*, 1901 *E, S, I*, 1905 *E, S, I*
Davies, G (Cambridge U, Pontypridd) 1947 *S, A*, 1948 *E, S, F, I*, 1949 *E, S, F*, 1951 *E, S*
Davies, G (Llanelli) 1921 *F, I*, 1925 *F*

Davies, H (Swansea) 1898 *I, E*, 1901 *S, I*
Davies, H (Swansea, Llanelli) 1939 *S, I*, 1947 *E, S, F, I*
Davies, H (Neath) 1912 *E, S*
Davies, H (Bridgend) 1984 *S, I, F, E*
Davies, H J (Cambridge U, Aberavon) 1959 *E, S*
Davies, H J (Newport) 1924 *S*
Davies, I T (Llanelli) 1914 *S, F, I*
Davies, J (Neath, Llanelli) 1985 *E, Fj*, 1986 *E, S, I, F, Fj, Tg, WS*, 1987 *F, E, S, I*, [*I, Tg* (R), *C, E, NZ, A*], 1988 *E, S, I, F, NZ* 1,2, *WS, R*
Davies, Rev J A (Swansea) 1913 *S, F, I*, 1914 *E, S, F, I*
Davies, J D (Neath) 1991 *I, F* 1, 1993 *F* (R), *Z* 2,2, *J, C*, 1994 *S, I, F, E, Pt, Sp, C, WS, R, It, SA*, 1995 *F, E*, [*J, NZ, I*] *SA*, 1996 *It, E, S, I, F*
Davies, J H (Aberavon) 1923 *I*
Davies, L (Swansea) 1939 *S, I*
Davies, L (Bridgend) 1966 *E, S, I*
Davies, L B (Neath) 1996 *It, E, S, I, F*
Davies, L M (Llanelli) 1954 *F, S*, 1955 *I*
Davies, M (Swansea) 1981 *A*, 1982 *I*, 1985 *Fj*
Davies, M J (Blackheath) 1939 *S, I*
Davies, N G (London Welsh) 1955 *E*
Davies, N G (Llanelli) 1988 *NZ* 2, *WS*, 1989 *S, I*, 1993 *F*, 1994 *S, I, E, Pt, Sp, C, Fj, Tg* (R), *WS, R, It*, 1995 *E, S, I, Fj*, 1996 *E, S, I, F*
Davies, P T (Llanelli) 1985 *E, Fj*, 1986 *E, S, I, F, Fj, Tg, WS*, 1987 *F, E, I*, [*Tg, C, NZ*], 1988 *WS, R*, 1989 *S, I, F, E, NZ*, 1990 *F, E, S*, 1991 *I, F* 1, *A, F* 2, [*WS, Arg, A*], 1993 *F, Z* 1, *Nm*, 1994 *S, I, F, E, C, Fj* (R), *WS, R, It*, 1995 *F, I*
Davies, R H (Oxford U, London Welsh) 1957 *S, I, F*, 1958 *A*, 1962 *E, S*
Davies, S (Treherbert) 1923 *I*
Davies, S (Swansea) 1992 *I, F, E, S, A*, 1993 *E, S, I, Z* 1 (R), 2, *Nm, J*, 1995 *F*, [*J, I*]
Davies, T G R (Cardiff, London Welsh) 1966 *A*, 1967 *S, I, F, E*, 1968 *E, S*, 1969 *S, I, F, NZ* 1,2, *A*, 1971 *E, S, I, F*, 1972 *E, S, F, NZ*, 1973 *E, S, I, F, A*, 1974 *S, F, E*, 1975 *F, E, S, I*, 1976 *E, S, I, F*, 1977 *I, F, E, S*, 1978 *E, S, I, A* 1,2
Davies, T J (Devonport Services, Swansea, Llanelli) 1953 *E, S, I, F*, 1957 *E, S, I, F*, 1958 *A, E, S, F*, 1959 *E, S, I, F*, 1960 *E, SA*, 1961 *E, S, F*
Davies, T M (London Welsh, Swansea) 1969 *S, I, F, E, NZ* 1,2, *A*, 1970 *SA, S, E, I, F*, 1971 *E, S, I, F*, 1972 *E, S, F, NZ*, 1973 *E, S, I, F, A*, 1974 *S, I, F, E*, 1975 *F, E, S, I, A*, 1976 *E, S, I, F*
Davies, W (Cardiff) 1896 *S*
Davies, W (Swansea) 1931 *SA*, 1932 *E, S, I*
Davies, W A (Aberavon) 1912 *S, I*
Davies, W G (Cardiff) 1978 *A* 1,2, *NZ*, 1979 *S, I, F, E*, 1980 *F, E, S, NZ*, 1981 *E, S, A*, 1982 *I, F, E, S*, 1985 *S, I, F*
Davies, W T H (Swansea) 1936 *I*, 1937 *E, I*, 1939 *E, S, I*
Davis, C E (Newbridge) 1978 *A* 2, 1981 *E, S*
Davis, M (Newport) 1991 *A*
Davis, W E N (Cardiff) 1939 *E, S, I*
Dawes, S J (London Welsh) 1964 *I, F, SA*, 1965 *E, S, I, F*, 1966 *A*, 1968 *I, F*, 1969 *E, NZ* 2, *A*, 1970 *SA, S, E, I, F*, 1971 *E, S, I, F*
Day, H C (Newport) 1930 *S, I, F*, 1931 *E, S*
Day, H T (Newport) 1892 *I*, 1893 *E, S*, 1894 *S, I*
Day, T B (Swansea) 1931 *E, S, F, I, SA*, 1932 *E, S, I*, 1934 *S, I*, 1935 *E, S, I*
Deacon, J T (Swansea) 1891 *I*, 1892 *E, S, I*
Delahay, W J (Bridgend) 1922 *E, S, I, F*, 1923 *E, S, F, I*, 1924 *NZ*, 1925 *E, S, F, I*, 1926 *S, I, F*, 1927 *S*
Delaney, L (Llanelli) 1989 *I, F, E*, 1990 *E*, 1991 *F* 2, [*WS, Arg, A*], 1992 *I, F, E*
Devereux, D (Neath) 1958 *A, E, S*
Devereux, J A (S Glamorgan Inst, Bridgend) 1986 *E, S, I, F, Fj, Tg, WS*, 1987 *F, E, S, I*, [*I, C, E, NZ, A*], 1988 *NZ* 1,2, *R*, 1989 *S, I*
Diplock, R (Bridgend) 1988 *R*
Dobson, G (Cardiff) 1900 *S*
Dobson, T (Cardiff) 1898 *I, E*, 1899 *E, S*
Donovan, A J (Swansea) 1978 *A* 2, 1981 *I* (R), *A*, 1982 *E, S*
Donovan, R (S Wales Police) 1983 *F* (R)
Douglas, M H J (Llanelli) 1984 *S, I, F*
Douglas, W M (Cardiff) 1886 *E, S*, 1887 *E, S*
Dowell, W H (Newport) 1907 *E, S, I*, 1908 *E, S, F, I*
Dyke, J C M (Penarth) 1906 *SA*
Dyke, L M (Penarth, Cardiff) 1910 *I*, 1911 *S, F, I*

Edmunds, D A (Neath) 1990 *I* (R), *Bb*
Edwards, A B (London Welsh, Army) 1955 *E, S*

Edwards, B O (Newport) 1951 *I*
Edwards, D (Glynneath) 1921 *E*
Edwards, G O (Cardiff, Cardiff Coll of Ed) 1967 *F, E, NZ,*
1968 *E, S, I, F,* 1969 *S, I, F, E, NZ* 1,2, A, 1970 *SA, S, E, I, F,*
1971 *E, S, I, F,* 1972 *E, S, F, NZ,* 1973 *E, S, I, F, A,* 1974 *S, I,*
F, E, 1975 *F, E, S, I, A,* 1976 *E, S, I, F,* 1977 *I, F, E, S,* 1978
E, S, I, F
Eidman, I H (Cardiff) 1983 *S, R,* 1984 *I, F, E, A,* 1985 *S, I,*
Fj, 1986 *E, S, I, F*
Elliott, J E (Cardiff) 1894 *I,* 1898 *I, E*
Elsey, W J (Cardiff) 1895 *E*
Emyr, Arthur (Swansea) 1989 *E, NZ,* 1990 *F, E, S, I, Nm*
1,2, 1991 *F* 1,2, [*WS, Arg, A*]
Evans, A (Pontypool) 1924 *E, I, F*
Evans, B (Swansea) 1933 *S*
Evans, B (Llanelli) 1933 *E, S,* 1936 *E, S, I,* 1937 *E*
Evans, B S (Llanelli) 1920 *E,* 1922 *E, S, I, F*
Evans, C (Pontypool) 1960 *E*
Evans, D (Penygraig) 1896 *S, I,* 1897 *E,* 1898 *E*
Evans, D B (Swansea) 1926 *E*
Evans, D D (Cheshire, Cardiff U) 1934 *E*
Evans, D P (Llanelli) 1960 *SA*
Evans, D W (Cardiff) 1889 *S, I,* 1890 *E, I,* 1891 *E*
Evans, D W (Oxford U, Cardiff, Treorchy) 1989 *F, E, NZ,*
1990 *F, E, S, I, Bb,* 1991 *A* (R), *F* 2 (R), [*A* (R)], 1995 [*J*
(R)]
Evans, E (Llanelli) 1937 *E,* 1939 *S, I*
Evans, F (Llanelli) 1921 *S*
Evans, G (Cardiff) 1947 *E, S, F, I, A,* 1948 *E, S, F, I,* 1949
E, S, I
Evans, G (Maesteg) 1981 *S* (R), *I, F, A,* 1982 *I, F, E, S,*
1983 *F, R*
Evans, G L (Newport) 1977 *F* (R), 1978 *F, A* 2 (R)
Evans, I (London Welsh) 1934 *S, I*
Evans, I (Swansea) 1922 *E, S, I, F*
Evans, I C (Llanelli) 1987 *F, E, S, I,* [*I, C, E, NZ, A*], 1988
E, S, I, F, NZ 1,2, 1989 *I, F, E,* 1991 *E, S, I, F* 1, *A, F* 2, [*WS,*
Arg, A], 1992 *I, F, E, S, A,* 1993 *E, S, I, F, J, C,* 1994 *S, I, E,*
Pt, Sp, C, Fj, Tg, WS, R, 1995 *E, S, I,* [*J, NZ, I*], *SA, Fj,* 1996
It, E, S, I, F
Evans, I L (Llanelli) 1991 *F* 2 (R)
Evans, J (Llanelli) 1896 *S, I,* 1897 *E*
Evans, J (Blaina) 1904 *E*
Evans, J (Pontypool) 1907 *E, S, I*
Evans, J D (Cardiff) 1958 *I, F*
Evans, J E (Llanelli) 1924 *S*
Evans, J R (Newport) 1934 *E*
Evans, O J (Cardiff) 1887 *E, S,* 1888 *S, I*
Evans, P D (Llanelli) 1951 *E, F*
Evans, R (Cardiff) 1889 *S*
Evans, R (Bridgend) 1963 *S, I, F*
Evans, R L (Llanelli) 1993 *E, S, I, F,* 1994 *S, I, F, E, Pt, Sp,*
C, Fj, WS, R, It, SA, 1995 *F,* [*NZ, I* (R)]
Evans, R T (Newport) 1947 *F, I,* 1950 *E, S, I, F,* 1951 *E, S,*
I, F
Evans, S (Swansea, Neath) 1985 *F, E,* 1986 *Fj, Tg, WS,*
1987 *F, E,* [*I, Tg*]
Evans, T (Swansea) 1924 *I*
Evans, T G (London Welsh) 1970 *SA, S, E, I,* 1972 *E, S, F*
Evans, T H (Llanelli) 1906 *I,* 1907 *E, S, I,* 1908 *I, A,* 1909
E, S, F, I, 1910 *F, E, S, I,* 1911 *E, S, F, I*
Evans, T P (Swansea) 1975 *F, E, S, I, A,* 1976 *E, S, I, F,*
1977 *I*
Evans, V (Neath) 1954 *I, F, S*
Evans, W (Llanelli) 1958 *A*
Evans, W F (Rhymney) 1882 *I,* 1883 *S*
Evans, W G (Brynmawr) 1911 *I*
Evans, W H (Llwynypia) 1914 *E, S, F, I*
Evans, W J (Pontypool) 1947 *S*
Evans, W R (Bridgend) 1958 *A, E, S, I, F,* 1960 *SA,* 1961
E, S, I, F, 1962 *E, S, I*
Everson, W A (Newport) 1926 *S*

Faulkner, A G (Pontypool) 1975 *F, E, S, I, A,* 1976 *E, S, I,*
F, 1978 *E, S, I, F, A* 1,2, *NZ,* 1979 *S, I, F*
Faull, J (Swansea) 1957 *I, F,* 1958 *A, E, S, I, F,* 1959 *E, S,*
I, 1960 *E, F*
Fauvel, T J (Aberavon) 1988 *NZ* 1 (R)
Fear, A G (Newport) 1934 *S, I,* 1935 *S, I*
Fender, N H (Cardiff) 1930 *I, F,* 1931 *E, S, F, I*
Fenwick, S P (Bridgend) 1975 *F, E, S, A,* 1976 *E, S, I, F,*
1977 *I, F, E, S,* 1978 *E, S, I, F, A* 1,2, 1979 *S, I, F, E,*
1980 *F, E, S, I, NZ,* 1981 *E, S*

Finch, E (Llanelli) 1924 *F, NZ,* 1925 *F, I,* 1926 *F,* 1927 *A,*
1928 *I*
Finlayson, A A J (Cardiff) 1974 *I, F, E*
Fitzgerald, D (Cardiff) 1894 *S, I*
Ford, F J V (Welch Regt, Newport) 1939 *E*
Ford, I (Newport) 1959 *E, S*
Ford, S P (Cardiff) 1990 *I, Nm* 1,2, *Bb,* 1991 *E, S, I, A*
Forward, A (Pontypool, Mon Police) 1951 *S, SA,* 1952 *E,*
S, I, F
Fowler, I J (Llanelli) 1919 *NZA*
Francis, D G (Llanelli) 1919 *NZA,* 1924 *S*
Francis, P (Maesteg) 1987 *S*

Gabe, R T (Cardiff, Llanelli) 1901 *I,* 1902 *E, S, I,* 1903 *E,*
S, I, 1904 *E, S, I,* 1905 *E, S, I, NZ,* 1906 *E, I, SA,* 1907 *E, S,*
I, 1908 *E, S, F, I*
Gale, N R (Swansea, Llanelli) 1960 *I,* 1963 *E, S, I, NZ,*
1964 *E, S, I, F, SA,* 1965 *E, S, I, F,* 1966 *E, S, I, F, A,* 1967 *E,*
NZ, 1968 *E,* 1969 *NZ* 1 (R), 2, *A*
Gallacher, I S (Llanelli) 1970 *F*
Garrett, R M (Penarth) 1888 *M,* 1889 *S,* 1890 *S, E, I,* 1891
S, I, 1892 *E*
Geen, W P (Oxford U, Newport) 1912 *SA,* 1913 *E, I*
George, E E (Pontypridd, Cardiff) 1895 *S, I,* 1896 *E*
George, G M (Newport) 1991 *E, S*
Gething, G I (Neath) 1913 *F*
Gibbs, A (Newbridge) 1995 *I, SA*
Gibbs, I S (Neath, Swansea) 1991 *E, S, I, F* 1, *A, F* 2, [*WS,*
Arg, A], 1992 *I, F, E, S, A,* 1993 *E, S, I, F, J, C*
Gibbs, R A (Cardiff) 1906 *S, I,* 1907 *E, S,* 1908 *E, S, F, I,*
1910 *F, E, S, I,* 1911 *E, S, F, I*
Giles, I (Aberavon) 1983 *R,* 1985 *Fj* (R), 1987 [*C*]
Girling, B E (Cardiff) 1881 *E*
Goldsworthy, S J (Swansea) 1884 *I,* 1885 *E, S*
Gore, J H (Blaina) 1924 *I, F, NZ,* 1925 *E*
Gore, W (Newbridge) 1947 *S, F, I*
Gould, A J (Newport) 1885 *E, S,* 1886 *E, S,* 1887 *E, S, I,*
1888 *S,* 1889 *I,* 1890 *S, E, I,* 1892 *E, S, I,* 1893 *E, S, I,* 1894
E, S, 1895 *E, S, I,* 1896 *E, S, I,* 1897 *E*
Gould, G H (Newport) 1892 *I,* 1893 *S, I*
Gould, R (Newport) 1882 *I,* 1883 *E, S,* 1884 *E, S, I,* 1885
E, S, 1886 *E,* 1887 *E, S*
Graham, T C (Newport) 1890 *I,* 1891 *S, I,* 1892 *E, S,* 1893
E, S, I, 1894 *E, S,* 1895 *E, S*
Gravell, R W R (Llanelli) 1975 *F, E, S, I, A,* 1976 *E, S, I, F,*
1978 *E, S, I, F, A* 1,2, *NZ,* 1979 *I, F,* 1981 *I, F,* 1982 *F, E, S*
Gray, A J (London Welsh) 1968 *E, S*
Greenslade, D (Newport) 1962 *S*
Greville, H G (Llanelli) 1947 *A*
Griffin, Dr J (Edinburgh U) 1883 *S*
Griffiths, C (Llanelli) 1979 *E* (R)
Griffiths, D (Llanelli) 1888 *M,* 1889 *I*
Griffiths, G (Llanelli) 1889 *I*
Griffiths, G M (Cardiff) 1953 *E, S, I, F, NZ,* 1954 *I, F, S,*
1955 *I, F,* 1957 *E, S*
Griffiths, J L (Llanelli) 1988 *NZ* 2, 1989 *S*
Griffiths, M (Bridgend, Cardiff) 1988 *WS, R,* 1989 *S, I, F,*
E, NZ, 1990 *F, E, Nm* 1,2, *Bb,* 1991 *I, F* 1,2, [*WS, Arg, A*],
1992 *I, F, E, S, A,* 1993 *Z* 1,2, *Nm, J, C,* 1995 *F* (R), *E, S, I,*
[*J, I*]
Griffiths, V M (Newport) 1924 *S, I, F*
Gronow, B (Bridgend) 1910 *F, E, S, I*
Gwilliam, J A (Cambridge U, Newport) 1947 *A,* 1948 *I,*
1949 *E, S, I, F,* 1950 *E, S, I, F,* 1951 *E, S, I, SA,* 1952 *E, S, I,*
F, 1953 *E, I, F, NZ,* 1954 *E*
Gwyn, D (Swansea) 1883 *E,* 1887 *S,* 1890 *E, I,* 1891 *E, S*
Gwynn, W H (Swansea) 1884 *E, S, I,* 1885 *E, S*

Hadley, A M (Cardiff) 1983 *R,* 1984 *S, I, F, E,* 1985 *F, E,*
Fj, 1986 *E, S, I, F, Fj, Tg,* 1987 *S* (R), *I,* [*I, Tg, C, E, NZ, A*],
US, 1988 *E, S, I, F*
Hall, I (Aberavon) 1967 *NZ,* 1970 *SA, S, E,* 1971 *S,* 1974
S, I, F
Hall, M R (Cambridge U, Bridgend, Cardiff) 1988 *NZ* 1
(R), 2, *WS, R,* 1989 *S, I, F, E, NZ,* 1990 *F, E, S,* 1991 *A, F* 2,
[*WS, Arg, A*], 1992 *I, F, E, S, A,* 1993 *E, S, I,* 1994 *S, I, F, E,*
Pt, Sp, C, Tg, R, It, SA, 1995 *F, S, I,* [*J, NZ, I*]
Hall, W H (Bridgend) 1988 *WS*
Hancock, F E (Cardiff) 1884 *I,* 1885 *E, S,* 1886 *S*
Hannan, J (Newport) 1888 *M,* 1889 *S, I,* 1890 *S, E, I,* 1891
E, 1892 *E, S, I,* 1893 *E, S, I,* 1894 *E, S, I,* 1895 *E, S, I*
Harding, A F (London Welsh) 1902 *E, S, I,* 1903 *E, S, I,*
1904 *E, S, I,* 1905 *E, S, I, NZ,* 1906 *E, S, I, SA,* 1907 *I,* 1908
E, S

Harding, G F (Newport) 1881 *E*, 1882 *I*, 1883 *E, S*
Harding, R (Swansea, Cambridge U) 1923 *E, S, F, I*, 1924 *I, F, NZ*, 1925 *F, I*, 1926 *E, I, F*, 1927 *E, S, F, I*, 1928 *E*
Harding, T (Newport) 1888 *M*, 1889 *S, I*
Harris, D J E (Pontypridd, Cardiff) 1959 *I, F*, 1960 *S, I, F, SA*, 1961 *E, S*
Harris, T (Aberavon) 1927 *A*
Hathway, G F (Newport) 1924 *I, F*
Havard, Rev W T (Llanelli) 1919 *NZA*
Hawkins, F (Pontypridd) 1912 *I, F*
Hayward, D (Newbridge) 1949 *E, F*, 1950 *E, S, I, F*, 1951 *E, S, I, F, SA*, 1952 *E, S, I, F*
Hayward, D J (Cardiff) 1963 *E, NZ*, 1964 *S, I, F, SA*
Hayward, G (Swansea) 1908 *S, F, I, A*, 1909 *E*
Hellings, R (Llwynypia) 1897 *E*, 1898 *I, E*, 1899 *S, I*, 1900 *E, I*, 1901 *E, S*
Herrerá, R C (Cross Keys) 1925 *S, F, I*, 1926 *E, S, I, F*, 1927 *E*
Hiams, H (Swansea) 1912 *I, F*
Hickman, A (Neath) 1930 *E*, 1933 *S*
Hiddlestone, D D (Neath) 1922 *E, S, I, F*, 1924 *NZ*
Hill, A F (Cardiff) 1885 *S*, 1886 *E, S*, 1888 *S, I, M*, 1889 *S*, 1890 *S, I*, 1893 *E, S, I*, 1894 *E, S, I*
Hill, S D (Cardiff) 1993 *Z 1,2, Nm*, 1994 *I* (R), *F, SA*, 1995 *F, SA*
Hinam, S (Cardiff) 1925 *I*, 1926 *E, S, I, F*
Hinton, J T (Cardiff) 1884 *I*
Hirst, G L (Newport) 1912 *S*, 1913 *S*, 1914 *E, S, F, I*
Hodder, W (Pontypool) 1921 *E, S, F*
Hodges, J J (Newport) 1899 *E, S, I*, 1900 *E, S, I*, 1901 *E, S*, 1902 *E, S, I*, 1903 *E, S, I*, 1904 *E, S*, 1905 *E, S, I, NZ*, 1906 *E, S, I*
Hodgson, G T R (Neath) 1962 *I*, 1963 *E, S, I, F, NZ*, 1964 *E, S, I, F, SA*, 1966 *S, I, F*, 1967 *I*
Hollingdale, H (Swansea) 1912 *SA*, 1913 *E*
Hollingdale, T H (Neath) 1927 *A*, 1928 *E, S, I, F*, 1930 *E*
Holmes, T D (Cardiff) 1978 *A 2, NZ*, 1979 *S, I, F, E*, 1980 *F, E, S, I, NZ*, 1981 *A*, 1982 *I, F, E*, 1983 *E, S, I, F*, 1984 *E*, 1985 *S, I, F, E, Fj*
Hopkin, W H (Newport) 1937 *S*
Hopkins, K (Cardiff, Swansea) 1985 *E*, 1987 *F, E, S*, [*Tg, C* (R)], *US*
Hopkins, P L (Swansea) 1908 *A*, 1909 *E, I*, 1910 *E*
Hopkins, R (Maesteg) 1970 *E* (R)
Hopkins, T (Swansea) 1926 *E, S, I, F*
Hopkins, W J (Aberavon) 1925 *E, S*
Howells, B (Llanelli) 1934 *E*
Howells, W G (Llanelli) 1957 *E, S, I, F*
Howells, W H (Swansea) 1888 *S, I*
Howley, R (Bridgend) 1996 *E, S, I, F*
Hughes, D (Newbridge) 1967 *NZ*, 1969 *NZ 2*, 1970 *SA, S, E, I*
Hughes, G (Penarth) 1934 *E, S, I*
Hughes, H (Cardiff) 1887 *S*, 1889 *S*
Hughes, K (Cambridge U, London Welsh) 1970 *I*, 1973 *A*, 1974 *S*
Hullin, W (Cardiff) 1967 *S*
Humphreys, J M (Cardiff) 1995 [*NZ, I*], *SA, Fj*, 1996 *It, E, S, I, F*
Hurrell, J (Newport) 1959 *F*
Hutchinson, F (Neath) 1894 *I*, 1896 *S, I*
Huxtable, R (Swansea) 1920 *F, I*
Huzzey, H V P (Cardiff) 1898 *I, E*, 1899 *E, S, I*
Hybart, A J (Cardiff) 1887 *E*

Ingledew, H M (Cardiff) 1890 *I*, 1891 *E, S*
Isaacs, I (Cardiff) 1933 *E, S*

Jackson, T H (Swansea) 1895 *E*
James, B (Bridgend) 1968 *E*
James, C R (Llanelli) 1958 *A, F*
James, D (Swansea) 1891 *I*, 1892 *S, I*, 1899 *E*
James, D R (Treorchy) 1931 *F, I*
James, E (Swansea) 1890 *S*, 1891 *I*, 1892 *S, I*, 1899 *E*
James, M (Cardiff) 1947 *A*, 1948 *E, S, F, I*
James, T O (Aberavon) 1935 *I*, 1937 *S*
James, W J (Aberavon) 1983 *E, S, I, F, R*, 1984 *S*, 1985 *S, I, F, E, Fj*, 1986 *E, S, I, F, Fj, Tg, WS*, 1987 *E, S, I*
James, W P (Aberavon) 1925 *E, S*
Jarman, H (Newport) 1910 *E, S, I*, 1911 *E*
Jarrett, K S (Newport) 1967 *E*, 1968 *E, S*, 1969 *S, I, F, E, NZ 1,2, A*
Jeffery, J J (Cardiff Coll of Ed, Newport) 1967 *NZ*
Jenkin, A M (Swansea) 1895 *I*, 1896 *E*

Jenkins, A (Llanelli) 1920 *E, S, F, I*, 1921 *S, F*, 1922 *F*, 1923 *E, S, F, I*, 1924 *NZ*, 1928 *S, I*
Jenkins, D M (Treorchy) 1926 *E, S, I, F*
Jenkins, D R (Swansea) 1927 *A*, 1929 *E*
Jenkins, E (Newport) 1910 *S, I*
Jenkins, E M (Aberavon) 1927 *S, F, I, A*, 1928 *E, S, I, F*, 1929 *F*, 1930 *E, S, I, F*, 1931 *E, S, F, I, SA*, 1932 *E, S, I*
Jenkins, G R (Pontypool, Swansea) 1991 *F 2*, [*WS* (R), *Arg, A*], 1992 *I, F, E, S, A*, 1993 *C*, 1994 *S, I, F, E, Pt, Sp, C, Tg, WS, R, It, SA*, 1995 *F, E, S, I*, [*J*], *SA* (R), *Fj* (t), 1996 *E* (R)
Jenkins, J C (London Welsh) 1906 *SA*
Jenkins, J L (Aberavon) 1923 *S, F*
Jenkins, L H (Mon TC, Newport) 1954 *I*, 1956 *E, S, I, F*
Jenkins, N R (Pontypridd) 1991 *E, S, I, F 1*, 1992 *I, F, E, S*, 1993 *E, S, I, F, Z 1,2, Nm, J, C*, 1994 *S, I, F, E, Pt, Sp, C, Tg, WS, R, It, SA*, 1995 *F, E, S, I*, [*J, NZ, I*], *SA, Fj*, 1996 *F*
Jenkins, V G J (Oxford U, Bridgend, London Welsh) 1933 *E, I*, 1934 *S, I*, 1935 *E, S, NZ*, 1936 *E, S, I*, 1937 *E*, 1938 *E, S*, 1939 *E*
Jenkins, W (Cardiff) 1912 *I, F*, 1913 *S, I*
John, B (Llanelli, Cardiff) 1966 *A*, 1967 *S, NZ*, 1968 *E, S, I, F*, 1969 *S, I, F, E, NZ 1,2, A*, 1970 *SA, S, E, I*, 1971 *E, S, I, F*, 1972 *E, S, F*
John, D A (Llanelli) 1925 *I*, 1928 *E, S, I*
John, D E (Llanelli) 1923 *F, I*, 1928 *E, S, I*
John, E R (Neath) 1950 *E, S, I, F*, 1951 *E, S, I, F, SA*, 1952 *E, S, I, F*, 1953 *E, S, I, F, NZ*, 1954 *E*
John G (St Luke's Coll, Exeter) 1954 *E, F*
John, J H (Swansea) 1926 *E, S, I, F*, 1927 *E, S, F, I*
John, P (Pontypridd) 1994 *Tg*
John, S C (Llanelli) 1995 *S, I*
Johnson, T A (Cardiff) 1921 *E, F, I*, 1923 *E, S, F*, 1924 *E, S, NZ*, 1925 *E, S, F*
Johnson, W D (Swansea) 1953 *E*
Jones, A H (Cardiff) 1933 *E, S*
Jones, B (Abertillery) 1914 *E, S, F*
Jones, Bert (Llanelli) 1934 *S, I*
Jones, Bob (Llwynypia) 1901 *I*
Jones, B J (Newport) 1960 *I, F*
Jones, B Lewis (Devonport Services, Llanelli) 1950 *E, S, I, F*, 1951 *E, S, SA*, 1952 *E, I, F*
Jones, C W (Cambridge U, Cardiff) 1934 *E, S, I*, 1935 *E, S, I, NZ*, 1936 *E, S, I*, 1938 *E, S, I*
Jones, C W (Bridgend) 1920 *E, S, F*
Jones, D (Neath) 1927 *A*
Jones, D (Aberavon) 1897 *E*
Jones, D (Swansea) 1947 *E, F, I*, 1949 *E, S, I, F*
Jones, D (Treherbert) 1902 *E, S, I*, 1903 *E, S, I*, 1905 *E, S, I, NZ*, 1906 *E, S, SA*
Jones, D (Newport) 1926 *E, S, I, F*, 1927 *E*
Jones, D (Llanelli) 1948 *E*
Jones, D (Cardiff) 1994 *SA*, 1995 *F, E, S*, [*J, NZ, I*], *SA, Fj*, 1996 *It, E, S, I, F*
Jones, D K (Llanelli, Cardiff) 1962 *E, S, F, I*, 1963 *E, F, NZ*, 1964 *E, S, SA*, 1966 *E, S, I, F*
Jones, D P (Pontypool) 1907 *I*
Jones, E H (Neath) 1929 *E, S*
Jones, E L (Llanelli) 1930 *F*, 1933 *E, S, I*, 1935 *E*
Jones, Elvet L (Llanelli) 1939 *S*
Jones, G (Ebbw Vale) 1963 *S, I, F*
Jones, G (Llanelli) 1988 *NZ 2*, 1989 *F, E, NZ*, 1990 *F*
Jones, G G (Cardiff) 1930 *S*, 1933 *I*
Jones, G H (Bridgend) 1995 *SA*
Jones, H (Penygraig) 1902 *S, I*
Jones, H (Neath) 1904 *I*
Jones, H (Swansea) 1930 *I, F*
Jones, Iorwerth (Llanelli) 1927 *A*, 1928 *E, S, I, F*
Jones, I C (London Welsh) 1968 *I*
Jones, Ivor E (Llanelli) 1924 *E, S*, 1927 *S, F, I, A*, 1928 *E, S, I, F*, 1929 *E, S, F, I*, 1930 *E, S*
Jones, J (Aberavon) 1901 *E*
Jones, J (Swansea) 1924 *F*
Jones, Jim (Aberavon) 1919 *NZA*, 1920 *E, S*, 1921 *S, F, I*
Jones, J A (Cardiff) 1883 *S*
Jones, J P (Tuan) (Pontypool) 1913 *S*
Jones, J P (Pontypool) 1908 *A*, 1909 *E, S, F, I*, 1910 *F, E*, 1912 *E, F*, 1913 *F, I*, 1920 *F, I*, 1921 *E*
Jones, K D (Cardiff) 1960 *SA*, 1961 *E, S, I*, 1962 *E, F*, 1963 *E, S, I, NZ*
Jones, K J (Newport) 1947 *E, S, F, I, A*, 1948 *E, S, F, I*, 1949 *E, S, I, F*, 1950 *E, S, I, F*, 1951 *E, S, I, F, SA*, 1952 *E, S, I, F*, 1953 *E, S, I, F, NZ*, 1954 *E, I, F, S*, 1955 *E, S, I, F*, 1956 *E, S, I, F*, 1957 *S*

Jones, K W J (Oxford U, London Welsh) 1934 *E*
Jones, M A (Neath) 1987 *S*, 1988 *NZ* 2 (R), 1989 *S, I, F, E,
NZ*, 1990 *F, E, S, I, Nm* 1,2, *Bb*
Jones, P (Newport) 1912 *SA*, 1913 *E, S, F*, 1914 *E, S, F, I*
Jones, P B (Newport) 1921 *S*
Jones, R (Swansea) 1901 *I*, 1902 *E*, 1904 *E, S, I*, 1905 *E*,
1908 *F, I, A*, 1909 *E, S, F, I*, 1910 *F, E*
Jones, R (London Welsh) 1929 *E*
Jones, R (Northampton) 1926 *E, S, F*
Jones, R (Swansea) 1927 *A*, 1928 *F*
Jones, R B (Cambridge U) 1933 *E, S*
Jones, R E (Coventry) 1967 *F, E*, 1968 *S, I, F*
Jones, R G (Llanelli) 1996 *It, E, S, I, F*
Jones, R L (Llanelli) 1993 *Z* 1,2, *Nm, J, C*
Jones, R N (Swansea) 1986 *E, S, I, F, Fj, Tg, WS*, 1987 *F,
E, S, I*, [*I, Tg, E, NZ, A*], *US*, 1988 *E, S, I, F, NZ* 1, *WS, R*,
1989 *I, F, E, NZ*, 1990 *F, E, S, I*, 1991 *E, S, F* 2, [*WS, Arg,
A*], 1992 *I, F, E, S, A*, 1993 *E, S, I*, 1994 *I* (R), *Pt*, 1995 *F, E,
S, I*, [*NZ, I*]
Jones, S T (Pontypool) 1983 *S, I, F, R*, 1984 *S*, 1988 *E, S, F,
NZ* 1,2
Jones, Tom (Newport) 1922 *E, S, I, F*, 1924 *E, S*
Jones, T B (Newport) 1882 *I*, 1883 *E, S*, 1884 *S*, 1885 *E, S*
Jones, W (Cardiff) 1898 *I, E*
Jones, W (Mountain Ash) 1905 *I*
Jones, W I (Llanelli, Cambridge U) 1925 *E, S, F, I*
Jones, W J (Llanelli) 1924 *I*
Jones, W K (Cardiff) 1967 *NZ*, 1968 *E, S, I, F*
Jones-Davies, T E (London Welsh) 1930 *E, I*, 1931 *E, S*
Jordan, H M (Newport) 1885 *E, S*, 1889 *S*
Joseph, W (Swansea) 1902 *E, S, I*, 1903 *E, S, I*, 1904 *E, S*,
1905 *E, S, I, NZ*, 1906 *E, S, I, SA*
Jowett, W F (Swansea) 1903 *E*
Judd, S (Cardiff) 1953 *E, S, I, F, NZ*, 1954 *E, F, S*, 1955 *E,
S*
Judson, J H (Llanelli) 1883 *E, S*

Kedzlie, Q D (Cardiff) 1888 *S, I*
Keen, L (Aberavon) 1980 *F, E, S, I*
Knight, P (Pontypridd) 1990 *Nm* 1,2, *Bb* (R), 1991 *E, S*
Knill, F M D (Cardiff) 1976 *F* (R)

Lamerton, A E H (Llanelli) 1993 *F, Z* 1,2, *Nm, J*
Lane, S M (Cardiff) 1978 *A* 1 (R), 2, 1979 *I* (R), 1980 *S, I*
Lang, J (Llanelli) 1931 *F, I*, 1934 *S, I*, 1935 *E, S, I, NZ*,
1936 *E, S, I*, 1937 *E*
Lawrence, S (Bridgend) 1925 *S, I*, 1926 *S, I, F*, 1927 *E*
Law, V J (Newport) 1939 *I*
Legge, W S G (Newport) 1937 *I*, 1938 *I*
Leleu, J (London Welsh, Swansea) 1959 *E, S*, 1960 *F, SA*
Lemon, A (Newport) 1929 *I*, 1930 *S, I, F*, 1931 *E, S, F, I, SA*,
1932 *E, S, I*, 1933 *I*
Lewis, A J L (Ebbw Vale) 1970 *F*, 1971 *E, I, F*, 1972 *E, S,
F*, 1973 *E, S, I, F*
Lewis, A L P (Cardiff) 1996 *It, E, S, I*
Lewis, A R (Abertillery) 1966 *E, S, I, F, A*, 1967 *I*
Lewis, B R (Swansea, Cambridge U) 1912 *I*, 1913 *I*
Lewis, C P (Llandovery Coll) 1882 *I*, 1883 *E, S*, 1884 *E, S*
Lewis, D H (Cardiff) 1886 *E, S*
Lewis, E J (Llandovery) 1881 *I*
Lewis, E W (Llanelli, Cardiff) 1991 *I, F* 1, *A, F* 2, [*WS,
Arg, A*], 1992 *I, F, S, A*, 1993 *E, S, I, F, Z* 1,2, *Nm, J, C*, 1994
S, I, F, E, Pt, Sp, Fj, WS, R, It, SA, 1995 *E, S, I*, [*J, I*], 1996
It, E, S, I, F
Lewis, G W (Richmond) 1960 *E, S*
Lewis, H (Swansea) 1913 *S, F, I*, 1914 *E*
Lewis, J G (Llanelli) 1887 *I*
Lewis, J M C (Cardiff, Cambridge U) 1912 *E*, 1913 *S, F, I*,
1914 *E, S, F, I*, 1921 *I*, 1923 *E, S*
Lewis, J R (S Glam Inst, Cardiff) 1981 *E, S, I, F*, 1982 *F,
E, S*
Lewis, M (Treorchy) 1913 *F*
Lewis, P I (Llanelli) 1984 *A*, 1985 *S, I, F, E*, 1986 *E, S, I*
Lewis, T W (Cardiff) 1926 *E*, 1927 *E, S*
Lewis, W (Llanelli) 1925 *F*
Lewis, W H (London Welsh, Cambridge U) 1926 *I*, 1927
E, F, I, A, 1928 *F*
Llewelyn, D B (Newport, Llanelli) 1970 *SA, S, E, I, F*,
1971 *E, S, I, F*, 1972 *E, S, F, NZ*
Llewellyn, G D (Neath) 1990 *Nm* 1,2, *Bb*, 1991 *E, S, I, F* 1,
A, F 2

Llewellyn, G O (Neath) 1989 *NZ*, 1990 *E, S, I*, 1991 *E, S,
A* (R), 1992 *I, F, E, S, A*, 1993 *E, S, I, F, Z* 1,2, *Nm, J, C*,
1994 *S, I, F, E, Pt, Sp, C, Tg, WS, R, It, SA*, 1995 *F, E, S, I*,
[*J, NZ, I*], 1996 *It, E, S, I, F*
Llewellyn, P D (Swansea) 1973 *I, F, A*, 1974 *S, E*
Llewellyn, W (Llwynypia) 1899 *E, S, I*, 1900 *E, S, I*, 1901
E, S, I, 1902 *E, S, I*, 1903 *I*, 1904 *E, S, I*, 1905 *E, S, I, NZ*
Lloyd, D J (Bridgend) 1966 *E, S, I, F, A*, 1967 *S, I, F, E*,
1968 *S, I, F*, 1969 *S, I, F, E, NZ* 1, *A*, 1970 *F*, 1972 *E, S, F*,
1973 *E, S*
Lloyd, E (Llanelli) 1895 *S*
Lloyd, G L (Newport) 1896 *I*, 1899 *S, I*, 1900 *E, S*, 1901 *E,
S*, 1902 *S, I*, 1903 *E, S, I*
Lloyd, P (Llanelli) 1890 *S, E*, 1891 *E, I*
Lloyd, R A (Pontypool) 1913 *S, F, I*, 1914 *E, S, F, I*
Lloyd, T (Maesteg) 1953 *I, F*
Lloyd, T C (Neath) 1909 *F*, 1913 *F, I*, 1914 *E, S, F, I*
Loader, C D (Swansea) 1995 *F, Fj*, 1996 *F*
Lockwood, T W (Newport) 1887 *E, S, I*
Long, E C (Swansea) 1936 *E, S, I*, 1937 *E, S*, 1939 *S, I*
Lyne, H S (Newport) 1883 *S*, 1884 *E, S, I*, 1885 *E*

McBryde, R C (Swansea, Llanelli) 1994 *Fj, SA* (t)
McCall, B E W (Welch Regt, Newport) 1936 *E, S, I*
McCarley, A (Neath) 1938 *E, S, I*
McCutcheon, W M (Swansea) 1891 *S*, 1892 *E, S*, 1893 *E,
S, I*, 1894 *E*
Maddock, H T (London Welsh) 1906 *E, S, I*, 1907 *E, S*,
1910 *F*
Maddocks, K (Neath) 1957 *E*
Main, D R (London Welsh) 1959 *E, S, I, F*
Mainwaring, H J (Swansea) 1961 *F*
Mainwaring, W T (Aberavon) 1967 *S, I, F, E, NZ*, 1968 *E*
Major, W C (Maesteg) 1949 *F*, 1950 *S*
Male, B O (Cardiff) 1921 *F*, 1923 *S*, 1924 *S, I*, 1927 *E, S*,
F, I, 1928 *S, I, F*
Manfield, L (Mountain Ash, Cardiff) 1939 *S, I*, 1947 *A*,
1948 *E, S, F, I*
Mann, B B (Cardiff) 1881 *E*
Mantle, J T (Loughborough Colls, Newport) 1964 *E, SA*
Margrave, F L (Llanelli) 1884 *E, S*
Marsden-Jones, D (Cardiff) 1921 *E*, 1924 *NZ*
Martin, A J (Aberavon) 1973 *A*, 1974 *S, I*, 1975 *F, E, S, I,
A*, 1976 *E, S, I, F*, 1977 *I, F, E, S*, 1978 *E, S, I, F, A* 1,2, *NZ*,
1979 *S, I, F, E*, 1980 *F, E, S, I, NZ*, 1981 *I, F*
Martin, W J (Newport) 1912 *I, F*, 1919 *NZA*
Mason, J (Pontypridd) 1988 *NZ* 2 (R)
Mathews, Rev A A (Lampeter) 1886 *S*
Mathias, R (Llanelli) 1970 *F*
Matthews, C (Bridgend) 1939 *I*
Matthews, J (Cardiff) 1947 *E, A*, 1948 *E, S, F*, 1949 *E, S,
I, F*, 1950 *E, S, I, F*, 1951 *E, S, I, F*
May, P S (Llanelli) 1988 *E, S, I, F, NZ* 1,2, 1991 [*WS*]
Meek, N N (Pontypool) 1993 *E, S, I*
Meredith, A (Devonport Services) 1949 *E, S, I*
Meredith, B V (St Luke's Coll, London Welsh, Newport)
1954 *I, F, S*, 1955 *E, S, I, F*, 1956 *E, S, I, F*, 1957 *E, S, I, F*,
1958 *A, E, S, I*, 1959 *E, S, I, F*, 1960 *E, S, F, SA*, 1961 *E, S,
I*, 1962 *E, S, F, I*
Meredith, C C (Neath) 1953 *S, NZ*, 1954 *E, I, F, S*, 1955 *E,
S, I, F*, 1956 *E, I*, 1957 *E, S*
Meredith, J (Swansea) 1888 *S, I*, 1890 *S, E*
Merry, A E (Pill Harriers) 1912 *I, F*
Michael, G (Swansea) 1923 *E, S, F*
Michaelson, R C B (Aberavon, Cambridge U) 1963 *E*
Miller, F (Mountain Ash) 1896 *I*, 1900 *E, S, I*, 1901 *E, S, I*
Mills, F M (Swansea, Cardiff) 1892 *E, S, I*, 1893 *E, S, I*,
1894 *E, S, I*, 1895 *E, S, I, F*, 1896 *E*
Moon, R H St J B (Llanelli) 1993 *F, Z* 1,2, *Nm, J, C*, 1994
S, I, F, E, Sp, C, Fj, WS, R, It, SA, 1995 *E* (R)
Moore, A P (Cardiff) 1995 [*J*], *SA, Fj*, 1996 *It*
Moore, A P (Swansea) 1995 *SA* (R), *Fj*
Moore, W J (Bridgend) 1933 *I*
Morgan, C H (Llanelli) 1957 *I, F*
Morgan, C I (Cardiff) 1951 *I, F, SA*, 1952 *E, S, I*, 1953 *S, I,
F, NZ*, 1954 *E, I, S*, 1955 *E, S, I, F*, 1956 *E, S, I, F*, 1957 *E,
S, I, F*, 1958 *E, S, I, F*
Morgan, D (Swansea) 1885 *S*, 1886 *E, S*, 1887 *E, S, I*,
1889 *I*
Morgan, D (Llanelli) 1895 *I*, 1896 *E*
Morgan, D R R (Llanelli) 1962 *E, S, F, I*, 1963 *E, S, I, F,
NZ*
Morgan, E (Llanelli) 1920 *I*, 1921 *E, S, F*
Morgan, Edgar (Swansea) 1914 *E, S, F, I*

Morgan, E T (London Welsh) 1902 *E, S, I*, 1903 *I*, 1904 *E, S, I*, 1905 *E, S, I, NZ*, 1906 *E, S, I, SA*, 1908 *F*
Morgan, F L (Llanelli) 1938 *E, S, I*, 1939 *E*
Morgan, H J (Abertillery) 1958 *E, S, I, F*, 1959 *I, F*, 1960 *E*, 1961 *E, S, I, F*, 1962 *E, S, F, I*, 1963 *S, I, F*, 1965 *E, S, I, F*, 1966 *E, S, I, F, A*
Morgan, H P (Newport) 1956 *E, S, I, F*
Morgan, I (Swansea) 1908 *A*, 1909 *E, S, F, I*, 1910 *F, E, S, I*, 1911 *E, F, I*, 1912 *S*
Morgan, J L (Llanelli) 1912 *SA*, 1913 *E*
Morgan, M E (Swansea) 1938 *E, S, I*, 1939 *E*
Morgan, N (Newport) 1960 *S, I, F*
Morgan, P E J (Aberavon) 1961 *E, S, F*
Morgan, P J (Llanelli) 1980 *S* (R), *I, NZ* (R), 1981 *I*
Morgan, R (Newport) 1984 *S*
Morgan, T (Llanelli) 1889 *I*
Morgan, W G (Cambridge U) 1927 *F, I*, 1929 *E, S, F, I*, 1930 *I, F*
Morgan, W L (Cardiff) 1910 *S*
Moriarty, R D (Swansea) 1981 *A*, 1982 *I, F, E, S*, 1983 *E*, 1984 *S, I, F, E*, 1985 *S, I, F*, 1986 *Fj, Tg, WS*, 1987 *[I, Tg, C* (R), *E, NZ, A]*
Moriarty, W P (Swansea) 1986 *I, F, Fj, Tg, WS*, 1987 *F, E, S, I, [I, Tg, C, E, NZ, A]*, *US*, 1988 *E, S, I, F, NZ 1*
Morley, J C (Newport) 1929 *E, S, F, I*, 1930 *E, I*, 1931 *E, S, F, I, SA*, 1932 *E, S, I*
Morris, G L (Swansea) 1882 *I*, 1883 *E, S*, 1884 *E, S*
Morris, H T (Cardiff) 1951 *F*, 1955 *I, F*
Morris, J I T (Swansea) 1924 *E, S*
Morris, M S (S Wales Police, Neath) 1985 *S, I, F*, 1990 *I, Nm* 1,2, *Bb*, 1991 *I, F* 1, *[WS* (R)], 1992 *E*
Morris, R R (Swansea, Bristol) 1933 *S*, 1937 *S*
Morris, S (Cross Keys) 1920 *E, S, F, I*, 1922 *E, S, I, F*, 1923 *E, S, F, I*, 1924 *E, S, F, NZ*, 1925 *E, S, F*
Morris, W (Abertillery) 1919 *NZA*, 1920 *F*, 1921 *I*
Morris, W (Llanelli) 1896 *S, I*, 1897 *E*
Morris, W D (Neath) 1967 *F, E*, 1968 *E, S, I, F*, 1969 *S, I, F, E, NZ* 1,2, *A*, 1970 *SA, S, E, I, F*, 1971 *E, S, I, F*, 1972 *E, S, F, NZ*, 1973 *E, S, I, A*, 1974 *S, I, F, E*
Morris, W J (Newport) 1965 *S*, 1966 *F*
Morris, W J (Pontypool) 1963 *S, I*
Moseley, K (Pontypool, Newport) 1988 *NZ* 2, *R*, 1989 *S, I*, 1990 *F, I* 2, *[WS, Arg, A]*
Murphy, C D (Cross Keys) 1935 *E, S, I*
Mustoe, L (Cardiff) 1995 *Fj*

Nash, D (Ebbw Vale) 1960 *SA*, 1961 *E, S, I, F*, 1962 *F*
Newman, C H (Newport) 1881 *E*, 1882 *I*, 1883 *E, S*, 1884 *E, S*, 1885 *E, S*, 1886 *E*, 1887 *E*
Nicholas, D L (Llanelli) 1981 *E, S, I, F*
Nicholas, T J (Cardiff) 1919 *NZA*
Nicholl, C B (Cambridge U, Llanelli) 1891 *I*, 1892 *E, S, I*, 1893 *E, S, I*, 1894 *E, S*, 1895 *E, S, I*, 1896 *E, S, I*
Nicholl, D W (Llanelli) 1894 *I*
Nicholls, E G (Cardiff) 1896 *S, I*, 1897 *E*, 1898 *I, E*, 1899 *E, S, I*, 1900 *S, I*, 1901 *E, S, I*, 1902 *E, S, I*, 1903 *I*, 1904 *E*, 1905 *I, NZ*, 1906 *E, S, I, SA*
Nicholls, F E (Cardiff Harlequins) 1892 *I*
Nicholls, H (Cardiff) 1958 *I*
Nicholls, S H (Cardiff) 1888 *M*, 1889 *S, I*, 1891 *S*
Norris, C H (Cardiff) 1963 *F*, 1966 *F*
Norster, R L (Cardiff) 1982 *S*, 1983 *E, S, I, F*, 1984 *S, I, F, E, A*, 1985 *S, I, F, E, Fj*, 1986 *Fj, Tg, WS*, 1987 *F, E, S, I, [I, C, E]*, *US*, 1988 *E, S, I, F, NZ* 1, *WS*, 1989 *F, E*
Norton, W B (Cardiff) 1882 *I*, 1883 *E, S*, 1884 *E, S, I*

O'Connor, A (Aberavon) 1960 *SA*, 1961 *E, S*, 1962 *F, I*
O'Connor, R (Aberavon) 1957 *E*
O'Neill, G (Cardiff) 1904 *S, I*, 1905 *E, S, I*, 1907 *E, I*, 1908 *E, S, F, I*
O'Shea, J P (Cardiff) 1967 *S, I*, 1968 *S, I, F*
Oliver, G (Pontypool) 1920 *E, S, F, I*
Osborne, W T (Mountain Ash) 1902 *E, S, I*, 1903 *E, S, I*
Ould, W J (Cardiff) 1924 *E, S*
Owen, A (Swansea) 1924 *E*
Owen, G D (Newport) 1955 *I, F*, 1956 *E, S, I, F*
Owen, R M (Swansea) 1901 *I*, 1902 *E, S, I*, 1903 *E, S, I*, 1904 *E, S, I*, 1905 *E, S, I, NZ*, 1906 *E, S, I, SA*, 1907 *E, S*, 1908 *F, I, A*, 1909 *E, S, F, I*, 1910 *F, E*, 1911 *E, S, F, I*, 1912 *E, S*

Packer, H (Newport) 1891 *E*, 1895 *S, I*, 1896 *E, S, I*, 1897 *E*
Palmer, F (Swansea) 1922 *E, S, I*

Parfitt, F C (Newport) 1893 *E, S, I*, 1894 *E, S, I*, 1895 *S*, 1896 *S, I*
Parfitt, S A (Swansea) 1990 *Nm* 1 (R), *Bb*
Parker, D S (Swansea) 1924 *I, F, NZ*, 1925 *E, S, F, I*, 1929 *F, I*, 1930 *E*
Parker, T (Swansea) 1919 *NZA*, 1920 *E, S, I*, 1921 *E, S, F, I*, 1922 *E, S, I, F*, 1923 *E, S, F*
Parker, W (Swansea) 1899 *E, S*
Parsons, G W (Newport) 1947 *E*
Pascoe, D (Bridgend) 1923 *F, I*
Pask, A E I (Abertillery) 1961 *F*, 1962 *E, S, F, I*, 1963 *E, S, I, F, NZ*, 1964 *E, S, I, F, SA*, 1965 *E, S, I, F*, 1966 *E, S, I, F, A*, 1967 *S, I*
Payne, G W (Army, Pontypridd) 1960 *E, S, I*
Payne, H (Swansea) 1935 *NZ*
Peacock, H (Newport) 1929 *S, F, I*, 1930 *S, I, F*
Peake, E (Chepstow) 1881 *E*
Pearce, G P (Bridgend) 1981 *I, F*, 1982 *I* (R)
Pearson, T W (Cardiff, Newport) 1891 *E, I*, 1892 *E, S*, 1894 *S, I*, 1895 *E, S, I*, 1897 *E*, 1898 *I, E*, 1903 *E*
Pegge, E V (Neath) 1891 *E*
Perego, M A (Llanelli) 1990 *S*, 1993 *F, Z* 1, *Nm* (R), 1994 *S, I, F, E, Sp*
Perkins, S J (Pontypool) 1983 *S, I, F, R*, 1984 *S, I, F, E, A*, 1985 *S, I, F, E, Fj*, 1986 *E, S, I, F*
Perrett, F L (Neath) 1912 *SA*, 1913 *E, S, F, I*
Perrins, V C (Newport) 1970 *SA, S*
Perry, W (Neath) 1911 *E*
Phillips, A J (Cardiff) 1979 *E*, 1980 *F, E, S, I, NZ*, 1981 *E, S, I, F, A*, 1982 *I, F, E, S*, 1987 *[C, E, A]*
Phillips, B (Aberavon) 1925 *E, S, F, I*, 1926 *E*
Phillips, D H (Swansea) 1952 *F*
Phillips, H P (Newport) 1892 *E*, 1893 *E, S, I*, 1894 *E, S*
Phillips, H T (Newport) 1927 *E, S, F, I, A*, 1928 *E, S, I, F*
Phillips, K H (Neath) 1987 *F, [I, Tg, NZ]*, *US*, 1988 *E, NZ* 1, 1989 *NZ*, 1990 *F, E, S, I, Nm* 1,2, *Bb*, 1991 *E, S, I, F* 1, *A*
Phillips, L A (Newport) 1900 *E, S, I*, 1901 *S*
Phillips, R (Neath) 1987 *US*, 1988 *E, S, I, F, NZ* 1,2, *WS*, 1989 *S, I*
Phillips, W D (Cardiff) 1881 *E*, 1882 *I*, 1884 *E, S, I*
Pickering, D F (Llanelli) 1983 *E, S, I, F, R*, 1984 *S, I, F, E, A*, 1985 *S, I, F, E, Fj*, 1986 *E, S, I, F, Fj*, 1987 *F, E, S*
Plummer, R C S (Newport) 1912 *S, I, F, SA*, 1913 *E*
Pook, T (Newport) 1895 *S*
Powell, G (Ebbw Vale) 1957 *I, F*
Powell, J (Cardiff) 1906 *I*
Powell, J (Cardiff) 1923 *I*
Powell, R W (Newport) 1888 *S, I*
Powell, W C (London Welsh) 1926 *S, I, F*, 1927 *E, F, I*, 1928 *S, I, F*, 1929 *E, S, F, I*, 1930 *S, I, F*, 1931 *E, S, F, I, SA*, 1932 *E, S, I*, 1935 *E, S, I*
Powell, W J (Cardiff) 1920 *E, S, F, I*
Price, B (Newport) 1961 *F, I*, 1962 *E, S*, 1963 *E, S, F, NZ*, 1964 *E, S, I, F, SA*, 1965 *E, S, I, F*, 1966 *E, S, I, F, A*, 1967 *S, I, F, E*, 1969 *S, I, F, E, NZ* 1,2, *A*
Price, G (Pontypool) 1975 *F, E, S, I, A*, 1976 *E, S, I, F*, 1977 *I, F, E, S*, 1978 *E, S, I, F, A* 1,2, *NZ*, 1979 *S, I, F, E*, 1980 *F, E, S, I, NZ*, 1981 *E, S, I, F, A*, 1982 *I, F, E, S*, 1983 *E, I, F*
Price, M J (Pontypool, RAF) 1959 *E, S, I, F*, 1960 *E, S, I, F*, 1962 *E*
Price, R E (Weston-s-Mare) 1939 *S, I*
Price, T G (Llanelli) 1965 *E, S, I, F*, 1966 *E, A*, 1967 *S, F*
Priday, A J (Cardiff) 1958 *I*, 1961 *I*
Pritchard, C (Pontypool) 1928 *E, S, I, F*, 1929 *E, S, F, I*
Pritchard, C C (Newport, Pontypool) 1904 *S, I*, 1905 *NZ*, 1906 *E, S*
Pritchard, C M (Newport) 1904 *I*, 1905 *E, S, NZ*, 1906 *E, S, I, SA*, 1907 *S, I*, 1908 *E*, 1910 *F, E*
Proctor, W T (Llanelli) 1992 *A*, 1993 *E, S, Z* 1,2, *Nm, C*, 1994 *I, C, Fj, WS, R, It, SA*, 1995 *S, I, [NZ]*, *Fj*, 1996 *It, E, S, I*
Prosser, D R (Neath) 1934 *S, I*
Prosser, G (Neath) 1934 *S, I*, 1935 *NZ*
Prosser, G (Pontypridd) 1995 *[NZ]*
Prosser, J (Cardiff) 1921 *I*
Prosser, T R (Pontypool) 1956 *S, F*, 1957 *E, S, I, F*, 1958 *A, E, S, I, F*, 1959 *E, S, I, F*, 1960 *E, S, I, F, SA*, 1961 *I, F*
Prothero, G J (Bridgend) 1964 *S, I, F*, 1965 *E, S, I, F*, 1966 *E, S, I, F*
Pryce-Jenkins, T J (London Welsh) 1888 *S, I*
Pugh, C (Maesteg) 1924 *E, S, I, F, NZ*, 1925 *E, S*
Pugh, J D (Neath) 1987 *US*, 1988 *S* (R), 1990 *S*
Pugh, P (Neath) 1989 *NZ*

269

Pugsley, J (Cardiff) 1910 *E, S, I*, 1911 *E, S, F, I*
Pullman, J J (Neath) 1910 *F*
Purdon, F T (Newport) 1881 *E*, 1882 *I*, 1883 *E, S*

Quinnell, D L (Llanelli) 1972 *F* (R), *NZ*, 1973 *E, S, A*, 1974 *S, F*, 1975 *E* (R), 1977 *I* (R), *F, E, S*, 1978 *E, S, I, F, A* 1, *NZ*, 1979 *S, I, F, E*, 1980 *NZ*
Quinnell, J C (Llanelli) 1995 *Fj*
Quinnell, L S (Llanelli) 1993 *C*, 1994 *S, I, F, E, Pt, Sp, C, WS*

Radford, W J (Newport) 1923 *I*
Ralph, A R (Newport) 1931 *F, I, SA*, 1932 *E, S, I*
Ramsey, S H (Treorchy) 1896 *E*, 1904 *E*
Randell, R (Aberavon) 1924 *I, F*
Raybould, W H (London Welsh, Cambridge U, Newport) 1967 *S, I, F, E, NZ*, 1968 *I, F*, 1970 *SA, E, I, F* (R)
Rayer, M A (Cardiff) 1991 [*WS* (R), *Arg, A* (R)], 1992 *E* (R), *A*, 1993 *E, S, I, Z* 1, *Nm, J* (R), 1994 *S* (R), *I* (R), *F, E, Pt, C, Fj, WS, R, It*
Rees, Aaron (Maesteg) 1919 *NZA*
Rees, Alan (Maesteg) 1962 *E, S, F*
Rees, A M (London Welsh) 1934 *E*, 1935 *E, S, I, NZ*, 1936 *E, S, I*, 1937 *E, S, I*, 1938 *E, S*
Rees, B I (London Welsh) 1967 *S, I, F*
Rees, C F W (London Welsh) 1974 *I*, 1975 *A*, 1978 *NZ*, 1981 *F, A*, 1982 *I, F, E, S*, 1983 *E, S, I, F*
Rees, D (Swansea) 1968 *S, I, F*
Rees, Dan (Swansea) 1900 *E*, 1903 *E, S*, 1905 *E, S*
Rees, E B (Swansea) 1919 *NZA*
Rees, H (Cardiff) 1937 *S, I*, 1938 *E, S, I*
Rees, H E (Neath) 1979 *S, I, F, E*, 1980 *F, E, S, I, NZ*, 1983 *E, S, I, F*
Rees, J (Swansea) 1920 *E, S, F, I*, 1921 *E, S, I*, 1922 *E*, 1923 *E, F, I*, 1924 *E*
Rees, J I (Swansea) 1934 *E, S, I*, 1935 *S, NZ*, 1936 *E, S, I*, 1937 *E, S, I*, 1938 *E, S, I*
Rees, L M (Cardiff) 1933 *I*
Rees, P (Llanelli) 1947 *F, I*
Rees, P M (Newport) 1961 *E, S, I*, 1964 *I*
Rees, T (Newport) 1935 *S, I, NZ*, 1936 *E, S, I*, 1937 *E, S*
Rees, T A (Llandovery) 1881 *E*
Rees, T E (London Welsh) 1926 *I, F*, 1927 *A*, 1928 *E*
Rees-Jones, G R (Oxford U, London Welsh) 1934 *E, S*, 1935 *I, NZ*, 1936 *E*
Reeves, F (Cross Keys) 1920 *F, I*, 1921 *E*
Reynolds, A (Swansea) 1990 *Nm* 1,2 (R), 1992 *A* (R)
Rhapps, J (Penygraig) 1897 *E*
Rice-Evans, W (Swansea) 1890 *S*, 1891 *E, S*
Richards, B (Swansea)1960 *F*
Richards, C (Pontypool) 1922 *E, S, I, F*, 1924 *I*
Richards, D S (Swansea) 1979 *F, E*, 1980 *F, E, S, I, NZ*, 1981 *E, S, I, F*, 1982 *I, F*, 1983 *E, S, I, R* (R)
Richards, E G (Cardiff) 1927 *S*
Richards, E S (Swansea) 1885 *E*, 1887 *S*
Richards, H D (Neath) 1986 *Tg* (R), 1987 [*Tg, E* (R), *NZ*]
Richards, I (Cardiff) 1925 *E, S, F*
Richards, K H L (Bridgend) 1960 *SA*, 1961 *E, S, I, F*
Richards, M C R (Cardiff) 1968 *I, F*, 1969 *S, I, F, E, NZ* 1,2, *A*
Richards, R (Aberavon) 1913 *S, F, I*
Richards, R (Cross Keys) 1956 *F*
Richards, T L (Maesteg) 1923 *I*
Richardson, S J (Aberavon) 1978 *A* 2 (R), 1979 *E*
Rickards, A R (Cardiff) 1924 *F*
Ring, J (Aberavon) 1921 *E*
Ring, M G (Cardiff, Pontypool) 1983 *E*, 1984 *A*, 1985 *S, I, F*, 1987 *I*, [*I, Tg, A*], *US*, 1988 *E, S, I, F, NZ* 1,2, 1989 *NZ*, 1990 *F, E, S, I, Nm* 1,2, *Bb*, 1991 *E, S, I, F* 1,2, [*WS, Arg, A*]
Ringer, P (Ebbw Vale, Llanelli) 1978 *NZ*, 1979 *S, I, F, E*, 1980 *F, E, NZ*
Roberts, C (Neath) 1958 *I, F*
Roberts, D E A (London Welsh) 1930 *E*
Roberts, E (Llanelli) 1886 *E*, 1887 *I*
Roberts, E J (Llanelli) 1888 *S, I*, 1889 *I*
Roberts, G J (Cardiff) 1985 *F* (R), *E*, 1987 [*I, Tg, C, E, A*]
Roberts, H M (Cardiff) 1960 *SA*, 1961 *E, S, I, F*, 1962 *S, F*, 1963 *I*
Roberts, J (Cardiff) 1927 *E, S, F, I, A*, 1928 *E, S, I, F*, 1929 *E, S, F, I*
Roberts, M G (London Welsh) 1971 *E, S, I, F*, 1973 *I, F*, 1975 *S*, 1979 *E*
Roberts, T (Newport, Risca) 1921 *S, F, I*, 1922 *E, S, I, F*, 1923 *E, S*

Roberts, W (Cardiff) 1929 *E*
Robins, J D (Birkenhead Park) 1950 *E, S, I, F*, 1951 *E, S, I, F*, 1953 *E, I, F*
Robins, R J (Pontypridd) 1953 *S*, 1954 *F, S*, 1955 *E, S, I*, 1956 *E, F*, 1957 *E, S, I, F*
Robinson, I R (Cardiff) 1974 *F, E*
Rocyn-Jones, D N (Cambridge U) 1925 *I*
Roderick, W B (Llanelli) 1884 *I*
Rosser, M A (Penarth) 1924 *S, F*
Rowland, E M (Lampeter) 1885 *E*
Rowlands, C F (Aberavon) 1926 *I*
Rowlands, D C T (Pontypool) 1963 *E, S, I, F, NZ*, 1964 *E, S, I, F, SA*, 1965 *E, S, I, F*
Rowlands, G (RAF, Cardiff) 1953 *NZ*, 1954 *E, F*, 1956 *F*
Rowlands, K A (Cardiff) 1962 *F, I*, 1963 *I*, 1965 *I, F*
Rowles, G R (Penarth) 1892 *E*
Roy, W S (Cardiff) 1995 [*J* (R)]
Russell, S (London Welsh) 1987 *US*

Samuel, D (Swansea) 1891 *I*, 1893 *I*
Samuel, F (Mountain Ash) 1922 *S, I, F*
Samuel, J (Swansea) 1891 *I*
Scourfield, T (Torquay) 1930 *F*
Scrine, G F (Swansea) 1899 *E, S*, 1901 *I*
Shanklin, J L (London Welsh) 1970 *F*, 1972 *NZ*, 1973 *I, F*
Shaw, G (Neath) 1972 *NZ*, 1973 *E, S, I, F, A*, 1974 *S, I, F, E*, 1977 *I, F*
Shaw, T W (Newbridge) 1983 *R*
Shea, J (Newport) 1919 *NZA*, 1920 *E, S*, 1921 *E*
Shell, R C (Aberavon) 1973 *A* (R)
Simpson, H J (Cardiff) 1884 *E, S, I*
Skrimshire, R T (Newport) 1899 *E, S, I*
Skym, A (Llanelli) 1928 *E, S, I, F*, 1930 *E, S, I, F*, 1931 *E, S, F, I, SA*, 1932 *E, S, I*, 1933 *E, S, I*, 1935 *E*
Smith, J S (Cardiff) 1884 *E, I*, 1885 *E*
Sparks, B (Neath) 1954 *I*, 1955 *E, F*, 1956 *E, S, I*, 1957 *S*
Spiller, W J (Cardiff) 1910 *S, I*, 1911 *E, S, F, I*, 1912 *E, F, SA*, 1913 *E*
Squire, J (Newport, Pontypool) 1977 *I, F*, 1978 *E, S, I, F, A* 1, *NZ*, 1979 *S, I, F, E*, 1980 *F, E, S, I, NZ*, 1981 *E, S, I, F, A*, 1982 *I, F, E*, 1983 *E, S, I, F*
Stadden, W J W (Cardiff) 1884 *I*, 1886 *E, S*, 1887 *I*, 1888 *S, M*, 1890 *S, E*
Stephens, C J (Llanelli) 1992 *I, F, E, A*
Stephens, G (Neath) 1912 *E, S, I, F, SA*, 1913 *E, S, F, I*, 1919 *NZA*
Stephens, I (Bridgend) 1981 *E, S, I, F, A*, 1982 *I, F, E, S*, 1984 *I, F, E, A*
Stephens, Rev J G (Llanelli) 1922 *E, S, I, F*
Stephens, J R G (Neath) 1947 *E, S, F, I*, 1948 *I*, 1949 *S, I, F*, 1951 *F, SA*, 1952 *E, S, I, F*, 1953 *E, S, I, F, NZ*, 1954 *E, I*, 1955 *E, S, I, F*, 1956 *S, I, F*, 1957 *E, S, I, F*
Stock, A (Newport) 1924 *F, NZ*, 1926 *E, S*
Stone, P (Llanelli) 1949 *F*
Strand-Jones, J (Llanelli) 1902 *E, S, I*, 1903 *E, S*
Summers, R H B (Haverfordwest) 1881 *E*
Sutton, S (Pontypool, S Wales Police) 1982 *F, E*, 1987 *F, E, S, I*, [*C, NZ* (R), *A*]
Sweet-Escott, R B (Cardiff) 1891 *S*, 1894 *I*, 1895 *I*

Tamplin, W E (Cardiff) 1947 *S, F, I, A*, 1948 *E, S, F*
Tanner, H (Swansea, Cardiff) 1935 *NZ*, 1936 *E, S, I*, 1937 *E, S, I*, 1938 *E, S, I*, 1939 *E, S, I*, 1947 *E, S, F, I*, 1948 *E, S, F, I*, 1949 *E, S, I, F*
Tarr, D J (Swansea, Royal Navy) 1935 *NZ*
Taylor, A R (Cross Keys) 1937 *I*, 1938 *I*, 1939 *F*
Taylor, C G (Ruabon) 1884 *E, S, I*, 1885 *E, S*, 1886 *E, S*, 1887 *E, I*
Taylor, H T (Cardiff) 1994 *Pt, C, Fj, Tg, WS* (R), *R, It, SA*, 1995 *E, S*, [*J, NZ, I*], *SA, Fj*, 1996 *It, E, S, I, F*
Taylor, J (London Welsh) 1967 *S, I, F, E, NZ*, 1968 *I, F*, 1969 *S, I, F, E, NZ* 1, *A*, 1970 *F*, 1971 *E, S, I, F*, 1972 *E, S, F, NZ*, 1973 *E, S, I, F*
Taylor, M (Pontypool, Swansea) 1994 *SA*, 1995 *F, E, SA* (R)
Thomas, A (Newport) 1963 *NZ*, 1964 *E*
Thomas, A (Bristol) 1996 *It, E, S, I*
Thomas, A G (Swansea, Cardiff) 1952 *E, S, I, F*, 1953 *S, I, F*, 1954 *E, I, F*, 1955 *S, I, F*
Thomas, Bob (Swansea) 1900 *E, S, I*, 1901 *E*
Thomas, Brian (Neath, Cambridge U) 1963 *E, S, I, F, NZ*, 1964 *E, S, I, F, SA*, 1965 *E*, 1966 *E, S, I*, 1967 *NZ*, 1969 *S, I, F, E, NZ* 1,2
Thomas, C (Bridgend) 1925 *E, S*

Thomas, C J (Newport) 1888 *I, M*, 1889 *S, I*, 1890 *S, E, I*, 1891 *E, I*
Thomas, D (Aberavon) 1961 *I*
Thomas, D (Llanelli) 1954 *I*
Thomas, Dick (Mountain Ash) 1906 *SA*, 1908 *F, I*, 1909 *S*
Thomas, D J (Swansea) 1904 *E*, 1908 *A*, 1910 *E, S, I*, 1911 *E, S, F, I*, 1912 *E*
Thomas, D J (Swansea) 1930 *S, I*, 1932 *E, S, I*, 1933 *E, S*, 1934 *E*, 1935 *E, S, I*
Thomas, D L (Neath) 1937 *E*
Thomas, E (Newport) 1904 *S, I*, 1909 *S, F, I*, 1910 *F*
Thomas, G (Llanelli) 1923 *E, S, F, I*
Thomas, G (Newport) 1888 *M*, 1890 *I*, 1891 *S*
Thomas, G (Bridgend) 1995 *[J, NZ, I]*, *SA, Fj*, 1996 *F*
Thomas, H (Llanelli) 1912 *F*
Thomas, H (Neath) 1936 *E, S, I*, 1937 *E, S, I*
Thomas, H W (Swansea) 1912 *SA*, 1913 *E*
Thomas, I (Bryncethin) 1924 *E*
Thomas, L C (Cardiff) 1885 *E, S*
Thomas, M C (Newport, Devonport Services) 1949 *F*, 1950 *E, S, I, F*, 1951 *E, S, I, F, SA*, 1952 *E, S, I, F*, 1953 *E*, 1956 *E, S, I, F*, 1957 *E, S*, 1958 *E, S, I, F*, 1959 *I, F*
Thomas, M G (St Bart's Hospital) 1919 *NZA*, 1921 *S, F, I*, 1923 *F*, 1924 *E*
Thomas, R (Pontypool) 1909 *F, I*, 1911 *S, F*, 1912 *E, S, SA*, 1913 *E*
Thomas, R C C (Swansea) 1949 *F*, 1952 *I, F*, 1953 *S, I, F, NZ*, 1954 *E, I, F, S*, 1955 *S, I*, 1956 *E, S, I*, 1957 *E*, 1958 *A, E, S, I, F*, 1959 *E, S, I, F*
Thomas, R L (London Welsh) 1889 *S, I*, 1890 *I*, 1891 *E, S, I*, 1892 *E*
Thomas, S (Llanelli) 1890 *S, E*, 1891 *I*
Thomas, W D (Llanelli) 1966 *A*, 1968 *S, I, F*, 1969 *E, NZ 2, A*, 1970 *SA, S, E, I, F*, 1971 *E, S, I, F*, 1972 *E, S, F, NZ*, 1973 *E, S, I, F*, 1974 *E*
Thomas, W G (Llanelli, Waterloo, Swansea) 1927 *E, S, F, I*, 1929 *E, S*, 1931 *E, S, SA*, 1932 *E, S, I*, 1933 *E, S, I*
Thomas, W H (Llandovery Coll, Cambridge U) 1885 *S*, 1886 *E, S*, 1887 *E, S*, 1888 *S, I*, 1890 *E, I*, 1891 *S, I*
Thomas, W J (Cardiff) 1961 *F*, 1963 *F*
Thomas, W J L (Llanelli) 1995 *SA, Fj*, 1996 *It, E, S, I, F*
Thomas, W L (Newport) 1894 *S*, 1895 *E, I*
Thomas, W T (Abertillery) 1930 *E*
Thompson, J F (Cross Keys) 1923 *E*
Thorburn, P H (Neath) 1985 *F, E, Fj*, 1986 *E, S, I, F*, 1987 *F*, *[I, Tg, C, E, NZ, A]*, *US*, 1988 *S, I, F, WS, R* (R), 1989 *S, I, F, E, NZ*, 1990 *F, E, S, I, Nm 1,2, Bb*, 1991 *E, S, I, F 1, A*
Titley, M H (Bridgend, Swansea) 1983 *R*, 1984 *S, I, F, E, A*, 1985 *S, I, Fj*, 1986 *F, Fj, Tg, WS*, 1990 *F, E*
Towers, W H (Swansea) 1887 *I*, 1888 *M*
Travers, G (Pill Harriers) 1903 *E, S, I*, 1905 *E, S, I, NZ*, 1906 *E, S, I, SA*, 1907 *E, S, I*, 1908 *E, S, F, I, A*, 1909 *E, S, I*, 1911 *S, F, I*
Travers, W H (Newport) 1937 *S, I*, 1938 *E, S, I*, 1939 *E, S, I*, 1949 *E, S, I, F*
Treharne, E (Pontypridd) 1881 *E*, 1883 *E*
Trew, W J (Swansea) 1900 *E, S, I*, 1901 *E, S*, 1903 *S*, 1905 *S*, 1906 *S*, 1907 *E, S*, 1908 *E, S, F, I, A*, 1909 *E, S, F, I*, 1910 *F, E, S*, 1911 *E, S, F, I*, 1912 *S*, 1913 *S, F*
Trott, R F (Cardiff) 1948 *E, S, F, I*, 1949 *E, S, I, F*
Truman, W H (Llanelli) 1934 *E*, 1935 *E*
Trump, L C (Newport) 1912 *E, S, I, F*
Turnbull, B R (Cardiff) 1925 *I*, 1927 *E, S*, 1928 *E, F*, 1930 *S*
Turnbull, M J L (Cardiff) 1933 *E, I*
Turner, P (Newbridge) 1989 *I* (R), *F, E*

Uzzell, H (Newport) 1912 *E, S, I, F*, 1913 *S, F, I*, 1914 *E, S, F, I*, 1920 *E, S, F, I*
Uzzell, J R (Newport) 1963 *NZ*, 1965 *E, S, I, F*

Vickery, W E (Aberavon) 1938 *E, S, I*, 1939 *E*
Vile, T H (Newport) 1908 *E, S*, 1910 *I*, 1912 *I, F, SA*, 1913 *E*, 1921 *S*
Vincent, H C (Bangor) 1882 *I*

Wakeford, J D M (S Wales Police) 1988 *WS, R*
Waldron, R (Neath) 1965 *E, S, I, F*
Walker, N (Cardiff) 1993 *I, F, J*, 1994 *S, F, E, Pt, Sp*, 1995 *F, E*
Waller, P D (Newport) 1908 *A*, 1909 *E, S, F, I*, 1910 *F*
Walters, N (Llanelli) 1902 *E*
Wanbon, R (Aberavon) 1968 *E*
Ward, W S (Cross Keys) 1934 *S, I*

Warlow, J (Llanelli) 1962 *I*
Waters, D R (Newport) 1986 *E, S, I, F*
Waters, K (Newbridge) 1991 *[WS]*
Watkins, D (Newport) 1963 *E, S, I, F, NZ*, 1964 *E, S, I, F, SA*, 1965 *E, S, I, F*, 1966 *E, S, I, F*, 1967 *I, F, E*
Watkins, E (Neath) 1924 *E, S, I, F*
Watkins, E (Blaina) 1926 *S, I, F*
Watkins, E (Cardiff) 1935 *NZ*, 1937 *S, I*, 1938 *E, S, I*, 1939 *E, S*
Watkins, H (Llanelli) 1904 *S, I*, 1905 *E, S, I*, 1906 *E*
Watkins, I J (Ebbw Vale) 1988 *E* (R), *S, I, F, NZ 2, R*, 1989 *S, I, F, E*
Watkins, L (Oxford U, Llandaff) 1881 *E*
Watkins, M J (Newport) 1984 *I, F, E, A*
Watkins, S J (Newport, Cardiff) 1964 *S, I, F*, 1965 *E, S, I, F*, 1966 *E, S, I, F, A*, 1967 *S, I, F, E, NZ*, 1968 *E, S*, 1969 *S, I, F, E, NZ 1*, 1970 *E, I, F*
Watkins, W R (Newport) 1959 *F*
Watts, D (Maesteg) 1914 *E, S, F, I*
Watts, J (Llanelli) 1907 *E, S, I*, 1908 *E, S, F, I, A*, 1909 *S, F, I*
Watts, W (Llanelli) 1914 *E*
Watts, W H (Newport) 1892 *E, S, I*, 1893 *E, S, I*, 1894 *E, S, I*, 1895 *E, I*, 1896 *E*
Weaver, D (Swansea) 1964 *E*
Webb, J (Abertillery) 1907 *S*, 1908 *E, S, F, I, A*, 1909 *E, S, F, I*, 1910 *F, E, S, I*, 1911 *E, S, F, I*, 1912 *E, S*
Webb, J E (Newport) 1888 *M*, 1889 *S*
Webbe, G M C (Bridgend) 1986 *Tg* (R), *WS*, 1987 *F, E, S*, *[Tg]*, *US*, 1988 *F* (R), *NZ 1, R*
Webster, R E (Swansea) 1987 *[A]*, 1990 *Bb*, 1991 *[Arg, A]*, 1992 *I, F, E, S, A*, 1993 *E, S, I, F*
Wells, G T (Cardiff) 1955 *E, S*, 1957 *I, F*, 1958 *A, E, S*
Westacott, D (Cardiff) 1906 *I*
Wetter, H (Newport) 1912 *SA*, 1913 *E*
Wetter, J J (Newport) 1914 *S, F, I*, 1920 *E, S, F, I*, 1921 *E*, 1924 *I, NZ*
Wheel, G A D (Swansea) 1974 *I, E* (R), 1975 *F, E, I, A*, 1976 *E, S, I, F*, 1977 *I, E, S*, 1978 *E, S, I, F, A 1,2, NZ*, 1979 *S, I*, 1980 *F, E, S, I*, 1981 *E, S, I, F, A*, 1982 *I*
Wheeler, P J (Aberavon) 1967 *NZ*, 1968 *E*
Whitefoot, J (Cardiff) 1984 *A* (R), 1985 *S, I, F, E, Fj*, 1986 *E, S, I, F, Fj, Tg, WS*, 1987 *F, E, S, I*, *[I, C]*
Whitfield, J (Newport) 1919 *NZA*, 1920 *E, S, F, I*, 1921 *E*, 1922 *E, S, I, F*, 1924 *S, I*
Whitson, G K (Newport) 1956 *F*, 1960 *S, I*
Wilkins, G (Bridgend) 1994 *Tg*
Williams, A (Bridgend, Swansea) 1990 *Nm 2* (R), 1995 *Fj* (R)
Williams, B (Llanelli) 1920 *S, F, I*
Williams, B L (Cardiff) 1947 *E, S, F, I, A*, 1948 *E, S, F, I*, 1949 *E, S, I*, 1951 *I, SA*, 1952 *S*, 1953 *E, S, I, F, NZ*, 1954 *S*, 1955 *E*
Williams, B R (Neath) 1990 *S, I, Bb*, 1991 *E, S*
Williams, C (Llanelli) 1924 *NZ*, 1925 *E*
Williams, C (Aberavon, Swansea) 1977 *E, S*, 1980 *F, E, S, I, NZ*, 1983 *E*
Williams, C D (Cardiff, Neath) 1955 *F*, 1956 *F*
Williams, D (Ebbw Vale) 1963 *E, S, I, F*, 1964 *E, S, I, F, SA*, 1965 *E, S, I, F*, 1966 *E, S, I, A*, 1967 *F, E, NZ*, 1968 *E*, 1969 *S, I, F, E, NZ 1,2, A*, 1970 *SA, S, E, I*, 1971 *E, S, I, F*
Williams, D B (Newport, Swansea) 1978 *A 1*, 1981 *E, S*
Williams, E (Neath) 1924 *NZ*, 1925 *F*
Williams, E (Aberavon) 1925 *E, S*
Williams, F L (Cardiff) 1929 *S, F, I*, 1930 *E, S, I, F*, 1931 *F, I, SA*, 1932 *E, S, I*, 1933 *I*
Williams, G (Aberavon) 1936 *E, S, I*
Williams, G (London Welsh) 1950 *I, F*, 1951 *E, S, I, F, SA*, 1952 *E, S, I, F*, 1953 *NZ*, 1954 *F*
Williams, G (Bridgend) 1981 *I, F*, 1982 *E* (R), *S*
Williams, G P (Bridgend) 1980 *NZ*, 1981 *E, S, A*, 1982 *I*
Williams, J (Blaina) 1920 *E, S, F, I*, 1921 *S, F, I*
Williams, J F (London Welsh) 1905 *I, NZ*, 1906 *S, SA*
Williams, J J (Llanelli) 1973 *F* (R), *A*, 1974 *S, I, F, E*, 1975 *F, E, S, I, A*, 1976 *E, S, I, F*, 1977 *I, F, E, S*, 1978 *E, S, I, F, A 1,2, NZ*, 1979 *S, I, F, E*
Williams, J L (Cardiff) 1906 *SA*, 1907 *E, S, I*, 1908 *E, S, I, A*, 1909 *E, S, F, I*, 1910 *I*, 1911 *E, S, F, I*
Williams, J P R (London Welsh, Bridgend) 1969 *S, I, F, E, NZ 1,2, A*, 1970 *SA, S, E, I, F*, 1971 *E, S, I, F*, 1972 *E, S, F, NZ*, 1973 *E, S, I, F, A*, 1974 *S, I, F*, 1975 *F, E, S, I, A*, 1976 *E, S, I, F*, 1977 *I, F, E, S*, 1978 *E, S, I, F, A 1,2, NZ*, 1979 *S, I, F, E*, 1980 *NZ*, 1981 *E, S*

271

Williams, L (Llanelli, Cardiff) 1947 *E, S, F, I, A*, 1948 *I*, 1949 *E*
Williams, L H (Cardiff) 1957 *S, I, F*, 1958 *E, S, I, F*, 1959 *E, S, I*, 1961 *F*, 1962 *E, S*
Williams, M (Newport) 1923 *F*
Williams, O (Bridgend) 1990 *Nm* 2
Williams, O (Llanelli) 1947 *E, S, A*, 1948 *E, S, F, I*
Williams, R (Llanelli) 1954 *S*, 1957 *F*, 1958 *A*
Williams, R D G (Newport) 1881 *E*
Williams, R F (Cardiff) 1912 *SA*, 1913 *E, S*, 1914 *I*
Williams, R H (Llanelli) 1954 *I, F, S*, 1955 *S, I, F*, 1956 *E, S, I*, 1957 *E, S, I, F*, 1958 *A, E, S, I, F*, 1959 *E, S, I, F*, 1960 *E*
Williams, S (Llanelli) 1947 *E, S, F, I*, 1948 *S, F*
Williams, S A (Aberavon) 1939 *E, S, I*
Williams, S M (Neath) 1994 *E*, 1996 *E* (t)
Williams, T (Pontypridd) 1882 *I*
Williams, T (Swansea) 1888 *S, I*
Williams, T (Swansea) 1912 *I*, 1913 *F*, 1914 *E, S, F, I*
Williams, T G (Cross Keys) 1935 *S, I, NZ*, 1936 *E, S, I*, 1937 *S, I*
Williams, W A (Crumlin) 1927 *E, S, F, I*
Williams, W A (Newport) 1952 *I, F*, 1953 *E*
Williams, W E O (Cardiff) 1887 *S, I*, 1889 *S*, 1890 *S, E*
Williams, W H (Pontymister) 1900 *E, S, I*, 1901 *E*
Williams, W O G (Swansea, Devonport Services) 1951 *F, SA*, 1952 *E, S, I, F*, 1953 *E, S, I, F, NZ*, 1954 *E, I, F, S*, 1955 *E, S, I, F*, 1956 *E, S, I*

Williams, W P J (Neath) 1974 *I, F*
Williams-Jones, H (S Wales Police, Llanelli) 1989 *S* (R), 1990 *F* (R), *I*, 1991 *A*, 1992 *S, A*, 1993 *E, S, I, F, Z* 1, *Nm*, 1994 *Fj, Tg, WS* (R), *It* (t), 1995 *E* (R)
Willis, W R (Cardiff) 1950 *E, S, I, F*, 1951 *E, S, I, F, SA*, 1952 *E, S*, 1953 *S, NZ*, 1954 *E, I, F, S*, 1955 *E, S, I, F*
Wiltshire, M L (Aberavon) 1967 *NZ*, 1968 *E, S, F*
Windsor, R W (Pontypool) 1973 *A*, 1974 *S, I, F, E*, 1975 *F, E, S, I, A*, 1976 *E, S, I, F*, 1977 *I, F, E, S*, 1978 *E, S, I, F, A* 1,2, *NZ*, 1979 *S, I, F*
Winfield, H B (Cardiff) 1903 *I*, 1904 *E, S, I*, 1905 *NZ*, 1906 *E, S, I*, 1907 *S, I*, 1908 *E, S, F, I, A*
Winmill, S (Cross Keys) 1921 *E, S, F, I*
Wintle, M E (Llanelli) 1996 *It*
Wintle, R V (London Welsh) 1988 *WS* (R)
Wooller, W (Sale, Cambridge U, Cardiff) 1933 *E, S, I*, 1935 *E, S, I, NZ*, 1936 *E, S, I*, 1937 *E, S, I*, 1938 *S, I*, 1939 *E, S, I*
Wyatt, M A (Swansea) 1983 *E, S, I, F*, 1984 *A*, 1985 *S, I*, 1987 *E, S, I*

Young, D (Swansea, Cardiff) 1987 [*E, NZ*], *US*, 1988 *E, S, I, F, NZ* 1,2, *WS, R*, 1989 *S, NZ*, 1990 *F*
Young, G A (Cardiff) 1886 *E, S*
Young, J (Harrogate, RAF, London Welsh) 1968 *S, I, F*, 1969 *S, I, F, E, NZ* 1, 1970 *E, I, F*, 1971 *E, S, I, F*, 1972 *E, S, F, NZ*, 1973 *E, S, I, F*

WELSH INTERNATIONAL RECORDS

Both team and individual records are for official Welsh international matches up to 30 April 1996.

TEAM RECORDS

Highest score
102 v Portugal (102-11) 1994 Lisbon

v individual countries
  16 v Argentina (16-7) 1991 Cardiff
  28 v Australia (28-3) 1975 Cardiff
  40 v Canada (40-9) 1987 Invercargill
  34 v England (34-21) 1967 Cardiff
  49 v France (49-14) 1910 Swansea
  40 v Fiji (40-3) 1985 Cardiff
  34 v Ireland (34-9) 1976 Dublin
  31 v Italy (31-26) 1996 Cardiff
  57 v Japan (57-10) 1995 Bloemfontein
  38 v Namibia (38-23) 1993 Windhoek
  16 v N Zealand (16-19) 1972 Cardiff
102 v Portugal (102-11) 1994 Lisbon
  16 v Romania (16-9) 1994 Bucharest
  12 v S Africa (12-20) 1994 Cardiff
  35 v Scotland (35-12) 1972 Cardiff
  54 v Spain (54-0) 1994 Madrid
  29 v Tonga (29-16) 1987 Palmerston North
  46 v United States (46-0) 1987 Cardiff
  32 v W Samoa (32-14) 1986 Apia
  42 v Zimbabwe (42-13) 1993 Harare

Biggest winning points margin
  91 v Portugal (102-11) 1994 Lisbon

v individual countries
  9 v Argentina (16-7) 1991 Cardiff

  25 v Australia (28-3) 1975 Cardiff
  31 v Canada (40-9) 1987 Invercargill
  25 v England (25-0) 1905 Cardiff
  42 v France (47-5) 1909 Colombes
  37 v Fiji (40-3) 1985 Cardiff
  29 v Ireland (29-0) 1907 Cardiff
  10 v Italy (29-19) 1994 Cardiff
  50 v Japan (55-5) 1993 Cardiff
  15 v Namibia (38-23) 1993 Windhoek
   5 v N Zealand (13-8) 1953 Cardiff
  91 v Portugal (102-11) 1994 Lisbon
   7 v Romania (16-9) 1994 Bucharest
  23 v Scotland { (35-12) 1972 Cardiff
                { (29-6) 1994 Cardiff
  54 v Spain (54-0) 1994 Madrid
  13 v Tonga (29-16) 1987 Palmerston North
  46 v United States (46-0) 1987 Cardiff
  22 v W Samoa (28-6) 1988 Cardiff
  29 v Zimbabwe (42-13) 1993 Harare
No wins v South Africa

Longest winning sequence
11 matches – 1907-10

Highest score by opposing team
63 Australia (6-63) 1991 Brisbane

v individual countries
   7 Argentina (16-7) 1991 Cardiff
  63 Australia (6-63) 1991 Brisbane
  26 Canada (24-26) 1993 Cardiff
  34 England (6-34) 1990 Twickenham

36 France (3-36) 1991 Paris
15 Fiji { (22-15) 1986 Suva
        { (19-15) 1995 Cardiff
30 Ireland (17-30) 1996 Dublin
26 Italy (31-26) 1996 Cardiff
10 Japan (57-10) 1995 Bloemfontein
30 Namibia (34-30) 1990 Windhoek
54 N Zealand (9-54) 1988 Auckland
11 Portugal (102-11) 1994 Lisbon
24 Romania (6-24) 1983 Bucharest
35 Scotland (10-35) 1924 Inverleith
40 S Africa (11-40) 1995 Johannesburg
 0 Spain (54-0) 1994 Madrid
16 Tonga (29-16) 1987 Palmerston North
 0 United States (46-0) 1987 Cardiff
34 W Samoa (9-34) 1994 Moamoa
13 Zimbabwe (42-13) 1993 Harare

Biggest losing points margin

57 v Australia (6-63) 1991 Brisbane
v individual countries
57 v Australia (6-63) 1991 Brisbane
 2 v Canada (24-26) 1993 Cardiff
28 v England (6-34) 1990 Twickenham
33 v France (3-36) 1991 Paris
16 v Ireland (3-19) 1925 Belfast
49 v N Zealand (3-52) 1988 Christchurch
18 v Romania (6-24) 1983 Bucharest
25 v Scotland (10-35) 1924 Inverleith
29 v S Africa (11-40) 1995 Johannesburg
25 v W Samoa (9-34) 1994 Moamoa
No defeats v Argentina, Fiji, Italy, Japan, Namibia, Portugal, Spain, Tonga, United States or Zimbabwe

Longest losing sequence

5 matches – 1989-90 and 1994-95

Most tries by Wales in an international

16 v Portugal (102-11) 1994 Lisbon

Most tries against Wales in an international

13 by England 1881 Blackheath

Most points by Wales in International Championship in a season – 102

in season 1975-76

Most tries by Wales in International Championship in a season – 21

in season 1909-10

INDIVIDUAL RECORDS

Most capped player

I C Evans   61   1987-96

in individual positions
Full-back
J P R Williams   54(55)[1]   1969-81
Wing
I C Evans   61   1987-96
Centre
M R Hall   32(42)[2]   1988-95
Fly-half
N R Jenkins   30(39)[3]   1991-96
Scrum-half
R N Jones   53(54)[4]   1986-95
G O Edwards   53   1967-78
Prop
G Price   41   1975-83
Hooker
B V Meredith   34   1954-62
Lock
G O Llewellyn   44(45)[5]   1989-96
Flanker
W D Morris   32(34)[6]   1967-74
No 8
T M Davies   38[7]   1969-76

[1] *Williams won one cap as a flanker*
[2] *Hall won 10 caps on the wing*
[3] *M G Ring, 32 caps, won 27 at centre, 4 at fly-half and 1 as a full-back. P Bennett, 29 caps, played 25 times as a fly-half. Jenkins has won 8 caps at centre and 1 at full-back*
[4] *Jones was capped once as a replacement threequarter*
[5] *Llewellyn has been capped once as a flanker*
[6] *Morris won his first two caps as a No 8*
[7] *P T Davies, 46 caps, has won 26 as a No 8, 2 as a flanker and 18 as a lock. E W Lewis, 41 caps, has won 26 as a flanker and 15 at No 8*

Longest international career

W J Trew
14 seasons 1899-1900 to 1912-13
T H Vile
14 seasons 1907-08 to 1920-21
H Tanner
14 seasons 1935-36 to 1948-49

Most consecutive internationals – 53★

G O Edwards 1967-78
★*entire career*

Most internationals as captain – 28

I C Evans 1991-95

Most points in internationals – 430

N R Jenkins (39 matches) 1991-96

Most points in International Championship in a season – 52
P H Thorburn (4 matches) 1985-86

Most points in an international – 24
N R Jenkins v Canada 1993 Cardiff
N R Jenkins v Italy 1994 Cardiff

Most tries in internationals – 27
I C Evans (61 matches) 1987-96

Most tries in International Championship in a season – 6
R A Gibbs (4 matches) 1907-08
M C R Richards (4 matches) 1968-69

Most tries in an international – 4
W M Llewellyn* v England 1899
   Swansea
R A Gibbs v France 1908 Cardiff
M C R Richards v England 1969
   Cardiff
I C Evans v Canada 1987 Invercargill
N Walker v Portugal 1994 Lisbon
* on first appearance

Most conversions in internationals – 47
N R Jenkins (39 matches) 1991-96

Most conversions in International Championship in a season – 11
J Bancroft (4 matches) 1908-09

Most conversions in an international – 11
N R Jenkins v Portugal 1994 Lisbon

Most dropped goals in internationals – 13
J Davies (27 matches) 1985-88

Most dropped goals in an international – 2
J Shea v England 1920 Swansea
A Jenkins v Scotland 1921 Swansea
B John v England 1971 Cardiff
M Dacey v England 1984 Twickenham
J Davies v Ireland 1987 Wellington
J Davies v Scotland 1988 Cardiff

Most penalty goals in internationals – 101
N R Jenkins (39 matches) 1991-96

Most penalty goals in International Championship in a season – 16
P H Thorburn (4 matches) 1985-86

Most penalty goals in an international – 8
N R Jenkins v Canada 1993 Cardiff

Most points on major overseas tour – 89
N R Jenkins (6 matches) Africa 1993

Most points in a tour match – 28
M Rayer v N Region 1990 Namibia
P Bennett scored 34 points v Japan in Tokyo in 1975, but this was not on a major tour

Most tries in a tour match – 3
M C R Richards v Otago 1969 Dunedin,
   NZ
S Fealey v Welwitschia 1990
   Swakopmund, Namibia
Several others have scored 3 in matches on non-major tours

MOTIVATING A NEW GENERATION

THE 1995-96 SEASON IN FRANCE
Bob Donahue *International Herald Tribune*

This was Toulouse's season. In January Stade Toulousain won the first European Cup; five months later they won the French club championship for a record 13th time. Ten Toulouse men played for France from the start of the World Cup to the end of the domestic season. And France's national coach from September was the former Toulouse international Jean-Claude Skrela, who had coached the club, alongside Pierre Villepreux, for most of the 1980s.

When, in early 1978, the selectors needed a captain to succeed scrum-half Jacques Fouroux, they chose Jean-Pierre Bastiat ahead of Skrela because Bastiat was deemed socially superior – he sold insurance, whereas Skrela was then a mere swimming instructor. How times change. Aged only 28, Skrela retired from international rugby in disgust. In 1995, the authorities entertained the notion, after they dropped the headstrong Pierre Berbizier as national coach, that Skrela, unlike Villepreux and some other fancy candidates, would be pliant. In fact, he is as stubborn as he is discreet.

While trying to maintain Berbizier's basics – possession, defence, discipline, counter-attack – Skrela wanted to free up play in the inspired manner that Toulouse sometimes achieve. He would do it with Berbizier's men, or he would see to it that the selectors called in the newcomers of his choice. So it was that Skrela used 45 players in ten tests, from the first Latin Cup, held in Argentina in October. By May, when a 30-man squad for a tour of Argentina was announced, only 11 members of the 1995 World Cup party remained: backs Jean-Luc Sadourny, Emile Ntamack, Yann Delaigue, Philippe Saint-André and Guy Accoceberry, and in the forwards, Philippe Benetton, Abdel Benazzi, Olivier Roumat, Olivier Merle, Marc de Rougemont and Christian Califano. Gone were, among others, Philippe Sella, Thierry Lacroix, Franck Mesnel, Christophe Deylaud, Laurent Bénézech and Marc Cecillon.

The season's results look successful in aggregate – seven victories in ten tests, with 43 tries scored and ten conceded – but deserved defeat followed flattering victory three times. It happened first against New Zealand, when the triumph in the First Test in Toulouse could not be repeated in Paris; then an English-style win against England in Paris was followed by limp humiliation in Edinburgh. And after an historic romp against Ireland came disaster in Cardiff, where the Five Nations trophy was there for the taking. Comfortable victories over Italy, Romania and Argentina at the start of the season, and against Romania again at the end, were merely sideshows to the main event.

The France team which played Wales in Cardiff. L-R, back row: O Brouzet (replacement), M Périé (replacement), R Ibanez (replacement), F Tournaire, J-M Gonzalez, C Califano, R Castel, L Cabannes, S Dispagne, A Benazzi, O Roumat; front row: F Galthié (replacement), R Dourthe (replacement), T Castaignède, S Glas, G Accoceberry, P Saint-André (capt), O Campan, E Ntamack, J-L Sadourny, A Penaud (replacement).

Skrela's models, he said, were the current New Zealanders, the Welsh teams of the 1970s and the Australia of the 1980s. Would he bring back from Argentina an attacking squad fit to beat the Springboks in France in the autumn of 1996?

France were by now, of course, a squad of professionals – the players' reported annual earnings approached or exceeded £100,000 – and the Fédération and its major clubs were at odds with each other, though less acrimoniously than in England. The challenge – Skrela's goal – was a telegenic performance on the pitch.

Supporting Skrela were manager Jo Maso, chairman of selectors André Herrero and an official 'reflection commission' grouping of Villepreux, Jean Trillo, Jean-Claude Ballatore and André Quilis. One of this commission's first puzzles was the inconsistency of the national side. How do you motivate the new generation in a professional era? It is a question that remains to be answered.

FRENCH CLUB CHAMPIONSHIP FINAL
1 June, Parc des Princes
Toulouse 20 (3PG 2DG 1T)   **Brive 13** (1G 2PG)

The four quarter-finals had produced a dreary tally of three tries and 30 penalty goals. The semi-finals, in which Dax and Pau were the losers, did better: nine tries and 11 penalties. The final, as so often, was an extraordinary fête for players and supporters but a disappointment for neutrals.

A third consecutive title for Toulouse was secured by David Berty's late try and Thomas Castaignède's dropped goal after Brive led twice: 10-6 at half-time and 13-12 near the end. The Toulouse pack started strongly, faded after ten minutes and recovered to close down a mundane match in the second half.

Toulouse: S Ougier; E Ntamack (*capt*), P Carbonneau, T Castaignède, D Berty; C Deylaud, J Cazalbou; C Califano, P Soula, C Portolan, H Miorin, F Belot, D Lacroix, S Dispagne, H Manent *Replacements* R Castel for Lacroix; E Artiguste for Deylaud; O Carbonneau for Cazalbou
Scorers *Try:* Berty   *Penalty Goals:* Castaignède (2), Deylaud   *Dropped Goals:* Deylaud, Castaignède
Brive: S Paillat; C Lucquiaud, R Paillat, J-M Soubira, J Carrat; A Penaud (*capt*), S Bonnet; D Casadéi, V Moscato, R Crespy, E Alegret, L Bonventre, L van der Linden, T Labrousse, A Carminati *Replacements* D Faugeron for Carrat; F Duboisset for Carminati; P Manhes for Alegret
Scorers *Try:* R Paillat   *Conversion:* S Paillat   *Penalty Goals:* S Paillat (2)
Referee P Thomas (Drôme-Ardèche)

FRENCH INTERNATIONAL PLAYERS
(up to 30 April 1996)

ABBREVIATIONS

A – Australia; *Arg* – Argentina; *B* – British Forces and Home Union Teams; *C* – Canada; *Cz* – Czechoslovakia; *E* – England; *Fj* – Fiji; *G* – Germany; *I* – Ireland; *It* – Italy; *Iv* – Ivory Coast; *J* – Japan; *K* – New Zealand Services; *M* – Maoris; *NZ* – New Zealand; *R* – Romania; *S* – Scotland; *SA* – South Africa; *Tg* – Tonga; *US* – United States of America; *W* – Wales; *Z* – Zimbabwe; (R) – Replacement; (t) – temporary replacement. Entries in square brackets [ ] indicate appearances in the World Cup.

Club Abbreviations: ASF – Association Sportive Française; BEC – Bordeaux Etudiants Club; CASG – Club Athlétique des Sports Généreaux; PUC – Paris Université Club; RCF – Racing Club de France; SB – Stade Bordelais; SBUC – Stade Bordelais Université Club; SCUF – Sporting Club Universitaire de France; SF – Stade Français; SOE – Stade Olympien des Etudiants; TOEC – Toulouse Olympique Employés Club.

Note: Years given for Five Nations matches are for second half of season, eg 1972 refers to season 1971-72. Years for all other matches refer to the actual year of the match. When a series has taken place, or more than one match has been played against a country in the same year, figures have been used to denote the particular matches in which players have featured. Thus 1967 *SA* 2,4 indicates that a player appeared in the second and fourth Tests of the 1967 series against South Africa. This list includes only those players who have appeared in FFR International Matches *'donnant droit au titre d'international'*.

Abadie, A (Pau) 1964 *I*
Abadie, A (Graulhet) 1965 *R*, 1967 *SA* 1, 3, 4, *NZ*, 1968 *S, I*
Abadie, L (Tarbes) 1963 *R*
Accoceberry, G (Bègles) 1994 *NZ* 1,2, *C* 2, 1995 *W, E, S, I, R* 1, [*Iv, S*], *It*, 1996 *I, W, R*
Aguerre, R (Biarritz O) 1979 *S*
Aguilar, D (Pau) 1937 *G*
Aguirre, J-M (Bagnères) 1971 *A* 2, 1972 *S*, 1973 *W, I, J, R*, 1974 *I, W, Arg* 2, *R, SA* 1, 1976 *W* (R), *E, US, A* 2, *R*, 1977 *W, E, S, I, Arg* 1,2, *NZ* 1,2, *R*, 1978 *E, S, I, W, R*, 1979 *I, W, E, S, NZ* 1,2, *R*, 1980 *W, I*
Ainciart, E (Bayonne) 1933 *G*, 1934 *G*, 1935 *G*, 1937 *G, It*, 1938 *G* 1
Albaladejo, P (Dax) 1954 *E, It*, 1960 *W, I, It, R*, 1961 *S, SA, E, W, I, NZ* 1,2, *A*, 1962 *S, E, W, I*, 1963 *S, I, E, W, It*, 1964 *S, NZ, W, It, I, SA, Fj*
Alvarez, A-J (Tyrosse) 1945 *B2*, 1946 *B, I, K, W*, 1947 *S, I, W, E*, 1948 *I, A, S, W, E*, 1949 *I, E, W*, 1951 *S, E, W*
Amand, H (SF) 1906 *NZ*
Ambert, A (Toulouse) 1930 *S, I, E, G, W*
Amestoy, J-B (Mont-de-Marsan) 1964 *NZ, E*
André, G (RCF) 1913 *SA, E, W, I*, 1914 *I, W, E*
Andrieu, M (Nîmes) 1986 *Arg* 2, *NZ* 1, *R* 2, *NZ* 2, 1987 [*R, Z*], *R*, 1988 *E, S, I, W, Arg* 1,2,3,4, *R*, 1989 *I, W, E, S, NZ* 2, *B, A* 2, 1990 *W, E, I* (R)
Anduran, J (SCUF) 1910 *W*
Araou, R (Narbonne) 1924 *R*
Arcalis, R (Brive) 1950 *S, I*, 1951 *I, E, W*
Arino, M (Agen) 1962 *R*
Aristouy, P (Pau) 1948 *S*, 1949 *Arg* 2, 1950 *S, I, E, W*
Arlettaz, P (Perpignan) 1995 *R* 2
Armary, L (Lourdes) 1987 [*R*], *R*, 1988 *S, I, W, Arg* 3,4, *R*, 1989 *W, S, A* 1,2, 1990 *W, E, S, I, A* 1,2,3, *NZ* 1, 1991 *W* 2, 1992 *S, I, R, Arg* 1,2, *SA* 1, 2, *Arg*, 1993 *E, S, I, W, SA* 1,2, *R* 2, *A* 1,2, 1994 *I, W, NZ* 1 (t), 2 (t), 1995 *I, R* 1 [*Tg, I, SA*]
Arnal, J-M (RCF) 1914 *I, W*
Arnaudet, M (Lourdes) 1964 *I*, 1967 *It, W*
Arotca, R (Bayonne) 1938 *R*
Arrieta, J (SF) 1953 *E, W*
Arthapignet, P (see Harislur-Arthapignet)
Astre, R (Béziers) 1971 *R*, 1972 *I* 1, 1973 *E* (R), 1975 *E, S, I, SA* 1,2, *Arg* 2, 1976 *A* 2, *R*
Augé, J (Dax) 1929 *S, W*
Augras-Fabre, L (Agen) 1931 *I, S, W*
Averous, J-L (La Voulte) 1975 *S, I, SA* 1,2, 1976 *I, W, E, US, A* 1,2, *R*, 1977 *W, E, S, I, Arg* 1, *R*, 1978 *E, S, I*, 1979 *NZ* 1,2, 1980 *E, S*, 1981 *A* 2
Azam, O (Montferrand) 1995 *R* 2, *Arg* (R)
Azarete, J-L (Dax, St Jean-de-Luz) 1969 *W, R*, 1970 *S, I, W, R*, 1971 *S, I, E, W, A* 1, *R*, 1973 *NZ, W, I, R*, 1974 *I, R, SA* 1,2, 1975 *W*

Bader, E (Primevères) 1926 *M*, 1927 *I, S*
Badin, C (Chalon) 1973 *W, I*, 1975 *Arg* 1
Baillette, M (Perpignan) 1925 *I, NZ, S*, 1926 *W, M*, 1927 *I, W, G* 2, 1929 *G*, 1930 *S, I, E, G*, 1931 *I, S, E*, 1932 *G*
Baladie, G (Agen) 1945 *B* 1,2, *W*, 1946 *B, I, K*
Ballarin, J (Tarbes) 1924 *E*, 1925 *NZ, S*

Baquey, J (Toulouse) 1921 *I*
Barbazanges, A (Roanne) 1932 *G*, 1933 *G*
Barrau, M (Beaumont, Toulouse) 1971 *S, E, W*, 1972 *E, W, A* 1,2, 1973 *S, NZ, E, I, J, R*, 1974 *I, S*
Barrère, P (Toulon) 1929 *G*, 1931 *W*
Barrière, R (Béziers) 1960 *R*
Barthe, E (SBUC) 1925 *W, E*
Barthe, J (Lourdes) 1954 *Arg* 1,2, 1955 *S*, 1956 *I, W, It, E, Cz*, 1957 *S, I, E, W, R* 1,2, 1958 *S, E, A, W, It, I, SA* 1,2, 1959 *S, E, It, W*
Basauri, R (Albi) 1954 *Arg* 1
Bascou, P (Bayonne) 1914 *E*
Basquet, G (Agen) 1945 *W*, 1946 *B, I, K, W*, 1947 *S, I, W, E*, 1948 *I, A, S, W, E*, 1949 *S, I, E, W, Arg* 1, 1950 *S, I, E, W*, 1951 *S, I, E, W*, 1952 *S, I, SA, W, E, It*
Bastiat, J-P (Dax) 1969 *R*, 1970 *S, I, W*, 1971 *S, I, SA* 2, 1972 *S, A* 1, 1973 *E*, 1974 *Arg* 1,2, *SA* 2, 1975 *W, Arg* 1,2, *R*, 1976 *S, I, W, E, A* 1,2, *R*, 1977 *W, E, S, I, R*, 1978 *E, S, I, W*
Baudry, N (Montferrand) 1949 *S, I, W, Arg* 1,2
Baulon, R (Vienne, Bayonne) 1954 *S, NZ, W, E, It*, 1955 *I, E, W, It*, 1956 *S, I, W, It, E, Cz*, 1957 *S, I, It*
Baux, J-P (Lannemezan) 1968 *NZ* 1,2, *SA* 1,2
Bavozet, J (Lyon) 1911 *S, E, W*
Bayard, J (Toulouse) 1923 *S, W, E*, 1924 *W, R, US*
Bayardon, J (Chalon) 1964 *S, NZ, E*
Beaurin-Gressier, C (SF) 1907 *E*, 1908 *E*
Bégu, J (Dax) 1982 *Arg* 2 (R), 1984 *E, S*
Béguerie, C (Agen) 1979 *NZ* 1
Beguet, L (RCF) 1922 *I*, 1923 *S, W, E, I*, 1924 *S, I, E, R, US*
Behoteguy, A (Bayonne, Cognac) 1923 *E*, 1924 *S, I, E, W, R, US*, 1926 *E*, 1927 *E, G* 1,2, 1928 *A, I, E, G, W*, 1929 *S, W, E*
Behoteguy, H (RCF, Cognac) 1923 *W*, 1928 *A, I, E, G, W*
Belascain, C (Bayonne) 1977 *R*, 1978 *E, S, I, W, R*, 1979 *I, W, E, S*, 1982 *W, E, S, I*, 1983 *E, S, I, W*
Belletante, G (Nantes) 1951 *I, E, W*
Benazzi, A (Agen) 1990 *A* 1,2,3, *NZ* 1,2, 1991 *E, US* 1 (R), 2, [*R, Fj, C*], 1992 *SA* 1 (R), 2, *Arg*, 1993 *E, S, I, W, A* 1,2, 1994 *I, W, E, S, C* 1, *NZ* 1,2, *C* 2, 1995 *W, E, S, I*, [*Tg, Iv, S, SA, E*], *NZ* 1, 2, 1996 *E, S, I, W*
Bénésis, R (Narbonne) 1969 *W, R*, 1970 *S, I, W, E*, 1971 *S, I, E, W, A* 2, *R*, 1972 *S, I* 1, *E, W, I* 2, *A* 1, *R*, 1973 *NZ, E, W, I, J, R*, 1974 *I, W, E, S*
Benetière, J (Roanne) 1954 *It, Arg* 1
Benetton, P (Agen) 1989 *B*, 1990 *NZ* 2, 1991 *US* 2, 1992 *Arg* 1,2 (R), *SA* 1 (R), 2, *Arg*, 1993 *E, S, I, W, SA* 1,2, *R* 2, *A* 1,2, 1994 *I, W, E, S, C* 1, *NZ* 1,2, *C* 2, 1995 *W, E, S, I*, [*Tg, Iv* (R), *S*], *It, R* 2 (R), *Arg, NZ* 1, 2
Benezech, L (RCF) 1994 *E, S, C* 1, *NZ* 1,2, *C* 2, 1995 *W, E*, [*Iv, S, E*], *R* 2, *Arg, NZ* 1, 2
Berbizier, P (Lourdes, Agen) 1981 *S, I, W, E, NZ* 1,2, 1982 *I, R*, 1983 *S, I*, 1984 *S* (R), *NZ* 1,2, 1985 *Arg* 1,2, 1986 *S, I, W, E, R* 1, *Arg* 1, *A, NZ* 1, *R* 2, *NZ* 2,3, 1987 *W, E, S, I*, [*S, R, Fj, A, NZ*], *R*, 1988 *E, S, I, W, Arg* 1,2,3, 1989 *I, W, E, S, NZ* 1,2, *B, A* 1, 1990 *W, I, W* 1, *E*
Berejnoi, J-C (Tulle) 1963 *R*, 1964 *S, W, It, I, SA, Fj, R*, 1965 *S, I, E, W, It, R*, 1966 *S, I, E, W, It, R*, 1967 *S, A, E, It, W, I, R*

278

Berges, B (Toulouse) 1926 *I*

Berges-Cau, R (Lourdes) 1976 *E* (R)

Bergese, F (Bayonne) 1936 *G* 2, 1937 *G, It*, 1938 *G* 1, *R, G* 2

Bergougnan, Y (Toulouse) 1945 *B* 1, *W*, 1946 *B, I, K, W*, 1947 *S, I, W, E*, 1948 *S, W, E*, 1949 *S, E, Arg* 1,2

Bernard, R (Bergerac) 1951 *S, I, E, W*

Bernat-Salles, P (Pau, Bègles-Bordeaux) 1992 *Arg*, 1993 *R* 1, *SA* 1,2, *R* 2, *A* 1,2, 1994 *I*, 1995 *E, S*, 1996 *E* (R)

Bernon, J (Lourdes) 1922 *I*, 1923 *S*

Bérot, J-L (Toulouse) 1968 *NZ* 3, *A*, 1969 *S, I*, 1970 *E, R*, 1971 *S, I, E, W, SA* 1,2, *A* 1,2, *R*, 1972 *S, I* 1, *E, W, A* 1, 1974 *I*

Bérot, P (Agen) 1986 *R* 2, *NZ* 2, 3, 1987 *W, E, S, I, R*, 1988 *E, S, I, Arg* 1, 2, 3, 4, *R*, 1989 *S, NZ* 1, 2

Bertrand, P (Bourg) 1951 *I, E, W*, 1953 *S, I, E, W, It*

Bertranne, R (Bagnères) 1971 *E, W, SA* 2, *A* 1,2, 1972 *S, I* 1, 1973 *NZ, E, J, R*, 1974 *I, W, E, S, Arg* 1,2, *R, SA* 1,2, 1975 *W, E, S, I, SA* 1,2, *Arg* 1,2, *R*, 1976 *S, I, W, E, US, A* 1,2, *R*, 1977 *W, E, S, I, Arg* 1,2, *NZ* 1,2, *R*, 1978 *E, S, I, W, R*, 1979 *I, W, E, S, R*, 1980 *W, E, S, I, SA, R*, 1981 *S, I, W, E, R, NZ* 1,2

Berty, D (Toulouse) 1990 *NZ* 2, 1992 *R* (R), 1993 *R* 2, 1995 *NZ* 1 (R)

Besset, E (Grenoble) 1924 *S*

Besset, L (SCUF) 1914 *W, E*

Besson, M (CASG) 1924 *I*, 1925 *I, E*, 1926 *S, W*, 1927 *I*

Besson, P (Brive) 1963 *S, I, E*, 1965 *R*, 1968 *SA* 1

Bianchi, J (Toulon) 1986 *Arg* 1

Bichindaritz, J (Biarritz O) 1954 *It, Arg* 1,2

Bidart, L (La Rochelle) 1953 *W*

Biemouret, P (Agen) 1969 *E, W*, 1970 *I, W, E*, 1971 *W, SA* 1,2, *A* 1, 1972 *E, W, I* 2, *A* 2, *R*, 1973 *S, NZ, E, W, I*

Biénès, R (Cognac) 1950 *S, I, E, W*, 1951 *S, I, E, W*, 1952 *S, I, SA, W, E, It*, 1953 *S, I, E*, 1954 *S, I, NZ, W, E, Arg* 1,2, 1956 *S, I, W, It, E*

Bigot, C (Quillan) 1930 *S, E*, 1931 *I, S*

Bilbao, L (St Jean-de-Luz) 1978 *I*, 1979 *I*

Billac, E (Bayonne) 1920 *S, E, W, I, US*, 1921 *S, W*, 1922 *W*, 1923 *E*

Billière, M (Toulouse) 1968 *NZ* 3

Bioussa, A (Toulouse) 1924 *W, US*, 1925 *I, NZ, S, E*, 1926 *S, I, E*, 1928 *E, G, W*, 1929 *I, S, W, E*, 1930 *S, I, E, G, W*

Bioussa, C (Toulouse) 1913 *W, I*, 1914 *I*

Biraben, M (Dax) 1920 *W, I, US*, 1921 *S, W, E, I*, 1922 *S, E, I*

Blain, A (Carcassonne) 1934 *G*

Blanco, S (Biarritz O) 1980 *SA, R*, 1981 *S, W, E, A* 1,2, *R, NZ* 1,2, 1982 *W, E, S, I, R, Arg* 1,2, 1983 *E, S, I, W*, 1984 *I, W, E, S, NZ* 1,2, *R*, 1985 *E, S, I, W, Arg* 1,2, 1986 *S, I, W, R, Arg* 2, *A, NZ* 1, *R* 2, *NZ* 2,3, 1987 *W, E, S, I*, [*S, R, Fj, A, NZ*], *R*, 1988 *E, S, I, W, Arg* 1,2,3,4, *R*, 1989 *I, W, E, S, NZ* 1,2, *B, A* 1, 1990 *E, S, I, R, A* 1,2,3, *NZ* 1,2, 1991 *S, I, W* 1, *E, R, US* 1,2, *W* 2, [*R, Fj, C, E*]

Blond, J (SF) 1935 *G*, 1936 *G* 2, 1937 *G*, 1938 *G* 1, *R, G* 2

Blond, X (RCF) 1990 *A* 3, 1991 *S, I, W* 1, *E*, 1994 *NZ* 2 (R)

Boffelli, V (Aurillac) 1971 *A* 2, *R*, 1972 *S, I* 1, 1973 *J, R*, 1974 *I, W, E, S, Arg* 1,2, *R, SA* 1,2, 1975 *W, S, I*

Bonal, J-M (Toulouse) 1968 *E, W, Cz, NZ* 2,3, *SA* 1,2, *R*, 1969 *S, I, E, R*, 1970 *W, E*

Bonamy, R (SB) 1928 *A, I*

Boniface, A (Mont-de-Marsan) 1954 *I, NZ, W, E, It, Arg* 1,2, 1955 *S, I*, 1956 *S, I, W, It, Cz*, 1957 *S, I, W, R* 2, 1958 *S, E*, 1959 *E*, 1961 *NZ* 1,3, *A, R*, 1962 *E, W, I, It, R*, 1963 *S, I, E, W, It, R*, 1964 *S, NZ, E, W, It*, 1965 *W, It, R*, 1966 *S, I, E, W*

Boniface, G (Mont-de-Marsan) 1960 *W, I, It, R, Arg* 1,2,3, 1961 *S, SA, E, W, It, I, NZ* 1,2,3, *R*, 1962 *R*, 1963 *S, I, E, W, It, R*, 1964 *S, I, E, W*, 1965 *S, I, E, W*, 1966 *S, I, E, W*

Bonnes, E (Narbonne) 1924 *W, R, US*

Bonneval, E (Toulouse) 1984 *NZ* 2 (R), 1985 *W, Arg* 1, 1986 *W, E, R* 1, *Arg* 1,2, *A, R* 2, *NZ* 2,3, 1987 *W, E, S, I*, [*Z*], 1988 *E*

Bonnus, F (Toulon) 1950 *S, I, E, W*

Bonnus, M (Toulon) 1937 *It*, 1938 *G* 1, *R, G* 2, 1940 *B*

Bontemps, D (La Rochelle) 1968 *SA* 2

Borchard, G (RCF) 1908 *E*, 1909 *E, W, I*, 1911 *I*

Borde, F (RCF) 1920 *I, US*, 1921 *S, W, E*, 1922 *S, W*, 1923 *S, I*, 1924 *E*, 1925 *I*, 1926 *E*

Bordenave, L (Toulon) 1948 *A, S, W, E*, 1949 *S*

Boubée, A (Tarbes) 1921 *S, E, I*, 1922 *E, W*, 1923 *E, I*, 1925 *NZ, S*

Boudreaux, R (SCUF) 1910 *W, S*

Bouet, D (Dax) 1989 *NZ* 1,2, *B, A* 2, 1990 *A* 3

Bouguyon, G (Grenoble) 1961 *SA, E, W, It, I, NZ* 1,2,3, *A*

Boujet, C (Grenoble) 1968 *NZ* 2, *A* (R), *SA* 1

Bouquet, J (Bourgoin, Vienne) 1954 *S*, 1955 *E*, 1956 *S, I, W, It, E, Cz*, 1957 *S, E, W, R* 2, 1958 *S, E*, 1959 *S, It, W, I*, 1960 *S, E, W, I, R*, 1961 *S, SA, E, W, It, I, R*, 1962 *S, E, W, I*

Bourdeu, J R (Lourdes) 1952 *S, I, SA, W, E, It*, 1953 *S, I, E*

Bourgarel, R (Toulouse) 1969 *R*, 1970 *S, I, E, R*, 1971 *W, SA* 1,2, 1973 *S*

Bourguignon, G (Narbonne) 1988 *Arg* 3, 1989 *I, E, B, A* 1, 1990 *R*

Bousquet, A (Béziers) 1921 *E, I*, 1924 *R*

Bousquet, R (Albi) 1926 *M*, 1927 *I, S, W, E, G* 1, 1929 *W, E*, 1930 *W*

Boyau, M (SBUC) 1912 *I, S, W, E*, 1913 *W, I*

Boyer, P (Toulon) 1935 *G*

Branca, G (SF) 1928 *S*, 1929 *I, S*

Branlat, A (RCF) 1906 *NZ, E*, 1908 *W*

Brejassou, R (Tarbes) 1952 *S, I, SA, W, E*, 1953 *W, E*, 1954 *S, I, NZ*, 1955 *S, I, E, W, It*

Brethes, R (St Sever) 1960 *Arg* 2

Bringeon, A (Biarritz O) 1925 *W*

Brouzet, O (Grenoble) 1994 *S, NZ* 2 (R), 1995 *E, S, I, R* 1, [*Tg, Iv, E* (t)], *It, Arg* (R), 1996 *W* (R)

Brun, G (Vienne) 1950 *E, W*, 1951 *S, E, W*, 1952 *S, I, SA, W, E, It*, 1953 *E, W, It*

Bruneau, M (SBUC) 1910 *W, E*, 1913 *SA, E*

Brunet, Y (Perpignan) 1975 *SA* 1, 1977 *Arg* 1

Buchet, E (Nice) 1980 *R*, 1982 *E, R* (R), *Arg* 1,2

Buisson, H (see Empereur-Buisson)

Buonomo, Y (Béziers) 1971 *A* 2, *R*, 1972 *I* 1

Burgun, M (RCF) 1909 *I*, 1910 *W, S, I*, 1911 *S, E*, 1912 *I, S*, 1913 *S, E*, 1914 *E*

Bustaffa, D (Carcassonne) 1977 *Arg* 1,2, *NZ* 1,2, 1978 *W, R*, 1980 *W, E, S, SA, R*

Buzy, C-E (Lourdes) 1946 *K, W*, 1947 *S, I, W, E*, 1948 *I, A, S, W, E*, 1949 *S, I, E, W, Arg* 1,2

Cabanier, J-M (Montauban) 1963 *R*, 1964 *S, Fj*, 1965 *S, I, W, It, R*, 1966 *S, I, E, W, It, R*, 1967 *S, A, E, It, W, I, SA* 1,3, *NZ, R*, 1968 *S, I*

Cabannes, L (RCF) 1990 *NZ* 2 (R), 1991 *S, I, W* 1, *E, US* 2, *W* 2, [*R, Fj, C, E*], 1992 *W, E, S, I, R, Arg* 2, *SA* 1,2, 1993 *E, S, I, W, R, SA* 1,2, 1994 *E, S, C* 1, *NZ* 1,2, 1995 *W, E, S, R* 1, [*Tg* (R), *Iv, S, I, SA, E*], 1996 *E, S, I, R*

Cabrol, H (Béziers) 1972 *A* 1 (R), 2, 1973 *J*, 1974 *SA* 2

Cadenat, J (SCUF) 1910 *S, E*, 1911 *W, I*, 1912 *W, E*, 1913 *I*

Cadieu, J-M (Toulouse) 1991 *R, US* 1, [*R, Fj, C, E*], 1992 *W, I, R, Arg* 1,2, *SA* 1

Cahuc, F (St Girons) 1922 *S*

Califano, C (Toulouse) 1994 *NZ* 1,2, *C* 2, 1995 *W, E, S, I*, [*Iv, S, I, SA, E*], *It, Arg, NZ* 1, 2, 1996 *E, S, I, W, R*

Cals, R (RCF) 1938 *G* 1

Calvo, G (Lourdes) 1961 *NZ* 1,3

Camberabero, D (La Voulte, Béziers) 1982 *R, Arg* 1,2, 1983 *E, W*, 1987 [*R* (R), *Z, Fj* (R), *A, NZ*], 1988 *I*, 1989 *B, A* 1, 1990 *W, S, I, E, R, A* 1,2, *NZ* 1, 1991 *S, I, W* 1, *E, R, US* 1,2, *W* 2, [*R, Fj, C*], 1993 *E, S, I*

Camberabero, G (La Voulte) 1961 *NZ* 3, 1962 *R*, 1964 *R*, 1967 *A, E, It, W, I, SA* 1,3,4, 1968 *S, E, W*

Camberabero, L (La Voulte) 1964 *R*, 1965 *S, I*, 1966 *E, W*, 1967 *A, E, It, W, I*, 1968 *S, E, W*

Cambré, T (Oloron) 1920 *E, W, I, US*

Camel, A (Toulouse) 1928 *S, A, I, E, G, W*, 1929 *W, E, G*, 1930 *S, I, E, G, W*, 1935 *G*

Camel, M (Toulouse) 1929 *S, W, E*

Camicas, F (Tarbes) 1927 *G* 2, 1928 *S, I, E, G, W*, 1929 *I, S, W, E*

Camo, E (Villeneuve) 1931 *I, S, W, E, G*, 1932 *G*

Campaes, A (Lourdes) 1965 *W*, 1967 *NZ*, 1968 *S, I, E, W, Cz, NZ* 1,2, *A*, 1969 *S, W*, 1972 *R*, 1973 *NZ*

Campan, O (Agen) 1993 *SA* 1 (R), 2 (R), 1996 *I, W, R*

Cantoni, J (Béziers) 1970 *W, R*, 1971 *S, I, E, W, SA* 1,2, *A* 1, *R*, 1972 *S, I* 1, 1973 *S, NZ, W, I*, 1975 *W* (R)

Capdouze, J (Pau) 1964 *SA, Fj, R*, 1965 *S, I, E*

Capendeguy, J-M (Bègles) 1967 *NZ, R*

Capitani, P (Toulon) 1954 *Arg* 1,2

Capmau, J-L (Toulouse) 1914 *E*

Carabignac, G (Agen) 1951 *S, I*, 1952 *SA, W, E*, 1953 *S, I*

Carbonne, J (Perpignan) 1927 *W*

Carbonneau, P (Toulouse) 1995 *R* 2, *Arg, NZ* 1, 2, 1996 *E, S, R* (R)

De Muizon, J J (SF) 1910 *I*
Delaigue, G (Toulon) 1973 *J, R*
Delaigue, Y (Toulon) 1994 *S, NZ* 2 (R), *C* 2, 1995 *I, R* 1, [*Tg, Iv*], *It, R* 2 (R)
Delque, A (Toulouse) 1937 *It*, 1938 *G* 1, *R, G* 2
De Rougemont, M (Toulon) 1995 *E* (t), *R* 1 (t), [*Iv*], *NZ* 1, 2, 1996 *I* (R)
Descamps, P (SB) 1927 *G* 2
Desclaux, F (RCF) 1949 *Arg* 1,2, 1953 *It*
Desclaux, J (Perpignan) 1934 *G*, 1935 *G*, 1936 *G* 1,2, 1937 *G, It*, 1938 *G* 1, *R, G* 2, 1945 *B* 1
Deslandes, C (RCF) 1990 *A* 1, *NZ* 2, 1991 *W* 1, 1992 *R, Arg* 1,2
Desnoyer, L (Brive) 1974 *R*
Destarac, L (Tarbes) 1926 *S, I, E, W, M*, 1927 *W, E, G* 1,2
Desvouges, R (SF) 1914 *W*
Detrez, P-E (Nîmes) 1983 *A* 2 (R), 1986 *Arg* 1 (R), 2, *A* (R), *NZ* 1
Devergie, T (Nîmes) 1988 *R*, 1989 *NZ* 1,2, *B, A* 2, 1990 *W, E, S, I, R, A* 1,2,3, 1991 *US* 2, *W* 2, 1992 *R* (R), *Arg* 2 (R)
Deygas, M (Vienne) 1937 *It*
Deylaud, C (Toulouse) 1992 *R, Arg* 1,2, *SA* 1, 1994 *C* 1, *NZ* 1,2, 1995 *W, E, S*, [*Iv* (R), *S, I, SA*], *It, Arg*
Dintrans, P (Tarbes) 1979 *NZ* 1,2, *R*, 1980 *E, S, I, SA, R*, 1981 *S, I, W, E, A* 1,2, *R, NZ* 1,2, 1982 *W, E, S, I, R, Arg* 1,2, 1983 *E, W, A* 1,2, *R*, 1984 *I, W, E, S, NZ* 1,2, *R*, 1985 *E, S, I, W, Arg* 1,2, 1987 [*R*], 1988 *Arg* 1,2,3, 1989 *W, E, S*, 1990 *R*
Dispagne, S (Toulouse) 1996 *I* (R), *W*
Dizabo, P (Tyrosse) 1948 *A, S, E*, 1949 *S, I, E, W, Arg* 2, 1950 *S, I*, 1960 *Arg* 1,2,3
Domec, A (Carcassonne) 1929 *W*
Domec, H (Lourdes) 1953 *W, It*, 1954 *S, I, NZ, W, E, It*, 1955 *S, I, E, W*, 1956 *I, W, It*, 1958 *E, A, W, It, I*
Domenech, A (Vichy, Brive) 1954 *W, E, It*, 1955 *S, I, E, W*, 1956 *S, I, W, It, E, Cz*, 1957 *S, I, E, W, It, R* 1,2, 1958 *S, E, It*, 1959 *It*, 1960 *S, E, W, I, It, R, Arg* 1,2,3, 1961 *S, SA, E, W, It, I, NZ* 1,2,3, *A, R*, 1962 *S, E, W, I, It, R*, 1963 *W, It*
Domercq, J (Bayonne) 1912 *I, S*
Dorot, J (RCF) 1935 *G*
Dospital, P (Bayonne) 1977 *R*, 1980 *I*, 1981 *S, I, W, E*, 1982 *I, R, Arg* 1,2, 1983 *E, S, I, W*, 1984 *E, S, NZ* 1,2, *R*, 1985 *E, S, I, W, Arg* 1
Dourthe, C (Dax) 1966 *R*, 1967 *S, A, E, W, I, SA* 1,2,3, *NZ*, 1968 *W, NZ* 3, *SA* 1,2, 1969 *W*, 1971 *SA* 2 (R), *R*, 1972 *I* 1,2, *A* 1,2, *R*, 1973 *S, NZ, E*, 1974 *I, Arg* 1,2, *SA* 1,2, 1975 *W, E, S*
Dourthe, R (Dax) 1995 *R* 2, *Arg, NZ* 1, 2, 1996 *E, R*
Doussau, E (Angoulême) 1938 *R*
Droitecourt, M (Montferrand) 1972 *R*, 1973 *NZ* (R), *E*, 1974 *E, S, Arg* 1, *SA* 2, 1975 *SA* 1,2, *Arg* 1,2, *R*, 1976 *S, I, W, A* 1, 1977 *Arg* 2
Dubertrand, A (Montferrand) 1971 *A* 2, *R*, 1972 *I* 2, 1974 *I, W, E, SA* 2, 1975 *Arg* 1,2, *R*, 1976 *S, US*
Dubois, D (Bègles) 1971 *S*
Dubroca, D (Agen) 1979 *NZ* 2, 1981 *NZ* 2 (R), 1982 *E, S*, 1984 *W, E, S*, 1985 *Arg* 2, 1986 *S, I, W, E, R* 1, *Arg* 2, *A, NZ* 1, *R* 2, *NZ* 2,3, 1987 *W, E, S, I*, [*S, Z, Fj, A, NZ*], *R*, 1988 *E, S, I, W*
Duché, A (Limoges) 1929 *G*
Duclos, A (Lourdes) 1931 *S*
Ducousso, J (Tarbes) 1925 *S, W, E*
Dufau, G (RCF) 1948 *I, A*, 1949 *I, W*, 1950 *S, E, W*, 1951 *S, I, E, W*, 1952 *SA, W*, 1953 *S, I, E, W*, 1954 *S, I, NZ, W, E, It*, 1955 *S, I, E, W, It*, 1956 *S, I, W, It*, 1957 *S, I, E, W, It, R* 1
Dufau, J (Biarritz) 1912 *I, S, W, E*
Duffaut, Y (Agen) 1954 *Arg* 1,2
Duffour, R (Tarbes) 1911 *W*
Dufourcq, J (SBUC) 1906 *NZ, E*, 1907 *E*, 1908 *W*
Duhard, Y (Bagnères) 1980 *E*
Duhau, J (SF) 1928 *I*, 1930 *I, G*, 1931 *I, S, W*, 1933 *G*
Dulaurens, C (Toulouse) 1926 *I*, 1928 *S*, 1929 *W*
Duluc, A (Béziers) 1934 *G*
Du Manoir, Y le P (RCF) 1925 *I, NZ, S, W, E*, 1926 *S*, 1927 *I, S*
Dupont, C (Lourdes) 1923 *S, W, I*, 1924 *S, I, W, R, US*, 1925 *S*, 1927 *E, G* 1,2, 1928 *A, G, W*, 1929 *I*
Dupont, J-L (Agen) 1983 *S*
Dupont, L (RCF) 1934 *G*, 1935 *G*, 1936 *G* 1,2, 1938 *R, G* 2
Dupouy, A (SB) 1924 *W, R*
Duprat, B (Bayonne) 1966 *E, W, It, R*, 1967 *S, A, E, SA* 2,3, 1968 *S, I*, 1972 *E, W, I* 2, *A* 1
Dupré, P (RCF) 1909 *W*

Dupuy, J (Tarbes) 1956 *S, I, W, It, E, Cz*, 1957 *S, I, E, W, It, R* 2, 1958 *S, E, SA* 1,2, 1959 *S, E, It, W, I*, 1960 *W, I, It, Arg* 1,3, 1961 *S, SA, E, NZ* 2, *R*, 1962 *S, E, W, I, It*, 1963 *W, It, R*, 1964 *S*
Du Souich, C J (see Judas du Souich)
Dutin, B (Mont-de-Marsan) 1968 *NZ* 2, *A, SA* 2, *R*
Dutour, F X (Toulouse) 1911 *E, I*, 1912 *S, W, E*, 1913 *S*
Dutrain, H (Toulouse) 1945 *W*, 1946 *B, I*, 1947 *E*, 1949 *I, E, W, Arg* 1
Dutrey, J (Lourdes) 1940 *B*
Duval, R (SF) 1908 *E, W*, 1909 *E*, 1911 *E, W, I*

Echavé, L (Agen) 1961 *S*
Elissalde, E (Bayonne) 1936 *G* 2, 1940 *B*
Elissalde, J-P (La Rochelle) 1980 *SA, R*, 1981 *A* 1,2, *R*
Empereur-Buisson, H (Béziers) 1931 *E, G*
Erbani, D (Agen) 1981 *A* 1,2, *NZ* 1,2, 1982 *Arg* 1,2, 1983 *S* (R), *I, W, A* 1,2, *R*, 1984 *W, E, R*, 1985 *E, W* (R), *Arg* 2, 1986 *S, I, W, E, R* 1, *Arg* 2, *NZ* 1,2 (R), 3, 1987 *W, E, S, I*, [*S, R, Fj, A, NZ*], 1988 *E, S*, 1989 *I* (R), *W, E, S, NZ* 1, *A* 2, 1990 *W, E*
Escaffre, P (Narbonne) 1933 *G*, 1934 *G*
Escommier, M (Montelimar) 1955 *It*
Esponda, J-M (RCF) 1967 *SA* 1,2, *R*, 1968 *NZ* 1,2, *SA* 2, *R*, 1969 *S, I* (R), *E*
Estève, A (Béziers) 1971 *SA* 1, 1972 *I* 1, *E, W, I* 2, *A* 2, *R*, 1973 *S, NZ, E, I*, 1974 *I, W, E, S, R, SA* 1,2, 1975 *W, E*
Estève, P (Narbonne, Lavelanet) 1982 *R, Arg* 1,2, 1983 *E, S, I, W, A* 1,2, *R*, 1984 *I, W, E, S, NZ* 1,2, *R*, 1985 *E, S, I, W*, 1986 *S, I*, 1987 [*S, Z*]
Etcheberry, J (Rochefort, Cognac) 1923 *W, I*, 1924 *S, I, E, W, R, US*, 1926 *S, I, E, M*, 1927 *I, S, W, G* 2
Etchenique, J-M (Biarritz O) 1974 *R, SA* 1, 1975 *E, Arg* 2
Etchepare, A (Bayonne) 1922 *I*
Etcheverry, M (Pau) 1971 *S, I*
Eutrope, A (SCUF) 1913 *I*

Fabre, E (Toulouse) 1937 *It*, 1938 *G* 1,2
Fabre, J (Toulouse) 1963 *S, I, E, W, It*, 1964 *S, NZ, E*
Fabre, L (Lezignan) 1930 *G*
Fabre, M (Béziers) 1981 *A* 1, *R, NZ* 1,2, 1982 *I, R*
Failliot, P (RCF) 1911 *S, W, I*, 1912 *I, S, E*, 1913 *E, W*
Fargues, G (Dax) 1923 *I*
Fauré, F (Tarbes) 1914 *I, W, E*
Fauvel, J-P (Tulle) 1980 *R*
Favre, M (Lyon) 1913 *E, W*
Ferrand, L (Chalon) 1940 *B*
Ferrien, R (Tarbes) 1950 *S, I, E, W*
Finat, R (CASG) 1932 *G*, 1933 *G*
Fite, R (Brive) 1963 *W, It*
Forestier, J (SCUF) 1912 *W*
Forgues, F (Bayonne) 1911 *S, E, W*, 1912 *I, W, E*, 1913 *S, SA, W*, 1914 *I, E*
Fort, J (Agen) 1967 *It, W, I, SA* 1,2,3,4
Fourcade, G (BEC) 1909 *E, W*
Foures, H (Toulouse) 1951 *S, I, E, W*
Fournet, F (Montferrand) 1950 *W*
Fouroux, J (La Voulte) 1972 *I* 2, *R*, 1974 *W, E, Arg* 1,2, *R, SA* 1,2, 1975 *W, Arg* 1, *R*, 1976 *S, I, W, E, US, A* 1, 1977 *W, E, S, I, Arg* 1,2, *NZ* 1,2, *R*
Francquenelle, A (Vaugirard) 1911 *S*, 1913 *W, I*
Furcade, R (Perpignan) 1952 *S*

Gabernet, S (Toulouse) 1980 *E, S*, 1981 *S, I, W, E, A* 1,2, *R, NZ* 1,2, 1982 *I*, 1983 *A* 2, *R*
Gachassin, J (Lourdes) 1961 *S, I*, 1963 *R*, 1964 *S, NZ, E, W, It, I, SA, Fj*, 1965 *S, I, E, W, It, R*, 1966 *S, I, E, W, It*, 1967 *S, A, It, W, I, NZ*, 1968 *I, E*, 1969 *S, I*
Galau, H (Toulouse) 1924 *S, I, E, W, US*
Galia, J (Quillan) 1927 *E, G* 1,2, 1928 *S, A, I, E, W*, 1929 *I, E, G*, 1930 *S, I, E, G, W*, 1931 *S, W, E, G*
Gallart, P (Béziers) 1990 *R, A* 1,2 (R), 3, 1992 *S, I, R, Arg* 1,2, *SA* 1,2, *Arg*, 1994 *I, W, E*, 1995 *I* (t), *R* 1, [*Tg*]
Gallion, J (Toulon) 1978 *E, S, I, W*, 1979 *I, W, E, S, NZ* 2, *R*, 1980 *W, E, S, I*, 1983 *A* 1,2, *R*, 1984 *I, W, E, S, R*, 1985 *E, S, I, W*, 1986 *Arg* 2
Galthié, F (Colomiers) 1991 *R, US* 1, [*R, Fj, C, E*], 1992 *W, E, S, R, Arg*, 1994 *I, W, E*, 1995 [*SA, E*], 1996 *W* (R)
Galy, J (Perpignan) 1953 *W*
Garuet-Lempirou, J-P (Lourdes) 1983 *A* 1,2, *R*, 1984 *I, NZ* 1,2, *R*, 1985 *E, S, I, W, Arg* 1, 1986 *R, W, E, Arg* 1, *A* 1, *NZ* 1, *R* 2, *NZ* 2,3, 1987 *W, E, S, I*, [*S, R, Fj, A, NZ*], 1988 *E, S, Arg* 1,2, *R*, 1989 *E* (R), *S, NZ* 1,2, 1990 *W, E*
Gasc, J (Graulhet) 1977 *NZ* 2

Gasparotto, G (Montferrand) 1976 *A* 2, *R*
Gauby, G (Perpignan) 1956 *Cz*
Gaudermen, P (RCF) 1906 *E*
Gayraud, W (Toulouse) 1920 *I*
Geneste, R (BEC) 1945 *B* 1, 1949 *Arg* 2
Genet, J-P (RCF) 1992 *S, I, R*
Gensane, R (Béziers) 1962 *S, E, W, I, It, R*, 1963 *S*
Gerald, G (RCF) 1927 *E, G* 2, 1928 *S*, 1929 *I, S, W, E, G*, 1930 *S, I, E, G, W*, 1931 *I, S, E, G*
Gerintes, G (CASG) 1924 *R*, 1925 *I*, 1926 *W*
Geschwind, P (RCF) 1936 *G* 1,2
Giacardy, M (SBUC) 1907 *E*
Gimbert, P (Bègles) 1991 *R, US* 1, 1992 *W, E*
Glas, S (Bourgoin) 1996 *S* (t), *I* (R), *W, R*
Gommes, J (RCF) 1909 *I*
Gonnet, C-A (Albi) 1921 *E, I*, 1922 *E, W*, 1924 *S, E*, 1926 *S, I, E, W, M*, 1927 *I, S, W, E, G* 1
Gonzalez, J-M (Bayonne) 1992 *Arg* 1,2, *SA* 1,2, *Arg*, 1993 *R* 1, *SA* 1,2, *R* 2, *A* 1,2, 1994 *I, W, E, S, C* 1, *NZ* 1,2, *C* 2, 1995 *W, E, S, I, R* 1, [*Tg, S, I, SA, E*], *It, Arg*, 1996 *E, S, I, W*
Got, R (Perpignan) 1920 *I, US*, 1921 *S, W*, 1922 *S, E, W, I*, 1924 *I, E, W, R, US*
Gourdon, J-F (RCF, Bagnères) 1974 *S, Arg* 1, 2, *R, SA* 1, 2, 1975 *W, E, S, I, R*, 1976 *S, I, W, E*, 1978 *E, S*, 1979 *W, E, S, R*, 1980 *I*
Gourragne, J-F (Béziers) 1990 *NZ* 2, 1991 *W* 1
Goyard, A (Lyon U) 1936 *G* 1,2, 1937 *G, It*, 1938 *G* 1, *R, G* 2
Graciet, R (SBUC) 1926 *I, W*, 1927 *S, G* 1, 1929 *E*, 1930 *W*
Graou, S (Auch, Colomiers) 1992 *Arg* (R), 1993 *SA* 1,2, *R* 2, *A* 2 (R), 1995 *R* 2, *Arg* (t), *NZ* 2 (R)
Gratton, J (Agen) 1984 *NZ* 2, 1985 *E, S, I, W, Arg* 1,2, 1986 *S, NZ* 1
Graule, V (Arl Perpignan) 1926 *I, E, W*, 1927 *S, W*, 1931 *G*
Greffe, M (Grenoble) 1968 *W, Cz, NZ* 1,2, *SA* 1
Griffard, J (Lyon U) 1932 *G*, 1933 *G*, 1934 *G*
Gruarin, A (Toulon) 1964 *W, It, I, SA, Fj, R*, 1965 *S, I, E, W, It*, 1966 *S, I, E, W, It, R*, 1967 *S, A, E, It, W, I, NZ*, 1968 *S, I*
Guelorget, P (RCF) 1931 *E, G*
Guichemerre, A (Dax) 1920 *E*, 1921 *E, I*, 1923 *S*
Guilbert, A (Toulon) 1975 *E, S, I, SA* 1,2, 1976 *A* 1, 1977 *Arg* 1,2, *NZ* 1,2, *R*, 1979 *I, W, E*
Guillemin, P (RCF) 1908 *E, W*, 1909 *E, I*, 1910 *W, S, E, I*, 1911 *S, E, W*
Guilleux, P (Agen) 1952 *SA, It*
Guiral, M (Agen) 1931 *G*, 1932 *G*, 1933 *G*
Guiraud, H (Nîmes) 1996 *R*

Haget, A (PUC) 1953 *E*, 1954 *I, NZ, E, Arg* 2, 1955 *E, W, It*, 1957 *I, E, It, R* 1, 1958 *It, SA* 2
Haget, F (Agen, Biarritz O) 1974 *Arg* 1,2, 1975 *SA* 2, *Arg* 1,2, *R*, 1976 *S*, 1978 *S, I, W, E*, 1979 *I, W, E, S, NZ* 1,2, *R*, 1980 *W, S, I*, 1984 *S, NZ* 1,2, *R*, 1985 *E, S, I*, 1986 *S, I, W, E, R* 1, *Arg* 1, *A, NZ* 1, 1987 *S, I*, [*R, Fj*]
Haget, H (CASG) 1928 *S*, 1930 *G*
Halet, R (Strasbourg) 1925 *NZ, S, W*
Harislur-Arthapignet, P (Tarbes) 1988 *Arg* 4 (R)
Harize, D (Cahors, Toulouse) 1975 *SA* 1,2, 1976 *A* 1,2, *R*, 1977 *W, E, S, I*
Hauc, J (Toulon) 1928 *E, G*, 1929 *I, S, G*
Hauser, M (Lourdes) 1969 *E*
Hedembaigt, M (Bayonne) 1913 *S, SA*, 1914 *W*
Hericé, D (Bègles) 1950 *I*
Herrero, A (Toulon) 1963 *R*, 1964 *NZ, E, W, It, I, SA, Fj, R*, 1965 *S, I, E, W*, 1966 *W, It, R*, 1967 *S, A, E, It, I, R*
Herrero, B (Nice) 1983 *I*, 1986 *Arg* 1
Heyer, F (Montferrand) 1990 *A* 2
Hiquet, J-C (Agen) 1964 *E*
Hoche, M (PUC) 1957 *I, E, W, It, R* 1
Hondagné-Monge, M (Tarbes) 1988 *Arg* 2 (R)
Hontas, P (Biarritz) 1990 *S, I, R*, 1991 *R*, 1992 *Arg*, 1993 *E, S, I, W*
Hortoland, J-P (Béziers) 1971 *A* 2
Houblain, H (SCUF) 1909 *E*, 1910 *W*
Houdet, R (SF) 1927 *S, W, G* 1, 1928 *G, W*, 1929 *I, S, E*, 1930 *S, E*
Hourdebaigt, A (SBUC) 1909 *I*, 1910 *W, S, E, I*
Hubert, A (ASF) 1906 *E*, 1907 *E*, 1908 *E, W*, 1909 *E, W, I*
Hueber, A (Lourdes, Toulon) 1990 *A* 3, *NZ* 1, 1991 *US* 2, 1992 *I, Arg* 1,2, *SA* 1,2, 1993 *E, S, I, W, R* 1, *SA* 1,2, *R* 2, *A* 1,2, 1995 [*Tg, S* (R), *I*]

Hutin, R (CASG) 1927 *I, S, W*
Hyardet, A (Castres) 1995 *It, Arg* (R)

Ibanez, R (Dax) 1996 *W* (R)
Icard, J (SF) 1909 *E, W*
Iguiniz, E (Bayonne) 1914 *E*
Ihingoué, D (BEC) 1912 *I, S*
Imbernon, J-F (Perpignan) 1976 *I, W, E, US, A* 1, 1977 *W, E, S, I, Arg* 1,2, *NZ* 1,2, 1978 *E, R*, 1979 *I*, 1981 *S, I, W, E*, 1982 *I*, 1983 *I, W*
Iraçabal, J (Bayonne) 1968 *NZ* 1,2, *SA* 1, 1969 *S, I, W, R*, 1970 *S, I, W, E, R*, 1971 *W, SA* 1,2, *A* 1, 1972 *E, W, I* 2, *A* 2, *R*, 1973 *S, NZ, E, W, I, J*, 1974 *I, W, E, S, Arg* 1,2, *SA* 2 (R)
Isaac, H (RCF) 1907 *E*, 1908 *E*
Ithurra, E (Biarritz O) 1936 *G* 1,2, 1937 *G*

Janeczek, T (Tarbes) 1982 *Arg* 1,2, 1990 *R*
Janik, K (Toulouse) 1987 *R*
Jarasse, A (Brive) 1945 *B* 1
Jardel, J (SB) 1928 *I, E*
Jaureguy, A (RCF, Toulouse, SF) 1920 *S, E, W, I, US*, 1922 *S, W*, 1923 *S, W, E, I*, 1924 *S, W, R, US*, 1925 *I, NZ*, 1926 *S, E, W, M*, 1927 *I, E*, 1928 *S, A, E, G, W*, 1929 *I, S, E*
Jaureguy, P (Toulouse) 1913 *S, SA, W, I*
Jeangrand, M-H (Tarbes) 1921 *I*
Jeanjean, P (Toulon) 1948 *I*
Jérôme, G (SF) 1906 *NZ, E*
Joinel, J-L (Brive) 1977 *NZ* 1, 1978 *R*, 1979 *I, W, E, S, NZ* 1,2, *R*, 1980 *W, E, S, I, SA*, 1981 *S, I, W, E, R, NZ* 1,2, 1982 *E, S, I, R*, 1983 *E, S, I, W, A* 1,2, *R*, 1984 *I, W, E, S*, 1985 *S, I, W, Arg* 1, 1986 *S, I, W, E, R* 1, *Arg* 1,2, *A*, 1987 [*Z*]
Jol, M (Biarritz O) 1947 *S, I, W, E*, 1949 *S, I, E, W, Arg* 1,2
Jordana, J-L (Pau) 1996 *R* (R)
Judas du Souich, C (SCUF) 1911 *W, I*
Juillet, C (Montferrand) 1995 *R* 2, *Arg*
Junquas, L (Tyrosse) 1945 *B* 1,2, *W*, 1946 *B, I, K, W*, 1947 *S, I, W, E*, 1948 *S, W*

Kaczorowski, D (Le Creusot) 1974 *I* (R)
Kaempf, A (St Jean-de-Luz) 1946 *B*

Labadie, P (Bayonne) 1952 *S, I, SA, W, E, It*, 1953 *S, I, It*, 1954 *S, I, NZ, W, E, Arg* 2, 1955 *S, I, E, W*, 1956 *I*, 1957 *I*
Labarthete, R (Pau) 1952 *S*
Labazuy, A (Lourdes) 1952 *I*, 1954 *S, W*, 1956 *E*, 1958 *A, W, I*, 1959 *S, E, It, W*
Laborde, C (RCF) 1962 *It, R*, 1963 *R*, 1964 *SA*, 1965 *E*
Labrousse, T (Brive) 1996 *R*
Lacans, P (Béziers) 1980 *SA*, 1981 *W, E, A* 2, *R*, 1982 *W*
Lacassagne, H (SBUC) 1906 *NZ*, 1907 *E*
Lacaussade, R (Bègles) 1948 *A, S*
Lacaze, C (Lourdes, Angoulême) 1961 *NZ* 2,3, *A, R*, 1962 *E, W, I, It*, 1963 *W, R*, 1964 *S, NZ, E*, 1965 *It, R*, 1966 *S, I, E, W, It, R*, 1967 *S, E, SA* 1,3,4, *R*, 1968 *S, E, W, Cz, NZ* 1, 1969 *E*
Lacaze, H (Périgueux) 1928 *I, G, W*, 1929 *I, W*
Lacaze, P (Lourdes) 1958 *SA* 1,2, 1959 *S, E, It, W, I*
Lacazedieu, C (Dax) 1923 *W, I*, 1928 *A, I*, 1929 *S*
Lacombe, B (Agen) 1989 *B*, 1990 *A* 2
Lacome, M (Pau) 1960 *Arg* 2
Lacoste, R (Tarbes) 1914 *I, W, E*
Lacrampe, F (Béziers) 1949 *Arg* 2
Lacroix, P (Mont-de-Marsan, Agen) 1958 *A*, 1960 *W, I, It, R, Arg* 1,2,3, 1961 *S, SA, E, W, I, NZ* 1,2,3, *A, R*, 1962 *S, E, W, I, R*, 1963 *S, I, E, W*
Lacroix, T (Dax) 1989 *A* 1 (R), 2, 1991 *W* 1 (R), 2 (R), [*R, C* (R), *E*], 1992 *SA* 2, 1993 *E, S, I, W, SA* 1,2, *R* 2, *A* 1,2, 1994 *I, W, E, S, C* 1, *NZ* 1,2, *C* 2, 1995 *W, E, S, R* 1 [*Tg, Iv, S, I, SA, E*], 1996 *E, S, I*
Lafarge, Y (Montferrand) 1978 *R*, 1979 *NZ* 1, 1981 *I* (R)
Laffitte, R (SCUF) 1910 *W, S*
Laffont, H (Narbonne) 1926 *W*
Lafond, A (Bayonne) 1922 *E*
Lafond, J-B (RCF) 1983 *A* 1, 1985 *Arg* 1,2 1986 *S, I, W, E, R* 1, 1987 *I* (R), 1988 *W*, 1989 *I, W, E*, 1990 *W, A* 3 (R), *NZ* 2, 1991 *S, I, W* 1, *E, R, US* 1, *W* 2, [*R* (R), *Fj, C, E*], 1992 *W, E, S, I* (R), *SA* 2, 1993 *E, S, I, W*
Lagisquet, P (Bayonne) 1983 *A* 1,2, *R*, 1984 *I, W, NZ* 1,2, 1986 *R* 1 (R), *Arg* 1,2, *A, NZ* 1, 1987 [*S, R, Fj, A, NZ*], *R*, 1988 *S, I, W, Arg* 1,2,3,4, *R*, 1989 *I, W, E, S, NZ* 1,2, *B, A* 1,2, 1990 *W, E, S, I, A* 1,2,3, 1991 *S, I, US* 2, [*R*]
Lagrange, J-C (RCF) 1966 *It*
Lalande, M (RCF) 1923 *S, W, I*

Lane, G (RCF) 1906 *NZ, E*, 1907 *E*, 1908 *E, W*, 1909 *E, W, I*, 1910 *W, E*, 1911 *S, W*, 1912 *I, W, E*, 1913 *S*
Langlade, J-C (Hyères) 1990 *R, A* 1, *NZ* 1
Laporte, G (Graulhet) 1981 *I, W, E, R, NZ* 1,2, 1986 *S, I, W, E, R* 1, *Arg* 1, *A* (R), 1987 [*R, Z* (R), *Fj*]
Larreguy, P (Bayonne) 1954 *It*
Larribau, J (Périgueux) 1912 *I, S, W, E*, 1913 *S*, 1914 *I, E*
Larrieu, J (Tarbes) 1920 *I, US*, 1921 *W*, 1923 *S, W, E, I*
Larrieux, M (SBUC) 1927 *G* 2
Larrue, H (Carmaux) 1960 *W, I, It, R, Arg* 1,2,3
Lasaosa, P (Dax) 1950 *I*, 1952 *S, I, E, It*, 1955 *It*
Lascubé, G (Agen) 1991 *S, I, W* 1, *E, US* 2, *W* 2, [*R, Fj, C, E*], 1992 *W, E*
Lassegue, J-B (Toulouse) 1946 *W*, 1947 *S, I, W*, 1948 *W*, 1949 *I, E, W, Arg* 1
Lasserre, F (René) (Bayonne, Cognac, Grenoble) 1914 *I*, 1920 *S*, 1921 *S, W, I*, 1922 *S, E, W, I*, 1923 *W, E*, 1924 *S, I, R, US*
Lasserre, J-C (Dax) 1963 *It*, 1964 *S, NZ, E, W, It, I, Fj*, 1965 *W, It, R*, 1966 *R*, 1967 *S*
Lasserre, M (Agen) 1967 *SA* 2,3, 1968 *E, W, Cz, NZ* 3, *A, SA* 1,2, 1969 *S, I, E*, 1970 *E*, 1971 *E, W*
Laterrade, G (Tarbes) 1910 *E, I*, 1911 *S, E, I*
Laudouar, J (Soustons, SBUC) 1961 *NZ* 1,2, *R*, 1962 *I, R*
Lauga, P (Vichy) 1950 *S, I, E, W*
Laurent, A (Biarritz O) 1925 *NZ, S, W, E*, 1926 *W*
Laurent, J (Bayonne) 1920 *S, E, W*
Laurent, M (Auch) 1932 *G*, 1933 *G*, 1934 *G*, 1935 *G*, 1936 *G* 1
Lavail, G (Perpignan) 1937 *G*, 1940 *B*
Lavaud, R (Carcassonne) 1914 *I, W*
Lavergne, P (Limoges) 1950 *S*
Lavigne, B (Agen) 1984 *R*, 1985 *E*
Lavigne, J (Dax) 1920 *E, W*
Lazies, H (Auch) 1954 *Arg* 2, 1955 *It*, 1956 *E*, 1957 *S*
Le Bourhis, R (La Rochelle) 1961 *R*
Lecointre, M (Nantes) 1952 *It*
Le Droff, J (Auch) 1963 *It, R*, 1964 *S, NZ, E*, 1970 *E, R*, 1971 *S, I*
Lefevre, R (Brive) 1961 *NZ* 2
Lefort, J-B (Biarritz O) 1938 *G* 1
Le Goff, R (Métro) 1938 *R, G* 2
Legrain, M (SF) 1909 *I*, 1910 *I*, 1911 *S, E, W, I*, 1913 *S, SA, E, I*, 1914 *I, W*

Lemeur, Y (RCF) 1993 *R* 1
Lenient, J-J (Vichy) 1967 *R*
Lepatey, J (Mazamet) 1954 *It*, 1955 *S, I, E, W*
Lepatey, L (Mazamet) 1924 *S, I, E*
Lescarboura, J-P (Dax) 1982 *W, E, S, I*, 1983 *A* 1,2, *R*, 1984 *I, W, E, S, NZ* 1,2, *R*, 1985 *E, S, I, W, Arg* 1,2, 1986 *Arg* 2, *A, NZ* 1, *R* 2, *NZ* 2, 1988 *S, W*, 1990 *R*
Lesieur, E (SF) 1906 *E*, 1908 *E, W*, 1909 *E, W, I*, 1910 *S, E, I*, 1911 *E, I*, 1912 *W*
Leuvielle, M (SBUC) 1908 *W*, 1913 *S, SA, E, W*, 1914 *W, E*
Levasseur, R (SF) 1925 *W, E*
Levée, H (RCF) 1906 *NZ*
Lewis, E W (Le Havre) 1906 *E*
Lhermet, J-M (Montferrand) 1990 *S, I*, 1993 *R* 1
Libaros, G (Tarbes) 1936 *G* 1, 1940 *B*
Lievremont, M (Perpignan) 1995 *It, R* 2, *Arg* (R), *NZ* 2 (R), 1996 *R*
Lira, M (La Voulte) 1962 *R*, 1963 *I, E, W, It, R*, 1964 *W, It, I, SA*, 1965 *S, I, R*
Llari, R (Carcassonne) 1926 *S*
Lobies, J (RCF) 1921 *S, W, E*
Lombard, F (Narbonne) 1934 *G*, 1937 *It*
Lombarteix, R (Montferrand) 1938 *R, G* 2
Londios, J (Montauban) 1967 *SA* 3
Loppy, L (Toulon) 1993 *R* 2
Lorieux, A (Grenoble, Aix) 1981 *A* 1, *R, NZ* 1,2, 1982 *W*, 1983 *A* 2, *R*, 1984 *I, W, E*, 1985 *Arg* 1,2 (R), 1986 *R* 2, *NZ* 2,3, 1987 *W, E*, [*S, Z, Fj, A, NZ*], 1988 *S, I, W, Arg* 1,2,4, 1989 *W, A* 2
Loury, A (RCF) 1927 *E, G* 1,2, 1928 *S, A, I*
Loustau, M (Dax) 1923 *E*
Lubin-Lebrère, M-F (Toulouse) 1914 *I, W, E*, 1920 *S, E, W, I, US*, 1921 *S*, 1922 *S, E, W*, 1924 *W, US*, 1925 *I*
Lubrano, A (Béziers) 1972 *A* 2, 1973 *S*
Lux, J-P (Tyrosse, Dax) 1967 *E, It, W, I, SA* 1,2,4, *R*, 1968 *I, E, Cz, NZ* 3, *A, SA* 1,2, 1969 *S, I, E*, 1970 *S, I, W, E, R*, 1971 *S, I, E, W, A* 1,2, 1972 *S, I* 1, *E, W, I* 2, *A* 1,2, *R*, 1973 *S, NZ, E*, 1974 *I, W, E, S, Arg* 1,2, 1975 *W*

Macabiau, A (Perpignan) 1994 *S, C* 1
Maclos, P (SF) 1906 *E*, 1907 *E*
Magnanou, C (RCF) 1923 *E*, 1925 *W, E*, 1926 *S*, 1929 *S, W*, 1930 *S, I, E, W*

Olivier Merle (29 caps) wins a line-out in the 15-12 victory over England at Parc des Princes.

Magnol, L (Toulouse) 1928 *S*, 1929 *S*, *W*, *E*
Magois, H (La Rochelle) 1968 *SA* 1,2, *R*
Majerus, R (SF) 1928 *W*, 1929 *I*, *S*, 1930 *S*, *I*, *E*, *G*, *W*
Malbet, J-C (Agen) 1967 *SA* 2,4
Maleig, A (Oloron) 1979 *W*, *E*, *NZ* 2, 1980 *W*, *E*, *SA*, *R*
Malquier, Y (Narbonne) 1979 *S*
Manterola, T (Lourdes) 1955 *It*, 1957 *R* 1
Mantoulan, C (Pau) 1959 *I*
Marcet, J (Albi) 1925 *I*, *NZ*, *S*, *W*, *E*, 1926 *I*, *E*
Marchal, J-F (Lourdes) 1979 *S*, *R*, 1980 *W*, *S*, *I*
Marchand, R (Poitiers) 1920 *S*, *W*
Marfaing, M (Toulouse) 1992 *R*, *Arg* 1
Marocco, P (Montferrand) 1968 *S*, *I*, *W*, *E*, *R* 1, *Arg* 1,2, *A*, 1988 *Arg* 4, 1989 *I*, 1990 *E* (R), *NZ* 1 (R), 1991 *S*, *I*, *W* 1, *E*, *US* 2, [*R*, *Fj*, *C*, *E*]
Marot, A (Brive) 1969 *R*, 1970 *S*, *I*, *W*, 1971 *SA* 1, 1972 *I* 2, 1976 *A* 1
Marquesuzaa, A (RCF) 1958 *It*, *SA* 1,2, 1959 *S*, *E*, *It*, *W*, 1960 *S*, *E*, *Arg* 1
Marracq, H (Pau) 1961 *R*
Martin, C (Lyon) 1909 *I*, 1910 *W*, *S*
Martin, H (SBUC) 1907 *E*, 1908 *W*
Martin, J-L (Béziers) 1971 *A* 2, *R*, 1972 *S*, *I* 1
Martin, L (Pau) 1948 *I*, *A*, *S*, *W*, *E*, 1950 *S*
Martine, R (Lourdes) 1952 *S*, *I*, *It*, 1953 *It*, 1954 *S*, *I*, *NZ*, *W*, *E*, *It*, *Arg* 2, 1955 *S*, *I*, *W*, 1958 *A*, *W*, *It*, *I*, *SA* 1,2, 1960 *S*, *E*, *Arg* 3, 1961 *S*, *It*
Martinez, G (Toulouse) 1982 *W*, *E*, *S*, *Arg* 1,2, 1983 *E*, *W*
Mas, F (Béziers) 1962 *R*, 1963 *S*, *I*, *E*, *W*
Maso, J (Perpignan, Narbonne) 1966 *It*, *R*, 1967 *S*, *R*, 1968 *S*, *W*, *Cz*, *NZ* 1,2,3, *A*, *R*, 1969 *S*, *I*, *W*, 1971 *SA* 1,2, *R*, 1972 *E*, *W*, *A* 2, 1973 *W*, *I*, *J*, *R*
Massare, J (PUC) 1945 *B* 1,2, *W*, 1946 *B*, *I*, *W*
Massé, A (SBUC) 1908 *W*, 1909 *E*, *W*, 1910 *W*, *S*, *E*, *I*
Masse, H (Grenoble) 1937 *G*
Matheu-Cambas, J (Agen) 1945 *W*, 1946 *B*, *I*, *K*, *W*, 1947 *S*, *I*, *W*, *E*, 1948 *I*, *A*, *S*, *W*, *E*, 1949 *S*, *I*, *E*, *W*, *Arg* 1,2, 1950 *E*, *W*, 1951 *S*, *I*
Mauduy, G (Périgueux) 1957 *It*, *R* 1,2, 1958 *S*, *E*, 1961 *W*, *It*
Mauran, J (Castres) 1952 *SA*, *W*, *E*, *It*, 1953 *I*, *E*
Mauriat, P (Lyon) 1907 *E*, 1908 *E*, *W*, 1909 *W*, *I*, 1910 *W*, *S*, *E*, *I*, 1911 *S*, *E*, *W*, *I*, 1912 *I*, *S*, 1913 *S*, *SA*, *W*, *I*
Maurin, G (ASF) 1906 *E*
Maury, A (Toulouse) 1925 *I*, *NZ*, *S*, *W*, *E*, 1926 *S*, *I*, *E*
Mayssonnié, A (Toulouse) 1908 *E*, *W*, 1910 *W*
Mazas, L (Colomiers) 1992 *Arg*
Melville, E (Toulon) 1990 *I* (R), *A* 1,2,3, *NZ* 1, 1991 *US* 2
Menrath, R (SCUF) 1910 *W*
Menthiller, Y (Romans) 1964 *W*, *It*, *SA*, *R*, 1965 *E*
Meret, F (Tarbes) 1940 *B*
Mericq, S (Agen) 1959 *I*, 1960 *S*, *E*, *W*, 1961 *I*
Merle, O (Grenoble, Montferrand) 1993 *SA* 1,2, *R* 2, *A* 1,2, 1994 *I*, *W*, *E*, *S*, *C* 1, *NZ* 1,2, *C* 2, 1995 *W*, *I*, *R* 1, [*Tg*, *S*, *I*, *SA*, *E*], *It*, *R* 2, *Arg*, *NZ* 1, 2, 1996 *E*, *S*, *R*
Merquey, J (Toulon) 1950 *S*, *I*, *E*, *W*
Mesnel, F (RCF) 1986 *NZ* 2 (R), 3, 1987 *W*, *E*, *S*, *I*, [*S*, *Z*, *Fj*, *A*, *NZ*], *R*, 1988 *E*, *Arg* 1,2,3,4, *R*, 1989 *I*, *W*, *E*, *NZ* 1, *A* 1,2, 1990 *E*, *S*, *I*, *A* 2,3, *NZ* 1,2, 1991 *S*, *I*, *W* 1, *E*, *R*, *US* 1,2, *W* 2, [*R*, *Fj*, *C*, *E*], 1992 *W*, *E*, *S*, *I*, *SA* 1,2, 1993 *E* (R), *W*, 1995 *I*, *R* 1, [*Iv*, *E*]
Mesny, P (RCF, Grenoble) 1979 *NZ* 1,2, 1980 *SA*, *R*, 1981 *I*, *W* (R), *A* 1,2, *R*, *NZ* 1,2, 1982 *I*, *Arg* 1,2
Meyer, G-S (Périgueux) 1960 *S*, *E*, *It*, *R*, *Arg* 2
Meynard, J (Cognac) 1954 *Arg* 1, 1956 *Cz*
Mias, L (Mazamet) 1951 *S*, *I*, *E*, *W*, 1952 *I*, *SA*, *W*, *E*, *It*, 1953 *S*, *I*, *W*, *It*, 1954 *S*, *I*, *NZ*, *W*, 1957 *R* 2, 1958 *S*, *E*, *A*, *W*, *I*, *SA* 1,2, 1959 *S*, *It*, *W*, *I*
Milliand, P (Grenoble) 1936 *G* 2, 1937 *G*, *It*
Minjat, R (Lyon) 1945 *B* 1
Miorin, H (Toulouse) 1996 *R*
Mir, J-H (Lourdes) 1967 *R*, 1968 *I*
Mir, J-P (Lourdes) 1967 *A*
Modin, R (Brive) 1987 [*Z*]
Moga, A-M-A (Bègles) 1945 *B* 1,2, *W*, 1946 *B*, *I*, *K*, *W*, 1947 *S*, *I*, *W*, *E*, 1948 *I*, *A*, *S*, *W*, *E*, 1949 *S*, *I*, *E*, *W*, *Arg* 1,2
Mommejat, B (Cahors, Albi) 1958 *It*, *I*, *SA* 1,2, 1959 *S*, *E*, *It*, *W*, *I*, 1960 *S*, *E*, *It*, *R*, 1962 *S*, *E*, *W*, *I*, *It*, *R*, 1963 *S*, *I*, *W*
Moncla, F (RCF, Pau) 1956 *Cz*, 1957 *I*, *E*, *W*, *It*, *R* 1, 1958 *SA* 1,2, 1959 *S*, *E*, *It*, *W*, *I*, 1960 *S*, *E*, *W*, *I*, *It*, *R*, *Arg* 1,2,3, 1961 *S*, *SA*, *E*, *W*, *It*, *I*, *NZ* 1,2,3
Moni, C (Nice) 1996 *R*
Monié, R (Perpignan) 1956 *Cz*, 1957 *E*
Monier, R (SBUC) 1911 *I*, 1912 *S*
Monniot, M (RCF) 1912 *W*, *E*

Montade, A (Perpignan) 1925 *I*, *NZ*, *S*, *W*, 1926 *W*
Montlaur, P (Agen) 1992 *E* (R), 1994 *S* (R)
Moraitis, B (Toulon) 1969 *E*, *W*
Morel, A (Grenoble) 1954 *Arg* 2
Morere, J (Toulouse) 1927 *E*, *G* 1, 1928 *S*, *A*
Moscato, V (Bègles) 1991 *R*, *US* 1, 1992 *W*, *E*
Mougeot, C (Bègles) 1992 *W*, *E*, *Arg*
Mouniq, P (Toulouse) 1911 *S*, *E*, *W*, *I*,1912 *I*, *E*, 1913 *S*, *SA*, *E*
Moure, H (SCUF) 1908 *E*
Moureu, P (Béziers) 1920 *I*, *US*, 1921 *W*, *E*, *I*, 1922 *S*, *W*, *I*, 1923 *S*, *W*, *E*, *I*, 1924 *S*, *I*, *E*, *W*, 1925 *E*
Mournet, A (Bagnères) 1981 *A* 1 (R)
Mouronval, F (SF) 1909 *I*
Muhr, A H (RCF) 1906 *NZ*, *E*, 1907 *E*
Murillo, G (Dijon) 1954 *It*, *Arg* 1

Namur, R (Toulon) 1931 *E*, *G*
Noble, J-C (La Voulte) 1968 *E*, *W*, *Cz*, *NZ* 3, *A*, *R*
Normand, A (Toulouse) 1957 *R* 1
Novès, G (Toulouse) 1977 *NZ* 1,2, *R*, 1978 *W*, *R*, 1979 *I*, *W*
Ntamack, E (Toulouse) 1994 *W*, *C* 1, *NZ* 1,2, *C* 2, 1995 *W*, *I*, *R* 1, [*Tg*, *S*, *I*, *SA*, *E*], *It*, *R* 2, *Arg*, *NZ* 1, 2, 1996 *E*, *S*, *I*, *W*, *R* (R)

Olive, D (Montferrand) 1951 *I*, 1952 *I*
Ondarts, P (Biarritz O) 1986 *NZ* 3, 1987 *W*, *E*, *S*, *I*, [*S*, *Z*, *Fj*, *A*, *NZ*], *R*, 1988 *E*, *I*, *W*, *Arg* 1,2,3,4, *R*, 1989 *I*, *W*, *E*, *NZ* 1,2, *A* 2, 1990 *W*, *E*, *S*, *I*, *R* (R), *NZ* 1,2, 1991 *S*, *I*, *W* 1, *E*, *US* 2, *W* 2, [*R*, *Fj*, *C*, *E*]
Orso, J-C (Nice, Toulon) 1982 *Arg* 1,2, 1983 *E*, *S*, *A* 1, 1984 *E* (R), *S*, *NZ* 1, 1985 *I* (R), *W*, 1988 *I*
Othats, J (Dax) 1960 *Arg* 2,3
Ougier, S (Toulouse) 1992 *R*, *Arg* 1, 1993 *E* (R)

Paco, A (Béziers) 1974 *Arg* 1,2, *R*, *SA* 1,2, 1975 *W*, *E*, *Arg* 1,2, *R*, 1976 *S*, *I*, *W*, *E*, *US*, *A* 1,2, *R*, 1977 *W*, *E*, *S*, *I*, *NZ* 1,2, *R*, 1978 *E*, *S*, *I*, *W*, *R*, 1979 *I*, *W*, *E*, *S*, 1980 *W*
Palat, J (Perpignan) 1938 *G* 2
Palmié, M (Béziers) 1975 *SA* 1,2, *Arg* 1,2, *R*, 1976 *S*, *I*, *W*, *E*, *US*, 1977 *W*, *E*, *S*, *I*, *Arg* 1,2, *NZ* 1,2, *R*, 1978 *E*, *S*, *I*, *W*
Paoli, R (see Simonpaoli)
Paparemborde, R (Pau) 1975 *SA* 1,2, *Arg* 1,2, *R*, 1976 *S*, *I*, *W*, *E*, *US*, *A* 1,2, *R*, 1977 *W*, *E*, *S*, *I*, *Arg* 1, *NZ* 1,2, 1978 *E*, *S*, *I*, *W*, *R*, 1979 *I*, *W*, *E*, *S*, *NZ* 1,2, *R*, 1980 *W*, *E*, *S*, *SA*, *R*, 1981 *S*, *I*, *W*, *E*, *A* 1,2, *R*, *NZ* 1,2, 1982 *W*, *I*, *R*, *Arg* 1,2 1983 *E*, *S*, *I*, *W*
Pardo, L (Hendaye) 1924 *I*, *E*
Pardo, L (Bayonne) 1980 *SA*, *R*, 1981 *S*, *I*, *W*, *E*, *A* 1, 1982 *W*, *E*, *S*, 1983 *A* 1 (R), 1985 *S*, *I*, *Arg* 2
Pardage, J-H (Lyon U) 1953 *It*
Paries, L (Biarritz O) 1968 *SA* 2, *R*, 1970 *S*, *I*, *W*, 1975 *E*, *S*, *I*
Pascalin, P (Mont-de-Marsan) 1950 *I*, *E*, *W*, 1951 *S*, *I*, *E*, *W*
Pascarel, J-R (TOEC) 1912 *W*, *E*, 1913 *S*, *SA*, *E*, *I*
Pascot, J (Perpignan) 1922 *S*, *E*, *I*, 1923 *S*, 1926 *I*, 1927 *G* 2
Paul, R (Montferrand) 1940 *B*
Pauthe, G (Graulhet) 1956 *E*
Pebeyre, E-J (Fumel, Brive) 1945 *W*, 1946 *I*, *K*, *W*, 1947 *S*, *I*, *W*, *E*
Pebeyre, M (Vichy, Montferrand) 1970 *E*, *R*, 1971 *I*, *SA* 1,2, *A* 1, 1973 *W*
Pecune, J (Tarbes) 1974 *W*, *E*, *S*, 1975 *Arg* 1,2, *R*, 1976 *I*, *W*, *E*, *US*
Pedeutour, P (Begles) 1980 *I*
Pellissier, L (RCF) 1928 *A*, *I*, *E*, *G*, *W*
Pelous, P (Dax) 1995 *R* 2, *Arg*, *NZ* 1, 2, 1996 *E*, *S*, *I*, *R* (R)
Penaud, A (Brive) 1992 *W*, *E*, *S*, *I*, *R*, *Arg* 1,2, *SA* 1,2, *Arg*, 1993 *R* 1, *SA* 1,2, *R* 2, *A* 1,2, 1994 *I*, *W*, *E*, 1995 *NZ* 1, 2, 1996 *S*, *R*
Périé, M (Toulon) 1996 *E*, *S*, *I* (R)
Peron, P (RCF) 1975 *SA* 1,2
Perrier, P (Bayonne) 1982 *W*, *E*, *S*, *I* (R)
Pesteil, J-P (Béziers) 1975 *SA* 1, 1976 *A* 2, *R*
Petit, C (Lorrain) 1931 *W*
Peyrelade, H (Tarbes) 1940 *B*
Peyroutou, G (Périgueux) 1911 *S*, *E*
Phliponeau, J-F (Montferrand) 1973 *W*, *I*
Piazza, A (Montauban) 1968 *NZ* 1, *A*
Picard, T (Montferrand) 1985 *Arg* 2, 1986 *R* 1 (R), *Arg* 2
Pierrot, G (Pau) 1914 *I*, *W*, *E*
Pilon, J (Périgueux) 1949 *E*, 1950 *E*

Piqué, J (Pau) 1961 *NZ* 2,3, *A*, 1962 *S, It*, 1964 *NZ, E, W, It, I, SA, Fj, R*, 1965 *S, I, E, W, It*
Piquemal, M (Tarbes) 1927 *I, S*, 1929 *I, G*, 1930 *S, I, E, G, W*
Piquiral, E (RCF) 1924 *S, I, E, W, R, US*, 1925 *E*, 1926 *S, I, E, W, M*, 1927 *I, S, W, E, G* 1,2, 1928 *E*
Piteu, R (Pau) 1921 *S, W, E, I*, 1922 *S, E, W, I*, 1923 *E*, 1924 *E*, 1925 *I, NZ, W, E*, 1926 *E*
Plantefol, A (RCF) 1967 *SA* 2,3,4, *NZ, R*, 1968 *E, W, Cz, NZ* 2, 1969 *E, W*
Plantey, S (RCF) 1961 *A*, 1962 *It*
Podevin, G (SF) 1913 *W, I*
Poeydebasque, F (Bayonne) 1914 *I, W*
Poirier, A (SCUF) 1907 *E*
Pomathios, M (Agen, Lyon U, Bourg) 1948 *I, A, S, W, E*, 1949 *S, I, E, W, Arg* 1,2, 1950 *S, I, W*, 1951 *S, I, E, W*, 1952 *W, E*, 1953 *S, I, W*, 1954 *S*
Pons, P (Toulouse) 1920 *S, E, W*, 1921 *S, W*, 1922 *S*
Porra, M (Lyon) 1931 *I*
Porthault, A (RCF) 1951 *S, E, W*, 1952 *I*, 1953 *S, I, It*
Portolan, C (Toulouse) 1986 *A*, 1989 *I, E*
Potel, A (Begles) 1932 *G*
Prat, J (Lourdes) 1945 *B* 1,2, *W*, 1946 *B, I, K, W*, 1947 *S, I, W, E*, 1948 *I, A, S, W, E*, 1949 *S, I, E, W, Arg* 1,2, 1950 *S, I, E, W*, 1951 *S, E, W*, 1952 *S, I, SA, W, E, It*, 1953 *S, I, E, W, It*, 1954 *S, I, NZ, W, E, It*, 1955 *S, I, E, W, It*
Prat, M (Lourdes) 1951 *I*, 1952 *S, I, SA, W, E*, 1953 *S, I, E*, 1954 *I, NZ, W, E, It*, 1955 *S, I, E, W, It*, 1956 *I, W, It, Cz*, 1957 *S, I, W, It, R* 1, 1958 *A, W, I*
Prevost, A (Albi) 1926 *M*, 1927 *I, S, W*
Prin-Clary, J (Cavaillon, Brive) 1945 *B* 1,2, *W*, 1946 *B, I, K, W*, 1947 *S, I, W*
Puech, L (Toulouse) 1920 *S, E, I*, 1921 *E, I*
Puget, M (Toulouse) 1961 *It*, 1966 *S, I, It*, 1967 *SA* 1,3,4, *NZ*, 1968 *Cz, NZ* 1,2, *SA* 1,2, *R*, 1969 *E, R*, 1970 *W*
Puig, A (Perpignan) 1926 *S, E*
Pujol, A (SOE Toulouse) 1906 *NZ*
Pujolle, M (Nice) 1989 *B, A* 1, 1990 *S, I, R, A* 1,2, *NZ* 2

Quaglio, A (Mazamet) 1957 *R* 2, 1958 *S, E, A, W, I, SA* 1,2, 1959 *S, E, It, W, I*
Quilis, A (Narbonne) 1967 *SA* 1,4, *NZ*, 1970 *R*, 1971 *I*

Ramis, R (Perpignan) 1922 *E, I*, 1923 *W*
Rancoule, H (Lourdes, Toulon, Tarbes) 1955 *E, W, It*, 1958 *A, W, It, I, SA* 1, 1959 *S, It, W*, 1960 *I, It, R, Arg* 1,2, 1961 *SA, E, W, It, NZ* 1,2, 1962 *S, E, W, I, It*
Rapin, A (SBUC) 1938 *R*
Raymond, F (Toulouse) 1925 *S*, 1927 *W*, 1928 *I*
Raynal, F (Perpignan) 1935 *G*, 1936 *G* 1,2, 1937 *G, It*
Raynaud, F (Carcassonne) 1933 *G*
Razat, J-P (Agen) 1962 *R*, 1963 *S, I, R*
Rebujent, R (RCF) 1963 *E*
Revailler, D (Graulhet) 1981 *S, I, W, E, A* 1,2, *R*, *NZ* 1,2, 1982 *W, S, I, R, Arg* 1
Revillon, J (RCF) 1926 *I, E*, 1927 *S*
Ribère, E (Perpignan, Quillan) 1924 *I*, 1925, *I*, *NZ, S*, 1926 *S, I, W, M*, 1927 *I, S, W, E, G* 1,2, 1928 *S, A, I, E, G, W*, 1929 *I, E, G*, 1930 *S, I, E, W*, 1931 *I, S, W, E, G*, 1932 *G*, 1933 *G*
Rives, J-P (Toulouse, RCF) 1975 *E, S, I, Arg* 1,2, *R*, 1976 *S, I, W, E, US, A* 1,2, *R*, 1977 *W, E, S, I, Arg* 1,2, *R*, 1978 *E, S, I, W, R*, 1979 *I, W, E, S, NZ* 1,2, *R*, 1980 *W, E, S, I, SA*, 1981 *S, I, W, E, A* 2, 1982 *W, E, S, I, R*, 1983 *E, S, I, W, A* 1,2, *R*, 1984 *I, W, E, S*
Rochon, A (Montferrand) 1936 *G* 1
Rodrigo, M (Mauléon) 1931 *I, W*
Rodriguez, L (Mont-de-Marsan, Montferrand, Dax) 1981 *A* 1,2, *R*, *NZ* 1,2, 1982 *W, E, S, I, R*, 1983 *E, S*, 1984 *I, NZ* 1,2, *R*, 1985 *E, S, I, W*, 1986 *Arg* 1, *A, R* 2, *NZ* 2,3, 1987 *W, E, S, I*, [*S, Z, Fj, A, NZ*], *R*, 1988 *E, S, I, W, Arg* 1,2,3,4, *R*, 1989 *I, E, S, NZ* 1,2, *B, A* 1, 1990 *W, E, S, I, NZ* 1
Rogé, L (Béziers) 1952 *I*, 1953 *E, W, It*, 1954 *S, Arg* 1,2, 1955 *S, I*, 1956 *W, It, E*, 1957 *S*, 1960 *S, E*
Rollet, J (Bayonne) 1960 *Arg* 3, 1961 *NZ* 3, *A*, 1962 *It*, 1963 *I*
Romero, H (Montauban) 1962 *S, E, W, I, It, R*, 1963 *E*
Romeu, J-P (Montferrand) 1972 *R*, 1973 *S, NZ, E, W, I, R*, 1974 *W, E, S, Arg* 1,2, *R*, *SA* 1,2 (R), 1975 *W, SA* 2, *Arg* 1,2, *R*, 1976 *S, I, W, E, US*, 1977 *W, E, S, I, Arg* 1,2, *NZ* 1,2, *R*
Roques, A (Cahors) 1958 *A, W, It, I, SA* 1,2, 1959 *S, E, W, I*, 1960 *S, E, W, I, It, Arg* 1,2,3, 1961 *S, SA, E, W, It, I*, 1962 *S, E, W, I, It*, 1963 *S*
Roques, J-C (Brive) 1966 *S, I, It, R*
Rossignol, J-C (Brive) 1972 *A* 2

Rouan, J (Narbonne) 1953 *S, I*
Roucaries, G (Perpignan) 1956 *S*
Rouffia, L (Narbonne) 1945 *B* 2, *W*, 1946 *W*, 1948 *I*
Rougerie, J (Montferrand) 1973 *J*
Rougé-Thomas, P (Toulouse) 1989 *NZ* 1,2
Roujas, F (Tarbes) 1910 *I*
Roumat, O (Dax) 1989 *NZ* 2 (R), *B*, 1990 *W, E, S, I, R, A* 1,2,3, *NZ* 1,2, 1991 *S, I, W* 1, *E, R, US* 1, *W* 2, [*R, Fj, C, E*], 1992 *W* (R), *E* (R), *S, I, SA* 1,2, *Arg*, 1993 *E, S, I, W, R* 1, *SA* 1,2, *R* 2, *A* 1,2, 1994 *I, W, E, C* 1, *NZ* 1,2, *C* 2, 1995 *W, E, S*, [*Iv, S, I, SA, E*], 1996 *E, S, I, W*
Rousie, M (Villeneuve) 1931 *S, G*, 1932 *G*, 1933 *G*
Rousset, G (Béziers) 1975 *SA* 1, 1976 *US*
Ruiz, A (Tarbes) 1968 *SA* 2, *R*
Rupert, J-J (Tyrosse) 1963 *R*, 1964 *S, Fj*, 1965 *E, W, It*, 1966 *S, I, E, W, It*, 1967 *It, R*, 1968 *S*

Sadourny, J-L (Colomiers) 1991 *W* 2 (R), [*C* (R)], 1992 *E* (R), *S, I, Arg* 1 (R), 2, *SA* 1,2, 1993 *R* 1, *SA* 1,2, *R* 2, *A* 1,2, 1994 *I, W, E, S, C* 1, *NZ* 1,2, *C* 2, 1995 *W, E, S, I, R* 1, [*Tg, S, I, SA, E*], *It, R* 2, *Arg, NZ* 1, 2, 1996 *E, S, I, W*
Sagot, P (SF) 1906 *NZ*, 1908 *E*, 1909 *W*
Sahuc, A (Métro) 1945 *B* 1,2
Sahuc, F (Toulouse) 1936 *G* 2
Saint-André, P (Montferrand) 1990 *R, A* 3, *NZ* 1,2, 1991 *I* (R), *W* 1, *E, US* 1,2, *W* 2, [*R, Fj, C, E*], 1992 *W, E, S, I, R, Arg* 1,2, *SA* 1,2, 1993 *E, S, I, W, SA* 1,2, *A* 1,2, 1994 *I, W, E, S, C* 1, *NZ* 1,2, *C* 2, 1995 *W, E, S, I, R* 1, [*Tg, Iv, S, I, SA, E*], *It, R* 2, *Arg, NZ* 1, 2, 1996 *E, S, I, W, R*
Saisset, O (Béziers) 1971 *R*, 1972 *S, I* 1, *A* 1,2, 1973 *S, NZ, E, W, I, J, R*, 1974 *I, Arg* 2, *SA* 1,2, 1975 *W*
Salas, P (Narbonne) 1979 *NZ* 1,2, *R*, 1980 *W, E*, 1981 *A* 1, 1982 *Arg* 2
Salinié, R (Perpignan) 1923 *E*
Sallefranque, M (Dax) 1981 *A* 2, 1982 *W, E, S*
Salut, J (TOEC) 1966 *R*, 1967 *S*, 1968 *I, E, Cz, NZ* 1, 1969 *I*
Samatan, R (Agen) 1930 *S, I, E, G, W*, 1931 *I, S, W, E, G*
Sanac, A (Perpignan) 1952 *It*, 1953 *S, I*, 1954 *E*, 1956 *Cz*, 1957 *S, I, E, W, It*
Sangalli, F (Narbonne) 1975 *I, SA* 1,2, 1976 *S, A* 1,2, *R*, 1977 *W, E, S, I, Arg* 1,2, *NZ* 1,2
Sanz, H (Narbonne) 1988 *Arg* 3,4, *R*, 1989 *A* 2, 1990 *S, I, R, A* 1,2, *NZ* 2, 1991 *W* 2
Sappa, M (Nice) 1973 *J, R*, 1977 *R*
Sarrade, R (Pau) 1929 *I*
Saux, J-P (Pau) 1960 *W, It, Arg* 1,2, 1961 *SA, E, W, It, I, NZ* 1,2,3, *A*, 1962 *S, E, W, I, It*, 1963 *S, I, E, It*
Savitsky, M (La Voulte) 1969 *R*
Savy, M (Montferrand) 1931 *I, S, W, E*, 1936 *G* 1
Sayrou, J (Perpignan) 1926 *W, M*, 1928 *E, G, W*, 1929 *S, W, E, G*
Scohy, R (BEC) 1931 *S, W, E, G*
Sébédio, J (Tarbes) 1913 *S, E*, 1914 *I*, 1920 *S, I, US*, 1922 *S, E*, 1923 *S*
Seguier, N (Béziers) 1973 *J, R*
Seigne, L (Agen, Merignac) 1989 *B, A* 1, 1990 *NZ* 1, 1993 *E, S, I, W, R* 1, *A* 1,2, 1994 *S, C* 1, 1995 *E* (R), *S*
Sella, P (Agen) 1982 *R, Arg* 1,2, 1983 *E, S, I, W, A* 1,2, *R*, 1984 *I, W, E, S, NZ* 1,2, *R*, 1985 *E, S, I, W, Arg* 1,2, 1986 *S, I, W, E, R* 1, *Arg* 1,2, *A, NZ* 1, *R* 2, *NZ* 2,3, 1987 *W, E, S, I*, [*S, R, Z* (R), *Fj, A, NZ*], 1988 *E, S, I, W, Arg* 1,2,3,4, *R*, 1989 *I, W, E, S, NZ* 1,2, *B, A* 1, 1990 *W, E, S, I, A* 1,2,3, 1991 *W* 1, *E, R, US* 1,2, *W* 2, [*Fj, C, E*], 1992 *W, E, S, I, Arg*, 1993 *E, S, I, W, R* 1, *SA* 1,2, *R* 2, *A* 1,2, 1994 *I, W, E, S, C* 1, *NZ* 1,2, *C* 2, 1995, 1996 *E, S, I*, [*Tg, S, I, SA, E*]
Semmartin, J (SCUF) 1913 *W, I*
Senal, G (Béziers) 1974 *Arg* 1,2, *R, SA* 1,2, 1975 *W*
Sentilles, J (Tarbes) 1912 *W, E*, 1913 *S, SA*
Serin, L (Béziers) 1928 *E*, 1929 *W, E, G*, 1930 *S, I, E, G, W*, 1931 *I, W, E*
Serre, P (Perpignan) 1920 *S, E*
Serrière, P (RCF) 1986 *A*, 1987 *R*, 1988 *E*
Servole, L (Toulon) 1931 *I, S, W, E, G*, 1934 *G*, 1935 *G*
Sicart, N (Perpignan) 1922 *I*
Sillières, J (Tarbes) 1968 *R*, 1970 *S, I*, 1971 *S, I, E*, 1972 *E, W*
Siman, M (Montferrand) 1948 *E*, 1949 *S*, 1950 *S, I, E, W*
Simon, S (Bègles) 1991 *R, US* 1
Simonpaoli, R (SF) 1911 *I*, 1912 *I, S*
Sitjar, M (Agen) 1964 *W, It, I, R*, 1965 *It, R*, 1967 *A, E, It, W, I, SA* 1,2
Skrela, J-C (Toulouse) 1971 *SA* 2, *A* 1,2, 1972 *I* 1 (R), *E, W, I* 2, *A* 1, 1973 *W, J, R*, 1974 *W, E, S, Arg* 1, *R*, 1975 *W* (R), *E, S, I, SA* 1,2, *Arg* 1,2, *R*, 1976 *S, I, W, E, US, A* 1,2, *R*, 1977 *W, E, S, I, Arg* 1,2, *NZ* 1,2, *R*, 1978 *E, S, I, W*

285

Soler, M (Quillan) 1929 *G*
Soro, R (Lourdes, Romans) 1945 *B* 1,2, *W*, 1946 *B, I, K*, 1947 *S, I, W, E*, 1948 *I, A, S, W, E*, 1949 *S, I, E, W, Arg* 1,2
Sorondo, L-M (Montauban) 1946 *K*, 1947 *S, I, W, E*, 1948 *I*
Soulié, E (CASG) 1920 *E, I, US*, 1921 *S, E, I*, 1922 *E, W, I*
Sourgens, J (Bègles) 1926 *M*
Spanghero, C (Narbonne) 1971 *E, W, SA* 1,2, *A* 1,2, *R*, 1972 *S, E, W, I* 2, *A* 1,2, 1974 *I, W, E, S, R, SA* 1, 1975 *E, S, I*
Spanghero, W (Narbonne) 1964 *SA, Fj, R*, 1965 *S, I, E, W, It, R*, 1966 *S, I, E, W, It, R*, 1967 *S, A, E, SA* 1,2,3,4, *NZ*, 1968 *S, I, E, W, NZ* 1,2,3, *A, SA* 1,2, *R*, 1969 *S, I, W*, 1970 *R*, 1971 *E, W, SA* 1, 1972 *E, I* 2, *A* 1,2, *R*, 1973 *S, NZ, E, W, I*
Stener, G (PUC) 1956 *S, I, E*, 1958 *SA* 1,2
Struxiano, P (Toulouse) 1913 *W, I*, 1920 *S, E, W, I, US*
Sutra, G (Narbonne) 1967 *SA* 2, 1969 *W*, 1970 *S, I*
Swierczinski, C (Bègles) 1969 *E*, 1977 *Arg* 2

Tachdjian, M (RCF) 1991 *S, I, E*
Taffary, M (RCF) 1975 *W, E, S, I*
Taillantou, J (Pau) 1930 *I, G, W*
Tarricq, P (Lourdes) 1958 *A, W, It, I*
Tavernier, H (Toulouse) 1913 *I*
Techoueyres, W (SBUC) 1994 *E, S*, 1995 *[Iv]*
Terreau, M-M (Bourg) 1945 *W*, 1946 *B, I, K, W*, 1947 *S, I, W, E*, 1948 *I, A, W, E*, 1949 *S, Arg* 1,2, 1951 *S*
Theuriet, A (SCUF) 1909 *E, W*, 1910 *S*, 1911 *W*, 1913 *E*
Thevenot, M (SCUF) 1910 *W, E, I*
Thierry, R (RCF) 1920 *S, E, W, US*
Thiers, P (Montferrand) 1936 *G* 1,2, 1937 *G, It*, 1938 *G* 1,2, 1940 *B*, 1945 *B*, 1,2
Tignol, P (Toulouse) 1953 *S, I*
Tilh, H (Nantes) 1912 *W, E*, 1913 *S, SA, E, W*
Tolot, J-L (Agen) 1987 *[Z]*
Tordo, J-F (Nice) 1991 *US* 1 (R), 1992 *W, E, S, I, R, Arg* 1,2, *SA* 1, *Arg*, 1993 *E, S, I, W, R* 1
Torreilles, S (Perpignan) 1956 *S*
Tournaire, F (Narbonne) 1995 *It*, 1996 *I, W, R*
Tourte, R (St Girons) 1940 *B*
Trillo, J (Bègles) 1967 *SA* 3,4, *NZ, R*, 1968 *S, I, NZ* 1,2,3, *A*, 1969 *I, E, W, R*, 1970 *E, R*, 1971 *S, I, SA* 1,2, *A* 1,2, 1972 *S, A* 1,2, *R*, 1973 *S, E*
Triviaux, R (Cognac) 1931 *E, G*
Tucco-Chala, M (PUC) 1940 *B*

Ugartemendia, J-L (St Jean-de-Luz) 1975 *S, I*

Vaills, G (Perpignan) 1928 *A*, 1929 *G*
Vallot, C (SCUF) 1912 *S*
Van Heerden, A (Tarbes) 1992 *E, S*
Vannier, M (RCF, Chalon) 1953 *W*, 1954 *S, I, Arg* 1,2, 1955 *S, I, E, W, It*, 1956 *S, I, W, It, E*, 1957 *S, I, E, W, It, R* 1,2, 1958 *S, E, A, W, It, I*, 1960 *S, E, W, I, It, R, Arg* 1,3, 1961 *SA, E, W, It, I, NZ* 1, *A*
Vaquer, F (Perpignan) 1921 *S, W*, 1922 *W*
Vaquerin, A (Béziers) 1971 *R*, 1972 *S, I* 1, *A* 1, 1973 *S*, 1974 *W, E, S, Arg* 1,2, *R, SA* 1,2, 1975 *W, E, S, I*, 1976 *US, A* 1 (R), 2, *R*, 1977 *Arg* 2, 1979 *W, E*, 1980 *S, I*
Vareilles, C (SF) 1907 *E*, 1908 *E, W*, 1910 *S, E*
Varenne, F (RCF) 1952 *S*
Varvier, T (RCF) 1906 *E*, 1909 *E, W*, 1911 *E, W*, 1912 *I*
Vassal, G (Carcassonne) 1938 *R, G* 2
Vaysse, J (Albi) 1924 *US*, 1926 *M*
Vellat, E (Grenoble) 1927 *I, E, G* 1,2, 1928 *A*
Venditti, D (Bourgoin) 1996 *R*
Vergé, L (Bègles) 1993 *R* 1 (R)
Verger, A (SF) 1927 *W, E, G* 1, 1928 *I, E, G, W*
Verges, S-A (SF) 1906 *NZ, E*, 1907 *E*
Viard, G (Narbonne) 1969 *W*, 1970 *S, R*, 1971 *S, I*
Viars, S (Brive) 1992 *W, E, I, R, Arg* 1,2, *SA* 1,2 (R), *Arg*, 1993 *R* 1, 1994 *C* 1 (R), *NZ* 1 (t), 1995 *E* (R), *[Iv]*
Vigerie, M (Agen) 1931 *W*
Vigier, R (Montferrand) 1956 *S, W, It, E, Cz*, 1957 *S, E, W, It, R* 1,2, 1958 *S, E, A, W, It, I, SA* 1,2, 1959 *S, E, It, W, I*
Vigneau, A (Bayonne) 1935 *G*
Vignes, C (RCF) 1957 *R* 1,2, 1958 *S, E*
Vila, E (Tarbes) 1926 *M*
Vilagra, J (Vienne) 1945 *B* 2
Villepreux, P (Toulouse) 1967 *It, I, SA* 2, *NZ*, 1968 *I, Cz, NZ* 1,2,3, *A*, 1969 *S, I, E, W, R*, 1970 *S, I, W, E, R*, 1971 *S, I, E, W, A* 1,2, *R*, 1972 *S, I* 1, *E, W, I* 2, *A* 1,2
Viviès, B (Agen) 1978 *E, S, I, W*, 1980 *SA, R*, 1981 *S, A* 1, 1983 *A* 1 (R)
Volot, M (SF) 1945 *W*, 1946 *B, I, K, W*

Weller, S (Grenoble) 1989 *A* 1,2, 1990 *A* 1, *NZ* 1
Wolf, J-P (Béziers) 1980 *SA, R*, 1981 *A* 2, 1982 *E*

Yachvili, M (Tulle, Brive) 1968 *E, W, Cz, NZ* 3, *A, R*, 1969 *S, I, R*, 1971 *E, SA* 1,2 *A* 1, 1972 *R*, 1975 *SA* 2

Zago, F (Montauban) 1963 *I, E*

FRENCH INTERNATIONAL RECORDS

Both team and individual records are for official French international matches up to 30 April 1996.

TEAM RECORDS

Highest score
70 v Zimbabwe (70-12) 1987 Auckland

v individual countries
47 v Argentina (47-12) 1995 Buenos Aires
34 v Australia (34-6) 1976 Parc des Princes
28 v Canada (28-9) 1994 Besançon
28 v Czechoslovakia (28-3) 1956 Toulouse
37 v England (37-12) 1972 Colombes
33 v Fiji (33-9) 1991 Grenoble
38 v Germany (38-17) 1933 Parc des Princes
45 v Ireland (45-10) 1996 Parc des Princes
60 v Italy (60-13) 1967 Toulon
54 v Ivory Coast (54-18) 1995 Rustenburg
30 v Japan (30-18) 1973 Bordeaux
24 v N Zealand (24-19) 1979 Auckland

64 v Romania (64-12) 1996 Aurillac
28 v Scotland (28-22) 1987 Parc des Princes
29 v S Africa (29-16) 1992 Parc des Princes
38 v Tonga (38-10) 1995 Pretoria
41 v United States (41-9) 1991 Denver
36 v Wales (36-3) 1991 Parc des Princes
70 v Zimbabwe (70-12) 1987 Auckland

Biggest winning points margin
58 v Zimbabwe (70-12) 1987 Auckland

v individual countries
35 v Argentina (47-12) 1995 Buenos Aires
28 v Australia (34-6) 1976 Parc des Princes
19 v Canada (28-9) 1994 Besançon
25 v Czechoslovakia (28-3) 1956 Toulouse
25 v England (37-12) 1972 Colombes
24 v Fiji (33-9) 1991 Grenoble

34 v Germany (34-0) 1931 Colombes
35 v Ireland (45-10) 1996 Parc des
  Princes
47 v Italy (60-13) 1967 Toulon
36 v Ivory Coast (54-18) 1995 Rustenburg
12 v Japan (30-18) 1973 Bordeaux
14 v N Zealand (22-8) 1994 Christchurch
56 v Romania (59-3) 1924 Colombes
20 v Scotland (23-3) 1977 Parc des
  Princes
13 v S Africa (29-16) 1992 Parc des
  Princes
28 v Tonga (38-10) 1995 Pretoria
32 v United States (41-9) 1991 Denver
33 v Wales (36-3) 1991 Parc des Princes
58 v Zimbabwe (70-12) 1987 Auckland

Longest winning sequence
10 matches – 1931-37

Highest score by opposing team
49 Wales (14-49) 1910 Swansea
*S Africa beat 'France' 55-6 at Parc des Princes on 3
January 1907, but this is not regarded as an official
international match*

by individual countries
27 Argentina (31-27) 1974 Buenos Aires
48 Australia (31-48) 1990 Brisbane
18 Canada (16-18) 1994 Ottawa
 6 Czechoslovakia (19-6) 1968 Prague
41 England (13-41) 1907 Richmond
16 Fiji (31-16) 1987 Auckland
17 Germany { (16-17) 1927 Frankfurt
            { (38-17) 1933 Parc des
            { Princes
25 Ireland { (5-25) 1911 Cork
           { (6-25) 1975 Dublin
22 Italy (34-22) 1995 Buenos Aires
18 Ivory Coast (54-18) 1995 Rustenburg
18 Japan (30-18) 1973 Bordeaux
38 N Zealand (8-38) 1906 Parc des
  Princes
21 Romania (33-21) 1991 Bucharest
31 Scotland (3-31) 1912 Inverleith
38 S Africa { (5-38) 1913 Bordeaux
           { (25-38) 1975
           { Bloemfontein
10 Tonga (38-10) 1995 Pretoria
17 United States (3-17) 1924 Colombes
49 Wales (14-49) 1910 Swansea
12 Zimbabwe (70-12) 1987 Auckland

Biggest losing points margin
42 v Wales (5-47) 1909 Colombes
*The 6-55 defeat by S Africa in Paris in 1907 is regarded
as unofficial*

v individual countries
12 v Argentina (6-18) 1988 Buenos Aires
21 v Australia (3-24) 1993 Parc des
  Princes

 2 v Canada (16-18) 1994 Ottawa
37 v England (0-37) 1911 Twickenham
 3 v Germany (0-3) 1938 Frankfurt
24 v Ireland (0-24) 1913 Cork
30 v N Zealand (8-38) 1906 Parc des
  Princes
15 v Romania (0-15) 1980 Bucharest
28 v Scotland (3-31) 1912 Inverleith
33 v S Africa (5-38) 1913 Bordeaux
14 v United States (3-17) 1924 Colombes
42 v Wales (5-47) 1909 Colombes
*No defeats v Czechoslovakia, Fiji, Italy, Ivory Coast,
Japan, Tonga or Zimbabwe*

Longest losing sequence
18 matches – 1911-20

**Most tries by France in an
international**
13 v Romania (59-3) 1924 Paris

**Most tries against France in an
international**
11 by Wales (5-47) 1909 Colombes

**Most points by France in
International Championship in a
season – 98**
in season 1985-86

**Most tries by France in
International Championship in a
season – 13**
in seasons 1975-76 and 1985-86

INDIVIDUAL RECORDS

Most capped player
P Sella   111   1982-95

in individual positions
Full-back
S Blanco   81(93)[1]   1980-91
Wing
P Saint-André   58(60)[2]   1990-96
Centre
P Sella   104(111)[3]   1982-95
Fly-half
J-P Romeu   33(34)[4]   1972-77
Scrum-half
P Berbizier   56   1981-91
Prop
R Paparemborde   55   1975-83
Hooker
P Dintrans   50   1979-90
Lock
J Condom   61[5]   1982-90

Flanker
J-P Rives   59[5]   1975-84
No 8
G Basquet   33[6]   1945-52

[1] *S Blanco won 12 caps as a wing*
[2] *Saint-André has won 2 caps as a centre*
[3] *Sella won 6 caps as a wing and 1 as a full-back*
[4] *Romeu was capped once as a replacement full-back. F Mesnel, 56 caps, won 32 as a centre and 24 at fly-half. D Camberabero, 36 caps, won 30 at fly-half, 3 on the wing and 3 at full-back*
[5] *B Dauga and M Crauste, 63 caps each, are France's most-capped forwards. Dauga was capped as a lock and No 8; Crauste as a flanker and No 8*
[6] *M Cecillon, 46 caps, won 31 as a No 8, 3 as a lock and 12 as a flanker*

Longest international career
F Haget 14 seasons 1974-87

Most consecutive Tests – 46
R Bertranne 1973-79

Most internationals as captain – 34
J-P Rives 1978-84

Most points in internationals – 357
T Lacroix (38 matches) 1989-96

Most points in International Championship in a season – 54
J-P Lescarboura (4 matches) 1983-84

Most points in an international – 30
D Camberabero v Zimbabwe 1987 Auckland

Most tries in internationals – 38
S Blanco (93 matches) 1980-91

Most tries in International Championship in a season – 5
P Estève (4 matches) 1982-83
E Bonneval (4 matches) 1986-87

Most tries in an international – 4
A Jauréguy v Romania 1924 Colombes
M Celhay v Italy 1937 Parc des Princes

Most conversions in internationals – 48
D Camberabero (36 matches) 1982-93

Most conversions in International Championship in a season – 7
P Villepreux (4 matches) 1971-72

Most conversions in an international – 9
G Camberabero v Italy 1967 Toulon
D Camberabero v Zimbabwe 1987 Auckland
Father and son

Most dropped goals in internationals – 15
J-P Lescarboura (28 matches) 1982-90

Most dropped goals in an international – 3
P Albaladejo v Ireland 1960 Paris
J-P Lescarboura v England 1985 Twickenham
J-P Lescarboura v New Zealand 1986 Christchurch
D Camberabero v Australia 1990 Sydney

Most penalty goals in internationals – 87
T Lacroix (38 matches) 1989-96

Most penalty goals in International Championship in a season – 10
J-P Lescarboura (4 matches) 1983-84

Most penalty goals in an international – 8
T Lacroix v Ireland 1995 Durban

Most points on major tour – 112
S Viars (7 matches) 1992 Argentina

Most points in any match on tour – 28
P Lagisquet v Paraguayan XV 1988 Asunción
P Estève scored 32 points against East Japan in 1984, but this was not on a major tour

Most tries in a tour match – 7
P Lagisquet v Paraguayan XV 1988 Asunción
P Estève scored 8 tries v East Japan in 1984, but this was not on a major tour

SUCCESS SPAWNS BONANZA

THE 1995 SEASON IN SOUTH AFRICA
Deon Viljoen

An abbreviated season delivered arguably more surprises – mostly innovative and far-reaching – than all of the previous ten terms put together. The World Cup and South Africa's unexpected success had an invigorating influence on the domestic game, instilling confidence and a gung-ho spirit at every level. It soon became obvious that despite Louis Luyt's vision – the South African president, drawing on his business acumen, was instrumental in engineering the unique SANZAR alignment and the ten-year, £360 million satellite television deal with Rupert Murdoch – a costly miscalculation had been made in terms of the immediate negotiating power of the players, especially the members of the World Cup squad. Led by François Pienaar and emboldened by the emergence of a rival world professional circuit (at the time said to have the financial backing of Kerry Packer), the players in effect held a gun to officialdom's head. Pienaar and the bulk of Transvaal's internationals rebelled and were omitted from the Union's Currie Cup tie with Eastern Province. The sorry affair ended in defeat on the paddock and foreshadowed what would ultimately be the team's downfall in the premier competition.

By the time the world professional circuit bluff, spearheaded by the Australian Russ Turnbull, had fizzled out, the entire World Cup squad were wealthy men, having signed lucrative individual contracts with the SARFU. The average monthly salary was rumoured to be £10,000. This did not prevent the Rugby League scouts from moving in to bag two notable internationals in Tiaan Strauss and Christian Stewart at the season's end. It was the first time South African rugby had lost two leading lights to Rugby League since Rob Louw and Ray Mordt joined Wigan in the mid-1980s, and it will surely not be the last.

The entire domestic landscape was rearranged with the drastic expansion of the Currie Cup competition from six to 14 teams. The adjustment precipitated the amalgamation of many small rural unions. No doubt the formation of large territorial entities will be cumbersome to administer, but in the end the lure of millions of rand of financial assistance brought the dawn of professionalism to even the farthest outposts.

In between these momentous developments, a bit of rugby was actually played. The Lion Cup knock-out competition disappeared in favour of a double round of Currie Cup matches. Free State, after topping the table in 1994, were a big disappointment, finishing with the wooden spoon, while Eastern Province remained true to form by finishing near the bottom. Northern Transvaal promised much, but finally succumbed to a rampant Western Province, who reached the final against Natal by winning their last four matches against all the odds.

For all Western Province's resurgence, however, the season ultimately belonged to Natal. Their prescience in securing two of France's best players – Thierry Lacroix (at centre or fly-half) and lock Olivier Roumat – after the World Cup paid rich dividends throughout an inspired campaign, and never more so than in the rain-affected final, played in October and won more convincingly by the home side at King's Park than the 25-17 result would suggest. Each was a towering presence in his own right, though it was Lacroix who commandeered the headlines with a flawless 20-point contribution via the boot. He also created Natal's try. Almost immediately after the Currie Cup climax, the SARFU moved decisively against the 'foreign legion' by imposing a stiff 180-day qualification period.

CURRIE CUP FINAL

Natal 25 (1G 6PG) **Western Province 17** (4PG 1T)
Natal *Try*: C van der Westhuizen *Conversion*: T Lacroix *Penalty Goals*: T Lacroix (6)
Western Province *Try*: C Strauss *Penalty Goals*: J Stransky (4)

CURRIE CUP	*P*	*W*	*D*	*L*	*F*	*A*	*Pts*
Natal	10	7	1	2	273	226	15
Western Province	10	7	0	3	256	199	14
Northern Transvaal	10	6	1	3	287	163	13
Transvaal	10	5	0	5	258	229	10
Eastern Province	10	2	1	7	162	302	5
Free State	10	1	1	8	203	320	3

BANKFIN CUP A	*P*	*W*	*D*	*L*	*F*	*A*	*Pts*
Griqualand West	10	9	0	1	457	117	18
Border	10	7	1	2	360	207	15
Western Transvaal	10	7	0	3	317	216	14
Northern Free State	10	2	2	6	177	281	6
Eastern Transvaal	10	2	0	8	215	442	4
Namibia	10	1	1	8	181	444	3

BANKFIN CUP B	*P*	*W*	*D*	*L*	*F*	*A*	*Pts*
South-Eastern Transvaal	10	9	0	1	464	149	18
Vaal Triangle	10	8	0	2	309	201	16
Boland	10	6	0	4	299	193	12
Stellaland	10	4	0	6	220	310	8
Zimbabwe	10	2	1	7	198	288	5
Far North	10	0	1	9	128	477	1

SUPER 10 SERIES FINAL: Transvaal 16, Queensland 30   **M-NET NIGHT SERIES FINAL:** Northern Transvaal 52, Western Samoa 16   **NATIONAL CLUB CHAMPIONSHIPS FINAL:** Pretoria Police 26, Durban Crusaders 12

SOUTH AFRICAN INTERNATIONAL PLAYERS
(*up to 30 April 1996*)

Ackermann, D S P (WP) 1955 *BI* 2,3,4, 1956 *A* 1,2, *NZ* 1,3, 1958 *F* 2
Albertyn, P K (SWD) 1924 *BI* 1,2,3,4
Alexander, F A (GW) 1891 *BI* 3
Allan, J (N) 1993 *A* 1 (R), *Arg* 1,2 (R), 1994 *E* 1,2, *NZ* 1,2,3
Allen, P B (EP) 1960 *S*
Allport, P H (WP) 1910 *BI* 2,3
Anderson, J W (WP) 1903 *BI* 3
Anderson, J H (WP) 1896 *BI* 1,3,4
Andrew, J B (Tvl) 1896 *BI* 2
Andrews, K S (WP) 1992 *E*, 1993 *F* 1,2, *A* 1 (R), 2,3, *Arg* 1 (R), 2, 1994 *NZ* 3
Andrews, M G (N) 1994 *E* 2, *NZ* 1,2,3, *Arg* 1,2, *S*, *W*, 1995 *WS*, [*A, WS, F, NZ*], *W, It, E*
Antelme, M J G (Tvl) 1960 *NZ* 1,2,3,4, 1961 *F*
Apsey, J T (WP) 1933 *A* 4,5, 1938 *BI* 2
Ashley, S (WP) 1903 *BI* 2
Aston, F T D (Tvl) 1896 *BI* 1,2,3,4
Atherton, S (N) 1993 *Arg* 1,2, 1994 *E* 1,2, *NZ* 1,2,3
Aucamp, J (WT) 1924 *BI* 1,2

Baard, A P (WP) 1960 *I*
Babrow, L (WP) 1937 *A* 1,2, *NZ* 1,2,3
Badenhorst, C (OFS) 1994 *Arg* 2, 1995 *WS* (R)
Barnard, A S (EP) 1984 *S Am* 1,2, 1986 *Cv* 1,2
Barnard, J H (Tvl) 1965 *S, A* 1,2, *NZ* 3,4
Barnard, R W (Tvl) 1970 *NZ* 2 (R)
Barnard, W H M (NT) 1949 *NZ* 4, 1951 *W*
Barry, J (WP) 1903 *BI* 1,2,3
Bartmann, W J (Tvl, N) 1986 *Cv* 1,2,3,4, 1992 *NZ, A, F*, 1,2
Bastard, W E (N) 1937 *A* 1, *NZ* 1,2,3, 1938 *BI* 1,3
Bates, A J (WT) 1969 *E*, 1970 *NZ* 1,2, 1972 *E*
Bayvel, P C R (Tvl) 1974 *BI* 2,4, *F* 1,2, 1975 *F* 1,2, 1976 *NZ* 1,2,3,4
Beck, J J (WP) 1981 *NZ* 2 (R), 3 (R), *US*
Bedford, T P (N) 1963 *A* 1,2,3,4, 1964 *W, F*, 1965 *I, A* 1,2, 1968 *BI* 1,2,3,4, *F* 1,2, 1969 *A* 1,2,3,4, *S, E*, 1970 *I, W*, 1971 *F* 1,2
Bekker, H J (WP) 1981 *NZ* 1,3
Bekker, H P J (NT) 1952 *E, F*, 1953 *A* 1,2,3,4, 1955 *BI* 2,3,4, 1956 *A* 1,2, *NZ* 1,2,3,4
Bekker, M J (NT) 1960 *S*
Bekker, R P (NT) 1953 *A* 3,4
Bergh, W F (SWD) 1931 *W, I*, 1932 *E, S*, 1933 *A* 1,2,3,4,5, 1937 *A* 1,2, *NZ* 1,2,3, 1938 *BI* 1,2,3
Bestbier, A (OFS) 1974 *F* 2 (R)
Bester, J J N (WP) 1924 *BI* 2,4
Bester, J L A (WP) 1938 *BI* 2,3
Beswick, A M (Bor) 1896 *BI* 2,3,4
Bezuidenhoudt, C E (NT) 1962 *BI* 2,3,4
Bezuidenhoudt, N S E (NT) 1972 *E*, 1974 *BI* 2,3,4, *F* 1,2, 1975 *F* 1,2, 1977 *Wld*
Bierman, J N (Tvl) 1931 *I*
Bisset, W M (WP) 1891 *BI* 1,3
Blair, R (WP) 1977 *Wld*
Bosch, G R (Tvl) 1974 *BI* 2, *F* 1,2, 1975 *F* 1,2, 1976 *NZ* 1,2,3,4

Bosman, N J S (Tvl) 1924 *BI* 2,3,4
Botha, D S (NT) 1981 *NZ* 1
Botha, H E (NT) 1980 *S Am* 1,2, *BI* 1,2,3,4, *S Am* 3,4, *F*, 1981 *I* 1,2, *NZ* 1,2,3, *US*, 1982 *S Am* 1,2, 1986 *Cv* 1,2,3,4, 1989 *Wld* 1,2, 1992 *NZ, A, F*, 1,2, *E*
Botha, J A (Tvl) 1903 *BI* 3
Botha, J P F (NT) 1962 *BI* 2,3,4
Botha, P H (Tvl) 1965 *A* 1,2
Boyes, H C (GW) 1891 *BI* 1,2
Brand, G H (WP) 1928 *NZ* 2,3, 1931 *W, I*, 1932 *E, S*, 1933 *A* 1,2,3,4,5, 1937 *A* 1,2, *NZ* 2,3, 1938 *BI* 1
Bredenkamp, M J (GW) 1896 *BI* 1,3
Breedt, J C (Tvl) 1986 *Cv* 1,2,3,4, 1989 *Wld* 1,2, 1992 *NZ, A*
Brewis, J D (NT) 1949 *NZ* 1,2,3,4, 1951 *S, I, W*, 1952 *E, F*, 1953 *A* 1
Briers, T P D (WP) 1955 *BI* 1,2,3,4, 1956 *NZ* 2,3,4
Brink, D J (WP) 1906 *S, W, E*
Brink, R (WP) 1995 [*R, C*]
Brooks, D (Bor) 1906 *S*
Brown, C B (WP) 1903 *BI* 1,2,3
Brynard, G S (WP) 1965 *A* 1, *NZ* 1,2,3,4, 1968 *BI* 3,4
Buchler, J U (Tvl) 1951 *S, I, W*, 1952 *E, F*, 1953 *A* 1,2,3,4, 1956 *A* 2
Burdett, A F (WP) 1906 *S, I*
Burger, J M (WP) 1989 *Wld* 1,2
Burger, M B (NT) 1980 *BI* 2 (R), *S Am* 3, 1981 *US* (R)
Burger, S W P (WP) 1984 *E* 1,2, 1986 *Cv* 1,2,3,4
Burger, W A G (Bor) 1906 *S, I, W*, 1910 *BI* 2

Carelse, G (EP) 1964 *W, F*, 1965 *I, S*, 1967 *F* 1,2,3, 1968 *F* 1,2, 1969 *A* 1,2,3,4, *S*
Carlson, R A (WP) 1972 *E*
Carolin, H W (WP) 1903 *BI* 3, 1906 *S, I*
Castens, H H (WP) 1891 *BI* 1
Chignell, T W (WP) 1891 *BI* 3
Cilliers, G D (OFS) 1963 *A* 1,3,4
Claassen, J T (WT) 1955 *BI* 1,2,3,4, 1956 *A* 1,2, *NZ* 1,2,3,4, 1958 *F* 1,2, 1960 *S, NZ* 1,2,3, *W, I*, 1961 *E, S, F, I, A* 1,2, 1962 *BI* 1,2,3,4
Claassen, W (N) 1981 *I* 1,2, *NZ* 2,3, *US*, 1982 *S Am* 1,2
Clark, W H G (Tvl) 1933 *A* 3
Clarkson, W A (N) 1921 *NZ* 1,2, 1924 *BI* 1
Cloete, H A (WP) 1896 *BI* 4
Cockrell, C H (WP) 1969 *S*, 1970 *I, W*
Cockrell, R J (WP) 1974 *F* 1,2, 1975 *F* 1,2, 1976 *NZ* 1,2, 1977 *Wld*, 1981 *NZ* 1,2 (R), 3, *US*
Coetzee, J H H (WP) 1974 *BI* 1, 1975 *F* 2 (R), 1976 *NZ* 1,2,3,4
Cope, D K (Tvl) 1896 *BI* 2
Cotty, W (GW) 1896 *BI* 3
Crampton, G (GW) 1903 *BI* 2
Craven, D H (WP) 1931 *W, I*, 1932 *S*, 1933 *A* 1,2,3,4,5, 1937 *A* 1,2, *NZ* 1,2,3, 1938 *BI* 1,2,3,
Cronje, P A (Tvl) 1971 *F* 1,2, *A* 1,2,3, 1974 *BI* 3,4
Crosby, J H (Tvl) 1896 *BI* 1
Crosby, N J (Tvl) 1910 *BI* 1,3
Currie, C (GW) 1903 *BI* 2

D'Alton, G (WP) 1933 *A* 1
Dalton, J (Tvl) 1994 *Arg* 1 (R), 1995 [*A, C*], *W, It, E*
Daneel, G M (WP) 1928 *NZ* 1,2,3,4, 1931 *W, I*, 1932 *E, S*
Daneel, H J (WP) 1906 *S, I, W, E*
Davison, P M (EP) 1910 *BI* 1
De Bruyn, J (OFS) 1974 *BI* 2
De Jongh, H P K (WP) 1928 *NZ* 3
De Klerk, I J (Tvl) 1969 *E*, 1970 *I, W*
De Klerk, K B H (Tvl) 1974 *BI* 1,2,3 (R), 1975 *F* 1,2, 1976 *NZ* 2 (R), 3,4, 1980 *S Am* 1,2, *BI* 2, 1981 *I* 1,2
De Kock, A N (GW) 1891 *BI* 2
De Kock, J S (WP) 1921 *NZ* 3, 1924 *BI* 3
Delport, W H (EP) 1951 *S, I, W*, 1952 *E, F*, 1953 *A* 1,2,3,4
De Melker, S C (GW) 1903 *BI* 2, 1906 *E*
Devenish, C E (GW) 1896 *BI* 2
Devenish, G St L (Tvl) 1896 *BI* 2
Devenish, M J (Tvl) 1891 *BI* 1
De Villiers, D I (Tvl) 1910 *BI* 1,2,3
De Villiers, D J (WP, Bol) 1962 *BI* 2,3, 1965 *I, NZ* 1,3,4, 1967 *F* 1,2,3,4, 1968 *BI* 1,2,3,4, *F* 1,2, 1969 *A* 1,4, *E*, 1970 *I, W, NZ* 1,2,3,4
De Villiers, H A (WP) 1906 *S, W, E*
De Villiers, H O (WP) 1967 *F* 1,2,3,4, 1968 *F* 1,2, 1969 *A* 1,2,3,4, *S, E*, 1970 *I, W*
De Villiers, P du P (WP) 1928 *NZ* 1,3,4, 1932 *E*, 1933 *A* 4, 1937 *A* 1,2, *NZ* 1
Devine, D (Tvl) 1924 *BI* 3, 1928 *NZ* 2
De Vos, D J J (WP) 1965 *S*, 1969 *A* 3, *S*
De Waal, A N (WP) 1967 *F* 1,2,3,4
De Waal, P J (WP) 1896 *BI* 4
De Wet, A E (WP) 1969 *A* 3,4, *E*
De Wet, P J (WP) 1938 *BI* 1,2,3
Dinkelmann, E E (NT) 1951 *S, I*, 1952 *E, F*, 1953 *A* 1,2
Dirksen, C W (NT) 1963 *A* 4, 1964 *W*, 1965 *I, S*, 1967 *F* 1,2,3,4, 1968 *BI* 1,2
Dobbin, F J (GW) 1903 *BI* 1,2, 1906 *S, W, E*, 1910 *BI* 1, 1912 *S, I, W*
Dobie, J A R (Tvl) 1928 *NZ* 2
Dormehl, P J (WP) 1896 *BI* 3,4
Douglass, F W (EP) 1896 *BI* 1
Drotské, A E (OFS) 1993 *Arg* 2, 1995 [*WS* (R)]
Dryburgh, R G (WP) 1955 *BI* 2,3,4, 1956 *A* 2, *NZ* 1,4, 1960 *NZ* 1,2
Duff, B R (WP) 1891 *BI* 1,2,3
Duffy, B A (Bor) 1928 *NZ* 1
Du Plessis, C J (WP) 1982 *S Am* 1,2, 1984 *E* 1,2, *S Am* 1,2, 1986 *Cv* 1,2,3,4, 1989 *Wld* 1,2
Du Plessis, D C (NT) 1977 *Wld*, 1980 *S Am* 2
Du Plessis, F (Tvl) 1949 *NZ* 1,2,3
Du Plessis, M (WP) 1971 *A* 1,2,3, 1974 *BI* 1,2, *F* 1,2, 1975 *F* 1,2, 1976 *NZ* 1,2,3,4, 1977 *Wld*, 1980 *S Am* 1,2, *BI* 1,2,3,4, *S Am* 4, *F*
Du Plessis, M J (WP) 1984 *S Am* 1,2, 1986 *Cv* 1,2,3,4, 1989 *Wld* 1,2
Du Plessis, N J (WT) 1921 *NZ* 2,3, 1924 *BI* 1,2,3
Du Plessis, P G (NT) 1972 *E*
Du Plessis, T D (NT) 1980 *S Am* 1,2
Du Plessis, W (WP) 1980 *S Am* 1,2, *BI* 1,2,3,4, *S Am* 3,4, *F*, 1981 *NZ* 1,2,3, 1982 *S Am* 1,2
Du Plooy, A J J (EP) 1955 *BI* 1
Du Preez, F C H (NT) 1961 *E, S, A* 1,2, 1962 *BI* 1,2,3,4, 1963 *A* 1, 1964 *W, F*, 1965 *I, A* 1,2, *NZ* 1,2,3,4, 1967 *F* 4, 1968 *BI* 1,2,3,4, *F* 1,2, 1969 *A* 1,2, *S*, 1970 *I, W, NZ* 1,2,3,4, 1971 *F* 1,2, *A* 1,2,3
Du Preez, J G H (WP) 1956 *NZ* 1
Du Preez, R J (N) 1992 *NZ, A*, 1993 *F* 1,2, *A* 1,2,3
Du Rand, J A (R, NT) 1949 *NZ* 2,3, 1951 *S, I, W*, 1952 *E, F*, 1953 *A* 1,2,3,4, 1955 *BI* 1,2,3,4, 1956 *A* 1,2, *NZ* 1,2,3,4
Du Randt, J P (OFS) 1994 *Arg* 1,2, *S, W*, 1995 *WS*, [*A, WS, F, NZ*]
Du Toit, A F (WP) 1928 *NZ* 3,4
Du Toit, B A (Tvl) 1938 *BI* 1,2,3
Du Toit, P A (NT) 1949 *NZ* 2,3,4, 1951 *S, I, W*, 1952 *E, F*
Du Toit, P G (WP) 1981 *NZ* 1, 1982 *S Am* 1,2, 1984 *E* 1,2
Du Toit, P S (WP) 1958 *F* 1,2, 1960 *NZ* 1,2,3,4, *W, I*, 1961 *E, S, F, I, A* 1,2
Duvenhage, F P (GW) 1949 *NZ* 1,3

Edwards, P (NT) 1980 *S Am* 1,2
Ellis, J H (SWA) 1965 *NZ* 1,2,3,4, 1967 *F* 1,2,3,4, 1968 *BI* 1,2,3,4, *F* 1,2, 1969 *A* 1,2,3,4, *S*, 1970 *I, W, NZ* 1,2,3,4, 1971 *F* 1,2, *A* 1,2,3, 1972 *E*, 1974 *BI* 1,2,3,4, *F* 1,2, 1976 *NZ* 1
Ellis, M C (Tvl) 1921 *NZ* 2,3, 1924 *BI* 1,2,3,4

Engelbrecht, J P (WP) 1960 *S, W, I*, 1961 *E, S, F, A* 1,2, 1962 *BI* 2,3,4, 1963 *A* 2,3, 1964 *W, F*, 1965 *I, S, A* 1,2, *NZ* 1,2,3,4, 1967 *F* 1,2,3,4, 1968 *BI* 1,2, *F* 1,2, 1969 *A* 1,2
Erasmus, F S (NT, EP) 1986 *Cv* 3,4, 1989 *Wld* 2
Etlinger, T E (WP) 1896 *BI* 4

Ferreira, C (OFS) 1986 *Cv* 1,2
Ferreira, P S (WP) 1984 *S Am* 1,2
Ferris, H H (Tvl) 1903 *BI* 3
Forbes, H H (Tvl) 1896 *BI* 2
Fourie, C (EP) 1974 *F* 1,2, 1975 *F* 1,2
Fourie, T T (SET) 1974 *BI* 3
Fourie, W L (SWA) 1958 *F* 1,2
Francis, J A J (Tvl) 1912 *S, I, W*, 1913 *E, F*
Frederickson, C A (Tvl) 1974 *BI* 2, 1980 *S Am* 1,2
Frew, A (Tvl) 1903 *BI* 1
Froneman, D C (OFS) 1977 *Wld*
Froneman, I L (Bor) 1933 *A* 1
Fuls, H T (Tvl, EP) 1992 *NZ* (R), 1993 *F* 1,2, *A* 1,2,3, *Arg* 1,2
Fry, S P (WP) 1951 *S, I, W*, 1952 *E, F*, 1953 *A* 1,2,3,4, 1955 *BI* 1,2,3,4

Gage, J H (OFS) 1933 *A* 1
Gainsford, J L (WP) 1960 *S, NZ* 1,2,3,4, *W, I*, 1961 *E, S, F, A* 1,2, 1962 *BI* 1,2,3,4, 1963 *A* 1,2,3,4, 1964 *W, F*, 1965 *I, S, A* 1,2, *NZ* 1,2,3,4, 1967 *F* 1,2,3
Geel, P A (OFS) 1949 *NZ* 3
Geere, V (Tvl) 1933 *A* 1,2,3,4,5
Geffin, A O (Tvl) 1949 *NZ* 1,2,3,4, 1951 *S, I, W*
Geldenhuys, A (EP) 1992 *NZ, A, F* 1,2
Geldenhuys, S B (NT) 1981 *NZ* 2,3, *US*, 1982 *S Am* 1,2, 1989 *Wld* 1,2
Gentles, T A (WP) 1955 *BI* 1,2,4, 1956 *NZ* 2,3, 1958 *F* 2
Geraghty, E M (Bor) 1949 *NZ* 4
Gerber, D M (EP, WP) 1980 *S Am* 3,4, *F*, 1981 *I* 1,2, *NZ* 1,2,3, *US*, 1982 *S Am* 1,2, 1984 *E* 1,2, *S Am* 1,2, 1986 *Cv* 1,2,3,4, 1992 *NZ, A, F* 1,2, *E*
Gerber, M C (EP) 1958 *F* 1,2, 1960 *S*
Gericke, F W (Tvl) 1960 *S*
Germishuys, J S (OFS, Tvl) 1974 *BI* 2, 1976 *NZ* 1,2,3,4, 1977 *Wld*, 1980 *S Am* 1,2, *BI* 1,2,3,4, *S Am* 3,4, *F*, 1981 *I* 1,2, *NZ* 2,3, *US*
Gibbs, B (GW) 1903 *BI* 2
Goosen, C P (OFS) 1965 *NZ* 2
Gorton, H C (Tvl) 1896 *BI* 1
Gould, R L (N) 1968 *BI* 1,2,3,4
Gray, B G (WP) 1931 *W*, 1932 *E, S*, 1933 *A* 5
Greenwood, C M (WP) 1961 *I*
Greyling, P J F (OFS) 1967 *F* 1,2,3,4, 1968 *BI* 1, *F* 1,2, 1969 *A* 1,2,3,4, *S, E*, 1970 *I, W, NZ* 1,2,3,4, 1971 *F* 1,2, *A* 1,2,3, 1972 *E*
Grobler, C J (OFS) 1974 *BI* 4, 1975 *F* 1,2
Guthrie, F H (WP) 1891 *BI* 1,3, 1896 *BI* 1

Hahn, C H L (Tvl) 1910 *BI* 1,2,3
Hamilton, F (EP) 1891 *BI* 1
Harris, T A (Tvl) 1937 *NZ* 2,3, 1938 *BI* 1,2,3
Hartley, A J (WP) 1891 *BI* 3
Hattingh, H (NT) 1992 *A* (R), *F* 2 (R), *E*, 1994 *Arg* 1,2
Hattingh, L B (OFS) 1933 *A* 2
Heatlie, B H (WP) 1891 *BI* 2,3, 1896 *BI* 1,4, 1903 *BI* 1,3
Hendriks, P (Tvl) 1992 *NZ, A*, 1994 *S, W*, 1995 [*A, R, C*]
Hepburn, T B (WP) 1896 *BI* 4
Heunis, J W (NT) 1981 *NZ* 3 (R), *US*, 1982 *S Am* 1,2, 1984 *E* 1,2, *S Am* 1,2, 1986 *Cv* 1,2,3,4, 1989 *Wld* 1,2
Hill, R A (R) 1960 *W, I*, 1961 *I, A* 1,2, 1962 *BI* 4, 1963 *A* 3
Hills, W G (NT) 1992 *F* 1,2, *E*, 1993 *F* 1,2, *A* 1
Hirsch, J G (EP) 1906 *I*, 1910 *BI* 1
Hobson, T E C (WP) 1903 *BI* 3
Hoffman, R S (Bol) 1953 *A* 3
Holton, D N (EP) 1960 *S*
Honiball, H W (N) 1993 *A* 3 (R), *Arg* 2, 1995 *WS* (R)
Hopwood, D J (WP) 1960 *S, NZ* 3,4, *W*, 1961 *E, S, F, I, A* 1,2, 1962 *BI* 1,2,3,4, 1963 *A* 1,2,4, 1964 *W, F*, 1965 *S, NZ* 3,4
Howe, B F (Bor) 1956 *NZ* 1,4
Howe-Browne, N R F G (WP) 1910 *BI* 1,2,3
Hugo, D P (WP) 1989 *Wld* 1,2
Hurter, M H (NT) 1995 [*R, C*], *W*

Immelman, J H (WP) 1913 *F*

Jackson, D C (WP) 1906 *I, W, E*

Jackson, J S (WP) 1903 *BI* 2
Jansen, E (OFS) 1981 *NZ* 1
Jansen, J S (OFS) 1970 *NZ* 1,2,3,4, 1971 *F* 1,2, *A* 1,2,3, 1972 *E*
Jennings, C B (Bor) 1937 *NZ* 1
Johnson, G K (Tvl) 1993 *Arg* 2, 1994 *NZ* 3, *Arg* 1, 1995 *WS*, [*R, C, WS*]
Johnstone, P G A (WP) 1951 *S, I, W*, 1952 *E, F*, 1956 *A* 1, *NZ* 1,2,4
Jones, C H (Tvl) 1903 *BI* 1,2
Jones, P S T (WP) 1896 *BI* 1,3,4
Jordaan, R P (NT) 1949 *NZ* 1,2,3,4
Joubert, A J (OFS, N) 1989 *Wld* 1 (R), 1993 *A* 3, *Arg* 1, 1994 *E* 1,2, *NZ* 1,2 (R), 3, *Arg* 2, *S, W*, 1995 [*A, C, WS, F, NZ*], *W, It, E*
Joubert, S J (WP) 1906 *I, W, E*

Kahts, W J H (NT) 1980 *BI* 1,2,3, *S Am* 3,4, *F*, 1981 *I* 1,2, *NZ* 2, 1982 *S Am* 1,2
Kaminer, J (Tvl) 1958 *F* 2
Kebble, G R (N) 1993 *Arg* 1,2, 1994 *NZ* 1 (R), 2
Kelly, E W (GW) 1896 *BI* 3
Kenyon, B J (Bor) 1949 *NZ* 4
Kipling, H G (GW) 1931 *W, I*, 1932 *E, S*, 1933 *A* 1,2,3,4,5
Kirkpatrick, A I (GW) 1953 *A* 2, 1956 *NZ* 2, 1958 *F* 1, 1960 *S, NZ* 1,2,3,4, *W, I*, 1961 *E, S, F*
Knight, A S (Tvl) 1912 *S, I, W*, 1913 *E, F*
Knoetze, F (WP) 1989 *Wld* 1,2
Koch, A C (Bol) 1949 *NZ* 2,3,4, 1951 *S, I, W*, 1952 *E, F*, 1953 *A* 1,2,4, 1955 *BI* 1,2,3,4, 1956 *A* 1, *NZ* 2,3, 1958 *F* 1,2, 1960 *NZ* 1,2
Koch, H V (WP) 1949 *NZ* 1,2,3,4
Kotze, G J M (WP) 1967 *F* 1,2,3,4
Krantz, E F W (OFS) 1976 *NZ* 1, 1981 *I* 1,
Krige, J D (Tvl) 1903 *BI* 1,3, 1906 *S, I, W*
Kritzinger, J L (Tvl) 1974 *BI* 3,4, *F* 1,2, 1975 *F* 1,2, 1976 *NZ* 4
Kroon, C M (EP) 1955 *BI* 1
Kruger, P E (Tvl) 1986 *Cv* 3,4
Kruger, R J (NT) 1993 *Arg* 1,2, 1994 *S, W*, 1995 *WS*, [*A, R, WS, F, NZ*], *W, It, E*
Kruger, T L (Tvl) 1921 *NZ* 1,2, 1924 *BI* 1,2,3,4, 1928 *NZ* 1,2
Kuhn, S P (Tvl) 1960 *NZ* 3,4, *W, I*, 1961 *E, S, F, I, A* 1,2, 1962 *BI* 1,2,3,4, 1963 *A* 1,2,3, 1965 *I, S*

La Grange, J B (WP) 1924 *BI* 3,4
Larard, A (Tvl) 1896 *BI* 2,4
Lategan, M T (WP) 1949 *NZ* 1,2,3,4, 1951 *S, I, W*, 1952 *E, F*, 1953 *A* 1,2
Laubscher, T G (WP) 1994 *Arg* 1,2, *S, W*, 1995 *It, E*
Lawless, M J (WP) 1964 *F*, 1969 *E* (R), 1970 *I, W*
Ledger, S H (GW) 1912 *S, I*, 1913 *E, F*
Le Roux, A H (OFS) 1994 *E* 1
Le Roux, H P (Tvl) 1993 *F* 1,2, 1994 *E* 1,2, *NZ* 1,2,3, *Arg* 2, *S, W*, 1995 *WS* [*A, R, C* (R), *WS, F, NZ*], *W, It, E*
Le Roux, J H S (Tvl) 1994 *E* 2, *NZ* 1,2
Le Roux, M (OFS) 1980 *BI* 1,2,3,4, *S Am* 3,4, *F*, 1981 *I* 1
Le Roux, P A (WP) 1906 *I, W, E*
Little, E M (GW) 1891 *BI* 1,3
Lochner, G P (WP) 1955 *BI* 3, 1956 *A* 1,2, *NZ* 1,2,3,4, 1958 *F* 1,2
Lochner, G P (EP) 1937 *NZ* 3, 1938 *BI* 1,2
Lockyear, R J (GW) 1960 *NZ* 1,2,3,4, 1960 *I*, 1961 *F*
Lombard, A C (EP) 1910 *BI* 2
Lötter, D (Tvl) 1993 *F* 2, *A* 1,2
Lotz, J W (Tvl) 1937 *A* 1,2, *NZ* 1,2,3, 1938 *BI* 1,2,3
Loubser, J A (WP) 1903 *BI* 3, 1906 *S, I, W, E*, 1910 *BI* 1,3
Lourens, M J (NT) 1968 *BI* 2,3,4
Louw, J S (Tvl) 1891 *BI* 1,2,3
Louw, M J (Tvl) 1971 *A* 2,3
Louw, M M (WP) 1928 *NZ* 3,4, 1931 *W, I*, 1932 *E, S*, 1933 *A* 1,2,3,4,5, 1937 *A* 1,2, *NZ* 2,3, 1938 *BI* 1,2,3
Louw, R J (WP) 1980 *S Am* 1,2, *BI* 1,2,3,4 *S Am* 3,4, *F*, 1981 *I* 1,2, *NZ* 1,3, 1982 *S Am* 1,2, 1984 *E* 1,2, *S Am* 1,2
Louw, S C (WP) 1933 *A* 1,2,3,4,5, 1937 *A* 1, *NZ* 1,2,3, 1938 *BI* 1,2,3
Luyt, F P (WP) 1910 *BI* 1,2,3, 1912 *S, I, W*, 1913 *E*
Luyt, J D (EP) 1912 *S, W*, 1913 *E, F*
Luyt, R R (W P) 1910 *BI* 2,3, 1912 *S, I, W*, 1913 *E, F*
Lyons, D J (EP) 1896 *BI* 1
Lyster, P J (N) 1933 *A* 2,5, 1937 *NZ* 1

McCallum, I D (WP) 1970 *NZ* 1,2,3,4, 1971 *F* 1,2, *A* 1,2,3, 1974 *BI* 1,2
McCallum, R J (WP) 1974 *BI* 1
McCulloch, J D (GW) 1913 *E, F*
MacDonald, A W (R) 1965 *A* 1, *NZ* 1,2,3,4
Macdonald, D A (WP) 1974 *BI* 2
Macdonald, I (Tvl) 1992 *NZ, A*, 1993 *F* 1, *A* 3, 1994 *E* 2, 1995 *WS* (R)
McDonald, J A J (WP) 1931 *W, I*, 1932 *E, S*
McEwan, W M C (Tvl) 1903 *BI* 1,3
McHardy, E E (OFS) 1912 *S, I, W*, 1913 *E, F*
McKendrick, J A (WP) 1891 *BI* 3
Malan, A S (Tvl) 1960 *NZ* 1,2,3,4, *W, I*, 1961 *E, S, F*, 1962 *BI* 1, 1963 *A* 1,2,3, 1964 *W*, 1965 *I, S*
Malan, A W (NT) 1989 *Wld* 1,2, 1992 *NZ, A, F* 1,2, *E*
Malan, E (NT) 1980 *BI* 3 (R), 4
Malan, G F (WP) 1958 *F* 2, 1960 *NZ* 1,3,4, 1961 *E, S, F*, 1962 *BI* 1,2,3, 1963 *A* 1,2,4, 1964 *W*, 1965 *A* 1,2, *NZ* 1,2
Malan, P (Tvl) 1949 *NZ* 4
Mallett, N V H (WP) 1984 *S Am* 1,2
Mans, W J (WP) 1965 *I, S*
Marais, F P (Bol) 1949 *NZ* 1,2, 1951 *S*, 1953 *A* 1,2
Marais, J F K (WP) 1963 *A* 3, 1964 *W, F*, 1965 *I, S, A* 2, 1968 *BI*, 1,2,3,4, *F* 1,2, 1969 *A* 1,2,3,4, *S, E*, 1970 *I, W, NZ* 1,2,3,4, 1971 *F* 1,2, *A* 1,2,3, 1974 *BI* 1,2,3,4, *F* 1,2
Maré, D S (Tvl) 1906 *S*
Marsberg, A F W (GW) 1906 *S, W, E*
Marsberg, P A (GW) 1910 *BI* 1
Martheze, W C (GW) 1903 *BI* 2, 1906 *I, W*
Martin, H J (Tvl) 1937 *A* 2
Mellet, T B (GW) 1896 *BI* 2
Mellish, F W (WP) 1921 *NZ* 1,3, 1924 *BI* 1,2,3,4
Merry, J (EP) 1891 *BI* 1
Metcalf, H D (Bor) 1903 *BI* 2
Meyer, C du P (WP) 1921 *NZ* 1,2,3
Meyer, P J (GW) 1896 *BI* 1
Michau, J M (Tvl) 1921 *NZ* 1
Michau, J P (WP) 1921 *NZ* 1,2,3
Millar, W A (WP) 1906 *E*, 1910 *BI* 2,3, 1912 *I, W*, 1913 *F*
Mills, W J (WP) 1910 *BI* 2
Moll, T (Tvl) 1910 *BI* 2
Montini, P E (WP) 1956 *A* 1,2
Moolman, L C (NT) 1977 *Wld*, 1980 *S Am* 1,2, *BI* 1,2,3,4, *S Am* 3,4, *F*, 1981 *I* 1,2, *NZ* 1,2,3, *US*, 1982 *S Am* 1,2, 1984 *S Am* 1,2, 1986 *Cv* 1,2,3,4
Mordt, R H (Z-R, NT) 1980 *S Am* 1,2, *BI* 1,2,3,4, *S Am* 3,4, *F*, 1981 *I* 2, *NZ* 1,2,3, *US*, 1982 *S Am* 1,2, 1984 *S Am* 1,2
Morkel, D A (Tvl) 1903 *BI* 1
Morkel, D F T (Tvl) 1906 *I, E*, 1910 *BI* 1,3, 1912 *S, I, W*, 1913 *E, F*
Morkel, H J (WP) 1921 *NZ* 1
Morkel, H W (WP) 1921 *NZ* 1,2
Morkel, J A (WP) 1921 *NZ* 2,3
Morkel, J W H (WP) 1912 *S, I, W*, 1913 *E, F*
Morkel, P G (WP) 1912 *S, I, W*, 1913 *E, F*, 1921 *NZ* 1,2,3
Morkel, P K (WP) 1928 *NZ* 4
Morkel, W H (WP) 1910 *BI* 3, 1912 *S, I, W*, 1913 *E, F*, 1921 *NZ* 1,2,3
Morkel, W S (Tvl) 1906 *S, I, W, E*
Moss, C (N) 1949 *NZ* 1,2,3,4
Mostert, P J (WP) 1921 *NZ* 1,2,3, 1924 *BI* 1,2,4, 1928 *NZ* 1,2,3,4, 1931 *W, I*, 1932 *E, S*
Mulder, J C (Tvl) 1994 *NZ* 2,3, *S, W*, 1995 *WS*, [*A, WS, F, NZ*], *W, It, E*
Muller, G H (WP) 1969 *A* 3,4, *S*, 1970 *W, NZ* 1,2,3,4, 1971 *F* 1,2, 1972 *E*, 1974 *BI* 1,3,4
Muller, H L (OFS) 1986 *Cv* 4 (R), 1989 *Wld* 1 (R)
Muller, H S V (Tvl) 1949 *NZ* 1,2,3,4, 1951 *S, I, W*, 1952 *E, F*, 1953 *A* 1,2,3,4
Muller, L J J (N) 1992 *NZ, A*
Muller, P G (N) 1992 *NZ, A, F* 1,2, *E*, 1993 *F* 1,2, *A* 1,2,3, *Arg* 1,2, 1994 *E* 1,2, *NZ* 1, *S, W*
Myburgh, F R (EP) 1896 *BI* 1
Myburgh, J L (NT) 1962 *BI* 1, 1963 *A* 4, 1964 *W, F*, 1968 *BI* 1,2,3, *F* 1,2, 1969 *A* 1,2, *E*, 1970 *I, W, NZ* 3,4
Myburgh, W H (WT) 1924 *BI* 1

Naude, J P (WP) 1963 *A* 4, 1965 *A* 1,2, *NZ* 1,3,4, 1967 *F* 1,2,3,4, 1968 *BI* 1,2,3,4
Neethling, J B (WP) 1967 *F* 1,2,3,4, 1968 *BI* 4, 1969 *S*, 1970 *NZ* 1,2
Nel, J A (Tvl) 1960 *NZ* 1,2, 1963 *A* 1,2, 1965 *A* 2, *NZ* 1,2,3,4, 1970 *NZ* 3,4

Nel, J J (WP) 1956 *A* 1,2, *NZ* 1,2,3,4, 1958 *F* 1,2
Nel, P A R O (Tvl) 1903 *BI* 1,2,3
Nel, P J (N) 1928 *NZ* 1,2,3,4, 1931 *W, I*, 1932 *E, S*, 1933 *A* 1,3,4,5, 1937 *A* 1,2, *NZ* 2,3
Nimb, C F (WP) 1961 *I*
Nomis, S H (Tvl) 1967 *F* 4, 1968 *BI* 1,2,3,4, *F* 1,2, 1969 *A* 1,2,3,4, *S, E*, 1970 *I, W, NZ* 1,2,3,4, 1971 *F* 1,2, *A* 1,2,3, 1972 *E*
Nykamp, J L (Tvl) 1933 *A* 2

Ochse, J K (WP) 1951 *I, W*, 1952 *E, F*, 1953 *A* 1,2,4
Oelofse, J S A (Tvl) 1953 *A* 1,2,3,4
Oliver, J F (Tvl) 1928 *NZ* 3,4
Olivier, E (WP) 1967 *F* 1,2,3,4, 1968 *BI* 1,2,3,4, *F* 1,2, 1969 *A* 1,2,3,4, *S, E*
Olivier, J (NT) 1992 *F* 1,2, *E*, 1993 *F* 1,2 *A* 1,2,3, *Arg* 1, 1995 *W, It* (R), *E*
Olver, E (EP) 1896 *BI* 1
Oosthuizen, J J (WP) 1974 *BI* 1, *F* 1,2, 1975 *F* 1,2, 1976 *NZ* 1,2,3,4
Oosthuizen, O W (NT, Tvl) 1981 *I* 1 (R), 2, *NZ* 2,3, *US*, 1982 *S Am* 1,2, 1984 *E* 1,2
Osler, B L (WP) 1924 *BI* 1,2,3, 1928 *NZ* 1,2,3,4, 1931 *W, I*, 1932 *E, S*, 1933 *A* 1,2,3,4,5
Osler, S G (WP) 1928 *NZ* 1
Otto, K (NT) 1995 [*R, C* (R), *WS* (R)]
Oxlee, K (N) 1960 *NZ* 1,2,3,4, *W, I*, 1961 *S, A* 1,2, 1962 *BI* 1,2,3,4, 1963 *A* 1,2,4, 1964 *W*, 1965 *NZ* 1,2

Pagel, G L (WP) 1995 [*A* (R), *R, C, NZ* (R)]
Parker, W H (EP) 1965 *A* 1,2
Partridge, J E C (Tvl) 1903 *BI* 1
Payn, C (N) 1924 *BI* 1,2
Pelser, H J M (Tvl) 1958 *F* 1, 1960 *NZ* 1,2,3,4, *W, I*, 1961 *F, I, A* 1,2
Pfaff, B D (WP) 1956 *A* 1
Pickard, J A J (WP) 1953 *A* 3,4, 1956 *NZ* 2, 1958 *F* 2
Pienaar, J F (Tvl) 1993 *F* 1,2, *A* 1,2,3, *Arg* 1,2, 1994 *E* 1,2, *NZ* 2,3, *Arg* 1,2, *S, W*, 1995 *WS*, [*A, C, WS, F, NZ*], *W, It, E*
Pienaar, Z M J (OFS) 1980 *S Am* 2 (R), *BI* 1,2,3,4, *S Am* 3,4, *F*, 1981 *I* 1,2, *NZ* 1,2,3
Pitzer, G (NT) 1967 *F* 1,2,3,4, 1968 *BI* 1,2,3,4, *F* 1,2, 1969 *A* 3,4
Pope, C F (WP) 1974 *BI* 1,2,3,4, 1975 *F* 1,2, 1976 *NZ* 2,3,4
Potgieter, H J (OFS) 1928 *NZ* 1,2
Potgieter, H L (OFS) 1977 *Wld*
Powell, A W (GW) 1896 *BI* 3
Powell, J M (GW) 1891 *BI* 2, 1896 *BI* 3, 1903 *BI* 2
Prentis, R B (Tvl) 1980 *S Am* 1,2, *BI* 1,2,3,4, *S Am* 3,4, *F*, 1981 *I* 1,2
Pretorius, N F (Tvl) 1928 *NZ* 1,2,3,4
Prinsloo, J (Tvl) 1958 *F* 1,2
Prinsloo, J (NT) 1963 *A* 3
Prinsloo, J P (Tvl) 1928 *NZ* 1
Putter, D J (WT) 1963 *A* 1,2,4

Raaff, J W E (GW) 1903 *BI* 1,2, 1906 *S, W, E*, 1910 *BI* 1
Ras, W J de Wet (OFS) 1976 *NZ* 1 (R), 1980 *S Am* 2 (R)
Reece-Edwards, H (N) 1992 *F* 1,2, 1993 *A* 2
Reid, A (WP) 1903 *BI* 3
Reid, B C (Bor) 1933 *A* 4
Reinach, J (OFS) 1986 *Cv* 1,2,3,4
Rens, I J (Tvl) 1953 *A* 3,4
Retief, D F (NT) 1955 *BI* 1,2,4, 1956 *A* 1,2, *NZ* 1,2,3,4
Reyneke, H J (WP) 1910 *BI* 3
Richards, A R (WP) 1891 *BI* 1,2,3
Richter, A (NT) 1992 *F* 1,2, *E*, 1994 *E* 2, *NZ* 1,2,3, 1995 [*R, C, WS* (R)]
Riley, N M (ET) 1963 *A* 3
Riordan, C A (Tvl) 1910 *BI* 1,2
Robertson, I W (R) 1974 *F* 1,2, 1976 *NZ* 1,2,4
Rodgers, P H (NT, Tvl) 1989 *Wld* 1,2, 1992 *NZ, F* 1,2
Rogers, C D (Tvl) 1984 *E* 1,2, *S Am* 1,2
Roos, G D (WP) 1910 *BI* 2,3
Roos, P J (WP) 1903 *BI* 3, 1906 *I, W, E*
Rosenberg, W (Tvl) 1955 *BI* 2,3,4, 1956 *NZ* 3, 1958 *F* 1
Rossouw, C L C (Tvl) 1995 *WS*, [*R, WS, F, NZ*]
Rossouw, D H (WP) 1953 *A* 3, 4
Rousseau, W P (WP) 1928 *NZ* 3,4
Roux, F du T (WP) 1960 *W*, 1961 *A* 1,2, 1962 *BI* 1,2,3,4, 1963 *A* 2, 1965 *A* 1,2, *NZ* 1,2,3,4, 1968 *BI* 3,4, *F* 1,2 1969 *A* 1,2,3,4, 1970 *I, NZ* 1,2,3,4

Roux, J P (Tvl) 1994 *E* 2, *NZ* 1,2,3, *Arg* 1, 1995 [*R, C, F* (R)]
Roux, O A (NT) 1969 *S, E*, 1970 *I, W*, 1972 *E*, 1974 *BI* 3,4

Samuels, T A (GW) 1896 *BI* 2,3,4
Sauermann, J T (Tvl) 1971 *F* 1,2, *A* 1, 1972 *E*, 1974 *BI* 1
Schlebusch, J J J (OFS) 1974 *BI* 3,4, 1975 *F* 2
Schmidt, L U (NT) 1958 *F* 2, 1962 *BI* 2
Schmidt, U L (NT, Tvl) 1986 *Cv* 1,2,3,4, 1989 *Wld* 1,2, 1992 *NZ, A*, 1993 *F* 1,2, *A* 1,2,3, 1994 *Arg* 1,2, *S, W*
Schoeman, J (WP) 1963 *A* 3,4, 1965 *I, S, A* 1, *NZ* 1,2
Scholtz, C P (WP, Tvl) 1994 *Arg* 1, 1995 [*R, C, WS*]
Scholtz, H H (WP) 1921 *NZ* 1,2
Schutte, P J W (Tvl) 1994 *S, W*
Scott, P A (Tvl) 1896 *BI* 1,2,3,4
Sendin, W D (GW) 1921 *NZ* 2
Serfontein, D J (WP) 1980 *BI* 1,2,3,4, *S Am* 3,4, *F*, 1981 *I* 1,2, *NZ* 1,2,3, *US*, 1982 *S Am* 1,2, 1984 *E* 1,2, *S Am* 1,2
Shand, R (GW) 1891 *BI* 2,3
Sheriff, A R (Tvl) 1938 *BI* 1,2,3
Shum, E H (Tvl) 1913 *E*
Sinclair, D J (Tvl) 1955 *BI* 1,2,3,4
Sinclair, J H (Tvl) 1903 *BI* 1
Skene, A L (WP) 1958 *F* 2
Slater, J T (EP) 1924 *BI* 3,4, 1928 *NZ* 1
Smal, G P (WP) 1986 *Cv* 1,2,3,4, 1989 *Wld* 1,2
Small, J T (Tvl, N) 1992 *NZ, A, F* 1,2, *E*, 1993 *F* 1,2, *A* 1,2,3, *Arg* 1,2, 1994 *E* 1,2, *NZ* 1,2,3 (t), *Arg* 1, 1995 *WS*, [*A, R, F, NZ*], *W, It, E* (R)
Smit, F C (WP) 1992 *E*
Smith, C M (OFS) 1963 *A* 3,4, 1964 *W, F*, 1965 *A* 1,2, *NZ* 2
Smith, C W (GW) 1891 *BI* 2, 1896 *BI* 2,3
Smith, D (GW) 1891 *BI* 2
Smith D J (Z-R) 1980 *BI* 1,2,3,4
Smith, G A C (EP) 1938 *BI* 3
Smollan, F C (Tvl) 1933 *A* 3,4,5
Snedden, R C D (GW) 1891 *BI* 2
Snyman, D S L (WP) 1972 *E*, 1974 *BI* 1,2 (R), *F* 1,2, 1975 *F* 1,2, 1976 *NZ* 2,3, 1977 *Wld*
Snyman, J C P (OFS) 1974 *BI* 2,3,4
Sonnekus, G H H (OFS) 1974 *BI* 3, 1984 *E* 1,2
Spies, J J (NT) 1970 *NZ* 1,2,3,4
Stander, J C J (OFS) 1974 *BI* 4 (R), 1976 *NZ* 1,2,3,4
Stapelberg, W P (NT) 1974 *F* 1,2
Starke, J J (WP) 1924 *NZ* 4
Starke, K T (WP) 1924 *BI* 1,2,3,4
Steenekamp, J G A (Tvl) 1958 *F* 1
Stegmann, A C (WP) 1906 *S, I*
Stegmann, J A (Tvl) 1912 *S, I, W*, 1913 *E, F*
Stewart, D A (WP) 1960 *S*, 1961 *E, S, F, I*, 1963 *A* 1,3,4, 1964 *W, F*, 1965 *I*
Stofberg, M T S (OFS, NT, WP) 1976 *NZ* 2,3, 1977 *Wld*, 1980 *S Am* 1,2, *BI* 1,2,3,4, *S Am* 3,4, *F*, 1981 *I* 1,2, *NZ* 1,2, *US*, 1982 *S Am* 1,2, 1984 *E* 1,2
Strachan, L C (Tvl) 1932 *E, S*, 1937 *A* 1,2, *NZ* 1,2,3, 1938 *BI* 1,2,3
Stransky, J (N, WP) 1993 *A* 1,2,3, *Arg* 1, 1994 *Arg* 1,2, 1995 *WS*, [*A, R* (t), *C, F, NZ*], *W, It, E*
Straeuli, R A W (Tvl) 1994 *NZ* 1, *Arg* 1,2, *S, W*, 1995 *WS*, [*A, WS, NZ* (R)], *E* (R)
Strauss, C P (WP) 1992 *F* 1,2, *E*, 1993 *F* 1,2, *A* 1,2,3, *Arg* 1,2, 1994 *E* 1, *NZ* 1,2, *Arg* 1,2
Strauss, J A (WP) 1984 *S Am* 1,2
Strauss, J H P (Tvl) 1976 *NZ* 3,4, 1980 *S Am* 1
Strauss, S S F (GW) 1921 *NZ* 3
Strydom, C F (OFS) 1955 *BI* 3, 1956 *A* 1,2, *NZ* 1,4, 1958 *F* 1,
Strydom, J (Tvl) 1993 *F* 2, *A* 1,2,3, *Arg* 1,2, 1994 *E* 1, 1995 [*A, C, F, NZ*]
Strydom, L J (NT) 1949 *NZ* 1,2
Styger, J J (OFS) 1992 *NZ* (R), *A, F* 1,2, *E*, 1993 *F* 2 (R), *A* 3 (R)
Suter, M R (N) 1965 *I, S*
Swart, J J N (SWA) 1955 *BI* 1
Swart, I S (Tvl) 1993 *A* 1,2,3, *Arg* 1, 1994 *E* 1,2, *NZ* 1,3, *Arg* 2, 1995 *WS*, [*A, WS, F, NZ*], *W*

Taberer, W S (GW) 1896 *BI* 2
Taylor, O B (N) 1962 *BI* 1
Teichmann, G H (N) 1995 *W*
Theunissen, D J (GW) 1896 *BI* 3
Thompson, G (WP) 1912 *S, I, W*
Tindall, J C (WP) 1924 *BI* 1, 1928 *NZ* 1,2,3,4

Tobias, E G (SARF, Bol) 1981 *I* 1,2, 1984 *E* 1,2, *S Am* 1,2
Tod, N S (N) 1928 *NZ* 2
Townsend, W H (N) 1921 *NZ* 1
Trenery, W E (GW) 1891 *BI* 2
Truter, D R (WP) 1924 *BI* 2,4
Truter, J T (N) 1963 *A* 1, 1964 *F*, 1965 *A* 2
Turner, F G (EP) 1933 *A* 1,2,3, 1937 *A* 1,2, *NZ* 1,2,3, 1938 *BI* 1,2,3
Twigge, R J (NT) 1960 *S*

Ulyate, C A (Tvl) 1955 *BI* 1,2,3,4, 1956 *NZ* 1,2,3
Uys, P de W (NT) 1960 *W*, 1961 *E, S, I, A* 1,2, 1962 *BI* 1,4, 1963 *A* 1,2, 1969 *A* 1 (R), 2

Van Aswegen, H J (WP) 1981 *NZ* 1, 1982 *S Am* 2 (R)
Van Broekhuizen, H D (WP) 1896 *BI* 4
Van Buuren, M C (Tvl) 1891 *BI* 1
Van de Vyver, D F (WP) 1937 *A* 2
Van den Berg, D S (N) 1975 *F* 1,2, 1976 *NZ* 1,2
Van den Berg, M A (WP) 1937 *A* 1, *NZ* 1,2,3
Van den Bergh, E (EP) 1994 *Arg* 2 (t & R)
Van der Linde, A (WP) 1995 *It, E*
Van der Merwe, A J (Bol) 1955 *BI* 2,3,4, 1956 *A* 1,2, *NZ* 1,2,3,4, 1958 *F* 1, 1960 *S, NZ* 2
Van der Merwe, A V (WP) 1931 *W*
Van der Merwe, B S (NT) 1949 *NZ* 1
Van der Merwe, H S (NT) 1960 *NZ* 4, 1963 *A* 2,3,4, 1964 *F*
Van der Merwe, J P (WP) 1970 *W*
Van der Merwe, P R (SWD, WT, GW) 1981 *NZ* 2,3, *US*, 1986 *Cv* 1,2, 1989 *Wld* 1
Vanderplank, B E (N) 1924 *BI* 3,4
Van der Schyff, J H (GW) 1949 *NZ* 1,2,3,4, 1955 *BI* 1
Van der Watt, A E (WP) 1969 *S* (R), *E*, 1970 *I*
Van der Westhuizen, C (WP) 1928 *NZ* 2,3,4, 1931 *I*
Van der Westhuizen, J H (WP) 1931 *I*, 1932 *E, S*
Van der Westhuizen, J H (NT) 1993 *Arg* 1,2, 1994 *E* 1,2 (R), *Arg* 2, *S, W*, 1995 *WS*, [*A, C* (R), *WS, F, NZ*], *W, It, E*
Van Druten, N J V (Tvl) 1924 *BI* 1,2,3,4, 1928 *NZ* 1,2,3,4
Van Heerden, A J (Tvl) 1921 *NZ* 1,3
Van Heerden, F J (WP) 1994 *E* 1,2 (R), *NZ* 3, 1995 *It, E*
Van Heerden, J L (NT, Tvl) 1974 *BI* 3,4, *F* 1,2, 1975 *F* 1,2, 1976 *NZ* 1,2,3,4, 1977 *Wld*, 1980 *BI* 1,3,4, *S Am* 3,4, *F*
Van Jaarsveld, C J (Tvl) 1949 *NZ* 1
Van Jaarsveldt, D C (R) 1960 *S*
Van Niekerk, J A (WP) 1928 *NZ* 4
Van Reenen, G L (WP) 1937 *A* 2, *NZ* 1
Van Renen, C G (WP) 1891 *BI* 3, 1896 *BI* 1,4
Van Renen, W (WP) 1903 *BI* 1,3
Van Rensburg, J T J (Tvl) 1992 *NZ, A, E*, 1993 *F* 1,2, *A* 1, 1994 *NZ* 2
Van Rooyen, G W (Tvl) 1921 *NZ* 2,3
Van Ryneveld, R C B (WP) 1910 *BI* 2,3
Van Schoor, R A M (R) 1949 *NZ* 2,3,4, 1951 *S, I, W*, 1952 *E, F*, 1953 *A* 1,2,3,4
Van Vollenhoven, K T (NT) 1955 *BI* 1,2,3,4, 1956 *A* 1,2, *NZ* 3
Van Vuuren, T F (EP) 1912 *S, I, W*, 1913 *E, F*
Van Wyk, C J (Tvl) 1951 *S, I, W*, 1952 *E, F*, 1953 *A* 1,2,3,4, 1955 *BI* 1

Van Wyk, J F B (NT) 1970 *NZ* 1,2,3,4, 1971 *F* 1,2, *A* 1,2,3, 1972 *E*, 1974 *BI* 1,3,4, 1976 *NZ* 3,4
Van Wyk, S P (WP) 1928 *NZ* 1,2
Van Zyl, B P (WP) 1961 *I*
Van Zyl, C G P (OFS) 1965 *NZ* 1,2,3,4
Van Zyl, G H (WP) 1958 *F* 1, 1960 *S, NZ* 1,2,3,4, *W, I*, 1961 *E, S, F, I, A* 1,2, 1962 *BI* 1,3,4
Van Zyl, H J (Tvl) 1960 *NZ* 1,2,3,4, *I*, 1961 *E, S, I, A* 1,2
Van Zyl, P J (Bol) 1961 *I*
Veldsman, P E (WP) 1977 *Wld*
Venter, B (OFS) 1994 *E* 1,2, *NZ* 1,2,3, *Arg* 1,2, 1995 [*R, C, WS* (R), *NZ* (R)]
Venter, F D (Tvl) 1931 *W*, 1932 *S*, 1933 *A* 3
Versfeld, C (WP) 1891 *BI* 3
Versfeld, M (WP) 1891 *BI* 1,2,3
Vigne, J T (Tvl) 1891 *BI* 1,2,3
Viljoen, J F (GW) 1971 *F* 1,2, *A* 1,2,3, 1972 *E*
Viljoen, J T (N) 1971 *A* 1,2,3
Villet, J V (WP) 1984 *E* 1,2
Visagie, P J (GW) 1967 *F* 1,2,3,4, 1968 *BI* 1,2,3,4, *F* 1,2, 1969 *A* 1,2,3,4, *S, E*, 1970 *NZ* 1,2,3,4, 1971 *F* 1,2, *A* 1,2,3
Visagie, R G (OFS, N) 1984 *E* 1,2, *S Am* 1,2, 1993 *F* 1
Visser, J de V (WP) 1981 *NZ* 2, *US*
Visser, M (WP) 1995 *WS* (R)
Visser, P J (Tvl) 1933 *A* 2
Viviers, S S (OFS) 1956 *A* 1,2, *NZ* 2,3,4
Vogel, M L (OFS) 1974 *BI* 2 (R)

Wagenaar, C (NT) 1977 *Wld*
Wahl, J J (WP) 1949 *NZ* 1
Walker, A P (N) 1921 *NZ* 1,3, 1924 *BI* 1,2,3,4
Walker, H N (OFS) 1953 *A* 3, 1956 *A* 2, *NZ* 1,4
Walker, H W (Tvl) 1910 *BI* 1,2,3
Walton, D C (N) 1964 *F*, 1965 *I, S, NZ* 3,4, 1969 *A* 1,2, *E*
Waring, F W (WP) 1931 *E*, 1932 *E*, 1933 *A* 1,2,3,4,5
Wegner, N (WP) 1993 *F* 2, *A* 1,2,3
Wessels, J J (WP) 1896 *BI* 1,2,3
Whipp, P J M (WP) 1974 *BI* 1,2, 1975 *F* 1, 1976 *NZ* 1,3,4, 1980 *S Am* 1,2
White, J (Bor) 1931 *W*, 1933 *A* 1,2,3,4,5, 1937 *A* 1,2, *NZ* 1,2
Wiese, J J (Tvl) 1993 *F* 1, 1995 *WS*, [*R, C, WS, F, NZ*], *W, It, E*
Williams, A E (GW) 1910 *BI* 1
Williams, A P (WP) 1984 *E* 1,2
Williams, C M (WP) 1993 *Arg* 2, 1994 *E* 1,2, *NZ* 1,2,3, *Arg* 1,2, *S, W*, 1995 *WS*, [*WS, F, NZ*], *It, E*
Williams, D O (WP) 1937 *A* 1,2, *NZ* 1,2,3, 1938 *BI* 1,2,3
Williams, J G (NT) 1971 *F* 1,2, *A* 1,2,3, 1972 *E*, 1974 *BI* 1,2,4, *F* 1,2, 1976 *NZ* 1,2
Wilson, L G (WP) 1960 *NZ* 3,4, *W, I*, 1961 *E, F, I, A* 1,2, 1962 *BI* 1,2,3,4, 1963 *A* 1,2,3,4, 1964 *W, F*, 1965 *I, S, A* 1,2, *NZ* 1,2,3,4
Wolmarans, B J (OFS) 1977 *Wld*
Wright, G D (EP, Tvl) 1986 *Cv* 3,4, 1989 *Wld* 1,2, 1992 *F* 1,2, *E*
Wyness, M R K (WP) 1962 *BI* 1,2,3,4, 1963 *A* 2

Zeller, W C (N) 1921 *NZ* 2,3
Zimerman, M (WP) 1931 *W, I*, 1932 *E, S*

SOUTH AFRICAN INTERNATIONAL RECORDS

Both team and individual records are for official South African international matches, up to 30 April 1996.

TEAM RECORDS

Highest score
60 v W Samoa (60-8) 1995 Johannesburg

v individual countries
52 v Argentina (52-23) 1993 Buenos Aires
30 v Australia (30-11) 1969 Johannesburg
34 v B Isles (34-14) 1962 Bloemfontein
20 v Canada (20-0) 1995 Port Elizabeth
35 v England (35-9) 1984 Johannesburg
38 v France { (38-5) 1913 Bordeaux
{ (38-25) 1975 Bloemfontein
38 v Ireland (38-0) 1912 Dublin
40 v Italy (40-21) 1995 Rome
24 v N Zealand { (24-12) 1981 Wellington
{ (24-27) 1992 Johannesburg
33 v NZ Cavaliers (33-18) 1986 Pretoria
21 v Romania (21-8) 1995 Cape Town
50 v S America (50-18) 1982 Pretoria

44 v Scotland (44-0) 1951 Murrayfield
38 v United States (38-7) 1981 New York
40 v Wales (40-11) 1995 Johannesburg
60 v W Samoa (60-8) 1995 Johannesburg

Biggest winning points margin
52 v W Samoa (60-8) 1995 Johannesburg

v individual countries
29 v Argentina (52-23) 1993 Buenos Aires
25 v Australia (28-3) 1961 Johannesburg
20 v B Isles (34-14) 1962 Bloemfontein
20 v Canada (20-0) 1995 Port Elizabeth
26 v England (35-9) 1984 Johannesburg
33 v France (38-5) 1913 Bordeaux
38 v Ireland (38-0) 1912 Dublin
19 v Italy (40-21) 1995 Rome
17 v N Zealand (17-0) 1928 Durban
15 v NZ Cavaliers (33-18) 1986 Pretoria
13 v Romania (21-8) 1995 Cape Town
44 v Scotland (44-0) 1951 Murrayfield
32 v S America (50-18) 1982 Pretoria
31 v United States (38-7) 1981 New York
29 v Wales (40-11) 1995 Johannesburg
52 v W Samoa (60-8) 1995 Johannesburg

Longest winning sequence
14 matches 1994-95

Highest score by opposing team
33 England (16-33) 1992 Twickenham

by individual countries
26 Argentina $\left\{\begin{array}{l}\text{(29-26) 1993 Buenos Aires} \\ \text{(46-26) 1994 Johannesburg}\end{array}\right.$
28 Australia (20-28) 1993 Brisbane
28 B Isles (9-28) 1974 Pretoria
 0 Canada (20-0) 1995 Port Elizabeth
33 England (16-33) 1992 Twickenham
29 France (16-29) 1992 Parc des Princes
15 Ireland (23-15) 1981 Cape Town
21 Italy (40-21) 1995 Rome
27 N Zealand (24-27) 1992 Johannesburg
19 NZ Cavaliers (18-19) 1986 Durban
 8 Romania (21-8) 1995 Cape Town
21 S America (12-21) 1982 Bloemfontein
10 Scotland $\left\{\begin{array}{l}\text{(18-10) 1960 Port Elizabeth} \\ \text{(34-10) 1994 Murrayfield}\end{array}\right.$
 7 United States (38-7) 1981 New York
12 Wales (20-12) 1994 Cardiff
14 W Samoa (42-14) 1995 Johannesburg

Biggest losing points margin
23 v Australia (3-26) 1992 Cape Town

v individual countries
23 v Australia (3-26) 1992 Cape Town
19 v B Isles (9-28) 1974 Pretoria
17 v England $\left\{\begin{array}{l}\text{(16-33) 1992 Twickenham} \\ \text{(15-32) 1994 Pretoria}\end{array}\right.$
13 v France (16-29) 1992 Parc des Princes
 3 v Ireland (6-9) 1965 Dublin
17 v N Zealand (3-20) 1965 Auckland
 1 v NZ Cavaliers (18-19) 1986 Durban
 9 v S America (12-21) 1982 Bloemfontein
 6 v Scotland (0-6) 1906 Glasgow
No defeats v Argentina, Canada, Italy, Romania, United States, Wales or W Samoa

Longest losing sequence
7 matches – 1964-65

Most tries by South Africa in an international
10 v Ireland (38-0) 1912 Dublin

Most tries against South Africa in an international
5 $\left\{\begin{array}{l}\text{by B Isles (22-23) 1955 Johannesburg} \\ \text{by N Zealand(3-20) 1965 Auckland} \\ \text{by B Isles (9-28) 1974 Pretoria}\end{array}\right.$

Most points on overseas tour (all matches)
753 in Australia/N Zealand (26 matches) 1937

Most tries on overseas tour (all matches)
161 in Australia/N Zealand (26 matches) 1937

INDIVIDUAL RECORDS

Most capped player
F C H du Preez   38   1961-71
J H Ellis   38   1965-76

in individual positions
Full-back
L G Wilson   27   1960-65
Wing
J P Engelbrecht   33   1960-69
Centre
J L Gainsford   33   1960-67
Fly-half
H E Botha   28   1980-92
Scrum-half
D J de Villiers   25   1962-70
Prop
J F K Marais   35   1963-74
Hooker
G F Malan   18   1958-65
Lock
F C H du Preez   31(38)[1]   1961-71
Flanker
J H Ellis   38   1965-76

No 8
D J Hopwood   22[2]   1960-65
[1] *Du Preez won 7 caps as a flanker*
[2] *T P Bedford, 25 caps, won 19 at No 8 and 6 as a flanker*

Longest international career
J M Powell 13 seasons 1891-1903
B H Heatlie 13 seasons 1891-1903
D M Gerber 13 seasons 1980-1992-93
H E Botha 13 seasons 1980-1992-93
Gerber's and Botha's careers ended during a Northern Hemisphere season

Most consecutive internationals – 25
S H Nomis 1967-72

Most internationals as captain
J F Pienaar   24   1993-95

Most points in internationals – 312
H E Botha (28 matches) 1980-92

Most points in an international – 28
G K Johnson v W Samoa 1995
   Johannesburg

Most tries in internationals – 19
D M Gerber (24 matches) 1980-92

Most tries in an international – 4
C M Williams v W Samoa 1995
   Johannesburg

Most conversions in internationals – 50
H E Botha (28 matches) 1980-92

Most conversions in an international – 7
A Geffin v Scotland 1951 Murrayfield

Most dropped goals in internationals – 18
H E Botha (28 matches) 1980-92

Most dropped goals in an international – 3
H E Botha   { v S America 1980 Durban
             { v Ireland 1981 Durban

Most penalty goals in internationals – 50
H E Botha (28 matches) 1980-92

Most penalty goals in an international – 6
G R Bosch v France 1975 Pretoria

Most points in international series – 69
H E Botha (4 appearances) v NZ Cavaliers 1986

Most points in international series on tour – 35
H E Botha (3 appearances) 1981 N Zealand

Most tries in international series on tour – 6
E E McHardy (5 appearances) 1912-13
   B Isles/France

Most points on overseas tour – 190
G H Brand (20 appearances) 1937
   Australia/N Zealand

Most tries on overseas tour – 22
J A Loubser (20 appearances) 1906-07
   B Isles/France

Most points in a tour match – 38
A J Joubert v Swansea 1994 St Helen's

Most tries in a tour match – 6
R G Dryburgh v Queensland 1956
   Brisbane

WAITING FOR THE PIECES TO SETTLE

THE 1995 SEASON IN NEW ZEALAND
Donald Cameron *New Zealand Herald*

As the sun set on the 1995 season, the mandarins of the NZRFU were once again talking about completely revamping the national administration, trimming the powerful council from 19 regional delegates to a nine-man mixture of elected delegates and high-profile businessmen. This would be a fitting end to a year which has seen the whole fabric of rugby in this country twisted – and sometimes ripped – to the extent that the 1996 weave will be completely different.

Some of the star players – including, of course, Jonah Lomu, the world player of 1995 – will be instant dollar millionaires under the new professional regime made possible by Newscorp's £360 million ten-year takeover. John Hart, who replaces Laurie Mains as All Black coach, is likely to command a £100,000 salary, marginally more than New Zealand's prime minister, Mr Bolger, earns. The scale of payments will go down to £40,000 for a run-of-the-mill All Black, if there is such a beast, and £10,000 for the average uncapped player hewing away in the National Provincial Championship.

The NZRFU is trying to come to terms with its status as an amateur administration running a professional game. As New Zealand, Australia and South Africa were patching together the huge Newscorp offer, most of the leading All Blacks were signing letters of intent allying them to the rival WCR enterprise.

This led to weeks of furious activity during which Jock Hobbs, the former All Black captain, covered the country in his quest to have all the players sign on the dotted line of the right document. Eventually most of them did.

Amid all these distractions, two men dominated the season. The first, not surprisingly, was Laurie Mains, the controversial All Black coach who maintained his prickly relations with the media and many of the administration moguls. As it turned out, Mains, and perhaps the All Blacks, too, were saved from a repetition of the embarrassments of 1994 by the appointment of Brian Lochore, the much-respected former All Black captain and coach, as a sort of father figure for the squad as they prepared for the World Cup.

Lochore immediately re-established his own warm relationship with the media and offered the new and younger players some old and earthy All Black wisdom. Best of all, he relieved the public pressure on Mains, who was then able to concentrate solely on developing the national side. In the countdown to the World Cup the omens were good. A 73-7 hammering of Canada was followed by a double win over Australia in the Bledisloe Cup series, the second match of which

298

launched the other man of the year, Jonah Lomu, into the world spotlight.

Mains had dropped Lomu quickly after New Zealand twice lost to France early in 1994, but he was persuaded that the giant wing was a new and fitter force in 1995. Various experts also warmly recommended Andrew Mehrtens at fly-half, and another piece of Mains' involved jigsaw fitted into place. The All Blacks lived up to Mains' high ambition in the World Cup, especially in the 45-29 crushing of England, but that stumble in the final lost them the title to South Africa in extra time. Nevertheless Lomu became a world figure of quite extraordinary potential as a player – not to mention as a target for the big-spending promoters and sponsors – and all this while still a youngster learning the rugby ropes.

Mains earned the final laurels he wanted when the All Blacks outplayed France in the Second Test at Parc des Princes in late November, after being hammered by their hosts in the First Test in Toulouse. Yet although he went out with a fanfare, the All Blacks' Test record – played 34, won 23, lost 10, drawn 1 – could only be described as spotty. This incongruity was in keeping with a year that turned New Zealand rugby upside down. We are still waiting for the pieces to settle.

NATIONAL CHAMPIONSHIP

Division 1	P	W	D	L	F	A	Pts
Auckland	8	7	0	1	236	118	29
Counties	8	6	0	2	233	208	25
Otago	8	5	0	3	215	220	22
N Harbour	8	4	1	3	247	159	20
Canterbury	8	4	1	3	259	232	19
Waikato	8	4	0	4	205	206	18
Wellington	8	3	0	5	165	230	13
King Country	8	2	0	6	150	221	8
Southland	8	0	0	8	136	222	6

Semi-finals: Auckland 60, North Harbour 26;
Otago 41, Counties 32
Final: Auckland 23, Otago 19

Division 2	P	W	D	L	F	A	Pts
Northland	8	8	0	0	351	101	32
Bay of Plenty	8	6	0	2	314	152	25
Taranaki	8	6	0	2	342	191	24
Hawke's Bay	8	5	0	3	242	196	20
Manawatu	8	4	0	4	258	165	19
Wairarapa-Bush	8	4	0	4	248	239	16
S Canterbury	8	2	0	6	135	303	9
Nelson Bays	8	1	0	7	114	436	6
Mid-C'bury	8	0	0	8	130	352	1

Semi-finals: Taranaki 37, Bay of Plenty 12;
Northland 36, Hawke's Bay 6
Final: Taranaki 22, Northland 18

Division 3	P	W	D	L	F	A	Pts
Thames Valley	8	7	0	1	306	169	28
Poverty Bay	8	6	0	2	233	156	25
Wanganui	8	5	0	3	184	128	21
Horowhenua	8	5	0	3	198	152	21
Marlborough	8	5	0	3	223	201	20
Buller	8	3	0	5	132	237	12
N Otago	8	2	0	6	182	226	10
W Coast	8	2	0	6	120	212	9
E Coast	8	1	0	7	147	244	6

Semi-finals: Thames Valley 32, Horowhenua 17;
Poverty Bay 26, Wanganui 19
Final: Thames Valley 47, Poverty Bay 8

RANFURLY SHIELD

Canterbury 64, Mid-Canterbury 19; Canterbury 43, Nelson Bays 17; Canterbury 79, Marlborough 0; Canterbury 72, South Canterbury 27; Canterbury 27, Southland 22; Canterbury 58, Waikato 30; Canterbury 66, Wellington 17; Auckland 35, Canterbury 0; Auckland 26, Waikato 17

NEW ZEALAND INTERNATIONAL PLAYERS
(*up to 30 April 1996*)

ABBREVIATIONS

A – Australia; *Arg* – Argentina; *AW* – Anglo-Welsh; *BI* – British Isles teams; *C* – Canada; *E* – England; *F* – France; *Fj* – Fiji; *I* – Ireland; *It* – Italy; *J* – Japan; *R* – Romania; *S* – Scotland; *SA* – South Africa; *US* – United States; *W* – Wales; *Wld* – World Invitation XV; *WS* – Western Samoa; (R) Replacement; (t) – temporary replacement. Entries in square brackets [ ] indicate appearances in the Rugby World Cup.

Note: When a series has taken place, figures denote the particular matches in which players featured. Thus 1959 *BI* 2,4 indicates that a player appeared in the second and fourth Tests of the 1959 series against the British Isles.

Abbott, H L (Taranaki) 1906 *F*
Aitken, G G (Wellington) 1921 *SA* 1,2
Allen, F R (Auckland) 1946 *A* 1,2, 1947 *A* 1,2, 1949 *SA* 1,2
Allen, M R (Taranaki) 1993 *WS* (t)
Allen, N H (Counties) 1980 *A* 3, *W*
Alley, G T (Canterbury) 1928 *SA* 1,2,3
Anderson, A (Canterbury) 1983 *S, E,* 1984 *A* 1,2,3, 1987 [*FJ*]
Anderson, B L (Wairarapa-Bush) 1986 *A* 1
Archer, W R (Otago, Southland) 1955 *A* 1,2, 1956 *SA* 1,3
Argus, W G (Canterbury) 1946 *A* 1,2, 1947 *A* 1,2
Arnold, D A (Canterbury) 1963 *I, W,* 1964 *E, F*
Arnold, K D (Waikato) 1947 *A* 1,2
Ashby, D L (Southland) 1958 *A* 2
Asher, A A (Auckland) 1903 *A*
Ashworth, B G (Auckland) 1978 *A* 1,2
Ashworth, J C (Canterbury, Hawke's Bay) 1978 *A* 1,2,3, 1980 *A* 1,2,3, 1981 *SA* 1,2,3, 1982 *A* 1,2, 1983 *BI* 1,2,3,4, *A,* 1984 *F* 1,2, *A* 1,2,3, 1985 *E* 1,2, *A*
Atkinson, H (West Coast) 1913 *A* 1
Avery, H E (Wellington) 1910 *A* 1,2,3

Bachop, G T M (Canterbury) 1989 *W, I,* 1990 *S* 1,2, *A* 1,2,3, *F* 1,2, 1991 *Arg* 1,2, *A* 1,2, [*E, US, C, A, S*], 1992 *Wld* 1, 1994 *SA* 1,2,3, *A,* 1995 *C,* [*I, W, E, SA*], *A* 1,2
Bachop, S J (Otago) 1994 *F* 2, *SA* 1,2,3, *A*
Badeley, C E O (Auckland) 1921 *SA* 1,2
Baird, J A S (Otago) 1913 *A* 2
Ball, N (Wellington) 1931 *A,* 1932 *A* 2,3, 1935 *W,* 1936 *E*
Barrett, J (Auckland) 1913 *A* 2,3
Barry, E F (Wellington) 1934 *A* 2
Barry, L J (North Harbour) 1995 *F* 2
Batty, G B (Wellington, Bay of Plenty) 1972 *W, S,* 1973 *E* 1, *I, F, E* 2, 1974 *A* 1,3, *I,* 1975 *S,* 1976 *SA* 1,2,3,4, 1977 *BI* 1
Batty, W (Auckland) 1930 *BI* 1,3,4, 1931 *A*
Beatty, G E (Taranaki) 1950 *BI* 1
Bell, R H (Otago) 1951 *A* 3, 1952 *A* 1,2
Bellis, E A (Wanganui) 1921 *SA* 1,2,3
Bennet, R (Otago) 1905 *A*
Berghan, T (Otago) 1938 *A* 1,2,3
Berry, M J (Wairarapa-Bush) 1986 *A* 3 (R)
Bevan, V D (Wellington) 1949 *A* 1,2, 1950 *BI* 1,2,3,4
Birtwistle, W M (Canterbury) 1965 *SA* 1,2,3,4, 1967 *E, W, S*
Black, J E (Canterbury) 1977 *F* 1, 1979 *A,* 1980 *A* 3
Black, N W (Auckland) 1949 *SA* 3
Black, R S (Otago) 1914 *A* 1
Blake, A W (Wairarapa) 1949 *A* 1
Boggs, E G (Auckland) 1946 *A* 2, 1949 *SA* 1
Bond, J G (Canterbury) 1949 *A* 2
Booth, E E (Otago) 1906 *F,* 1907 *A* 1,3
Boroevich, K G (Wellington) 1986 *F* 1, *A* 1, *F* 3 (R)
Botica, F M (North Harbour) 1986 *F* 1, *A* 1,2,3, *F* 2,3, 1989 *Arg* 1 (R)
Bowden, N J G (Taranaki) 1952 *A* 2
Bowers, R G (Wellington) 1954 *I, F*
Bowman, A W (Hawke's Bay) 1938 *A* 1,2,3
Braid, G J (Bay of Plenty) 1983 *S, E*
Bremner, S G (Auckland, Canterbury) 1952 *A* 2, 1956 *SA* 2
Brewer, M R (Otago, Canterbury) 1986 *F* 1, *A* 1,2,3, *F* 2,3, 1988 *A* 1, 1989 *A, W, I,* 1990 *S* 1,2, *A* 1,2,3, *F* 1,2, 1992 *I* 2, *A* 1, 1994 *F* 1,2, *SA* 1,2,3, *A,* 1995 *C,* [*I, W, E, SA*], *A* 1,2

Briscoe, K C (Taranaki) 1959 *BI* 2, 1960 *SA* 1,2,3,4, 1963 *I, W,* 1964 *E, S*
Brooke, R M (Auckland) 1992 *I* 2, *A* 1,2,3, *SA,* 1993 *BI* 1,2,3, *A, WS,* 1994 *SA* 2,3, 1995 *C,* [*J, S, E, SA*], *A* 1,2, *It, F* 1,2
Brooke, Z V (Auckland) 1987 [*Arg*], 1989 *Arg* 2 (R), 1990 *A* 1,2,3, *F* 1 (R), 1991 *Arg* 2, *A* 1,2, [*E, It, C, A, S*], 1992 *A* 2,3, *SA,* 1993 *BI* 1,2,3 (R), *WS* (R), *S, E,* 1994 *F* 2, *SA* 1,2,3, *A,* 1995 [*J, S, E, SA*], *A* 1,2, *It, F* 1,2
Brooke-Cowden, M (Auckland) 1986 *F* 1, *A* 1, 1987 [*W*]
Brown, C (Taranaki) 1913 *A* 2,3
Brown, O M (Auckland) 1992 *I* 2, *A* 1,2,3, *SA,* 1993 *BI* 1,2,3, *A, S, E,* 1994 *F* 1,2, *SA* 1,2,3, *A,* 1995 *C,* [*I, W, S, E, SA*], *A* 1,2, *It, F* 1,2
Brown, R H (Taranaki) 1955 *A* 3, 1956 *SA* 1,2,3,4, 1957 *A* 1,2, 1958 *A* 1,2,3, 1959 *BI* 1,3, 1961 *F* 1,2,3, 1962 *A* 1
Brownlie, C J (Hawke's Bay) 1924 *W,* 1925 *E, F*
Brownlie, M J (Hawke's Bay) 1924 *I, W,* 1925 *E, F,* 1928 *SA* 1,2,3,4
Bruce, J A (Auckland) 1914 *A* 1,2
Bruce, O D (Canterbury) 1976 *SA* 1,2,4, 1977 *BI* 2,3,4, *F* 1,2, 1978 *A* 1,2, *I, W, E, S*
Bryers, R F (King Country) 1949 *A* 1
Budd, T A (Southland) 1946 *A* 2, 1949 *A* 2
Bullock-Douglas, G A H (Wanganui) 1932 *A* 1,2,3, 1934 *A* 1,2
Bunce, F E (North Harbour) 1992 *Wld* 1,2,3, *I* 1,2, *A* 1,2,3, *SA,* 1993 *BI* 1,2,3, *A, WS, S, E,* 1994 *F* 1,2, *SA* 1,2,3, *A,* 1995 *C,* [*I, W, S, E, SA*], *A* 1,2, *It, F* 1,2
Burgess, G A J (Auckland) 1981 *SA* 2
Burgess, G F (Southland) 1905 *A*
Burgess, R E (Manawatu) 1971 *BI* 1,2,3, 1972 *A* 3, *W,* 1973 *I, F*
Burke, P S (Taranaki) 1955 *A* 1, 1957 *A* 1,2
Burns, P J (Canterbury) 1908 *AW* 2, 1910 *A* 1,2,3, 1913 *A* 3
Bush, R G (Otago) 1931 *A*
Bush, W K (Canterbury) 1974 *A* 1,2, 1975 *S,* 1976 *I, SA,* 2,4, 1977 *BI* 2,3,4 (R), 1978 *I, W,* 1979 *A*
Buxton, J B (Canterbury) 1955 *A* 3, 1956 *SA* 1

Cain, M J (Taranaki) 1913 *US,* 1914 *A* 1,2,3
Callesen, J A (Manawatu) 1974 *A* 1,2,3, 1975 *S*
Cameron, D (Taranaki) 1908 *AW* 1,2,3
Cameron, L M (Manawatu) 1980 *A* 3, 1981 *SA* 1 (R), 2,3, *R*
Carleton, S R (Canterbury) 1928 *SA* 1,2,3, 1929 *A* 1,2,3
Carrington, K R (Auckland) 1971 *BI* 1,3,4
Carter, M P (Auckland) 1991 *A* 2, [*It, A*]
Casey, S T (Otago) 1905 *S, I, E, W,* 1907 *A* 1,2,3, 1908 *AW* 1
Catley, E H (Waikato) 1946 *A* 1, 1947 *A* 1,2, 1949 *SA* 1,2,3,4
Caughey, T H C (Auckland) 1932 *A* 1,3, 1934 *A* 1,2, 1935 *S, I,* 1936 *E, A* 1, 1937 *SA* 3
Cherrington, N P (North Auckland) 1950 *BI* 1
Christian, D L (Auckland) 1949 *SA* 4
Clamp, M (Wellington) 1984 *A* 2,3
Clark, D W (Otago) 1964 *A* 1,2
Clark, W H (Wellington) 1953 *W,* 1954 *I, E, S,* 1955 *A* 1,2, 1956 *SA* 2,3,4
Clarke, A H (Auckland) 1958 *A* 3, 1959 *BI* 4, 1960 *SA* 1

Clarke, D B (Waikato) 1956 *SA* 3,4, 1957 *A* 1,2, 1958 *A* 1,3, 1959 *BI* 1,2,3,4, 1960 *SA* 1,2,3,4, 1961 *F* 1,2,3, 1962 *A* 1,2,3,4,5, 1963 *E* 1,2, *I, W,* 1964 *E, S, F, A* 2,3
Clarke, E (Auckland) 1992 *Wld* 2,3, *I* 1,2, 1993 *BI* 1,2, *S* (R), *E*
Clarke, I J (Waikato) 1953 *W,* 1955 *A* 1,2,3, 1956 *SA* 1,2,3,4, 1957 *A* 1,2, 1958 *A* 1,3, 1959 *BI* 1,2, 1960 *SA* 2,4, 1961 *F* 1,2,3, 1962 *A* 1,2,3, 1963 *E* 1,2
Clarke, R L (Taranaki) 1932 *A* 2,3
Cobden, D G (Canterbury) 1937 *SA* 1
Cockerill, M S (Taranaki) 1951 *A* 1,2,3
Cockroft, E A P (South Canterbury) 1913 *A* 3, 1914 *A* 2,3
Codlin, B W (Counties) 1980 *A* 1,2,3
Collins, A H (Taranaki) 1932 *A* 2,3, 1934 *A* 1
Collins, J L (Poverty Bay) 1964 *A* 1, 1965 *SA* 1,4
Colman, J T H (Taranaki) 1907 *A* 1,2, 1908 *AW* 1,3
Connor, D M (Auckland) 1961 *F* 1,2,3, 1962 *A* 1,2,3,4,5, 1963 *E* 1,2, 1964 *A* 2,3
Conway, R J (Otago, Bay of Plenty) 1959 *BI* 2,3,4, 1960 *SA* 1,3,4, 1965 *SA* 1,2,3,4
Cooke, A E (Auckland, Wellington) 1924 *I, W,* 1925 *E, F,* 1930 *BI* 1,2,3,4
Cooke, R J (Canterbury) 1903 *A*
Cooksley, M S B (Counties, Waikato) 1992 *Wld* 1, 1993 *BI* 2,3 (R), *A,* 1994 *F* 1,2, *SA* 1,2
Cooper, G J L (Auckland, Otago) 1986 *F* 1, *A* 1,2, 1992 *Wld* 1,2,3, *I* 1
Cooper, M J A (Waikato) 1992 *I* 2, *SA* (R), 1993 *BI* 1 (R), 3 (t), *WS* (t), 1994 *F* 1,2
Corner, M M N (Auckland) 1930 *BI* 2,3,4, 1931 *A,* 1934 *A* 1, 1936 *E*
Cossey, R R (Counties) 1958 *A* 1
Cottrell, A I (Canterbury) 1929 *A* 1,2,3, 1930 *BI* 1,2,3,4, 1931 *A,* 1932 *A* 1,2,3
Cottrell, W D (Canterbury) 1968 *A* 1,2, *F* 2,3, 1970 *SA* 1, 1971 *BI* 1,2,3,4
Couch, M B R (Wairarapa) 1947 *A* 1, 1949 *A* 1,2
Coughlan, T D (South Canterbury) 1958 *A* 1
Creighton, J N (Canterbury) 1962 *A* 4
Crichton, S (Wellington) 1983 *S, E*
Cross, T (Canterbury) 1904 *BI,* 1905 *A*
Crowley, K J (Taranaki) 1985 *E* 1,2, *A, Arg* 1,2, 1986 *A* 3, *F* 2,3, 1987 *[Arg],* 1990 *S* 1,2, *A* 1,2,3, *F* 1,2, 1991 *Arg* 1,2, *[A]*
Crowley, P J B (Auckland) 1949 *SA* 3,4, 1950 *BI* 1,2,3,4
Culhane, S D (Southland) 1995 *[J], It, F* 1,2
Cummings, W (Canterbury) 1913 *A* 2,3
Cundy, R T (Wairarapa) 1929 *A* 2 (R)
Cunningham, G R (Auckland) 1979 *A, S, E,* 1980 *A* 1,2
Cunningham, W (Auckland) 1905 *S, I,* 1906 *F,* 1907 *A* 1,2,3, 1908 *AW* 1,2,3
Cupples, L F (Bay of Plenty) 1924 *I, W*
Currie, C J (Canterbury) 1978 *I, W*
Cuthill, J E (Otago) 1913 *A* 1, *US*

Dalley, W C (Canterbury) 1924 *I,* 1928 *SA* 1,2,3,4
Dalton, A G (Counties) 1977 *F* 2, 1978 *A* 1,2,3, *I, W, E, S,* 1979 *F* 1,2, *S,* 1981 *S* 1,2, *SA* 1,2,3, *R, F* 1,2, 1982 *A* 1,2,3, 1983 *BI* 1,2,3,4, *A,* 1984 *F* 1,2, *A* 1,2,3, 1985 *E* 1,2, *A*
Dalton, D (Hawke's Bay) 1935 *I, W,* 1936 *A* 1,2, 1937 *SA* 1,2,3, 1938 *A* 1,2
Dalton, R A (Wellington) 1947 *A* 1,2
Dalzell, G N (Canterbury) 1953 *W,* 1954 *I, E, S, F*
Davie, M G (Canterbury) 1983 *E* (R)
Davies, W A (Auckland, Otago) 1960 *SA* 4, 1962 *A* 4,5
Davis, K (Auckland) 1952 *A* 2, 1953 *W,* 1954 *I, E, S, F,* 1955 *A* 2, 1958 *A* 1,2,3
Davis, L J (Canterbury) 1976 *I,* 1977 *BI* 3,4
Davis, W L (Hawke's Bay) 1967 *A, E, W, F, S,* 1968 *A* 1,2, *F* 1, 1969 *W* 1,2, 1970 *SA* 2
Deans, I B (Canterbury) 1988 *W* 1,2, *A* 1,2,3, 1989 *F* 1,2, *Arg* 1,2, *A*
Deans, R G (Canterbury) 1905 *S, I, E, W,* 1908 *AW* 3
Deans, R M (Canterbury) 1983 *S, E,* 1984 *A* 1 (R), 2,3
Delamore, G W (Wellington) 1949 *SA* 4
Dewar, H (Taranaki) 1913 *A* 1, *US*
Diack, E S (Otago) 1959 *BI* 2
Dick, J (Auckland) 1937 *SA* 1,2, 1938 *A* 3
Dick, M J (Auckland) 1963 *I, W,* 1964 *E, S, F,* 1965 *SA* 3, 1966 *BI* 4, 1967 *A, E, W, F,* 1969 *W* 1,2, 1970 *SA* 1,4
Dixon, M J (Canterbury) 1954 *I, E, S, F,* 1956 *SA* 1,2,3,4, 1957 *A* 1,2
Dobson, R L (Auckland) 1949 *A* 1
Dodd, E H (Wellington) 1905 *A*

Donald, A J (Wanganui) 1983 *S, E,* 1984 *F* 1,2, *A* 1,2,3
Donald, J G (Wairarapa) 1921 *SA* 1,2
Donald, Q (Wairarapa) 1924 *I, W,* 1925 *E, F*
Donaldson, M W (Manawatu) 1977 *F* 1,2, 1978 *A* 1,2,3, *I, E, S,* 1979 *F* 1,2, *A, S* (R), 1981 *SA* 3 (R)
Dougan, J P (Wellington) 1972 *A* 1, 1973 *E* 2
Dowd, C W (Auckland) 1993 *BI* 1,2,3, *A, WS, S, E,* 1994 *SA* 1 (R), 1995 *C, [I, W, J, E, SA], A* 1,2, *It, F* 1,2
Dowd, G W (North Harbour) 1992 *I* 1 (R)
Downing, A J (Auckland) 1913 *A* 1, *US,* 1914 *A* 1,2,3
Drake, J A (Auckland) 1986 *F* 2,3, 1987 *[Fj, Arg, S, W, F], A*
Duff, R H (Canterbury) 1951 *A* 1,2,3, 1952 *A* 1,2, 1955 *A* 2,3, 1956 *SA* 1,2,3,4
Duncan, J (Otago) 1903 *A*
Duncan, M G (Hawke's Bay) 1971 *BI* 3 (R), 4
Duncan, W D (Otago) 1921 *SA* 1,2,3
Dunn, E J (Auckland) 1979 *S,* 1981 *S* 1
Dunn, I T W (North Auckland) 1983 *BI* 1,4, *A*
Dunn, J M (Auckland) 1946 *A* 1

Earl, A T (Canterbury) 1986 *F* 1, *A* 1, *F* 3 (R), 1987 *[Arg],* 1989 *W, I,* 1991 *Arg* 1 (R), 2, *A* 1, *[E* (R), *US, S],* 1992 *A* 2,3 (R)
Eastgate, B P (Canterbury) 1952 *A* 1,2, 1954 *S*
Elliott, K G (Wellington) 1946 *A* 1,2
Ellis, M C G (Otago) 1993 *S, E,* 1995 *C, [I* (R), *W, J, S, SA* (R)]
Elsom, A E G (Canterbury) 1952 *A* 1,2, 1953 *W,* 1955 *A* 1,2,3
Elvidge, R R (Otago) 1946 *A* 1,2, 1949 *SA* 1,2,3,4, 1950 *BI* 1,2,3
Erceg, C P (Auckland) 1951 *A* 1,2,3, 1952 *A* 1
Evans, D A (Hawke's Bay) 1910 *A* 2
Eveleigh, K A (Manawatu) 1976 *SA* 2,4, 1977 *BI* 1,2

Fanning, A H N (Canterbury) 1913 *A* 3
Fanning, B J (Canterbury) 1903 *A,* 1904 *BI*
Farrell, C P (Auckland) 1977 *BI* 1,2
Fawcett, C L (Auckland) 1976 *SA* 2,3
Fea, W R (Otago) 1921 *SA* 3
Finlay, B E L (Manawatu) 1959 *BI* 1
Finlay, J (Manawatu) 1946 *A* 1
Finlayson, I (North Auckland) 1928 *SA* 1,2,3,4, 1930 *BI* 1,2
Fitzgerald, J T (Wellington) 1952 *A* 1
Fitzpatrick, B B J (Wellington) 1953 *W,* 1954 *I, F*
Fitzpatrick, S B T (Auckland) 1986 *F* 1, *A* 1, *F* 2,3, 1987 *[It, Fj, Arg, S, W, F], A,* 1988 *W* 1,2, *A* 1,2,3, 1989 *F* 1,2, *Arg* 1,2, *A, W, I,* 1990 *S* 1,2, *A* 1,2,3, *F* 1,2, 1991 *Arg* 1,2, *A* 1,2, *[E, US, It, C, A, S],* 1992 *Wld* 1,2,3, *I* 1,2, *A* 1,2,3, *SA,* 1993 *BI* 1,2,3, *A, WS, S, E,* 1994 *F* 1,2, *SA* 1,2,3, *A,* 1995 *C, [I, W, S, E, SA], A* 1,2, *It, F* 1,2
Fleming, J K (Wellington) 1979 *S, E,* 1980 *A* 1,2,3
Fletcher, C J C (North Auckland) 1921 *SA* 3
Fogarty, R (Taranaki) 1921 *SA* 1,3
Ford, B R (Marlborough) 1977 *BI* 3,4, 1978 *I,* 1979 *E*
Forster, S T (Otago) 1993 *S, E,* 1994 *F* 1,2, 1995 *It, F* 1
Fox, G J (Auckland) 1985 *Arg* 1, 1987 *[It, Fj, Arg, S, W, F], A,* 1988 *W* 1,2, *A* 1,2,3, 1989 *F* 1,2, *Arg* 1,2, *A, W, I,* 1990 *S* 1,2, *A* 1,2,3, *F* 1,2, 1991 *Arg* 1,2, *A* 1,2, *[E, It, C, A],* 1992 *Wld* 1,2 (R), *A* 1,2,3, *SA,* 1993 *BI* 1,2,3, *A, WS*
Francis, A R H (Auckland) 1905 *A,* 1907 *A* 1,2,3, 1908 *AW* 1,2,3, 1910 *A* 1,2,3
Francis, W C (Wellington) 1913 *A* 2,3, 1914 *A* 1,2,3
Fraser, B G (Wellington) 1979 *S, E,* 1980 *A* 3, *W,* 1981 *S* 1,2, *SA* 1,2,3, *R, F* 1,2, 1982 *A* 1,2,3, 1983 *BI* 1,2,3,4, *A, S, E,* 1984 *A* 1
Frazer, H F (Hawke's Bay) 1946 *A* 1,2, 1947 *A* 1,2, 1949 *SA* 2
Fryer, F C (Canterbury) 1907 *A* 1,2,3, 1908 *AW* 2
Fuller, W B (Canterbury) 1910 *A* 1,2
Furlong, B D M (Hawke's Bay) 1970 *SA* 4

Gallagher, J A (Wellington) 1987 *[It, Fj, S, W, F], A,* 1988 *W* 1,2, *A* 1,2,3, 1989 *F* 1,2, *Arg* 1,2, *A, W, I*
Gallaher, D (Auckland) 1903 *A,* 1904 *BI,* 1905 *S, E, W,* 1906 *F*
Gard, P C (North Otago) 1971 *BI* 4
Gardiner, A J (Taranaki) 1974 *A* 3
Geddes, J H (Southland) 1929 *A* 1
Geddes, W McK (Auckland) 1913 *A* 2
Gemmell, B McL (Auckland) 1974 *A* 1,2
George, V L (Southland) 1938 *A* 1,2,3

Gilbert, G D M (West Coast) 1935 *S, I, W,* 1936 *E*
Gillespie, C T (Wellington) 1913 *A* 2
Gillespie, W D (Otago) 1958 *A* 3
Gillett, G A (Canterbury, Auckland) 1905 *S, I, E, W,* 1907 *A* 2,3, 1908 *AW* 1,3
Gillies, C C (Otago) 1936 *A* 2
Gilray, C M (Otago) 1905 *A*
Glasgow, F T (Taranaki, Southland) 1905 *S, I, E, W,* 1906 *F,* 1908 *AW* 3
Glenn, W S (Taranaki) 1904 *BI,* 1906 *F*
Goddard, M P (South Canterbury) 1946 *A* 2, 1947 *A* 1,2, 1949 *SA* 3,4
Going, S M (North Auckland) 1967 *A, F,* 1968 *F* 3, 1969 *W* 1,2, 1970 *SA* 1 (R), 4, 1971 *BI* 1,2,3,4, 1972 *A* 1,2,3, *W, S,* 1973 *E* 1, *I, F, E* 2, 1974 *I,* 1975 *S,* 1976 *I* (R), *SA* 1,2,3,4, 1977 *BI* 1,2
Gordon, S B (Waikato) 1993 *S, E*
Graham, D J (Canterbury) 1958 *A* 1,2, 1960 *SA* 2,3, 1961 *F* 1,2,3, 1962 *A* 1,2,3,4,5, 1963 *E* 1,2, *I, W,* 1964 *E, S, F, A* 1,2,3
Graham, J B (Otago) 1913 *US,* 1914 *A* 1,3
Graham, W G (Otago) 1979 *F* 1 (R)
Grant, L A (South Canterbury) 1947 *A* 1,2, 1949 *SA* 1,2
Gray, G D (Canterbury) 1908 *AW* 2, 1913 *A* 1, *US*
Gray, K F (Wellington) 1963 *I, W,* 1964 *E, S, F, A* 1,2,3, 1965 *SA* 1,2,3,4, 1966 *BI* 1,2,3,4, 1967 *W, F, S,* 1968 *A* 1, *F* 2,3, 1969 *W* 1,2
Gray, W N (Bay of Plenty) 1955 *A* 2,3, 1956 *SA* 1,2,3,4
Green, C I (Canterbury) 1983 *S* (R), *E,* 1984 *A* 1,2,3, 1985 *E* 1,2, *A, Arg* 1,2, 1986 *A* 2,3, *F* 2,3, 1987 *[It, Fj, S, W, F], A*
Grenside, B A (Hawke's Bay) 1928 *SA* 1,2,3,4, 1929 *A* 2,3
Griffiths, J L (Wellington) 1934 *A* 2, 1935 *S, I, W,* 1936 *A* 1,2, 1938 *A* 3
Guy, R A (North Auckland) 1971 *BI* 1,2,3,4

Haden, A M (Auckland) 1977 *BI* 1,2,3,4, *F* 1,2, 1978 *A* 1,2,3, *I, W, E, S,* 1979 *F* 1,2, *A, S, E,* 1980 *A* 1,2,3, *W,* 1981 *S* 2, *SA* 1,2,3, *R, F* 1,2, 1982 *A* 1,2,3, 1983 *BI* 1,2,3,4, *A,* 1984 *F* 1,2, 1985 *Arg* 1,2
Hadley, S (Auckland) 1928 *SA* 1,2,3,4
Hadley, W E (Auckland) 1934 *A* 1,2, 1935 *S, I, W,* 1936 *E, A* 1,2
Haig, J S (Otago) 1946 *A* 1,2
Haig, L S (Otago) 1950 *BI* 2,3,4, 1951 *A* 1,2,3, 1953 *W,* 1954 *E, S*
Hales, D A (Canterbury) 1972 *A* 1,2,3, *W*
Hamilton, D C (Southland) 1908 *AW* 2
Hammond, I A (Marlborough) 1952 *A* 2
Harper, E T (Canterbury) 1904 *BI,* 1906 *F*
Harris, P C (Manawatu) 1976 *SA* 3
Hart, A H (Taranaki) 1924 *I*
Hart, G F (Canterbury) 1930 *BI* 1,2,3,4, 1931 *A,* 1934 *A* 1, 1935 *S, I, W,* 1936 *A* 1,2
Harvey, B A (Wairarapa-Bush) 1986 *F* 1
Harvey, I H (Wairarapa) 1928 *SA* 4
Harvey, L R (Otago) 1949 *SA* 1,2,3,4, 1950 *BI* 1,2,3,4
Harvey, P (Canterbury) 1904 *BI*
Hasell, E W (Canterbury) 1913 *A* 2,3
Hayward, H O (Auckland) 1908 *AW* 3
Hazlett, E J (Southland) 1966 *BI* 1,2,3,4, 1967 *A, E*
Hazlett, W E (Southland) 1928 *SA* 1,2,3,4, 1930 *BI* 1,2,3,4
Heeps, T R (Wellington) 1962 *A* 1,2,3,4,5
Heke, W R (North Auckland) 1929 *A* 1,2,3
Hemi, R C (Waikato) 1953 *W,* 1954 *I, E, S, F,* 1955 *A* 1,2,3, 1956 *SA* 1,3,4, 1957 *A* 1,2, 1959 *BI* 1,3,4
Henderson, P (Wanganui) 1949 *SA* 1,2,3,4, 1950 *BI* 2,3,4
Henderson, P W (Otago) 1991 *Arg* 1, *[C],* 1992 *Wld* 1,2,3, *I* 1, 1995 *[J]*
Herewini, M A (Auckland) 1962 *A* 5, 1963 *I,* 1964 *S, F,* 1965 *SA* 4, 1966 *BI* 1,2,3,4, 1967 *A*
Hewett, J A (Auckland) 1991 *[It]*
Hewitt, N J (Southland) 1995 *[I* (t), *J]*
Hewson, A R (Wellington) 1981 *S* 1,2, *SA* 1,2,3, *R, F* 1,2, 1982 *A* 1,2,3, 1983 *BI* 1,2,3,4, *A,* 1984 *F* 1,2, *A* 1
Higginson, G (Canterbury, Hawke's Bay) 1980 *W,* 1981 *S* 1, *SA* 1, 1982 *A* 1,2, 1983 *A*
Hill, S F (Canterbury) 1955 *A* 3, 1956 *SA* 1,3,4, 1957 *A* 1,2, 1958 *A* 3, 1959 *BI* 1,2,3,4
Hines, G R (Waikato) 1980 *A* 3
Hobbs, M J B (Canterbury) 1983 *BI* 1,2,3,4, *A, S, E,* 1984 *F* 1,2, *A* 1,2,3, 1985 *E* 1,2, *A, Arg* 1,2, 1986 *A* 2,3, *F* 2,3
Holder, E C (Buller) 1934 *A* 2
Hook, L S (Auckland) 1929 *A* 1,2,3

Hooper, J A (Canterbury) 1937 *SA* 1,2,3
Hopkinson, A E (Canterbury) 1967 *S,* 1968 *A* 2, *F* 1,2,3, 1969 *W* 2, 1970 *SA* 1,2,3
Hore, J (Otago) 1930 *BI* 2,3,4, 1932 *A* 1,2,3, 1934 *A* 1,2, 1935 *S,* 1936 *E*
Horsley, R H (Wellington) 1960 *SA* 1,2,3
Hotop, J (Canterbury) 1952 *A* 1,2, 1955 *A* 3
Howarth, S P (Auckland) 1994 *SA* 1,2,3, *A*
Hughes, A M (Auckland) 1949 *A* 1,2, 1950 *BI* 1,2,3,4
Hughes, E (Southland, Wellington) 1907 *A* 1,2,3, 1908 *AW* 1, 1921 *SA* 1,2
Hunter, B A (Otago) 1971 *BI* 1,2,3
Hunter, J (Taranaki) 1905 *S, I, E, W,* 1906 *F,* 1907 *A* 1,2,3, 1908 *AW* 1,2,3
Hurst, I A (Canterbury) 1973 *I, F, E* 2, 1974 *A* 1,2

Ieremia, A I (Wellington) 1994 *SA* 1,2,3, 1995 *[J]*
Ifwersen, K D (Auckland) 1921 *SA* 3
Innes, C R (Auckland) 1989 *W, I,* 1990 *A* 1,2,3, *F* 1,2, 1991 *Arg* 1,2, *A* 1,2, *[E, US, It, C, A, S]*
Innes, G D (Canterbury) 1932 *A* 2
Irvine, I B (North Auckland) 1952 *A* 1
Irvine, J G (Otago) 1914 *A* 1,2,3
Irvine, W R (Hawke's Bay, Wairarapa) 1924 *I, W,* 1925 *E, F,* 1930 *BI* 1
Irwin, M W (Otago) 1955 *A* 1,2, 1956 *SA* 1, 1958 *A* 2, 1959 *BI* 3,4, 1960 *SA* 1

Jackson, E S (Hawke's Bay) 1936 *A* 1,2, 1937 *SA* 1,2,3, 1938 *A* 3
Jaffray, J L (Otago, South Canterbury) 1972 *A* 2, 1975 *S,* 1976 *I, SA* 1, 1977 *BI* 2, 1979 *F* 1,2
Jarden, R A (Wellington) 1951 *A* 1,2, 1952 *A* 1,2, 1953 *W,* 1954 *I, E, S, F,* 1955 *A* 1,2,3, 1956 *SA* 1,2,3,4
Jefferd, A C R (East Coast) 1981 *S* 1,2, *SA* 1
Jessep, E M (Wellington) 1931 *A,* 1932 *A* 1
Johnson, L M (Wellington) 1928 *SA* 1,2,3,4
Johnston, W (Otago) 1907 *A* 1,2,3
Johnstone, B R (Auckland) 1976 *SA* 2, 1977 *BI* 1,2, *F* 1,2, 1978 *I, W, E, S,* 1979 *F* 1,2, *S, E*
Johnstone, P (Otago) 1949 *SA* 2,4, 1950 *BI* 1,2,3,4, 1951 *A* 1,2,3
Jones, I D (North Auckland, North Harbour) 1990 *S* 1,2, *A* 1,2,3, *F* 1,2, 1991 *Arg* 1,2, *A* 1,2, *[E, US, It, C, A, S],* 1992 *Wld* 1,2,3, *I* 1,2, *A* 1,2,3, *SA,* 1993 *I* 2 (R), 3, *WS, S, E,* 1994 *F* 1,2, *SA* 1,3, *A* 1995 *C, [I, W, S, E, SA], A* 1,2, *It, F* 1,2
Jones, M G (North Auckland) 1973 *E* 2
Jones, M N (Auckland) 1987 *[It, Fj, S, F], A,* 1988 *W* 1,2, *A* 2,3, 1989 *F* 1,2, *Arg* 1,2, 1990 *F* 1,2, 1991 *Arg* 1,2, *A* 1,2, *[E, US, S],* 1992 *Wld* 1,3, *I* 2, *A* 1,3, *SA,* 1993 *BI* 1,2,3, *A, WS,* 1994 *SA* 3 (R), *A,* 1995 *A* 1 (R), 2, *It, F* 1,2
Jones, P F H (North Auckland) 1954 *E, S,* 1955 *A* 1,2, 1956 *SA* 3,4, 1958 *A* 1,2,3, 1959 *BI* 1, 1960 *SA* 1
Joseph, H T (Canterbury) 1971 *BI* 2,3
Joseph, J W (Otago) 1992 *Wld* 2,3 (R), *I* 1, *A* 1 (R), 3, *SA,* 1993 *BI* 1,2,3, *A, WS, S, E,* 1994 *SA* 2 (t), 1995 *C, [I, W, J* (R), *S, SA* (R)]

Karam, J F (Wellington, Horowhenua) 1972 *W, S,* 1973 *E* 1, *I, F,* 1974 *A* 1,2,3, *I,* 1975 *S*
Katene, T (Wellington) 1955 *A* 2
Kearney, J C (Otago) 1947 *A* 2, 1949 *SA* 1,2,3
Kelly, J W (Auckland) 1949 *A* 1,2
Kember, G F (Wellington) 1970 *SA* 4
Ketels, R C (Counties) 1980 *W,* 1981 *S* 1,2, *R, F* 1
Kiernan, H A D (Auckland) 1903 *A*
Kilby, F D (Wellington) 1932 *A* 1,2,3, 1934 *A* 2
Killeen, B A (Auckland) 1936 *A* 1
King, R R (West Coast) 1934 *A* 2, 1935 *S, I, W,* 1936 *E, A* 1,2, 1937 *SA* 1,2,3, 1938 *A* 1,2,3
Kingstone, C N (Taranaki) 1921 *SA* 1,2,3
Kirk, D E (Auckland) 1985 *E* 1,2, *A, Arg* 1, 1986 *F* 1, *A* 1,2,3, *F* 2,3, 1987 *[It, Fj, Arg, S, W, F], A*
Kirkpatrick, I A (Canterbury, Poverty Bay) 1967 *F,* 1968 *A* 1 (R), 2, *F* 1,2,3, 1969 *W* 1,2, 1970 *SA* 1,2,3,4, 1971 *BI* 1,2,3,4, 1972 *A* 1,2,3, *W, S,* 1973 *E* 1, *I, F, E* 2, 1974 *A* 1,2,3, *I* 1975 *S,* 1976 *I, SA* 1,2,3,4, 1977 *BI* 1,2,3,4
Kirton, E W (Otago) 1967 *E, W, F, S,* 1968 *A* 1,2, *F* 1,2,3, 1969 *W* 1,2, 1970 *SA* 2,3
Kirwan, J J (Auckland) 1984 *F* 1,2, 1985 *E* 1,2, *A, Arg* 1,2, 1986 *F* 1, *A* 1,2,3, *F* 2,3, 1987 *[It, Fj, Arg, S, W, F], A,* 1988 *W* 1,2, *A* 1,2,3, 1989 *F* 1,2, *A, Arg* 1,2, 1990 *S* 1,2, *A* 1,2,3, *F* 1,2, 1991 *Arg* 2, *A* 1,2, *[E, It, C, A, S],* 1992 *Wld* 1,2 (R), 3, *I* 1,2, *A* 1,2,3, *SA,* 1993 *BI* 2,3, *A, WS,* 1994 *F* 1,2, *SA* 1,2,3

302

Smith, J B (North Auckland) 1946 *A* 1, 1947 *A* 2, 1949 *A* 1,2
Smith, R M (Canterbury) 1955 *A* 1
Smith, W E (Nelson) 1905 *A*
Smith, W R (Canterbury) 1980 *A* 1, 1982 *A* 1,2,3, 1983 *BI* 2,3, *S, E,* 1984 *F* 1,2, *A* 1,2,3, 1985 *E* 1,2, *A, Arg* 2
Snow, E M (Nelson) 1929 *A* 1,2,3

Solomon, F (Auckland) 1931 *A,* 1932 *A* 2,3
Sonntag, W T C (Otago) 1929 *A* 1,2,3
Speight, M W (Waikato) 1986 *A* 1
Spencer, J C (Wellington) 1905 *A,* 1907 *A* 1 (R)
Spiers, J E (Counties) 1979 *S, E,* 1981 *R, F* 1,2
Spillane, A P (South Canterbury) 1913 *A* 2,3

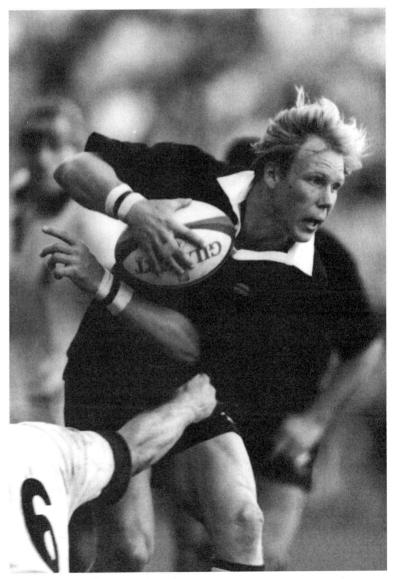

Jeff Wilson: 13 caps for New Zealand since his first appearance against Scotland in 1993.

NEW ZEALAND INTERNATIONAL RECORDS

Both team and individual records are for official New Zealand international matches, up to 30 April 1996.

TEAM RECORDS

Highest score
145 v Japan (145-17) 1995 Bloemfontein

v individual countries
- 60 v Argentina (60-9) 1989 Dunedin
- 38 v Australia { (38-13) 1936 Dunedin
  { (38-3) 1972 Auckland
- 38 v B Isles (38-6) 1983 Auckland
- 73 v Canada (73-7) 1995 Auckland
- 45 v England (45-29) 1995 Cape Town
- 74 v Fiji (74-13) 1987 Christchurch
- 38 v France (38-8) 1906 Paris
- 59 v Ireland (59-6) 1992 Wellington
- 70 v Italy { (70-6) 1987 Auckland
  { (70-6) 1995 Bologna
- 145 v Japan (145-17) 1995 Bloemfontein
- 14 v Romania (14-6) 1981 Bucharest
- 27 v S Africa (27-24) 1992 Johannesburg
- 51 v Scotland (51-15) 1993 Murrayfield
- 51 v United States (51-3) 1913 Berkeley
- 54 v Wales (54-9) 1988 Auckland
- 35 v W Samoa (35-13) 1993 Auckland

Biggest winning points margin
128 v Japan (145-17) 1995 Bloemfontein

v individual countries
- 51 v Argentina (60-9) 1989 Dunedin
- 35 v Australia (38-3) 1972 Auckland
- 32 v B Isles (38-6) 1983 Auckland
- 66 v Canada (73-7) 1995 Auckland
- 27 v England (42-15) 1985 Wellington
- 61 v Fiji (74-13) 1987 Christchurch
- 30 v France (38-8) 1906 Paris
- 53 v Ireland (59-6) 1992 Wellington
- 64 v Italy { (70-6) 1987 Auckland
  { (70-6) 1995 Bologna
- 128 v Japan (145-17) 1995 Bloemfontein
- 8 v Romania (14-6) 1981 Bucharest
- 17 v S Africa (20-3) 1965 Auckland
- 36 v Scotland (51-15) 1993 Murrayfield
- 48 v United States (51-3) 1913 Berkeley
- 49 v Wales (52-3) 1988 Christchurch
- 22 v W Samoa (35-13) 1993 Auckland

Longest winning sequence
17 matches – 1965-69

Highest score by opposing team
30 Australia (16-30) 1978 Auckland

by individual countries
- 21 Argentina (21-21) 1985 Buenos Aires
- 30 Australia (16-30) 1978 Auckland
- 20 B Isles (7-20) 1993 Wellington
- 13 Canada (29-13) 1991 Lille
- 29 England (45-29) Cape Town
- 13 Fiji (74-13) 1987 Christchurch
- 24 France (19-24) 1979 Auckland
- 21 Ireland (24-21) 1992 Dunedin
- 21 Italy (31-21) 1991 Leicester
- 17 Japan (145-17) 1995 Bloemfontein
- 6 Romania (14-6) 1981 Bucharest
- 24 S Africa { (12-24) 1981 Wellington
  { (27-24) 1992 Johannesburg
- 30 Scotland (48-30) 1995 Pretoria
- 6 United States (46-6) 1991 Gloucester
- 16 Wales (19-16) 1972 Cardiff
- 13 W Samoa (35-13) 1993 Auckland

Biggest losing points margin
17 v S Africa (0-17) 1928 Durban

v individual countries
- 16 v Australia (10-26) 1980 Sydney
- 13 v B Isles (7-20) 1993 Wellington
- 13 v England (0-13) 1936 Twickenham
- 14 v France (8-22) 1994 Christchurch
- 17 v S Africa (0-17) 1928 Durban
- 5 v Wales (8-13) 1953 Cardiff

No defeats v Argentina, Canada, Fiji, Ireland, Italy, Japan, Romania, Scotland, United States or Western Samoa

Longest losing sequence
6 matches – 1949

Most tries by New Zealand in an international
21 v Japan (145-17) 1995 Bloemfontein

Most tries against New Zealand in an international
5 { by S Africa (6-17) 1937 Auckland
  { by Australia (16-30) 1978 Auckland
  { by World XV (54-26) 1992 Wellington

Most points on overseas tour (all matches)
868 in B Isles/France (33 matches) 1905-06

Most tries on overseas tour
215 in B Isles/France (33 matches) 1905-06

INDIVIDUAL RECORDS

Most capped player
S B T Fitzpatrick 73   1986-95
in individual positions
Full-back
D B Clarke   31   1956-64
Wing
J J Kirwan   63   1984-94
Centre (includes 2nd five-eighth)
B J Robertson   34[1]   1972-81
1st five-eighth
G J Fox   46   1985-93
Scrum-half
G T M Bachop   31   1989-95
Prop
R W Loe   48(49)[2]   1987-95
Hooker
S B T Fitzpatrick   73   1986-95
Lock
G W Whetton   58   1981-91
Flanker
M N Jones   38(40)[3]   1987-95
No 8
M G Mexted   34[4]   1979-85

[1] *W K Little, 36 caps, has won 32 as a centre and 4 as a fly-half.*
[2] *One of Loe's appearances was as a temporary replacement.*
[3] *Two of Jones' appearances were at No 8.*
[4] *Z V Brooke, 37 caps, won 31 at No 8 and 6 as a flanker.*

Longest international career
E Hughes 15 seasons 1907-21
C E Meads 15 seasons 1957-71

Most consecutive internationals – 63
S B T Fitzpatrick 1986-95

Most internationals as captain – 33
S B T Fitzpatrick 1992-95

Most points in internationals – 645
G J Fox (46 matches) 1985-93

Most points in an international – 45
S D Culhane v Japan 1995 Bloemfontein

Most tries in internationals – 35
J J Kirwan (63 matches) 1984-94

Most tries in an international – 6
M C G Ellis v Japan 1995 Bloemfontein

Most conversions in internationals – 118
G J Fox (46 matches) 1985-93

Most conversions in an international – 20
S D Culhane v Japan 1995 Bloemfontein

Most dropped goals in internationals – 7
G J Fox (46 matches) 1985-93

Most dropped goals in an international – 2
O D Bruce v Ireland 1978 Dublin
F M Botica v France 1986 Christchurch
A P Mehrtens v Australia 1995 Auckland

Most penalty goals in internationals – 128
G J Fox (46 matches) 1985-93

Most penalty goals in an international – 7
G J Fox v W Samoa 1993 Auckland

Most points in international series – 46
A R Hewson (4 appearances) v B Isles 1983

Most points in international series on tour – 38
G J Fox (2 appearances) 1990 France

Most tries in international series on tour – 5
K Svenson (4 appearances) 1924-25 B Isles/France
Svenson scored in each match of the international series

Most points on tour – 230
W J Wallace (25 appearances) 1905-06 B Isles/France

Most tries on tour – 42
J Hunter (23 appearances) 1905-06 B Isles/France

Most points in a tour match – 43
R M Deans v South Australia 1984 Adelaide

Most tries in a tour match – 8
T R Heeps v Northern NSW 1962 Quirindi

WARS DRAIN THE WALLABIES

THE 1995 SEASON IN AUSTRALIA
Greg Campbell

For a year which dawned with such high hopes and expectations, 1995 ended as one of Australian rugby's most turbulent on record with very strained relationships between players and administrators, sackings among players and coaches, officials' resignations and retirements, and with the Wallabies losing both the World Cup and Bledisloe Cup titles. It was a season which demanded inner strength, harmony and team-work but which plummeted into weakness, anarchy and near piracy.

The football revolution encompassed both Rugby Union and Rugby League. Rugby Union had to wage war on three fronts, taking on the anti-establishment Super League and the proposed rebel World Rugby Corporation as well as the traditional Australian Rugby League competition.

Ironically, Rupert Murdoch's News Corporation proved to be the saviour of Australian rugby after his Super League plans had loomed as a major threat only months earlier. Newscorp's £360 million ten-year deal with the Australian, New Zealand and South African Rugby Unions for provincial and international rugby television rights ultimately provided the Australian game with the necessary funding to retain its players.

The Ross Turnbull-led and Kerry Packer-backed WRC became the most perilous battlefront as it threatened to buy the majority of the country's best and most promising players rather than a specially selected handful. The roles of several leading Australian players who actively recruited colleagues while serving as Wallaby team members bordered on treason.

Amid all the skirmishes individual and team performances suffered, and the Wallabies completed the year with four wins and four losses – Australia's worst record since 1989. Yet the warning signs of a decline in form had already surfaced with their inconsistent displays in 1994. This slide had been masked by spasmodic bursts of brilliant play. The wars left many scars and several casualties. The principle victim was Bob Dwyer, who was sacked as Wallaby coach later in the year and replaced by Greg Smith of New South Wales. Dwyer ended his second term as national coach with an overall record of 45 wins, 25 losses and two draws from 72 Tests. Sadly, the national coaching appointment once again became shamefully political among the member state unions and Smith's election was largely the result of the NSW Rugby Union's disproportionate five votes on the 14-man ARFU council. By the end of the year, the ARFU had taken measures to give the Union a more corporate look by electing a ten-man board which will include two players' representatives – one of whom will have full voting rights.

There were many battles within the ARFU administration itself, which resulted in the resignations of volatile chairman Leo Williams and chief executive Bruce Hayman, who left less than 18 months after taking office. Dick McGruther makes a welcome return as the new chairman while highly qualified businessman John O'Neill becomes joint chief executive and managing director under the new corporate structure. While peace between the players and the Union over WRC was finally brokered, it was an uneasy truce: the players' association claimed that the ARFU had reneged on promises regarding the distribution of the players' 95 per cent share of Newscorp's television rights payment.

The year saw four new Wallaby caps in winger Joe Roff, flanker Daniel Manu, scrum-half Steve Merrick and hooker Michael Foley, while record-breaking fly-half Michael Lynagh announced his retirement from international rugby after the World Cup. Lynagh's brilliant match-winning performances since he was first capped in 1983 will see his name etched into the record books as one of Australia's greatest-ever players. The mercurial David Campese was another victim, dropped from the team for the two Tests against the All Blacks.

Despite exhaustive and expensive preparations, the Wallabies failed to perform at anywhere near the levels of the previous all-conquering four years. Too many players were crocked with crippling injuries, the forwards lost their dominance and muscle, ball-retention was dreadful and back-line play was hesitant and stagnant. The record-breaking 53-7 and 31-13 Test wins over Argentina prior to the World Cup were flawed, while the World Cup itself saw the Wallabies well beaten in their first match by ultimate champions South Africa and subsequent unconvincing pool victories over Romania and Canada. The quarter-final loss to England in such dramatic, heart-breaking circumstances delivered the final, cruel blow to Australia's four-year term as world champions. The All Blacks further underlined the Wallabies' decline when they swept to a 2-0 Bledisloe Cup series win.

Amid the gloom which enveloped the year, there were some highlights, such as John Eales' superb displays, Tim Horan's remarkable comeback from a horrific knee injury and Queensland's successful defence of the Super-10 championship.

MAJOR PROVINCIAL MATCHES: NSW 33, Queensland 21; NSW 30, Queensland 23
SYDNEY GRAND FINAL: Gordon 24, Canberra 11
BRISBANE GRAND FINAL: Southern Districts 28, Eastern Districts 11

AUSTRALIAN INTERNATIONAL PLAYERS
(up to 30 April 1996)

ABBREVIATIONS

Arg – Argentina; *BI* – British Isles teams; *C* – Canada; *E* – England; *F* – France; *Fj* – Fiji; *I* – Ireland; *It* – Italy; *J* – Japan; *M* – Maoris; *NZ* – New Zealand; *R* – Romania; *S* – Scotland; *SA* – South Africa; *SK* – South Korea; *Tg* – Tonga; *US* – United States of America; *W* – Wales; *WS* – Western Samoa; (R) – Replacement; (t) – temporary replacement. Entries in square brackets [ ] indicate appearances in the Rugby World Cup.

STATE ABBREVIATIONS

ACT – Australian Capital Territory; NSW – New South Wales; Q – Queensland; V – Victoria; WA – Western Australia.

N.B. In the summer of 1986, the ARU retrospectively granted full Australian Test status to the five international matches played by the 1927-28 touring team to Europe. In 1988 Test status was extended to all those who played overseas in the 1920s.

Note: When a series has taken place, figures denote the particular matches in which players featured. Thus 1963 *SA* 2,4 indicates that a player appeared in the second and fourth Tests of the 1963 series against South Africa.

Abrahams, A M F (NSW) 1967 *NZ*, 1968 *NZ* 1, 1969 *W*
Adams, N J (NSW) 1955 *NZ* 1
Adamson, R W (NSW) 1912 *US*
Allan, T (NSW) 1946 *NZ* 1, *M*, *NZ* 2, 1947 *NZ* 2, *S*, *I*, *W*, 1948 *E*, *F*, 1949 *M* 1,2,3, *NZ* 1,2
Anlezark, E A (NSW) 1905 *NZ*
Armstrong, A R (NSW) 1923 *NZ* 1,2
Austin, L R (NSW) 1963 *E*

Baker, R L (NSW) 1904 *BI* 1,2
Baker, W H (NSW) 1914 *NZ* 1,2,3
Ballesty, J P (NSW) 1968 *NZ* 1,2, *F, I, S*, 1969 *W, SA* 2,3,4,
Bannon, D P (NSW) 1946 *M*
Bardsley, E J (NSW) 1928 *NZ* 1,3, *M* (R)
Barker, H S (NSW) 1952 *Fj* 1,2, *NZ* 1,2, 1953 *SA* 4, 1954 *Fj* 1,2
Barnett, J T (NSW) 1907 *NZ* 1,2,3, 1908 *W*, 1909 *E*
Barry, M J (Q) 1971 *SA* 3
Barton, R F D (NSW) 1899 *BI* 3
Batch, P G (NSW) 1975 *S, W*, 1976 *E, Fj* 1,2,3, *F* 1,2, 1978 *W* 1,2, *NZ* 1,2,3, 1979 *Arg* 2
Batterham, R P (NSW) 1967 *NZ*, 1970 *S*
Battishall, B R (NSW) 1973 *E*
Baxter, A J (NSW) 1949 *M* 1,2,3, *NZ* 1,2, 1951 *NZ* 1,2, 1952 *NZ* 1,2
Baxter, T J (NSW) 1958 *NZ* 3
Beith, B McN (NSW) 1914 *NZ* 3
Bell, K R (Q) 1968 *S*
Bennett, W G (Q) 1931 *M*, 1933 *SA* 1,2,3,
Bermingham, J V (Q) 1934 *NZ* 1,2, 1937 *SA* 1
Berne, J E (NSW) 1975 *S*
Besomo, K S (NSW) 1979 *I* 2
Betts, T N (Q) 1951 *NZ* 2,3, 1954 *Fj* 2
Biilmann, R R (NSW) 1933 *SA* 1,2,3,4
Birt, R (Q) 1914 *NZ* 2
Black, J W (NSW) 1985 *C* 1,2, *NZ*, *Fj* 1
Blackwood, J G (NSW) 1923 *NZ* 1,2,3, 1925 *NZ*, 1927 *I*, *W, S*, 1928 *E, F*
Blair, M R (NSW) 1928 *F*, 1931 *M*, *NZ*
Bland, G V (NSW) 1928 *NZ* 3, *M*, 1932 *NZ* 1,2,3, 1933 *SA* 1,2,4,5
Blomley, J (NSW) 1949 *M* 1,2,3, *NZ* 1,2, 1950 *BI* 1,2
Boland, S B (Q) 1899 *BI* 3,4, 1903 *NZ*
Bond, J H (NSW) 1921 *NZ*
Bonis, E T (Q) 1929 *NZ* 1,2,3, 1930 *BI*, 1931 *M*, *NZ*, 1932 *NZ* 1,2,3, 1933 *SA* 1,2,3,4,5, 1934 *NZ* 1,2, 1936 *NZ* 1,2, *M*, 1937 *SA* 1, 1938 *NZ* 1
Bosler, J M (NSW) 1953 *SA* 1
Bouffler, R G (NSW) 1899 *BI* 3
Bourke, T K (Q) 1947 *NZ* 2
Bowen, S (NSW) 1993 *SA* 1,2,3, 1995 [*R*], *NZ* 1,2
Bowers, A J A (NSW) 1923 *NZ* 3, 1925 *NZ*, 1927 *I*
Boyce, E S (NSW) 1962 *NZ* 1,2, 1964 *NZ* 1,2,3, 1965 *SA* 1,2, 1966 *W, S*, 1967 *E, I* 1, *F, I* 2
Boyce, J S (NSW) 1962 *NZ* 3,4,5, 1963 *E*, *SA* 1,2,3,4, 1964 *NZ* 1,3, 1965 *SA* 1,2
Boyd, A (NSW) 1899 *BI* 3

Boyd, A F McC (Q) 1958 *M* 1
Brass, J E (NSW) 1966 *BI* 2, *W, S*, 1967 *E, I* 1, *F, I* 2, *NZ*, 1968 *NZ* 1, *F, I, S*
Breckenridge, J W (NSW) 1927 *I, W, S*, 1928 *E, F*, 1929 *NZ* 1,2,3, 1930 *BI*
Brial, M C (NSW) 1993 *F* 1 (R), 2
Bridle, O L (V) 1931 *M*, 1932 *NZ* 1,2,3, 1933 *SA* 3,4,5, 1934 *NZ* 1,2, 1936 *NZ* 1,2, *M*
Broad, E G (Q) 1949 *M* 1
Brockhoff, J D (NSW) 1949 *M* 2,3, *NZ* 1,2, 1950 *BI* 1,2, 1951 *NZ* 2,3
Brown, B R (Q) 1972 *NZ* 1,3
Brown, J V (NSW) 1956 *SA* 1,2, 1957 *NZ* 1,2, 1958 *W, I, E, S, F*
Brown, R C (NSW) 1975 *E* 1,2
Brown, S W (NSW) 1953 *SA* 2,3,4
Bryant, H (NSW) 1925 *NZ*
Buchan, A J (NSW) 1946 *NZ* 1,2, 1947 *NZ* 1,2, *S, I, W*, 1948 *E, F*, 1949 *M* 3
Bull, D (NSW) 1928 *M*
Buntine, H (NSW) 1923 *NZ* 1 (R)
Burdon, A (NSW) 1903 *NZ*, 1904 *BI* 1,2, 1905 *NZ*
Burge, A B (NSW) 1907 *NZ* 3, 1908 *W*
Burge, P H (NSW) 1907 *NZ* 1,2,3
Burge, R (NSW) 1928 *NZ* 1,2,3 (R), *M* (R)
Burke, B T (NSW) 1988 *S* (R)
Burke, C T (NSW) 1946 *NZ* 2, 1947 *NZ* 2, *S, I, W*, 1948 *E, F*, 1949 *M* 2,3, *NZ* 1,2, 1950 *BI* 1,2, 1951 *NZ* 1,2,3, 1953 *SA* 2,3,4, 1954 *Fj* 1, 1955 *NZ* 1,2,3, 1956 *SA* 1,2,
Burke, M (NSW) 1993 *SA* 3 (R), *F* 1, 1994 *I* 1,2, *It* 1,2, 1995 [*C, R, E*], *NZ* 1,2
Burke, M P (NSW) 1984 *E* (R), *I*, 1985 *C* 1,2, *NZ, Fj* 1,2, 1986 *It* (R), *F, Arg* 1,2, *NZ* 1,2,3, 1987 *SK*, [*US, J, I, F, W*], *NZ, Arg* 1,2
Burnet, D R (NSW) 1972 *F* 1,2, *NZ* 1,2,3, *Fj*
Butler, O F (NSW) 1969 *SA* 1,2, 1970 *S*, 1971 *SA* 2,3, *F* 1,2

Calcraft, W J (NSW) 1985 *C* 1, 1986 *It, Arg* 2
Caldwell, B C (NSW) 1928 *NZ* 3
Cameron, A S (NSW) 1951 *NZ* 1,2,3, 1952 *Fj* 1,2, *NZ* 1,2, 1953 *SA* 1,2,3,4, 1954 *Fj* 1,2, 1955 *NZ* 1,2,3, 1956 *SA* 1,2, 1957 *NZ* 1, 1958 *I*
Campbell, J D (NSW) 1910 *NZ* 1,2,3
Campbell, W A (Q) 1984 *Fj*, 1986 *It, F, Arg* 1,2, *NZ* 1,2,3, 1987 *SK*, [*E, US, J* (R), *I, F*], *NZ*, 1988 *E*, 1989 *BI* 1,2,3, *NZ*, 1990 *NZ* 2,3
Campese, D I (ACT, NSW) 1982 *NZ* 1,2,3, 1983 *US, Arg* 1,2, *NZ, It, F* 1,2, 1984 *Fj, NZ* 1,2,3, *E, I, W, S*, 1985 *Fj* 1,2, 1986 *It, F, Arg* 1,2, *NZ* 1,2,3, 1987 [*E, US, J, I, F, W*], *NZ, Arg* 1,2, 1988 *E* 1,2, *NZ* 1,2,3, *E, S*, *It*, 1989 *BI* 1,2,3, *NZ, F* 1,2, 1990 *F* 2,3, *US, NZ* 1,2,3, 1991 *W, E, NZ* 1,2, [*Arg, WS, W, I, NZ, E*], 1992 *S* 1,2, *NZ* 1,2,3, *SA, I, W*, 1993 *Tg, NZ, SA* 1,2,3, *C, F* 1,2, 1994 *I* 1,2, *It* 1,2, *WS, NZ*, 1995 *Arg* 1,2, [*SA, C, E*], *NZ* 2 (R)
Canniffe, W D (Q) 1907 *NZ* 2

Carberry, C M (NSW, Q) 1973 *Tg* 2, *E*, 1976 *I*, *US*, *Fj* 1,2,3, 1981 *F* 1,2, *I*, *W*, *S*, 1982 *E*
Cardy, A M (NSW) 1966 *BI* 1,2, *W*, *S*, 1967 *E*, *I* 1, *F*, 1968 *NZ* 1,2
Carew, P J (Q) 1899 *BI* 1,2,3,4
Carmichael, P (Q) 1904 *BI* 2, 1907 *NZ* 1, 1908 *W*, 1909 *E*
Carozza, P V (Q) 1990 *F* 1,2,3, *NZ* 2,3, 1992 *S* 1,2, *NZ* 1,2,3, *SA*, *I*, *W*, 1993 *Tg*, *NZ*
Carpenter, M G (V) 1938 *NZ* 1,2,
Carr, E T A (NSW) 1913 *NZ* 1,2,3, 1914 *NZ* 1,2,3
Carr, E W (NSW) 1921 *NZ* 1 (R)
Carroll, D B (NSW) 1908 *W*, 1912 *US*
Carroll, J C (NSW) 1953 *SA* 1
Carroll, J H (NSW) 1958 *M* 2,3, *NZ* 1,2,3, 1959 *BI* 1,2
Carson, J (NSW) 1899 *BI* 1
Carson, P J (NSW) 1979 *NZ*, 1980 *NZ* 3
Carter, D G (NSW) 1988 *E* 1,2, *NZ* 1, 1989 *F* 1,2
Casey, T V (NSW) 1963 *SA* 2,3,4, 1964 *NZ* 1,2,3
Catchpole, K W (NSW) 1961 *Fj* 1,2,3, *SA* 1,2, *F*, 1962 *NZ* 1,2,4, 1963 *SA* 2,3,4, 1964 *NZ* 1,2,3, 1965 *SA* 1,2, 1966 *BI* 1,2, *W*, *S*, 1967 *E*, *I* 1, *F*, *I* 2, *NZ*, 1968 *NZ* 1
Cawsey, R M (NSW) 1949 *M* 1, *NZ* 1,2
Cerutti, W H (NSW) 1928 *NZ* 1,2,3, *M*, 1929 *NZ* 1,2,3, 1930 *BI*, 1931 *M*, *NZ*, 1932 *NZ* 1,2,3, 1933 *SA* 1,2,3,4,5, 1936 *M*, 1937 *SA* 1,2
Challoner, R L (NSW) 1899 *BI* 2
Chapman, G A (NSW) 1962 *NZ* 3,4,5
Clark, J G (Q) 1931 *M*, *NZ*, 1932 *NZ* 1,2, 1933 *SA* 1
Clarken, J C (NSW) 1905 *NZ*, 1910 *NZ* 1,2,3
Cleary, M A (NSW) 1961 *Fj* 1,2,3, *SA* 1,2, *F*
Clements, P (NSW) 1982 *NZ* 3
Clifford, M (NSW) 1938 *NZ* 3
Cobb, W G (NSW) 1899 *BI* 3,4
Cocks, M R (NSW, Q) 1972 *F* 1,2, *NZ* 2,3, *Fj*, 1973 *Tg* 1,2, *W*, *E*, 1975 *J* 1
Codey, D (NSW Country, Q) 1983 *Arg* 1, 1984 *E*, *W*, *S*, 1985 *C* 2, *NZ*, 1986 *F*, *Arg* 1, 1987 [*US*, *J*, *F* (R), *W*], *NZ*
Cody, E W (NSW) 1913 *NZ* 1,2,3
Colbert, R (NSW) 1952 *Fj* 2, *NZ* 1,2, 1953 *SA* 2,3,4
Cole, J W (NSW) 1968 *NZ* 1,2, *F*, *I*, *S*, 1969 *W*, *SA* 1,2,3,4, 1970 *S*, 1971 *SA* 1,2,3, *F* 1,2, 1972 *NZ* 1,2,3, 1973 *Tg* 1,2, 1974 *NZ* 1,2,3
Collins, P K (NSW) 1937 *SA* 2, 1938 *NZ* 2,3
Colton, A J (Q) 1899 *BI* 1,3
Colton, T (Q) 1904 *BI* 1,2
Comrie-Thomson, I R (NSW) 1928 *NZ* 1,2,3 *M*
Connor, D M (Q) 1958 *W*, *I*, *E*, *S*, *F*, *M* 2,3, *NZ* 1,2,3, 1959 *BI* 1,2
Constable, R (Q) 1994 *I* 2 (t & R)
Cook, M T (Q) 1986 *F*, 1987 *SK*, [*J*], 1988 *E* 1, *NZ* 1,2,3, *E*, *S*, *It*
Cooke, B P (Q) 1979 *I* 1
Cooke, G M (Q) 1932 *NZ* 1,2,3, 1933 *SA* 2,3, 1946 *NZ* 2, 1947 *NZ* 2, *S*, *I*, *W*, 1948 *E*, *F*
Coolican, J E (NSW) 1982 *NZ* 1, 1983 *It*, *F* 1,2
Corfe, A C (Q) 1899 *BI* 2
Cornelsen, G (NSW) 1974 *NZ* 2,3, 1975 *J* 2, *S*, *W*, 1976 *E*, *F* 1,2, 1978 *W* 1,2, *NZ* 1,2,3, 1979 *I* 1,2, *NZ*, *Arg* 1,2, 1980 *NZ* 1,2,3, 1981 *I*, *W*, *S*, 1982 *E*
Cornes, J R (Q) 1972 *Fj*
Cornforth, R G W (NSW) 1947 *NZ* 1, 1950 *BI* 2
Cornish, P (ACT) 1990 *F* 2,3, *NZ* 1
Costello, P P S (Q) 1950 *BI* 2
Cottrell, N V (Q) 1949 *M* 1,2,3, *NZ* 1,2, 1950 *BI* 1,2, 1951 *NZ* 1,2,3, 1952 *Fj* 1,2, *NZ* 1,2
Cowper, D L (V) 1931 *NZ*, 1932 *NZ* 1,2,3, 1933 *SA* 1,2,3,4,5
Cox, B P (NSW) 1952 *Fj* 1,2, *NZ* 1,2, 1954 *Fj* 2, 1955 *NZ* 1, 1956 *SA* 2, 1957 *NZ* 1,2
Cox, M H (NSW) 1981 *W*, *S*
Cox, P A (NSW) 1979 *Arg* 1,2, 1980 *Fj*, *NZ* 1,2, 1981 *W* (R), *S*, 1982 *S* 1,2, *NZ* 1,2,3, 1984 *Fj*, *NZ* 1,2,3
Craig, R R (NSW) 1908 *W*
Crakanthorp, J S (NSW) 1923 *NZ* 3
Cremin, J F (NSW) 1946 *NZ* 1,2, 1947 *NZ* 1
Crittle, C P (NSW) 1962 *NZ* 4, 5, 1963 *SA* 2,3,4, 1964 *NZ* 1,2,3, 1965 *SA* 1,2, 1966 *BI* 1,2, *S*, 1967 *E*, *I*
Croft, B H D (NSW) 1928 *M*
Cross, J R (NSW) 1955 *NZ* 1,2,3

Cross, K A (NSW) 1949 *M* 1, *NZ* 1,2, 1950 *BI* 1,2, 1951 *NZ* 2,3, 1952 *NZ* 1, 1953 *SA* 1,2,3,4, 1954 *Fj* 1,2, 1955 *NZ* 3, 1956 *SA* 1,2, 1957 *NZ* 1,2
Crossman, O C (NSW) 1925 *NZ*, 1929 *NZ* 2, 1930 *BI*
Crowe, P J (NSW) 1976 *F* 2, 1978 *W* 1,2, 1979 *I* 2, *NZ*, *Arg* 1
Crowley, D J (Q) 1989 *BI* 1,2,3, 1991 [*WS*], 1992 *I*, *W*, 1993 *C* (R), 1995 *Arg* 1,2, [*SA*, *E*], *NZ* 1
Curley, T G P (NSW) 1957 *NZ* 1,2, 1958 *W*, *I*, *E*, *S*, *F*, *M* 1, *NZ* 1,2,3
Curran, D J (NSW) 1980 *NZ* 3, 1981 *F* 1,2, *W*, 1983 *Arg* 1
Currie, E W (Q) 1899 *BI* 2
Cutler, S A G (NSW) 1982 *NZ* 2 (R), 1984 *NZ* 1,2,3, *E*, *I*, *W*, *S*, 1985 *C* 1,2, *NZ*, *Fj* 1, 1986 *It*, *F*, *NZ* 1,2,3, 1987 *SK*, [*E*, *J*, *I*, *F*, *W*], *NZ*, *Arg* 1,2, 1988 *E* 1,2, *NZ* 1,2,3, *E*, *S*, *It*, 1989 *BI* 1,2,3, *NZ*, 1991 [*WS*]

Daly, A J (NSW) 1989 *NZ*, *F* 1,2, 1990 *F* 1,2,3, *US*, *NZ* 1,2,3, 1991 *W*, *E*, *NZ* 1,2, [*Arg*, *W*, *I*, *NZ*, *E*], 1992 *S* 1,2, *NZ* 1,2,3, *SA*, 1993 *Tg*, *NZ*, *SA* 1,2,3, *C*, *F* 1,2, 1994 *I* 1,2, *It* 1,2, *WS*, *NZ*, 1995 [*C*, *R*]
D'Arcy, A M (Q) 1980 *Fj*, *NZ* 3, 1981 *F* 1,2, *I*, *W*, *S*, 1982 *E*, *S* 1,2
Darveniza, P (NSW) 1969 *W*, *SA* 2,3,4
Davidson, R A L (NSW) 1952 *Fj* 1,2, *NZ* 1,2, 1953 *SA* 1, 1957 *NZ* 1,2, 1958 *W*, *I*, *E*, *S*, *F*, *M* 1
Davis, C C (NSW) 1949 *NZ* 1, 1951 *NZ* 1,2,3
Davis, E H (V) 1947 *S*, *W*, 1949 *M* 1,2
Davis, G V (NSW) 1963 *E*, *SA* 1,2,3,4, 1964 *NZ* 1,2,3, 1965 *SA* 1, 1966 *BI* 1,2, *W*, *S*, 1967 *E*, *I* 1, *F*, *I* 2, *NZ*, 1968 *NZ* 1,2, *F*, *I*, *S*, 1969 *W*, *SA* 1,2,3,4, 1970 *S*, 1971 *SA* 1,2,3, *F* 1,2, 1972 *F* 1,2, *NZ* 1,2,3
Davis, G W G (NSW) 1955 *NZ* 2,3
Davis, R A (NSW) 1974 *NZ* 1,2,3
Davis, T S R (NSW) 1921 *NZ*, 1923 *NZ* 1,2,3
Davis, W (NSW) 1899 *BI* 1,3,4
Dawson, W L (NSW) 1946 *NZ* 1,2
Diett, L J (NSW) 1959 *BI* 1,2
Dix, W (NSW) 1907 *NZ* 1,2,3, 1909 *E*
Dixon, E J (Q) 1904 *BI* 3
Donald, K J (Q) 1957 *NZ* 1, 1958 *W*, *I*, *E*, *S*, *M* 2,3, 1959 *BI* 1,2
Dore, E (Q) 1904 *BI* 1
Dore, M J (Q) 1905 *NZ*
Dorr, R W (V) 1936 *M*, 1937 *SA* 1
Douglas, J A (V) 1962 *NZ* 3,4,5
Dowse, J H (NSW) 1961 *Fj* 1,2, *SA* 1,2
Dunbar, A R (NSW) 1910 *NZ* 1,2,3, 1912 *US*
Dunlop, E E (V) 1932 *NZ* 3, 1934 *NZ* 1
Dunn, P K (NSW) 1958 *NZ* 1,2,3, 1959 *BI* 1,2
Dunn, V A (NSW) 1921 *NZ*
Dunworth, D A (Q) 1971 *F* 1,2, 1972 *F* 1,2, 1976 *Fj* 2
Dwyer, L J (NSW) 1910 *NZ* 1,2,3, 1912 *US*, 1913 *NZ* 3, 1914 *NZ* 1,2,3

Eales, J A (Q) 1991 *W*, *E*, *NZ* 1,2, [*Arg*, *WS*, *W*, *I*, *NZ*, *E*], 1992 *S* 1,2, *NZ* 1,2,3, *SA*, *I*, 1994 *I* 1,2, *It* 1,2, *WS*, *NZ*, 1995 *Arg* 1,2, [*SA*, *C*, *R*, *E*], *NZ* 1,2
Eastes, C C (NSW) 1946 *NZ* 1,2, 1947 *NZ* 1,2, 1949 *M* 1,2
Egerton, R H (NSW) 1991 *W*, *E*, *NZ* 1,2, [*Arg*, *W*, *I*, *NZ*, *E*]
Ella, G A (NSW) 1982 *NZ* 1,2, 1983 *F* 1,2, 1988 *E* 2, *NZ* 1
Ella, G J (NSW) 1982 *S* 1, 1983 *It*, 1985 *C* 2 (R), *Fj* 2
Ella, M G (NSW) 1980 *NZ* 1,2,3, 1981 *F* 2, *S*, 1982 *E*, *S* 1, *NZ* 1,2,3, 1983 *US*, *Arg* 1,2, *NZ*, *It*, *F* 1,2, 1984 *Fj*, *NZ* 1,2,3, *E*, *I*, *W*, *S*
Ellem, M A (NSW) 1976 *Fj* 3 (R)
Elliott, F M (NSW) 1957 *NZ* 1
Elliott, R E (NSW) 1921 *NZ*, 1923 *NZ* 1,2,3
Ellis, C S (NSW) 1899 *BI* 1,2,3,4
Ellis, K J (NSW) 1958 *NZ* 1,2,3, 1959 *BI* 1,2
Ellwood, B J (NSW) 1958 *NZ* 1,2,3, 1961 *Fj* 2,3, *SA* 1, *F*, 1962 *NZ* 1,2,3,4,5, 1963 *SA* 1,2,3,4, 1964 *NZ* 3, 1965 *SA* 1,2, 1966 *BI* 1,2
Emanuel, D M (NSW) 1957 *NZ* 2, 1958 *W*, *I*, *E*, *S*, *F*, *M* 1,2,3
Emery, N A (NSW) 1947 *NZ* 2, *S*, *I*, *W*, 1948 *E*, *F*, 1949 *M* 2,3, *NZ* 1,2
Erasmus, D J (NSW) 1923 *NZ* 1,2
Erby, A B (NSW) 1923 *NZ* 2,3
Evans, L J (Q) 1903 *NZ*, 1904 *BI* 1,3
Evans, W T (Q) 1899 *BI* 1,2

Fahey, E J (NSW) 1912 *US*, 1913 *NZ* 1,2, 1914 *NZ* 3

Fairfax, R L (NSW) 1971 *F* 1,2, 1972 *F* 1,2, NZ 1, *Fj,* 1973 *W, E*
Farmer, E H (Q) 1910 *NZ* 1
Farr-Jones, N C (NSW) 1984 *E, I, W, S,* 1985 *C* 1,2, *NZ, Fj* 1,2, 1986 *It, F, Arg* 1,2, *NZ* 1,2,3, 1987 *SK,* [*E, I, F, W* (R)], *NZ, Arg* 2, 1988 *E* 1,2, *NZ* 1,2,3, *E, S, It,* 1989 *BI* 1,2,3, *NZ, F* 1,2, 1990 *F* 1,2,3, *US, NZ* 1,2,3, 1991 *W, E, NZ* 1,2, [*Arg, WS, I, NZ, E*], 1992 *S* 1,2, *NZ* 1,2,3, *SA,* 1993 *NZ, SA* 1,2,3
Fay, G (NSW) 1971 *SA* 2, 1972 *NZ* 1,2,3, 1973 *Tg* 1,2, *W, E,* 1974 *NZ* 1,2,3, 1975 *E* 1,2, *J* 1, *S, W,* 1976 *I, US,* 1978 *W* 1,2, *NZ* 1,2,3, 1979 *I* 1
Fenwicke, P T (NSW) 1957 *NZ* 1, 1958 *W, I, E,* 1959 *BI* 1,2
Ferguson, R T (NSW) 1923 *NZ* 3
Fihelly, J A (Q) 1907 *NZ* 2
Finlay, A N (NSW) 1927 *I, W, S,* 1928 *E, F,* 1929 *NZ* 1,2,3, 1930 *BI*
Finley, F G (NSW) 1904 *BI* 3
Finnane, S C (NSW) 1975 *E* 1, *J* 1,2, 1976 *E,* 1978 *W* 1,2
FitzSimons, P (NSW) 1989 *F* 1,2, 1990 *F* 1,2,3, *US, NZ* 1
Flanagan, P (Q) 1907 *NZ* 1,2
Flett, J A (NSW) 1990 *US, NZ* 2,3, 1991 [*WS*]
Flynn, J P (Q) 1914 *NZ* 1,2
Fogarty, J R (Q) 1949 *M* 2,3
Foley, M A (Q) 1995 [*C* (R), *R*]
Forbes, C F (Q) 1953 *SA* 2,3,4, 1954 *Fj* 1, 1956 *SA* 1,2
Ford, B (Q) 1957 *NZ* 2
Ford, E E (NSW) 1927 *I, W, S,* 1928 *E, F,* 1929 *NZ* 1,3
Ford, J A (NSW) 1925 *NZ,* 1927 *I, W, S,* 1928 *E,* 1929 *NZ* 1,2,3, 1930 *BI*
Forman, T R (NSW) 1968 *I, S,* 1969 *W, SA* 1,2,3,4
Fox, C L (NSW) 1921 *NZ,* 1928 *F*
Fox, O G (NSW) 1958 *F*
Francis, E (Q) 1914 *NZ* 1,2
Frawley, D (Q, NSW) 1986 *Arg* 2 (R), 1987 *Arg* 1,2, 1988 *E* 1,2, *NZ* 1,2,3, *S, It*
Freedman, J E (NSW) 1962 *NZ* 3,4,5, 1963 *SA* 1
Freeman, E (NSW) 1946 *NZ* 1 (R), *M*
Freney, M E (Q) 1972 *NZ* 1,2,3, 1973 *Tg* 1, *W, E* (R)
Furness, D C (NSW) 1946 *M*
Futter, F C (NSW) 1904 *BI* 3

Gardner, J M (Q) 1987 *Arg* 2, 1988 *E* 1, *NZ* 1, *E*
Gardner, W C (NSW) 1950 *BI* 1
Garner, R L (NSW) 1949 *NZ* 1,2
Gavin, K A (NSW) 1909 *E*
Gavin, T B (NSW) 1988 *NZ* 2,3, *S, It* (R), 1989 *NZ* (R), *F* 1,2, 1990 *F* 1,2,3, *US, NZ* 1,2,3, 1991 *W, E, NZ* 1, 1992 *S* 1,2, *SA, I, W,* 1993 *Tg, NZ, SA* 1,2,3, *C, F* 1,2, 1994 *I* 1,2, *It* 1,2, *WS, NZ,* 1995 *Arg* 1,2, [*SA, C, R, E*], *NZ* 1,2
Gelling, A M (NSW) 1972 *NZ* 1, *Fj*
George, H W (NSW) 1910 *NZ* 1,2,3, 1912 *US,* 1913 *NZ* 1,3, 1914 *NZ* 1,3
George, W G (NSW) 1923 *NZ* 1,2, 1928 *NZ* 1,2,3, *M*
Gibbons, E de C (NSW) 1936 *NZ* 1,2, *M*
Gibbs, P R (V) 1966 *S*
Gilbert, H (NSW) 1910 *NZ* 1,2,3
Girvan, B (ACT) 1988 *E*
Gordon, G C (NSW) 1929 *NZ* 1
Gordon, K M (NSW) 1950 *BI* 1,2
Gould, R G (Q) 1980 *NZ* 1,2,3, 1981 *I, W, S,* 1982 *S* 2, *NZ* 1,2,3, 1983 *US, Arg* 1, *F* 1,2, 1984 *NZ* 1,2,3, *E, I, W, S,* 1985 *NZ,* 1986 *It,* 1987 *SK,* [*E*]
Gourley, S R (NSW) 1988 *S, It,* 1989 *BI* 1,2,3
Graham, C S (Q) 1899 *BI* 2
Graham, R (NSW) 1973 *Tg* 1,2, *W, E,* 1974 *NZ* 2,3, 1975 *E* 2, *J* 1,2, *S, W,* 1976 *I, US, Fj* 1,2,3, *F* 1,2
Gralton, A S I (Q) 1899 *BI* 1,4, 1903 *NZ*
Grant, J C (NSW) 1988 *E* 1, *NZ* 2,3, *E*
Graves, R H (NSW) 1907 *NZ* 1 (R)
Greatorex, E N (NSW) 1923 *NZ* 3, 1928 *E, F*
Gregan, G M (ACT) 1994 *It* 1,2, *WS, NZ,* 1995 *Arg* 1,2, [*SA, C* (R), *R, E*]
Gregory, S C (Q) 1968 *NZ* 3, *F, I, S,* 1969 *SA* 1,3, 1971 *SA* 1,3, *F* 1,2, 1972 *F* 1,2, 1973 *Tg* 1,2, *W, E*
Grey, G O (NSW) 1972 *F* 2 (R), *NZ* 1,2,3, *Fj* (R)
Griffin, T S (NSW) 1907 *NZ* 1,3, 1908 *W,* 1910 *NZ* 1,2, 1912 *US*
Grigg, P C (Q) 1980 *NZ* 3, 1982 *S* 2, *NZ* 1,2,3, 1983 *Arg* 2, *NZ,* 1984 *Fj, W, S,* 1985 *C* 1,2, *NZ, Fj* 1,2, 1986 *Arg* 1,2, *NZ* 1,2, 1987 *SK,* [*E, J, I, F, W*]
Grimmond, D N (NSW) 1964 *NZ* 2
Gudsell, K E (NSW) 1951 *NZ* 1,2,3

Centre Tim Horan of Queensland, who has made 38 appearances for the Wallabies.

313

Little, J S (Q) 1989 *F* 1,2, 1990 *F* 1,2,3, *US*, 1991 *W, E, NZ* 1,2, [*Arg, W, I, NZ, E*], 1992 *NZ* 1,2,3, *SA, I, W*, 1993 *Tg, NZ, SA* 1,2,3, *C, F* 1,2, 1994 *WS, NZ*, 1995 *Arg* 1,2, [*SA, C, E*], *NZ* 1,2
Livermore, A E (Q) 1946 *NZ* 1, *M*
Loane, M E (Q) 1973 *Tg* 1,2, 1974 *NZ* 1, 1975 *E* 1,2, *J* 1, 1976 *E, I, Fj* 1,2,3, *F* 1,2, 1978 *W* 1,2, 1979 *I* 1,2, *NZ, Arg* 1,2, 1981 *F* 1,2, *I, W, S*, 1982 *E, S* 1,2
Logan, D L (NSW) 1958 *M* 1
Loudon, D B (NSW) 1921 *NZ*
Loudon, R B (NSW) 1923 *NZ* 1 (R), 2,3, 1928 *NZ* 1,2,3, *M*, 1929 *NZ* 2, 1933 *SA* 2,3,4,5, 1934 *NZ* 2
Love, E W (NSW) 1932 *NZ* 1,2,3
Lowth, D R (NSW) 1958 *NZ* 1
Lucas, B C (Q) 1905 *NZ*
Lucas, P W (NSW) 1982 *NZ* 1,2,3
Lutge, D (NSW) 1903 *NZ*, 1904 *BI* 1,2,3
Lynagh, M P (Q) 1984 *Fj, E, I, W, S*, 1985 *C* 1,2, *NZ*, 1986 *It, F, Arg* 1,2, *NZ* 1,2,3, 1987 [*E, US, J, I, F, W*], *Arg* 1,2, 1988 *E* 1,2, *NZ* 1,3 (R), *E, S, It*, 1989 *BI* 1,2,3, *NZ, F* 1,2, 1990 *F* 1,2,3, *US, NZ* 1,2,3, 1991 *W, E, NZ* 1,2, [*Arg, WS, W, I, NZ, E*], 1992 *S* 1,2, *NZ* 1,2,3, *SA, I*, 1993 *Tg, C, F* 1,2, 1994 *I* 1,2, *It* 1, 1995 *Arg* 1,2, [*SA, C, E*]

McArthur, M (NSW) 1909 *E*
McBain, M I (Q) 1983 *It, F* 1, 1985 *Fj* 2, 1986 *It* (R), 1987 [*J*], 1988 *E* 2 (R), 1989 *BI* 1 (R)
MacBride, J W T (NSW) 1946 *NZ* 1, *M, NZ* 2, 1947 *NZ* 1,2, *S, I, W*, 1948 *E, F*
McCabe, A J M (NSW) 1909 *E*
McCall, R J (Q) 1989 *F* 1,2, 1990 *F* 1,2,3, *US, NZ* 1,2,3, 1991 *W, E, NZ* 1,2, [*Arg, W, I, NZ, E*], 1992 *S* 1,2, *NZ* 1,2,3, *SA, I, W*, 1993 *Tg, NZ, SA* 1,2,3, *C, F* 1,2, 1994 *It* 2, 1995 *Arg* 1,2, [*SA, R, E*]
McCarthy, F J C (Q) 1950 *BI* 1
McCowan, R H (Q) 1899 *BI* 1,2,4
McCue, P A (NSW) 1907 *NZ* 1,3, 1908 *W*, 1909 *E*
McDermott, L C (Q) 1962 *NZ* 1,2
McDonald, B S (NSW) 1969 *SA* 4, 1970 *S*
McDonald, J C (Q) 1938 *NZ* 2,3
Macdougall, D G (NSW) 1961 *Fj* 1, *SA* 1
Macdougall, S G (NSW, ACT) 1971 *SA* 3, 1973 *E*, 1974 *NZ* 1,2,3, 1975 *E* 1,2, 1976 *E*
McGhie, G H (Q) 1929 *NZ* 2,3, 1930 *BI*
McGill, A N (NSW) 1968 *NZ* 1,2, *F*, 1969 *W, SA* 1,2,3,4, 1970 *S*, 1971 *SA* 1,2,3, *F* 1,2, 1972 *F* 1,2, *NZ* 1,2,3, 1973 *Tg* 1,2
McIntyre, A J (Q) 1982 *NZ* 1,2,3, 1983 *F* 1,2, 1984 *Fj, NZ* 1,2,3, *E, I, W, S*, 1985 *C* 1,2, *NZ*, *Fj* 1,2, 1986 *It, F, Arg* 1,2, 1987 [*E, US, I, F, W*], *NZ, Arg* 2, 1988 *E* 1,2, *NZ* 1,2,3, *E, S, It*, 1989 *NZ*
McKenzie, E J A (NSW) 1990 *F* 1,2,3, *US, NZ* 1,2,3, 1991 *W, E, NZ* 1,2, [*Arg, W, I, NZ, E*], 1992 *S* 1,2, *NZ* 1,2,3, *SA, I, W*, 1993 *Tg, NZ, SA* 1,2,3, *C, F* 1,2, 1994 *I* 1,2, *It* 1, 2, *WS, NZ*, 1995 *Arg* 1,2, [*SA, C* (R), *R, E*], *NZ* 2
McKid, W A (NSW) 1976 *E, Fj* 1, 1978 *NZ* 2,3, 1979 *I* 1,2
McKinnon, A (Q) 1904 *BI* 2
McKivat, C H (NSW) 1907 *NZ* 1,3, 1908 *W*, 1909 *E*
McLaughlin, R E M (NSW) 1936 *NZ* 1,2
McLean, A D (Q) 1933 *SA* 1,2,3,4,5, 1934 *NZ* 1,2, 1936 *NZ* 1,2, *M*
McLean, J D (Q) 1904 *BI* 2,3, 1905 *NZ*
McLean, J J (Q) 1971 *SA* 2,3, *F* 1,2, 1972 *F* 1,2, *NZ* 1,2,3, *Fj*, 1973 *W, E*, 1974 *NZ* 1
McLean, P E (Q) 1974 *NZ* 1,2,3, 1975 *J* 1,2, *S, W*, 1976 *E, I, Fj* 1,2,3, *F* 1,2, 1978 *W* 1,2, *NZ* 2, 1979 *I* 1,2, *NZ, Arg* 1,2, 1980 *Fj*, 1981 *F* 1,2, *I, W, S*, 1982 *E, S* 2
McLean, P W (Q) 1978 *NZ* 1,2,3, 1979 *I* 1,2, *NZ, Arg* 1,2, 1980 *Fj* (R), *NZ* 3, 1981 *I, W, S*, 1982 *E, S* 1,2
McLean, R A (NSW) 1971 *SA* 1,2,3, *F* 1,2
McLean, W M (Q) 1946 *NZ* 1, *M, NZ* 2, 1947 *NZ* 1,2
McMahon, M J (Q) 1913 *NZ* 1
McMaster, R E (Q) 1946 *NZ* 1, *M, NZ* 2, 1947 *NZ* 1,2, *I, W*
MacMillan, D I (Q) 1950 *BI* 1,2
McMullen, K V (NSW) 1962 *NZ* 3,5, 1963 *E, SA* 1
McShane, J M S (NSW) 1937 *SA* 1,2
Mackney, W A R (NSW) 1933 *SA* 1,5, 1934 *NZ* 1,2
Magrath, E (NSW) 1961 *Fj* 1, *SA* 2, *F*
Maguire, D J (Q) 1989 *BI* 1,2,3
Malcolm, S J (NSW) 1927 *S*, 1928 *E, F, NZ* 1,2, *M*, 1929 *NZ* 1,2,3, 1930 *BI*, 1931 *NZ*, 1932 *NZ* 1,2,3, 1933 *SA* 4,5, 1934 *NZ* 1,2
Malone, J H (NSW) 1936 *NZ* 1,2, *M*, 1937 *SA* 2
Malouf, B P (NSW) 1982 *NZ* 1

Mandible, E F (NSW) 1907 *NZ* 2,3, 1908 *W*
Manning, J (NSW) 1904 *BI* 2
Manning, R C S (Q) 1967 *NZ*
Mansfield, B W (NSW) 1975 *J* 2
Manu, D T (NSW) 1995 [*R* (t)], *NZ* 1,2
Marks, H (NSW) 1899 *BI* 1,2
Marks, R J P (Q) 1962 *NZ* 4,5, 1963 *E, SA* 2,3,4, 1964 *NZ* 1,2,3, 1965 *SA* 1,2, 1966 *W, S*, 1967 *E, I* 1, *F, I* 2
Marrott, W J (NSW) 1923 *NZ* 1,2
Marshall, J S (NSW) 1949 *M* 1
Martin, G J (Q) 1989 *BI* 1,2,3, *NZ, F* 1,2, 1990 *F* 1,3 (R), *NZ* 1
Martin, M C (NSW) 1980 *Fj, NZ* 1,2, 1981 *F* 1,2, *W* (R)
Massey-Westropp, M (NSW) 1914 *NZ* 3
Mathers, M J (NSW) 1980 *Fj, NZ* 2 (R)
Maund, J W (NSW) 1903 *NZ*
Meadows, J E C (V, Q) 1974 *NZ* 1, 1975 *S, W*, 1976 *I, US, Fj* 1,3, *F* 1,2, 1978 *NZ* 1,2,3, 1979 *I* 1,2, 1981 *I, S*, 1982 *E, NZ* 2,3, 1983 *US, Arg* 2, *NZ*
Meadows, R W (NSW) 1958 *M* 1,2,3, *NZ* 1,2,3
Meagher, F W (NSW) 1923 *NZ* 3, 1925 *NZ*, 1927 *I, W*
Meibusch, J H (Q) 1904 *BI* 3
Meibusch, L S (Q) 1912 *US*
Melrose, T C (NSW) 1978 *NZ* 3, 1979 *I* 1,2, *NZ, Arg* 1,2
Merrick, S (NSW) 1995 *NZ* 1,2
Messenger, H H (NSW) 1907 *NZ* 2,3
Middleton, S A (NSW) 1909 *E*, 1910 *NZ* 1,2,3
Miller, A R (NSW) 1952 *Fj* 1,2, *NZ* 1,2, 1953 *SA* 1,2,3,4, 1954 *Fj* 1,2, 1955 *NZ* 1,2,3, 1956 *SA* 1,2, 1957 *NZ* 1,2, 1958 *W, E, S, F, M* 1,2,3, 1959 *BI* 1,2, 1961 *Fj* 1,2,3, *SA* 2, *F*, 1962 *NZ* 1,2, 1966 *BI* 1,2, *W, S*, 1967 *I* 1, *F, I* 2, *NZ*
Miller, J M (NSW) 1962 *NZ* 1, 1963 *E, SA* 1, 1966 *W, S*, 1967 *E*
Miller, J S (Q) 1986 *NZ* 2,3, 1987 *SK*, [*US, I, F*], *NZ, Arg* 1,2, 1988 *E* 1,2, *NZ* 2,3, *E, S, It*, 1989 *BI* 1,2,3, *NZ*, 1990 *F* 1,3, 1991 *W*, [*WS, W, I*]
Miller, S W J (NSW) 1899 *BI* 3
Mingey, N (NSW) 1923 *NZ* 1,2
Monaghan, L E (NSW) 1973 *E*, 1974 *NZ* 1,2,3, 1975 *E* 1,2, *S, W*, 1976 *E, I, US, F* 1, 1978 *W* 1,2, *NZ* 1, 1979 *I* 1,2
Monti, C I A (Q) 1938 *NZ* 2
Moon, B J (Q) 1978 *NZ* 2,3, 1979 *I* 1,2, *NZ, Arg* 1,2, 1980 *Fj, NZ* 1,2,3, 1981 *F* 1,2, *I, W, S*, 1982 *E, S* 1,2, 1983 *US, Arg* 1,2, *NZ, It, F* 1,2, 1984 *Fj, NZ* 1,2,3, *E*, 1986 *It, F, Arg* 1,2
Mooney, T P (Q) 1954 *Fj* 1,2
Moran, H M (NSW) 1908 *W*
Morgan, G (Q) 1992 *NZ* 1 (R), 3 (R), *W*, 1993 *Tg, NZ, SA* 1,2,3, *C, F* 1,2, 1994 *I* 1,2, *It* 1, *WS, NZ*
Morrissey, C V (NSW) 1925 *NZ*
Morrissey, W (Q) 1914 *NZ* 2
Morton, A R (NSW) 1957 *NZ* 1,2, 1958 *F, M* 1,2,3, *NZ* 1,2,3, 1959 *BI* 1,2
Mossop, R P (NSW) 1949 *NZ* 1,2, 1950 *BI* 1,2, 1951 *NZ* 1
Moutray, I E (NSW) 1963 *SA* 2
Munsie, A (NSW) 1928 *NZ* 2
Murdoch, A (NSW) 1993 *F* 1
Murphy, P J (Q) 1910 *NZ* 1,2,3, 1913 *NZ* 1,2,3, 1914 *NZ* 1,2,3
Murphy, W (Q) 1912 *US*

Nasser, B P (Q) 1989 *F* 1,2, 1990 *F* 1,2,3, *US, NZ* 2, 1991 [*WS*]
Nicholson, F C (Q) 1904 *BI* 3
Nicholson, F V (Q) 1903 *NZ*, 1904 *BI* 1
Niuqila, A S (NSW) 1988 *S, It*, 1989 *BI* 1
Nothling, O E (NSW) 1921 *NZ*, 1923 *NZ* 1,2,3
Nucifora, D V (Q) 1991 [*Arg* (R)], 1993 *C* (R)

O'Brien, F W H (NSW) 1937 *SA* 2, 1938 *NZ* 3
O'Connor, J A (NSW) 1928 *NZ* 1,2,3, *M*
O'Connor, M (ACT) 1994 *I* 1
O'Connor, M D (ACT, Q) 1979 *Arg* 1,2, 1980 *Fj, NZ* 1,2,3, 1981 *F* 1,2, *I*, 1982 *E, S* 1,2
O'Donnell, C (NSW) 1913 *NZ* 1,2
O'Donnell, I C (NSW) 1899 *BI* 3,4
O'Donnell, J B (NSW) 1928 *NZ* 1,3, *M*
O'Donnell, J M (NSW) 1899 *BI* 4
O'Gorman, J F (NSW) 1961 *Fj* 1, *SA* 1,2, *F*, 1962 *NZ* 2, 1963 *E, SA* 1,2,3,4, 1965 *SA* 1,2, 1966 *W, S*, 1967 *E, I* 1, *F, I* 2
O'Neill, D J (Q) 1964 *NZ* 1,2
O'Neill, J M (Q) 1952 *NZ* 1,2, 1956 *SA* 1,2

Ofahengaue, V (NSW) 1990 NZ 1,2,3, 1991 W, E, NZ 1,2, [Arg, W, I, NZ, E], 1992 S 1,2, SA, I, W, 1994 WS, NZ, 1995 Arg 1,2 (R), [SA, C, E], NZ 1,2
Osborne, D H (V) 1975 E 1,2, J 1
Outterside, R (NSW) 1959 BI 1,2
Oxenham, A McE (Q) 1904 BI 2, 1907 NZ 2
Oxlade, A M (Q) 1904 BI 2,3, 1905 NZ, 1907 NZ 2
Oxlade, B D (Q) 1938 NZ 1,2,3

Palfreyman, J R L (NSW) 1929 NZ 1, 1930 BI, 1931 NZ, 1932 NZ 3
Papworth, B (NSW) 1985 Fj 1,2, 1986 It, Arg 1,2, NZ 1,2,3, 1987 [E, US, J (R), I, F], NZ, Arg 1,2
Parker, A J (Q) 1983 Arg 1 (R), 2, NZ
Parkinson, C E (Q) 1907 NZ 2
Pashley, J J (NSW) 1954 Fj 1,2, 1958 M 1,2,3
Pauling, T P (NSW) 1936 NZ 1, 1937 SA 1
Pearse, G K (NSW) 1975 W (R), 1976 I, US, Fj 1,2,3, 1978 NZ 1,2,3
Penman, A P (NSW) 1905 NZ
Perrin, P D (Q) 1962 NZ 1
Perrin, T D (NSW) 1931 M, NZ
Phelps, R (NSW) 1955 NZ 2,3, 1956 SA 1,2, 1957 NZ 1,2, 1958 W, I, E, S, F, M 1, NZ 1,2,3, 1961 Fj 1,2,3, SA 1,2, F, 1962 NZ 1,2
Phipps, J A (NSW) 1953 SA 1,2,3,4, 1954 Fj 1,2, 1955 NZ 1,2,3, 1956 SA 1,2
Phipps, W J (NSW) 1928 NZ 2
Pilecki, S J (Q) 1978 W 1,2, NZ 1,2, 1979 I 1,2, NZ, Arg 1,2, 1980 Fj, NZ 1,2, 1982 S 1,2, 1983 US, Arg 1,2
Pini, M (Q) 1994 I 1, It 2, WS, NZ, 1995 Arg 1,2, [SA, R (t)]
Piper, B J C (NSW) 1946 NZ 1, M, NZ 2, 1947 NZ 1, S, I, W, 1948 E, F, 1949 M, 1,2,3
Poidevin, S P (NSW) 1980 Fj, NZ 1,2,3, 1981 F 1,2, I, W, S, 1982 E, NZ 1,2,3, 1983 US, Arg 1,2, NZ, It, F 1,2, 1984 Fj, NZ 1,2,3, E, I, W, S, 1985 C 1,2, NZ, Fj 1,2, 1986 It, F, Arg 1,2, NZ 1,2,3, 1987 SK, [E, J, I, F, W], Arg 1, 1988 NZ 1,2,3, 1989 NZ, 1991 E, NZ 1,2, [Arg, W, I, NZ, E]
Pope, A M (Q) 1968 NZ 2 (R)
Potter, R T (Q) 1961 Fj 2
Potts, J M (NSW) 1957 NZ 1,2, 1958 W, I, 1959 BI 1
Prentice, C W (NSW) 1914 NZ 3
Prentice, W S (NSW) 1908 W, 1909 E, 1910 NZ 1,2,3, 1912 US
Price, R A (NSW) 1974 NZ 1,2,3, 1975 E 1,2, J 1,2, 1976 US
Primmer, C J (Q) 1951 NZ 1,3
Proctor, I J (NSW)) 1967 NZ
Prosser, R B (NSW) 1967 E, I 1,2, NZ, 1968 NZ 1,2, F, I, S, 1969 W, SA 1,2,3,4, 1971 SA 1,2,3, F 1,2, 1972 F 1,2, NZ 1,2,3, Fj
Pugh, G H (NSW) 1912 US
Purcell, M P (Q) 1966 W, S, 1967 I 2
Purkis, E M (NSW) 1958 S, M 1

Ramalli, C (NSW) 1938 NZ 2,3
Ramsay, K M (NSW) 1936 M, 1937 SA 1, 1938 NZ 1,3
Rankin, R (NSW) 1936 NZ 1,2, M, 1937 SA 1,2, 1938 NZ 1,2
Rathie, D S (Q) 1972 F 1,2
Raymond, R L (NSW) 1921 NZ
Redwood, C (Q) 1903 NZ, 1904 BI 1,2,3
Reid, E J (NSW) 1925 NZ
Reid, T W (NSW) 1961 Fj 1,2,3, SA 1, 1962 NZ 1
Reilly, N P (Q) 1968 NZ 1,2, F, I, S, 1969 W, SA 1,2,3,4
Reynolds, L J (NSW) 1910 NZ 2 (R), 3
Reynolds, R J (NSW) 1984 Fj, NZ 1,2,3, 1985 Fj 1,2, 1986 Arg 1,2, NZ 1, 1987 [J]
Richards, E W (Q) 1904 BI 1,3, 1905 NZ, 1907 NZ 1 (R), 2
Richards, G (NSW) 1978 NZ 2 (R), 3, 1981 F 1
Richards, T J (Q) 1908 W, 1909 E, 1912 US
Richards, V S (NSW) 1936 NZ 1,2 (R), M, 1937 SA 1, 1938 NZ 1
Richardson, G C (Q) 1971 SA 1,2,3, 1972 NZ 2,3, Fj, 1973 Tg 1,2, W
Rigney, W A (NSW) 1925 NZ
Riley, S A (NSW) 1903 NZ
Roberts, B T (NSW) 1956 SA 2
Roberts, H F (Q) 1961 Fj 1,3, SA 2, F
Robertson, I J (NSW) 1975 J 1,2
Roche, C (Q) 1982 S 1,2, NZ 1,2,3, 1983 US, Arg 1,2, NZ, It, F 1,2, 1984 Fj, NZ 1,2,3, I

Rodriguez, E E (NSW) 1984 Fj, NZ 1,2,3, E, I, W, S, 1985 C 1,2, NZ, Fj 1, 1986 It, F, Arg 1,2, NZ 1,2,3, 1987 SK, [E, J, W (R)], NZ, Arg 1,2
Roebuck, M C (NSW) 1991 W, E, NZ 1,2, [Arg, WS, W, I, NZ, E], 1992 S 1,2, NZ 2,3, SA, I, W, 1993 Tg, SA 1,2,3, C, F 2
Roff, J W (ACT) 1995 [C, R], NZ 1,2
Rose, H A (NSW), 1967 I 2, NZ, 1968 NZ 1,2, F, I, S, 1969 W, SA 1,2,3,4, 1970 S
Rosenblum, M E (NSW) 1928 NZ 1,2,3, M
Rosenblum, R G (NSW) 1969 SA 1,3, 1970 S
Rosewell, J S H (NSW) 1907 NZ 1,3
Ross, A W (NSW) 1927 I, W, S, 1928 E, F, 1929 NZ 1, 1930 BI, 1931 M, NZ, 1932 NZ 2,3, 1933 SA 5, 1934 NZ 1,2
Ross, W S (Q) 1979 I 1,2, Arg 2, 1980 Fj, NZ 1,2,3, 1982 S 1,2, 1983 US, Arg 1,2, NZ
Rothwell, P R (NSW) 1951 NZ 1,2,3, 1952 Fj 1
Row, F L (NSW) 1899 BI 1,3,4
Row, N E (NSW) 1907 NZ 1,3, 1909 E, 1910 NZ 1,2,3
Rowles, P G (NSW) 1972 Fj, 1973 E
Roxburgh, J R (NSW) 1968 NZ 1,2, F, 1969 W, SA 1,2,3,4, 1970 S
Ruebner, G (NSW) 1966 BI 1,2
Russell, C J (NSW) 1907 NZ 1,2,3, 1908 W, 1909 E
Ryan, J R (NSW) 1975 J 2, 1976 I, US, Fj 1,2,3
Ryan, K J (Q) 1958 E, M 1, NZ 1,2,3
Ryan, P F (NSW) 1963 E, SA 1, 1966 BI 1,2

Sampson, J H (NSW) 1899 BI 4
Sayle, J L (NSW) 1967 NZ
Schulte, B G (Q) 1946 NZ 1, M
Scott, P R I (NSW) 1962 NZ 1,2
Scott-Young, S J (Q) 1990 F 2,3 (R), US, NZ 3, 1992 NZ 1,2,3
Shambrook, G G (Q) 1976 Fj 2,3
Shaw, A A (Q) 1973 W, E, 1975 E 1,2, J 2, S, W, 1976 E, I, US, Fj 1,2,3, F 1,2, 1978 W 1,2, NZ 1,2,3, 1979 I 1,2, NZ, Arg 1,2, 1980 Fj, NZ 1,2,3, 1981 F 1,2, I, W, S, 1982 S 1,2
Shaw, C (NSW) 1925 NZ (R)
Shaw, G A (NSW) 1969 W, SA 1 (R), 1970 S, 1971 SA 1,2,3, F 1,2, 1973 W, E, 1974 NZ 1,2,3, 1975 E 1,2, J 1,2, W, 1976 E, I, US, Fj 1,2,3, F 1,2, 1979 NZ
Sheehan, W B J (NSW) 1923 NZ 1,2,3, 1927 W, S
Shehadie, N M (NSW) 1947 NZ 2, 1948 E, F, 1949 M 1,2,3, NZ 1,2, 1950 BI 1,2, 1951 NZ 1,2,3, 1952 Fj 1,2, NZ 2, 1953 SA 1,2,3,4, 1954 Fj 1,2, 1955 NZ 1,2,3, 1956 SA 1,2, 1957 NZ 2, 1958 W, I
Sheil, A G R (Q) 1956 SA 1
Shepherd, D J (V) 1964 NZ 3, 1965 SA 1,2, 1966 BI 1,2
Simpson, R J (NSW) 1913 NZ 2
Skinner, A J (NSW) 1969 W, SA 4, 1970 S
Slack, A G (Q) 1978 W 1,2, NZ 1,2, 1979 NZ, Arg 1,2, 1980 Fj, 1981 I, W, S, 1982 E, S 1, NZ 3, 1983 US, Arg 1,2 NZ, It, 1984 Fj, NZ 1,2,3, E, I, W, S, 1986 It, F, NZ 1,2,3, 1987 SK, [E, US, J, I, F, W]
Slater, S H (NSW) 1910 NZ 3
Slattery, P J (Q) 1990 US (R), 1991 W (R), E (R), [WS (R), W, I (R)], 1992 I, W, 1993 Tg, C, F 1,2, 1994 I 1,2, It 1 (R), 1995 [C, R (R)]
Smairl, A M (NSW) 1928 NZ 1,2,3
Smith, B A (Q) 1987 SK, [US, J, I (R), W], Arg 1
Smith, D P (Q) 1993 SA 1,2,3, C, F 2, 1994 I 1,2, It 1,2, WS, NZ, 1995 Arg 1,2, [SA, R, E], NZ 1,2
Smith, F B (NSW) 1905 NZ, 1907 NZ 1,2,3
Smith, L M (NSW) 1905 NZ
Smith, N C (NSW) 1923 NZ 1
Smith, P V (NSW) 1967 NZ, 1968 NZ 1,2, F, I, S, 1969 W, SA 1
Smith, R A (NSW) 1971 SA 1,2, 1972 F 1,2, NZ 1,2 (R), 3, Fj, 1975 E 1,2, J 1,2, S, W, 1976 E, I, US, Fj 1,2,3, F 1,2
Smith, T S (NSW) 1921 NZ, 1925 NZ
Snell, H W (NSW) 1928 NZ 3
Solomon, H J (NSW) 1949 M 3, NZ 2, 1950 BI 1,2, 1951 NZ 1,2, 1952 Fj 1,2, NZ 1,2, 1953 SA 1,2,3, 1955 NZ 1
Spragg, S A (NSW) 1899 BI 1,2,3,4
Stanley, R G (NSW) 1921 NZ, 1923 NZ 1,2,3
Stapleton, E T (NSW) 1951 NZ 1,2,3, 1952 Fj 1,2, NZ 1,2, 1953 SA 1,2,3,4, 1954 Fj 1, 1955 NZ 1,2,3, 1958 NZ 1
Steggall, J C (Q) 1931 M, NZ, 1932 NZ 1,2,3, 1933 SA 1,2,3,4,5
Stegman, T R (NSW) 1973 Tg 1,2
Stephens, O G (NSW) 1973 Tg 1,2, W, 1974 NZ 2,3
Stewart, A A (NSW) 1979 NZ, Arg 1,2
Stone, A H (NSW) 1937 SA 2, 1938 NZ 2,3

Stone, C G (NSW) 1938 *NZ* 1
Stone, J M (NSW) 1946 *M, NZ* 2
Storey, G P (NSW) 1927 *I, W, S*, 1928 *E, F*, 1929 *NZ* 3 (R), 1930 *BI*
Storey, K P (NSW) 1936 *NZ* 2
Storey, N J D (NSW) 1962 *NZ* 1
Strachan, D J (NSW) 1955 *NZ* 2,3
Street, N O (NSW) 1899 *BI* 2
Streeter, S F (NSW) 1978 *NZ* 1
Stuart, R (NSW) 1910 *NZ* 2,3
Stumbles, B D (NSW) 1972 *NZ* 1 (R), 2,3, *Fj*
Sturtridge, G S (V) 1929 *NZ* 2, 1932 *NZ* 1,2,3, 1933 *SA* 1,2,3,4,5
Sullivan, P D (NSW) 1971 *SA* 1,2,3, *F* 1,2, 1972 *F* 1,2, *NZ* 1,2, *Fj*, 1973 *Tg* 1,2, *W*
Summons, A J (NSW) 1958 *W, I, E, S, M* 2, *NZ* 1,2,3, 1959 *BI* 1,2
Suttor, D C (NSW) 1913 *NZ* 1,2,3
Swannell, B I (NSW) 1905 *NZ*
Sweeney, T L (Q) 1953 *SA* 1

Taafe, B S (NSW) 1969 *SA* 1, 1972 *F* 1,2
Tabua, I (Q) 1993 *SA* 2,3, *C, F* 1, 1994 *I* 1,2, *It* 1,2, 1995 [*C, R*]
Tancred, A J (NSW) 1927 *I, W, S*
Tancred, J L (NSW) 1928 *F*
Tanner, W H (Q) 1899 *BI* 1,2
Tasker, W G (NSW) 1913 *NZ* 1,2,3, 1914 *NZ* 1,2,3
Tate, M J (NSW) 1951 *NZ* 3, 1952 *Fj* 1,2, *NZ* 1,2, 1953 *SA* 1, 1954 *Fj* 1,2
Taylor, D A (Q) 1968 *NZ* 1,2, *F, I, S*
Taylor, H C (NSW) 1923 *NZ* 1,2,3
Taylor, J I (NSW) 1971 *SA* 1, 1972 *F* 1,2, *Fj*
Teitzel, R G (Q) 1966 *W, S*, 1967 *E, I* 1, *F, I* 2, *NZ*
Thompson, C E (NSW) 1923 *NZ* 1
Thompson, E G (Q) 1929 *NZ* 1,2,3, 1930 *BI*
Thompson, F (NSW) 1913 *NZ* 1,2,3, 1914 *NZ* 1,2,3
Thompson, J (Q) 1914 *NZ* 1
Thompson, P D (Q) 1950 *BI* 1
Thompson, R J (WA) 1971 *SA* 3, *F* 2 (R), 1972 *Fj*
Thorn, A M (NSW) 1921 *NZ*
Thorn, E J (NSW) 1923 *NZ* 1,2,3
Thornett, J E (NSW) 1955 *NZ* 1,2,3, 1956 *SA* 1,2, 1958 *W, I, S, F, M* 2,3, *NZ* 2,3, 1959 *BI* 1,2, 1961 *Fj* 2,3, *SA* 1,2, *F*, 1962 *NZ* 2,3,4,5, 1963 *E, SA* 1,2,3,4, 1964 *NZ* 1,2,3, 1965 *SA* 1,2, 1966 *BI* 1,2, 1967 *F*
Thornett, R N (NSW) 1961 *Fj* 1,2,3, *SA* 1,2, *F*, 1962 *NZ* 1,2,3,4,5
Thorpe, A C (NSW) 1929 *NZ* 1 (R)
Timbury, F R V (Q) 1910 *NZ* 1,2,
Tindall, E N (NSW) 1973 *Tg* 2
Toby, A E (NSW) 1925 *NZ*
Tolhurst, H A (NSW) 1931 *M, NZ*
Tombs, R C (NSW) 1992 *S* 1,2, 1994 *I* 2, *It* 1
Tonkin, A E J (NSW) 1947 *S, I, W*, 1948 *E, F*, 1950 *BI* 2
Tooth, R M (NSW) 1951 *NZ* 1,2,3, 1954 *Fj* 1,2, 1955 *NZ* 1,2,3, 1957 *NZ* 1,2
Towers, C H T (NSW) 1927 *I*, 1928 *E, F, NZ* 1,2,3, *M*, 1929 *NZ* 1,3, 1930 *BI*, 1931 *M, NZ*, 1934 *NZ* 1,2, 1937 *SA* 1,2
Trivett, R K (Q) 1966 *BI* 1,2
Turnbull, A (V) 1961 *Fj* 3
Turnbull, R V (NSW) 1968 *I*
Tuynman, S N (NSW) 1983 *F* 1,2, 1984 *E, I, W, S*, 1985 *C* 1,2, *NZ, Fj* 1,2, 1986 *It, F, Arg* 1,2, *NZ* 1,2,3, 1987 *SK*, [*E, US, J, I, W*], *NZ, Arg* 1 (R), 2, 1988 *E, It*, 1989 *BI* 1,2,3, *NZ*, 1990 *NZ* 1
Tweedale, E (NSW) 1946 *NZ* 1,2, 1947 *NZ* 2, *S, I*, 1948 *E, F*, 1949 *M* 1,2,3

Vaughan, D (NSW) 1983 *US, Arg* 1, *It, F* 1,2
Vaughan, G N (V) 1958 *E, S, F, M* 1,2,3
Verge, A (NSW) 1904 *BI* 1,2

Walden, R J (NSW) 1934 *NZ* 2, 1936 *NZ* 1,2, *M*
Walker, A K (NSW) 1947 *NZ* 1, 1948 *E, F*, 1950 *BI* 1,2
Walker, A S B (NSW) 1912 *US*, 1921 *NZ*
Walker, L F (NSW) 1988 *NZ* 2,3, *S, It*, 1989 *BI* 1,2,3, *NZ*
Walker, L R (NSW) 1982 *NZ* 2,3
Wallace, A C (NSW) 1921 *NZ*, 1927 *I, W, S*, 1928 *E, F*
Wallace, T M (NSW) 1994 *It* 1 (R), 2
Wallach, C (NSW) 1913 *NZ* 1,3, 1914 *NZ* 1,2,3
Walsh, J J (NSW) 1953 *SA* 1,2,3,4
Walsh, P B (NSW) 1904 *BI* 1,2,3
Walsham, K P (NSW) 1962 *NZ* 3, 1963 *E*
Ward, P G (NSW) 1899 *BI* 1,2,3,4
Ward, T (Q) 1899 *BI* 2
Watson, G W (Q) 1907 *NZ* 1
Watson, W T (NSW) 1912 *US*, 1913 *NZ* 1,2,3, 1914 *NZ* 1
Waugh, W W (NSW) 1993 *SA* 1, 1995 [*C*], *NZ* 1,2
Weatherstone, L J (ACT) 1975 *E* 1,2, *J* 1,2, *S* (R), 1976 *E, I*
Webb, W (NSW) 1899 *BI* 3,4
Wells, B G (NSW) 1958 *M* 1
Westfield, R E (NSW) 1928 *NZ* 1,2,3, *M*, 1929 *NZ* 2,3
White, C J B (NSW) 1899 *BI* 1, 1903 *NZ*, 1904 *BI* 1
White, J M (NSW) 1904 *BI* 3
White, J P L (NSW) 1958 *NZ* 1,2,3, 1961 *Fj* 1,2,3, *SA* 1,2, *F*, 1962 *NZ* 1,2,3,4,5, 1963 *E, SA* 1,2,3,4, 1964 *NZ* 1,2,3, 1965 *SA* 1,2
White, M C (Q) 1931 *M, NZ* 1932 *NZ* 1,2, 1933 *SA* 1,2,3,4,5
White, S W (NSW) 1956 *SA* 1,2, 1958 *I, E, S, M* 2,3
White, W G S (Q) 1933 *SA* 1,2,3,4,5, 1934 *NZ* 1,2, 1936 *NZ* 1,2, *M*
White, W J (NSW) 1928 *NZ* 1, *M*, 1932 *NZ* 1
Wickham, S M (NSW) 1903 *NZ*, 1904 *BI* 1,2,3, 1905 *NZ*
Williams, D (Q) 1913 *NZ* 3, 1914 *NZ* 1,2,3
Williams, I M (NSW) 1987 *Arg* 1,2, 1988 *E* 1,2, *NZ* 1,2,3, 1989 *BI* 2,3, *NZ, F* 1,2, 1990 *F* 1,2,3, *US, NZ* 1
Williams, J L (NSW) 1963 *SA* 1,3,4
Williams, S A (NSW) 1980 *Fj, NZ* 1,2, 1981 *F* 1,2, 1982 *E, NZ* 1,2,3, 1983 *US, Arg* 1 (R), 2, *NZ, It, F* 1,2, 1984 *NZ* 1,2,3, *E, I, W, S*, 1985 *C* 1,2, *NZ, Fj* 1,2
Wilson, B J (NSW) 1949 *NZ* 1,2
Wilson, C R (Q) 1957 *NZ* 1, 1958 *NZ* 1,2,3
Wilson, D J (Q) 1992 *S* 1,2, *NZ* 1,2,3, *SA, I, W*, 1993 *Tg, NZ, SA* 1,2,3, *C, F* 1,2, 1994 *I* 1,2, *It* 1,2, *WS, NZ*, 1995 *Arg* 1,2, [*SA, R, E*]
Wilson, V W (Q) 1937 *SA* 1,2, 1938 *NZ* 1,2,3
Windon, C J (NSW) 1946 *NZ* 1,2, 1947 *NZ* 1, *S, I, W*, 1948 *E, F*, 1949 *M* 1,2,3, *NZ* 1,2, 1951 *NZ* 1,2,3, 1952 *Fj* 1,2, *NZ* 1,2
Windon, K S (NSW) 1937 *SA* 1,2, 1946 *M*
Windsor, J C (Q) 1947 *NZ* 2
Winning, K C (Q) 1951 *NZ* 1
Wogan, L W (NSW) 1913 *NZ* 1,2,3, 1914 *NZ* 1,2,3, 1921 *NZ*
Wood, F (NSW) 1907 *NZ* 1,2,3, 1910 *NZ* 1,2,3, 1913 *NZ* 1,2,3, 1914 *NZ* 1,2,3
Wood, R N (Q) 1972 *Fj*
Woods, H F (NSW) 1925 *NZ*, 1927 *I, W, S*, 1928 *E*
Wright, K J (NSW) 1975 *E* 1,2, *J* 1, 1976 *US, F* 1,2, 1978 *NZ* 1,2,3

Yanz, K (NSW) 1958 *F*

AUSTRALIAN INTERNATIONAL RECORDS

Both team and individual records are for official international matches, up to 30 April 1996.

TEAM RECORDS

Highest score
73 v Western Samoa (73-3) 1994 Sydney

v individual countries
53 v Argentina (53-7) 1995 Brisbane
30 v British Isles (30-12) 1989 Sydney

59 v Canada (59-3) 1985 Sydney
40 v England (40-15) 1991 Sydney
52 v Fiji (52-28) 1985 Brisbane
48 v France (48-31) 1990 Brisbane
42 v Ireland (42-17) 1992 Dublin
55 v Italy (55-6) 1988 Rome
50 v Japan (50-25) 1975 Brisbane
30 v N Zealand (30-16) 1978 Auckland
42 v Romania (42-3) 1995 Stellenbosch
37 v Scotland $\begin{cases} (37\text{-}12)\ 1984\ \text{Murrayfield} \\ (37\text{-}13)\ 1992\ \text{Brisbane} \end{cases}$
28 v South Africa (28-20) 1993 Brisbane
65 v South Korea (65-18) 1987 Brisbane
52 v Tonga (52-14) 1993 Brisbane
67 v United States (67-9) 1990 Brisbane
63 v Wales (63-6) 1991 Brisbane
73 v Western Samoa (73-3) 1994 Sydney

Biggest winning points margin
70 v Western Samoa (73-3) 1994 Sydney

v individual countries
46 v Argentina (53-7) 1995 Brisbane
18 v British Isles (30-12) 1989 Sydney
56 v Canada (59-3) 1985 Sydney
25 v England (40-15) 1991 Sydney
24 v Fiji (52-28) 1985 Brisbane
21 v France (24-3) 1993 Parc des Princes
25 v Ireland (42-17) 1992 Dublin
49 v Italy (55-6) 1988 Rome
30 v Japan (37-7) 1975 Sydney
16 v N Zealand (26-10) 1980 Sydney
39 v Romania (42-3) 1995 Stellenbosch
25 v Scotland (37-12) 1984 Murrayfield
23 v South Africa (26-3) 1992 Cape Town
47 v South Korea (65-18) 1987 Brisbane
38 v Tonga (52-14) 1993 Brisbane
58 v United States (67-9) 1990 Brisbane
57 v Wales (63-6) 1991 Brisbane
70 v Western Samoa (73-3) 1994 Sydney

Longest winning sequence
10 matches 1991-1992

Highest score by opposing team
38 N Zealand $\begin{cases} (13\text{-}38)\ 1936\ \text{Dunedin} \\ (3\text{-}38)\ 1972\ \text{Auckland} \end{cases}$

by individual countries
27 Argentina (19-27) 1987 Buenos Aires
31 British Isles (0-31) 1966 Brisbane
16 Canada (43-16) 1993 Calgary
28 England (19-28) 1988 Twickenham
28 Fiji (52-28) 1985 Brisbane
34 France (6-34) 1976 Paris
27 Ireland (12-27) 1979 Brisbane
20 Italy (23-20) 1994 Brisbane
25 Japan (50-25) 1975 Brisbane
38 N Zealand $\begin{cases} (13\text{-}38)\ 1936\ \text{Dunedin} \\ (3\text{-}38)\ 1972\ \text{Auckland} \end{cases}$
 3 Romania (42-3) 1995 Stellenbosch

24 Scotland (15-24) 1981
  Murrayfield
30 South Africa (11-30) 1969
  Johannesburg
18 South Korea (65-18) 1987
  Brisbane
16 Tonga (11-16) 1973 Brisbane
12 United States (47-12) 1987
  Brisbane
28 Wales (3-28) 1975 Cardiff
 3 Western Samoa $\begin{cases} (9\text{-}3)\ 1991\ \text{Pontypool} \\ (73\text{-}3)\ 1994\ \text{Sydney} \end{cases}$

Biggest losing points margin
35 v N Zealand (3-38) 1972 Auckland

v individual countries
15 v Argentina (3-18) 1983 Brisbane
31 v British Isles (0-31) 1966 Brisbane
17 v England $\begin{cases} (3\text{-}20)\ 1973\ \text{Twickenham} \\ (6\text{-}23)\ 1976\ \text{Twickenham} \end{cases}$
 2 Fiji $\begin{cases} (15\text{-}17)\ 1952\ \text{Sydney} \\ (16\text{-}18)\ 1954\ \text{Sydney} \end{cases}$
28 v France (6-34) 1976 Paris
15 v Ireland (12-27) 1979 Brisbane
35 v New Zealand (3-38) 1972 Auckland
 9 v Scotland (15-24) 1981 Murrayfield
25 v South Africa (3-28) 1961
  Johannesburg
 5 v Tonga (11-16) 1973 Brisbane
25 v Wales (3-28) 1975 Cardiff
No defeats v Canada, Italy, Japan, Romania, South Korea, United States or Western Samoa.

Longest losing sequence
10 matches $\begin{cases} 1899\text{-}1907 \\ 1937\text{-}47 \end{cases}$

Most tries by Australia in an international
13 v South Korea (65-18) 1987
  Brisbane

Most tries against Australia in an international
9 by N Zealand (13-38) 1936
  Dunedin

Most points on overseas tour (all matches)
500 in B Isles/France (35 matches)
  1947-48

Most tries on overseas tour (all matches)
115 in B Isles/France (35 matches)
  1947-48

INDIVIDUAL RECORDS

Most capped player
D I Campese   92   1982-95
in individual positions
Full-back
R G Gould   25   1980-87
Wing
D I Campese   76(92)[1]   1982-95
Centre
A G Slack   39   1978-87
Fly-half
M P Lynagh   64(72)[2]   1984-95
Scrum-half
N C Farr-Jones   62(63)[3]   1984-93
Prop
E J A McKenzie   45   1990-95
Hooker
P N Kearns   49   1989-95
Lock
{S A G Cutler   40   1982-91
{R J McCall   40   1989-95
Flanker
S P Poidevin   59   1980-91
No 8
T B Gavin   42(44)[4]   1988-95
[1] *Campese has played 16 times as a full-back*
[2] *Lynagh has played 7 times as a centre and once as a replacement full-back*
[3] *Farr-Jones was capped once as a replacement wing*
[4] *Gavin has been capped twice as a lock*

Longest international career
G M Cooke 16 seasons 1932-1947/8
A R Miller 16 seasons 1952-1967
Cooke's career ended during a Northern hemisphere season

Most consecutive internationals – 46
P N Kearns 1989-95

Most internationals as captain – 36
N C Farr-Jones   1988-92
Includes wins against the British Isles and all senior IB nations

Most points in internationals – 911
M P Lynagh (72 matches) 1984-95

Most points in an international – 28
M P Lynagh v Argentina 1995 Brisbane

Most tries in internationals – 63
D I Campese (92 matches) 1982-95

Most tries in an international – 4
G Cornelsen v N Zealand 1978 Auckland
D I Campese v United States 1983 Sydney

Most conversions in internationals – 140
M P Lynagh (72 matches) 1984-95

Most conversions in an international – 8
M P Lynagh v Italy 1988 Rome
M P Lynagh v United States 1990 Brisbane

Most dropped goals in internationals – 9
P F Hawthorne (21 matches) 1962-67
M P Lynagh (72 matches) 1984-95

Most dropped goals in an international – 3
P F Hawthorne v England 1967 Twickenham

Most penalty goals in internationals – 177
M P Lynagh (72 matches) 1984-95

Most penalty goals in an international – 6
M P Lynagh v France 1986 Sydney
M P Lynagh v England 1988 Brisbane

Most points in international series on tour – 42
M P Lynagh (4 appearances) 1984 B Isles

Most tries in international series on tour – 4
G Cornelsen (3 appearances) 1978 N Zealand
M G Ella (4 appearances) 1984 B Isles
Ella scored in each match of the international series

Most points on overseas tour – 154
P E McLean (18 appearances) B Isles 1975-76

Most tries on overseas tour – 23
C J Russell B Isles 1908-09

Most points in a tour match – 26
A J Leeds v Buller (NZ) 1986 Westport

Most tries in a tour match – 6
J S Boyce v Wairarapa (NZ) 1962 Masterton

319

BRITISH ISLES TOURS
(up to 30 April 1996)

* Indicates replacement during tour, throughout this section

BRITISH ISLES TEAMS TO AUSTRALIA AND NEW ZEALAND

1888

Full record						
in Australia	Played 16	Won 14	Lost 0	Drawn 2	Points for 210	Against 65
in New Zealand	Played 19	Won 13	Lost 2	Drawn 4	Points for 82	Against 33

Players

Full-backs: J T Haslam (Batley), A G Paul (Swinton)
Threequarters: H C Speakman (Runcorn), Dr H Brooks (Edinburgh U & Durham), J Anderton (Salford), A E Stoddart (Blackheath)
Half-backs: W Bumby (Swinton), J Nolan (Rochdale Hornets), W Burnett (Hawick)
Forwards: C Mathers (Bramley), S Williams (Salford), T Banks (Swinton), R L Seddon (Swinton), H Eagles (Swinton), A J Stuart (Dewsbury), W H Thomas (Cambridge U), T Kent (Salford), A P Penketh (Douglas, IOM), R Burnett (Hawick), A J Laing (Hawick), Dr J Smith (Edinburgh U), J P Clowes (Halifax)
Captains †R L Seddon, A E Stoddart **Managers** A Shaw, A Shrewsbury

† *Stoddart took over as captain after Seddon was drowned in Australia*

1899 (Australia only)

Full record	Played 21	Won 18	Lost 3	Drawn 0	Points for 333	Against 90
International record	Played 4	Won 3	Lost 1			
International details	Jun 24	Australia 13		British Isles 3	(Sydney)	
	Jul 22	Australia 0		British Isles 11	(Brisbane)	
	Aug 5	Australia 10		British Isles 11	(Sydney)	
	Aug 12	Australia 0		British Isles 13	(Sydney)	

Players

Full-backs: E Martelli (Dublin U), C E K Thompson (Lancashire)
Threequarters: A B Timms (Edinburgh U), E T Nicholson (Birkenhead Park), A M Bucher (Edinburgh Acads), E G Nicholls (Cardiff), G P Doran (Lansdowne)
Half-backs: Rev M Mullineux (Blackheath), G Cookson (Manchester), C Y Adamson (Durham)
Forwards: F M Stout (Gloucester), J W Jarman (Bristol), H G S Gray (Scottish Trials), G R Gibson (Northern), W Judkins (Coventry), F C Belson (Bath), J S Francomb (Manchester), B I Swannell (Northampton), G V Evers (Moseley), T M W McGown (N of Ireland), A Ayre-Smith (Guy's Hospital)
Captain and Manager Rev M Mullineux

1904

Full record						
in Australia	Played 14	Won 14	Lost 0	Drawn 0	Points for 265	Against 51
in New Zealand	Played 5	Won 2	Lost 2	Drawn 1	Points for 22	Against 33
International record						
v Australia	Played 3	Won 3				
v New Zealand	Played 1	Lost 1				

International details

v Australia	Jul 2	Australia	0	British Isles 17	(Sydney)
	Jul 23	Australia	3	British Isles 17	(Brisbane)
	Jul 30	Australia	0	British Isles 16	(Sydney)
v New Zealand	Aug 13	New Zealand	9	British Isles 3	(Wellington)

Players

Full-back: C F Stanger-Leathes (Northern)
Threequarters: J L Fisher (Hull and E Riding), R T Gabe (Cardiff), W F Jowett (Swansea), W Llewellyn (Llwynypia & Newport), E Morgan (London Welsh & Guy's Hospital), P F McEvedy (Guy's Hospital), A B O'Brien (Guy's Hospital)
Half-backs: P F Bush (Cardiff), F C Hulme (Birkenhead Park), T H Vile (Newport)
Forwards: D R Bedell-Sivright (Cambridge U), T S Bevan (Swansea), S N Crowther (Lennox), J T Sharland (Streatham), D D Dobson (Oxford U), C D Patterson (Malone), R W Edwards (Malone), A F Harding (Cardiff & London Welsh), B S Massey (Hull and E Riding), R J Rogers (Bath), F McK Saunders (Guy's Hospital), D H Traill (Guy's Hospital), B I Swannell (Northampton)
Captain D R Bedell-Sivright   **Manager** A B O'Brien

1908 (Anglo-Welsh)

Full record

| in Australia | Played 9 | Won 7 | Lost 2 | Drawn 0 | Points for 139 | Against 48 |
| in New Zealand | Played 17 | Won 9 | Lost 7 | Drawn 1 | Points for 184 | Against 153 |

International record

| v New Zealand | Played 3 | Lost 2 | Drawn 1 |

International details	Jun 6	New Zealand 32	British Isles 5	(Dunedin)
	Jun 27	New Zealand 3	British Isles 3	(Wellington)
	Jul 25	New Zealand 29	British Isles 0	(Auckland)

Players

Full-backs: J C M Dyke (Cardiff), E J Jackett (Falmouth & Leicester)
Threequarters: F E Chapman (Westoe & West Hartlepool), R A Gibbs (Cardiff), J L Williams (Cardiff), R B Griffiths (Newport), J P 'Ponty' Jones (Pontypool & London Welsh), J P 'Tuan' Jones (Guy's Hospital), Dr P F McEvedy (Guy's Hospital), H H Vassall (Oxford U & Blackheath)
Half-backs: J Davey (Redruth), H Laxon (Cambridge U), W L Morgan (Cardiff), G L Williams (Liverpool)
Forwards: H Archer (Guy's Hospital), R Dibble (Bridgwater and Albion), P J Down (Bristol), G V Kyrke (Marlborough Nomads), R K Green (Neath), E Morgan (Swansea), L S Thomas (Penarth), A F Harding (Cardiff & London Welsh), J F Williams (London Welsh), G R Hind (Guy's Hospital), F S Jackson (Leicester), W L Oldham (Coventry), J A S Ritson (Northern), T W Smith (Leicester)
Captain A F Harding   **Manager** G H Harnett

1930

Full record

| in New Zealand | Played 21 | Won 15 | Lost 6 | Drawn 0 | Points for 420 | Against 205 |
| in Australia | Played 7 | Won 5 | Lost 2 | Drawn 0 | Points for 204 | Against 113 |

International record

| v New Zealand | Played 4 | Won 1 | Lost 3 |
| v Australia | Played 1 | Lost 1 |

International details

v New Zealand	Jun 21	New Zealand 3	British Isles 6	(Dunedin)
	Jul 5	New Zealand 13	British Isles 10	(Christchurch)
	Jul 26	New Zealand 15	British Isles 10	(Auckland)

	Aug 9	New Zealand 22	British Isles 8	(Wellington)
v Australia	Aug 30	Australia 6	British Isles 5	(Sydney)

Players

Full-backs: J Bassett (Penarth), W G McG Bonner (Bradford)
Threequarters: C D Aarvold (Cambridge U & Blackheath), J S R Reeve (Harlequins),
J C Morley (Newport), A L Novis (Blackheath & Army), R Jennings (Redruth),
H M Bowcott (Cambridge U & Cardiff), T E Jones-Davies (London Welsh),
P F Murray (Wanderers)
Half-backs: R S Spong (Old Millhillians), W H Sobey (Old Millhillians),
T C Knowles (Birkenhead Park), H Poole (Cardiff)
Forwards: F D Prentice (Leicester), H Rew (Blackheath & Army), D Parker
(Swansea), W B Welsh (Hawick), B H Black (Oxford U & Blackheath), M J Dunne
(Lansdowne), G R Beamish (Leicester & RAF), J L Farrell (Bective Rangers),
J McD Hodgson (Northern), H O'H O'Neill (Queen's U, Belfast), Ivor Jones
(Llanelli), H Wilkinson (Halifax), S A Martindale (Kendal), D A Kendrew
(Woodford, Leicester and Army), H C S Jones (Manchester)
Captain F D Prentice   **Manager** J Baxter

1950

Full record						
in New Zealand	Played 23	Won 17	Lost 5	Drawn 1	Points for 420	Against 162
in Australia	Played 6	Won 5	Lost 1	Drawn 0	Points for 150	Against 52
International record						
v New Zealand	Played 4	Lost 3	Drawn 1			
v Australia	Played 2	Won 2				
International details					
v New Zealand	May 27	New Zealand 9	British Isles 9	(Dunedin)
	Jun 10	New Zealand 8	British Isles 0	(Christchurch)
	Jul 1	New Zealand 6	British Isles 3	(Wellington)
	Jul 29	New Zealand 11	British Isles 8	(Auckland)
v Australia	Aug 19	Australia 6	British Isles 19	(Brisbane)
	Aug 26	Australia 3	British Isles 24	(Sydney)

Players

Full-backs: G W Norton (Bective Rangers), W B Cleaver (Cardiff), B Lewis Jones★
(Devonport Services & Llanelli)
Threequarters: D W C Smith (London Scottish), M F Lane (UC Cork), K J Jones
(Newport), M C Thomas (Devonport Services & Newport), B L Williams (Cardiff), J
Matthews (Cardiff), N J Henderson (Queen's U, Belfast), R Macdonald (Edinburgh U)
Half-backs: J W Kyle (Queen's U, Belfast), I Preece (Coventry), W R Willis (Cardiff),
G Rimmer (Waterloo), A W Black (Edinburgh U)
Forwards: V G Roberts (Penryn), J S McCarthy (Dolphin), R T Evans (Newport),
J W McKay (Queen's U, Belfast), J R G Stephens (Neath), E R John (Neath),
P W Kininmonth (Oxford U & Richmond), J E Nelson (Malone), D J Hayward
(Newbridge), J D Robins (Birkenhead Park), T Clifford (Young Munster), C Davies
(Cardiff), G M Budge (Edinburgh Wands), D M Davies (Somerset Police),
Dr K D Mullen (Old Belvedere)
Captain Dr K D Mullen   **Manager** Surgeon-Captain (D) L B Osborne (RN)
Assistant Manager E L Savage

1959

Full record						
in Australia	Played 6	Won 5	Lost 1	Drawn 0	Points for 174	Against 70
in New Zealand	Played 25	Won 20	Lost 5	Drawn 0	Points for 582	Against 266

International record

v Australia	Played	2	Won	2		
v New Zealand	Played	4	Won	1	Lost 3	

International details

v Australia	Jun 6	Australia	6	British Isles 17	(Brisbane)
	Jun 13	Australia	3	British Isles 24	(Sydney)
v New Zealand	Jul 18	New Zealand 18		British Isles 17	(Dunedin)
	Aug 15	New Zealand 11		British Isles 8	(Wellington)
	Aug 29	New Zealand 22		British Isles 8	(Christchurch)
	Sept 19	New Zealand 6		British Isles 9	(Auckland)

Players

Full-backs: T J Davies (Llanelli), K J F Scotland (Cambridge U)

Threequarters: J R C Young (Oxford U), P B Jackson (Coventry), A J F O'Reilly (Old Belvedere), N H Brophy (UC Dublin), M J Price (Pontypool), W M Patterson★ (Sale), D Hewitt (Queen's U, Belfast), J Butterfield (Northampton), M C Thomas (Newport), G H Waddell (Cambridge U)

Half-backs: J P Horrocks-Taylor★ (Leicester), A B W Risman (Manchester U), M A F English (Limerick Bohemians), R E G Jeeps (Northampton), S Coughtrie (Edinburgh Acads), A A Mulligan★ (Wanderers & London Irish)

Forwards: B V Meredith (Newport), R Prosser (Pontypool), A R Dawson (Wanderers), H F McLeod (Hawick), G K Smith (Kelso), S Millar (Ballymena), B G M Wood (Garryowen), R H Williams (Llanelli), W A Mulcahy (UC Dublin), W R Evans (Cardiff), R W D Marques (Harlequins), A Ashcroft (Waterloo), N A A Murphy (Cork Const), H J Morgan (Abertillery), J Faull (Swansea)

Captain A R Dawson   **Manager** A Wilson   **Assistant Manager** O B Glasgow

1966

Full record

in Australia	Played	8	Won	7	Lost 0	Drawn 1	Points for 202	Against 48
in New Zealand	Played 25		Won 15		Lost 8	Drawn 2	Points for 300	Against 281

International record

v Australia	Played	2	Won	2	
v New Zealand	Played	4	Lost	4	

International details

v Australia	May 28	Australia	8	British Isles 11	(Sydney)
	Jun 4	Australia	0	British Isles 31	(Brisbane)
v New Zealand	Jul 16	New Zealand 20		British Isles 3	(Dunedin)
	Aug 6	New Zealand 16		British Isles 12	(Wellington)
	Aug 27	New Zealand 19		British Isles 6	(Christchurch)
	Sept 10	New Zealand 24		British Isles 11	(Auckland)

Players

Full-backs: D Rutherford (Gloucester), S Wilson (London Scottish), T G Price★ (Llanelli)

Threequarters: D I E Bebb (Swansea), A J W Hinshelwood (London Scottish), K F Savage (Northampton), S J Watkins (Newport), D K Jones (Cardiff), F P K Bresnihan★ (UC Dublin), M P Weston (Durham City), C W McFadyean (Moseley), J C Walsh (Sunday's Well)

Half-backs: C M H Gibson (Cambridge U), D Watkins (Newport), A R Lewis (Abertillery), R M Young (Queen's U, Belfast)

Forwards: R A Lamont (Instonians), A E I Pask (Abertillery), N A A Murphy (Cork Const), D Grant (Hawick), G J Prothero (Bridgend), J W Telfer (Melrose), W J McBride (Ballymena), M J Campbell-Lamerton (London Scottish), W D Thomas (Llanelli), B Price (Newport), R J McLoughlin (Gosforth), D L Powell

(Northampton), C H Norris (Cardiff), D Williams (Ebbw Vale), K W Kennedy (CIYMS), F A L Laidlaw (Melrose)
Captain M J Campbell-Lamerton   **Manager** D J O'Brien
Assistant Manager J D Robins

1971

Full record

in Australia	Played 2	Won 1	Lost 1	Drawn 0	Points for 25	Against 27
in New Zealand	Played 24	Won 22	Lost 1	Drawn 1	Points for 555	Against 204

International record

v New Zealand	Played 4	Won 2	Lost 1	Drawn 1

International details

v New Zealand	Jun 26	New Zealand 3	British Isles 9	(Dunedin)
	Jul 10	New Zealand 22	British Isles 12	(Christchurch)
	Jul 31	New Zealand 3	British Isles 13	(Wellington)
	Aug 14	New Zealand 14	British Isles 14	(Auckland)

Players

Full-backs: R Hiller (Harlequins), J P R Williams (London Welsh)
Threequarters: D J Duckham (Coventry), A G Biggar (London Scottish), T G R Davies (London Welsh), J C Bevan (Cardiff Coll of Education), A J Lewis (Ebbw Vale), J S Spencer (Headingley), S J Dawes (London Welsh), C W W Rea (Headingley)
Half-backs: C M H Gibson (NIFC), B John (Cardiff), G O Edwards (Cardiff), R Hopkins (Maesteg)
Forwards: T M Davies (London Welsh), P J Dixon (Harlequins), J Taylor (London Welsh), J F Slattery (UC Dublin), M L Hipwell (Terenure Coll), D L Quinnell (Llanelli), R J Arneil★ (Leicester), W D Thomas (Llanelli), W J McBride (Ballymena), M G Roberts (London Welsh), G L Brown (West of Scotland), T G Evans★ (London Welsh), A B Carmichael (West of Scotland), R J McLoughlin (Blackrock Coll), J McLauchlan (Jordanhill Coll), J F Lynch (St Mary's Coll), C B Stevens★ (Harlequins & Penzance-Newlyn), J V Pullin (Bristol), F A L Laidlaw (Melrose)
Captain S J Dawes   **Manager** Dr D W C Smith   **Assistant Manager** C R James

1977 (New Zealand and Fiji only)

Full record	Played 26	Won 21	Lost 5	Drawn 0	Points for 607	Against 320
in New Zealand	Played 25	Won 21	Lost 4	Drawn 0	Points for 586	Against 295
in Fiji	Played 1	Won 0	Lost 1	Drawn 0	Points for 21	Against 25

International record

v New Zealand	Played 4	Won 1	Lost 3

International details

v New Zealand	Jun 18	New Zealand 16	British Isles 12	(Wellington)
	Jul 9	New Zealand 9	British Isles 13	(Christchurch)
	Jul 30	New Zealand 19	British Isles 7	(Dunedin)
	Aug 13	New Zealand 10	British Isles 9	(Auckland)

Players

Full-backs: A R Irvine (Heriot's FP), B H Hay (Boroughmuir)
Threequarters: P J Squires (Harrogate), H E Rees (Neath), J J Williams (Llanelli), G L Evans (Newport), C M H Gibson (NIFC), S P Fenwick (Bridgend), D H Burcher (Newport), I R McGeechan (Headingley)
Half-backs: P Bennett (Llanelli), J D Bevan (Aberavon), D W Morgan (Stewart's-Melville FP), D B Williams (Cardiff), A D Lewis★ (Cambridge U & London Welsh)
Forwards: W P Duggan (Blackrock Coll), J Squire (Newport), T J Cobner (Pontypool), T P Evans (Swansea), A Neary (Broughton Park), D L Quinnell (Llanelli), G L Brown (West of Scotland), N E Horton (Moseley), A J Martin

(Aberavon), M I Keane (Lansdowne), W B Beaumont★ (Fylde), F E Cotton (Sale),
P A Orr (Old Wesley), G Price (Pontypool), C Williams (Aberavon), A G Faulkner★
(Pontypool), R W Windsor (Pontypool), P J Wheeler (Leicester)
Captain P Bennett **Manager** G Burrell **Assistant Manager** S J Dawes

1983 (New Zealand only)

Full record	Played 18	Won 12	Lost 6	Drawn 0	Points for 478	Against 276
International record	Played 4		Lost 4			
International details	Jun 4	New Zealand 16	British Isles 12	(Christchurch)		
	Jun 18	New Zealand 9	British Isles 0	(Wellington)		
	Jul 2	New Zealand 15	British Isles 8	(Dunedin)		
	Jul 16	New Zealand 38	British Isles 6	(Auckland)		

Players

Full-backs: H P MacNeill (Oxford U), W H Hare (Leicester), G Evans (Maesteg)
Threequarters: J Carleton (Orrell), G R T Baird (Kelso), T M Ringland (Ballymena),
D G Irwin (Instonians), M J Kiernan (Dolphin), R A Ackerman (London Welsh),
C R Woodward (Leicester)
Half-backs: S O Campbell (Old Belvedere), J Y Rutherford (Selkirk), T D Holmes
(Cardiff), R J Laidlaw (Jedforest), N D Melville★ (Wasps), S J Smith★ (Sale)
Forwards: S T Jones (Pontypool), I Stephens (Bridgend), G A J McLoughlin★
(Shannon), G Price (Pontypool), I G Milne (Heriot's FP), C T Deans (Hawick),
C F Fitzgerald (St Mary's Coll), S B Boyle (Gloucester), R L Norster (Cardiff),
M J Colclough (Angoulême), D G Lenihan★ (Cork Const), S J Bainbridge
(Gosforth), J H Calder (Stewart's-Melville FP), J B O'Driscoll (London Irish),
P J Winterbottom (Headingley), J Squire (Pontypool), N C Jeavons★ (Moseley),
J R Beattie (Glasgow Acads), I A M Paxton (Selkirk), E T Butler★ (Pontypool)
Captain C F Fitzgerald **Manager** W J McBride **Assistant Manager** J W Telfer

1989 (Australia only)

Full record	Played 12	Won 11	Lost 1	Drawn 0	Points for 360	Against 192
International record	Played 3	Won 2	Lost 1			
International details	Jul 1	Australia 30	British Isles 12	(Sydney)		
	Jul 8	Australia 12	British Isles 19	(Brisbane)		
	Jul 15	Australia 18	British Isles 19	(Sydney)		

Players

Full-backs: A G Hastings (London Scottish), P W Dods (Gala)
Threequarters: I C Evans (Llanelli), M R Hall (Bridgend), C Oti (Wasps),
R Underwood (Leicester & RAF), J A Devereux (Bridgend), J C Guscott (Bath),
S Hastings (Watsonians), B J Mullin (London Irish)
Half-backs: C M Chalmers (Melrose), P M Dean (St Mary's Coll), C R Andrew★
(Wasps), A Clement★ (Swansea), R N Jones (Swansea), G Armstrong (Jedforest)
Forwards: B C Moore (Nottingham), S J Smith (Ballymena), D M B Sole (Edinburgh
Acads), M Griffiths (Bridgend), G J Chilcott (Bath), D Young (Cardiff),
D G Lenihan (Cork Const), W A Dooley (Preston Grasshoppers), P J Ackford
(Harlequins), R L Norster (Cardiff), J Jeffrey (Kelso), R A Robinson (Bath),
M C Teague (Gloucester), D Richards (Leicester), D B White (London Scottish),
F Calder (Stewart's-Melville FP)
Captain F Calder **Manager** D C T Rowlands **Coach** I R McGeechan

1993 (New Zealand only)

Full record	Played 13	Won 7	Lost 6	Points for 314	Against 285
International record	Played 3	Won 1	Lost 2		

International details	Jun 12	New Zealand 20	British Isles 18	(Christchurch)
	Jun 26	New Zealand 7	British Isles 20	(Wellington)
	Jul 3	New Zealand 30	British Isles 13	(Auckland)

Players

Full-backs: A G Hastings (Watsonians), A Clement (Swansea)

Threequarters: R Underwood (Leicester & RAF), T Underwood (Leicester), I Hunter (Northampton), I C Evans (Llanelli), W D C Carling (Harlequins), J C Guscott (Bath), I S Gibbs (Swansea), S Hastings (Watsonians), V J G Cunningham* (St Mary's Coll), R M Wallace* (Garryowen)

Half-backs: S Barnes (Bath), C R Andrew (Wasps), R N Jones (Swansea), C D Morris (Orrell), A D Nicol* (Dundee HSFP)

Forwards: J Leonard (Harlequins), N J Popplewell (Greystones), A P Burnell (London Scottish), P H Wright (Boroughmuir), B C Moore (Harlequins), K S Milne (Heriot's FP), W A Dooley (Preston Grasshoppers), M C Bayfield (Northampton), M O Johnson* (Leicester), D F Cronin (London Scottish), A I Reed (Bath), M J Galwey (Shannon), M C Teague (Moseley), P J Winterbottom (Harlequins), R E Webster (Swansea), D Richards (Leicester), B B Clarke (Bath)

Captain A G Hastings   **Manager** G Cooke   **Coach** I R McGeechan

BRITISH ISLES TEAMS TO SOUTH AFRICA

1891

Full record	Played 19	Won 19	Lost 0	Drawn 0	Points for 224	Against 1
International record	Played 3	Won 3				
International details	Jul 30	South Africa 0	British Isles 4	(Port Elizabeth)		
	Aug 29	South Africa 0	British Isles 3	(Kimberley)		
	Sept 5	South Africa 0	British Isles 4	(Cape Town)		

Players

Full-backs: W G Mitchell (Cambridge U & Richmond), E Bromet (Cambridge U)

Threequarters: P R Clauss (Oxford U), R L Aston (Cambridge U), W E Maclagan (London Scottish)

Half-backs: H Marshall (Blackheath), B G Roscoe (Lancashire), A Rotherham (Cambridge U), W Wotherspoon (Cambridge U)

Forwards: W E Bromet (Oxford U), J H Gould (Old Leysians), J Hammond (Cambridge U), P F Hancock (Somerset), W J Jackson (Gloucester), R G MacMillan (London Scottish), E Mayfield (Cambridge U), C P Simpson (Cambridge U), A A Surtees (Cambridge U), R Thompson (Cambridge U), W H Thorman (Cambridge U), T Whittaker (Lancashire)

Captain W E Maclagan   **Manager** E H Ash

1896

Full record	Played 21	Won 19	Lost 1	Drawn 1	Points for 310	Against 45
International record	Played 4	Won 3	Lost 1			
International details	Jul 30	South Africa 0	British Isles 8	(Port Elizabeth)		
	Aug 22	South Africa 8	British Isles 17	(Johannesburg)		
	Aug 29	South Africa 3	British Isles 9	(Kimberley)		
	Sept 5	South Africa 5	British Isles 0	(Cape Town)		

Players

Full-back: J F Byrne (Moseley)

Threequarters: C A Boyd (Dublin U), J T Magee (Bective Rangers), L Q Bulger

(Dublin U & Lansdowne), C O Robinson (Northumberland), O G Mackie (Cambridge U & Wakefield Trinity)
Half-backs: Rev M Mullineux (Blackheath), S P Bell (Cambridge U), L M Magee (Bective Rangers & London Irish)
Forwards: J Hammond (Blackheath & Cambridge U), T J Crean (Dublin Wands), A W D Meares (Dublin U), R Johnston (Dublin Wands), A D Clinch (Dublin U), J Sealy (Dublin U), W J Carey (Oxford U), P F Hancock (Blackheath & Somerset), W Mortimer (Marlborough Nomads), A F Todd (Blackheath), R C Mullins (Oxford U), G W Lee★ (Rockcliff)
Captain J Hammond   **Manager** R Walker

1903

Full record	Played 22	Won 11	Lost 8	Drawn 3	Points for 231	Against 138
International record	Played 3	Lost 1	Drawn 2			
International details	Aug 26	South Africa 10		British Isles 10	(Johannesburg)	
	Sept 5	South Africa 0		British Isles 0	(Kimberley)	
	Sept 12	South Africa 8		British Isles 0	(Cape Town)	

Players

Full-back: E M Harrison (Guy's Hospital)
Threequarters: A E Hind (Cambridge U), I G Davidson (N of Ireland), G F Collet (Gloucestershire), R T Skrimshire (Newport & Blackheath), E F Walker (Lennox)
Half-backs: L L Greig (United Services), J I Gillespie (Edinburgh Acads), R M Neill (Edinburgh Acads), P S Hancock (Richmond)
Forwards: M C Morrison (Royal HSFP), W P Scott (West of Scotland), D R Bedell-Sivright (Cambridge U), W T C Cave (Cambridge U), J C Hosack (Edinburgh Wands), A Tedford (Malone), R S Smyth (Dublin U), Joseph Wallace (Dublin Wands), James Wallace (Dublin Wands), F M Stout (Richmond), T A Gibson (Cambridge U)
Captain M C Morrison   **Manager** J Hammond

1910

Full record	Played 24	Won 13	Lost 8	Drawn 3	Points for 290	Against 236
International record	Played 3	Won 1	Lost 2			
International details	Aug 6	South Africa 14		British Isles 10	(Kimberley)	
	Aug 27	South Africa 3		British Isles 8	(Port Elizabeth)	
	Sept 3	South Africa 21		British Isles 5	(Cape Town)	

Players

Full-back: S H Williams (Newport)
Threequarters: A Melville Baker (Newport), R C S Plummer (Newport), M E Neale (Bristol), A R Foster (Derry), C G Timms (Edinburgh U), J P Jones (Pontypool & Newport), J A Spoors (Bristol), K B Wood (Leicester)
Half-backs: N F Humphreys (Tynedale), A N McClinton (North of Ireland), G A M Isherwood (Cheshire, Sale & Old Alleynians), E Milroy★ (Watsonians)
Forwards: Dr T Smyth (Newport), W Tyrrell (Queen's U, Belfast), D F Smith (Richmond), P D Waller (Newport), J Reid-Kerr (Greenock Wands), R Stevenson (St Andrew's U), L M Speirs (Watsonians), E O'D Crean (Liverpool), H Jarman (Newport), O J S Piper (Cork Const), Dr W A Robertson (Edinburgh U & Hartlepool Rovers), C H Pillman (Blackheath), W J Ashby (Queen's Coll, Cork), F G Handford★ (Kersal), T J Richards★ (Bristol), J Webb★ (Abertillery)
Captain Dr T Smyth   **Managers** W Cail, Walter E Rees

1924

Full record	Played 21	Won 9	Lost 9	Drawn 3	Points for 175	Against 155
International record	Played 4	Lost 3	Drawn 1			
International details	Aug 16	South Africa 7	British Isles 3	(Durban)		
	Aug 23	South Africa 17	British Isles 0	(Johannesburg)		
	Sept 13	South Africa 3	British Isles 3	(Port Elizabeth)		
	Sept 20	South Africa 16	British Isles 9	(Cape Town)		

Players

Full-backs: D Drysdale (Heriot's FP), W F Gaisford (St Bart's Hospital),
T E Holliday (Aspatria)
Threequarters: R Harding (Swansea), I S Smith (Oxford U), S W Harris (Blackheath),
W Wallace (Percy Park), R M Kinnear (Heriot's FP), J H Bordass (Cambridge U),
R B Maxwell (Birkenhead Park)
Half-backs: H J Davies* (Newport), V M Griffiths (Newport), H Waddell (Glasgow
Acads), W A Cunningham* (Lansdowne), A T Young (Blackheath), H Whitley
(Northern)
Forwards: Dr R Cove-Smith (Old Merchant Taylors'), A F Blakiston (Blackheath),
A T Voyce (Gloucester), N C Macpherson (Newport), R G Henderson (Northern),
K G P Hendrie (Heriot's FP), D S Davies (Hawick), R A Howie (Kirkcaldy), A Ross
(Kilmarnock), J D Clinch (Dublin U), Dr W J Roche (UC Cork & Newport),
J McVicker (Belfast Collegians), D Marsden-Jones (Cardiff & London Welsh),
M J Bradley (Dolphin), T N Brand (North of Ireland)
Captain Dr R Cove-Smith   **Manager** H Packer

1938

Full record	Played 23	Won 17	Lost 6	Drawn 0	Points for 407	Against 272
International record	Played 3	Won 1	Lost 2			
International details	Aug 6	South Africa 26	British Isles 12	(Johannesburg)		
	Sept 3	South Africa 19	British Isles 3	(Port Elizabeth)		
	Sept 10	South Africa 16	British Isles 21	(Cape Town)		

Players

Full-backs: V G J Jenkins (London Welsh), C F Grieve (Oxford U)
Threequarters: E J Unwin (Rosslyn Park), W H Clement (Llanelli), E L Jones (Llanelli),
C V Boyle (Dublin U), R Leyland (Waterloo), D J Macrae (St Andrew's U), H R
McKibbin (Queen's U, Belfast), B E Nicholson (Old Whitgiftians & Harlequins)
Half-backs: F J Reynolds (Old Cranleighans), G E Cromey (Queen's U, Belfast),
J L Giles (Coventry), H Tanner (Swansea), G J Morgan (Clontarf)
Forwards: S Walker (Belfast Instonians), M E Morgan (Swansea), W G Howard (Old
Birkonians), W H Travers (Newport), C R A Graves (Dublin Wands), R B Mayne
(Queen's U, Belfast), G T Dancer (Bedford), S R Couchman (Old Cranleighans),
A G Purchas (Coventry), J A Waters (Selkirk), P L Duff (Glasgow Acads), I Williams
(Cardiff), A R Taylor (Cross Keys), R Alexander (North of Ireland)
Captain S Walker   **Manager** Col B C Hartley
Assistant Manager H A Haigh-Smith

1955

Full record	Played 24	Won 18	Lost 5	Drawn 1	Points for 418	Against 271
International record	Played 4	Won 2	Lost 2			
International details	Aug 6	South Africa 22	British Isles 23	(Johannesburg)		
	Aug 20	South Africa 25	British Isles 9	(Cape Town)		
	Sept 3	South Africa 6	British Isles 9	(Pretoria)		
	Sept 24	South Africa 22	British Isles 8	(Port Elizabeth)		

Players

Full-backs: A Cameron (Glasgow HSFP), A G Thomas (Llanelli)
Threequarters: A R Smith (Cambridge U), F D Sykes (Northampton), H Morris (Cardiff), A C Pedlow (Queen's U, Belfast), J Butterfield (Northampton), W P C Davies (Harlequins), A J F O'Reilly (Old Belvedere), J P Quinn (New Brighton), G Griffiths★ (Cardiff)
Half-backs: C I Morgan (Cardiff), D G S Baker (Old Merchant Taylors'), J E Williams (Old Millhillians), R E G Jeeps (Northampton), T Lloyd (Maesteg)
Forwards: R H Thompson (Instonians), C C Meredith (Neath), B V Meredith (Newport), H F McLeod (Hawick), W O Williams (Swansea), R Roe (Lansdowne), T Elliot (Gala), E J S Michie (Aberdeen U), T E Reid (Garryowen), R H Williams (Llanelli), J T Greenwood (Dunfermline), R J Robins (Pontypridd), R Higgins (Liverpool), D S Wilson (Metropolitan Police), R C C Thomas (Swansea)
Captain R H Thompson   **Manager** J A E Siggins   **Assistant Manager** D E Davies

1962

Full record	Played 24	Won 15	Lost 5	Drawn 4	Points for 351	Against 208
International record	Played 4	Lost 3	Drawn 1			
International details	Jun 23	South Africa 3	British Isles 3	(Johannesburg)		
	Jul 21	South Africa 3	British Isles 0	(Durban)		
	Aug 4	South Africa 8	British Isles 3	(Cape Town)		
	Aug 25	South Africa 34	British Isles 14	(Bloemfontein)		

Players

Full-backs: T J Kiernan (UC Cork), J G Willcox (Oxford U)
Threequarters: N H Brophy (Blackrock), D I E Bebb (Swansea), R C Cowan (Selkirk), A R Smith (Edinburgh Wands), J M Dee (Hartlepool Rovers), W R Hunter (CIYMS), M P Weston (Durham City), D K Jones (Llanelli), D Hewitt (Queen's U, Belfast)
Half-backs: R A W Sharp (Oxford U), R E G Jeeps (Northampton), G H Waddell (London Scottish), A O'Connor (Aberavon), H J C Brown★ (RAF & Blackheath)
Forwards: S Millar (Ballymena), K D Jones (Cardiff), D M D Rollo (Howe of Fife), T P Wright (Blackheath), B V Meredith (Newport), A E I Pask (Abertillery), S A M Hodgson (Durham City), M J Campbell-Lamerton (Army & Halifax), W J McBride (Ballymena), W A Mulcahy (Bohemians), K A Rowlands (Cardiff), H J Morgan (Abertillery), D P Rogers (Bedford), J Douglas (Stewart's Coll FP), D Nash (Ebbw Vale), H O Godwin★ (Coventry), G D Davidge★ (Newport)
Captain A R Smith   **Manager** Instructor-Commander D B Vaughan RN
Assistant Manager H R McKibbin

1968

Full record	Played 20	Won 15	Lost 4	Drawn 1	Points for 377	Against 181
International record	Played 4	Lost 3	Drawn 1			
International details	Jun 8	South Africa 25	British Isles 20	(Pretoria)		
	Jun 22	South Africa 6	British Isles 6	(Port Elizabeth)		
	Jul 13	South Africa 11	British Isles 6	(Cape Town)		
	Jul 27	South Africa 19	British Isles 6	(Johannesburg)		

Players

Full-backs: T J Kiernan (Cork Const), R Hiller (Harlequins)
Threequarters: A J W Hinshelwood (London Scottish), W K Jones (Cardiff), M C R Richards (Cardiff), K F Savage (Northampton), F P K Bresnihan (UC Dublin), T G R Davies (Cardiff), K S Jarrett (Newport), W H Raybould (London Welsh), J W C Turner (Gala)
Half-backs: C M H Gibson (North of Ireland), B John (Cardiff), G O Edwards (Cardiff), R M Young (Queen's U, Belfast), G C Connell★ (London Scottish)

Forwards: A L Horton (Blackheath), M J Coulman (Moseley), S Millar (Ballymena), J P O'Shea (Cardiff), P J Larter (Northampton), W J McBride (Ballymena), P K Stagg (Sale), W D Thomas (Llanelli), J V Pullin (Bristol), J Young (Harrogate), M G Doyle (Blackrock Coll), J Taylor (London Welsh), K G Goodall* (City of Derry), R J Arneil (Edinburgh Acads), R B Taylor (Northampton), J W Telfer (Melrose), B R West* (Northampton)
Captain T J Kiernan   **Manager** D K Brooks   **Assistant Manager** A R Dawson

1974

Full record	Played 22	Won 21	Lost 0	Drawn 1	Points for 729	Against 207
International record	Played 4	Won 3	Drawn 1			
International details	Jun 8	South Africa 3		British Isles 12	(Cape Town)	
	Jun 22	South Africa 9		British Isles 28	(Pretoria)	
	Jul 13	South Africa 9		British Isles 26	(Port Elizabeth)	
	Jul 27	South Africa 13		British Isles 13	(Johannesburg)	

Players
Full-backs: A R Irvine (Heriot's FP), J P R Williams (London Welsh)
Threequarters: T O Grace (St Mary's Coll), C F W Rees (London Welsh), W C C Steele (Bedford & RAF), J J Williams (Llanelli), A J Morley* (Bristol), R T E Bergiers (Llanelli), G W Evans (Coventry), I R McGeechan (Headingley), R A Milliken (Bangor)
Half-backs: P Bennett (Llanelli), A G B Old (Leicester), C M H Gibson* (NIFC), G O Edwards (Cardiff), J J Moloney (St Mary's Coll)
Forwards: T M Davies (Swansea), A G Ripley (Rosslyn Park), T P David (Llanelli), S A McKinney (Dungannon), A Neary (Broughton Park), J F Slattery (Blackrock Coll), G L Brown (West of Scotland), W J McBride (Ballymena), C W Ralston (Richmond), R M Uttley (Gosforth), M A Burton (Gloucester), A B Carmichael (West of Scotland), F E Cotton (Coventry), J McLauchlan (Jordanhill), K W Kennedy (London Irish), R W Windsor (Pontypool)
Captain W J McBride   **Manager** A G Thomas   **Assistant Manager** S Millar

1980

Full record	Played 18	Won 15	Lost 3	Drawn 0	Points for 401	Against 244
International record	Played 4	Won 1	Lost 3			
International details	May 31	South Africa 26		British Isles 22	(Cape Town)	
	Jun 14	South Africa 26		British Isles 19	(Bloemfontein)	
	Jun 28	South Africa 12		British Isles 10	(Port Elizabeth)	
	Jul 12	South Africa 13		British Isles 17	(Pretoria)	

Players
Full-backs: B H Hay (Boroughmuir), R C O'Donnell (St Mary's Coll), A R Irvine* (Heriot's FP)
Threequarters: J Carleton (Orrell), H E Rees (Neath), M A C Slemen (Liverpool), P Morgan (Llanelli), R W R Gravell (Llanelli), J M Renwick (Hawick), D S Richards (Swansea), C R Woodward (Leicester), P W Dodge* (Leicester)
Half-backs: S O Campbell (Old Belvedere), W G Davies (Cardiff), A J P Ward* (Garryowen), T D Holmes (Cardiff), C S Patterson (Instonians), J C Robbie* (Greystones), S J Smith* (Sale)
Forwards: J R Beattie (Glasgow Acads), D L Quinnell (Llanelli), S M Lane (Cardiff), J B O'Driscoll (London Irish), J Squire (Pontypool), C C Tucker (Shannon), G P Williams* (Bridgend), W B Beaumont (Fylde), M J Colclough (Angoulême), A J Martin (Aberavon), A J Tomes (Hawick), P J Blakeway (Gloucester), G Price (Pontypool), F E Cotton (Sale), C Williams (Swansea), I Stephens* (Bridgend), P A Orr* (Old Wesley), A J Phillips (Cardiff), P J Wheeler (Leicester)
Captain W B Beaumont   **Manager** S Millar   **Assistant Manager** N A A Murphy

INTERNATIONAL MATCH APPEARANCES FOR BRITISH ISLES TEAMS
(up to 30 April 1996)

From 1910 onwards, when British Isles teams first became officially representative of the four Home Unions. (*Uncapped when first selected to play in a Test match for the British Isles.)

ABBREVIATIONS

A – Australia; NZ – New Zealand; SA – South Africa; (R) – Replacement; (t) – temporary replacement.

CLUB ABBREVIATIONS

NIFC – North of Ireland Football Club; CIYMS – Church of Ireland Young Men's Society

Note: When a series has taken place, figures have been used to denote the particular matches in which players have featured. Thus 1962 SA 1,4 indicates that a player appeared in the first and fourth Tests of a series.

Aarvold, C D (Cambridge U, Blackheath and England) 1930 NZ 1,2,3,4, A
Ackerman, R A (London Welsh and Wales) 1983 NZ 1,4 (R)
Ackford, P J (Harlequins and England) 1989 A 1,2,3
Alexander, R (NIFC and Ireland) 1938 SA 1,2,3
Andrew, C R (Wasps and England) 1989 A 2,3, 1993 NZ 1,2,3
Arneil, R J (Edinburgh Acads and Scotland) 1968 SA 1,2,3,4
Ashcroft, A (Waterloo and England) 1959 A 1, NZ 2

Bainbridge, S J (Gosforth and England) 1983 NZ 3,4
Baird, G R T (Kelso and Scotland) 1983 NZ 1,2,3,4
Baker, A M (Newport and Wales) 1910 SA 3
Baker, D G S (Old Merchant Taylors' and England) 1955 SA 3,4
Bassett, J (Penarth and Wales) 1930 NZ 1,2,3,4, A
Bayfield, M C (Northampton and England) 1993 NZ 1,2,3
Beamish, G R (Leicester, RAF and Ireland) 1930 NZ 1,2,3,4, A
Beattie, J R (Glasgow Acads and Scotland) 1983 NZ 2 (R)
Beaumont, W B (Fylde and England) 1977 NZ 2,3,4, 1980 SA 1,2,3,4
Bebb, D I E (Swansea and Wales) 1962 SA 2,3, 1966 A 1,2, NZ 1,2,3,4
Bennett, P (Llanelli and Wales) 1974 SA 1,2,3,4, 1977 NZ 1,2,3,4
Bevan, J C (Cardiff Coll of Ed, Cardiff and Wales) 1971 NZ 1
Black, A W (Edinburgh U and Scotland) 1950 NZ 1,2
Black, B H (Oxford U, Blackheath and England) 1930 NZ 1,2,3,4, A
Blakiston, A F (Northampton and England) 1924 SA 1,2,3,4
Bowcott, H M (Cambridge U, Cardiff and Wales) 1930 NZ 1,2,3,4, A
Boyle, C V (Dublin U and Ireland) 1938 SA 2,3
Brand, T N (NIFC and *Ireland) 1924 SA 1,2
Bresnihan, F P K (UC Dublin and Ireland) 1968 SA 1,2,4
Brophy, N H (UC Dublin and Ireland) 1962 SA 1,4
Brown, G L (W of Scotland and Scotland) 1971 NZ 3,4, 1974 SA 1,2,3, 1977 NZ 2,3,4
Budge, G M (Edinburgh Wands and Scotland) 1950 NZ 4
Burcher, D H (Newport and Wales) 1977 NZ 3
Burnell, A P (London Scottish and Scotland) 1993 NZ 1
Butterfield, J (Northampton and England) 1955 SA 1, 2,3,4

Calder, F (Stewart's-Melville FP and Scotland) 1989 A 1,2,3
Calder, J H (Stewart's-Melville FP and Scotland) 1983 NZ 3
Cameron, A (Glasgow HSFP and Scotland) 1955 SA 1,2
Campbell, S O (Old Belvedere and Ireland) 1980 SA 2 (R), 3,4, 1983 NZ 1,2,3,4
Campbell-Lamerton, M J (Halifax, Army and Scotland) 1962 SA 1,2,3,4, 1966 A 1,2, NZ 1,3

Carleton, J (Orrell and England) 1980 SA 1,2,4, 1983 NZ 2,3,4
Carling, W D C (Harlequins and England) 1993 NZ 1
Chalmers, C M (Melrose and Scotland) 1989 A 1
Clarke, B B (Bath and England) 1993 NZ 1,2,3
Cleaver, W B (Cardiff and Wales) 1950 NZ 1,2,3
Clifford, T (Young Munster and Ireland) 1950 NZ 1,2,3, A 1,2
Cobner, T J (Pontypool and Wales) 1977 NZ 1,2,3
Colclough, M J (Angoulême and England) 1980 SA 1,2,3,4, 1983 NZ 1,2,3,4
Connell, G C (Trinity Acads and Scotland) 1968 SA 4
Cotton, F E (Loughborough Colls, Coventry and England) 1974 SA 1,2,3,4, 1977 NZ 2,3,4
Coulman, M J (Moseley and England) 1968 SA 3
Cove-Smith, R (Old Merchant Taylors' and England) 1924 SA 1,2,3,4
Cowan, R C (Selkirk and Scotland) 1962 SA 4
Cromey, G E (Queen's U, Belfast and Ireland) 1938 SA 3
Cunningham, W A (Lansdowne and Ireland) 1924 SA 3

Dancer, G T (Bedford) 1938 SA 1,2,3
Davies, C (Cardiff and Wales) 1950 NZ 4
Davies, D M (Somerset Police and Wales) 1950 NZ 3,4, A 1
Davies, D S (Hawick and Scotland) 1924 SA 1,2,3,4
Davies, H J (Newport and Wales) 1924 SA 2
Davies, T G R (Cardiff, London Welsh and Wales) 1968 SA 3, 1971 NZ 1,2,3,4
Davies, T J (Llanelli and Wales) 1959 NZ 2,4
Davies, T M (London Welsh, Swansea and Wales) 1971 NZ 1,2,3,4, 1974 SA 1,2,3,4
Davies, W G (Cardiff and Wales) 1980 SA 2
Davies, W P C (Harlequins and England) 1955 SA 1,2,3
Dawes, S J (London Welsh and Wales) 1971 NZ 1,2,3,4
Dawson, A R (Wanderers and Ireland) 1959 A 1,2, NZ 1,2,3,4
Dixon, P J (Harlequins and England) 1971 NZ 1,2,4
Dodge, P W (Leicester and England) 1980 SA 3,4
Dooley, W A (Preston Grasshoppers and England) 1989 A 2,3
Doyle, M G (Blackrock Coll and Ireland) 1968 SA 1
Drysdale, D (Heriot's FP and Scotland) 1924 SA 1,2,3,4
Duckham, D J (Coventry and England) 1971 NZ 2,3,4
Duggan, W P (Blackrock Coll and Ireland) 1977 NZ 1,2,3,4
Duff, P L (Glasgow Acads and Scotland) 1938 SA 2,3

Edwards, G O (Cardiff and Wales) 1968 SA 1,2, 1971 NZ 1,2,3,4, 1974 SA 1,2,3,4
Evans, G (Maesteg and Wales) 1983 NZ 3,4
Evans, G L (Newport and Wales) 1977 NZ 2,3,4
Evans, I C (Llanelli and Wales) 1989 A 1,2,3, 1993 NZ 1,2,3
Evans, R T (Newport and Wales) 1950 NZ 1,2,3,4, A 1,2
Evans, T P (Swansea and Wales) 1977 NZ 1
Evans, W R (Cardiff and Wales) 1959 A 2, NZ 1,2,3

331

O'Donnell, R C (St Mary's Coll and Ireland) 1980 *SA* 1
O'Driscoll, J B (London Irish and Ireland) 1980 *SA* 1,2,3,4, 1983 *NZ* 2,4
O'Neill, H O'H (Queen's U, Belfast and Ireland) 1930 *NZ* 1,2,3,4, *A*
O'Reilly, A J F (Old Belvedere and Ireland) 1955 *SA* 1,2,3,4, 1959 *A* 1,2, *NZ* 1,2,3,4
Orr, P A (Old Wesley and Ireland) 1977 *NZ* 1
O'Shea, J P (Cardiff and Wales) 1968 *SA* 1

Parker, D (Swansea and Wales) 1930 *NZ* 1,2,3,4, *A*
Pask, A E I (Abertillery and Wales) 1962 *SA* 1,2,3, 1966 *A* 1,2, *NZ* 1,3,4
Patterson, C S (Instonians and Ireland) 1980 *SA* 1,2,3
Patterson, W M (Sale and *England) 1959 *NZ* 2
Paxton, I A M (Selkirk and Scotland) 1983 *NZ* 1,2,3,4
Pedlow, A C (CIYMS and Ireland) 1955 *SA* 1,4
Pillman, C H (Blackheath and England) 1910 *SA* 2,3
Piper, O J S (Cork Const and Ireland) 1910 *SA* 1
Poole, H (Cardiff) 1930 *NZ* 3
Popplewell, N J (Greystones and Ireland) 1993 *NZ* 1,2,3
Preece, I (Coventry and England) 1950 *NZ* 1
Prentice, F D (Leicester and England) 1930 *NZ* 2, *A*
Price, B (Newport and Wales) 1966 *A* 1,2, *NZ* 1,4
Price, G (Pontypool and Wales) 1977 *NZ* 1,2,3,4, 1980 *SA* 1,2,3,4, 1983 *NZ* 1,2,3,4
Price, M J (Pontypool and Wales) 1959 *A* 1,2, *NZ* 1,2,3
Prosser, T R (Pontypool and Wales) 1959 *NZ* 4
Pullin, J V (Bristol and England) 1968 *SA* 2,3,4, 1971 *NZ* 1,2,3,4

Quinnell, D L (Llanelli and *Wales) 1971 *NZ* 3, 1977 *NZ* 2,3, 1980 *SA* 1,2

Ralston, C W (Richmond and England) 1974 *SA* 4
Reed, A I (Bath and Scotland) 1993 *NZ* 1
Rees, H E (Neath and *Wales) 1977 *NZ* 4
Reeve, J S R (Harlequins and England) 1930 *NZ* 1,3,4, *A*
Reid, T E (Garryowen and Ireland) 1955 *SA* 2,3
Renwick, J M (Hawick and Scotland) 1980 *SA* 1
Rew, H (Blackheath, Army and England) 1930 *NZ* 1,2,3,4
Reynolds, F J (Old Cranleighans and England) 1938 *SA* 1,2
Richards, D (Leicester and England) 1989 *A* 1,2,3, 1993 *NZ* 1,2,3
Richards, D S (Swansea and Wales) 1980 *SA* 1
Richards, M C R (Cardiff and Wales) 1968 *SA* 1,3,4
Richards, T J (Bristol and Australia) 1910 *SA* 1,2
Rimmer, G (Waterloo and England) 1950 *NZ* 3
Ringland, T M (Ballymena and Ireland) 1983 *NZ* 1
Risman, A B W (Loughborough Colls and England) 1959 *A* 1,2, *NZ* 1,4
Robbie, J C (Greystones and Ireland) 1980 *SA* 4
Robins, J D (Birkenhead Park and Wales) 1950 *NZ* 1,2,3, *A* 1,2
Robins, R J (Pontypridd and Wales) 1955 *SA* 1,2,3,4
Rogers, D P (Bedford and England) 1962 *SA* 1,4
Rowlands, K A (Cardiff and Wales) 1962 *SA* 1,2,4
Rutherford, D (Gloucester and England) 1966 *A* 1
Rutherford, J Y (Selkirk and Scotland) 1983 *NZ* 3

Savage, K F (Northampton and England) 1968 *SA* 1,2,3,4
Scotland, K J F (Cambridge U, Heriot's FP and Scotland) 1959 *A* 1,2, *NZ* 1,3,4
Sharp, R A W (Oxford U, Redruth and England) 1962 *SA* 3,4
Slattery, J F (Blackrock Coll and Ireland) 1974 *SA* 1,2,3,4
Slemen, M A C (Liverpool and England) 1980 *SA* 1
Smith, A R (Edinburgh Wands, London Scottish and Scotland) 1962 *SA* 1,2,3
Smith, D F (Richmond and England) 1910 *SA* 1,2,3
Smith, D W C (London Scottish and Scotland) 1950 *A* 1
Smith, G K (Kelso and Scotland) 1959 *A* 1,2, *NZ* 1,3
Smith, I S (Oxford U, London Scottish and Scotland) 1924 *SA* 1,2
Smyth, T (Malone, Newport and Ireland) 1910 *SA* 2,3
Sole, D M B (Edinburgh Acads and Scotland) 1989 *A* 1,2,3
Spong, R S (Old Millhillians and England) 1930 *NZ* 1,2,3,4, *A*
Spoors, J A (Bristol) 1910 *SA* 1,2,3
Squire, J (Newport, Pontypool and Wales) 1977 *NZ* 4, 1980 *SA* 1,2,3,4, 1983 *NZ* 1
Squires, P J (Harrogate and England) 1977 *NZ* 1
Stagg, P K (Oxford U, Sale and Scotland) 1968 *SA* 1,3,4

Steele, W C C (Bedford, RAF and Scotland) 1974 *SA* 1,2
Stephens, I (Bridgend and Wales) 1983 *NZ* 1
Stephens, J R G (Neath and Wales) 1950 *A* 1,2
Stevenson, R C (St Andrew's U and Scotland) 1910 *SA* 1,2,3

Tanner, H (Swansea and Wales) 1938 *SA* 2
Taylor, A R (Cross Keys and Wales) 1938 *SA* 1,2
Taylor, J (London Welsh and Wales) 1971 *NZ* 1,2,3,4
Taylor, R B (Northampton and England) 1968 *SA* 1,2,3,4
Teague, M C (Gloucester, Moseley and England) 1989 *A* 2,3, 1993 *NZ* 2 (t)
Telfer, J W (Melrose and Scotland) 1966 *A* 1,2, *NZ* 1,2,4, 1968 *SA* 2,3
Thomas, M C (Devonport Services, Newport and Wales) 1950 *NZ* 2,3, *A* 1, 1959 *NZ* 2
Thomas, R C C (Swansea and Wales) 1955 *SA* 3,4
Thomas, W D (Llanelli and *Wales) 1966 *NZ* 2,3, 1968 *SA* 3 (R), 4, 1971 *NZ* 1,2,4 (R)
Thompson, R H (Instonians, London Irish and Ireland) 1955 *SA* 1,2,4
Travers, W H (Newport and Wales) 1938 *SA* 2,3
Tucker, C C (Shannon and Ireland) 1980 *SA* 3,4
Turner, J W C (Gala and Scotland) 1968 *SA* 1,2,3,4

Underwood, R (RAF, Leicester and England) 1989 *A* 1,2,3, 1993 *NZ* 1,2,3
Unwin, E J (Rosslyn Park, Army and England) 1938 *SA* 1,2
Uttley, R M (Gosforth and England) 1974 *SA* 1,2,3,4

Voyce, A T (Gloucester and England) 1924 *SA* 3,4

Waddell, G H (Cambridge U, London Scottish and Scotland) 1962 *SA* 1,2
Waddell, H (Glasgow Acads and Scotland) 1924 *SA* 1,2,4
Walker, S (Instonians and Ireland) 1938 *SA* 1,2,3
Wallace, W (Percy Park) 1924 *SA* 1
Waller, P D (Newport and Wales) 1910 *SA* 1,2,3
Ward, A J P (Garryowen and Ireland) 1980 *SA* 1
Waters, J A (Selkirk and Scotland) 1938 *SA* 3
Watkins, D (Newport and Wales) 1966 *A* 1,2, *NZ* 1,2,3,4
Watkins, S J (Newport and Wales) 1966 *A* 1,2, *NZ* 3
Webb, J (Abertillery and Wales) 1910 *SA* 1,2,3
Welsh, W B (Hawick and Scotland) 1930 *NZ* 4
Weston, M P (Richmond, Durham City and England) 1962 *SA* 1,2,3,4, 1966 *A* 1,2
Wheeler, P J (Leicester and England) 1977 *NZ* 2,3,4, 1980 *SA* 1,2,3,4
White, D B (London Scottish and Scotland) 1989 *A* 1
Whitley, H (Northern and *England) 1924 *SA* 1,3,4
Willcox, J G (Oxford U, Harlequins and England) 1962 *SA* 1,2,4
Williams, B L (Cardiff and Wales) 1950 *NZ* 2,3,4, *A* 1,2
Williams, C (Swansea and Wales) 1980 *SA* 1,2,3,4
Williams, D (Ebbw Vale and Wales) 1966 *A* 1,2, *NZ* 1,2,4
Williams, D B (Cardiff and *Wales) 1977 *NZ* 1,2,3
Williams, J J (Llanelli and Wales) 1974 *SA* 1,2,3,4, 1977 *NZ* 1,2,3
Williams, J P R (London Welsh and Wales) 1971 *NZ* 1,2,3,4, 1974 *SA* 1,2,3,4
Williams, R H (Llanelli and Wales) 1955 *SA* 1,2,3,4, 1959 *A* 1,2, *NZ* 1,2,3,4
Williams, S H (Newport and *England) 1910 *SA* 1,2,3
Williams, W O G (Swansea and Wales) 1955 *SA* 1,2,3,4
Willis, W R (Cardiff and Wales) 1950 *NZ* 4, *A* 1,2
Wilson, S (London Scottish and Scotland) 1966 *A* 2, *NZ* 1,2,3,4
Windsor, R W (Pontypool and Wales) 1974 *SA* 1,2,3,4, 1977 *NZ* 1
Winterbottom, P J (Headingley, Harlequins and England) 1983 *NZ* 1,2,3,4, 1993 *NZ*, 1,2,3
Wood, B G M (Garryowen and Ireland) 1959 *NZ* 1,3
Wood, K B (Leicester) 1910 *SA* 1,3
Woodward, C R (Leicester and England) 1980 *SA* 2,3

Young, A T (Cambridge U, Blackheath and England) 1924 *SA* 2
Young, D (Cardiff and Wales) 1989 *A* 1,2,3
Young, J (Harrogate, RAF and Wales) 1968 *SA* 1
Young, J R C (Oxford U, Harlequins and England) 1959 *NZ* 2
Young, R M (Queen's U, Belfast, Collegians and Ireland) 1966 *A* 1,2, *NZ* 1, 1968 *SA* 3

RESULTS OF BRITISH ISLES MATCHES
(*up to 30 April 1996*)

From 1910 onwards – the tour to South Africa in that year was the first fully representative one in which the four Home Unions co-operated.

v SOUTH AFRICA
Played 30   British Isles won 8, South Africa won 18, Drawn 4

1910 *1* Johannesburg
South Africa 1G 3T (14) to 1DG 2T (10)

2 Port Elizabeth
British Isles 1G 1T (8) to 1T (3)

3 Cape Town
South Africa 3G 1PG 1T (21) to 1G (5)
South Africa won series 2-1

1924 *1* Durban
South Africa 1DG 1T (7) to 1T (3)

2 Johannesburg
South Africa 1G 1PG 3T (17) to 0

3 Port Elizabeth
Drawn 1T (3) each

4 Cape Town
South Africa 1DG 4T (16) to 1PG 2T (9)
South Africa won series 3-0, with 1 draw

1938 *1* Johannesburg
South Africa 4G 2PG (26) to 4PG (12)

2 Port Elizabeth
South Africa 2G 2PG 1T (19) to 1T (3)

3 Cape Town
British Isles 1G 1PG 1DG 3T (21)
to 2G 1PG 1T (16)
South Africa won series 2-1

1955 *1* Johannesburg
British Isles 4G 1T (23)
to 2G 2PG 2T (22)

2 Cape Town
South Africa 2G 5T (25) to 1PG 2T (9)

3 Pretoria
British Isles 1PG 1DG 1T (9) to 2PG (6)

4 Port Elizabeth
South Africa 2G 1DG 3T (22)
to 1G 1T (8)
Series drawn 2-2

1962 *1* Johannesburg
Drawn 1T (3) each

2 Durban
South Africa 1PG (3) to 0

3 Cape Town
South Africa 1G 1PG (8) to 1DG (3)

4 Bloemfontein
South Africa 5G 2PG 1T (34)
to 1G 1PG 2T (14)
South Africa won series 3-0, with 1 draw

1968 *1* Pretoria
South Africa 2G 4PG 1T (25)
to 1G 5PG (20)

2 Port Elizabeth
Drawn 2PG (6) each

3 Cape Town
South Africa 1G 2PG (11) to 2PG (6)

4 Johannesburg
South Africa 2G 1DG 2T (19) to 2PG (6)
South Africa won series 3-0, with 1 draw

1974 *1* Cape Town
British Isles 3PG 1DG (12) to 1DG (3)

2 Pretoria
British Isles 1G 1PG 1DG 4T (28)
to 2PG 1DG (9)

3 Port Elizabeth
British Isles 1G 2PG 2DG 2T (26)
to 3PG (9)

4 Johannesburg
Drawn British Isles 1G 1PG 1T (13)
South Africa 3PG 1T (13)
British Isles won series 3-0, with 1 draw

1980 *1* Cape Town
South Africa 3G 2T (26)
to 5PG 1DG 1T (22)

2 Bloemfontein
South Africa 2G 2PG 2T (26)
to 1G 3PG 1T (19)

3 Port Elizabeth
South Africa 1G 1PG 1DG (12)
to 2PG 1T (10)

4 Pretoria
British Isles 1G 1PG 2T (17)
to 3PG 1T (13)
South Africa won series 3-1

v NEW ZEALAND
Played 31   British Isles won 6, New Zealand won 23, Drawn 2

1930 *1* Dunedin
British Isles 2T (6) to 1T (3)

2 Christchurch
New Zealand 2G 1GM (13) to 2G (10)

3 Auckland
New Zealand 1G 1DG 2T (15) to 2G (10)

4 Wellington
New Zealand 2G 4T (22) to 1G 1PG (8)
New Zealand won series 3-1

1950 *1* Dunedin
Drawn 1PG 2T (9) each

2 Christchurch
New Zealand 1G 1T (8) to 0

3 Wellington
New Zealand 1PG 1T (6) to 1PG (3)

4 Auckland
New Zealand 1G 1DG 1T (11)
to 1G 1PG (8)
New Zealand won series 3-0, with 1 draw

1959 *1* Dunedin
New Zealand 6PG (18) to 1G 1PG 3T (17)

2 Wellington
New Zealand 1G 2T (11) to 1G 1PG (8)

3 Christchurch
New Zealand 2G 1PG 1DG 2T (22)
to 1G 1PG (8)

4 Auckland
British Isles 3T (9) to 2PG (6)
New Zealand won series 3-1

1966 *1* Dunedin
New Zealand 1G 2PG 1DG 2T (20)
to 1PG (3)

2 Wellington
New Zealand 2G 1PG 1T (16)
to 3PG 1DG (12)

3 Christchurch
New Zealand 2G 2PG 1T (19) to 2T (6)

4 Auckland
New Zealand 3G 1PG 1DG 1T (24)
to 1G 1PG 1T (11)
New Zealand won series 4-0

1971 *1* Dunedin
British Isles 2PG 1T (9) to 1PG (3)

2 Christchurch
New Zealand 2G 1PG 3T (22)
to 1PG 1DG 2T (12)

3 Wellington
British Isles 2G 1DG (13) to 1T (3)

4 Auckland
Drawn British Isles 1G 2PG 1DG (14)
New Zealand 1G 2PG 1T (14)
British Isles won series 2-1, with 1 draw

1977 *1* Wellington
New Zealand 2G 1T (16) to 4PG (12)

2 Christchurch
British Isles 3PG 1T (13) to 3PG (9)

3 Dunedin
New Zealand 1G 2PG 1DG 1T (19)
to 1PG 1T (7)

4 Auckland
New Zealand 2PG 1T (10) to 1G 1PG (9)
New Zealand won series 3-1

1983 *1* Christchurch
New Zealand 3PG 1DG 1T (16)
to 3PG 1DG (12)

2 Wellington
New Zealand 1G 1PG (9) to 0

3 Dunedin
New Zealand 1G 3PG (15) to 2T (8)

4 Auckland
New Zealand 4G 2PG 2T (38) to 2PG (6)
New Zealand won series 4-0

1993 *1* Christchurch
New Zealand 5PG 1T (20) to 6PG (18)

2 Wellington
British Isles 4PG 1DG 1T (20) to 1G (7)

3 Auckland
New Zealand 3G 3PG (30) to 1G 2PG (13)
New Zealand won series 2-1

v AUSTRALIA

Played 10   British Isles won 8, Australia won 2, Drawn 0

1930 *1* Sydney
Australia 2T (6) to 1G (5)

1950 *1* Brisbane
British Isles 2G 2PG 1DG(19) to 2PG (6)

2 Sydney
British Isles 3G 1PG 2T (24) to 1T (3)
British Isles won series 2-0

1959 *1* Brisbane
British Isles 1G 2PG 1DG 1T (17)
to 2PG (6)

2 Sydney
British Isles 3G 1PG 2T (24) to 1PG (3)
British Isles won series 2-0

1966 *1* Sydney
British Isles 1G 1PG 1T (11)
to 1G 1PG (8)

2 Brisbane
British Isles 5G 1PG 1DG (31) to 0
British Isles won series 2-0

1989 *1* Sydney
Australia 4G 1PG 1DG (30)
to 3PG 1DG (12)

2 Brisbane
British Isles 1G 2PG 1DG 1T (19)
to 1G 2PG (12)

3 Sydney
British Isles 5PG 1T (19) to 1G 4PG (18)
British Isles won series 2-1

BRITISH ISLES RECORDS
(*up to 30 April 1996*)

From 1910 onwards – the tour to South Africa in that year was the first fully representative one in which the four Home Unions co-operated.

TEAM RECORDS

Highest score
31 v Australia (31-0) 1966 Brisbane

v individual countries
28 v S Africa (28-9) 1974 Pretoria
20 v New Zealand (20-7) 1993 Wellington
31 v Australia (31-0) 1966 Brisbane

Biggest winning points margin
31 v Australia (31-0) 1966 Brisbane

v individual countries
19 v S Africa (28-9) 1974 Pretoria
13 v New Zealand (20-7) 1993 Wellington
31 v Australia (31-0) 1966 Brisbane

Highest score by opposing team
38 New Zealand (6-38) 1983 Auckland

by individual countires
34 S Africa (14-34) 1962 Bloemfontein
38 New Zealand (6-38) 1983 Auckland
30 Australia (12-30) 1989 Sydney

Biggest losing points margin
32 v New Zealand (6-38) 1983 Auckland

v individual countries
20 v S Africa (14-34) 1962 Bloemfontein
32 v New Zealand (6-38) 1983 Auckland
18 v Australia (12-30) 1989 Sydney

Most tries by B Isles in an international
5 {
v Australia (24-3) 1950 Sydney
v S Africa (23-22) 1955 Johannesburg
v Australia (24-3) 1959 Sydney
v Australia (31-0) 1966 Brisbane
v S Africa (28-9) 1974 Pretoria
}

Most tries against B Isles in an international
7 by South Africa (9-25) 1955 Cape Town

Most points on overseas tour (all matches)
842 in Australia, New Zealand and Canada (33 matches) 1959
(includes 582 points in 25 matches in New Zealand)

Most tries on overseas tour (all matches)
165 in Australia, New Zealand and Canada (33 matches) 1959
(includes 113 tries in 25 matches in New Zealand)

INDIVIDUAL RECORDS

Most capped player
W J McBride 17 1962-74

in individual positions
Full-back
J P R Williams   8[1]   1971-74
Wing
A J F O'Reilly   9(10)[2]   1955-59
Centre
C M H Gibson   8(12)[3]   1966-71
Fly-half
P Bennett   8   1974-77
Scrum-half
R E G Jeeps   13   1955-62
Prop
G Price   12   1977-83
Hooker
B V Meredith   8   1955-62
Lock
W J McBride   17   1962-74
Flanker
N A A Murphy   8   1959-66
No 8
T M Davies   8[4]   1971-74

[1] *A R Irvine, 9 Tests, played 7 time at full-back and twice as a wing*
[2] *O'Reilly played once as a centre*
[3] *Gibson played 4 times as a fly-half. I R McGeechan, 8 Tests, played 7 times as a centre and once, as a replacement, on the wing*
[4] *Both A E I Pask and J W Telfer (8 Tests each), played 4 Tests at No 8 and 4 Tests at flanker*

Longest international career
W J McBride   13 seasons   1962-74

Most consecutive Tests – 15
W J McBride 1966-74

Most internationals as captain – 6
A R Dawson 1959

Most points in internationals – 66
A G Hastings (6 appearances) 1989-93

Most points in an international – 18
A J P Ward v S Africa 1980 Cape Town
A G Hastings v New Zealand 1993
   Christchurch

Most tries in internationals – 6
A J F O'Reilly (10 appearances) 1955-59

Most tries in an international – 2
C D Aarvold v New Zealand 1930
   Christchurch
J E Nelson v Australia 1950 Sydney
M J Price v Australia 1959 Sydney
M J Price v New Zealand 1959 Dunedin
D K Jones v Australia 1966 Brisbane
T G R Davies v New Zealand 1971
   Christchurch
J J Williams v S Africa 1974 Pretoria
J J Williams v S Africa 1974 Port Elizabeth

Most conversions in internationals – 6
S Wilson (5 matches) 1966

Most conversions in an international – 5
S Wilson v Australia 1966 Brisbane

Most dropped goals in internationals – 2
D Watkins (6 matches) 1966
B John (5 matches) 1968-71
P Bennett (8 matches) 1974-77
C R Andrew (5 matches) 1989-93
(P F Bush also dropped 2 goals in Tests played by British teams prior to 1910)

Most dropped goals in an international – 2
P Bennett v S Africa 1974 Port Elizabeth

Most penalty goals in international – 20
A G Hastings (6 matches) 1989-93

Most penalty goals in an international – 6
A G Hastings v New Zealand 1993
   Christchurch

Most points for B Isles on overseas tour – 188
B John (17 appearances) 1971 Australia/
   N Zealand
(including 180 points in 16 appearances in
   N Zealand)

Most tries for B Isles on overseas tour – 22*
A J F O'Reilly (23 appearances) 1959
   Australia/N Zealand/Canada
(includes 17* tries in 17 appearances in N
   Zealand)
* Includes one penalty try

Most points for B Isles in international series – 38
A G Hastings (3 appearnaces) 1993
   New Zealand

Most tries for B Isles in international series – 4
J J Williams (4 appearances) 1974 S Africa

Most points for B Isles in any match on tour – 37
A G B Old v South Western Districts 1974
   Mossel Bay, S Africa

Most tries for B Isles in any match on tour – 6
D J Duckham v West Coast-Buller 1971
   Greymouth, N Zealand
J J Williams v South Western Districts
   1974 Mossel Bay, S Africa
(A R Irvine scored 5 tries from full-back v
   King Country-Wanganui 1977
   Taumarunui, N Zealand)

LEADING CAP-WINNERS
(up to 30 April 1996)

ENGLAND

R Underwood	85
C R Andrew	70
W D C Carling	66
B C Moore	64
P J Winterbottom	58
W A Dooley	55
J Leonard	49
D Richards	48
J C Guscott	45
A Neary	43
J V Pullin	42
P J Wheeler	41
J A Probyn	37
D J Duckham	36
G S Pearce	36
D P Rogers	34
W B Beaumont	34
J P Scott	34
J M Webb	33
P W Dodge	32
W W Wakefield	31
F E Cotton	31
M A C Slemen	31
M C Bayfield	31
E Evans	30
R Cove-Smith	29
C R Jacobs	29
M P Weston	29
P J Squires	29
R J Hill	29
J Butterfield	28
S J Smith	28
P A G Rendall	28
B B Clarke	28
A T Voyce	27
J S Tucker	27
M C Teague	27
J Carleton	26
C D Morris	26
C N Lowe	25
J D Currie	25
M S Phillips	25
C B Stevens	25
W H Hare	25
M J Colclough	25
T A K Rodber	25

SCOTLAND

A G Hastings	61
S Hastings	61
J M Renwick	52
C T Deans	52
A R Irvine	51
A B Carmichael	50
A J Tomes	48
R J Laidlaw	47
C M Chalmers	47
A F McHarg	44
K W Robertson	44
I G Milne	44
D M B Sole	44
J McLauchlan	43
J Y Rutherford	42
D B White	41
A P Burnell	41
J Jeffrey	40
H F McLeod	40
D M D Rollo	40
K S Milne	39
A G Stanger	38
J MacD Bannerman	37
I Tukalo	37
G W Weir	37
I A M Paxton	36
D F Cronin	36
F Calder	34
A R Smith	33
I S Smith	32
F A L Laidlaw	32
I R McGeechan	32
D G Leslie	32
N S Bruce	31
I H P Laughland	31
G L Brown	30
G Armstrong	30
W I D Elliot	29
S R P Lineen	29
W M Simmers	28
P K Stagg	28
J W Y Kemp	27
K J F Scotland	27
P C Brown	27
J H Calder	27
D I Johnston	27
G R T Baird	27
W E Maclagan	26
D Drysdale	26
J C McCallum	26
G P S Macpherson	26
J B Nelson	25
J P Fisher	25
J R Beattie	25
J W Telfer	25

IRELAND

C M H Gibson	69
W J McBride	63
J F Slattery	61
P A Orr	58
B J Mullin	55
T J Kiernan	54
D G Lenihan	52
M I Keane	51
J W Kyle	46
K W Kennedy	45
M J Kiernan	43
G V Stephenson	42
N A A Murphy	41
W P Duggan	41
K D Crossan	41
N J Henderson	40
R J McLoughlin	40
M T Bradley	40
N J Popplewell	39
P M Matthews	38
S Millar	37
H P MacNeill	37
S P Geoghegan	37
N P J Francis	36
J R Kavanagh	35
W A Mulcahy	35
E O'D Davy	34
T M Ringland	34
D C Fitzgerald	34
P M Dean	32
A C Pedlow	30
G T Hamlet	30
W E Crawford	30
J D Clinch	30
J L Farrell	29
B G M Wood	29
A J F O'Reilly	29
T J Kingston	29
M Sugden	28
J S McCarthy	28
P P A Danaher	28
P S Johns	28
A M Magee	27
A R Dawson	27
M G Molloy	27
J J Moloney	27
W A Anderson	27
J C Walsh	26
R M Young	26
J B O'Driscoll	26
G R Beamish	25
K D Mullen	25

F P K Bresnihan 25
A T A Duggan 25
B J McGann 25
T O Grace 25
S A McKinney 25
C F Fitzgerald 25
D G Irwin 25
S J Smith 25
B F Robinson 25
W D McBride 25

WALES

I C Evans 61
J P R Williams 55
R N Jones 54
G O Edwards 53
T G R Davies 46
P T Davies 46
G O Llewellyn 45
K J Jones 44
M R Hall 42
G Price 41
E W Lewis 41
N R Jenkins 39
T M Davies 38
P H Thorburn 37
A Clement 37
D Williams 36
R M Owen 35
B V Meredith 34
D I E Bebb 34
W D Morris 34
A J Martin 34
R L Norster 34
M Griffiths 34
W J Bancroft 33
B Price 32
J R G Stephens 32
G A D Wheel 32
M G Ring 32
J J Williams 30
S P Fenwick 30
G R Jenkins 30
W J Trew 29
C I Morgan 29
P Bennett 29
J Squire 29
R W Windsor 28
R G Collins 28
J D Davies 28
A J Gould 27
W C Powell 27
M C Thomas 27
H J Morgan 27
A M Hadley 27
J Davies 27
R C C Thomas 26

A E I Pask 26
S J Watkins 26
J Taylor 26
G Travers 25
H Tanner 25
B John 25
N R Gale 25
W D Thomas 25
T D Holmes 25

FRANCE

P Sella 111
S Blanco 93
R Bertranne 69
M Crauste 63
B Dauga 63
J Condom 61
P Saint-André 60
J-P Rives 59
O Roumat 59
P Berbizier 56
L Rodriguez 56
F Mesnel 56
R Paparemborde 55
A Domenech 52
J Prat 51
W Spanghero 51
J-L Joinel 51
M Celaya 50
P Dintrans 50
A Boniface 48
J-P Lux 47
L Armary 47
J-C Skréla 46
D Erbani 46
P Lagisquet 46
M Cecillon 46
L Cabannes 45
A Benazzi 44
M Vannier 43
J-P Garuet 42
E Champ 42
P Ondarts 42
J-L Sadourny 42
J Dupuy 40
C Darrouy 40
F Haget 40
J-M Aguirre 39
G Dufau 38
T Lacroix 38
P Benetton 37
D Camberabero 36
J-B Lafond 36
G Boniface 35
E Cester 35
A Paco 35
J-M Gonzalez 35

E Ribère 34
J Bouquet 34
P Villepreux 34
J Iraçabal 34
J-P Romeu 34
G Basquet 33
C Lacaze 33
C Dourthe 33
D Dubroca 33
J Gachassin 32
J-P Bastiat 32
A Cassayet 31
A Jauréguy 31
M Prat 31
F Moncla 31
G Cholley 31
D Codorniou 31
P Albaladéjo 30
A Roques 30
R Bénésis 30
A Lorieux 30
R Biénès 29
L Mias 29
O Merle 29
J Trillo 28
J-P Lescarboura 28
H Rancoule 27
P Lacroix 27
J-C Berejnoi 27
C Carrère 27
J Fouroux 27
J Gallion 27
B Chevallier 26
J Barthe 26
J-M Cabanier 26
A Gruarin 26
J-L Azarète 26
A Vaquerin 26
M Andrieu 26
R Martine 25
J Maso 25
J-L Averous 25
P Estève 25

SOUTH AFRICA

F C H du Preez 38
J H Ellis 38
J F K Marais 35
J P Engelbrecht 33
J L Gainsford 33
J T Claassen 28
H E Botha 28
F du T Roux 27
L G Wilson 27
J T Small 26
T P Bedford 25
D J de Villiers 25

P J F Greyling	25	O M Brown	28	T J Horan	38
S H Nomis	25	R W Norton	27	J S Little	38
P J Visagie	25	J T Stanley	27	J E Thornett	37
L C Moolman	24	M J Pierce	26	J N B Hipwell	36
D M Gerber	24	J K R Timu	26	A A Shaw	36
J F Pienaar	24	B J Lochore	25	B J Moon	35
D J Hopwood	22	B E McLeod	24	S N Tuynman	34
A C Koch	22	K F Gray	24	J A Eales	31
M du Plessis	22	I J Clarke	24	N M Shehadie	30
J A du Rand	21	J C Ashworth	24	P E McLean	30
M T S Stofberg	21	D S Loveridge	24	M E Loane	28
J S Germishuys	20	W T Taylor	24	S A Williams	28
H P le Roux	20	R A White	23	K W Catchpole	27

NEW ZEALAND

		B G Fraser	23	G A Shaw	27
S B T Fitzpatrick	73	D J Graham	22	D J Wilson	27
J J Kirwan	63	D Young	22	C T Burke	26
G W Whetton	58	W T Shelford	22	E E Rodriguez	26
C E Meads	55	R M Brooke	22	J S Miller	26
R W Loe	49	G N K Mourie	21	V Ofahengaue	26
I D Jones	48	M J B Hobbs	21	R B Prosser	25
S C McDowell	46	K L Skinner	20	G Cornelsen	25
G J Fox	46	C R Laidlaw	20	M G Ella	25
A M Haden	41	I N MacEwan	20	R G Gould	25
M N Jones	40	P J Whiting	20	P C Grigg	25
I A Kirkpatrick	39	C I Green	20	M J Hawker	25
K R Tremain	38	J W Joseph	20	J K Lenehan	24
B G Williams	38			J P L White	24
Z V Brooke	37	## AUSTRALIA		J W Cole	24
G A Knight	36			G Fay	24
W K Little	36	D I Campese	92	R Phelps	23
A G Dalton	35	M P Lynagh	72	M P Burke	23
A J Whetton	35	N C Farr-Jones	63	M C Roebuck	23
B J Robertson	34	S P Poidevin	59	R A Smith	22
S S Wilson	34	P N Kearns	49	J E C Meadows	22
M G Mexted	34	E J A McKenzie	45	W A Campbell	22
F E Bunce	33	B T Gavin	45	E T Bonis	21
W J Whineray	32	P G Johnson	42	P F Hawthorne	21
M R Brewer	32	A R Miller	41	R J Heming	21
D B Clarke	31	T A Lawton	41	A N McGill	21
G T M Bachop	31	A J Daly	41	W H Cerutti	21
M W Shaw	30	S A G Cutler	40	A S Cameron	20
T J Wright	30	R J McCall	40	B J Ellwood	20
S M Going	29	G V Davis	39	C J Windon	20
		A G Slack	39	M N Hartill	20
		A J McIntyre	38		

WORLD'S LEADING CAP-WINNERS

(up to 30 April 1996)

The following list includes appearances for individual countries in major international matches.

P Sella	France	111	G W Whetton	New Zealand	58
S Blanco	France	93	P J Winterbottom	England	58
D I Campese	Australia	92	L Rodriguez	France	56
R Underwood	England	85	P Berbizier	France	56
S B T Fitzpatrick	New Zealand	73	F Mesnel	France	56
M P Lynagh	Australia	72	C E Meads	New Zealand	55
C R Andrew	England	70	J P R Williams	Wales	55
C M H Gibson	Ireland	69	R Paparemborde	France	55
R Bertranne	France	69	W A Dooley	England	55
W D C Carling	England	66	B J Mullin	Ireland	55
B C Moore	England	64	T J Kiernan	Ireland	54
M Crauste	France	63	R N Jones	Wales	54
W J McBride	Ireland	63	G O Edwards	Wales	53
B Dauga	France	63	A Domenech	France	52
N C Farr-Jones	Australia	63	J M Renwick	Scotland	52
J J Kirwan	New Zealand	63	C T Deans	Scotland	52
J Condom	France	61	D G Lenihan	Ireland	52
J F Slattery	Ireland	61	J Prat	France	51
A G Hastings	Scotland	61	W Spanghero	France	51
S Hastings	Scotland	61	A R Irvine	Scotland	51
I C Evans	Wales	61	M I Keane	Ireland	51
P Saint-André	France	60	J-L Joinel	France	51
J-P Rives	France	59	M Celaya	France	50
S P Poidevin	Australia	59	A B Carmichael	Scotland	50
O Roumat	France	59	P Dintrans	France	50
P A Orr	Ireland	58			

The following list incorporates appearances by home countries players for British Isles teams (the Lions) in international matches against New Zealand, Australia and South Africa (up to 30 April 1996). The number of Lions appearances is shown in brackets.

P Sella	France	111		N C Farr-Jones	Australia	63	
S Blanco	France	93		J J Kirwan	New Zealand	63	
D I Campese	Australia	92		J Condom	France	61	
R Underwood	England	91	(6)	A R Irvine	Scotland	60	(9)
C M H Gibson	Ireland	81	(12)	P Saint-André	France	60	
W J McBride	Ireland	80	(17)	T J Kiernan	Ireland	59	(5)
C R Andrew	England	75	(5)	J-P Rives	France	59	
S B T Fitzpatrick	New Zealand	73		P A Orr	Ireland	59	(1)
M P Lynagh	Australia	72		S P Poidevin	Australia	59	
B C Moore	England	69	(5)	O Roumat	France	59	
R Bertranne	France	69		G W Whetton	New Zealand	58	
W D C Carling	England	67	(1)	R N Jones	Wales	57	(3)
A G Hastings	Scotland	67	(6)	W A Dooley	England	57	(2)
I C Evans	Wales	67	(6)	B J Mullin	Ireland	56	(1)
J F Slattery	Ireland	65	(4)	L Rodriguez	France	56	
P J Winterbottom	England	65	(7)	P Berbizier	France	56	
G O Edwards	Wales	63	(10)	F Mesnel	France	56	
J P R Williams	Wales	63	(8)	C E Meads	New Zealand	55	
S Hastings	Scotland	63	(2)	R Paparemborde	France	55	
M Crauste	France	63		D Richards	England	54	(6)
B Dauga	France	63		J M Renwick	Scotland	53	(1)

G Price	Wales	53	(12)	**J McLauchlan**	Scotland	51	(8)
A Domenech	France	52		**J-L Joinel**	France	51	
C T Deans	Scotland	52		**R J Laidlaw**	Scotland	51	(4)
J W Kyle	Ireland	52	(6)	**J Leonard**	England	51	(2)
M I Keane	Ireland	52	(1)	**M Celaya**	France	50	
D G Lenihan	Ireland	52		**A B Carmichael**	Scotland	50	
J Prat	France	51		**P Dintrans**	France	50	
W Spanghero	France	51		**J C Guscott**	England	50	(5)
T G R Davies	Wales	51	(5)				

Most appearances for the Lions are by W J McBride (Ireland) 17, R E G Jeeps (England) 13, C M H Gibson (Ireland) 12, G Price (Wales) 12, and A J F O'Reilly (Ireland), R H Williams (Wales), and G O Edwards (Wales) 10 each, up to 30 April 1996.

In addition to heading the Welsh list with 61 caps for his country, Ieuan Evans has made six international appearances for the British Lions, three against Australia in 1989 and three in New Zealand in 1993.

INTERNATIONAL REFEREES 1995-96

Leading Referees

Up to 30 April 1996, in major international matches. These include all matches for which senior members of the International Board have awarded caps, and also all matches played in the World Cup final stages.

12 or more internationals

W D Bevan	Wales	30	F Palmade	France	17
C Norling	Wales	25	S R Hilditch	Ireland	17
D J Bishop	New Zealand	24	B S Cumberlege	England	16
K D Kelleher	Ireland	23	O E Doyle	Ireland	16
D G Walters	Wales	23	E F Morrison	England	16
J M Fleming	Scotland	23	D I H Burnett	Ireland	15
M Joseph	Wales	22	C H Gadney	England	15
R C Williams	Ireland	21	I David	Wales	14
K V J Fitzgerald	Australia	21	Dr I R Vanderfield	Australia	14
F A Howard	England	20	R G Byres	Australia	13
A M Hosie	Scotland	19	J P Murphy	New Zealand	13
Capt M J Dowling	Ireland	18	N R Sanson	Scotland	13
A E Freethy	Wales	18	K H Lawrence	New Zealand	13
R C Quittenton	England	18	R F Johnson	England	12
J R West	Ireland	18	T D Schofield	Wales	12
J B Anderson	Scotland	18	T H Vile	Wales	12
R Hourquet	France	18	W Williams	England	12
D P D'Arcy	Ireland	17	A R MacNeill	Australia	12

Major international match appearances 1995-96

Matches controlled between 1 April 1995 and 30 April 1996

1995				
R v F	G Simmonds (Wales)		Tg v Iv	D Reordan (United States)
SA v WS	*J Meuwesen (Namibia)		A v R	*N Saito (Japan)
NZ v C	W J Erickson (Australia)		F v S	W J Erickson (Australia)
S v R	*N Lasaga (France)		SA v C	D T M McHugh (Ireland)
A v Arg	C J Hawke (New Zealand)		Arg v It	C Thomas (Wales)
A v Arg	D J Bishop (New Zealand)		NZ v J	*G Gadjovich (Canada)
It v I	A J Spreadbury (England)		W v I	I Rogers (South Africa)
SA v A	W D Bevan (Wales)		E v WS	P Robin (France)
S v Iv	*F Vito (Western Samoa)		F v I	E F Morrison (England)
F v Tg	S Lander (England)		SA v WS	J M Fleming (Scotland)
C v R	C J Hawke (New Zealand)		A v E	D J Bishop (New Zealand)
WS v It	J Dumé (France)		NZ v S	W D Bevan (Wales)
W v J	E J Sklar (Argentina)		SA v F	W D Bevan (Wales)
E v Arg	J M Fleming (Scotland)		E v NZ	S R Hilditch (Ireland)
NZ v I	W J Erickson (Australia)		E v F	D J Bishop (New Zealand)
WS v Arg	D J Bishop (New Zealand)		SA v NZ	E F Morrison (England)
SA v R	K W McCartney (Scotland)		NZ v A	R J Megson (Scotland)
F v Iv	*H Moon-Soo (South Korea)		A v NZ	B W Stirling (Ireland)
S v Tg	B Leask (Australia)		SA v W	J Dumé (France)
A v C	P Robin (France)		F v It	*N Chiciu (Romania)
I v J	S Neethling (South Africa)		F v R	E J Sklar (Argentina)
E v It	S R Hilditch (Ireland)		Arg v F	*J Morandin (Italy)
NZ v W	E F Morrison (England)		It v NZ	G Gadjovich (Canada)
			F v NZ(2)	*P Marshall (Australia)

W v Fj	*P D O'Brien (New Zealand)		I v S	*B Campsall (England)
It v SA	S Lander (England)		E v W	K W McCartney (Scotland)
E v SA	J M Fleming (Scotland)		S v F	C Thomas (Wales)
S v WS	*T Henning (South Africa)		F v I	E F Morrison (England)
I v Fj	P D O'Brien (New Zealand)		W v S	J Dumé (France)
E v WS	I Rogers (South Africa)		S v E	W D Bevan (Wales)
1996			I v W	D Méné (France)
US v I	G Gadjovich (Canada)		W v F	B W Stirling (Ireland)
W v It	*G Black (Ireland)		E v I	*E Murray (Scotland)
F v E	D T M McHugh (Ireland)		F v R	*J Atorasagasti (Spain)

Denotes debut in a major international

Referees dismissing players in a major international

A E Freethy	E v NZ	1925		F A Howard	Nm v W	1990
K D Kelleher	S v NZ	1967		A J Spreadbury	A v F	1990
R T Burnett	A v E	1975		C Norling	A v F	1990
W M Cooney	A v Fj	1976		C J Hawke	E v Arg	1990
N R Sanson (2)	W v I	1977		E F Morrison	R v F	1991
D I H Burnett	E v W	1980		J M Fleming (2)	Arg v WS	1991*
C Norling	F v I	1984		S R Hilditch (2)	F v E	1992
K V J Fitzgerald	NZ v W	1987*		D J Bishop	NZ v Wld	1992
F A Howard	A v W	1987*		E F Morrison	A v SA	1993
K V J Fitzgerald	Fj v E	1988		I Rogers (2)	C v F	1994
O E Doyle	Arg v F	1988		D Méné	W v E	1995
B W Stirling (2)	E v Fj	1989		S Lander	F v Tg	1995*
F A Howard	W v F	1990		D T M McHugh (3)	SA v C	1995*
F A Howard	S v F	1990		J Dumé	SA v W	1995

World Cup matches

INTERNATIONAL REFEREES

The list which follows shows referees who have controlled major internationals (i.e. games for which a senior member country of the IB has awarded caps, or the final stages of the official World Cup) since 1876, when referees were first appointed, up to 30 April 1996.

ABBREVIATIONS

A – Australia; *Arg* – Argentina; *AW* – Anglo-Welsh; *B* – British Forces and Home Union Teams; *Bb* – Barbarians; *BI* – British Isles; *C* – Canada; *Cv* – New Zealand Cavaliers; *Cz* – Czechoslovakia; *E* – England; *F* – France; *Fj* – Fiji; *GB* – Great Britain; *G* – Germany; *I* – Ireland; *It* – Italy; *Iv* – Ivory Coast; *J* – Japan; *K* – New Zealand Kiwis; *M* – New Zealand Maoris; *Nm* – Namibia; *NZ* – New Zealand; *NZA* – New Zealand Army; *P* – President's XV; *Pt* – Portugal; *R* – Romania; *S* – Scotland; *SA* – South Africa; *SAm* – South America; *SK* – South Korea; *Sp* – Spain; *Tg* – Tonga; *US* – United States of America; *W* – Wales; *Wld* – World XV; *WS* – Western Samoa; *Z* – Zimbabwe; (C) – Special Centenary Match; (R) – Replacement. Entries in square brackets [ ] indicates matches in the World Cup final stages.

NB The Australian Rugby Union now recognises the internationals played by the New South Wales touring teams of the 1920s as cap matches.

Ackermann, C J (South Africa) 1953 *SA v A* (2), 1955 *SA v BI*, 1958 *SA v F*
Acton, W H (Ireland) 1926 *W v E, E v S*
Adams, A (South Africa) 1991 *US v F* (2)
Alderson, F H R (England) 1903 *S v I*
Allan, M A (Scotland) 1931 *I v W, I v SA*, 1933 *E v I, I v W*, 1934 *I v E*, 1935 *E v I, I v W*, 1936 *I v E*, 1937 *I v W*, 1947 *I v E*, 1948 *I v W*
Allen, J W (Ireland) 1906 *W v S, S v E*
Anderson, C (Scotland) 1928 *I v F*
Anderson, I (South Africa) 1993 *Z v W*
Anderson, J B (Scotland) 1981 *W v E, I v A*, 1982 *R v F*, 1983 *I v E, A v NZ*, 1984 *E v W*, 1986 *W v F, NZ v A*, 1987 [*A v US, A v I, F v A*], 1988 *A v NZ* (2), 1989 *I v F, R v E, F v B*, 1991 [*E v It, Arg v WS*]

Anderson, J H (South Africa) 1903 *SA v GB*
Angus, A W (Scotland) 1924 *W v E*, 1927 *I v A*
Ashmore, H L (England) 1890 *S v I*, 1891 *S v W*, 1892 *S v I*, 1894 *I v S*, 1895 *S v I*
Atorasagasti, J (Spain) 1996 *F v R*
Austin, A W C (Scotland) 1952 *W v F*, 1953 *I v E*, 1954 *I v W*
Austry, R (France) 1972 *E v I*

Badger, Dr (England) 1900 *I v S*
Baise, M (South Africa) 1967 *SA v F* (2), 1968 *SA v BI* (2), 1969 *SA v A*, 1974 *SA v BI* (2)
Baise, S (South Africa) 1969 *SA v A*
Barnes, P (Australia) 1938 *A v NZ*
Baxter, J (England) 1913 *F v S, S v I*, 1914 *I v S*, 1920 *S v I*, 1921 *W v S, I v S*, 1923 *W v S*, 1925 *W v S, I v W*

Bean, A S (England) 1939 *W v S*, 1945 *W v F*, 1946 *F v W*, 1947 *F v W*, *W v A*, 1948 *S v F*, *W v F*, 1949 *S v I*
Beattie, R A (Scotland) 1937 *E v W*, 1938 *W v E*, 1945 *B v F*, 1947 *W v E*, *I v A*, 1948 *E v W*, 1949 *I v E*, 1950 *E v I*, *I v W*
Beattie, W H (Australia) 1899 *A v GB*, 1904 *A v GB*
Bell, T (Ireland) 1932 *S v W*, 1933 *E v W*
Bevan, W D (Wales) 1985 *E v R*, 1986 *F v E*, *NZ v A* (2), 1987 *[NZ v Fj*, *F v Z]*, *A v NZ*, 1988 *I v WS*, 1990 *NZ v S*, 1991 *I v F*, *[F v Fj*, *S v WS*, *E v A]*, 1992 *S v E*, *E v I*, *NZ v Wld* (2), 1993 *F v S*, *NZ v A*, *C v A*, *Arg v SA* (2), 1994 *S v F*, *NZ v F* (2), 1995 *S v I*, *[SA v A*, *NZ v S*, *SA v F]*, 1996 *S v E*
Beves, G (South Africa) 1896 *SA v GB*
Bezuidenhout, G P (South Africa) 1976 *SA v NZ* (3)
Bishop, D J (New Zealand) 1986 *Fj v W*, *R v F*, *I v R*, 1987 *[W v Tg*, *W v C]*, 1988 *A v E* (2), *E v A*, *S v A*, 1990 *S v E*, *I v W*, 1991 *S v W*, *W v I*, *[A v Arg*, *F v E]*, 1992 *NZ v Wld*, *SA v A*, 1993 *F v A* (2), 1994 *Sp v W*, 1995 *A v Arg*, *[WS v Arg*, *E v A*, *F v E]*
Bisset, W M (South Africa) 1896 *SA v GB*
Black, G (Ireland) 1996 *W v It*
Bonnet, J-P (France) 1979 *W v E*, 1980 *S v E*, *SA v BI* (2), 1981 *I v E*, *Arg v E* (2), 1982 *W v S*
Bott, J G (Scotland) 1931 *W v S*, 1933 *W v S*
Boundy, L M (England) 1955 *S v I*, 1956 *W v S*, 1957 *F v S*, *I v F*, *S v I*, *R v F*, 1958 *S v F*, 1959 *S v I*, 1961 *S v SA*
Bowden, G (Scotland) 1910 *F v E*
Bowen, D H (Wales) 1905 *E v S*
Bradburn, T J (England) 1928 *F v A*, 1929 *F v G*
Bressy, Y (France) 1988 *W v It*
Brook, P G (England) 1963 *F v W*, 1964 *W v S*, 1965 *W v I*, *I v SA*, 1966 *F v I*, *It v F*, *R v F*
Brown, A (Australia) 1907 *A v NZ*
Brown, D A (England) 1960 *I v W*, *It v F*
Brunton, J (England) 1924 *W v NZ*
Buchanan, A (Scotland) 1877 *I v S*, 1880 *S v I*
Bullerwell, I M (England) 1988 *W v R*, 1990 *F v R*
Burger, F (South Africa) 1989 *F v A* (2), 1990 *S v Arg*, 1992 *S v F*, *F v I*, *Arg v F* (2), 1993 *S v NZ*, *E v NZ*
Burmeister, R D (South Africa) 1949 *SA v NZ* (2), 1953 *SA v A*, 1955 *SA v BI* (2), 1960 *SA v NZ* (2), 1961 *SA v A*
Burnand, F W (England) 1890 *I v W*
Burnet, W (Scotland) 1932 *I v E*, 1934 *W v I*
Burnett, D I H (Ireland) 1977 *W v E*, 1979 *F v W*, 1980 *E v W*, 1981 *S v W*, *E v S*, 1982 *W v F*, *F v Arg*, 1983 *E v F*, 1984 *S v E*, *A v NZ*, 1985 *E v F*, *NZ v A*, 1986 *S v F*, 1987 *[S v Z*, *NZ v S]*
Burnett, R T (Australia) 1973 *A v Tg*, 1974 *A v NZ*, 1975 *A v E*, *A v J*, 1978 *A v W*
Burrell, G (Scotland) 1958 *E v I*, 1959 *W v I*
Burrell, R P (Scotland) 1966 *I v W*, 1967 *I v F*, *F v NZ*, 1969 *I v E*, *F v W*
Butt, C C (Australia) 1914 *A v NZ*
Byres, R G (Australia) 1976 *A v Fj*, 1978 *A v W*, 1979 *A v I* (2), *A v NZ*, 1980 *A v NZ*, 1981 *NZ v S*, 1982 *A v S* (2), 1983 *NZ v BI* (2), 1984 *I v W*, *W v F*

Calitz, M (South Africa) 1961 *SA v I*
Calmet, R (France) 1970 *E v W*
Calver, E W (England) 1914 *F v I*
Camardon, A (Argentina) 1960 *Arg v F*
Campbell, A (New Zealand) 1908 *NZ v AW* (2)
Campsall, B (England) 1996 *I v S*
Carlson, K R V (South Africa) 1962 *SA v BI*
Cartwright, V H (England) 1906 *I v S*, 1909 *S v I*, 1910 *I v S*, *F v I*, 1911 *S v I*
Castens, H H (South Africa) 1891 *SA v GB*
Ceccon, A (France) 1991 *I v E*, *R v S*
Chambers, J (Ireland) 1888 *W v S*, *I v M*, 1890 *S v E*, 1891 *E v S*
Chapman, W S (Australia) 1938 *A v NZ* (2)
Charman, R (England) 1919 *W v NZA*
Chevrier, G (France) 1980 *I v S*
Chiciu, N (Romania) 1995 *F v It*
Chiene, Dr J (Scotland) 1879 *I v S*
Clark, K H (Ireland) 1973 *E v F*, 1974 *S v F*, 1976 *F v E*
Cochrane, C B (Australia) 1907 *A v NZ*
Coffey, J J (Ireland) 1912 *S v F*
Colati, L (Fiji) 1991 *[I v J]*
Coles, E (England) 1903 *W v I*, 1905 *S v I*
Collett, C K (Australia) 1981 *NZ v S*
Combe, A (Ireland) 1876 *I v E*
Cook, H G (Ireland) 1886 *S v E*
Cooney, R C (Australia) 1929 *A v NZ*, 1930 *A v BI*, 1932 *A v NZ*, 1934 *A v NZ*

Cooney, W M (Australia) 1972 *A v F*, 1975 *A v E*, *A v J*, 1976 *A v Fj*
Cooper, Dr P F (England) 1952 *I v W*, 1953 *S v W*, *W v I*, *F v It*, *W v NZ*, 1954 *I v NZ*, *W v S*, *It v F*, 1956 *F v I*, *W v F*, *It v F*, 1957 *F v W*
Corley, H H (Ireland) 1906 *S v SA*, 1908 *S v E*
Corr, W S (Australia) 1899 *A v GB* (2)
Costello, J (Fiji) 1972 *Fj v A*
Craven, W S D (England) 1920 *F v W*
Crawford, S H (Ireland) 1913 *W v E*, *S v W*, 1920 *S v W*, 1921 *S v E*
Cross, W (Scotland) 1877 *S v E*
Crowe, K J (Australia) 1965 *A v SA*, 1966 *A v BI*, 1968 *A v NZ*, 1976 *A v Fj*
Cumberlege, B S (England) 1926 *S v I*, *W v I*, 1927 *S v F*, *I v S*, *I v W*, 1928 *S v I*, 1929 *F v I*, *S v F*, *I v S*, 1930 *I v F*, *S v I*, 1931 *I v S*, 1932 *S v SA*, *S v I*, 1933 *I v S*, 1934 *S v I*
Cunningham, J G (Scotland) 1913 *W v I*, 1921 *F v I*
Cuny, Dr A (France) 1976 *W v S*
Curnow, J (Canada) 1976 *US v F*
Currey, F I (England) 1887 *S v W*

Dallas, J D (Scotland) 1905 *W v NZ*, 1908 *I v W*, 1909 *W v E*, *I v E*, 1910 *E v W*, *I v W*, 1911 *I v E*, 1912 *I v W*
D'Arcy, D P (Ireland) 1967 *E v F*, *E v S*, *F v W*, *F v R*, 1968 *E v W*, *S v E*, *F v SA*, 1969 *E v F*, *W v E*, 1970 *W v S*, 1971 *W v E*, 1973 *F v NZ*, *F v W*, *F v R*, 1975 *E v S*, *F v Arg*, *W v A*
David, I (Wales) 1938 *E v S*, 1939 *S v E*, 1947 *E v S*, 1952 *S v F*, *I v S*, *E v I*, 1953 *S v I*, 1954 *S v F*, *E v NZ*, *S v NZ*, *F v NZ*, *F v E*, 1955 *I v F*, 1956 *F v E*
Davidson, I G (Ireland) 1911 *S v W*
Day, H L V (England) 1934 *S v W*
Day, P W (South Africa) 1903 *SA v GB*
Dedet, L (France) 1906 *F v NZ*, *F v E*
De Bruyn, C J (South Africa) 1969 *SA v A*, 1974 *SA v BI* (2)
Delany, M G (Ireland) 1899 *S v W*, 1900 *S v E*
Desclaux, M (France) 1992 *W v S*
Dickie, A I (Scotland) 1954 *F v I*, *E v I*, *W v F*, 1955 *I v E*, *W v I*, 1956 *E v I*, *I v W*, 1957 *W v E*, *I v E*, 1958 *W v A*, *W v F*
Dodds, J (Ireland) 1898 *S v E*
Domercq, G (France) 1972 *S v NZ*, 1973 *W v E*, 1976 *E v W*, 1977 *S v W*, 1978 *I v W*
Donaldson, S (Ireland) 1937 *S v E*
Donaldson, W P (South Africa) 1903 *SA v GB*
Don Wauchope, A R (Scotland) 1889 *W v I*, 1890 *E v I*, 1893 *I v E*
Doocey, T F (New Zealand) 1976 *NZ v I*, 1983 *E v S*, *F v W*
Douglas, W M (Wales) 1891 *I v E*, 1894 *E v I*, 1896 *S v E*, 1903 *E v S*
Doulcet, J-C (France) 1989 *S v W*
Dowling, M J (Ireland) 1947 *S v W*, 1950 *W v S*, *S v E*, *W v F*, 1951 *W v E*, *S v W*, *F v W*, *E v S*, *S v SA*, 1952 *W v S*, *F v SA*, *S v E*, 1953 *W v E*, *E v S*, 1954 *E v W*, 1955 *S v W*, 1956 *S v F*, *S v E*
Downes, A D (New Zealand) 1913 *NZ v A*
Doyle, O E (Ireland) 1984 *W v S*, *R v S*, *W v A*, 1987 *E v S*, 1988 *F v E*, *Arg v F* (2), *W v WS*, 1989 *F v S*, 1990 *F v E*, 1991 *[It v US*, *Fj v R]*, 1992 *W v F*, 1993 *F v W*, *W v C*, 1994 *S v SA*
Drennan, V (Ireland) 1914 *W v S*
Duffy, B (Ireland) 1977 *NZ v BI*
Dumé, J (France) 1993 *W v E*, *S v W*, 1994 *A v I* (2), 1995 *[WS v It]*, *SA v W*, 1996 *W v S*
Duncan, J (New Zealand) 1908 *NZ v AW*
Durand, C (France) 1969 *E v S*, 1970 *I v S*, 1971 *E v S*

Eckhold, A E (New Zealand) 1923 *NZ v A*
Elliott, H B (England) 1955 *F v S*, *F v It*, 1956 *I v S*
Engelbrecht, Dr G K (South Africa) 1964 *SA v W*
Erickson, W J (Australia) 1994 *Arg v S* (2), *E v C*, 1995 *NZ v C*, *[NZ v I*, *F v S]*
Evans, F T (New Zealand) 1904 *NZ v GB*
Evans, G (England) 1905 *E v NZ*, 1908 *W v A*
Evans, W J (Wales) 1958 *I v A*, *F v E*

Farquhar, A B (New Zealand) 1961 *NZ v F* (3), 1962 *NZ v A* (2), 1964 *NZ v A*
Faull, J W (Wales) 1936 *E v NZ*, *S v I*, 1937 *E v I*
Ferguson, C F (Australia) 1963 *A v E*, 1965 *A v SA*, 1968 *A v F*, 1969 *A v W*, 1971 *A v SA* (2)
Ferguson, P (Australia) 1914 *A v NZ*
Findlay, D G (Scotland) 1895 *I v E*, 1896 *E v W*, *E v I*, 1897 *I v E*, 1898 *E v I*, 1899 *I v E*, 1900 *E v I*

345

Findlay, J C (Scotland) 1902 *I v W*, 1903 *I v E*, 1904 *E v W*, *I v W*, 1905 *I v NZ*, 1911 *I v F*
Finlay, A K (Australia) 1961 *A v Fj*, 1962 *A v NZ*
Fitzgerald, K V J (Australia) 1985 *I v F*, *W v I*, *NZ v E* (2), *Arg v NZ* (2), 1987 *[I v W*, *E v US*, *NZ v W*, *NZ v F]*, 1988 *Fj v E*, 1989 *S v I*, *W v E*, *SA v Wld* (2), 1990 *A v US*, 1991 *F v W*, *S v I*, *[Fj v C*, *NZ v It*, *S v E]*
Fleming, G R (Scotland) 1879 *S v E*
Fleming, J M (Scotland) 1985 *I v E*, 1986 *A v Arg* (2), 1987 *E v F*, *[A v J*, *Fj v Arg]*, *F v R*, 1989 *F v W*, 1990 *NZ v A*, 1991 *W v F*, *[E v NZ*, *Arg v WS* (R), *I v A*, *NZ v A]*, 1992 *A v NZ*, 1993 *E v F*, *NZ v WS*, *F v R*, 1994 *F v I*, *E v W*, 1995 *[E v Arg*, *SA v WS]*, *E v SA*
Fleury, A L (New Zealand) 1959 *NZ v BI*
Fong, A S (New Zealand) 1946 *NZ v A*, 1950 *NZ v BI*
Fordham, R J (Australia) 1986 *E v W*, *F v I*, *Arg v F* (2), 1987 *[NZ v It*, *F v R]*
Fornès, E (Argentina) 1954 *Arg v F* (2)
Forsyth, R A (New Zealand) 1958 *NZ v A*
Frames, P R (South Africa) 1891 *SA v GB*
Francis, R C (New Zealand) 1984 *E v A*, *I v A*, 1985 *Arg v F* (2), 1986 *W v S*, *S v E*, *WS v W*
Freeman, W L (Ireland) 1932 *E v SA*
Freethy, A E (Wales) 1923 *F v E*, 1924 *E v F*, *I v NZ*, *F v US*, 1925 *E v NZ*, *I v S*, *S v E*, *F v E*, 1926 *E v F*, 1927 *F v E*, 1928 *I v E*, *E v F*, *I v F*, *F v E*, 1930 *I v E*, *E v F*, *F v E*, 1931 *E v I*, *F v E*
Fright, W H (New Zealand) 1956 *NZ v SA* (2)
Frood, J (New Zealand) 1952 *NZ v A*
Fry, H A (England) 1945 *F v B*
Furness, D C (Australia) 1952 *A v Fj* (2), 1954 *A v Fj*

Gadjovich, G (Canada) 1995 *[NZ v J]*, *It v NZ*, 1996 *US v J*
Gadney, C H (England) 1935 *S v NZ*, *W v NZ*, 1936 *S v W*, *W v I*, 1937 *W v S*, *I v S*, 1938 *S v W*, *I v W*, 1939 *I v S*, 1940 *F v B*, 1946 *F v B*, 1947 *F v S*, *S v I*, 1948 *F v A*, *I v S*
Games, J (Wales) 1909 *E v A*, 1913 *E v F*, 1914 *F v E*
Gardiner, F (Ireland) 1912 *S v E*, *I v SA* (R)
Gardner, J A (Scotland) 1884 *E v W*, 1887 *W v I*
Garling, A F (Australia) 1981 *A v NZ* (2)
Garrard, W G (New Zealand) 1899 *A v GB*
Gilchrist, N R (New Zealand) 1936 *M v A*
Gillespie, J I (Scotland) 1907 *W v E*, 1911 *W v E*
Gilliard, P (England) 1902 *W v S*
Gillies, C R (New Zealand) 1958 *NZ v A* (2), 1959 *NZ v BI* (2)
Gilliland, R W (Ireland) 1964 *It v F*, 1965 *S v W*, *E v F*, *F v W*, *F v R*, 1966 *E v W*, 1967 *F v A*
Gillmore, W N (Ireland) 1956 *F v Cz*, 1958 *I v S*, *It v F*
Glasgow, O B (Ireland) 1953 *F v S*, *F v W*, 1954 *S v E*, 1955 *W v E*, *F v W*
Goulding, W J (Ireland) 1882 *I v W*
Gourlay, I W (South Africa) 1976 *SA v NZ*
Gouws, Dr J (South Africa) 1977 *SA v Wld*
Greenlees, Dr J R C (Scotland) 1913 *I v E*, 1914 *E v W*
Grierson, T F E (Scotland) 1970 *I v SA*, 1971 *F v R*, 1972 *F v E*, 1973 *W v I*, 1975 *E v F*
Griffin, Dr J (South Africa) 1891 *SA v GB*
Griffiths, A A (New Zealand) 1946 *M v A*, 1952 *NZ v A*
Guillemard, A G (England) 1877 *E v I*, 1878 *E v S*, 1879 *E v I*, 1880 *E v S*, 1881 *E v I*, *E v W*
Gurdon, E T (England) 1898 *I v S*, 1899 *S v I*

Hamilton, F M (Ireland) 1902 *S v E*
Harland, R W (Ireland) 1922 *F v W*, 1925 *W v F*, 1926 *F v W*, 1928 *W v E*, *S v W*, *F v W*, 1929 *E v W*, 1931 *W v F*
Harnett, G H (Ireland) 1896 *W v S*, 1901 *S v I*, *W v I*
Harris, G A (Ireland) 1910 *S v F*
Harrison, G L (New Zealand) 1980 *Fj v A*, 1981 *A v F*, 1983 *A v US*, *F v A* (2), 1984 *Fj v A*
Harrison, H C (England) 1922 *F v S*
Hartley, A (England) 1900 *W v S*
Haslett, F W (Ireland) 1934 *W v E*, *E v S*, 1935 *E v W*, *W v S*, 1936 *W v E*
Hawke, C J (New Zealand) 1990 *I v Arg*, *E v Arg*, 1992 *A v S*, 1994 *SA v E* (2), 1995 *A v Arg*, *[C v R[*
Haydon, N V (Australia) 1957 *A v NZ*
Helliwell, D (England) 1926 *S v W*, 1927 *W v A*, 1929 *W v S*, 1930 *F v S*, *W v I*, *G v F*, *F v W*
Henning, T (South Africa) 1995 *S v WS*
Herbert, D (Wales) 1883 *W v E*
Herck, M (Romania) 1938 *F v G*
High, C J (England) 1987 *F v W*, *W v US*, 1990 *NZ v S*

Hilditch, S R (Ireland) 1984 *S v A*, 1985 *W v Fj*, 1987 *[R v Z*, *S v R]*, 1988 *E v W*, 1989 *E v F*, *NZ v A*, *S v R*, 1991 *E v S*, *[F v C*, *S v NZ]*, 1992 *F v E*, *E v SA*, 1993 *SA v F*, 1994 *F v E*, 1995 *[E v It*, *NZ v E]*
Hill, A (England) 1902 *I v S*
Hill, E D (New Zealand) 1949 *NZ v A*
Hill, G R (England) 1883 *S v W*, 1884 *S v I*, *W v I*, 1885 *S v W*, 1886 *S v I*, 1887 *W v E*, *I v S*, 1888 *I v W*, 1889 *E v M*, 1891 *I v S*, 1893 *I v S*
Hill, W W (Australia) 1913 *US v NZ*
Hinton, W P (Ireland) 1921 *S v F*
Hodgson, J (England) 1892 *W v S*
Hofmeyr, E W (South Africa) 1949 *SA v NZ* (2), 1961 *SA v A*, 1963 *SA v A*
Hollander, S (New Zealand) 1930 *NZ v BI* (3), 1931 *NZ v A*
Hollis, M (England) 1931 *F v G*
Holmes, E (England) 1931 *W v SA*, 1932 *W v I*
Holmes, E B (England) 1892 *I v W*, 1894 *W v S*, 1895 *S v W*, *W v I*, 1896 *I v S*, *I v W*, 1897 *S v I*
Horak, A T (South Africa) 1938 *SA v BI*
Hosie, A M (Scotland) 1973 *I v E*, 1974 *F v I*, 1975 *W v E*, 1976 *E v I*, *F v A*, 1977 *F v W*, *I v F*, 1979 *W v I*, *I v E*, 1980 *W v F*, *F v I*, 1981 *E v F*, *R v NZ*, 1982 *E v I*, *NZ v A* (2), 1983 *I v F*, *E v NZ*, 1984 *F v E*
Hourquet, R (France) 1983 *S v NZ*, 1984 *E v I*, *SA v E* (2), *SA v SAm* (2), 1985 *S v W*, 1987 *I v E*, *[E v J*, *W v E]*, 1988 *I v E*, 1989 *A v BI* (2), 1990 *W v S*, *NZ v A* (2), 1991 *[W v Arg*, *Z v J]*
Howard, F A (England) 1984 *I v S*, 1986 *I v W*, *A v F*, *NZ v F*, 1987 *[F v S*, *I v C*, *A v W]*, 1988 *W v F*, *A v NZ*, 1989 *NZ v F* (2), 1990 *W v F*, *S v F*, *Nm v W* (2), *W v Bb*, 1991 *A v W*, *[S v I*, *NZ v C]*, 1992 *I v W*
Hughes, D M (Wales) 1965 *F v It*, 1966 *S v F*, *I v S*, 1967 *I v E*, *S v I*
Hughes, J (England) 1935 *I v S*
Hughes, P E (England) 1977 *F v R*, 1978 *I v S*
Humphreys, W H (England) 1893 *S v W*, *W v I*

Ireland, J C H (Scotland) 1938 *I v E*, *W v I*, 1939 *E v W*, *E v I*, *I v W*
Irving, A L C (Australia) 1934 *A v NZ*, 1937 *A v SA*

Jackson, W H (England) 1926 *F v M*, 1927 *W v S*, *W v F*, *v G*, *G v F*
Jamison, G A (Ireland) 1972 *W v S*
Jardine, A (Scotland) 1906 *E v W*
Jeffares, R W (Ireland) 1930 *W v E*, *E v S*, 1931 *S v F*, 1935 *S v E*, *I v NZ*
Jeffares, R W (Sen) (Ireland) 1901 *S v W*, *E v S*, 1902 *E v W*, 1909 *S v W*
Jeffreys, M (England) 1920 *F v US*
Johns, E A (Wales) 1911 *E v F*
Johnson, R F (England) 1969 *F v R*, 1970 *F v I*, *E v W* (R), 1971 *W v I*, 1972 *I v F*, *W v NZ*, 1973 *I v F*, 1974 *W v S*, *I v NZ*, *F v SA*, 1975 *S v I*, *S v A*
Jones, A O (England) 1906 *W v SA*, 1907 *S v I*, 1911 *F v S*, 1912 *F v I*, *W v F*
Jones, T (Wales) 1947 *E v F*, 1948 *E v I*, *F v E*, 1949 *E v F*, 1950 *S v F*, 1951 *I v E*
Jones, W (Wales) 1984 *S v F*, *NZ v F* (2), 1988 *S v E*
Jones, W K M (Wales) 1968 *I v A*, 1970 *F v E*, 1971 *S v I*
Joseph, M (Wales) 1966 *S v A*, 1967 *I v A*, 1968 *I v S*, *E v I*, *R v F*, 1969 *S v I*, *S v SA*, 1970 *S v E*, 1971 *I v E*, *S v E* (C), 1972 *S v F*, *S v E*, 1973 *I v NZ*, *S v P* (C), *F v J*, 1974 *E v I*, 1975 *F v Arg*, 1976 *E v A*, *F v A*, 1977 *E v S*, *S v I*, *F v S*
Joynson, D C (Wales) 1955 *E v S*

Keenan, H (England) 1962 *It v F*, 1963 *I v NZ*
Kelleher, J C (Wales) 1973 *I v S*, 1974 *F v E*, 1976 *R v F*, 1977 *E v F*
Kelleher, K D (Ireland) 1960 *W v S*, 1961 *W v E*, *E v S*, 1962 *S v E*, *W v F*, 1963 *W v E*, *F v It*, 1964 *E v W*, *R v F*, 1965 *F v S*, *W v E*, 1966 *S v E*, *W v F*, *W v A*, 1967 *E v A*, *F v S*, *S v W*, *S v NZ*, 1968 *S v F*, 1969 *S v W*, *E v SA*, 1970 *W v F*, 1971 *F v S*
Kelly, H C (Ireland) 1881 *I v S*, 1883 *I v S*, *S v E*, 1885 *S v I*
Kemsley, H B (South Africa) 1896 *SA v GB*
Kennedy, G H B (Ireland) 1905 *S v W*, 1910 *W v S*, *S v E*
Kennedy, W (Ireland) 1905 *S v NZ*
Kilner, W F B (Australia) 1937 *A v SA*
King, J S (New Zealand) 1937 *NZ v SA* (2)
King, M H R (England) 1961 *S v I*
Kinsey, B (Australia) 1986 *Tg v W*, 1990 *Arg v E* (2), 1991 *Fj v E*, 1992 *F v SA* (2), 1993 *NZ v BI*
Knox, J (Argentina) 1949 *Arg v F*

Krembs, M (Germany) 1938 *G v F*

Lacroix, M (Belgium) 1962 *R v F*
Laidlaw, H B (Scotland) 1963 *I v E*, 1964 *W v F*, 1965 *I v E*, 1968 *F v E*, *W v F*
Lamb, G C (England) 1968 *F v I*, *W v S*, *F v SA*, 1969 *F v S*, *I v F*, 1970 *S v F*, *W v SA*, *I v W*, *R v F*, 1971 *I v F*, *F v A*
Lambert, N H (Ireland) 1947 *S v A*, 1948 *E v A*, *S v E*, 1949 *W v E*, *S v W*, *E v S*, *F v W*, 1950 *E v W*, *F v E*, 1951 *W v SA*, 1952 *E v W*
Lander, S (England) 1995 *S v W*, [*F v Tg*], *It v SA*
Lang, J S (Scotland) 1884 *I v E*
Larkin, F A (Australia) 1932 *A v NZ*
Lasaga, N (France) 1995 *S v R*
Lathwell, H G (England) 1946 *I v F*
Lawrence, K H (New Zealand) 1985 *A v C* (2), 1986 *A v It*, 1987 *F v S*, *S v W* [*Fj v It*, *A v E*], *Arg v A* (2), 1989 *A v BI*, 1991 *A v E*, [*I v Z*, *W v A*]
Lawrie, A A (Scotland) 1924 *I v F*, 1925 *E v W*, 1926 *I v F*
Leask, B (Australia) 1993 *A v Tg*, 1994 *Pt v W*, *WS v W*, *F v C*, 1995 [*S v Tg*]
Lee, S (Ireland) 1904 *S v E*
Lefevre, C (Ireland) 1905 *W v E*, 1907 *S v W*
Leith, H S (New Zealand) 1928 *M v A*
Leslie, D (Scotland) 1990 *E v W*, 1993 *I v F*
Lewis, C P (Wales) 1885 *W v E*
Lewis, E M (Wales) 1971 *F v A*
Lewis, M S (Wales) 1975 *F v S*, 1976 *I v S*
Lewis, R (Wales) 1970 *E v I*, 1971 *E v F*, 1972 *F v I*, 1973 *S v I*, *E v A*, 1974 *Arg v F* (2)
Lieprand, M (Germany) 1934 *G v F*
Llewellyn, A (Wales) 1906 *E v I*
Llewellyn, V S (Wales) 1951 *E v F*
Llewellyn, W J (Wales) 1926 *F v S*, *I v E*, 1927 *S v A*
Lloyd, D M (Wales) 1975 *I v F*, 1976 *S v E*
Lloyd, R A (Ireland) 1922 *S v W*, *E v S*
Louw, L L (South Africa) 1953 *SA v A*
Luff, A C (England) 1963 *W v I*, 1964 *I v S*, *I v W*
Lyle, T R (Ireland) 1887 *E v S*
Lyne, H S (Wales) 1885 *E v I*

McAllister, E (Ireland) 1889 *S v W*, 1890 *W v S*
Macassey, L E (New Zealand) 1937 *NZ v SA*
McAuley, C J (New Zealand) 1962 *NZ v A*
McCartney, K W (Scotland) 1990 *F v I*, 1991 *NZ v A*, 1992 *F v R*, 1993 *Nm v W*, 1994 *W v It*, 1995 *E v F*, [*SA v R*], 1996 *E v W*
McDavitt, P A (New Zealand) 1972 *NZ v A*, 1975 *NZ v S*, 1977 *NZ v BI*
McEwan, M C (Scotland) 1892 *E v W*
McGill, J (Scotland) 1925 *F v I*, 1929 *I v W*
McGowan, J B (Ireland) 1923 *W v F*, 1924 *S v W*
McHugh, D T M (Ireland) 1994 *R v W*, 1995 *F v S*, [*SA v C*], 1996 *F v E*
McKenzie, E (New Zealand) 1921 *NZ v SA*
McKenzie, G (New Zealand) 1928 *NZ v A*
McKenzie, H J (New Zealand) 1936 *NZ v A*
McLachlan, L L (New Zealand) 1992 *A v S*, 1993 *A v SA*, 1994 *S v E*, *W v F*
MacLaren, J S (England) 1884 *W v S*, 1888 *S v I*
McMahon, D C J (Scotland) 1961 *W v I*, 1963 *E v F*, 1964 *E v NZ*, 1967 *E v NZ*, *W v E*, 1969 *W v I*
McMullen, R F (New Zealand) 1973 *NZ v E*
MacNeill, A R (Australia) 1988 *F v Arg* (2), 1989 *W v NZ*, *I v NZ*, 1990 *F v NZ* (2), 1991 [*C v R*], 1992 *NZ v I* (2), *SA v NZ*, 1993 *W v I*, *I v E*
Magee, J T (Ireland) 1897 *W v S*, *E v S*, 1898 *E v W*, 1899 *E v S*
Magrath, R M (Ireland) 1928 *F v S*
Mailhan, L (France) 1933 *F v G*, 1935 *F v G*, 1937 *F v G*
Malan, Dr W C (South Africa) 1970 *SA v NZ*, 1971 *SA v F* (2)
Marie, B (France) 1960 *Arg v F* (2), 1965 *F v W* (R), 1966 *E v I*
Marsh, F W (England) 1907 *W v I*
Marshall, P (Australia) 1995 *F v NZ* (2)
Martelli, E (Ireland) 1903 *S v W*
Martin, N B (Australia) 1910 *A v NZ* (2)
Matheson, A M (New Zealand) 1946 *NZ v A*
Maurette, G (France) 1987 *W v I*, [*J v US*, *I v Tg*], 1988 *NZ v W* (2), 1989 *E v S*
Mayne, A V (Australia) 1929 *A v NZ* (2), 1932 *A v NZ*
Megson, R J (Scotland) 1987 *W v E*, 1988 *I v W*, *I v It*, 1991 *W v E*, *A v NZ*, 1992 *E v W*, *F v Arg*, 1995 *W v I*, *NZ v A*
Méné, D (France) 1994 *W v SA*, 1995 *W v E*, 1996 *I v W*

Meuwesen, J (Namibia) 1995 *SA v WS*
Miles, J H (England) 1913 *F v W*, *I v F*, 1914 *W v F*
Millar, D H (New Zealand) 1965 *NZ v SA*, 1968 *NZ v F*, 1977 *NZ v BI* (2), 1978 *NZ v A* (3)
Millar, W A (South Africa) 1924 *SA v BI* (2)
Mitchell, R (Ireland) 1955 *E v F*, 1956 *E v W*, 1957 *E v S*
Moffat, F J C (Scotland) 1932 *W v E*
Moffitt, J (New Zealand) 1936 *NZ v A*
Moolman, Dr J (South Africa) 1972 *SA v E*
Moon-Soo, H (South Korea) 1995 [*F v Iv*]
Moore, D F (Ireland) 1886 *E v W*, *W v S*
Moore, T W (Australia) 1947 *A v NZ*, 1950 *A v BI*, 1951 *A v NZ*, 1954 *A v Fj*, 1956 *A v SA*
Morandin, J (Italy) 1995 *Arg v F*
Morgan, C E (Australia) 1907 *A v NZ*, 1910 *A v NZ*
Morgan, K (Wales) 1967 *F v It*
Morrison, D (USA) 1981 *US v SA*
Morrison, E F (England) 1991 *F v S*, *R v F*, [*S v I*, *A v WS*], 1992 *I v A*, 1993 *S v I*, *SA v F*, *A v SA* (2), *W v J*, 1994 *I v S*, *A v NZ*, 1995 [*NZ v W*, *F v I*, *SA v NZ*], 1996 *F v I*
Mortimer, S (England) 1888 *W v M*
Morton, D S (Scotland) 1893 *W v E*
Muller, F (South Africa) 1982 *SA v SAm*, 1988 *S v F*, *F v I*
Mullock, R (Wales) 1886 *I v E*
Muntz, C J (France) 1924 *F v R*
Murdoch, W C W (Scotland) 1951 *W v I*, *I v SA*, 1952 *E v SA*, *F v E*
Murphy, J P (New Zealand) 1959 *NZ v BI*, 1963 *NZ v E*, 1964 *NZ v A* (2), 1965 *NZ v SA* (3), 1966 *NZ v BI* (3), 1968 *NZ v F*, 1969 *NZ v W* (2)
Murray, E (Scotland) 1996 *E v I*
Myburgh, P A (South Africa) 1962 *SA v BI*, 1963 *SA v A* (3)

Neethling, S (South Africa) 1994 *E v R*, 1995 [*I v J*]
Neilson, A E (New Zealand) 1921 *NZ v SA* (2)
Neser, V H (South Africa) 1924 *SA v BI*, 1928 *SA v NZ* (4), 1933 *SA v A* (4)
Neville, Dr W C (Ireland) 1882 *I v E*
Nicholls, E G (Wales) 1909 *E v S*
Nicholls, F (England) 1904 *W v S*
Nicholson, G W (New Zealand) 1913 *NZ v A*
Noon, O (Argentina) 1949 *Arg v F*
Norling, C (Wales) 1978 *I v NZ*, 1979 *E v S*, 1980 *F v E*, 1981 *I v F*, *NZ v SA* (2), *F v NZ*, 1982 *I v S*, 1983 *A v Arg* (2), 1984 *F v I*, 1985 *E v S*, 1986 *E v I*, 1987 *I v F*, [*C v Tg*, *F v Fj*], 1988 *E v I*, *R v F*, 1989 *NZ v Arg* (2), 1990 *I v S*, *A v F* (2), 1991 *Nm v I* (2)
Nugent, G P (Ireland) 1880 *I v E*

Oakley, L D (South Africa) 1924 *SA v BI*
O'Brien, P D (New Zealand) 1995 *W v Fj*, *I v Fj*
O'Callaghan, B J (Australia) 1959 *A v BI*
O'Leary, J (Australia) 1958 *A v M*

Palmade, F (France) 1973 *F v S* (R), *S v W*, 1974 *I v S*, 1975 *I v E*, 1977 *I v E*, 1978 *E v I*, 1979 *S v W*, 1980 *SA v BI* (2), 1981 *W v I*, *SA v I* (2), 1982 *E v W*, 1983 *NZ v BI* (2), 1985 *W v E*, 1986 *I v S*
Parfitt, V J (Wales) 1953 *E v F*, 1954 *I v S*
Parkes, Dr N M (England) 1958 *W v S*, *F v A*, *I v W*, *F v I*, 1959 *F v It*, *F v W*, 1960 *W v F*, 1961 *F v W*, 1962 *W v S*, *I v S*
Parkinson, F G M (New Zealand) 1955 *NZ v A*, 1956 *NZ v SA* (2)
Paton, R J (New Zealand) 1931 *M v A*
Pattinson, K A (England) 1973 *F v S*, *W v A*, 1974 *I v W*, *R v F*, 1975 *F v W*, 1976 *S v F*
Pattisson, A S (Scotland) 1883 *E v I*
Pauling, T G (Australia) 1904 *A v GB* (2), 1914 *A v NZ*
Peake, J F (New Zealand) 1923 *NZ v A*
Pearce, T N (England) 1948 *F v I*, *W v S*, 1949 *F v S*, *I v F*, *W v I*, 1950 *F v I*, *I v S*, 1951 *F v S*, *I v F*, *S v I*, 1952 *F v I*
Peard, L J (Wales) 1989 *I v E*, 1991 *E v F*, [*F v R*, *E v US*]
Pearson, J J M (England) 1995 *F v W*
Petrie, A G (Scotland) 1882 *S v I*
Phillips, T H (Wales) 1936 *E v S*
Phillips, W D (Wales) 1887 *I v E*, 1889 *I v S*
Pontin, A C (USA) 1976 *US v A*
Potter-Irwin, F C (England) 1909 *W v I*, 1911 *W v I*, 1912 *W v S*, *I v S*, *S v SA*, *I v SA*, *W v SA*, 1920 *F v S*, *W v I*
Pozzi, S (Italy) 1957 *F v R*, 1960 *R v F*
Pretorius, N F (South Africa) 1938 *SA v BI*
Price, F G (Wales) 1963 *I v F*
Prideaux, L (England) 1980 *W v S*, *I v W*, *SAm v SA* (2), 1981 *S v I*, *NZ v SA*, 1985 *F v S*

WORLD INTERNATIONAL RECORDS

Both team and individual records are for official cap matches played by senior members of the International Board, up to 30 April 1996.

TEAM RECORDS

Highest score – 145
New Zealand (145-17) v Japan 1995
Bloemfontein

Biggest winning margin – 128
New Zealand (145-17) v Japan 1995
Bloemfontein

Most tries by a team in an international – 21
New Zealand v Japan 1995 Bloemfontein

Most conversions by a team in an international – 20
New Zealand v Japan 1995 Bloemfontein

Most penalty goals in an international – 8
Wales v Canada 1993 Cardiff
Scotland v Tonga 1995 Pretoria
France v Ireland 1995 Durban

Most consecutive international victories – 17
New Zealand between 1965 and 1969

Most consecutive internationals undefeated – 23
New Zealand between 1987 and 1990

Most points in an international series – 109
New Zealand v Argentina (2 matches)
1989 in New Zealand

Most tries in an international series – 18
New Zealand v Wales (2 matches) 1988
in New Zealand

Most points in Five Nations Championship in a season – 118
England 1991-92

Most tries in Five Nations Championship in a season – 21
Wales 1909-10

Most points on an overseas tour (all matches) – 868
New Zealand to B Isles/France
(33 matches) 1905-06

Most tries on an overseas tour (all matches) – 215
New Zealand to B Isles/France
(33 matches) 1905-06

Biggest win on a major tour (all matches)
117-6 New Zealand v S Australia 1974
Adelaide

INDIVIDUAL RECORDS

Including appearances for British Isles, shown in brackets.

Most capped player
P Sella (France) 111 1982-95
in individual positions
Full-back
S Blanco (France) 81[1] 1980-91
Wing
R Underwood (England) 91(6)[2] 1984-96
Centre (includes 2nd five-eighth)
P Sella (France) 104[3] 1982-95
Fly-half (includes 1st five-eighth)
C R Andrew (England) 74(5)[4] 1985-95
Scrum-half
G O Edwards (Wales) 63(10)[5] 1967-78
Prop
P A Orr (Ireland) 59(1) 1976-87
Hooker
S B T Fitzpatrick (New Zealand) 73
1986-95
Lock
W J McBride (Ireland) 80(17) 1962-75
Flanker
J F Slattery (Ireland) 65(4) 1970-84
P J Winterbottom (England) 65(7)
1982-93
No 8
D Richards (England) 53(6)[6] 1986-96

[1] *Blanco also played 12 times as a wing*
[2] *D I Campese (Australia) 92 caps, has won 76 as a wing*
[3] *Sella also played 6 times on the wing and once at full-back*

[4] *Andrew also played once for England as a full-back*
[5] *N C Farr-Jones, 63 caps for Australia, won 62 as a scrum-half and one as a replacement wing*
[6] *Several French utility forwards won more caps than Richards, but none has played as frequently at No 8. Richards' figure excludes 1 cap as a temporary replacement*

J-P Lescarboura (France) v England 1985 Twickenham
J-P Lescarboura (France) v New Zealand 1986 Christchurch
D Camberabero (France) v Australia 1990 Sydney

Most consecutive internationals for a country – 63
S B T Fitzpatrick (New Zealand) 1986-95

Most internationals as captain – 59
W D C Carling (England) 1988-96

Most points in internationals – 911
M P Lynagh (Australia) (72 matches) 1984-95

Most points in an international – 45
S D Culhane (New Zealand) v Japan 1995 Bloemfontein

Most tries in internationals – 63
D I Campese (Australia) (92 matches) 1982-95

Most tries in an international – 6
M C G Ellis (New Zealand) v Japan 1995 Bloemfontein

Most conversions in internationals – 140
M P Lynagh (Australia) (72 matches) 1984-95

Most conversions in an international – 20
S D Culhane (New Zealand) v Japan 1995 Bloemfontein

Most dropped goals in internationals – 23
C R Andrew (England) (70 matches) and (B Isles) (5 matches) 1985-95

Most dropped goals in an international – 3
P Albaladejo (France) v Ireland 1960 Paris
P F Hawthorne (Australia) v England 1967 Twickenham
H E Botha (South Africa) v S America 1980 Durban
H E Botha (South Africa) v Ireland 1981 Durban

Most penalty goals in internationals – 177
M P Lynagh (Australia) (72 matches) 1984-95

Most penalty goals in an international – 8
N R Jenkins (Wales) v Canada 1993 Cardiff
A G Hastings (Scotland) v Tonga 1995 Pretoria
T Lacroix (France) v Ireland 1995 Durban

Fastest player to 100 points in internationals
A P Mehrtens (New Zealand) in his 5th match

Fastest player to 200 points in internationals
G J Fox (New Zealand) in his 13th match

Fastest player to 10 tries in internationals
M C G Ellis (New Zealand) in his 6th match

Most points in a Five Nations match – 24
S Viars (France) v Ireland 1992
C R Andrew (England) v Scotland 1995

Most points in Five Nations Championship in a season – 67
J M Webb (England) (4 matches) 1991-92

Most tries in Five Nations Championship in a season – 8
C N Lowe (England) (4 appearances) 1913-14
I S Smith (Scotland) (4 appearances) 1924-25

Tries in each match of a Five Nations Championship
H C Catcheside (England) 1923-24
A C Wallace (Scotland) 1924-25
P Estève (France) 1982-83
P Sella (France) 1985-86

Most penalty goals in Five Nations Championship in a season – 18

S D Hodgkinson (England) (4 matches) 1990-91

Most conversions in Five Nations Championship in a season – 11

J Bancroft (Wales) (4 appearances) 1908-09

J M Webb (England) (4 matches) 1991-92

Most dropped goals in Five Nations Championship in a season – 5

G Camberabero (France) (3 appearances) 1966-67

J-P Lescarboura (France) dropped a goal in each Championship match in 1983-84, a unique feat

Most points on an overseas tour – 230

W J Wallace (New Zealand) (25 appearances) in B Isles/France 1905-06

Jeremy Guscott and Will Carling, record-holding partners at centre, celebrate Guscott's try against Wales in the 1996 Five Nations Championship.

351

Most tries on an overseas tour – 42
J Hunter (New Zealand) (23 appearances)
in B Isles/France 1905-06

**Most points in any match on tour –
43**
R M Deans (New Zealand) v South
Australia 1984 Adelaide

Most tries in any match on tour – 8
T R Heeps (New Zealand) v Northern
NSW 1962
*P Estève scored 8 for France v East Japan in 1984, but this
was not on a major tour*

PARTNERSHIP RECORDS

Centre threequarters
W D C Carling and J C Guscott (England)
44 (includes 1 Test for B Isles)
Half-backs
M P Lynagh and N C Farr-Jones
(Australia) 47
Front row
A J Daly, P N Kearns and E J A McKenzie
(Australia) 37
Second row
A J Martin and G A D Wheel (Wales) 27
Back row
J Matheu, G Basquet and J Prat
(France) 22

OTHER INTERNATIONAL MATCH RECORDS

*Up to 30 April 1996. These are included for comparison and cover performances since 1971 by teams and players in Test
matches for nations which are not senior members of the International Board.*

Most points in a match
By a team
164 Hong Kong v Singapore 1994 Kuala
Lumpar
By a player
50 A Billington Hong Kong v Singapore
1994

Most tries in a match
By a team
26 Hong Kong v Singapore 1994 Kuala
Lumpar
By a player
10 A Billington Hong Kong v Singapore
1994

Most conversions in a match
By a team
17 Hong Kong v Singapore 1994 Kuala
Lumpar
By a player
17 J McKee Hong Kong v Singapore 1994

Most penalty goals in a match
By a team
8 Canada v Scotland 1991 St John
8 Italy v Romania 1994 Catania
8 Argentina v Canada 1995 Buenos Aires
By a player
8 M A Wyatt Canada v Scotland 1991
St John
8 D Dominguez Italy v Romania 1994
Catania
8 S E Meson Argentina v Canada 1995
Buenos Aires

Most dropped goals in a match
By a team

3 Argentina v SA Gazelles 1971 Pretoria
3 Argentina v Australia 1979 Buenos
Aires
3 Argentina v New Zealand 1985 Buenos
Aires
By a player
3 T A Harris-Smith Argentina v SA
Gazelles 1971
3 H Porta Argentina v Australia 1979
3 H Porta Argentina v New Zealand 1985

Most points in matches
530 H Porta (Argentina/S America)
483 S Bettarello (Italy)

Most tries in matches
24 Marcello Cuttitta (Italy)

Most conversions in matches
54 H Porta (Argentina/S America)
46 S Bettarello (Italy)

Most penalty goals in matches
109 H Porta (Argentina/S America)
104 S Bettarello (Italy)

Most dropped goals in matches
25 H Porta (Argentina/S America)
17 S Bettarello (Italy)

Most matches as captain
43 H Porta (Argentina/S America)

Biggest win on a major tour
128-0 W Samoa v Marlborough
(New Zealand) 1993 Blenheim

INTERNATIONAL SCENE EXPANDS

WOMEN'S RUGBY 1995-96
Alice Cooper

The Home Nations tournament was held for the first time this season, and there are whispers about France joining next year, resulting in more international fixtures at all levels and providing good preparation for the next World Cup, to be held in Holland in 1998. Annual fixtures with New Zealand and the USA would be more beneficial health checks, but such long-distance events remain beyond the financial means of the women's game.

ENGLAND

On the positive side, the creation of 35 new clubs brought the total to 227, but the RFUW was dealt a body blow right at the beginning of the season with the withdrawal of Vladivar Vodka from sponsorship of the National Cup after just one season. Happily, NCP continued to sponsor the Divisional Championship, won again by the North.

At international level, England won the inaugural Home Nations tournament with their best performance, 56-3, against the Welsh at Leicester, their first really cohesive display since the 1994 World Cup final. Captain Gill Burns continued the trend of introducing new blood: the dynamic centre Julie Twigg emerged from Division 3 anonymity and lock Karen Henderson gained a deserved first-team place after several seasons in the team.

At club level, Saracens and Richmond slugged it out again leaving Wasps a poor third. Saracens won the double – League Division 1 and the National Cup – utilising their international talent to the full. Division 1 newcomers Novocastrians struggled and returned to Division 2, topped this season by Richmond II. As the latter cannot be promoted, Blackheath go back up. The Division 3 play-offs promoted Crawley and St Albans.

No student leagues were played so as to allow teams to concentrate on the BUSA Cup, won by Loughborough, and National Student Cup, in which Loughborough were beaten by new rivals Brunel. England developed North and South squads to provide a stepping stone between club and international stages. At youth level, a National Under-18s tournament at Chorley, won by Chinnor, emerged as the showpiece. Young talent is now reaching the top: there were 15-year-olds playing in the English Students and Saracens and Richmond each fielded a 16-year-old in their Cup final team.

RFUW National Cup: *21 April:* Saracens 35, Richmond 15 (Staines)
National Sevens: *4-5 May:* CUP: Richmond I   PLATE: Cheltenham   BEST OF THE REST: Richmond II (Banbury) **NCP Divisional Championship:** Midlands 5, North

37; South 13, London 5; South 34, Midlands 5; London 7, North 23; North 26, South 0; London v Midlands cancelled **Winners:** The North **RFUW Regional Competition:** Midlands West 7, North-West 27; Midlands East 5, North-East 27; South-West 0, London Region 17; South-West 49, Midlands East 0; South-East 57, Midlands West 11; London 20, North-East 11; North-West 17, South-East 12; North-East 0, South-West 0; London v Midlands East cancelled **Regional Student Matches:** *18 February:* North Students 0, South Students 29 (Waterloo) *13 April:* South Students 15, East Midlands Region 14 (Wrexham) *24 April:* North Students 31, North Wales Region 0 (Bethesda) **BUSA final:** *29 March:* Loughborough 25, Birmingham 5 (Twickenham) **Student National Cup:** *21 April:* Brunel 17, Loughborough 5 (Staines) **National Under-18s Tournament:** *21 April:* Chinnor 5, St Brendans 0 (Chorley)

IRELAND

The game continued to expand in Ireland with five new clubs this season and more already registered for next. The IWRFU have appointed development officers in each region with the welcome support of the IRFU, which has provided both technical and financial assistance. The next stage is to set up inter-provincial rugby to bridge the gap between club and country.

The first Home Nations tournament was not a success for Ireland. Despite the guidance of Des Beirne, coach of leading English club Wasps, the national side still lack experience at top level, as illustrated by a dismal 35-0 defeat of the A side by Wasps. But the talent is certainly there, as was seen in Ireland's game against England.

Sligo Sevens: *26-27 August:* FINAL: Sligo 12, Creggs 7 (*aet*) (Sligo) **4th Annual Blackrock Festival:** *12 November:* PERPETUAL TROPHY WINNERS: Blackrock **Irish Senior Cup:** *24 April:* Creggs 9, Blackrock 3 (North Kildare) **Irish Senior Plate:** *24 April:* Cooke 5, Shannon 0 (North Kildare) **Division 2 Play-offs:** *27 April:* Corrib 5, Sligo 0 (Creggs) **Kinsale Sevens:** *4-5 May:* CUP WINNERS: Creggs LEAGUE WINNERS: Blackrock

SCOTLAND

Scotland started their season with the inaugural district tournament between North, South, East, West and Exiles, won by the North, during which the national selectors evaluated skills.

At club level, the new league structure evolved to accommodate new clubs and attracted sponsorship from Keyline Builders Merchants. All the Leagues were fiercely contested and produced new winners. In the Cup, Edinburgh Wanderers knocked out last year's champions Edinburgh Academicals in the second round and went right through to the final, where they defeated Aberdeen in a tense, close game.

At international level, Scotland started to show what they are capable of. Their finest performance was against a rattled English side who had been dogged by misfortune just getting to the ground. The Scottish Universities side is producing a useful development squad. Indeed, expansion continues apace north of the border. More new clubs will mean eight teams in Divisions 1 and 2 next season while Division 3 will continue on a district basis. The SWRU are formulating a structure to develop the growing youth game.

District Competition winners: North **National Sevens winners:** *28 April:* Edinburgh Academicals (Aberdeenshire) **National Cup final:** *21 April:* Edinburgh Wanderers (Kirkcaldy)

WALES

Division 1 was strengthened by the return of Cardiff Harlequins, who had been playing in RFUW Division 1. Cardiff went on to win the League, the National Sevens and the National Cup. Previous winners Swansea Uplands were dogged by injury and unavailability, while Blaenau Gwent, Ystradgynlais and Whitland all finished their seasons strongly. Division 2, won convincingly by Llantwit Fardre, will be much enlarged next season to accommodate several new clubs.

At international level, Sue Ellis (née Butler) continued to captain Wales, who benefited from the coaching of Gwyn Griffiths and former international Paul Ringer. Performances against England and Scotland showed sparks of remarkable talent that could come to fruition next season. Amanda Bennett at fly-half provided steady tactical decision-making and kicking.

National Sevens final: *5 May:* Cardiff Harlequins 12, Swansea Uplands 5 **Heno National Cup final:** *28 April:* Blaenau Gwent 23, Cardiff Harlequins 29 (Ystradgynlais) **Plate final:** *28 April:* Lefn Coed 5, Llantwit Fardre 35 (Ystradgynlais)

EXILES MATCHES

29 October: Scottish Exiles 12, Welsh Exiles 10 (Alton) *19 November:* Scottish Exiles 15, Welsh Counties 5 (Old Leamingtonians) *4 December:* Welsh Counties 15, Welsh Exiles 13 (Cardiff Harlequins) *17 March:* Emerging England 10, Scottish Exiles 20 (Richmond College)

HOME NATIONS COMPETITION WINNERS: England

21 January: Ireland 3, Scotland 21 (Old Belvedere)
4 February: England 56, Wales 3 (Leicester)
18 February: Wales 11, Scotland 6 (Bridgend)
3 March: Scotland 8, England 12 (Boroughmuir) Wales 22, Ireland 6 (Cardiff RFC)
17 March: England 43, Ireland 8 (London Irish)

OTHER INTERNATIONALS

2 September: England 40, Nomads 0 (Rosslyn Park) *22 September:* Scotland A 44, Holland A 0 (Utrecht) *24 September:* Holland 5, Scotland 3 (Utrecht) *11 November:* England A 25, Central Army Club, Kazachstan 5 (Luton) *7 January:* England A 5, Spain 7 (Banbury) *17 February:* France 6, England 15 (Villard Bonnot) *18 February:* Wales A 8, Scotland A 18 (Bridgend) *3 March:* Scotland A 8, England A 7 (Boroughmuir) *21 April:* Holland 12, England A 27 (Utrecht)

STUDENT MATCHES

29 October: Scottish Universities 37, Tyneside Universities 0 (Edinburgh University) *19 January:* Ulster District 0, Scottish Universities 17 (Antrim) *18 February:* English

Students 20, Welsh Students 5 (Waterloo) *11 March:* Scottish Universities 12, Barcelona University 5 (Edinburgh Academicals) *23 March:* Scottish Universities 29, Welsh Universities 3 (Edinburgh University) *26 April:* Scottish Universities 7, English Students 13 (Murrayfield)

LEAGUE TABLES

RFUW National Division 1

	P	W	D	L	F	A	Pts
Saracens	14	13	0	1	410	110	26
Richmond	14	11	1	2	298	89	23
Wasps	14	9	0	5	255	175	18
Waterloo	14	7	0	7	211	181	14
Clifton	14	6	2	6	145	157	14
O Leams	14	3	1	10	118	316	7
Leeds	14	2	2	10	71	276	6
Novocastrians	14	1	1	12	104	308	3

RFUW National Division 2

	P	W	D	L	F	A	Pts
Richmond II	10	10	0	0	231	57	18
Blackheath	10	6	1	3	104	61	12
Alton	10	4	3	3	92	117	9
Eton Manor	10	4	1	5	91	176	9
Sale	10	2	1	7	68	129	5
Cheltenham	10	2	0	8	65	121	4

RFUW Division 3 South-West

	P	W	D	L	F	A	Pts
Clifton	10	9	0	1	252	47	28
Hornets	10	5	1	4	127	76	20
Tavistock	10	4	1	5	127	90	19
Exeter	10	4	1	5	133	128	19
Hereford	10	3	1	6	47	236	17
Lydney*	10	3	0	6	46	132	15

*1 game defaulted

RFUW Division 3 Midlands

	P	W	D	L	F	A	Pts
St Albans	14	13	1	0	467	55	41
Northampton	14	8	4	2	290	68	34
Nottingham	14	8	3	3	270	79	33
Shelford	14	7	3	4	250	109	31
Sudbury	14	8	0	6	244	167	30
Colchester	14	3	0	11	39	576	20
Newbold on A*	14	1	0	12	51	521	15
Selly Oak**	14	2	3	6	106	147	18

*1 game defaulted, **3 games defaulted

356

RFUW Division 3 South-East

	P	W	D	L	F	A	Pts
Crawley	14	13	0	1	501	42	40
Wimbledon	14	10	0	4	333	101	34
Medway	14	9	0	5	166	156	31
Saracens II	14	7	2	5	142	87	30
Teddington	14	7	1	6	181	171	29
Richmond III	14	4	0	10	171	260	22
Camberley	14	2	0	12	56	341	18
Wasps II*	14	1	1	11	55	501	16

*1 game defaulted

RFUW Division 3 North

	P	W	D	L	F	A	Pts
Liverpool St H	12	12	0	0	425	43	36
Wharfedale	12	9	0	3	280	68	30
Northern	12	8	0	4	139	104	28
Whitchurch	12	5	0	7	133	171	22
Hull	12	5	0	7	95	248	22
Bury & Bolton*	12	1	0	8	5	193	11
N Ribblesdale**	12	1	0	6	5	240	8

*3 games defaulted **5 games defaulted

Irish Division 1

	P	W	D	L	F	A	Pts
Blackrock	9	8	1	0	205	8	26
Old Crescent	9	6	0	3	72	16	18
Creggs	8	4	1	3	78	46	14
Shannon	5	1	0	4	19	132	3
Old Belvedere	10	1	0	9	18	145	3
Cooke	5	1	0	4	15	63	3

Irish Division 2: *Section A winners:* Corrib *Section B winners:* Sligo *Play-offs:* Sligo 13, Corrib 5

SWRU Keyline League Division 1

	P	W	D	L	F	A	Pts
Edinburgh W	8	8	0	0	426	6	24
Edinburgh A	9	7	0	2	342	36	23
W of Scotland	8	4	0	4	186	166	16
Edinburgh U	8	2	0	6	40	381	12
Aberdeen U*	6	1	0	5	22	320	8
Biggar*	5	1	0	4	20	127	7

*1 game defaulted

SWRU Keyline League Division 2

	P	W	D	L	F	A	Pts
Haddington	10	9	0	1	497	54	28
Glasgow S	8	7	0	1	182	58	22
W of Scotland II	9	4	1	4	108	219	18
Stirling U	7	1	1	5	70	180	10
Ed Acads II	8	1	0	7	59	233	10
Perthshire*	5	1	0	4	33	205	7

*1 game defaulted

**SWRU Keyline League Division 3
North & West**

	P	W	D	L	F	A	Pts
Aberdeenshire	7	7	0	0	183	5	21
Dundee HSFP	7	6	0	1	167	94	19
Kirkcaldy	7	5	0	2	263	73	17
Inverness CD	7	3	0	4	131	110	13
Mull*	6	3	0	3	20	146	12

*1 game defaulted

**SWRU Keyline League Division 3
South & Edinburgh**

	P	W	D	L	F	A	Pts
Melrose	8	8	0	0	372	24	24
Hawick	8	6	0	2	324	65	20
RDVC	8	6	0	2	209	73	20
Lismore*	7	4	0	3	183	93	15

Edinburgh Ws II*	5	3	0	2	249	69	11
Dalkeith	7	2	0	5	133	184	11
Duns	6	2	0	4	31	106	10
Berwick	6	1	0	5	7	373	8
Edinburgh U II*	6	0	0	6	5	526	6

Overall winner of Division 3 after play-offs:
Aberdeenshire

WWRU Division 1

	P	W	D	L	F	A	Pts
Cardiff Quins	14	14	0	0	489	19	42
Swansea Uplands	14	12	0	2	405	77	38
Blaenau Gwent	14	10	0	4	250	79	34
Ystradgynlais*	13	7	0	5	147	158	25
Aberystwyth**	14	6	0	6	85	254	24
Whitland**	14	3	0	9	66	341	18
Tumble****	14	2	0	7	88	220	13
N'castle E***	13	1	0	9	39	399	12

*conceded 1 match **conceded 2 matches
***conceded 3 matches ****conceded 4 matches

WWRU Division 2

	P	W	D	L	F	A	Pts
Llantwit Fardre	6	6	0	0	121	10	18
Carmarthen Quins	6	3	0	3	69	57	12
St Athan	6	3	0	3	59	47	12
Cefn Coed	6	0	0	6	20	155	6

*Results do not include Brynaman, who dropped out
mid-season*

CLUBS SECTION

Records of most-capped players are complete up to 30 April 1996.

ENGLAND
Bath

Year of formation 1865
Ground Recreation Ground, London Road, Bath   Tel: Bath (01225) 465328
Colours Blue, white and black
Most capped player J C Guscott (England) 45 caps
Captain 1995-96 P R de Glanville
Courage Leagues 1995-96 Div 1 *Winners*   **Pilkington Cup 1995-96** *Winners* – beat Leicester 16-15 (final)

League Record 1995-96

Date	Venue	Opponents	Result	Scorers
9 Sept	A	West Hartlepool	20-15	*T:* Sleightholme *C:* Callard (5)
16 Sept	H	Gloucester	37-11	*T:* Lumsden, Nicol, Sleightholme *C:* Callard (2) *PG:* Callard (5) *DG:* Catt
23 Sept	A	Leicester	14-9	*T:* Adebayo *PG:* Callard (3)
30 Sept	H	Orrell	55-20	*T:* Adebayo (2), Callard (2), Catt, Ubogu, De Glanville, Guscott *C:* Callard (6) *PG:* Callard
7 Oct	A	Wasps	15-6	*T:* Adebayo (2) *C:* Callard *PG:* Callard
14 Oct	H	Bristol	52-19	*T:* Guscott (3), Catt, Clarke, Geoghegan, Ojomoh *C:* Callard (4) *PG:* Callard (3)
21 Oct	A	Harlequins	19-13	*T:* Lumsden *C:* Callard *PG:* Callard (4)
28 Oct	H	Saracens	52-16	*T:* Geoghegan (2), Sanders (2), Guscott, De Glanville, Lumsden, pen try *C:* Callard (6)
4 Nov	A	Sale	30-18	*T:* Lumsden (2), Callard *C:* Callard (3) *PG:* Callard (3)
11 Nov	H	West Hartlepool	34-22	*T:* Clarke, Guscott, Lumsden, pen try *C:* Callard (4) *PG:* Callard (2)
6 Jan	H	Leicester	14-15	*T:* Adebayo *PG:* Callard (3)
17 Feb	H	Wasps	36-12	*T:* Dawe, De Glanville, Nicol, Yates, Sleightholme *C:* Callard (4) *PG:* Callard
30 Mar	A	Bristol	43-5	*T:* Geoghegan (2), Guscott (2), De Glanville, Hilton, Lumsden *C:* Callard (4)
6 Apr	H	Harlequins	41-15	*T:* De Glanville, Guscott, Sleightholme *C:* Callard *PG:* Callard (6) *DG:* Catt, Nicol
10 Apr	A	Gloucester	10-16	*T:* De Glanville *C:* Butland *PG:* Butland
13 Apr	A	Saracens	21-15	*T:* Adebayo, Dawe *C:* Callard *PG:* Callard (3)
20 Apr	A	Orrell	44-11	*T:* Haag (2), Sleightholme (2), De Glanville, Nicol *C:* Callard (4) *PG:* Callard (2)
27 Apr	H	Sale	38-38	*T:* Catt, Lumsden, Nicol, Sleightholme, Waters *C:* Callard (2) *PG:* Callard (3)

Bedford

Year of formation 1886
Ground Goldington Road, Bedford   Tel: Bedford (01234) 347511
Colours Oxford and Cambridge blue
Most capped player D P Rogers (England) 34 caps
Captain 1995-96 P Alston
Courage Leagues 1995-96 Div 2 10th   **Pilkington Cup 1995-96** Lost 0-37 to Bristol (5th round)

Adedayo Adebayo races away from Leicester's Niall Malone to score Bath's only try in the first encounter between the two giants, in September at Welford Road, which Bath won 14-9.

League Record 1995-96

Date	Venue	Opponents	Result	Scorers
9 Sept	A	Wakefield	23-32	*T:* Oliver, Subbiani *C:* Finnie (2) *PG:* Finnie (3)
16 Sept	H	Waterloo	10-10	*T:* Subbiani *C:* Finnie *PG:* Finnie
23 Sept	H	Blackheath	21-18	*T:* Oliver, Finnie *C:* Finnie *PG:* Finnie (3)
30 Sept	A	Newcastle	30-23	*T:* Oliver, Skingsley, Subbiani, Thomson *C:* Finnie (2) *DG:* Finnie (2)
7 Oct	H	Northampton	17-49	*T:* Whetstone (2), Farr *C:* Finnie
14 Oct	A	London Scottish	10-50	*T:* Farr *C:* Finnie *DG:* Finnie
21 Oct	H	London Irish	29-46	*T:* Alston (2), Oliver, Whetstone *C:* Finnie (3) *PG:* Finnie
28 Oct	A	Moseley	18-27	*T:* Oliver, Subbiani *C:* Finnie *PG:* Finnie (2)
4 Nov	H	Nottingham	20-12	*T:* Oliver, Roach *C:* Finnie (2) *PG:* Finnie (2)
11 Nov	H	Wakefield	20-13	*T:* Alston, Deans, Oliver, Stone
6 Jan	A	Blackheath	8-23	*T:* Rennell *PG:* Finnie
13 Jan	A	Waterloo	24-48	*T:* Clough (2), Goldsmith, Stone *C:* Finnie (2)
9 Mar	H	Newcastle	6-24	*PG:* Tapper (2)
23 Mar	A	Northampton	0-48	
30 Mar	H	London Scottish	21-19	*T:* Allen, Cook *C:* Tapper *PG:* Tapper (2) *DG:* Cook
6 Apr	A	London Irish	13-25	*T:* Chandler *C:* Smith *PG:* Smith (2)
13 Apr	H	Moseley	8-23	*T:* Mansell *PG:* Smith
27 Apr	A	Nottingham	11-30	*T:* Oliver *PG:* Smith (2)

Blackheath

Year of formation 1858
Ground Rectory Field, Charlton Road, Blackheath, London SE3   Tel: 0181-858 1578
Colours Red and black
Most capped player C N Lowe (England) 25 caps
Captain 1995-96 M Friday
Courage Leagues 1995-96 Div 2 7th   **Pilkington Cup 1995-96** Lost 9-19 Coventry (4th round)

League Record 1995-96

Date	Venue	Opponents	Result	Scorers
9 Sept	A	Nottingham	17-31	*T:* Codling, Harris *C:* Howard (2) *PG:* Howard
16 Sept	H	Wakefield	20-16	*T:* Aldridge *PG:* Howard (4) *DG:* Howard
23 Sept	A	Bedford	18-21	*T:* Hanslip, Friday *C:* Howard *PG:* Howard (2)
30 Sept	H	Waterloo	21-9	*T:* Hanslip, Ridgway *C:* Howard *PG:* Howard (3)
7 Oct	H	Newcastle	39-19	*T:* Hanslip (2), Barham (2), White, Griffiths, Ridgway *C:* Howard (2)
14 Oct	A	Northampton	14-69	*T:* Hanslip *PG:* Howard (2) *DG:* Howard
21 Oct	H	London Scottish	16-16	*T:* Ticehurst *C:* Howard *PG:* Howard (2) *DG:* Howard
28 Oct	A	London Irish	9-32	*PG:* Howard (3)
4 Nov	H	Moseley	9-27	*PG:* Howard (2) *DG:* Howard
11 Nov	H	Nottingham	25-16	*T:* Howard (2), Stewart *C:* Howard (2) *PG:* Howard *DG:* Howard
6 Jan	H	Bedford	23-8	*T:* Coyne, Smith *C:* Harris (2) *PG:* Harris (3)
13 Jan	A	Wakefield	0-17	
10 Feb	A	Waterloo	10-32	*T:* Harris *C:* Howard *PG:* Howard

17 Feb	A	Newcastle	10-25	*T:* Harris *C:* Howard *PG:* Howard
30 Mar	H	Northampton	10-24	*T:* Walton *C:* Howard *PG:* Howard
6 Apr	A	London Scottish	26-27	*T:* Friday (2), Neil-Dwyer *C:* Howard *PG:* Howard (3)
13 Apr	H	London Irish	23-46	*T:* Shadbolt (2), Jarrett *C:* Howard *PG:* Howard (2)
27 Apr	A	Moseley	51-36	*T:* Coyne, Essenhigh, Jowett, Shadbolt, Stewart, Walton, White *C:* Howard (5) *PG:* Howard (2)

Bristol

Year of formation 1888
Ground Memorial Ground, Filton Avenue, Horfield, Bristol   Tel: Bristol (0117) 951448
Colours Navy blue and white
Most capped player J V Pullin (England) 42 caps
Captain 1995-96 P A Hull
Courage Leagues 1995-96 Div 1 6th   **Pilkington Cup 1995-96** Lost 12-19 to Bath
(quarter-final)

League Record 1995-96

Date	Venue	Opponents	Result	Scorers
9 Sept	A	Wasps	5-33	*T:* Regan
16 Sept	H	West Hartlepool	12-3	*PG:* Tainton (4)
23 Sept	H	Harlequins	25-31	*T:* Bracken, Corry, Hull *C:* Tainton (2) *PG:* Tainton (2)
30 Sept	A	Saracens	24-11	*T:* Maggs, Shaw *C:* Tainton *PG:* Tainton (4)
7 Oct	H	Sale	30-6	*T:* Corry, Wring *C:* Tainton *PG:* Tainton (5), Hull
14 Oct	A	Bath	19-52	*T:* Archer *C:* Tainton *PG:* Tainton (4)
21 Oct	H	Gloucester	22-16	*T:* Hull *C:* Hull *PG:* Hull (4) *DG:* Thomas
28 Oct	A	Leicester	6-43	*PG:* Hull (2)
4 Nov	H	Orrell	33-14	*T:* Shaw, Corry, Thomas *C:* Thomas (3) *PG:* Thomas (3) *DG:* Thomas
11 Nov	H	Wasps	9-17	*PG:* Thomas (3)
6 Jan	A	Harlequins	3-28	*DG:* Thomas
17 Feb	A	Sale	6-15	*PG:* Tainton *DG:* Tainton
30 Mar	H	Bath	5-43	*T:* Thomas
6 Apr	A	Gloucester	14-18	*T:* G Sharp *PG:* Thomas (3)
13 Apr	H	Leicester	29-43	*T:* Bracken, Rollitt *C:* Tainton (2) *PG:* Tainton (5)
20 Apr	H	Saracens	21-7	*T:* Bracken, Regan *C:* Tainton *PG:* Tainton (3)
27 Apr	A	Orrell	29-26	*T:* Tiueta (2), Bracken, Thomas *C:* Thomas (3) *PG:* Thomas
5 May	A	West Hartlepool	37-15	*T:* Rollitt (2), Breeze, Corry *C:* Tainton (4) *PG:* Tainton (2) *DG:* Tainton

Gloucester

Year of formation 1873
Ground Kingsholm, Kingsholm Road, Gloucester   Tel: Gloucester (01452) 381087
Colours Cherry and white
Most capped player A T Voyce (England) & M C Teague (England) 27 caps
Captain 1995-96 D Sims
Courage Leagues 1995-96 Div 1 8th   **Pilkington Cup 1995-96** Lost 10-19 to Bath
(semi-final)

League Record 1995-96

Date	Venue	Opponents	Result	Scorers
9 Sept	H	Sale	17-22	*T:* Sims *PG:* Osborne (3) *DG:* T Smith
16 Sept	A	Bath	11-37	*T:* Holford *PG:* Osborne *DG:* Kimber
23 Sept	A	West Hartlepool	27-19	*T:* Holford (2), Sims, Deacon *C:* Kimber (2) *PG:* Kimber
30 Sept	H	Leicester	14-27	*T:* Holford *PG:* Kimber (3)
7 Oct	A	Orrell	3-21	*PG:* T Smith
14 Oct	H	Wasps	15-26	*PG:* T Smith (4) *DG:* Kimber
21 Oct	A	Bristol	16-22	*T:* Kimber *C:* T Smith *PG:* T Smith (3)
28 Oct	H	Harlequins	13-24	*T:* Fenley *C:* T Smith *PG:* T Smith (2)
4 Nov	A	Saracens	16-19	*T:* Windo *C:* T Smith *PG:* T Smith (2) *DG:* Kimber
11 Nov	A	Sale	13-21	*T:* Sims, Miles *PG:* T Smith
6 Jan	H	West Hartlepool	17-16	*T:* Beim *PG:* T Smith (3), Osborne
17 Feb	H	Orrell	27-0	*T:* Roberts, Windo *C:* Fenwick *PG:* Fenwick (4) *DG:* Kimber
30 Mar	A	Wasps	10-21	*T:* pen try *C:* Fenwick *PG:* Fenwick
6 Apr	H	Bristol	18-14	*PG:* Fenwick (3), Mapletoft (2) *DG:* Kimber
10 Apr	H	Bath	16-10	*T:* Holford *C:* T Smith *PG:* T Smith (3)
13 Apr	A	Harlequins	19-33	*T:* Raymond, T Smith *PG:* T Smith (3)
24 Apr	A	Leicester	6-28	*PG:* Mapletoft (2)
27 Apr	H	Saracens	17-10	*T:* Windo *PG:* Mapletoft (3) *DG:* Kimber

Harlequins

Year of formation 1866
Ground Stoop Memorial Ground, Craneford Way, Twickenham, Middlesex
Tel: 0181-892 0822
Colours Light blue, magenta, chocolate, French grey, black and light green
Most capped player W D C Carling (England) 66 caps
Captain 1995-96 J Leonard
Courage Leagues 1995-96 Div 1 3rd **Pilkington Cup 1995-96** Lost 9-24 to Leicester
(quarter-final)

League Record 1995-96

Date	Venue	Opponents	Result	Scorers
9 Sept	A	Orrell	23-9	*T:* Kitchin, Mitchell, O'Leary *C:* Pears *PG:* Pears *DG:* Pears
16 Sept	H	Wasps	29-20	*T:* Bromley, Sheasby *C:* Pears (2) *PG:* Pears (2) *DG:* Pears (3)
23 Sept	A	Bristol	31-25	*T:* O'Leary (2), Greenwood, Bromley *C:* Pears *PG:* Pears (3)
30 Sept	H	West Hartlepool	34-18	*T:* Bromley, Brown, Carling, Kitchin, Sheasby *C:* Pears (3) *PG:* Pears
7 Oct	H	Saracens	23-15	*T:* Allison, O'Leary *C:* Pears (2) *PG:* Pears (2) *DG:* Pears
14 Oct	A	Sale	11-29	*T:* Staples *PG:* Pears (2)
21 Oct	H	Bath	13-19	*T:* O'Leary *C:* Pears *PG:* Pears *DG:* Pears
28 Oct	A	Gloucester	24-13	*T:* Bromley, Challinor, Staples, Wright *C:* Staples
4 Nov	H	Leicester	25-29	*T:* Sheasby, Mensah, O'Leary *C:* Challinor (2) *PG:* Challinor (2)
11 Nov	H	Orrell	21-25	*T:* Kitchin, Mensah *C:* Pears *PG:* Pears (3)
6 Jan	H	Bristol	28-3	*T:* Bromley, Watson, Kitchin (3) *PG:* Carling

17 Feb	A	Saracens	13-6	*T:* Mensah *C:* Challinor *PG:* Challinor (2)
9 Mar	A	Wasps	34-3	*T:* O'Leary (2), Bromley, Challinor *C:* Walshe *PG:* Challinor (3) *DG:* Challinor
23 Mar	A	West Hartlepool	91-21	*T:* Allison (2), Bromley (2), Greenwood (2), O'Leary (2), Staples (2), Watson (2), Challinor, Mullins *C:* Challinor (9) *PG:* Challinor
30 Mar	H	Sale	55-0	*T:* Bromley (3), Staples (2), Watson (2), O'Leary *C:* Challinor (3) *PG:* Challinor *DG:* Challinor, Staples
6 Apr	A	Bath	15-41	*T:* Challinor, Kitchin *C:* Challinor *PG:* Challinor
13 Apr	H	Gloucester	33-19	*T:* Challinor, Greenwood, O'Leary (2), Staples *C:* Challinor *PG:* Challinor *DG:* Challinor
27 Apr	A	Leicester	21-19	*T:* Greenwood, O'Leary *C:* Challinor *PG:* Challinor *DG:* Challinor (2)

Leicester

Year of formation 1880
Ground Welford Road, Leicester   Tel: Leicester (0116) 2540276 or 2541607
Colours Scarlet, green and white
Most capped player R Underwood (England) 85 caps
Captain 1995-96 D Richards
Courage Leagues 1995-96 Div 1 2nd   **Pilkington Cup 1995-96** Lost 15-16 to Bath (final)

League Record 1995-96

Date	Venue	Opponents	Result	Scorers
9 Sept	H	Saracens	31-3	*T:* Hackney, Robinson, R Underwood *C:* Liley (2) *PG:* Liley (4)
16 Sept	A	Sale	16-12	*T:* Potter *C:* Liley *PG:* Liley (2), Malone
23 Sept	H	Bath	9-14	*PG:* Liley (3)
30 Sept	A	Gloucester	27-14	*T:* Back, Kilford *C:* Liley *PG:* Liley (5)
7 Oct	A	West Hartlepool	19-12	*T:* Cockerill, Garforth *PG:* Liley (3)
14 Oct	H	Orrell	22-3	*T:* Hackney *C:* Liley *PG:* Liley (5)
21 Oct	A	Wasps	21-11	*T:* Liley, Tarbuck *C:* Liley *PG:* Liley (2) *DG:* Liley
28 Oct	H	Bristol	43-6	*T:* Cockerill, Hackney, R Underwood *C:* Liley (2) *PG:* Liley (8)
4 Nov	A	Harlequins	29-25	*T:* R Underwood, pen try *C:* Liley (2) *PG:* Liley (5)
11 Nov	A	Saracens	21-25	*T:* Hackney, Robinson *C:* Liley *PG:* Liley (3)
6 Jan	A	Bath	15-14	*PG:* Liley (5)
17 Feb	H	West Hartlepool	48-15	*T:* Kardooni (3), Hackney (2), Back *C:* Liley (6) *PG:* Liley *DG:* Harris
30 Mar	A	Orrell	38-10	*T:* R Underwood (2), Liley, Wells *C:* Liley (3) *PG:* Liley (4)
6 Apr	H	Wasps	15-12	*PG:* Liley (4) *DG:* Malone
13 Apr	A	Bristol	43-29	*T:* R Underwood (2), Liley, Potter *C:* Liley (4) *PG:* Liley (4) *DG:* Harris
17 Apr	H	Sale	32-10	*T:* Kardooni (3), Richards, Back *C:* Harris (2) *PG:* Harris
24 Apr	H	Gloucester	28-6	*T:* Garforth, Liley, R Underwood *C:* Liley (2) *PG:* Liley (3)
27 Apr	H	Harlequins	19-21	*T:* Back, Liley *PG:* Liley (3)

London Irish

Year of formation 1898
Ground The Avenue, Sunbury-on-Thames, Middlesex   Tel: Sunbury (01932) 783034
Colours Emerald green
Most capped player B J Mullin (Ireland) 55 caps
Captain 1995-96 G F Halpin
Courage Leagues 1995-96 Div 2 2nd – *promoted*   **Pilkington Cup 1995-96** Lost 21-46 to
Leicester (semi-final)

League Record 1995-96

Date	Venue	Opponents	Result	Scorers
9 Sept	H	Northampton	32-65	*T:* O'Shea (2), Corcoran, Nolan *C:* Corcoran (3) *PG:* Corcoran *DG:* Cathcart
16 Sept	A	London Scottish	15-19	*T:* Nolan, pen try *C:* Corcoran *PG:* Cobbe
23 Sept	A	Waterloo	50-16	*T:* Corcoran (2), Dougan (2), O'Shea, Henderson *C:* Corcoran (4) *PG:* Corcoran (4)
30 Sept	H	Moseley	49-8	*T:* O'Shea (3), Bishop, Corcoran, Halpin, Neary, Kellam *C:* Corcoran (3) *PG:* Corcoran
7 Oct	A	Nottingham	22-9	*T:* Walsh *C:* Corcoran *PG:* Corcoran (5)
14 Oct	H	Wakefield	31-7	*T:* Corcoran, Flood, O'Shea *C:* Corcoran (2) *PG:* Corcoran (4)
21 Oct	A	Bedford	46-29	*T:* Walsh (2), Bishop, Corcoran, pen try *C:* Corcoran (3) *PG:* Corcoran (5)
28 Oct	H	Blackheath	32-9	*T:* Corcoran, Flood, Walsh *C:* Corcoran *PG:* Corcoran (5)
4 Nov	A	Newcastle	23-19	*T:* Burns *PG:* Corcoran (5) *DG:* Flood
11 Nov	A	Northampton	24-52	*T:* Corcoran, Halpin, Henderson *C:* Corcoran (3) *DG:* Haly
6 Jan	H	Waterloo	39-16	*T:* Ewington, Haly, Henderson (3) *C:* Corcoran (4) *PG:* Corcoran (2)
13 Jan	H	London Scottish	21-20	*PG:* Corcoran (7)
17 Feb	H	Nottingham	39-27	*T:* O'Shea (2), Dougan, Henderson *C:* Corcoran (2) *PG:* Corcoran (5)
9 Mar	A	Moseley	29-26	*T:* Peters, Walsh *C:* Corcoran (2) *PG:* Corcoran (5)
30 Mar	A	Wakefield	31-19	*T:* Bird, Briers, Humphreys *C:* Corcoran (2) *PG:* Corcoran (4)
6 Apr	H	Bedford	25-13	*T:* Bishop, Briers, Halpin, Humphreys *C:* Corcoran *PG:* Corcoran
13 Apr	A	Blackheath	46-23	*T:* Halpin (2), Bird, Dougan, Henderson, O'Shea *C:* Corcoran (2) *PG:* Corcoran (4)
27 Apr	H	Newcastle	29-28	*T:* Henderson (2) *C:* Corcoran (2) *PG:* Corcoran (4) *DG:* Humphreys

London Scottish

Year of formation 1878
Ground Richmond Athletic Ground, Richmond, Surrey   Tel: 0181-332 2473
Colours Blue jersey with red lion crest
Most capped player A G Hastings (Scotland) 61 caps
Captain 1995-96 S Holmes
Courage Leagues 1995-96 Div 2 3rd   **Pilkington Cup 1995-96** Lost 16-32 to Nottingham
(4th round)

League Record 1995-96

Date	Venue	Opponents	Result	Scorers
9 Sept	A	Waterloo	11-3	*T:* Rowland *PG:* Steele (2)
16 Sept	H	London Irish	19-15	*T:* Millard (2), Holmes *C:* Steele (2)

23 Sept	A	Moseley	21-19	*T:* Steele, Jackson, Millard *C:* Steele (3)
30 Sept	H	Nottingham	17-9	*T:* Fraser *PG:* Steele (4)
7 Oct	A	Wakefield	20-16	*T:* Watson, Withers-Green, pen try *C:* Steele *PG:* Steele
14 Oct	H	Bedford	50-10	*T:* Burnell, Fraser, Millard, Nisbet, Steele, Watson *C:* Steele (4) *PG:* Steele (3) *DG:* Steele
21 Oct	A	Blackheath	16-16	*T:* Watson *C:* Steele *PG:* Steele (2) *DG:* Steele
28 Oct	H	Newcastle	28-8	*T:* Eriksson, Harrold, Mair *C:* Russell (2) *PG:* Russell (3)
4 Nov	A	Northampton	11-54	*T:* Signorini *PG:* Russell (2)
11 Nov	H	Waterloo	16-16	*T:* Withers-Green *C:* Russell *PG:* Russell (3)
6 Jan	H	Moseley	17-8	*T:* Withers-Green *PG:* Stent (4)
13 Jan	A	London Irish	20-21	*T:* N Robinson (2), Thompson *C:* Stent *PG:* Stent
17 Feb	H	Wakefield	22-31	*T:* Harrold *C:* Steele *PG:* Steele (5)
9 Mar	A	Nottingham	19-12	*T:* Orr-Ewing *C:* Steele *PG:* Steele (4)
30 Mar	A	Bedford	19-21	*T:* Duthie, Robinson, Holmes *C:* Harrold (2)
6 Apr	H	Blackheath	27-26	*T:* Walker, Clarke, Millard *C:* Steele (3) *PG:* Steele (2)
13 Apr	A	Newcastle	11-45	*T:* Walker *PG:* Steele (2)
27 Apr	H	Northampton	17-59	*T:* Steele (2) *C:* Steele (2) *PG:* Steele

Moseley

Year of formation 1873
Ground The Reddings, Reddings Road, Moseley, Birmingham Tel: 0121-499 2149
Colours Red and black
Most capped player M C Teague (England) 27 caps
Captain 1995-96 N Martin
Courage Leagues 1995-96 Div 2 6th **Pilkington Cup 1995-96** Lost 5-26 to Newcastle (4th round)

League Record 1995-96

Date	Venue	Opponents	Result	Scorers
9 Sept	H	Newcastle	9-0	*PG:* Kerr (3)
16 Sept	A	Northampton	7-50	*T:* Purdy *C:* Kerr
23 Sept	H	London Scottish	19-21	*T:* Kerr, Bonney *PG:* Kerr (2) *DG:* Kerr
30 Sept	A	London Irish	8-49	*T:* Miles *DG:* Kerr
7 Oct	A	Waterloo	17-22	*T:* Corbett *PG:* Miles (3) *DG:* Houston
14 Oct	H	Nottingham	18-6	*T:* Bright, Houston *C:* Corbett *PG:* Corbett (2)
21 Oct	A	Wakefield	11-9	*T:* Bonney *PG:* Kerr (2)
28 Oct	H	Bedford	27-18	*T:* Kerr (2), Fuller, Owen *C:* Kerr (2) *PG:* Kerr
4 Nov	A	Blackheath	27-9	*T:* Kerr, Anderson *C:* Kerr *PG:* Kerr (2) *DG:* Bonney, Houston (2)
11 Nov	A	Newcastle	9-8	*PG:* Kerr (3)
6 Jan	A	London Scottish	8-17	*T:* Kerr *PG:* Dossett
17 Feb	H	Waterloo	24-30	*PG:* Kerr (8)
24 Feb	H	Northampton	16-46	*T:* pen try *C:* Kerr *PG:* Kerr (3)
9 Mar	H	London Irish	26-29	*T:* Chudleigh, Ball *C:* Kerr (2) *PG:* Kerr (4)
30 Mar	A	Nottingham	27-48	*T:* Bonney, Kerr, pen try *C:* Kerr (3) *PG:* Kerr (2)
6 Apr	H	Wakefield	15-26	*T:* Chudleigh, Jones *C:* Kerr *PG:* Kerr

13 Apr	A	Bedford	23-8	*T:* Binns, Smallcombe *C:* Binns (2)
				PG: Binns (2) *DG:* Binns
27 Apr	H	Blackheath	36-51	*T:* Hanson, Houston, Johal, Kerr *C:* Kerr (2)
				PG: Kerr (4)

Newcastle

Year of formation 1877
Ground Kingston Park, Brunton Road, Kenton Bank Foot, Newcastle-upon-Tyne
Tel: 0191-214 0422
Colours Green and white
Most capped player R J McLoughlin (Ireland) 40 caps
Captain 1995-96 R Wilkinson
Courage Leagues 1995-96 Div 2 8th   **Pilkington Cup 1995-96** Lost 22-44 to Harlequins
(5th round)

League Record 1995-96

Date	*Venue*	*Opponents*	*Result*	*Scorers*
9 Sept	A	Moseley	0-9	
16 Sept	H	Nottingham	31-24	*T:* Chandler, Robson, Holder *C:* Clark (2)
				PG: Clark (4)
23 Sept	A	Wakefield	7-26	*T:* pen try *C:* Clark
30 Sept	H	Bedford	23-30	*T:* Fletcher, Penn *C:* Cramb (2) *PG:* Clark (2)
				DG: Frankland
7 Oct	A	Blackheath	19-39	*T:* Fletcher *C:* Cramb *PG:* Cramb (4)
14 Oct	H	Waterloo	26-29	*T:* Brummitt (2), R Wilkinson *C:* Clark
				PG: Clark (3)
21 Oct	H	Northampton	9-52	*PG:* Cramb (3)
28 Oct	A	London Scottish	8-28	*T:* J Wilkinson *PG:* Cramb
4 Nov	H	London Irish	19-23	*T:* J Wilkinson *C:* Cramb *PG:* Cramb (4)
11 Nov	H	Moseley	8-9	*T:* J Wilkinson *PG:* Chandler
6 Jan	H	Wakefield	11-17	*T:* Metcalfe *PG:* Cramb (2)
13 Jan	A	Nottingham	24-24	*T:* Arnold, Frankland *C:* Cramb
				PG: Cramb (4)
17 Feb	H	Blackheath	25-10	*T:* Cramb, Fletcher, Wilson *C:* Andrew (2)
				PG: Andrew (2)
9 Mar	A	Bedford	24-6	*T:* Armstrong, Cassidy, Underwood
				C: Andrew (3) *PG:* Andrew
30 Mar	A	Waterloo	36-13	*T:* Armstrong (3), Popplewell (2)
				C: Andrew (2), Cramb (2) *PG:* Andrew
6 Apr	A	Northampton	5-26	*T:* Underwood
13 Apr	H	London Scottish	45-11	*T:* Belgian, Popplewell, Ryan (2), Underwood,
				Walton, Vanzandvliet *C:* Belgian (2)
				PG: Belgian (2)
27 Apr	A	London Irish	28-29	*T:* Brummitt (2), pen try *C:* Belgian (2)
				PG: Belgian (3)

Northampton

Year of formation 1880
Ground Franklins Gardens, Weedon Road, Northampton
Tel: Northampton (01604) 751543
Colours Black, green and gold
Most capped player G S Pearce (England) 36 caps
Captain 1995-96 T A K Rodber
Courage Leagues 1995-96 Div 2 *Winners – promoted*   **Pilkington Cup 1995-96** Lost 3-12 to
Bath (4th round)

Harvey Thorneycroft scores for Northampton against Newcastle in April. On their way back to Division 1 for 1996-97, Northampton averaged close to 50 points a match.

367

League Record 1995-96

Date	Venue	Opponents	Result	Scorers
9 Sept	A	London Irish	65-32	*T:* Allen (3), Moir (2), Dawson, Rodber, Thorneycroft, Seely *C:* Grayson (7) *PG:* Grayson (2)
16 Sept	H	Moseley	50-7	*T:* Dods (2), Seely (2), Moir, M Allen, Grayson, Bayfield *C:* Grayson (5)
23 Sept	A	Nottingham	43-7	*T:* M Allen (2), Moir, Dawson, Seely, Dods, Thorneycroft *C:* Grayson (4)
30 Sept	H	Wakefield	23-0	*T:* Pountney, Merlin *C:* Grayson (2) *PG:* Grayson (3)
7 Oct	A	Bedford	49-17	*T:* Bell, Townsend, Moir, Seely, Merlin, pen try *C:* Grayson (5) *PG:* Grayson (3)
14 Oct	H	Blackheath	69-14	*T:* Seely (3), Townsend (3), Bell (2), Dods, M Allen, Phillips *C:* Dods (7)
21 Oct	A	Newcastle	52-9	*T:* M Allen (3), Dawson, Beddow, Rodber, Merlin, pen try *C:* Grayson (6)
28 Oct	A	Waterloo	69-3	*T:* M Allen (3), Dods (2), Seely (2), Townsend (2), Merlin, Pountney *C:* Grayson (6), Dods
4 Nov	H	London Scottish	54-11	*T:* Townsend (3), Thorneycroft (2), Dawson, Seely, Phillips *C:* Grayson (7)
11 Nov	H	London Irish	52-24	*T:* Townsend (3), Dods, Grayson, Pountney, Thorneycroft, Seely *C:* Dods (4), Grayson (2)
6 Jan	H	Nottingham	35-5	*T:* Allen, Beal, Dawson, Pountney, pen try *C:* Grayson (5)
24 Feb	A	Moseley	46-16	*T:* Beal (2), Allen, Bayfield, Grayson, Dawson (2), Thorneycroft *C:* Grayson (3)
23 Mar	H	Bedford	48-0	*T:* Bell (2), Pountney (2), Beal, Rodber, Seely, Townsend *C:* Grayson (4)
30 Mar	A	Blackheath	24-10	*T:* Bayfield, Clarke, Phillips, Pountney *C:* Grayson (2)
6 Apr	H	Newcastle	26-5	*T:* Allen, Thorneycroft *C:* Grayson (2) *PG:* Grayson (2) *DG:* Grayson (2)
13 Apr	H	Waterloo	69-5	*T:* Moir (4), Pountney (2), Beal (2), Dawson, Allen, Hunter *C:* Grayson (7)
20 Apr	A	Wakefield	34-21	*T:* Beal, Dawson, Morgan *C:* Grayson (2) *PG:* Grayson (4) *DG:* Grayson
27 Apr	A	London Scottish	59-17	*T:* Allen (3), Beal, Foale, Rodber, Seely, Morgan (2) *C:* Grayson (7)

Nottingham

Year of formation 1877
Ground Ireland Avenue, Beeston, Nottingham   Tel: Nottingham (0115) 9254238
Colours White and green
Most capped player C R Andrew (England) 70 caps
Captain 1995-96 C Gray
Courage Leagues 1995-96 Div 2 9th   **Pilkington Cup 1995-96** Lost 10-36 to Gloucester (5th round)

League Record 1995-96

Date	Venue	Opponents	Result	Scorers
9 Sept	H	Blackheath	31-17	*T:* Royer, Reed, Beese *C:* Stent (2) *PG:* Stent (4)
16 Sept	A	Newcastle	24-31	*T:* Beese (2), Parsonage *C:* Hodgkinson (3) *PG:* Hodgkinson
23 Sept	H	Northampton	7-43	*T:* Smallwood *C:* Gallagher
30 Sept	A	London Scottish	9-17	*PG:* Hodgkinson (2) *DG:* Hodgkinson

7 Oct	H	London Irish	9-22	*PG:* Hodgkinson (3)
14 Oct	A	Moseley	6-18	*PG:* Hodgkinson (2)
21 Oct	H	Waterloo	12-18	*PG:* Hodgkinson (4)
28 Oct	H	Wakefield	22-18	*T:* Reed *C:* Hodgkinson *PG:* Hodgkinson (5)
4 Nov	A	Bedford	12-20	*T:* Royer, Ireland *C:* Hodgkinson
11 Nov	A	Blackheath	16-25	*T:* Claydon *C:* Hodgkinson *PG:* Hodgkinson (3)
6 Jan	A	Northampton	5-35	*T:* Gallagher
13 Jan	H	Newcastle	24-24	*T:* Reed, pen try *C:* Hodgkinson *PG:* Hodgkinson (4)
17 Feb	A	London Irish	27-39	*T:* Bygrave, Byrom *C:* Hodgkinson *PG:* Hodgkinson (3) *DG:* Hodgkinson (2)
9 Mar	H	London Scottish	12-19	*PG:* Hodgkinson (4)
30 Mar	H	Moseley	48-27	*T:* Royer (3), Reed (2), Gallagher, Carroll *C:* Gallagher, Hodgkinson (4) *PG:* Hodgkinson
6 Apr	A	Waterloo	24-13	*T:* Brennan, Hodgkinson, Smallwood *C:* Hodgkinson (3) *PG:* Hodgkinson
13 Apr	A	Wakefield	15-36	*T:* Gallagher, Smallwood *C:* Hodgkinson *DG:* Hodgkinson
27 Apr	H	Bedford	30-11	*T:* Bradley, Byrom, Royer (2) *C:* Hodgkinson (2) *PG:* Hodgkinson (2)

Orrell

Year of formation 1927
Ground Edge Hall Road, Orrell, Lancashire   Tel: Upholland (01695) 623193
Colours Black and amber
Most capped player C D Morris & J Carleton (England) 26 caps
Captain 1995-96 P Johnson
Courage Leagues 1995-96 Div 1 7th   **Pilkington Cup 1995-96** Lost 17-19 to Harlequins
(4th round)

League Record 1995-96

Date	Venue	Opponents	Result	Scorers
9 Sept	H	Harlequins	9-23	*PG:* Mason (3)
16 Sept	A	Saracens	9-12	*PG:* Mason (3)
23 Sept	H	Sale	12-6	*PG:* Mason (4)
30 Sept	A	Bath	20-55	*T:* Johnson, Scott *C:* Mason (2) *PG:* Mason (2)
7 Oct	H	Gloucester	21-3	*T:* Mason, Smith *C:* Mason *PG:* Mason (2) *DG:* Johnson
14 Oct	A	Leicester	3-22	*PG:* Mason
21 Oct	H	West Hartlepool	20-10	*T:* Bibby, Healey *C:* Mason (2) *PG:* Mason (2)
28 Oct	H	Wasps	32-29	*T:* Smith (3), Healey *C:* Mason (3) *PG:* Mason (2)
4 Nov	A	Bristol	14-33	*T:* Wynn *PG:* Mason (3)
11 Nov	A	Harlequins	25-21	*T:* Mason, Taberner *PG:* Mason (5)
6 Jan	A	Sale	13-39	*T:* Luger, Wynn *PG:* Mason
13 Jan	H	Saracens	38-13	*T:* Mason, Smith (3) *C:* Mason (3) *PG:* Mason (4)
17 Feb	A	Gloucester	0-27	
30 Mar	H	Leicester	10-38	*T:* Smith *C:* Mason *PG:* Mason
6 Apr	A	West Hartlepool	44-22	*T:* Anglesey, Huxley, Mason, Winstanley, Wynn (2) *C:* Mason (4) *PG:* Mason (2)
13 Apr	A	Wasps	16-51	*T:* Hamer, Tuigamala *PG:* Mason (2)

20 Apr	H	Bath	11-44	T: Wynn PG: Healey, Mason
27 Apr	H	Bristol	26-29	T: Smith (2), Tuigamala, Healey
				C: Healey (2), Peacock

Sale

Year of formation 1861
Ground Heywood Road, Brooklands, Sale, Cheshire Tel: 0161-973 6348
Colours Blue and white
Most capped player F E Cotton (England) 31 caps
Captain 1995-96 J Mallinder
Courage Leagues 1995-96 Div 1 5th **Pilkington Cup 1995-96** Lost 9-18 to Wasps
(4th round)

League Record 1995-96

Date	Venue	Opponents	Result	Scorers
9 Sept	A	Gloucester	22-17	T: Saverimutto, Vyvyan, Yates C: Liley (2) PG: Liley
16 Sept	H	Leicester	12-16	PG: Liley (2) DG: Liley, Stocks
23 Sept	A	Orrell	6-12	PG: Liley DG: Liley
30 Sept	H	Wasps	18-25	PG: Liley (5) DG: Turner
7 Oct	A	Bristol	6-30	PG: Liley (2)
14 Oct	H	Harlequins	29-11	T: Ashurst, Baldwin C: Liley (2) PG: Liley (5)
21 Oct	A	Saracens	24-9	T: Ashurst, Baxendell, Saverimutto C: Liley (3) PG: Liley
28 Oct	A	West Hartlepool	29-11	T: Baldwin, Baxendell, Liley, Yates PG: Liley (3)
4 Nov	H	Bath	18-30	T: Mallinder, Baxendell C: Liley PG: Liley (2)
11 Nov	H	Gloucester	21-13	T: Liley, Rees C: Liley PG: Liley (2) DG: Turner
6 Jan	H	Orrell	39-13	T: Baldwin, C Yates, Higginbotham, Vyvyan, Warr C: Liley (4) DG: Turner (2)
17 Feb	H	Bristol	15-6	T: Vyvyan (2) C: Liley PG: Turner
23 Mar	A	Wasps	16-25	T: Saverimutto C: Liley PG: Liley (3)
30 Mar	A	Harlequins	0-55	
6 Apr	H	Saracens	18-15	T: Liley, Ryan, Warr PG: Liley
13 Apr	H	West Hartlepool	44-13	T: Ashurst, Baxendell, Fowler, Hewitt, Mallinder, O'Grady C: Liley (4) PG: Liley (2)
17 Apr	A	Leicester	10-32	T: Mallinder C: Liley PG: Liley
27 Apr	A	Bath	38-38	T: Baxendell (2), Yates, Ashurst, O'Grady C: Liley (2) PG: Liley (3)

Saracens

Year of formation 1876
Ground Bramley Sports Ground, Green Road, Southgate, London N14
Tel: 0181-449 3770
Colours Black with red star and crescent
Most capped player J Leonard (England) 49 caps
Captain 1995-96 B Davies
Courage Leagues 1995-96 Div 1 9th **Pilkington Cup 1995-96** Lost 16-40 to Leicester
(5th round)

League Record 1995-96

Date	Venue	Opponents	Result	Scorers
9 Sept	A	Leicester	3-31	PG: Tunningley
16 Sept	H	Orrell	12-6	PG: Tunningley (4)

23 Sept	A	Wasps	16-38	*T:* Tunningley *C:* Tunningley *PG:* Tunningley (3)
30 Sept	H	Bristol	11-24	*T:* Holmes *PG:* Tunningley (2)
7 Oct	A	Harlequins	15-23	*T:* Gregory, Lee *C:* Lee *PG:* Lee
14 Oct	H	West Hartlepool	31-30	*T:* Harries *C:* Lee *PG:* Lee (6) *DG:* Lee (2)
21 Oct	H	Sale	9-24	*PG:* Lee (2) *DG:* Tunningley
28 Oct	A	Bath	16-52	*T:* Harries, Tunningley *PG:* Lee (2)
4 Nov	H	Gloucester	19-16	*T:* Gregory *C:* Lee *PG:* Lee (3) *DG:* Lee
11 Nov	H	Leicester	25-21	*T:* Harries *C:* Lee *PG:* Lee (5) *DG:* Lee
6 Jan	H	Wasps	20-24	*T:* Tunningley *PG:* Lee (5)
13 Jan	A	Orrell	13-38	*T:* Chesney, Harries *PG:* Tunningley
17 Feb	H	Harlequins	6-13	*PG:* Lee (2)
30 Mar	A	West Hartlepool	41-31	*T:* Botterman, Diprose, Langley, Lee *C:* Lee (3) *PG:* G Hughes, Lee (3) *DG:* Lee
6 Apr	A	Sale	15-18	*T:* Chesney, G Hughes *C:* G Hughes *PG:* G Hughes
13 Apr	H	Bath	15-21	*T:* Diprose, Halvey *C:* G Hughes *PG:* G Hughes
20 Apr	A	Bristol	7-21	*T:* Hill *C:* Singer
27 Apr	A	Gloucester	10-17	*T:* Hill *C:* Singer *PG:* Singer

Wakefield

Year of formation 1901
Ground Pinderfields Road, College Grove, Wakefield   Tel: Wakefield (01924) 374801
Colours Black and gold
Most capped player M E Harrison (England) 15 caps
Captain 1995-96 M Jackson
Courage Leagues 1995-96 Div 2 4th   **Pilkington Cup 1995-96** Lost 12-16 to Bath
(5th round)

League Record 1995-96

Date	Venue	Opponents	Result	Scorers
9 Sept	H	Bedford	32-23	*T:* White, Metcalfe, Yates, Maynard *C:* Jackson (3) *PG:* Jackson (2)
16 Sept	A	Blackheath	16-20	*T:* pen try *C:* Jackson *PG:* Jackson (3)
23 Sept	H	Newcastle	26-7	*T:* Green, Petyt *C:* Jackson (2) *PG:* Jackson (4)
30 Sept	A	Northampton	0-23	
7 Oct	H	London Scottish	16-20	*T:* Rushworth *C:* Jackson *PG:* Jackson (3)
14 Oct	A	London Irish	7-31	*T:* Miller *C:* Jackson
21 Oct	H	Moseley	9-11	*PG:* Jackson (2) *DG:* Shuttleworth
28 Oct	A	Nottingham	18-22	*T:* Maynard, Shuttleworth *C:* Jackson *PG:* Jackson (2)
4 Nov	H	Waterloo	14-6	*T:* Falkingham *PG:* Jackson (3)
11 Nov	A	Bedford	13-20	*T:* Scully *C:* Jackson *PG:* Jackson (2)
6 Jan	A	Newcastle	17-11	*T:* Green *PG:* Jackson (4)
13 Jan	H	Blackheath	17-0	*T:* Petyt, Scully *C:* Jackson (2) *DG:* Metcalfe
17 Feb	A	London Scottish	31-22	*T:* Green, Scully, Stewart, White *C:* Jackson *PG:* Jackson (3)
30 Mar	H	London Irish	19-31	*T:* Metcalfe *C:* Jackson *PG:* Jackson (4)
6 Apr	A	Moseley	26-15	*T:* Rushforth, Scully *C:* Jackson (2) *PG:* Jackson (4)
13 Apr	H	Nottingham	36-15	*T:* Scully (2), Maynard, Jackson, Rushforth *C:* Jackson *PG:* Jackson (3)
20 Apr	H	Northampton	21-34	*T:* Jackson, Scully *C:* Jackson *PG:* Jackson (3)
27 Apr	A	Waterloo	10-20	*T:* Adams *C:* Jackson *PG:* Jackson

Wasps

Year of formation 1867
Ground Repton Avenue (off Rugby Road), Sudbury, Middlesex Tel: 0181-902 4220
Colours Black with gold wasp on left breast
Most capped player C R Andrew (England) 70 caps
Captain 1995-96 D Ryan/L Dallaglio
Courage Leagues 1995-96 Div 1 4th **Pilkington Cup 1995-96** Lost 9-22 to Gloucester
(quarter-final)

League Record 1995-96

Date	Venue	Opponents	Result	Scorers
9 Sept	H	Bristol	33-5	*T:* D Hopley (2), Roiser (2), Ryan *C:* Andrew *PG:* Andrew (2)
16 Sept	A	Harlequins	20-29	*T:* Dunston *PG:* Andrew (5)
23 Sept	H	Saracens	38-16	*T:* Scrivener, D Hopley, White, Ryan *C:* Andrew (3) *PG:* Andrew (2) *DG:* Ufton (2)
30 Sept	A	Sale	25-18	*T:* Scrivener, Ryan *PG:* Andrew (3) *DG:* Andrew (2)
7 Oct	H	Bath	6-15	*PG:* Andrew *DG:* Andrew
14 Oct	A	Gloucester	26-15	*T:* Dallaglio (2), Ryan *C:* Andrew *PG:* Andrew (3)
21 Oct	H	Leicester	11-21	*T:* Ufton *PG:* Ufton (2)
28 Oct	A	Orrell	29-32	*T:* Braithwaite (2), Scrivener (2), Gomarsall *C:* Ufton (2)
11 Nov	A	Bristol	17-9	*T:* Roiser *PG:* Gregory (4)
6 Jan	A	Saracens	24-20	*T:* pen try, Gomarsall, P Hopley *C:* Gregory (3) *PG:* Gregory
17 Feb	A	Bath	12-36	*T:* Gomarsall, pen try *C:* Gregory
9 Mar	H	Harlequins	3-34	*PG:* Gregory
23 Mar	H	Sale	25-16	*T:* Greenstock, Scrase, White *C:* Gregory (2) *PG:* Gregory (2)
30 Mar	H	Gloucester	21-10	*T:* Roiser (2), White *C:* Braithwaite (3)
6 Apr	A	Leicester	12-15	*PG:* Gregory (2) *DG:* Gregory (2)
13 Apr	H	Orrell	51-16	*T:* Dallaglio (2), Gregory, Roiser, Scrase, Greenstock, Braithwaite *C:* Gregory (5) *PG:* Gregory (2)
20 Apr	H	West Hartlepool	52-12	*T:* Gregory (2), Roiser (2), Gomarsall, Greenstock, Greenwood, Molloy *C:* Gregory (6)
27 Apr	A	West Hartlepool	34-3	*T:* Gomarsall, Greenwood, Ufton, White, pen try *C:* Ufton (3) *DG:* Braithwaite

Waterloo

Year of formation 1882
Ground St Anthony's Road, Blundellsands, Liverpool Tel: 0151-924 4552
Colours Green, red and white
Most capped player H G Periton (England) 21 caps
Captain 1995-96 P Buckton
Courage Leagues 1995-96 Div 2 5th **Pilkington Cup 1995-96** Lost 15-20 to Leeds
(4th round)

League Record 1995-96

Date	Venue	Opponents	Result	Scorers
9 Sept	H	London Scottish	3-11	*PG:* Emmett
16 Sept	A	Bedford	10-10	*T:* Kay, Wright
23 Sept	H	London Irish	16-50	*T:* Smith *C:* Aitchison *PG:* Aitchison (3)

30 Sept	A	Blackheath	9-21	*PG:* Ryan (3)
7 Oct	H	Moseley	22-17	*T:* Wright *C:* Emmett *PG:* Emmett (4) *DG:* Ryan
14 Oct	A	Newcastle	29-26	*T:* Wolfenden, Wright *C:* Emmett (2) *PG:* Emmett (3) *DG:* Ryan (2)
21 Oct	A	Nottingham	18-12	*PG:* Emmett (5), Aitchison
28 Oct	H	Northampton	3-69	*DG:* Ryan
4 Nov	A	Wakefield	6-14	*PG:* Emmett (2)
11 Nov	A	London Scottish	16-16	*T:* Buckton *C:* Emmett *PG:* Emmett (3)
6 Jan	A	London Irish	16-39	*T:* Beckett, Smith *PG:* Handley *DG:* Handley
13 Jan	H	Bedford	48-24	*T:* Bruce, Emmett, Kay, McCaugheran, Buckton (2) *C:* Emmett (3) *PG:* Emmett (4)
10 Feb	H	Blackheath	32-10	*T:* Bruce (2), Blyth, Allott *C:* Emmett (3) *PG:* Emmett (2)
17 Feb	A	Moseley	30-24	*T:* Blyth, McCaugheran *C:* Emmett *PG:* Emmett (6)
30 Mar	H	Newcastle	13-36	*T:* McCaugheran *C:* Emmett *PG:* Emmett (2)
6 Apr	H	Nottingham	13-24	*T:* White *C:* Thompson *PG:* Thompson (2)
13 Apr	A	Northampton	5-69	*T:* Fletcher
27 Apr	H	Wakefield	20-10	*T:* McCaugheran, Hackett *C:* Thompson (2) *PG:* Thompson (2)

West Hartlepool

Year of formation 1881
Ground Brierton Lane, Hartlepool   Tel: Hartlepool (01429) 272640
Colours Red, white and green
Most capped player R I Wainwright (Scotland) 22 caps
Captain 1995-96 P Lancaster/T Stimpson
Courage Leagues 1995-96 Div 1 10th **Pilkington Cup 1995-96** Lost 10-11 to London Irish (quarter-final)

League Record 1995-96

Date	Venue	Opponents	Result	Scorers
9 Sept	H	Bath	15-20	*PG:* Stimpson (4) *DG:* Hodder
16 Sept	A	Bristol	3-12	*PG:* Stimpson
23 Sept	H	Gloucester	19-27	*T:* Brown *C:* Stimpson *PG:* Stimpson (4)
30 Sept	A	Harlequins	18-34	*T:* Hodder, Stimpson *C:* Stimpson *PG:* Stimpson, Parker
7 Oct	H	Leicester	12-19	*PG:* Stimpson (4)
14 Oct	A	Saracens	30-31	*T:* Blyth, O Evans, Shelley, Stimpson *C:* Stimpson (2) *PG:* Stimpson (2)
21 Oct	A	Orrell	10-20	*T:* Mitchell *C:* Stimpson *PG:* Stimpson
28 Oct	H	Sale	11-29	*T:* Wainwright *PG:* Stimpson (2)
11 Nov	A	Bath	22-34	*T:* O Evans, P Evans, Shelley *C:* Stimpson (2) *PG:* Stimpson
6 Jan	A	Gloucester	16-17	*T:* Shelley, Stimpson *PG:* Stimpson (2)
17 Feb	A	Leicester	15-48	*T:* Stimpson (2) *C:* Stimpson *PG:* Stimpson
23 Mar	H	Harlequins	21-91	*T:* O Evans, Herbert, Wood *PG:* Parker (2)
30 Mar	H	Saracens	31-41	*T:* Ions, Lee, Wood *C:* Oliphant (2) *PG:* Oliphant (3) *DG:* Oliphant
6 Apr	H	Orrell	22-44	*T:* Blyth, Shelley, Thompson *C:* Parker (2) *PG:* Parker
13 Apr	A	Sale	13-44	*T:* pen try *C:* Benson *PG:* Benson (2)
20 Apr	A	Wasps	12-52	*T:* Patterson, Thompson *C:* Oliphant
27 Apr	H	Wasps	3-34	*PG:* Parker
5 May	H	Bristol	15-37	*T:* Parker, Patterson *C:* Oliphant *PG:* Oliphant

SCOTLAND
Biggar

Year of formation 1975
Ground Hartree Mill, Biggar   Tel: Biggar (01899) 221219
Colours Black jersey with red collar and cuffs
Captain 1995-96 L Graham
SRU Tennents Championship 1995-96 Div 3 2nd – *promoted*   **SRU Tennents Cup 1995-96** Lost 17-52 to Hawick (5th round)

League Record 1995-96

Date	Venue	Opponents	Result	Scorers
2 Sept	A	Preston Lodge FP	21-17	*T:* Harrison (2) *C:* Lavery *PG:* Bruce, Lavery (2)
9 Sept	H	Grangemouth	27-19	*T:* Read (2) *C:* Lavery *PG:* Lavery (5)
13 Sept	H	Peebles	13-12	*T:* Harvey *C:* Lavery *PG:* Lavery (2)
16 Sept	A	Musselburgh	27-3	*T:* Graham, Read (2), Steele *C:* Lavery (2) *PG:* Lavery
23 Sept	H	Kirkcaldy	15-12	*PG:* Lavery (5)
30 Sept	A	Glasgow Acads	9-17	*PG:* Lavery (3)
7 Oct	H	Corstorphine	50-13	*T:* Harvey, S Jack, E McAlpine, R McAlpine, Read (3) *C:* Bruce (3) *PG:* Bruce (2) *DG:* Watson
14 Oct	H	Preston Lodge FP	15-9	*PG:* Lavery (5)
21 Oct	A	Grangemouth	25-11	*T:* Steele *C:* Lavery *PG:* Lavery (6)
28 Oct	A	Peebles	13-15	*T:* Read *C:* Lavery *PG:* Lavery (2)
4 Nov	H	Musselburgh	16-13	*T:* Read *C:* Lavery *PG:* Lavery (3)
11 Nov	A	Kirkcaldy	10-21	*T:* E McAlpine *C:* Lavery *PG:* Lavery
19 Nov	H	Glasgow Acads	19-16	*T:* Harrison, Steele *PG:* Lavery (3)
25 Nov	A	Corstorphine	64-3	*T:* Abernethy, Harrison (2), Harvey, E McAlpine, Read (2), Steele, Watson (2) *C:* Lavery *PG:* Lavery (3) *DG:* R Young

Boroughmuir

Year of formation 1919 (Boroughmuir FP until 1974)
Ground Meggetland, Colinton Road, Edinburgh EH14 1AS   Tel: 0131-443 7571
Colours Blue and green quarters
Most capped player S R P Lineen (Scotland) 29 caps
Captain 1995-96 P H Wright
SRU Tennents Championship 1995-96 Div 1 4th   **SRU Tennents Cup 1995-96** Lost 22-50 to Melrose (5th round)

League Record 1995-96

Date	Venue	Opponents	Result	Scorers
2 Sept	H	Edinburgh Acads	3-18	*PG:* Knight
9 Sept	A	Melrose	16-9	*T:* Lineen, Stark *PG:* Knight (2)
13 Sept	H	Gala	25-10	*T:* Macrae, Stark, Wands *C:* Knight (2) *PG:* Knight (2)
16 Sept	A	Hawick	23-14	*T:* Reid *PG:* Knight (6)
23 Sept	H	Stirling County	10-16	*T:* Reid *C:* Knight *PG:* Knight
30 Sept	H	Watsonians	21-21	*T:* Easson, Lineen *C:* Easson *PG:* Easson (3)
7 Oct	A	Heriot's FP	30-21	*T:* Beveridge, Stark *C:* Easson *PG:* Easson (6)
14 Oct	A	Edinburgh Acads	35-19	*T:* Beveridge, Stark, Wallace, pen try *C:* Easson (3) *PG:* Easson (3)
21 Oct	H	Melrose	31-15	*T:* Beveridge, Reid, Tukalo *C:* Easson (2) *PG:* Easson (3), Knight

28 Oct	A	Gala	26-18	*T:* G Dickson, Stark *C:* Easson (2)
				PG: Easson (4)
4 Nov	H	Hawick	18-19	*T:* Stark, Wallace *C:* Easson *PG:* Easson (2)
19 Nov	A	Watsonians	35-48	*T:* N G B Dickson, Easson, Laird, Stark
				C: Easson (3) *PG:* Easson (3)
25 Nov	H	Heriot's FP	40-40	*T:* Lineen (2), Tukalo (2) *C:* Easson (4)
				PG: Easson (4)
2 Dec	A	Stirling County	14-33	*T:* McKinlay, Thom *C:* Easson (2)

Corstorphine

Year of formation 1921
Ground Union Park, Carricknowe, Corstorphine, Edinburgh   Tel: 0131-334 8063
Colours Navy blue and scarlet quarters
Captain 1995-96 S R Maclean
SRU Tennents Championship 1995-96 Div 3 8th – *relegated*   **SRU Tennents Cup 1995-96**
Lost 8-27 to Kilmarnock (5th round)

League Record 1995-96

Date	Venue	Opponents	Result	Scorers
2 Sept	H	Peebles	9-11	*PG:* Pollock (3)
9 Sept	A	Musselburgh	20-39	*T:* Johnston, Zavaroni *C:* Pollock (2)
				PG: Pollock (2)
13 Sept	H	Kirkcaldy	18-35	*PG:* Pollock (6)
16 Sept	A	Glasgow Acads	16-67	*T:* Pilkington *C:* Pollock *PG:* Pollock (3)
23 Sept	A	Grangemouth	9-25	*PG:* Pollock (3)
30 Sept	H	Preston Lodge FP	12-23	*T:* Cockburn, Pilkington *C:* Threadgall
7 Oct	A	Biggar	13-50	*T:* Chisholm *C:* S R Maclean
				PG: S R Maclean (2)
14 Oct	A	Peebles	5-36	*T:* Williamson
21 Oct	H	Musselburgh	10-14	*T:* Pilkington *C:* S R Maclean
				PG: S R Maclean
28 Oct	A	Kirkcaldy	10-47	*T:* Zavaroni *C:* Liddle *PG:* Liddle
4 Nov	H	Glasgow Acads	5-60	*T:* Bezett
11 Nov	H	Grangemouth	16-25	*T:* McDonald, M Maclean *PG:* Liddle,
				S R Maclean
19 Nov	A	Preston Lodge FP	8-48	*T:* M Maclean *PG:* Liddle
25 Nov	H	Biggar	3-64	*PG:* Threadgall

Currie

Year of formation 1970
Ground Malleny Park, Balerno, Edinburgh EH14 5HA   Tel: 0131-449 2432
Colours Amber and black
Captain 1995-96 A Donaldson
SRU Tennents Championship 1995-96 Div 2 *Winners – promoted*   **SRU Tennents Shield**
Winners – beat Stirling County 75-20 (final)

League Record 1995-96

Date	Venue	Opponents	Result	Scorers
2 Sept	H	Kelso	28-16	*T:* Hardie, Sheppard *PG:* Donaldson (5)
				DG: Donaldson
9 Sept	A	GHK	28-22	*T:* Donaldson, Ellis, Robertson
				C: Donaldson (2) *PG:* Donaldson (3)

13 Sept	H	Dundee HSFP	22-12	T: Russell C: Donaldson PG: Donaldson (4) DG: Donaldson
16 Sept	A	West of Scotland	33-16	T: Plumb, Robertson, Thomson C: Donaldson (3) PG: Donaldson (4)
23 Sept	H	Selkirk	32-24	T: Hardie (2), Wilson (2) C: Donaldson (3) PG: Donaldson (2)
30 Sept	H	Stewart's-Melville	33-9	T: Eagle, Ellis, Logan, Russell C: Donaldson (2) PG: Donaldson (3)
7 Oct	A	Jedforest	16-32	T: Ward, Wilson PG: Donaldson (2)
14 Oct	A	Kelso	17-36	T: Blair PG: Donaldson (4)
21 Oct	H	GHK	34-17	T: Forrester (2), Keen, Ward C: Donaldson (4) PG: Donaldson (2)
28 Oct	A	Dundee HSFP	22-16	T: Sheppard C: Donaldson PG: Donaldson (4) DG: Donaldson
4 Nov	H	West of Scotland	25-14	T: Donaldson (2), Sheppard, Ward C: Donaldson PG: Donaldson
11 Nov	A	Selkirk	12-9	PG: Donaldson (2) DG: Donaldson, Sheppard
19 Nov	A	Stewart's-Melville	48-12	T: Forrester (2), Keen, Logan, Plumb, Rogerson, Sheppard, Wilson C: Donaldson (4)
25 Nov	H	Jedforest	7-31	T: Blair C: Morrison

Dundee High School FP

Year of formation 1880
Ground Mayfield, Arbroath Road, Dundee   Tel: Dundee (01382) 453517 (ground); 451045 (clubhouse)
Colours Blue and red
Most capped player D G Leslie (Scotland) 32 caps
Captain 1995-96 D R Hamilton
SRU Tennents Championship 1995-96 Div 2 5th **SRU Tennents Cup 1995-96** Lost 7-57 to Watsonians (semi-final)

League Record 1995-96

Date	Venue	Opponents	Result	Scorers
2 Sept	H	Stewart's-Melville	14-17	T: Lamont, S Newton C: S Newton (2)
9 Sept	A	Kelso	20-9	T: Campbell, Robinson C: Robinson (2) PG: Robinson (2)
13 Sept	A	Currie	12-22	PG: Robinson (4)
16 Sept	H	Selkirk	19-0	T: Cousin, Hayter, Milne C: Robinson (2)
23 Sept	A	Jedforest	25-17	T: Hamilton, S Newton, Robinson C: Robinson (2) PG: Robinson (2)
30 Sept	H	GHK	16-10	T: Cousin, McWhirter PG: Robinson (2)
7 Oct	A	West of Scotland	12-21	T: Hope, James C: Robinson
14 Oct	A	Stewart's-Melville	32-23	T: D Gray, Pearson, Rouse, Sandford C: Robinson (3) PG: Robinson DG: Robinson
21 Oct	H	Kelso	13-23	T: Robinson C: Robinson PG: Robinson DG: Robinson
28 Oct	H	Currie	16-22	T: Milne C: Robinson PG: Robinson (2), Whitney
4 Nov	A	Selkirk	16-21	T: Rouse C: Robinson PG: Robinson (3)
11 Nov	H	Jedforest	16-17	T: Milne, Rouse PG: Robinson (2)
19 Nov	A	GHK	12-37	PG: Robinson (3), Whitney
25 Nov	H	West of Scotland	36-0	T: Longstaff, McWhirter, Robinson, Rouse C: Robinson (2) PG: Robinson (4)

Edinburgh Academicals

Year of formation 1857
Ground Raeburn Place, Stockbridge, Edinburgh EH4 1HQ   Tel: 0131-332 1070
Colours Blue and white hoops
Most capped player D M B Sole (Scotland) 44 caps
Captain 1995-96 D J McIvor
SRU Tennents Championship 1995-96 Div 1 7th – *relegated*   **SRU Tennents Cup 1995-96**
Lost 6-33 to Watsonians (3rd round) **SRU Tennents Bowl** *Winners* – beat Selkirk 28-21
(final)

League Record 1995-96

Date	Venue	Opponents	Result	Scorers
2 Sept	A	Boroughmuir	18-3	*PG:* Hay-Smith (3) *DG:* Hay-Smith (3)
9 Sept	H	Gala	13-13	*T:* Troup *C:* Hay-Smith *PG:* Hay-Smith (2)
13 Sept	A	Stirling County	6-17	*PG:* Hay-Smith (2)
16 Sept	H	Heriot's FP	28-10	*T:* Allan, McKinlay, Waite *C:* Hay-Smith (2) *PG:* Hay-Smith (3)
23 Sept	A	Melrose	3-22	*PG:* Hay-Smith
30 Sept	A	Hawick	13-30	*T:* pen try *C:* Duncan *PG:* Duncan (2)
7 Oct	A	Watsonians	31-23	*T:* Baillie, Burns, Day, Stewart, Waite *C:* Hay-Smith (3)
14 Oct	H	Boroughmuir	19-35	*T:* Waite *C:* Barber *PG:* Barber, Hay-Smith (2) *DG:* Hay-Smith
21 Oct	A	Gala	35-14	*T:* McVie, Simmers, Stewart, Waite, pen try *C:* Duncan (5)
28 Oct	H	Stirling County	13-16	*T:* McKinlay *C:* Duncan *PG:* Duncan (2)
4 Nov	A	Heriot's FP	21-34	*T:* Simmers, Troup, Waite *C:* Hay-Smith (3)
11 Nov	H	Melrose	15-18	*T:* Hoole, Waite *C:* Hay-Smith *PG:* Hay-Smith
19 Nov	A	Hawick	13-19	*T:* Waite *C:* Hay-Smith *PG:* Hay-Smith (2)
25 Nov	H	Watsonians	15-28	*T:* Burns (2) *C:* Duncan *PG:* Duncan

Gala

Year of formation 1875
Ground Netherdale, Nether Road, Galashiels TD1 3HE   Tel: Galashiels (01896) 755145
Colours Maroon
Most capped player P C Brown (Scotland) 27 caps
Captain 1995-96 G R Isaac
SRU Tennents Championship 1995-96 Div 1 8th – *relegated*   **SRU Tennents Cup 1995-96**
Lost 6-29 to Glasgow Academicals (5th round)

League Record 1995-96

Date	Venue	Opponents	Result	Scorers
2 Sept	H	Watsonians	6-37	*PG:* D Changleng (2)
9 Sept	A	Edinburgh Acads	13-13	*T:* D Changleng *C:* D Changleng *PG:* D Changleng (2)
13 Sept	A	Boroughmuir	10-25	*T:* Amos *C:* D Changleng *PG:* D Changleng
16 Sept	H	Stirling County	28-22	*T:* D Changleng, Moncrieff, S W Paterson *C:* D Changleng (2) *PG:* D Changleng (3)
23 Sept	A	Heriot's FP	10-59	*T:* Stoltz, Swan
30 Sept	H	Melrose	12-29	*PG:* D Changleng (4)
7 Oct	A	Hawick	10-20	*T:* Swan *C:* D Changleng *PG:* D Changleng
14 Oct	A	Watsonians	17-29	*T:* G S Dalgleish, Moncrieff *C:* G S Dalgleish (2) *PG:* G S Dalgleish
21 Oct	H	Edinburgh Acads	14-35	*T:* Stoltz *PG:* G S Dalgleish (3)

28 Oct	H	Boroughmuir	18-26	T: G S Dalgleish, S W Paterson
				C: G S Dalgleish PG: D S Dalgleish (2)
4 Nov	A	Stirling County	6-45	PG: G S Dalgleish (2)
25 Nov	H	Hawick	24-23	T: C S Dalgleish, Hogg C: G S Dalgleish
				PG: G S Dalgleish (4)
2 Dec	A	Melrose	11-31	T: Moncrieff PG: G S Dalgleish (2)

Glasgow High/Kelvinside

Year of formation 1982 (on amalgamation of Glasgow High RFC and Kelvinside Academicals)
Ground Old Anniesland, 637 Crow Road, Glasgow   Tel: 0141-959 1154
Colours Navy blue, green and white
Most capped player D S Munro (Scotland) 6 caps (before amalagmation J M Bannerman [Glasgow HSFP] was capped 37 times and D M White [Kelvinside Academicals] 4 times, both for Scotland)
Captain 1995-96 S N Hirini
SRU Tennents Championship 1995-96 Div 2 3rd   **SRU Tennents Cup 1995-96** Lost 15-25 to Boroughmuir (4th round)

League Record 1995-96

Date	Venue	Opponents	Result	Scorers
2 Sept	A	Jedforest	5-9	T: M I Wallace
9 Sept	H	Currie	22-28	T: Breckenridge, McIlwham PG: Bassi (4)
13 Sept	H	West of Scotland	11-22	T: Breckenridge PG: Bassi (2)
16 Sept	A	Stewart's-Melville	93-5	T: Agnew, Breckenridge (4), Docherty, Du Plessis, Hawkes, Hirini (2), Hutton, C E Little (2), McIlwham C: Bassi (10) PG: Bassi
23 Sept	H	Kelso	35-5	T: Breckenridge (2), Hawkes (2), Hutton, M I Wallace C: Bassi PG: Bassi
30 Sept	A	Dundee HSFP	10-16	T: Agnew (2)
7 Oct	H	Selkirk	0-17	
14 Oct	H	Jedforest	30-26	T: Breckenridge (2), Hawkes, M I Wallace C: Bassi (2) PG: Bassi (2)
21 Oct	A	Currie	17-34	T: Breckenridge, Gay, M I Wallace C: Breckenridge
28 Oct	A	West of Scotland	10-9	T: Breckenridge C: Bassi PG: Breckenridge
4 Nov	H	Stewart's-Melville	49-23	T: Agnew (2), Breckenridge, Hawkes, Ness, Sanderson (2) C: Breckenridge (4) PG: Breckenridge (2)
11 Nov	A	Kelso	16-13	T: Du Plessis, M I Wallace PG: Breckenridge (2)
19 Nov	H	Dundee HSFP	37-12	T: Agnew (2), Bassi, Breckenridge, C E Little C: Breckenridge (3) PG: Breckenridge (2)
25 Nov	A	Selkirk	40-20	T: Agnew (2), Bassi, C E Little, M I Wallace (2) C: McLeod (5)

Glasgow Academicals

Year of formation 1867
Ground New Anniesland, Helensburgh Drive, Glasgow   Tel: 0141-959 1101
Colours Navy blue and white hoops
Most capped player W M Simmers (Scotland) 28 caps
Captain 1995-96 S M Simmers
SRU Tennents Championship 1995-96 Div 2 *Winners – promoted*   **SRU Tennents Cup 1995-96** Lost 8-14 to Melrose (quarter-final)

League Record 1995-96

Date	Venue	Opponents	Result	Scorers
2 Sept	H	Musselburgh	39-9	T: Boundy, C G MacGregor (2), Mathewson (2), Richmond, S M Simmers C: C G MacGregor (2)
9 Sept	A	Kirkcaldy	13-15	T: C G MacGregor, Mathewson PG: C G MacGregor
13 Sept	A	Grangemouth	27-3	T: M Begley, Mathewson, Williams C: C G MacGregor (3) PG: C G MacGregor (2)
16 Sept	H	Corstorphine	67-16	T: S Begley, Boundy (2), Davis, J F Mason (2), Mathewson (5) C: C G MacGregor (6)
23 Sept	A	Preston Lodge FP	30-9	T: Davis, J F Mason, Mathewson C: C G MacGregor (3) PG: C G MacGregor (3)
30 Sept	H	Biggar	17-9	T: J F Mason PG: C G MacGregor (4)
7 Oct	A	Peebles	32-0	T: Davis, Mathewson (2), Richmond C: C G MacGregor (3) PG: C G MacGregor (2)
14 Oct	A	Musselburgh	47-9	T: Davis, C G MacGregor (3), A S Mason, Mathewson (2) C: C G MacGregor (3) PG: C G MacGregor DG: C G MacGregor
21 Oct	H	Kirkcaldy	22-8	T: S Begley, C G MacGregor, Simmers, Williams C: C G MacGregor
28 Oct	H	Grangemouth	33-10	T: Davis, C G MacGregor, Williams C: C G MacGregor (3) PG: C G MacGregor (4)
4 Nov	A	Corstorphine	60-5	T: M Begley, Hart (2), C G MacGregor, J F Mason (2), Mathewson (3), Simmers C: C G MacGregor (5)
11 Nov	H	Preston Lodge FP	21-8	T: M Begley, Simmers C: C G MacGregor PG: C G MacGregor (3)
19 Nov	A	Biggar	16-19	T: Hart C: C G MacGregor PG: Hart, C G MacGregor (2)
25 Nov	H	Peebles	37-12	T: Davis (2), McFadzean, J F Mason, Mathewson C: C G MacGregor (3) PG: C G MacGregor (2)

Grangemouth

Year of formation 1929
Ground Glensburgh, Glensburgh Road, Grangemouth   Tel: Grangemouth (01324) 486142
Colours Red and black hoops
Captain 1995-96 G Jesty
SRU Tennents Championship 1995-96 Div 3 7th – *relegated*   **SRU Tennents Cup 1995-96**
Lost 16-22 to Kilmarnock (4th round)

League Record 1995-96

Date	Venue	Opponents	Result	Scorers
2 Sept	H	Kirkcaldy	3-9	PG: Halliday
9 Sept	A	Biggar	19-27	T: Smith C: Halliday PG: Halliday (4)
13 Sept	H	Glasgow Acads	3-27	PG: Halliday
16 Sept	A	Peebles	8-16	T: Howard PG: Crossan
23 Sept	H	Corstorphine	25-9	T: Crossan, Innes, Kennet, Penman C: Halliday DG: Halliday
30 Sept	H	Musselburgh	17-15	T: Parsons, pen try C: Halliday (2) PG: Halliday
7 Oct	A	Preston Lodge FP	9-29	PG: Halliday (2) DG: Halliday
14 Oct	A	Kirkcaldy	10-20	T: Tuckerman (2)

21 Oct	H	Biggar	11-25	*T:* Parsons *PG:* Halliday (2)
28 Oct	A	Glasgow Acads	10-33	*T:* Tuckerman *C:* Halliday *PG:* Halliday
4 Nov	H	Peebles	27-17	*T:* Horne, Howard, Kennet, Parsons *C:* Halliday (2) *PG:* Halliday
11 Nov	A	Corstorphine	25-16	*T:* Howard, Kennet, Penman *C:* Halliday (2) *PG:* Halliday (2)
19 Nov	A	Musselburgh	17-19	*T:* Horne *PG:* Halliday (4)
25 Nov	H	Preston Lodge FP	18-11	*T:* Parsons, Penman *C:* Halliday *PG:* Halliday (2)

Hawick

Year of formation 1873
Ground Mansfield Park, Mansfield Road, Hawick, Roxburghshire
Tel: Hawick (01450) 737429
Colours Dark green
Most capped player J M Renwick (Scotland) & C T Deans (Scotland) 52 caps
Captain 1995-96 B L Renwick
SRU Tennents Championship 1995-96 Div 1 5th   **SRU Tennents Cup 1995-96** *Winners –* beat Watsonians 17-15 (final)

League Record 1995-96

Date	Venue	Opponents	Result	Scorers
2 Sept	A	Stirling County	12-9	*PG:* Welsh (2) *DG:* Welsh (2)
9 Sept	H	Heriot's FP	24-25	*T:* Graham, Murray (2) *PG:* C W Turnbull (2) *DG:* Welsh
13 Sept	A	Melrose	3-31	*PG:* Welsh
16 Sept	H	Boroughmuir	14-23	*T:* B L Renwick *PG:* C W Turnbull, Welsh *DG:* Welsh
23 Sept	H	Watsonians	17-33	*T:* Murray *PG:* C W Turnbull (4)
30 Sept	A	Edinburgh Acads	30-13	*T:* Grant, Hay, Murray, Stanger, Suddon *C:* Welsh *PG:* Welsh
7 Oct	H	Gala	20-10	*T:* Welsh *PG:* Welsh (5)
14 Oct	H	Stirling County	23-15	*T:* Welsh (2) *C:* Welsh (2) *PG:* Welsh (3)
21 Oct	A	Heriot's FP	23-26	*T:* Suddon, C W Turnbull, Welsh *C:* Welsh *PG:* Welsh (2)
28 Oct	H	Melrose	10-9	*T:* Reid *C:* Welsh *PG:* Welsh
4 Nov	A	Boroughmuir	19-18	*T:* Sharp, Suddon *PG:* Welsh (3)
19 Nov	H	Edinburgh Acads	19-13	*T:* Murrray *C:* Welsh *PG:* Welsh (3) *DG:* Welsh
25 Nov	A	Gala	23-24	*T:* Suddon (2) *C:* C W Turnbull, Welsh *PG:* C W Turnbull, Welsh (2)
2 Dec	A	Watsonians	6-39	*PG:* Welsh (2)

Heriot's FP

Year of formation 1890
Ground Goldenacre, Bangholm Terrace, Edinburgh EH3 5QN   Tel: 0131-552 4097 (groundstaff); 0131-552 5925 (clubhouse)
Colours Blue and white horizontal stripes
Most capped player A R Irvine (Scotland) 51 caps
Captain 1995-96 S W Paul
SRU Tennents Championship 1995-96 Div 1 6th   **SRU Tennents Cup 1995-96** Lost 6-23 to Watsonians (quarter-final)

League Record 1995-96

Date	Venue	Opponents	Result	Scorers
2 Sept	H	Melrose	10-17	*T:* Elliot *C:* Aitken *PG:* Smith
9 Sept	A	Hawick	25-24	*T:* Officer *C:* Rahui *PG:* Rahui (5) *DG:* Lawrie
13 Sept	H	Watsonians	0-43	
16 Sept	A	Edinburgh Acads	10-28	*T:* Lawrie *C:* Smith *PG:* Smith
23 Sept	H	Gala	59-10	*T:* Aitken (2), Lawrie (2), Officer (2), Young *C:* Rahui (6) *PG:* Rahui (4)
30 Sept	A	Stirling County	6-38	*PG:* Rahui (2)
7 Oct	H	Boroughmuir	21-20	*T:* Lang, Officer *C:* Aitken *PG:* Rahui (3)
14 Oct	A	Melrose	10-38	*T:* pen try *C:* Aitken *PG:* Aitken
21 Oct	H	Hawick	26-23	*T:* H R Gilmour, I C Glasgow *C:* Rahui (2) *PG:* Rahui (4)
28 Oct	A	Watsonians	23-14	*T:* Milne, Stoddart *C:* I C Glasgow, Rahui *PG:* I C Glasgow, Rahui (2)
4 Nov	H	Edinburgh Acads	34-21	*T:* A Glasgow, I C Glasgow (2), Livingstone (2) *C:* Rahui (3) *PG:* Rahui
25 Nov	A	Boroughmuir	40-40	*T:* H R Gilmour (2), I C Glasgow, Lang *C:* Rahui (4) *PG:* Rahui (4)
16 Dec	H	Stirling County	14-34	*T:* Milne *PG:* Aitken (2), Smith

Jedforest

Year of formation 1885
Ground Riverside Park, Jedburgh Tel: Jedburgh (01835) 862855
Colours Royal blue
Most capped player R J Laidlaw (Scotland) 47 caps
Captain 1995-96 R M Kirkpatrick
SRU Tennents Championship 1995-96 Div 2 2nd – *promoted* **SRU Tennents Cup 1995-96** Lost 6-17 to Dundee HSFP (5th round)

League Record 1995-96

Date	Venue	Opponents	Result	Scorers
2 Sept	H	GHK	9-5	*PG:* Richards (3)
9 Sept	A	West of Scotland	21-16	*PG:* Richards (6) *DG:* Hogg
13 Sept	H	Stewart's-Melville	43-0	*T:* Amos, Hogg, Hynd, Richards, D H A Scott, Turnbull, Yule *C:* Richards (4)
16 Sept	A	Kelso	8-16	*T:* Richards *PG:* Richards
23 Sept	H	Dundee HSFP	17-25	*T:* K Armstrong *PG:* Richards (3) *DG:* Hogg
30 Sept	A	Selkirk	33-13	*T:* C J Brown (3) *C:* Richards (3) *PG:* Richards (4)
7 Oct	H	Currie	32-16	*T:* Amos (2), G Armstrong *C:* Richards *PG:* Richards (5)
14 Oct	A	GHK	26-30	*T:* K Armstrong, Hemming, Renwick *C:* Richards *PG:* Richards (3)
21 Oct	H	West of Scotland	11-7	*T:* Hynd *PG:* Richards (2)
28 Oct	A	Stewart's-Melville	12-20	*PG:* Richards (4)
4 Nov	H	Kelso	23-11	*T:* G Armstrong (2), Liddle *C:* Richards *PG:* Richards (2)
11 Nov	A	Dundee HSFP	17-16	*T:* C Laidlaw, pen try *C:* Richards (2) *PG:* Richards
19 Nov	H	Selkirk	19-3	*T:* G Armstrong, C J Brown *PG:* Richards (3)
25 Nov	A	Currie	31-7	*T:* Barrie, C J Brown (2), Kerr *C:* Amos (4) *PG:* Amos

Kelso

Year of formation 1876
Ground Poynder Park, Bowmont Street, Kelso, Roxburghshire   Tel: Kelso (01573) 224300
and 223773
Colours Black and white
Most capped player J Jeffrey (Scotland) 40 caps
Captain 1995-96 S Bennet
SRU Tennents Championship 1995-96 Div 2 6th   **SRU Tennents Cup 1995-96** Lost
26-29 to Preston Lodge FP (4th round)

League Record 1995-96

Date	Venue	Opponents	Result	Scorers
2 Sept	A	Currie	16-28	*T:* Bennet *C:* Aitchison *PG:* Aitchison (3)
9 Sept	H	Dundee HSFP	9-20	*PG:* Aitchison (3)
13 Sept	A	Selkirk	7-15	*T:* Ross *C:* Aitchison
16 Sept	H	Jedforest	16-8	*T:* Lang *C:* Aitchison *PG:* Aitchison (3)
23 Sept	A	GHK	5-35	*T:* Pearson
30 Sept	H	West of Scotland	17-32	*T:* Robertson *PG:* Aitchison (4)
7 Oct	A	Stewart's-Melville	33-17	*T:* Aitchison, Mannion, Roxburgh *C:* Aitchison (3) *PG:* Aitchison (4)
14 Oct	H	Currie	36-17	*T:* Baird, Mannion, Tait *C:* Aitchison (3) *PG:* Aitchison (5)
21 Oct	A	Dundee HSFP	23-13	*T:* Fairley, Jeffrey, Mead *C:* Aitchison *PG:* Aitchison (2)
28 Oct	H	Selkirk	30-11	*T:* Bennet, Ross, Roxburgh (2) *C:* Aitchison (2) *PG:* Aitchison (2)
4 Nov	A	Jedforest	11-23	*T:* J Thomson *PG:* Aitchison (2)
11 Nov	H	GHK	13-16	*T:* G Laing *C:* Aitchison *PG:* Aitchison (2)
19 Nov	A	West of Scotland	19-35	*T:* Rowley, Tait, J Thomson *C:* Aitchison (2)
25 Nov	H	Stewart's-Melville	40-0	*T:* Bennet, Jeffrey, Roxburgh (2), A Stewart *C:* Aitchison (3) *PG:* Aitchison (3)

Kirkcaldy

Year of formation 1873
Ground Beveridge Park, Balwearie Road, Kirkcaldy   Tel: Kirkcaldy (01592) 263470
Colours Royal blue
Most capped player D D Howie (Scotland) & R Howie (Scotland) 9 caps
Captain 1995-96 J W Thomson
SRU Tennents Championship 1995-96 Div 3 3rd   **SRU Tennents Cup 1995-96** Lost
12-18 to Heriot's FP (4th round)

League Record 1995-96

Date	Venue	Opponents	Result	Scorers
2 Sept	A	Grangemouth	9-3	*PG:* J R Mitchell (3)
9 Sept	H	Glasgow Acads	15-13	*PG:* J R Mitchell (5)
13 Sept	A	Corstorphine	35-18	*T:* J R Mitchell (2), Murray, Renton *C:* J R Mitchell (3) *PG:* J R Mitchell (2) *DG:* Ferguson
16 Sept	H	Preston Lodge FP	28-12	*T:* Lang, J R Mitchell, Renton (2) *C:* J R Mitchell *PG:* J R Mitchell (2)
23 Sept	A	Biggar	12-15	*PG:* J R Mitchell (4)
30 Sept	H	Peebles	21-10	*T:* Imrie, J R Mitchell *C:* J R Mitchell *PG:* J R Mitchell (3)
7 Oct	A	Musselburgh	18-21	*T:* J R Mitchell, Renton *C:* J R Mitchell *PG:* J R Mitchell (2)
14 Oct	H	Grangemouth	20-10	*T:* R R Dewar, Renton *C:* J R Mitchell (2) *PG:* J R Mitchell (2)

21 Oct	A	Glasgow Acads	8-22	*T:* Murray *PG:* J R Mitchell
28 Oct	H	Corstorphine	47-10	*T:* Brocklebank, Carruthers, R R Dewar, Ferguson (2), J R Mitchell (2) *C:* J R Mitchell (3) *PG:* J R Mitchell (2)
4 Nov	A	Preston Lodge FP	27-17	*T:* Macdonald (2), J R Mitchell *PG:* J R Mitchell (4)
11 Nov	H	Biggar	21-10	*T:* Hannah (2) *C:* J R Mitchell *PG:* J R Mitchell (3)
19 Nov	A	Peebles	5-9	*T:* J R Mitchell
25 Nov	H	Musselburgh	50-12	*T:* Ferguson, J R Mitchell (3), R Mitchell (2), Thomson *C:* J R Mitchell (6) *PG:* J R Mitchell

Melrose

Year of formation 1877
Ground The Greenyards, Melrose, Roxburghshire TD6 9SA   Tel: Melrose (0189682) 2993 (office); 2559 (clubrooms)
Colours Yellow and black hoops
Most capped player K W Robertson (Scotland) 44 caps
Captain 1995-96 B W Redpath
SRU Tennents Championship 1995-96 Div 1 *Winners* – **SRU Tennents Cup 1995-96** Lost 15-28 to Hawick (semi-final)

League Record 1995-96

Date	Venue	Opponents	Result	Scorers
2 Sept	A	Heriot's FP	17-10	*T:* Chalmers, Parker, A G Shiel *C:* Chalmers
9 Sept	H	Boroughmuir	9-16	*PG:* Parker (3)
13 Sept	H	Hawick	31-3	*T:* Broughton, Chalmers, Parker *C:* Chalmers (2) *PG:* Chalmers (4)
16 Sept	A	Watsonians	41-16	*T:* Broughton, R R Brown, Shepherd, Turnbull *C:* Chalmers (3) *PG:* Chalmers (4) *DG:* Chalmers
23 Sept	H	Edinburgh Acads	22-3	*T:* Browne (2), Feaunati, Parker *C:* Chalmers
30 Sept	A	Gala	29-12	*T:* Parker, B W Redpath *C:* Chalmers (2) *PG:* Chalmers (5)
7 Oct	H	Stirling County	26-27	*T:* Parker, Shepherd, Turnbull *C:* Parker *PG:* Chalmers, Parker (2)
14 Oct	H	Heriot's FP	38-10	*T:* Broughton, Feaunati, Purves (2), Shiel, Turnbull *C:* Parker (4)
21 Oct	A	Boroughmuir	15-31	*PG:* Parker (5)
28 Oct	A	Hawick	9-10	*PG:* Parker (3)
4 Nov	H	Watsonians	25-20	*T:* Bain, R R Brown, Chalmers *C:* Parker (2) *PG:* Parker (2)
11 Nov	A	Edinburgh Acads	18-15	*T:* Brotherstone, B W Redpath *C:* Chalmers *PG:* Chalmers, Parker
25 Nov	A	Stirling County	15-15	*T:* Chalmers, Joiner *C:* Parker *PG:* Parker
2 Dec	H	Gala	31-11	*T:* Joiner (3), Parker *C:* Parker *PG:* Parker (3)

Musselburgh

Year of formation 1921
Ground Stoneyhill, Stoneyhill Farm Road, Musselburgh   Tel: 0131-665 3435
Colours Navy blue with narrow white hoop
Captain 1995-96 J Hawkins
SRU Tennents Championship 1995-96 Div 3 joint 4th   **SRU Tennents Cup 1995-96** Lost 17-20 to Preston Lodge FP (5th round)

League Record 1995-96

Date	Venue	Opponents	Result	Scorers
2 Sept	A	Glasgow Acads	9-39	*PG:* Livingstone (3)
9 Sept	H	Corstorphine	39-20	*T:* Easingwood, Horsburgh, Lindsay, Livingstone, McLeod *C:* Livingstone (4) *PG:* Livingstone (2)
13 Sept	A	Preston Lodge FP	15-26	*PG:* Walker (5)
16 Sept	H	Biggar	3-27	*PG:* Rowberry
23 Sept	A	Peebles	26-19	*T:* Bonthron, Pow, Young *C:* Lockhart *PG:* Livingstone, Lockhart (2)
30 Sept	A	Grangemouth	15-17	*T:* Bonthron, Livingstone *C:* Livingstone *PG:* Livingstone
7 Oct	H	Kirkcaldy	21-18	*T:* Campbell, Lindsay *C:* Lockhart *PG:* Lockhart (3)
14 Oct	H	Glasgow Acads	9-47	*PG:* Lockhart (3)
21 Oct	A	Corstorphine	14-10	*T:* McLeod *PG:* Livingstone (2), Lockhart
28 Oct	H	Preston Lodge FP	21-8	*T:* McLeod *C:* Livingstone *PG:* Lockhart *DG:* Livingstone (2)
4 Nov	A	Biggar	13-16	*T:* pen try *C:* Livingstone *PG:* Livingstone, Lockhart
11 Nov	H	Peebles	13-22	*T:* McLeod *C:* Lockhart *PG:* Lockhart (2)
19 Nov	H	Grangemouth	19-17	*T:* McLeod *C:* Lockhart *PG:* Lockhart (3) *DG:* Lockhart
25 Nov	A	Kirkcaldy	12-50	*T:* McLeod (2) *C:* Lockhart

Peebles

Year of formation 1923
Ground Gytes Leisure Centre, Peebles EH45 8NN   Tel: Peebles (01721) 720494 (clubrooms); 723688 (ground)
Colours Red and white hoops
Captain 1995-96 N McIver
SRU Tennents Championship 1995-96 Div 3 joint 4th   **SRU Tennents Cup 1995-96** Lost 19-30 to Duns (3rd round)

League Record 1995-96

Date	Venue	Opponents	Result	Scorers
2 Sept	A	Corstorphine	11-9	*T:* M Smith *PG:* R Wilson (2)
9 Sept	H	Preston Lodge FP	9-15	*PG:* Bell (3)
13 Sept	A	Biggar	12-13	*PG:* Bell (4)
16 Sept	H	Grangemouth	16-8	*T:* Jeffrey *C:* Bell *PG:* Bell (3)
23 Sept	H	Musselburgh	19-26	*T:* Kerr *C:* Bell *PG:* Bell (4)
30 Sept	A	Kirkcaldy	10-21	*T:* Fletcher *C:* Bell *PG:* Bell
7 Oct	H	Glasgow Acads	0-32	
14 Oct	H	Corstorphine	36-5	*T:* Gray, Napier, Nisbet, G Wilson, R Wilson, pen try *C:* Bell (2), R Wilson
21 Oct	A	Preston Lodge FP	12-13	*PG:* Bell (4)
28 Oct	H	Biggar	15-13	*PG:* Bell (5)
4 Nov	A	Grangemouth	17-27	*T:* Farmer, Raeburn *C:* Bell (2) *PG:* Bell
11 Nov	A	Musselburgh	22-13	*T:* Clapperton, Flannery, Gray *C:* Bell (2) *PG:* Bell
19 Nov	H	Kirkcaldy	9-5	*PG:* Bell (3)
25 Nov	A	Glasgow Acads	12-37	*T:* Greenshields, pen try *C:* Bell

Preston Lodge FP

Year of formation 1931
Ground Pennypit Park, Rope Walk, Prestonpans, East Lothian EH32 9BN   Tel: 01875 810309
Colours Black with maroon band edged in white
Captain 1995-96 G Henderson
SRU Tennents Championship 1995-96 Div 3 joint 4th   **SRU Tennents Cup 1995-96** Lost 11-26 to Hawick (quarter-final)

League Record 1995-96

Date	Venue	Opponents	Result	Scorers
2 Sept	H	Biggar	17-21	*T:* Payne *PG:* Gibbs (4)
9 Sept	A	Peebles	15-9	*T:* Fairweather, Gibbs *C:* Redpath *PG:* Redpath
13 Sept	H	Musselburgh	26-15	*T:* John, Payne (2) *C:* Melvin *PG:* Melvin, Redpath (2)
16 Sept	A	Kirkcaldy	12-28	*PG:* S Gilliland (3), G Stewart
23 Sept	H	Glasgow Acads	9-30	*PG:* Sandilands (3)
30 Sept	A	Corstorphine	23-12	*T:* D Allan, Clyde, Hastie *C:* D Allan *PG:* D Allan (2)
7 Oct	H	Grangemouth	29-9	*T:* Fairweather, Michie *C:* Gibb (2) *PG:* Gibb (4) *DG:* D Allan
14 Oct	A	Biggar	9-15	*PG:* Gibb (3)
21 Oct	H	Peebles	13-12	*T:* McMillan *C:* Gibb *PG:* Gibb (2)
28 Oct	A	Musselburgh	8-21	*T:* S Gilliland *PG:* Gibb
4 Nov	H	Kirkcaldy	17-27	*T:* Hastie, Suttie *C:* Gibb (2) *PG:* Gibb
11 Nov	A	Glasgow Acads	8-21	*T:* McDonald *PG:* Sandilands
19 Nov	H	Corstorphine	48-8	*T:* Fairweather (2), Grant, Hastie, McMillan, Payne (2), Sandilands *C:* Sandilands (4)
25 Nov	A	Grangemouth	11-18	*T:* Redpath *PG:* Sandilands (2)

Selkirk

Year of formation 1907
Ground Philiphaugh, Ettrickhaugh Road, Selkirk   Tel: Selkirk (01750) 20403
Colours Navy blue
Most capped player J Y Rutherford (Scotland) 42 caps
Captain 1995-96 K D McConnell
SRU Tennents Championship 1995-96 Div 2 7th – *relegated*   **SRU Tennents Cup 1995-96** Lost 10-21 to Gala (3rd round)

League Record 1995-96

Date	Venue	Opponents	Result	Scorers
2 Sept	H	West of Scotland	24-18	*T:* Hulme, Hunter, Jaffray, S A Nichol *C:* Brett, Hunter
9 Sept	A	Stewart's-Melville	18-20	*T:* Hulme, B Johnston *C:* Pow *PG:* Pow (2)
13 Sept	H	Kelso	15-7	*T:* Hunter, S A Nichol *C:* Pow *PG:* Pow
16 Sept	A	Dundee HSFP	0-19	
23 Sept	A	Currie	24-32	*T:* Gentleman, Jaffray, S A Nichol *C:* Pow (3) *PG:* Pow
30 Sept	H	Jedforest	13-33	*T:* McConnell *C:* Pow *PG:* Pow (2)
7 Oct	A	GHK	17-0	*T:* Gentleman *PG:* Pow (4)
14 Oct	A	West of Scotland	14-39	*T:* Brett, Jaffray *C:* Pow (2)
21 Oct	H	Stewart's-Melville	26-22	*T:* K G Johnston (2), Pow *C:* Pow *PG:* Pow (3)
28 Oct	A	Kelso	11-30	*T:* Hulme *PG:* Brett (2)

385

4 Nov	H	Dundee HSFP	21-16	*T:* Hunter, Pow *C:* Pow *PG:* Pow (2)
				DG: S A Nichol
11 Nov	H	Currie	9-12	*PG:* Pow (3)
19 Nov	A	Jedforest	3-19	*PG:* Hunter
25 Nov	H	GHK	20-40	*T:* Hulme *PG:* Pow (5)

Stewart's-Melville FP

Year of formation 1973 (on amalgamation of Daniel Stewart's College FP and Melville College FP)
Ground Inverleith, Ferry Road, Edinburgh EH5 2DW   Tel: 0131-552 1515
Colours Scarlet with broad black and narrow gold bands
Most capped player F Calder (Scotland) 38 caps
Captain 1995-96 L A B Hamilton
SRU Tennents Championship 1995-96 Div 2 8th – *relegated*   **SRU Tennents Cup 1995-96** Lost 20-25 to Heriot's FP (5th round)

League Record 1995-96

Date	Venue	Opponents	Result	Scorers
2 Sept	A	Dundee HSFP	17-14	*T:* Stirling *PG:* Thomson (4)
9 Sept	H	Selkirk	20-18	*T:* Bull (2), Thomson *C:* Thomson
				PG: Thomson
13 Sept	A	Jedforest	0-43	
16 Sept	H	GHK	5-93	*T:* Stirling
23 Sept	A	West of Scotland	14-24	*T:* Conlin *PG:* Stirling (3)
30 Sept	A	Currie	9-33	*PG:* Stirling (3)
7 Oct	H	Kelso	17-33	*T:* Tweedie (2) *C:* Stirling (2) *PG:* Stirling
14 Oct	H	Dundee HSFP	23-32	*T:* Scott, Wyllie *C:* Stirling (2) *PG:* Stirling (3)
21 Oct	A	Selkirk	22-26	*T:* Penny, Wyllie *PG:* Stirling (4)
28 Oct	H	Jedforest	20-12	*T:* Gallagher, Stirling, Tweedie *C:* Stirling
				PG: Stirling
4 Nov	A	GHK	23-49	*T:* Stirling, Tweedie (2) *C:* Stirling
				PG: Stirling (2)
11 Nov	H	West of Scotland	11-25	*T:* Penny *PG:* Stirling (2)
19 Nov	H	Currie	12-48	*T:* Penny, Rennie *C:* G Pollock
25 Nov	A	Kelso	0-40	

Stirling County

Year of formation 1904
Ground Bridgehaugh, Causewayhead Road, Stirling   Tel: Stirling (01786) 474827
Colours Red, white and black
Most capped player K M Logan (Scotland) 22 caps
Captain 1995-96 K D McKenzie
SRU Tennents Championship 1995-96 Div 1 2nd (beaten by Melrose on points difference)
SRU Tennents Cup 1995-96 Lost to Dundee HSFP 3-5 (4th round)

League Record 1995-96

Date	Venue	Opponents	Result	Scorers
2 Sept	H	Hawick	9-12	*PG:* M McKenzie *DG:* M McKenzie (2)
9 Sept	A	Watsonians	16-29	*T:* Fraser *C:* M McKenzie
				PG: M McKenzie (3)
13 Sept	H	Edinburgh Acads	17-6	*T:* Fraser *PG:* M McKenzie (3)
				DG: M McKenzie
16 Sept	A	Gala	22-28	*T:* Norval *C:* M McKenzie
				PG: M McKenzie (4) *DG:* M McKenzie
23 Sept	A	Boroughmuir	16-10	*T:* Jardine *C:* M McKenzie
				PG: M McKenzie (3)

30 Sept	H	Heriot's FP	38-6	*T:* MacRobert, Sangster, Turner *C:* M McKenzie *PG:* M McKenzie (6) *DG:* M McKenzie
7 Oct	A	Melrose	27-26	*T:* Flockhart, Logan (2), pen try *C:* M McKenzie (2) *PG:* M McKenzie
14 Oct	A	Hawick	15-23	*PG:* M McKenzie (5)
21 Oct	H	Watsonians	17-13	*T:* Hamilton *PG:* M McKenzie (4)
28 Oct	A	Edinburgh Acads	16-13	*T:* Flockhart, MacRobert *PG:* M McKenzie (2)
4 Nov	H	Gala	45-6	*T:* Elliot, Jardine (2), Logan, McGrandles, MacRobert (2) *C:* M McKenzie (2) *PG:* M McKenzie (2)
25 Nov	H	Melrose	15-15	*T:* Flockhart, Jardine *C:* M McKenzie *PG:* M McKenzie
2 Dec	H	Boroughmuir	33-14	*T:* Elliot, Logan (2), MacRobert *C:* M McKenzie (2) *PG:* M McKenzie (2) *DG:* M McKenzie
16 Dec	A	Heriot's FP	34-14	*T:* Flockhart, Jardine, K D McKenzie, M McKenzie *C:* M McKenzie (4) *PG:* M McKenzie (2)

Watsonians

Year of formation 1875
Ground Myreside, Myreside Road, Edinburgh EH10 5DB   Tel: 0131-447 5200
Colours Maroon and white hoops
Most capped player A G Hastings (Scotland) & S Hastings (Scotland) 61 caps
Captain 1995-96 F M Henderson
SRU Tennents Championship 1995-96 Div 1 3rd   **SRU Tennents Cup 1995-96** Lost to
Hawick 15-17 (final)

League Record 1995-96

Date	Venue	Opponents	Result	Scorers
2 Sept	A	Gala	37-6	*T:* Farland, Hannah, S Hastings, MacDonald *C:* Hodge (4) *PG:* Hodge (2) *DG:* Hodge
9 Sept	H	Stirling County	29-16	*T:* Garry, S Hastings *C:* Hodge (2) *PG:* Hodge (5)
13 Sept	A	Heriot's FP	43-0	*T:* Burnett, Garry, Henderson (2), Hodge *C:* Hodge (3) *PG:* Hodge (4)
16 Sept	H	Melrose	16-41	*T:* Weston *C:* Hodge *PG:* Hodge (3)
23 Sept	A	Hawick	33-17	*T:* Hannah, Henderson, Kerr, Smith, Weston *C:* Hodge *PG:* Hodge *DG:* Hodge
30 Sept	A	Boroughmuir	21-21	*T:* Hodge, Weston *C:* Hodge *PG:* Hodge (3)
7 Oct	H	Edinburgh Acads	23-31	*T:* Kerr (2), Te Whaiti *C:* A G Hastings *PG:* A G Hastings (2)
14 Oct	H	Gala	29-17	*T:* Hannah, Kerr *C:* A G Hastings (2) *PG:* A G Hastings (5)
21 Oct	A	Stirling County	13-17	*T:* Kerr *C:* A G Hastings *PG:* A G Hastings (2)
28 Oct	H	Heriot's FP	14-23	*T:* Henderson *PG:* A G Hastings (3)
4 Nov	A	Melrose	20-25	*T:* C Mather, Weston *C:* A G Hastings (2) *PG:* A G Hastings (2)
19 Nov	H	Boroughmuir	48-35	*T:* Garry, A G Hastings, S Hastings, Kerr, Sinclair *C:* A G Hastings (4) *PG:* A G Hastings (5)
25 Nov	A	Edinburgh Acads	28-15	*T:* Garry, A G Hastings, Stanaway *C:* A G Hastings (2) *PG:* A G Hastings (3)
2 Dec	H	Hawick	39-6	*T:* Farland, S Hastings, Henderson, Kerr, Kittle, Mayer *C:* A G Hastings (3) *PG:* A G Hastings

West of Scotland

Year of formation 1865
Ground Burnbrae, Glasgow Road, Milngavie, Glasgow G62 6HX   Tel: 0141-956 3116
Colours Red and yellow hoops
Most capped player A B Carmichael (Scotland) 50 caps
Captain 1995-96 F H Stott
SRU Tennents Championship 1995-96 Div 2 4th   **SRU Tennents Cup 1995-96** Lost to Melrose 12-89 (4th round)

League Record 1995-96

Date	Venue	Opponents	Result	Scorers
2 Sept	A	Selkirk	18-24	*T:* G C Bulloch, Riding *C:* Barrett *PG:* Barrett *DG:* Barrett
9 Sept	H	Jedforest	16-21	*T:* A J Bulloch *C:* Barrett *PG:* Barrett (3)
13 Sept	A	GHK	22-11	*T:* Barrett *C:* Barrett *PG:* Barrett (5)
16 Sept	H	Currie	16-33	*T:* Riding *C:* Barrett *PG:* Barrett (3)
23 Sept	H	Stewart's-Melville	24-14	*T:* Barrett, Lonergan, Williamson *PG:* Barrett, Williamson (2)
30 Sept	A	Kelso	32-19	*T:* Barrett, Lonergan (2), Shaw *C:* Barrett (2), Williamson *PG:* Barrett (2)
7 Oct	H	Dundee HSFP	21-12	*T:* G C Bulloch, Jamieson *C:* Barrett *PG:* Barrett (2) *DG:* Barrett
14 Oct	H	Selkirk	39-14	*T:* A J Bulloch, G C Bulloch, Little, McLeish, Riding, Williamson *C:* Barrett (3) *PG:* Barrett
21 Oct	A	Jedforest	7-11	*T:* Jamieson *C:* Wallace
28 Oct	H	GHK	9-10	*PG:* Barrett, Williamson (2)
4 Nov	A	Currie	14-25	*T:* A J Bulloch *PG:* Barrett (2) *DG:* Little
11 Nov	A	Stewart's-Melville	25-11	*T:* G C Bulloch (2), Riding *C:* D N Barrett (2) *PG:* D N Barrett (2)
19 Nov	H	Kelso	25-19	*T:* Barrett, J M Craig, Jamieson, Riding *C:* A C D Greenshields *PG:* Barrett
25 Nov	A	Dundee HSFP	0-36	

IRELAND
Ballymena

Year of formation 1922
Ground Eaton Park, Raceview Road, Ballymena   Tel: Ballymena 656746
Colours Black
Most capped player W J McBride (Ireland) 63 caps
Captain 1995-96 P Millar
Insurance Corporation League Div 1 7th   **First Trust Bank Ulster Senior Cup** Lost 13-18 to Dungannon (quarter-final)

League Record 1995-96

Date	Venue	Opponents	Result	Scorers
16 Sept	H	Old Wesley	13-13	*T:* Topping *C:* McAleese *PG:* Humphreys (2)
23 Sept	A	Old Belvedere	5-14	*T:* Peake
30 Sept	H	Instonians	8-30	*T:* Tweed *PG:* McAleese
14 Oct	A	Garryowen	21-28	*T:* Longwell, Smyth *C:* McAleese *PG:* McAleese (3)
21 Oct	H	St Mary's Coll	13-12	*T:* Topping *C:* McAleese *PG:* McAleese (2)
23 Mar	A	Shannon	12-25	*T:* Topping, McAleese *C:* McIlmoyle
30 Mar	H	Blackrock Coll	30-12	*T:* Longwell, Richie, McAleese, McCartney *C:* McIlmoyle (2) *PG:* McIlmoyle (2)

6 Apr	A	Cork Const	16-11	*T:* Tweed *C:* McAleese *PG:* McAleese *DG:* McAleese (2)
13 Apr	H	Young Munster	15-19	*PG:* McAleese (5)
20 Apr	A	Lansdowne	24-17	*T:* Wallace, Coulter, Rainey *C:* McAleese (3) *PG:* McAleese

Bective Rangers

Year of formation 1881
Ground Donnybrook, Dublin 4   Tel: Dublin 2693894
Colours Red, green and white hoops
Most capped player J L Farrell (Ireland) 29 caps
Captain 1995-96 P McNamara
Insurance Corporation League Div 2 4th   **Aluset Leinster Senior Cup** Lost 13-14 to Greystones (1st round)

League Record 1995-96

Date	Venue	Opponents	Result	Scorers
16 Sept	H	Greystones	22-12	*T:* Mortell *C:* Barrett *PG:* Barrett (3) *DG:* Barrett, McQuilkin
23 Sept	A	Clontarf	15-13	*PG:* Barrett (4) *DG:* Barrett
30 Sept	A	Dungannon	8-23	*T:* McNamara *PG:* Barrett
7 Oct	A	Old Crescent	9-20	*PG:* Barrett (3)
14 Oct	H	Dolphin	16-8	*T:* Dwyer *C:* Barrett *PG:* Barrett (2) *DG:* Barrett
21 Oct	A	Terenure Coll	9-16	*PG:* Barrett (3)
23 Mar	H	NIFC	17-6	*T:* Fitzgerald *PG:* Buckley (4)
6 Apr	H	Sunday's Well	21-24	*PG:* Buckley (5) *DG:* Buckley (2)
13 Apr	A	Wanderers	27-13	*T:* Poole, Dwyer *C:* Buckley *PG:* Buckley (5)
20 Apr	H	Malone	42-12	*T:* Bolger (2), Cusack, Purcell, Dwyer, Fitzgerald *C:* Buckley (3) *PG:* Buckley (2)

Blackrock College

Year of formation 1882
Ground Stradbrook Road, Blackrock, Dublin   Tel: Dublin 2805967
Colours Royal blue and white hoops
Most capped player J F Slattery (Ireland) 61 caps
Captain 1995-96 S Byrne
Insurance Corporation League Div 1 9th   **Aluset Leinster Senior Cup** Lost 8-11 to Wanderers (1st round)

League Record 1995-96

Date	Venue	Opponents	Result	Scorers
16 Sept	A	Young Munster	15-3	*PG:* A McGowan (4) *DG:* A McGowan
23 Sept	H	Lansdowne	29-23	*T:* Woods (2), Wallace, Guinan *C:* A McGowan (3) *PG:* A McGowan
30 Sept	A	Garryowen	22-23	*T:* Guinan *C:* A McGowan *PG:* A McGowan (5)
7 Oct	H	Cork Const	13-23	*T:* Oswald *C:* A McGowan *PG:* A McGowan (2)
14 Oct	A	Shannon	6-7	*PG:* A McGowan (2)
23 Mar	H	St Mary's Coll	7-11	*T:* pen try *C:* Harvey
30 Mar	A	Ballymena	12-30	*PG:* Harvey (4)
6 Apr	H	Old Wesley	6-39	*PG:* Hunt *DG:* Kearns
13 Apr	A	Old Belvedere	16-24	*T:* Rolland, Doyle *PG:* J McGowan (2)
20 Apr	H	Instonians	34-25	*T:* Rogers, O'Neill, Connolly, Rolland *C:* J McGowan *PG:* J McGowan (4)

Clontarf

Year of formation 1876
Ground Castle Avenue, Clontarf, Dublin   Tel: Dublin 8332621
Colours Royal blue and scarlet
Most capped player G J Morgan (Ireland) 19 caps
Captain 1995-96 T Hannigan
Insurance Corporation League Div 2 9th   **Aluset Leinster Senior Cup** Lost 18-31 to
Terenure College (quarter-final)

League Record 1995-96

Date	Venue	Opponents	Result	Scorers
16 Sept	A	Dungannon	6-35	*PG:* Roche (2)
23 Sept	H	Bective Rangers	13-15	*T:* Smith *C:* Roche *PG:* Roche (2)
30 Sept	A	Terenure Coll	3-0	*PG:* Woods
14 Oct	A	Greystones	19-21	*T:* Lawless *C:* Woods *PG:* Woods (4)
21 Oct	H	Wanderers	9-25	*PG:* Woods (3)
23 Mar	A	Sunday's Well	12-9	*PG:* Woods (4)
30 Mar	H	Dolphin	27-24	*T:* Woods, Lawless, Aherne, Kyne *C:* Woods (2) *PG:* Woods
6 Apr	A	Old Crescent	5-31	*T:* Fitzsimonds
13 Apr	H	Malone	18-33	*T:* Mullany, pen try *C:* Woods *PG:* Woods (2)
20 Apr	H	NIFC	18-19	*T:* Dunne, O'Brien, Aherne *PG:* Woods

Cork Constitution

Year of formation 1892
Ground Temple Hill, Ballintemple, Cork   Tel: Cork 292563
Colours White
Most capped player T J Kiernan (Ireland) 54 caps
Captain 1995-96 D O'Mahony
Insurance Corporation League Div 1 3rd   **Carling Munster Senior Cup** Lost 13-15 to
Shannon (final)

League Record 1995-96

Date	Venue	Opponents	Result	Scorers
23 Sept	H	Young Munster	17-14	*T:* K Murphy *PG:* Burke (4)
30 Sept	A	Lansdowne	20-13	*T:* Casey *PG:* Burke (5)
7 Oct	A	Blackrock Coll	23-13	*T:* Casey *PG:* Burke (6)
14 Oct	H	Instonians	21-10	*PG:* Burke (7)
21 Oct	A	Shannon	10-19	*T:* Donnelly *C:* Burke *PG:* Burke
23 Mar	H	Garryowen	11-23	*T:* O'Dowd *PG:* Burke (2)
6 Apr	H	Ballymena	11-16	*T:* Corkery *PG:* O'Brien (2)
13 Apr	A	Old Wesley	23-6	*T:* Dineen, Murray *C:* Burke (2) *PG:* Burke (2) *DG:* Burke
20 Apr	H	Old Belvedere	47-12	*T:* O'Callaghan (2), Byrne, O'Brien, O'Dowd, pen try *C:* Burke (4) *PG:* Burke (2) *DG:* Walsh
27 Apr	A	St Mary's Coll	25-23	*T:* Murray, O'Brien, O'Meara *C:* O'Mahony (2) *PG:* O'Mahony (2)

Dolphin

Year of formation 1902
Ground Musgrave Park, Cork   Tel: Cork 962435
Colours Navy blue, yellow and white
Most capped player M J Kiernan (Ireland) 43 caps

Captain 1995-96 B O'Neill
Insurance Corporation League Div 2 10th   **Carling Munster Senior Cup** Lost 16-23 to Sunday's Well (quarter-final)

League Record 1995-96

Date	Venue	Opponents	Result	Scorers
23 Sept	H	Old Crescent	0-25	
30 Sept	H	Greystones	12-25	*PG:* Keary (4)
7 Oct	H	Sunday's Well	20-44	*T:* Scott, Keogh, Keary *C:* Keary *PG:* Keary
14 Oct	A	Bective Rangers	8-16	*T:* Murray *PG:* C Mahony
21 Oct	H	Dungannon	7-10	*T:* Farrelly *C:* Keary
23 Mar	A	Malone	24-29	*T:* Keary, O'Mahony *C:* Keary *PG:* Keary (4)
30 Mar	A	Clontarf	24-27	*T:* Keary, O'Neill, Clarke, C Mahony *C:* Keary, O'Neill
6 Apr	H	NIFC	35-18	*T:* Farrelly (2), Taylor, O'Shea *C:* C Mahony (3) *PG:* C Mahony (2) *DG:* L Mahony
13 Apr	A	Terenure Coll	19-34	*T:* O'Donoghue, Walsh, Kingston *C:* C Mahony (2)
21 Apr	A	Wanderers	16-17	*T:* Mahony, O'Neill *PG:* O'Neill (2)

Dungannon

Year of formation 1873
Ground Stevenson Park, Dungannon   Tel: Dungannon 22387
Colours Blue and white hoops
Most capped player P S Johns (Ireland) 28 caps
Captain 1995-96 H McCaughey
Insurance Corporation League Div 2 2nd – *promoted*   **First Trust Bank Ulster Senior Cup** *Winners* – beat Malone 22-10 (final)

League Record 1995-96

Date	Venue	Opponents	Result	Scorers
16 Sept	H	Clontarf	35-6	*T:* Sandford, Johns, Blair, McGarry *C:* McGarry (3) *PG:* McGarry (3)
23 Sept	A	NIFC	36-12	*T:* Johns, Patterson, Gamble *C:* McGarry (3) *PG:* McGarry (5)
30 Sept	H	Bective Rangers	23-8	*T:* Davidson, Patterson *C:* McGarry (2) *PG:* McGarry (3)
7 Oct	A	Malone	25-24	*T:* Redpath *C:* McGarry *PG:* McGarry (5) *DG:* McGarry
14 Oct	H	Old Crescent	20-30	*T:* Assaf *PG:* McGarry (5)
21 Oct	A	Dolphin	10-7	*T:* McCaughey *C:* McGarry *PG:* McGarry
23 Mar	H	Terenure Coll	9-31	*PG:* Blair (3)
30 Mar	A	Sunday's Well	27-27	*T:* Dunne (2), Weir, Hastings *C:* Blair (2) *PG:* Blair
6 Apr	H	Wanderers	44-17	*T:* McCaughey (2), Assaf, Davidson, Stanford, Dunne *C:* Blair (4) *PG:* Blair (2)
13 Apr	A	Greystones	25-9	*T:* Blair (2), Hastings, Cowan *C:* Blair *PG:* Blair

Garryowen

Year of formation 1884
Ground Dooradoyle, Limerick   Tel: Limerick 303099
Colours Light blue with white five-pointed star
Most capped player B G M Wood (Ireland) 29 caps
Captain 1995-96 D O'Sullivan

Insurance Corporation League Div 1 2nd   **Carling Munster Senior Cup** Lost 16-17 to Young Munster (quarter-final)

League Record 1995-96

Date	Venue	Opponents	Result	Scorers
16 Sept	H	Instonians	23-17	*T:* Larkin, Wallace, O'Sullivan *C:* Everett *PG:* Everett, Keane
23 Sept	A	Shannon	3-9	*PG:* Smith
30 Sept	H	Blackrock Coll	23-22	*T:* Smith *PG:* Smith (5) *DG:* Keane
7 Oct	A	Old Belvedere	12-11	*T:* Wallace, O'Grady *C:* Smith
14 Oct	H	Ballymena	28-21	*T:* Spain *C:* Smith *PG:* Smith (5) *DG:* Everett (2)
21 Oct	A	Old Wesley	16-13	*T:* Smith *C:* Smith *PG:* Smith (3)
23 Mar	A	Cork Const	23-11	*T:* Larkin, Wallace *C:* Smith (2) *PG:* Smith (3)
6 Apr	A	Lansdowne	20-15	*T:* Coughlin, Wallace *C:* Smith (2) *PG:* Smith (2)
20 Apr	H	St Mary's Coll	11-9	*T:* Wallace *PG:* Smith (2)
27 Apr	H	Young Munster	12-37	*PG:* Smith (4)

Greystones

Year of formation 1937
Ground Dr J J Hickey Park, Delgany Road, Greystones, Co Wicklow   Tel: Dublin 2874640
Colours Green and white narrow hoops
Most capped player N Popplewell (Ireland) 39 caps
Captain 1995-96 D Rigney
Insurance Corporation League Div 2 5th   **Aluset Leinster Senior Cup** Lost 15-22 to Old Belvedere (quarter-final)

League Record 1995-96

Date	Venue	Opponents	Result	Scorers
16 Sept	A	Bective Rangers	12-22	*PG:* R Murphy (4)
23 Sept	H	Sunday's Well	11-22	*T:* McAree *PG:* Vance (2)
30 Sept	A	Dolphin	25-12	*T:* Dowling *C:* R Murphy *PG:* R Murphy (6)
7 Oct	A	NIFC	23-19	*T:* McLeane *PG:* R Murphy (4) *DG:* R Murphy, Dowling
14 Oct	H	Clontarf	21-19	*PG:* R Murphy (6) *DG:* R Murphy
23 Mar	A	Wanderers	22-9	*T:* Hogan *C:* R Murphy *PG:* R Murphy (5)
30 Mar	H	Old Crescent	12-12	*PG:* R Murphy (3) *DG:* R Murphy
6 Apr	A	Malone	19-16	*T:* L Murphy *C:* R Murphy *PG:* R Murphy (4)
13 Apr	H	Dungannon	9-25	*PG:* R Murphy (3)
20 Apr	H	Terenure Coll	10-17	*T:* Mullins *C:* R Murray *PG:* R Murphy

Instonians

Year of formation 1919
Ground Shane Park, Stockmans Lane, Belfast   Tel: Belfast 660629
Colours Purple, yellow and black
Most capped player K D Crossan (Ireland) 41 caps
Captain 1995-96 B Cornelius
Insurance Corporation League Div 1 11th   **First Trust Bank Ulster Senior Cup** Lost 7-15 to Malone (2nd round)

League Record 1995-96

Date	Venue	Opponents	Result	Scorers
16 Sept	A	Garryowen	17-23	*T:* Cornelius *PG:* Laing (4)
23 Sept	H	St Mary's Coll	16-34	*T:* Robson *C:* Laing *PG:* Laing (3)
30 Sept	A	Ballymena	30-8	*T:* Robson, Collins, McCloskey (2) *C:* Laing (2) *PG:* Laing (2)
7 Oct	H	Lansdowne	9-24	*PG:* Laing (3)
14 Oct	A	Cork Const	10-21	*T:* McCausland *C:* Laing *PG:* Laing
21 Oct	H	Young Munster	12-19	*PG:* Laing (4)
23 Mar	H	Old Wesley	3-12	*PG:* Laing
30 Mar	A	Old Belvedere	20-23	*T:* Parker, Adair, McCloskey *C:* Gartside *PG:* Gartside
13 Apr	H	Shannon	3-35	*PG:* Laing
20 Apr	A	Blackrock Coll	25-34	*T:* Adair, Irvine, Cornelius *C:* Gartside (2) *PG:* Gartside (2)

Lansdowne

Year of formation 1872
Ground Lansdowne Road, Dublin   Tel: Dublin 6689300
Colours Red, yellow and black
Most capped player M I Keane (Ireland) 51 caps
Captain 1995-96 B Glennon
Insurance Corporation League Div 1 6th   **Aluset Leinster Senior Cup** Lost 7-17 to Terenure College (final)

League Record 1995-96

Date	Venue	Opponents	Result	Scorers
16 Sept	H	Shannon	11-17	*T:* Glennon *PG:* Elwood (2)
23 Sept	A	Blackrock Coll	23-29	*T:* Hennessy, O'Sullivan *C:* Elwood (2) *PG:* Elwood (3)
30 Sept	H	Cork Const	13-20	*T:* Hennessy *C:* Elwood *PG:* Elwood (2)
7 Oct	A	Instonians	24-9	*T:* Hennessy (2) *C:* Elwood *PG:* Elwood (4)
15 Oct	A	Old Wesley	33-18	*T:* O'Mahony, Sharkey, Glennon, Kearin *C:* Elwood (2) *PG:* Elwood (3)
21 Oct	H	Old Belvedere	22-14	*T:* Elwood *C:* Elwood *PG:* Elwood (5)
23 Mar	A	Young Munster	14-13	*T:* Farrell *PG:* Aherne (3)
6 Apr	H	Garryowen	15-20	*T:* Corrigan, McEntee *C:* Aherne *PG:* Aherne
13 Apr	A	St Mary's Coll	8-8	*T:* Geraghty *PG:* Aherne
20 Apr	H	Ballymena	17-24	*T:* Kearin, Corrigan, O'Mahony *C:* Aherne

Malone

Year of formation 1892
Ground Gibson Park, Gibson Park Avenue, Belfast   Tel: Belfast 451312
Colours White
Most capped player W D McBride (Ireland) 25 caps
Captain 1995-96 B Harbison
Insurance Corporation League Div 2 7th   **First Trust Bank Ulster Senior Cup** Lost 10-22 to Dungannon (final)

League Record 1995-96

Date	Venue	Opponents	Result	Scorers
16 Sept	H	NIFC	18-16	*T:* Wilkinson, Mackie *C:* Wilkinson *PG:* Wilkinson (2)

23 Sept	A	Terenure Coll	6-17	*PG:* Pattison (2)
30 Sept	H	Sunday's Well	23-14	*T:* Field (2), McBride *C:* Wilkinson *PG:* Wilkinson (2)
7 Oct	H	Dungannon	24-25	*T:* Burns, Wilkinson, Porter *C:* Wilkinson (3) *PG:* Wilkinson
21 Oct	A	Old Crescent	20-25	*T:* Wilkinson, McBride *C:* Wilkinson (2) *PG:* Wilkinson (2)
23 Mar	H	Dolphin	29-24	*T:* Carroll, Wilkinson *C:* Wilkinson (2) *PG:* Wilkinson (4) *DG:* Wilkinson
6 Apr	H	Greystones	16-19	*T:* Carroll, Harbison *PG:* Wilkinson (2)
13 Apr	A	Clontarf	33-18	*T:* Carroll (2), Potter, Ellis *C:* Wilkinson (2) *PG:* Wilkinson (3)
20 Apr	A	Bective Rangers	12-42	*T:* Field, Potter *C:* Cullen
27 Apr	A	Wanderers	24-20	*T:* Wilkinson, Willis, Hewitt, McBride *C:* Wilkinson (2)

NIFC

Year of formation 1859
Ground Shaftesbury Avenue, Ormeau Road, Belfast   Tel: Belfast 321096
Colours Red, black and blue
Most capped player C M H Gibson (Ireland) 69 caps
Captain 1995-96 N Doak
Insurance Corporation League Div 2 11th   **First Trust Bank Ulster Senior Cup** Lost 9-15 to Bangor (1st round)

League Record 1995-96

Date	Venue	Opponents	Result	Scorers
16 Sept	A	Malone	16-18	*T:* Wilson *C:* Wilson *PG:* Wilson (3)
23 Sept	H	Dungannon	12-36	*T:* Park (2) *C:* Wilson
7 Oct	H	Greystones	19-23	*T:* Wilson *C:* Wilson *PG:* Wilson (3) *DG:* Wilson
14 Oct	A	Wanderers	13-26	*T:* Higginson *C:* Wilson *PG:* Wilson (2)
21 Oct	H	Sunday's Well	25-39	*T:* Park *C:* Lamont *PG:* Lamont (6)
23 Mar	A	Bective Rangers	6-17	*PG:* Doak (2)
30 Mar	H	Terenure Coll	22-34	*T:* Megarry, Parke, Wilson *C:* Doak (2) *PG:* Doak
6 Apr	A	Dolphin	18-35	*T:* Logan (2) *C:* Doak *PG:* Doak (2)
13 Apr	H	Old Crescent	7-53	*T:* Wilson *C:* Doak
20 Apr	A	Clontarf	19-18	*T:* Logan, Megarry *PG:* Doak (3)

Old Belvedere

Year of formation 1930
Ground Anglesea Road, Ballsbridge, Dublin   Tel: Dublin 6689748
Colours Black and white hoops
Most capped player N P J Francis (Ireland) 36 caps
Captain 1995-96 M Feely
Insurance Corporation League Div 1 10th   **Aluset Leinster Senior Cup** Lost 21-32 to Lansdowne (semi-final)

League Record 1995-96

Date	Venue	Opponents	Result	Scorers
16 Sept	A	St Mary's Coll	12-24	*PG:* Murphy (4)
23 Sept	H	Ballymena	14-5	*T:* Gavin *PG:* Murphy (2), Philpott
30 Sept	A	Old Wesley	11-19	*T:* Mark-McCarthy *PG:* Murphy *DG:* Philpott
7 Oct	H	Garryowen	11-12	*T:* Maloney *PG:* Murphy (2)

14 Oct	H	Young Munster	14-16	*T:* Norse *PG:* Murphy (2) *DG:* Philpott
21 Oct	A	Lansdowne	14-22	*T:* Spicer *PG:* Murphy (3)
30 Mar	H	Instonians	23-20	*T:* O'Reilly (2), Spicer *C:* Murphy *PG:* Murphy *DG:* McKenna
6 Apr	A	Shannon	0-8	
13 Apr	H	Blackrock Coll	24-16	*T:* Francis, Spicer, McKenna *C:* Murphy (3) *PG:* Murphy
20 Apr	A	Cork Const	12-47	*T:* Johnston, McDonnell *C:* Murphy

Old Crescent

Year of formation 1947
Ground Rosbrien, Limerick   Tel: Limerick 228083
Colours Navy blue and white stripes
Most capped player P Lane (Ireland) 1 cap
Captain 1995-96 D Reddan
Insurance Corporation League Div 2 *Winners – promoted*   **Carling Munster Senior Cup**
Lost 19-30 to Cork Constitution (quarter-final)

League Record 1995-96

Date	Venue	Opponents	Result	Scorers
16 Sept	H	Terenure Coll	13-6	*T:* Doyle *C:* Begley *PG:* Begley *DG:* Tuohy
23 Sept	A	Dolphin	25-0	*T:* Madigan (2), O'Sullivan *C:* Begley (2) *PG:* Begley *DG:* Tuohy
30 Sept	H	Wanderers	18-15	*PG:* Begley (6)
7 Oct	H	Bective Rangers	20-9	*T:* O'Sullivan, Toland *C:* Begley (2) *PG:* Begley *DG:* Tuohy
14 Oct	A	Dungannon	30-20	*T:* McLoughlin, Madigan *C:* Begley *PG:* Begley (5) *DG:* Tuohy
21 Oct	H	Malone	25-20	*T:* McDonagh *C:* Begley *PG:* Begley (4) *DG:* Tuohy (2)
30 Mar	A	Greystones	12-12	*PG:* Begley (3) *DG:* Tuohy
6 Apr	H	Clontarf	31-5	*T:* Doyle (2), Madigan, O'Malley *C:* Begley (4) *PG:* Begley
13 Apr	A	NIFC	53-7	*T:* Madigan (3), Kirby, McDonagh, Meenan, O'Meara, Forde *C:* Begley (3), Tuohy (2) *PG:* Begley
21 Apr	A	Sunday's Well	19-9	*T:* O'Sullivan (2) *PG:* Tuohy (3)

Old Wesley

Year of formation 1891
Ground Donnybrook, Dublin   Tel: Dublin 6609893
Colours White with blue and red band
Most capped player P A Orr (Ireland) 58 caps
Captain 1995-96 G Duffy
Insurance Corporation League Div 1 8th   **Aluset Leinster Senior Cup** Lost 20-21 to
Clontarf (1st round)

League Record 1995-96

Date	Venue	Opponents	Result	Scorers
16 Sept	A	Ballymena	13-13	*T:* Wolfe *C:* Farren *PG:* Farren (2)
30 Sept	H	Old Belvedere	19-11	*T:* Bursey *C:* Farren *PG:* Farren (4)
7 Oct	A	St Mary's Coll	9-12	*PG:* Hawe (3)
15 Oct	H	Lansdowne	18-33	*T:* O'Sullivan, Bursey *C:* Hawe *PG:* Hawe *DG:* Hawe
21 Oct	H	Garryowen	13-16	*T:* Wilson *C:* Wilson *PG:* Wilson *DG:* Wilson

23 Mar	A	Instonians	12-3	*PG:* Farren (4)
30 Mar	H	Shannon	12-22	*PG:* Farren (3) *DG:* Wilson
6 Apr	A	Blackrock Coll	39-6	*T:* Johnston (2), Wilson *C:* Farren (3)
				PG: Farren (6)
13 Apr	H	Cork Const	6-23	*PG:* Farren (2)
20 Apr	A	Young Munster	15-25	*PG:* Hawe (4) *DG:* Hawe

St Mary's College

Year of formation 1900
Ground Templeville Road, Templeogue, Dublin   Tel: Dublin 4900440
Colours Royal blue with white five-pointed star
Most capped player P M Dean (Ireland) 32 caps
Captain 1995-96 B Browne
Insurance Corporation League Div 1 5th   **Aluset Leinster Senior Cup** Lost 13-26 to
Lansdowne (1st round)

League Record 1995-96

Date	Venue	Opponents	Result	Scorers
16 Sept	H	Old Belvedere	24-12	*T:* Costello, Potts *C:* Campion
				PG: Campion (2), Barry *DG:* Campion
23 Sept	A	Instonians	34-16	*T:* O'Kelly, Halpin, Lynch, Lavin *C:* Barry (4)
				PG: Barry (2)
30 Sept	H	Shannon	9-6	*PG:* Barry *DG:* Campion (2)
7 Oct	H	Old Wesley	12-9	*PG:* Barry (3), Campion
21 Oct	A	Ballymena	12-13	*PG:* Barry (3) *DG:* Campion
23 Mar	A	Blackrock Coll	11-7	*T:* Hickie *PG:* Campion (2)
6 Apr	A	Young Munster	5-12	*T:* O'Kelly
14 Apr	H	Lansdowne	8-8	*T:* Hickie *PG:* Campion
20 Apr	A	Garryowen	9-11	*PG:* Quigley (3)
27 Apr	H	Cork Const	23-25	*T:* Gillen, Hickie, O'Kelly *C:* Quigley
				PG: Quigley (2)

Shannon

Year of formation 1884
Ground Thomond Park, Limerick   Tel: Limerick 452350
Colours Black and blue hoops
Most capped player G A J McLoughlin (Ireland) 18 caps
Captain 1995-96 P Murray
Insurance Corporation League Div 1 *Winners*   **Carling Munster Senior Cup** *Winners* –
beat Cork Constitution 15-13 (final)

League Record 1995-96

Date	Venue	Opponents	Result	Scorers
16 Sept	A	Lansdowne	17-11	*T:* Foley *PG:* Thompson (3) *DG:* Murray
23 Sept	H	Garryowen	9-3	*PG:* Thompson *DG:* Murray
30 Sept	A	St Mary's Coll	6-9	*PG:* Thompson (2)
7 Oct	A	Young Munster	8-12	*T:* O'Shea *PG:* Thompson
14 Oct	H	Blackrock Coll	7-6	*T:* Halvey *C:* Thompson
21 Oct	H	Cork Const	19-10	*T:* Maher *C:* Murray *PG:* Murray,
				Thompson (2) *DG:* Murray
23 Mar	H	Ballymena	25-12	*T:* Foley, O'Shea, Thompson *C:* Murray (2)
				PG: Murray (2)
30 Mar	A	Old Wesley	22-12	*T:* Foley, Maher *PG:* Murray (4)
6 Apr	H	Old Belvedere	8-0	*T:* O'Shea *PG:* Murray
13 Apr	A	Instonians	35-3	*T:* Thompson, O'Shea, McGrath, McDermott
				C: Thompson (3) *PG:* Thompson (3)

Sunday's Well

Year of formation 1923
Ground Musgrave Park, Tramore Road, Cork   Tel: Cork 965735
Colours Red, green and white hoops
Most capped player J C Walsh (Ireland) 26 caps
Captain 1995-96 J Curtiss
Insurance Corporation League Div 2 6th   **Carling Munster Senior Cup** Lost 18-22 to Cork Constitution (semi-final)

League Record 1995-96

Date	Venue	Opponents	Result	Scorers
16 Sept	H	Wanderers	16-17	*T:* McCahill *C:* Crotty *PG:* Crotty (3)
23 Sept	A	Greystones	22-11	*T:* Lacey (2), Whelhan *C:* Hogan-O'Connell (2) *PG:* Hogan-O'Connell
30 Sept	A	Malone	14-23	*T:* Lacey (2) *C:* Crotty (2)
7 Oct	H	Dolphin	44-20	*T:* Crotty, Lacey, O'Neill, McCahill, Burke *C:* Hogan-O'Connell (5) *PG:* Hogan-O'Connell (2) *DG:* Burke
14 Oct	H	Terenure Coll	19-19	*T:* Curtiss *C:* Hogan-O'Connell *PG:* Hogan-O'Connell (3) *DG:* Crotty
21 Oct	A	NIFC	39-25	*T:* O'Neill (2), McCahill, Burke, Lacey, O'Connell *C:* Hogan-O'Connell (3) *PG:* Hogan-O'Connell
23 Mar	H	Clontarf	9-12	*PG:* Burke (3)
30 Mar	H	Dungannon	27-27	*T:* Lacey, O'Neill, Whelan *C:* Burke (3) *PG:* Burke (2)
6 Apr	A	Bective Rangers	24-21	*T:* Murray, Curtiss, Tuohy, O'Neill *C:* Murray (2)
21 Apr	H	Old Crescent	9-19	*PG:* Daly (3)

Terenure College

Year of formation 1940
Ground Lakelands Park, Greenlea, Terenure, Dublin   Tel: Dublin 4907572
Colours Purple, black and white
Most capped player M L Hipwell (Ireland) 12 caps
Captain 1995-96 P Bruce
Insurance Corporation League Div 2 3rd – *promoted*   **Aluset Leinster Senior Cup** *Winners* – beat Lansdowne 17-7 (final)

League Record 1995-96

Date	Venue	Opponents	Result	Scorers
16 Sept	A	Old Crescent	6-13	*PG:* Walsh *DG:* Muldowney
23 Sept	H	Malone	17-6	*T:* Clarke *PG:* Walsh (4)
30 Sept	H	Clontarf	0-3	
7 Oct	H	Wanderers	17-8	*T:* James *PG:* Walsh (2), O'Farrell *DG:* O'Farrell
14 Oct	A	Sunday's Well	19-19	*T:* Corkery, Walsh *PG:* O'Farrell (2) *DG:* O'Farrell
21 Oct	H	Bective Rangers	16-9	*T:* Hogan *C:* O'Farrell *PG:* O'Farrell (3)
23 Mar	A	Dungannon	31-9	*T:* James, Coleman, Hogan, Hennebry *C:* Dempsey (4) *PG:* Dempsey
30 Mar	A	NIFC	34-22	*T:* Walsh, Bruce, O'Brien, Hennebry *C:* Dempsey *PG:* Walsh (3) *DG:* Hennebry
13 Apr	H	Dolphin	34-19	*T:* Walsh, Clarke, Muldowney *C:* Walsh (2) *PG:* Walsh (5)
20 Apr	A	Greystones	17-10	*T:* Coleman *PG:* Walsh (2), McCarthy *DG:* Hennebry

Wanderers

Year of formation 1870
Ground Lansdowne Road, Dublin   Tel: Dublin 6689277
Colours Blue, black and white
Most capped player J R Kavanagh (Ireland) 35 caps
Captain 1995-96 M Leahy
Insurance Corporation League Div 2 8th **Aluset Leinster Senior Cup** Lost 5-22 to Lansdowne (quarter-final)

League Record 1995-96

Date	Venue	Opponents	Result	Scorers
16 Sept	A	Sunday's Well	17-16	*T:* Leahy *PG:* Wyse (4)
30 Sept	A	Old Crescent	15-18	*PG:* Wyse (5)
7 Oct	A	Terenure Coll	8-17	*T:* Leahy *PG:* Wyse
14 Oct	H	NIFC	26-13	*T:* Leahy, Culliton *C:* Wyse (2) *PG:* Wyse (3) *DG:* Wyse
21 Oct	A	Clontarf	25-9	*T:* Mahon, Culliton, McEntee *C:* Wyse (2) *PG:* Wyse (2)
23 Mar	H	Greystones	9-22	*PG:* Wyse (3)
6 Apr	A	Dungannon	17-44	*T:* O'Riordan, Culliton, Mahon *C:* Wyse
13 Apr	H	Bective Rangers	13-27	*T:* O'Callaghan *C:* Wyse *PG:* Wyse (2)
21 Apr	H	Dolphin	17-16	*T:* Leahy *C:* Wyse (2) *PG:* Wyse
27 Apr	H	Malone	20-24	*T:* McEntee, Wyse *C:* Wyse (2) *PG:* Wyse (2)

Young Munster

Year of formation 1895
Ground Tom Clifford Park, Greenfields, Limerick   Tel: Limerick 228433
Colours Black and amber hoops
Most capped player P M Clohessy (Ireland) 16 caps
Captain 1995-96 J Fitzgerald
Insurance Corporation League Div 1 4th   **Carling Munster Senior Cup** Lost 10-11 to Shannon (semi-final)

League Record 1995-96

Date	Venue	Opponents	Result	Scorers
16 Sept	H	Blackrock Coll	3-15	*PG:* O'Halloran
23 Sept	A	Cork Const	14-17	*T:* Clohessy *PG:* Lynch (2) *DG:* O'Halloran
7 Oct	H	Shannon	12-8	*PG:* O'Halloran (3) *DG:* O'Halloran
14 Oct	A	Old Belvedere	16-14	*T:* McNamara *C:* O'Halloran *PG:* O'Halloran (2) *DG:* O'Halloran
21 Oct	A	Instonians	19-12	*T:* McNamara *C:* O'Halloran *PG:* O'Halloran (3) *DG:* O'Halloran
23 Mar	H	Lansdowne	13-14	*T:* Boland, McNamara *PG:* O'Halloran
6 Apr	H	St Mary's Coll	12-5	*PG:* O'Halloran (3), Lynch
13 Apr	A	Ballymena	19-15	*T:* Earls *C:* O'Halloran *PG:* O'Halloran (4)
20 Apr	H	Old Wesley	25-15	*T:* Edwards, Boland, McNamara *C:* O'Halloran (2) *PG:* O'Halloran (2)
27 Apr	A	Garryowen	37-12	*T:* D Clohessy, Fitzgerald, Walsh *C:* O'Halloran (2) *PG:* O'Halloran (3) *DG:* O'Halloran (3)

WALES
Aberavon

Year of formation 1876
Ground Talbot Athletic Ground, Manor Street, Port Talbot, West Glamorgan
Tel: Port Talbot (01639) 886038 and 882427
Colours Red and black hoops
Most capped player A J Martin (Wales) 34 caps
Captain 1995-96 B Shenton
Heineken Leagues 1995-96 Div 1 11th – *relegated* **SWALEC Cup 1995-96** Lost 0-27 to
Caerphilly (4th round)

League Record 1995-96

Date	Venue	Opponents	Result	Scorers
2 Sept	A	Newport	9-30	*PG:* M Watts (3)
9 Sept	H	Bridgend	16-31	*T:* M Codd *C:* M Watts *PG:* M Watts (3)
16 Sept	A	Pontypridd	25-70	*T:* G Baber, P Clapham, N Stork, C Laity *C:* M Watts *DG:* M Watts
23 Sept	H	Neath	10-20	*T:* B Shenton *C:* D Davies *PG:* D Davies
30 Sept	A	Swansea	5-66	*T:* D Davies
7 Oct	H	Llanelli	16-39	*T:* D Davies, B Grabham *PG:* D Davies (2)
14 Oct	A	Treorchy	39-28	*T:* D Austin, M Bernard, D Davies, P Wintle, B Grabham *C:* D Davies (4) *PG:* D Davies (2)
28 Oct	H	Ebbw Vale	11-18	*T:* S Hutchinson *PG:* D Davies (2)
5 Nov	A	Cardiff	9-57	*PG:* D Davies (3)
18 Nov	A	Abertillery	11-28	*T:* P Wintle *PG:* N Stork (2)
25 Nov	H	Newbridge	3-22	*PG:* M Watts
2 Dec	H	Newport	8-6	*T:* C Laity *DG:* M Watts
9 Dec	A	Bridgend	16-19	*T:* B Shenton, B Grabham *PG:* N Stork (2)
6 Jan	H	Swansea	6-12	*PG:* N Stork (2)
10 Feb	H	Pontypridd	3-19	*PG:* N Stork
9 Mar	H	Treorchy	16-17	*T:* S Barclay *C:* N Stork *PG:* N Stork (3)
30 Mar	A	Ebbw Vale	12-21	*T:* J Jardine, S Barclay *C:* C Laity
3 Apr	A	Neath	17-95	*T:* C Laity (2), S Barclay *C:* N Stork
8 Apr	H	Cardiff	13-41	*T:* P Wintle, R Diplock *PG:* M Watts
16 Apr	A	Llanelli	0-39	
20 Apr	H	Abertillery	33-24	*T:* G Baber, C Kinsey, J Jardine, R Jasper, H Merrett *C:* M Watts (4)
27 Apr	A	Newbridge	34-41	*T:* N Stork (3), A Miers (2), M Watts *C:* M Watts (2)

Abercynon

Year of formation 1896
Ground Y Parc, Abercynon, Mid Glamorgan CF45 4RE Tel: Abercynon (01443) 740586
Colours Red and black
Captain 1995-96 S Pascoe
Heineken Leagues 1995-96 Div 2 8th **SWALEC Cup 1995-96** Lost 16-26 to South Wales
Police (5th round)

League Record 1995-96

Date	Venue	Opponents	Result	Scorers
2 Sept	A	Cross Keys	12-13	*T:* G Davies, T Williams *C:* R Savage
9 Sept	H	Tenby Utd	27-12	*T:* G Thomas, K McDonald *C:* R Savage *PG:* R Savage (5)
16 Sept	H	Ystradgynlais	14-10	*T:* D Jones *PG:* R Savage (3)
23 Sept	A	Llanharan	10-9	*T:* A Haines *C:* R Savage *PG:* R Savage

30 Sept	H	Maesteg	22-7	*T:* N Mills, K McDonald, M Cotter
				C: R Savage (2) *PG:* R Savage
7 Oct	A	Caerphilly	0-23	
14 Oct	H	South Wales Police	27-11	*T:* G Thomas (2), D Jones, C van Rensburgh
				C: R Savage (2) *PG:* R Savage
28 Oct	A	Llandovery	14-21	*T:* A Keepings *PG:* G Davies (3)
4 Nov	H	Dunvant	10-36	*T:* A Keepings *C:* G Davies *PG:* G Dixon
18 Nov	A	Pontypool	26-31	*T:* D Kathrens, G Thomas, K Lynch, G Phillips
				C: C van Rensburgh (3)
25 Nov	H	Bonymaen	17-5	*T:* P Cummings (2) *C:* C van Rensburgh (2)
				PG: C van Rensburg
2 Dec	H	Cross Keys	15-29	*T:* P Cummings, K Lynch
				C: C van Rensburgh *PG:* C van Rensburgh
9 Dec	A	Tenby Utd	8-22	*T:* S Pascoe *PG:* C van Rensburgh
23 Dec	A	Ystradgynlais	11-16	*T:* R Savage *PG:* R Savage (2)
6 Jan	A	Maesteg	9-11	*PG:* R Savage (3)
13 Jan	H	Caerphilly	6-14	*PG:* R Savage *DG:* R Savage
9 Mar	A	South Wales Police	19-16	*T:* L Winder, N Edwards, pen try
				C: R Savage (2)
30 Mar	H	Llandovery	13-9	*T:* P Cummings, A Keepings *DG:* R Savage
6 Apr	A	Dunvant	6-41	*PG:* R Savage (2)
13 Apr	H	Llanharan	17-24	*T:* L Winder, M Owen *C:* R Savage (2)
				PG: R Savage
20 Apr	H	Pontypool	26-16	*T:* N Edwards, P Cummings *C:* G Davies (2)
				PG: G Davies (3) *DG:* G Davies
27 Apr	A	Bonymaen	35-7	*T:* N Edwards, A Haines, P Cummings,
				S Pascoe, G Kathrens *C:* G Davies (2)
				PG: G Davies (2)

Abertillery

Year of formation 1884
Ground The Park, Abertillery, Gwent   Tel: Abertillery (01495) 212555
Colours Green and white
Most capped player H J Morgan (Wales) 27 caps
Captain 1995-96 M Rossiter
Heineken Leagues 1995-96 Div 1 12th – *relegated*   **SWALEC Cup 1995-96** Lost 3-32 to
Bridgend (5th round)

League Record 1995-96

Date	Venue	Opponents	Result	Scorers
2 Sept	H	Newbridge	10-15	*T:* D Duly *C:* M Williams *PG:* M Williams
9 Sept	A	Llanelli	5-40	*T:* R Gladwyn
16 Sept	A	Newport	12-31	*PG:* M Williams (4)
23 Sept	H	Treorchy	24-21	*T:* I Lewis, S Connor *C:* M Williams
				PG: M Williams (2), S Connor (2)
30 Sept	A	Bridgend	3-56	*PG:* M Williams
7 Oct	H	Ebbw Vale	9-16	*PG:* S Connor (3)
14 Oct	A	Pontypridd	17-55	*T:* A Hillman, M Williams *C:* M Williams (2)
				PG: M Williams
21 Oct	H	Cardiff	19-60	*T:* S Connor, R Roberts *PG:* M Williams (2)
				DG: S Connor
4 Nov	A	Neath	17-63	*T:* S Connor, D Duly, M Williams
				C: S Connor
18 Nov	H	Aberavon	28-11	*T:* M Williams, D Duly, J Cicero
				C: M Williams (2) *PG:* M Williams (3)
25 Nov	A	Swansea	13-71	*T:* M Griffiths *C:* M Williams
				PG: M Williams *DG:* S Connor
2 Dec	A	Newbridge	13-15	*T:* S Connor *C:* S Connor *PG:* S Connor (2)

23 Dec	H	Newport	33-50	*T:* M Williams, G Gladwyn, L Phillips *C:* M Williams (3) *PG:* M Williams (3) *DG:* S Connor
6 Jan	H	Bridgend	15-37	*T:* M Picton, L Phillips *C:* M Williams *PG:* M Williams
13 Jan	A	Ebbw Vale	13-16	*T:* M Williams, J Cicero *DG:* S Connor
9 Mar	H	Pontypridd	10-70	*T:* N Prest *C:* M Williams *PG:* M Williams
23 Mar	A	Treorchy	12-20	*PG:* M Williams (4)
30 Mar	A	Cardiff	25-95	*T:* S Connor (2), M Picton, B Corlett, M Williams
3 Apr	H	Llanelli	29-39	*T:* D Wright (2), S Connor, J Powell *C:* M Williams (3) *PG:* M Williams
6 Apr	H	Neath	24-50	*T:* R McCorduck, A Richards, M Picton, M Williams *C:* M Williams (2)
20 Apr	A	Aberavon	24-33	*T:* B Corlett (2), M Williams, D Caswell *C:* M Williams (2)
27 Apr	H	Swansea	14-64	*T:* S Connor, L Phillips *C:* M Williams (2)

Bonymaen

Year of formation 1914
Ground Parc Mawr, Cefn Hengoed Road, Bonymaen, Swansea
Tel: Bonymaen (01792) 652859
Colours Red and black hoops
Captain 1995-96 A Sturgess
Heineken Leagues 1995-96 Div 2 5th **SWALEC Cup 1995-96** Lost 24-26 to Maesteg
(4th round)

League Record 1995-96

Date	Venue	Opponents	Result	Scorers
2 Sept	H	Ystradgynlais	16-3	*T:* I Jones, S Marney *PG:* P Roberts (2)
9 Sept	A	Llanharan	14-17	*T:* M Dacey *PG:* P Roberts (2), P Rees
16 Sept	H	Maesteg	31-26	*T:* Lewis, P Roberts, P John *C:* P Rees (2) *PG:* P Rees (4)
23 Sept	A	Caerphilly	8-17	*T:* P John *PG:* P Rees
30 Sept	H	South Wales Police	35-18	*T:* M John (2), P John *C:* P Rees *PG:* P Rees (6)
7 Oct	A	Llandovery	19-23	*T:* C Haste *C:* P Roberts *PG:* P Roberts (4)
14 Oct	H	Dunvant	6-38	*PG:* P Rees (2)
28 Oct	A	Pontypool	16-27	*T:* M Dacey *C:* P Roberts *PG:* P Roberts (3)
4 Nov	H	Tenby Utd	40-12	*T:* S Bowling (3), P John (2), P Roberts *C:* P Roberts (2) *PG:* P Roberts (2)
18 Nov	H	Cross Keys	36-21	*T:* G Alexander, N Davies, P John, M Dacey, D Thomas *C:* S Bowling (4) *PG:* S Bowling
25 Nov	A	Abercynon	5-17	*T:* M John
2 Dec	A	Ystradgynlais	12-14	*T:* P John, D Charles *C:* P Roberts
9 Dec	H	Llanharan	37-23	*T:* S Bowling (2), M John, G Alexander, D Thomas *C:* P Roberts (3) *PG:* P Roberts (2)
23 Dec	A	Maesteg	14-27	*T:* J Williams, S Bowling *C:* P Roberts (2)
6 Jan	A	South Wales Police	0-35	
13 Jan	H	Llandovery	44-19	*T:* M John (2), P Roberts, P John, P Rees, S Bowling *C:* P Rees (4) *PG:* P Rees *DG:* P Rees
9 Mar	A	Dunvant	13-6	*T:* P Roberts *C:* P Roberts *PG:* P Roberts (2)
30 Mar	H	Pontypool	22-15	*T:* P Roberts, G Alexander, I Jones, M Dacey *C:* P Roberts

401

6 Apr	A	Tenby Utd	38-5	*T:* M John (2), C Lewis, C Jenkins, D Squires, S Bowling *C:* P Roberts (4)
13 Apr	H	Caerphilly	10-27	*T:* D Charles *C:* P Roberts *PG:* P Roberts
20 Apr	A	Cross Keys	24-39	*T:* P John, P Roberts, Andrew Davies *C:* P Roberts (3) *PG:* P Roberts
27 Apr	H	Abercynon	7-35	*T:* M McComas *C:* P Roberts

Bridgend

Year of formation 1878
Ground Brewery Field, Tondu Road, Bridgend, Mid Glamorgan
Tel: Bridgend (01656) 652707 and 659032
Colours Blue and white hoops
Most capped player J P R Williams (Wales) 55 caps
Captain 1995-96 R Howley
Heineken Leagues 1995-96 Div 1 5th **SWALEC Cup 1995-96** Lost 15-18 to Llanelli
(6th round)

League Record 1995-96

Date	Venue	Opponents	Result	Scorers
9 Sept	A	Aberavon	31-16	*T:* G Wilkins (2), N Spender, J Reynolds, J Forster *C:* M Lewis (3)
16 Sept	H	Newbridge	28-29	*T:* D James (2), G Jones, M Lewis, R Howley *PG:* M Lewis
23 Sept	A	Newport	12-27	*T:* A Williams, L Manning *C:* M Lewis
30 Sept	H	Abertillery	56-3	*T:* G Jones, J Forster, M Lewis, L Manning, G Thomas, A Durston, D James, P Jones *C:* M Lewis (5) *PG:* M Lewis (2)
4 Oct	H	Cardiff	32-19	*T:* G Thomas, M Lewis, G Wilkins *C:* M Lewis *PG:* M Lewis (4) *DG:* M Lewis
7 Oct	H	Pontypridd	12-17	*T:* M Lewis *PG:* M Lewis (3) *DG:* M Lewis
14 Oct	A	Neath	7-34	*T:* G Wilkins *C:* M Lewis
28 Oct	H	Swansea	31-16	*T:* G Wilkins (2), A Jones *C:* A Durston (2) *PG:* A Durston (4)
4 Nov	A	Llanelli	24-30	*T:* M Lewis, A Jones, N Jones, C Bradshaw *C:* M Lewis, A Durston
18 Nov	H	Treorchy	33-17	*T:* C Bradshaw, M Lewis, J Reynolds, L Griffiths *C:* L Griffiths (2) *PG:* L Griffiths (3)
25 Nov	A	Ebbw Vale	8-10	*T:* P Manning *PG:* A Durston
2 Dec	A	Cardiff	19-18	*T:* A Durston *C:* M Lewis *PG:* M Lewis (4)
9 Dec	H	Aberavon	19-16	*T:* A Williams *C:* M Lewis *PG:* M Lewis (3) *DG:* M Lewis
23 Dec	A	Newbridge	22-25	*T:* J Ball, S Gale, I Greenslade, P Jones *C:* M Lewis
6 Jan	A	Abertillery	37-15	*T:* A Williams (3), P Jones (2), G Rowlands, D James *C:* M Lewis
13 Jan	A	Pontypridd	11-48	*T:* A Williams *PG:* M Lewis (2)
9 Mar	H	Neath	8-45	*T:* G Wilkins *PG:* L Griffiths
23 Mar	A	Swansea	38-29	*T:* G Thomas (2), M Back, D James *C:* L Griffiths (3) *PG:* L Griffiths (4)
6 Apr	H	Llanelli	29-21	*T:* P Jones, G Thomas *C:* L Griffiths (2) *PG:* L Griffiths (3), M Lewis *DG:* M Lewis
20 Apr	A	Treorchy	20-20	*T:* J Forster (2), R Jones *C:* L Griffiths *PG:* L Griffiths
24 Apr	H	Newport	48-17	*T:* G Thomas (2), M Lewis, C Bradshaw, D James, R Jones, N Thomas *C:* L Griffiths (5) *PG:* L Griffiths

| 27 Apr | H | Ebbw Vale | 46-6 | *T:* A Williams (2), G Rowlands, M Lewis, J Forster, P Jones *C:* L Griffiths (3), M Lewis, G Thomas *PG:* L Griffiths (2) |

Caerphilly

Year of formation 1886
Ground Virginia Park, Pontygwindy Road, Caerphilly   Tel: Caerphilly (01222) 882573
Colours Green and white hoops
Captain 1995-96 I Evans
Heineken Leagues 1995-96 Div 2 2nd – *promoted*   **SWALEC Cup 1995-96** Lost 10-16 to Newport (quarter-final)

League Record 1995-96

Date	Venue	Opponents	Result	Scorers
2 Sept	A	Llandovery	7-9	*T:* R Scrivens *C:* P Phillips
9 Sept	H	Dunvant	9-23	*PG:* R Scrivens (3)
16 Sept	A	Pontypool	8-31	*T:* K Hever *PG:* R Scrivens
23 Sept	H	Bonymaen	17-8	*T:* S Law *PG:* C Conway (2) *DG:* D Phillips (2)
30 Sept	A	Cross Keys	13-11	*T:* I Jones *C:* C Conway *PG:* C Conway (2)
7 Oct	H	Abercynon	23-0	*T:* R Bidgood, D Phillips, W Bray *C:* C Conway *PG:* C Conway (2)
14 Oct	A	Ystradgynlais	36-30	*T:* D Phillips (2), W Bray, M Lewis, D Starr *C:* R Scrivens *PG:* C Conway, R Scrivens *DG:* D Phillips
28 Oct	H	Llanharan	20-17	*T:* R Hammond, S Law *C:* C Conway (2) *PG:* C Conway *DG:* D Phillips
4 Nov	A	Maesteg	22-12	*T:* M Lewis, R Bidgood, J Lougher *C:* C Conway (2) *PG:* C Conway
18 Nov	A	Tenby Utd	25-7	*T:* R Hammond, D Starr, B Bolderson, J Lougher *C:* B Bolderson *PG:* B Bolderson
25 Nov	H	South Wales Police	16-12	*T:* D Phillips, R Hammond *PG:* B Bolderson *DG:* D Phillips
2 Dec	H	Llandovery	32-8	*T:* M Lewis (2), J Lougher, A Evans, D Starr *C:* C Conway (2) *PG:* B Bolderson
9 Dec	A	Dunvant	13-16	*T:* D Phillips *C:* B Bolderson *PG:* B Bolderson (2)
23 Dec	H	Pontypool	13-6	*T:* R Hammond *C:* C Conway *PG:* C Conway (2)
6 Jan	H	Cross Keys	22-13	*T:* D Phillips, P Phillips, R Hammond *C:* C Conway (2) *PG:* C Conway
13 Jan	A	Abercynon	14-6	*T:* C Conway *PG:* C Conway (3)
9 Mar	H	Ystradgynlais	21-3	*T:* P Phillips, D Hawthorne, R Hammond *PG:* P Phillips, C Conway
30 Mar	A	Llanharan	22-16	*T:* D Starr (2), D Hawthorne *C:* C Conway, P Phillips *PG:* C Conway
6 Apr	H	Maesteg	24-9	*T:* R Bidgood, W Evans *C:* P Phillips *PG:* P Phillips (4)
13 Apr	A	Bonymaen	27-10	*T:* C Ferris, I Phillips *C:* D Phillips *PG:* D Phillips (5)
20 Apr	H	Tenby U	59-5	*T:* R Bidgood (3), W Bray (3), R Hammond (3), D Starr *C:* D Phillips (3) *PG:* D Phillips
27 Apr	A	South Wales Police	15-12	*T:* D Phillips, P Phillips, L Tomlins

Cardiff

Year of formation 1876
Ground Cardiff Arms Park, Westgate Street, Cardiff CF1 1JA
Tel: Cardiff (01222) 383546
Colours Cambridge blue and black
Most capped player G O Edwards (Wales) 53 caps
Captain 1995-96 H Taylor
Heineken Leagues 1995-96 Div 1 2nd   **SWALEC Cup 1995-96** Lost 10-11 to Llanelli
(quarter-final)

League Record 1995-96

Date	Venue	Opponents	Result	Scorers
9 Sept	H	Pontypridd	36-31	*T:* S Ford (3), pen try *C:* C John (2) *PG:* C John (4)
16 Sept	A	Neath	11-8	*T:* O Williams *PG:* C John (2)
23 Sept	H	Swansea	50-13	*T:* S Ford (2), S Hill, M Ring, Si Davies, M Hall, V Davies *C:* A Davies (5), C John *PG:* A Davies
30 Sept	A	Llanelli	16-12	*T:* J Humphreys *C:* A Davies *PG:* A Davies (3)
4 Oct	A	Bridgend	19-32	*T:* M Bennett *C:* A Davies *PG:* A Davies (4)
7 Oct	H	Treorchy	67-3	*T:* S Ford (2), S Hill (2), V Davies, J Humphreys, A Moore, H Taylor, S John *C:* A Davies (8) *PG:* A Davies (2)
14 Oct	A	Ebbw Vale	16-10	*T:* S Davies *C:* A Davies *PG:* A Davies (3)
21 Oct	A	Abertillery	60-19	*T:* S Ford (3), C John (2), O Williams, H Stone, P Booth, A Lewis *C:* C John (6) *PG:* C John
5 Nov	H	Aberavon	57-9	*T:* M Ring (3), M Rayer (2), S Ford, A Davies, O Williams, A Booth *C:* A Davies (6)
18 Nov	A	Newbridge	30-18	*T:* S John, P Young, A Booth, N Walker *C:* A Davies (2) *PG:* A Davies (2)
25 Nov	H	Newport	18-22	*PG:* C John (6)
2 Dec	H	Bridgend	18-19	*T:* A Booth, G Jones *C:* C John *PG:* C John (2)
23 Dec	H	Neath	28-8	*T:* A Davies, A Moore, O Williams *C:* A Davies (2) *PG:* A Davies (3)
9 Mar	H	Ebbw Vale	16-13	*T:* G Jones *C:* J Davies *PG:* J Davies (3)
30 Mar	H	Abertillery	95-25	*T:* S Ford (5), M Hall (2), G Jones (2), A Lewis, A Davies, O Williams, K Stewart, C John, S Hill *C:* M Rayer (7), S Ford, O Williams, A Booth
8 Apr	A	Aberavon	41-13	*T:* S Ford (3), J Humphreys, A Davies, A Booth, O Williams *C:* A Davies (3)
13 Apr	A	Swansea	59-0	*T:* N Walker (2), G Jones (2), S Hill (2), C John, A Moore, M Rayer *C:* M Rayer (2), A Davies (2), H Stone, O Williams, C John
20 Apr	H	Newbridge	78-7	*T:* M Rayer (2), S Hill (2), G Jones (2), N Walker (2), O Williams, A Lewis, A Davies, P Young *C:* M Rayer (8), O Williams
27 Apr	A	Newport	29-19	*T:* M Rayer (2), A Davies, N Walker, G Jones *C:* M Rayer (2)
2 May	A	Treorchy	31-10	*T:* A Davies (2), M Rayer, S Hill, J Davies *C:* M Rayer (3)
10 May	A	Pontypridd	27-27	*T:* N Walker (2), A Moore *C:* M Rayer (3) *PG:* M Rayer (2)
14 May	H	Llanelli	65-13	*T:* G Jones (3), A Davies (2), M Hall, O Williams, C Mills, A Moore, S Ford, N Walker *C:* M Rayer (5)

Cross Keys

Year of formation 1885
Ground Pandy Park, Cross Keys, Gwent   Tel: Cross Keys (01495) 270289
Colours Black and white hoops
Most capped player S Morris (Wales) 19 caps
Captain 1995-96 M Wysocki
Heineken Leagues 1995-96 Div 2 3rd   **SWALEC Cup 1995-96** Lost 8-24 to Newbridge
(5th round)

League Record 1995-96

Date	Venue	Opponents	Result	Scorers
2 Sept	H	Abercynon	13-12	*T:* J Reid, D Rees *PG:* D Rees
9 Sept	A	Ystradgynlais	19-16	*T:* D Rees *C:* D Rees *PG:* D Rees (4)
16 Sept	H	Llanharan	57-13	*T:* C Bushell (2), A Bunny (2), R Nicholls (2), J Reid, pen try *C:* D Rees (7) *PG:* D Rees
23 Sept	A	Maesteg	13-15	*T:* G Emyr, M Isherwood *PG:* D Rees
30 Sept	H	Caerphilly	11-13	*T:* S Jenks *PG:* D Rees (2)
7 Oct	A	South Wales Police	20-21	*T:* R Nicholls *PG:* I Bebb (5)
14 Oct	H	Llandovery	30-22	*T:* S W Davies, G Stroud, R Nicholls, P Ovey *C:* I Bebb (2) *PG:* I Bebb (2)
28 Oct	A	Dunvant	3-11	*PG:* C Bushell
4 Nov	H	Pontypool	29-23	*T:* D Grant, S Phillips *C:* I Bebb (2) *PG:* I Bebb (5)
18 Nov	A	Bonymaen	21-36	*T:* M Wysocki, S W Davies *C:* I Bebb *PG:* I Bebb (3)
25 Nov	H	Tenby Utd	46-0	*T:* D Harris (2), D Rees, R Nicholls, A Price, G Stroud, I Bebb *C:* I Bebb (4) *PG:* I Bebb
2 Dec	A	Abercynon	29-15	*T:* P Ovey, T Griffin, S Phillips, R Nicholls, I Bebb *C:* I Bebb (2)
9 Dec	H	Ystradgynlais	13-18	*T:* I Bebb, G Emyr *PG:* I Bebb
6 Jan	A	Caerphilly	13-22	*T:* J Powell *C:* I Bebb *PG:* I Bebb (2)
13 Jan	H	South Wales Police	25-28	*T:* D Grant, M Isherwood, M Price *C:* I Bebb (2) *PG:* I Bebb (2)
24 Feb	A	Llanharan	3-6	*PG:* D Rees
9 Mar	A	Llandovery	10-29	*T:* M Wysocki *C:* I Bebb *PG:* I Bebb
23 Mar	H	Maesteg	35-20	*T:* M Wysocki, D Harris, J Powell, G Emyr, R Nicholls *C:* I Bebb (2) *PG:* I Bebb (2)
30 Mar	H	Dunvant	22-16	*T:* I Bebb *C:* I Bebb *PG:* I Bebb (5)
6 Apr	A	Pontypool	20-29	*T:* D Rees (2), D Harris *C:* D Rees *PG:* D Rees
20 Apr	H	Bonymaen	39-24	*T:* J Reid (2), J Powell, C Bushell, L Gardner, A Price *C:* I Bebb (3) *PG:* I Bebb
27 Apr	A	Tenby Utd	63-22	*T:* T Griffin (2), C Clements (2), P Ovey, R Lewis, S Jenks, J Reid, A Bunney, M Price, J Powell *C:* D Rees (4)

Dunvant

Year of formation 1888
Ground Broadacre, Killay, Swansea SA2 7RU   Tel: 01792 207291
Colours Red and green hoops
Captain 1995-96 D Evans
Heineken Leagues 1995-96 Div 2 *Winners – promoted*   **SWALEC Cup 1995-96** Lost 17-44
to Neath (quarter-final)

League Record 1995-96

Date	Venue	Opponents	Result	Scorers
2 Sept	H	Maesteg	17-14	*T:* D Evans, P Farnworth, R Greenwood *C:* D Evans
9 Sept	A	Caerphilly	23-9	*T:* M Sutton, S Dixon, R Hopkins *C:* A Snell *PG:* A Snell *DG:* A Snell
16 Sept	H	South Wales Police	16-7	*T:* M Sutton, M Davies *PG:* A Snell (2)
23 Sept	A	Llandovery	14-15	*T:* S Dixon *PG:* W Booth (3)
30 Sept	H	Tenby Utd	51-8	*T:* R Hopkin (2), D Morgan (2), D Niblo (2), R Llewellyn, R Williams, pen try *C:* R Hopkin, D Morgan (2)
7 Oct	H	Pontypool	26-10	*T:* R Llewellyn, M Davies, C Hutchings *C:* R Hopkin *PG:* D Morgan (2) *DG:* D Morgan
14 Oct	A	Bonymaen	38-6	*T:* S Dixon (2), M Sutton, D Niblo, M Davies *C:* D Morgan (2) *PG:* D Morgan (2)
28 Oct	H	Cross Keys	11-3	*T:* G Davies *PG:* D Morgan *DG:* D Morgan
4 Nov	A	Abercynon	36-10	*T:* P Farnworth, W Lloyd, G Davies, A Snell *C:* D Morgan (2) *PG:* D Morgan (4)
18 Nov	H	Ystradgynlais	19-21	*T:* S Wake (2), B Taylor *C:* D Morgan (2)
25 Nov	A	Llanharan	50-11	*T:* K Davies (2), M Sutton, D Morgan, S Wake, R Greenwood, C Butler, pen try *C:* M Thomas (5)
2 Dec	A	Maesteg	14-6	*T:* M Thomas, W Lloyd *C:* M Thomas (2)
9 Dec	H	Caerphilly	16-13	*T:* D Morgan *C:* M Thomas *PG:* M Thomas (3)
13 Jan	A	Pontypool	21-20	*T:* M Davies (2), C Davies *C:* M Thomas (3)
10 Feb	A	South Wales Police	27-10	*T:* B Taylor, M Sutton, M Davies, D Morgan *C:* M Thomas, D Morgan *PG:* M Thomas
9 Mar	H	Bonymaen	6-13	*PG:* M Thomas (2)
30 Mar	A	Cross Keys	16-22	*T:* D Morgan *C:* D Morgan *PG:* D Morgan (3)
6 Apr	H	Abercynon	41-6	*T:* M Davies (2), D Evans, B Taylor, S Dixon, R Greenwood *C:* D Morgan (3), D Evans *PG:* D Morgan
13 Apr	H	Llandovery	25-5	*T:* D Evans (2), M Sutton *C:* D Evans, D Morgan *PG:* D Morgan *DG:* D Morgan
16 Apr	A	Tenby Utd	36-5	*T:* M Davies, B Taylor, R Greenwood, B Taylor, D Chick, P Farnworth *C:* D Morgan (3)
20 Apr	A	Ystradgynlais	42-27	*T:* B Taylor, R Llewellyn, R Greenwood, M Davies, D Evans *C:* M Thomas (4) *PG:* M Thomas (3)
27 Apr	H	Llanharan	31-22	*T:* B Taylor, D Morgan, W Lloyd, G Davies, M Sutton *C:* M Thomas (3)

Ebbw Vale

Year of formation 1880
Ground Eugene Cross Park, Ebbw Vale, Gwent   Tel: Ebbw Vale (01495) 302995
Colours Red, white and green
Most capped player D Williams (Wales) 36 caps
Captain 1995-96 K Jones
Heineken Leagues 1995-96 Div 1 7th **SWALEC Cup 1995-96** Lost 11-30 to Penarth (4th round)

League Record 1995-96

Date	Venue	Opponents	Result	Scorers
2 Sept	A	Pontypridd	18-35	T: B Watkins, N Morgan C: B Hayward PG: B Hayward (2)
9 Sept	H	Neath	6-17	PG: B Hayward (2)
16 Sept	A	Swansea	20-53	T: D Worgan, D Llewellyn C: B Hayward (2) PG: B Hayward (2)
23 Sept	H	Llanelli	15-60	T: N Morgan, P Hudson C: B Hayward PG: B Hayward
30 Sept	A	Treorchy	29-20	T: P Hudson, D Llewellyn C: B Hayward (2) PG: B Hayward (4) DG: B Hayward
7 Oct	A	Abertillery	16-9	T: D Llewellyn C: B Hayward PG: B Hayward DG: B Hayward (2)
14 Oct	H	Cardiff	10-16	T: D Llewellyn C: B Hayward PG: B Hayward
28 Oct	A	Aberavon	18-11	T: J Williams, D Llewellyn C: B Hayward PG: B Hayward (2)
4 Nov	H	Newbridge	24-12	T: B Hayward, D Llewellyn, C Price DG: B Hayward (3)
18 Nov	A	Newport	22-25	T: A Phillips, N Morgan, M Chapman C: B Hayward (2) PG: B Hayward
25 Nov	H	Bridgend	10-8	T: B Watkins C: B Hayward PG: M Chapman
2 Dec	H	Pontypridd	3-7	PG: B Hayward
9 Dec	A	Neath	29-76	T: W Ford (2), I Lewis, J Williams C: B Hayward (3) PG: B Hayward
23 Dec	H	Swansea	25-0	T: I Lewis, N Morgan, pen try C: B Hayward (2) PG: B Hayward (2)
6 Jan	H	Treorchy	40-6	T: B Watkins, I Jeffreys, J Williams, D Worgan, P Hudson C: B Hayward (3) PG: B Hayward (3)
13 Jan	H	Abertillery	16-13	T: B Hayward C: B Hayward PG: B Hayward (3)
23 Jan	A	Llanelli	8-39	T: D Llewellyn PG: B Hayward
9 Mar	A	Cardiff	13-16	T: I Jeffreys C: B Hayward PG: B Hayward DG: B Hayward
30 Mar	H	Aberavon	21-12	T: C Price, P Hudson C: B Hayward PG: B Hayward (2) DG: B Hayward
6 Apr	A	Newbridge	32-16	T: P Hudson (2), N Morgan, D Worgan C: B Hayward (3) PG: B Hayward (2)
20 Apr	H	Newport	27-12	T: B Hayward (2), D Llewellyn, K Jones C: B Hayward (2) PG: B Hayward
27 Apr	A	Bridgend	6-46	PG: B Hayward DG: B Hayward

Llandovery

Year of formation 1878
Ground Church Bank, Llandovery, Dyfed   Tel: Llandovery (01550) 721110
Colours Red and white hoops
Most capped player C P Lewis (Wales) 5 caps
Captain 1995-96 I Jones
Heineken Leagues 1995-96 Div 2 6th   **SWALEC Cup 1995-96** Lost 5-25 to Newport
(6th round)

League Record 1995-96

Date	Venue	Opponents	Results	Scorers
2 Sept	H	Caerphilly	9-7	PG: D Lloyd-Jones (3)
9 Sept	A	South Wales Police	18-8	T: N Griffiths, S Davies C: N Griffiths PG: N Griffiths DG: N Griffiths

16 Sept	H	Tenby Utd	16-10	*T:* D Giles *C:* N Griffiths *PG:* N Griffiths (3)
23 Sept	H	Dunvant	15-14	*PG:* N Griffiths (3) *DG:* N Griffiths, D Lloyd-Jones
30 Sept	A	Pontypool	13-22	*T:* H James, A Davies *DG:* N Griffiths
7 Oct	H	Bonymaen	23-19	*T:* D Williams, pen try *C:* N Griffiths (2) *PG:* N Griffiths (3)
14 Oct	A	Cross Keys	22-30	*T:* N Griffiths, H Thomas, S Davies *C:* N Griffiths (2) *PG:* N Griffiths
28 Oct	H	Abercynon	21-14	*T:* C Davies, J Griffiths *C:* N Griffiths *PG:* N Griffiths (3)
4 Nov	A	Ystradgynlais	3-7	*PG:* N Griffiths
18 Nov	H	Llanharan	20-13	*T:* G Davies, J Griffiths *C:* C Williams (2) *PG:* C Williams (2)
25 Nov	A	Maesteg	23-28	*T:* J Griffiths (2), C Davies *C:* D Lloyd-Jones *PG:* D Lloyd-Jones (2)
2 Dec	A	Caerphilly	8-32	*T:* A Rowlands *PG:* D Lloyd-Jones
9 Dec	H	South Wales Police	15-13	*T:* C Davies, A Evans *C:* N Griffiths *DG:* N Griffiths
23 Dec	A	Tenby Utd	12-9	*T:* D Giles, A Davies *C:* N Griffiths
6 Jan	H	Pontypool	13-10	*T:* pen try *C:* D Lloyd-Jones *PG:* D Lloyd-Jones (2)
13 Jan	A	Bonymaen	19-44	*T:* C Davies, G John, D Morgan *C:* N Griffiths, D Lloyd-Jones
9 Mar	H	Cross Keys	29-10	*T:* A Rowlands (2), D Williams, G Davies *C:* D Lloyd-Jones (3) *PG:* D Lloyd-Jones
30 Mar	A	Abercynon	9-13	*PG:* D Lloyd-Jones (3)
6 Apr	H	Ystradgynlais	18-18	*T:* C Davies, C Williams *C:* S Richards *PG:* S Richards (2)
13 Apr	A	Dunvant	5-25	*T:* N Clarke
20 Apr	A	Llanharan	21-36	*T:* J Griffiths, A Davies, A Williams *C:* S Richards (3)
27 Apr	H	Maesteg	17-17	*T:* A Rowlands *PG:* S Richards (4)

Llanelli

Year of formation 1872
Ground Stradey Park, Llanelli, Dyfed SA15 4BT
Tel: Llanelli (01554) 774060 and 0891 660221
Colours Scarlet with white collar
Most capped player I C Evans (Wales) 61 caps
Captain 1995-96 P Davies
Heineken Leagues 1995-96 Div 1 4th   **SWALEC Cup 1995-96** Lost 17-35 to Pontypridd
(semi-final)

League Record 1995-96

Date	Venue	Opponents	Result	Scorers
9 Sept	H	Abertillery	40-5	*T:* J Thomas, P Jones, H Harries, N Boobyer, O Lloyd *C:* M McCarthy (3) *PG:* M McCarthy (3)
16 Sept	H	Treorchy	52-7	*T:* W Proctor (3), J Thomas, R Moon, O Lloyd, C Quinnell, pen try *C:* S Pearce (3) *PG:* S Pearce (2)
23 Sept	A	Ebbw Vale	60-15	*T:* I Evans (3), N Davies (2), G Evans, J Williams, J Thomas, L Williams *C:* M McCarthy (6) *PG:* M McCarthy
30 Sept	H	Cardiff	12-16	*PG:* M McCarthy (4)
7 Oct	A	Aberavon	39-16	*T:* N Davies (2), J Thomas (2), W Proctor, P Morris *C:* S Pearce (3) *PG:* S Pearce
14 Oct	H	Newbridge	17-9	*T:* W Proctor (2), J Thomas *C:* M McCarthy

28 Oct	A	Newport	8-21	*T:* I Evans *PG:* M McCarthy
4 Nov	H	Bridgend	30-24	*T:* N Boobyer, I Evans, S John *C:* S Pearce (3) *PG:* S Pearce (2) *DG:* S Pearce
18 Nov	A	Pontypridd	18-31	*T:* W Proctor, M Wintle *C:* S Pearce *PG:* S Pearce (2)
25 Nov	H	Neath	18-6	*T:* J Thomas, J Williams *C:* M McCarthy *PG:* M McCarthy (2)
2 Dec	H	Swansea	13-3	*T:* J Williams *C:* M McCarthy *PG:* M McCarthy (2)
12 Dec	A	Swansea	20-26	*T:* G Jones, J Thomas, I Evans, W Proctor
23 Dec	A	Treorchy	43-10	*T:* W Proctor (2), H Harries (2), C Wyatt, P Jones, D Evans *C:* S Pearce (4)
23 Jan	H	Ebbw Vale	39-8	*T:* I Evans (2), W Proctor, N Davies, M Wintle *C:* S Pearce (4) *PG:* S Pearce (2)
9 Mar	A	Newbridge	10-6	*T:* M Wintle *C:* J Thomas *PG:* J Thomas
3 Apr	A	Abertillery	39-29	*T:* M Wintle (2), J Thomas (2), R Evans, H Harries, N Boobyer *C:* J Thomas (2)
6 Apr	A	Bridgend	21-29	*T:* R Evans, N Boobyer, G Jones *C:* J Thomas (3)
16 Apr	H	Aberavon	39-0	*T:* I Evans (2), J Williams, P Davies, R Moon, M Wintle, R Evans *C:* M McCarthy (2)
20 Apr	H	Pontypridd	23-13	*T:* M Wintle, P Davies, W Proctor *C:* M McCarthy *PG:* M McCarthy (2)
26 Apr	A	Neath	0-41	
11 May	H	Newport	56-22	*T:* W Proctor (4), D Evans (3), N Boobyer, R Moon, G Evans *C:* S Pearce (3)
14 May	A	Cardiff	13-65	*T:* W Proctor *C:* M McCarthy *PG:* M McCarthy (2)

Llanharan

Year of formation 1891
Ground Dairy Field, Bridgend Road, Llanharan, Mid Glamorgan
Tel: Llanharan (01443) 222209
Colours Black and sky blue hoops
Captain 1995-96 M Reynolds
Heineken Leagues 1995-96 Div 2 11th – *relegated*   **SWALEC Cup 1995-96** Lost 5-102 to Pontypridd (4th round)

League Record 1995-96

Date	Venue	Opponents	Result	Scorers
2 Sept	A	Pontypool	17-29	*T:* P John *PG:* W Jervis (3) *DG:* W Jervis
9 Sept	H	Bonymaen	17-14	*T:* P John *PG:* W Jervis (3) *DG:* W Jervis
16 Sept	A	Cross Keys	13-57	*T:* R Phillips *C:* D Griffiths *PG:* W Jervis (2)
23 Sept	H	Abercynon	9-10	*PG:* W Jervis (3)
30 Sept	A	Ystradgynlais	19-20	*T:* R Phillips *C:* W Jervis *PG:* W Jervis (3) *DG:* W Jervis
7 Oct	A	Tenby Utd	15-31	*T:* R Phillips (2) *C:* W Jervis *PG:* W Jervis
14 Oct	H	Maesteg	27-25	*T:* A Davies, W Brooks, J Morris, S Jenkins *C:* W Jervis (2) *PG:* W Jervis
28 Oct	A	Caerphilly	17-20	*T:* D Benjamin, P Ager, S Jenkins *C:* W Jervis
4 Nov	H	South Wales Police	24-27	*T:* G Pritchard, A Orrell *C:* W Jervis *PG:* W Jervis (2) *DG:* W Jervis
18 Nov	A	Llandovery	13-20	*T:* G Pritchard *C:* W Jervis *PG:* W Jervis (2)
25 Nov	H	Dunvant	11-50	*T:* S Jenkins *PG:* J Morris (2)
2 Dec	H	Pontypool	15-13	*T:* G Pritchard, P Ager *C:* W Jervis *PG:* W Jervis
9 Dec	A	Bonymaen	23-37	*T:* G Pritchard, P Ager *C:* W Jervis (2) *PG:* W Jervis (3)

6 Jan	H	Ystradgynlais	26-18	*T:* A Donovan, M Reynolds *C:* W Jervis (2) *PG:* W Jervis (4)
13 Jan	H	Tenby United	20-13	*T:* P John, W Jervis *C:* W Jervis (2) *PG:* W Jervis (2)
24 Feb	H	Cross Keys	6-3	*PG:* W Jervis (2)
9 Mar	A	Maesteg	10-21	*T:* D Martin *C:* W Jervis *PG:* W Jervis
30 Mar	H	Caerphilly	16-22	*T:* D Evans *C:* W Jervis *PG:* W Jervis (3)
6 Apr	A	South Wales Police	22-10	*T:* D Martin, D Griffiths, S Jenkins *C:* W Jervis (2) *PG:* W Jervis
13 Apr	A	Abercynon	24-17	*T:* A Donovan, A Davies *C:* W Jervis *PG:* W Jervis (4)
20 Apr	H	Llandovery	36-21	*T:* S Jenkins (2), A Evans, M Harry, A Tucker *C:* A Donovan *PG:* A Donovan (3)
27 Apr	A	Dunvant	22-31	*T:* M Griffiths, A Evans, D Evans, A Davies *C:* W Jervis

Maesteg

Year of formation 1877
Ground Old Parish Ground, Llynfi Road, Maesteg, Mid Glamorgan
Tel: Maesteg (01656) 732283
Colours Black and amber hoops
Most capped player G Evans (Wales) 10 caps
Captain 1995-96 G Davies
Heineken Leagues 1995-96 Div 2 7th   **SWALEC Cup 1995-96** Lost 13-41 to Pontypridd
(6th round)

League Record 1995-96

Date	Venue	Opponents	Result	Scorers
2 Sept	A	Dunvant	14-17	*T:* C Stephens *PG:* M Pearce (2) *DG:* M Pearce
9 Sept	H	Pontypool	3-28	*PG:* M Pearce
16 Sept	A	Bonymaen	26-31	*T:* R Gregory (2), I Strange, M Jones *C:* D Morris (3)
23 Sept	H	Cross Keys	15-13	*PG:* M Pearce (4) *DG:* M Pearce
30 Sept	A	Abercynon	7-22	*T:* L Harvey *C:* M Pearce
7 Oct	H	Ystradgynlais	18-7	*T:* D Morris, pen try *C:* D Morris *PG:* D Morris, M Pearce
14 Oct	A	Llanharan	25-27	*T:* C Stephens (2), D Neill, R Gregory *C:* M Pearce *PG:* M Pearce
28 Oct	A	Tenby Utd	15-7	*T:* C Stephens, M Morgans *C:* M Pearce *DG:* M Pearce
4 Nov	H	Caerphilly	12-22	*PG:* M Pearce (2) *DG:* M Pearce (2)
18 Nov	A	South Wales Police	14-10	*T:* M Morgans, C Stephens *C:* M Pearce (2)
25 Nov	H	Llandovery	28-23	*T:* P Watkin, C Stephens, H Lewis, pen try *C:* M Pearce *PG:* M Pearce (2)
2 Dec	H	Dunvant	6-14	*PG:* M Pearce (2)
23 Dec	H	Bonymaen	27-14	*T:* L Morgan (2), B Davey *PG:* M Pearce (3) *DG:* M Pearce
6 Jan	H	Abercynon	11-9	*T:* C Stephens *PG:* M Pearce (2)
13 Jan	A	Ystradgynlais	9-18	*PG:* M Pearce (3)
9 Mar	H	Llanharan	21-10	*T:* R Gregory, M Morgans *C:* D Morris *PG:* D Morris, M Pearce *DG:* M Pearce
15 Mar	A	Pontypool	17-48	*T:* S Jenkins (2), M Brown *C:* B Davey
23 Mar	A	Cross Keys	20-35	*T:* M Morgans, St J Towell *C:* M Pearce (2) *PG:* M Pearce (2)
30 Mar	H	Tenby Utd	26-14	*T:* D Neill, H Lewis, B Davey *C:* M Pearce *PG:* M Pearce (3)
6 Apr	A	Caerphilly	9-24	*PG:* M Pearce (3)

20 Apr	H	South Wales Police	17-11	*T:* R Gregory *PG:* M Pearce (4)
27 Apr	A	Llandovery	17-17	*T:* B Davey, St J Towell, P Watkin
				C: D Morris

Neath

Year of formation 1871
Ground The Gnoll, Gnoll Park Road, Neath, West Glamorgan   Tel: Neath (01639) 636547
Colours All black with white Maltese cross
Most capped player G O Llewellyn (Wales) 45 caps
Captain 1995-96 G O Llewellyn
Heineken Leagues 1995-96 Div 1 *Winners*   **SWALEC Cup 1995-96** Lost 22-29 to Pontypridd (final)

League Record 1995-96

Date	Venue	Opponents	Result	Scorers
9 Sept	A	Ebbw Vale	17-6	*T:* J Burnell, M Morgan *C:* G Davies (2) *PG:* G Davies
16 Sept	H	Cardiff	8-11	*T:* K Allen *PG:* C Beukes
23 Sept	A	Aberavon	20-10	*T:* L Davies, A Flowers, G D Llewellyn *C:* P Williams *PG:* P Williams
30 Sept	H	Newbridge	42-12	*T:* C Higgs, G D Llewellyn, C Scott, P Thorburn, J Funnell, S Williams, Ro Jones *C:* P Thorburn, C Beukes *PG:* C Beukes
7 Oct	A	Newport	10-10	*T:* C Higgs *C:* C Beukes *PG:* C Beukes
14 Oct	H	Bridgend	34-7	*T:* S Williams, H Woodland, J Davies, L Davies *C:* P Williams (4) *PG:* P Williams (2)
28 Oct	A	Pontypridd	5-22	*T:* Ri Jones
4 Nov	H	Abertillery	63-17	*T:* L Davies (3), I Boobyer (2), C Beukes (2), M Morgan, P Horgan, D Morris, R Wintle *C:* C Beukes (2), P Williams (2)
18 Nov	H	Swansea	18-11	*T:* G O Llewellyn, Ri Jones *C:* P Williams *PG:* P Williams (2)
25 Nov	A	Llanelli	6-18	*PG:* C Bridges (2)
2 Dec	H	Treorchy	42-13	*T:* C Higgs (2), H Woodland, Ro Jones, G Evans, J Davies, S Williams *C:* P Horgan (2) *PG:* P Horgan
9 Dec	H	Ebbw Vale	76-29	*T:* G Evans (2), R Jones (2), C Scott, J Davies, C Bridges, L Davies, R Wintle, D Morris, K Allen, C Higgs *C:* C Bridges (8)
23 Dec	A	Cardiff	8-28	*T:* C Scott *PG:* C Bridges
6 Jan	A	Newbridge	20-3	*T:* G D Llewellyn (2), P Horgan *C:* P Horgan *PG:* P Horgan
9 Mar	A	Bridgend	45-8	*T:* C Higgs (2), I Boobyer (2), Ri Jones, Ro Jones, G Evans, J Funnell *C:* J Funnell *PG:* P Horgan
30 Mar	H	Newport	65-23	*T:* Ri Jones (2), G Evans (2), J Davies, P Horgan, S Williams, pen try *C:* P Horgan (8) *PG:* P Horgan (3)
3 Apr	H	Aberavon	95-17	*T:* C Higgs (4), J Burnell (4), Ri Jones (2), G O Llewellyn, G Davies, L Davies, J Funnell, B Williams *C:* C Bridges (10)
6 Apr	A	Abertillery	50-24	*T:* C Scott (2), J Burnell (2), L Davies, P Williams, G D Llewellyn, C Higgs *C:* C Bridges (5)
20 Apr	A	Swansea	25-21	*T:* J Davies (2), G Evans *C:* C Bridges (2) *PG:* C Bridges (2)

411

26 Apr	H	Llanelli	41-0	*T:* C Higgs (2), L Davies, J Funnell, G O Llewellyn, A Kembery, R Wintle *C:* P Horgan (3)
11 May	A	Treorchy	58-31	*T:* I Boobyer (2), D Case (2), L Gerard, G D Llewellyn, H Woodland, Ro Jones, P Thorburn, M Morris *C:* P Horgan (2), P Thorburn, I Boobyer
14 May	H	Pontypridd	45-25	*T:* I Boobyer, J Davies, C Bridges, C Higgs, P Horgan, H Woodland, S Williams *C:* C Bridges (3), P Horgan, I Boobyer

Newbridge

Year of formation 1888
Ground The Welfare Ground, Bridge Street, Newbridge, Gwent
Tel: Newbridge (01495) 243247
Colours Blue and black hoops
Most capped player D Hayward (Wales) 15 caps
Captain 1995-96 P Kawulok
Heineken Leagues 1995-96 Div 1 9th   **SWALEC Cup 1995-96** Lost 15-20 to Pontypridd (quarter-final)

League Record 1995-96

Date	Venue	Opponents	Result	Scorers
2 Sept	A	Abertillery	15-10	*T:* G Taylor, J Hawker *C:* P Withers *PG:* P Withers
9 Sept	H	Newport	12-16	*T:* S Marshall, M Silva *C:* J Strange
16 Sept	A	Bridgend	29-28	*T:* P Watkins, S Hill, I Jones, R Smith, G Taylor *C:* J Strange (2)
23 Sept	H	Pontypridd	9-14	*T:* P Withers (2) *DG:* P Withers
30 Sept	A	Neath	12-42	*T:* R Smith, S Reed *C:* J Strange
7 Oct	H	Swansea	15-10	*PG:* P Withers (4) *DG:* P Withers
14 Oct	A	Llanelli	9-17	*PG:* J Strange (3)
28 Oct	H	Treorchy	30-26	*T:* D Dunn (2), P Withers, pen try *C:* P Withers (2) *PG:* P Withers (2)
4 Nov	A	Ebbw Vale	12-24	*T:* J Hawker, S Reed *C:* P Withers
18 Nov	H	Cardiff	18-30	*T:* D Dunn, R Smith, M Silva *PG:* P Withers
25 Nov	A	Aberavon	22-3	*T:* P Withers, J Derrick, G Taylor *C:* P Withers (2) *PG:* P Withers
2 Dec	H	Abertillery	15-13	*T:* D Dunn, R Williams, A Lucas
9 Dec	A	Newport	20-13	*T:* A Lucas, S Marshall, A Gibbs, R Smith
23 Dec	H	Bridgend	25-22	*T:* S Marshall (2), J Derrick *C:* J Strange (2) *PG:* J Strange (2)
6 Jan	H	Neath	3-20	*PG:* J Strange
13 Jan	A	Swansea	15-20	*T:* G Taylor, R Smith *C:* P Withers *PG:* P Withers
9 Mar	H	Llanelli	6-10	*PG:* P Withers (2)
30 Mar	A	Treorchy	10-12	*T:* D Rees, I Jones
6 Apr	H	Ebbw Vale	16-32	*T:* J Derrick *C:* J Strange *PG:* J Strange (3)
20 Apr	A	Cardiff	7-78	*T:* P Sedgemore *C:* J Strange
23 Apr	A	Pontypridd	5-75	*T:* P Withers
27 Apr	H	Aberavon	41-34	*T:* J Hawker (2), A Gibbs, P Withers, R Smith, S Marshall, pen try *C:* P Withers (3)

Newport

Year of formation 1874
Ground Rodney Parade, Rodney Road, Newport, Gwent
Tel: Newport (01633) 258193 or 267410

Colours Black and amber
Most capped player K J Jones (Wales) 44 caps
Captain 1995-96 R Goodey
Heineken Leagues 1995-96 Div 1 8th   **SWALEC Cup 1995-96** Lost 22-24 to Neath (semi-final)

League Record 1995-96

Date	Venue	Opponents	Result	Scorers
2 Sept	H	Aberavon	30-9	*T:* M Yendle, M Williams *C:* G Rees *PG:* G Rees (5) *DG:* G Rees
9 Sept	A	Newbridge	16-12	*T:* M Roderick *C:* G Rees *PG:* G Rees (3)
16 Sept	H	Abertillery	31-12	*T:* P Young, M Yendle, D Hughes, A Carter *C:* G Rees *PG:* G Rees (3)
23 Sept	H	Bridgend	27-12	*T:* G Rees, M Workman, C Brown *C:* G Rees (3) *PG:* G Rees (2)
30 Sept	A	Pontypridd	3-38	*PG:* G Rees
7 Oct	H	Neath	10-10	*T:* R Rees *C:* G Rees *PG:* G Rees
14 Oct	A	Swansea	6-78	*PG:* G Rees (2)
28 Oct	H	Llanelli	21-8	*T:* R Goodey, R Rees *C:* G Rees *PG:* G Rees (2) *DG:* J Hewlett
4 Nov	A	Treorchy	31-25	*T:* R Goodey, D Edwards, C Arnold *C:* G Rees (2) *PG:* G Rees (4)
18 Nov	H	Ebbw Vale	25-22	*T:* R Rees, J Hewlett, M Voyle *C:* G Rees (2) *PG:* G Rees (2)
25 Nov	A	Cardiff	22-18	*T:* O Thomas *C:* G Rees *PG:* G Rees (5)
2 Dec	A	Aberavon	6-8	*PG:* G Rees (2)
9 Dec	H	Newbridge	13-20	*T:* D Gray *C:* G Rees *PG:* G Rees (2)
23 Dec	A	Abertillery	50-33	*T:* G Rees (2), C Arnold, D Hughes, pen try *C:* G Rees (4), D Hughes *PG:* G Rees (5)
6 Jan	H	Pontypridd	29-30	*T:* G Rees (2) *C:* G Rees (2) *PG:* G Rees (5)
9 Mar	H	Swansea	27-16	*T:* A Palfrey, D Hughes, R Rees *C:* G Rees (3) *PG:* G Rees (2)
30 Mar	A	Neath	23-65	*T:* R Rees, S Davies *C:* G Rees (2) *PG:* G Rees (3)
6 Apr	H	Treorchy	30-36	*T:* D Hughes, M Llewellyn, J Hewlett, R Rees *C:* G Rees (2) *PG:* G Rees *DG:* G Rees
20 Apr	A	Ebbw Vale	12-27	*PG:* G Rees (4)
24 Apr	A	Bridgend	17-48	*T:* G Rees, R Snow *C:* G Rees (2) *PG:* G Rees
27 Apr	H	Cardiff	19-29	*T:* J Lowry *C:* G Rees *PG:* G Rees (3) *DG:* J Hewlett
11 May	A	Llanelli	22-56	*T:* S Davies, G Rees, A Palfrey *C:* G Rees (2) *PG:* G Rees

Pontypool

Year of formation 1868 (reconstituted 1901)
Ground The Park, Pontypool, Gwent   Tel: Pontypool (01495) 763492
Colours Red, white and black hoops
Most capped player G Price (Wales) 41 caps
Captain 1995-96 W Morris
Heineken Leagues 1995-96 Div 2 4th   **SWALEC Cup 1995-96** Lost 12-22 to Rumney (4th round)

League Record 1995-96

Date	Venue	Opponents	Result	Scorers
2 Sept	H	Llanharan	29-17	*T:* D Meredith (2), G Pugh *C:* J Williams *PG:* J Williams (3) *DG:* J Williams

413

9 Sept	A	Maesteg	28-3	*T:* K Walker (2), D Lynch, M Hayter *C:* J Williams *PG:* J Williams (2)
16 Sept	H	Caerphilly	31-8	*T:* D Meredith (2), P Taylor, W Morris, M Squire *C:* J Williams (3)
23 Sept	A	South Wales Police	29-17	*T:* W Morris (2), J Williams, G Pugh *C:* J Williams (3) *PG:* J Williams
30 Sept	H	Llandovery	22-13	*T:* P Taylor, J Williams *PG:* J Williams (4)
7 Oct	A	Dunvant	10-26	*T:* P Taylor, K Walker
14 Oct	H	Tenby Utd	36-10	*T:* C West, J Williams, K Walker *C:* J Williams (3) *PG:* J Williams (5)
28 Oct	H	Bonymaen	27-16	*T:* J Williams, J Rhead, R Harvey, C Billen *C:* J Williams (2) *PG:* J Williams
4 Nov	A	Cross Keys	23-29	*T:* I Calder, J Thomas *C:* J Williams (2) *PG:* J Williams (3)
18 Nov	H	Abercynon	31-26	*T:* J Rhead (2), C Billen, W Morris, D Lynch *C:* J Williams (3)
25 Nov	A	Ystradgynlais	20-15	*T:* D Lynch, N Hope *C:* J Williams (2) *PG:* J Williams (2)
2 Dec	A	Llanharan	13-15	*T:* W Morris, P Taylor *PG:* J Williams
23 Dec	A	Caerphilly	6-13	*PG:* J Williams (2)
6 Jan	A	Llandovery	10-13	*T:* K Walker *C:* J Williams *PG:* J Williams
13 Jan	H	Dunvant	20-21	*T:* A Ward *PG:* J Williams (5)
9 Mar	A	Tenby Utd	28-14	*T:* K Walker (2), J Rhead (2) *C:* J Williams *PG:* J Williams (2)
15 Mar	H	Maesteg	48-17	*T:* W Morris (3), K Walker (2), P Armstrong, C West *C:* J Williams (5) *PG:* J Williams
23 Mar	H	South Wales Police	25-38	*T:* J Rhead, A Ward, C West, W Morris *C:* J Williams *PG:* J Williams
30 Mar	A	Bonymaen	15-22	*T:* W Morris, J Rhead *C:* J Williams *PG:* J Williams
6 Apr	H	Cross Keys	29-20	*T:* D Lynch, J Williams, L Mruk *C:* J Williams *PG:* J Williams (4)
20 Apr	A	Abercynon	16-26	*T:* A Carr, L Mruk *PG:* J Williams (2)
27 Apr	H	Ystradgynlais	14-16	*T:* S Cross *PG:* J Williams (3)

Pontypridd

Year of formation 1876
Ground Sardis Road Ground, Pwllgwaun, Pontypridd
Tel: Pontypridd (01443) 405006 and 407170
Colours Black and white hoops
Most capped player N R Jenkins (Wales) 39 caps
Captain 1995-96 N Bezani
Heineken Leagues 1995-96 Div 1 3rd **SWALEC Cup 1995-96** *Winners* – beat Neath 29-22 (final)

League Record 1995-96

Date	Venue	Opponents	Result	Scorers
2 Sept	H	Ebbw Vale	35-18	*T:* D McIntosh (2), C Thomas, G Jones, N Lloyd *C:* C Cormack (2) *PG:* C Cormack, L Jarvis
9 Sept	A	Cardiff	31-36	*T:* Paul John (2), D Manley *C:* N Jenkins (2) *PG:* N Jenkins (4)
16 Sept	H	Aberavon	70-25	*T:* J Lewis (2), L Lewis, N Jenkins, Phil John, C Cormack, M Spiller, D Manley, N Eynon, G Jones *C:* N Jenkins (7) *PG:* N Jenkins (2)
23 Sept	A	Newbridge	14-9	*T:* Phil John *PG:* N Jenkins (3)
30 Sept	H	Newport	38-3	*T:* N Jenkins, R Collins, G Jones *C:* N Jenkins *PG:* N Jenkins (7)

7 Oct	A	Bridgend	17-12	*T:* S McIntosh *PG:* N Jenkins (4)
14 Oct	H	Abertillery	55-17	*T:* N Jenkins (3), D Manley (2), Paul John, C Cormack, M Williams, S McIntosh *C:* N Jenkins (5)
28 Oct	H	Neath	22-5	*T:* M Lloyd *C:* N Jenkins *PG:* N Jenkins (5)
18 Nov	H	Llanelli	31-18	*T:* Paul John, N Bezani, D Manley *C:* N Jenkins (2) *PG:* N Jenkins (3) *DG:* N Jenkins
25 Nov	A	Treorchy	9-11	*PG:* N Jenkins (3)
2 Dec	A	Ebbw Vale	7-3	*T:* M Rowley *C:* N Jenkins
6 Jan	A	Newport	30-29	*T:* D Manley, J Lewis *C:* L Jarvis *PG:* L Jarvis (6)
13 Jan	H	Bridgend	48-11	*T:* D Manley (2), G Lewis (2), S Lewis, pen try *C:* L Jarvis (3) *PG:* L Jarvis (3) *DG:* L Jarvis
23 Jan	A	Swansea	9-13	*PG:* L Jarvis (3)
10 Feb	A	Aberavon	19-3	*T:* Paul John, D Manley, G Lewis *C:* N Jenkins (2)
9 Mar	A	Abertillery	70-10	*T:* D Manley (2), Paul John (2), G Lewis (2), S Lewis, C Cormack, N Jenkins, M Lloyd, J Lewis *C:* N Jenkins (5), C Cormack *PG:* N Jenkins
6 Apr	H	Swansea	54-22	*T:* G Lewis (3), R Collins, J Lewis, N Jenkins, C Cormack *C:* N Jenkins (5) *PG:* N Jenkins (3)
20 Apr	A	Llanelli	13-23	*T:* Paul John *C:* N Jenkins *PG:* N Jenkins (2)
23 Apr	H	Newbridge	75-5	*T:* S Enoch (2), M Lloyd (2), S Lewis (2), G Lewis, N Jenkins, D McIntosh, N Lloyd, M Rowley *C:* N Jenkins (10)
27 Apr	H	Treorchy	80-12	*T:* Paul John (5), G Jones (3), N Jenkins, G Prosser, S Lewis, S Enoch *C:* N Jenkins (10)
10 May	H	Cardiff	27-27	*T:* N Jenkins, G Lewis, Paul John, M Spiller *C:* N Jenkins (2) *PG:* N Jenkins
14 May	A	Neath	25-45	*T:* S Lewis, G Prosser, J Lewis, N Jenkins *C:* N Jenkins *PG:* N Jenkins

South Wales Police

Year of formation 1969
Ground Waterton Cross, Bridgend, Mid Glamorgan
Tel: Bridgend (01656) 655555 ext 218
Colours Red, white and royal blue with blue shorts
Most capped player R G Collins (Wales) 28 caps
Captain 1995-96 S Legge
Heineken Leagues 1995-96 Div 2 10th   **SWALEC Cup 1995-96** Lost 13-29 to Caerphilly (6th round)

League Record 1995-96

Date	Venue	Opponents	Result	Scorers
2 Sept	A	Tenby Utd	6-24	*PG:* J Price (2)
9 Sept	H	Llandovery	8-18	*T:* P Lloyd *PG:* J Price
16 Sept	A	Dunvant	7-16	*T:* D Thomas *C:* J Price
23 Sept	H	Pontypool	17-29	*T:* D Thomas (2) *C:* J Price (2) *PG:* J Price
30 Sept	A	Bonymaen	18-35	*T:* S Rees, I Hemburrow, A Davies *PG:* D Connick
7 Oct	H	Cross Keys	21-20	*T:* R James, S Pritchard *C:* J Price *PG:* J Price (3)
14 Oct	A	Abercynon	11-27	*T:* R James *PG:* J Price (2)
28 Oct	H	Ystradgynlais	35-21	*T:* R James (3), I Hemburrow (2) *C:* J Price (2) *PG:* J Price *DG:* S Pritchard

4 Nov	A	Llanharan	27-24	*T:* S Legge (2), I Hemburrow *C:* M Cox (3) *PG:* M Cox (2)
18 Nov	H	Maesteg	10-14	*T:* G Hiscocks *C:* M Cox *PG:* M Cox
25 Nov	A	Caerphilly	12-16	*T:* A Patterson, pen try *C:* J Price
2 Dec	H	Tenby Utd	30-14	*T:* A Hughes, G Jones, pen try *C:* J Price (3) *PG:* J Price (3)
9 Dec	A	Llandovery	13-15	*T:* A Davies *C:* J Price *PG:* J Price (2)
6 Jan	H	Bonymaen	35-0	*T:* S Evans (2), I Hemburrow (2), M Poole, A Davies *C:* J Price *PG:* J Price
13 Jan	A	Cross Keys	28-25	*T:* M Cox (2), A Hughes *C:* J Price (2) *PG:* J Price (3)
10 Feb	H	Dunvant	10-27	*T:* I Hemburrow *C:* J Price *PG:* J Price
9 Mar	H	Abercynon	16-19	*T:* J Price *C:* J Price *PG:* J Price (3)
23 Mar	A	Pontypool	38-25	*T:* J Price (2), M Cox, S Evans, S Parfitt *C:* J Price (5) *PG:* J Price
30 Mar	A	Ystradgynlais	22-25	*T:* Alan Davies, Alun Davies, pen try *C:* J Price (2) *PG:* J Price
6 Apr	H	Llanharan	10-22	*T:* D Thomas, S Rees
20 Apr	A	Maesteg	11-17	*T:* G Pritchard *PG:* J Price *DG:* A Hughes
27 Apr	H	Caerphilly	12-15	*T:* S Evans, P Ashby *C:* J Price

Swansea

Year of formation 1873
Ground St Helen's Ground, Bryn Road, Swansea, West Glamorgan SA2 0AR
Tel: Swansea (01792) 466593
Colours All white
Most capped player R N Jones (Wales) 54 caps
Captain 1995-96 A Clement/Stuart Davies
Heineken Leagues 1995-96 Div 1 6th   **SWALEC CUP 1995-96** Lost 9-20 to Cardiff (6th round)

League Record 1995-96

Date	Venue	Opponents	Result	Scorers
9 Sept	A	Treorchy	16-12	*T:* Simon Davies *C:* L Griffiths *PG:* L Griffiths (3)
16 Sept	H	Ebbw Vale	53-20	*T:* A Harris (3), M Taylor, Simon Davies, A Moore, C Charvis, D Weatherley, M Thomas *C:* A Williams (2), L Griffiths (2)
23 Sept	A	Cardiff	13-50	*T:* Simon Davies, A Williams *PG:* A Williams
30 Sept	H	Aberavon	66-5	*T:* Rh Jones (3), A Harris, A Clement, A Moore, C Charvis, R Appleyard, M Taylor *C:* A Williams (6) *PG:* A Williams (3)
7 Oct	A	Newbridge	10-15	*T:* Stuart Davies, R Appleyard
14 Oct	H	Newport	78-6	*T:* C Charvis (4), A Harris (3), Simon Davies (2), A Williams (2) *C:* A Williams (7) *PG:* A Williams (3)
28 Oct	A	Bridgend	16-31	*T:* Stuart Davies *C:* A Williams *PG:* A Williams (3)
18 Nov	A	Neath	11-18	*T:* R Boobyer *PG:* A Williams (2)
25 Nov	H	Abertillery	71-13	*T:* A Harris (3), A Williams (2), M Taylor (2), D Weatherley (2), Simon Davies, M Thomas *C:* A Williams (4), A Harris (4)
2 Dec	A	Llanelli	3-13	*PG:* A Williams
9 Dec	H	Treorchy	46-24	*T:* Simon Davies (2), R Boobyer (2), A Harris, M Taylor, C Anthony *C:* A Williams (4) *PG:* A Williams
12 Dec	H	Llanelli	26-20	*T:* A Williams, A Harris, Simon Davies *C:* A Williams *PG:* A Williams (3)

23 Dec	A	Ebbw Vale	0-25	
6 Jan	A	Aberavon	12-6	*PG:* A Williams (4)
13 Jan	H	Newbridge	20-15	*T:* W Leach (2), M Taylor, M Thomas
23 Jan	H	Pontypridd	13-9	*T:* R Boobyer *C:* L Davies *PG:* L Davies, A Williams
9 Mar	A	Newport	16-27	*T:* Rh Jones, Simon Davies *PG:* L Davies (2)
23 Mar	H	Bridgend	29-38	*T:* D Thomas (2), Ro Jones, M Evans *C:* A Williams (3) *PG:* A Williams
6 Apr	A	Pontypridd	22-54	*T:* R Boobyer, R Shaw, C Charvis *C:* A Williams (2) *PG:* A Williams
13 Apr	H	Cardiff	0-59	
20 Apr	H	Neath	21-25	*T:* E Evans, R Boobyer *C:* A Williams *PG:* A Williams (3)
27 Apr	A	Abertillery	64-14	*T:* A Williams (3), Simon Davies, C Charvis, Stuart Davies, D Hawkins, R Jones, R Boobyer, pen try *C:* A Williams (5), A Harris, Simon Davies

Tenby United

Year of formation 1901
Ground Heywood Lane, Tenby, Dyfed   Tel: Tenby (01834) 842909 and 843501
Colours Black and scarlet hoops
Captain 1995-96 M Evans
Heineken Leagues 1995-96 Div 2 12th – *relegated*   **SWALEC Cup 1995-96** Lost 9-46 to Swansea (4th round)

League Record 1995-96

Date	Venue	Opponents	Result	Scorers
2 Sept	H	South Wales Police	24-6	*T:* S Hartland (2), D Hadley *C:* D Bowen (2), D Bevan *PG:* D Bowen
9 Sept	A	Abercynon	12-27	*PG:* D Bowen (4)
16 Sept	A	Llandovery	10-16	*T:* D Lawrence *C:* D Bowen *PG:* D Bowen
23 Sept	H	Ystradgynlais	18-14	*T:* D Lawrence (2) *C:* D Bowen *PG:* D Bowen (2)
30 Sept	A	Dunvant	8-51	*T:* D Thomas *PG:* D Bowen
7 Oct	H	Llanharan	31-15	*T:* D Bevan, M Evans, A Phillips *C:* D Bowen (2) *PG:* D Bowen (4)
14 Oct	A	Pontypool	10-36	*T:* M Evans, D Thomas
28 Oct	H	Maesteg	7-15	*T:* E Lewis *C:* D Bowen
4 Nov	A	Bonymaen	12-40	*T:* M Evans, A McPherson *C:* D Bowen
18 Nov	H	Caerphilly	7-25	*T:* S Hartland *C:* D Bowen
25 Nov	A	Cross Keys	0-46	
2 Dec	A	South Wales Police	14-30	*T:* L Anson, D Balkwill *C:* D Bowen (2)
9 Dec	H	Abercynon	22-8	*T:* D Balkwill, S Hartland, D Hadley *C:* D Bowen (2) *PG:* D Bowen
23 Dec	H	Llandovery	9-12	*PG:* D Bowen (3)
13 Jan	A	Llanharan	13-20	*T:* pen try *C:* D Bowen *PG:* D Bowen (2)
10 Feb	A	Ystradgynlais	10-17	*T:* D Balkwill *C:* G Davies *PG:* G Davies
9 Mar	H	Pontypool	14-28	*T:* L Anson, E Lewis *C:* D Bowen (2)
30 Mar	A	Maesteg	14-26	*T:* D Bowen *PG:* D Bowen (3)
6 Apr	H	Bonymaen	5-38	*T:* P Morris
13 Apr	H	Dunvant	5-36	*T:* C Miles
20 Apr	A	Caerphilly	5-59	*T:* D Balkwill

27 Apr	H	Cross Keys	22-63	*T:* S Williams, G Davies, D Balkwill, D Hadley *C:* G Davies

Treorchy

Year of formation 1886
Ground The Oval, Treorchy, Rhondda   Tel: Treorchy (01443) 434671
Colours Black and white hoops
Most capped player D W Evans (Wales) 12 caps
Captain 1995-96 G Owen
Heineken Leagues 1995-96 Div 1 10th   **SWALEC Cup 1995-96** Lost 5-41 to Pontypridd
(5th round)

League Record 1995-96

Date	Venue	Opponents	Result	Scorers
9 Sept	H	Swansea	12-16	*PG:* D Lloyd (4)
16 Sept	A	Llanelli	7-52	*T:* R Morgan *C:* A Harries
23 Sept	A	Abertillery	21-24	*T:* A Thomas, D Owen *C:* D Evans *PG:* D Evans (3)
30 Sept	H	Ebbw Vale	20-29	*T:* A Thomas (2) *C:* D Evans (2) *PG:* D Evans (2)
7 Oct	A	Cardiff	3-67	*PG:* D Evans
14 Oct	H	Aberavon	28-39	*T:* I Davies, K Jones, A Lewis *C:* D Evans (2) *PG:* D Evans (3)
28 Oct	A	Newbridge	26-30	*T:* A Lewis, S Eggar, I Davies, pen try *C:* D Evans (3)
4 Nov	H	Newport	25-31	*T:* M Smith, A Thomas, C Hammans, D Owen *C:* D Evans *PG:* D Evans
18 Nov	A	Bridgend	17-33	*T:* D Lloyd (2), A Freeman *C:* D Evans
25 Nov	H	Pontypridd	11-9	*T:* D Davies *PG:* W Booth *DG:* W Booth
2 Dec	A	Neath	13-42	*T:* S Eggar *C:* D Evans *PG:* D Evans (2)
9 Dec	A	Swansea	24-46	*T:* D Evans, P Jones, C Hammans *C:* D Evans (3) *PG:* D Evans
23 Dec	H	Llanelli	10-43	*T:* A Thomas, C Hammans
6 Jan	A	Ebbw Vale	6-40	*PG:* D Evans (2)
9 Mar	A	Aberavon	17-16	*T:* R Morgan *PG:* D Evans (4)
23 Mar	H	Abertillery	20-12	*T:* A Harries *PG:* D Evans (4) *DG:* D Evans
30 Mar	H	Newbridge	12-10	*PG:* D Evans (2) *DG:* D Evans (2)
6 Apr	A	Newport	36-30	*T:* A Lewis, G Owen, N Jones, D Lloyd, D Evans, J Riggs *C:* D Evans (3)
20 Apr	H	Bridgend	20-20	*T:* J Riggs, C Hammans, A Thomas *C:* D Evans *PG:* D Evans
27 Apr	A	Pontypridd	12-80	*T:* R Morgan, A Thomas *C:* D Evans
2 May	H	Cardiff	10-31	*T:* K Jones *C:* D Evans *PG:* D Evans
11 May	H	Neath	31-58	*T:* D Evans, P Jones, R Pask, D Lloyd, A Lewis *C:* D Evans (2), P Jones

Ystradgynlais

Year of formation 1890
Ground Ynyscedwyn Road, Ystradgynlais   Tel: Ystradgynlais (01639) 842948
Colours Blue and white
Captain 1995-96 D Love
Heineken Leagues 1995-96 Div 2 9th   **SWALEC Cup 1995-96** Lost 5-49 to Newport
(5th round)

League Record 1995-96

Date	Venue	Opponents	Result	Scorers
2 Sept	A	Bonymaen	3-16	*PG:* D Love
9 Sept	H	Cross Keys	16-19	*T:* J Hopkins *C:* D Love *PG:* D Love (3)
16 Sept	A	Abercynon	10-14	*T:* pen try *C:* D Love *PG:* D Love
23 Sept	A	Tenby Utd	14-18	*T:* B Howells *PG:* M Healey (3)
30 Sept	H	Llanharan	20-19	*T:* C Thomas, S Donovan *C:* K Jones (2) *PG:* M Healey *DG:* A Davies
7 Oct	A	Maesteg	7-18	*T:* pen try *C:* K Jones
14 Oct	H	Caerphilly	30-36	*T:* C Hopkins (2), H Davies, J Morgan *C:* J Richards (2) *PG:* J Richards (2)
21 Oct	A	South Wales Police	21-35	*T:* R Woodley, A Davies, M Harris *C:* D Love (3)
4 Nov	H	Llandovery	7-3	*T:* D Griffiths *C:* D Love
18 Nov	A	Dunvant	21-19	*T:* B Howells, pen try *C:* D Love *PG:* D Love (2) *DG:* M Nottingham
25 Nov	H	Pontypool	15-20	*T:* D Griffiths, D Love *C:* D Love *PG:* D Love
2 Dec	H	Bonymaen	14-12	*T:* D Griffiths *PG:* M Nottingham (3)
9 Dec	A	Cross Keys	18-13	*T:* D Love, pen try *C:* D Love *PG:* M Nottingham, D Love
23 Dec	H	Abercynon	16-11	*T:* S Donovan *C:* D Love *PG:* D Love (3)
6 Jan	A	Llanharan	18-26	*T:* D Griffiths (3) *DG:* M Nottingham
13 Jan	H	Maesteg	18-9	*T:* D Griffiths (2) *C:* M Nottingham *PG:* M Nottingham (2)
10 Feb	H	Tenby Utd	17-10	*T:* D Love (2), S Donovan *C:* M Nottingham
9 Mar	A	Caerphilly	3-21	*DG:* M Nottingham
30 Mar	H	South Wales Police	25-22	*T:* G Jones, J Hopkins, D Love *C:* M Nottingham (2) *PG:* M Nottingham (2)
6 Apr	A	Llandovery	18-18	*T:* A Williams, D Griffiths *C:* D Love *DG:* M Nottingham (2)
20 Apr	H	Dunvant	27-42	*T:* A Williams, pen try *C:* M Nottingham *PG:* M Nottingham (5)
27 Apr	A	Pontypool	16-14	*T:* D Love *C:* M Nottingham *PG:* M Nottingham (3)

OBITUARY 1995-96 *(up to 1 May 1996)*

Joseph Richard AUTY (Headingley, Leicester), an outside-half renowned in the thirties for his sidestep, died in Leeds on 7 June 1995, aged 84. Dick Auty made his sole England appearance against Scotland at Murrayfield in 1935 with Bernard Gadney, later his club scrum-half, as partner.

Dewi Iorwerth Ellis BEBB (Carmarthen Training College, Swansea), one of Wales' all-time quickest wings, made a fairy-tale start to his 34-cap career. Catapulted into the Welsh XV in 1959 after only a handful of first-class games, he scored the winning try of a match against England played in awful conditions. Blessed with long legs and a raking stride, he went on to make the most of the few chances which came his way in international rugby and collected 11 tries, six of them against England. He was a Lion in South Africa in 1962 and in Australasia in 1966. He died on 14 March 1996 in Cardiff, aged 57.

Graham BEVAN (Newport), the hooker in Newport's famous 3-0 triumph over the Fifth All Blacks of 1963-64, died in May 1995.

Leonard Grist BLYTH (Swansea) collapsed and died in Johannesburg on 25 June 1995 after attending the Rugby World Cup. He was 74. First capped as a 30-something against South Africa in 1951, he won three caps for Wales as a flanker in a side which went on to win the Grand Slam. He was later chairman of selectors at Swansea. His son Roger won six Welsh caps between 1974 and 1980.

Gerhard Hamilton BRAND (Western Province) won 16 caps for South Africa and scored 55 points as a wing-cum-full-back between 1928 and 1938. Arguably one of rugby's best-ever kickers, he landed 30 goals on the 1931-32 Springbok tour to Britain and Ireland. The range of his successful drop-kick in the international against England on that tour was 85 yards – easily the longest such kick in the history of Test rugby. He died on 4 February 1996 at the age of 89.

Peter Robert BROMAGE, the Birmingham solicitor who was an RFU committee member for 15 years, died at his home on 20 July 1995, aged 62. Only one week before his death he had become the first chairman of the Union's new executive committee.

Massimiliano CAPUZZONI (Milan) died in a diving accident off the Sicilian coast on 5 August 1995. Only 26, he had played in the winning Italian side against Ireland in Treviso two months earlier and was a member of the national squad at the Rugby World Cup in South Africa.

Sir John CARMICHAEL (St Andrews University), a distinguished civil servant, businessman and golfer who died aged 85 on 6 January 1996, was a noted rugby footballer in his student days. He had a Scotland trial and was a reserve for the national side more than a dozen times.

Henri CLARAC (St Girons) was capped once for France as a wing forward in 1938. During the war he fought in the Resistance and was decorated for his bravery. He died in October 1995 at the age of 82.

Douglas DALTON (Hawke's Bay, Wellington), a tough-as-teak front-rower, appeared in nine Tests for New Zealand between 1935 and 1938. After the war he served Hawke's Bay and North Island as a selector. He died in Napier on 28 July 1995, aged 82.

Geoffrey John DEAN (Harlequins, Army), England's scrum-half against Ireland in 1931, died in January 1996 at the age of 86. 'Tinny' Dean belonged to the small band of Cambridge internationals who failed to win his rugby Blue. He captained the Army from 1936 to 1938.

Paul DESCAMPS (SBUC), who died at Léon on 2 September 1995, was, at 92, one of the last survivors of the French XVs of the 1920s. He won his only cap in the back row against Germany at Frankfurt in 1927.

Sir Thomas Gordon DEVITT (Cambridge University, Blackheath), whose death was announced at Christmas 1995, won Blues for rugby and athletics at Cambridge before playing four times on the wing for England between 1926 and 1928. Aged 92, he was the second-oldest surviving England international at the time of his death.

Allan Burdett FARQUHAR created history in 1961 by becoming the first New Zealander to referee an entire Test series: the three-match rubber between New Zealand and France. Altogether he controlled six Tests up to 1964 and his other representative appointments included the game between Otago and the 1959 Lions. He died in Auckland on 21 November 1995 at 72.

Murray FLETCHER (Bedford), the East Midlands scrum-half in three County Championship finals in the early 1950s, died in March 1996, aged 72. A pupil and later master at Bedford School, he played 148 matches for the town's club.

Graeme Lester HARRISON, the NZRFU director of rugby refereeing, died suddenly at work on 12 March 1996, aged 62. He controlled six major internationals between 1980 and 1984.

Derek Peter HEPBURN (Woodford) died at Milton on Stour, Dorset, on 30 April 1996. He was 76. As an outside-half and later centre, he won nine Scotland caps between 1947 and 1949. He dropped a goal on his international debut against Australia in November 1947 when Scotland were beaten 16-7 at Murrayfield.

Francis Melville HEYWOOD (Cambridge University), a former master of Marlborough College, died on 2 November 1995 at the age of 87. At Cambridge, where he took a double first in Classics, he appeared on the wing in the side which won the 1928 Varsity Match.

Paul Geoffrey Allen JOHNSTONE (Western Province, Oxford University, Transvaal) died in Hermanus on 22 April 1996, aged 65. His nine caps for South Africa between 1951 and 1956 included all five Test wins of the Fourth Springboks tour of Europe in 1951-52. He returned to England to win three Oxford Blues between 1952 and 1954 and captained the university in his final year.

Pierre LACAZE (Lourdes) was the inspirational full-back who made his debut for France in South Africa in 1958 when the Springboks were defeated in a home series for the first time this century. 'Papillon' kept his place for the 1959 Five Nations, when he helped France to win their first outright title, but transferred to Rugby League soon afterwards, winning further international honours. He died at Pontacq on 8 July 1995, aged 61.

George Phillipus LOCHNER (Eastern Province) died at Somerset West on 30 January 1996 at the age of 82. He appeared as a utility back in South Africa's triumphant march through Australia and New Zealand in 1937, but played at centre in three winning Tests for the Springboks in 1937 and 1938. 'Flappie' Lochner later became the president of Boland RFU.

Henare Pawhara MILNER (East Coast, Wanganui, Counties) won his only New Zealand cap as a wing in the Third Test of the 1970 visit to South Africa. 'Buff' Milner died suddenly on 2 March 1996 while touring England as coach of Osaka University. He was 50.

Peter Henry MURDOCH (Auckland) died in Auckland on 16 October 1995, aged 54. As a five-eighth he represented the All Blacks in 1964 and 1965, scoring tries in the first two of his five New Zealand Test matches.

Bruce Alan NEALE (Rosslyn Park, Army) won three caps for England as a lock in 1951. He was an Army stalwart for many seasons after the war and captained the soldiers in 1952. He died in Ipswich on 28 January 1996, aged 72.

Brig Donald NOTT DSO, OBE, MC (Army), the well-known career soldier who died on 5 February 1996 at the age of 87, played in the back row of the Army XVs of 1929 and 1930. He also turned out for Devon and Kent in the County Championship and was a county-standard hockey player.

John Michael O'NEILL (Queensland) was a talented utility back whose Test career for Australia was restricted to four matches, owing to his medical studies. Dr O'Neill died at Gold Coast on 16 August 1995, aged 63.

Sir John Henry ORR OBE (Heriot's FP, Edinburgh City Police), a former chief constable for Lothian and Borders who died at 77 in Edinburgh on 26 September 1995, was a strapping forward in his youth. On the verge of Scotland honours in 1939, he was originally deprived of a cap by the war. He eventually appeared twice for Scotland in 1947 and was president of the SRU in 1975-76.

Grahame Wilshaw PARKER OBE (Cambridge University, Blackheath, Gloucester) was England's full-back twice in 1938, scoring 24 points (including six conversions – still the series record – in blustery conditions against Ireland). He was also a noted Gloucestershire cricketer and served the county as secretary/manager and president. He died in Sidmouth on 11 November 1995, aged 83.

Alun Edward Islwyn PASK (Abertillery) was 20 years ahead of his time when he won his 26 Welsh caps in the 1960s. Athletic, mobile and with good hands, he was a master of all the game's skills in an era when loose forwards were generally expected to do no more than push, forage and defend. Indeed, a criticism of his play was that it was too showy. Yet he was undoubtedly the best back-row man of his generation – a fact recognised by the Lions selectors, who chose him for eight Tests on the 1962 and 1966 tours overseas. The former Welsh captain died in a fire at his Blackwood home on 1 November 1995. He was 58.

Harry PEACOCK (Newport), a forward first capped as a teenager, died in France in March 1996, aged 87. He played for Wales six times in 1929 and 1930.

Maixent PIQUEMAL (Tarbes), whose death at the age of 88 was reported in August 1995, played full-back for France nine times between 1927 and 1930.

John REED, rugby union correspondent of the *Sunday Express* from 1958 until his retirement in 1984, died in Esher in November 1995, aged 76. He was a founding member of the Rugby Union Writers' Club, a longstanding Surrey County member and author of their centenary history.

James Vere RICHARDSON (Oxford University, Birkenhead Park), who died at Padstowe on 1 May 1995, aged 91, was on the winning side as a centre in all five of his England internationals in 1928 and topped the scoring list as place-kicker that season, collecting 23 points.

David Edward Arfon ROBERTS (Oxford University, London Welsh) was at Oxford (where he missed out on his Blue) at the time of his only Welsh cap: at scrum-half against England at Cardiff in 1930. He died on 16 November 1995 at the age of 86.

Dr Edward Keith SCOTT (Oxford University, St Mary's Hospital, Redruth) won an early wartime Blue before forming with Nim Hall and Norman Bennett a dynamic midfield for the successful St Mary's Hospital side of the mid-1940s. All three later played for England, and Scott captained his country three times in 1948. His father had also played for England, in 1907. Keith Scott died on 3 June 1995. He was 76.

John Allen Edgar SIGGINS (Collegians) died at 86 in Belfast on 24 December 1995. He won 24 consecutive caps for Ireland and was captain on ten occasions between 1935 and 1937. Post-war he became a widely respected administrator. In 1955 he managed the successful Lions tour of South Africa and later served the IRFU as president.

Desmond John SINCLAIR (Transvaal) won his Springbok rugby colours on the 1951-52 tour of Europe, scoring five tries in his 13 games as a centre. Test honours followed in 1955, when he appeared in all four internationals against the Lions. He died in Johannesburg on 29 April 1996 at the age of 68.

Lou SORENSEN, manager of the successful Queensland team which won the inaugural Super-10 tournament, died in Brisbane on 17 July 1995. He was 37.

Tommy STONE (Cardiff), one of the unluckiest of Welsh players, died in October 1995, aged 85. In 1937 he was selected to play full-back for Wales against Ireland in Belfast. Snow necessitated a postponement, and by the time the match was rearranged he had transferred to Barrow BL for £300.

Brian Maurice STONEMAN (Oxford University, Richmond), who died at Torbay Hospital on 15 June 1995, aged 58, won a Blue as a No 8 in 1962. In club rugby he made his name as an uncompromising prop and appeared in England trials between 1964 and 1967.

William Richard TECTOR (Dublin University, Wanderers) died aged 67 in Dublin on 28 April 1996. He won three caps as Ireland's full-back in 1955.

Ifor THOMAS (Bryncethin) was, at 95, the oldest surviving Welsh international up to his death in

Bridgend on 12 May 1995. His only international appearance was against England at Swansea in 1924 when, unusually, he was capped from a village club.

Paul TIGNOL (Toulouse, Mont-de-Marsan) died in Limoges in September 1995 at the age of 62. While at Toulouse he was twice capped in the 1953 Five Nations tournament. After transferring to Mont-de-Marsan, he appeared at lock in the 1959 and 1963 French championship finals.

Ivan Matthew Henry VODANOVICH (Wellington) won three caps as an All Blacks prop in the 1955 Bledisloe Cup series and was New Zealand's coach from 1969 to 1971. He died in Wellington on 2 September 1995, aged 65.

Edward Verdun WATKINS (Cardiff) made his debut for Wales in the famous 13-12 win over the All Blacks in December 1935. He went on to play eight times for his country as a forward before joining Wigan RL club in 1939. He died in Cardiff on 28 June 1995 at the age of 79.

John Peter WILD, who died aged 70 in Papakura on 17 June 1995, was a former NZRFU Council member who acted as liaison officer to several visiting international teams between 1972 and 1985.

Frederick William WILLIAMSON (Dolphin, Wanderers), Ireland's full-back in three matches in 1930, died in Richmond on 20 May 1995, aged 89. He was also a past president of the London Irish club.

John WINTERBOTTOM, Headingley's 'Mr Rugby' and father of Peter, died in South Africa in March 1996. He was 74. From 1978 to 1981 he was president of the club and more recently helped forge the link with Roundhay to form the new Leeds club.

It is with sadness that we also record the death of George Abbott, who compiled the Schools section of this Yearbook from 1972 to 1990.

FIXTURES 1996-97

*Venues and fixtures are understood to be correct at time of going to press, but are subject to alteration. We should like to thank all those who have assisted in the compilation of this list, especially those at the various headquarters of the Home Unions. *Fixtures to be rearranged.*

Saturday, 17 August 1996

SOUTH AFRICA v NEW ZEALAND (Durban)
SCOTLAND v BARBARIANS (Murrayfield)

Saturday, 24 August

SOUTH AFRICA v NEW ZEALAND (Pretoria)
WALES v BARBARIANS (Cardiff)

Saturday, 31 August

SOUTH AFRICA v NEW ZEALAND (Johannesburg)

Anglo-Welsh Challenge
Bath v Neath (Twickenham)

RFU Courage Leagues
Division 1
Bristol v London Irish
Harlequins v Gloucester
Northampton v West Hartlepool
Orrell v Bath*
Sale v Wasps
Saracens v Leicester*
Division 3
Exeter v Rosslyn Park
Harrogate v Reading
Leeds v Otley
London Welsh v Liverpool St Helens
Lydney v Havant
Morley v Clifton
Redruth v Fylde
Walsall v Wharfedale

SRU Tennents Premiership
Division 1
Boroughmuir v Hawick
Currie v Heriot's FP
Jedforest v Watsonians
Melrose v Stirling County
Division 2
Dundee HSFP v Glasgow Acads
Edinburgh Acads v Biggar
GHK v West of Scotland

Kelso v Gala
Division 3
Kilmarnock v Kirkcaldy
Musselburgh v Stewart's-Melville FP
Peebles v Preston Lodge FP
Selkirk v Glasgow Southern
Division 4
Glenrothes v Ayr
Gordonians v Grangemouth
Haddington v Langholm
Hillhead/Jordanhill v Corstorphine

WRU Leagues
Division 1
Bridgend v Llanelli
Dunvant v Ebbw Vale
Neath v Pontypridd*
Newport v Caerphilly
Newbridge v Treorchy
Swansea v Cardiff

Sunday, 1 September

Anglo-Welsh Challenge
Pontypridd v Leicester (Cardiff)

Tuesday, 3 September

WRU Leagues
Division 1
Caerphilly v Dunvant
Ebbw Vale v Newbridge
Llanelli v Neath
Pontypridd v Cardiff
Swansea v Newport
Treorchy v Bridgend

Saturday, 7 September

RFU Courage Leagues
Division 1
Bristol v Orrell
Gloucester v Sale
Leicester v Bath
London Irish v Northampton
Wasps v Saracens
West Hartlepool v Harlequins

Division 2
Bedford v Nottingham
Blackheath v Rotherham
Coventry v Richmond
London Scottish v Rugby
Moseley v Wakefield
Newcastle v Waterloo
Division 3
Clifton v Walsall
Fylde v Morley
Havant v Redruth
Liverpool St Helens v Lydney
Otley v London Welsh
Reading v Leeds
Rosslyn Park v Harrogate
Wharfedale v Exeter

SRU Tennents Premiership
Division 1
Hawick v Jedforest
Heriot's FP v Boroughmuir
Stirling County v Currie
Watsonians v Melrose
Division 2
Biggar v Dundee HSFP
Gala v GHK
Glasgow Acads v Kelso
West of Scotland v Edinburgh Acads
Division 3
Glasgow Southern v Musselburgh
Kirkcaldy v Selkirk
Preston Lodge FP v Kilmarnock
Stewart's-Melville FP v Peebles
Division 4
Ayr v Gordonians
Corstorphine v Glenrothes
Grangemouth v Haddington
Langholm v Hillhead/Jordanhill

SRU Cup: *1st round*

WRU Leagues
Division 1
Bridgend v Ebbw Vale
Caerphilly v Swansea
Cardiff v Llanelli
Neath v Treorchy
Newbridge v Dunvant
Newport v Pontypridd
Division 2
Aberavon v Pontypool
Abertillery v Ystradgynlais
Bonymaen v Abercynon

Cross Keys v Blackwood
South Wales Police v Maesteg
UWIC v Llandovery

Saturday, 14 September
**PAN-AMERICAN
  CHAMPIONSHIP
ARGENTINA v URUGUAY**
  (Toronto)
CANADA v USA (Toronto)

RFU Courage Leagues
Division 1
Bath v Wasps
Harlequins v London Irish
Northampton v Bristol
Orrell v Leicester
Sale v West Hartlepool
Saracens v Gloucester
Division 2
Blackheath v Bedford
Nottingham v Newcastle
Richmond v Rotherham
Rugby v Coventry
Wakefield v London Scottish
Waterloo v Moseley
Division 3
Clifton v Fylde
Harrogate v Wharfedale
Leeds v Rosslyn Park
London Welsh v Reading
Lydney v Otley
Morley v Havant
Redruth v Liverpool St Helens
Walsall v Exeter

RFU Cup: *1st Round*

SRU Tennents Premiership
Division 1
Heriot's FP v Jedforest
Melrose v Currie
Stirling County v Hawick
Watsonians v Boroughmuir
Division 2
Dundee HSFP v West of Scotland
Edinburgh Acads v Gala
Glasgow Acads v Biggar
Kelso v GHK
Division 3
Glasgow Southern v Kirkcaldy
Kilmarnock v Stewart's-Melville FP
Musselburgh v Peebles
Selkirk v Preston Lodge FP

Division 4
Glenrothes v Langholm
Gordonians v Corstorphine
Grangemouth v Ayr
Haddington v Hillhead/Jordanhill

WRU Leagues
Division 1
Dunvant v Swansea
Ebbw Vale v Neath
Llanelli v Newport
Newbridge v Bridgend
Pontypridd v Caerphilly
Treorchy v Cardiff
Division 2
Aberavon v South Wales Police
Abercynon v Cross Keys
Blackwood v Abertillery
Llandovery v Bonymaen
Maesteg v UWIC
Ystradgynlais v Pontypool

Tuesday, 17 September

PAN-AMERICAN CHAMPIONSHIP
CANADA v URUGUAY (Hamilton)
USA v ARGENTINA (Hamilton)

WRU Leagues
Division 2
Abercynon v UWIC
Aberavon v Cross Keys
Blackwood v Llandovery
Maesteg v Abertillery
South Wales Police v Pontypool
Ystradgynlais v Bonymaen

Wednesday, 18 September

WRU Leagues
Division 1
Bridgend v Dunvant
Caerphilly v Llanelli
Cardiff v Ebbw Vale
Neath v Newbridge
Newport v Treorchy
Swansea v Pontypridd

Saturday, 21 September

PAN-AMERICAN CHAMPIONSHIP
CANADA v ARGENTINA (Ottawa)
USA v URUGUAY (Ottawa)

IRFU Provincial Championship
Munster v Connacht
Ulster v Leinster

RFU Courage Leagues
Division 1
Bristol v Harlequins
Gloucester v Bath
London Irish v Sale
Northampton v Orrell
Wasps v Leicester
West Hartlepool v Saracens
Division 2
Bedford v Richmond
Coventry v Wakefield
London Scottish v Waterloo
Moseley v Nottingham
Newcastle v Blackheath
Rotherham v Rugby
Division 3
Exeter v Harrogate
Fylde v Walsall
Havant v Clifton
Liverpool St Helens v Morley
Otley v Redruth
Reading v Lydney
Rosslyn Park v London Welsh
Wharfedale v Leeds

SRU Tennents Premiership
Division 1
Boroughmuir v Melrose
Hawick v Watsonians
Heriot's FP v Stirling County
Jedforest v Currie
Division 2
Biggar v Kelso
Gala v Dundee HSFP
GHK v Edinburgh Acads
West of Scotland v Glasgow Acads
Division 3
Kirkcaldy v Musselburgh
Peebles v Kilmarnock
Preston Lodge FP v Glasgow Southern
Stewart's-Melville FP v Selkirk
Division 4
Ayr v Haddington
Corstorphine v Grangemouth
Hillhead/Jordanhill v Glenrothes
Langholm v Gordonians

WRU Leagues
Division 1
Bridgend v Neath
Dunvant v Pontypridd
Ebbw Vale v Newport
Llanelli v Swansea
Newbridge v Cardiff
Treorchy v Caerphilly
Division 2
Abertillery v Abercynon
Bonymaen v UWIC
Cross Keys v Llandovery
Maesteg v Aberavon
Pontypool v Blackwood
South Wales Police v Ystradgynlais

Saturday, 28 September

IRFU Provincial Championship
Leinster v Munster
Ulster v Connacht

RFU Courage Leagues
Division 1
Bath v West Hartlepool
Harlequins v Northampton
Leicester v Gloucester
Orrell v Wasps
Sale v Bristol
Saracens v London Irish
Division 2
Blackheath v Moseley
Nottingham v London Scottish
Richmond v Newcastle
Rugby v Bedford
Wakefield v Rotherham
Waterloo v Coventry
Division 3
Clifton v Liverpool St Helens
Fylde v Havant
Leeds v Exeter
London Welsh v Wharfedale
Lydney v Rosslyn Park
Morley v Otley
Redruth v Reading
Walsall v Harrogate

SRU Tennents Premiership
Division 1
Currie v Boroughmuir
Jedforest v Stirling County
Melrose v Hawick
Watsonians v Heriot's FP

Division 2
Biggar v West of Scotland
Dundee HSFP v GHK
Glasgow Acads v Gala
Kelso v Edinburgh Acads
Division 3
Glasgow Southern v Stewart's-Melville FP
Kirkcaldy v Preston Lodge FP
Musselburgh v Kilmarnock
Selkirk v Peebles
Division 4
Ayr v Corstorphine
Gordonians v Hillhead/Jordanhill
Grangemouth v Langholm
Haddington v Glenrothes

WRU Leagues
Division 1
Cardiff v Bridgend
Caerphilly v Ebbw Vale
Neath v Dunvant
Newport v Newbridge
Pontypridd v Llanelli
Swansea v Treorchy
Division 2
Abercynon v Pontypool
Blackwood v South Wales Police
Bonymaen v Cross Keys
Llandovery v Abertillery
UWIC v Aberavon
Ystradgynlais v Maesteg

Tuesday, 1 October

WRU Leagues
Division 2
Aberavon v Llandovery
Blackwood v UWIC
Maesteg v Bonymaen
Pontypool v Abertillery
South Wales Police v Cross Keys
Ystradgynlais v Abercynon

Saturday, 5 October

ITALY v WALES (Rome)
IRFU Provincial Championship
Leinster v Connacht
Munster v Ulster

427

RFU Courage Leagues
Division 1
Bristol v Saracens
Gloucester v Wasps
Harlequins v Orrell
London Irish v Bath
Northampton v Sale
West Hartlepool v Leicester
Division 2
Bedford v Wakefield
Coventry v Nottingham
London Scottish v Blackheath
Moseley v Richmond
Newcastle v Rugby
Rotherham v Waterloo
Division 3
Exeter v London Welsh
Harrogate v Leeds
Havant v Walsall
Liverpool St Helens v Fylde
Otley v Clifton
Reading v Morley
Rosslyn Park v Redruth
Wharfedale v Lydney

SRU Tennents Premiership
Division 1
Boroughmuir v Jedforest
Hawick v Currie
Heriot's FP v Melrose
Stirling County v Watsonians
Division 2
Edinburgh Acads v Dundee HSFP
Gala v Biggar
GHK v Glasgow Acads
Kelso v West of Scotland
Division 3
Kilmarnock v Selkirk
Musselburgh v Preston Lodge FP
Peebles v Glasgow Southern
Stewart's-Melville FP v Kirkcaldy
Division 4
Glenrothes v Gordonians
Haddington v Corstorphine
Hillhead/Jordanhill v Grangemouth
Langholm v Ayr

WRU Leagues
Division 2
Aberavon v Ystradgynlais
Abertillery v Bonymaen
Cross Keys v UWIC
Maesteg v Blackwood

Pontypool v Llandovery
South Wales Police v Abercynon

Saturday, 12 October
Air France Paris Sevens (Charlety)

Heineken Championships
European Cup
Pool A
Bath v Edinburgh
Pontypridd v Treviso
Pool B
Llanelli v Leinster
Pau v South of Scotland
Pool C
Brive v Neath
Scottish North & Midlands v Ulster
Pool D
Munster v Milan
Wasps v Cardiff
European Conference
Pool A
Agen v Newport
Newbridge v Glasgow
Sale v Montferrand
Pool B
Bridgend v Castres
Bristol v Treorchy
Narbonne v Dinamo Bucharest
Pool C
Connacht v Padova
Orrell v Dunvant
Toulon v Northampton
Pool D
Bourgoin v Bègles-Bordeaux
Gloucester v Ebbw Vale
Swansea v London Irish

RFU Courage Leagues
Division 2
Blackheath v Coventry
Nottingham v Rotherham
Richmond v London Scottish
Rugby v Moseley
Wakefield v Newcastle
Waterloo v Bedford
Division 3
Clifton v Reading
Fylde v Otley
Havant v Liverpool St Helens
London Welsh v Harrogate
Lydney v Exeter
Morley v Rosslyn Park

Redruth v Wharfedale
Walsall v Leeds

RFU Cup: *2nd round*

WRU Leagues
Division 2
Abercynon v Maesteg
Blackwood v Aberavon
Bonymaen v Pontypool
Cross Keys v Abertillery
Llandovery v South Wales Police
UWIC v Ystradgynlais

Tuesday, 15 October

WRU Leagues
Division 2
Abertillery v Blackwood
Bonymaen v Llandovery
Cross Keys v Abercynon
Pontypool v Ystradgynlais
South Wales Police v Aberavon
UWIC v Maesteg

Wednesday, 16 October

Heineken Championships
European Cup
Pool A
Edinburgh v Pontypridd
Treviso v Dax
Pool B
Leinster v Leicester
South of Scotland v Llanelli
Pool C
Neath v Scottish North & Midlands
Ulster v Harlequins
Pool D
Cardiff v Munster
Milan v Toulouse
European Conference
Pool A
Agen v Montferrand
Glasgow v Sale
Newport v Newbridge
Pool B
Dinamo Bucharest v Bristol
Narbonne v Castres
Treorchy v Bridgend
Pool C
Dunvant v Connacht
Northampton v Orrell
Toulon v Padova

Pool D
Ebbw Vale v Swansea
Gloucester v Bègles-Bordeaux
London Irish v Bourgoin

Saturday, 19 October

Italian Selection v Australians

Heineken Championships
European Cup
Pool A
Dax v Edinburgh
Pontypridd v Bath
Pool B
Leicester v South of Scotland
Llanelli v Pau
Pool C
Harlequins v Neath
Scottish North & Midlands v Brive
Pool D
Munster v Wasps
Toulouse v Cardiff
European Conference
Pool A
Montferrand v Glasgow
Newbridge v Agen
Sale v Newport
Pool B
Bridgend v Dinamo Bucharest
Bristol v Narbonne
Castres v Treorchy
Pool C
Connacht v Northampton
Orrell v Toulon
Padova v Dunvant
Pool D
Bègles-Bordeaux v London Irish
Bourgoin v Ebbw Vale
Swansea v Gloucester

RFU Courage Leagues
Division 2
Bedford v Rotherham
Coventry v London Scottish
Moseley v Newcastle
Nottingham v Blackheath
Richmond v Rugby
Wakefield v Waterloo
Division 3
Exeter v Redruth
Harrogate v Lydney
Leeds v London Welsh
Liverpool St Helens v Walsall

Otley v Havant
Reading v Fylde
Rosslyn Park v Clifton
Wharfedale v Morley

WRU Leagues
Division 2
Aberavon v Abercynon
Abertillery v UWIC
Maesteg v Llandovery
Pontypool v Cross Keys
South Wales Police v Bonymaen
Ystradgynlais v Blackwood

Wednesday, 23 October

ITALY v AUSTRALIA (*provisional*)

Saturday, 26 October
Heineken Championships
European Cup
Pool A
Bath v Dax
Edinburgh v Treviso
Pool B
Pau v Leicester
South of Scotland v Leinster
Pool C
Brive v Harlequins
Neath v Ulster
Pool D
Cardiff v Milan
Wasps v Toulouse
European Conference
Pool A
Agen v Sale
Newbridge v Montferrand
Newport v Glasgow
Pool B
Bristol v Castres
Dinamo Bucharest v Treorchy
Narbonne v Bridgend
Pool C
Northampton v Dunvant
Orrell v Padova
Toulon v Connacht
Pool D
Ebbw Vale v London Irish
Gloucester v Bourgoin
Swansea v Bègles-Bordeaux

RFU Courage Leagues
Division 2
Blackheath v Richmond
London Scottish v Moseley
Newcastle v Bedford
Rotherham v Coventry
Rugby v Wakefield
Waterloo v Nottingham
Division 3
Clifton v Wharfedale
Fylde v Rosslyn Park
Havant v Reading
Liverpool St Helens v Otley
Lydney v Leeds
Morley v Exeter
Redruth v Harrogate
Walsall v London Welsh

WRU Leagues
Division 2
Abercynon v Ystradgynlais
Abertillery v Pontypool
Bonymaen v Maesteg
Cross Keys v South Wales Police
Llandovery v Aberavon
UWIC v Blackwood

Tuesday, 29 October
WRU Leagues
Division 2
Abercynon v Bonymaen
Blackwood v Cross Keys
Llandovery v UWIC
Maesteg v South Wales Police
Pontypool v Aberavon
Ystradgynlais v Abertillery

Wednesday, 30 October
Scotland A v Australians (Gala)

RFU Courage Leagues
Division 1
Bath v Bristol
Leicester v London Irish
Orrell v Gloucester
Sale v Harlequins
Saracens v Northampton
Wasps v West Hartlepool

Saturday, 2 November
Combined Scottish Districts v Australians (Glasgow)

Heineken Championships
European Cup
Pool A
Dax v Pontypridd
Treviso v Bath
Pool B
Leicester v Llanelli
Leinster v Pau
Pool C
Harlequins v Scottish North &
Midlands
Ulster v Brive
Pool D
Milan v Wasps
Toulouse v Munster
European Conference
Pool A
Glasgow v Agen
Montferrand v Newport
Sale v Newbridge
Pool B
Bridgend v Bristol
Castres v Dinamo Bucharest
Treorchy v Narbonne
Pool C
Connacht v Orrell
Dunvant v Toulon
Padova v Northampton
Pool D
Bègles-Bordeaux v Ebbw Vale
Bourgoin v Swansea
London Irish v Gloucester

RFU Courage Leagues
Division 2
Bedford v Moseley
Blackheath v Rugby
Coventry v Newcastle
Nottingham v Wakefield
Richmond v Waterloo
Rotherham v London Scottish

RFU Cup: *3rd round*

WRU Leagues
Division 2
Aberavon v Bonymaen
Blackwood v Abercynon
Maesteg v Cross Keys
Pontypool v UWIC
South Wales Police v Abertillery
Ystradgynlais v Llandovery

Sunday, 3 November

SRU Cup: *2nd round*

Tuesday, 5 November

**Scottish Districts Selection v
Australians** (Perth)
Mendoza v South Africans
(Mendoza)

Friday, 8 November

Scotland A v Junior Springboks

Saturday, 9 November

SCOTLAND v AUSTRALIA
(Murrayfield)
ARGENTINA v SOUTH AFRICA
(Buenos Aires)

RFU Courage Leagues
Division 1
Bristol v Leicester
Harlequins v Saracens
London Irish v Wasps
Northampton v Bath
Sale v Orrell
West Hartlepool v Gloucester
Division 2
London Scottish v Bedford
Moseley v Coventry
Newcastle v Rotherham
Rugby v Nottingham
Wakefield v Richmond
Waterloo v Blackheath
Division 3
Exeter v Clifton
Harrogate v Morley
Leeds v Redruth
London Welsh v Lydney
Otley v Walsall
Reading v Liverpool St Helens
Rosslyn Park v Havant
Wharfedale v Fylde

WRU Leagues
Division 1
Bridgend v Newport
Dunvant v Llanelli
Ebbw Vale v Swansea
Neath v Cardiff
Newbridge v Caerphilly
Treorchy v Pontypridd

Division 2
Abertillery v Maesteg
Bonymaen v Ystradgynlais
Cross Keys v Aberavon
Llandovery v Blackwood
Pontypool v South Wales Police
UWIC v Abercynon

Tuesday, 12 November
Rosario v South Africans (Rosario)

Wednesday, 13 November
Leinster v Australians (Dublin)

Saturday, 16 November
ARGENTINA v SOUTH AFRICA
(Buenos Aires)
Ulster v Australians (Belfast)
Heineken Championships:
Semi-finals

RFU Courage Leagues
Division 2
Bedford v Coventry
Blackheath v Wakefield
London Scottish v Newcastle
Nottingham v Richmond
Rotherham v Moseley
Rugby v Waterloo
Division 3
Clifton v Harrogate
Fylde v Exeter
Havant v Wharfedale
Liverpool St Helens v Rosslyn Park
Morley v Leeds
Otley v Reading
Redruth v London Welsh
Walsall v Lydney

SRU Tennents Premiership
Division 1
Hawick v Boroughmuir
Heriot's FP v Currie
Stirling County v Melrose
Watsonians v Jedforest
Division 2
Biggar v GHK
Dundee HSFP v Kelso
Glasgow Acads v Edinburgh Acads
West of Scotland v Gala

Division 3
Glasgow Southern v Kilmarnock
Kirkcaldy v Peebles
Preston Lodge FP v Stewart's-Melville
FP
Selkirk v Musselburgh
Division 4
Ayr v Hillhead/Jordanhill
Corstorphine v Langholm
Gordonians v Haddington
Grangemouth v Glenrothes

WRU Leagues
Division 1
Caerphilly v Bridgend
Cardiff v Dunvant
Llanelli v Treorchy
Newport v Neath
Pontypridd v Ebbw Vale
Swansea v Newbridge
Division 2
Aberavon v Abertillery
Abercynon v Llandovery
Blackwood v Bonymaen
Maesteg v Pontypool
South Wales Police v UWIC
Ystradgynlais v Cross Keys

Thursday, 21 November
RWC Sevens Qualifying Round
(Dubai)

Friday, 22 November
RWC Sevens Qualifying Round
(Dubai)

Wednesday, 20 November
Connacht v Australians (Galway)
London Division v Argentinians
(Twickenham)

Saturday, 23 November
ENGLAND v ITALY (Twickenham)
London Division v Junior
Springboks (Twickenham)
French Barbarians v South
Africans (Brive)
Munster v Australians (Limerick)
RFU Cup: *4th round*

SRU Tennents Premiership
Division 1
Boroughmuir v Heriot's FP
Currie v Stirling County
Jedforest v Hawick
Melrose v Watsonians
Division 2
Biggar v Edinburgh Acads
Gala v Kelso
Glasgow Acads v Dundee HSFP
West of Scotland v GHK
Division 3
Glasgow Southern v Selkirk
Kirkcaldy v Kilmarnock
Preston Lodge FP v Peebles
Stewart's-Melville FP v Musselburgh
Division 4
Ayr v Glenrothes
Corstorphine v Hillhead/Jordanhill
Grangemouth v Gordonians
Langholm v Haddington

Sunday, 24 November

South-West Division v Argentinians
(Bristol)

Tuesday, 26 November

French Selection v South Africans
(Lyons)
Ireland A v Australians (Belfast)

Wednesday, 27 November

Midlands Division v Argentinians
(Leicester)

Saturday, 30 November

IRELAND v AUSTRALIA (Dublin)
FRANCE v SOUTH AFRICA
(Bordeaux)
England XV v NZ Barbarians
(Twickenham)

RFU County Championship
Northern Group
Cumbria v Lancashire
East Midlands v Leicestershire
Northumberland v Cheshire
(Northern)
**Notts, Lincs & Derbys v
Warwickshire**
Staffordshire v North Midlands
Yorkshire v Durham

Southern Group
Cornwall v Sussex (Camborne)
Dorset & Wilts v Berkshire
Hampshire v Eastern Counties (US
Portsmouth)
Kent v Gloucestershire (Maidstone)
Middlesex v Buckinghamshire
(Croxley Green)
Oxfordshire v Hertfordshire
Somerset v Devon
(Weston-super-Mare)

SRU Tennents Premiership
Division 1
Heriot's FP v Hawick
Melrose v Jedforest
Stirling County v Boroughmuir
Watsonians v Currie
Division 2
Dundee HSFP v Biggar
Edinburgh Acads v West of Scotland
GHK v Gala
Kelso v Glasgow Acads
Division 3
Kilmarnock v Preston Lodge FP
Musselburgh v Glasgow Southern
Peebles v Stewart's-Melville FP
Selkirk v Kirkcaldy
Division 4
Glenrothes v Corstorphine
Gordonians v Ayr
Haddington v Grangemouth
Hillhead/Jordanhill v Langholm

WRU Leagues
Division 1
Bridgend v Swansea
Cardiff v Newport
Dunvant v Treorchy
Ebbw Vale v Llanelli
Neath v Caerphilly
Newbridge v Pontypridd

Sunday, 1 December

Northern Division v Argentinians
(Huddersfield)

Tuesday, 3 December

French Selection v South Africans
(Lille)

Wednesday, 4 December
Combined Services v Argentinians

Saturday, 7 December
FRANCE v SOUTH AFRICA (Paris)
Barbarians v Australians
(Twickenham)

RFU County Championship
Northern Group
Cheshire v Warwickshire
(Birkenhead Park)
Cumbria v East Midlands
Durham v North Midlands
Lancashire v Leicestershire
(Waterloo)
Northumberland v Notts, Lincs & Derbys (Tynedale)
Yorkshire v Staffordshire
Southern Group
Berkshire v Eastern Counties
Buckinghamshire v Devon
Dorset & Wilts v Hampshire
(Bournemouth)
Gloucestershire v Sussex
Hertfordshire v Surrey (Hertford)
Kent v Cornwall (US Chatham)
Middlesex v Somerset (Croxley Green)

RFU Courage Leagues
Division 1
Bath v Harlequins
Gloucester v London Irish
Leicester v Northampton
Orrell v West Hartlepool
Saracens v Sale
Wasps v Bristol

SRU Tennents Premiership
Division 1
Boroughmuir v Watsonians
Currie v Melrose
Hawick v Stirling County
Jedforest v Heriot's FP
Division 2
Biggar v Glasgow Acads
Gala v Edinburgh Acads
GHK v Kelso
West of Scotland v Dundee HSFP

Division 3
Kirkcaldy v Glasgow Southern
Peebles v Musselburgh
Preston Lodge FP v Selkirk
Stewart's-Melville FP v Kilmarnock
Division 4
Ayr v Grangemouth
Corstorphine v Gordonians
Hillhead/Jordanhill v Haddington
Langholm v Glenrothes

IRFU Insurance Corporation Leagues
Division 1
Ballymena v Terenure Coll
Cork Const v Instonians
Garryowen v Blackrock Coll
Lansdowne v Dungannon
Old Wesley v Old Belvedere
St Mary's Coll v Old Crescent
Young Munster v Shannon
Division 2
Clontarf v UC Cork
Dolphin v Wanderers
Greystones v Malone
Highfield v Bective Rangers
Monkstown v DLSP
NIFC v Sunday's Well
Skerries v Derry
Division 3
Bangor v Queen's U, Belfast
Bohemians v UC Dublin
Buccaneers v Waterpark
Collegians v Dublin U
Corinthians v Galwegians

WRU Leagues
Division 1
Caerphilly v Cardiff
Llanelli v Newbridge
Newport v Dunvant
Pontypridd v Bridgend
Swansea v Neath
Treorchy v Ebbw Vale

Tuesday, 10 December
England A v Argentinians
(Northampton)
Oxford U v Cambridge U
(Twickenham)
Scotland Development XV v Queensland

Saturday, 14 December

ENGLAND v ARGENTINA
(Twickenham)
SCOTLAND v ITALY (Murrayfield)

RFU County Championship
Northern Group
East Midlands v Lancashire
Leicester v Cumbria
North Midlands v Yorkshire
Notts, Lincs & Derbys v Cheshire
Staffordshire v Durham
Warwickshire v Northumberland
(Rugby)
Southern Group
Cornwall v Gloucestershire
(Redruth)
Devon v Middlesex (Barnstaple)
Eastern Counties v Dorset & Wilts
(Braintree)
Hampshire v Berkshire
(Basingstoke)
Somerset v Buckinghamshire
(Bridgwater)
Surrey v Oxfordshire (Imber Court)
Sussex v Kent (Worthing)

IRFU Insurance Corporation
Leagues
Division 1
Blackrock Coll v Old Wesley
Dungannon v Ballymena
Instonians v St Mary's Coll
Old Belvedere v Young Munster
Old Crescent v Lansdowne
Shannon v Cork Const
Terenure Coll v Garryowen
Division 2
Bective Rangers v NIFC
Derry v Monkstown
DLSP v Dolphin
Malone v Clontarf
Sunday's Well v Skerries
UC Cork v Highfield
Wanderers v Greystones
Division 3
Buccaneers v Corinthians
Dublin U v Queen's U, Belfast
Galwegians v Portadown
UC Dublin v Bangor
Waterpark v Collegians

Sunday, 15 December

WALES v SOUTH AFRICA
(Cardiff)

Saturday, 21 December

RFU Cup: *5th round*

RFU Courage Leagues
Division 3
Exeter v Havant
Harrogate v Fylde
Leeds v Clifton
London Welsh v Morley
Lydney v Redruth
Reading v Walsall
Rosslyn Park v Otley
Wharfedale v Liverpool St Helens

IRFU Insurance Corporation
Leagues
Division 1
Ballymena v Old Crescent
Garryowen v Dungannon
Lansdowne v Instonians
Old Belvedere v Blackrock Coll
Old Wesley v Terenure Coll
St Mary's Coll v Shannon
Young Munster v Cork Const
Division 2
Clontarf v Highfield
Dolphin v Derry
Greystones v DLSP
Malone v Wanderers
Monkstown v Sunday's Well
NIFC v UC Cork
Skerries v Bective Rangers
Division 3
Bangor v Waterpark
Collegians v Buccaneers
Corinthians v Bohemians
Portadown v UC Dublin
Queen's U, Belfast v Galwegians

WRU Leagues
Division 1
Caerphilly v Newport
Cardiff v Swansea
Ebbw Vale v Dunvant
Llanelli v Bridgend
Pontypridd v Neath
Treorchy v Newbridge

Division 2
Aberavon v Maesteg
Abercynon v Abertillery
Blackwood v Pontypool
Llandovery v Cross Keys
UWIC v Bonymaen
Ystradgynlais v South Wales Police

Sunday, 22 December
SRU Districts Championship
Edinburgh District v Glasgow District
Scottish North & Midlands v South of Scotland

Saturday, 28 December
RFU Courage Leagues
Division 1
Bristol v Gloucester
Harlequins v Leicester
London Irish v West Hartlepool
Northampton v Wasps
Sale v Bath
Saracens v Orrell
Division 2
Nottingham v Bedford
Richmond v Coventry
Rotherham v Blackheath
Rugby v London Scottish
Wakefield v Moseley
Waterloo v Newcastle
Division 3
Clifton v London Welsh
Fylde v Leeds
Havant v Harrogate
Liverpool St Helens v Exeter
Morley v Lydney
Otley v Wharfedale
Reading v Rosslyn Park
Redruth v Walsall

WRU Leagues
Division 1
Bridgend v Treorchy
Cardiff v Pontypridd
Dunvant v Caerphilly
Neath v Llanelli
Newbridge v Ebbw Vale
Newport v Swansea
Division 2
Aberavon v UWIC
Abertillery v Llandovery

Cross Keys v Bonymaen
Maesteg v Ystradgynlais
Pontypool v Abercynon
South Wales Police v Blackwood

Sunday, 29 December
SRU Districts Championship
Glasgow District v South of Scotland
Scottish North & Midlands v Edinburgh District

Saturday, 4 January 1997
IRELAND v ITALY (Dublin)
RWC Sevens Qualifying Round (Punta del Este)
Heineken Championships: *Finals*

RFU Courage Leagues
Division 1
Bath v Saracens
Gloucester v Northampton
Leicester v Sale
Orrell v London Irish
Wasps v Harlequins
West Hartlepool v Bristol
Division 2
Bedford v Blackheath
Coventry v Rugby
London Scottish v Wakefield
Moseley v Waterloo
Newcastle v Nottingham
Rotherham v Richmond
Division 3
Exeter v Otley
Harrogate v Liverpool St Helens
Leeds v Havant
London Welsh v Fylde
Lydney v Clifton
Redruth v Morley
Walsall v Rosslyn Park
Wharfedale v Reading

WRU Leagues
Division 1
Dunvant v Newbridge
Ebbw Vale v Bridgend
Llanelli v Cardiff
Pontypridd v Newport
Swansea v Caerphilly
Treorchy v Neath

Division 2
Abercynon v South Wales Police
Blackwood v Maesteg
Bonymaen v Abertillery
Llandovery v Pontypool
UWIC v Cross Keys
Ystradgynlais v Aberavon

Sunday, 5 January

RWC Sevens Qualifying Round
  (Punta del Este)

SRU District Championship
Glasgow District v Scottish North &
  Midlands
South of Scotland v Edinburgh
  District

Saturday, 11 January

RFU Courage Leagues
Division 1
Bristol v Wasps
Harlequins v Bath
London Irish v Gloucester
Northampton v Leicester
Sale v Saracens
West Hartlepool v Orrell
Division 2
Blackheath v Newcastle
Nottingham v Moseley
Richmond v Bedford
Rugby v Rotherham
Wakefield v Coventry
Waterloo v London Scottish
Division 3
Clifton v Redruth
Fylde v Lydney
Havant v London Welsh
Liverpool St Helens v Leeds
Morley v Walsall
Otley v Harrogate
Reading v Exeter
Rosslyn Park v Wharfedale

SRU Tennents Premiership
Division 1
Currie v Jedforest
Melrose v Boroughmuir
Stirling County v Heriot's FP
Watsonians v Hawick

Division 2
Dundee HSFP v Gala
Edinburgh Acads v GHK
Glasgow Acads v West of Scotland
Kelso v Biggar
Division 3
Glasgow Southern v Preston Lodge FP
Kilmarnock v Peebles
Musselburgh v Kirkcaldy
Selkirk v Stewart's-Melville FP
Division 4
Glenrothes v Hillhead/Jordanhill
Gordonians v Langholm
Grangemouth v Corstorphine
Haddington v Ayr

IRFU Insurance Corporation
  Leagues
Division 1
Blackrock Coll v Young Munster
Cork Const v St Mary's Coll
Dungannon v Old Wesley
Instonians v Ballymena
Old Crescent v Garryowen
Shannon v Lansdowne
Terenure Coll v Old Belvedere
Division 2
Bective Rangers v Monkstown
Derry v Greystones
DLSP v Malone
Highfield v NIFC
Sunday's Well v Dolphin
UC Cork v Skerries
Division 3
Dublin U v Bangor
Galwegians v Collegians
Queen's U, Belfast v Portadown
UC Dublin v Corinthians
Waterpark v Bohemians

WRU Leagues
Division 2
Aberavon v Blackwood
Abertillery v Cross Keys
Maesteg v Abercynon
Pontypool v Bonymaen
South Wales Police v Llandovery
Ystradgynlais v UWIC

Friday, 17 January

Scotland A v Wales A
Scotland U-21 v Wales U-21

Saturday, 18 January
SCOTLAND v WALES (Murrayfield)
IRELAND v FRANCE (Dublin)
RFU County Championship:
Quarter-finals

RFU Courage Leagues
Division 1
Bath v Northampton
Gloucester v West Hartlepool
Leicester v Bristol
Orrell v Sale
Saracens v Harlequins
Wasps v London Irish
Division 2
Bedford v Rugby
Coventry v Waterloo
London Scottish v Nottingham
Moseley v Blackheath
Newcastle v Richmond
Rotherham v Wakefield
Division 3
Clifton v Morley
Fylde v Redruth
Havant v Lydney
Liverpool St Helens v London Welsh
Otley v Leeds
Reading v Harrogate
Rosslyn Park v Exeter
Wharfedale v Walsall

Sunday, 19 January
SRU Cup: *3rd round*

Wednesday, 22 January
IRFU Insurance Corporation
  Leagues
Division 2
Wanderers v Clontarf

Saturday, 25 January
RFU Cup: *6th round*

RFU Courage Leagues
Division 3
Exeter v Wharfedale
Harrogate v Rosslyn Park
Leeds v Reading
London Welsh v Otley
Lydney v Liverpool St Helens
Morley v Fylde
Redruth v Havant

Walsall v Clifton

SRU Tennents Premiership
Division 1
Boroughmuir v Stirling County
Currie v Watsonians
Hawick v Heriot's FP
Jedforest v Melrose
Division 2
Edinburgh Acads v Kelso
Gala v Glasgow Acads
GHK v Dundee HSFP
West of Scotland v Biggar
Division 3
Kilmarnock v Musselburgh
Peebles v Selkirk
Preston Lodge FP v Kirkcaldy
Stewart's-Melville FP v Glasgow
  Southern
Division 4
Corstorphine v Ayr
Glenrothes v Haddington
Hillhead/Jordanhill v Gordonians
Langholm v Grangemouth

IRFU Insurance Corporation
  Leagues
Division 1
Ballymena v Shannon
Blackrock Coll v Terenure Coll
Garryowen v Instonians
Lansdowne v Cork Const
Old Belvedere v Dungannon
Old Wesley v Old Crescent
Young Munster v St Mary's Coll
Division 2
Clontarf v NIFC
Dolphin v Bective Rangers
Greystones v Sunday's Well
Malone v Derry
Monkstown v UC Cork
Skerries v Highfield
Division 3
Bangor v Galwegians
Bohemians v Buccaneers
Collegians v UC Dublin
Corinthians v Waterpark
Portadown v Dublin U

WRU SWALEC Cup: *5th round*

Tuesday, 28 January
Scotland Development XV v Otago

Wednesday, 29 January

IRFU Insurance Corporation Leagues
Division 2
Wanderers v DLSP

Friday, 31 January

Wales A v Ireland A
Wales U-21 v Ireland U-21
England A v Scotland A

Saturday, 1 February

ENGLAND v SCOTLAND
(Twickenham)
WALES v IRELAND (Cardiff)

RFU Courage Leagues
Division 3
Exeter v Walsall
Fylde v Clifton
Havant v Morley
Liverpool St Helens v Redruth
Otley v Lydney
Reading v London Welsh
Rosslyn Park v Leeds
Wharfedale v Harrogate

Saturday, 8 February

RFU Courage Leagues
Division 1
Bristol v Bath
Gloucester v Orrell
Harlequins v Sale
London Irish v Leicester
Northampton v Saracens
West Hartlepool v Wasps
Division 2
Blackheath v London Scottish
Nottingham v Coventry
Richmond v Moseley
Rugby v Newcastle
Wakefield v Bedford
Waterloo v Rotherham
Division 3
Clifton v Havant
Harrogate v Exeter
Leeds v Wharfedale
London Welsh v Rosslyn Park
Lydney v Reading
Morley v Liverpool St Helens
Redruth v Otley
Walsall v Fylde

SRU Tennents Premiership
Division 1
Boroughmuir v Currie
Hawick v Melrose
Heriot's FP v Watsonians
Stirling County v Jedforest
Division 2
Biggar v Gala
Dundee HSFP v Edinburgh Acads
Glasgow Acads v GHK
West of Scotland v Kelso
Division 3
Glasgow Southern v Peebles
Kirkcaldy v Stewart's-Melville FP
Preston Lodge FP v Musselburgh
Selkirk v Kilmarnock
Division 4
Ayr v Langholm
Corstorphine v Haddington
Gordonians v Glenrothes
Grangemouth v Hillhead/Jordanhill

IRFU Insurance Corporation Leagues
Division 1
Cork Const v Ballymena
Dungannon v Blackrock Coll
Instonians v Old Wesley
Old Crescent v Old Belvedere
Shannon v Garryowen
St Mary's Coll v Lansdowne
Terenure Coll v Young Munster
Division 2
Bective Rangers v Greystones
Derry v Wanderers
DLSP v Clontarf
Highfield v Monkstown
NIFC v Skerries
Sunday's Well v Malone
UC Cork v Dolphin
Division 3
Dublin U v Corinthians
Galwegians v Bohemians
Portadown v Bangor
Queen's U, Belfast v Collegians
UC Dublin v Buccaneers

WRU Leagues
Division 1
Bridgend v Newbridge
Caerphilly v Pontypridd
Cardiff v Treorchy
Neath v Ebbw Vale

Newport v Llanelli
Swansea v Dunvant
Division 2
Abercynon v Aberavon
Blackwood v Ystradgynlais
Bonymaen v South Wales Police
Cross Keys v Pontypool
Llandovery v Maesteg
UWIC v Abertillery

Friday, 14 February

France A v Wales A (Paris)
France Students v Wales Students

Saturday, 15 February

IRELAND v ENGLAND (Dublin)
FRANCE v WALES (Paris)

RFU Courage Leagues
Division 3
Exeter v Leeds
Harrogate v Walsall
Havant v Fylde
Liverpool St Helens v Clifton
Otley v Morley
Reading v Redruth
Rosslyn Park v Lydney
Wharfedale v London Welsh

SRU Tennents Premiership
Division 1
Currie v Hawick
Jedforest v Boroughmuir
Melrose v Heriot's FP
Watsonians v Stirling County
Division 2
Edinburgh Acads v Glasgow Acads
Gala v West of Scotland
GHK v Biggar
Kelso v Dundee HSFP
Division 3
Kilmarnock v Glasgow Southern
Musselburgh v Selkirk
Peebles v Kirkcaldy
Stewart's-Melville FP v Preston Lodge
   FP
Division 4
Glenrothes v Grangemouth
Haddington v Gordonians
Hillhead/Jordanhill v Ayr
Langholm v Corstorphine

440

Saturday, 22 February

RFU Cup: *Quarter-finals*

RFU Courage Leagues
Division 3
Clifton v Otley
Fylde v Liverpool St Helens
Leeds v Harrogate
London Welsh v Exeter
Lydney v Wharfedale
Morley v Reading
Redruth v Rosslyn Park
Walsall v Havant

IRFU Insurance Corporation
   Leagues
Division 1
Ballymena v St Mary's Coll
Blackrock Coll v Old Crescent
Garryowen v Cork Const
Old Belvedere v Instonians
Old Wesley v Shannon
Terenure Coll v Dungannon
Young Munster v Lansdowne
Division 2
Clontarf v Skerries
DLSP v Derry
Malone v Bective Rangers
Dolphin v Highfield
Greystones v UC Cork
Monkstown v NIFC
Wanderers v Sunday's Well
Division 3
Bohemians v Dublin U
Buccaneers v Galwegians
Collegians v Portadown
Corinthians v Queen's U, Belfast
Waterpark v UC Dublin

WRU SWALEC Cup: *6th round*

Friday, 28 February

Scotland A v Ireland A
Scotland U-21 v Ireland U-21

Saturday, 1 March

SCOTLAND v IRELAND
   (Murrayfield)
ENGLAND v FRANCE
   (Twickenham)

RFU Courage Leagues
Division 3
Exeter v Lydney
Harrogate v London Welsh
Leeds v Walsall
Liverpool St Helens v Havant
Otley v Fylde
Reading v Clifton
Rosslyn Park v Morley
Wharfedale v Redruth

WRU Leagues
Division 1
Dunvant v Bridgend
Ebbw Vale v Cardiff
Llanelli v Caerphilly
Newbridge v Neath
Pontypridd v Swansea
Treorchy v Newport

Saturday, 8 March

RFU County Championship:
Semi-finals

RFU Courage Leagues
Division 1
Bath v London Irish
Leicester v West Hartlepool
Orrell v Harlequins
Sale v Northampton
Saracens v Bristol
Wasps v Gloucester
Division 2
Bedford v Waterloo
Coventry v Blackheath
London Scottish v Richmond
Moseley v Rugby
Newcastle v Wakefield
Rotherham v Nottingham
Division 3
Clifton v Rosslyn Park
Fylde v Reading
Havant v Otley
London Welsh v Leeds
Lydney v Harrogate
Morley v Wharfedale
Redruth v Exeter
Walsall v Liverpool St Helens

IRFU Insurance Corporation Leagues
Division 1
Cork Const v Old Wesley
Dungannon v Young Munster
Instonians v Blackrock Coll
Lansdowne v Ballymena
Old Crescent v Terenure Coll
St Mary's Coll v Garryowen
Shannon v Old Belvedere
Division 2
Bective Rangers v Wanderers
Derry v Clontarf
Highfield v Greystones
NIFC v Dolphin
Skerries v Monkstown
Sunday's Well v DLSP
UC Cork v Malone
Division 3
Bangor v Collegians
Dublin U v Buccaneers
Galwegians v Waterpark
Portadown v Corinthians
Queen's U, Belfast v Bohemians

WRU Leagues
Division 1
Caerphilly v Treorchy
Cardiff v Newbridge
Neath v Bridgend
Newport v Ebbw Vale
Pontypridd v Dunvant
Swansea v Llanelli
Division 2
Abercynon v Blackwood
Abertillery v South Wales Police
Bonymaen v Aberavon
Cross Keys v Maesteg
Llandovery v Ystradgynlais
UWIC v Pontypool

Friday, 14 March

France A v Scotland A
Wales Students v England Students
France U-21 v Scotland U-21

Saturday, 15 March

WALES v ENGLAND (Cardiff)
FRANCE v SCOTLAND (Paris)

RFU Courage Leagues
Division 3
Exeter v Morley
Harrogate v Redruth
Leeds v Lydney
London Welsh v Walsall
Otley v Liverpool St Helens
Reading v Havant
Rosslyn Park v Fylde
Wharfedale v Clifton

**IRFU Insurance Corporation
  Leagues**
Division 1
Blackrock Coll v Shannon
Dungannon v Old Crescent
Garryowen v Lansdowne
Old Belvedere v Cork Const
Old Wesley v St Mary's Coll
Terenure Coll v Instonians
Young Munster v Ballymena
Division 2
Clontarf v Monkstown
Derry v Sunday's Well
DLSP v Bective Rangers
Dolphin v Skerries
Greystones v NIFC
Malone v Highfield
Wanderers v UC Cork
Division 3
Bohemians v Portadown
Buccaneers v Queen's U, Belfast
Corinthians v Bangor
UC Dublin v Galwegians
Waterpark v Dublin U

Saturday, 22 March
RUGBY WORLD CUP SEVENS
  (Hong Kong)

RFU Courage Leagues
Division 1
Bristol v Sale
Gloucester v Leicester
London Irish v Saracens
Northampton v Harlequins
Wasps v Orrell
West Hartlepool v Bath
Division 2
Blackheath v Nottingham
London Scottish v Coventry
Newcastle v Moseley
Rotherham v Bedford

Rugby v Richmond
Waterloo v Wakefield
Division 3
Clifton v Exeter
Fylde v Wharfedale
Havant v Rosslyn Park
Liverpool St Helens v Reading
Lydney v London Welsh
Morley v Harrogate
Redruth v Leeds
Walsall v Otley

SRU Cup: *4th round*

**IRFU Insurance Corporation
  Leagues**
Division 1
Ballymena v Garryowen
Cork Const v Blackrock Coll
Instonians v Dungannon
Lansdowne v Old Wesley
Old Crescent v Young Munster
Shannon v Terenure Coll
St Mary's Coll v Old Belvedere
Division 2
Bective Rangers v Derry
Highfield v Wanderers
Monkstown v Dolphin
NIFC v Malone
Skerries v Greystones
Sunday's Well v Clontarf
UC Cork v DLSP
Division 3
Bangor v Bohemians
Collegians v Corinthians
Dublin U v UC Dublin
Portadown v Buccaneers
Queen's U, Belfast v Waterpark

WRU SWALEC Cup: *Quarter-finals*

Sunday, 23 March
RUGBY WORLD CUP SEVENS
  (Hong Kong)

Saturday, 29 March
RFU Cup: *Semi-finals*

RFU Courage Leagues
Division 1
Bath v Gloucester
Harlequins v Bristol

Leicester v Wasps
Orrell v Northampton
Sale v London Irish
Saracens v West Hartlepool

**IRFU Insurance Corporation
  Leagues**
Division 1
Blackrock Coll v St Mary's Coll
Dungannon v Shannon
Old Belvedere v Lansdowne
Old Crescent v Instonians
Old Wesley v Ballymena
Terenure Coll v Cork Const
Young Munster v Garryowen
Division 2
Clontarf v Dolphin
Derry v UC Cork
DLSP v Highfield
Greystones v Monkstown
Malone v Skerries
Sunday's Well v Bective Rangers
Wanderers v NIFC
Division 3
Bohemians v Collegians
Buccaneers v Bangor
Galwegians v Dublin U
UC Dublin v Queen's U, Belfast
Waterpark v Portadown

WRU Leagues
Division 1
Bridgend v Cardiff
Dunvant v Neath
Ebbw Vale v Caerphilly
Llanelli v Pontypridd
Newbridge v Newport
Treorchy v Swansea

Saturday, 5 April

RFU Courage Leagues
Division 1
Bristol v Northampton
Gloucester v Saracens
Leicester v Orrell
London Irish v Harlequins
Wasps v Bath
West Hartlepool v Sale
Division 2
Bedford v Newcastle
Coventry v Rotherham
Moseley v London Scottish
Nottingham v Waterloo

Richmond v Blackheath
Wakefield v Rugby
Division 3
Exeter v Fylde
Harrogate v Clifton
Leeds v Morley
London Welsh v Redruth
Lydney v Walsall
Reading v Otley
Rosslyn Park v Liverpool St Helens
Wharfedale v Havant

**IRFU Insurance Corporation
  Leagues**
Division 1
Ballymena v Old Belvedere
Cork Const v Dungannon
Garryowen v Old Wesley
Instonians v Young Munster
Lansdowne v Blackrock Coll
Shannon v Old Crescent
St Mary's Coll v Terenure Coll
Division 2
Bective Rangers v Clontarf
Dolphin v Greystones
Highfield v Derry
Monkstown v Malone
NIFC v DLSP
Skerries v Wanderers
UC Cork v Sunday's Well

WRU Leagues
Division 1
Caerphilly v Newbridge
Cardiff v Neath
Llanelli v Dunvant
Newport v Bridgend
Pontypridd v Treorchy
Swansea v Ebbw Vale

Sunday, 6 April

SRU Cup: *5th round*

Saturday, 12 April

Army v Royal Navy (Twickenham)

RFU Courage Leagues
Division 1
Bath v Leicester
Harlequins v West Hartlepool
Northampton v London Irish
Orrell v Bristol

Sale v Gloucester
Saracens v Wasps
Division 2
London Scottish v Rotherham
Moseley v Bedford
Newcastle v Coventry
Rugby v Blackheath
Wakefield v Nottingham
Waterloo v Richmond
Division 3
Clifton v Leeds
Fylde v Harrogate
Havant v Exeter
Liverpool St Helens v Wharfedale
Morley v London Welsh
Otley v Rosslyn Park
Redruth v Lydney
Walsall v Reading

IRFU Insurance Corporation Leagues
Division 1
Blackrock Coll v Ballymena
Cork Const v Old Crescent
Dungannon v St Mary's Coll
Instonians v Shannon
Old Belvedere v Garryowen
Terenure Coll v Lansdowne
Young Munster v Old Wesley
Division 2
Bective Rangers v UC Cork
Clontarf v Greystones
Derry v NIFC
DLSP v Skerries
Malone v Dolphin
Sunday's Well v Highfield
Wanderers v Monkstown

WRU SWALEC Cup: *Semi-finals*

Wednesday, 16 April
Army v Royal Air Force
  (Twickenham)

Saturday, 19 April
RFU County Championship: *Final*
  (Twickenham)

RFU Courage Leagues
Division 1
Bath v Orrell
Gloucester v Harlequins

Leicester v Saracens
London Irish v Bristol
Wasps v Sale
West Hartlepool v Northampton
Division 2
Bedford v London Scottish
Blackheath v Waterloo
Coventry v Moseley
Richmond v Wakefield
Rotherham v Newcastle
Nottingham v Rugby
Division 3
Exeter v Liverpool St Helens
Harrogate v Havant
Leeds v Fylde
London Welsh v Clifton
Lydney v Morley
Rosslyn Park v Reading
Walsall v Redruth
Wharfedale v Otley

IRFU Provincial Cups: *1st rounds*

WRU Leagues
Division 1
Bridgend v Caerphilly
Dunvant v Cardiff
Ebbw Vale v Pontypridd
Neath v Newport
Newbridge v Swansea
Treorchy v Llanelli
Division 2
Abertillery v Aberavon
Bonymaen v Blackwood
Cross Keys v Ystradgynlais
Llandovery v Abercynon
Pontypool v Maesteg
UWIC v South Wales Police

Sunday, 20 April
SRU Cup: *Quarter-finals*

Wednesday, 23 April
Royal Air Force v Royal Navy
  (Twickenham)

Saturday, 26 April
RFU Courage Leagues
Division 1
Bath v Sale
Gloucester v Bristol
Leicester v Harlequins

Orrell v Saracens
Wasps v Northampton
West Hartlepool v London Irish
Division 2
Coventry v Bedford
Moseley v Rotherham
Newcastle v London Scottish
Richmond v Nottingham
Wakefield v Blackheath
Waterloo v Rugby
Division 3
Clifton v Lydney
Fylde v London Welsh
Havant v Leeds
Liverpool St Helens v Harrogate
Morley v Redruth
Otley v Exeter
Reading v Wharfedale
Rosslyn Park v Walsall

IRFU Provincial Cups: *Quarter-finals*

WRU Leagues
Division 1
Caerphilly v Neath
Llanelli v Ebbw Vale
Newport v Cardiff
Pontypridd v Newbridge
Swansea v Bridgend
Treorchy v Dunvant

Sunday, 27 April
SRU Cup: *Semi-finals*

Saturday, 3 May
RFU Courage Leagues
Division 1
Bristol v West Hartlepool
Harlequins v Wasps
London Irish v Orrell
Northampton v Gloucester

Sale v Leicester
Saracens v Bath
Division 3
Exeter v Reading
Harrogate v Otley
Leeds v Liverpool St Helens
London Welsh v Havant
Lydney v Fylde
Redruth v Clifton
Walsall v Morley
Wharfedale v Rosslyn Park

RFU Intermediate Clubs Cup: *Final*
  (Twickenham)
RFU Junior Shield: *Final*
  (Twickenham)
IRFU Provincial Cups: *Semi-finals*

WRU Leagues
Division 1
Bridgend v Pontypridd
Cardiff v Caerphilly
Dunvant v Newport
Ebbw Vale v Treorchy
Neath v Swansea
Newbridge v Llanelli

Saturday, 10 May
RFU CUP: *Final* (Twickenham)
SRU CUP: *Final* (Murrayfield)
Connacht Cup: *Final*
Leinster Cup: *Final*
Munster Cup: *Final*
Ulster Cup: *Final*
WRU SWALEC CUP: *Final* (Cardiff)

Saturday, 17 May
Middlesex Sevens (Twickenham)

Sunday, 18 May
ANGLO-WELSH CUP: *Final*

MAJOR TOURS 1996-97

AUSTRALIANS TO ITALY, IRELAND AND BRITAIN

October 1996
19	**Italian Selection**
23	**ITALY** (Rome)
30	**Scotland A** (Gala)

November
2	**Combined Scottish Districts** (Glasgow)
5	**Scottish Districts Selection** (Perth)
9	**SCOTLAND** (Murrayfield)
13	**Leinster** (Dublin)

16 **Ulster** (Belfast)
20 **Connacht** (Galway)
23 **Munster** (Limerick)
26 **Ireland A** (Belfast)
30 **IRELAND**   (Dublin)

December

7   **Barbarians** (Twickenham)

ARGENTINIANS TO ENGLAND

November 1996

20 **London Division** (Twickenham)
24 **South-West Division** (Bristol)
27 **Midlands Division** (Leicester)

December

1   **Northern Division**
    (Huddersfield)
4   **Combined Services**
10 **England A** (Northampton)
14 **ENGLAND** (Twickenham)

SOUTH AFRICANS TO ARGENTINA, FRANCE AND WALES

November 1996

5   **Mendoza** (Mendoza)
9   **ARGENTINA** (Buenos Aires)
12 **Rosario** (Rosario)
16 **ARGENTINA** (Buenos Aires)
23 **French Barbarians** (Brive)

26 **French Selection** (Lyons)
30 **FRANCE** (Bordeaux)

December

3   **French Selection** (Lille)
7   **FRANCE** (Paris)
15 **WALES** (Cardiff)

BRITISH LIONS TO SOUTH AFRICA

May 1997

24 **Eastern Province XV**
    (Port Elizabeth)
28 **Western Province** (Cape Town)
31 **Free State** (Bloemfontein)

June

4   **Transvaal** (Johannesburg)
7   **Northern Transvaal** (Pretoria)
11 **South-Eastern Transvaal**
    (Witbank)
14 **Natal** (Durban)
17 **Emerging Springboks**
    (Wellington)
21 **SOUTH AFRICA** (Cape Town)
24 **Border** (East London)
28 **SOUTH AFRICA** (Durban)

July

1   **SA Barbarians** (Welkom)
5   **SOUTH AFRICA**
    (Johannesburg)

MAJOR FIXTURES 1996-97

August 1996

17 **SOUTH AFRICA v NEW
    ZEALAND** (Durban)
    SCOTLAND v BARBARIANS
    (Murrayfield)
24 **SOUTH AFRICA v NEW
    ZEALAND** (Pretoria)
    WALES v BARBARIANS
    (Cardiff)
31 **SOUTH AFRICA v NEW
    ZEALAND** (Johannesburg)

September

14 **ARGENTINA v URUGUAY**
    (Toronto)
    CANADA v UNITED STATES
    (Toronto)
17 **CANADA v URUGUAY**
    (Hamilton)
    **UNITED STATES v
    ARGENTINA** (Hamilton)
21 **CANADA v ARGENTINA**
    (Ottawa)
    **UNITED STATES v
    URUGUAY** (Ottawa)

October

5   **ITALY v WALES** (Rome)
23 **ITALY v AUSTRALIA**
30 **Scotland A v Australians**

November

8   **Scotland A v Junior Springboks**
9   **ARGENTINA v SOUTH AFRICA** (Buenos Aires)
    SCOTLAND v AUSTRALIA (Murrayfield)
16 **ARGENTINA v SOUTH AFRICA** (Buenos Aires)
23 **ENGLAND v ITALY** (Twickenham)
26 **Ireland A v Australians** (Belfast)
30 **IRELAND v AUSTRALIA** (Dublin)
    FRANCE v SOUTH AFRICA (Bordeaux)
    England XV v NZ Barbarians (Twickenham)

December

7   **FRANCE v SOUTH AFRICA** (Paris)
    Barbarians v Australians (Twickenham)
10 **England A v Argentinians** (Northampton)
    Oxford U v Cambridge U (Twickenham)
14 **ENGLAND v ARGENTINA** (Twickenham)
    SCOTLAND v ITALY (Murrayfield)
15 **WALES v SOUTH AFRICA** (Cardiff)

January 1997

4   **IRELAND v ITALY** (Dublin)
    Heineken European Finals
17 **Scotland A v Wales A**
18 **SCOTLAND v WALES** (Murrayfield)
    IRELAND v FRANCE (Dublin)

31 **England A v Scotland A**
    Wales A v Ireland A

February

1   **ENGLAND v SCOTLAND** (Twickenham)
    WALES v IRELAND (Cardiff)
14 **France A v Wales A**
15 **IRELAND v ENGLAND** (Dublin)
    FRANCE v WALES (Paris)
28 **Scotland A v Ireland A**

March

1   **SCOTLAND v IRELAND** (Murrayfield)
    ENGLAND v FRANCE (Twickenham)
14 **France A v Scotland A**
15 **WALES v ENGLAND** (Cardiff)
    FRANCE v SCOTLAND (Paris)
21- **RUGBY WORLD CUP SEVENS**
23 **FINALS** (Hong Kong)

April

19 **RFU County Championship Final** (Twickenham)

May

10 **RFU Cup Final** (Twickenham)
    SRU Cup Final (Murrayfield)
    WRU Cup Final (Cardiff)
17 **Middlesex Sevens** (Twickenham)
18 **Anglo-Welsh Cup Final**

June

21 **SOUTH AFRICA v LIONS** (Cape Town)
28 **SOUTH AFRICA v LIONS** (Durban)

July

5   **SOUTH AFRICA v LIONS** (Johannesburg)

A selection of non-fiction
from Headline

ROTHMANS FOOTBALL YEARBOOK 1996-97	Glenda Rollin	£17.99	☐
PLAYFAIR RUGBY UNION ANNUAL	Day/Gallagher	£4.99	☐
PLAYFAIR FOOTBALL ANNUAL 1996-97	Glenda Rollin	£4.99	☐
THE ILLUSTRATED CANTONA	Eric Cantona	£18.99	☐
LIVERPOOL'S GREATEST PLAYERS	David Walmsley	£17.99	☐
OFFICIAL ILLUSTRATED HISTORY OF THE FA CUP	Bryon Butler	£25.00	☐
STATTO'S ULTIMATE FOOTBALL TRIVIA BOOK	Statto	£7.99	☐

All Headline books are available at your local bookshop or newsagent, or can be ordered direct from the publisher. Just tick the titles you want and fill in the form below. Prices and availability subject to change without notice.

Headline Book Publishing Ltd, Cash Sales Department, Bookpoint, 39 Milton Park, Abingdon, OXON OX14 4TD, UK. If you have a credit card you may order by telephone – 01235 400400.

Please enclose a cheque or postal order made payable to Bookpoint Ltd to the value of the cover price and allow the following for postage and packing:

UK & BFPO: £1.00 for the first book, 50p for the second book and 30p for each additional book ordered up to a maximum charge of £3.00.

OVERSEAS & EIRE: £2.00 for the first book, £1.00 for the second book, and 50p for each additional book.

Name ....

Address ....

....

....

If you would prefer to pay by credit card, please complete:

Please debit my Visa/Access/Diner's Card/American Express (delete as applicable) card no:

Signature .... Expiry date ....